R. Gupta's®

POPULAR MASTER GUIDE

JUNIOR ENGINEERS ELECTRICAL

Recruitment Exam

by

RPH Editorial Board

RAMESH PUBLISHING HOUSE, NEW DELHI

Published by
O.P. Gupta *for* Ramesh Publishing House

Admin. Office
12-H, New Daryaganj Road, Opp. Officers' Mess,
New Delhi-110002 ✆ 23275224, 23245124

E-mail: info@rameshpublishinghouse.com
For Online Shopping: www.rameshpublishinghouse.com

Showroom
- Balaji Market, Nai Sarak, Delhi-6 ✆ 23253720, 23282525
- 4457, Nai Sarak, Delhi-6, ✆ 23918938

Book Code: R-150

ISBN: 978-81-7812-607-4

Price: ₹ 495

Printed at: Deepak Offset, Delhi

CONTENTS

Previous Paper (Solved)

JUNIOR ENGINEER—ELECTRICAL

Examination, 2023*

(Exam held on 09-10-2023)

Section-I : General Intelligence and Reasoning

1. Select the word-pair in which the two words are related in the same way as are the two words in the given pair.

(The words must be considered as meaningful English words and must not be related to each other based on the number of letters/number of consonants/vowels in the word.)

Hamper : Retard

A. Hamstrung : Encourage
B. Jovial : Solemn
C. Insipid : Tedious
D. Hypocrisy : Frankness

2. Select the correct mirror image of the given figure when the mirror is placed at MN as shown below.

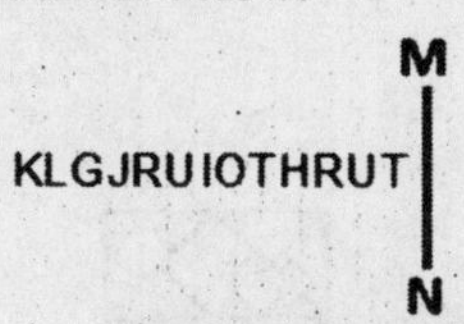

A. 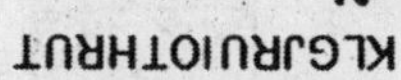
B. 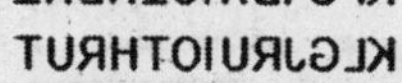
C. 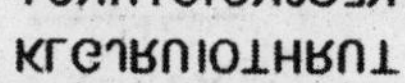
D. KLIOTHGJRURUT

3. 'OU22' is related to 'LF11' in a certain way. In the same way, 'TN12' is related to 'GM6'. Which of the following is related to 'AP22' using the same logic?

A. YK44
B. ZL44
C. ZK44
D. ZK88

4. Select the option in which the given figure is embedded (rotation is NOT allowed).

A. 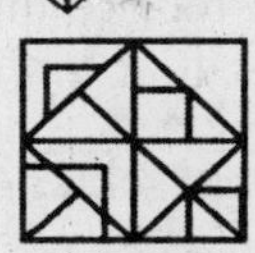
B. 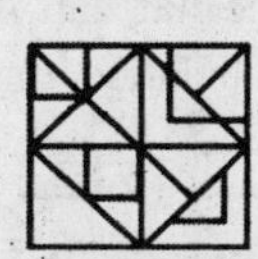
C. 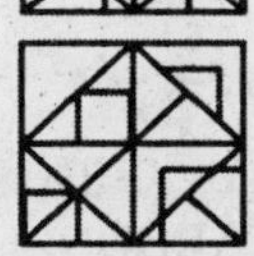
D. 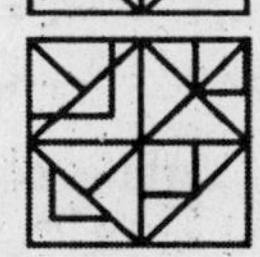

5. In a certain code language, 'LIGHTS' is written as '93' and 'BATTER' is written as '102'. How will 'BRING' be written in that language?

A. 90
B. 95
C. 85
D. 63

1. C	2. B	3. C	4. D	5. A

* *Conducted by SSC.*

6. Select the word-pair in which the two words are related in the same way as are the two words in the given pair.

(The words must be considered as meaningful English words and must not be related to each other based on the number of letters/number of consonants/vowels in the word.)

Seismology : Earthquake

A. Taxonomy : Taxation
B. Haematology : Hydrogen
C. Physiology : Physics
D. Herpetology : Amphibians

7. In a certain code language, 'PETS' is coded as '48', and 'FARM' is coded as '70'. How will 'DAIRY' be coded in that language?

A. 78 B. 74
C. 47 D. 22

8. A is B's wife. F is the grandson of B. D is the father of F. C is A's daughter. How is F related to C?

A. Brother's son
B. Mother
C. Brother
D. Mother's sister

9. Select the correct combination of mathematical signs that can sequentially replace the boxes and balance the given equation.

30 □ 13 □ 21 □ 3 □ 2 □ 4 □ 2

A. –, +, ÷, ×, =, + B. –, +, ×, =, ÷, +
C. –, –, ÷, =, ×, + D. +, –, ÷, ×, =, +

10. In a certain code language, 'BRANCH' is coded as DUCQEK and 'CARBON' is coded as EDTEQQ. How will 'DRIVEN' be coded in that language?

A. FUKYGQ
B. GUKYGQ
C. GUKZGR
D. FUJYHQ

11. Select the option that represents the letters that, when sequentially placed from left to right in the blanks below, will complete the letter series.

R_ _ KU_ I N_ URI _ K_ RI _ _ U

A. I N K R N U N K
B. I N R K U N N K
C. I N R K N U N K
D. I N R K N U U K

12. Which letter cluster will replace the question mark (?) to complete the given series?

MKXB, OOAC, QSDD, ?

A. SWGE B. SWGF
C. SWHE D. SWHF

13. Which letter-cluster will replace the question mark (?) to complete the given series?

TTIR, PHMJ, LVQB, ?, DXYL

A. HJUT B. GJUT
C. HKUT D. GKUT

14. Which two signs should be interchanged to make the given equation correct?

$11 - 8 + 78 \div 6 \times 37 = 64$

A. × and + B. ÷ and ×
C. – and × D. ÷ and –

15. Select the option in which the given figure is embedded (rotation is NOT allowed).

A. 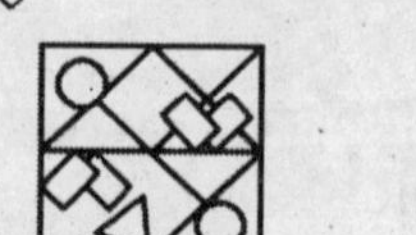

B. 

C. 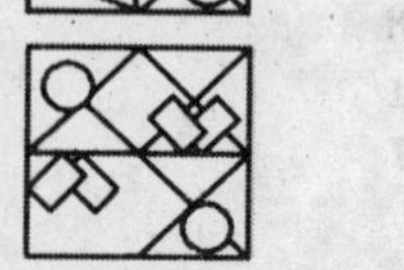

D. 

6. D	7. A	8. A	9. C	10. A	11. C	12. A	13. A	14. C	15. D

16. Select the option in which the given figure is embedded (rotation is NOT allowed).

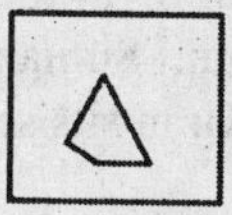

A. 
B. 
C. 
D. 

17. Select the option that is related to the third term in the same way as the second term is related to the first term and the sixth term is related to the fifth term.

3 : 20 :: 7 : ? :: 11 : 68

A. 37
B. 39
C. 41
D. 44

18. Select the figure from the options that can replace the question mark (?) and complete the given pattern.

A. 
B. 
C. 
D. 

19. Select the option that is related to the third word in the same way as the second word is related to the first word. (The words must be considered as meaningful English words and must not be related to each other based on the number of letters/number of consonants/vowels in the word)

Persuade : Discourage : : Profound : ?

A. Clever
B. Sincere
C. Superficial
D. Intense

20. Select the option that represents the letters that, when sequentially placed from left to right in the blanks below, will complete the letter series.

A_ _ J L _ DG_ LAD_ J _ AD_ _ L

A. D GAL GL GJ
B. D GAJ GL GJ
C. D GAL GJ GJ
D. D AGJ GL GL

21. Select the option in which the given figure is embedded (rotation is NOT allowed).

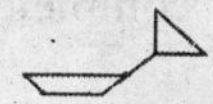

A. 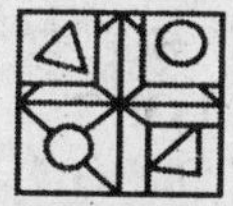
B. 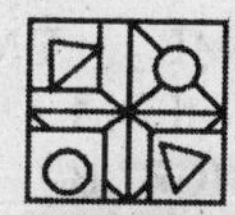
C. 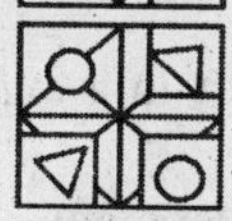
D. 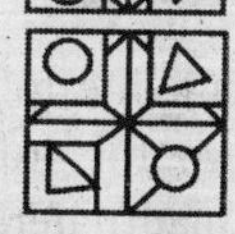

22. Select the option that represents the correct order of the given words as they would appear in an English dictionary.

1. Object
2. Obey
3. Obligation
4. Obedience
5. Obligatory

A. 4, 2, 3, 1, 5
B. 4, 2, 1, 3, 5
C. 2, 4, 1, 3, 5
D. 4, 2, 1, 5, 3

23. Two statements are given followed by two conclusions numbered I and II. Assuming the statements to be true, even if they seem to be at variance with commonly known facts, decide which of the conclusions logically follow(s) from the statements.

Statements:

All dogs are cats.

Some cows are cats but not dogs

Conclusions:

I. Some dogs are cows.

II. Some cats are both dogs and cows.

A. Both conclusions I and II follow
B. Only conclusion I follows
C. Only conclusion II follows
D. Neither conclusion I nor II follows

16. C **17.** D **18.** A **19.** C **20.** B **21.** C **22.** B **23.** D

24. Select the option that is related to the fourth number in the same way as the first number is related to the second number and the fifth number is related to the sixth number.

10 : 7 :: ? : 12 :: 32 : 18

A. 22 B. 15
C. 18 D. 20

25. Select the option that represents the letters which, when sequentially placed from left to right in the blanks below, will complete the letter series.

L _ MB_ _ GM _ OL _ M BO

A. BGLOM B. GLOBG
C. MGBLB D. GOLBG

26. Arrange the following words in a logical and meaningful order.

1. Quadrilateral 2. Heptagon
3. Pentagon 4. Hexadecagon
5. Dodecagon

A. 1, 3, 5, 2, 4 B. 1, 5, 3, 2, 4
C. 4, 2, 3, 5, 1 D. 4, 5, 2, 3, 1

27. Which of the following options will replace the question mark (?) in the given series?

$\frac{1}{289}, \frac{1}{17}$, ?, 17

A. $\frac{1}{85}$ B. $\frac{1}{34}$
C. 1 D. $\frac{1}{119}$

28. A & B means 'A is the wife of B'.
A # B means 'A is the father of B'.
A @ B means 'A is the Son B'.
A % B means 'A is the husband of B'.
A + B means 'A is the mother of B'.
If A & B # C & D @ E % F + G, then how is C related to G?

A. Father's mother B. Sister
C. Mother D. Brother's wife

29. Six friends are sitting in a circle. All of them are facing the centre. Samir is an immediate neighbour of Kiran. Gagan is an immediate neighbour of Pran and Vyom. Suman sits second to the right of Gagan. Kiran sits second to the right of Vyom.
Who sits third to the right of Suman?

A. Kiran B. Vyom
C. Pran D. Samir

30. Select the set in which the numbers are related in the same way as are the numbers of the following sets.
(NOTE: Operations should be performed on the whole numbers, without breaking down the numbers into its constituent digits. E.g., 13 – Operations on 13 such as adding/ subtraction/multiplying etc. to 13 can be performed. Breaking down 13 into 1 and 3 and then performing mathematical operations on 1 and 3 is not allowed)
(33, 6, 54)
(22, 7, 30)

A. (14, 4, 26) B. (18, 3, 42)
C. (24, 2, 66) D. (26, 8, 36)

31. Select the option that represents the correct order of the given words as they would appear in an English dictionary.

1. Whisker 2. Whistle
3. Wistful 4. Wither
5. Whisper 6. Wishful

A. 5, 1, 2, 3, 4, 6 B. 1, 5, 2, 6, 3, 4
C. 5, 1, 2, 6, 3, 4 D. 1, 5, 2, 3, 6, 4

32. A man departs from his house and walks 10 m towards north. He then turns left and walks 15 m. Now, he turns right and walks 7 m and stops. A pole is placed exactly 15 m east from where he stands. How far and in which direction is his house from the pole? (Assuming that all turns are 90 degree turns only.)

A. 27 m, north B. 17 m, south
C. 7 m, north D. 15 m, south

24. D	25. D	26. D	27. C	28. D	29. C	30. D	31. B	32. B

33. Select the option that is related to the third term in the same way as the second term is related to the first term and the sixth term is related to the fifth term.

17 : 374 :: 14 : ? :: 13 : 234

A. 266 B. 296
C. 299 D. 269

34. Two dimensions of the same dice are given below. Which of the following faces is opposite to the face having digit 3?

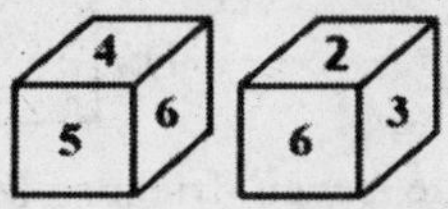

A. 1 B. 5
C. 2 D. 4

35. Daisy starts walking from her house and goes 20 m west. From there she turns right and walks a certain distance called P m. Then she turns right and walks 30 m. She turns right again and walks 40 m. After that, she takes a final right turn and walks 10 m. If Daisy's current position is 5 m south of her home, then what is the value of P?

A. 35 B. 45
C. 15 D. 40

36. If A denotes '+', B denotes '×', C denotes '–', and D denotes '÷', then what will come in place of '?' in the following equation?

89 C 8 A (18 B 2) D 4 = ?

A. 146 B. 81
C. 90 D. 89

37. Select the number from among the given options that can replace the question mark (?) in the following series.

1, 6, 28, 71, 139, 236, ?

A. 366 B. 333
C. 335 D. 363

38. If '+' means '–', '–' means '×', '×' means '÷', '÷' means '+', then what will come in place of the question mark (?) in the following equation?

41 ÷ 18 – 7 + 322 × 23 = ?

A. 167 B. 153
C. 169 D. 144

39. Ten people are sitting in two parallel rows containing 5 people each, in such a way that there is equal distance between adjacent persons.

In Row 1 – A, B, C, D and E are seated and all of them are facing the south.

In Row 2 – P, Q, R, S and T are seated and all of them are facing the north.

Thus, each person is facing another person from the other row.

B is sitting third to the left of A. P is facing an immediate neighbour of A. Q is sitting third to the right of P. C is facing S. D is sitting second to the right of the person who is facing T.

Who amongst the following is NOT sitting at any of the extreme ends of the row?

A. C B. R
C. Q D. E

40. Select the option that is embedded in the given figure (rotation is NOT allowed).

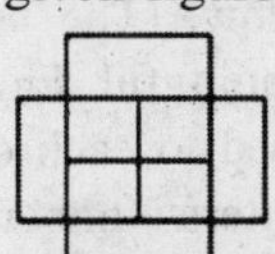

A. 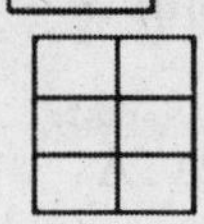
B. 

C. 
D. 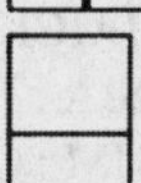

33. A	**34.** D	**35.** A	**36.** C	**37.** A	**38.** B	**39.** A	**40.** D

41. Three statements are followed by three conclusions numbered I, II and III. You have to consider these statements to be true, even if they seem to be at variance with commonly known facts. Decide which of the given conclusions logically follow(s) from the given statements.

Statements:

Few mountains are rivers.

Most rivers are valleys.

All valleys are hills.

Conclusions:

I. Few mountains are valleys.

II. Some hills are mountains.

III. Some rivers are hills.

A. Only conclusion I follows

B. All the conclusions I, II and III follow

C. Only conclusion III follows

D. Either conclusion I or II and conclusion III follow

42. Select the option that is related to the fourth term in the same way as the first term is related to the second term and the fifth term is related to the sixth term?

54 : 3 :: ? : 9 :: 432 : 6

A. 729 B. 1458

C. 477 D. 1089

43. Select the word-pair that best represents a similar relationship to the one expressed in the pair of words given below. (The words must be considered as meaningful English words and must not be related to each other based on the number of letters/numbers of consonants/vowels in the word)

INDIA : NEW DELHI

A. WEST BENGAL : KOLKATA

B. UP : LUCKNOW

C. RUSSIA : MOSCOW

D. SIKKIM : GANGTOK

44. In a certain code language, "DILQ" is written as "FKNS" and "SBGK" is written as "UDIM". How will "FORA" be written in that language?

A. HRSC B. GPSD

C. GRTD D. HQTC

45. Select the option that is embedded in the given figure (rotation is NOT allowed).

A. 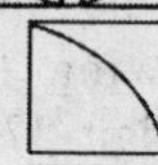 B. 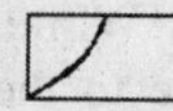

C.  D. 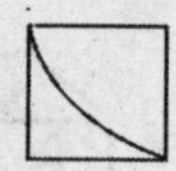

46. Each of the seven friends, Misha, Minshu, Mohi, Priya, Veer, Pari and Krishi, has a different height. Krishi is taller than only three people. Pari is taller than only Veer. Misha is taller than Minshu but not Mohi. Priya is taller than Mohi.

Who is tallest among them?

A. Priya B. Minshu

C. Krishi D. Mohi

47. Select the correct option that indicates the arrangement of the following words in a logical and meaningful order.

1. Shelf 2. Wood

3. Plank 4. Tree

5. Cupboard

A. 4, 2, 3, 1, 5 B. 2, 4, 5, 1, 3

C. 4, 2, 1, 5, 3 D. 2, 4, 3, 5, 1

48. Select the word-pair that best represents a similar relationship to the one expressed in the pair of words given below.

(The words must be considered as meaningful English words and must not be related to each other based on the number of letters/number of consonants/vowels in the word.)

Mustang : Horse

A. Stag : Deer B. Panthera Leo : Lion

C. Turkey : Fowl D. Burmese : Cat

41. C	**42.** B	**43.** C	**44.** D	**45.** B	**46.** A	**47.** A	**48.** D

49. How many triangles are there in the given figure?

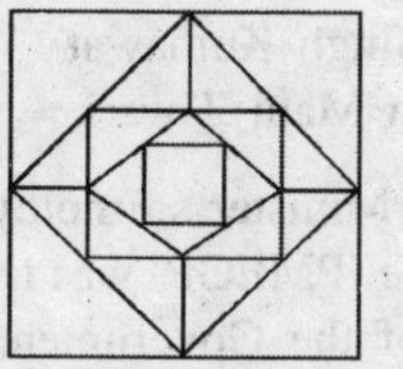

A. 24 B. 26
C. 28 D. 30

50. Which of the following numbers will replace the question marks (?) in the given series?

20, 30, 42, 56, ?, 90

A. 58 B. 72
C. 36 D. 78

Section-II : General Awareness

51. Which of the following refers to the net money value of all the final goods and services produced by the normal residents of a country, during a period of one year?

A. Gross National Product at market price
B. Net National Product at market price
C. Gross National Product at factor cost
D. Net National Product at factor cost

52. The 11th Fundamental Duty was added to the Constitution of India by the________ Constitutional Amendment Act.

A. 88th B. 81st
C. 86th D. 83rd

53. Which of the following is NOT an Alicyclic compound?

A. Cyclohexene B. Cyclopropane
C. Cyclohexane D. Isobutane

54. The White Paper on the five themes of Youth 20 (Y20) was launched by ______ in Guwahati in February 2023.

A. Nitin Gadkari B. Anurag Thakur
C. Amit Shah D. Piyush Goyal

55. In which of the following dance forms the faces of dancers are made up to look like painted masks and the costume consists of a full skirt, a heavy jacket, numerous garlands and necklaces and a towering headdress?

A. Mohiniyattam B. Odissi
C. Kathakali D. Kathak

56. Plants of which family have a highly compressed inflorescence branching system called a capitulum or flower head in which all the flowers are attached to a receptacle surrounded by unbranched bracts?

A. Sapindaceae B. Asteraceae
C. Ericaceae D. Ranunculaceae

57. Which of the following is an example of good netiquette when participating in online discussion or forums?

A. Reading the discussion thread before posting to avoid repeating previous points
B. Using all caps
C. Attacking other users
D. Posting irrelevant or off-topic comments

58. Identify an allotrope of carbon that is smooth and slippery.

A. Graphite B. Lead
C. Fullerene D. Diamond

59. Which vitamin deficiency in the diet causes Korsakoff syndrome, a chronic memory disorder that damages your brain?

A. Thiamine B. Niacin
C. Tocopherol D. Phylloquinone

60. The Bhitari Pillar inscription of which Gupta ruler narrates his fight with the Pushyamitras?

A. Skandagupta B. Chandragupta I
C. Samudragupta D. Chandragupta II

49. A **50.** B **51.** D **52.** C **53.** D **54.** B **55.** C **56.** B **57.** A **58.** A **59.** A **60.** A

61. _________ will be declared if the umpire thinks the batsman did NOT have a reasonable opportunity to score off the delivery.
A. Leg Bye B. Bye
C. No Ball D. Wide

62. According to NITI Aayog's Multidimensional Poverty Index (MPI) based on NFHS-4 (2015-16), 51.91 per cent of the population of which state is multidimensionally poor?
A. Uttar Pradesh B. Arunachal Pradesh
C. Bihar D. Meghalaya

63. Which of the following terminologies describes the areas where ecological communities, ecosystems or biotic regions coincide?
A. Benthos B. Ecotones
C. Permafrost D. Ecocline

64. EV Ramaswamy Naicker founded the ______ Movement.
A. Self-Respect
B. Prarthana Samaj
C. Satyashodhak Samaj
D. Ghadar

65. Where can you find solid form of water?
A. Oceans B. Forest
C. Polar region D. Desert

66. What does the word Gopuram mean in the context of temple architecture of South India?
A. Top edge of the shikhara of the temple
B. Platform of the temple to place deity
C. Entrance gateway in front wall of the temple
D. Place to keep cows near the temple

67. R–X is the general formula of which functional group in which one or more hydrogen atoms are replaced by Group 17 elements?
A. Alkyl halides B. Amide
C. Nitrile D. Imines

68. Who has cracked the Panini code in his thesis?
A. Rishi Rajpopat
B. Prasann K. Sharma
C. Udai Singh Kumawat
D. Manish Mani Tiwari

69. The Prime Minister's Employment Generation Programme (PMEGP) was launched by which Ministry of the Government of India during 2008-09?
A. Ministry of Agriculture and Farmers Welfare
B. Ministry of Home Affairs
C. Ministry of Micro, Small and Medium Enterprises
D. Ministry of Skill Development and Entrepreneurship

70. Famous musician Ustad Amjad Ali Khan was born in 1945 in ________.
A. Agra B. Lucknow
C. Gwalior D. Jhansi

71. At maturity, ______ is a non-conductive cell composed of heavily thick-walled dead cells with lignin and high cellulose content (60%–80%), and it serves to provide structural support in plants.
A. sclerenchyma cell
B. meristematic cell
C. reproductive cell
D. parenchyma cell

72. Which 19th century German chemist visualised the ring structure of benzene in 1865?
A. Robert Bunsen
B. Marguerite Perey
C. Emil Fischer
D. Friedrich August Kekule

73. Al Biruni wrote famous book "Kitab ul Hind" in __________ language.
A. Sanskrit B. Arabic
C. Persian D. Mongolian

61. D **62.** C **63.** B **64.** A **65.** C **66.** C **67.** A **68.** A **69.** C **70.** C
71. A **72.** D **73.** B

74. Which of the following diseases is caused by Rhino viruses?
A. Malaria B. Amoebiasis
C. Common cold D. Ascariasis

75. These volcanoes are mostly made up of basalt, a type of lava that is very fluid when erupted. For this reason, these volcanoes are not steep.

Which of the following volcano is an example of the above given type of volcano?
A. Mount Shasta Volcano
B. Hawaiian Volcano
C. Mount Rainier Volcano
D. Mayon Volcano

76. According to Koeppen's Scheme of climate division of India, match the following climates of India with their respective regions.

Climate	**Region**
(*a*) Cold humid winter with short summer	1. Coromandel coast of Tamil Nadu
(*b*) Hot desert	2. Arunachal Pradesh
(*c*) Monsoon with dry summer	3. Extreme Western Rajasthan

	(*a*)	(*b*)	(*c*)
A.	1	3	2
B.	2	1	3
C.	3	2	1
D.	2	3	1

77. A provision has been inserted to empower the Assessing Officer to require a ______ for inventory valuation before tax assessment in case of appeals as per Finance Bill 2023.
A. secretarial audit
B. legal audit
C. cost audit
D. statutory audit

78. What are thunderstorms in Assam during the month of 'Baisakhi' called?
A. Ghorisila B. Kal Baisakhi
C. Nor Westers D. Bardoisila

79. NABARD came into being in 1982. With how much initial capital was it set up?
A. ₹ 100 crore B. ₹ 200 crore
C. ₹ 50 crore D. ₹ 150 crore

80. Which field should be used when you want to send a copy of the email to someone else without the original recipient knowing?
A. From B. CC
C. To D. BCC

81. Which of the following is NOT a former name of Lakshadweep?
A. Amindivi Island
B. Minicoy Island
C. Kavaratti Island
D. Laccadive Island

82. The second five-year plan introduced to the concept of public sector of state-run enterprises based on the _____ model of industrialisation.
A. French B. Japanese
C. Russian D. German

83. Which of the following is a rabi crop?
A. Watermelon B. Groundnut
C. Maize D. Wheat

84. The idea of 'Fundamental Rights' was taken from the constitution of which of the following countries?
A. Constitution of Switzerland
B. Constitution of France
C. Constitution of the United States
D. Constitution of the Ireland

85. Bishop is used in which of the following games?
A. Badminton B. Chess
C. Billiards D. Cricket

86. Who was responsible for causing the partition of Bengal?
A. Lord Dufferin B. Lord Wellesly
C. Lord Curzon D. Lord Lytton

74. C **75.** B **76.** D **77.** C **78.** D **79.** A **80.** D **81.** C **82.** C **83.** D
84. C **85.** B **86.** C

87. The Gram Nyayalay Act was passed in the year ________.
A. 1992 B. 2006
C. 1996 D. 2008

88. Pandit Shiv Kumar Sharma, a renowned instrumentalist, published which of the following books as his autobiography?
A. My Life My Music
B. Journey with a Hundred Strings : My Life in Music
C. Raag Mala
D. Yours in Music

89. According the Census of India 2011, which state is the most densely populated?
A. Uttar Pradesh B. Kerala
C. Bihar D. Haryana

90. The Central Board of Direct Taxes (CBDT) has implemented the Income-tax (25th Amendment) Rule 2021 which states that any interest accrued in a PF account for contributions of more than ______ per financial year will be taxed.
A. 10 lakhs B. 2.5 lakhs
C. 7.5 lakhs D. 5 lakhs

91. Arjun Singh Dhurve, a Baiga folk dance teacher received the Padma Shri in 2021-22. To which state do the Baigas mainly belong?
A. Chhattisgarh B. Maharashtra
C. Madhya Pradesh D. Gujarat

92. Identify the organism that does NOT belong to the first level trophic level.
A. Grass B. Trees
C. Zooplankton D. Phytoplankton

93. Article 44 of the Indian Constitution is related to __________.
A. organisation of agriculture
B. living wage for workers
C. uniform civil code for the citizens
D. equal justice and free legal aid

94. Manoj Sinha, who is the second Lieutenant Governor of the Union territory of Jammu and Kashmir, hails from ________.
A. Uttar Pradesh B. Madhya Pradesh
C. Jharkhand D. Odisha

95. Which Act abolished the powers so long enjoyed by the Board of Control?
A. Act of 1813
B. Act of 1858
C. Act of 1853
D. Act of 1786

96. The salary and allowance of the Prime Minister of India is determined by the __________.
A. President of India
B. PMO
C. Cabinet Secretariat
D. Parliament

97. Heal in India is an initiative of the Indian Government aimed at promoting ________ in the country.
A. spiritual enlightenment
B. yoga
C. spiritual healing
D. medical tourism

98. In which form have earth forming materials been distributed?
A. Parts B. Layers
C. Clusters D. Regions

99. According to Census of India 2011, how much per cent of the total population were Sikhs?
A. 0.4% B. 1.7%
C. 2.3% D. 0.7%

100. Which iron and steel plant was established near the confluence of the rivers Subarnarekha and Kharkai?
A. Bokaro Steel Plant
B. Tata Iron and Steel Company Limited
C. Indian Iron and Steel Company Limited
D. Bhilai Steel Plant

87. D **88.** B **89.** C **90.** B **91.** C **92.** C **93.** C **94.** A **95.** B **96.** D
97. D **98.** B **99.** B **100.** B

Section-III : General Engineering (Electrical)

101. A supply of 200 V can be obtained from a source of 600 V by means of a two-winding transformer or an auto transformer.

The ratio of weights of conductor material in the auto transformer with respect to the two-winding transformer is ________.

A. 1 : 2
B. 1 : 1.5
C. 2 : 1
D. 1.5 : 1

102. Choose the most efficient generator for wind power generation.

A. Doubly-fed induction generator
B. Permanent magnet synchronous generator
C. Induction generators
D. Squirrel cage induction generators

103. Why is the hold-on coil connected in series with the shunt field in a three-point starter of a DC motor?

A. To provide the lubricant for the motor
B. To disconnect the supply when the motor is in normal operation
C. To control the speed of the motor
D. To prevent the motor from running away in case of an open-field circuit

104. Find the estimated current taken by the primary side if a single-phase transformer with a voltage ratio of 440/110 V takes a no-load current of 5 A at 0.2 power factor lagging and the secondary supplies a current of 120 A at a power factor of 0.8 lagging.

Given that cos(41°36′) = 0.748.

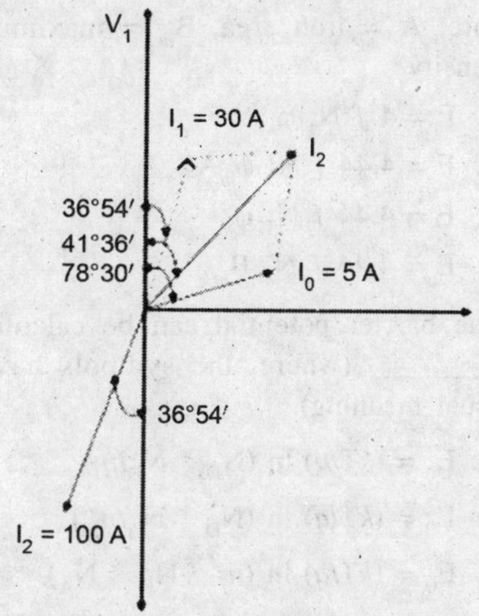

A. 30 A
B. $\sqrt{1140.4}$ A
C. $\sqrt{1149.4}$ A
D. $\sqrt{1178}$ A

105. Which of the following is NOT a type of tender, depending on the type of contract?

A. Selected tender
B. Percentage rate tender
C. Lum-sum tender
D. Item rate tender

106. In AC series motor, power factor is low because of ________.

A. high resistance of the field and armature circuit
B. high inductance of the field and armature circuit
C. low inductance of the field and armature circuit
D. high capacitance of the field and armature circuit

101. B **102.** A **103.** D **104.** C **105.** A **106.** B

107. Which expression is right about EMF equation of a transformer if f = frequency, N_1 = number of turns in primary, φ_m = maximum flux in a core, A = iron area, B_m = maximum flux density?

A. $E = 4 f N_1 \varphi_m A$
B. $E = 4.44 f N_1 \varphi_m A$
C. $E = 4.44 f N_1 \varphi_m$
D. $E = 4.44 f N_1 B_m$

108. The barrier potential can be calculated by ________ (where, the symbols have their usual meaning).

A. $E_0 = (kT/q) \ln (N_D * N_D/n_i)$
B. $E_0 = (kT/q) \ln (N_D * N_A/n_i^2)$
C. $E_0 = (kT/q) \ln (n_i^2 / N_D * N_A)$
D. $E_0 = (kT/q) \ln (N_A * N_A/n_i^2)$

109. Reciprocity theorem CANNOT be applied to the circuit having ______.
A. bilateral elements
B. linear elements
C. non-linear elements and multi-sources
D. only one independent sources

110. The horizontal amplifier should be designed for ____________.
A. low amplitude signals with a fast rise time
B. high amplitude signals with a fast rise time
C. high amplitude signals with a slow rise time
D. high frequency signals with a fast rise time

111. With respect to measuring the current in a circuit using the CRO, which of the following statements is/are correct?
I. A low-resistance standard resistor is connected in series with the circuit whose current is being measured.
II. The CRO is connected across the standard resistor to measure the voltage drop across it.
III. A high-resistance standard resistor is connected in parallel with the circuit where the current is being measured.
IV. The CRO is connected in series with the circuit whose current is being measured.

A. Only IV
B. Only I and IV
C. Only III and IV
D. Only I and II

112. In the circuit shown below, the current I in the circuit is:

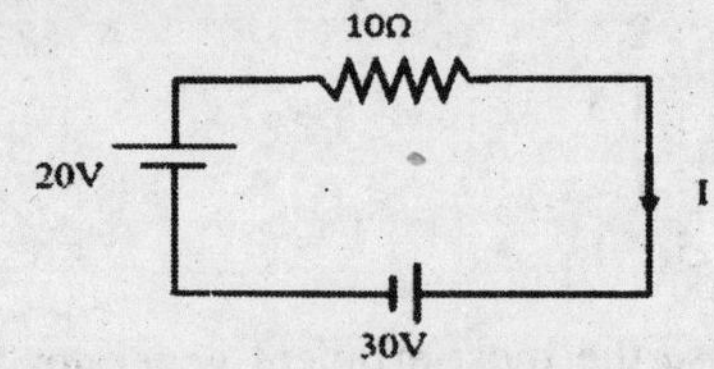

A. 0 A
B. 1 A
C. –1 A
D. 2 A

113. Three-point lighting is usually employed in film lighting schemes. Which of the following does NOT form a part of the scheme?
A. Bounce lighting
B. Key lighting
C. Back lighting
D. Fill lighting

114. Which of the following statements is NOT correct about active power in an AC circuit?
A. Active power is the power dissipated in the pure inductance.
B. Active power is the power dissipated in the pure resistance.
C. Active power can be measured in terms of kilo watt.
D. Active power depends on power factor.

115. Repulsion start induction run motors are used in applications such as ________.
A. fans
B. vacuum cleaners
C. hair dryers
D. compressors

116. A 25 V, 800 W bulb is connected to a 10 V source. The power consumed by the bulb is ________.
A. 100 W
B. 64 W
C. 400 W
D. 128 W

107. C	108. B	109. C	110. C	111. D	112. C	113. A	114. A	115. D	116. D

117. Which of the following statements is accurate regarding wires and cables?
A. Wires are made by stranding together many cables.
B. Wires and cables are the same thing.
C. Cables are made by stranding together many wires.
D. Wires and cables are never insulated.

118. The deflecting torque in a PMMC instrument is proportional to ________ .
A. the resistance of the coil
B. the area of the coil
C. the current flowing through the coil
D. the square of the current flowing through the coil

119. At the leading power factor, the armature reaction of an alternator is:
A. partially cross magnetising and partially magnetising
B. partially cross magnetising and partially demagnetising
C. wholly magnetising
D. wholly demagnetising

120. The standard percentage of the tender amount for the security deposit is ____.
A. 2.5 B. 5
C. 10 D. 2

121. The ability of a capacitor to store charge does NOT depend on the ______.
A. distance between the plates
B. areas of the plates
C. nature of the insulating material
D. amount of charge

122. A 2500 watts refrigerator works for 4 hours per day. Find the total unit of electricity used in 40 days.
A. 400 units B. 10 units
C. 40 units D. 400000 units

123. Which law gives the direction of induced EMF?
A. Maxwell's law B. Gauss's law
C. Lenz's law D. Newton's law

124. A switched reluctance motor can produce torque at a speed ________.
A. equal to synchronous speed
B. less than synchronous speed
C. double than synchronous speed
D. triple than synchronous speed

125. What is the use of encoder in the DC servomotor?
A. Determines the magnetic field strength inside the motor
B. Determines the temperature of the windings of the motor
C. Determines the rotational speed of the motor
D. Determines the input voltage of the motor

126. Which of the following is the correct interrelation between the variables x_1 and x_2 used in the expression to calculate the sag in a transmission conductor with different heights, where, variables x_1 and x_2 represent the horizontal distances of support at lower and higher levels from the lowest point of the conductor, respectively?
A. $x_1 < x_2$ B. $x_1 >> x_2$
C. $x_1 > x_2$ D. $x_1 = x_2$

127. An LC circuit with inductance L = 2 H and capacitance C = 8 μF is connected to an AC source. Find the value of the power factor of combination.
A. 0 B. 10
C. 2 D. 8

128. For providing controlling torque to a horizontally mounted MI instrument, which of the following methods is used?
A. Water control B. Spring control
C. Eddy current D. Electrostatic field

117. C **118.** C **119.** A **120.** C **121.** D **122.** A **123.** C **124.** A **125.** C **126.** A **127.** A **128.** B

129. A permanent magnetic material has ________ retentivity.

A. low B. high
C. zero D. constant

130. In the context of electromagnetic induction, if the magnetic fluxes of two coils oppose each other, then the connection is called _______.

A. parallel opposing
B. mutually opposing
C. series opposing
D. self-opposing

131. The wavelength of a sodium vapour lamp is _________.

A. 673 nm B. 326 nm
C. 254 nm D. 589 nm

132. The Norton's equivalent current between the load terminal A-B will be:

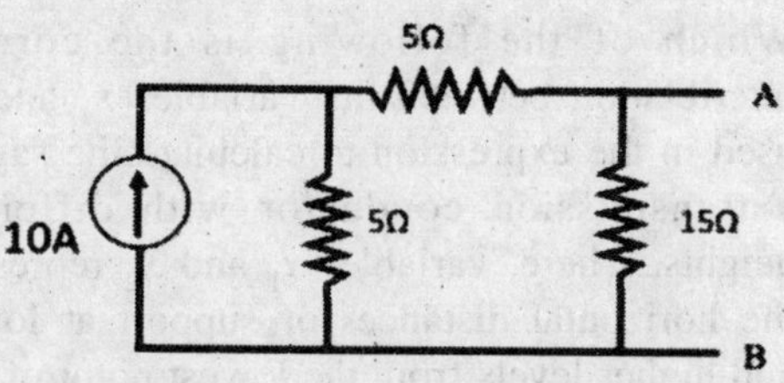

A. 5 A B. 20 A
C. 10 A D. 0 A

133. Which of the following is the correct expression for eddy current (W_e) loss if B_{max} = Maximum flux density, f = Frequency of magnetic reversal, t = Thickness of each lamination and V = Volume of the armature core?

A. $W_e = kB^2_{max} f t^2 V^2$ watts

B. $W_e = kB^2_{max} f^2 t^2 V^2$ watts

C. $W_e = kB^2_{max} f^2 t^2 V$ watts

D. $W_e = kB^2_{max} f^2 t V^2$ watts

134. Which of the following lighting calculation methods is handy and quick?

A. Watts per square metre method
B. Point by point method
C. Flux method
D. Lumen method

135. In case of magnetic circuits, the force that tends to create magnetic flux is called ______.

A. absolute permeability
B. reluctance
C. relative permeability
D. MMF

136. Which of the following connections is used as distribution transformer?

A. Delta-star B. Star-star
C. Delta-delta D. Star-delta

137. The power consumed by the 30 Ω resistor is:

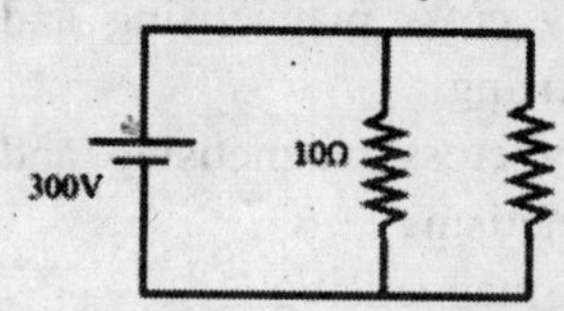

A. 300 W B. 9000 W
C. 10 W D. 3000 W

138. Which phase of the project management life-cycle often takes the longest to wrap up?

A. Planning B. Estimation
C. Execution D. Conceptualisation

139. In an electrical circuit, the current that changes periodically, both in magnitude and direction, at regular intervals of time is called ______.

A. phase current B. direct current
C. leading current D. alternating current

140. What type of rotor is used in alternators driven by hydro-turbines?

A. Shaded pole type
B. Salient pole type
C. Non-salient pole type
D. Smooth cylindrical type

129. B **130.** C **131.** D **132.** A **133.** C **134.** A **135.** D **136.** A **137.** D **138.** C **139.** D **140.** B

141. Identify the correct voltage range of medium transmission line.
A. > 100 kV < 200 kV
B. > 20 kV < 100 kV
C. > 1 kV < 5 kV
D. > 5 kV < 10 kV

142. In motor applications, efficiency of the motor is always less than 100% due to conversion of the ______.
A. output energy into current
B. input energy into heat
C. output energy into heat
D. input energy into voltage

143. Calculate the respective values of magnetising force and flux density at a distance of 10 cm from a long circular conductor carrying a current of 100 πA, placed in air?
A. 6.28×10^{-7} AT/m and 500 Wb/m^2
B. 1500 Wb/m^2 and 3.14×10^{-4} AT/m
C. 500 AT/m and 6.28×10^{-4} Wb/m^2
D. 50 Wb/m^2 and 6.28×10^{-7} AT/m

144. A coal-fired thermal power plant generates 750 MW of electricity with a thermal efficiency of 30%. The coal has a heating value of 30,000 kJ/kg. Find the mass flow rate of the coal required to generate the required electricity.
A. 0.833 kg/s B. 83.33 kg/s
C. 8.33 kg/s D. 0.0833 kg/s

145. The transfer characteristic of JFET is drawn between:
A. I_{DSS} and V_{DS} B. I_B and V_{DS}
C. I_B and V_{GS} D. I_{DSS} and V_{GS}

146. Consider two MOSFET's A and B with the same over drive voltage and sizes. MOSFET A is *p*-type MOSFET while MOSFET B is *n*-type MOSFET. Which of the following statements is true?
(*a*) MOSFET A has a higher transconductance
(*b*) MOSFET B has a higher transconductance
(*c*) MOSFET A and B have same transconductance due to same dimensions
(*d*) MOSFET A has a higher transconductance due to less mobility
A. Only (*c*) B. Only (*a*) and (*d*)
C. Only (*b*) D. Only (*a*)

147. Which of the following types of steel is used to make the core of a transformer?
A. Stainless steel B. Silicon steel
C. High-carbon steel D. Tool steel

148. Which of the following should NOT be prioritised when making a comparison statement for the tender evaluation sheet/format?
A. Cost of packaging and shipping
B. Confidence that faulty goods will be replaced
C. Conditions of supply
D. Supplier's name

149. Find the equivalent resistance across terminal *a-b*:

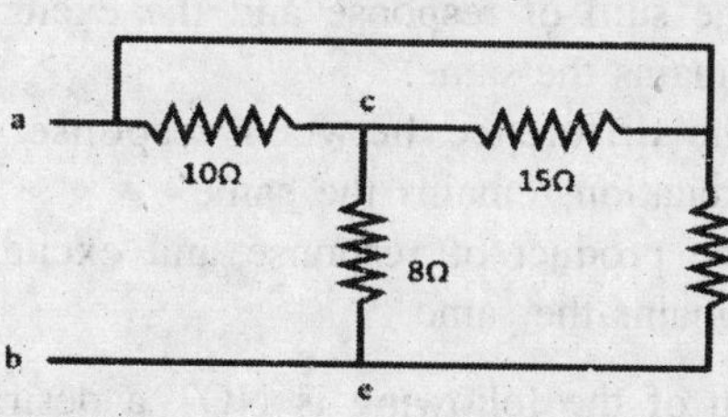

A. 20 Ω B. 14 Ω
C. 7 Ω D. 28 Ω

150. The following test results were obtained from a 6 kVA, 200/400 V, 50 Hz single-phase transformer: Data for no-load low-voltage side: 200 V, 0.5 A and 50 W. At normal voltage and frequency, determine the magnetising current of the transformer.
A. 0 A B. 0.433 A
C. 0.569 A D. 0.236 A

141. B **142.** B **143.** C **144.** B **145.** D **146.** C **147.** B **148.** D **149.** C **150.** B

151. In electromagnetic induction, the energy is supplied to the circuit and a part of this supplied energy is spent to meet ____.

A. hysteresis loss B. iron losses
C. eddy current loss D. I^2R losses

152. Which of the following statements is true about selection of the size of units in electrical energy generation?

A. The size should be selected such that the unit operates close to the load curve of the station.
B. The size should be selected independent of both the maximum demand curve and the load curve.
C. The size must be selected such that the unit operates close to the maximum demand curve of the station.
D. The size of units must match both the maximum demand curve and the load curve.

153. Which of the following is true regarding reciprocity theorem?

A. The ratio of the response to the excitation remains the same.
B. The sum of response and the excitation remains the same.
C. The difference between response and excitation remains the same.
D. The product of response and excitation remains the same.

154. Which of the following is NOT a desirable property for the insulating materials used in an underground cable?

A. High insulation resistance
B. Non-inflammable
C. Hygroscopic
D. High dielectric strength

155. If V-I characteristics is plotted for forward current by increasing the temperature, it has been seen that plot for V-I characteristics _________ as temperature increases.

A. does not change
B. is moved to the left
C. is moved down
D. is moved to the right

156. A balanced star connected load of 4 + j3 Ω per phase connected to a 3-phase, 230 V (phase value) supply. Find the value of active power.

A. 25.4 kW B. 19.13 kW
C. 22.45 kW D. 15.34 kW

157. In a pure inductive circuit, if the frequency of the AC source is doubled, then its inductive reactance will:

A. remain the same B. be halved
C. become zero D. be doubled

158. For measuring the earth resistance by the fall-of-potential method, how many auxiliary electrodes are used?

A. 2 B. 1
C. 3 D. 4

159. For an ideal short transmission line with zero voltage regulation, if receiving end voltage is 150 kV, then the sending end voltage will be:

A. 150 kV B. 125 kV
C. 200 kV D. 300 kV

160. If the frequency of supply in a three core underground cable is doubled, the charging current will be ______.

A. four times B. half
C. double D. three times

161. What is the function of the phosphor-coated screen in a CRT?

A. It is the part that moves the direction of the electron beam
B. It is the part that generates a beam of electrons
C. It is the part that regulates the intensity of the electron beam
D. It is the part that emits light

151. D **152.** A **153.** A **154.** C **155.** B **156.** A **157.** D **158.** A **159.** A **160.** C **161.** D

162. Consider the following statements about the working of a hysteresis motor and choose the suitable combination of correct choices.

(*a*) The stator of the hysteresis motor has a main winding along with an auxiliary winding.

(*b*) When the stator winding is fed from a single phase supply, it produces a synchronously revolving magnetic field.

(*c*) The rotor material has low retentivity so hysteresis loss is low.

(*d*) The rotor of the hysteresis motor consists of a smooth cylinder of magnetically hard steel, without winding

A. Only (*b*), (*c*) and (*d*) are correct.
B. Only (*a*), (*b*) and (*d*) are correct.
C. Only (*d*) is correct.
D. Only (*c*) is correct.

163. Which of the following is NOT an advantage of shell type transformers over core type transformers?

A. Less copper requirement
B. Easy maintenance
C. Reduced loss
D. High mechanical strength

164. The deflection sensitivity in a cathode ray oscilloscope (CRO) is ___ the mass of electron.

A. inversely proportional to
B. directly proportional to
C. directly proportional to the square root of
D. inversely proportional to the square root of

165. The load on the transformer changes every day, with a daily production of 120 kWh and a cumulative loss of 5 kWh. What is the all-day efficiency of the transformer?

A. 96% B. 95%
C. 92% D. 90%

166. Calculate the apparent power of a circuit if the circuit has a power factor of 0.8 and the active power of the circuit is 40 W.

A. 100 VA B. 40 VA
C. 75 VA D. 50 VA

167. In the split-phase induction motor, both main winding and starting winding are displaced _________ in space.

A. 180 degrees B. 270 degrees
C. 90 degrees D. 360 degrees

168. In an electrical signal waveform, if each value on the curve is proportional to sine of the angle of rotation of the coil, then such a wave is called _______.

A. ramp wave B. square wave
C. sine wave D. triangular wave

169. If a power station supplies 1000 MWh of electricity to its consumers for a period of two months, then the average demand during the period will be:

A. 1.39 MW B. 1.39 kW
C. 0.694 MW D. 0.694 kW

170. If the synchronous speed of a motor is 1000 rpm and the rotor speed is 970 rpm, then percentage slip is _______.

A. 3% B. 7%
C. 5% D. 9%

171. For the circuit shown below, the voltage across 10 F and 40 F capacitors are:

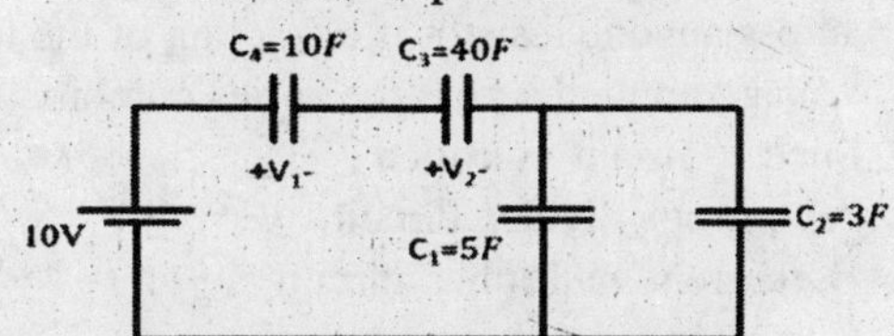

A. 10 V and 40 V, respectively
B. 400 V and 1600 V, respectively
C. 4 V and 1 V, respectively
D. 1 V and 4 V, respectively

172. A voltage of 230 ∠60° is applied to a current offering an impedance of 10 + j10 Ω. Find the expression for the current flowing through the circuit in polar form.

A. 23 ∠45° leading B. 16.3 ∠15° lagging
C. 16.3 ∠15° leading D. 23 ∠45° lagging

162. B	**163.** B	**164.** D	**165.** A	**166.** D	**167.** C	**168.** C	**169.** C	**170.** A	**171.** C	**172.** C

173. The height between the two supports of a transmission and distribution overhead line can be determined as:

A. $\frac{1}{2} \times$ (Vertical distance between the lower height support point of the conductor and lowest point of the conductor)

B. (Vertical distance between the lower height support point of the conductor and Lowest point of the conductor) + (Vertical distance between the higher height support point of the conductor and lowest point of the conductor)

C. $\frac{1}{2} \times$ (Vertical distance between the higher height support point of the conductor and lowest point of the conductor)

D. (Vertical distance between the higher height support point of the conductor and Lowest point of the conductor) – (Vertical distance between the lower height support point of the conductor and lowest point of the conductor)

174. In an electronic circuit, the potential difference across anyone resistor is a fraction of the total voltage applied across the series combination. Such a circuit is called ______.

A. current divider circuit
B. current multiplier circuit
C. voltage divider circuit
D. voltage multiplier circuit

175. The value of the current I in the circuit is:

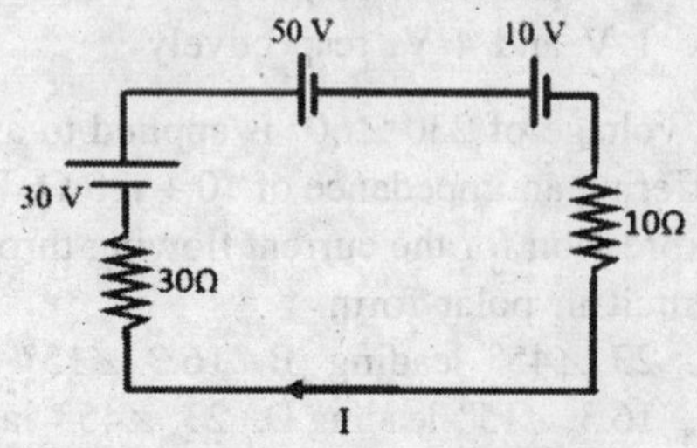

A. –0.75 A B. 0.75 A
C. 2.25 A D. –2.25 A

176. The advantage of the stationary armature of a synchronous machine is:

A. stator weight is less compared to rotor weight
B. perfect mechanical balance is obtained on stator winding
C. stator winding voltage rating can be decreased
D. commutator is present

177. Which of the following statements accurately describes voltage drop due to armature leakage reactance in an alternator on load?

A. The voltage drop due to armature leakage reactance decreases with increasing load.
B. The voltage drop due to armature leakage reactance increases with increasing load.
C. The voltage drop due to armature leakage reactance is independent of the load.
D. The voltage drop due to armature leakage reactance only occurs when the alternator is operating at no load.

178. In case of thermal efficiency, by using which of the following relations can 1 kWh of electrical energy be converted into joules?

A. 1 kWh = 36×10^5 joules
B. 1 kWh = 3.6×10^3 joules
C. 1 kWh = 3.6×10^5 joules
D. 1 kWh = 36×10^6 joules

179. Which of the following overhead conductor materials is preferred for the harmful gas (like ammonia) atmosphere?

A. Galvanized steel
B. Cadmium copper
C. Phosphor bronze
D. Aluminium

173. D	**174.** C	**175.** A	**176.** B	**177.** B	**178.** A	**179.** C

180. During working of a permanent magnet synchronous motor, ______________.

A. stator and rotor both produce rotating magnetic field

B. rotor produces rotating magnetic field and stator produces constant magnetic field

C. stator and rotor both produce constant magnetic field

D. rotor produces constant magnetic field and stator produces rotating magnetic field

181. The current through the 2 Ω resistor is:

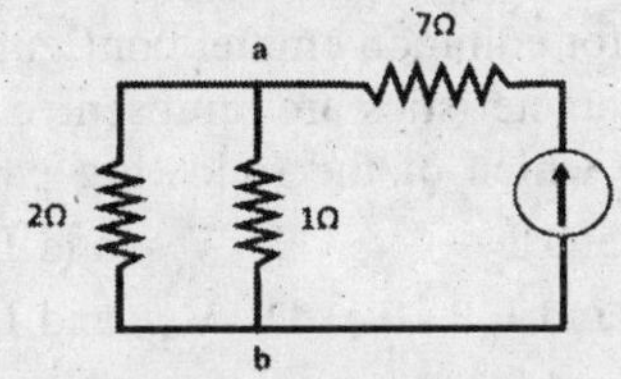

A. 1 A from *a* to *b* B. 10 A from *b* to *a*

C. 12 A from *a* to *b* D. 25 A from *b* to *a*

182. The split-phase induction motor is NOT used for drives that require more than ________.

A. 1000 kW B. 100 kW

C. 10 kW D. 1 kW

183. For an AC circuit, the voltage and the current are given as V = (100 + j10) V and I = (20 – j10) A, respectively. The active power of the circuit is:

A. P = 1800 W B. P = 1000 W

C. P = 1900 W D. P = 1500 W

184. Which of the following is a ferromagnetic material?

A. Water B. Oxygen

C. Nickel D. Gold

185. In the circuit shown below, the value of the current I is ________.

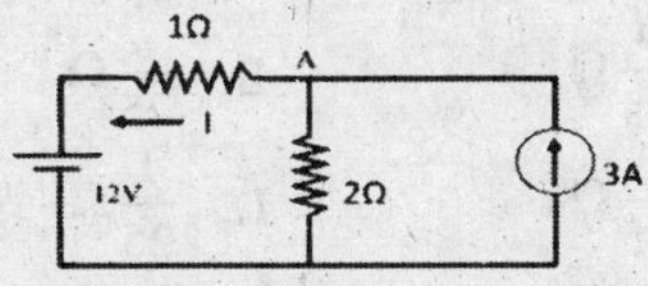

A. –2 A B. 4 A

C. 0 A D. 2 A

186. The change in current through a junction diode is 1.5 mA when the forward bias voltage is changed by 0.6 V. The dynamic resistance is ________.

A. 600 Ω B. 500 Ω

C. 400 Ω D. 300 Ω

187. A substation is a facility that transmits and distributes electricity. It serves as an intermediary between electricity plants and end users. Which of the following statements about substations is INCORRECT?

A. Rotary converters are also used in railway substations.

B. Domestic consumers may also connect directly to the main transmission network.

C. All of the options

D. At the point of inter-connection between two distinct transmission voltages, transformers may be installed in a substation.

188. In an electrical network, if the quantity of a source is controlled by another voltage or current present in the circuit, such a source is called ______.

A. ideal source B. dependent source

C. non-ideal source D. independent source

189. What is the main reason of placing field winding on the stationary rotor?

A. Insulation of high voltage is made easy on stator than on rotor.

B. Stator is associated with more power.

C. Stator is associated with more current.

D. Field circuit possesses less power.

190. The electrical pressure measured between any two points in an electrical circuit is called ______.

A. work done B. energy

C. voltage D. resistivity

180. D **181.** C **182.** D **183.** C **184.** C **185.** A **186.** C **187.** B **188.** B **189.** A **190.** C

191. In a capacitor-start capacitor-run induction motor, under standstill condition forward and backward voltages are ________.
A. infinite
B. unequal in magnitude
C. zero
D. equal in magnitude

192. Which of the following statements is/are correct regarding black liquor?
(*a*) It retains more than 50% of the biomass energy of wood.
(*b*) It is a non-toxic substance produced when wood is burned into paper.
(*a*) Tall oil is an important by-product separated from black liquor by skimming.
A. (*b*) and (*c*) B. (*a*) and (*c*)
C. Only (*c*) D. (*a*) and (*b*)

193. Which of the following statements is FALSE in association with synchronous motor applications?
A. Synchronous motor is used in constant load drive application.
B. Voltage regulation can be done using synchronous motor.
C. Synchronous motor is expensive in low power output application.
D. Synchronous motor is highly suitable for low power output below 40 kW in medium speed range.

194. Which of the following statements is NOT correct about the significance of stationary armature alternator?
A. The rotating field type alternator has a smaller size than the rotating armature type.
B. The armature windings of the rotating field alternator are not subjected to centrifugal forces.
C. The output current can be easily taken from rotor winding.
D. The armature windings can be braced better mechanically against the high electromagnetic force.

195. The actual efficiency of a solar power plant is lower than its theoretical efficiency. Which of the following can be reasons for this?
I. Recombination of electrons and holes
II. Internal resistance of the cell
A. Neither I nor II B. Only I
C. Both I and II D. Only II

196. Find the electrical energy consumed in 10 Ω resistance when 100 mA current flows for 2 minutes.
A. 100 J B. 1200 J
C. 12 J D. 120 J

197. In BJT, for common emitter configuration, the input characteristics are represented by a plot between which of the following parameters?
A. V_{EE} and I_B B. V_{CE} and I_C
C. V_{BE} and I_B D. V_{BE} and I_E

198. A rectifier type instrument uses a bridge rectifier and has its scale calibrated in terms of rms value of a sine wave. It indicates a voltage of 3.33 V when measuring a voltage of a triangular wave shape. Calculate the peak value of the applied voltage?
A. 6.66 Volts B. 9 Volts
C. 6 Volts D. 9.99 Volts

199. The phasing out test on a three-phase transformer is carried out to find ________.
A. primary winding belonging to the same phase
B. primary and secondary windings belonging to a different phase
C. primary and secondary windings belonging to the same phase
D. secondary winding belonging to a different phase

200. The admittance of an electric circuit is represented by Y = (3 + j4). What is the value of resistance in this circuit?
A. $\frac{4}{25}\Omega$ B. $\frac{2}{25}\Omega$
C. $\frac{3}{25}\Omega$ D. $\frac{1}{25}\Omega$

191. D	192. B	193. D	194. C	195. C	196. C	197. C	198. C	199. C	200. C

EXPLANATORY ANSWERS

3. (C): Position of letter in reverse letter series:
Z = A, Y = B, X = C, U = F, O = L, J = Q, E = V, A = Z

∴ O U 22 → L P 11 (22 ×½ = 11) and T N 12 → G M 6 (12 ×½ = 6)

Similarly, Z K 44 → A P 22 (44 ×½ = 22)

Therefore, 'ZK44 is related to 'AP22' using the same logic.

5. (A): In reverse letter series:
ZYXW ..... CBA
Z = 1, Y = 2, X = 3, W = 4, ... B = 25, A = 26
Now, LIGHTS = 93
⇒ (15 + 18 + 20 + 19 + 7 + 8) + Number of letters
= 87 + 6 = 93
and BATTER = 102
⇒ (25 + 26 + 7 + 7 + 22 + 9) + 6
= 96 + 6 = 102
Similarly,
BRING = (25 + 9 + 18 + 13 + 20) + 5
= 85 + 5 = 90
⇒ BRING = 90.

7. (A): In reverse letter series,
A = 26, B = 25, E = 22, J = 17, O = 12, T = 7, Z = 1
∴ PETS = 78
⇒ 11 + 22 + 7 + 8 = 48
and FARM = 70
⇒ 21 + 26 + 9 + 14 = 70
Similarly, DAIRY = 23 + 26 + 18 + 9 + 2
= 78
Therefore, 'DAIRY" will be coded as 78.

8. (A):

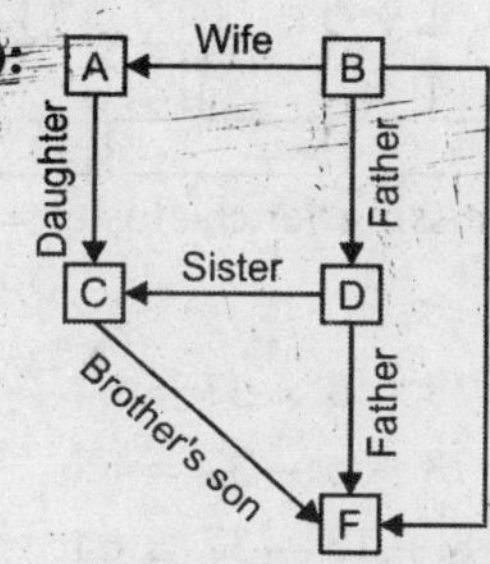

Here, F is the Brother's son of C.

9. (C): –, –, ÷, =, ×, +

∴ 30 [–] 13 [–] 21 [÷] 3 [=] 2 [×] 4 [+] 2
⇒ 30 – 13 – 21 ÷ 3 = 2 × 4 + 2
⇒ 30 – 13 – 7 = 8 + 2
⇒ 30 – 20 = 10
⇒ 10 = 10
∴ Option (C) is the correct combination.

10. (A): Given, B R A N C H → (+2, +3, +2, +3, +2, +3) → D U C Q E K

and C A R B O N → (+2, +3, +2, +3, +2, +3) → E D T E Q Q

Similarly, D R I V E N → (+2, +3, +2, +3, +2, +3) → F U K Y G Q

∴ DRIVEN will be coded as FUKYGQ.

11. (C): INRKNUNK
∴ R I N K U, R I N K U, R I N K U, R I N K U
Section RINKU repeated in the series
∴ Option (C) is correct combination.

12. (A):

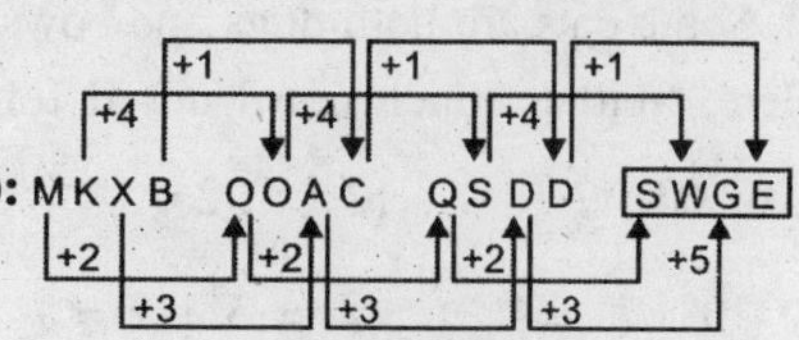

Here, ? = the missing letter-cluster = SWGE.

13. (A):

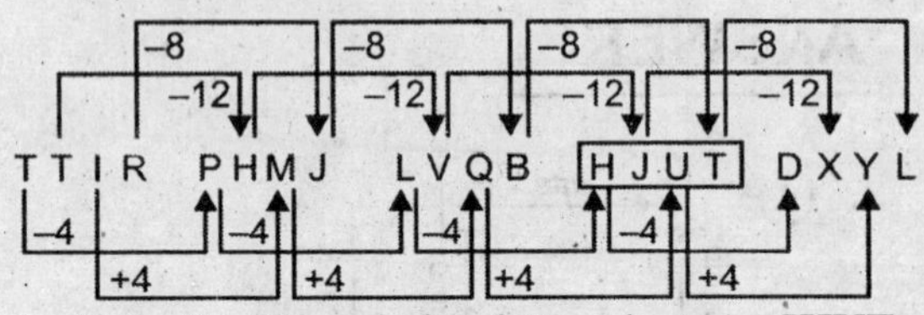

Here, ? = the missing letter-cluster = HJUT.

14. (C): – and ×

$\therefore \quad 11 - 8 + 78 \div 6 \times 37 = 64$

$\Rightarrow \quad 11 \times 8 + 78 \div 6 - 37 = 64$

$\Rightarrow \quad 11 \times 8 + 13 - 37 = 64$

$\Rightarrow \quad 88 + 13 - 37 = 64$

$\Rightarrow \quad 101 - 37 = 64$

$\Rightarrow \quad 64 = 64.$

17. (D): $3 : 20 \Rightarrow (3 + 2) \times 4 = 20$

$7 : ? \Rightarrow (7 + 4) \times 4 = 44$

$11 : 68 \Rightarrow (11 + 6) \times 4 = 68$

$\therefore$ 3 : 20 : : 7 : $\boxed{44}$: : 11 : 68.

20. (B): DGAJGLGJ

A D G J L, A D G J L, A D G J L, A D G J L

Section ADGJL is repeated in the series.

$\therefore$ Option (B) is correct combination.

22. (B): Given word: According to English dictionary,

Obedience → Obey → Object → Obligation → Obligatory.

23. (D): From given statement:

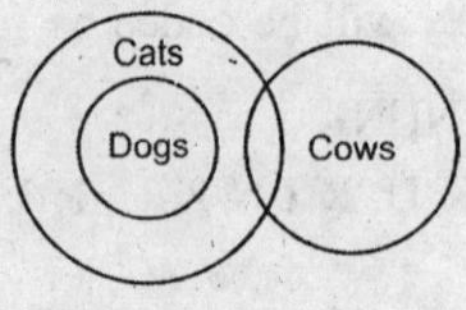

Conclusions:

I. Some dogs are cows. (False)

II. Some cats are both dogs and cows. (False)

Here, Neither conclusion I nor II follows.

24. (D): 10 : 7 : : ? : 12 : : 32 : 18

$\because 10 : 7 \Rightarrow \frac{10}{2} + 2 = 5 + 2 = 7$

$? : 12 \Rightarrow \frac{x}{2} + 2 = 12$

$\Rightarrow x = 20 \Rightarrow ? = 20$

$32 : 18 \Rightarrow \frac{32}{2} + 2 = 18 = 16 + 2 = 18$

Therefore, 10 : 7 : : $\boxed{20}$: 12 : : 32 : 18.

25. (D): GOLBG

$\therefore$ L G M B O, L G M B O, L G M B O

Section LGMBO is repeated in the series.

Here, option (D) complete the letter series.

26. (D): Arranging the given words in a logical and meaningful order:

Hexadecagon → Dodecagon → Heptagon → Pentagon → Quadrilateral.

27. (C):

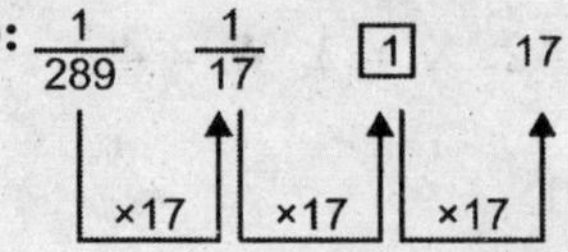

Here, ? = the missing number = 1.

28. (D): Given, A & B # C & D @ E % F + G

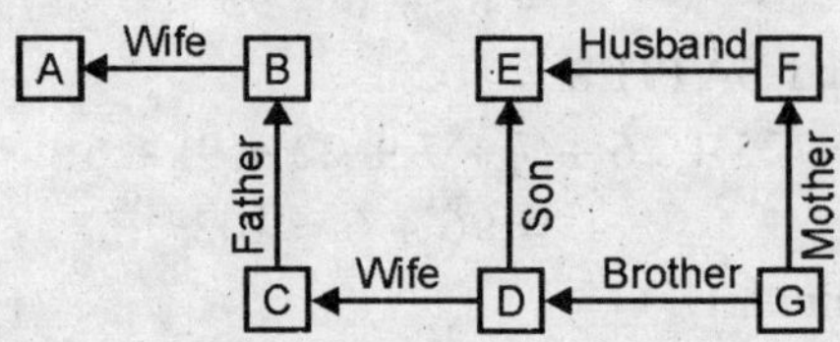

Here, C is the Brother's wife of G.

29. (C): 6 friends are sitting in a circle and facing in the centre.

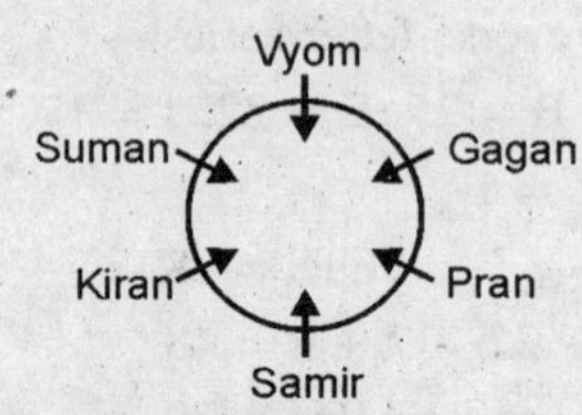

Here, Pran sits third to the right of Suman.

30. (D): Given, set

(33, 6, 54) $\Rightarrow (33 - 6) \times 2 = 27 \times 2 = 54$

(22, 7, 30) $\Rightarrow (22 - 7) \times 2 = 15 \times 2 = 30$

(D) (26, 8, 36) $\Rightarrow$ (26 – 8) × 2 = 18 × 2 = 36

Hence, option (D) are related in the same way as are the number of the given sets.

31. **(B):** Given words: According to English dictionary,

Whisker → Whisper → Whistle → Wishful → Wistful → Wither.

32. **(B):** Here, A = House = Starting point

E = Pole

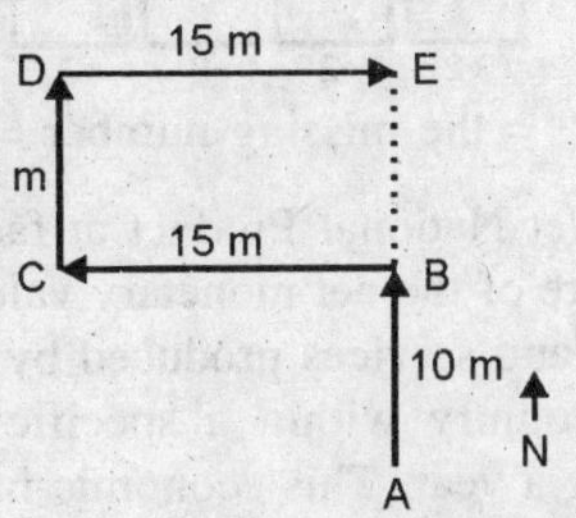

$$AB = 10 \text{ m}$$

$$BC = DE = 15 \text{ m}$$

$$\therefore \quad CD = EB = 7 \text{ m}$$

$$\text{and } EA = EB + BA$$

$$= 7 + 10$$

$$= 17 \text{ m}$$

Hence, A (House) is 17 m, South from the pole.

33. **(A):** 17 : 374 : : 14 : ? : : 13 : 234

17 : 374 $\Rightarrow$ 17 × (17 + 5) = 17 × 22 = 374

14 : ? $\Rightarrow$ 14 × (14 + 5) = 14 × 19 = $\boxed{266}$

13 : 234 $\Rightarrow$ 13 × (13 + 5) = 13 × 18 = 234

$\therefore$ 17 : 374 : : 14 : $\boxed{266}$: : 13 : 234.

34. **(D):** From, given two dimensions of the same dice taking clockwise from common digit 6

$$\therefore \begin{matrix} 6 & 5 & 4 \\ 6 & 2 & 3 \end{matrix} \Rightarrow \boxed{\begin{matrix} 6 \\ 6 \end{matrix}} \boxed{\begin{matrix} 5 \\ 2 \end{matrix}} \boxed{\begin{matrix} 4 \\ 3 \end{matrix}}$$

$$\Rightarrow \quad 6 \leftrightarrow 1$$

$$5 \leftrightarrow 2$$

$$4 \leftrightarrow 3$$

Here, 4 is opposite to the face having digit 3.

35. **(A):**

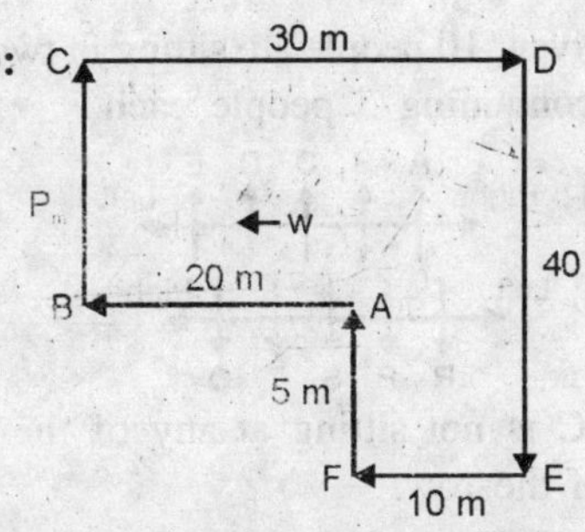

Here, A = Starting point = House and final point = F

AB = 20 m, BC = P_m, CD = 30 m, DE = 40 m, EF = 10 m, AF = 5 m

$$\because \quad EF + AB = CD = 30 \text{ m}$$

$$\therefore \quad FA + BC = DE = 40 \text{ m}$$

$$\Rightarrow \quad FA + BC = 40$$

$$\Rightarrow \quad 5 + P = 40$$

$$\Rightarrow \quad P = 40 - 5$$

$$\Rightarrow \quad P = 35 \text{ m.}$$

36. **(C):** Given, A = +, B = ×, C = – and D = ÷

$\therefore$ 89 C 8 A (18 B 2) D 4

= 89 – 8 + (18 × 2) ÷ 4

= 89 – 8 + 36 ÷ 4

= 89 – 8 + 9

= 98 – 8 = 90.

37. **(A):**

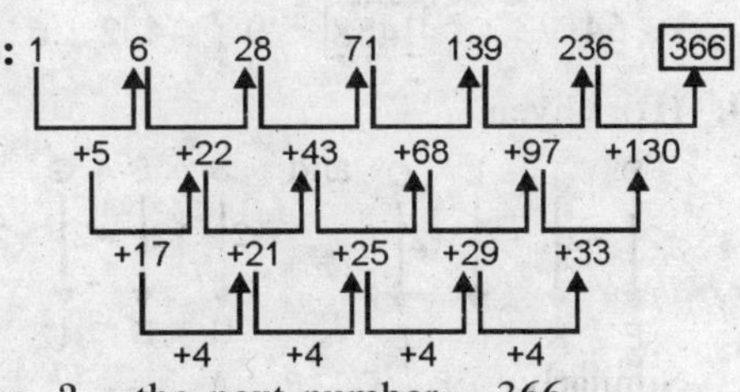

Here, ? = the next number = 366.

38. **(B):** Given, + = –, – = ×, × = ÷, ÷ = +

$\therefore$ 41 ÷ 18 – 7 + 322 × 23

= 41 + 18 × 7 – 322 ÷ 23

$= 41 + 18 \times 7 - 322 \times \dfrac{1}{23}$

= 41 + 18 × 7 – 14

= 41 + 126 – 14

= 167 – 14 = 153.

39. (A): Given, 10 people are sitting in two parallel rows containing 5 people each

Row–1:
Row–2:

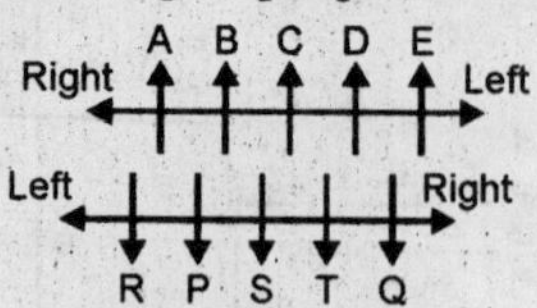

Here, C is not sitting at any of the extreme ends of the row.

41. (C): From given statements:

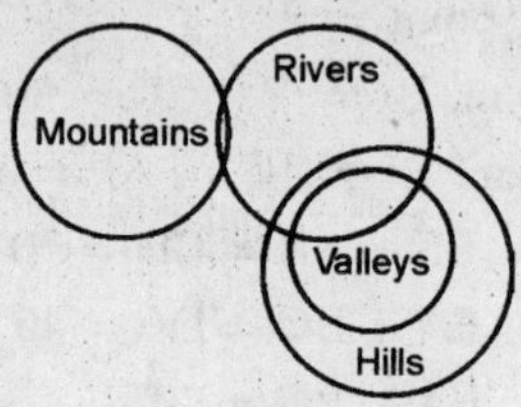

Conclusion:

I. Few mountains are valleys. (False)

II. Some hills are mountains. (False)

III. Some rivers are hills. (True)

Here, Only conclusion III follows.

42. (B): 54 : 3 : : ? : 9 : : 432 : 6

Now, 54 : 3 ⇒ $3^2 \times 3 \times 2 = 54$

? : 9 ⇒ $9^2 \times 9 \times 2 = 81 \times 18 = \boxed{1458}$

432 : 6 ⇒ $6^2 \times 6 \times 2 = 36 \times 12 = 432$

∴ 54 : 3 : : $\boxed{1458}$: 9 : : 432 : 6

44. (D): Given,

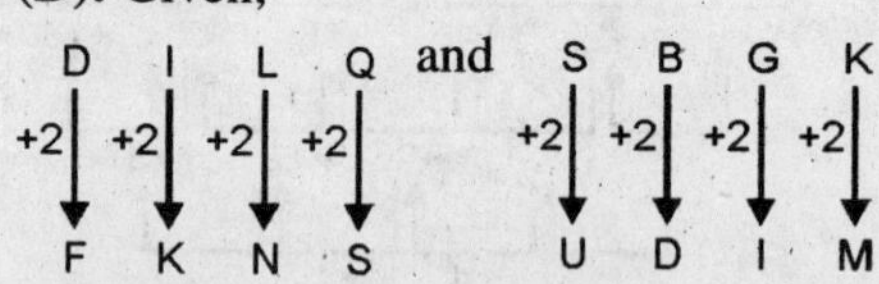

Similarly,

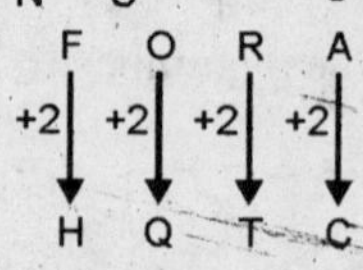

∴ 'FORA' will be written as HQTC in that language.

46. (A): Given, Each of 7 friends has a different height

Krishi > – > Pari > Veer

Priya > Mohi > Misha > Minshu

⇒ Priya > Mohi > Misha > Krishi > Minshu > Pari > Veer

Here, Priya is tallest among them.

47. (A): Arranging the given words in a logical and meaningful order.

Tree → Wood → Plank → Shelf → Cupboard.

50. (B):

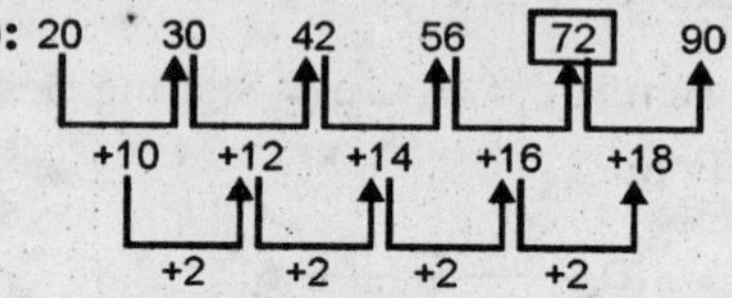

Here, ? = the missing number = 72.

51. (D): Net National Product at factor cost is a measure of the net monetary value of all final goods and services produced by the residents of a country within a specific time frame, usually a year. This economic indicator takes into account depreciation, providing a net figure. The term "at factor cost" means that it considers the costs incurred in the production process, including wages, rent, interest, and profits, while excluding indirect taxes and incorporating subsidies. In essence, it represents the net contribution of the country's residents to the economy, factoring in only the actual production costs without the influence of indirect taxes but considering subsidies in the overall calculation.

52. (C): The 86th Constitutional Amendment Act of 2002 introduced the 11th Fundamental Duty to the Constitution of India. This amendment aimed to reinforce the sense of responsibility and commitment among citizens towards the preservation of India's rich heritage and environment. The newly added duty states that every citizen should value and preserve the heritage of the nation, including its culture, traditions, and natural resources. The inclusion of this duty reflects the constitutional intent to promote a holistic understanding of citizenship that goes beyond individual rights, emphasizing the importance of contributing to the collective well-being and cultural heritage of the nation.

53. (D): Isobutane is not an alicyclic compound; instead, it belongs to the category of alkanes. Isobutane is a branched, saturated hydrocarbon with the molecular formula C_4H_{10}. It is specifically an isomer of butane, characterized by a branched structure in which the carbon atoms are arranged in a chain with one methyl (CH_3) group attached to the second carbon atom. Unlike alicyclic compounds, which form closed-ring structures, isobutane has an open-chain configuration. As an alkane, isobutane contains only single bonds between carbon atoms and is commonly used as a fuel and refrigerant due to its stable and inert nature.

54. (B): Anurag Thakur, India's Union Minister for Youth Affairs and Sports, launched the White Paper on the five themes of Youth 20 (Y20) in February 2023 during the Y20 Inception Meeting in Guwahati. This paper outlined key areas for youth engagement with the G20, including future of work, climate change, peace building, democracy, and health. His involvement highlights the importance placed on youth voices in shaping global dialogue on these crucial issues.

55. (C): Kathakali is a traditional dance form originating from the southern Indian state of Kerala. In Kathakali, the dancers' faces are elaborately made up to resemble painted masks, often portraying characters from mythology or ancient stories. The costume is opulent and distinctive, featuring a full skirt, a heavy jacket, numerous garlands, and necklaces, creating a visually striking and vibrant ensemble. The headdress worn by Kathakali dancers is particularly noteworthy, often towering and elaborate, adding to the grandeur of the performance. This dance form is characterized by its expressive and intricate hand and facial gestures, intricate footwork, and the elaborate use of costumes and makeup, making it a captivating and culturally rich art form.

56. (B): The Asteraceae family, commonly known as the composite or sunflower family, is recognized for its distinctive inflorescence structure called a capitulum or flower head. This inflorescence arrangement is characterized by a highly compressed system where numerous tiny individual flowers are densely packed onto a common receptacle. What sets Asteraceae apart is the presence of unbranched bracts surrounding the receptacle, creating the appearance of a single flower. These bracts are often mistaken for petals and contribute to the overall structure of what seems like a single, large flower. The family includes a vast array of plants with diverse forms and sizes, ranging from the iconic sunflowers and daisies to asters and chrysanthemums, all sharing this distinctive floral arrangement.

57. (A): Adhering to good netiquette in online discussions involves practices that foster positive and constructive communication. Reading the discussion thread before posting is an essential aspect of this etiquette as it ensures that participants are well-informed about the ongoing conversation, preventing the repetition of points already addressed. This not only demonstrates respect for the contributions of others but also contributes to a more coherent and valuable discussion. By staying informed and avoiding redundancy, participants can collectively enhance the quality of the conversation, creating a more engaging and respectful online environment.

58. (A): Graphite is an allotrope of carbon that exhibits a unique structure, forming layers of hexagonally arranged carbon atoms. Within each layer, the carbon atoms are bonded in a flat, two-dimensional lattice, and the layers themselves are held together by relatively weak van der Waals forces. This arrangement imparts distinct properties to graphite, making it smooth and slippery. The weak forces between the layers allow them to slide past each other easily, giving graphite its lubricating and slippery characteristics. Additionally, the hexagonal lattice structure provides graphite with excellent conductivity, making it a versatile material widely used as a lubricant, in pencils, and in various industrial applications.

59. **(A):** Korsakoff syndrome, a chronic memory disorder that damages the brain, is primarily associated with a deficiency of vitamin B1, also known as thiamine. Thiamine plays a crucial role in energy metabolism, particularly in the conversion of glucose into energy within the brain. Inadequate thiamine levels, often linked to prolonged alcohol abuse or malnutrition, can lead to neurological complications. Korsakoff syndrome is characterized by severe memory impairment, confabulation (the production of fabricated, distorted memories), and difficulty learning new information. The condition is commonly observed in individuals with alcohol use disorder, where poor dietary intake and impaired thiamine absorption contribute to the neurological damage underlying Korsakoff syndrome. Thiamine supplementation is a key component in the treatment and prevention of this disorder.

60. **(A):** The Bhitari Pillar inscription is attributed to the Gupta ruler Skandagupta. This inscription provides historical insights into the military achievements and battles of Skandagupta, particularly highlighting his confrontation with the Pushyamitras. The Pushyamitras were a tribal group challenging the authority of the Gupta Empire. Skandagupta's successful military campaign against the Pushyamitras is documented in this inscription, shedding light on the strategic and martial prowess of the Gupta ruler. The Bhitari Pillar inscription contributes valuable information to our understanding of the political and military landscape during the Gupta period in ancient Indian history.

61. **(D):** In cricket, a wide is called by the umpire when the bowler delivers the ball, and it is deemed to be too wide for the batsman to play a shot at it. This can occur if the ball is delivered too far to the off side or leg side of the batsman. When a wide is called, the batting team is awarded an extra run, and the delivery is bowled again. The primary rationale behind awarding an extra run is to penalize the bowler for delivering a ball that is considered unfair or not within the acceptable playing limits. The re-bowling of the delivery provides the batsman with another opportunity to score, ensuring fairness in the game. This rule is designed to maintain a balance between the batsman and the bowler and contributes to the overall integrity of the cricket match.

62. **(C):** Bihar tops the list with a staggering 51.91% of its population trapped in multidimensional poverty, according to the NITI Aayog's Multidimensional Poverty Index (MPI) based on NFHS-4 data. This means over half of Bihar's residents face deprivations in several crucial areas like education, health, and living standards. Imagine a state where basic necessities like clean water, proper sanitation, and nutritious food are out of reach for over half the population. The situation demands urgent attention and a multi-pronged strategy to uplift these communities from the clutches of poverty.

63. **(B):** Ecotones refer to transitional zones or boundaries where distinct ecological communities, ecosystems, or biotic regions meet and interact. These areas exhibit a blend of characteristics from the adjoining ecosystems, creating a unique and often diverse environment. Ecotones can result from various factors, including changes in soil composition, climate, or topography. They play a crucial role in promoting biodiversity by providing habitats for species adapted to both adjacent ecosystems. The dynamics within ecotones are influenced by the interplay of species from different ecological niches, making them ecologically significant zones where the diversity of life is rich and complex. Understanding ecotones is essential for comprehending the broader ecological processes that shape landscapes and influence the distribution of species.

64. (A): E.V. Ramasamy Naicker, popularly known as Periyar, was a social reformer and politician who founded the Self-Respect Movement in South India during the early 20th century. The Self-Respect Movement, initiated in the Madras Presidency (now Tamil Nadu) in the 1920s, aimed to uplift and empower marginalized communities, particularly the non-Brahmin Dravidian population. Periyar advocated for social justice, equality, and the eradication of caste-based discrimination. The movement emphasized the importance of self-respect for individuals and communities, challenging societal norms that perpetuated inequality. Periyar's efforts laid the groundwork for the Dravidian movement and influenced the political landscape in the region, leading to the formation of the Dravida Munnetra Kazhagam (DMK) and contributing to the socio-political transformation of Tamil Nadu.

65. (C): The solid form of water, which is ice, is prominently found in Polar Regions. Regions near the North Pole (Arctic) and South Pole (Antarctic) experience frigid temperatures, often well below the freezing point of water. In these extreme cold conditions, water undergoes a phase transition from liquid to solid, forming vast expanses of ice sheets, glaciers, and sea ice. The Polar Regions are characterized by a unique landscape shaped by frozen water, with icebergs, ice shelves, and frozen tundras defining these environments. The presence of ice in the Polar Regions has significant implications for global climate systems, sea levels, and the ecology of these areas.

66. (C): In the context of temple architecture in South India, the term "Gopuram" refers to the entrance gateway prominently positioned at the front wall of a Hindu temple. Gopurams are characterized by their towering and ornate structures, adorned with intricate carvings, sculptures, and vibrant paintings that depict religious narratives and deities. Serving as both a symbolic and functional element, the Gopuram signifies the transition from the secular to the sacred space, guiding devotees into the temple premises. The elaborate and often tiered design of Gopurams showcases the rich artistic and architectural traditions prevalent in South Indian temples, and their grandeur adds to the spiritual and cultural significance of the temple complex.

67. (A): The general formula R-X corresponds to alkyl halides in organic chemistry, where alkane hydrogens (represented by R) are replaced by halogen atoms from Group 17 elements (X). Alkyl halides are a class of organic compounds that include substances like alkyl fluorides, alkyl chlorides, alkyl bromides, and alkyl iodides. The introduction of halogen atoms imparts distinct chemical properties to these compounds, affecting factors such as reactivity and polarity. Alkyl halides find applications in various chemical processes and reactions, and their properties are crucial in organic synthesis and medicinal chemistry. The nomenclature and classification of alkyl halides are based on the type of halogen attached and the specific carbon atoms in the alkyl chain where the substitution occurs.

68. (A): In December 2022, Dr. Rishi Rajpopat, a 27-year-old PhD candidate at Cambridge University, cracked the Panini code. The Panini code is a 2,500-year-old Sanskrit grammar problem that has puzzled scholars since the 5th century BC. The Panini code is a prescriptive and generative grammar with algebraic rules that govern all aspects of

Sanskrit. It has 3,959 sutras (aphoristic threads) in 8 chapters, with each chapter subdivided into four sections. Rajpopat's breakthrough came when he decoded a rule taught by Panini, known as the father of linguistics. His thesis, titled "In Panini, We Trust: Discovering the Algorithm for Rule Conflict Resolution in the Astadhyayi", encapsulates his findings. Rajpopat rejected the traditional interpretation of the metarule. Instead, he argued that Panini wanted us to choose the rule applicable to the right side of a word.

69. **(C):** The Prime Minister's Employment Generation Programme (PMEGP) was initiated by the Ministry of Micro, Small and Medium Enterprises (MSME) of the Government of India during the fiscal year 2008-09. This program aims to promote entrepreneurship and generate employment opportunities in the micro and small business sector. PMEGP provides financial assistance for setting up new projects or expanding existing ones, encouraging the establishment of micro-enterprises across various sectors. By facilitating access to credit, the program plays a crucial role in fostering entrepreneurship, particularly in rural and economically weaker sections of society. PMEGP reflects the government's commitment to supporting small and medium enterprises, contributing to economic development and job creation.

70. **(C):** Ustad Amjad Ali Khan, the distinguished Indian classical musician, was born in 1945 in Gwalior, Madhya Pradesh. He hails from a family with a rich musical lineage, being the sixth generation in a line of illustrious sarod players. Amjad Ali Khan is celebrated for his mastery of the sarod, a classical string instrument, and has made significant contributions to the world of Indian classical music. His style is marked by a combination of tradition and innovation, and he has earned numerous accolades and awards for his outstanding contributions to the cultural heritage of India. Ustad Amjad Ali Khan's performances and compositions have garnered international acclaim, and he continues to be a prominent figure in the realm of classical music.

71. **(A):** At maturity, sclerenchyma cells play a vital role in providing structural support to plants. These cells are characterized by heavily thickened and lignified cell walls, which contribute to their non-conductive nature. The thickening is primarily composed of cellulose, making up a significant portion (60%-80%) of the cell wall composition. Sclerenchyma cells are often found in mature plant tissues, such as the stems, branches, and seed coats, where their rigid structure aids in providing mechanical support and protection. Due to the presence of lignin, these cells are dead at maturity but retain their strength, contributing to the overall structural integrity of plant tissues.

72. **(D):** In 1865, the German chemist Friedrich August Kekulé proposed the ring structure for benzene, a breakthrough that revolutionized the understanding of aromatic compounds. Prior to Kekulé's proposal, the structure of benzene was a subject of speculation. Kekulé's insight came to him in a dream of a snake biting its own tail, inspiring him to suggest that benzene consists of a hexagonal ring of six carbon atoms with alternating single and double bonds. This representation resolved the long standing mystery of benzene's unique stability and explained its characteristic aromatic properties. Kekulé's ring structure for benzene laid the foundation for the modern understanding of aromatic compounds and contributed significantly to the development of organic chemistry.

73. **(B):** Al-Biruni, the renowned Persian scholar and polymath, wrote the famous book "Kitab ul Hind" in the Arabic language during the 11th century. "Kitab ul Hind," meaning the

Book of India, is a comprehensive work that reflects Al-Biruni's extensive studies and observations on the Indian subcontinent's culture, geography, astronomy, and mathematics. Al-Biruni's linguistic versatility allowed him to compose his influential works in various languages, but "Kitab ul Hind" stands out as a valuable historical and cultural record of India during that period. In this extensive treatise, Al-Biruni explored the traditions, scientific achievements, and societal nuances of the Indian subcontinent, making enduring contributions to the fields of history, anthropology, and the study of cultures.

74. **(C):** Rhino viruses are a predominant cause of the common cold, a widespread respiratory infection characterized by symptoms such as a runny or stuffy nose, sneezing, coughing, and a sore throat. These viruses, belonging to the Picornaviridae family, specifically the Enterovirus genus, are highly contagious and can be transmitted through respiratory droplets when an infected person coughs or sneezes. Rhino viruses account for a significant proportion of cold infections, and due to their genetic diversity, multiple strains contribute to the variability in symptoms experienced by individuals. Although the common cold is generally a mild and self-limiting illness, the prevalence and ease of transmission make it a frequent occurrence, particularly in colder months, leading to its designation as one of the most prevalent infectious diseases in humans.

75. **(B):** Hawaiian volcanoes, such as those found on the Big Island of Hawaii, are classic examples of shield volcanoes characterized by their gently sloping profiles. These volcanoes are predominantly composed of basaltic lava, which is fluid and low in viscosity when erupted. The term "shield" reflects the broad, shield-like shape of these volcanoes, formed by the accumulation of successive, thin layers of lava flows. Due to the low viscosity of basaltic lava, eruptions are typically non-explosive, allowing the lava to travel long distances and create wide, gentle slopes. The Hawaiian volcanoes, including notable examples like Kilauea and Mauna Loa, are known for their effusive eruptions and are in stark contrast to the more explosive stratovolcanoes, such as Mount St. Helens, which are composed of more viscous lava types like andesite.

76. **(D):** According to Köppen's Scheme of climate division of India, the matching of climates with their respective regions is as follows:

1. **Cold humid winter with short summer: Arunachal Pradesh:** According to Koeppen's climatic classification, Arunachal Pradesh has a cold, humid winter with a short summer. This climate type is known as Dfc. In Arunachal Pradesh, the average winter temperature is between 15° and 21°C, while the average temperature during the monsoon season is between 22° and 30°C. The state experiences heavy rainfall from May to September. Due to its high altitude, Arunachal Pradesh gets cold in the winter. In the summer, from April to June, the temperature becomes bearable.
2. **Hot desert: Extreme Western Rajasthan:** The western part of Rajasthan is a desert because of high summer temperatures and the Aravallis' parallel path to the Arabian Sea Branch of the southwest monsoons. The Thar Desert is an arid region of rolling sand hills in the Indian subcontinent. It is located partly in Rajasthan state, northwestern India, and partly in Punjab. The region has an arid-hot desert climate with very scanty rainfall. During summers, the temperature in Rajasthan is very high and it ranges somewhere between 32 degree Celsius and 46 degree Celsius. The place has an average temperature of 38 degree Celsius. Jaisalmer is a place located

in Rajasthan that is known to be the driest place in India. It is located at the heart of the Thar Desert.

3. **Monsoon with dry summer: Coromandel Coast of Tamil Nadu:** The Coromandel Coast of Tamil Nadu has a monsoon climate with a dry summer, according to Koeppen's classification. The Coromandel Coast is also known as the Eastern Ghats and includes coastal Tamil Nadu and parts of Andhra Pradesh, Kerala, and Karnataka. The Coromandel Coast receives rainfall during the winter due to the north-east monsoons. During the summer, the Indian coastline remains dry.

77. **(C):** The Finance Bill 2023 aims to amend Section 142 of the Income Tax Act relating to inquiry before assessment. The proposed amendment to Sub-section (2A) will empower Assessing Officers to request a valuation of assesses inventory by a cost accountant. Finance Bill 2023 introduces a new amendment to Section 142(2A) of the Income Tax Act, empowering Assessing Officers to require a cost audit for inventory valuation in certain cases. This applies specifically to situations involving appeals against tax assessments. The cost audit will be performed by a cost accountant, who is nominated by the Principal Chief Commissioner or Chief Commissioner of Income Tax. The cost accountant conducting the audit is appointed by the tax authorities, ensuring impartiality and objectivity. The cost audit report plays a crucial role in guiding the final tax assessment by the Assessing Officer.

78. **(D):** Thunderstorms in Assam during the month of 'Baisakhi' are locally known as Bardoisila. These storms are a meteorological phenomenon unique to the region, particularly occurring during the pre-monsoon season around the month of Baisakhi, which is part of the Assamese calendar. Bardoisila is characterized by intense thunder, lightning, and heavy rainfall. The storms often bring relief from the rising temperatures, marking the onset of the monsoon season. The term "Bardoisila" is a regional reference, reflecting the local significance and impact of these storms in the cultural and climatic context of Assam.

79. **(A):** NABARD, established in 1982, emerged as a key financial institution in India with the primary objective of fostering rural development, particularly in the agriculture sector. At its inception, NABARD was endowed with an initial capital of ₹ 100 crore. The institution plays a crucial role in providing financial support, credit facilities, and developmental assistance to various initiatives aimed at uplifting rural economies. NABARD channels funds into agriculture and allied activities, rural infrastructure, and agri-business, contributing significantly to the economic empowerment of rural communities across the country. Over the years, NABARD has become a cornerstone in the implementation of policies and programs directed at rural development, ensuring financial inclusion and sustainability in the agricultural and rural sectors.

80. **(D):** In email communication, the BCC (Blind Carbon Copy) field is employed when you want to send a copy of the email to someone else without the knowledge of the original recipients. When you use the BCC field, the email addresses entered in this field remain hidden from the primary recipients, ensuring that they are unaware of who else received a copy. This is particularly useful for maintaining privacy and discretion, preventing unintended disclosure of email addresses and respecting the confidentiality of certain communications. BCC is commonly utilized in professional and personal email correspondence when it is necessary to include additional recipients without revealing their identities to others in the email chain.

81. (C): Kavaratti Island is actually one of the main islands of the Lakshadweep archipelago and has not served as a former name for the entire region. The former name of the Lakshadweep group of islands collectively was Laccadive Islands. The islands underwent a name change to Lakshadweep, and this transition reflected a more accurate representation of the various islands that make up the archipelago, including Laccadive, Amindivi, and Minicoy. Kavaratti, on the other hand, is one of the inhabited islands within the Lakshadweep group, known for its administrative and cultural significance in the union territory.

82. (C): The second five-year plan in India, initiated in 1956, marked a significant shift in economic policy by introducing the concept of the public sector and state-run enterprises. This approach was influenced by the Russian model of industrialization, emphasizing a socialist pattern of development. The plan aimed at achieving self-sufficiency in key sectors through the establishment of public sector units. The state-led industrialization, inspired by the Soviet Union's centralized economic planning, sought to reduce dependence on the private sector and promote strategic government intervention in key industries. The Russian model emphasized state ownership and control as a means to achieve rapid industrial growth and economic development, shaping the trajectory of India's economic policies during this period.

83. (D): Wheat is a prime example of a rabi crop. Rabi crops are those sown in the winter season and harvested in the spring. Wheat cultivation typically begins in the months of October to December and reaches maturity for harvest in March to April. This crop is well-suited to the cooler temperatures of the winter season, requiring a period of low temperature for proper growth and development. Wheat is a major staple food in many parts of the world, and its cultivation during the rabi season contributes significantly to agricultural productivity and food security.

84. (C): The idea of 'Fundamental Rights' in the Indian Constitution was drawn from the Constitution of the United States. The framers of the Indian Constitution, led by Dr. B.R. Ambedkar and the Constituent Assembly, were inspired by the American Bill of Rights and the principles of individual liberties enshrined in the U.S. Constitution. The inclusion of Fundamental Rights in the Indian Constitution, as articulated in Part III, reflects a commitment to safeguarding and ensuring certain essential rights and freedoms for the citizens of India. These rights encompass a range of civil, political, and social liberties, providing a constitutional guarantee against arbitrary state actions and upholding the principles of justice, equality, and dignity for all citizens. The influence of the U.S. Constitution on this aspect of the Indian Constitution underscores the global impact of constitutional ideas and the quest for protecting the inherent rights of individuals.

85. (B): In the game of chess, the term "Bishop" refers to one of the pieces positioned on the board. Each player begins the game with two bishops, and they are distinguished by their ability to move diagonally across the chess-board. The bishop's movement is unrestricted by the distance it can cover diagonally, allowing it to traverse the board in a unique manner. Unlike some other chess pieces, the bishop can only move along squares of a single color. Its strategic value lies in its potential to control specific diagonals and contribute to complex tactical maneuvers on the chess-board. The presence of bishops adds depth to the game, as players strategically position these pieces to control key areas of the board and influence the course of the game.

86. (C): The partition of Bengal in 1905 was orchestrated by Lord Curzon, who served as the Viceroy of India. The decision was implemented on October 16, 1905, with the aim of administrative efficiency, but it had profound political and social implications. Bengal, as it existed, was a large province, and the partition was intended to create two separate entities: East Bengal and Assam with a majority Muslim population, and the rest of Bengal, which included a Hindu majority. The move was met with strong opposition and protests, particularly from the Bengali intelligentsia and nationalist leaders, who perceived it as a divisive strategy employed by the British to weaken the growing unity among Hindus and Muslims in Bengal. The protests eventually led to the annulment of the partition in 1911, with Bengal being reunified. The episode had lasting consequences and contributed to the socio-political consciousness of the Indian independence movement.

87. **(D):** The Gram Nyayalay Act, enacted in 2008, was a significant legislative measure aimed at enhancing access to justice at the grassroots level in India. Also known as the Village Courts Act, it sought to establish Gram Nyayalays or village courts to adjudicate on specified civil and criminal matters in rural areas. These village courts were intended to provide a swift and cost-effective mechanism for dispute resolution, bringing justice closer to the doorstep of rural communities. The Act aimed to address the challenges of judicial delays and accessibility in rural areas by establishing local courts with jurisdiction over a defined geographical area. Gram Nyayalays were empowered to handle disputes related to agriculture, rural indebtedness, and other local matters, contributing to the broader goal of ensuring justice for all, including those residing in remote and underserved regions of the country.

88. **(B):** In his autobiography "Journey with a Hundred Strings: My Life in Music," Pandit Shiv Kumar Sharma, the celebrated santoor player, shares the remarkable story of his life and musical career. The book provides insights into the artist's journey, spanning his early experiences, artistic evolution, and the challenges and triumphs he encountered along the way. Pandit Shiv Kumar Sharma reflects on the profound impact of his pioneering work in popularizing the santoor, a unique Indian classical instrument. The autobiography offers readers a glimpse into the world of classical music, providing a personal narrative that intertwines with the broader cultural and musical landscape of India. "Journey with a Hundred Strings" stands as a testament to Pandit Shiv Kumar Sharma's contribution to the rich tapestry of Indian classical music and his enduring legacy as a maestro of the santoor.

89. **(C):** According to the Census of India 2011, the most densely populated state is Bihar, with a staggering 1106 people per square kilometer. This translates to over 11 people occupying the same space as one football field. Densely populated areas are characterized by a high concentration of people per unit of land. Bihar's population density is influenced by factors such as its geographical size and the substantial population residing within its boundaries. The state's fertile plains, coupled with historical and cultural factors, contribute to a higher concentration of people. Population density is a crucial demographic indicator, reflecting the distribution of people across different regions and states. In the case of Bihar, its status as the most densely populated state highlights the demographic challenges and the need for effective urban and rural planning to accommodate and sustain a large population.

90. **(B):** In Budget 2021, the Finance Minister had proposed taxability of interest on various provident funds, where the specified limit exceeds. As per this new rule, interest earned on an employee's contribution above ₹ 2.5

lakh in a year will become taxable in the hands of the employee. That means if you contribute more than this per year, the interest on the exceeding amount will be added to your taxable income. This applies only to your contributions, not your employer's.

91. (C): The Baigas, to whom Arjun Singh Dhurve belongs, mainly belong to the state of Madhya Pradesh. The Baigas are an indigenous community, and their presence is particularly prominent in the central Indian states of Madhya Pradesh and Chhattisgarh. Known for their unique cultural heritage, the Baigas have distinct traditions, including folk dances that are integral to their identity. Arjun Singh Dhurve, as a Baiga folk dance teacher, has made significant contributions to preserving and promoting the rich cultural heritage of the Baiga community. His recognition with the Padma Shri in 2021-22 reflects not only his personal achievements but also acknowledges the cultural significance and diversity of the indigenous communities in the region, particularly in Madhya Pradesh.

92. (C): In a trophic level hierarchy, organisms are classified based on their position in the food chain. The first trophic level, also known as the primary producers, comprises autotrophic organisms that produce their own food through photosynthesis. In this context, both grass and trees are examples of primary producers as they harness sunlight to synthesize their own nutrients. Phytoplankton, which consists of microscopic algae found in aquatic environments, is also a primary producer. However, zooplanktons, such as tiny animals like krill, are consumers that feed on phytoplankton and other smaller organisms. Therefore, zooplankton belongs to a higher trophic level, specifically the primary consumer level. The first trophic level is fundamental as it forms the basis of the food chain, with subsequent levels representing different stages of energy transfer as organisms consume and are consumed within an ecosystem.

93. (C): Article 44 of the Indian Constitution pertains to the directive principles of state policy and specifically addresses the concept of a uniform civil code for the citizens of India. The objective behind Article 44 is to promote a sense of unity and commonality among the diverse population of the country by advocating for a standardized set of personal laws governing matters such as marriage, divorce, inheritance, and adoption, applicable to all citizens irrespective of their religious affiliations. However, the implementation of a uniform civil code has been a subject of debate and discussion due to the diverse religious and cultural practices in India, and its enforcement remains a goal that the state shall strive to achieve. The provision reflects the constitutional vision of fostering a more unified and egalitarian legal framework for personal laws in the country.

94. (A): Manoj Sinha, the second Lieutenant Governor of the Union Territory of Jammu and Kashmir, hails from the state of Uttar Pradesh. Born on July 1, 1959, in Mohanpura, Ghazipur, Uttar Pradesh, he has had a distinguished political career. Manoj Sinha has been associated with the Bharatiya Janata Party (BJP) and has held various significant positions within the party and in government. His appointment as the Lieutenant Governor of Jammu and Kashmir underscores his administrative and political experience. Manoj Sinha has been actively involved in public service, representing the people of Ghazipur in the Lok Sabha and contributing to the development and welfare initiatives in the region.

95. (B): The Act of 1858, also known as the Government of India Act 1858, played a pivotal role in restructuring the governance of British India. It was a consequential legislative measure following the Indian Rebellion of 1857, also known as the Sepoy Mutiny. The Act marked the end of the East

India Company's rule and transferred the powers and responsibilities of the company to the British Crown. Notably, it abolished the powers that the Board of Control, a body overseeing the company's affairs, had long enjoyed. The Act of 1858 ushered in a new era with direct governance by the British Crown, symbolizing a shift from the East India Company's dominance to more direct imperial control over India.

96. **(D):** The salary and allowances of the Prime Minister of India are determined by the Parliament. The emoluments of the Prime Minister, including the salary, allowances, and other perks, are specified and approved through legislation and budgetary allocations. The Prime Minister's remuneration is subject to periodic reviews and adjustments, and any changes or revisions in the Prime Minister's salary and allowances require approval from the Parliament. This parliamentary oversight ensures transparency and accountability in the determination of the Prime Minister's financial compensation, aligning with democratic principles and the checks and balances inherent in India's political system.

97. **(D):** "Heal in India" is an initiative by the Indian Government designed to foster and promote medical tourism in the country. Medical tourism involves individuals traveling to another country to receive medical treatment, and India, with its world-class healthcare facilities, highly skilled medical professionals, and advanced technologies, has emerged as a key destination for such purposes. The initiative focuses on attracting international patients seeking quality healthcare services at comparatively lower costs. By showcasing India's medical expertise and infrastructure, the government aims to position the country as a preferred choice for individuals seeking various medical treatments and procedures, thereby contributing to the growth of the healthcare sector and the economy as a whole.

98. **(B):** Earth-forming materials have been distributed in the form of layers, creating a complex and stratified structure. This layering is a result of the processes that shaped the Earth over geological time. The Earth's composition is differentiated into distinct layers, with the outermost layer being the solid crust, followed by the mantle, outer core, and inner core. Each layer has unique properties, composition, and characteristics. The layering is a consequence of various geological and planetary processes, including differentiation during the early stages of the Earth's formation, gravitational settling, and the dynamic movements of materials over time. The distribution of earth-forming materials into layers is fundamental to understanding the planet's structure and its dynamic geophysical processes.

99. **(B):** As per the Census of India 2011, Sikhs accounted for approximately 1.7% of the total population. Sikhs, followers of Sikhism, a monotheistic religion founded in the 15th century by Guru Nanak, have a distinctive identity marked by their beliefs, practices, and the adherence to the principles enshrined in the Guru Granth Sahib. The majority of India's Sikhs live in the northern state of Punjab, where they make up about 57% of the population. Total Population in 2011 is 121.09 crores and Sikhs were 2.08 crores (1.7%).

100. **(B):** Tata Iron and Steel Company Limited (TISCO) was established in 1907 at Sakchi, near the confluence of the Subarnarekha and Kharkai rivers in Jharkhand. Sakchi was later renamed Jamshedpur. TISCO is India's first large-scale iron and steel manufacturing plant. It is a private sector company founded by Jamshedji Tata in 1868. It is now owned by TATA sons. Tata Steel Limited, formerly TISCO, is an Indian multinational steel-making company headquartered in Kolkata, West Bengal. It operates in 26 countries with key operations in India, Netherlands, and United Kingdom.

101. (B): From Question, we have

$$a_{auto} = \frac{V_H}{V_L} = 3$$

$$(\text{Cu} - \text{weight})_{auto}$$

$$= \left(1 - \frac{1}{a_{auto}}\right)(\text{Cu} - \text{weight})_{2-wdg}$$

$$\frac{(\text{Cu} - \text{weight})_{auto}}{(\text{Cu} - \text{weight})_{2-wdg}} = \left(1 - \frac{1}{3}\right) = \frac{2}{3} = \frac{1}{1.5}$$

$$(\text{Cu} - \text{weight})_{auto} : (\text{Cu} - \text{weight})_{2-wdg} = 1 : 1.5.$$

102. (A): Doubly fed induction generator (DFIG), a generating principle widely used in wind turbines. It is based on an induction generator with a multiphase wound rotor and a multiphase slip ring assembly with brushes for access to the rotor windings. It is possible to avoid the multiphase slip ring assembly, but there are problems with efficiency, cost and size. A better alternative is a brushless wound-rotor doubly fed electric machine.

103. (D): The hold on coil connected in series with the shunt field in a three-point starter of a DC motor to prevent the motor from running away in case of an open field circuit.

Hold on coil also known as NVC hold. NVC is designed in such a way that it holds the handle in 'RUN' position against the force of the spring as long as supply is given to the motor.

104. (C):

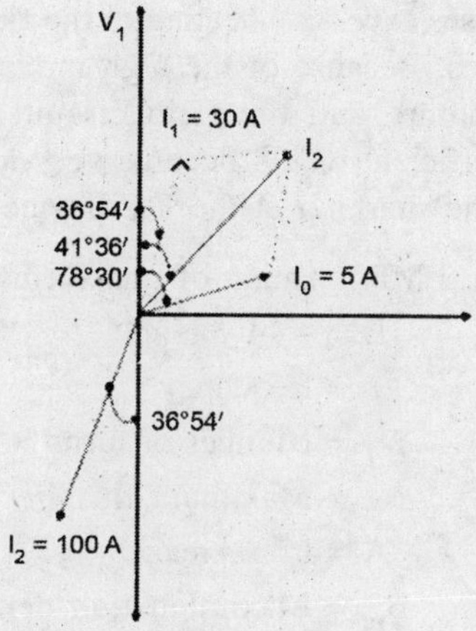

Given,

$$I_2' = 30 \text{ A}; \; I_0 = 5\text{A}$$

$$I_1 = \sqrt{(I_2')^2 + (I_0)^2 + 2I_2' \times I_0 \cos\phi}$$

$$= \sqrt{(30)^2 + (5)^2 + 2 \times 30 \times 5 \times \cos 41°36'}$$

$$= \sqrt{1149.4 \text{ A}}.$$

105. (A):

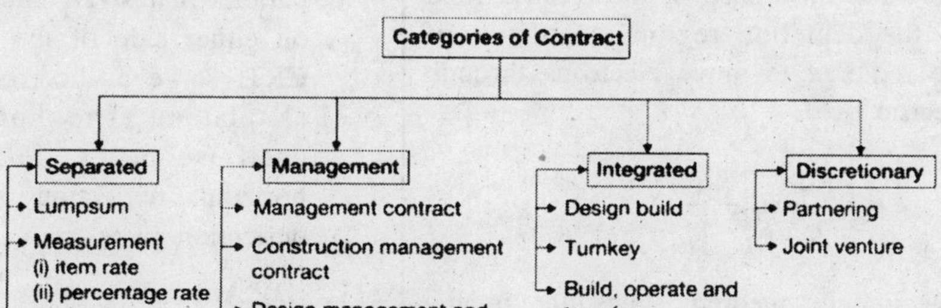

Tenders based on measurement (Item rate and % rate): The tender form contains all items of work included in bill of quantities excluding lump sum items and those items which are to be executed through another agency. In percentage rate tender, the owner gives both rates and quantities and amount. The contractor quotes % above or at par or % below the estimated cost.

Lump sum tenders: The tenderer quotes a fixed price. However, if the quote is varied, it involves contractual problems and methodology to arrive at the rates for addition, deletion and alterations would be necessary and it is to be built in tender document. This is to facilitate release of interim and final payments.

106. (B): An AC source will generate a unidirectional torque since the direction of both the currents (i.e. field current and armature current) reverse at the same time.

Due to the alternating current, eddy currents are produced in the field and yoke cores which causes excessive heating of the field and yoke cores. Because of the high inductance of the armature and the field circuits, the power coefficient would become very low. There is some sparking at the DC device brushes.

107. (C): EMF equation of transformer,

$E = 4.44\ f\ N_1\varphi_m$

f = frequency

N_1 = Number of turns in primary

φ_m = Maximum flux in core

A = Iron Area,

B_m = Maximum flux density.

108. (B): Barrier Potential: The electric field formed in the depletion region acts as a barrier. External energy must be applied to get the electrons to move across the barrier of the electric field. The potential difference required to move the electrons through the electric field is called the barrier potential.

The potential difference of the electric field across the depletion region is amount of voltage required to move electrons through the electric field.

$$E_0 = \frac{KT}{q}\ln\left(\frac{N_D^* N_A}{n_i^2}\right).$$

109. (C): Reciprocity theorem states that in any branch of a network, the current (I) due to a single source of voltage (V) elsewhere in the network is equal to the current through the branch in which the source was originally placed when the source is placed in the branch in which the current (I) was originally obtained.

In the circuit (a), the value I_a is obtained for a voltage source V. According to reciprocity theorem, this current is equivalent to I_b in the circuit B.

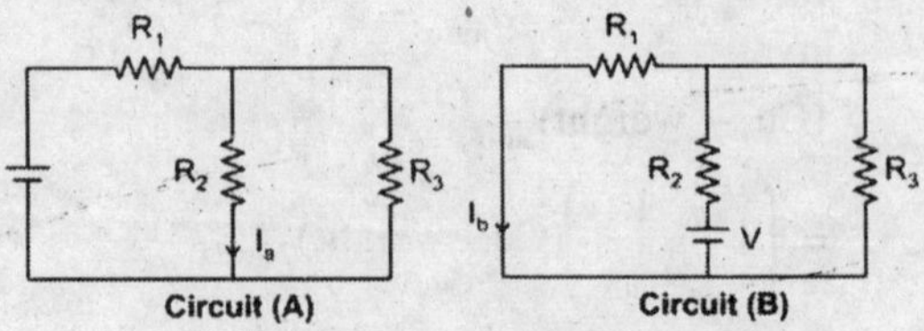

Limitations of reciprocity theorem:

- The network should be bilateral linear and time-invariant.
- It can apply only to the single-source network and not for multisource.
- It is also applicable for passive networks consisting L, C.
- Not applicable for circuits containing dependent sources even if it is linear.

110. (C): In a Cathode Ray Oscilloscope (CRO), the horizontal amplifier is designed for high amplitude signals with slow rise time. The horizontal amplifier amplifies the sweep generator output when the oscilloscope is being used in the ordinary mode of operation to display a signal applied to the vertical input. The horizontal deflection voltage is derived from a saw-tooth signal. A pair of parallel plates (H_1 and H_2) placed vertically on either side of the electron beam in the CRT, serve as horizontal deflection plates (X-plates). The horizontal axis of an oscilloscope is deflected by applying horizontal deflection voltage to the horizontal deflection plates.

111. (D): Ammeter:

- It is a device used to measure the current in a circuit.
- It is generally connected in series in a circuit.
- This is because the current remains the same when devices are connected in series.
- The ideal ammeter has low resistance because the reading will change as an extra resistance is added in series.

The cathode ray oscilloscope (CRO) may be used to observe waveforms and to measure voltages and currents,. The display of a CRO involves a spot of light moving across a screen. The amount by which the spot is deflected from its initial position depends on the p.d. applied to the terminals of the CRO and the range selected. The displacement is calibrated in 'volts per cm'.

The CRO is connected across the standard resistor to measure the voltage drop across it.

112. **(C):** In this circuit, V= I.R

$$(20 - 30) = I.(10)$$

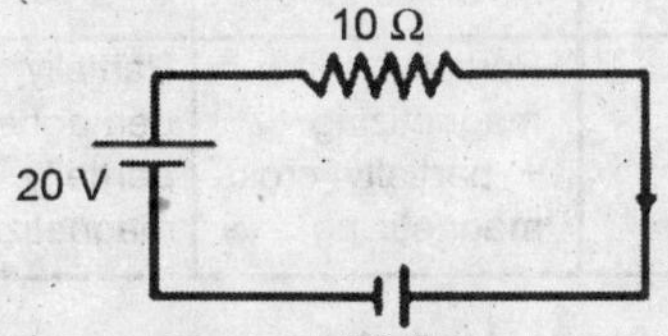

$$\therefore \quad I = \frac{-10}{10} = -1\,A.$$

113. **(A):**

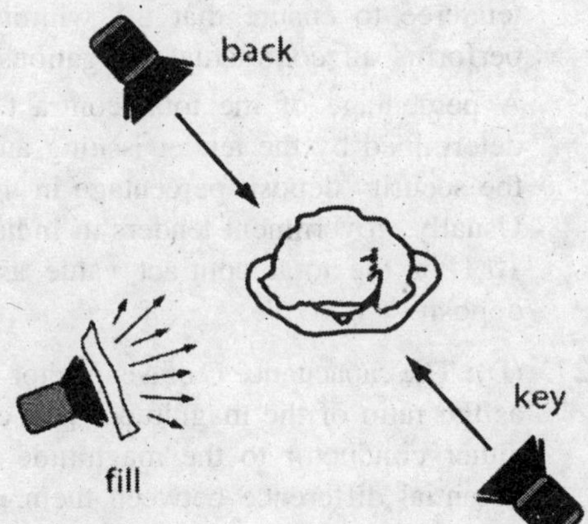

Three-Point Lighting: Three-point lighting refers to a specific and commonly used lighting strategy that employs a key light (usually a 3/4 frontal light, positioned at 45° from the camera and at a 45° vertical angle), a fill light (usually opposite the key), and a backlight (usually a 3/4 back) (Figure). You can see three-point lighting used extensively in television dramas and interviews.

Three-point lighting is quick and efficient and occasionally a good starting point for a lighting approach.

However, it's important not to think of three-point lighting as a rule that must be observed in every shot, and it's especially problematic to think that one should always light people with the three-point lighting scheme. Automatically following conventional approaches by rote can only lead to bland images.

114. **(A):** Yes, active power is the power dissipated in a pure resistance. It is also known as true power or real power.

In a purely resistive circuit, the current and voltage are in-phase. The resistance consumes all the electrical power, usually as heat. None of the electrical power is returned to the source supply or circuit.

Active power is measured in watts (W). Larger units of active power include kilowatt (kW), megawatt (MW), and gigawatt (GW).

The power factor value depends on the active power and the nonactive power, while the THD value depends on the fundamental signal magnitude and the nonfundamental signal magnitude.

115. **(D):** Repulsion start induction run motors are used in compressors. They are also used in other applications, such as:

Large air compressors, Refrigeration equipment, Large hoists, Baker's machinery, Concrete mixers, Pumps.

Repulsion start induction run motors are typically rated from 1/3 kW to 12 kW, but can be as high as 30 kW for special applications. They are useful in areas with low line voltage problems.

Repulsion start motors rely on shorted brush pairs. If the brushes aren't shorted, it's a traditional brushed motor instead of a repulsion start.

116. (D):

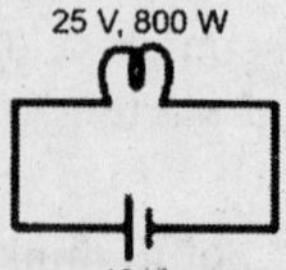

Resistance of bulb (R_b) = $\frac{V_b^2}{P_b} = \frac{(25)^2}{800}$

$= \frac{25}{8 \times 4} = \frac{25}{32}$

Power consumed by the bulb (P)

$= \frac{V^2}{R_b} = \frac{(10)^2}{25} \times 32 = 4 \times 32 = 128$ W.

117. (C): A strand is two or more wires wrapped around a center wire. Strands can have one or more layers, and typically have 7, 19, or 37 wires. A group of strands wrapped around a core is called a cable or wire rope.

Stranded cables are more flexible than solid cables and are better for applications that require reshaping and flexibility. Stranded cables are also better for shorter distances due to higher attenuation.

118. (C): In moving-coil—the deflecting torque is directly proportional to the current flowing through it.

$$T_d = BINA$$

$$T_d \propto I$$

- Deflection torque is directly proportional to the current flowing through the coil and it is independent of flux density (B) because flux density is constant. Therefore, the relationship between coil current and deflection is not governed by the pole shape of the magnet.
- Deflection torque is directly proportional to the current flowing through the coil, therefore it measured only the average value of the electrical response.
- The current is led into and out of the coil by means of two control hair-springs hence, instruments can measure the sum of two currents using two co-planar coils.

119. (A): At leading power factor, the armature reaction of an alternator is partially cross magnetizing and partially magnetizing.

Power factor	Alternator	Motor
Unity	Purely cross magnetizing	Purely cross magnetizing
ZPF lag	Purely demagnetizing	Purely magnetizing
ZPF lead	Purely magnetizing	Purely demagnetizing
Lagging	Partially demagnetizing + partially cross magnetizing	Partially magnetizing + partially cross magnetizing
Leading	Partially magnetizing + partially cross magnetizing	Partially demagnetizing + partially cross magnetizing

120. (C): Security deposit for government tenders is a mandatory part of the tender agreement. It is the money paid by the winning bidder/ tenderer to the tender issuing authority/ tenderee to ensure that the winning bidder performs all contractual obligations.

A percentage of the total contract value as determined by the tender issuing authority is the security deposit percentage in the tender. Usually, government tenders in India demand 10% of the total contract value as security deposit.

121. (D): The capacitance C of a capacitor is defined as the ratio of the magnitude Q of charge on either conductor to the magnitude V of the potential difference between them.

- The capacitance depends on the particular geometry of the two conductors constituting the capacitor and does not depend on the charge Q or the potential difference V. The capacitance reflects the ability of the capacitor to store charge, in the sense that a larger capacitance C allows more charge Q to be put onto the conductors for a given value of the potential difference V. The ability of a capacitor to store charge lies at the heart of the random-access memory (RAM) chips used in computers.

- The SI unit of capacitance is coulomb per volt, called farad (F).

$$1 \text{ F} = 1 \text{ CV}^{-1}$$

122. **(A):** From question, we have,

$$P = 2500 \text{ watts}$$

$$t = 40 \times 4 = 160 \text{ hours}$$

$$E = p \times t$$

$$= 2500 \times 160$$

$$E = \frac{400,000 \text{ kW}}{1000}$$

$$E = 400 \text{ units.}$$

123. **(C):** Lenz's law is consequence of the law of conservation of energy, specifically the law of conservation of energy for electromagnetic fields. Lenz's law states that when an electromagnetic field is induced by a changing magnetic field, the direction of the induced current in a conductor will be such that it creates a magnetic field that opposes the change in the original magnetic field that produceds it.

124. **(A):** When the rotor speed is about synchronous, stator magnetic field pulls rotor into synchronism i.e. minimum reluctance position and keeps it magnetically locked. Then rotor continues to rotate with a speed equal to synchronous speed. Such a torque exerted on the rotor is called the reluctance torque. Thus finally the reluctance motor runs as a synchronous motor. The resistance of the rotor must be very small and the combined inertia of the rotor and the load should be small to run the motor as a synchronous motor.

125. **(C):** A DC servomotor encoder detects the rotation speed, angle, and travel distance of a moving machine part. The encoder then sends this information to the controller, which sends electrical signals to the driver. The driver amplifies and translates these signals for the servo motor. The encoder's role is to keep the motor's rotation speed constant. If the detected speed is slower than the set rotation speed, the servo amplifier will rotate the motor faster. If the detected speed is faster, the amplifier will rotate the motor slower.

126. **(A):**

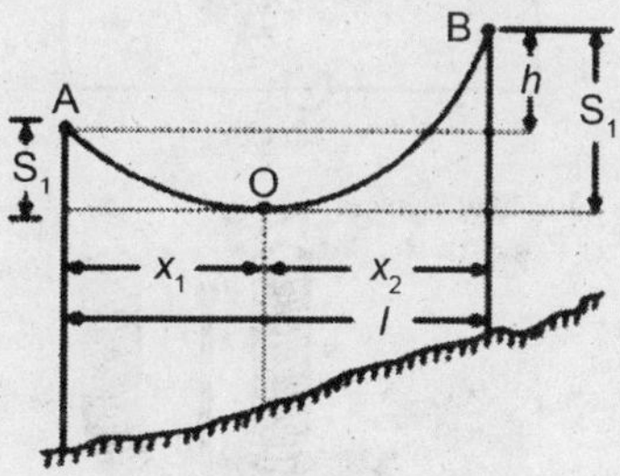

Suppose that, l = Span length

h = Difference in level b/w two support

x_1 = Distance of support at lower level (*i.e.,* A from 0)

x_2 = Distance of support of higher level (*i.e.,* B from 0)

T = Tension in conductor

If weight of conductor's per unit length is 'W', then

$$S_1 = \frac{h}{W}\left[\cos h\left(\frac{WX_1}{h}\right) - 1\right]$$

$$S_1 = \frac{h}{W}\left[\cos h\left(\frac{WX_2}{h}\right) - 1\right]$$

If tension is A and B, then:

$$T_A = h\cos h\frac{WX_1}{h}$$

$$T_B = h\cos h\frac{WX_2}{h}$$

Hence, maximum tension will be at B, as shown in above figure,

$$X_1 < X_2$$

Hence, tension will be maximum at higher level.

127. **(A):** An LC circuit with inductance, L = 2H and capacitance, C = 8μF is connected to an AC source, then value of the power factor of combination is 0 because power factor is $\cos\phi = \frac{R}{Z}$ and resistance in the circuit is 0.

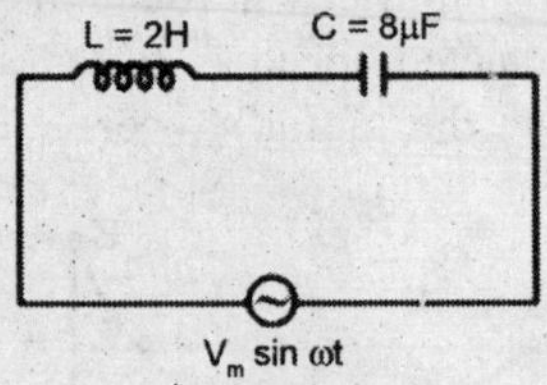

128. (B):

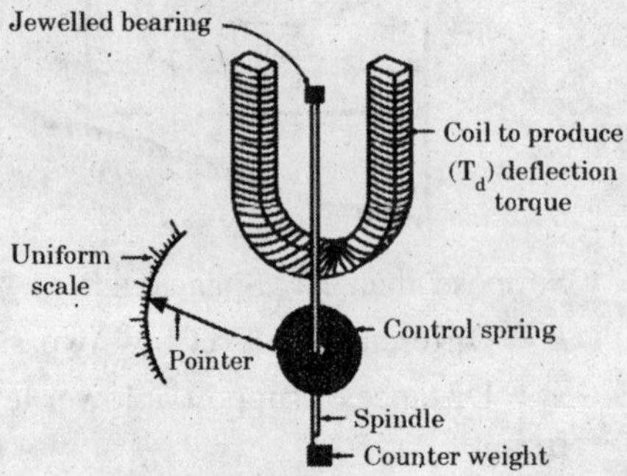

Fig.: *Spring control*

A helical hair spring usually made of Phosphor Bronze is attached to the moving system in such away that its one end is fixed to the moving system while the outer end to a rigid body. As the angle of deflection increases, the stress in the spring increases due to which it exerts a torque on the moving mechanism opposite to the motion of the moving mechanism. This torque is proportional to the angle of deflection.

$$T_c \propto \theta$$

$$I \propto \theta \quad [\text{when at } T_d = T_c]$$

$$T_c = \frac{Edt^3}{i2l}\theta \text{ kg-m}.$$

129. (B): A permanent magnetic material has high retentivity, which means it can retain its magnetic properties for a long time without losing strength.

Materials with high retentivity, like iron, will keep some magnetic properties and become permanent magnets. Materials with low or no retentivity will not keep their magnetic properties and will lose their magnetization. Some materials used for permanent magnets include: Steel, Alnico, Ticonal, Cobalt steel.

130. (C): In the context of electromagnetic induction, if magnetic fluxes of two coils oppose each other, then the connection is called series opposing.

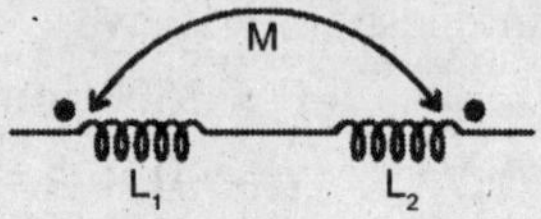

$$L_{eq} = L_1 + L_2 - 2M$$

$$M = K\sqrt{L_1 L_2}$$

K → Coupling factor

L_1, L_2 → Self inductance

M → Mutual inductance.

131. (D): A sodium-vapor lamp is a gas-discharge lamp that uses sodium in an excited state to produce light at a characteristic wavelength near 589 nm. Two varieties of such lamps exist : low pressure and high pressure. Sodium lamp emits just two wavelengths of 589 and 589.56 nm and hence its spectra will be a line spectra with only two lines.

132. (A):

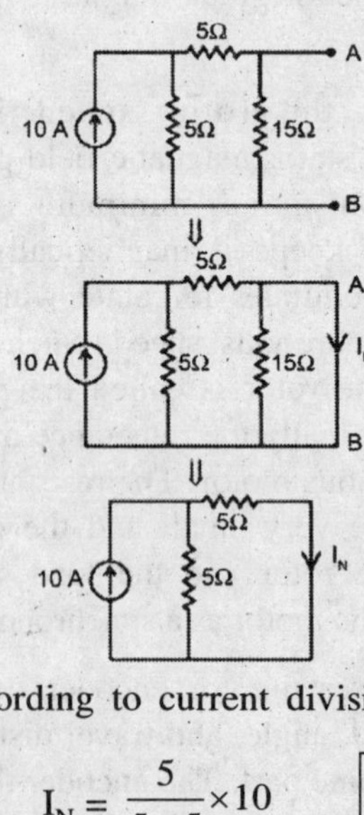

According to current division rule:

$$I_N = \frac{5}{5+5} \times 10 \qquad \left[I_2 = \frac{R_1}{R_1 + R_2} \times I\right]$$

$$I_N = 5A$$

133. (C): Eddy current losses: These are basically I^2R losses present in the core due to the production of eddy current in the core.

$$W_e = kB_{max}^2 f^2 t^2$$

where, k = Steinmetz constant

B_{max} = maximum flux density

f = frequency of magnetization or supply frequency

t = thickness of the core

maximum flux density (B_{max}) is directly proportional to the V/f ratio.

$$B_{max} \propto \frac{V}{f}.$$

134. (A): The watts per square meter method is a rule of thumb for rough calculations and checking purposes. It involves allocating watts per square meter of the area to be illuminated, based on an average figure of overall system efficiency.

The watts per square meter method is easy to calculate the requirements but it is outdated and less used in the calculations.

For example, if your room measures 4 m × 5 m it has an area of 20 square meters. If you are using conventional bulbs, multiply this by 25, giving a total wattage of 500 watts, or a light level of around 5000 lumens is required.

135. (D): Magnetomotive force (MMF) is the force that creates magnetic flux in a magnetic circuit. It is also known as magnetic potential. MMF is the product of the current and the number of turns of a coil. Mathematically, it is represented as MMF = N × I, where N is the number of turns of the coil and I is the current through the coil. The unit of MMF is ampere-turn (AT).

MMF is analogous to electromotive force (EMF) in an electric circuit.

136. (A): Delta-star (D_Y) connection: This type of connection is used for stepping up the voltage to a high level. For example these are used in the beginning of HV transmission lines so that insulation is stressed to about 57.74% of line voltage. Delta-star (D_Y) connection is shown in figure. Star connection is also called as *y*-connection.

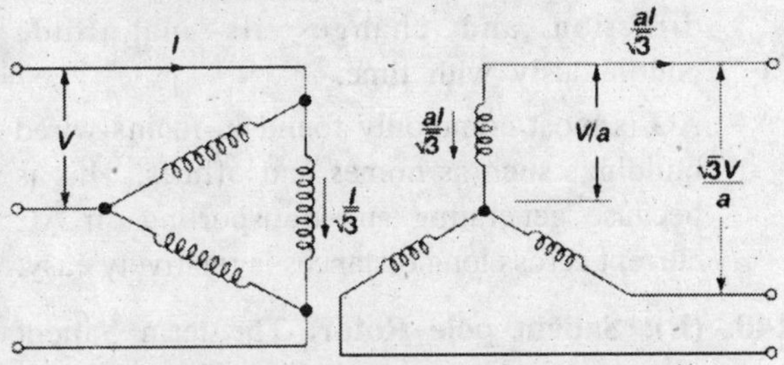

Fig. *Delta-star (D_Y) connection*

Delta-star transformers are also generally used as distribution transformers for providing mixed line to line voltage to high power equipment. For example, 1 KV/400 V Delta-star distribution transformers is used to distribute power to consumers by 3-phase four wire system.

138. (C): A standard project typically has the following four major phases (each with its own agenda of tasks and issues): initiation, planning, implementation, and closure.

Implementation (Execution) Phase:

- During the third phase, the implementation phase, the project plan is put into motion and the work of the project is performed.
- It is important to maintain control and communicate as needed during implementation. Progress is continuously monitored and appropriate adjustments are made and recorded as variances from the original plan. In any project, a project manager spends most of the time in this step.
- During project implementation, people are carrying out the tasks, and progress information is being reported through regular team meetings. The project manager uses this information to maintain control over the direction.

139. (D): Alternating current (AC) is an electric current that changes its magnitude and direction at regular intervals of time.

In contrast to direct current (DC), which flows only in one direction, AC periodically reverses direction and changes its magnitude continuously with time.

AC is most commonly found in mains-wired buildings such as homes and offices. This is because generating and transporting an AC current across long distances is relatively easy.

140. (B): Salient pole Rotor: The term Salient means projecting or protruding. Thus, a salient pole rotor consists of poles projecting out from the surface of the rotor core as shown in the Figure.

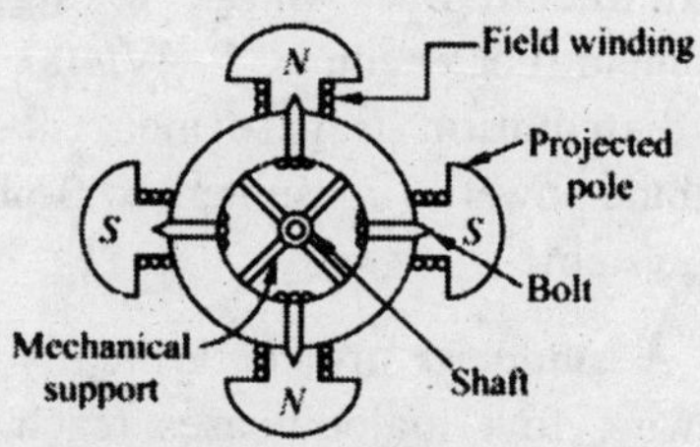

Fig. *Salient Pole Type Rotor*

The poles are built up of thick steel laminations. The poles are bolted to the rotor as shown in the Figure. The pole face has been given a specific shape. The field winding is provided on the pole shoe. These rotors have large diameters and small axial lengths. The limiting factor for the size of the rotor is the centrifugal force acting on the rotating member of the machine. As mechanical strength of salient pole type is less, this is preferred for low speed alternators ranging from 125 r.p.m. to 500 r.p.m. The prime movers used to drive such rotor are generally water turbines and I.C. engines.

142. (B): The efficiency of an electric motor is less than 100% for a number of reasons, including friction, electrical losses, and heat generation.

Here are some reasons why a motor's efficiency is less than 100%:

- **Friction:** Friction within the motor's moving parts, such as bearings and brushes, results in energy loss.
- **Resistance:** Some energy is lost in the winding by the resistance in the winding to the movement of the magnetic fields through them.
- **Air resistance:** Other forms of energy loss such as heat or sound.

The portion of electric energy that is not converted to mechanical power is converted to heat, which is mostly unusable.

Motor efficiency varies between 70 and 96%.

143. (C): $r = 10 \text{ cm} = 10 \times 10^{-2}$ m

$I = 100\pi$ A

Magnetising force (H)

$$= \frac{NI}{2\pi r} = \frac{100\pi}{2\times\pi\times10\times10^{-2}} = 500 \text{ AT/m}$$

Flux density (B) = μH

$= 4\pi \times 10^{-7} \times 500$

$= 6.28 \times 10^{-4}$ wb/m^2.

144. (B): Output power = 750 MW

$\eta = 30\%$

$E/m = 30{,}000$ KJ/kg

$\therefore$ Input power $= \frac{750}{30}\times100 = 2500$ MW

$$P_{in} = \frac{E}{t} = \frac{F\times x}{t} = \frac{max}{t}$$

$$\therefore \frac{E}{m} = ax = 30 \times 10^6 \text{ J/kg}$$

then, $$\frac{m}{t} = \frac{P_{in}}{ax} = \frac{2500\times10^6}{30\times10^6}$$

$= 83.33$ kg/s.

145. (D): The transfer characteristics can be determined by observing different values of drain current with variation in gate-source voltage provided that the drain-source voltage should be constant. The transfer characteristics are just opposite to drain characteristics.

One just needs to remember the concept that in drain characteristics we are keeping the gate-source voltage constant and determining the values of drain current at different values of drain-source voltage while in transfer characteristics we are keeping the value of drain-source voltage constant.

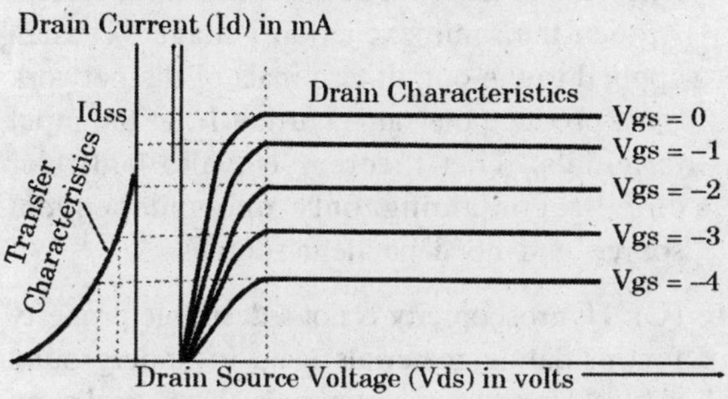

The characteristic curve of transfer characteristics of JFET is described above; it can be easily observed that the value of drain current varies inversely with respect to gate-source voltage when the drain-source voltage is constant.

147. **(B):** Silicon steel is also a good electrical conductor and has a high magnetic permeability, which helps to increase the transformer's efficiency. It helps to reduce energy losses through eddy currents. Here are some other reasons why silicon steel is used to make the core of a transformer:

- Low hysteresis loss
- High resistance
- Virtually eliminated aging
- Lower the thickness of the lamination.

148. **(D): Terms and conditions for the tender evaluation sheet**

- The name of the supplier is not mentioned, as it is decided after the opening of technical bids.
- The list of materials put up for sale by tender may please be seen in Annexure 'A'.
- The rates are to be submitted only in Annexure - 'B'.
- Ministry of Defence, Government of India, shall be hereinafter referred to as stockholder.
- The tender must be submitted by Specified Times on the date mentioned on the first page of tender documents at MSTC Ltd. New Delhi.
- All tender should be kept open for acceptance for a period of 45 (Forty-Five) days from the date of opening.
- Tenders received with Earnest Money less than the requisite amount will be rejected.
- The tender should be accompanied by Earnest Money @ 20% of the total sale value of each lot quoted by way of a Demand Draft/Pay Order on any Nationalised Bank in Favour of MSTC Ltd. New Delhi Payable at New Delhi.
- The earnest money of unsuccessful tenders is refunded to the tenderers as soon as possible after disposal of the tenders.
- The successful tenderer shall remove each lot allotted to them by employing their own labour and transport at their own cost from the area allotted to them within 30 (thirty) days from the date of issue of sale-cum-Delivery Order and assurance to replace defective supplies.

150. **(B):** From question, we have,

No-load voltage, $(V_1) = 200$ V

No-load current, $(I_0) = 0.5$ A

Power, $(P_0) = 50$ W

Magnetic current, $I_\mu = ?$

$$P_0 = V_1 I_0 \cos\phi_0$$

$$\cos\phi = \frac{50}{200\times0.5} = \frac{1}{2}$$

$$\cos\phi_0 = \cos 60^\circ$$

$$\phi_0 = 60^\circ$$

Magnetic current, $I_\mu = I_0 \sin\phi_0$

$$I_\mu = 0.5\times\frac{\sqrt{3}}{2}$$

Magnetic current, $I_\mu = 0.433$ A.

151. (D): In an electric magnetic circuit, for establishing a magnetic field, energy must be spent, through no energy is required to maintain it.

Let us take on the example of exciting coils of electromagnetic as shown in the figure

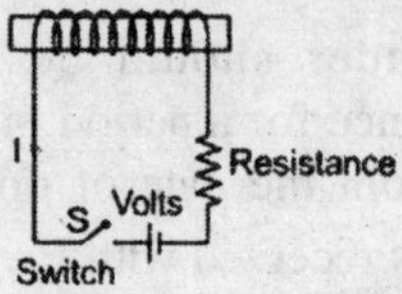

The energy supplied to it is spent in two ways:

- Part of it goes to meet I^2R losses and is lost once for all.
- Part of it goes to create a flux and is solved in the form of the magnetic field as "potential energy" and is similar to the potental energy of a raised weight when a mass 'M' is raised through height H, the potential energy solved it is MgH.

152. (A): Following are the factors which need to be considered for selecting unit size and rating of generators in a power station.

- The combined capacity of all generators must be able to meet the peak demand of the station.
- The number and sizes of units should be so selected that they approximately fit the annual load curve of the station.
- The size of the unit selected should be such that it should work at near full load.
- To meet future load requirement, the plant capacity should be 15-20% more than expected maximum demand.
- Additional units as reserve capacity should be maintained so as to take care of breakdown or scheduled maintenance of running units.
- Unit with equal capacity and same make be selected so that spare parts can be interchanged and maintenance is easier. This will reduce spare parts inventory.

153. (A): The reciprocity theorem states that "In a linear, bilateral, active, single-source network, the ratio of excitation to response remains same when the positions of excitation and response are interchanged". That means, if an excitation voltage V_S applied to the input terminals of a network results in output current I_1, then the same excitation voltage V_S when applied to the output terminals of the network must produce the same current I_1, at the input terminals. This theorem is valid only for circuits containing only one independent source and no dependent sources.

154. (C): Hygroscopicity is not a desirable property for insulating materials used in underground cables. Hygroscopic materials absorb and store moisture from the air. This moisture can decrease the insulation resistance and cause the cable to break down.

Insulating materials for cables should also have the following properties:

- High insulation resistance
- High dielectric strength
- Low permittivity
- High mechanical strength
- Non-inflammable
- High flexibility
- Unaffected by acids and alkalis
- Electrical and chemical properties not affected by temperature
- Low cost.

155. (B): If V-I characteristic is plotted for forward current by increasing the temperature it has been seen that plot for V-I characteristic is moved to the left as temperature increases.

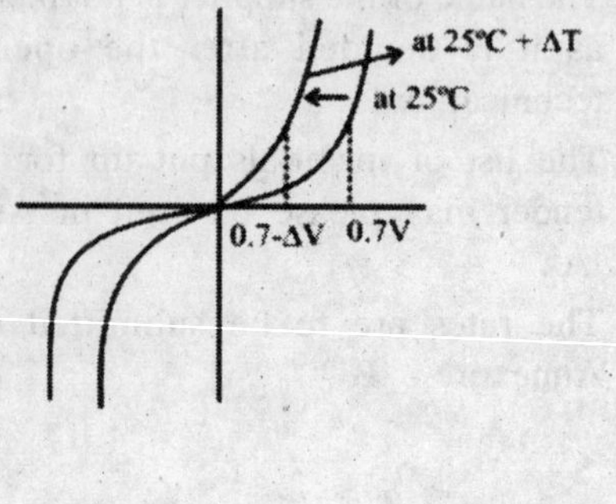

157. (D): Inductive reactance $(X_L) = 2\pi f L$

$$X_L \propto f$$

if the frequency of AC source is doubled then its inductive reactance will be doubled.

158. (A): This method measures grounding electrode resistance based upon the principle of potential drop across the resistance. It also uses two auxiliary electrodes (one current rod and the other a potential rod) that are placed at a sufficient distance from the test electrodes; a current of known magnitude is passed through the electrode under test and one of the auxiliary electrodes (current rod). The drop in potential between the electrode under the test and the second auxiliary electrode (potential rod) is measured. The ratio of voltage drop (V) to the known current (I) will indicate the resistance of the grounding circuit. Either a DC or AC voltage source may be used for conducting this test.

159. (A):

$$V.R. = 0$$

$$V_R = 150 \text{ kV}$$

$$V_S = ?$$

Formula,

$$V.R. = \frac{V_S - V_R}{V_R}$$

$$0 = \frac{V_S - V_R}{V_R}$$

$$V_S = V_R = 150 \text{ kV}.$$

160. (C): When the frequency of supply in a three-core underground cable is doubled, the charging current is also doubled. This occurs because frequency and charging current have a direct relationship due to their reliance on the change in voltage over time in the equation I = CdV/dt. It is also important to note that in actuality, cable resistance could impact this but the core principle remains the same.

161. (D): A cathode-ray tube (CRT) is a vacuum tube containing one or more electron guns, which emit electron beams that are manipulated to display images on a phosphorescent screen. The images may represent electrical waveforms (oscilloscope), pictures (television set, computer monitor), radar targets, or other phenomena. A CRT on a television set is commonly called a picture tube.

In CRT television sets and computer monitors, the entire front area of the tube is scanned repeatedly and systematically in a fixed pattern called a raster.

162. (B):

- A hysteresis motor is a synchronous motor.
- It has a cylindrical rotor and works on hysteresis losses induced in the rotor of hardened steel with high retentivity.
- It is a single-phase motor.
- It has a rotor is made of ferromagnetic material with non-magnetic support over the shaft.
- A hysteresis motor is constructed of five main components Stator, Single-phase stator winding, Rotor, Shaft, Shading coil.
- The stator of the hysteresis motor has a main winding along with an auxiliary or starting winding. When the stator winding is fed from a single-phase supply, it produces a synchronously revolving magnetic field.
- In the hysteresis motor, hysteresis torque remains practically constant.
- The revolving magnetic field is accomplished by using a permanent split capacitor type construction of the motor. As a result, both the starting and the main windings of the motor remain connected in the motor circuit during running as well as at starting.
- The value of the capacitor is so adjusted that it results in a flux revolving at synchronous speed. The rotor of the hysteresis motor consists of a smooth cylinder of magnetically hard steel, without winding or rotor teeth.

- In the hysteresis motor, hysteresis torque remains practically constant.

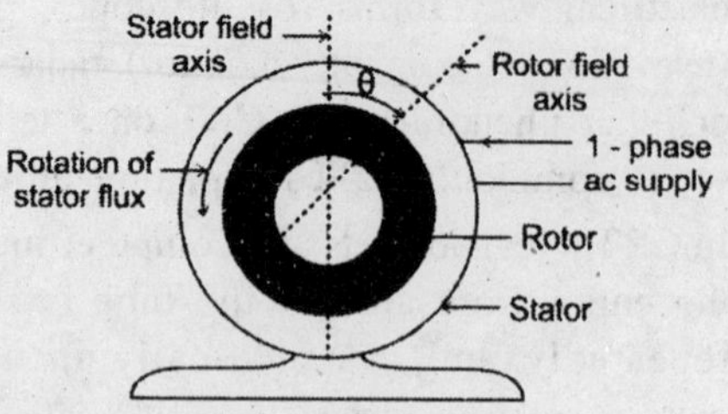

163. (B):

- The shell-type transformer has two yokes and three limbs.
- Only the middle limb is provided with winding and windings are surrounded by the core.
- Outer limbs and middle limbs have a different cross-sectional area.
- Leakage flux is less, and power transfer capability is more.
- Less amount of copper is required for windings.
- More amount of insulating material is required.
- The shell-type transformer provides a shorter magnetic path when compared to the core type. In shell-type transformer leakage, flux and magnetizing current are lesser than in the core type, and power transfer capability is more in shell-type transformers.
- This transformer is also called a sandwich otherwise disc winding. Maintaining these transformers is difficult and mechanical strength is high.

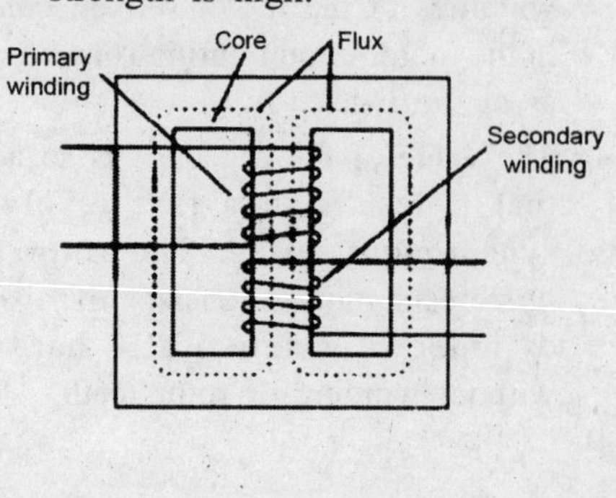

- The core losses are comparatively less in a shell-type transformer because half of the total flux flows in the entire core, the shell-type transformer is shown in fig.

164. (D): The deflection sensitivity in a cathode ray oscilloscope (CRO) is inversely proportional to the square root of the mass of electron.

Electrostatics deflection sensitivity,

$$S = \frac{L\ell_d}{2dV_a}$$

Magnetic deflection sensitivity,

$$S = LI\sqrt{\frac{q}{m}}\frac{\ell}{\sqrt{2V_a}}$$

165. (A): Output load = 120 kWh

loss (W) = 5 kWh

all day Efficiency (η)

$$= \frac{\text{Output in kWh for 24 hours}}{\text{Input in kWh for 24 hours}}$$

$$= \frac{120}{120+5}\times 100$$

$$= \frac{120}{125}\times 100 = 96\%.$$

166. (D): Power factor = 0.8

Active power (P) = 40 W

Active power = Apparent power × power factor

40 = Apparent power × 0.8

Apparent power = 50 VA

167. (C): The Split Phase Motor is also known as a Resistance Start Motor. It has a single cage rotor and its stator has two windings known as main winding and starting winding. Both the windings are displaced 90 degrees in space. The main winding has very low resistance and a high inductive reactance whereas the starting winding has high resistance and low inductive reactance.

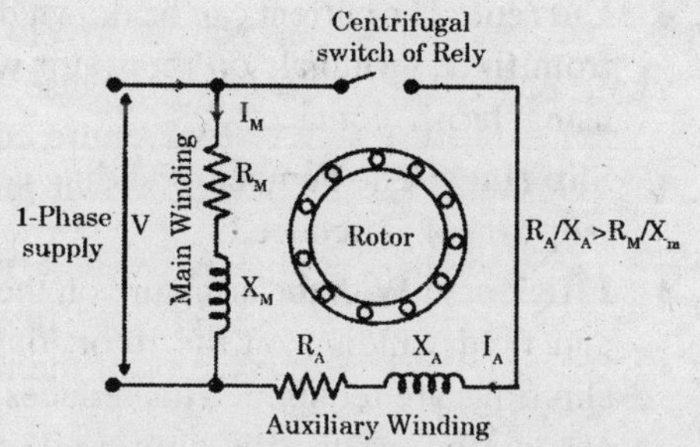

A resistor is connected in series with the auxiliary winding. The current in the two windings is not equal as a result the rotating field is not uniform.

168. (C): In an electrical signal waveform, if each value on the curve is proportional to sine of angle or rotations of the coil, then such a wave is called sine wave.

169. (C): Power station supplies energy (E)

= 1000 MWh

Time (t) = 2 month

= 60 day

= 60 × 24 hours

Average demand

$$= \frac{\text{Energy supplied by power station}}{\text{Total duration}}$$

$$= \frac{1000}{60 \times 24} = 0.694 \text{ MW.}$$

170. (A): Mathematically, Percentage slip,

$$\% \text{ S} = \left[\frac{N_S - N}{N_S}\right] \times 100$$

$$\text{or fractional slip, S} = \frac{N_S - N}{N_S}$$

$$N_S = 1000 \text{ rpm}$$

$$N_r = 970 \text{ rpm}$$

$$\text{Percentage slip (s)} = \frac{N_S - N_r}{N_S} \times 100$$

$$= \frac{1000 - 970}{1000} \times 100$$

$$= 3\%.$$

171. (C):

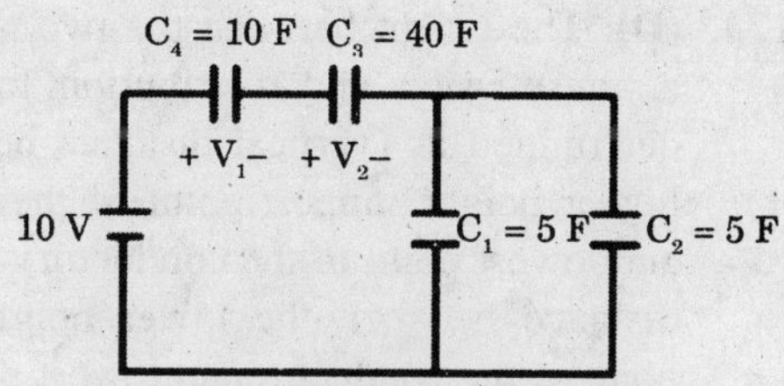

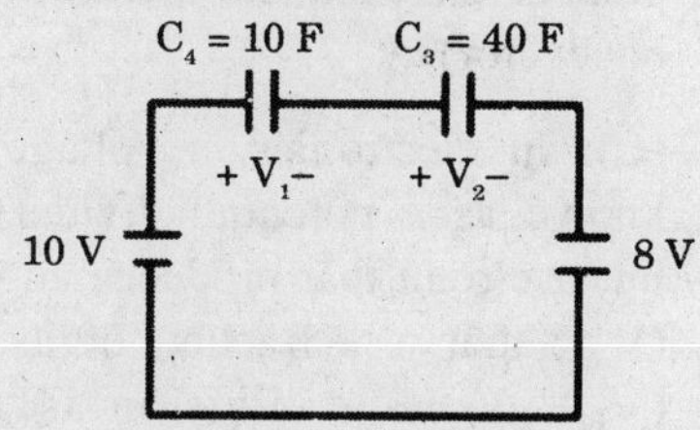

Applying voltage division rule:

$$V_1 = \frac{\frac{1}{10}}{\frac{1}{10} + \frac{1}{40} + \frac{1}{8}} \times 10$$

$$= \frac{\frac{1}{10}}{\frac{4+1+5}{40}} \times 10 = \frac{40}{100} \times 10 = 4\,\text{V}$$

$$V_2 = \frac{\frac{1}{40}}{\frac{4+1+5}{40}} \times 10 = \frac{10}{10} = 1\,\text{V.}$$

172. (C): From question, we have

$$V = 230\angle 60^\circ$$

$$Z = 10 + j10$$

$$= 10\sqrt{2}\angle 45^\circ$$

$$Z = \sqrt{(10)^2 + (10)^2} = 10\sqrt{2}$$

$$\cos\phi = \frac{R}{Z} = \frac{10}{10\sqrt{2}}$$

$$\phi = 45^\circ$$

$$Z = 10\sqrt{2}\angle 45^\circ$$

$$I = \frac{V}{Z} = \frac{230\angle 60^\circ}{10\sqrt{2}\angle 45^\circ}$$

$$= 16.3\angle 15^\circ \text{ (Leading).}$$

173. (D): The height between the two supports of a transmission and distribution line can be determined as (vertical distance between the higher height support point of the conductor and lowest point of the conductor) – (Vertical distance between the lower height support point of the conductor and lowest point of the conductor).

174. (C): In electronics, a voltage divider (also known as a potential divider) is a passive linear circuit that produces an output voltage (V_{out}) that is a fraction of its input voltage (V_{in}). Voltage division is the result of distributing the input voltage among the components of the divider. A simple example of a voltage divider is two resistors connected in series, with the input voltage applied across the resistor pair and the output voltage emerging from the connection between them.

175. (A):

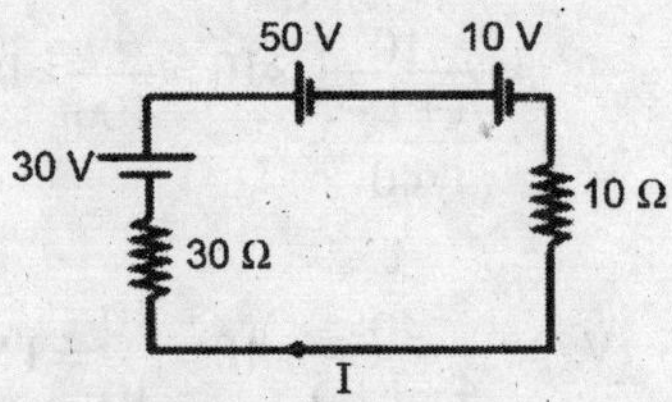

Applying KVL in loop:

$$30 - 50 - 10 = 10\,I + 30\,I$$
$$-30 = 40\,I$$
$$I = -0.75\text{ A.}$$

176. (B): Stationary armatures have several advantages, including:

- **Mechanical balance:** Stationary armatures can better brace armature windings against high electromagnetic forces.
- **Stability:** Stationary armature generators are more stable and less prone to wear and tear than moving armature generators.
- **Maintenance:** Stationary armature generators are easier to maintain and repair because the armature remains stationary.
- **Insulation:** It's easier to insulate stationary windings for high voltages.
- **Current:** The current can be drawn directly from fixed terminals on the stator without using brush contacts.
- **Slip rings:** The number of sliding contacts (slip rings) is reduced.
- **Efficiency:** With the armature on the stator and field winding on the rotor, only two slip rings are required. This reduces losses associated with slip ring and carbon brushes, increasing efficiency.

177. (B): Whenever the load on the alternator is varied, the terminal voltage will also vary this variation in terminal voltage is mainly due to three reasons-voltage drop due to armature resistance IR_a, the voltage drop due to armature leakage reactance IX_a, and voltage drop due to armature reaction.

The voltage drop due to armature leakage reactance increases with increasing load.

178. (A):
$$1\text{ kWh} = 10^3\text{ Wh}$$
$$= 10^3 \times 60 \times 60\text{ W.S}$$
$$= 36 \times 10^5\text{ Joule.}$$

179. (C): Phosphor bronze is a preferred overhead conductor material for harmful gas atmospheres like ammonia when the spans are extremely long.

Here are some reasons why phosphor bronze is a good conductor material:

- **Corrosion resistance:** Phosphor bronze is resistant to corrosion and humidity, unlike pure copper.
- **Strength:** Phosphor bronze is stronger than copper but has lower conductivity.
- **Electrical conductivity:** Phosphor bronze has high electrical conductivity and low elasticity.
- **Cryogenic environments:** Phosphor bronze has good strength in cryogenic environments and can make electrical connections to devices at ultra low temperatures.

180. **(D):** Synchronous motors, which transform electrical energy into mechanical energy are the most extensively used steady-state 3-phase AC motors in an electrical system. This motor rotates at a constant synchronous speed that is synchronized with the supply frequency, and the period of rotation is equal to the integral number of AC cycles. That is, the motor's rotational speed is equal to the spinning magnetic field's rotational speed. This motor is primarily used to increase the power factor in power systems. There are two types of synchronous motors: non excited and DC excited, which function based on the magnetic power of the motor. Nonexcited synchronous motors include reluctance motors, hysteresis motors, and permanent magnet motors.

The interaction of the rotating magnetic field of the stator and the constant magnetic field of the rotor provides the basis for synchronous motor functioning. The rotating magnetic field of a synchronous motor's stator is analogous to that of a three-phase induction motor.

According to Ampere's Law, the magnetic field of the rotor interacts with the synchronous alternating current of the stator windings to produce torque, which causes the rotor to rotate (more).

181. **(C):** According to current division rule:

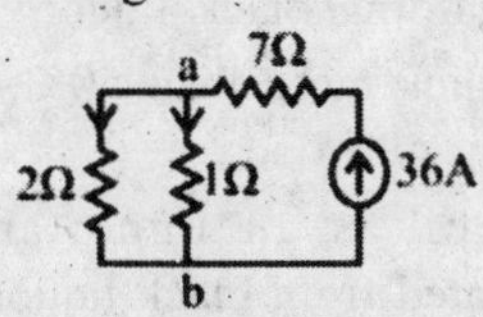

Current in 2Ω resistor ($I_{2\Omega}$)

$$= \frac{1}{2+1} \times 36 = 12 \text{ A}$$

$I_{2\Omega}$ = 12 A (from *a* to *b*).

182. **(D):** As a single-phase induction motor is not self-starting some techniques must be employed to start these types of motors. Often, single-phase motors are classified according to the method used to start the motor.

The torque-speed curve of this type of motor is shown in Fig.

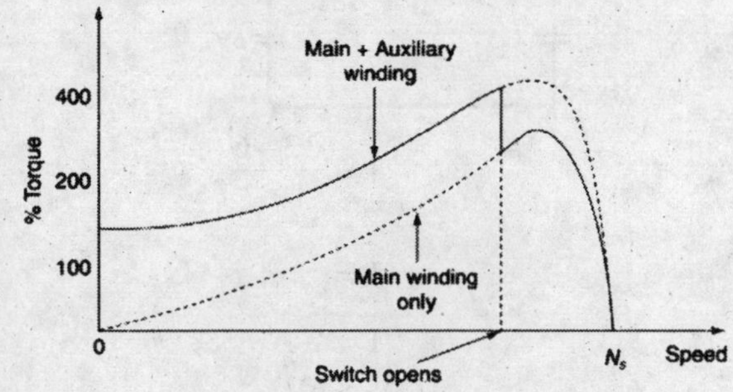

Fig. *Torque-speed curve of a split phase induction motor*

- The starting torque –1.5 to 2 times the full load torque.
- The maximum or pull out torque –2.5 times full load torque at about 75% of synchronous speed.
- Starting current –7 to 8 times the full load current.

Applications: These motors are very cheap and are most suitable for washing machines, fans, blowers, small drills, centrifugal pumps, grinders, mixers etc. This motor is rarely used for drives requiring more than 1 kW.

183. **(C):** From question, we have

$$V = (100 + j10)\text{V}$$

$$I = (20 - j10)\text{A}$$

Apparent power (S) = VI*

= (100 + *j*10) (20 + *j*10)

= 2000 – 100 + *j*(1000 + 200)

= 1900 + *j* 1200

= P + *j*Q

Active power (P) = 1900 watt.

184. **(C):** The element Nickel (Ni) is one of the few ferromagnetic metals. Ferromagnetic means they are attracted to magnets and can be magnetized themselves. Most metals aren't magnetic with the exception of iron, nickel, cobalt, gadolinium, neodymium and samarium.

185. (A):

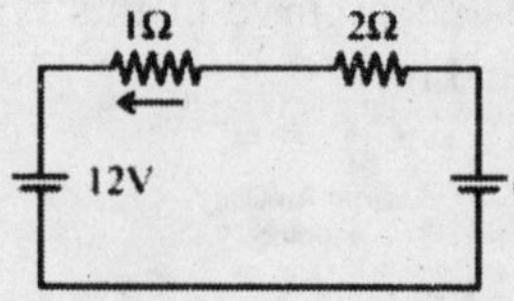

$$I = \frac{12-6}{1+2},$$

$$I = \frac{6}{3}$$

$$I = 2\ A$$

$$\because \quad 12V > 6V,$$

Hence, the value of current (I) is negative.

$$I = -2A.$$

186. (C): Given,

Change in current $(\Delta I) = 1.5 \times 10^{-3}$ A

Change in voltage $(\Delta V) = 0.6$

$$\text{Dynamic resistance} = \frac{\text{Change in voltage}}{\text{Change in current}}$$

$$= \frac{\Delta V}{\Delta I}$$

$$= \frac{0.6}{1.5\times10^{-3}} = 400\,\Omega.$$

187. (B): A substation is a facility that transmits and distributes electricity. It serves as an intermediary between electrically plants and end user.

The following statements about substation is correct:

- Domestic consumers may also connect directly to the main transmission network.
- Rotary converters are also used in railway substations.
- At the point of interconnection between two distinct transmission voltages, transformers may be installed in substation.

188. (B): In an electrical network, a dependent source is a voltage or current source whose value depends on another voltage or current in the network.

Dependent sources are useful for modeling the behaviour of amplifiers. For example, a bipolar junction transistor can be modeled as a dependent current source.

189. (A): The main reason for placing field winding on the stationary rotor is that it's easier to insulate high voltage on the stator than on the rotor.

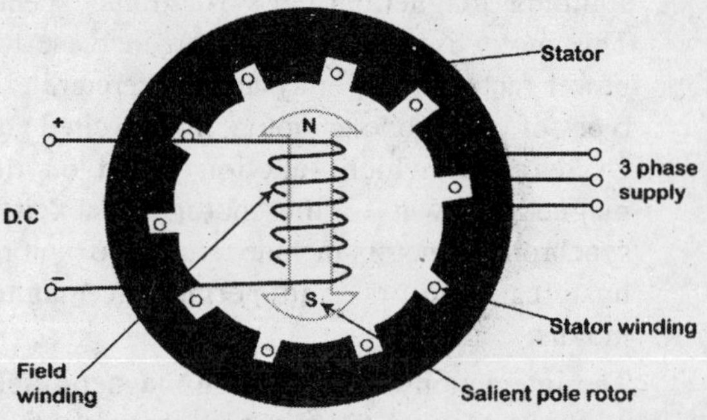

190. (C): Voltage is the pressure from an electrical circuit's power source that pushes charged electrons (current) through a conducting loop, enabling them to do work such as illuminating a light. In brief, voltage = pressure, and it is measured in volts (V).

191. (D): In a capacitor start capacitor run induction motor, under standstill condition forward and backward voltage are equal in magnitude.

192. (B): Regarding black liquor

(*i*) It retains more than 50% of the biomass energy of wood.

(*ii*) Tall oil is an important by-product separated from black liquor by skimming.

(*iii*) It is a toxic substance produced when wood is burned into paper.

193. (D): Synchronous motor:

- For industrial, squirrel cage induction motors are used mostly for motor and drive systems applications.
- Synchronous motors are very rarely used below 40 kW output because of the higher cost compared to induction motors.

- In addition to the higher initial cost synchronous motors needs dc excitation source and starting and control devices are usually more expensive.
- However, for particular output range and speed, the high initial cost of synchronous motor varnishes is economical compared to the induction motor, where applications involve high kW output and low-speed synchronous motors are economical compared to induction motors.
- It runs at a constant speed (at synchronous speed).
- It can run over a wide range of power factors both lagging and leading.
- Its torque is less sensitive to change in supply frequency.

194. (C):

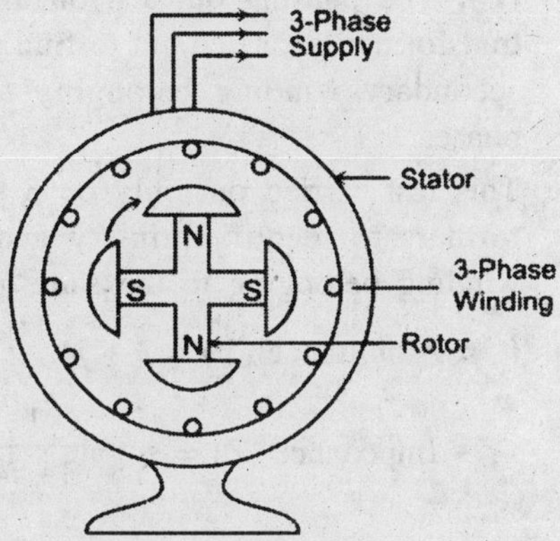

The alternator consists of a stator and a rotor. The 3ϕ AC supply is given on the stator while a DC supply is provided on the rotor. Hence, it is a doubly exciting machine.

In an alternator, the armature windings are placed on the stator while the field winding is placed on the rotor. This is done due to the following advantages:

1. When a stationary armature is used in the alternator, the output current can be taken directly from the fixed terminals on the stationary armature without using slip rings, brushes, etc. Hence, sparking at brushes is completely avoided.
2. The armature windings of the rotating field alternator, being stationary, are not subjected to vibration and centrifugal forces.
3. When the stationary armature is used, the armature windings can be braced better mechanically against the high electromagnetic forces due to large short circuit currents.
4. A stationary armature can be easily insulated for the high voltage for which the alternator is designed. This generated voltage may be as high as 33 kV.
5. The rotating field is supplied with the direct current. Thus, only two slip rings are required to provide direct current for the rotating field.
6. A stationary armature may be cooled easily because the size of the armature can be increased to provide more cooling ducts.

195. (C): Solar-cell efficiency refers to the portion of energy in the form of sunlight that can be converted via photovoltaics into electricity by the solar cell.

The efficiency of the solar cells used in a photovoltaic system, in combination with latitude and climate, determines the annual energy output of the system.

Several factors affect a cell's conversion efficiency, including its reflectance, thermodynamic efficiency, charge carrier separation efficiency, charge carrier collection efficiency and conduction efficiency values.

Reflectance losses are accounted for by the quantum efficiency value, as they affect "external quantum efficiency". Recombination losses are accounted for by the quantum efficiency, V_{OC} ratio, and fill factor values.

Resistive losses are predominantly accounted for by the fill factor value, but also contribute to the quantum efficiency and V_{OC} ratio values.

196. **(C):** Current (I) = 100 mA

Resistance (R) = 10 Ω

Time (t) = 2 min = 120 sec

Electrical energy (E) = I^2Rt

$= (100 \times 10^{-3})^2 \times 10 \times 120 = 12$ J.

197. **(C):** The input current is the base current in CE configuration and it is expressed as

$$I_B = f(V_{BE}, V_{CE})$$

The plot of the input current I_B versus changing input voltage V_{BE} for three fixed values of V_{CE} = 1 V, 10 V, 20 V are shown in Fig. The input dc resistance is the ratio of dc-input voltage and dc input current.

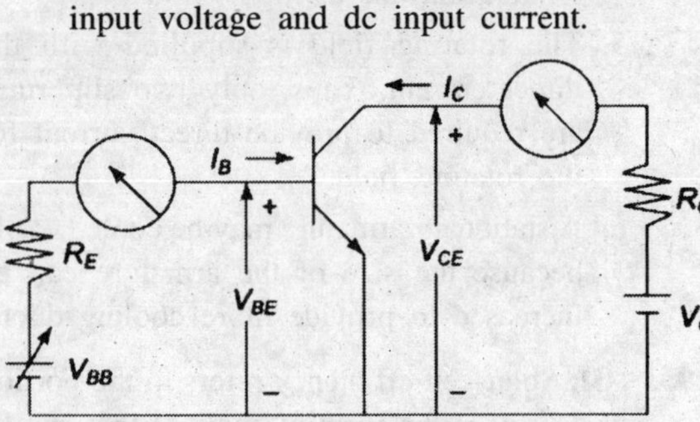

Fig. *CE circuit*

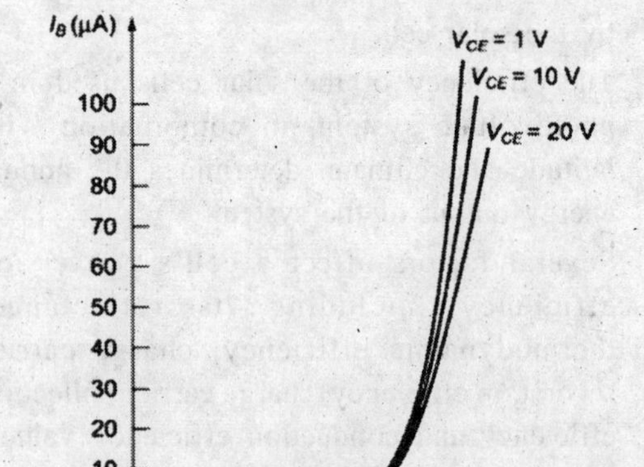

Fig. *Input characteristics of BJT in CE*

The dynamic input resistance in CE configuration of transistor is defined as

$$r_{in} = h_{ie} = \left.\frac{\Delta V_{BE}}{\Delta I_B}\right|_{V_{CE}=K}$$

198. **(C):** V_{rms} = 3.33V (Sine wave)

$$FF = \frac{V_{rms}}{V_{avg}} \text{ (Sine wave)}$$

$$1.11 = \frac{3.33}{V_{avg}}$$

$$V_{avg} = 3$$

$$3 = V_m/2$$

$$V_{avg} = \frac{V_m}{2} \text{ (Triangular wave shape)}$$

$$V_m = 3 \times 2 = 6 \text{ V.}$$

199. **(C):** The phasing out test on a three phase transformer is carried out to find primary and secondary winding belonging to the same phase.

This test carried out only on 3 phase transformers to identify primary and secondary winding belonging to the same phase.

200. **(C):** Admittance (Y) = 3 + j4

$$\text{Impedance (Z)} = \frac{1}{Y} = \frac{1}{3+j4} \times \frac{3-j4}{3-j4}$$

$$= \frac{3-j4}{9+16}$$

$$= \frac{3}{25} - \frac{j4}{25}$$

Compare-Z = R − jX

$$R = \frac{3}{25}\Omega.$$

Previous Paper (Solved)

Junior Engineers (Electrical)

Recruitment Exam 2021*

General Knowledge

1. Who among the following authorities chaired the 22nd meeting of Financial Stability and Development Council held in May 2020?
A. Governor of RBI
B. Union Finance Minister
C. Union Home Affairs Minister
D. Prime Minister

2. The Khelo India Youth Games 2020 was held in which city?
A. Pune B. Guwahati
C. Jaipur D. Nagpur

3. Who was the first Indian to become Governor General of independent India?
A. Jawaharlal Nehru B. Vallabhbhai Patel
C. Rajagopalachari D. Rajendra Prasad

4. Which one of the following is an example of sedimentary rocks?
A. Sandstone B. Basalt
C. Granite D. Marble

5. The simultaneous presence of high rate of inflation and high rate of unemployment is called __________.
A. Disinflation B. Stagflation
C. Deflation D. Depression

6. Under which field Abhijit Banerjee got Nobel Prize?
A. Economics B. Medicine
C. Peace D. Literature

7. Where is the India's research station called Bharati' located?
A. Europe B. Antarctica
C. South America D. Arctic

8. In February 2020, the fourth East Asia Summit conference on maritime security cooperation was held in__________.
A. Berlin B. Dubai
C. Oslo D. Chennai

9. What is the full form of 'SSC', a recruitment governing agency for Government of India?
A. Staff Standardised Commission
B. Staff Scrutiny Commission
C. Staff Selection Commission
D. Staff Screening Commission

10. What is the full form of 'RAM', a type of computer memory?
A. Relative Access Memory
B. Ready Access Memory
C. Random Access Memory
D. Read Access Memory

English Knowledge

11. Rearrange the following to form a meaningful sentence and find the most logical order from the given options.
P : criterion for buying refurbished
Q : price and affordability is the key
R : smartphones amid the pandemic
S : a survey by Cashify suggests that
A. SQPR B. PSRQ
C. SQRP D. PQRS

12. Fill in the blanks with suitable Preposition from the given alternatives.

* *Exam held on 06/01/2021.*

There is a fruit shop just _____ the road.

A. about B. across

C. besides D. since

13. Replace the underlined phrase grammatically and conceptually with the help of the given options. If the given sentence is correct then select the option 'The given sentence is correct'.

The Indian government wants its citizens **to delete the listed apps over** national security concerns.

A. to deleted the listed apps over

B. to delete a listed apps over

C. to deleted a listed apps over

D. The given sentence is correct

14. Find the word which is correctly spelt from the given options.

A. Fractare B. Necessary

C. Weathar D. Spectakular

15. Fill in the blanks with suitable Article from the given alternatives.

March and April are ________ most popular months for holidays.

A. an B. a

C. the D. No Article

16. Choose the best option from the given alternatives which can be substituted for the given word/sentence.

One who collects coins.

A. Mint B. Numismatist

C. Misogynist D. Incredible

17. Find the word which is correctly spelt from the given options.

A. Credibel B. Subtantive

C. Hypothatical D. Stringent

18. Choose the word which expresses nearly the opposite meaning of the given word "INCUMBENT".

A. Unnecessary

B. Necessary

C. Binding

D. Urgent

19. Choose the word which best expresses the similar meaning of the given word "TRIVIAL".

A. Large B. Important

C. Avoid D. Small

20. In the following question, one part of the sentence may have an error. Find out which part of the sentence has an error and select the option corresponding to it. If the sentence does not have any error then select the option 'NO ERROR'. (Avoid punctuation errors)

(A) Every boy and girl / (B) were ready to attend / (C) the function. / (D) NO ERROR.

A. A B. D

C. B D. C

Post Specific Subject Related Questions (Electrical)

21. The given impulse response $h(n)$ of the LTI system is stable when _____.

$$h(n) = \begin{cases} a^n, & n < 0 \\ b^n, & n \geq 0 \end{cases}$$

A. $|a| > 1$ and $|b| > 1$

B. $|a| < 1$ and $|b| < 1$

C. $|a| > 1$ and $|b| < 1$

D. $|a| < 1$ and $|b| > 1$

22. A 25-bus power system has 5 generator buses and 20 load buses. For the load flow analysis using Newton-Raphson method in polar coordinates, the size of the Jacobian matrix is _____.

A. 48 × 48 B. 25 × 25

C. 28 × 28 D. 44 × 44

23. Consider the following two statements and identify the correct option.

Statement 1: The proportional (P) controller completely eliminates a steady state error.

Statement 2: The derivative controller reduces the rate of change of error.

A. Both Statement–1 and Statement–2 are FALSE
B. Statement–1 is TRUE and Statement–2 is FALSE
C. Both Statement–1 and Statement–2 are TRUE
D. Statement–1 is FALSE and Statement–2 is TRUE

24. The bus admittance matrix of a simple four bus system is shown in fig. is given as:

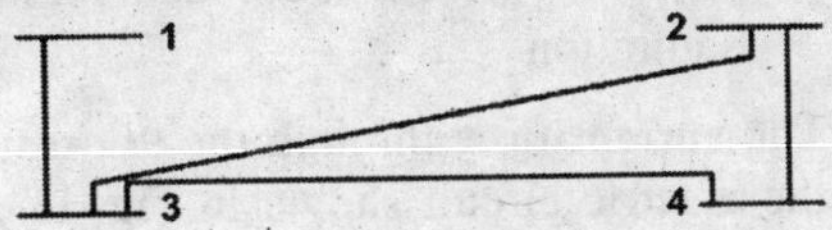

$$Y_{bus} = \begin{bmatrix} 1-j3 & 0 & -1+j3 & 0 \\ 0 & 1.666-j5 & -0.666+j2 & -1+j3 \\ -1+j3 & -0.666+j2 & 3.666-j11 & -2+j6 \\ 0 & -1+j3 & -2+j6 & 3-j9 \end{bmatrix}$$

The shunt admittance at all the buses is assumed to be negligible. If the line of admittance $(2 - j6)$ p.u. is connected between bus 1 and bus 2, the new bus admittance matrix is:

A. $Y_{bus} = \begin{bmatrix} 3-j9 & -2+j6 & -1+j3 & 0 \\ -2+j6 & 3.666-j11 & -0.666+j2 & -1+j3 \\ -1+j3 & -0.666+j2 & 3.666-j11 & -2+j6 \\ 0 & -1+j3 & -2+j6 & 3-j9 \end{bmatrix}$

B. $Y_{bus} = \begin{bmatrix} 3+j3 & 0 & -1+j3 & 0 \\ 0 & 3.666+j1 & -0.666+j2 & -1+j3 \\ -1+j3 & -0.666+j2 & 3.666-j11 & -2+j6 \\ 0 & -1+j3 & -2+j6 & 3-j9 \end{bmatrix}$

C. $Y_{bus} = \begin{bmatrix} 3-j9 & 0 & -1+j3 & 0 \\ 0 & 3.666-j11 & -0.666+j2 & -1+j3 \\ -1+j3 & -0.666+j2 & 3.666-j11 & -2+j6 \\ 0 & -1+j3 & -2+j6 & 3-j9 \end{bmatrix}$

D. $Y_{bus} = \begin{bmatrix} 3+j3 & 2-j6 & -1+j3 & 0 \\ 2-j6 & 3.666+j1 & -0.666+j2 & -1+j3 \\ -1+j3 & -0.666+j2 & 3.666-j11 & -2+j6 \\ 0 & -1+j3 & -2+j6 & 3-j9 \end{bmatrix}$

25. The particular integral of the differential equation $(D^3 + D)y = e^x + e^{-x}$ is ______.

A. $\frac{1}{2}(e^x + e^{-x})$ B. $\frac{1}{2}(e^x - e^{-x})$

C. $\frac{1}{2}(e^x + xe^{-x})$ D. $\frac{1}{2}(e^x - xe^{-x})$

26. Consider the two point particles separated by a distance '*d*' have charges Q_1 and Q_2 respectively. Particle Q_2 experiences an electrostatic force of 20 mN due to particle Q_1. If the charges of both particles are doubled and distance between them is also doubled, what is the magnitude of the electrostatic force between them?

A. 10 mN B. 30 mN
C. 40 mN D. 20 mN

27. The synchronous reactance of the synchronous machine 'X_s' is given as ______ where X_a and X_l are the armature reactance and leakage reactance of the synchronous machine.

A. $X_s = X_a + X_l$ B. $X_s = \frac{X_a - X_l}{2}$

C. $X_s = \frac{X_a + X_l}{2}$ D. $X_s = X_a - X_l$

28. If the severity of single line-to-ground fault at the terminals of an unloaded synchronous generator is lesser than that of 3-phase faults, then ______ where, X_1 is the positive sequence reactance of the generator, X_{g0} is the zero sequence reactance of the generator and X_n is the neutral reactance.

A. $X_n = 3(X_1 - X_{g0})$

B. $X_n < \frac{1}{3}(X_1 - X_{g0})$

C. $X_n = \frac{1}{3}(X_1 - X_{g0})$

D. $X_n > \frac{1}{3}(X_1 - X_{g0})$

29. A transformer has 3% resistance and 6% reactance drop. The voltage regulation at full-load, 0.8 power factor lagging is ______.

A. 6% B. –1.20%
C. –6% D. 1.20%

30. In the two-wattmeter method of power measurement for a three-phase load, the readings of the wattmeter are 2000 W and 1000 W. What is the power factor of the load?

A. 1 B. Zero
C. 0.866 D. 0.5

31. A 25 MVA, 4-pole, 50 Hz turbo-alternator has an inertia constant H = 5 kW sec/kVA. The stored kinetic energy in the rotor at synchronous speed is ________.

A. 100 MJ B. 62.5 MJ
C. 125 MJ D. 50 MJ

32. What is the magnitude of the uniform magnetic field that contains as much energy per unit volume as a uniform 6000 V/m electric field?

A. 1×10^{-5} T
B. 4×10^{-5} T
C. 3×10^{-5} T
D. 2×10^{-5} T

33. What is the time constant of an RL circuit shown in Fig.?

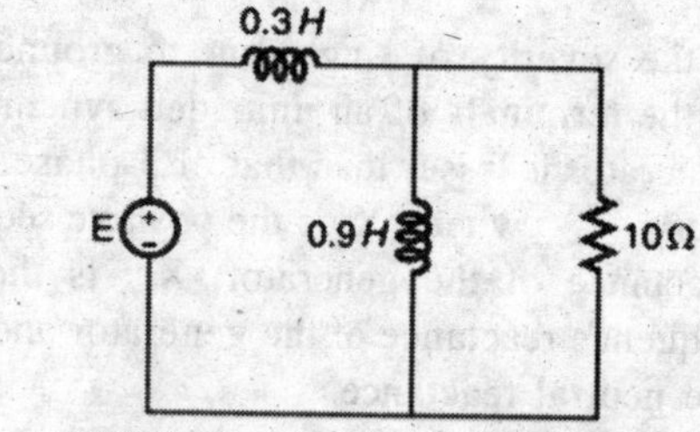

A. 22.5 ms B. 30 ms
C. 60 ms D. 120 ms

34. The value of $\int_0^a \int_0^b \int_0^c xyz\,dx\,dy\,dz$ is equal to:

A. $\frac{a^2c^2c^2}{2}$ B. $\frac{a^2c^2c^2}{2^2}$

C. $\frac{a^2c^2c^2}{8}$ D. $\frac{abc}{2}$

35. The value of $\oint_C \frac{\sin^2 z}{(z-2)^2} dz$, where C is the circle $|z| = 1$ is equal to ______.

A. $\frac{1}{2}$ B. 1

C. 0 D. $\frac{Z}{2}$

36. Synchronous generator voltage obtained by the synchronous impedance method is ________.

A. nearly accurate as the generator is normally operated in the unsaturated region of magnetization
B. higher than actual as it does not account for magnetic saturation
C. lower than actual as it does not account for magnetic saturation
D. nearly accurate as it accounts for magnetic saturation

37. The current flow through the 9Ω resistor for the electric circuit shown in Fig. is ______.

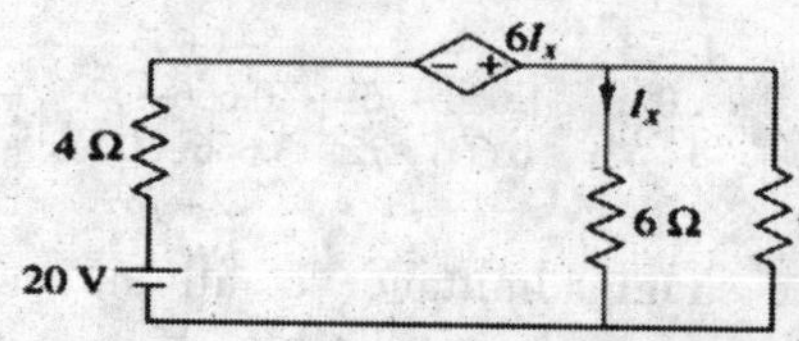

A. 1 A B. 3 A
C. 4 A D. 2 A

38. Consider two DC machines A and B having identical armature and four numbers of poles. If the machine A is wave wound and the machine B is lap wound, then ______.

A. Machine B will have more rated current and more voltage
B. Machine B will have less rated current and less voltage
C. Machine A will have more rated current and less voltage
D. Machine A will have less rated current and more voltage

39. The electromagnetic torque developed in a motor is 200 Nm. If the field flux is decreased by 20% and armature current is increased by 20%, find the new electromagnetic torque developed.

A. 128 Nm B. 240 Nm
C. 288 Nm D. 192 Nm

40. The singular Solution of $z = px + qy + p^2 - q^2$ is ______.

A. $2z = y^2 + x^2$ B. $4z = y^2 + x^2$
C. $4z = y^2 - x^2$ D. $2z = y^2 - x^2$

41. A three phase, 10 kW, 4-pole, 50 Hz induction motor has full load speed of 1440 rpm. The friction and windage loss of the motor at this speed is 500 W. Calculate the rotor copper loss.

A. 295 W B. 395 W
C. 327.5 W D. 437.5 W

42. The coefficient of a_0 in the Fourier series expansion of the function $f(x) = x$ in $-\pi < x < \pi$ is ________.

A. $\frac{\pi^2}{4}$ B. $\frac{\pi^2}{2}$
C. 0 D. π^2

43. In an RS-flip flop, if R and S are set to logic-1 and logic-0 respectively, then the flip flop gives _____.

A. Set state
B. Indeterminate state
C. Hold state
D. Reset state

44. If the flux density is $\vec{D} = (x+3)\hat{a}_x$, find the total charge inside a cubical volume of 1 m on a side situated in the positive octant with three edges coincident with the x, y and z axis and one corner of the origin.

A. 3 Coulombs
B. Zero
C. 4 Coulombs
D. 1 Coulomb

45. Consider a series RLC circuit excited by a sinusoidal source of 20 V resonates at a frequency of 50 Hz. If the bandwidth is 4 Hz, what will be the voltage across the capacitor?

A. 150 V B. 250 V
C. 100 V D. 200 V

46. The radius of curvature of the curve $y = 2x + 3$ at $x = 0$ is equal to _______.

A. ∞ B. 1
C. x D. 0

47. For the electrical circuit shown in Fig., the total current supplied by the 24 V battery is _______.

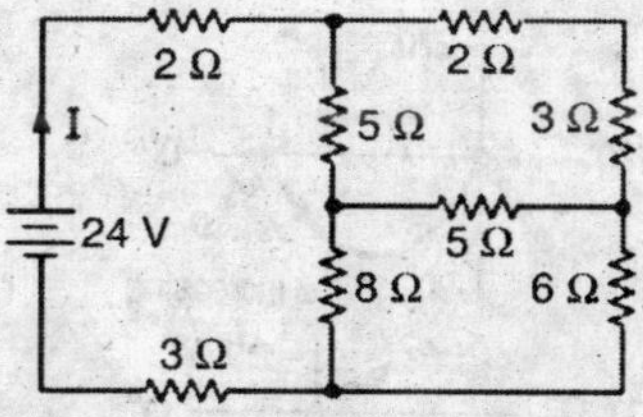

A. 1.1 A B. 4.4 A
C. 2.2 A D. 3.3 A

48. If $L(f(t)) = F(s)$, then $L(t^2 f(t)) =$

A. $-\frac{d^2F(s)}{ds^2}$ B. $2\frac{d^2F(s)}{ds^2}$
C. $\frac{1}{2}\frac{d^2F(s)}{ds^2}$ D. $\frac{d^2F(s)}{ds^2}$

49. For the circuit shown in Fig., the equivalent inductance seen at terminals A and B is ________.

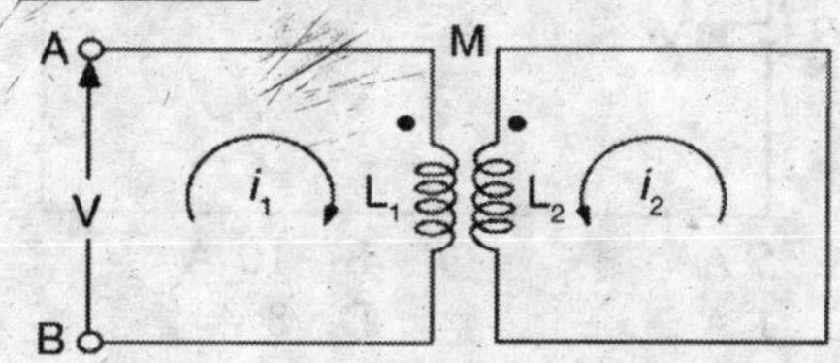

A. $L_{eq} = L_2 - \frac{M^2}{L_1}$ B. $L_{eq} = L_1 + \frac{M^2}{L_2}$
C. $L_{eq} = L_1 - \frac{M^2}{L_2}$ D. $L_{eq} = L_2 + \frac{M^2}{L_1}$

50. The polar plot for the open loop transfer function of a unity feedback system $G(s) = \frac{1}{(1+sT_1)(1+sT_2)(1+sT_3)}$ is given by ____.

A.
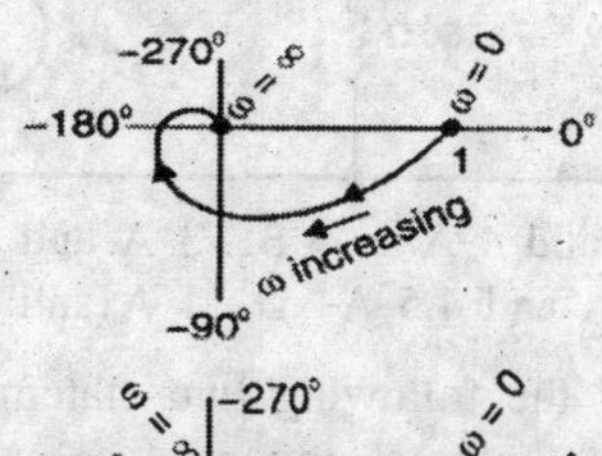

B.
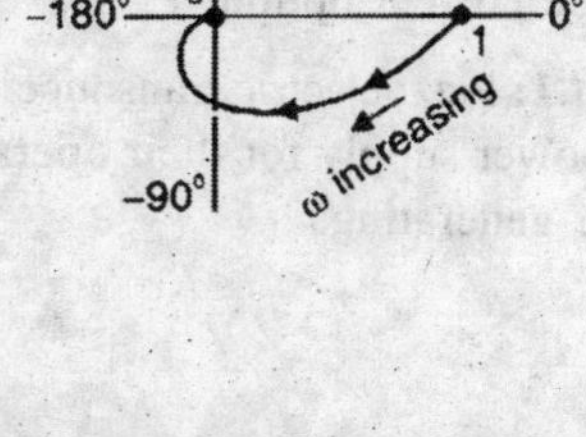

C. 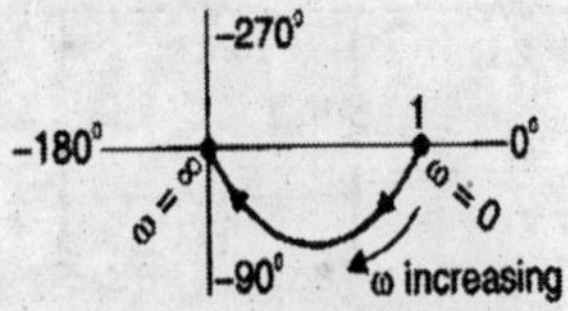

D. 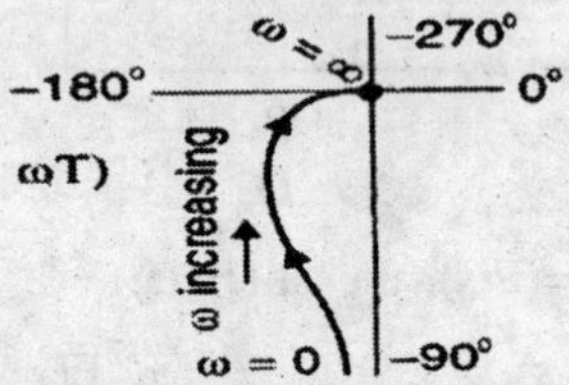

51. Determine the total current in the circuit shown in Fig.

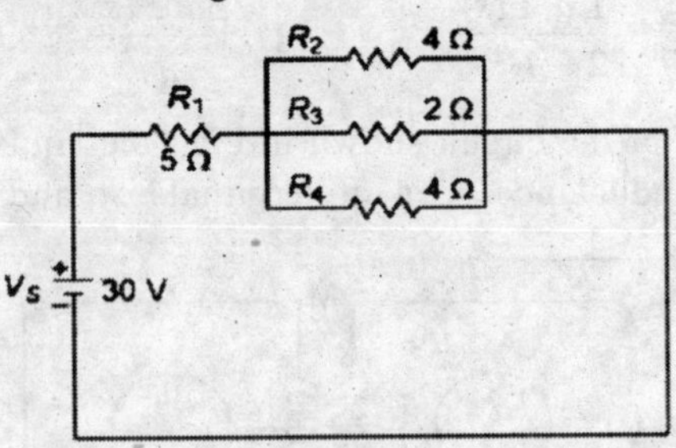

A. 5 A B. 10 A
C. 1 A D. 8 A

52. The symmetric impulse response having even number of samples cannot be used to design ________.

A. Highpass filter B. Bandstop filter
C. Bandpass filter D. Lowpass filter

53. The current 'i_1' and 'i_2' in the circuit shown in Fig. is ______.

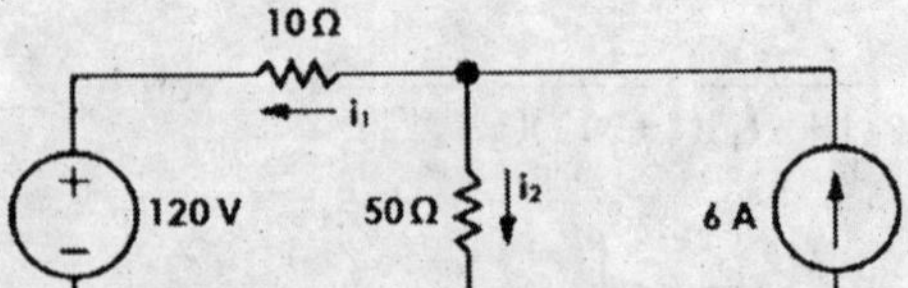

A. 2 A and 4 A B. 3 A and 3 A
C. 1.5 A and 4.5 A D. 1 A and 5 A

54. Consider the following two statements and identify the correct option.

Statement 1: Piezoelectric transducer requires external power supply for their operation and is not self-generating.

Statement 2: Thermistor do not require any external source of supply for their operation and is self-generating.

A. Statement-1 is FALSE and Statement-2 is TRUE
B. Both Statement-1 and Statement-2 are TRUE
C. Both Statement-1 and Statement-2 are FALSE
D. Statement-1 is TRUE and Statement-2 is FALSE

55. A single phase current source inverter (CSI) has a capacitor 'C' as the load. For the constant source current, the voltage across the capacitor is ______.

A. square wave B. pulsed wave
C. step function D. triangular wave

56. An AC voltage controller has a pure resistive load of 10 Ω and input voltage is 150 V(RMS), 50 Hz. The thyristor switch is ON for 25 cycles and OFF for 75 cycles. Determine the RMS output voltage and input power factor.

A. 75 V and 0.5 B. 150 V and 0.5
C. 150 V and 0.866 D. 75 V and 0.866

57. In DC chopper, the load voltage is controlled by ________.

A. number of thyristors used in the circuit
B. DC voltage applied to the circuit
C. duty cycle of the circuit
D. None of the above

58. Determine the value of K for stability of unity feedback system whose open loop transfer function is given by______.

$$G(s) = \frac{K}{s(s+1)(s+5)}$$

A. $0 < K < 45$ B. $K > 30$
C. $0 < K < 30$ D. $K > 45$

59. If $F(f(x)) = \frac{1}{\sqrt{2\pi}}\int_{-\infty}^{\infty} f(x)e^{isx}\,dx = F(s)$, then

$F[f(x - a)] =$

A. e^{-ias} F(s) B. e^{ias} F(s)
C. F(s + a) D. F(s − a)

60. Find the incident average power of an electric field wave travelling in air and incident normally on a boundary between air and a dielectric having permeability μ0 and permittivity $\varepsilon_r = 4$.

A. $P_i = \dfrac{E_i^2}{2\sqrt{\dfrac{\varepsilon_0}{\mu_0}}}$ B. $P_i = \dfrac{E_i^2}{\sqrt{\dfrac{\mu_0}{\varepsilon_0}}}$

C. $P_i = \dfrac{E_i^2}{2\sqrt{\dfrac{\mu_0}{\varepsilon_0}}}$ D. $P_i = \dfrac{E_i^2}{\sqrt{\mu_0 \varepsilon_0}}$

61. Consider the system defined by

$\dot{x} = Ax + Bu$

$y = Cx$

where, $A = \begin{bmatrix} 0 & 1 & 0 \\ 0 & 0 & 1 \\ -6 & -11 & -6 \end{bmatrix}$

$B = \begin{bmatrix} 1 \\ 0 \\ 1 \end{bmatrix}$ and $C = \begin{bmatrix} 10 & 5 & 1 \end{bmatrix}$

Check the system for complete state controllability and complete observability and choose the correct option.

A. The system is completely observable but not completely state controllable
B. The system is not completely state controllable and not completely observable
C. The system is completely state controllable and completely observable
D. The system is completely state controllable but not completely observable

62. Determine the effective inductance of the series-connected coupled coils shown in Fig.

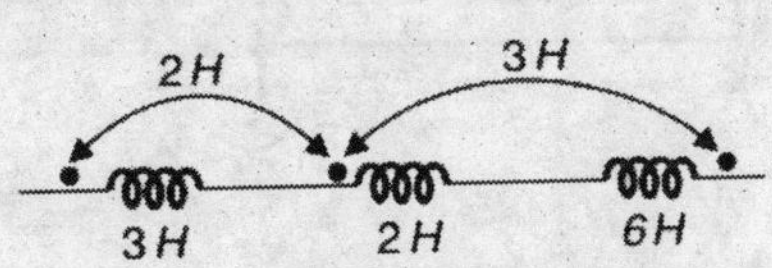

A. 12 H B. 16 H
C. 9 H D. 3 H

63. Consider the following two statements and identify the correct option.

Statement 1: Both MOSFET and BJT have positive temperature coefficient.

Statement 2: MOSFET can be used as a voltage controlled capacitor.

A. Statement-1 is FALSE and Statement-2 is TRUE
B. Statement-1 is TRUE and Statement-2 is FALSE
C. Both Statement-1 and Statement-2 are FALSE
D. Both Statement-1 and Statement-2 are TRUE

64. The transfer function C(s)/R(s) for the block diagram shown in Fig. is:

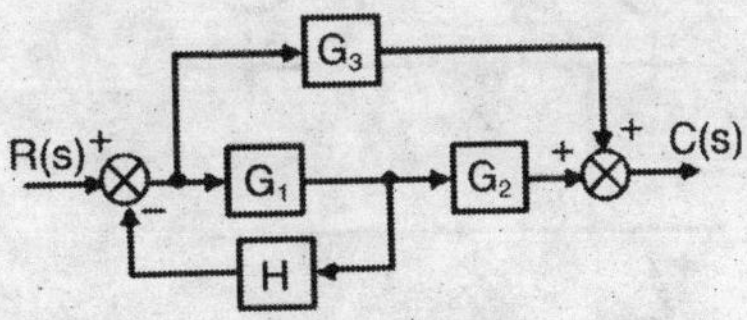

A. $\dfrac{C(s)}{R(s)} = \dfrac{G_1G_2 + G_3}{1 + G_1H}$

B. $\dfrac{C(s)}{R(s)} = \dfrac{G_1 + G_2G_3}{1 + G_1H}$

C. $\dfrac{C(s)}{R(s)} = \dfrac{1 + G_1G_2G_3}{1 + G_1G_2G_3H}$

D. $\dfrac{C(s)}{R(s)} = \dfrac{G_1G_2G_3}{1 + G_1G_2H}$

65. The rotor of a four-pole, 50 Hz slip-ring induction motor has a resistance of 0.2 Ω per phase and runs at 1425 rpm at full-load. Determine the external resistance per phase which must be added to reduce the speed to 1200 rpm, the torque remaining same in both the cases.

A. 0.8 Ω B. 0.2 Ω
C. 0.4 Ω D. 0.6 Ω

66. The zero-sequence network equivalent for the transformer connected between buses 1 and 2 as shown in Fig. is:

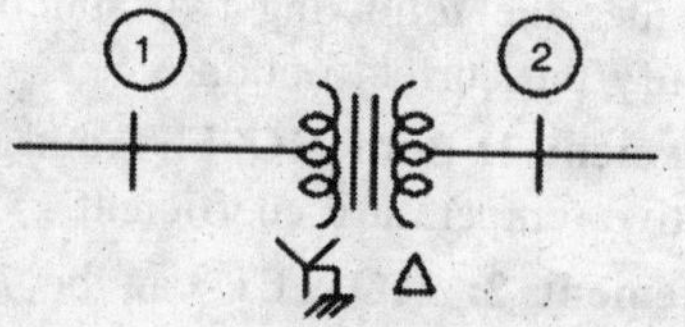

A.

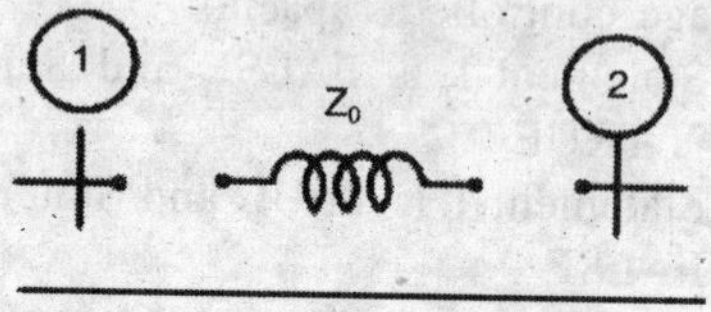

B.

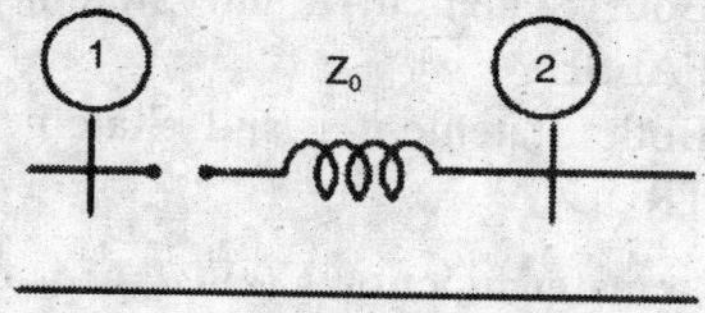

C.

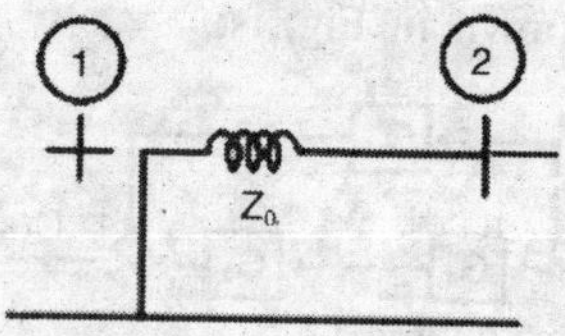

D.

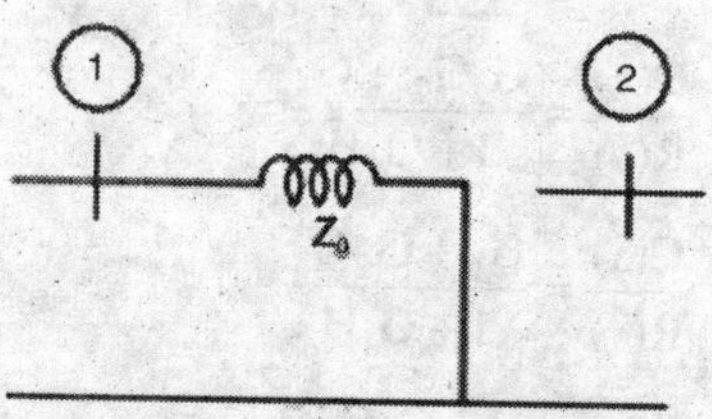

67. A three phase, 4-pole, 50 Hz induction motor has full load speed of 1455 rpm. What will be the frequency of the rotor-induced EMF?

A. 1.5 Hz B. 2 Hz
C. 1 Hz D. 3 Hz

68. Determine the Nyquist sampling frequency and Nyquist interval for the signal, $x(t) = \left[\frac{\sin 200\pi t}{\pi t}\right]^2$

A. 200 Hz, 2.5 ms
B. 200 Hz, 5 ms
C. 400 Hz, 5 ms
D. 400 Hz, 2.5 ms

69. The output expression 'F' for the combinational logic circuit shown in Fig. is given by:

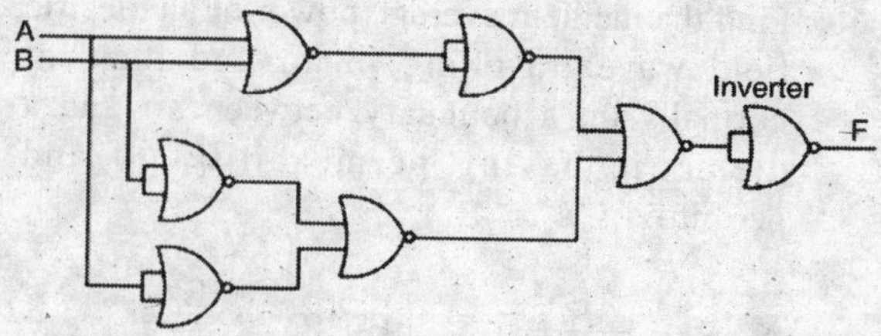

A. $F = AB$ B. $F = \bar{A}\bar{B} + AB$
C. $F = A + B$ D. $F = \bar{A}B + A\bar{B}$

70. If the sum of two eigen values of a 3×3 matrix is equal to the trace of the matrix, then the product of the eigen values is equal to ______.

A. 0 B. 1
C. 9 D. 3

71. In the bridge circuit shown in Fig. when $X_c/R = 1$, the voltmeter reads:

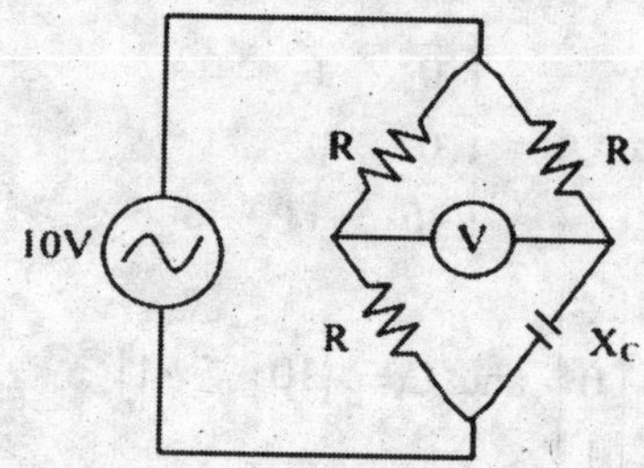

A. 10 V B. 0 V
C. 2.5 V D. 5 V

72. Determine the minimum and maximum closed loop voltage gain for the non-inverting amplifier circuit shown in Fig. Assume an ideal op-amp and the variable resistance varies from 0 to 100 kΩ.

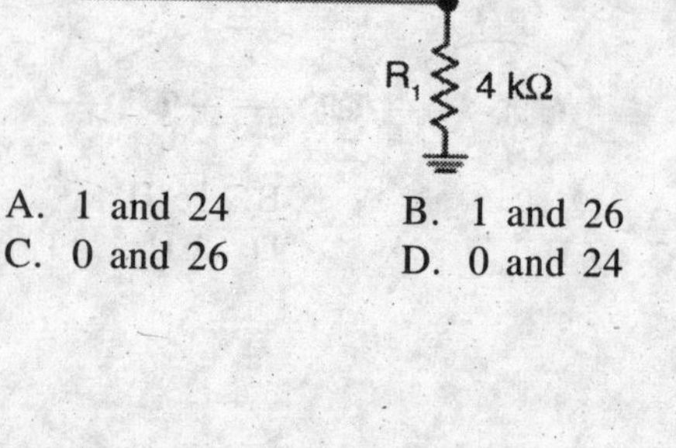

A. 1 and 24 B. 1 and 26
C. 0 and 26 D. 0 and 24

73. A 4-pole wave connected armature of a DC machine has 600 conductors and is driven at 650 rev/min. If the flux per pole is 25mWb, determine the generated emf.

A. 500 V
B. 650 V
C. 162.5 V
D. 325 V

74. Which of the following circuit diagrams represents an average reading AC voltmeter?

A. 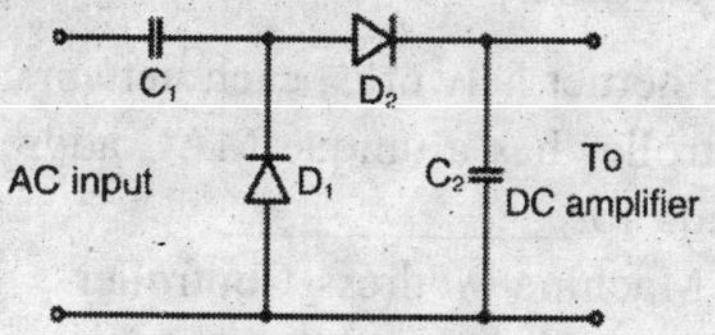

B. 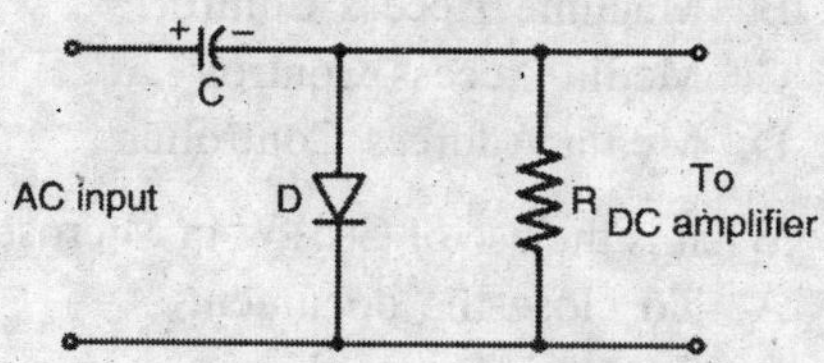

C. 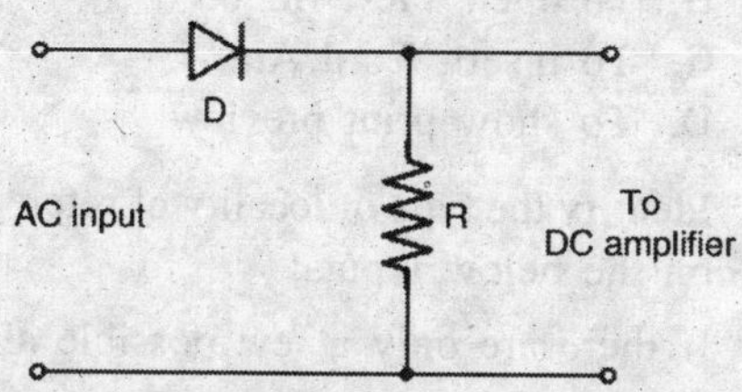

D. None of the above

75. Consider a 3-phase half-wave rectifier circuit shown in the figure. The source is a symmetrical, 3-phase four wire system. The line-to-line voltage of the source is 150 V and the supply frequency is 300 Hz. The ripple frequency at the output is ______.

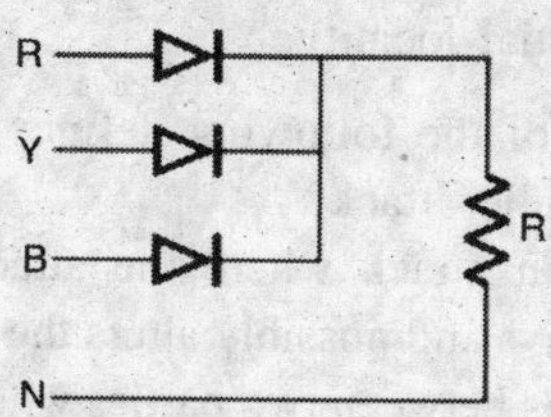

A. 1200 Hz
B. 900 Hz
C. 300 Hz
D. 150 Hz

76. The capacitance measured between terminals B and Y for the circuit shown in Fig. is ________.

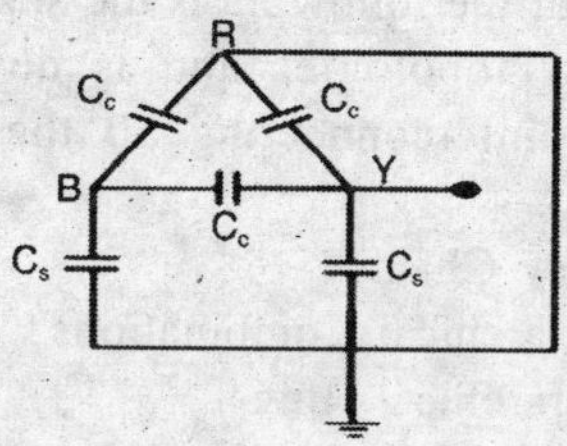

A. $\dfrac{C_c + 2C_s}{3}$
B. $\dfrac{C_s + 3C_c}{2}$
C. $\dfrac{C_s + 2C_c}{3}$
D. $\dfrac{C_c + 3C_s}{2}$

77. If $u = f(x - y, y - z, z - x)$, then $\dfrac{\partial u}{\partial x} + \dfrac{\partial u}{\partial y} + \dfrac{\partial u}{\partial z} =$

A. $2\dfrac{1}{9}$
B. u
C. 0
D. $2u$

78. Which of the following gates is represented by the Boolean expression:

F = A + B + C + D

A. 4-input NAND gate
B. 4-input OR gate
C. 4-input NOR gate
D. 4-input AND gate

79. The full-load copper loss of a transformer is twice its core loss. The efficiency will be maximum at ________.

A. 141% of full load
B. 25% of full load
C. 50% of full load
D. 70.7% of full load

80. Consider a 3-phase, 3-wire system with star connected load of impedance (4 + *j*3) Ω per phase. If the line voltage is 240 V, the power absorbed by each phase is ______.

A. 1775 W
B. 3072 W
C. 5320 W
D. 2944 W

Computer Knowledge

81. Which of the following is the simplest of the complex topologies and is developed by serially interconnecting all the hubs of a network?

A. Daisy Chains
B. Hierarchical Combinations
C. Hierarchical Rings
D. Hierarchical Stars

82. Which of the following is false about Trojan horse?

A. Trojan horse refers to tricking someone into inviting an attacker into a securely protected area.
B. Trojan horse is a software that is designed to be spread from one computer to another, often sent as email attachment.
C. Trojan horse can inject themselves into other files or otherwise propagate themselves.
D. Trojan horse is a malicious bit of attacking code or software that tricks users into running it willingly, by hiding behind a legitimate program.

83. ________ replaced vacuum tubes in computer designs, giving rise to the second generation of computers.

A. Large scale Integration chips
B. Microprocessors
C. Transistors
D. Integrated Chips

84. Which of the following is the only memory management method that does not provide the user's programwith a linear and contiguous address space?

A. Paged Memory Management
B. Partitioned Allocation
C. Single Contiguous Allocation
D. Segmented Memory Management

85. Which of the following is not true about process and thread?

A. A process will need certain resources such as CPU time, memory, etc.
B. A thread may contain multiple processes.
C. A process can be thought of as a program in execution.
D. If multiple threads attempt to access the synchronization objects, deadlock is possible.

86. In Ethernet networks, each network interface controller has a unique MAC address. MAC stands for_____________.

A. Machine Address Controller
B. Machine Access Control
C. Media Access Control
D. Media Address Controller

87. What is the use of Ctrl+W in Microsoft Word?

A. To close the document
B. To open View ribbon
C. To insert Word Art
D. To show print preview

88. Identify the type of locality of reference based on the below inputs:

If there are only a few possible alternatives for the prospective part of the path, when an instruction loop has a simple structure or restricted to a small set of possibilities and the possibilities can be located far away from each other.

A. Branch locality
B. Temporal locality
C. Equidistant locality
D. Spatial locality

89. Which of the following defines the Man-in-the-middle attack?

A. is an attack where the attacker secretly relays and possibly alters the communications between two parties who believe that they are directly communicating with each other.

B. is a cyber-attack in which the perpetrator seeks to make a machine or network resource unavailable to its intended users by temporarily or indefinitely disrupting services of a host connected to the Internet.

C. is a form of computer security hacking in which corrupt Domain Name System data is introduced into the DNS resolver's cache, causing the name server to return an incorrect result record.

D. a technique by which an attacker sends Address Resolution Protocol messages onto a local area network.

90. Which of the following MS Excel functions will produce random number integers > = 1 and < = 5 (ignore single quote in front)?

A. '=int(rand()*6)

B. '=randbetween(1,5)

C. '=randbetween(0,6)

D. '=rand()*5

ANSWERS

1	**2**	**3**	**4**	**5**	**6**	**7**	**8**	**9**	**10**
B	B	C	A	B	A	B	D	C	C
11	**12**	**13**	**14**	**15**	**16**	**17**	**18**	**19**	**20**
A	B	D	B	C	B	D	A	D	C
21	**22**	**23**	**24**	**25**	**26**	**27**	**28**	**29**	**30**
C	D	D	A	B	D	A	D	A	C
31	**32**	**33**	**34**	**35**	**36**	**37**	**38**	**39**	**40**
C	D	A	*	C	B	D	D	D	C
41	**42**	**43**	**44**	**45**	**46**	**47**	**48**	**49**	**50**
D	C	D	D	B	A	C	D	C	A
51	**52**	**53**	**54**	**55**	**56**	**57**	**58**	**59**	**60**
A	A	B	C	D	A	C	C	B	C
61	**62**	**63**	**64**	**65**	**66**	**67**	**68**	**69**	**70**
C	C	A	A	D	D	A	D	C	A
71	**72**	**73**	**74**	**75**	**76**	**77**	**78**	**79**	**80**
B	B	D	C	B	B	C	B	D	B
81	**82**	**83**	**84**	**85**	**86**	**87**	**88**	**89**	**90**
A	B	C	D	B	C	A	A	A	B

Previous Paper (Solved)

Junior Engineers (Electrical)

Recruitment Exam 2020*

Post Specific Subject Related Questions (Technical)

1. Which of the following function is not performed by a transformer?

A. Transfers electric energy from one circuit to another

B. Transfers electric energy with a change of frequency

C. Transfers electric energy by electro-magnetic induction

D. Transfers electric energy where the two electric circuits are in mutual inductive influence of each other.

2. The ratio of rotor copper loss with rotor output is:

A. (1 – s)   B. 1/s

C. S   D. s/(1 – s)

3. Demand Factor =

A. Average load / Maximum load during a given period

B. Sum of Individual Max. Demand / Max. Demand on Power Station

C. The time that an equipment is in use / The total time that it could be in use

D. Maximum demand of a system / Total connected load on the system

4. It is a single-crystal semiconductor material with no other types of atoms within the crystal.

A. extrinsic semiconductors

B. intrinsic semiconductors

C. insulators

D. conductors

5. The amount of electrical energy stored for every kilogram of battery mass is defined as ________.

A. specific energy

B. self-discharge rates

C. energy density

D. specific power

6. A ________ is an *npn* or *pnp* sandwich of semiconductor materials.

A. BJT   B. FET

C. Gate   D. UJT

7. Which of the following is NOT a part of automatic control systems?

A. A controller which affects the actuator

B. A sensor for the process variable

C. The fluid to be controlled

D. A Transformer system

8. In which of the following motors is torque produced due to the tendency of the rotor to align itself in the minimum reluctance position when the speed of the motor is close to the synchronous speed?

A. Hysteresis motor

B. Repulsion motor

C. Reluctance motor

D. Universal motor

9. _______ is the flux-producing ability of an electric current in a magnetic circuit.

A. Electromotive force

B. Flux density

C. Magnetomotive force

D. Magnetic field strength

10. _______ are used in control systems to attain the mechanical matching of the motor to the load.

A. Synchros   B. DC servomotors

C. Gear trains   D. Stepper motors

* *Exam held on 22/01/2020 (Conducted by UP Metro Rail Corporation Limited)*

11. In simple Series RLC circuit, _________ corresponds to infinite capacitance C = ∞ and zero inductance L = 0.
A. RLC Series Circuit
B. Purely inductive circuit
C. Purely resistive circuit
D. Purely capacitive circuit

12. Convert $(0.7854)_{10}$ to binary.
A. $(0.1010)_2$ B. $(0.1110)_2$
C. $(0.1100)_2$ D. $(0.1101)_2$

13. Which law states: The sum of voltages around a closed loop circuit is equal to zero.
A. Voltage divider rule
B. Current division rule
C. Kirchhoffs Voltage Law
D. Kirchhoffs Current Law

14. In _______, the susceptibility will decrease with increase in temperature and they have relatively small susceptibility at all temperatures.
A. Anti ferromagnetic materials
B. Ferrimagnetic materials
C. Superparamagnetic materials
D. Ferromagnetic materials

15. _______ possess NO free-charge carriers and thus are non-conductive.
A. Salts B. Conductors
C. Insulators D. Semiconductors

16. The cosine of the angle between useful power and total power is _______.
A. diversity factor B. load factor
C. power factor D. demand factor

17. _______ has the property of storing potential energy.
A. A spring B. A damper
C. Friction D. Mass

18. A register capable of incrementing and/or decrementing its contents.
A. Counter B. Decoder
C. Multiplexer D. Demultiplexer

19. What is the motor load factor when a motor of 20 hp drives a constant 15 hp load whenever it is on?
A. 75% B. 65%
C. 85% D. 95%

20. Following type control system uses the concept of an open loop system as its forward path but has one or more feedback loops or paths between its output and its input.
A. Adaptive control system
B. Automatic control system
C. Closed loop control system
D. Optimal control system

21. The difference between the tooth space and tooth width in mechanical systems which is essential for rapid working gear transmission is known as ______.
A. dead zone B. friction
C. backlash D. relay

22. A series RLC circuit with L = 160 mH, C = 100 μF and R = 40.0 Ω is connected to a sinusoidal voltage $V(t) = 40.0 \sin \omega t$, with ω = 200 rad/s. What is the impedance and phase ϕ of the circuit?
A. 43.9 Ω, –24.2° B. 33.9 Ω, 35.2°
C. 54.0 Ω, –42.2° D. 65.9 Ω, –80.2°

23. Which of the following type of motors has the armature placed in rotor and the field winding replaced by permanent magnet poles fixed due to the stator to produce the required magnetic field?
A. Armature controlled DC servomotors
B. Electromagnetic field DC motors
C. Permanent magnet DC motors
D. Field controlled DC servomotors

24. Fermi energy level for *n*-type extrinsic semiconductors lies _______ .
A. close to the conduction band
B. None of these options
C. in the middle of the band gap
D. close to the valence band

25. Which of the following is an advantage of an AC transmission system?
A. Problems of skin effects and proximity effects are found only in AC systems.
B. The alternating voltages can easily be stepped up and down

C. The reactance of the line affects the voltage regulation of the electrical power transmission system.
D. Construction of AC electrical power transmission network is more complicated than DC systems.

26. The systems which control the motion of electrical machines are known as ______.
A. electroforming B. electric heating
C. electrical motors D. electrical drives

27. ________ are those whose field magnets are energized from an independent external source of DC current.
A. Series generator
B. Shunt generator
C. Compound generator
D. Separately excited generator

28. For ________, the output C(s) of the system is equal to transfer function of the system.
A. Impulse response
B. Step response
C. Parabolic response
D. Ramp response

29. A three phase IM, six poles, 50 Hz is supplied by a three phase source. The rotor rotates at 800 rpm. Calculate the slip.
A. 0.2 B. 0.3
C. 0.1 D. 0.4

30. ______ is defined as maximum current can flow through the breaker from time of occurring short circuit to the time of clearing the short circuit without any permanent damage in the Circuit breaker.
A. short time current
B. short circuit breaking current
C. short circuit making capacity
D. operating sequence of a circuit breaker

31. Radar tracking systems, missile tracking systems and machine tool position control are applications of _______.
A. AC closed loop control system
B. DC closed loop control system
C. a position control system
D. automatic tank level control system

32. ________ is equal to the current passing through short circuited output terminals.
A. Thevenin's voltage
B. Load current
C. Load resistance
D. Norton's current

33. _______ of measurement is a measure of the change in instrument output that occurs when the quantity being measured changes by a given amount.
A. Sensitivity B. Linearity
C. Hysteresis D. Resolution

34. In a split phase machine, the main winding has low resistance but high reactance whereas the starting winding has a _______ resistance, but ______ reactance:
A. Low, High B. High, Low
C. Low, Low D. High, High

35. Which among the following is an electro-magnetic transducer commonly used to convert an angular position of shaft into electric signal and which produces an output voltage depending upon the angular position of the rotor.
A. synchro B. gear train
C. stepper motor D. DC servomotor

36. Which of the following is a measure of the flow of electric charge over time?
A. Power B. Voltage
C. Energy D. Current

37. Which of the following acts as a covering and it provides protection and mechanical strength to all the inner parts of the induction motor?
A. Stator frame
B. Stator winding
C. Squirrel cage rotor
D. Stator core

38. A _______ is a combined unit of ampere meter, voltmeter and ohmmeter.
A. clip-on meter
B. power factor meter
C. tongue tester
D. multi-meter

39. In motor operations, if at any time ______, the motor will accelerate

A. $T_e > T_L$ B. $T_e = T_L$
C. $T_e = -T_L$ D. $T_e < T_L$

40. ________ is performed when the diode is forward biased during the negative half-cycle of the input in Negative Diode Clipping Circuits.

A. No rectification
B. Full wave rectification
C. Positive half wave rectification
D. Negative half wave rectification

41. Servomechanisms are _______ where the feedback signals are used to control position, speed, velocity, acceleration, etc.

A. adaptive control systems
B. open loop control systems
C. closed loop control systems
D. optimal control systems

42. ________ is the process of plating one metal onto another by hydrolysis, most commonly for decorative purposes or to prevent corrosion of a metal.

A. Illumination B. Electric welding
C. Electric heating D. Electroplating

43. The amount of electrical energy consumed by a circuit over a period of time is ______.

A. angular frequency
B. decibel
C. time constant
D. watt-hour

44. The function of this element is to manipulate the signal presented to it preserving the original nature of the signal.

A. Data presentation element
B. Variable conversion element
C. Primary sensing element
D. Variable manipulation element

45. ______ consists of a high-performance permanent magnet motor, often with an integral tachogenerator, and a chopper-type power amplifier module in DC motor.

A. Thyristor DC drives
B. Chopper-fed DC motor drives
C. Digitally controlled drives
D. DC servo drives

46. Which of the following is the most common protection device that can make or break the circuit either manually or through remote control under normal operating conditions?

A. Protective relay
B. Fuse
C. Circuit breaker
D. Lighting arrestor

47. ________ are usually difficult to treat mathematically and there are no general methods available for solving a wide class of these systems.

A. Non-linear control systems
B. Time-invariant control systems
C. Time-varying control systems
D. Linear control systems

48. It is defined as the degree of the measurement system. It indicates changes in the measure and without any dynamic error.

A. Respond time B. Dynamic error
C. Measuring lag D. Fidelity

49. Which of the following is a unit of voltage?

A. Joule / Coulomb B. Joule / second
C. Joule D. Coulomb / second

50. Which of the following provides leading current which neutralize (totally or approximately) the lagging inductive component of load current (*i.e.* leading component neutralize or eliminate the lagging component of load current) thus power factor of the load circuit is improved?

A. Multipliers
B. Static Capacitors
C. Phase Advancers
D. Synchronous Condensers

51. ________ is an instrument used for measuring electrical potential difference between two points in an electric circuit.

A. Voltmeter B. Potentiometer
C. Ammeter D. Galvanometer

52. In intrinsic semiconductors, the number of electrons is _______ the number of holes.
A. less than B. greater than
C. equal to D. Can not define

53. _______ can be defined as an abnormal connection of very low impedance between two points of different potential, whether made intentionally or accidentally.
A. Symmetrical faults
B. Short circuit faults
C. Open circuit faults
D. Unsymmetrical faults

54. Mixed Node is defined as:
A. A node which has neither incoming nor outgoing branches
B. A node which has only outgoing branches
C. A node which has both incoming and outgoing branches
D. A node which has only incoming branches

55. The function of the _______ is to facilitate collection of current from the armature conductors.
A. Yoke B. Commutator
C. Pole D. Brush

56. In a capacitor filter rectifier circuit, _____ the capacitance value, higher will be the power factor.
A. Lower B. Higher
C. Unaffected D. Equal

57. _______ employs mesh analysis to find the different mesh currents by finding the IR products in each mesh.
A. KCL
B. Current divider rule
C. KVL
D. Voltage divider rule

58. In which of the following, vibration galvanometer, tuneable amplifier and headphones are used?
A. Triangular wave bridges
B. DC bridges
C. Trapezoidal wave bridges
D. AC bridges

59. _______ is also known as Inverter.
A. NOT Gate B. OR Gate
C. NAND Gate D. AND Gate

60. In industries, _______ is required for the melting of metals, moulding of glass, enamelling of copper, baking of insulator and welding etc.
A. electroplating B. illumination
C. electric heating D. electric welding

61. High resistances are provided with a guard terminal. This guard terminal used to:
A. To eliminate the effect of leads
B. Guard the resistance against stray electrostatic fields
C. Bypass the leakage current
D. Guard the resistance against overloads

62. _________ of the consumers may be either connected to the distributors or sub-distributors depending upon the position and agreement of consumers.
A. Distribution sub-station
B. Service mains
C. Primary distribution feeder
D. Distribution transformer

63. The pole faces shaped to fit the curvature of the armature are known as the _______.
A. armature winding
B. pole core
C. pole shoe
D. field winding

64. Control system in which the output has no influence or effect on the control action of the input signal is called:
A. closed loop control system
B. open loop control system
C. automatic control system
D. optimal control system

65. Some metals lose all resistivity abruptly and completely at some low temperatures, above 0 K. This phenomenon is called:
A. Semiconductivity
B. Superconductivity
C. Ferro-electricity
D. Piezo-electricity

66. Drain current vs gate-source voltage characteristics of n-channel enhancement type MOSFET is:

A. 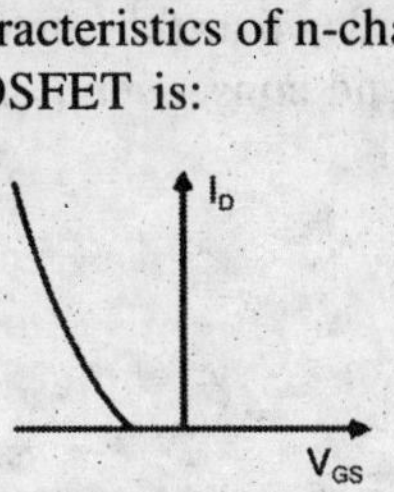

B. 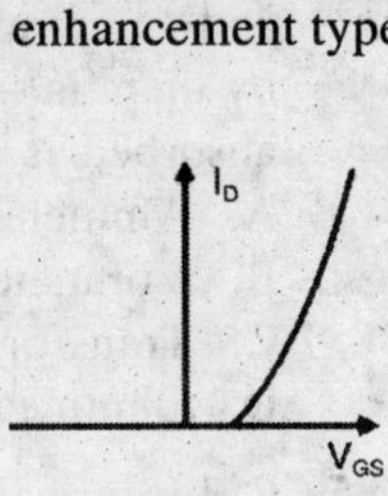

C. 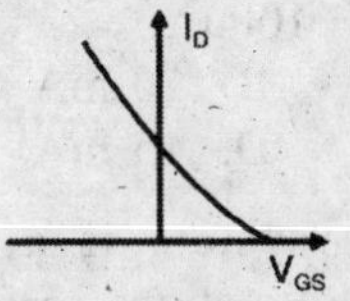

D. 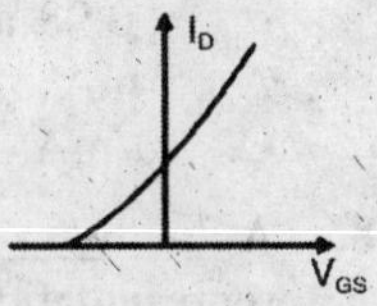

67. The most conventional method of generating electric power with reasonably high efficiency:

A. Thermal power
B. Solar energy
C. Hydro-electric power
D. Nuclear power

68. The ratio of electrical energy supplied by a battery to the amount of electrical energy required to return it to the state before discharge is defined as _______.

A. energy efficiency
B. energy density
C. self-discharge rates
D. Ahr (or charge) efficiency

69. Which of the following is NOT an example of a secondary instrument?

A. Ammeter
B. Tangent galvanometer
C. Voltmeter
D. Wattmeter

70. The instruments which use a permanent magnet for creating a stationary magnetic field between which the coil moves is known as a ________.

A. PMMC instrument
B. transformer
C. generator
D. galvanometer

71. Which of the following welding processes uses a continuously fed electrode through a welding gun and the operator needs to pull a trigger in order to feed the consumable electrode through?

A. Flux-cored arc welding
B. Gas tungsten arc welding
C. Gas metal arc welding
D. Stick-shielded metal arc welding

72. Which part of the induction motor among the following carries a 3-phase winding and is fed from a 3-phase supply?

A. Commutator B. Stator
C. Air Gap D. Rotor

73. Conduction of current in both directions in an element (example: Resistance: Inductance: Capacitance) with the same magnitude is termed as ________.

A. bilateral element B. passive element
C. active element D. unilateral element

74. Which of the below is not a merit of static relay?

A. Fast response
B. Compact size
C. Sensitive to voltage transients
D. Long life

75. ______ finds the voltage potentials at different nodes that provide a common connection for two or more circuit components in a circuit.

A. Norton's theorem
B. Mesh current analysis
C. Nodal voltage analysis
D. Thevenin's theorem

76. The ________ determines the ability of the transformer to provide the constant voltage for variable loads.

A. transformation ratio
B. voltage regulation of a transformer
C. transformer losses
D. efficiency of a transformer

77. ______ is a machine that converts mechanical energy into electrical energy.

A. transformer B. wattmeter
C. generator D. motor

78. _________ is an analytical method used to change a complex circuit into a simple equivalent circuit consisting of a single resistance in series with a source voltage.
A. Superposition theorem
B. Thevenin's theorem
C. Maximum power transfer theorem
D. Norton's theorem

79. A voltmeter has resistance of 2000 Ω, when it is connected across a DC circuit its power consumption is 2mW. Suppose this voltmeter is replaced by a voltmeter of 4000 Ω resistance, the power consumption will be:
A. 2mW B. 4mW
C. 3mW D. 1mW

80. In ________ materials each atom has a relatively large dipole moment, caused primarily by uncompensated electron spin moment.
A. ferrimagnetic
B. superparamagnetic
C. ferromagnetic
D. anti-ferromagnetic

81. Due to its smooth rotor, the following motor operates quietly and does not suffer from magnetic pulsations caused by slots/salient poles that are present in the rotors of other motors.
A. hysteresis motor B. stepper motor
C. universal motor D. reluctance motor

82. Faraday's Law of Induction is represented as _________.
A. $\phi_B = \int \vec{B}d\vec{A}$ B. $\vec{F} = I\vec{L} \times \vec{B}$
C. $\vec{F} = q\vec{v} \times \vec{B}$ D. $\varepsilon = -\frac{d\phi_B}{dt}$

83. For percentage differential protection or normal differential protection, the _______ in the primary and secondary winding should be same.
A. magnetising inrush current
B. transformer phase shift
C. length of the pilot wire
D. current transformer ratio

84. The following have a high electrical resistance and essential in order that the current drawn by them is small and consequently the power absorbed is small.
A. Ammeters
B. Voltmeters
C. Transformers
D. Ohmmeters

85. Calculate I_E for a transistor that has $\alpha_{dc} = 0.98$ and $I_B = 100\mu A$.
A. 5 mA B. 20 mA
C. 10 mA D. 15 mA

86. A ________ of a system is a pictorial representation of the functions performed by each component and of the flow of signals.
A. signal flow graph
B. block diagram
C. test signal
D. transfer function

87. In which material, a magnetic field induces a magnetic moment that opposes the very magnetic field that actually causes it.
A. Ferromagnetic
B. Ferrimagnetic
C. Diamagnetic
D. Anti ferromagnetic

88. A good insulating material should not possess:
A. Non-uniform viscosity
B. High dielectic strength
C. Least thermal expansion
D. Large insulating resistance

89. A ______ is a device used in electrical power systems and telecommunication systems to protect the insulation and conductors of the system from the damaging effects of lightning.
A. lightning arrester
B. bus bar
C. buchholz relay
D. feeder

90. Which of the following class of insulating materials include cotton, silk, paper, cellulose, wood, etc.
A. Class E B. Class A
C. Class B D. Class Y

Quantitative Aptitude & Logical Ability

91. 10 men do a work in 15 days. 7 men and 3 women do the same work in 20 days. The number of days taken by a woman to do the work is:

A. 300 B. 600
C. 900 D. 150

92. Select an option that most suitably relates to 'Court' in the same manner as 'Skating' is related to 'Rink'.

A. Hockey B. Tennis
C. Justice D. Judge

93. A lion prowled 900 m north from its den. It took a right turn and prowled 800 m. It, then took a right turn and prowled 700 m. It, again, took a right turn and prowled 600 m. Which direction is the lion facing now?

A. North B. West
C. East D. South

94. The bar graph given below shows the total number of productions of a certain product X by different brands: P, LG, S, E and H (in thousand numbers) sold by a supplier in 2017 and 2018.

Study the graph carefully and answer the following question.

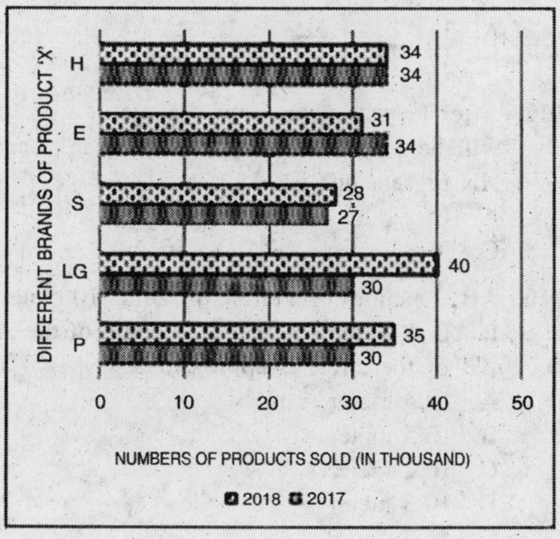

Total number of product X sold in 2017 and 2018 together was equal in case of which of the following pairs of brand of product X?

A. P & E B. H & LG
C. E & H D. S & H

95. Select an option that is different from the rest in a certain way.

A. Paper : Oil
B. Sack : Jute
C. Rubber : Latex
D. Metal : Ore

96. Two circles having centers at A and B have radii 4 and 5. If AB = 9, the number of common tangents to them is:

A. 1 B. 4
C. 2 D. 3

97. From the top of a tower of height 100 meter, the angles of depression of two houses A and B on two opposite sides of the tower are 30 and 60 degree respectively. The distance between A and B is approximately:

A. 210 meter
B. 230 meter
C. 220 meter
D. 200 meter

98. If '+' means 'divided by', '–' means 'add', '×' means 'minus' and '÷' means 'multiplied by', what will be the value of the following expression?

$[\{(5 \times 1) \div 2\} + (1 - 1)]/1$

A. 8 B. 2
C. 6 D. 4

99. Ram, Shyam, and Mohan start a business with investments of ₹ 50000, 100000, and 150000 respectively. After the end of one year, Shyam withdraws ₹ 50000, and after the end of two year. Mohan withdraws ₹ 100000. At the end of three years, the profit is 350000. The share of Mohan will be:

A. ₹ 175000 B. ₹ 150000
C. ₹ 180000 D. ₹ 125000

100. The value of $-20 \div (36 \div 3^2 \times 6 \div 6) \times 5 - 3$ is:

A. –2 B. –28

C. –4 D. –22

101. If in a certain code, 'VIXEN' is written as 'ERCVM', how will 'MAGIC' be written using the same code?

A. NYSRY B. NZTRX

C. LYTRU D. NXRSY

102. There are five students- A, B, C, D and E having different heights in Class. A's height is more than only one student. B's height is more than D and A but not more than C. D's height is more than A. C is not the smallest. Who has the maximum height in the class?

A. D B. B

C. C D. E

103. In the expansion of $(a + b)^8$, the coefficient of a^5b^3 is:

A. 64 B. 56

C. 40 D. 72

104. Two pipes A and B are such that the pipe B alone can fill a tank in 12 hours more time than the time taken to fill it by the pipe A alone. If A and B together fill the tank in 8 hours, then the time taken by A to fill the tank is:

A. 10 hours B. 16 hours

C. 12 hours D. 15 hours

105. Select the option that is different from the rest in a certain manner.

A. 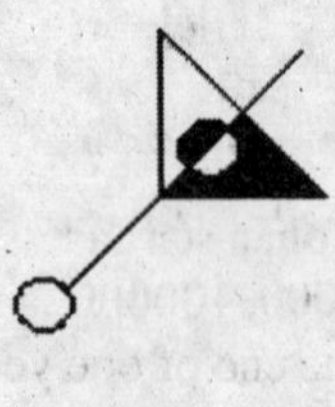

B. 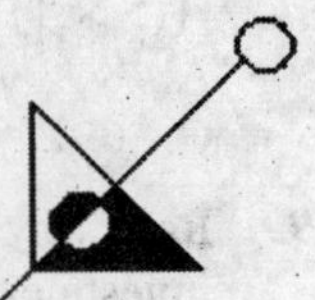

C. 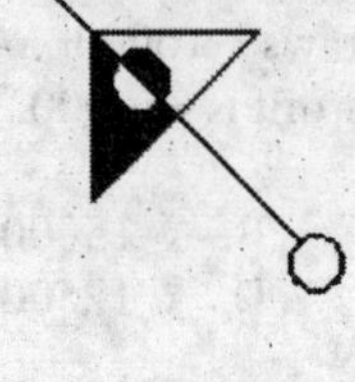

D. 

106. A car covers certain distance in certain time at the speed of 40 km/hr. At the speed of 56 km/hr, it can cover 80 km more in the same time. The original distance travelled by the car is:

A. 200 km B. 240 km

C. 245 km D. 225 km

107. Consider the given statement and decide which of the given assumptions is/are implicit in the statement.

Statement: The government has made an appeal to all the citizens to honestly pay income tax and contribute in the developmental process of the country.

Assumptions:

I. The appeal will cause people to realise their responsibilities as the citizens of the country.

II. A larger number of citizens will start paying income tax.

A. Only assumptions II implicit

B. Neither assumption I nor II implicit.

C. Both assumptions I and II implicit

D. Only assumptions I implicit

108. Understand the pattern of the following series then find the next number from the following options.

1, 3, 7, 13, 21, ?

A. 31 B. 25

C. 37 D. 28

109. After 10 years from now, the age of a person will be square of his age at 10 years back. His present age is:

A. 15 B. 12

C. 18 D. 16

110. AB is a chord of a circle of radius 10 meters. If AB = 10 meters, then the length of the arc AB of the circle is approximately:

A. 10.4 meter

B. 10.5 meter

C. 10.2 meter

D. 10.3 meter

General English

111. Parts of the following sentence are given as options. Identify the part that has an error.

I would have helped you if I had know.

A. helped you
B. had know
C. if I
D. I would have

112. Select the most appropriate ANTONYM of the given word.

DEPART

A. emerge B. arrive
C. leave D. receive

113. Select the most appropriate synonym of the given word.

ACQUIRE

A. give B. get
C. lend D. destroy

114. Select the option that can be used as a one-word substitute for the given phrase.

A person who sells glasses and contact lenses

A. eye doctor
B. ophthalmologist
C. optical dispenser
D. optician

115. Parts of a sentence are given below in jumbled order. Arrange the parts in the right order to form a meaningful sentence.

Use snake hand your enemy's to catch a

A. Use your enemy's hand to catch a snake.
B. Use hand your to catch an enemy's snake.
C. Use your snake enemy's to catch a hand.
D. Use a snake catch to your enemy's hand.

116. Select the option that expresses the given sentence in indirect speech.

Sam told me, "You can take the weekend off."

A. Sam told me that he could take the weekend off.
B. Sam told me that I could take the weekend off.
C. Sam told me that I can take the weekend off.
D. Sam told me that I could take off the weekend.

117. Select the most appropriate meaning of the underlined idiom in the given sentence.

Shyam had extensive surgery, but he is not yet <u>out of the woods</u>.

A. lost among the trees
B. out of luck
C. on the mend
D. out of danger

118. Select the correctly spelt word.

A. seperate
B. sepperate
C. separate
D. seperrate

119. Select the most appropriate option to fill in the blank.

I want to get some apples and pears, _______ the usual bananas.

A. besides B. beside
C. but D. be side

120. Select the option that expresses the given sentence in passive voice.

The committee will send out invitation letters next week.

A. Invitation letters will be sent out next week by the committee.
B. Invitation letters will be sending out next week by the committee.
C. Invitation letters will be send out next week by the committee.
D. Invitation letters will sent out next week by the committee.

General Awareness

121. Which of the following countries is known for Marsupial Animals?
A. Australia B. Brazil
C. South Africa D. Russia

122. The "Taka" is an official national currency and used in which of the following countries?
A. Indonesia B. Sri Lanka
C. Malaysia D. Bangladesh

123. "Bahai Temple" situated in Delhi is also commonly known as _______.
A. Yogmaya Temple
B. Akshardham Temple
C. Lotus Temple
D. Shree Sidh Shakti Peeth Shani Dham

124. Besides PAN card as per the budget 2019 now Income Tax return can be filed by using which of the following identification?
A. Driving License Number
B. Ration Card Number
C. Credit Card Number
D. Aadhaar Number

125. As per the Ministry of Home Affairs, which of the following countries shares the shortest border with India?
A. Myanmar B. Afghanistan
C. Bhutan D. Nepal

126. Dengue fever is a ________ disease.
A. Mosquito-borne B. Air-borne
C. Parasite-borne D. Food-borne

127. In which of the following months the Indian government approved the higher minimum support prices for Kharif crop 2019-20?
A. June 2019 B. August 2019
C. July 2019 D. May 2019

128. The world ocean day is observed on which of the following dates of the year?
A. 9 June B. 11 June
C. 8 June D. 10 June

129. The festival 'Bali Yatra' that is considered as one of Asia's largest open trade fair is organized in which of the following states of India?
A. Bihar B. Odisha
C. Chhattisgarh D. Karnataka

130. Which of the following books was the winner of the Booker Prize 2019 (together with The Testaments)?
A. Girl, Woman, Other
B. Midnight's Children
C. The Blind Assassin
D. Milkman

131. Who was the last viceroy of British India until 15 August 1947?
A. Lord Mountbatten
B. Lord Willingdon
C. Lord Wavell
D. Lord Linlithgow

132. Under which of the following schemes, income support of ₹ 6000 per year is provided to all farmers families across the country in three equal installments of ₹ 2000 each every four months?
A. Pradhan Mantri Kisan Suvidha Nidhi
B. Pradhan Mantri Kisan Samman Nidhi
C. Pradhan Mantri Kisan Social Nidhi
D. Pradhan Mantri Kisan Surksha Nidhi

133. The total market value of the final goods and services produced by a nation's economy during a specific period of time (usually a year) is known as ________.
A. Net National Income (NNI)
B. Balance of Payment (BOP)
C. Gross Domestic Product (GDP)
D. Current Account Deficit (CAD)

134. In which of the following cities, for the first time in six decades, Filmfare will host its annual gala Filmfare awards ceremony outside Mumbai in February 2020?

A. Agra B. Guwahati
C. Indore D. Jaipur

135. The 25th United Nations Climate Change Conference was held in which of the following cities in December 2019?
A. Chicago B. New Delhi
C. Madrid D. Hanoi

136. Recently, against which of the following countries India won test match by an innings and 46 runs that was also a record 12th successive series win at home?
A. Sri Lanka B. Australia
C. South Africa D. Bangladesh

137. Who among them was the former President of India who proclaimed national emergency across India in 1975?
A. Fakhruddin Ali Ahmed
B. Kocheril Raman Narayanan
C. Mohammad Hidayatullah
D. Zakir Husain

138. Famous "Indian Institute of Science" is located in which of the following cities of India?
A. Bangalore B. New Delhi
C. Mumbai D. Bhubaneshwar

139. "Polio" or "Poliomyelitis" is a crippling and potentially deadly infectious disease is caused by:
A. Virus B. Insects
C. Protozoa D. Bacteria

140. Ingestion of excess "Fluoride" through drinking-water, can cause "Fluorosis" which mainly affects ______.
A. Heart B. Teeth and bones
C. Eyes D. Liver

ANSWERS

1	2	3	4	5	6	7	8	9	10
B	D	D	B	A	A	D	C	C	C
11	**12**	**13**	**14**	**15**	**16**	**17**	**18**	**19**	**20**
C	C	C	A	C	C	A	A	A	C
21	**22**	**23**	**24**	**25**	**26**	**27**	**28**	**29**	**30**
C	A	C	A	B	D	D	A	A	B
31	**32**	**33**	**34**	**35**	**36**	**37**	**38**	**39**	**40**
C	D	A	B	A	D	A	D	A	D
41	**42**	**43**	**44**	**45**	**46**	**47**	**48**	**49**	**50**
C	D	D	D	D	C	A	D	A	B
51	**52**	**53**	**54**	**55**	**56**	**57**	**58**	**59**	**60**
A	C	B	C	B	A	C	D	A	C
61	**62**	**63**	**64**	**65**	**66**	**67**	**68**	**69**	**70**
C	B	C	B	B	B	A	A	B	A
71	**72**	**73**	**74**	**75**	**76**	**77**	**78**	**79**	**80**
C	B	A	D	C	B	C	B	D	C
81	**82**	**83**	**84**	**85**	**86**	**87**	**88**	**89**	**90**
A	D	D	B	A	B	C	A	A	D
91	**92**	**93**	**94**	**95**	**96**	**97**	**98**	**99**	**100**
C	B	B	A	A	D	B	D	A	B
101	**102**	**103**	**104**	**105**	**106**	**107**	**108**	**109**	**110**
B	C	B	C	A	A	C	A	A	B

111	112	113	114	115	116	117	118	119	120
B	B	B	D	A	B	D	C	A	A
121	122	123	124	125	126	127	128	129	130
A	D	C	D	B	A	C	A	B	A
131	132	133	134	135	136	137	138	139	140
A	B	C	B	C	D	A	A	A	B

EXPLANATORY ANSWERS

91. Let 1 woman can do a work in x days

Then, 1 woman's 1 day's work = $\frac{1}{x}$

$\therefore$ 1 man's 1 day's work = $\frac{1}{15 \times 10}$

According to question

$$\frac{7}{15\times10}+\frac{3}{x}=\frac{1}{20}$$

$$\Rightarrow \frac{3}{x}=\frac{1}{20}-\frac{7}{150}$$

$$\Rightarrow \frac{3}{x}=\frac{15-14}{300}=\frac{1}{300}$$

$$\Rightarrow x = 900$$

Hence, the number of days taken by a woman to do the work is 900.

93. Here,

Starting point = A

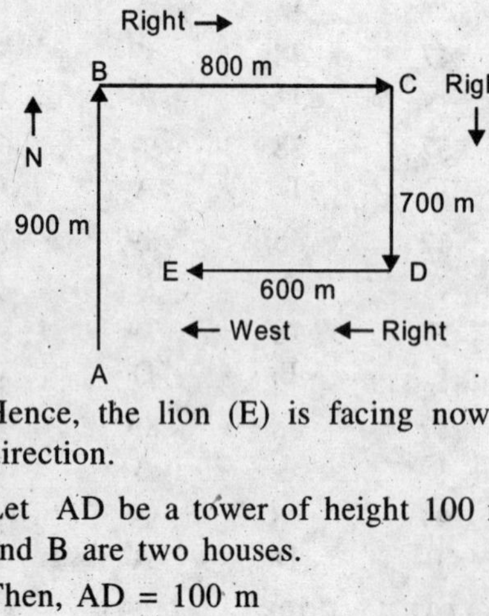

Hence, the lion (E) is facing now in west direction.

97. Let AD be a tower of height 100 m and A and B are two houses.

Then, AD = 100 m

$\angle ABD = 30°$, $\angle ACD = 60°$

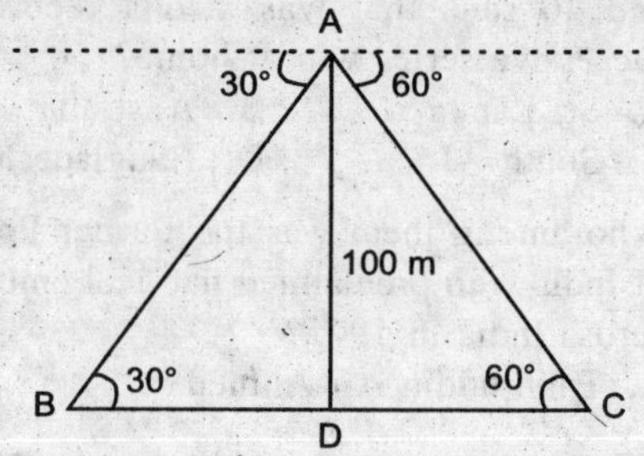

In ΔADB,

$$\tan 30° = \frac{AD}{DB} \Rightarrow \frac{1}{\sqrt{3}}=\frac{100}{DB}$$

$$\Rightarrow DB = 100\sqrt{3}\text{ m}$$

and in ΔADC

$$\tan 60° = \frac{AD}{DC} \Rightarrow \sqrt{3}=\frac{100}{DC}$$

$$\Rightarrow DC = \frac{100}{\sqrt{3}}$$

Hence, the distance between A and B

$$= DB + DC = 100\sqrt{3}+\frac{100}{\sqrt{3}}$$

$$= \frac{100\sqrt{3}\cdot\sqrt{3}+100}{\sqrt{3}}$$

$$= \frac{100\times3+100}{\sqrt{3}}=\frac{400}{\sqrt{3}}$$

$$= \frac{400}{1.732} = 230.9468$$

= 230 m (Approximately)

98. Given, + = ÷, − = +, × = −, ÷ = ×

$\therefore$ [{(5 × 1) ÷ 2} + (1 − 1)]/1

= [{(5 − 1) × 2} ÷ (1 + 1)]/1

= [{4 × 2} ÷ 2]/1

= [8 ÷ 2]/1 = 4/1 = 4.

Previous Paper (Solved)

Junior Engineers (Electrical)
Recruitment Exam 2019*

Post Specific Subject Related Questions (Electrical)

1. In the circuit shown below the voltage across 100 Ω resistance is:

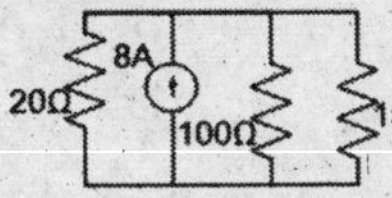

A. 50 V B. 100 V
C. 60 V D. 120 V

2. Current in A in an inductor is given by $10 + 10\,t$ where t is the time in seconds. If the self-induced emf in the coil is 20 mV, then its self-inductance is:

A. 10 mH B. 1 mH
C. 2 mH D. 20 mH

3. Equivalent resistance of the circuit shown below between X and Y:

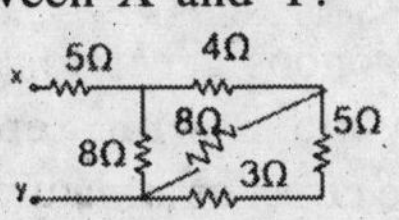

A. 6 Ω B. 9 Ω
C. 18 Ω D. 12 Ω

4. Equivalent resistance seen between the terminals a and b for the circuit shown below is:

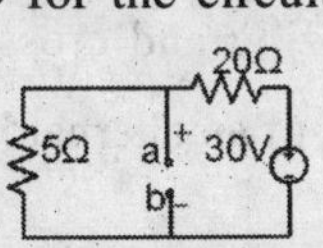

A. 20 Ω B. 4 Ω
C. 25 Ω D. 5 Ω

5. Reciprocal of reluctance is:

A. Hysteresis B. Permeability
C. Susceptibility D. Permeance

6. An average voltage of 40 V is induced in a 1000 turn coil due to a change in flux which occurs in 0.5 seconds. The total flux change in webers is:

A. 0.02 B. 0.05
C. 0.01 D. 0.04

7. Two filament lamps rated 200 W/200 V and 50 W/200 V are connected in series across a 200 V, 50 Hz, ac supply. Then, the total power supplied by the source is:

A. 160 W B. 80 W
C. 20 W D. 40 W

8. A battery having an open circuit voltage of 2 V has a terminal voltage of 1 V when supplying a current of 5 A. Its internal resistance is:

A. 0.6 Ω B. 0.4 Ω
C. 0.2 Ω D. 0.1 Ω

9. An iron cored choke coil has an equivalent resistance of 4 Ω. It draws 10 A from a single phase ac source of voltage 200 V, 50 Hz. Then, power consumed by the coil and its power factor respectively are:

A. 200 W, 0.2 lag B. 400 W, 0.2 lag
C. 200 W, 0.2 lead D. 400 W, 0.2 lead

10. Mutual inductance between two closely coupled coils is 2 H. Now, if the number of turns in one coil is reduced by 50 per cent and those of the other coil is doubled then, new value of mutual inductance is:

A. 2 H B. 8 H
C. 1 H D. 4 H

11. In the circuit below, the value of resistance R is:

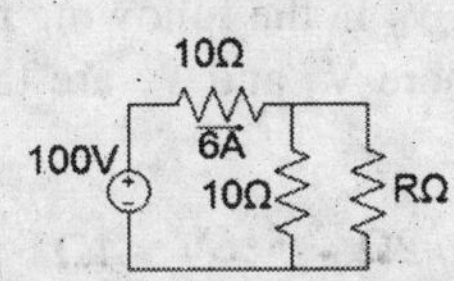

A. 20 Ω B. 30 Ω
C. 10 Ω D. 40 Ω

* *Exam conducted by DSSSB.*

12. A conductor 0.2 m long is carrying a current of 20 A at right angles to a magnetic field of 0.5 Tesla. What will be force on the conductor of the current is increased by 50 per cent?

A. 1 N B. 4 N
C. 6 N D. 3 N

13. When applied with a unidirectional voltage, an inductor behaves virtually like a:

A. Depends on the magnitude of voltage applied
B. Short circuit
C. Depends on the polarity of voltage applied
D. Open circuit

14. A non-ideal current source of 25 mA is supplying a resistive load of 5 kΩ. If the actual current flowing through the load is 20 mA, then the internal resistance of the source is:

A. 1 kΩ B. 10 kΩ
C. 5 kΩ D. 20 kΩ

15. Three resistances are connected in parallel. Total circuit current is 6A. Individual conductance of each parallel circuit are $G^1 = 1S$, $G^2 = 3S$ and $G^3 = 2S$. Then, current through G^3 is:

A. 4 A B. 1 A
C. 6 A D. 2 A

16. In the circuit shown below, the current drawn by the 6 Ω resistor is 2 A, then the value of resistance R is:

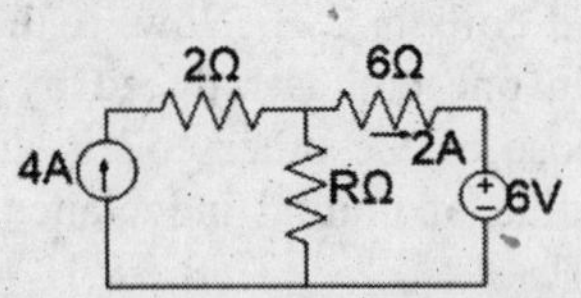

A. 9 Ω B. 18 Ω
C. 3 Ω D. 6 Ω

17. Find $V_a - V_b$ in the following part of a closed circuit where V_a and V_b are the potentials at *a* and *b*.

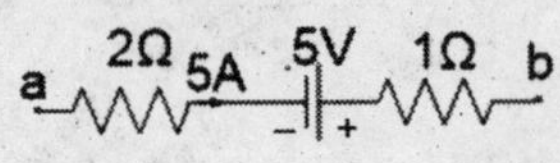

A. 10 V B. 15 V
C. 5 V D. 20 V

18. Certain number of resistors having equal resistances offers an equivalent resistance of 1 Ω when connected in parallel and 100 Ω if they are connected in series. Then, the number of resistors and the resistance of each are ______.

A. 20, 10 Ω B. 5, 20 Ω
C. 20, 5 Ω D. 10, 10 Ω

19. RMS value of a half wave rectified symmetrical square wave current of 2 A is:

A. 2 A B. 1 A
C. $2\sqrt{2}$ D. $\sqrt{2}$

20. In the circuit below, the voltage across 9 Ω resistor is:

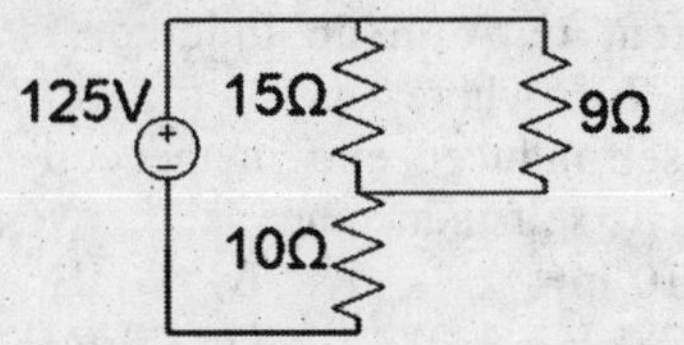

A. 54 V B. 50 V
C. 75 V D. 45 V

21. In a synchronous generator supplying power at rated voltage with zero power factor lagging, the effect of armature reaction ampere turns is:

A. Demagnetising
B. Cross magnetising
C. Magnetising
D. Magnetizing and cross magnetising

22. Field system of an alternator is usually excited from:

A. Single phase ac voltage
B. Square wave voltage
C. Three phase ac voltage
D. DC voltage

23. Scott connected transformers can convert (*a*) three phase to two phase (*b*) two phase to three phase (*c*) two phase to four phase (*d*) three phase to four phase. From the above options correct answer is:

A. (*a*) and (*c*) B. (*b*) and (*c*)
C. (*b*) and (*d*) D. (*a*) and (*b*)

24. Torque developed by a motor while running at 1000 rpm is 106 N-m and the shaft torque available is 100 N-m, then the iron and mechanical losses in watts are:

A. 300 π B. 50 π
C. 200 π D. 100 π

25. In a low power factor wattmeter compensating coil is connected:

A. In series with the current coil
B. In series with the pressure coil
C. In parallel with the pressure coil
D. In parallel with the current coil

26. Loss of charge method is used for the measurement of:

A. High inductance B. Low resistance
C. Low inductance D. High resistance

27. During plugging of a three-phase induction motor:

A. Rotor circuit is opened
B. Phase sequence of the stator voltage is reversed
C. One phase of stator is short circuited
D. DC source is connected to stator

28. A transformer is supplying a unity power factor load. Power factor on primary side will be:

A. About 0.95 lag B. Unity
C. About 0.95 lead D. Zero

29. A dc shunt generator has a critical field resistance of 400 Ω at 1200 rpm. Now if the speed of the generator is increased to 1800 rpm what is the change in the critical resistance?

A. Increases to 900 Ω B. Remains the same
C. Increases to 600 Ω D. Decreases to 267 Ω

30. A three phase star connected alternator develops an rms voltage of V_1 per phase at the fundamental frequency. It also generates a third harmonic component whose rms value is V_3. What is the line voltage of the alternator?

A. $\sqrt{3\left(V_1^2+V_3^2\right)}$ B. $\sqrt{V_1^2+V_3^2}$

C. $\dfrac{\sqrt{V_1^2+V_3^2}}{\sqrt{3}}$ D. $\sqrt{2\left(V_1^2+V_3^2\right)}$

31. In hydro-electric plants the type of alternator used is:

A. Turbo generator
B. Non salient pole
C. Salient pole
D. Steam turbine generator

32. A current transformer has a phase error of +5 degree. The phase angle between the primary and secondary current is:

A. 5 degree B. 95 degree
C. 175 degree D. 85 degree

33. Ferranti effect on long overhead lines is experienced when:

A. Power factor is unity
B. Line is lightly loaded
C. Line is heavily loaded
D. Line is fully loaded

34. A 400 V three phase 50 Hz balanced source is supplying power to a balanced three phase load. Line current flowing through the load is 5 A at a power factor angle of 30 degrees lagging. Reading of two wattmeters used to measure the load power are:

A. 1000 W, 2000 W B. 2000 W 4000 W
C. 2000 W, 3000 W D. 1000 W, 3000 W

35. An industrial consumer has a load pattern of 2000 kW at 0.8 lagging for 12 hours and 1000 kW at unity power factor for 12 hours. Its load factor is

A. 0.6 B. 0.8
C. 0.5 D. 0.75

36. Current flowing in a circuit is i = (18 + 10 sin ωt + 7 sin $2\omega t$). A moving iron ammeter is connected in the circuit to measure this current. The reading of the meter will be approximately:

A. 28 A B. 35 A
C. 18 A D. 20 A

37. Moving coil permanent magnet instrument can be used for the measurement of:

A. AC and DC
B. DC only
C. AC only
D. Half wave rectified DC

38. Form factor of sinusoidal ac signal is:
A. 1.11 B. 0.11
C. 2.11 D. 3.11

39. Voltage applied to a load is $100\sqrt{2}\sin 500t$ ·

Current through the load is $10\sqrt{2}\sin\left(500t+\frac{\pi}{3}\right)$.

The power consumed by the load is:
A. 500 W B. 200 W
C. 1000 W D. 2000 W

40. A three-phase induction motor is running at 5 per cent slip with certain load. If at this load the power input to the rotor is 2000 W, then the mechanical power developed by the motor is:
A. 2000 W B. 2100 W
C. 1700 W D. 1900 W

41. In a particular circuit, a coil having a self-inductance of 2 H is required to carry a current of 4 A. A capacitor rated for 400 V is used across the coil in order to prevent sparking during breaking of the circuit. The value of capacitor needed is:
A. 120 μF B. 100 μF
C. 400 μF D. 200 μF

42. Unit of reluctance is:
A. Henry B. Weber
C. Weber/m^2 D. (Henry)$^{-1}$

43. In a transmission system if V is the transmission voltage, weight of copper needed is proportional to ________.
A. V B. 1/V^2
C. V^2 D. 1/V

44. Cost of power generation will be low if:
A. Load factor is low and diversity factor is high
B. Load factor is high and diversity factors is low
C. Load factor and diversity factor are low
D. Load factor and diversity factor are high

45. Energy produced in a power station is 1440 MWh per day. What is the maximum demand of the station if its load factor is 0.5?
A. 120 MW
B. 280 MW
C. 60 MW
D. 140 MW

46. Sag of the conductors of a transmission line is 2 m when the span is 200 m. Now if the height of the supporting tower is increased by 25 per cent sag will ____.
A. Increase by 25 per cent
B. Reduce by 25 per cent
C. Reduce by 12.5 per cent
D. Remains unchanged

47. In dielectric heating current flows through _____.
A. Ionic discharge between dielectric medium and metallic conductor.
B. Metallic conductor
C. Air
D. Dielectric

48. A motor has to be selected for following load cycle. Load uniformly rising from zero to 100 hp in 10 minutes after which it is constant at 100 hp for the next 10 minutes, followed by no load period of 30 minutes. Suitable size of continuous rated motor is:
A. 100 hp B. 25 hp
C. 50 hp D. 200 hp

49. Gain of a buffer amplifier is:
A. Dependent on the circuit parameters
B. Unity
C. Infinity
D. Zero

50. The most economical method of electric braking is:
A. Dynamic braking with separate excitation
B. Dynamic braking with self-excitation
C. Plugging
D. Regenerative braking

51. Voltage of a bus can be controlled by controlling the _____.
A. Apparent power of the bus
B. Active power of the bus
C. Reactive power of the bus
D. Apparent power and phase angle

52. The transistor configuration that is most commonly used as a switching device is:
A. Common base
B. Common emitter
C. Common collector
D. Common emitter shorted

53. A three phase 4 wire system is commonly used for ______.
A. Primary distribution
B. Primary transmission
C. Secondary distribution
D. Secondary transmission

54. An elevator drive is required to operate ______.
A. Three quadrants B. Two quadrants
C. All four quadrants D. One quadrant only

55. Bundled conductors are mainly used in HV transmission line to ______.
A. Reduce sag
B. Increase the mechanical strength of line
C. Reduce transmission line loss
D. Reduce corona

56. A lamp takes 5 A at 250 V and emits 8000 lumens. Its MSCP is:
A. 2000 π B. 1400 π
C. $\frac{2000}{\pi}$ D. 1250 π

57. Surge impedance loading of a lossless 400 kV three phase 50 Hz overhead line of average surge impedance of 400 Ω is:
A. 200 MW B. 400 MW
C. 1600 MW D. 100 MW

58. If L_1 is the total inductance when two mutually coupled coils are connected in series such that mutual inductance is aiding the self-inductance and L_2 is the total inductance when connected in series opposition, then mutual inductance between them is given by:
A. $\frac{(L_1 - L_2)}{2}$ B. $\frac{(L_1 + L_2)}{2}$
C. $\frac{(L_1 + L_2)}{4}$ D. $\frac{(L_1 - L_2)}{4}$

59. In the circuit shown below 18 V zener diode has zero zener resistance and a knee current of 2 mA. The minimum value of R so that voltage across it does not fall below 18 V is:

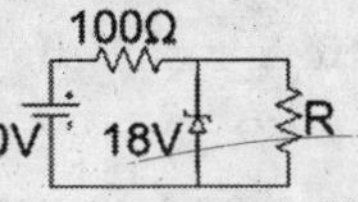

A. 1000 Ω B. 500 Ω
C. 9000 Ω D. 2000 Ω

60. Bulk power transmission over long HVDC lines is preferred because of:
A. No harmonics
B. Low cost HVDC terminals
C. Simple protection
D. Minimum line power loss

61. What is the energy stored in 1 second in an inductor while carrying a current $i = 20 + 10t$ where t is the time in seconds if the electro motive force induced in the coil due to self-induction is 40 mV?
A. 1.8 J B. 0.45 J
C. 0.9 J D. 1.2 J

62. Power dissipated in the circuit given is 9 W. Value of E will be:

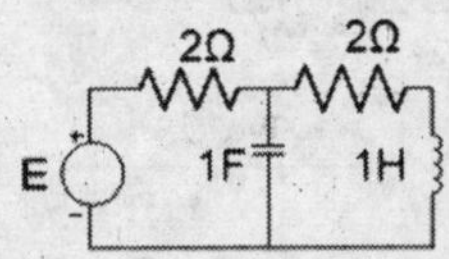

A. 2 V B. 4 V
C. 6 V D. 8 V

63. A three-phase delta connected symmetrical load consumes 3000 W of power from a balanced supply. If the same load is connected in star to the same supply then power consumption will be:
A. $\frac{3000}{\sqrt{3}}$ B. $\frac{3000}{\sqrt{2}}$
C. 3000 W D. 1000 W

64. A RLC series circuit has a resistance of 1 kΩ. Its half power frequencies are 10 and 90 kHz. Quality factor of the circuit is:
A. 43469 B. 43532
C. 43593 D. 43467

65. A current of $i = -6 + 8\sqrt{2}\sin(\omega t + 30)$ is passed through a center zero PMMC meter and a moving iron meter. The two meters will read:

A. 6 A, 10 A B. –6 A, 8 A
C. –6 A, 10 A D. 6 A, 8 A

66. The circuit shown is used to measure the power consumed by the load. Resistance of the current and potential coils of the wattmeter are 0.02 Ω and 1000 Ω respectively. With this circuit measured power compared to load power will be:

A. 2 per cent less B. 4 per cent more
C. 4 per cent less D. 2 per cent more

67. When a unit impulse voltage is applied to an inductor of 4 H, energy supplied by the source is:

A. 8 J B. 2 J
C. 4 J D. 1 J

68. In the circuit shown the switch is opened at $t = 0$ after having been closed for a long time. Current through the resistor for $t > 0$ is given by:

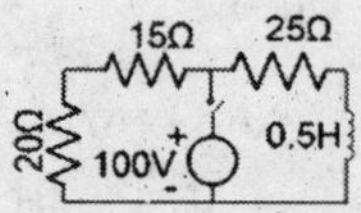

A. $4e^{-50t}$ B. $5e^{-50t}$
C. $4e^{-120t}$ D. $3e^{-120t}$

69. If all the sequence voltages at the fault point in a power system are equal, then the fault is a ______.

A. Line to ground fault
B. Three phase fault
C. Double line to ground fault
D. Line to line fault

70. Relative permeability is less than 1.0 in case of:

A. Dia-magnet material
B. Non-ferrous material
C. Ferro-magnet material
D. Ferrites

71. What will the zero-sequence current when line to ground fault occurs and the current in faulted phase is 300 A?

A. 100 A B. 300 A
C. 50 A D. 150 A

72. Two coils having self-inductance of 10 mH and 15 mH give an effective inductance of 20 mH when connected in series opposition. What will be the effective inductance if they are connected in series aiding?

A. 80 mH B. 30 mH
C. 60 mH D. 40 mH

73. For a fully transposed transmission line ______.

A. Negative and zero sequence impedances are equal.
B. Positive and zero sequence impedances are equal
C. Positive, negative and zero sequence impedances are equal.
D. Positive and negative sequence impedances are equal.

74. A long wire carrying a certain current produces a magnetic field of 0.8 Tesla at a distance 0.5 cm. Then magnetic field at a distance of 1 cm is:

A. 0.16 Tesla B. 0.2 Tesla
C. 0.8 Tesla D. 0.4 Tesla

75. For a fixed receiving end and sending end voltages in a transmission system, locus of constant power is a ______.

A. Straight line B. Ellipse
C. Circle D. Parabola

76. A 200 V single phase ac source is connected to a load with an impedance of magnitude 10 Ω and phase angle +60 degrees. A capacitor is connected across the load and supplies 1000 Var. The real power supplied by the source is:

A. 2000 W B. 4000 W
C. 1000 W D. 3000 W

77. A two terminal network is connected to a resistive load whose resistance is equal to Norton resistance of the network. What will be the load current if Norton current is I_n?

A. $2I_n/3$ B. $I_n/2$
C. $2I_n$ D. I_n

78. Energy stored in an iron cored coil is 500 Joules when carrying a certain current and at that current its copper loss is 1000 W. Time constant of the coil in seconds is:

A. 4 B. 2
C. 1 D. 0.5

79. In the circuit shown below power delivered by the source is:

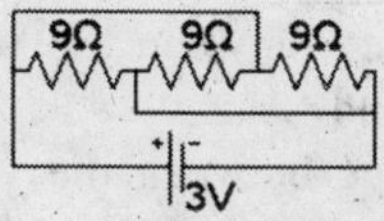

A. 12 W B. 6 W
C. 3 W D. 9 W

80. A shunt resistance of 50 Ω is required for extending the range of an ammeter from 100 to 500 μA. The value of internal resistance of the ammeter is:

A. 400 Ω B. 200 Ω
C. 800 Ω D. 100 Ω

81. A 720 kVA, $240\sqrt{3}$ V, star connected synchronous machine generates rated open circuit voltage at a field current of 20 A. A field current of 10 A produces rated armature current under short circuit condition. Per unit saturated synchronous reactance is:

A. 2 B. 0.5
C. 0.4 D. 1.5

82. A heater operated from a 250 V, 50 Hz single phase supply consumes 2.5 kWh in one hour. If it is now connected to a square wave generator of 400 V peak to peak voltage and frequency 150 Hz the power dissipated by the heater will be:

A. 1.6 kW B. 2.8 kW
C. 3.2 kW D. 6.4 kW

83. The locked rotor current in a three-phase star connected 15 kW, 4 pole, 250 V, 50 Hz induction motor at rated conditions is 50 A. Neglecting losses what will be the locked current when motor is connected to 240 V, 60 Hz supply is:

A. 48 A B. 52 A
C. 40 A D. 50 A

84. For a transmission line with resistance R and reactance X and negligible capacitance generalized constant A is:

A. 1 B. R – jX
C. R + jX D. 0

85. A dc potentiometer is designed to measure up-to about 2 V with a slide wire of 1600 m. Standard cell of emf 1.2 V balances at 1200 mm a test cell is seen to balance at 1400 mm, the emf of the test cell is:

A. 1.1 V B. 1.2 V
C. 1.7 V D. 1.4 V

86. An amplifier circuit has a voltage gain of 500. If the output voltage is 5 V, then the input voltage is:

A. $\frac{1}{2500}$ V B. 2500 V
C. 100 mV D. 10 mV

87. In a three-phase induction motor regenerative braking occurs when:

A. Load is lowered by a hoisting machine
B. Motor speed falls due to overload
C. Load is raised by a hoisting machine
D. Number of poles is reduced in a pole changing machine

88. A three-phase slip ring induction motor develops full load torque at a slip of 0.04 when the slip rings are short circuited. If the rotor resistance is increased 3 times by inserting external resistance in the rotor circuit, then the slip will be:

A. 0.04 B. 0.01
C. 0.12 D. 0.06

89. For heating non conducting materials following heating method can be used:

A. Induction heating
B. Dielectric heating
C. Resistance heating
D. Electric arc heating

90. In a center tap full wave rectifier, if the peak voltage applied between the center tap and one of the secondary 200 V, then the reverse biased diode is applied with a maximum voltage of:

A. 200 V B. 100 V
C. $200\sqrt{2}$ V D. 400 V

91. The dc base bias voltage of a *npn* transistor made of silicon is 10 V and input base resistor is 100 kΩ. Then the value of base current into the transistor:
A. 9.3 μA B. 0.93 μA
C. 930 μA D. 93 μA

92. A 10 kVA, 400/200 V single phase transformer with resistance 4 per cent and reactance 6 per cent supplies a current of 50 A a resistive load. Voltage across the load is:
A. 190 V B. 188 V
C. 192 V D. 194 V

93. A 150 kW, 1200 rpm, $240\sqrt{3}$ V, three phase delta connected synchronous motor has synchronous reactance of 1 Ω per phase. If the excitation voltage is fixed at 400 V per phase, power output at a torque angle of 30 degrees is:
A. 75 kW B. 25 kW
C. 87 kW D. 50 kW

94. Two insulator discs of identical capacitance value C makes up a string for 2.2 kV, 50 Hz single phase overhead line insulating system. If the pin to earth capacitance is also C, then string efficiency is:
A. 75 per cent B. 50 per cent
C. 80 per cent D. 90 per cent

95. A power system has two synchronous generators whose governor turbine characteristics are given by P1 = 50(50 – *f*) and P2 = 100(52 – *f*), where *f* is the system frequency. When the total load supplied is 1000 MW, what is the system frequency if the operation is lossless.
A. 58 Hz B. 44.66 Hz
C. 52.4 Hz D. 48 Hz

96. A voltmeter connected across 15 kΩ resistor reads 10 V in the circuit given. Voltmeter is rated at 500 Ω/volt and has a full-scale reading of 20 V. The supply voltage is:

A. 60 V B. 45 V
C. 30 V D. 90 V

97. The inductance of a single phase two wire power transmission line per km gets doubled when the _____.
A. Distance between the wires is increased four-fold
B. Distance between the wires is increased as the square of the original distance.
C. Distance between the wires is doubled
D. Radius of the wire is doubled

98. A generating station has an installed capacity of 400 MW. Plan capacity factor is 0.6 and annual load factor is 0.8. Capital cost is ₹ 10^{10} and annual running charges are ₹ 10^9. What is the cost per unit generated if the annual interest and depreciation is 20 per cent?
A. 42 paise B. 242 paise
C. 14.2 paise D. 142 paise

99. In order to minimize the inrush current in a single-phase transformer, the supply switch should be closed at the instant when:
A. supply voltage is $\frac{1}{2}$ times the maximum voltage
B. supply voltage is $\frac{1}{\sqrt{2}}$ times the maximum voltage
C. supply voltage is maximum
D. supply voltage is zero

100. A light source having an intensity of 400 candle power is fitted with a reflector so that it directs 70 per cent of its light along a beam having a divergence angle of 5 degrees. Total flux emitted along the beam is:
A. $\frac{1600}{\pi}$ B. 1120 π
C. 1600 π D. $\frac{1120}{\pi}$

General Intelligence and Reasoning Ability

101. Choose the odd one from the given alternatives.
A. PRT B. SUV
C. JLN D. TVX

102. Which of the following figure is exactly the mirror image of the question figure, when the mirror is held at AB?

A.  B. 

C.  D. 

103. Find out the next term: JL22, OQ32, TV42, ?
A. YZ51 B. YB28
C. YA52 D. YZ52

104. Find the missing number from the given responses in the following question.

9	6	8
5	8	4
7	4	?
11	2	7

A. 6 B. 7
C. 3 D. 4

105. In the question below a statement followed by two courses of action numbered I and II is given. On the basis of the information given in the statement, you have to assume everything in the statement to be true, then decide which of the suggested courses of action logically follow(s) first pursuing.

Statement : A huge fire broke out due to damage done to the gas pipeline. While laying pipes for one of the utility companies.

Courses of action:

I. All the licenses of the utility companies should immediately be suspended pending enquiry into the incidence.

II. People residing in the area should be advised to stay indoors to avoid burn injuries.

A. If neither Course of Action (I) nor (II) follows
B. If either Course of Action (I) or (II) follows
C. If only Course of Action (I) follows
D. If only Course of Action (II) follows

106. Select the related letter group from the given alternatives.
YQ : VN :: KN : ?
A. HL B. HK
C. HJ D. GK

107. Which of the following interchanges of numbers would make the given equation correct?
$8 \times 20 \div 3 + 9 - 5 = 38$
A. 3, 5 B. 8, 9
C. 3, 9 D. 3, 8

108. Which figure does not belong to the group in the following question?

A.  B. 

C.  D. 

109. In a certain code PROGRESS is written as '3' and DEVELOPMENT is written as '16'. How is MANAGEMENT written in that code?
A. 7 B. 6
C. 9 D. 8

110. A lady plans to visit five Stores to buy her stuff. The shops are Reebok, Puma, Addidas, HRX and Nike which she visits exactly once. She decided:
(*i*) She must visit Reebok before Puma and Nike.
(*ii*) She must visit Puma before HRX.

(*iii*) The third shop she visited must be Addidas which is just after Puma.

Which is the Fourth store she visited?

A. Nike
B. Puma
C. HRX or Nike
D. HRX

111. In this question given below which of the four option figures should come after the question figures, if the sequence were continued?

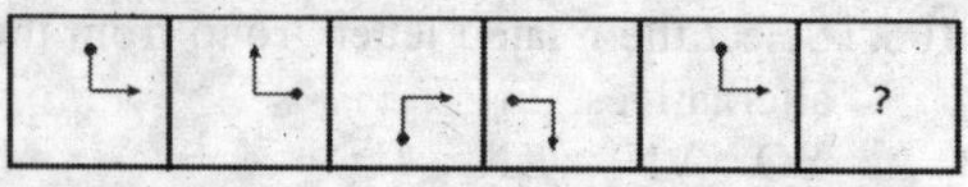

A.  B. 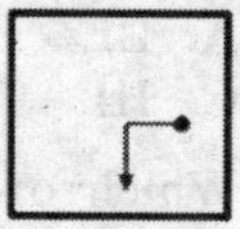

C. 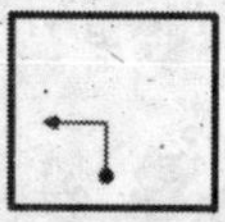 D. 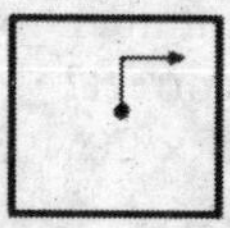

112. Seven friends, P, Q, R, S, T and U are sitting in a straight line facing north. Q sits fifth to the right of T. Q does not sit at any of extreme ends. Two people sit between U and R. S sits third to the left of V. S sits exactly in the middle. U is not an immediate neighbour of P.

How many people sit between R and V?

A. One B. Three
C. Four D. Two

113. According to the following venn diagram how many people's hobby is dancing and reading and travelling but not playing cricket?

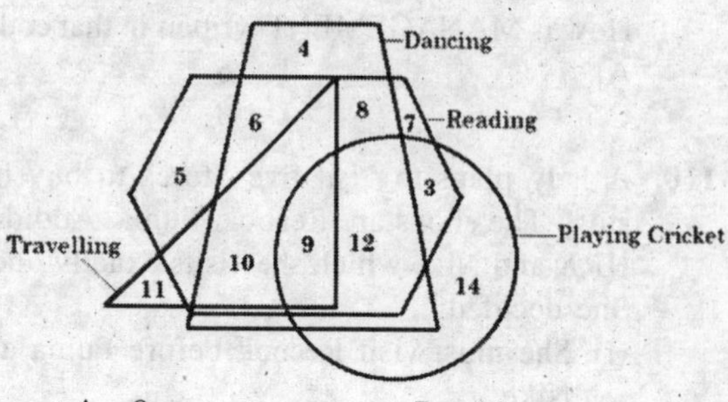

A. 9 B. 11
C. 10 D. 12

114. Which of the following answer figure will complete the given figure?

A.  B. 

C.  D. 

115. Select a suitable figure from the four alternatives that would complete the figure matrix.

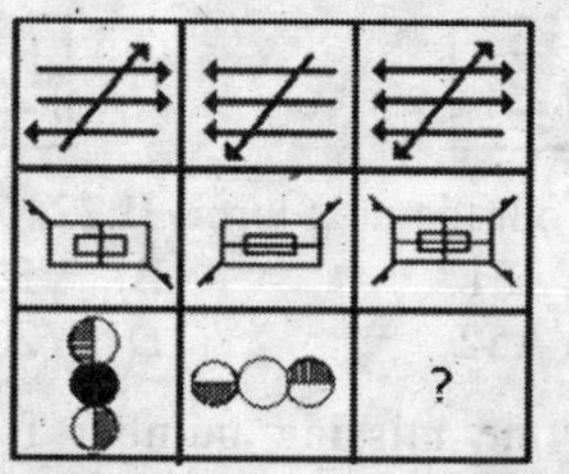

A.  B. 

C.  D. 

116. In question below is given a statement followed by two assumptions numbered I, II and III. An assumption is something supposed or taken for granted. You have to consider the statement and the following assumptions and decide which of the assumptions is implicit in the statement.

Statement : "Wanted a three bedroom flat in the court area for immediate possession"—an advertisement

Assumptions:

I. Flats are available in court area.
II. Some people will respond to the advertisement.
III. It is a practice to give such an advertisement.

A. None is implicit
B. Only I and II are implicit

C. Only II is implicit
D. All are implicit

117. Select the term that will come next in the following series.
FZ, IB, OF, XL, ?
A. IT B. JT
C. JU D. IS

118. Four pair of words are given and three of them share a certain similarity. Choose the pair which is different from the other three.
A. Right Livelihood Award : Environment
B. Sahitya Akademy Awards : Writing
C. Vyas Samman : English Literature
D. R.D. Birla Award : Medical Sciences

119. Which of the following is the water image of the question figure?

A. 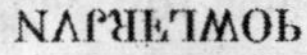
B. 
C. 
D. 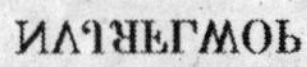

120. Select the related word from the given alternatives.
Godavari : Nasik :: Rapti :?
A. Varanasi
B. Kanpur
C. Lucknow
D. Gorakhpur

General Awareness

121. Which of the following physical quantity is responsible for opening the lid of a bottle?
A. Velocity B. Acceleration
C. Torque D. Pressure

122. Which of the following is traditional folk theatre form of Maharashtra?
A. Jatra B. Tamaasha
C. Krishnattam D. Yakshagaana

123. Who originally built the Meenakshi Temple at Madurai?
A. Pulakeshin I
B. Karikala Chola
C. Kulashekarar Pandyan
D. Mahendravarman I

124. With which of the following sport sheesh mahal tournament is associated?
A. Boat racing B. Badminton
C. Football D. Cricket

125. In which of the following field, 'Fields medal' is given?
A. Physics B. Mathematics
C. Architecture D. Peace mission

126. Srikanth Kidambi is associated with which of the following fields?
A. Dance B. Science
C. Music D. Sports

127. Which article of Indian Constitution defines the money bill?
A. Article 114 B. Article 112
C. Article 116 D. Article 110

128. Who among the following is not a citizen of India according to Indian Constitution?
A. A person who has voluntarily acquired the citizenship of any foreign State
B. A person either of whose parents was born in the territory of India
C. A person who has been ordinarily resident in the territory of India for not less than five years immediately preceding such commencement
D. A person who was born in the territory of India

129. Alvars were devotees of which Indian deity?
A. Shakti B. Shiva
C. Vishnu D. Brahma

130. Which of the following dam is not constructed on Chambal River?
A. Indira Sagar Dam
B. Gandhi Sagar Dam
C. Jawahar Sagar Dam
D. Rana Pratap Sagar Dam

131. What is the national sport of China?
A. Cricket B. Table tennis
C. Swimming D. Hockey

132. In acidic solution China rose indicator turns which of the following colour?
A. Orange
B. Green
C. Magenta (Dark Pink)
D. Colourless

133. Under which dynasty Delhi became the capital of a Kingdom for the first time?
A. Tughluq Dynasty B. Chauhans
C. Khalji Dynasty D. Tomara Rajput

134. What kind of virus causes cancer?
A. Oncogenic virus B. Variola virus
C. Rubella virus D. Rhino virus

135. Who among the following is associated with widow remarriage?
A. Ishwarchandra Vidyasagar
B. Jyotirao Phule
C. E.V. Ramaswamy Naicker
D. Shri Narayana Guru

136. _________ are known as excludable goods.
A. Merit Goods B. Demerit Goods
C. Public Goods D. Private Goods

137. Who is the author of the book 'The Coalition Years'?
A. Shashi Tharoor
B. Satya Nadella
C. Pranab Mukharjee
D. Raghuram G Rajan

138. Jawadi hills are part of which of the following?
A. Eastern Ghat
B. Arunachal Himalayas
C. Northwestern Himalayas
D. Western Ghat

139. Who is the present governor of Maharashtra?
A. Anandiben Patel B. C. Vidyasagar Rao
C. Lalji Tandon D. Mridula Sinha

140. _________ is defined as the market price of the good (p) multiplied by the firm's output (q).
A. Average revenue B. Total revenue
C. Price Line D. Marginal revenue

Arithmetical and Numerical Ability

141. The respective ratio of the marks of three students A, B and C is 3 : 4 : 6. If average marks of A and B is 77. Find the marks of C.
A. 132 B. 125
C. 88 D. 102

142. A man's age is 125% of what it was 10 years ago, but $83\frac{1}{3}\%$ of what it will be after 10 years. His present age is:
A. 49 years B. 51 years
C. 48 years D. 50 years

143. In what ratio should water be mixed with wine, that costs ₹ 60 per litre, so that the price of the resultant mixture is ₹ 40 per litre?
A. 2 : 3 B. 3 : 4
C. 1 : 2 D. 4 : 5

144. A train covers a certain distance in 50 minutes, if it runs at a speed of 48 km/hr on an average. The speed at which the train must run so that time of journey becomes 40 minutes?
A. 10 km/hr B. 40 km/hr
C. 60 km/hr D. 20 km/hr

145. The ratio of the speeds of a boat in still water and the speed of the river is 3 : 1. The boat takes 45 minutes for a round trip journey. Find the distance of the whole trip if the speed of the stream is 4 km/hr.
A. 4 km B. 16 km
C. 8 km D. 12 km

146. Given below is a bar graph showing the details of cars manufactured and sold by company "ABC Limited" for the period of 2010 to 2014. Study the graph carefully and answer the question.

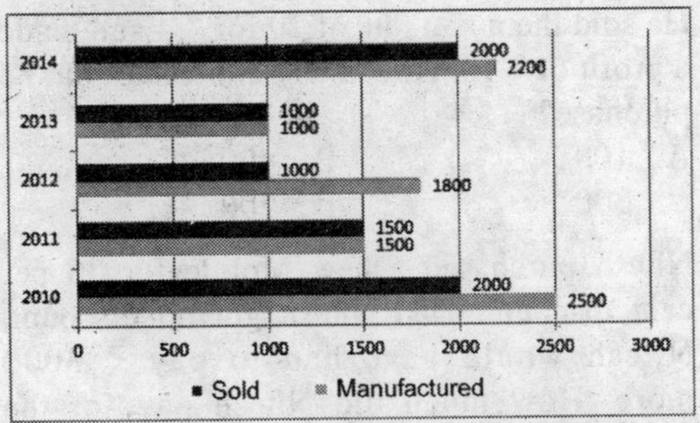

$\left(\text{Sale \%} = \frac{\text{No of cars sold}}{\text{No of cars manufactured}} \times 100\right)$

In which year sale percentage was least?

A. 2014 B. 2012

C. 2011 D. 2010

147. Study the following bar graph carefully to answer the given question. The graph shows the monthly income and expenditure of three persons A, B and C.

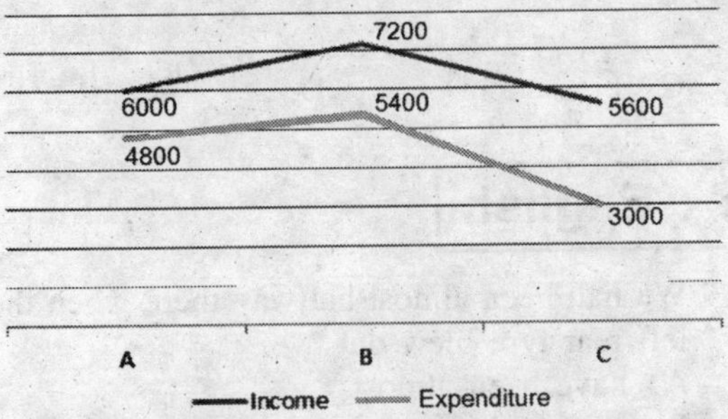

Note: Savings = Income – Expenditure

The difference between the savings of A and C is what percentage less than that of savings of B?

A. $16\frac{2}{9}\%$ B. $22\frac{2}{9}\%$

C. $33\frac{1}{3}\%$ D. 25%

148. Simplify the following expression.

12624 + 15285 – 16234 + 90724 + 13381 = ?

A. 116784 B. 112564

C. 115780 D. 116850

149. If $\frac{a}{b} = \frac{2}{3}$, then the value of $5a^3 - 2a^2b : 3ab^2 - b^3$ is:

A. 32 : 29 B. 16 : 27

C. 27 : 16 D. 34 : 19

150. Which of the following fractions is the smallest?

$\frac{13}{14}, \frac{14}{15}, \frac{15}{16}, \frac{16}{17}$

A. $\frac{16}{17}$ B. $\frac{15}{16}$

C. $\frac{14}{15}$ D. $\frac{13}{14}$

151. If 40 per cent of a number is 75 more than 20 per cent of 1500, the value of the number is:

A. 912.5 B. 937.5

C. 952.5 D. 962.5

152. Monthly expenditures (in ₹) of an average household on rent, food, clothing and other miscellaneous items are 1000, 1500, 350 and 750 respectively. If this information is presented with the help of a pie chart, then the angle for clothing is:

A. 35° B. 60°

C. 15° D. 45°

153. 15 men or 18 women can complete a piece of work in 45 days. If 5 men and 6 women work together then the work will be completed in:

A. $53\frac{1}{2}$ days B. 75 days

C. 48 days D. $67\frac{1}{2}$ days

154. Following pie chart shows the modes of transport for 1000 students of a regional college of engineering in Delhi.

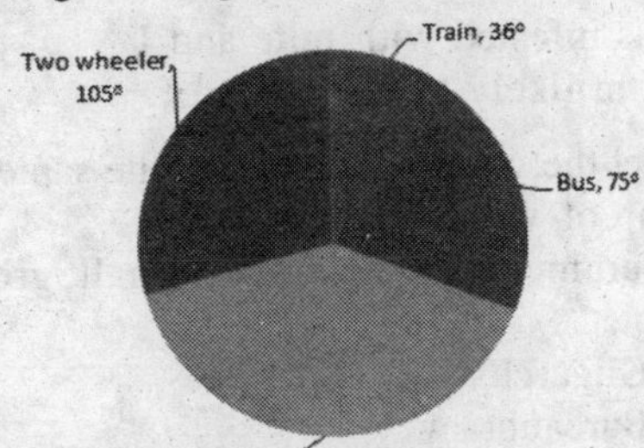

The number of students who come college by car is what per cent of the number of students who come by train:

A. 150 per cent B. 25 per cent

C. 200 per cent D. 400 per cent

155. What is the greatest number that will divide 580 and 679 and leave remainders 4 and 7 respectively?

A. 16 B. 8

C. 32 D. 96

156. In how many years will a sum of ₹ 1875 amount to ₹ 2187 at 8 per cent p.a. compound interest?

A. 2 B. 4

C. 3 D. 1

157. A takes $5\frac{1}{3}$ days and B takes $8\frac{1}{3}$ days more than the time taken by A and B together to complete a work. In how many days will they finish the work together?

A. $3\frac{1}{3}$ B. $9\frac{2}{3}$

C. $6\frac{2}{3}$ D. $8\frac{2}{3}$

158. Rakesh bought some chocolates at 10 for ₹ 1.50 and an equal number at 20 paise each. He sold them at a rate of 20 for ₹ 4 and made a profit of ₹ 10. How many chocolates did he purchase?

A. 100 B. 400

C. 300 D. 200

159. Nitesh purchased a new Mobile for 30 per cent discount. Had Nitesh got no discount, Nitesh would have had to pay ₹ 3000 more. How much did Nitesh pay for the Mobile?

A. ₹ 7000 B. ₹ 8500

C. ₹ 8000 D. ₹ 7500

160. Find the volume of a right circular cone formed by joining the edges of a sector of a circle of radius 4 cm where the angle of the sector is 90°.

A. $\frac{2\sqrt{3}}{\pi}$ cm³ B. $\frac{\pi\sqrt{5}}{\sqrt{3}}$ cm³

C. $\frac{12\sqrt{3}}{\pi}$ cm³ D. $\frac{2\sqrt{2}\pi}{3}$ cm³

Test of Language : English

161. Find out which part of the sentence has an error. If there is no error, mark your answer as 'No error'.

The table's wood (A) / is infested with mite and I (B) / am likely to dispose it of. (C) / No error (D).

A. The table's wood

B. No error

C. is infested with mite and I

D. am likely to dispose it of.

162. Select the word which means the same as the group of words given.

Government by few or a small group of people.

A. Oligarchy

B. Bureaucracy

C. Ochlocracy

D. Aristocracy

163. Select the most appropriate option to substitute the underlined segment in the given sentence. If there is no need to substitute it, select option No substitution required.

We <u>had been almost</u> halfway there when the left rear tyre blew out.

A. have been almost

B. were going to be almost

C. No substitution required

D. were almost

164. In the following question, there are six parts marked S1, S6, P, Q, R and S. The position of S1 and S6 is fixed. Some parts of the sentence have been jumbled up. Rearrange these parts and choose the proper sequence from the given options.

S1. Two partridges (quail-like birds) lived in a certain tree in the jungle. While one of them lived on the branches, the other lived inside a hole at the foot of the tree.

P. One day, one of them went away with some more partridges in search of food.

Q. They became good friends, and they would spend long hours with each other telling each other stories and events of their lives.

R. In this manner, the partridges spent their time in happiness.
S. As was usual, when he did not return back even at sunset, the other partridge started worrying.
S6. He thought, "He has not done this ever. Why has the partridge not returned home today? Has been trapped by some hunter? Or maybe even killed? I cannot live without him. I am certain there is some reason why he has not returned even at nightfall."

A. QRPS B. SPRQ
C. SPQR D. QRSP

165. Identify the incorrect sentence or sentences.
(*a*) Tamil Nadu will be the most wired state from the perspective of e-learning.
(*b*) At the core of ₹ 20 crore project is a Knowledge Data Centre at the Anna University.
(*c*) The K.D.C. will house information in digital format.
(*d*) It can be accessed by students through the state.

A. Only (*a*) B. (*b*) and (*d*)
C. (*a*) and (*c*) D. Only (*b*)

166. Select the most appropriate option to fill in the blank.
When light ________ through a spectroscope it breaks into bands of unique colours.

A. passed B. passing
C. passes D. pass

167. Select the most appropriate option to substitute the underlined segment in the given sentence. If there is no need to substitute it, select option No substitution required.
The man spent a lot because <u>he had so large amount of money.</u>

A. he had a large lot of money
B. No substitution required
C. he had a large amount of money
D. he had a large number of money

168. Select the synonym of the given word.
Morose

A. Delectable B. Meagre
C. Gloomy D. Concealed

169. Select the most appropriate option to fill in the blank.

You never know how much you rely on your friends _______ they are beyond your reach.

A. still B. in case
C. until D. unless

170. Select the meaning of the given idiom.
To the backbone:

A. With flexibility B. Farthest point
C. Thoroughly D. Physically

171. Select the meaning of the given idiom.
A bird's eye view:

A. Lacking clarity B. A quick look
C. A general view D. Unrealistic

172. Select the antonym of the given word.
Proximity

A. Remoteness B. Expedite
C. Pardon D. Adjacent

173. Out of the given four words only one is not spelt correctly. Find the word that is not correctly spelt.

A. Judgement B. Laboratory
C. Librality D. Knowledge

174. In each of the questions given below, rearrange the parts of the sentence in the correct order, and choose the correct option.
When botanists endeavoured by means of the microscope
P. to see the cells multiplying and producing actual growth
Q. it was discovered that this phenomenon took place for the most part .
R. at night during the absence of light

A. RPQ B. QRP
C. RQP D. PQR

175. Find the correctly spelt word.

A. Assecment B. Assessment
C. Asessment D. Asessmente

Directions (Qs. No. 176-180): *Read the passage carefully and choose the best answer to each question out of the four alternatives.*

Comprehension

The word 'routine' is not a very adored term. It has often been substituted for anything that is ordinary or mundane. Routines are regular procedures and practices that are almost performed as second nature. If you look up the net there are even sites which help to get out of routines and make life more exciting. If you're bored with routines they can offer help.

Reality is a bit different though. In reality routines form the backbone of our lives. Traffic rules are routine but imagine one fine day we said, dump those rules. You can imagine the chaos. Which shoe do you wear first? The left or the right? Check next time, you've probably been doing it all your life (wearing the left or right first) without the slightest thought to it. Most of us marvel at Army marches. We are amazed how their legs and arms move in such synchronised manner. To them, that's routine. For us, it's a wonder. They have been trained for it and they practice it every day. It is in that sense that Secularism is a routine. Being a backbone of our lives, secularism needs to be maintained and practiced. Soldiers don't fight big battles with their marching skills. Do they? At best that routine organises them for the battle. In much similar fashion secularism by itself does not win any battles. But many of our fraudulent politicians have been selling this product (in a fake form). Excessive secularism, which feeds the fire of people who like to present India as a country that does not respect its majority, is just as dangerous as religious "fundamentalism". This is the outcome of fake secularism practiced by all the parties.

Secularism demands that people be seen as one nation under one roof. Politicians may act divisively but why should media morons act divisively? And when rapped for such illegitimate behaviour all that these fools can do is cry abuse.

Secularism is a routine practice and not an issue on which any election should have ever been contested but the sickulars and the corrupt media have brought it down to this level. I consider myself a secular person but except for the media discussions or election season it doesn't cross my mind even once. People brush their teeth and have a bath every day. It makes them feel good, clean and freshened up. But that doesn't guarantee them luck, job or food. Routine hygiene is a "maintenance" job for the body. Secularism is a maintenance job for a society. It need not get any premium. No one deserves to be rewarded for being secular; certainly not with a vote.

176. Out of the given options, which word can replace the word 'Moron' as used in the passage?

A. Puppet B. Sickulars
C. Fool D. Gloomy

177. In what sense secularism is a routine?

A. Secularism is simply a notion that is a lip service to the nation.
B. Secularism demands that people be seen as one nation under one roof.
C. Secularism is a routine in a sense that it needs to be practiced and maintained.
D. Secularism is a maintenance job for a society.

178. According to the passage, what exactly is a routine?

A. Routine is a boring term used for an act repeated over a period of time
B. Routine is an everyday practice that puts people at ease since it provides a sense of consistency and repetition
C. They are regular procedures and practices that are performed as second nature
D. Routine is a safe haven for people who are averse to change

179. All except one is true according to the passage:

A. Secularism is not a maintenance job for the society.
B. Secularism is not an issue to form the basis of contesting an election.
C. Secularism being a backbone of our life needs to be practiced and maintained.
D. Absence of routine in our life will lead to chaos.

180. What can be an appropriate title for the passage?

A. Divisive Secularism
B. Is secularism a reality?
C. Fake Secularism
D. A fool's secularism

ANSWERS

1	2	3	4	5	6	7	8	9	10
D	C	B	B	D	A	D	C	B	A
11	**12**	**13**	**14**	**15**	**16**	**17**	**18**	**19**	**20**
A	D	B	D	D	A	A	D	D	D
21	**22**	**23**	**24**	**25**	**26**	**27**	**28**	**29**	**30**
A	D	D	C	B	D	B	A	C	A
31	**32**	**33**	**34**	**35**	**36**	**37**	**38**	**39**	**40**
C	C	B	A	D	D	B	A	A	D
41	**42**	**43**	**44**	**45**	**46**	**47**	**48**	**49**	**50**
D	D	B	D	A	D	D	C	B	D
51	**52**	**53**	**54**	**55**	**56**	**57**	**58**	**59**	**60**
C	B	C	C	D	C	B	D	A	D
61	**62**	**63**	**64**	**65**	**66**	**67**	**68**	**69**	**70**
A	C	D	B	C	D	B	C	C	A
71	**72**	**73**	**74**	**75**	**76**	**77**	**78**	**79**	**80**
A	B	D	D	C	A	B	C	C	B
81	**82**	**83**	**84**	**85**	**86**	**87**	**88**	**89**	**90**
B	A	C	A	D	D	A	C	B	D
91	**92**	**93**	**94**	**95**	**96**	**97**	**98**	**99**	**100**
D	C	D	A	B	A	B	D	C	B
101	**102**	**103**	**104**	**105**	**106**	**107**	**108**	**109**	**110**
B	B	C	C	C	B	A	C	A	C
111	**112**	**113**	**114**	**115**	**116**	**117**	**118**	**119**	**120**
B	C	C	C	D	C	B	C	A	D
121	**122**	**123**	**124**	**125**	**126**	**127**	**128**	**129**	**130**
C	B	C	D	B	D	D	A	C	A
131	**132**	**133**	**134**	**135**	**136**	**137**	**138**	**139**	**140**
B	C	D	A	A	C	C	A	B	B
141	**142**	**143**	**144**	**145**	**146**	**147**	**148**	**149**	**150**
A	D	C	C	C	B	B	C	B	D
151	**152**	**153**	**154**	**155**	**156**	**157**	**158**	**159**	**160**
B	A	D	D	D	A	C	B	A	B
161	**162**	**163**	**164**	**165**	**166**	**167**	**168**	**169**	**170**
A	A	D	A	B	C	C	C	C	C
171	**172**	**173**	**174**	**175**	**176**	**177**	**178**	**179**	**180**
C	A	C	D	B	C	C	C	A	D

EXPLANATORY ANSWERS

101. 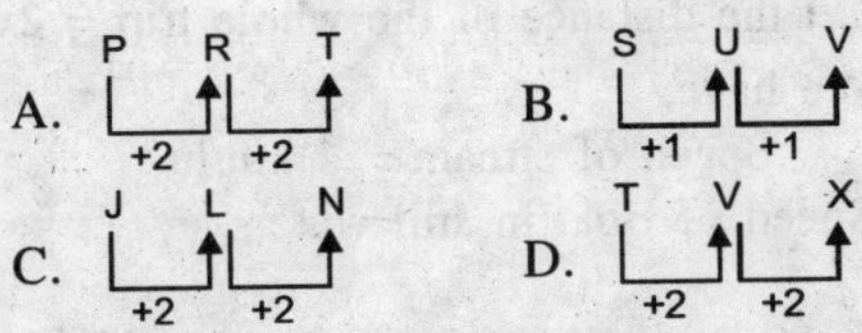

Hence, option (B) is the odd one from the given alternatives.

103. 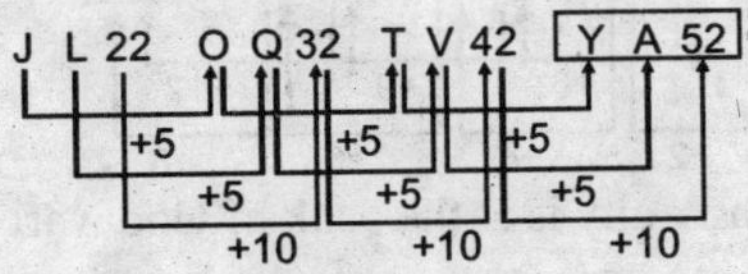

104. As, In column I, 9 + 7 = 5 + 11 (16) and Column II, 6 + 4 = 8 + 2 (10)

Similarly,

Column III, $8 + ? = 4 + 7$

$8 + ? = 11$

$? = 3$

Hence, the missing number is '3'.

106. 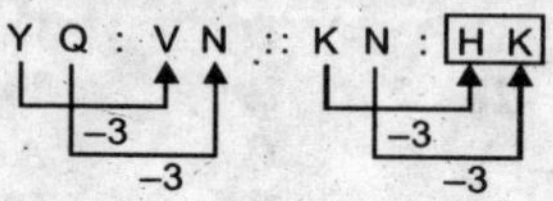

107. $8 \times 20 \div 3 + 9 - 5 = 38$

Check the option, (A), 3, 5

$8 \times 20 \div 5 + 9 - 3 = 38$

L.H.S., Apply BODMAS Rule, we get,

$= 8 \times 4 + 9 - 3$

$= 32 + 9 - 3$

$= 41 - 3$

$= 38 = \text{RHS}$

Hence, option (A) is correct.

109. As, PROGRESS = 19 – 16 = 3

↑ ↑

16 19

DEVELOPMENT = 20 – 4 = 16

↑ ↑

4 20

Similarly,

MANAGEMENT = 20 – 13 = 7

↑ ↑

13 20

110. Visiting order of the stores is following
1. Reebok 2. Puma 3. Addidas 4. Nike/HRX
Hence, fourth store will be either Nike or HRX.

112. 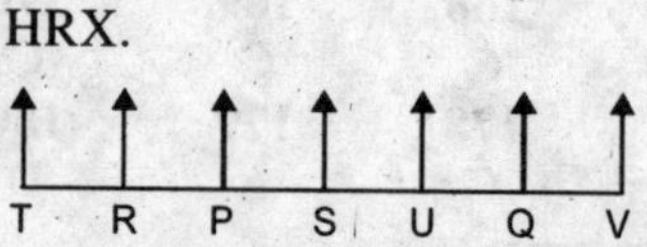

There are four people sit between R and V.

117. 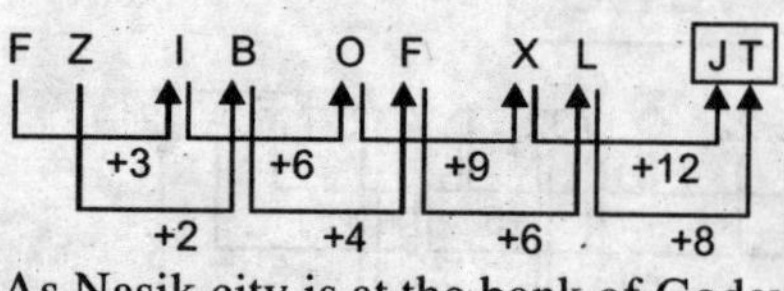

120. As Nasik city is at the bank of Godavari river. Similarly, Gorakhpur city is at the bank of Rapti river.

141. Let the marks of three students A, B and C are $3x$, $4x$ and $6x$ respectively.

According to question,

$$\frac{3x+4x}{2} = 77$$

$$7x = 2 \times 77$$

$$x = 22$$

Then, The marks of Student C $= 6x$

$= 6 \times 22 = 132.$

142. Let the man's present age be x years

According to question,

$$x = 125\% \ (x - 10)$$

$$x = \frac{5}{4}(x-10)$$

$$4x = 5x - 50$$

$$\therefore \quad x = 50$$

Hence, the present age of man be 50 years.

143. By Alligation Rule,

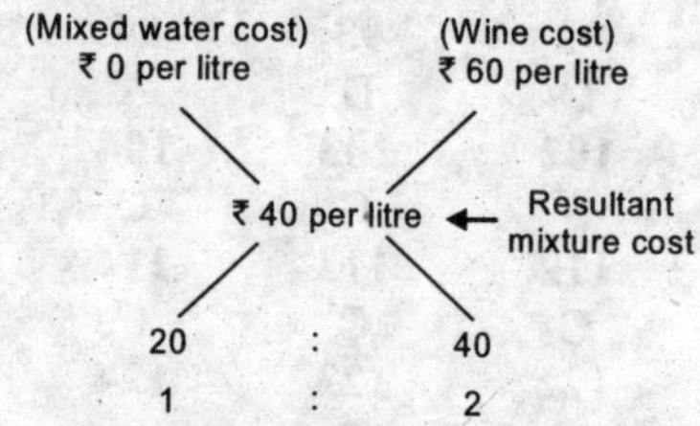

Required Ratio be 1 : 2.

144. Let the distance be x km

Then, Distance = Speed × Time

$$\therefore \quad x = 48 \times \frac{50}{60} = 4 \times \frac{50}{5}$$

$= 40$ km

$$\text{Required Speed} = \frac{\text{Distance}}{\text{Time}} = \frac{40 \text{ km}}{40 \text{ min}}$$

$$= \frac{40 \times 60 \text{ km}}{40 \text{ hour}}$$

$= 60$ km/h.

145. Let the distance of the whole trip $= 2x$ km

We have,

Speed of stream = 4 km/hr

Speed of Boat in still water

$$= 4 \times \frac{3}{1} = 12 \text{ km/hr}$$

Then, Boat's downstream speed

$= 12 + 4 = 16$ km/h

Boat's upstream speed $= 12 - 4 = 8$ km/h

According to question,

$$\frac{x}{16}+\frac{x}{8} = \frac{45}{60}$$

$$\frac{x+2x}{16} = \frac{45}{60}$$

$$3x \times 60 = 16 \times 45$$

$$x = \frac{16\times45}{180} = 4 \text{ km}$$

Then, the distance of whole trip $= 2x$

$= 2 \times 4 = 8$ km.

146. $\because$ % sale $= \frac{\text{Number of cars sold}}{\text{Number of cars manufactured}}\times100$

In 2010, % sale $= \frac{2000}{2500}\times100 = 80\%$

In 2011, % sale $= \frac{1500}{1500}\times100 = 100\%$

In 2012, % sale $= \frac{1000}{1800}\times100 = 55.56\%$

In 2013, % sale $= \frac{1000}{1000}\times100 = 100\%$

In 2014, % sale $= \frac{2000}{2200}\times100 = 90.90\%$

Hence, In 2012 the sale percentage was least.

147. $\because$ Savings = Income – Expenditure

Savings of A = 6000 – 4800 = 1200

Savings of C = 5600 – 3000 = 2600

Difference between A's and C's Savings

= 2600 – 1200 = 1400

Savings of B = 7200 – 5400 = 1800

Required Percentage

$$= \frac{1800-1400}{1800}\times100$$

$$= \frac{400}{1800}\times100 = \frac{400}{18} = \frac{200}{9} = 22\frac{2}{9}\%.$$

148. 12624 + 15285 – 16234 + 90724 + 13381 = ?

= 132014 – 16234 = 115780.

149. We have, $\frac{a}{b} = \frac{2}{3}$

Let $a = 2x$ and $b = 3x$

$$\frac{5a^3-2a^2b}{3ab^2-b^3} = \frac{5(2x)^3-2(2x)^2 3x}{3(2x)(3x)^2-(3x)^3}$$

$$= \frac{40x^3-24x^3}{54x^3-27x^3} = \frac{16x^3}{27x^3} = \frac{16}{27}.$$

150. $\frac{13}{14}, \frac{14}{15}, \frac{15}{16}, \frac{16}{17}$

$\frac{13}{14} = 0.928;$ $\frac{14}{15} = 0.933;$ $\frac{15}{16} = 0.937$

$\frac{16}{17} = 0.941$

$$\therefore \frac{13}{14}<\frac{14}{15}<\frac{15}{16}<\frac{16}{17}$$

Hence, the smallest fraction is $\frac{13}{14}$.

151. Let the value of number be x

According to question,

$$x \times 40\% = 1500 \times 20\% + 75$$

$$\frac{2x}{5} = 300 + 75 \Rightarrow x = \frac{375\times5}{2} = 937.5$$

Hence, the value of number be 937.5.

152. Required Angle

$$= \frac{350}{1000+1500+350+750}\times360°$$

$$= \frac{350\times360°}{3600} = 35°.$$

153. We have, 15 M = 18 W

$$\frac{M}{W} = \frac{6}{5}$$

Let one man efficiency $= 6x$

and one woman efficiency $= 5x$

$\therefore$ 15 M × 45 = (5M + 6W) × D

$15 \times 6x \times 45 = (5 \times 6x + 6 \times 5x) \times D$

$4050x = 60x \times D$

$\therefore$ Required days,

$$D = \frac{4050x}{60x} = \frac{135}{2} = 67\frac{1}{2} \text{ days.}$$

154. The number of students who come college

by car $= \frac{1000}{360°} \times 144° = \frac{1200}{3} = 400$

The number of students who come college

by train $= \frac{1000}{360°} \times 36° = 100$

Required percentage $= \frac{400}{100} \times 100 = 400\%$.

155. Required number

$= \text{HCF}(|580 - 4|, |679 - 7|)$

$= \text{HCF}(576, 672) = 96$

By Division Method,

```
576 ) 672 ( 1
      576
      -----
       96 ) 576 ( 6
            576
            ---
             ×
            ---
```

Hence, the required number is 96.

156. We have, $P = ₹\ 1875$

$A = ₹\ 2187$

$r = 8\%$

$\because \quad A = P\left(1 + \frac{r}{100}\right)^t$

$2187 = 1875\left(1 + \frac{8}{100}\right)^t$

$\frac{2187}{1875} = \left(\frac{27}{25}\right)^t$

$\left(\frac{27}{25}\right)^t = \frac{729}{625}$

$\left(\frac{27}{25}\right)^t = \left(\frac{27}{25}\right)^2$

On Comparing both sides, we get,

$t = 2$ years.

158. Let Rakesh purchased $2x$ chocolates

Then, Total cost price

$= \frac{1.5}{10} \times x + \frac{20}{100} \times x$

$= 0.15x + 0.2x = 0.35x$

Total selling price $= \frac{4}{20} \times 2x = 0.4x$

$\because$ Profit = Selling Price – Cost Price

$\therefore \quad 0.4x - 0.35x = ₹\ 10$

$0.05x = 10$

$x = \frac{10}{0.05} = 200$

Required number of chocolates

$= 2x = 2 \times 200 = 400.$

159. Let the marked price of mobile is $₹\ x$

According to question,

$x - x \times 70\% = 3000$

$30\% x = 3000$

$x = \frac{3000 \times 100}{30} = ₹\ 10{,}000$

Nitesh pay for the mobile

$= x \times \left(1 - \frac{30}{100}\right) = 10{,}000\left(\frac{70}{100}\right) = ₹\ 7000.$

160.

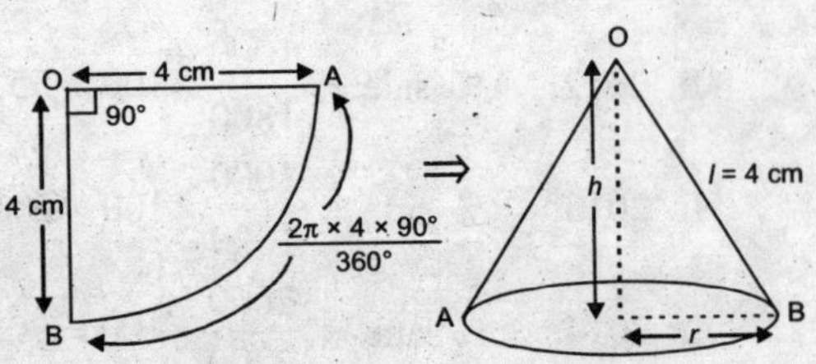

Perimeter of Sector AB = Perimeter of Base of cone

$\therefore \quad 2\pi r = \frac{2\pi \times 4 \times 90°}{360°}$

$r = 1$ cm

Height of cone, $h = \sqrt{l^2 - r^2}$

$= \sqrt{(4)^2 - (1)^2} = \sqrt{15}$ cm

Volume of cone

$= \frac{1}{3}\pi r^2 h = \frac{1}{3} \times \pi(1)^2 \times \sqrt{15}$

$= \frac{\sqrt{15}}{3} \times \pi = \sqrt{\frac{15}{9}} \times \pi = \frac{\sqrt{5}}{\sqrt{3}} \times \pi$ cm^3.

Previous Paper (Solved)

Assistant Engineer Electrical Examination–2018*

SUBJECT : ELECTRICAL ENGINEERING

1. The frequency response of $G(s) = \frac{1}{s(s+1)(s+2)}$ plotted in the complex $G(j\omega)$ plane (for $0 < \omega < \infty$) is:

A.
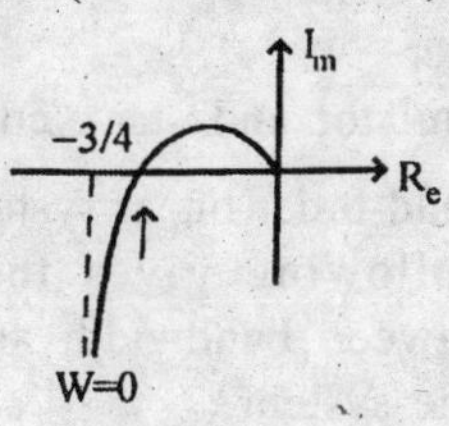

B.
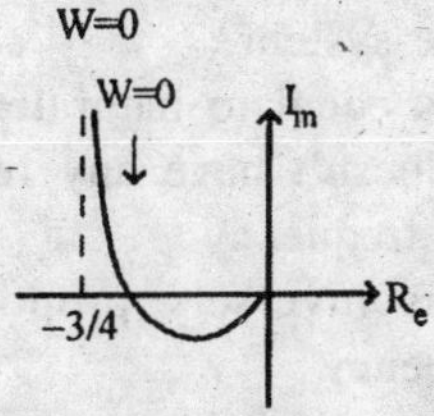

C.
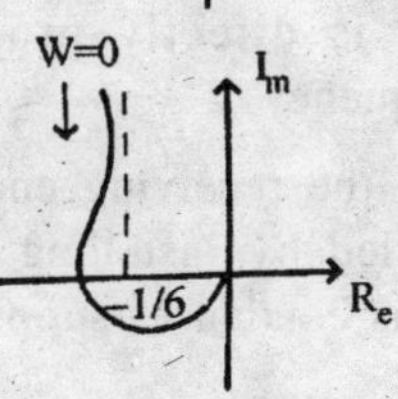

D.
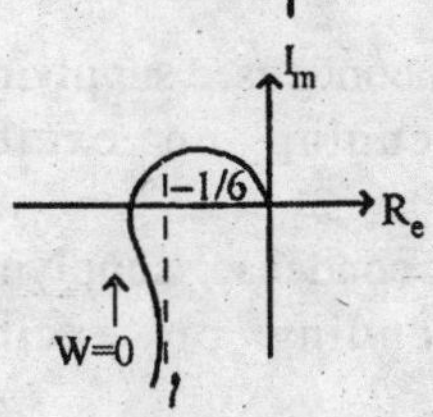

2. The constant M loci plot is symmetrical with respect to:

A. real axis and imaginary axis
B. M = 1 straight line and the real axis
C. M = 1 straight line and the imaginary axis
D. M = 1 straight line

3. Consider the state space model of a system, as given below:

$$\begin{bmatrix} \dot{x}_1 \\ \dot{x}_2 \\ \dot{x}_3 \end{bmatrix} = \begin{bmatrix} -1 & 1 & 0 \\ 0 & -1 & 0 \\ 0 & 0 & -2 \end{bmatrix} \begin{bmatrix} x_1 \\ x_2 \\ x_3 \end{bmatrix} + \begin{bmatrix} 0 \\ 4 \\ 0 \end{bmatrix} u$$

$$y = [1 \quad 1 \quad 1] \begin{bmatrix} x_1 \\ x_2 \\ x_3 \end{bmatrix}$$

The system is ________

A. Controllable and observable
B. Uncontrollable and observable
C. Uncontrollable and unobservable
D. Controllable and unobservable

4. High voltage Schering bridge is used for the measurement of:

A. Resistance and inductance of a coil
B. Frequency of the ac source
C. Loss angle of a capacitor
D. Q of a coil

5. An ammeter of 0.1 Ω resistance is connected across the secondary of a 400/5 A current transformer (CT). The CT burden is:

A. 0.5 VA B. 2.5 VA
C. 5.0 VA D. 25 VA

6. An aquadag is used in a CRO to collect ________

* *Held on 11 March 2018 (Conducted by TSTRANSCO)*

A. Primary electrons
B. Secondary emission electrons
C. Both primary and secondary emission electrons
D. The frequency of the signal

7. A PMMC meter has an internal resistance 200 Ω and the current required for its full scale deflection is 50 μA. The meter is capable of measuring, on its own, a maximum voltage of_________

A. 5 μV B. 10 μV
C. 5 mV D. 10 mV

8. Errors which may be variable both in magnitude and nature (positive or negative) are classified as

A. Hysteresis error
B. Random errors
C. Systematic errors
D. Interaction errors

9. The input voltage to a full wave bridge rectifier is $v(t)$ = 200 sin wt volts. The peak inverse voltage of the diodes is:

A. 200 volt B. $\sqrt{2} \times 200$ volt
C. $\sqrt{2} \times 100$ volt D. 400 volt

10. As the temperature is increased, the voltage across a semiconductor diode carrying a constant current:

A. increases
B. decreases
C. remains constant
D. may increase or decrease depending upon the doping levels in the junction

11. The frequency of ac voltage in a single phase PWM converter is regulated by:

A. increasing the amplitude of sine wave
B. varying the frequency of sine wave
C. varying the frequency of triangular wave
D. amplitude of the triangular wave

12. A single phase half wave converter with freewheeling diode fed separately excited DC drive operates at 1000 rpm at firing angle $\alpha = 45°$. If single phase half wave converter is replaced by single phase semi converter, the motor rotates at:

A. 2000 rpm B. 1500 rpm
C. 1000 rpm D. 500 rpm

13. A three phase full wave controlled rectifier is connected to a separately excited DC motor and the machine has the following data: T_e = 150 N–m; ω = 75 rad/sec and I_a = 50 A; What will be the back emf of the motor?

A. 200 V B. 225 V
C. 250 V D. 275 V

14. Which of the following is an 8-bit register in Intel 8085 microprocessor

A. Accumulator
B. Programme counter
C. Stack counter
D. Both accumulator and stack counter

15. Consider a second-order linear system. Which one of the following gives the correct relationship between bandwidth and natural frequency of the system?

A. Bandwidth is equal to natural frequency
B. Bandwidth doesn't have any relationship with natural frequency
C. Bandwidth is inversely proportional to natural frequency
D. Bandwidth is directly proportional to natural frequency

16. The voltage at the receiving end of the line can be controlled by installing

A. Synchronous condenser supplying leading kVAR
B. Synchronous condenser supplying lagging kVAR depending on excitation of condenser
C. Synchronous condenser supplying leading kVAR depending on excitation of condenser
D. Synchronous condenser supplying lagging kVAR

17. The power transformer having a capacity of 10 MVA with 132/66 kV (Star-Delta) configuration is protected by circulating current protection system. Calculate the CT

ratios on both sides of the transformer for a circulating current of 5A in the pilot wires.
A. 43.71/5, 87.4/5
B. 43.71/(5/1.732), 87.4/5
C. 87.4/5, 43.71/(5/1.732)
D. 43.71/5, 87.4(5/1.732)

18. BJT amplifier configuration which acts as buffer is:
A. Common emitter
B. Common base
C. Common collector
D. Cascode amplifier

19. Hexa decimal equivalent value of decimal number 757.25 is:
A. 7B2.2B B. 2F5.40
C. 3E4.60 D. 42A.8

20. Frequency of oscillation of Colpitt's oscillator is:

A. $f = \dfrac{1}{2\pi\sqrt{L\left(\dfrac{C_1C_2}{C_1+C_2}\right)}}$

B. $f = \dfrac{1}{2\pi\sqrt{L(C_1+C_2)}}$

C. $f = \dfrac{1}{2\pi\sqrt{(L_1+L_2)C}}$

D. $f = \dfrac{1}{2\pi\sqrt{(L_1+L_2+2M)C}}$

21. The type of feedback used in wien bridge oscillator is:
A. Negative feedback only
B. Positive feedback only
C. No feedback
D. Both negative and positive feedback

22. The clock frequency of an 8-bit successive approximation type A to D converter is 2MHz. The conversion time for an analog signal sample to be converted to digital equivalent value is:
A. 2μs B. 1 μs
C. 4 μs D. 16 μs

23. The present outputs of the flip-flops of a 3 bit synchronous down converter are 110. After 7 clock pulses the outputs change to:
A. 110 B. 111
C. 101 D. 100

24. The highest priority interrupt in Intel 8085 microprocessor is:
A. INTR B. RST 7.5
C. TRAP D. RST 6.5

25. The figure shows a circuit with an ideal operational amplifier $V_{in} = 5 \sin \omega t$ mV. The V_{out} is _______ mV.

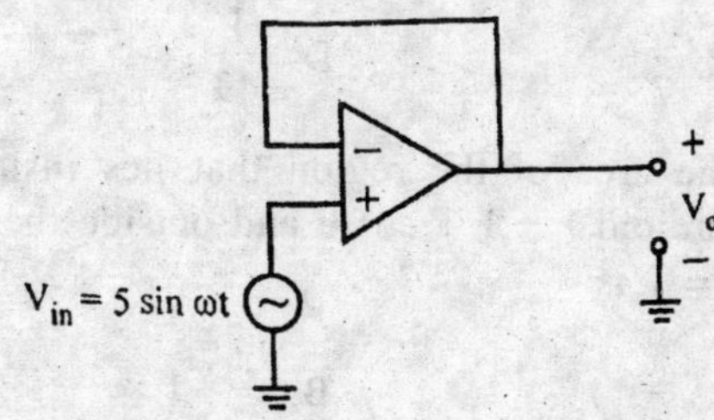

A. $5 \sin \omega t$ B. $-5 \sin \omega t$
C. $10 \sin \omega t$ D. $2.5 \sin \omega t$

26. $\int_{|z+1|=2} \dfrac{z^2}{4-z^2}\,dz =$
A. 0 B. $2\pi i$
C. $-2\pi i$ D. 1

27. Which of the following is not an Eigen vector of the matrix $\begin{bmatrix} 1 & 1 & 3 \\ 1 & 5 & 1 \\ 3 & 1 & 1 \end{bmatrix}$?

A. $\begin{bmatrix} 1 \\ 0 \\ -1 \end{bmatrix}$ B. $\begin{bmatrix} -3 \\ 0 \\ 3 \end{bmatrix}$

C. $\begin{bmatrix} 3 \\ 0 \\ -3 \end{bmatrix}$ D. $\begin{bmatrix} 1 \\ 0 \\ 1 \end{bmatrix}$

28. The Fourier transform of the function $f(x) = xe^{4x^2}$ is:

A. 0 B. $\frac{\sqrt{\pi}}{2}e^{\frac{w^2}{16}}$

C. $-i\frac{\sqrt{\pi}}{16}we^{-\frac{w^2}{16}}$ D. $i\frac{\sqrt{\pi}}{8}we^{-\frac{w^2}{8}}$

29. Let X be a random variable that follows Binomial distribution with expectation E(X) = 7 and variance V(X) = 6. Then the probability of success p is:

A. $\frac{6}{7}$ B. $\frac{36}{49}$

C. $\frac{1}{7}$ D. $\frac{1}{49}$

30. The area of the region that lies inside the cardioid $r = 1 + \cos\theta$ and outside the circle $r = 1$ is:

A. $\frac{\pi}{4}$ B. $\frac{\pi}{4}+1$

C. $\frac{\pi}{4}+2$ D. $\frac{\pi}{4}+4$

31. A coil with a certain number of turns has a specified time constant. If the number of turns is doubled, its time constant would be:

A. Remain unaffected
B. Become doubled
C. Become fourfold
D. Get halved

32. The instantaneous power of a balanced three-phase load is 2000 W when phase A is at its peak voltage. What will be the instantaneous power 30° later?

A. 1 kW B. 4 kW
C. $\sqrt{3}$ kW D. 2 kW

33. A balanced three phase delta connected load is supplied by a balanced 3-phase, 400 V supply. The phase current is 10 A at a 0.8 power factor lagging. The total reactive power absorbed by the load is:

A. 7.2 kVAR B. 2.4 kVAR
C. 3.2 kVAR D. 9.6 kVAR

34. The Thevenin's equivalent of the circuit shown in figure is a voltage source of:

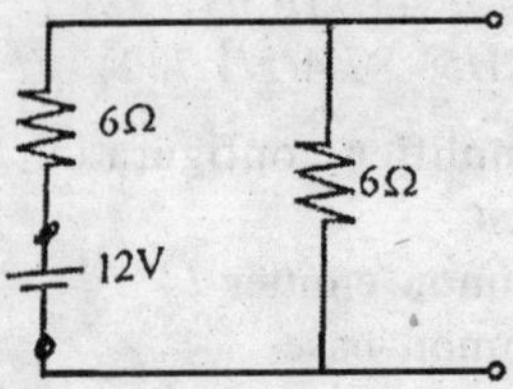

A. 6V in series with a resistance of 3 Ω
B. 12V in series with a resistance of 3 Ω
C. 6V in series with a resistance of 6 Ω
D. 6V in series with a resistance of 12 Ω

35. The combined inductance of two coils connected in series is 0.6H or 0.1 H, depending upon the relative directions of the currents in the coils. How much is the mutual inductance between the coils?

A. 0.25 H B. 0.3 H
C. 0.05 H D. 0.125 H

36. An initially relaxed RC-series network with R = 2M ohm and C = 1 micro Farad is switched on to a 10 V step input. The voltage across the capacitor after 2 seconds will be:

A. Zero B. 3.68 V
C. 6.32 V D. 10 V

37. The parameter Z_{11} of the below circuit is ________.

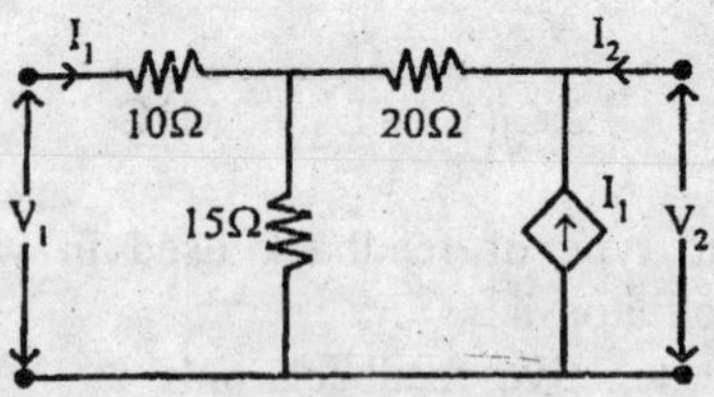

A. 50 Ω B. 15 Ω
C. 35 Ω D. 40 Ω

38. The network function $f(s) = \frac{(s+2)}{((s+1)(s+3))}$, represents:

A. RC impedance

B. RL impedance
C. RC impedance and RL admittance
D. RC admittance and RL impedance

39. For a series RLC circuit, the power factor at the lower half power frequency is:
A. 0.5 lagging
B. 0.5 leading
C. Unity
D. 0.707 leading

40. An electric field is given as $E = 6y^2z\hat{x} + 12xyz\hat{y} + 6xy^2\hat{z}$ V/m. An incremental path is represented by $\Delta L = -3\hat{x} + 5\hat{y} - 2\hat{z}$ μm. How much is the work done in moving a 2μC charge along this path if the location of the path is at (0, 2, 5)?
A. 360 pJ
B. 720 pJ
C. 180 pJ
D. 1440 pJ

41. A point charge of 500 pC is located at the origin of the coordinate system. How much is the potential difference between two points A and B, which are at radial distances of 5 m and 15 m, respectively, from the charge?
A. 0.9 V
B. 0.6 V
C. 0.3 V
D. 1.2 V

42. The unit of relative permeability is ______
A. a Number
B. $\frac{AT}{m^2}$
C. $\frac{AT}{m}$
D. $\frac{N}{wb}$

43. A circular-loop conductor, having a radius of 0.1 m and a resistance of 5Ω, lies in the $z = 0$ plane with its center at the origin of the coordinate system. The magnetic flux density in the region is $0.2 \sin 1000t\ \hat{z}$ Wb/m^2. How much is the current flowing in the conductor?
A. $0.4\pi \cos 1000t$ A
B. $0.02\pi \sin 1000t$ A
C. $-0.4\pi \cos 1000t$ A
D. $-0.02\pi \sin 1000t$ A

44. The magnetic field strength in a region is given as $H = y \cos ax\,\hat{x} + (y + e^x)\hat{z}$. What is the value of $\nabla \times H$ at the origin?
A. $\hat{x} + \hat{y} + \hat{z}$
B. $\hat{x} + \hat{y} - \hat{z}$
C. $-\hat{x} - \hat{y} - \hat{z}$
D. $\hat{x} - \hat{y} - \hat{z}$

45. A hollow metal sphere of radius 5 cm is charged such that the potential on its surface is 10 V. The potential at a distance of 2 cm from the centre of the sphere is ______
A. 4 V
B. 10 V
C. $\frac{10}{3}$ V
D. Zero

46. The Maxwell equation for time varying field is ________
A. $\nabla \times H = J + \frac{\partial D}{\partial t}$
B. $\nabla \cdot H = J + \frac{\partial D}{\partial t}$
C. $\nabla \cdot H = J \frac{\partial D}{\partial t}$
D. $\nabla \times H = J - \frac{\partial D}{\partial t}$

47. How much is the energy of the discrete-time signal $x[n]$ given by:
$x[n] = (-0.5)^n\, u[n]$, where $u[n]$ is the unit step sequence.
A. $\frac{3}{4}$
B. $\frac{1}{2}$
C. $\frac{4}{3}$
D. 2

48. The Laplace transform of signal $x(t) = -e^{-2t} u(-t)$ is ______ , where $u(t)$ is the unit step signal.
A. $\frac{1}{s-2}$
B. $\frac{1}{s+2}$
C. $-\frac{1}{s+2}$
D. $-\frac{1}{s-2}$

49. The amplitude spectrum $|X(j\omega)|$ of a real signal $x(t)$ is ______
A. an even function
B. an odd function

C. an even and odd function both
D. neither even nor odd function

50. Which of the following discrete time system is not causal
A. $y[n] = x[-n]$
B. $y[n] = \sum_{k=-\infty}^{n} x[k]$
C. $y[n] = x[n-1]$
D. $y[n] = y[n-1] + x[n]$

51. The fundamental period N of a discrete time signal $e^{j\left(\frac{3\pi}{4}\right)n}$ is:

A. N = 1	B. N = 2
C. N = 4	D. N = 8

52. A single-phase 200/125 volt autotransformer delivers 40 kVA to a load at 0.8 power factor lagging. Neglect leakage reactance and magnetizing current. For this loading condition the transformed kVA is:

A. 15	B. 40
C. 25	D. 32

53. A 3-phase induction motor runs at 3% slip and develops mechanical power equal to 10 kW. The air gap power is

A. 9.7 kW	B. $\left(\frac{10}{0.97}\right)$ kW
C. 10.30 kW	D. 10.03 kW

54. A three-phase, 2000-volt, Y-connected wound rotor induction motor has the following no-load test data:
2000 volt, 15.3 amp and 10.1 kW

The core loss resistance r_c of the approximate equivalent circuit is nearly

A. 396 Ω	B. 686 Ω
C. 329 Ω	D. 666 Ω

55. A 230 V dc series motor has an armature circuit resistance of 0.2 Ω and field resistance of 0.1 Ω. At rated voltage, the motor draws a line current of 40 A and runs at speed of 1000 rpm. Assume that the flux at 20 A line current is 60% of flux at 40 A line current. What is the speed of motor for a line current of 20 A at 230 V.

A. 1317 rpm	B. 1713 rpm
C. 1137 rpm	D. 3117 rpm

56. A three-phase Y-connected synchronous generator has synchronous reactance $X_s = 5\ \Omega$ per phase. It delivers 12 kVA load at unity power factor. The terminal voltage is 200 volts/phase. The induced emf per phase of the generator is:
A. $\sqrt{5} \times 100$ volts
B. $\sqrt{3} \times 100$ volts
C. $\sqrt{2} \times 100$ volts
D. 200 volts

57. The emf induced per phase in the rotor winding of a 3-phase induction motor is 100 V at stand still. Under full-load condition, this emf would be normally:

A. 100 V	B. 50 V
C. 4 V	D. 0.2 V

58. A 3-phase induction motor has a starting torque of 200 N-m when switched on-directly to supply. If an auto-transformer with 50% tapping is used for starting, the starting torque would be

A. 400 N-m	B. 200 N-m
C. 100 N-m	D. 50 N-m

59. A 3-phase synchronous generator is operating at 0.8 of lagging with respect to the excitation voltage. The nature of armature reaction mmf produced by the armature currents is
A. Magnetizing
B. Demagnetizing
C. Cross-magnetizing and partly demagnetizing
D. Partly demagnetizing and partly cross-magnetizing

60. When speed becomes more than the synchronous speed during hunting, the damper bars develop
A. Synchronous motor torque
B. Induction motor torque

C. DC motor torque
D. Induction generator torque

61. Rotor slot of the squirrel cage induction motor are skewed slightly, so as to:
A. Increase the mechanical strength of rotor
B. Make the rotor construction simple
C. Eliminate locking tendency of the rotor and to reduce the noise
D. Save the amount of copper required

62. Maximum torque developed by a three-phase induction motor
A. increases with increase in rotor resistance
B. decreases with increase in rotor resistance
C. is independent of rotor resistance
D. increases with decrease in rotor resistance

63. A synchronous machine has its field winding on the stator and armature winding on the rotor. When running under steady conditions, its air gap field is
A. Stationary with respect to stator
B. Stationary with respect to rotor
C. Rotating at synchronous speed with respect to stator
D. Rotating at synchronous speed in the direction of rotor rotating

64. A long transmission line is energized at the sending end and is kept open circuited at the receiving end. The magnitude of receiving end line voltage is 400 kV. The magnitude of the sending end line voltage is:
A. < 400 kV B. = 400 kV
C. > 400 kV D. ≥ 400 kV

65. The string efficiency of a string of suspension insulators of a 400 kV, 3-phase transmission line is 80%. The voltage across the string is:
A. 400 kV B. $(400\sqrt{3})$ kV
C. $(500\sqrt{3})$ kV D. 320 kV

66. A 3-phase, 11 kV, induction motor draws 100 kVA at 0.8 pf lagging from the system. A 3-phase capacitor bank rated 60 kVAR is installed across the motor in order to increase the power factor to unity. The apparent power supplied by the system to the motor with capacitor bank is:
A. 100 kVA B. 40 kVA
C. 160 kVA D. 80 kVA

67. As the moisture content in the air increases, the disruptive critical voltage:
A. Decreases
B. Increases
C. Remains constant
D. Infinite

68. The arc resistance causes distance relay:
A. under reach
B. over reach
C. under reach or over reach depending on the length of the line
D. reach unchanged

69. Figure shows the single phase equivalent circuit for analyzing circuit breaker operation. The frequency of re-striking voltage is:

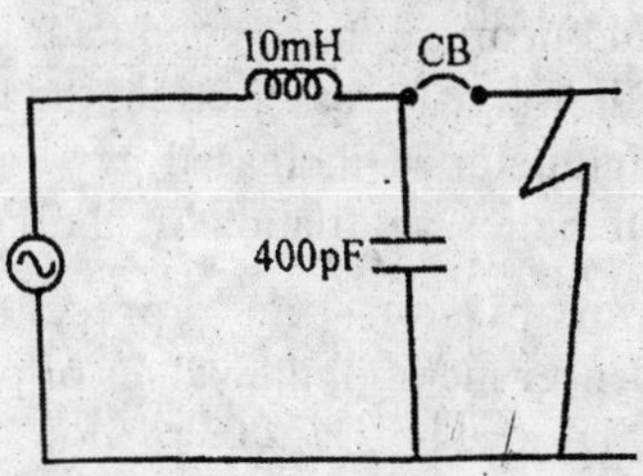

A. 1000 kHz
B. 5000 kHz
C. 500×10^3 radians/sec
D. 200×10^3 radians/sec

70. One line diagram of a 3-bus power system is given in figure. The line admittances are marked in per unit. The first row of the Y_{Bus}

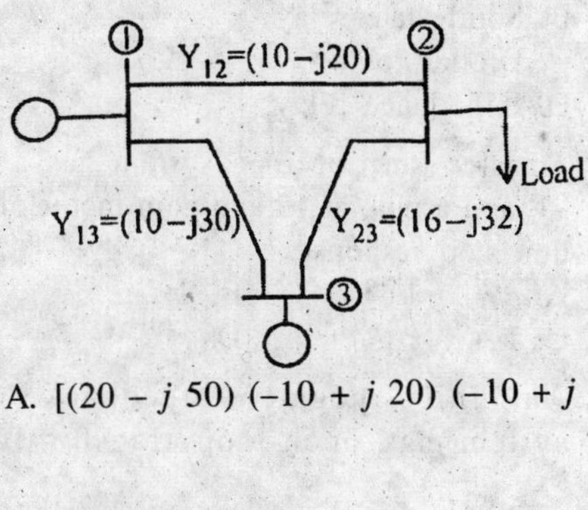

A. [(20 − *j* 50) (−10 + *j* 20) (−10 + *j* 30)]

B. [(20 – j 50) (10 – j 20) (10 – j 30)]
C. [(10 – j 20) (–10 + j 20) (–10 + j 30)]
D. [(20 + j 50) (–10 + j 20) (–10 + j 30)]

71. Number of iterations required for convergence of a load flow algorithm increases significantly with increase of number of buses with
A. G-S load flow algorithm
B. N-R load flow algorithm
C. both G-S and N-R load flow algorithms
D. Fast decoupled load flow algorithm

72. For low head and high discharge, the hydraulic turbine used is:
A. Francis turbine
B. Kaplan turbine
C. Pelton wheel
D. Impulse turbine

73. Corona loss can be reduced by the use of hollow conductors because,
A. The current density is reduced
B. Eddy current in the conductor is eliminated
C. For a given cross-section, the radius of the conductor is increased
D. Of better ventilation in the conductor

74. A transmission line represented in End condenser method, the values of parameters A and D are ________ and ________ respectively.
A. A = 1 + ZY; D = 1 + ZY
B. A = 1 + ZY; D = 1
C. A = 1 – ZY; D = 1 + ZY
D. A = 1; D = 1 + ZY

75. Overreaching of distance relay due to the decaying DC component is avoided by
A. Electromechanical relay
B. Solid state relay
C. Digital relay
D. Impedance relay

76. Transfer function of a system has a zero at –1, and a pole at –2 and gain factor of 2. The unit step response is:
A. $e^{-2t} - 1$
B. $1 - e^{-2t}$
C. $1 + e^{-2t}$
D. e^{-2t}

77. An unity negative feedback control system has open-loop transfer function $G(s) = \dfrac{4}{s(s+1)}$. The damped natural frequency ω_d in radians/sec is:
A. $2 \times \sqrt{1-(0.5)^2}$
B. $4 \times \sqrt{1-(0.25)^2}$
C. $2 \times \sqrt{1+(0.25)^2}$
D. $2 \times \sqrt{1-(0.25)^2}$

78. For a feedback control system of type-2, the steady state error for a ramp input is:
A. infinite
B. constant
C. zero
D. indeterminate

79. The overall transfer function of the system shown below is ________

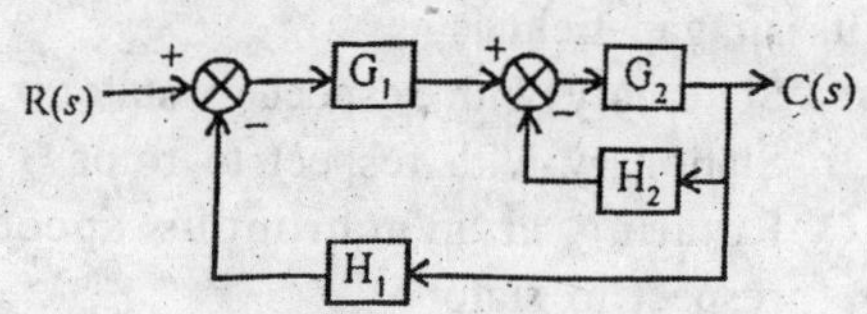

A. $\dfrac{G_1G_2}{1+G_1H_1+G_1G_2H_2}$

B. $\dfrac{G_1G_2}{1+G_2H_2+G_1G_2H_1}$

C. $\dfrac{G_1G_2}{1+G_2H_2+G_1G_2H_2}$

D. $\dfrac{G_1G_2}{1-G_2H_2-G_1G_2H_1}$

80. An electric motor with high torque/inertia ratio has ______
A. Lower motor time constant and faster dynamic response
B. Higher motor time constant and slow dynamic response
C. Lower motor time constant and slow dynamic response
D. Higher motor time constant and faster dynamic response

GENERAL AWARENESS AND NUMERICAL ABILITY

81. Conventional Rainfall occurs in:
A. Equatorial Region
B. Temperate Region
C. Tropical Region
D. Polar Region

82. Eden Garden stadium in Kolkata is associated with:
A. Basket Ball B. Foot Ball
C. Cricket D. Hockey

83. Which in the following is a stringed instrument?
A. Tabla B. Shehnai
C. Santoor D. Mridangam

84. Someone is sitting ________ the shade of a tree today because someone planted it a long time ago.
A. Under B. On
C. Above D. In

85. The teacher ______ us some advice on taking tests.
A. Did B. Gave
C. Made D. Took

86. If you were the Prime Minister of India, what _______ you _______?
A. Would, do
B. Would, have done
C. Will, do
D. Had, done

87. Sachin retired from his ________ cricket career in 2013.
A. Illustrate B. Illustrious
C. Illustrations D. Illusive

88. Who of the following has called Hyderabad as Bagh City?
A. Thevenot B. Methold
C. Tavernier D. Manucci

89. Who was the principal deity of Kakatiyas?
A. Goddess Laxmi
B. Lord Vishnu
C. Swamyambhu Shiva
D. Goddess Durga

90. Who wrote the book The Tragedy of Hyderabad?
A. Mir Laiq Ali
B. Mohammed Hyder
C. Narendra Luther
D. John Zubrzyki

91. Who was the first Martyr of Telangana Struggle?
A. M.A. Rasheed
B. B. Narsi Reddy
C. K. Venkateshwar Rao
D. Mir Laiq Ali

92. Which of the following is not a valid IP address?
A. 192.10.9.20 B. 192.30.23.189
C. 192.10.23.350 D. 192.10.50.230

93. Which of the following is not class of IP addresses?
A. Class A B. Class C
C. Class E D. Class F

94. Process of inserting an element in an array is called ______
A. Create B. Push
C. Pop D. Evaluate

95. DNS is stands for _________
A. Domain Name Server
B. Domain Name System
C. Dynamic Name System
D. Domain Network Service

96. Find the missing term in the following series:

2, 5, 10, 17, 26, 37, ?, 65
A. 48 B. 49
C. 50 D. 51

97. Complete the analogous pair, Terrible : Serene : : Roof : ?
A. Door B. Floor
C. Walls D. Pillars

98. The price of a commodity increases first by 20% and then by 10%. What is the net increase in the price?

A. 28% B. 30%
C. 32% D. 34%

99. Find the average of the first 97 natural numbers?
A. 47 B. 48
C. 49 D. 50

100. Who is empowered to transfer a Judge from one High court to another High court:
A. Chief Justice of India
B. President of India
C. Law Minister of India
D. The Union Cabinet

ANSWERS

1	2	3	4	5	6	7	8	9	10
A	B	B	C	B	B	D	B	A	B
11	**12**	**13**	**14**	**15**	**16**	**17**	**18**	**19**	**20**
B	A	B	A	D	C	D	C	B	A
21	**22**	**23**	**24**	**25**	**26**	**27**	**28**	**29**	**30**
D	C	B	C	A	B	D	C	C	C
31	**32**	**33**	**34**	**35**	**36**	**37**	**38**	**39**	**40**
B	D	A	A	D	C	D	C	D	B
41	**42**	**43**	**44**	**45**	**46**	**47**	**48**	**49**	**50**
B	A	C	D	B	A	C	B	A	A
51	**52**	**53**	**54**	**55**	**56**	**57**	**58**	**59**	**60**
D	B	B	A	B	A	C	D	D	D
61	**62**	**63**	**64**	**65**	**66**	**67**	**68**	**69**	**70**
C	C	A	A	B	D	A	A	C	A
71	**72**	**73**	**74**	**75**	**76**	**77**	**78**	**79**	**80**
A	B	C	B	C	C	D	C	B	A
81	**82**	**83**	**84**	**85**	**86**	**87**	**88**	**89**	**90**
A	C	C	D	B	A	B	A	C	A
91	**92**	**93**	**94**	**95**	**96**	**97**	**98**	**99**	**100**
D	C	D	B	B	C	B	C	C	B

Previous Paper (Solved)

Junior Engineer Electrical

Examination–2017*

SUBJECT : ELECTRICAL ENGINEERING

1. The emf induced in a coil of N turns is given by:

A. $e = \frac{Ndt}{d\varnothing}$ B. $e = -\frac{Nd\varnothing}{dt}$

C. $e = \frac{Nd\varnothing}{dt}$ D. $e = \frac{d\varnothing}{dt}$

2. The element which is capable of delivering energy by its own is known as:

A. Non-Linear element

B. Unilateral element

C. Active element

D. Passive element

3. When a high voltage overhead line passes over or adjacent to any building the vertical clearance between the highest part of the building immediately under such lines, recommended in IE rules is of not less than:

A. 1.2 m B. 2.8 m

C. 6 m D. 3.7 m

4. A billion electrons pass through a conductor of cross-section in 10^{-3} sec. The current is:

A. 10^{-7}A B. 2.6×10^{-3}A

C. 2×10^{-4}A D. 1.6×10^{-7}A

5. In a star connected balanced circuit the phase difference between the line voltage V_{RY} and the phase voltage V_{RN} is equal to:

A. 30° – Φ B. 60°

C. 120° D. 30°

6. In a CRO, when set for internal trigger (INT) ________.

A. Trigger circuit will input vertical amplifier

B. Trigger circuit receives input from the horizontal amplifier

C. Trigger circuit will input horizontal amplifier

D. Trigger circuit receives input from the vertical amplifier

7. The schematic symbol for a PN junction diode is:

A.  B. 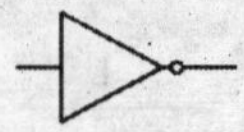

C. 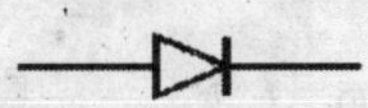 D. 

8. A 8H choke is carrying a current of 500 mA. The energy supplied by inductor is:

A. 2 J B. 4 J

C. 0.5 J D. 1 J

9. The type of wattmeter commonly used for measurement of power in AC circuits is:

A. Moving iron type

B. Thermocouple type

C. Rectifier type

D. Dynamometer type

10. The wave forms shown below indicate:

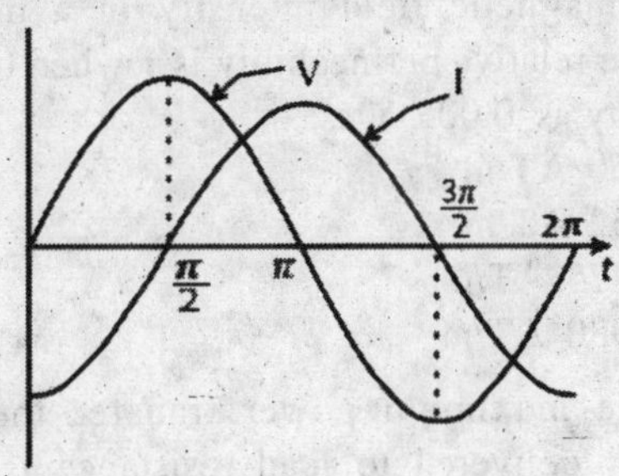

* Held on 5 March 2017 (Conducted by Noida Metro)

A. V lags I by π
B. V leads I by π
C. V lags I by $\frac{\pi}{2}$
D. V leads I by $\frac{\pi}{2}$

11. An alternating voltage is given by V = 20 sin 157*t*, the frequency of the alternating voltage is:
A. 75 Hz B. 100 Hz
C. 50 Hz D. 25 Hz

12. A silicon PN junction in forward conduction has a voltage drop closer to:
A. 1.7 V B. 2.1 V
C. 0.1 V D. 0.7 V

13. Resonance in RLC series circuit occurs at a frequency:
A. $f_r = \frac{1}{\pi\sqrt{LC}}$ B. $f_r = 2\pi\sqrt{LC}$
C. $f_r = \frac{R}{2\pi\sqrt{LC}}$ D. $f_r = \frac{1}{2\pi\sqrt{LC}}$

14. A fuse material should possess the following properties:
A. Low melting point and low specific resistance
B. High melting point and low specific resistance
C. Low melting point and high specific resistance
D. High melting point and high specific resistance

15. The magnetic field intensity in a material whose relative permeability is 1 when the flux density is 0.005 T is:
A. 250 AT/m
B. 452 AT/m
C. 1775 AT/m
D. 3980 AT/m

16. In the maximum power transfer theorem, power delivered to load resistance is given by:
A. $P_{max} = \frac{V_{TH}^2}{4R_{TH}}$ B. $P_{max} = \frac{V_{TH}}{4R_{TH}}$
C. $P_{max} = \frac{V_{TH}^2}{4R_{TH}^2}$ D. $P_{max} = \frac{V_{TH}}{4R_{TH}^2}$

17. The method of speed control of DC shunt motors used for applications where a very wide range sensitive speed control is required is:
A. Ward-Leonard system
B. Multiple voltage control
C. Tapped field control
D. Rheostatic control

18. The DC shunt motor is running with a certain load. The effect of adding an external resistance in field circuit is to:
A. Increase the motor speed
B. Stop the motor
C. Reduce the motor speed
D. Reduce the armature current of the motor

19. In the circuit shown in figure the voltage at the node B with respect to node D is calculated to be 15 V. Then the current in 30 Ω resistor will be:

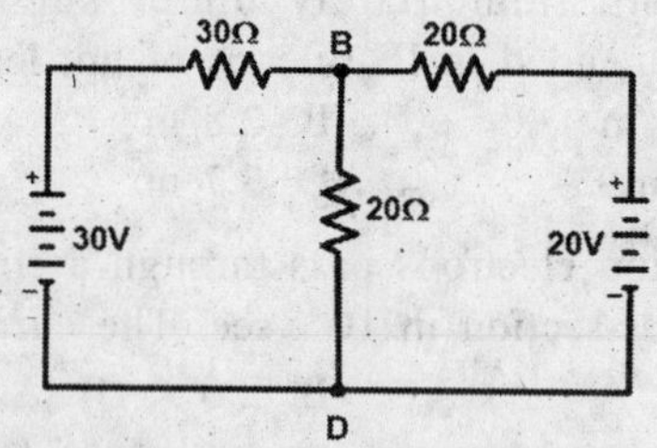

A. 2.5 A B. 2 A
C. 10A D. 0.5 A

20. The type of single phase induction motor having the highest power factor at full load is
A. Capacitor run type
B. Capacitor start type
C. Shaded pole type
D. Split phase type

21. The following generating station has the minimum running cost:

A. Diesel power station
B. Nuclear power station
C. Hydroelectric power station
D. Thermal power station

22. ______ remains same in all parts of a series circuit.

A. Current B. Resistance
C. Voltage D. Power

23. In DC motor, the speed depends upon:

A. Applied voltage alone
B. Back emf alone
C. Back emf and flux
D. Flux only

24. The parallel circuit consists of an inductive branch with R and L as its resistance and inductance, and a capacitance branch with C farad. The impedance offered by this circuit under resonance condition is given by:

A. Z = LCR B. $Z = \frac{R}{LC}$

C. $Z = \frac{L}{CR}$ D. $Z = \frac{LC}{R}$

25. A spherical conductor of radius 'a' with charge 'q' is placed concentrically inside an uncharged and unearthed spherical conducting shell of inner and outer radii r_1 and r_2 respectively. Taking potential to be zero at infinity. The potential at any point within the shell ($r_1 < r < r_2$) will be?

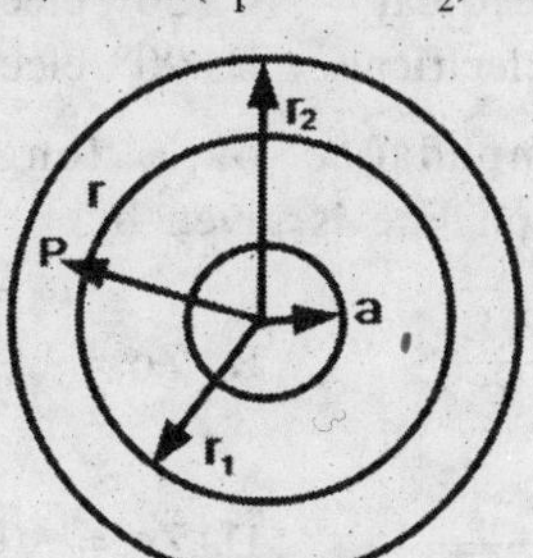

A. $\frac{q}{4\pi\varepsilon_o a}$ B. $\frac{q}{4\pi\varepsilon_o r_2}$

C. $\frac{q}{4\pi\varepsilon_o r}$ D. $\frac{q}{4\pi\varepsilon_o r_1}$

26. Convert the Delta network into equivalent star network:

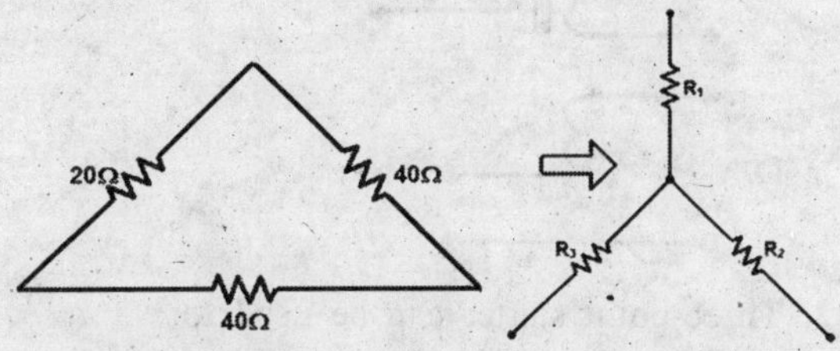

A. $R_1 = 8\ \Omega$, $R_2 = 8\ \Omega$, $R_3 = 8\ \Omega$
B. $R_1 = 8\ \Omega$, $R_2 = 16\ \Omega$, $R_3 = 16\ \Omega$
C. $R_1 = 8\ \Omega$, $R_2 = 8\ \Omega$, $R_3 = 16\ \Omega$
D. $R_1 = 8\ \Omega$, $R_2 = 16\ \Omega$, $R_3 = 8\ \Omega$

27. A 2000/200V, 20 kVA transformer has 66 turns in the secondary. The number of primary turns are:

A. 660 B. 440
C. 770 D. 330

28. Induction type energy meter measures energy in ______ .

A. Joules B. kW
C. kWh D. kWs

29. Open circuit test on a transformer gives:

A. Total loss
B. Insulation resistance
C. Core loss
D. Cu loss

30. Compensating winding is used in:

A. Capacitor start motor
B. Shaded pole motor
C. AC series motor
D. Capacitor run motor

31. Identify the symbol of isolation transformer among the following:

A. 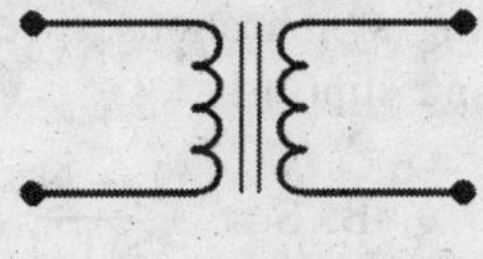

B. 

C. 

D. 

32. Three-point starter can be used for:
A. Both shunt and compound motors
B. Shunt motor only
C. Series motor only
D. Compound motor only

33. In a PNP transistor, electrons flow:
A. Out of the transistor, at the collector and base leads
B. Out of the transistor, at the emitter and base leads
C. Into the transistor, at the emitter and base leads
D. Into the transistor, at the collector and base leads

34. The normal phase sequence of a 3 phase AC supply is:
A. RBY B. RYB
C. BRY D. YBR

35. High silicon content steel is used for transformer core construction to:
A. Improve cooling of core and yoke
B. Reduce hysteresis loss
C. Reduce eddy current loss
D. Reduce weight of steel

36. The ratio of average load to the maximum demand during a given period is _______ .
A. Demand factor B. Diversity factor
C. Load factor D. Connected load

37. The relation among synchronous speed (N_s) rotor speed (N) and slip(s) is:

A. $S = \frac{N - N_s}{N}$ B. $S = \frac{N_s - N}{N_s}$

C. $S = \frac{N_s - N}{N}$ D. $S = \frac{N - N_s}{N_s}$

38. In a nuclear power station, the moderator is used to:
A. Accelerate the speed of neutrons
B. Stop the chain reaction
C. Absorb neutrons
D. Reduce the speed of neutrons

39. When the collector-to-base junction in transistor is biased in the reverse direction and the emitter-to-base junction in the forward direction, then the transistor is in:
A. Active region
B. Cut off region
C. Break down region
D. Saturation region

40. Mixture preferred for filling around the earth electrode for effective earthing is:
A. Paper salt mixture
B. Saw dust mixture
C. Coal-salt mixture
D. Lime-sand mixture

41. Most suitable circuit breakers for short line fault without switching resistors is:
A. Minimum oil circuit breaker
B. Vacuum circuit breaker
C. SF_6 circuit breaker
D. Air blast circuit breaker

42. The three-phase induction motor stator windings is displaced by ________ from each other.
A. 45° electrical B. 30° electrical
C. 120° electrical D. 90° electrical

43. Surge impedance of a long loss-less transmission line is given by:

A. $Zo = \frac{\sqrt{L}}{C}$ B. $Zo = \sqrt{\frac{L}{C}}$

C. $Zo = \frac{1}{\sqrt{LC}}$ D. $Zo = \sqrt{LC}$

44. A magnetizing force of 800 AT/m will produce a flux density of ______ in air.
A. 0.5 Wb/m^2 B. 1 Wb/m^2
C. 10 mWb/m^2 D. 1 mWb/m^2

45. If a DC supply of 180 V is connected across terminals AB in figure, then current in 6 Ω resistor will be:

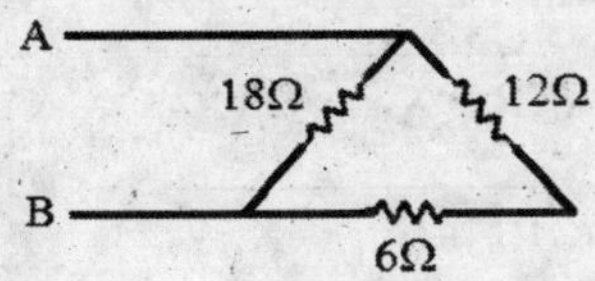

A. 6 A B. 5 A
C. 12 A D. 10 A

46. The control parameter of JFET is:
A. Gate current B. Drain voltage
C. Gate voltage D. Source voltage

47. A sine wave has a maximum value of 20V. Its value at 30° is ______.
A. 17.32 V B. 10 V
C. 15 V D. 14.14 V

48. A three-phase induction motor is wound for 4 pole and is supplied from 50 Hz system. Calculate synchronous speed.
A. 1550 rpm B. 1500 rpm
C. 1440 rpm D. 1400 rpm

49. A 4 pole, 50 Hz induction motor operates at 5% slip. The frequency of emf induced in the rotor will be:
A. 25 Hz B. 2 Hz
C. 2.5 Hz D. 50 Hz

50. In a star connected 3 phase system, relationship between line voltage and phase voltage is given by:
A. $V_L = V_{ph}$
B. $V_L = 3V_{ph}$
C. $V_L = \sqrt{3}\, V_{ph}$
D. $V_L = \sqrt{2}\, V_{ph}$

51. Voltage equation of DC motor is given by:
A. $V = E_b + I_a R_a$
B. $V = E_b - I_a R_a$
C. $V = E_b I_a - R_a$
D. $V = E_b I_a + R_a$

52. A transformer has an efficiency of 80% and works at 100 V and 4 kW. If the secondary voltage is 240 V, find the primary current:
A. 16.67 A B. 40 A
C. 30 A D. 10 A

53. The depletion region of PN junction is consist of:
A. Atoms
B. Passive component
C. Mobile charges
D. Immobile charges

54. Generally used motor in domestic food mixer is:
A. Capacitor start motor
B. Shaded pole motor
C. Universal motor
D. Reluctance motor

55. If the rotor emf per phase at standstill is E_2 and the motor is operating at a slip (S), the generated rotor emf per phase under running condition will be
A. s^2E_2 B. E_2
C. SE_2 D. $\frac{E_2}{S}$

56. DC motor recommended for locomotive drive is:
A. DC series motor
B. DC long shunt compound motor
C. DC Shunt motor
D. DC short shunt compound motor

57. Two wattmeter method can be used to measure the total power delivered to:
A. Star connected with neutral loads
B. Delta connected load only
C. Star connected load only
D. Star as well as delta connected loads

58. In case of 3 phase induction motors, plugging is done by:
A. Starting the motor on load which is more than the rated load
B. Pulling the motor directly on line without a starter
C. Interchanging connections of any two phases of stator for quick stopping
D. Locking of rotor due to harmonics

59. Cables in power transmission line are provided with inter sheaths to:
A. Minimize charging current
B. Minimize stress
C. Provide uniform stress distribution
D. Minimize high voltage

60. The active and apparent powers of an inductive circuit are 60 W and 100 KVA respectively. The power factor of a circuit is:
A. 0.6 leading B. 0.6 lagging
C. 0.5 lagging D. 0.75 lagging

61. A current of 2A flows in the circuit shown in figure. The potential difference $V_A - V_B$ is:

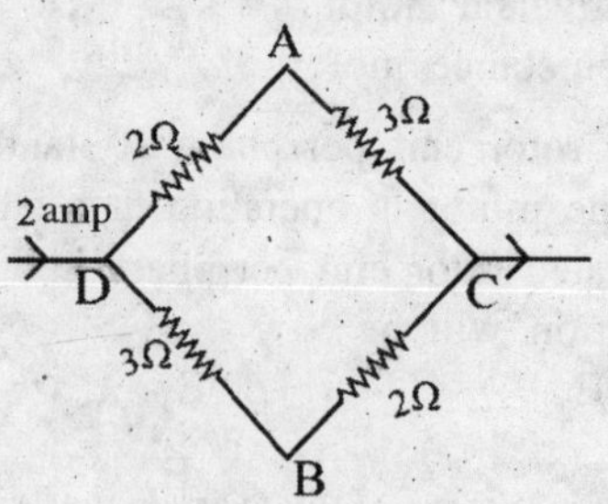

A. –1 V B. 1 V
C. 2V D. 4V

62. When the supply voltage to an induction motor is reduced by 10%, the maximum torque will decrease approximately by:
A. 10% B. 20%
C. 5% D. 40%

63. In an RLC series circuit the condition below the resonant frequency is:
A. $X_C > X_L$ B. $X_C + X_L$
C. $X_C < X_L$ D. $X_C = X_L$

64. The total electric flux through any closed surface is equal to the amount of charge enclosed. The above statement is based on:
A. Gauss's law
B. Ampere's law
C. Maxwell's law
D. Coulomb's law

65. Brushes are provided in DC machine for:
A. Smooth rotation
B. Preventing sparking
C. Providing a path for flow of current
D. Reducing the losses

66. In a RLC series circuit, impedance is given by:
A. $Z = \sqrt{(R + X_L)^2 + X_C^2}$
B. $Z = \sqrt{R^2 + (X_L - X_C)^2}$
C. $Z = R - X_L + X_C$
D. $Z = R + X_L - X_C$

67. When all the resistance in the given circuit are 1 Ω each, the equivalent resistance across the points A and B will be?

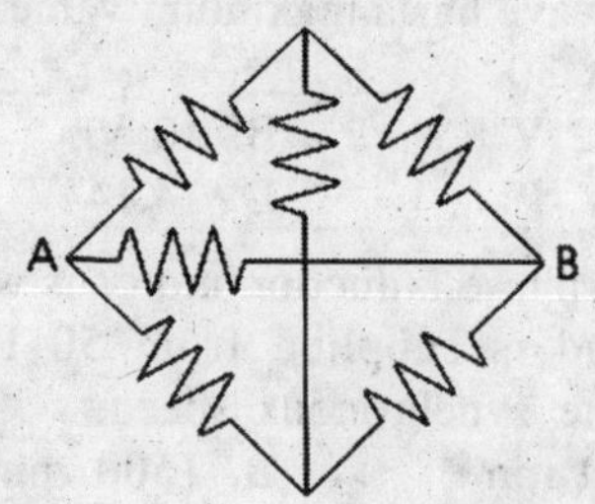

A. 1 Ω B. 0.5 Ω
C. 3 Ω D. 2 Ω

68. When two coils having coefficient of self-inductance L_1 and L_2 are coupled through a mutual inductance M. The coefficient of coupling K is given by:
A. $K = \frac{M}{\sqrt{L_1 L_2}}$ B. $K = \frac{M}{\sqrt{2 L_1 L_2}}$
C. $K = \frac{2M}{\sqrt{2 L_1 L_2}}$ D. $K = \frac{4 L_1 L_2}{\sqrt{M}}$

69. A transistor connected in common base configuration has:
A. a high input resistance and low output resistance
B. a high input resistance and high output resistance
C. a low input resistance and high output resistance
D. a low input resistance and low output resistance

70. Damping winding in a synchronous motor:
A. improves power factor of the motor
B. increases hunting of the motor
C. reduces windage losses
D. increases starting torque

71. For the given circuit, the value of Norton's equivalent Resistance is:

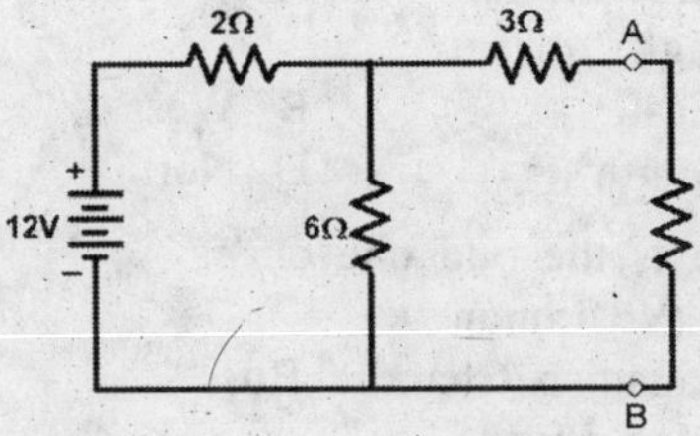

A. 4.5 Ω B. 5 Ω
C. 6 Ω D. 10 Ω

72. Method of heating in which the supply circuit is likely to have a leading power factor:
A. Induction heating
B. Dielectric heating
C. Resistance heating
D. Electric arc

73. Bridge suited for measurement of low Q-factor inductance is:
A. Hay's bridge
B. Maxwell's bridge
C. Schering bridge
D. Anderson's bridge

74. The rating of transformer is expressed in:
A. kVA B. kW
C. HP D. kWh

75. An alternating voltage is given by V = 200 sin314t. Its rms value will be:
A. 110 V B. 282.8 V
C. 121.4 V D. 141.4 V

76. Where is tehri hydroelectric project located in India?
A. Madhya Pradesh B. Uttrakhand
C. Rajasthan D. Jammu & Kashmir

77. Which coin was introduced in 2010 to commemorate the centenary birth anniversary of mother Teresa?
A. Twenty-Ruppe coin
B. Five Rupee coin
C. Thousand-Rupee coin
D. Ten Rupee coin

78. Where were the first Asian Games (Asiad) held?
A. Lahore B. Mumbai
C. New Delhi D. Beijing

79. Which article of Indian constitution says that 'It is the duty of Union to protect states against external aggression and internal disturbance'?
A. Article 356 B. Article 355
C. Article 255 D. Article 155

80. The king of which dynasty was described as 'Son of God'?
A. Maurya dynasty
B. Kushan dynasty
C. Chola dynasty
D. Saka

81. Which committee proposed removal of subsidy to small scale industries?
A. Abid Hussain committee
B. Khelkar committee
C. Parikh committee
D. Rangarajan committee

82. Which part of the Indian constitution contains Fundamental rights?
A. Part II B. Part IV
C. Part III D. Part I

83. What is the total number of medals won by India in 2016 Rio Olympics?
A. 4 B. 3
C. 1 D. 2

84. International Bank of Reconstruction and Development is presently known as?
A. Reserve Bank of India
B. International Monetary Fund
C. Swiss Bank
D. World Bank

85. Who is the current Union Minister of Textiles in the cabinet of PM Narendra Modi?
A. Ram Kripal Yadav
B. Giriraj Singh
C. Smriti Irani
D. M.J. Akbar

86. Where is Gol Gumbaz located in India?
A. Raipur B. Nagpur
C. Bellary D. Bijapur

87. The Anamudi peak is the highest mountain peak of which of the following mountain ranges?
A. Himalayas B. Sahayadri
C. Aravalli D. Vindhya

88. Who is considered as the Greatest ruler in the Mauryan Empire?
A. Kautilya B. Ashoka
C. Samudragupta D. Bindusara

89. Which state was on the basis of Doctine of lapse evicted firstly?
A. Hyderabad B. Satara
C. Nagpur D. Sambalpur

90. Who is the civil aviation minister in at present cabinet of P.M. Narendra Modi Government?
A. Giriraj Singh
B. B.K. Singh
C. Jyant Sinha
D. Santosh Kumar Gangwar

91. Complete the series:
Z, R, V, O, R, L, N, I, ?, ?
A. J, H B. J, D
C. O, D D. J, F

92. In a certain code, ORIENTAL is written as ATNEIROL. How is INACTIVE written in the same code?
A. VITNICAE B. VACTINIE
C. VITCANIE D. CVAITENI

93. Identify the number that fits the analogy:
6 : 18 : : 7 : ?
A. 102 B. 42
C. 516 D. 21

94. Five participants A, B, C, D and E are standing in a line. Their heights are as follows. A is shorter than B but taller than C. D is shorter than C. E is taller than D. A is taller than E.
Who among the five participants is the shortest?
A. C B. E
C. D D. B

95. Complete the series:
1, 4, 10, 22, 46, ?
A. 94 B. 96
C. 98 D. 92

96. One morning after sunrise, Vivek and suresh were standing in a lawn with their backs towards each other. Vivek's shadow fell exactly towards the left. Which direction was Suresh facing?
A. East B. West
C. South D. North

97. Who is the odd one out?
A. C.V. Raman
B. Jagadish Chandra Bose
C. Max Plank
D. Stephen William Hawking

98. Complete the series:
M, N, P, S, W, ?
A. D B. K
C. B D. A

99. If 'C' is coded as 6, 'F' is coded as 8, 'H' is coded as 4, 'A' is coded as 3, 'P' is coded as 2, 'U' is coded as 5, 'N' is coded as 7, what is the coded form of 'ACFPUN'?
A. 368257 B. 365728
C. 358527 D. 465827

100. Five friends A, B, C, D and E are standing in a line. A is shorter than B but taller than C. D is shorter than C. E is taller than D. A is taller than E.
Who among the five friends is the tallest?
A. A B. D
C. B D. C

101. Pointing to a boy, Namita said, "He is the son of my grandfather's only child." How is the boy related to Namita?
A. Cousin B. Uncle
C. Father D. Brother

102.

Look at the pattern above. Fill in the missing number.

A. 14 B. 12
C. 16 D. 15

103. 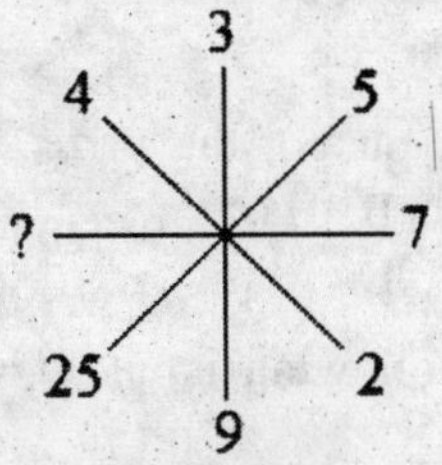

Look at the pattern above. Fill in the missing number.

A. 64 B. 49
C. 29 D. 39

104. If SWITCH can be written as 192392038, how can SUGAR be written?

A. 1821187 B. 19275118
C. 19217118 D. 20217518

105. Complete the series:

24, 12, 48, 24, 96, 48, ?

A. 24 B. 12
C. 192 D. 48

106. A milk vendor has 2 cans of milk. The first contains 25% water and the rest milk. The second contains 50% of water. How much milk should be mixed from each of the containers so as to get 10 litres of milk such that the ratio of water to milk is 2 : 3?

A. 3 litres, 7 litres B. 2 litres, 8 litres
C. 4 litres, 6 litres D. 5 litres, 5 litres

107. At the rate of 5% per annum simple interest, a sum of ₹ 3,000 will earn how much interest by the end of 5 years?

A. ₹ 725 B. ₹ 800
C. ₹ 750 D. ₹ 700

108. A shopkeeper loses 20%, if an article is sold for ₹ 100. What should be the selling price of the article to gain 30%?

A. ₹ 162.5 B. ₹ 170.5
C. ₹ 165.5 D. ₹ 160.5

109. Which of the following pairs of numbers are co-primes?

A. (31, 93) B. (18, 25)
C. (14, 35) D. (32, 62)

110. Find the greatest 6 digit number which is exactly divisible by 6, 12, 18, 24.

A. 999963 B. 999936
C. 999863 D. 999639

111. Find the value of $4(\sin^4 60° + \cos^4 60°) - 3(\cos^2 45° + \sin^2 90°)$.

A. –3 B. 4
C. –2 D. 3

112. The current birth rate per thousand is 40, whereas corresponding death rate is 20 per thousand. The net growth rate in terms of population increase in percentage is given by:

A. 2 B. 4
C. 1 D. 3

113. Simplify:

$$\frac{5.32 \times 56 + 5.32 \times 44}{(7.66)^2 - (2.34)^2}$$

A. 15 B. 5
C. 20 D. 10

114. How many terms of A.P. series $-6, \frac{-11}{2}, -5,$ .... are needed to obtain the sum (–25)?

A. 10 or 15 B. 5 or 20
C. 15 or 18 D. 8 or 12

115. The average of all odd numbers up to 50 is:

A. 20 B. 30
C. 25 D. 15

116. Moving at $\frac{8}{9}$ of its usual speed, a train is 5 minutes late. Find its usual time to cover the journey.

A. 30 min B. 45 min
C. 35 min D. 40 min

117. A certain amount was divided between Salim and Rahim in the ratio of 3 : 2. If Rahim's share was ₹ 3,000, the total amount was:

A. ₹ 7,500 B. ₹ 5,000
C. ₹ 8,500 D. ₹ 8,000

118. The sum of two numbers is 27 and their product is 50. Find the sum of 2nd power of each number.

A. 404 B. 650
C. 529 D. 629

119. If the height of a pole is $4\sqrt{3}$ m and the length of its shadow is 4 m. Find the angle of elevation of the sun.

A. 60° B. 45°
C. 30° D. 90°

120. Raviteja runs at 17.6 kmph. How many metres does he run in 3 minutes?

A. 900 m B. 800 m
C. 980 m D. 880 m

121. Complete the sentence.

My friend said: "I thought you did not see the movie." I replied: "No. _______."

A. I said I saw the movie
B. I will see the movie
C. I see the movie
D. I have not seen the movie

122. Give the passive form of the sentence.

"My husband has promised me a present"

A. A present was promised by my husband.
B. A present has been promised by my husband.
C. A present had been promised by my husband.
D. A present will be given by husband.

123. Identify the preposition.

"I sat beneath the shady tree"

A. tree B. sat
C. shady D. beneath

124. Give the reported speech form of the sentence.

She said, "It was a wonderful day"

A. She tells it was a wonderful day
B. She told it is a wonderful day
C. She told me that it is a wonderful day
D. She said that it was a wonderful day

125. Use the right preposition to fill in the blank.

" White tigers are found _______ Sunderbans"

A. from B. in
C. by D. with

126. Complete the sentence using the right interjection.

"_______" I knew you got the prize"

A. No B. Ha
C. Yes D. Alas

127. Which among the following is an adverb of frequency?

A. How B. When
C. Twice D. Then

128. Use the right preposition to fill in the blank.

"She jumped _______ the wall"

A. in B. of
C. off D. among

129. If you are 'encouraging' a person then you are _______ him.

A. cheering B. telling
C. disallowing D. stopping

130. Complete the sentence.

The customs officer said to me: "______ the goods?"

A. Declared goods
B. Goods declared
C. Did you declare
D. Goods you declared

131. What is the opposite of 'Rich'?

A. Unhappy B. Luxurious
C. Happy D. Poor

132. What is the mood of the verb 'prays' in the following sentence?

"My mother prays"

A. Intransitive B. Indicative
C. Imperative D. Passive

133. Find the word equivalent in meaning to 'defy'.

A. Obey B. Agree
C. Disagree D. Disobey

134. The other adjectival form of *hard* is:

A. Harder B. Hardest
C. Tough D. Hardly

135. Complete the sentence.

This road is 'zigzag'; but that one is _____.

A. long B. narrow

C. broad D. straight

136. Complete the sentence.

His behaviour did not bring 'credit' to the school. Instead it brought ______.

A. reputation B. pride

C. discredit D. honour

137. Identify the adverb in the sentence.

'I remember the college where I studied'

A. college B. where

C. remember D. studied

138. What is the opposite of 'Workaholic'?

A. Active B. Lazy

C. Workhorse D. Hardworking

139. Give the reported speech form of the sentence.

My friend said "How beautiful you are!"

A. My friend says I am beautiful.

B. My friend told to me I am beautiful.

C. My friend exclaimed that I was beautiful.

D. My friend reports I am beautiful.

140. Complete the sentence.

He said, "I am dining out."

I said, "I thought you said _____."

A. that he had dinined out

B. that he is not dining out

C. that you are dining out

D. tha you were not dining out

141. Give the passive form of the sentence.

"The tsunami almost destroyed Chennai"

A. Chennai was almost being destroyed by the tsunami

B. Chennai is almost destroyed by the tsunami

C. Chennai has been almost destroyed by the tsunami

D. Chennai was almost destroyed by the tsunami

142. Identify the adverb in the sentence.

"please stand near me John"

A. near B. me

C. please D. John

143. Identify the opposite of 'Liberal'.

A. Intolerate B. Intolerantly

C. Intolerance D. Intolerant

144. Give the passive form of the sentence.

"He will give you the boarding pass"

A. You will be given the boarding pass by him

B. You will have to be given the boarding pass

C. He will be given the boarding pass by you

D. The boarding pass will be given by him

145. Which among the following is not a synonym of 'Lie'?

A. Untrue B. Truth

C. False D. Wrong

146. She said she is 'fond' of her daughter, that is she _______ her daughter.

A. disapproves B. hates

C. dislikes D. likes

147. The word opposite in meaning to 'Degrade' is:

A. Demean B. Increase

C. Discredit D. Respect

148. Give the direct speech form of the sentence.

"He requested me to open my briefcase"

A. He tells, "Open the briefcase"

B. He said, "Open you briefcase?"

C. He told, "Can you open your briefcase?"

D. He said, "Can you open your briefcase, please?"

149. What is the role of the adverb in the given sentence?

"The then principal of the college"

A. Noun B. Preposition

C. Verb D. Adjective

150. What would you call the 'come' in the following sentence?

"Come here"

A. Simple

B. Imperative

C. Subjunctive

D. Participle

151. Which word is nearest in meaning to 'Crack'?
A. End B. Open
C. Close D. Break

152. Change the voice of the sentence.
"The room was filled with laughter"
A. Laughter was filling the room
B. Laughter will fill the room
C. Laughter is filling the room
D. Laughter filled the room

153. Identify the preposition
"In addition to laddu, I ate ice-cream"
A. to B. in addition to
C. In D. addition

154. 'Kindness' is an:
A. Countable noun
B. Uncountable noun
C. Abstract noun
D. Collective noun

155. What type of pronoun is used in the sentence?
"That is the Taj Mahal"
A. Compound
B. Demonstrative
C. Relative
D. Reflexive

156. Identify the preposition.
"She came from her home"
A. her B. home
C. from D. came

157. When she said she is 'focusing' on the problam she meant that she was ________ on the problem.
A. seeing B. concentrating
C. looking at D. watching

158. The word equivalent meaning to 'Give' is:
A. Offer B. Try
C. Take back D. Approve

159. The adverb used in the given sentence is called:
"How many poems did you read"
A. Interrogative adverb of reason
B. Interrogative adverb of number
C. Interrogative adverb of manner
D. Interrogative adverb of degree

160. Which among the following adverbs has two forms?
A. Often B. Early
C. When D. Pretty

161. Give the passive form of the sentence.
"Little strokes fell the oaks"
A. The oaks are felled by little strokes.
B. The oaks were fallen by little strokes.
C. The oaks were fell by little strokes.
D. The oaks were felled by little strokes.

162. Give the direct speech form of the sentence.
"The teacher asked me where I came from."
A. Teacher asked, "Where are you coming from?"
B. The teacher says, "Coming from where?"
C. Teacher asked, "You are coming from?"
D. Teacher asked, "You coming from?"

163. What is the opposite of 'Zenith'?
A. Top B. End
C. Peak D. Nadir

164. Change the voice of the sentence.
"The secret was known to the officer".
A. The officer has been knowing the secret
B. The officer knows the secret
C. The officer has known the secret
D. The officer knew the secret

165. Identify the preposition.
"I found the gold chain underneath the bed."
A. gold B. bed
C. chain D. underneath

166. Combine the sentence using the right conjunction.
"He is handsome. He is haughty"
A. Although B. Though
C. That D. But

167. Give the reported speech form of the sentence.
The doctor said to me "Don't travel".
A. The doctor says me not to travel
B. The doctor tell to me not to travel

C. The doctor told me not to travel
D. The doctor said not to travel

168. What do you call 'himself' in the following sentence?

"The President himself visited the site"

A. Indefinite pronoun
B. Distributive pronoun
C. Demonstrative pronoun
D. Emphatic pronoun

169. Give the active form of the sentence.

"Who were you taught dance by?"

A. Who had taught you dance
B. Who taught you dance?
C. Who has taught you dance?
D. Who taught you dance by?

170. 'Generate' means:

A. Destroy B. Electricity
C. Donate D. Create

171. What form of noun is 'St/Paul's' in the following sentence?

"I went to St. Paul's"

A. Plural
B. Singular
C. Uncountable
D. Possessive case

172. Use the right preposition to fill in the blank.

"The temple is _____ huge trees"

A. above B. amidst
C. inside D. outside

173. Identify the preposition.

"She borrowed money in order to give the poor"

A. in order to B. to
C. order D. in

174. Give the active form of the sentence.

"Why should you be trusted by me?"

A. Why should I trust?
B. Why should I trust you?
C. Why I should?
D. Why should you trust I?

175. Which word will be similar in meaning to 'Resolve'?

A. Simple B. Solve
C. Entangle D. Complicate

Directions (Qs. 176-180): *Read the passage and answer the following questions accordingly.*

Cox & Kings the world's oldest travel company had started in 1758 as a regiment agent to the British Army. The company had arranged the transport of Arthur Wllesley's troops to the Battle of Waterloo and had even organized Mahatma Gandhi's trip to London.

Peter Kerkar (53) is now spearheading the company's growth from the U.K. In 1986, Mr. Kerkar, the son of former Taj Group boss Ajit Kerkar, fresh out of Stanford University joined Cox & Kings as General Manager. At the time, he had 8 employees and 12 clients. He has led the firm to become a leading player in the leisure, accommodation and education service areas beyound just travel, through a series of mergers, acquisition and asset disposals.

176. Where was Peter Karkar educated?

A. Harvard B. Cambridge
C. Stanford D. Oxford

177. What was the initial assignment taken up by Cox & Kings?

A. Be regiment agent to British Army
B. Launch space ship
C. Start a Chemistry laboratory
D. Start a University

178. Where did it transport the British Army?

A. Hiroshima B. New York
C. Waterloo D. Belgium

179. Which among the following is not in the service agenda of Cox & Kings?

A. Agriculture
B. Leisure
C. Education
D. Travel & accommodation

180. 'Spearhead' means:

A. Lead
B. Break with a spear
C. Work efficiently
D. Open

ANSWERS

1	2	3	4	5	6	7	8	9	10
B	C	D	D	D	D	C	D	D	D
11	12	13	14	15	16	17	18	19	20
D	D	D	A	D	A	A	A	D	A
21	22	23	24	25	26	27	28	29	30
C	A	C	C	D	D	A	C	C	C
31	32	33	34	35	36	37	38	39	40
A	A	D	B	B	C	B	D	A	C
41	42	43	44	45	46	47	48	49	50
C	C	B	D	D	C	B	B	C	C
51	52	53	54	55	56	57	58	59	60
A	B	C	C	C	A	D	C	C	B
61	62	63	64	65	66	67	68	69	70
C	B	A	A	C	B	B	A	C	D
71	72	73	74	75	76	77	78	79	80
A	B	D	A	D	B	B	C	B	B
81	82	83	84	85	86	87	88	89	90
A	C	D	D	C	D	B	B	B	C
91	92	93	94	95	96	97	98	99	100
D	C	D	C	A	C	D	C	A	C
101	102	103	104	105	106	107	108	109	110
D	C	B	C	C	C	C	A	B	B
111	112	113	114	115	116	117	118	119	120
C	A	D	B	C	D	A	D	A	D
121	122	123	124	125	126	127	128	129	130
A	B	D	D	B	B	C	C	A	C
131	132	133	134	135	136	137	138	139	140
D	B	D	D	D	C	B	B	C	D
141	142	143	144	145	146	147	148	149	150
D	A	D	A	B	D	D	D	D	B
151	152	153	154	155	156	157	158	159	160
D	D	B	C	B	C	B	A	B	D
161	162	163	164	165	166	167	168	169	170
A	A	D	D	D	D	C	D	B	D
171	172	173	174	175	176	177	178	179	180
D	B	A	B	B	C	A	C	A	A

Previous Paper (Solved)

Junior Engineer Electrical Examination—2016*

1. Given that.

1. A is the brother of B
2. C is the father of A
3. D is the brother of E
4. E is the daughter of B

Then the uncle of 'D' is:

A. E B. B
C. C D. A

2. Study the following figure:

A person goes from A to B always moving to right or downwards along the lines. How many different routes he can adopt?

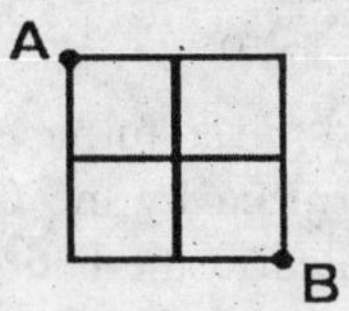

Select the correct answer:

A. 5 B. 4
C. 6 D. 7

Directions: *Given below are three positions of the same dice having names of six institutions inscribed on six faces. The names of these institutions are, ICA, ICWA, ICSI, ICFAI, IIT, BHU.*

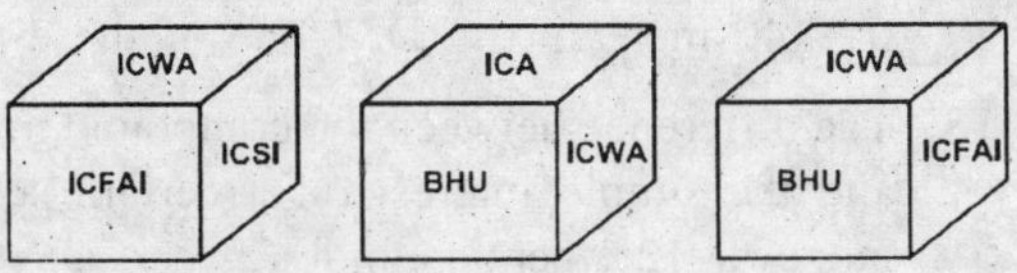

3. Which name occurs on the face opposite to that of ICA?

A. ICSI B. ICFAI
C. IIT D. None of these

4. Bidhya Devi Bhandari's is the?

A. First female President of Nepal
B. First female Prime Minister of Nepal
C. First female Vice President of Nepal
D. First female Chief Justice of Nepal

5. The Gulf Stream is an ocean current which begins:

A. Off the coast of Florida
B. From the Bay of Bengal
C. Gulf countries coastline
D. In the Philippines

6. Who recently became 161st member of WTO?

A. Yemen B. Seychelles
C. Tajikistan D. Ukraine

Directions: *In the following question a number series is given. After the series a number is given followed by (a), (b), (c), (d) and (e). You have to complete the series starting with the number given following the sequence of the given series and answer the question given below the series.*

7. 3 4 16 75 364 1945
1 (*a*) (*b*) (*c*) (*d*) (*e*)

What will come in place of (*c*)

A. 63 B. 64
C. 65 D. None of these

8. How many triangles are there in the given figure?

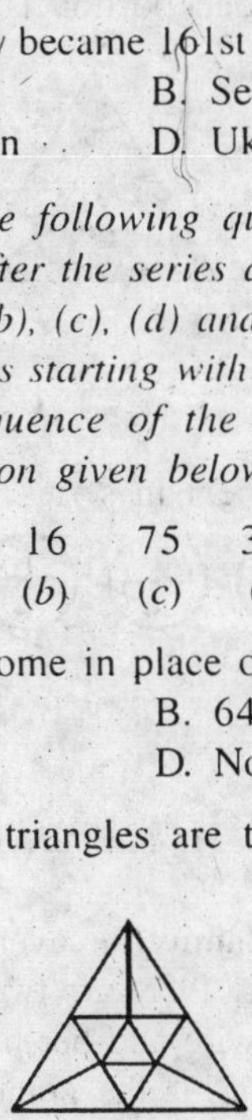

A. 16 B. 14
C. 15 D. None of these

---

* *Held on 20-03-2016.*

9. A frog tries to come out of a dried well 9 m deep with slippery walls. Every time the frog jumps 60 cm, he slides back by 30 cm. How many jumps will the frog have to take to come out of the well?

A. 20 B. 29
C. 30 D. 31

10. How many minutes will it take to completely fill a water tank with a capacity of 3750 cuft, if the water is being pumped at the rate of 800 cuft. per minute and being drained out of tank at the rate of 300 cuft per minute:

A. 3 minutes 36 seconds
B. 6 minutes
C. 7 minutes 30 seconds
D. 8 minutes

11. Triangle ABC and triangle DEF are equilaterals triangles with shaded portions of equal width throughout. If AB = 4 and EF = 2, Area of the shaded portion is:

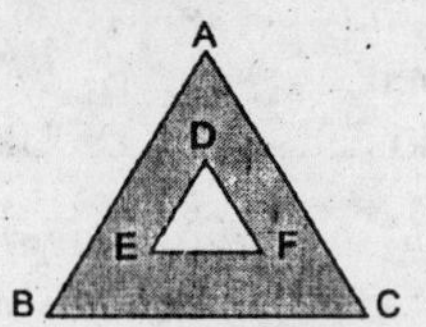

A. $4\sqrt{3}$ B. $3\sqrt{3}$
C. $\sqrt{3}$ D. None of these

12. Which is next in series?

A.  B. 

C.  D. 

13. In a joint family of seven persons F, E, N, J, P, M and L, there are two married couples. F is a housewife and her husband is E. J is the wife of N. L is the granddaughter of F. E is the father in law of J and father of P. M is the son of N and brother of L. How is J related to P?

A. Sister B. Sister-in-law
C. Niece D. Cousin sister

Directions: *Answer the following question according to the instructions given.*

A$B means A is not smaller than B
A#B means A is not greater than B
A@B means A is neither smaller nor equal to B
*A*B means A is neither greater than nor smaller than B*
A%B means A is neither greater than nor equal to B

14. Statement: M@J, J$T, T*N

Conclusion:

I. N#J II. T%M III. M@N

A. Only I and II are true
B. Only II is true
C. Only I and III are true
D. All are true

15. One of the following is not a winner of Confucius Peace Prize of China?

A. Robert Mugabe
B. Vladimir Putin
C. Tony Abbot
D. Fidel Castro

16. The largest blast furnace steel plant which was modernized by the Central Government and dedicated to the nation recently is in the state of:

A. Bihar B. West-Bengal
C. Odisha D. Jharkhand

17. If a runner takes as much time in running 20 meters as the car takes in covering 50 meters, the distance covered by the runner during the time the car covers 1 km is:

A. 400 meters B. 40 meters
C. 440 meters D. None of these

18. The difference between the compound interest and the simple interest on a certain sum of money at 12% per annum for 2 years is ₹ 1800. Find the principal sum when the interest is compounded annually:

A. ₹ 1,20,000
B. ₹ 1,25,000
C. ₹ 1,28,000
D. None of these

Directions (Q. No. 19-22): *Read the information given and answer the questions based on it.*

Seven boys namely Prashant, Rajesh, Salman, Tarun, Umar, Varun and Wasim go for tuitions to study different subjects namely Mathematics, Physics, Sociology, Chemistry, Biology, Economics and Accounts (not necessarily in the same order). Each student studies only one subject and each subject's tuition is only once a week. Two subjects cannot be taught in the same day. Also-

I. Prashant studies chemistry and goes on Sunday.

II. Umar goes for tuition on Friday.

III. The student who studies biology goes on Thursday

IV. Rajesh goes on Monday

V. Tarun goes on Wednesday but does not study Sociology

VI. Varun studies mathematics

VII. The student who studies economics goes on Tuesday. Wasim and Tarun do not study economics

19. Mathematics tuitions are on which day of the week?

A. Wednesday B. Saturday
C. Friday D. Monday

20. Umar studies which subject?

A. Sociology
B. Accounts
C. Physics
D. Cannot be determined

21. If Umar studies accounts then on which day is sociology tuition?

A. Wednesday B. Friday
C. Monday D. Thursday

22. If Rajesh studies sociology then Umar studies?

A. Mathematics
B. Physics
C. Accounts
D. Cannot be determined

23. A group of ten persons can do a particular task in 10 days. Another group can do the same job in 20 days. In how many days will the job be finished if the groups works together (each group does part of the task in proportion to its total ability):

A. $5\frac{1}{3}$ B. $6\frac{2}{3}$
C. $7\frac{1}{3}$ D. $8\frac{1}{2}$

24. In a certain code language LESSON is coded as NGUQML. How will PUZZLE be coded in that code language?

A. RWXBJP B. RVBXJC
C. RWBXJC D. RUBJXC

25. In the given figure AB and CD are two parallel chords of a circle with center O and radius 5 cm. Also AB = 8 cm and CD = 6 cm. If OP ⊥ AB and OQ ⊥ CD, determine the length of PQ:

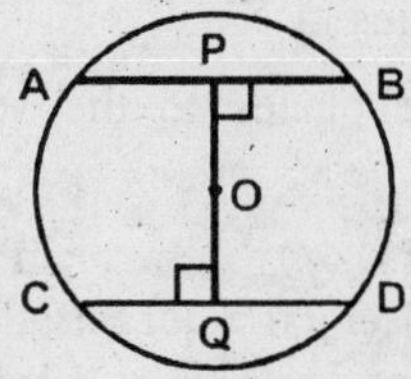

A. 7 cm B. 10 cm
C. 8 cm D. None of these

26. A well of inner diameter 14 m is dug to a depth of 15m. Earth taken out of it has been evenly spread all around it to a width of 7 m to form an embankment. Find the height of embankment so formed:

A. 7 m B. 5 m
C. 14 m D. None of these

27. Dr. APJ Abdul Kalam Collapsed only 5 minutes into his lecture at IIM, Shillong. Name this lecture.

A. Creating a livable planet earth
B. Ignited minds
C. Forge your future
D. Transforming dreams into actions

28. A hall 50 m long and 45 m broad is to be paved with square tiles. Find the largest tile as well as its number in the given options so that the tiles exactly fit in the hall?
A. 36 sq m and 80 tiles
B. 16 sq m and 80 tiles
C. 25 sq m and 90 tiles
D. 36 sq m and 90 tiles

29. A metal cube of edge 12 cm is melted and formed into three smaller cubes. If the edges of two smaller cubes are 6 cm and 8 cm, find the edge of the third smaller cube?
A. 8 cm B. 10 cm
C. 12 cm D. None of these

30. Silk Route–2015 is a:
A. Joint military training exercise between China & Sri Lanka
B. A route defined for smuggling of gold between India & Dubai
C. Silk trade agreement between India & Silk producing countries
D. Anti terrorism agreement between SAARC countries

31. Match the places to the state to which it belongs.

STATE	PLACES
(*a*) West Bengal	1. Badrinath Temple
(*b*) Tripura	2. Ujjayanta Palace
(*c*) Uttarakhand	3. Hajo
(*d*) Assam	4. Kalimpong

A. (*a*)-1, (*b*)-2, (*c*)-3, (*d*)-4
B. (*a*)-4, (*b*)-2, (*c*)-1, (*d*)-3
C. (*a*)-2, (*b*)-3, (*c*)-1, (*d*)-4
D. (*a*)-1, (*b*)-2, (*c*)-4, (*d*)-3

32. Match the following in the given sequence in context of memory:

(*a*) Very High Speed	1. DVD
(*b*) Non-Volatile & high storage	2. ROM
(*c*) External & cheaper	3. Cache
(*d*) Read only	4. Hard Disk

A. (*a*)-1, (*b*)-2, (*c*)-3, (*d*)-4
B. (*a*)-1, (*b*)-3, (*c*)-4, (*d*)-2
C. (*a*)-3, (*b*)-4, (*c*)-2, (*d*)-1
D. (*a*)-3, (*b*)-4, (*c*)-1, (*d*)-2

33. The temples of Halebid and Belur were built by:
A. Cholas B. Hoysalas
C. Rashtrakutas D. Pallavas

34. The perimeters of a square and a regular hexagon are equal. The ratio of the area of the hexagon to the area of the square is:
A. $2\sqrt{3}:1$ B. $2\sqrt{3}:3$
C. $3\sqrt{3}:2$ D. $\sqrt{2}:3$

35. Which of the following ports of India is on the eastern Coast:
A. Cochin B. Tuticorin
C. Kandla D. Mumbai

36. Which of the following are included in the original jurisdiction of the Supreme Court?
1. A dispute between the Government of India and one or more states.
2. A dispute regarding elections to either house of the parliament or that of legislative of a state.
3. A dispute between the Government of India and a union territory.
4. A dispute between two or more states.

Select the correct answers using the codes.
A. 1 & 2 B. 2 & 3
C. 1 & 4 D. 3 & 4

37. Two trains moving in opposite directions cross each other in 7.5 seconds. If the length of one train is 150 m, what is the length of the other train if the trains are travelling at 50 & 70 km. per hour respectively:
A. 100 m B. 150 m
C. 125 m D. 200 m

38. Three pipes A, B, C can fill a tank from empty to full in 30 minutes, 20 minutes, and 10 minutes respectively. When the tank is empty, all three pipes are opened. A B & C discharge chemical solution 'Q', 'R', 'S' respectively. What is the proportion of solution 'S' in the liquid in the tank after 3 minutes:
A. $\frac{7}{11}$ B. $\frac{5}{11}$
C. $\frac{6}{11}$ D. $\frac{8}{11}$

39. Recently Government of India has constituted a committee under the chairmanship of Justice R.V. Easwar to look into?

A. To look into the implementation of goods & service tax

B. To look into the affairs of Physically challenged person

C. To look into the affairs of Niti Aaayog

D. The simplification of provisions of Income Tax Act

40. Identify the odd one out (refer to National Sports Awards for 2014–15):

A. Harbans Singh B. Sandeep Kumar

C. Anoop Singh D. Naval Singh

41. 2022 Common Wealth Games will be hosted by:

A. Durban B. Gold Coast

C. Victoria D. Kingston

42. There are two clocks, both set to show 10 pm on 21st January 2010. One clock gains 2 minutes in an hour and the other clock loses 5 minutes in an hour. Then by how many minutes do the two clocks differ at 4 pm on 22nd January 2010?

A. 126 minutes B. 136 minutes

C. 96 minutes D. 106 minutes

43. A publisher sells copies of books to a retail dealer at ₹ 5 per copy but allows 25 copies to be counted as 24. If the retailer sells each of the 25 copies at ₹ 6, his profit % is:

A. 20% B. 24%

C. 25% D. 40%

Directions (Q. No. 44 & 45): *Each question below is followed by two statement I and II. You are to determine whether the data given in the statement is sufficient for answering the question. You should use the data and your knowledge of mathematics to choose between the possible answers.*

(*a*) If the statement I alone is sufficient to answer the question but the statement II alone is not sufficient.

(*b*) If the statement II alone is sufficient to answer the question but statement I alone is not sufficient.

(*c*) If both statements I and II together are needed to answer the question.

(*d*) If either the statement I alone or statement II alone is sufficient to answer the question.

(*e*) If you can not get the answer from statement I and II together but need even more data.

44. X, Y and Z are three consecutive odd number (not necessary in this order). What is the sum of these number?

I. The difference of Y & Z is 4

II. One third of X is 33

A. (*a*) B. (*b*)

C. (*c*) D. (*d*)

45. What is the number?

I. 25% of that number is one fourth of that number

II. 3/4 of that number is less by 14 of that number.

A. (*a*) B. (*b*)

C. (*d*) D. (*e*)

46. Impedance Z is as shown in fig:

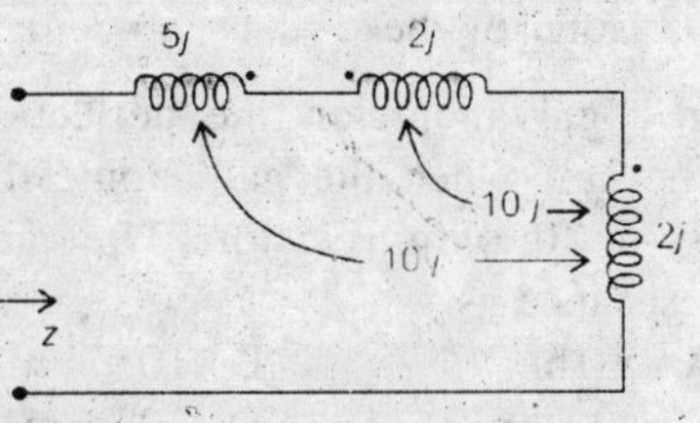

A. 29j ohm B. 9j ohm

C. 19j ohm D. 39j ohm

47. For highest power gain, what configuration is used?

A. CC B. CE

C. CB D. CS

48. An SCR has ...... PN junctions:

A. Two B. Four

C. Three D. One

49. A pole pitch in electrical machine is:

A. Equal to 180° electrical

B. Equal to 180° mechanical

C. Less than 180° electrical

D. Greater than 180° electrical

50. Which of the following compensator will increase the bandwidth of the system?
A. Phase lag
B. Phase lead
C. Lag-lead
D. None of these

51. To increase power transfer capability of a long transmission line, we should:
A. Increase line resistance
B. Increase transmission voltage
C. Decrease line reactance
D. Both B & C

52. The instantaneous voltage and current across a load is given by $v = 50 \sin (314t - \pi/6)$ volts and $i = 10 \sin (314t - \pi/2)$ amperes, respectively. The active power consumed by the load is:
A. 500 watts B. 125 watts
C. 1000 watts D. None of these

53. Drop in alternator frequency is corrected by:
A. Damper winding
B. Increased prime mover output
C. Automatic voltage regulator
D. None of these

54. In a galvanometer, the deflection becomes one half when the galvanometer is shunted by a 20 ohm resistor. The galvanometer resistance is:
A. 5 ohm B. 10 ohm
C. 40 ohm D. 20 ohm

55. In a three phase half wave rectifier feeding resistive load, if the input source is a three phase 4 wire system and line to line voltage is 100 V. The supply frequency is 400 Hz. The ripple frequency at the output is:
A. 400 Hz
B. 800 Hz
C. 1200 Hz
D. None of these

56. Ripple in output current of a step-down chopper feeding RLE load is maximum, when duty cycle is equal to:
A. 1 B. 0.5
C. 0.75 D. 0.33

57. Which of the following are constant losses in Transformers?
A. Winding losses
B. Core losses
C. Both winding & core losses
D. None of these

58. Deep bar rotor construction is used in three phase induction motors to mainly:
A. Control speed
B. Control power factor
C. Increase starting torque
D. None of these

59. Two transformers with identical voltage ratings are working in parallel to supply common load. The percentage impedance of one transformer is higher compared to that of other. The load sharing between the two transformer will:
A. Be proportional to their percentage impedance
B. Be independent of their percentage impedance
C. Be inversely proportional to their respective impedance
D. Depend on the resistance to leakage reactance ratio of each transformer

60. Number of comparators required for an 8 bit flash ADC is:
A. 8 B. 16
C. 255 D. 256

61. A 35 V dc supply is connected across a resistance of 600 ohm in series with an unknown resistance R. A voltmeter having a resistance of 1.2 kΩ is connected across 600 ohm resistances and reads 5 V. The value of resistance R shall be:
A. 1.2 kΩ B. 2.4 kΩ
C. 120 kΩ D. 400 kΩ

62. A three phase slip ring induction motor is fed from the rotor side with stator winding short circuited stator is:
A. Slip frequency
B. Supply frequency
C. Frequency corresponding to rotor speed
D. Zero

63. In the circuit given below, the value of R required for the transfer of maximum power to the load having a resistance of 3Ω will be?

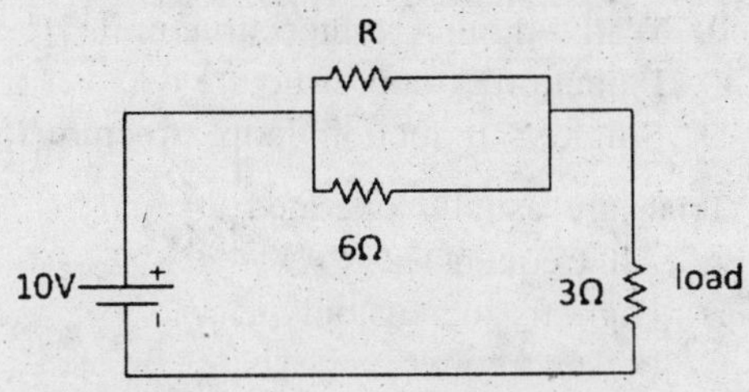

A. 3 Ω B. 10 Ω
C. 6 Ω D. 9 Ω

64. In the following given circuit what will be the value of current *i* in the 5 Ω resistor?

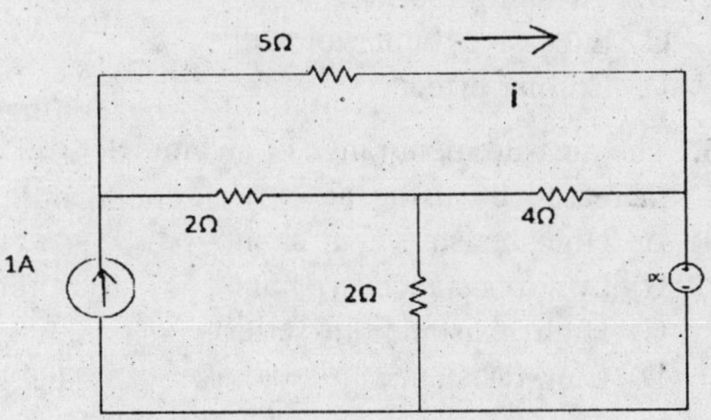

A. 5 A B. 4 A
C. 2 A D. 0 A

65. From source V_s = 200 cos ωt, a load draws current I_m = 2.5 at power factor 0.6 lagging. The load impedance is:
A. 48 + 64j B. 40 + 50j
C. 30 + 64j D. 48 + 50j

66. Two capacitor C_1 and C_2 have C_1 = 20 μF and C_2 = 30 μF, are connected in parallel across a 100V source. The net capacitance of the circuit is?
A. 50 μF B. 10 μF
C. 12 μF D. 60 μF

67. Power-factor of industrial arc and induction furnace is:
A. High lagging
B. High leading
C. Low lagging
D. Very low lagging

68. A 100 mA meter has accuracy of ± 2%. Its accuracy while reading 50 mA will be:
A. ± 1% B. ± 2%
C. ± 4% D. ± 20%

69. A series inductor is normally added in a thyrister circuit for achieving protection against:
A. High current B. High voltage
C. High *di/dt* D. High *dv/dt*

70. Clamp on ammeter is used for measurement of:
A. Large alternating currents
B. Small direct currents
C. Small alternating currents
D. Large direct currents

71. Consider the following statements:
Over head transmission lines are provided with earth wires:
1. To protect the transmission line from direct lightning strike
2. To protect the transmission line insulation from the indirect lightning strike
3. To balance the line currents
4. To provide path for neutral current

Which of these statement/s is/are correct?
A. 1 and 3 B. 1 and 4
C. 1 only D. 2 only

72. An ammeter has a current range of 0–5 A, and its internal resistance is 0.2 Ω. In order to change the range to 0–25 A, what should be the value of resistance added and how it would connect with meter (i.e. series/parallel)?
A. (0.05 Ω/series)
B. (0.05 Ω/parallel)
C. (0.20 Ω/parallel)
D. (0.20 Ω/series)

73. Power consumed by a balanced 3-phase, 3-wire load is measured by two wattmeter method. The first wattmeter reads twice that of the second. Then what will be the load impedance angle in radian?
A. (π/6) B. (π/3)
C. (π/2) D. (π/4)

74. The X/R ratio for distribution lines is:
A. Less than unity
B. More than unity
C. Equal to unity
D. None of these is necessary

75. Corona loss is minimum in:
A. Monopolar HVDC line
B. Bipolar HVDC line
C. Both in Monopolar& Bipolar HVDC lines
D. EHV AC lines

76. The potential transformers' Nominal Ratio is defined as the ratio of:
A. Primary winding voltage and secondary winding voltage
B. Rated primary winding voltage and rated secondary winding voltage
C. Primary winding turns and secondary winding turns
D. Any of the above

77. Whenever a 3-phase fault takes place at the terminals of an induction generator, the sustained fault current is:
A. Equal to the full load current
B. About 20 times the full load current
C. Much less than full load current
D. About 10 times the full load current

78. For complete protection of a 3-phase line:
A. Three-phase and three-earth fault relays are required
B. Three-phase and two-earth fault relays are required
C. Two-phase and two-earth fault relays are required
D. Two-phase and one-earth fault relays are required

79. When two transformer of different kVA rating are connected in parallel they share the load in proportion to their respective kVA rating only when their:
A. kVA rating are identical
B. Efficiencies are equal
C. Pu impedance are equal
D. Equivalent impedance are equal

80. The most efficient torque – producing actuating structure for induction – type relay is:
A. Shaded pole structure
B. Watt – hour – meter structure
C. Induction – cup structure
D. Single – induction loop structure

81. Triac are usually operated at:
A. All frequencies
B. High frequency only
C. Power frequency
D. None of these

82. Earth wire on EHV overhead transmission line is provided to protect the line against:
A. Lightning surge
B. Switching surge
C. Excessive fault voltage
D. Corona effect

83. The measurement range of an ammeter can be increased by using a:
A. High resistance in shunt
B. Low resistance in shunt
C. High resistance in series
D. Low resistance in series

84. Three equal resistors, connected in series across a source of emf, dissipated 10W of power. What would be the power dissipated in the same resistor when they are connected in parallel across the same source?
A. 10 W B. 30 W
C. 90 W D. 270 W

85. If a 3-pahse, 400 V, 50 Hz, 4 pole induction motor is running at a slip of 5% then the relative speed of rotor field with respect to stator filed is:
A. Zero B. 75 rpm
C. 142.5 rpm D. 1500 rpm

86. A 3-phase induction motor is running at slip 's'. If its two supply leads are interchanged, then the operating slip at that instant will be:
A. 2s B. (1–s)
C. (2–s) D. Zero

87. In a 3-phase voltage source inverter used for speed control of induction motor, anti-parallel diodes are used across each switching device. The main purpose of diodes is to:
A. Protect the switching devices against over voltage
B. Provide path for freewheeling current
C. Allow the motor to return energy during regeneration
D. Help in switching off the devices

88. Skewing of rotor bars eliminate the:
A. Effect of space harmonics
B. Entire effect of crawling
C. Magnetic noise
D. Vibration due to unequal force developed on rotor

89. Out of the followings, which one is correct in case of a circuit breaker?
A. Making capacity = 2.55 × braking capacity
B. Braking capacity = 2.55 × making capacity
C. Making capacity = 1.8 × braking capacity
D. Braking capacity = 1.8 × making capacity

90. The steady-state fault current during a 3-phase terminal fault on a generator is limited by:
A. Transient reactance of the generator
B. Sub-transient reactance of the generator
C. Synchronous reactance of the generator
D. DC off-set during the instant of the fault

91. A 3-phase delta connected squirrel cage induction motor when started with a DOL starter has a starting torque of 600 NM. Its starting torque when star delta starter is used:
A. 600 NM
B. 200 NM
C. 300 NM
D. 1200 NM

92. Making current of a circuit breaker refers to:
A. Steady state rated current
B. Average value of transient short circuit current
C. R.M.S. value of the short circuit current at the time of major peak
D. Equal to the fault current

93. In case of a 'High Voltage DC' transmission, how many minimum conductors are required?
A. One
B. Two
C. Three
D. Four

94. Which of the following motor has squirrel cage winding on the stator?
A. 3-phase squirrel cage induction motor
B. Single phase squirrel cage pump motor
C. Single phase ceiling fan induction motor
D. Single phase table fan induction motor

95. In order to switch-off and EHV circuit for maintenance, the following sequence is adopted:
A. Open the circuit breaker, open the isolator, operate the earth switch
B. Operate the earth switch, open the isolator, open the circuit breaker
C. Open the isolator, operate the earth switch, open the circuit breaker
D. Open the isolator, open the circuit breaker, operate the earth switch

96. For the circuit given in the fig, the Thevenis's voltage and resistance as seen at AB are represented by:

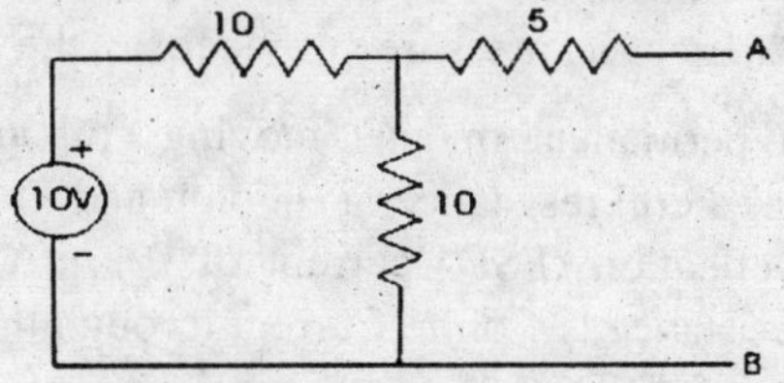

A. 5 V, 10 Ω
B. 10 V, 10 Ω
C. 5 V, 5 Ω
D. 54 V, 15 Ω

97. Why are shunt reactors connected at the receiving end of long transmission line system:
A. To increase the terminal voltage
B. To compensate voltage rise caused by capacitive charging at light load
C. To improve power factor
D. None of these

98. A 10 Ω resistor is connected in parallel with a 15 Ω resistor and the combination in series with a 12 Ω resistor. The equivalent resistance of the circuit is:
A. 37 Ω
B. 27 Ω
C. 18 Ω
D. None of these

99. A nickel coil has a resistance of 13 Ω at 50°C. If the temperature coefficient of resistance at 0°C is 0.006/ °C, the resistance at 0°C is:
A. 16.9 Ω B. 10 Ω
C. 43.3 Ω D. None of these

100. The energy used by a 1.5 kW heater in 5 minutes is:
A. 450000 J
B. 450 J
C. 7500 J
D. None of these

101. What is called the Electro Motive Force (EMF) of a voltage source?
A. Terminal voltage when load is applied
B. Internal voltage when no load is applied
C. Product of internal resistance and load current
D. Electric pressure provided to the load

102. A permanent magnet moving coil ammeter has a coil resistance of 99 ohm and Full Scale Deflection (FSD) current of 0.1 mA. Shunt resistance is 1 ohm. Current through the meter at 0.5 FSD is:
A. 0.007 mA B. 0.05 mA
C. 0.023 mA D. None of these

103. For power measurement of three phase circuit by two wattmeter method, when the value of power factor is less than 0.5 lagging:
A. One of the wattmeters will read zero
B. Both give the same readings
C. One of the wattmeter connections will have to be reversed
D. Pressure coil of the wattmeter will become ineffective

104. Find the node voltage V_A:

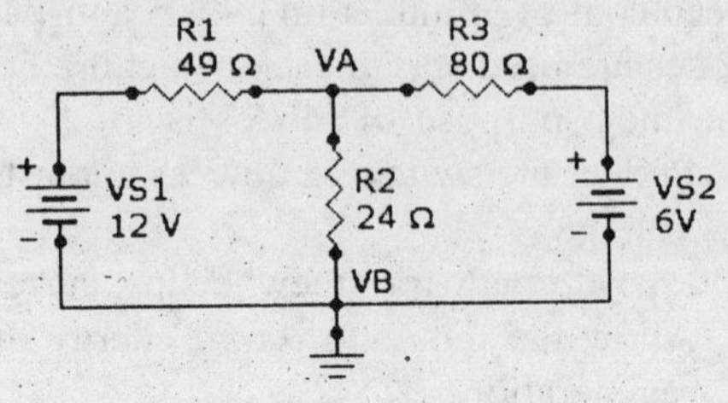

A. 6 V B. 12 V
C. 4.25 V D. None of these

105. One international ohm is equal to:
A. 1.00049 absolute ohm
B. 0.99951 absolute ohm
C. 0.969 absolute ohm
D. 1.049 absolute ohm

106. In a uniform electric field, field lines and equipotentials:
A. Are parallel to one another
B. Intersect at 45°
C. Intersect at 30°
D. Are orthogonal

107. During forward blocking state, the SCR has:
A. Low current, medium voltage
B. Low current, large voltage
C. Medium current, large voltage
D. Large current, low voltage

108. Turn on time of an SCR can be reduced by using a:
A. Rectangular pulse of high amplitude and narrow width
B. Rectangular pulse of low amplitude and wide width
C. Triangular pulse
D. Trapezoidal pulse

109. The disruptive critical voltage will:
A. Decrease with the increase of moisture content in air
B. Increase with the increase of moisture content in air
C. Increase with the decrease of moisture content in air
D. Decrease with the decrease of moisture content in air

110. What type of insulator will be used if the direction of the transmission line is to be changed?
A. Pin-type B. Suspension type
C. Strain type D. Shakle type

111. Which statement is correct:
A. SF_6 gas is toxic
B. SF_6 gas is lighter than air
C. SF_6 gas is yellow in colour
D. SF_6 gas has pungent smell

112. One coulomb of electrical charge is contributed by how many electrons?
A. 0.625×10^{19} B. 1.6×10^{19}
C. 10^{19} D. None of these

113. A dynamic system with input $x(t)$ and output $y(t)$ is represented by the following:
A. $y(t) = f(x(t), t)$
B. $y(t) = ax(t) + bx^2(t)$
C. $y(t) = ax \sin(t)$
D. None of these

114. Three equal resistors each equal to R ohm are connected as shown in fig. The equivalent resistance between points A and B is:

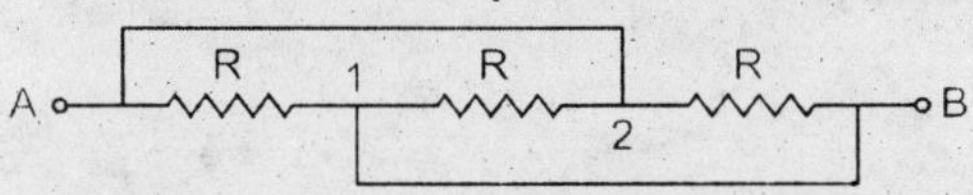

A. R B. 3R
C. R/3 D. 2R/3

115. The time constant of the circuit shown in fig. is:

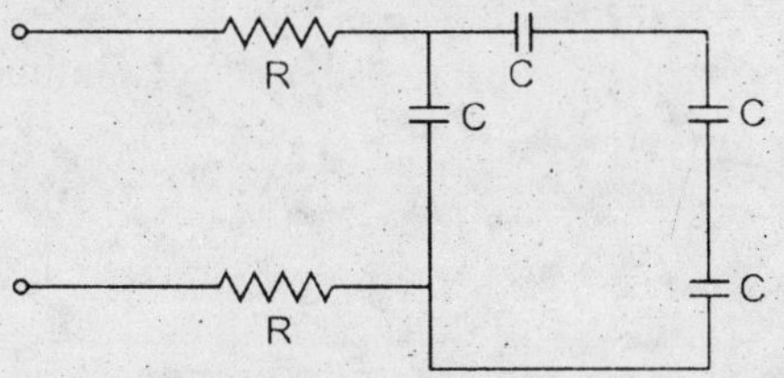

A. RC/3
B. 4RC/3
C. 2RC/3
D. 8RC/3

116. If the current in the armature of d.c series motor is reduced to 5%, the torque of the motor will become:
A. 50% of the previous value
B. 25% of the previous value
C. 150% of the previous value
D. 125% of the previous value

117. If the excitation of an alternator operating in parallel with other alternators decreased, its:
A. Power factor becomes more leading
B. Output Kw will change
C. Power factor becomes more lagging
D. Power factor becomes unity

118. The output signal of a common-collector amplifier always:
A. Larger than the input signal
B. In phase with the input signal
C. Out of phase with the input signal
D. Exactly equal to the input signal

119. A current is said to be alternating when it changes in:
A. Magnitude
B. Direction
C. Both magnitude and direction
D. None of these

120. Hysteresis loss in a transformer depends upon:
A. Frequency
B. Supply voltage
C. Square of the frequency alone
D. Square of the voltage alone

ANSWERS

1	2	3	4	5	6	7	8	9	10
D	C	B	A	A	B	A	C	B	C
11	**12**	**13**	**14**	**15**	**16**	**17**	**18**	**19**	**20**
B	D	B	D	C	B	A	B	B	D

21	22	23	24	25	26	27	28	29	30
C	D	B	C	A	B	A	C	B	A
31	32	33	34	35	36	37	38	39	40
B	D	B	B	B	C	A	C	D	B
41	42	43	44	45	46	47	48	49	50
A	A	C	C	B	B	B	C	A	A
51	52	53	54	55	56	57	58	59	60
D	B	B	B	C	B	B	C	C	C
61	62	63	64	65	66	67	68	69	70
B	A	C	D	A	A	D	C	C	A
71	72	73	74	75	76	77	78	79	80
C	B	A	B	A	B	C	D	C	C
81	82	83	84	85	86	87	88	89	90
C	A	B	C	A	C	C	A	A	C
91	92	93	94	95	96	97	98	99	100
B	C	A	C	A	A	B	C	B	A
101	102	103	104	105	106	107	108	109	110
B	B	C	C	A	D	B	A	A	B
111	112	113	114	115	116	117	118	119	120
A	A	A	C	D	B	A	B	C	A

Previous Paper (Solved)

Junior Engineer Electrical Examination–2015*

GENERAL INTELLIGENCE AND REASONING

Directions (Q. No. 1 to 8): *Find the odd word/number/letters/number pair from the given alternatives*

1. A. 96 B. 8 C. 111 D. 87

2. A. egghjj B. prrsuu C. mnnoqq D. accdff

3. A. 997 B. 778 C. 895 D. 976

4. A. RLSK B. TGUF C. NMOK D. PKQJ

5. A. Cycling B. Analogy C. Decoding D. Reasoning

6. A. XZCG B. JMNQ C. EGJN D. OQTX

7. A. Entomology B. Nephrology C. Astrology D. Pathology

8. A. look B. stare C. hug D. glance

9. Two cars started from a particular spot. The car A ran straight at the speed of 30 kmph for 2 hours north and then took a right turn. It ran 40 km and again turned right. It stopped after 30 km. The car B ran straight towards east at the speed of 20 kmph for 2 hours and turned left. It ran for 10 km and then stopped. How far were these two cars from each other when both of them stopped at last?

A. 17 km B. 20 km C. 18 km D. 19 km

Directions (Q. No. 10 to 12): *Which one of the given responses would be a meaningful order of the following?*

10. 1. Branches 2. Root 3. Trunk 4. Leaf 5. Flower

A. 4, 1, 3, 2, 5 B. 4, 3, 1, 2, 5 C. 2, 3, 1, 4, 5 D. 1, 2, 3, 4, 5

11. 1. Village 2. State 3. Nation 4. District

A. 2, 3, 1, 4 B. 1, 4, 2, 3 C. 1, 2, 4, 3 D. 4, 2, 3, 1

12. 1. Adulthood 2. Babyhood 3. Childhood 4. Infancy

A. 4, 3, 2, 1 B. 4, 2, 3, 1 C. 4, 1, 2, 3 D. 4, 3, 1, 2

13. How many triangles are there in the figure?

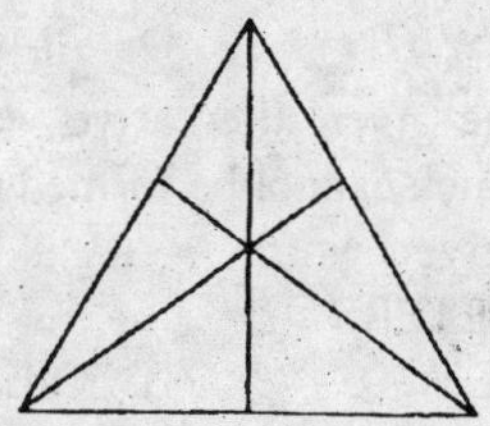

A. 10 B. 16 C. 20 D. 7

Directions (Q. No. 14 to 22): *Select the related word/letters/number from the given alternatives.*

14. BOOK : LIBRARY :: ? : FILE

A. DATA B. BYTES C. FOLDER D. COMPUTER

* *Held on 31-01-2016.*

15. CHAIR : FURNITURE :: FORK : ?

A. CROCKERY B. CUTLERY
C. FOOD D. SPOON

16. 21 : 65 :: 31 : ?

A. 85 B. 78
C. 95 D. 80

17. 25 : 36 :: ?

A. 81 : 121 B. 9 : 25
C. 25 : 49 D. 16 : 25

18. COMPASS : SHIP :: VAASTU : ?

A. FLAT B. BUILDING
C. HOME D. LAND

19. 17 : 102 :: 23 : ?

A. 138 B. 112
C. 216 D. 413

20. ABB : EGJ :: FHL : ?

A. JMT B. BDH
C. FHH D. JJL

21. q : d :: b : ?

A. p B. b
C. q D. d

22. EV : KP :: TG : ?

A. AA B. AZ
C. ZZ D. ZA

23. If in a certain code 'Education' is written as 365798214 then how 'Conduct' can be written?

A. 6547871 B. 1458776
C. 6485767 D. 7146578

24. From the given alternative words, select the word which cannot be formed using the letters of the given word.

KILOMETERS

A. MEET B. OIL
C. TREES D. STREET

25. From the given answer figures, select the one in which the question figure is hidden/ embedded.

Question figure

Answer figures

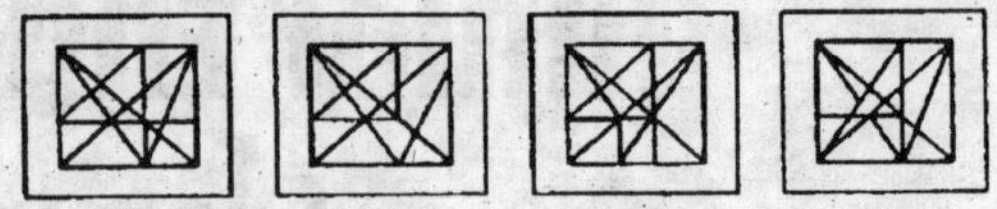

A B C D

26. If a mirror is placed on the line MN, then which of the answer figures is the right image of the given figure?

Question figure

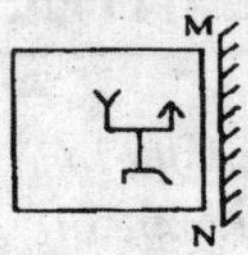

Answer figures

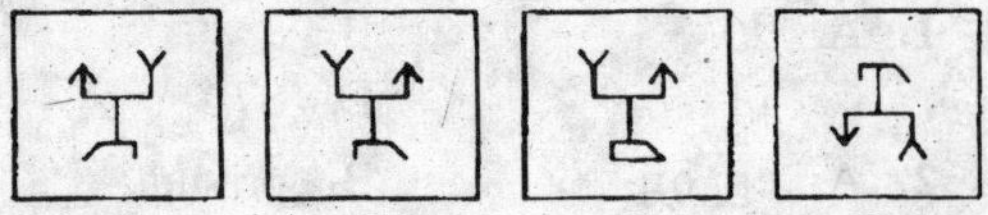

A B C D

27. In the given figure, the circle stands for intelligent, square for hard working, triangle for Postgraduate and the rectangle for loyal employees. Study the figure and answer the following questions.

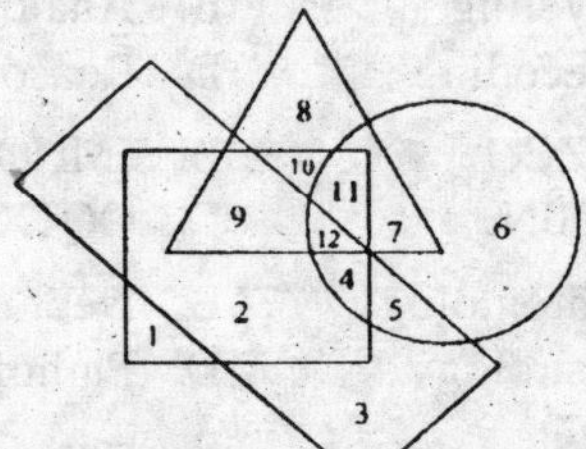

Employees who are intelligent, hard working and loyal but not Postgraduate are represented by:

A. 4 B. 11
C. 5 D. 3

Directions (Qs. Nos. 28 and 29): *Select the missing number from the given responses.*

28.

13	15	12
02	04	05
04	05	08
30	65	?

A. 69 B. 65
C. 68 D. 64

29. 20 30 12
3 4 8
80 ? 116

A. 100 B. 60
C. 140 D. 120

30. Find the number of minimum straight lines required to make figure?

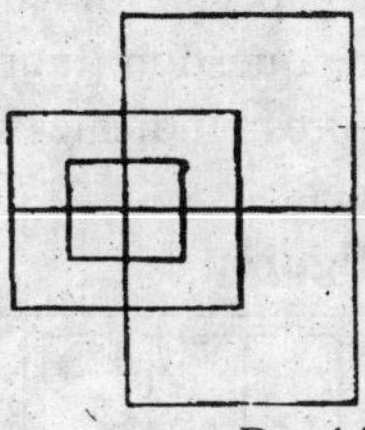

A. 19 B. 15
C. 17 D. 13

31. Ramu's mother has three sons. The eldest one is called Onekari, the second one is called Twokari. Then the third son's name is:

A. Sandu B. Ramu
C. Nokari D. Teenkari

32. If 44 + 12 = 30, 77 + 14 = 61, 84 + 16 = 66 then what should be for following:

A. 20 B. 32
C. 24 D. 28

33. Pick the odd number from the sequence below:
2, 3, 6, 7, 11, 15, 30

A. 30 B. 11
C. 7 D. 6

Directions (Q. No. 34 to 39): *In questions, a series is given, with one term missing. Choose the correct alternative from the given ones that will complete the series.*

34. CDDP DEER EFFT FGGV GHHX ?

A. HJJY B. HIIZ
C. ZIIH D. HIJZ

35. $\left(\frac{1}{8}\right), \left(\frac{1}{4}\right), \left(\frac{1}{2}\right)$, 1, ?, 4

A. $\left(\frac{3}{8}\right)$ B. 2
C. 6 D. $\left(\frac{2}{8}\right)$

36. 3, 9, 21, 45, ?

A. 78 B. 87
C. 93 D. 54

37. R I A T N I E ?

A. C B. D
C. A D. B

38. Lmnmnopnopqr?

A. opqrs B. Lmnop
C. npqrs D. pqrst

39. 11, 12, 16, 25, ?

A. 45 B. 43
C. 49 D. 41

40. Which answer figure will complete the pattern in the question figure?

Question figure

Answer figures

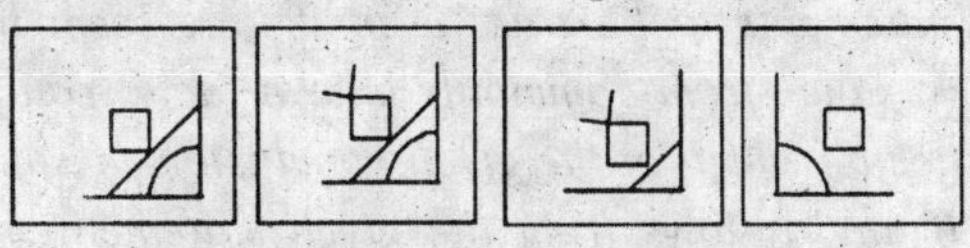

A B C D

41. Write the number of space enclosed by rectangle and circle but not by triangle.

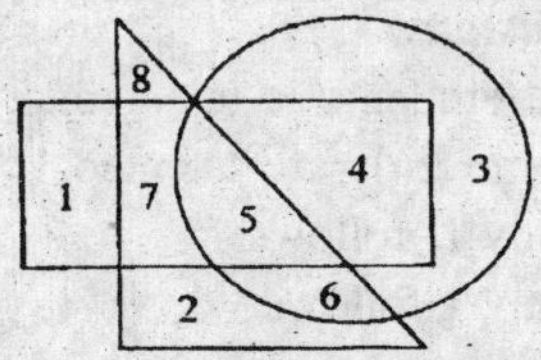

A. 4 B. 3
C. 2 D. 1

42. A word is represented by only one set of numbers as given in any one of the alternatives. The sets of numbers given in the alternatives are represented by two classes of alphabets as in two matrices given below. The columns and rows of Matrix I are numbered from 0 to 4 and that of Matrix II are numbered from 5 to 9. A letter from these matrices can be represented first by its row and next by its column, e.g., 'M' can be represented by 01, 14 etc., and 'S' can be represented by 58, 77 etc. Similarly, you have to identify the set for the word 'ROHAN'.

MATRIX-I

	0	1	2	3	4
0	H	M	X	W	K
1	N	R	N	Y	M
2	K	V	H	P	W
3	Y	Z	R	M	N
4	W	V	H	J	P

MATRIX-II

	5	6	7	8	9
5	A	D	E	S	B
6	T	U	O	G	Q
7	O	Q	S	D	A
8	S	E	U	E	D
9	Q	B	A	T	O

A. 32, 67, 41, 55, 12
B. 11, 57, 00, 55, 12
C. 11, 75, 00, 55, 10
D. 32, 75, 21, 55, 10

Directions (Q. No. 43 & 44): *In questions, one/two statements are given, followed by two conclusions/ assumptions, I and II. You have to consider the statements to be true, even if they seem to be at variance from commonly known facts. You have to decide which of the given conclusions/assumptions, if any, follows from the given statements.*

43. ***Statements:***
1. All students are girls.
2. Some students are not talented.

Conclusions:
I. No students is talented.
II. Some girls are talented.

A. Only II follows
B. Only I follows
C. Neither I nor II follows
D. Both I and II follow

44. ***Statements:***
1. Tigers donot fly.
2. Hens donot fly.

Conclusions:
I. Tigers are birds.
II. All birds can not fly.

A. Either I or II follows
B. Only II follows
C. Neither I nor II follows
D. Only I follows

45. In a certain code language, if the word 'RHOMBUS' is coded as TJQODWU, then how is the word 'RECTANGLE' in that language?

A. TGEWDPING B. TGEVCPIMG
C. TGFWEPING D. TGEVCPING

46. A piece of paper is folded and cut as shown below in the question figures. From the given answer figures, Indicate how it will appear when opened.

Question figure:

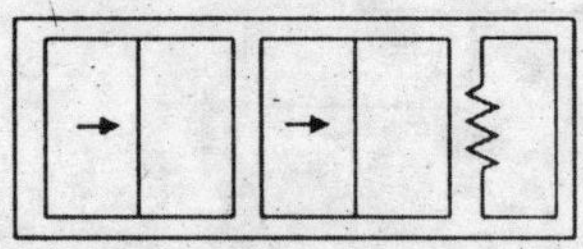

Answer figures:

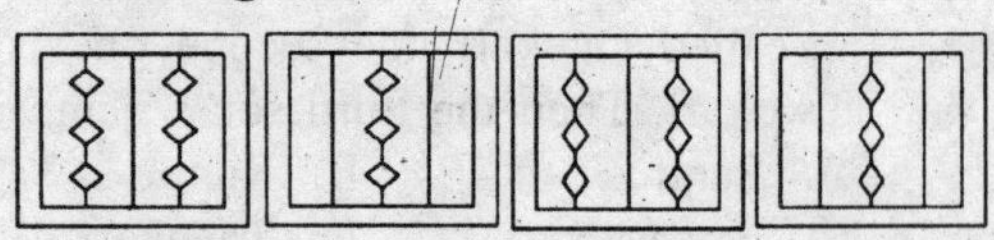

A. B. C. D.

47. If $7x = 8k$ and $5y = 6k$, then the value of ratio x is to y is:

A. 35 : 48 B. 48 : 35
C. 21 : 20 D. 20 : 21

48. Select the set of symbols which can be fitted correctly in the following equation:

8__4__2__6__3 = 32

A. +, ÷, ×, − B. −, ×, ÷, +
C. +, ×, ÷, − D. ×, −, +, ÷

49. Ashok is heavier than Gopal. Mahesh is lighter than Jayesh. Prashant is heavier than Jayesh but lighter then Gopal. Who among them is heavier?

A. Prashant B. Ashok
C. Mahesh D. Gopal

50. Hospital is 12 km towards east of Rupin's house. His school is 5 km towards south of hospital. What is the shortest distance between Rupin's house and school?

A. 17 km B. 13 km
C. 16 km D. 12 km

GENERAL AWARENESS

51. The Phenomenon of light splits up into seven distinct colours when it panes through Prism is:
A. Dispersion B. Polarisation
C. Oliffraction D. Reflection

52. Which of the following is an allied activity of agriculture?
A. Livestock
B. Money lending
C. Insurance
D. Small Scale Industry

53. The murder of Archduke Ferdinand and his wife triggered off which of the following events?
A. First World War
B. Crimean War
C. Balkan War
D. Second World War

54. Ms Florence Nightingale was associated with:
A. Seven Years War
B. Thirty Years War
C. Crimean War
D. Hundred Years War

55. When salt is added to water, the boiling point of water is?
A. Unaffected B. Increased
C. Lowered D. Constant

56. Who among the following Gupta emperor was known as 'Vikramaditya'?
A. Samudra Gupta
B. Chandra Gupta II
C. Chandra Gupta I
D. Kumara Gupta

57. Name the biggest employer in India:
A. Food Corporation of India (FCI)
B. Steel Authority of India Ltd (SAIL)
C. Indian Railways
D. Post & Telecom Department

58. The disadvantage of self-pollination is:
A. Seeds are less in number
B. No wastage of pollengrains
C. Mechanism is too simple
D. No dependence of pollinating agents

59. Second Ozone hole was detected over:
A. Northern Hemisphere
B. Antarctica
C. Arctica
D. Sweden

60. The green house gases, otherwise called radioactively active gases includes:
A. All of the given options
B. Carbon dioxide
C. CH_4
D. N_2O

61. .com represents:
A. Educational domain
B. Government domain
C. Commercial domain
D. Communication domain

62. Which one of the following is First multipurpose project constructed in India?
A. Thungabadra B. Farakka Barrage
C. Rihand D. Domodar

63. The most serious environmental effect posed by hazardous wastes is:
A. Increased use of land for landfills
B. None of the options
C. Air pollution
D. Contamination of ground water

64. The hydrogen ion concentration of a solution is measured using a:
A. Thermometer B. Hydrometer
C. pH meter D. Barometer

65. Glycolysis during fermentation results in net gain of:
A. 1 ATP B. 3 ATPs
C. 4 ATPs D. 2 ATPs

66. Thigmotropism is the response of the plant to:
A. Contact B. Light
C. Gravity D. Water

67. The Election Commission of India is:
A. Executive body
B. An independent body
C. Quasi-legislative body
D. Quasi-judicial body

68. When was the first All India Postage Stamp issued?
A. 1854 B. 1850
C. 1856 D. 1858

69. World "No Tobacco Day" was observed globally as:
A. 2 June B. 20 June
C. 15 June D. 31 May

70. Disguised Unemployment means:
A. Marginal Productivity is zero
B. Working as Self-employed
C. Not working whole day
D. Production is less

71. The storage form of glucose is:
A. Glucagea B. Insulin
C. Fructose D. Glycogen

72. Cartel is a part of:
A. Mono Polistic Competition
B. Oligopoly
C. Perfect Competition
D. Monopoly

73. Usain Bolt is famous as:
A. A boxer B. An athlete
C. An astronaut D. A cricketer

74. The Chief Election Commissioner of India is appointed by:
A. Chief Justice of India
B. Prime Minister
C. President
D. Parliament

75. Articles 23 and 24 of the Indian Constitution deal with:
A. Right to Freedom of Religion
B. Right against Exploitation
C. Right to Freedom
D. Right to Education

76. A plumb bob is hanging from the ceiling of a car. If the car moves with an acceleration 'a', the angle made by the string with the vertical is:

A. $\sin^{-1}\left(\frac{a}{g}\right)$ B. $\tan^{-1}\left(\frac{g}{a}\right)$

C. $\tan^{-1}\left(\frac{a}{g}\right)$ D. $\sin^{-1}\left(\frac{g}{a}\right)$

77. The gas dissolved in water that makes it acidic is:
A. Nitrogen B. Ammonia
C. Hydrogen D. Carbon dioxide

78. When is the World Earth Day celebrated?
A. 23 March B. 4 April
C. 1 May D. 22 April

79. Which Delhi Sultan resorted to price control and rationing?
A. Allauddin Khilji
B. Bahlol Lodi
C. Balban
D. Mohammad-bin-Tughlaq

80. Market Gardening comes in this category:
A. Horticulture
B. Monoculture
C. Sericulture
D. Subsistence Farming

81. Non-bonding valence electrons are:
A. Not involved in covalent bond formation
B. Involved in both ionic and covalent bond formation
C. Involved only in ionic bond formation
D. Involved only in covalent bond formation

82. Name the Co-operative society that provides housing loan facility at reasonable rates:
A. Housing Co-operatives
B. Consumer Co-operatives
C. Producer's Co-operatives
D. Credit Co-operatives

83. Which of the following ideologies aims at the spiritualization of politics?
A. Sarvodaya B. Socialism
C. Pluralism D. Marxism

84. Root hairs are produced from:
A. Trichoblasts B. Rhizodermis
C. Trichomes D. Epidermis

85. The Maratha ruler Shivaji ruled his kingdom with the help of a Council of Ministers called:
A. Ashtadigajas B. Mantriparishad
C. Navaratnas D. Ashtapradhan

86. A deep or trench in the ocean floor is called:
A. Trough B. Continental shelf
C. Ridges D. Crest

87. Which is the best type of cotton grown in the world?
A. Long staple B. Short staple
C. Thick staple D. Medium staple

88. Aung San Sui Kyi, a pro democracy campaigner is from which of the following countries:
A. Bangladesh B. Nepal
C. China D. Myanmar

89. Who is called the 'Father of Indian Cinema'?
A. Raj Kapoor
B. Dada Saheb Phalke
C. Mehboob Khan
D. Dilip Kumar

90. A block placed on an inclined plane of slope angle θ slides down with a constant speed. The coefficient of kinetic friction is equal to?
A. sin θ B. tan θ
C. cot θ D. cos θ

91. By increasing the intensity of incident light on the surface, the photo electric current:
A. Decreases
B. Increases initially and then decreases
C. Unchanged
D. Increases

92. IKE stands for?
A. Information Key Exchange
B. Information Key Execution
C. Internet Key Exchange
D. Infrastructure Key Encryption

93. Which of the following is the morning 'Raag' in music?
A. Sohini B. Malhaar
C. Bhairavi D. Sarang

94. Name the first Indian woman to climb Mount Everest:
A. Bachhendri Pal B. Leela Seth
C. Rita Faria D. Santosh Yadav

95. In the Presidential system of government, the President is:
A. Head of the Executive
B. Head of the state and Head of the Government
C. Head of the Government
D. Head of the state

96. Which IPL Team won the eighth edition of the Indian Premier League?
A. Kolkata Knight Rider's
B. Delhi Daredevils
C. Mumbai Indians
D. Chennai Super Kings

97. Nehru Trophy is associated with which sport in India?
A. None of the options
B. Football
C. Hockey
D. Cricket

98. What is the symbol of (WWF) World Wildlife Fund?
A. Rhododendron B. Red Panda
C. Bear D. White Tiger

99. In which country was paper currency first used?
A. Japan B. China
C. Egypt D. India

100. The finely painted cotton fabric made in Golkonda was called:
A. Muslin B. Palampore
C. Calico D. Kalamkari

GENERAL ENGINEERING (ELECTRICAL)

101. For the circuit shown below, find the resistance between points P & Q.

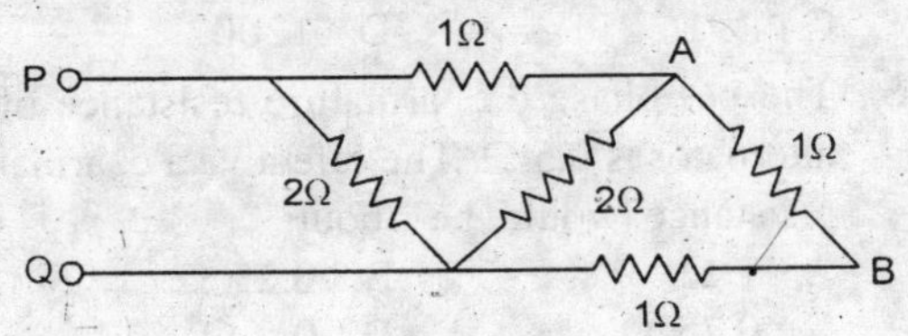

A. 4 Ω B. 1 Ω
C. 2 Ω D. 3 Ω

102. Synchronous impedance method of finding voltage regulation of an alternator is called pessimistic method because:
A. It is simplest to perform and compute
B. It gives regulation value lower than its actual found by direct loading

C. armature reaction is wholly magnetising
D. it gives regulation value higher than its actual found by direct loading

103. A 200 V lamp takes a current of 1 A, it produces a total flux of 2860 lumens. The efficiency of the lamp is:
A. 8.9 lumens/W B. 10.9 lumens/W
C. 9.9 lumens/W D. 14.3 lumens/W

104. The Ta Vs Ia graph of a dc series motor is a:
A. Parabola from no load to over load
B. Parabola up to full load and a straight line at over load
C. Straight line throughout
D. Parabola throughout

105. Which of the following motor is non-self starting?
A. Synchronous motor
B. Squirrel cage induction motor
C. DC series motor
D. Slip ring induction motor

106. Leakage flux in a transformer occurs because:
A. Air is not a good magnetic insulator
B. Applied voltage is sinusoidal
C. Transformer is not an efficient device
D. Iron core has high permeability

107. A dc voltmeter has a sensitivity of 1000 Ω/volt. When it measures half full scale in 100V range, the current through the voltmeter will be:
A. 1 mA B. 50 mA
C. 0.5 mA D. 100 mA

108. If two capacitances C_1 and C_2 are connected in parallel then the equivalent capacitance is given by:
A. $C_1 + C_2$ B. $C_1 | C_2$
C. C_1C_2 D. $\frac{C_1C_2}{C_1 + C_2}$

109. If the co-efficient of coupling between two coils is increased, mutual inductance between the coils:
A. Is decreased
B. Changes depend on current only
C. Is increased
D. Remains unchanged

110. The permissible voltage drop from supply terminal to any point on the wiring system should not exceed:
A. 4% + 1 volt B. 2% + 1 volt
C. 1% + 1 volt D. 3% + 1 volt

111. When the current through the coil of an electromagnet reverses, the:
A. Magnetic field collapses
B. Direction of the magnetic field reverses
C. Direction of the magnetic field remains unchanged
D. Magnetic field expands

112. A 10 pole 25 Hz alternator is directly coupled to and is driven by 60 Hz synchronous motor then the number of poles in a synchronous motor are:
A. None of the options
B. 48 poles
C. 24 poles
D. 12 poles

113. For the circuit shown in figure, the Norton's equivalent current source at terminals A & B is given by:

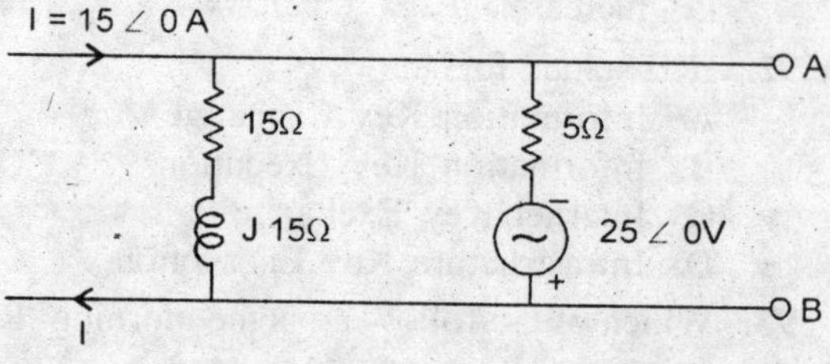

A. 14 ∠ 36.86 A B. 16 ∠ 36.86 A
C. 20 ∠ 0 A D. 10 ∠ 0 A

114. A current of 2A passes through a coil of 350 kms wound on a ring of mean diameter 12 cm. The flux density established in the ring is 1-4 wb/m^2. Find the value of relative permeability of Iron:
A. 210×10^3 B. 600
C. 191 D. 1200

115. The per phase d.c. armature resistance of an alternator is 0.5 Ω. The effective a.c. armature resistance would be about:
A. 1 Ω B. 0.25 Ω
C. 0.75 Ω D. 0.5 Ω

116. An electric heater draws 3.5 A from a 110 V source. The resistance of the heating element is approximately:

A. 38.5 Ω B. 385 Ω
C. 31 Ω D. 3.1 Ω

117. For cleat wiring and 250 volts supply, the cables will be placed .... a part centre to centre for single core cables:

A. 2.5 cm B. 4 cm
C. 3 cm D. 4.5 cm

118. If the power factor is high, then the consumer maximum KVA demand:

A. Becomes zero B. Remains constant
C. Increases D. Decreases

119. The current 'I' in the electric circuit shown below is:

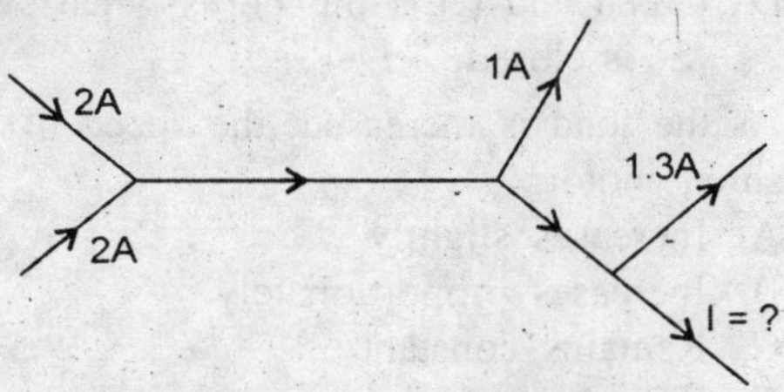

A. 3.7 A B. 1 A
C. 1.7 A D. 2.7 A

120. For painful shock, what is the range of electric shock current at 50 Hz?

A. 0 - 1 mA B. 0 - 3 mA
C. 5 - 10 mA D. 3 - 5 mA

121. In a Parallel RLC circuit if the lower cut-off frequency is 2400 Hz and the upper cut off frequency is 2800 Hz. What is the band width?

A. 5200 Hz B. 2400 Hz
C. 400 Hz D. 2800 Hz

122. The minimum area of cross section of a three and half core cable should be:

A. 40 cm^2 B. 30 cm^2
C. 50 cm^2 D. 60 cm^2

123. An RLC series circuit has R = 10 Ω, L = 2H. What value of capacitance will make the circuit critically damped?

A. 0.08 F B. 0.2 F
C. 0.02 F D. 0.4 F

124. The Superposition theorem is used when the circuit contains:

A. Passive elements only
B. A single voltage source
C. Active elements only
D. A number of voltage sources

125. Each of the following statements regarding a shaded pole motor is true except:

A. Its direction of rotation is from unshaded to shaded portion of poles.
B. It has high starting torque.
C. It has very poor power factor.
D. It has very poor efficiency.

126. An amplifier has a gain of 10,000 expressed in decibels the gain is:

A. 80 B. 40
C. 10 D. 100

127. In Bipolar Junction transistors, the type of configuration which will give both voltage gain and current gain is:

A. CB B. CE
C. CC D. None of the options

128. The magnitude of AT required to establish a given value of flux in the air gap will be much greater than that required for Iron part of a magnetic circuit, because:

A. Air is a good conductor of magnetic flux
B. Air has the lowest relative permeability
C. Iron has the lowest permeability
D. Air is a gas

129. Three wattmeter method of power measurement can be used to measure power in:

A. None of the options
B. Unbalanced Circuits
C. Both balanced and unbalanced Circuits
D. Balanced Circuits

130. A 150 V moving iron voltmeter of accuracy class 1.0 reads 75 V when used in a circuit under standard conditions. The maximum possible percentage error in the reading is:

A. 4.0 B. 0.5
C. 2.0 D. 1.0

131. The no load input power to a transformer is practically equal to .... loss in the transformer:

A. Copper B. Eddy current
C. Windage D. Iron

132. The primary and secondary windings of a transformer are wound on the top of each other in order to reduce .... ?

A. Copper losses
B. Iron losses
C. Reakage reactance
D. Winding resistance

133. The e.m.f. induced in a coil of N turns is given by:

A. $N\frac{d\phi}{dt}$ B. $\frac{d\phi}{dt}$

C. $N\frac{dt}{d\phi}$ D. $-N\frac{d\phi}{dt}$

134. If span length is doubled with no change in other factors, the sag of the line will become:

A. 8 times B. 2 times
C. 0.5 times D. 4 times

135. The internal resistance of a voltage source is 10 Ω and has 10 volts at its terminals. Find the max. power that can be transferred to the load:

A. 2.5 W B. 0.25 W
C. 25 W D. 5 W

136. When a series RL circuit is connected to a voltage source V at $t = 0$, the current passing through the inductor L at $t = 0^+$ is:

A. $\frac{V}{R}$ B. Zero

C. Infinite D. $\frac{V}{L}$

137. Two lamps, Green (G) and Red (R) are connected in a motor circuit as shown in the fig. The conditions under which the lamps will burn are? (Supply is available at terminals A & B)

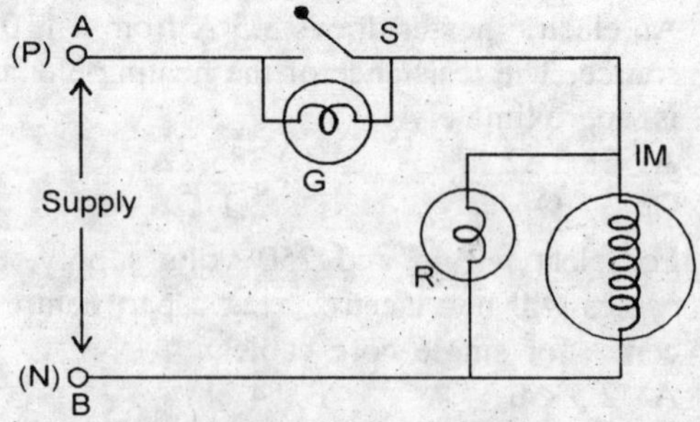

A. Green lamp will not burn always, red lamp burns only when switch 'S' is closed.
B. Green lamp burns only when 'S' is open and red lamp burns only when 'S' is closed.
C. Green lamp burns always, red lamp burns only when switch 'S' is closed.
D. Green and red lamp burns when switch 'S' is closed.

138. As the load is increased, the speed of a dc shunt motor:

A. Increases slightly
B. Increases proportionately
C. Remains constant
D. Reduces slightly

139. A resistor is connected across a 50 V source. The current in the resistor if the colour code is red, orange, orange, silver, is:

A. 2 mA B. 214 mA
C. 2.2 mA D. 21.4 mA

140. One sine wave has a period of 2 ms, another has a period of 5 ms and other has a period of 10 ms. Which sine wave is changing at a faster rate?

A. Sine wave with period 2 ms
B. All are at the same rate
C. Sine wave with period of 10 msec
D. Sine wave with period 5 ms

141. Locked rotor current of a shaded pole motor is:

A. Slightly more than full load current
B. Less than full load current
C. Equal to full load current
D. Several times the full load current

142. To prepare a P type semiconducting material the impurities to be added to silicon are:

A. Gallium, Arsenic
B. Arsenic, Antimony
C. Gallium, Phosphorous
D. Boron, Gallium

143. With the positive probe on an NPN base, an ohmmeter reading between the other transistor terminals should be:
A. High resistance B. Open
C. Low resistance D. Infinite

144. If 750 μA is flowing through 11 kΩ of resistance, what is the voltage drop across the resistor?
A. 82.5 V B. 14.6 V
C. 8.25 V D. 146 V

145. The unit for permeability is:
A. $\frac{At}{Wb}$ B. $\frac{Wb}{At \times m}$
C. Wb D. $\frac{At}{m}$

146. Base load of a power station stands for:
A. 12 - 24 hours/day
B. 8 - 12 hours/day
C. 4 - 8 hours/day
D. 2 - 4 hours/day

147. In a three phase system, the volt ampere rating is given by:
A. $V_{ph} I_{ph}$ B. $3 V_L I_L$
C. $V_L I_L$ D. $\sqrt{3} V_L I_L$

148. What is the maximum number of point of light, fan and socket-outlets that can be connected in one sub-circuit?
A. Twelve B. Ten
C. Four D. Six

149. What is the power consumed by the resistor of 20 Ω connected across 100 V source?
A. 50 W B. 100 W
C. 500 W D. 300 W

150. The no load primary current I_0 is about .... of full load primary current of a transformer.
A. 3 - 5% B. 30 - 40%
C. Above 40% D. 15 - 30%

151. An alternator is supplying a load of 300 kw at a power factor of 0.6 lagging. If the power factor is raised to unity, how many more kw can alternator supply?
A. 150 kw B. 200 kw
C. 300 kw D. 100 kw

152. If static voltage of a squirrel cage induction motor is reduced to 50 percent of its rated value, torque developed is reduced by how many percentage of its full load value?
A. 57.7% B. 25%
C. 75% D. 50%

153. The reactive power generated by a synchronous alternator can be controlled by:
A. Changing the alternator speed
B. Changing the field excitation
C. Changing the terminal voltage
D. Changing the prime move input

154. A circuit breaker is rated as follows: 1500 A, 33 KV, 3 sec, 3-phase oil circuit breaker. Determine the making current:
A. 35 KA B. 89 KA
C. 110 KA D. 1.5 KA

155. If the number of turns of a coil is increased, its inductance:
A. Remains the same
B. Is increased
C. Is decreased
D. None of the options

156. The area of the hysteresis loop will be least for one of the following materials. It is:
A. Hard steel B. Wrought iron
C. Silicon steel D. Soft iron

157. A bar of Iron 1 cm^2 in cross section has 10^{-4} wb of Magnetic flux in it. If μr = 2000. What is the Magnetic field intensity in the bar?
A. $398 \times 10^{-4} \frac{AT}{m}$ B. $398 \frac{AT}{m}$
C. $796 \times 10^{3} \frac{AT}{m}$ D. $398 \times 10^{4} \frac{AT}{m}$

158. Mutual inductance between two coils is 4 H. If current in one coil changes at the rate of 2A/sec, then emf induced in the other coil is:
A. 0.5 V B. 8 V
C. 2 V D. 5.0 V

159. The aluminium conductor of size .... is used for a subcircuit in domestic wiring:

A. $\frac{1}{1.8}$ mm B. $\frac{1}{1.2}$ mm

C. $\frac{1}{1.4}$ mm D. $\frac{1}{2.24}$ mm

160. A CRO Screen has ten divisions on the horizontal scale. If a voltage signal 5 sin(314t + 45°) is examined with a line base setting of 5 msec/div, the number of cycle of signal displayed on the screen will be?

A. 5 cycles B. 2.5 cycle
C. 10 cycles D. 0.5 cycle

161. A salient-pole synchronous motor is operating at $\frac{1}{4}$ full load. If its field current is suddenly switched off, it would?

A. Run at sub-synchronous speed
B. Stop running
C. Continue to run at synchronous speed
D. Run at super-synchronous speed

162. The electric driver posses the following drawback:

A. Not available with various rating
B. Requires at continuous power supply
C. Not adoptable to various environments
D. Requires hazardous fuel requirement

163. Find the node voltage V_A:

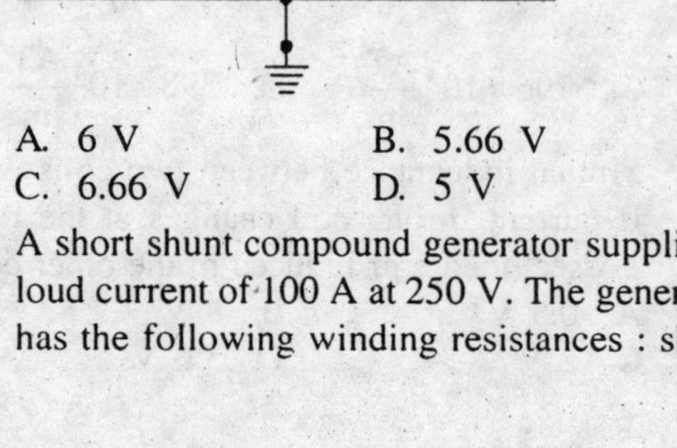

A. 6 V B. 5.66 V
C. 6.66 V D. 5 V

164. A short shunt compound generator supplies a loud current of 100 A at 250 V. The generator has the following winding resistances : shunt field = 130Ω, Armature = 0.1Ω and series field = 0.1Ω. Find the Emf generated if the brush drop is IV per brush:

A. 272.0 volt B. 262.2 volt
C. 272.2 volt D. 262.0 volt

165. The errors in Current Transformers can be reduced by designing them with:

A. High permeability and low loss core materials, avoiding any joints in the core and also keeping the flux density to a low value.
B. All of the given options
C. Using primary and secondary winding as close to each other as possible.
D. Using large cross section for both primary and secondary winding conductors.

166. When a source is delivering maximum power to the load, the efficiency will be?

A. 50% B. Above 50%
C. Below 50% D. Maximum

167. A lissajous pattern on an oscilloscope has 5 horizontal tangencies and 2 vertical tangencies. The frequency of the horizontal input is 100 Hz. The frequency of the vertical input will be:

A. 2500 Hz B. 400 Hz
C. 5000 Hz D. 4000 Hz

168. If a dynamometer type wattmeter is connected in an ac circuit, the power indicated by the wattmeter will be:

A. Peak power
B. Average power
C. Instantaneous power
D. Volt ampere product

169. An eight pole wound rotor induction motor operating on 60 Hz supply is driven at 1800 rpm by a prime mover in the opposite direction of revolving magnetic field. The frequency of rotor current is:

A. 200 Hz B. 120 Hz
C. 60 Hz D. 180 Hz

170. The acceptable value of grounding resistance for domestic applications is:

A. 2 Ω B. 0.5 Ω
C. 1.5 Ω D. 1 Ω

171. How much energy is stored by a 100 mH inductance when a current of 1A is flowing through it?
A. 0.05 J B. 0.5 J
C. 0.005 J D. 5.0 J

172. Which instrument is used to measure the high resistance?
A. Carey-Foster bridge
B. Megger
C. Kelvin's Double bridge
D. Wheatstone bridge

173. Humans are more vulnerable to electric shock current at:
A. 45 Hz B. 50 Hz
C. 40 Hz D. 48 Hz

174. Which of the following motors is used in mixies?
A. Universal motors
B. Hysteresis motor
C. Repulsion motor
D. Reluctance motor

175. A linear circuit is one whose parameters:
A. Change with change in current
B. Change with change in voltage
C. None of the options
D. Do not change with voltage and current

176. The voltage across the $1k\Omega$ resistor of the network shown in the given figure is:

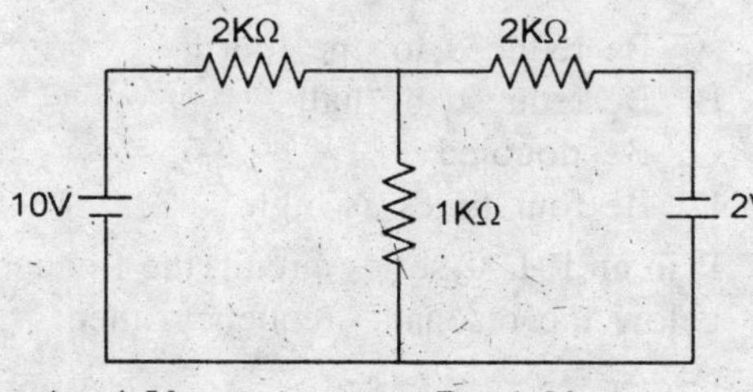

A. 4 V B. 1 V
C. 2 V D. 6 V

177. Which of the following fault is coming under symmetrical fault?
A. LLG fault B. LLLG fault
C. LL fault D. LG fault

178. To operate properly a transistor's base-emitter junction must be forward biased with reverse bias applied to which junction?
A. Collector-base B. Collector-emitter
C. Base-collector D. Base-emitter

179. During the resistance welding, the heat produced at the joint is proportional to:
A. Volt-ampere B. I^2R
C. Voltage D. Current

180. A Primary cell has an emf of 1.5 V. When short circuited, it gives a current of 3A. The internal resistance of cell is:
A. 4.5 Ω B. 0.2 Ω
C. 0.5 Ω D. 2 Ω

181. The purpose of starting winding in a single-phase induction motor is to:
A. Reduce losses
B. Limit temperature rise of the machine
C. Produce rotating flux in conjunction with main winding
D. Increase losses

182. In the Maxwell bridge as shown in the figure below the values of resistance Rx and inductance Lx of a coil are to be calculated after balancing the bridge. The component values are shown in the fig. at balance. The values of Rx and Lx will respectively be:

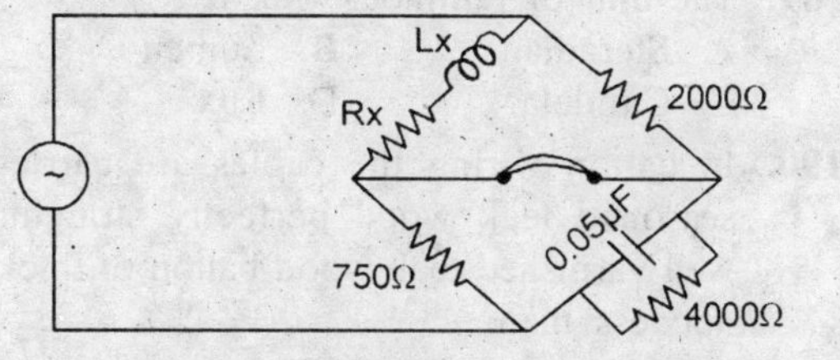

A. 75 ohm, 150 mH
B. 375 ohm, 75 mH
C. 75 ohm, 75 mH
D. 37.5 ohm, 75 mH

183. The motor used on small lathes is usually:
A. 3-phase synchronous motor.
B. Universal motor.
C. Single phase capacitor run motor.
D. D.C. shunt motor

184. An arc blow is a welding defect that is countered with the help of carrying:
A. The arc welding using DC supply.
B. The resistance welding.
C. The arc welding using AC supply.
D. The thermit welding.

185. Thevenin's theorem cannot be applied to:
A. Active circuit B. Passive circuit
C. Nonlinear circuit D. Linear circuit

186. Modern electronic multimeters measure resistance by:
A. Using an electronic bridge compensator for melting
B. Using a bridge circuit
C. Forcing a constant current and measuring the voltage across the unknown resistance
D. Using a electrical bridge circuit

187. Silicon has a preference in IC technology because:
A. It is an indirect semiconductor
B. It is a covalent semiconductor
C. Of the availability of nature oxide SiO
D. It is an elemental semiconductor

188. Creeping in a single phase induction type energy meter may be due to:
A. All of the given options
B. Over compensation for friction
C. Over voltage
D. Vibrations

189. The unit of luminous flux is:
A. Steradian B. Lumen
C. Candela D. Lux

190. In batton wiring the cables are carried on seasoned teak wood perfectly straight and well varnished teak wood batton of thickness not less than:
A. 4 cm B. 3 cm
C. 1 cm D. 2 cm

191. In dc operation of flourescent tube, the life of the tube:
A. Remain same
B. May increase or decrease
C. Increases by about 80% as that with ac operation.
D. Decreases by about 80% as that with ac operation.

192. A node in a circuit is defined as a:
A. Junction of two or more elements.
B. Group of interconnected elements.
C. Closed path.
D. Open terminal of an element.

193. There are 3 lamps 40 W, 100 W and 60 W. To realise the full rated power of the lamps they are to be connected in:
A. Parallel only B. Series-parallel
C. Series or parallel D. Series only

194. Which of the following motors is preferred for tape-recorders?
A. Two valve capacitor motor
B. Hysteresis motor
C. Universal motor
D. Shaded pole motor

195. The rate of change of current in a 4 H inductor is 2 Amps/sec. Find the voltage across inductor:
A. 16 V B. 8 V
C. 2 V D. 0.8 V

196. An active element in a circuit is one which:
A. Both receives and supplies energy
B. Dissipates energy
C. Receives energy
D. Supplies energy

197. Electrical Resistivity ρ is:
A. Low for copper as well as for alloy
B. Low for copper and high for alloy
C. High for copper as well as for alloy
D. High for copper and low for alloy

198. In a pure inductive circuit if the supply frequency is reduced to $\frac{1}{2}$, the current will:
A. Be reduced to one fourth
B. Be reduced by half
C. Be doubled
D. Be four times as high

199. If in an R-L-C series circuit, the frequency is below the resonant frequency, then:
A. $X_C = X_L$
B. $X_C < X_L$
C. None of the options
D. $X_C > X_L$

200. Which of the following braking is not suitable for motors?
A. Plugging
B. Friction braking
C. Dynamic braking
D. Regenerative braking

ANSWERS

1	2	3	4	5	6	7	8	9	10
B	C	A	C	A	B	C	C	B	C
11	**12**	**13**	**14**	**15**	**16**	**17**	**18**	**19**	**20**
B	B	B	A	B	C	D	B	A	A
21	**22**	**23**	**24**	**25**	**26**	**27**	**28**	**29**	**30**
A	D	D	D	A	A	A	C	C	D
31	**32**	**33**	**34**	**35**	**36**	**37**	**38**	**39**	**40**
B	A	B	B	B	C	D	A	D	B
41	**42**	**43**	**44**	**45**	**46**	**47**	**48**	**49**	**50**
A	C	A	B	D	A	D	D	B	B
51	**52**	**53**	**54**	**55**	**56**	**57**	**58**	**59**	**60**
A	A	A	C	B	B	C	A	A	A
61	**62**	**63**	**64**	**65**	**66**	**67**	**68**	**69**	**70**
C	D	D	C	D	A	B	A	D	A
71	**72**	**73**	**74**	**75**	**76**	**77**	**78**	**79**	**80**
D	B	B	C	B	C	D	D	A	A
81	**82**	**83**	**84**	**85**	**86**	**87**	**88**	**89**	**90**
A	A	A	A	D	A	A	D	B	B
91	**92**	**93**	**94**	**95**	**96**	**97**	**98**	**99**	**100**
D	C	C	A	B	C	C	B	B	D
101	**102**	**103**	**104**	**105**	**106**	**107**	**108**	**109**	**110**
B	D	D	B	A	A	B	A	C	B
111	**112**	**113**	**114**	**115**	**116**	**117**	**118**	**119**	**120**
B	C	D	B	C	C	A	D	C	C
121	**122**	**123**	**124**	**125**	**126**	**127**	**128**	**129**	**130**
C	C	A	D	B	A	B	B	C	C
131	**132**	**133**	**134**	**135**	**136**	**137**	**138**	**139**	**140**
D	C	D	D	A	B	B	D	C	A
141	**142**	**143**	**144**	**145**	**146**	**147**	**148**	**149**	**150**
A	D	C	C	B	A	D	B	C	A
151	**152**	**153**	**154**	**155**	**156**	**157**	**158**	**159**	**160**
B	B	B	B	B	C	B	B	C	B
161	**162**	**163**	**164**	**165**	**166**	**167**	**168**	**169**	**170**
C	B	A	C	A	A	A	B	D	D
171	**172**	**173**	**174**	**175**	**176**	**177**	**178**	**179**	**180**
A	B	B	A	D	C	B	A	B	C
181	**182**	**183**	**184**	**185**	**186**	**187**	**188**	**189**	**190**
C	B	C	A	C	C	C	A	B	C
191	**192**	**193**	**194**	**195**	**196**	**197**	**198**	**199**	**200**
D	A	A	B	B	D	B	C	D	B

EXPLANATORY ANSWERS

13.

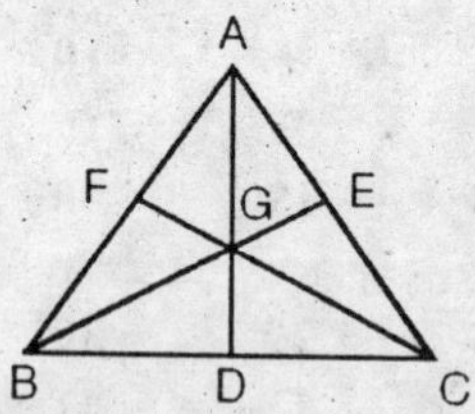

Number of triangles in the given figures are 16 *i.e.,*

ΔAGF, ΔBGF, ΔBDG, ΔCDG, ΔCEG, ΔAEG, ΔABD, ΔACD, ΔBCE, ΔABE, ΔAFC, ΔBCF, ΔABG, ΔBCG, ΔACG and ΔABC.

27. There are two numbers 4 and 5 enclosed by rectangle and circle. But 5 is enclosed by all the three figures circle, triangle and rectangle. So, required number is 4.

28.

13	15	12
02	04	05
04	05	08
13 × 2 + 04 = 30	15 × 4 + 05 = 65	12 × 5 + 08 = 68

29.

20	30	12
3	4	8
80	140	116
(= 20 × 3 + 20)	(= 30 × 4 + 20)	(= 12 × 8 + 20)

30. Number of straight lines required are 13. *i.e.,* Number of straight lines required to draw two squares are 8 and 4 straight lines are required to draw rectangles. There is one more line required to bisect all the three figures.

31. Ramu's mother has three sons. They are Onekari, Twokari and Ramu.

32. $44 + 12 \Rightarrow 44 - 12 - 2 = 30$

$77 + 14 \Rightarrow 77 - 14 - 2 = 61$

$84 + 16 \Rightarrow 84 - 16 - 2 = 66$

$44 + 22 \Rightarrow 44 - 22 - 2 = 20.$

34.

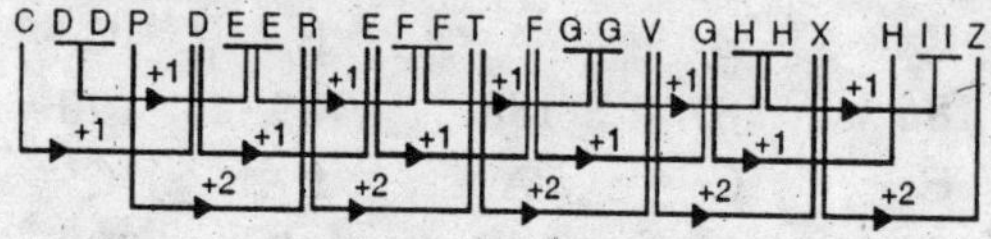

35.

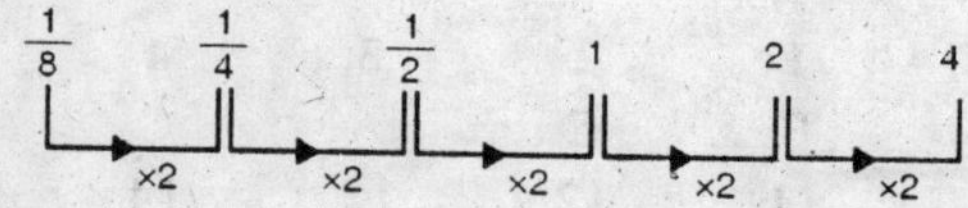

36.

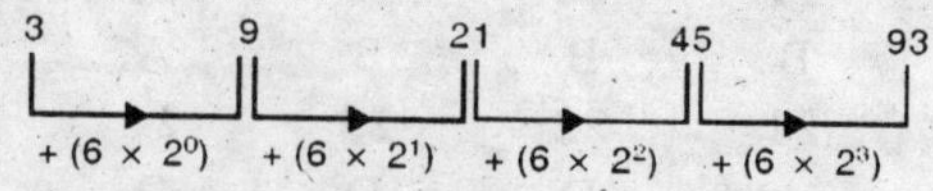

39.

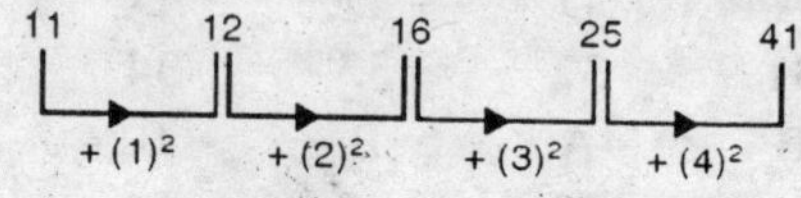

42. R → (11), 32

O → (75), 67, 99

H → (00), 22, 42

A → (55), 79, 97

N → (10), 12, 34

43.

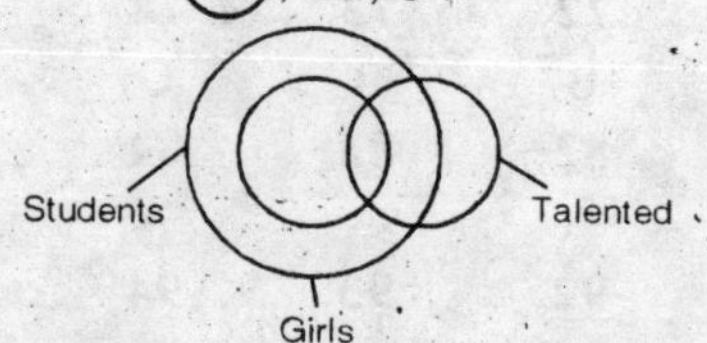

All students are girls and some students are talented so, some girls are also talented.

44. Hens, are birds that can't fly. So, all birds can't fly is a right conclusion.

45.

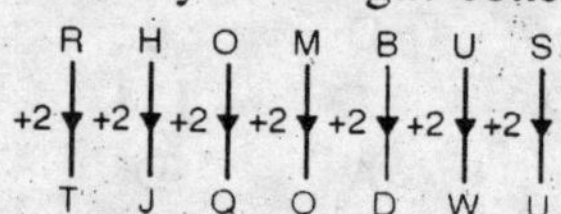

Similarly,

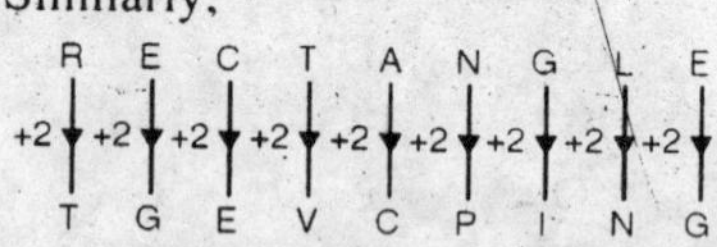

47.

$$7x = 8k \Rightarrow x = \frac{8k}{7}$$

$$5y = 6k \Rightarrow y = \frac{6k}{5}$$

$$\frac{x}{y} = \frac{\frac{8k}{7}}{\frac{6k}{5}} = \frac{20}{21}$$

$$\therefore \quad x : y = 20 : 21.$$

Previous Paper (Solved)

JUNIOR ENGINEER ELECTRICAL EXAMINATION—2014*

1. Ward-Leonard controlled DC drives are generally used for:
   A. Light duty excavators
   B. Medium duty excavators
   C. Heavy duty excavators
   D. Low duty excavators

2. Bohr Magneton is unit of:
   A. Magnetic energy
   B. Permanent dipole moment due to spin
   C. Polarisability
   D. Hysteresis

3. What is the required connection for an enhancement type N-MOSFET to function as a resistor?
   A. Gate connected to sources
   B. Gate connected to drain
   C. Drain connected to sources
   D. Source open-circuited

4. What is the Output voltage of Op-amp for input voltage of V_{i1} = 150 μV, V_{i2} = 140 μV if the amplifier has differential gain of A_d = 4000 and value of CMRR is 100.
   A. 45.8 mV B. 40.006 mV
   C. 10 μV D. 145 μV

5. What happens when the shunt resistance of a galvanometer circuit is increased?
   A. Its current sensitivity increases
   B. Its current sensitivity decreases
   C. It's damping increases
   D. It's controlling torque increases

6. A DC shunt generator supplies 450 A at 230 V. The resistances of shunt field and armature are 50 Ω and 0.025 Ω respectively. What will be the armature voltage drop?
   A. 11.24 V B. 22.7 V
   C. 31.6 V D. 38.4 V

7. A single phase 60 Hz generator supplies an inductive load of 4500 kW at a power factor of 0.80 lagging by means of a 20 km long overhead transmission line. The line resistance and inductance are 0.0195 ohm and 0.60 mH per km. The voltage at the receiving end is required to be kept constant at 10.2 kV. Find the voltage regulation of the line.
   A. 12.59% B. 16.34%
   C. 32.68% D. 41.15%

8. What is the energy stored in the magnetic field at a solenoid of 40 cm long and 4 cm diameter wound with 100 turns of wire carrying a current at 20A?
   A. 0.705 Joule B. 0.789 Joule
   C. 0.587 Joule D. 0.658 Joule

9. What does the maximum Surge current rating of an SCR specify?
   A. Repetitive current with sine wave.
   B. Non-repetitive current with rectangular wave.
   C. Non-repetitive current with sine wave.
   D. Repetitive current with rectangular wave.

10. If α = 0.995, I_E = 10 mA and I_{CO} = 0.5 mA, then I_{CEO} will be
    A. 100 μA B. 25 μA
    C. 10.1 μA D. 10.5 μA

11. An electromechanical closed loop control system has the transfer function

    $C(s)/R(s) = k/s\,(s^2 + s + 1)\,(s + 4) + k$. Which one of the following is correct?
    A. The system is stable for all positive values of k
    B. The system is unstable for all values of k

C. The system is stable for values of k between zero and 3.36
D. The system is stable for values of k between 1.6 and 2.45

12. A large transformer operating at no load draws an exciting current I_o of 5A, when the primary is connected to a 120 V, 60 Hz source. From a wattmeter test, it is known that iron losses are equal to 180 W. Calculate the reactive power absorbed by the core.
A. 600 var B. 572 var
C. 180 var D. 360 var

13. A 60 Hz, 4 pole turbo generator rated 100 MVA, 13.8 KV has an inertia constant of 10 MJ/MVA. Find the stored energy in the rotor at synchronous speed.
A. 10 MJ B. 100 J
C. 1000 J D. 1000 MJ

14. Error detector is also called as
A. Multiplexer B. Decoder
C. Comparator D. Integrator

15. For measuring the frequency of an unknown A.C. source. Which of the following device is necessary to obtain a standard waveform?
A. Operational amplifier
B. Astable multivibrator
C. Schmitt trigger
D. Monostable multivibrator

16. The reciprocal of resistance is called
A. Impedance B. Conductance
C. Inductance D. Susceptance

17. A 150 kW electric motor has an efficiency of 92%, when it operates at full load. Calculate the losses in the machine.
A. 92 kW B. 150 kW
C. 163 kW D. 13 kW

18. What does the discharge transistor do in the 555 timer circuit?
A. Discharge the external capacitor to stop the timing
B. Charge the external capacitor to stop the timing
C. Discharge the external capacitor to start the timing over again
D. Charge the external capacitor to start the timing over again

19. The differential coupling of two coils in series connection has self-inductance of 2 mH & 4 mH and a mutual inductance of 0.15 mH. The equivalent inductance of the combination is:
A. 5.7 mH B. 5.85 mH
C. 6 mH D. 6.15 mH

20. Two's complement of – 8 is
A. 1000 B. 1010
C. 110 D. 1110

21. Which among the following is the equation for the number of independent loops for a network with n nodes and β branches?
A. $n - 1$ B. $b + n - 1$
C. $b - n + 1$ D. $b - n$

22. A Lissajous pattern on an oscilloscope has 5 horizontal tangencies and 2 vertical tangencies. The frequency of the horizontal input is 1000 Hz. What is the frequency of the vertical input?
A. 400 Hz B. 5000 Hz
C. 4000 Hz D. 2500 Hz

23. For a transient stability analysis, as long as equal area criterion is satisfied, the maximum angle to which rotor angle can oscillate is:
A. 0° to 20°
B. 45° to 50°
C. Greater than 90°
D. 65° to 85°

24. What is the equivalent resistance of one limb A when delta connection is transformed into star?
A. $R_1R_3/R_1 + R_2 + R_3$
B. $R_2R_3/R_1 + R_2 + R_3$
C. $R_1R_2R_3/R_1 + R_2 + R_3$
D. $R_1 + R_2 + R_3$

25. Calculate the power loss, if power generated by two plants are P_1 = 50 MW and P_2 = 40 MW and the loss coefficients are B_{11} = 0.001, B_{22} = 0.0025 and B_{12} = –0.0005.
A. 4.5 MW B. 5.5 MW
C. 6.5 MW D. 8.5 MW

26. Q factor is defined as the ratio of
A. Resistance/inductance of reactive element
B. Resistance/capacitance of reactive element
C. Resistance to reactance of reactive element
D. Resistance to susceptance of reactive element

27. A 0.5 Hp, 6 pole wound-rotor induction motor is excited by a 3 phase 60 Hz source. Calculate the frequency of the rotor current at standstill.
A. 50 Hz B. 30 Hz
C. 60 Hz D. 120 Hz

28. A 30 MVA, 15 KV, 1500 rpm, 3 phase synchronous generator connected to a power grid has a synchronous reactance of 9 ohm per phase. If the exciting voltage is 12 kV (line to neutral) and the system voltage is 17.3 kV (line to line), Calculate the maximum power that generator can deliver before it falls out of step (losses synchronous).
A. 39.952 MW B. 78.349 MW
C. 16.67 MW D. 112.89 MW

29. Byte is string of how many bits?
A. Eight B. Four
C. Two D. Sixteen

30. What is the nature of supply current in parallel RC circuit with reference to the voltage?
A. In phase
B. Lags by 90 degree
C. Leads by 90 degree
D. Compensates and becomes zero

31. Calculate the approximate locked rotor current of a 3 phase induction motor having a rating of 500 Hp, 2300 V.
A. 130 A B. 39 A
C. 390 A D. 780 A

32. A Power system has a total load of 1260 MW at 50 Hz. The load varies 1.5% for every 1% change in frequency. Find the steady state frequency deviation, when a 60 MW load is suddenly dripped if there is no speed control.
A. 1.667 Hz B. 50 Hz
C. No change D. 3.32 Hz

33. For a two port symmetric bilateral network, if A = 3Ω and B = 1Ω, the value of parameter C will be
A. 4s B. 6s
C. 8s D. 16s

34. In order to recover the original signal from the Sampled one, what is the condition to be satisfied for sampling frequency ω_s and highest frequency component ω_m?
A. $\omega_m < \omega_s \leq 2\,\omega_m$
B. $\omega_s \geq 2\,\omega_m$
C. $\omega_s < \omega_m$
D. $\omega_s = \omega_m$

35. In the measurement of three phase power by two wattmeter method, if the two wattmeter readings are equal then power factor of the circuit is
A. 0.8 lag B. Unity
C. 0.8 lead D. Zero

36. When a resistor R is connected to a current source, it consumes a power of 18 W. When the same R is connected to a voltage source having the same magnitude as the current source, the power absorbed by R is 4.5 W. The magnitude of the current source and the value of R are
A. $\sqrt{18}$ A and 1Ω
B. 3A and 2Ω
C. 1A and 18Ω
D. 6A and 0.5Ω

37. In a control system, moving a summing point right side to the block yields in
A. Multiplication of the G(s) in the feedback path
B. Multiplication of the 1/G(s) in the feedback path
C. Addition of gain block
D. Subtraction of gain block

38. What is the order of the characteristic equation of an armature controlled DC motor?
A. First order equation
B. Second order equation
C. Zero order equation
D. Third order equation

39. Internal resistance of a cell depends on
A. Terminal voltage B. Torque
C. Current D. Area of the plates

40. Q-meter is based on characteristics of
A. Shunt resonant circuit
B. Series-parallel circuit
C. Series resonant circuit
D. Inductive reactance circuit

41. A 3 Phase, 60 Hz generator connected in Y connection, generates a line to line voltage of 23900 V. Calculate the peak line voltage.
A. 13800 V B. 33800 V
C. 42300 V D. 23900 V

42. A practical voltage source consists of an ideal voltage source in
A. Series with internal resistance
B. Parallel with internal resistance
C. Series with impedance
D. Series with capacitance

43. The AC source shown in the figure has an effective voltage of 120 V, 60 Hz. The load draws a DC current of 20 A. Calculate the average DC current in each diode.

Peak voltage = E_m

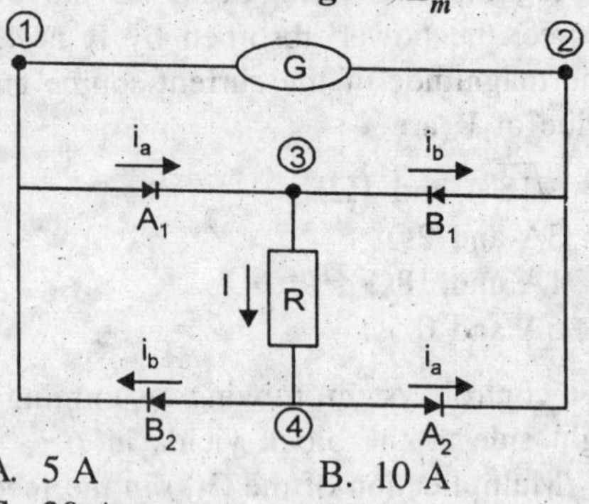

A. 5 A B. 10 A
C. 20 A D. 0

44. If the load current and flux of a DC motor are held constant, and voltage applied across its armature is increased by 10%, its speed will:
A. Decrease by 10%.
B. Remain unchanged.
C. Increase by 10%.
D. Increase by 20%.

45. The meter constant of a single phase 240 V induction watt hour meter is 400 revolutions per KWhr. The speed of the meter disc for a current of 10 A of 0.8 pf, lagging will be
A. 12.8 rpm B. 16.02 rpm
C. 18.2 rpm D. 21.1 rpm

46. For a class A operation, the biasing resistor should be adjusted such that
A. Q-point never lies
B. Q-point lies in the middle of the load line
C. Q-point lies in the cut off region
D. Q-point lies on the operating region

47. A single phase transformer rated at 3000 kVA, 69 kV, 4.16 kV, 60 Hz has a total internal impedance Z_p of 127 ohm, referred to the primary side. Calculate the primary current if the secondary is accidentally short circuited.
A. 43.5 A B. 543 A
C. 9006 A D. 721 A

48. For a fault at terminals of the synchronous generator, the fault current is maximum for a:
A. Three phase fault
B. Double line to ground fault
C. Line to line fault
D. Line to ground fault

49. The measurement of dielectric loss and power factor is done using
A. Weins Bridge
B. Hays Bridge
C. Schering Bridge
D. Wheatstone Bridge

50. A choke coil having resistance RΩ and of inductance L Henry is shunted by a capacitor of C farads. The dynamic impedance of the resonant circuit would be:
A. R/LC B. C/RL
C. L/RC D. 1/RLC

51. If the characteristics equation of a closed loop system is $s^2 + 2s + 2 = 0$, then the system is
A. Over damped B. Critically damped
C. Under damped D. Undamped

52. What would be the total power drawn from the supply, when two heaters, rated at 1000 W, 250 V each are connected in series across a 250 V, 50 Hz supply?
A. 1000 W B. 500 W
C. 250 W D. 2000 W

53. In case of four pole, lap wound machine if the air gap under each pole is the same, then what will be the result?
A. There will be reduced eddy currents
B. There will be reduced hysteresis loss
C. Current in each path will not be the same
D. It will result in higher terminal voltage

54. A thyristor power converter is said to be in discontinuous when:
A. The load current is zero even though the load voltage is present.
B. Both load voltage and load current are zero simultaneously.
C. The load current is present even though load voltage is zero.
D. When load current is ripple free.

55. What is the basic principle of operation of a transformer?
A. Self-induction
B. Mutual-induction
C. Static-induction
D. Dynamic-induction

56. The technique of using stair case ramp in DVM (Digital Volt Meter) is called
A. Deflecting torque technique
B. Null balancing technique
C. Controlling torque technique
D. Detaching torque technique

57. What is the clock cycle time for a system that uses a clock with frequency of 150 kHz?
A. 55 μ sec B. 5.5 μ sec
C. 202 sec D. 6.6 μ sec

58. Norton's Theorem is a way to reduce a network to
A. An equivalent circuit composed of a single current source, series resistance, and series load
B. An equivalent circuit composed of a single voltage source, parallel resistance, and parallel load
C. An equivalent circuit composed of a single voltage source, series resistance, and series load
D. An equivalent circuit composed of a single current source, parallel resistance, and parallel load

59. The usual value of slip of a 3Φ induction motor at full load is about:
A. 0.05 B. 0.1
C. 0.3 D. 0.8

60. A system function has a pole at s = 0 and a zero at s = −1. The constant multiplier is unity. For an excitation cos(t). What is the steady-state response?
A. $\sqrt{2}\sin(t + 45°)$ B. $\sqrt{2}\sin(t - 45°)$
C. $\sin(t - 45°)$ D. $\sin(t)$

61. Which of the following gate is called universal gate?
A. AND B. NOT
C. NOR D. EX-OR

62. When '*n*' resistances each of value '*r*' are connected in parallel, then the resultant resistance is '*x*'. When these '*n*' resistances are connected in series, total resistance is
A. n^2X B. X/n
C. n^2/X D. nX^2

63. According to Biot-Savart's laws the magnetic field at a point due to incremental element of length *dl* carrying a current is
A. Inversely proportional to the current carried by the element
B. Directly proportional to the current carried by the element
C. Directly proportional to the square of the distance
D. Inversely proportional to the length of the element

64. A Transformer rated 250 kVA, 4160 V/480 V, 60 Hz has an impedance of 5.1%. Calculate the total impedance of the transformer referred to the primary side.
A. 69 ohm B. 0.92 ohm
C. 3.52 ohm D. 0.51 ohm

65. Maximum power developed in a synchronous motor occurs at a coupling angle of:
A. 120° B. 60°
C. 90° D. 0°

66. If each branch of a Delta circuit has impedance $\sqrt{3}$ Z, then each branch of the equivalent Y circuit has impedance:

A. $Z/\sqrt{3}$ B. 3Z

C. $3\sqrt{3}$ Z D. Z/3

67. Metallic copper is a:

A. Paramagnetic substance
B. Diamagnetic substance
C. Ferromagnetic substance
D. Ferrimagnetic substance

68. An op-amp having a slew rate of 62.8 V/msec, is connected in a voltage follower configuration. If the maximum amplitude of the sinusoidal input is 10 V, then the minimum frequency at which the slew rate limited distortion would set in at the output is

A. 1 MHz B. 6.28 MHz
C. 10 MHz D. 62.8 MHz

69. A galvanised steel tower member has original length of 22 cm and cross-sectional area of 13 cm^2. With working axial tensile load of 125 KN, the change in length was 0.2 mm. Calculate the percentage of elongation.

A. 0.0712% B. 0.00612%
C. 0.0909% D. 0.19%

70. Which loss has least proportion in DC machines?

A. Armature copper loss
B. Field copper loss
C. Magnetic loss
D. Mechanical loss

71. Fermi level is the measure of

A. Doping of electrons
B. Probability of occupancy of electrons or holes
C. Probability of occupancy of photons
D. Probability of occupancy of wavelength

72. Which of the following testing methods is a direct testing of DC machine?

A. Swinburne's Test
B. Field Test
C. Hopkinson's Test
D. Brake Test

73. The radix of binary number is

A. 1 B. 0
C. 2 D. 8

74. We wish to build a 135 V, 20 A, DC power supply using a single phase bridge rectifier and an inductive filter. The peak to peak current ripple should be about 10%. If a 60 Hz AC source is available. Calculate the peak to peak current ripple.

A. 19 A B. 20 A
C. 2 A D. 1 A

75. The per unit impedance of a circuit element is 0.30. If the base kV and base MVA are halved, then the new value of the per unit impedance of the circuit element will be:

A. 0.3 B. 0.6
C. 0.003 D. 0.006

76. The transfer function of a phase lead compensator is found to be the form $(s + z_1)/(s + p_1)$ and that of a lag compensator to be of the form $(s + z_2) / (s + p_2)$. Then which of the following conditions must be satisfied?

A. $z_1 > p_1$ and $z_2 > p_2$
B. $z_1 > p_1$ and $z_2 < p_2$
C. $z_1 < p_1$ and $z_2 < p_2$
D. $z_1 < p_1$ and $z_2 > p_2$

77. A Transmission line conductor has been suspended freely from two towers and has taken the form of a catenary that has c = 487.68 m. The span between the two towers is 152 m, and the weight of the conductor is 1160 kg/km. Calculate the length of the conductor.

A. 487.68 m B. 152.614 m
C. 5.934 m D. 11.9 m

78. What is a load cell?

A. A strain gauge
B. A photo voltaic cell
C. A thermistor
D. A pressure pick up device

79. Signal flow graph is a

A. Polar plot
B. Bode plot
C. Topological representation of set of differential equations
D. Truth table

80. A 16 kV DC source having an internal resistance of 1 ohm supplies 900 A to a 12 kV, 3 phase 6 pulse 60 Hz inverter. Calculate the DC voltage generated by the inverter.

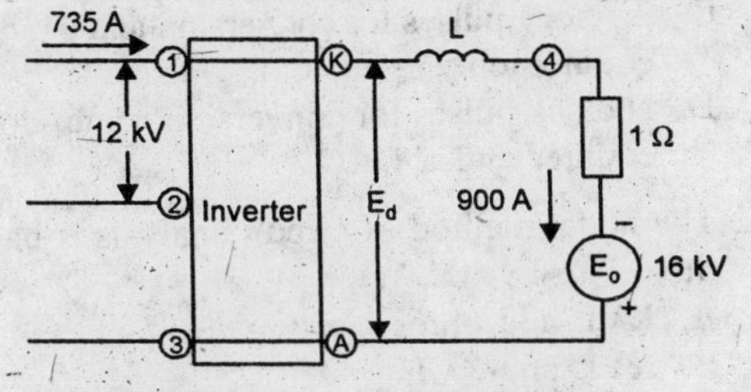

A. 27000 V B. 15100 V
C. 16000 V D. 16400 V

81. In an instrument transformer the errors can be reduced by
A. Using high reluctance core
B. Using small cross sectional area
C. Using low permeability materials
D. Using low reluctance core

82. An energy meter has a constant of 600 rev/kWh. If the meter makes 10 revolutions in 20 s. What is the load in kW?
A. 0.75 kW B. 1.5 kW
C. 3 kW D. 6 kW

83. Which one among these is an example for trivalent impurity?
A. Phosphorus B. Antimony
C. Gallium D. Arsenic

84. A 750 Hp, 250 V, 1200 r/min DC motor is connected to a 208 V, 3 phase, 60 Hz, line using a 3 phase bridge converter. The full load armature current is 2500 A and the armature resistance is 4 m ohm. Calculate the required firing angle under rated full load conditions.
A. 45 deg. B. 208 deg.
C. 27 deg. D. 32 deg.

85. In the solution of load flow equation, Newton Raphson (NR) method is superior to the Gauss-Seidal (GS) Method, because the:
A. Convergence characteristic of the NR methods are not affected by selection of slack bus
B. Number of iterations required in the NR method is not independent of the size of the system
C. Time taken to perform one iteration in the NR method is less when compared to the GS method
D. Number of iteration required in the NR method is more than compared to that in the GS method

86. A three phase 50 Hz, 400 kV transmission line is 300 km long. The line inductance is 0.97 mH/km per phase and capacitance is 0.0115 mF/km per phase. Assume a loss less line. Determine the line wavelength (a line phase constant).
A. 1250 km B. 6578 km
C. 4990 km D. 2445 km

87. A Phase shift transformer is designed to control 150 MVA on a 230 kV, 3 phase line. The phase angle is variable between zero and ±15 deg. Calculate the approximate basic power rating of the transformer.
A. 150 MVA B. 56 MVA
C. 75 MVA D. 750 MVA

88. What is the most effective way to reduce the cost of power generation in a power station?
A. By increasing the diversity factor and decreasing the load factor
B. By increasing both the diversity factor and the load factor
C. By decreasing both the diversity factor and the load factor
D. By decreasing the diversity factor and increasing the load factor

89. What happens to the angle between current and voltage, when a small capacitance is added in series with a highly inductive circuit?
A. Increases
B. Remains same as earlier angle
C. Decreases
D. Becomes indeterminant

90. The generator shown in the figure rotates at 6000 r/min and generates an effective sinusoidal voltage of 170 V per winding. Calculate the output frequency.

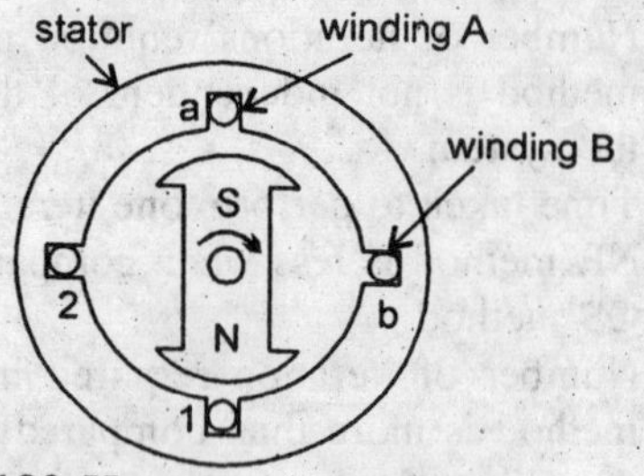

A. 100 Hz B. 10 Hz
C. 1 Hz D. 1 kHz

91. Three resistors of 4 Ω, 6 Ω and 9 Ω are connected in parallel. Which resistor consumes the maximum power?
A. 4 Ω B. 6 Ω
C. 9 Ω D. 17 Ω

92. A 30 MVA, 13.2 KV synchronous generator has a solidly grounded neutral. Its positive, negative and zero sequence impedances are 0.30, 0.40 and 0.05 pu respectively. What value of reactance must be placed in the generator neutral so that the fault current for a line to ground fault of zero fault impedance shall not exceed the rated line current.
A. 4.416 ohm B. 8.8 ohm
C. 2.08 ohm D. 10.2 ohm

93. What is the time constant of an RC series circuit?
A. R/C B. C/R
C. 1/RC D. RC

94. Which of the following is a scalar quantity?
A. Electric field strength
B. Electric displacement density
C. Electric potential
D. Force

95. An alternator is feeding an infinite bus bar. Its prime mover is suddenly shut down. The alternator will:
A. Continue to work as alternator but the direction of rotation will reverse.
B. Come to stand still.
C. Continue to work as synchronous motor and direction of rotation will also be same.
D. Will work as an induction motor.

96. What is essential for a successive approximation N-bit ADC?
A. 2^N clock pulses for conversion, an up-down counter and a DAC.
B. N clock pulses for conversion, a binary counter and a comparator.
C. 2^N clock pulses for conversion and a binary counter only.
D. N clock pulses for conversion, an up-down counter and a DAC.

97. The nodal method of circuit analysis is based on
A. KVL and ohms law
B. KVL and KCL
C. KCL and ohms law
D. Thevenins theorem

98. What is the dimensional representation of Power?
A. ML^2T^{-3} B. $M^2L^2T^{-3}$
C. MLT^{-3} D. M^2LT^{-2}

99. A pulse transformer is used in a driver circuit to:
A. Prevent DC triggering.
B. Shape trigger signal.
C. Generate high frequency pulses.
D. Provide isolation.

100. The direction of rotation of hysteresis motor is determined by the:
A. Resistivity of the rotor material.
B. Amount of hysteresis loss.
C. Permeability of rotor material.
D. Position of shaded pole w.r.t main pole.

101. The power in a 3 phase circuit is measured with the help of 2 wattmeters. The reading of one of wattmeters is positive and that of the others is negative. The magnitude of readings is different. It can be concluded that the power factor of the circuit is
A. Unity
B. 2 (lagging)
C. 5 (lagging)
D. Less than 0.5 (lagging)

102. Copper shading is provided in energy meter to
A. Bring flux exactly in quadrature with applied voltage
B. To increase speed of aluminium disc

C. To count the rotation
D. To balance the system from vibration

103. What is the Bode amplitude plot of a first-order low-pass system?
A. Line with slope −40 dB/decade
B. Line with slope −20 dB/decade
C. Line with slope +20 dB/decade
D. Straight line parallel to the frequency axis

104. A 200 V, 50 Hz inductive circuit takes a current of 10 A at 30 degree lagging pf, what is the inductive reactance of the circuit?
A. 17.8 Ω B. 100 Ω
C. 178 Ω D. 10 Ω

105. What type of insulators are used whenever the conductors are dead ended and there is a change in the direction of transmission line?
A. Shackle type B. Strain type
C. Pin type D. Suspension type

106. A ramp voltage V(t) = 100 V is applied to an RC differentiating circuit with R = 5 kΩ and C = 4 μF. The maximum output voltage is
A. 0.2 V B. 2 V
C. 10 V D. 50 V

107. What is the equivalent resistance of a network having 5 resistors of each 10 ohms connected in parallel?
A. 10 ohms B. 50 ohms
C. 500 ohms D. 2 ohms

108. What language is understood by 'Micro Processor'?
A. Binary B. FORTRAN
C. Instruction D. C++

109. The current I(t), through a 10Ω resistor in series with an inductance, is given by
I(t) = 3 + 4 sin (100t + 450) + 4 sin(300t + 600) amperes. The RMS values of the current and power dissipation in the circuit are:
A. $\sqrt{41}$ A, 410 W respectively
B. $\sqrt{35}$ A, 350 W respectively
C. 5 A, 250 W respectively
D. 11 A, 1210 W respectively

110. What is peak factor of a sinusoidal wave?
A. 1.11 B. 1.414
C. 3.142 D. 4.44

111. Which test is used to determine the magnetizing impedance of a transformer?
A. Short-circuit test B. Impulse test
C. Load test D. Open-circuit test

112. The capacitance of 0-1000V electrostatic voltmeter increases from 36-42 pF from zero to full scale deflection. It is required to extend the range of voltmeter to 10000 V by using an external series capacitor. What should be the value of series capacitor?
A. 0.8 pF B. 1.00 pF
C. 6.644 pF D. 4.667 pF

113. A single phase motor draws a current of 5 A from a 120 V, 60 Hz line. The power factor of the motor is 65%. Calculate the active power absorbed by the motor.
A. 600 W B. 390 W
C. 456 W D. 650 W

114. A parallel combination of capacitance C and resistance R is connected in series with inductance L and small resistance *r*. Under what condition will the circuit be non-reactive?
A. C = LR B. C = LR^2
C. C = L/R^2 D. C = L/R

115. A shunt motor rotating at 1500 r/min is fed by a 120 V source. The line current is 51 A and the shunt field resistance is 120 ohm. If the armature resistance is 0.1 ohm, calculate the current in the armature.
A. 1 A B. 51 A
C. 50 A D. 12 A

116. To charge a 120 V battery from a 600 V DC source using a DC chopper, the average battery current should be 20 A, with a peak to peak ripple of 2 A. If the chopper frequency is 200 Hz, calculate the duty cycle.
A. 0.2 B. 0.1
C. 0.5 D. 0.6

117. A conductor is composed of seven identical copper strands, each having a radius 'R'. Then what is self GMD (Geometric Mean Distance) of the conductor?
A. 2.645 R B. 2.177 R
C. 2.141 R D. 1.21 R

118. What type of excitation is given to the rotor winding of a synchronous motor?
A. DC supply at 100-250 V
B. AC supply at 400 V
C. Revolving field
D. Induction from stator currents

119. For a two port network to be reciprocal:
A. $Z_{11} = Z_{22}$ B. $Y_{21} = Y_{21}$
C. $h_{21} = h_{22}$ D. AD-BC = 0

120. A metal oxide varistor (MOV) is used for protecting:
A. Gate circuit against over currents
B. Gate circuit against over voltages
C. Anode circuit against over currents
D. Anode circuit against over voltages

121. What is the decimal equivalent of hexa decimal no (8A6)?
A. 1422 B. 1242
C. 2122 D. 2214

122. The sending and receiving end voltages of a three phase transmission line at 100 MW load are equal at 230 KV. The phase line impedance is $j14$ ohm. Calculate the maximum steady state power that can be transmitted over the line.
A. 3778.5 MW B. 2234.56 MW
C. 1784.19 MW D. 512.37 MW

123. Which of the following power plants involves high initial cost in erecting?
A. Hydro-electric power plant
B. Steam power plant
C. Gas turbine power plant
D. Nuclear power plant

124. A 220 kV, 3 phase transmission line is 60 km long. The resistance is 0.15 ohm / km and the inductance is 1.4 mH / km. Use the short line model to find the power at the sending end when the line is supplying a three phase load of 300 MVA at 0.8 pf lagging at 220 kV.
A. 5.58 MW B. 80 MW
C. 85.58 MW D. 74.42 MW

125. What is the value of total electric flux coming out of closed surface?
A. Zero
B. Equal to volume charge density
C. Equal to the total charge enclosed by the surface
D. Equal to the surface charge density

126. A Reactor having an inductive reactance of 4 ohm is connected to the terminals of a 120 V AC generator. Calculate the power associated with the reactor.
A. 3.6 kvar B. 30 kvar
C. 7.2 kvar D. 4.16 kvar

127. A coil having 90 turns is connected to a 120 V, 60 Hz source. If the effective value of the magnetizing current is 4 A. Calculate the inductance of the coil.
A. 79.6 mH B. 121.2 mH
C. 32.2 mH D. 83.16 mH

128. A 1mA D' Arsonval movement has resistance of 100Ω. It is to be converted to a 10 V voltmeter. The value of multiplier resistance is
A. 999 Ω B. 9999 Ω
C. 9900 Ω D. 990 Ω

129. Three single phase transformers are connected in delta-delta to step down a line voltage of 138 kV to 4160 V to supply power to a production plant. The plant draws 21 MW at a lagging power factor of 86%. Calculate the apparent power furnished by the HV line.
A. 24.4 MVA B. 48.8 MVA
C. 12.2 MVA D. 6.1 MVA

130. A three phase breaker is rated at 2000 MVA, 33 kV, its making current is
A. 70 kA B. 89 kA
C. 49 kA D. 35 kA

131. What is the minimum clearance of HV lines from ground across streets?
A. 3 meters B. 8 meters
C. 6 meters D. 5 meters

132. The stator of a 3 phase, 10 pole induction motor possesses 120 slots. If a lap winding is used, calculate the coil pitch, if the coil width extends from slot 1 to slot 11.
A. 72.12% B. 83.30%
C. 12% D. 42%

133. What is the pitch factor of a 4 pole alternator having 36 slots and a coil span of 1 to 8?
A. 140° B. 80°
C. 20° D. 40°

134. What is the main drawback of the underground transmission system compared to the overhead transmission system?
A. Exposure to lightning
B. Heavy initial cost
C. Exposure to atmospheric hazards such as smoke, ice, wind
D. Induction interference between power and communication circuits

135. Which of the following plants is suitable for peak load?
A. Diesel engine plant
B. Steam power plant
C. Nuclear power plant
D. Hydro-electric plant

136. Which of the following serves as donor impurity in Silicon?
A. Boron B. Indium
C. Germanium D. Antimony

137. The phase voltages across a certain load are given as $V_a = (176 - j132)$ V, $V_b = (-128 - j96)$ V and $V_c = (-160 + j100)$ V. Compute positive sequence component of voltage.
A. 0 B. 163.24 – j35.1 V
C. 50.1 – j53.9 V D. 25.1 – j53.9 V

138. What is the power factor of a cable of loss angle "θ"?
A. sin θ B. cos θ
C. tan θ D. Independent of θ

139. Which of the following gate is inverted OR gate?
A. NAND B. NOR
C. AND D. EX-OR

140. Determine the transformer tap ratios when the receiving end voltage is equal to the sending end voltage, the high voltage line operates at 220 kV and transmit 80 MW at 0.8 pf and the impedance of the line is (40 + j140)ohm. Assume $t_s t_r = 1.0$
A. 0.8 B. 0.9
C. 0.7 D. 0.6

141. RMS value of rectangular wave of period T, having a value of +V for a duration T_1(<T) and –V for the duration $T - T_1 = T_2$ equals
A. V B. $T_1 - T_2 / T$
C. $V/\sqrt{2}$ D. T_1/T_2

142. The hysteresis loop of magnetic material has an area of 5 cm² with the scales given as 1 cm = 2AT and 1 cm = 50 mWb, at 50 Hz, the total hysteresis loss is
A. 15 W B. 20 W
C. 25 W D. 50 W

143. What does the region around the stationary electric charge has?
A. Electric field
B. Magnetic field
C. Semipermeable region
D. Insulating field

144. Which of the following statements is CORRECT?
A. A grid-connected induction generator always supplies lagging reactive power to the bus.
B. An overexcited synchronous motor draws current at a lagging power factor.
C. An under excited synchronous generator connected to an infinite bus works at a leading power factor.
D. The load angle of a synchronous machine is the angle between the excitation voltage and the load current.

145. In which type of the faults given below, all of the three components I_{a0}, I_{a1} and I_{a2} are equal?
A. Single line to ground fault
B. Double line to ground fault
C. Line to line fault
D. 3 phase faults

146. One 200 KVA transformer has an iron loss of 1 KW and full load Cu loss of 2 KW. Its load KVA corresponding to maximum efficiency is:
A. 100 KVA B. 141.4 KVA
C. 50 KVA D. 200 KVA

147. A three phase transmission line delivers a load of 5 MW at 0.8 power factor lagging.

Resistance of each conductor is 0.5 ohm / km. Receiving end voltage is 33 kV. If the line loss is not to exceed 10%, determine the length of the line.

A. 7 km B. 27.9 km
C. 56.8 km D. 13.9 km

148. Which among the following is the dual of Boolean expression X + YZ = (X + Y) (X + Z)?

A. X(Y + Z) = XY + YZ
B. X.(Y + Z) = X.Y + X.Z
C. X + (Y + Z) = X.Y + Z
D. X + (YZ) = X + Y + Z

149. What is the purpose of providing a fuse in an electric circuit?

A. To safe guard the installation against heavy current
B. To reduce the current flowing in the circuit
C. To reduce the power consumption
D. To improve power factor

150. FET belongs to which of the following type of device?

A. Current controlled device
B. Magnetic device
C. Power controlled device
D. Voltage controlled device

ANSWERS

1	2	3	4	5	6	7	8	9	10
C	B	B	A	B	A	B	B	C	A
11	**12**	**13**	**14**	**15**	**16**	**17**	**18**	**19**	**20**
C	B	D	C	C	B	D	C	A	A
21	**22**	**23**	**24**	**25**	**26**	**27**	**28**	**29**	**30**
C	D	C	A	B	C	C	A	A	C
31	**32**	**33**	**34**	**35**	**36**	**37**	**38**	**39**	**40**
D	A	C	B	B	B	A	D	D	C
41	**42**	**43**	**44**	**45**	**46**	**47**	**48**	**49**	**50**
B	A	B	C	A	B	C	D	C	C
51	**52**	**53**	**54**	**55**	**56**	**57**	**58**	**59**	**60**
C	D	B	B	B	B	D	D	A	A
61	**62**	**63**	**64**	**65**	**66**	**67**	**68**	**69**	**70**
C	A	B	C	C	A	B	A	C	D
71	**72**	**73**	**74**	**75**	**76**	**77**	**78**	**79**	**80**
B	D	C	C	B	D	B	A	C	B
81	**82**	**83**	**84**	**85**	**86**	**87**	**88**	**89**	**90**
D	C	C	C	A	C	B	B	C	A
91	**92**	**93**	**94**	**95**	**96**	**97**	**98**	**99**	**100**
A	A	C	C	C	D	C	A	D	D
101	**102**	**103**	**104**	**105**	**106**	**107**	**108**	**109**	**110**
D	A	B	D	B	B	D	A	C	B
111	**112**	**113**	**114**	**115**	**116**	**117**	**118**	**119**	**120**
D	D	B	C	C	A	B	A	B	D
121	**122**	**123**	**124**	**125**	**126**	**127**	**128**	**129**	**130**
D	A	D	C	C	A	A	C	A	B
131	**132**	**133**	**134**	**135**	**136**	**137**	**138**	**139**	**140**
C	B	D	B	A	D	B	A	B	B
141	**142**	**143**	**144**	**145**	**146**	**147**	**148**	**149**	**150**
A	C	A	C	A	B	B	B	A	D

OBJECTIVE ELECTRICAL ENGINEERING

1. POWER SYSTEM

INTRODUCTION

Energy exists in various forms like mechanical energy, electrical energy, thermal energy and so on. One form of energy can be converted into another form by suitable arrangements. Out of these forms, electrical energy is preferred due to the following reasons.

(i) It can be easily transported from one place to another,

(ii) Losses in energy transportation are minimum,

(iii) It can be easily controlled and regulated to suit requirements,

(iv) It can be easily converted into other forms of energy particularly mechanical and thermal,

(v) It can be easily sub-divided.

Sources of Energy

Some of the sources of energy are

1. Fuels:

(a) Solid fuels: wood, charcoal, peat, coke, briquetted coal, pulverised coal.

(b) Liquid fuels: petroleum based like petrol, diesel, etc. Non-petroleum fuels like ethyl alcohol, methyl alcohol, benzene etc.

(c) Gaseous fuels: producer gas, blast furnace gas, coke oven gas, water gas.

*2. **Energy of water*** as used in hydroelctric plants where potential energy of water is converted into electrical energy.

3. Nuclear energy
4. Solar energy
5. Wind power
6. Wave power
7. Tidal power
8. Geothermal energy
9. Fuel cells
10. Thermo electric power
11. Thermionic converter
12. Magneto hydrodynamic (MHD) generator.

In all power stations, electric energy is generated from other forms of energy, e.g.,

(i) Chemical energy of fuel (thermal energy)

(ii) Energy of falling water (hydraulic energy)

(iii) Atomic energy (nuclear energy)

TRANSMISSION

Several generating stations can be inter connected (as shown in Fig. 1). The main advantages are:

(i) reduction in the number of spare plants required as one station can assist the other at the time of emergency.

(ii) during light loads one station or some generators can be shut off, thus affecting operational economy.

Primary Transmission

High voltages of the order of 66 kV, 132 kV, 220kV and 400 kV are used for transmitting power by 3 phase 3 wire overhead system. This is supplied to substations usually at the out skirts of major distribution centre or city.

Secondary Transmission

The primary voltage is reduced to low values of the order of 3.3 kV, 11 kV or 33 kV for secondary transmission.

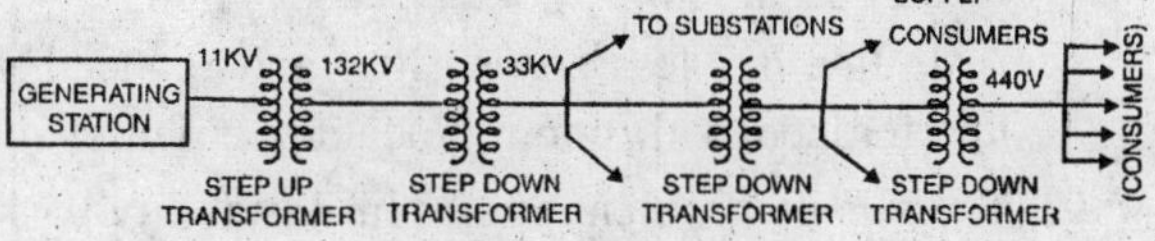

Fig. 1

Primary Distribution

The transmission lines or inner connectors terminate at large main substations from which the power is distributed to small secondary substations scattered throughout the load area. The voltage may range from 11 kV to 132 kV.

Secondary Distribution

This consists of the low-voltage network laid along the streets, localities and over the rural areas. From these sources connections to individual customers are provided. The circuit used for this purpose is 3 phase 4 wire, 440 V/220 V from which either 3 phase 440 V or single phase 220 V supply to the consumers may be provided.

System Layout

From the power stations *PS*, emanate 3 phase feeder supplying secondary distributions substations located at points throughout the supply area. The normal voltages are 132 kV, 33 kV and 11 kV.

Comparison of AC and DC Transmission

(A) Advantages of DC Transmission

1. It requires only two conductors.
2. There is no problem of inductance, capacitance and phase displacement which is common in ac transmission.
3. For the same load and sending end voltage, the voltage drop in dc transmission lines is less than that in ac transmission.
4. As there is no skin effect on conductors, therefore entire cross-section of conductor is usefully utilised thereby affecting saving in material.
5. For the same value of voltage insulating materials on dc lines experience less stress as compared to those on ac transmission lines.
6. A dc line has less corona loss and reduced interference with communication circuits.
7. There is no problem of system instability so common in ac transmission.

Disadvantages of DC Transmission

1. Generation of power at high dc voltages is difficult due to commutation problems and cannot be usefully utilised at consumer ends.
2. Step up or step-down transformation of dc voltages is not possible in equipment like transformer.

(B) Advantages of AC Transmission

1. Power can be generated at high voltages as there is no commutation problem.
2. AC voltages can be conveniently stepped up or stepped down.
3. High voltage transmission of AC power reduces losses.

Disadvantages of AC Transmission

1. Problems of inductances and capacitances exist in transmission lines.
2. Due to skin effect, more copper is required.
3. Construction of AC transmission lines is more complicated as well as costly.
4. Effective resistance of AC transmission lines is increased due to skin effect.

CONDUCTOR MATERIALS

A material for conducting electrical power should have the following properties.

1. High electrical conductivity
2. Low cost
3. Low specific gravity
4. High tensile strength

Commonly used materials for conductors are:

1. Copper
2. Aluminium
3. Aluminium Conductor Steel Reinforced (ACSR)
4. Galvanised steel
5. Cadmium copper

Economic Size of Conductor: Kelvin's Law

The most economical size of conductor is that for which the variable part of the annual charges is equal to the cost of energy losses per year.

Limitations of Kelvin's Law

1. The law assumes a linear relation between the cost on account of interst and depreciation on the capital outlay which is not necessarily always valid. Moreover, it is difficult to calculate these values.
2. Actual energy loss on a transmission line cannot be estimated without actual load curves. Load curves are not available at the planning stages.
3. The conductor size estimated according to this law may not be the optimum as various aspects of safety etc., have not been taken into account.
4. The law does not take into account some of the aspects like safe current density, mechanical strength, corona loss, etc.

TRANSMISSION LINES

Transmission lines are used to transfer electrical power from one place to another. The requirements of transmission lines are

1. transmission loses should be least
2. power must be delivered at the specified voltage
3. no radio interference
4. high availability.

The common transmission voltage in India is 132 kV, 220 kV and 400 kV rms value, phase to phase capacitance.

Classification of Overhead Lines

1. Short transmission lines: When the length of an overhead transmission line is upto 540 km and the line voltage less than 20kV, it is known as short transmission line. Due to smaller length and lower voltage, the capacitance effects are small and hence can be neglected. Thus, resistance and inductance are the major parameters considered for these lines.

2. Medium transmission lines: These lines are 50 km to 150 km and the range of voltage is 20 kV to 100 kV. Due to sufficient length and voltage of the line, the capacitive effects are not neglected.

3. Long transmission lines: These lines are more than 150 km in length and carry voltage higher than 100 kV.

Parameters of a Transmission Line

1. Resistance: Aluminium Conductors Steel Reinforced (ACSR) are used for transmission of power over long distance. The acceptable limits of current density for aluminium is around 95 A in a conductor of 1 cm diameter. In case of copper it is 160 A in a 1 cm diameter conductor. Thus size of a conductor for a transmission line is given by

Diameter of aluminium conductor

$$= \left[\frac{\text{Current to be carried}}{95}\right]^{1/2} \text{cm}$$

As aluminium has got low tensile strength therefore steel cored (ACSR) conductors are used.

2. Inductance of a phase single circuit overhead line is given by

$$L = \frac{\mu_0}{2\pi}\left(\frac{1}{4} + \log_e \frac{S}{r}\right) \text{ henry/metre}$$

where μ_0 = Permeability of air

$= 4\pi \times 10^{-7}$ henry/metre

$$S = D_{eq} = 3\sqrt{D_{ab}\, D_{bc}\, D_{ca}}$$

D_{eq} is equivalent equilateral spacing between 3 conductors *a*, *b* and *c*. D_{ab}, D_{bc} and D_{ca} are distances between conductors *a*, *b* and *c*.

r = radius of the conductor

3. Capacitance of a three phase line: C_A is given by

$$C_A = \frac{2\pi\varepsilon_0}{S} \text{ Farads per metre,}$$

phase to $\log_e \frac{S}{r}$ neutral

where ε_0 = permittivity of free air

(8.85×10^{-12} Farads/m)

S and *r* have same meaning as in the estimation of inductance.

Transmission Line Constants

The transmission lines upto 50 kilometre length and voltages upto 33 kV are considered as short lines. Lines more than 50 kilometres in length and carrying voltages above 33 kV are called long transmission lines. If V_s and V_r be respectively the sending end and receiving end voltages (corresponding currents being I_s and I_r) then

$$V_s = AV_r + B\,I_r$$

and $$I_s = CV_r + DI_r$$

The values of constants *A*, *B*, *C* and *D* primarily depend on the *R*, *L*, *C* parameters of the line.

For Short Lines

$$V_s = V_r + LZ\,I_r,\ I_s = I_r,\ A = D = 1,\ B = Z$$

and $$C = 0,\ AD - BC = 1,\ A = D$$

For Medium Lines (T-network)

$$A = D = 1 + \frac{YZ}{2}$$

$$B = Z + \frac{YZ^2}{4}$$

$$C = Y$$

$$AD - BC = 1,\ A = D$$

(π–network)

$$A = 1 + \frac{YZ}{2}\quad B + Z,\ C = Y + \frac{Y^2Z}{4}$$

$$D = 1 + \frac{YZ}{2}$$

Long Lines

$$A = \cosh\sqrt{(YZ)}$$

$$B = \sqrt{Z/Y}\,\sinh\sqrt{YZ}$$

$$C = \sqrt{Y/Z}\,\sinh\sqrt{YZ}$$

$$D = \cosh\sqrt{YZ}$$

$$AD - BC = 1,\ A = D$$

SKIN EFFECT

When alternating current flows through a conductor it is always linked with flux. The flux linking the central portion of the conductor is always more than that at the surface. This results in higher current density at the surface of the conductor as compared to that at the core of the conductor. This is known as skin effect. This has following effects.

(i) Skin effect causes increase in dc resistance of the effective dc resistance

(ii) Skin effect is high for conductors of magnetic materials

(iii) Skin effect is more predominant at higher frequencies

(iv) In case of dc, skin effect does not exist.

PROXIMITY EFFECT

For a conductor carrying alternating current, the current density in the conductor depends on the internal flux distribution. When two ac current carrying conductors run parallel, the internal current distribution in both the conductors gets rearranged in such a way so that ac current density on the side nearer to the other conductor is lesser than that at the other end. The effect is known as proximity effect. As a result of this effect, the effective dc resistance of the conductors increases.

CORONA

Conductors carrying electric power at higher voltage have strong electrostatic field around them. This results in a violet visible discharge, called corona. It is accompanied by hissing sound, vibrations, power loss and radio interference.

The voltage between the conductors at which the surrounding air is ionised is called the break down voltage or disruptive voltage. Break down voltage depends on atmospheric conditions and also surface conditions of the conductor.

The electrical stress at the surface of a conductor is given by

$$E = \frac{V}{r_0 \log_e \dfrac{S}{r_0}}$$

where V = phase to earth voltage,

r_0 = radius of conductor

S = equivalent equilateral spacing between 3 phase conductors

The factors affective corona are—

1. Atmosphere: There is more tendency during stormy weather.

2. Conductor size: Rough and irregular surfaces give rise to more corona because unevenness of the surface decreases the value of breakdown voltage stranded conductors having rough surface have more tendency for corona.

3. Spacing between conductors: Shorter distance between conductors increases tendency for corona.

4. Line voltage: Higher voltages have increased chances of corona.

INSULATORS

An insulator should have high mechanical and electrical strength and should be non-porous free from impurities and cracks and should have high ratio of puncture strength to flash over.

Pin type insulators are used upto 33 kV. Suspension type insulators are used for voltages higher than 33 kV. Strain insulators are installed at the dead end of the line or whenever there is corner or sharp curve.

All electric circuits need a switching device and also a protective device. Switchgear is the general term covering a wide range of equipment connected with switching and protection. A circuit breaker is a switching and circuit interrupting device. A circuit breaker serves two purposes:

(i) Switching on and off during normal operation for maintenance etc.

(ii) Switching during abnormal conditions—short circuits, earthing etc., to protect the associated equipment.

In short, a circuit breaker is a sort of automatic switch which can interrupt the fault currents. Two important parts of a circuit breaker that need consideration are:

(i) Arc extinction system

(ii) Relay for operation

ARC EXTINCTION

Whenever a circuit carrying current is interrupted by a circuit breaker an arc is inevitably formed between the contacts which prolongs the current interrupting process for a duration ranging from 10 to 100 or more milliseconds (see Fig. 2).

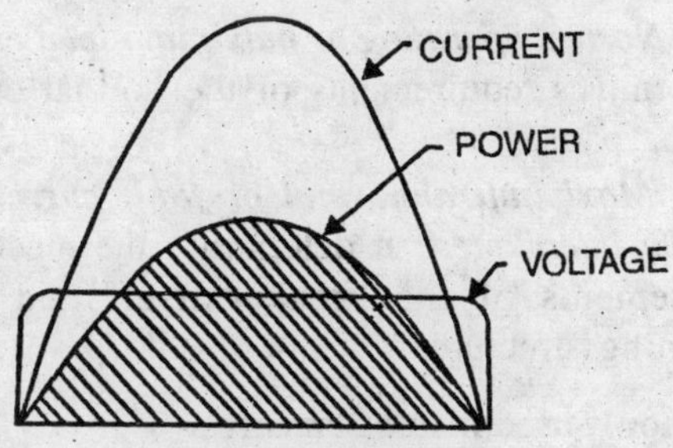

Fig. 2

Since arc is produced in every circuit breaker, therefore a suitable energy dissipating device must be incorporated in the design of circuit breaker. Unless carefully controlled, arc can lead to danger of fire or explosion.

The arc consists of a column of ionised gas, *i.e.*, gas in which the molecules have lost one or more of their negative electrons, leaving positive ions. The negative electrons are attracted towards the positive contact and being light, more towards it very rapidly. The positive ions attract towards the negative contact. Due to electron movement the current flows.

The ionisation process is accompanied by the emission of light and heat. Also some portion of power is dissipated as heat. The temperature of arc may be as high as 6000ºC.

CIRCUIT BREAKERS

These are heavy-duty devices capable of interrupting comparatively large electric currents safely. They are designed not only to carry and interrupt the normal load currents flowing in circuit but also to interrupt any abnormally high current that may flow under fault conditions such as short circuit. Circuit breakers are constructed mechanically strong enough to withstand the forces set-up by enormous short-circuit currents.

The ability of a breaker to withstand short circuit forces is expressed in Volt-Amperes, *i.e.*, product of nominal circuit voltage and the short-circuit current for which the breaker is designed.

The specification of a circuit breaker are :

1. Operating voltage of the circuit: It determines the insulating requirements.

2. Normal operating or maximum load current: It determines requirements of the normal or load-carrying parts.

3. Maximum abnormal or fault current that must be interrupted: It determines the mechanical requirements of the breaker itself and of its supporting structure.

Commonly used insulations are

1. Oil
2. Vacuum
3. Inert gas, *e.g.*, sulphur hexafluoride

Principle of operation: The circuit breaker actually makes a physical separation in the current-carrying or conducting element by inserting an insulating medium sufficient to prevent current from continuing to flow. In so doing, the persistence of an arc across the gap is prevented (Fig. 3).

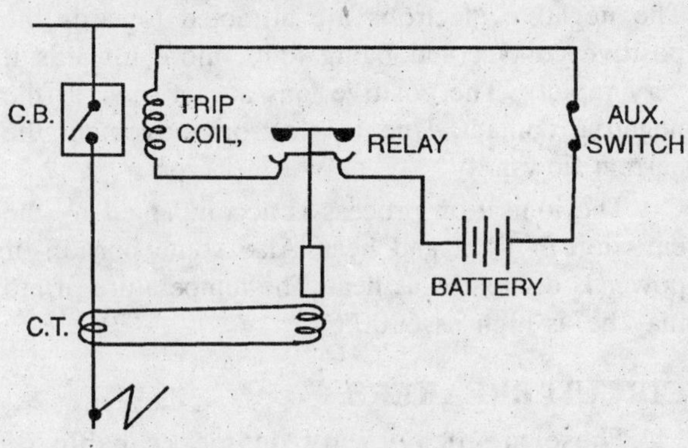

Fig. 3

The circuit is usually opened by drawing out an arc between contacts until the arc can no longer support itself. The arc formed when the contacts of a circuit breaker move apart to interrupt a circuit is a conductor made up of ionized particles of the insulating materials.

Whenever voltages and currents are large other forms of insulation are used in place or air to extinguish the arc as quickly as possible.

Whenever fault occurs in the circuit breaker, relay connected to the current transformer CT actuates and closes its contacts. Current flows from the battery in the trip circuit. As soon as the trip coil of the circuit breaker gets energized the circuit breaker operating mechanism is actuated and it operates for the opening mechanism.

Types of Circuit Breakers
(C.B. = Circuit Breaker)

Type	*Medium*	*Range*
1. Air break C.B.	Air at atmospheric pressure	Low voltage upto 1000 V
2. Tank type oil circuit breaker	Dielectric oil	upto 33 kV
3. Minimum oil circuit breaker	Dielectric oil	36 kV, 1500 MVA 132 kV, 3000 MVA
4. Air blast C.B.	Compressed air (pressure 20 to 30 atmospheres)	132 kV, 220 kV 400 kV, 760 kV
5. SF_6 C.B.	SF_6 gas	132 kV, 220 kV 400 kV, 760 kV
6. Vacuum C.B.	Vacuum	11 kV, 33 kV
7. High voltage direct current C.B.	Vacuum of SF_6	±500 kV DC.

Some Terms Associated with Circuit Breakers are Given Below

1. Arcing time: Time between separation of circuit breaker contacts and final current zero.

2. Dead time: Time between final current zero of first opening and contact touch during subsequent reclosing.

3. Deionizing time: Time for deionizing the arc space after opening of circuit breaker.

4. Fault clearing time: Time between occurrence of fault and closing of tripping contacts or energizing of shunt trip release.

5. Opening time: Time between energizing of shunt trip release and opening of circuit breaker contacts.

6. Rated short circuit breaking circuit: The rated short circuit breaker current of a circuit breaker is the highest value of short circuit which a circuit breaker is capable of breaking under specified conditions of recovery voltage and power frequency recovery voltage.

7. Relay time: Time between occurrence of fault and closure of relay contacts.

Consider a single phase overhead line consisting of two parallel conductors *A* and *B*, each of radii *r* metres and spaced *d* metres apart (*d* being very large as compared to *r*).

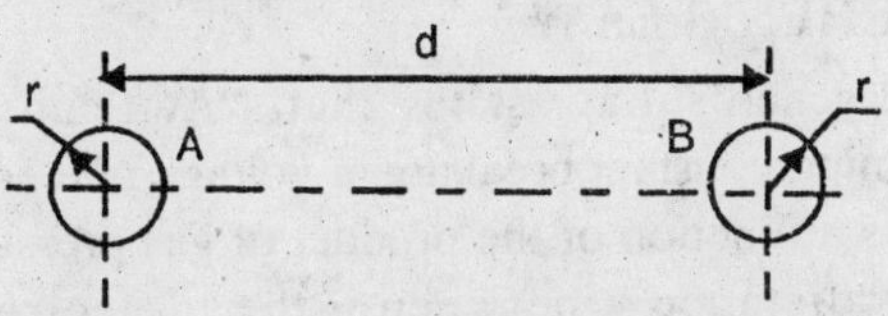

Fig. 4

Conductors *A* and *B* carry the same current (*i.e.* $I_1 = I_2$) in magnitude but opposite in directions, as one forms the return path for the other.

Inductance of conductor *A*

$$L_A = 2 \times 10^{-7} \log_e \frac{d}{re^{-1/4}} \text{ H/m}$$

Similarly, inductance of conductor *B*,

$$L_B = 2 \times 10^{-7} \log_e \frac{d}{r'} \text{ H/m}$$

and Loop inductance,

$$L = 4 \times 10^{-7} \log_e \frac{d}{r'} \text{ H/m}$$

We know that any two conductors separated by an insulating medium constitute a condenser or a *capacitor*. In the case of the overhead line the two conductors form the plates of a capacitor, as they are separated by air from one another. This capacitance is uniformly distributed over the total length of the line and may be regarded as a uniform series of consumers connected between the conductors, as shown.

Consider a single phase overhead line with two parallel conductors, each of radius *r* metre placed at a distance of *d* metres in air (assuming *d* very large compared to *r*).

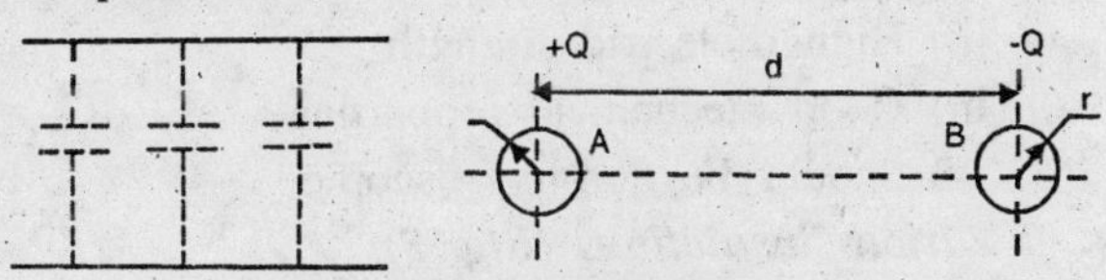

Fig. 5

If conductor *A* has a charge of + *Q* coulombs per metre length, the conductor B will have a charge of –*Q* coulombs per metre length.

Potential of conductor *A*

$$V_A = \frac{Q}{2\pi\varepsilon_0} \log_e \frac{d}{r} \text{ volts}$$

Similarly potential of conductor *B*,

$$V_B = \frac{-Q}{2\pi\varepsilon_0} \left(\log_e \frac{d}{r} \right) \text{volts}$$

Potential difference between the conductors A and *B*

$$V = V_A - V_B$$

$$= \frac{Q}{2\pi\varepsilon_0} \log_e \frac{d}{r} - \left(\frac{-Q}{2\pi\varepsilon_0} \right) \log_e \frac{d}{r}$$

$$= \frac{Q}{\pi\varepsilon_0} \log_e \frac{d}{r} \text{ volts}$$

Capacitance

$$C = \frac{Q}{V} = \frac{Q}{\frac{Q}{\pi\varepsilon_0} \log_e \frac{d}{r}} \text{ Farads/m}$$

$$= \pi \varepsilon_0 / \log_e \frac{d}{r} \text{ Farads/m}$$

CABLES

These consist of

(i) Conductor for transmitting electric power which provides conducting path for electric currents

(ii) Insulation which prevents direct contact between conductor and other objects.

(iii) External protection against mechanical damage chemical attack, fire etc.

Requirements for insulations:

(i) High insulation resistance
(ii) High dielectric strength
(iii) Good mechanical properties
(iv) Should be non-hydroscopic

Various insulations (Fig. 5):

(i) Vulcanized rubber
(ii) Butyl rubber
(iii) Silicone rubber
(iv) Neoprene rubber
(v) Polyvinyl chloride
(vi) Impregnated paper

According to voltage rating cables are classified as:

(i) Low tension cables upto 1000 volts
(ii) High tension cables upto 11 kV
(iii) High tension cables for 22 and 33 kV
(iv) Extra high tension cables

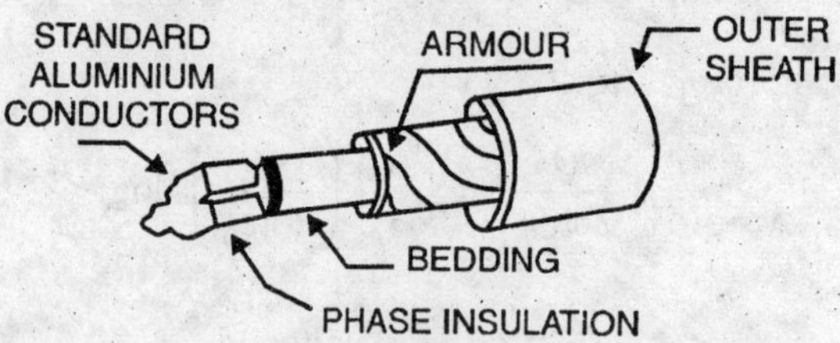

Fig. 5

Expression of Isulation Resistance

A single core metal sheathed cable, r and R be the inner and outer radii of insulating material and l metres is the length of the cable, ρ is specific resistance of the insulating material. The path of leakage current is radial through the insulation. Consider an infinitely small layer of insulation of thickness x (see Fig. 6). The length through which leakage current flows = dx. Cross-sectional area offered to this flow of current = $2\pi xl$

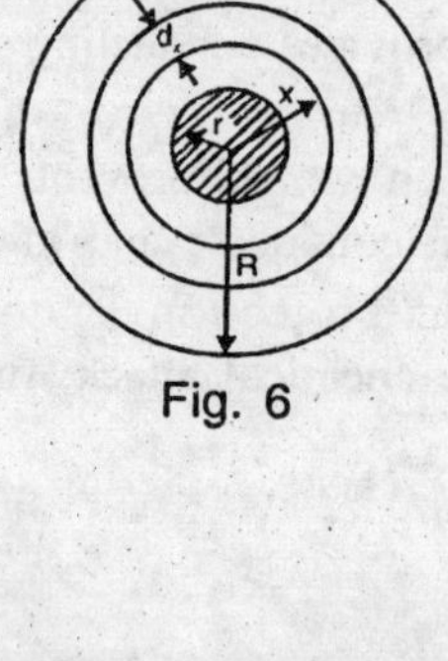

Fig. 6

The insulation resistance dr of this layer is

$$dr = \frac{\rho\, dx}{2\pi x l}$$

where ρ is the volume resistivity.

The insulation resistance R of the whole length of cable is

$$R = \int_r^R \frac{\rho\, dx}{2\pi x l} = \frac{\rho}{2\pi l}\left[\log_e x\right]_r^R$$

$$= \frac{\rho}{2\pi l}\log_e R_r$$

Thus, insulation resistance is inversely proportional to the length of the cable.

PASCHEN'S LAW

Paschen's Law states that, "At temperature remaining constant breakdown voltage in a uniform field is a function of the product of gas pressure (p) and distance between the electrodes." Mathematically,

$$V_0 = f(p, s)$$

BREAKDOWN VOLTAGE

The electric strength of a gap in a uniform field is same for direct and power frequency voltages and can be determined from the formula

$$V_0 = 6.66\sqrt{\delta S} + 24.55\,\delta S$$

where

S = distance between the electrodes in cm
δ = relative air density

CORONA DISCHARGE

In high voltage systems corona discharges have to be taken into account. For a smoothly polished conductor of radius r situated along the axis of a cylinder $R >> r$, the critical intensity can be determined from the relation

$$E_c = 31\,\delta\left(1 + \frac{0.308}{\sqrt{r\delta}}\right)$$

and the corresponding critical voltage from

$$V_c = E_c\, r \log_e \frac{R}{r}$$

POWER LOSS DUE TO CORONA

$$P_C = 244\ (25 + f)\ \sqrt{\frac{r}{D}}\ (E - E_0)^2 \times 10^{-5}$$

kW/phase/km

where f = frequency in Hz

E = voltage in kV to neutral (rms).

DISTRUPTIVE VOLTAGE

$$E_0 = m\delta rg \ln \frac{D}{r}\ kV \text{ to neutral}$$

$$g = 21.1 \text{ kV (rms)}$$

$$E_0 = 21.1\ m\delta r \ln \frac{D}{r}\ kV \text{ to normal}$$

where D = distance between conductors in cm.

INSULATING MATERIALS

These are encountered in every electric and electronic device and piece of equipment. They are vital for isolating conductors and for their performance. These have extremely high resistivities and high dielectric strengths below certain temperatures. The electrical properties are dielectric constant, electrical resistivity and dielectric strength of material. Traditional materials include cellulosics such as paper and organic fabrics. They also include mica, glass and ceramics. Cellulosic materials suffer from hygroscopicity and are bound to contain gas voids.

Mica has been used where high temperatures and/or surface discharges are experienced (e.g., in vacuum tubes, heaters and dc machine commutators). Mica powder mixed with finely ground glass in a hot-pressing process yields a dense machinable material with excellent electrical qualities, particularly suitable for insulators in high-voltage high-frequency equipment.

Porcelain and glass are used in insulating overhead power lines and bus-bars. Several newly developed insulating materials fall within the classification as polymers. Their molecular arrangements are either linear or cross-linked, the former including elastomers and thermoplastics and are generally very flexible and yield with time under a given mechanical load. The higher the temperature, the greater the yield. They include polyethylene (PE), poly vinyl chloride (PVC), and polyamides (nylons). Polytetrafluoroethylene (PTFE), which is a linear polymer, is not flexible nor does it yield and melt at high temperatures. Because of the high binding energies of fluorine atoms, the polymer is about 95% crystalline. At temperatures as high as 400°C, it decomposes.

TABLE : Potential, Field, Maximum Field and Ratio n of Average

Configuration	*Potential*	*E*	E_{max}	$n = E_{av}/E_{max}$	*Field of Application*
Concentric spheres	$\phi(r) = \frac{a}{b}\frac{V}{r}(b-r)$;	$E(r) = \frac{Vba}{r^2\,(b-a)}$	$E_{max} = \frac{Vb}{a\,(b-a)}$	$\frac{a}{b}$	Spherical capacitors,
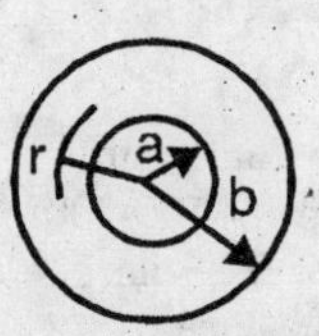					capacitance representation of the dome of a Van de Graaff generator and the structure of the room
Coaxial cylinders	$\phi(r) = \frac{V \ln (b/r)}{\ln (b/a)}$;	$E(r) = \frac{V}{r \ln (b/a)}$	$E_{max} = \frac{V}{a \ln (b/a)}$	$\frac{a \ln (b/a)}{b-a}$	Cable bushing and GIS
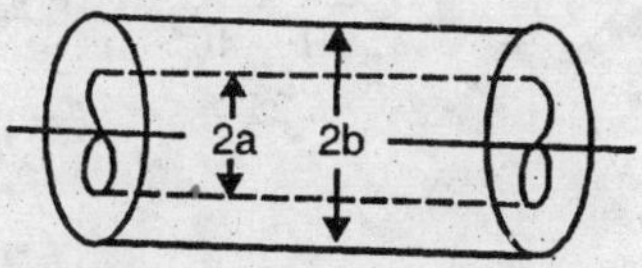					

Separated equal 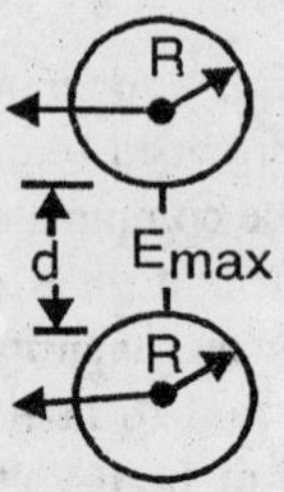	Two-dimensional field	Two-dimensional field	$E_{max} = \frac{V}{2R}$ if $d >> R$	$\frac{2R}{d}$ if $\frac{d}{r} >> 1$	Sphere gap for HV measurements, etc.
Equal parallel cylinders 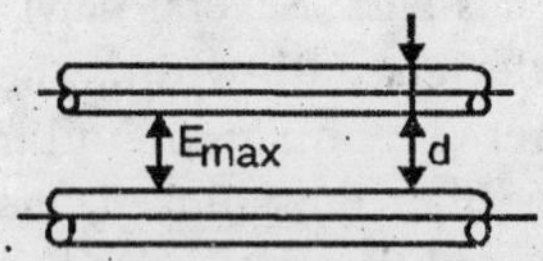	Two-dimensional	Two-dimensional	$E_{max} = \frac{V}{2R \ln [(d+2R)/R]}$	$\frac{2R \ln (d/R)}{d}$ if $\frac{d}{R} >> 4$	Overhead transmission-line arrangements

GROUNDING SYSTEMS

Use of electricity brings with it an electric shock hazard for humans and animals particularly in case defective electrical apparatus. It is therefore necessary to connect the system to ground at suitable points. In case of fault, sufficient current will flow through and operate the protective system isolating the faulty circuit. Hence the connection to ground should be of low resistance.

TABLE : Electrical Properties of Some Insulating Materials

Material	ε_r	*tan δ at 25°C 1 MHz (average)*	*ρv at 25°C (Ω.cm)*	*Breakdown Stress (kV/mm)*
Quartz glass	3.8	5×10^{-4}	10^{17}	
Lead glass	9			
Soda-lime glass	7	0.01		10 – 40
Glass ceramic	5-7	0.001 – 0.1	10^{12} – 10^{14}	20 – 80
Porcelain	5	0.04	10^{12} – 10^{15}	20 – 30
Zirconium ceramic	7-12	0.003		20 – 30
Alumina ceramic	10	0.0005		
Barium titanate ceramic	2000-8000	0.1		
Micanite	5-11	0.003	10^{14} – 10^{16}	50 (for 1-mm specimen) 100-200 (for 0.1- mm specimen)
PVC	6	0.1		
PE	2.3	0.0001	10^{15} – 10^{18}	40
Polystyrene	2.6	0.0001	10^{16} – 10^{18}	30 – 40
PTFE	2	0.0002	10^{16} – 10^{18}	25
Bakelite	4.5	0.1	10^{13}	
Vulcanized natural rubber	3.5	0.05		
Methyl methacrylate	3.6	0.01		

Resistance of a Grounding Point Electrode

The ground resistance of a hemisphere electrode is sum of resistances of an infinite number of thin hemispherical shells of soil (see Fig. 7).

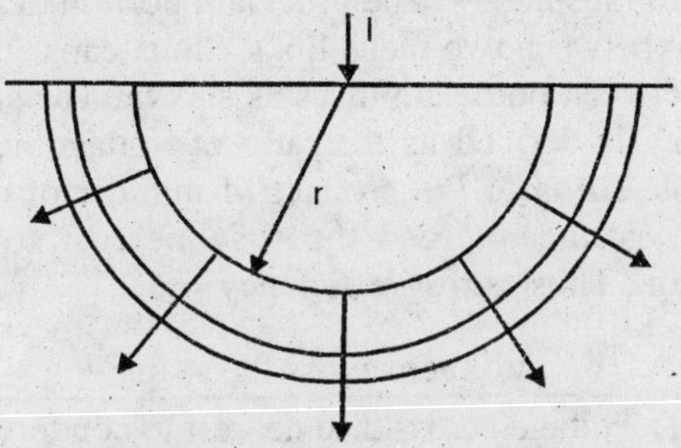

Fig. 7 : *Current entering ground through a hemispherical electrode*

$$R = \int_r^{r_1} \frac{\rho\, dx}{2\pi x^2}$$

$$= \frac{\rho}{2\pi}\left(\frac{1}{r} - \frac{1}{r_1}\right)$$

where ρ is earth resistivity.

As $r_1 = \infty$

$$R_\infty = \frac{\rho}{2\pi r}$$

Resistance of Driven Rods

Driven rod is one of the simplest and most economical forms of electrodes (Fig. 7).

$$R = \frac{\rho}{2\pi l} \ln \frac{4l}{d}$$

If rod is cylindrical with hemispherical end,

$$R = \frac{\rho}{2\pi l} \ln \frac{2l}{d}$$

when rod carries current uniformly along its length

$$R = \frac{\rho}{2\pi l}\left[\ln\left(\frac{8l}{d}\right) - 1\right]$$

The resistance of n rods in parallel is found to exceed $\left(\frac{1}{n}\right)$ of that of a single rod because of their mutual screening. The screening coefficient η for n electrodes in parallel is defined as

$$\eta = \frac{\text{Resistance of one electrode}}{n\text{ (resistance of } n \text{ electrodes in parallel)}}$$

Grounding Grids

To obtain a low ground resistance at high voltage sub-stations we used inter connected ground grids. Size of the grid conductors required to avoid fusing under fault current I is

$$a = I\sqrt{\frac{76\,t}{\ln[(234+T_m)/(234+T_a)]}}$$

where a = copper cross section,

t = fault duration (secs),

T_m = Maximum allowable temperature

T_a = Ambient temperature

Such a grid not only effectively grounds the equipment but has the advantage of controlling the voltage gradients at the surface of the earth to values safe for human contact.

Neutral Grounding

Grounding of the neutral points of generators, transformers, and transmission schemes is an important item in the design of power systems. It has a considerable bearing on the levels of transient and dynamic over-voltages stressing the equipment insulation. It also directly affects the levels of short-circuit currents in the power network and accordingly, the ratings of switchgear needed to cope with them (see Fig. 8).

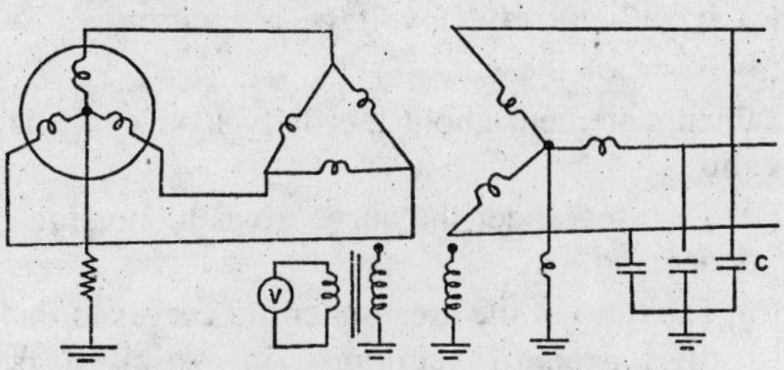

Fig. 8 : *Examples of power system neutral grounding*

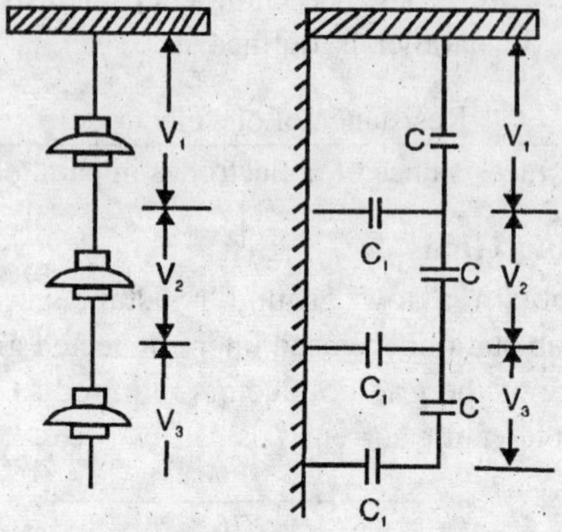

Fig. 9

The methods of system neutral grounding include resistance and low reactance for effective grounding.

String Efficiency

A string of suspension insulators consists of a number of porcelain discs connected in series through metallic links. Fig. 9 shows 3 strings of suspension insulators. The procelain portion of each disc is in between two metal links. Shunt capacitance exists between porcelain discs as shown. The string efficiency is defined as the ratio of voltage across the whole string to the product of number of discs and the voltage across the disc nearest to the conductor. Thus, string efficiency

$$= \frac{\text{Voltage across the string}}{n \times \text{voltage across disc nearest to conductor}}$$

where n is the number of discs in the string.

(i) using longer cross-arms

(ii) grading the insulators

(iii) using a guard ring

EXERCISE

1. Which fault gives rise to symmetrical fault currents?
(a) Single line to ground fault
(b) Line to line fault
(c) Double line to ground fault
(d) Three phase fault

2. Resistance switching is normally resorted in case of
(a) Air blast CB (b) Bulk oil CB
(c) Minimum oil CB (d) All types of CBs.

3. By transmitting power at high voltage
(a) it will give poor voltage regulation
(b) it will give better voltage regulation
(c) it will not effect voltage regulation
(d) None of these

4. Which statement about the daily load curve is valid?
(a) The area under the curve gives the average demand.
(b) The ratio of the area under the curves to the total area of rectangle in which it is contained gives the load factor for the day.
(c) The peak of the curve gives the installed capacity of the plant.
(d) The area of the curves divided by the number of hours gives load factor.

5. High voltage Schring bridge is used to measure
(a) large capacitance without additional element
(b) small capacitance without additional element
(c) medium value capacitance
(d) None of these

6. Draw-in-system of laying underground cables has the drawback(s) of
(a) higher cost
(b) reduced current carrying capacity of the cables
(c) requirements of much deeper and wider trenches
(d) repairs, alterations or additions difficult
(e) all of the above except (d).

7. Surge impedance of a transmission line is
(a) independent of its length
(b) dependent on its length
(c) independent on its temperature
(d) none of the above

8. If two synchronous generators connected in parallel loose synchronism, it will lead to
(a) stalling of generators
(b) wild fluctuations in current
(c) wild fluctuations in current and voltage
(d) None of these

9. A differential relay responds to
(a) algebraic difference of two or more similar electrical quantities
(b) vector difference of two or more similar electrical quantities
(c) algebraic difference between two currents
(d) algebraic difference between two voltages

10. The conductor carries more current on the surface in comparison to its core. This phenomenon is called the
(a) Skin effect (b) Corona
(c) Ferranti effect (d) Lenz's effect

11. A booster is connected in
(a) series with the feeder
(b) parallel with the feeder
(c) both (a) and (b) are correct
(d) none of these

12. Fuses have got advantages of
(a) cheapest type of protection
(b) inverse time-current characteristic
(c) no maintenance
(d) current limiting effect under short-circuit conditions
(e) all of the above

13. The power transmitted will be maximum when
(a) line reactance is high
(b) corona losses are minimum
(c) sending end voltage is more
(d) receiving end voltage is more

14. The connected load of a consumer is 2 kW and his maximum demand is 1.5 kW. The load factor of the consumer is
(a) 0.75 (b) 0.375
(c) 1.33 (d) None of these

15. In a transformer, the exciting current will be in phase quadrature with the impressed voltage provided
(a) only the leakage impedance drop is ignored
(b) only the core loss is ignored
(c) both the leakage impedance drop and the core loss are ignored
(d) only the no-load copper loss is ignored

16. Which of the following techniques is used for the measurements of a.c. high frequency voltages?
(a) Peak voltmeter
(b) Series resistance mircro-ammeter
(c) Resistance potential divider
(d) All of these

17. Use of additional shunt capacitor can be made for increasing the capability of line as it
(a) reduces surge impedance Z_0
(b) increases phase shift β
(c) increase in α
(d) all of the above

18. The sag of a transmission line is least affected owing to
(a) weight of the conductor
(b) current through the conductor
(c) atmospheric temperature
(d) ice deposited on the conductor

19. In case of Impulse Thermal break down of solid insulating materials, the critical electric field is proportional to
(a) critical absolute temperature
(b) square of critical absolute temperature
(c) square of T_0
(d) none of these

20. The insulation of the modern EHV lines is designed based on
(a) corona
(b) switching voltages
(c) lightning voltage
(d) all of these

21. For constant voltage transmission, the voltage drop along the line is maintained constant by installing
(a) capacitors
(b) inductors
(c) resistors
(d) synchronous phase modifiers at the receiving end

22. AC network analyser is employed for solving the problems of
(a) load flow
(b) load flow and stability
(c) load flow and short-circuit
(d) load flow, stability and short-circuit

23. The change in excitation in an alternator connected to an infinite line provides a corresponding change in
(a) terminal voltage (b) speed of rotor
(c) power generated (d) power factor

24. Different types of insulators used for transmission lines are
(a) pin type only
(b) suspension type only
(c) strain type only
(d) pin type, suspension type and shackle type

25. The conductor connecting consumer's terminals to the distributor is called the
(a) feeder (b) distributor
(c) service main (d) none of the above

26. Which of the following method or techniques can be used for the measurement of high d.c. voltages?
(a) Generating voltmeter
(b) Electrostatic voltmeter
(c) Peak voltmeter
(d) Half effect generators

27. The ripple voltage in dc output is small if
(a) frequency of supply voltage is small
(b) the filtering capacitor is small
(c) load current is small
(d) none of these

28. The voltage measurements using uniform spark gap are
(a) affected by dust particles
(b) affected by polarity of supply
(c) affected by temperature
(d) none of these

29. Neutral earthing is provided for
(a) the safety of personnel from electric shock
(b) the safety of equipment and personnel against lightning and voltage surges
(c) reducing the voltage stress on lines and equipment with respect to earth under various operating and fault conditions
(d) controlling the earth fault currents for protective relaying
(e) both (c) and (d)

30. The function of Lightning arrester is
(a) to limiting the short-circuit fault current
(b) to provide path to high voltage surge to earth
(c) to reduce arcing
(d) none of these

31. In which of the following cases are delay fuses used?
(a) For the protection of light circuits
(b) For the protection of power out-let circuits
(c) For the protection of fluorescent lamps
(d) For the protection of motors

32. In order to improve the voltage profile of the line, compensation is resorted by providing
(a) capacitors at the receiving end
(b) reactors at the receiving end
(c) resistors at the receiving end
(d) none of these

33. Skin effect in conductor is proportional to
(a) $(\text{diameter of conductor})^{1/2}$
(b) diameter of conductor
(c) $(\text{diameter of conductor})^2$
(d) $(\text{diameter of conductor})^4$

34. The function of steel wire in an ACSR conductor is to
(a) compensate for skin effect
(b) take care of surges
(c) provide additional mechanical strength
(d) reduce inductance

35. A fault is more severe from the view point of RRRV if it is a
(a) Short length fault
(b) Medium length line fault
(c) Long length line fault
(d) None of these

36. Protective resistance to be connected between the sphere gap and the test equipment is required while measuring
(a) power frequency and higher frequency a.c. voltage
(b) power frequency and impulse voltage
(c) all kinds of voltages
(d) none of these

37. Series capacitor is used in a transmission line to
(a) compensate the voltage drop
(b) reduce line loss
(c) limit short circuit current
(d) improve load power factor

38. The passive element that is used as interconnecting element for the stable operation of interconnected system is
(a) reactor
(b) resistor
(c) capacitor
(d) resistor and capacitor

39. Corona loss in a transmission line is dependent on
(a) diameter of the conductor
(b) material of the conductor
(c) height of the conductor
(d) none of these

40. In a minimum oil circuit breaker the oil is used
(a) to act as circuit breaking medium only
(b) for circuit breaking and providing insulation
(c) for providing insulation only
(d) for none of the above purposes

41. Skin effect is
(a) proportional to frequency
(b) proportional to square of frequency
(c) inversely proportional to frequency
(d) independent of frequency

42. Rated making capacity of breaker is equal to
(a) $\sqrt{2} \times$ rated symmetrical breaking capacity
(b) 2.55 × rated symmetrical breaking capacity
(c) 1 × rated symmetrical breaking capacity
(d) none of these

43. The main reason for using high voltage for long distance power transmission is
(a) reduction in transmission losses
(b) reduction in time of transmission
(c) increase in system reliability
(d) none of the above

44. Bus-coupler is very essential in
(a) single bus-bar arrangement
(b) ring bus-bar arrangement
(c) double bus, double breaker arrangement
(d) main and transfer bus

45. With the rise in temperature, the insulation resistivity
(a) remains unchanged
(b) decreases linearly
(c) increases linearly
(d) reduces exponentially

46. The effect of bonding the cable is
(a) to increase the effective resistance and inductance
(b) to increase the effective resistance but reduce inductance
(c) to reduce the effective resistance and inductance
(d) to reduce the effective resistance but increase the inductance

47. Increase in temperature in overhead transmission lines causes
(a) increase in stress and length
(b) decrease in stress and length
(c) decrease in stress but increase in length
(d) none of the above

48. The insulation resistance of the cable decreases with the
(a) increase in length of cable
(b) decrease in length of cable
(c) electric stresses
(d) none of these

49. Corona has the disadvantage(s) of
(a) power loss
(b) interference with neighbouring communication circuits
(c) introducing the harmonics, predominately third harmonics, into the transmission lines
(d) all of the above

50. In a load duration curve for an intergrated power system the uppermost crest represents the energy contributed by
(a) base power stations
(b) major thermal stations
(c) peaking hydro or gas turbine stations
(d) non-conventional power stations

51. At bridge crossing and near the railway track ternary lead cables are used because they
(a) are of high tensile strength
(b) are of low coefficient of thermal expansion
(c) are of low specific gravity
(d) can withstand shocks and vibrations

52. The heat produced at the contact point owing to flow of electric current is least affected by
(a) temperature of the surrounding medium
(b) contact resistance
(c) magnitude of electric current flowing
(d) duration of flow of current

53. A stationary alternator should not be connected to the live bus-bar because
(a) it is likely to operate as a synchronous motor
(b) it will get short-circuited
(c) it will reduce bus-bar voltage
(d) all of the above

54. In a transmission system the feeder supplies power to
(a) transformer substations (step-up)
(b) service mains
(c) distributors
(d) all of the above

55. For a given amount of power to be transmitted over a certain distance with fixed power loss, the volume of copper required is
(a) directly proportional to voltage
(b) inversely proportional to voltage
(c) inversely proportional to the square of voltage and pf of the load
(d) directly proportional to the square of the voltage and pf of the load

56. Power despatch through a line can be increased by
(a) installing series capacitors
(b) installing shunt capacitors
(c) installing series reactor
(d) installing shunt reactor

57. In the figure shown which curve represents the variation of cost of generation per kWh with the load factor, for a thermal power plant?

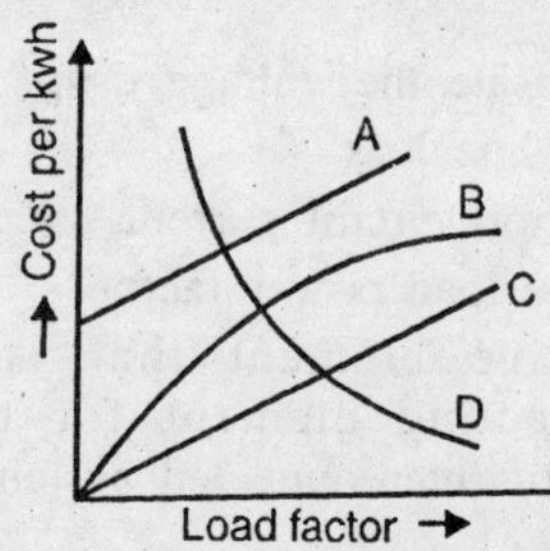

(a) Curve A (b) Curve B
(c) Curve C (d) Curve D

58. Under no load conditions the current in a transmission line is because of
(a) capacitance effect
(b) corona effect
(c) proximity effect
(d) back flow from earth

59. The only advantage of corona is that it
(a) produces a pleasing luminous glow
(b) makes line current sinusoidal
(c) works as a safety valve for surges
(d) ozone gas is produced

60. Earth wires are made of
(a) copper
(b) aluminium
(c) iron
(d) galvanised stranded steel

61. The connected load of a consumer is 2 kW and his maximum demand is 1.5 kW. The demand factor of the consumer is
(a) 0.75 (b) 0.375
(c) 1.33 (d) none of the above

62. A lightning arrester connected between the line and earth in a power system
(a) protects the terminal equipment against travelling surges
(b) protects the terminal equipment against direct lightning stroke
(c) suppresses high frequency oscillations in the line
(d) reflects back the travelling waves approaching it

63. Oil filled cables have the advantage(s) of
(a) smaller overall size
(b) most perfect impregnation
(c) easy detection of fault
(d) all of the above

64. A bus coupler circuit breaker is utilised in a substation for
(a) joining the transmission line with station bus-bar
(b) joining main and transfer bus in a substation
(c) joining the generator with transfer
(d) joining the neutral of the generator with earth

65. The fluids used in circuit breakers should be of
(a) high dielectric strength and thermal stability
(b) non-inflammability
(c) arc extinguishing ability
(d) all of the above

66. Feeder is designed mainly from the point of view of
(a) its current carrying capacity
(b) voltage drop in it
(c) operating voltage
(d) operating frequency

67. Power output per unit volume of an MHD generator is proportional to
(a) specific electrical conductivity of gas
(b) square of the magnetic field strength
(c) square of the fluid velocity
(d) all of the above

68. Increase in frequecy of transmission line causes
(a) no change in line resistance
(b) increase in line resistance
(c) decrease in line resistance
(d) decrease in line series reactance

69. Earth fault relays are
(a) directional relays
(b) non-directional relays
(c) short operate time relays
(d) none of these

70. A dc series generator can excite itself
(a) only on zero load current
(b) only when load current is not zero
(c) irrespective of the value of load current
(d) none of the above

71. Thermal relays are used for protection of motors against over-current owing to
(a) short-circuits (b) heavy loads
(c) earth fault (d) all of these

72. Transmission efficiency of a transmission line increases with the
(a) decrease in power factor and voltage
(b) increase in power factor and voltage
(c) increase in power factor but decrease in voltage
(d) increase in voltage but decrease in power factor

73. While using air-blast circuit breaker, current chopping is a phenomenon often observed when
(a) a long overhead line is switched off
(b) a bank of capacitors is switched off
(c) a trasformer on no-load is switched off
(d) none of these

74. The contact resistance of a circuit breaker is about
(a) 20 Ω (b) 2 Ω
(c) 20 mΩ (d) 20 μΩ

75. Metallic shielding is provided on underground cables to
(a) reduce thermal resistance
(b) reduce corona effect
(c) control the electrostatic voltage stress
(d) all of the above

76. The most economical limit of power factor correcting is governed by
(a) original power factor
(b) relative costs of the supply and power factor correction equipment
(c) both (a) and (b)
(d) none of the above

77. A short-circuit current is identified by
(a) heavy current flow
(b) voltage rise
(c) voltage drop
(d) none of these

78. Which of the following materials is not used for transmission and distribution of electrical power?
(a) Tungsten (b) Copper
(c) Aluminium (d) Cadmium copper

79. Which of the following alternators will have maximum number of poles?
(a) Alternator coupled to hydraulic turbine
(b) Alternator coupled to steam turbine
(c) Alternator coupled to gas turbine
(d) All will have same number of poles

80. In humid weather, the corona occurs at a voltage
(a) much less than the needed in fair weather
(b) much higher than that needed in fair weather
(c) equal to that needed in fair weather
(d) none of the above

81. Short-circuit currents are due to
(a) single phase to earth fault
(b) phase to phase fault
(c) all the three phases to earth fault
(d) all the three phases short-circuited
(e) any of the above

82. Over-current protection respond to
(a) increase in current above pick-up value
(b) single line to earth faults
(c) double line to earth faults
(d) all of the above

83. A fuse is
(a) always connected in series with the circuit
(b) always connected in parallel with the circuit
(c) normally connected in series with the circuit
(d) none of these

84. Standard impulse testing of power transformer requires
(a) one application of chopped wave followed by one application of full-wave
(b) two applications of chopped wave followed by an application of a full-wave
(c) one application of chopped wave followed by two application of a full-wave
(d) none of these

85. The presence of earth in case of overhead lines
(a) increases the capacitance
(b) increases the inductance
(c) decreases the capacitance and increases the inductance
(d) does not effect any of the line constants

86. Partial discharge measurement on a cable gives
(a) p.f of the cable
(b) loss angle of the cable
(c) location of fault
(d) None of these

87. Any leakage of air into the condenser destroys the vacuum and causes
(a) an increase in air pressure in the condenser limiting the useful heat drop in the steam turbine
(b) lowering of the partial pressure of the steam and of the saturation temperature along with it
(c) undercooling of the condensate more severe
(d) all of the above

88. The intersheaths in cables are used to
(a) provide proper stress distribution
(b) minimize the stress
(c) provide protection against moisture and voltage surges
(d) provide protection against current and voltage surges

89. The string efficiency of insulators can be increased by
(a) reducing the number of strings
(b) increasing the number of strings
(c) correct grading of insulators of various strings
(d) none of these

90. Which one of the following statements regarding the position of minimum copper loss in a phase of rotary convertor is true?
(a) The position of minimum copper loss is in the middle of the phase whatever may be the power factor
(b) The position of minimum copper loss varies with the variation in power factor and this position is displaced from the middle of the phase by the power factor angle
(c) The position of minimum copper loss is the tapping point whatever may be the power factor
(d) None of the above

91. In order to have lower cost of electrical generation
(a) the load factor and diversity factor should be high
(b) the load factor should be low but diversity factor high
(c) the load factor should be high but diversity factor low
(d) the load factor and diversity factor should be low

92. The stability limit of system is defined as the value of power below which
(a) the system is stable and above which also stable
(b) the system is unstable and above which it is stable
(c) the system is stable and above which it is unstable
(d) none of these

93. Swing equation represents
(a) the variation of power with respect to time
(b) the variation of torque angle with respect to time
(c) the variation of input power with respect to time
(d) none of these

94. In case of Impulse Thermal breakdown of insulating materials, the critical time to breakdown is
(a) proportional to critical electric field
(b) inversely proportional to critical electric field
(c) proportional to square of critical absolute temperature
(d) none of these

95. Economiser in a steam power plant
(a) improves the boiler efficiency by 10-12%
(b) saves fuel consumption by 5-15%
(c) becomes a necessity for pressure
(d) none of these

96. Conductor configuration determine
(a) inductance (b) sag
(c) voltage (d) current

97. If the length of the arc of circuit breaker increases, its resistance
(a) be extinguished (b) decreases
(c) remains same (d) none of these

98. If the frequency of a transmission system is changed from 50 Hz to 100 Hz, the string efficiency
(a) will increase
(b) will decrease
(c) remain unchanged
(d) may increase or decrease depending on the line parameters

99. The pressurised water reactors employ
(a) light water and natural uranium
(b) heavy water and enriched uranium
(c) light water and enriched uranium
(d) none of the above combinations

100. The suitable turbine used for harnessing tidal power is
(a) Francis turbine (b) Pelton turbine
(c) Kaplan turbine (d) None of these

101. In an AC Transmission line, difference in phase of voltages at the two ends of the line is due to
(a) resistance of line (b) system voltage
(c) reactance of line (d) insulators

102. Steam power plants work closely on
(a) Binary vapour cycle
(b) Brayton cycle
(c) Rankine cycle
(d) Carnot cycle

103. If the tariff for electrical energy charges provides incentive by way of reduced charges for higher consumption, then it may be concluded that the
(a) load factor is high
(b) power factor is high
(c) plant has sufficient reserve capacity
(d) power is generated through hydro-power plant

104. In overhead lines, the presence of earth wire causes
(a) increase in the capacitance
(b) increase in the inductance
(c) decrease in the capacitance
(d) decrease in the inductance

105. The use of reactors permits installation of circuit breakers of the
(a) lower rating (b) higher rating
(c) same rating (d) none of these

106. In power plants, the condenser normally used is
(a) Surface type
(b) Jet type
(c) Both surface and jet type
(d) Regenerative type

107. The critical mass of a nuclear reactor depends upon
(a) the enrichment of the fuel used
(b) the moderator material used
(c) both the enrichment of fuel and moderator material
(d) none of these

108. When the load on a transmission line is equal to the surge impedance loading
(a) the receiving end voltage is less than the sending end voltage
(b) the sending end voltage is less than the receiving end voltage
(c) the receiving end voltage is equal to the sending end voltage
(d) none of these

109. In a power plant, a reserve generating capacity which is not in service but is in operation is known as
(a) hot reserve (b) cold reserve
(c) firm power (d) spinning reserve

110. What is the advantage of hydro-electric power stations over thermal power stations?
(a) The initial cost of hydro-electric power stations is low.
(b) Their operating cost is low.
(c) Hydro-electric power stations can supply the same power throughout the year.
(d) Hydro-electric power stations can be constructed where electric energy is required.

111. Galvanised steel wire is usually used as
(a) stay wire
(b) earth wire
(c) structural components
(d) all of the above

112. It is always economical to improve the p.f. of an installation to
(a) zero
(b) unity
(c) a little less than unity
(d) a little more than unity

113. The efficiency of a transmission line
(a) increases with the decrease in load p.f.
(b) is independent of load p.f.
(c) increases with the increase in load p.f.
(d) decreases with the increase in load p.f.

114. If the source is not able to supply charging current required by the test cable, it is desirable to use
(a) shunt capacitor (b) series capacitor
(c) series inductor (d) none of these

115. Isolated neutral transmission system is not recommended as the
(a) system insulation is overstressed due to over-voltages
(b) insulation overstress may lead to its failure resulting in phase to phase faults
(c) system is not adequately protected against earth fault
(d) all of the above

116. The power loss in an overload transmission line is mainly due
(a) impedance of the line conductor
(b) resistance of each conductor
(c) inductance of each conductor
(d) capacitance of each conductor

117. Sulphur hexafluoride cable is insulated by
(a) impregnated paper
(b) polyvinyl chloride
(c) high pressure oil
(d) compressed gas

118. The voltage of a bus can be controlled by controlling the
(a) phase angle
(b) reactive power of the bus
(c) active power of the bus
(d) phase angle and the reactive power

119. A three phase breaker is rated at 2000 MVA, 33 kV, its making current will be
(a) 35 kA (b) 70 kA
(c) 89 kA (d) 160 kA

120. The insulation used in a cable designed for use on 1000 kV is usually
(a) impregnated paper
(b) compressed SF_6 gas
(c) PVC
(d) any of the above

121. The main function of under voltage protective device generally employed with a motor starter is to
(a) open the supply circuit on failure of power supply
(b) control the motor voltage
(c) prevent the opening of supply circuit
(d) none of the above

122. Which of the following power plants is free from environmental problems?
(a) Diesel engine (b) Nuclear
(c) Hydro-electric (d) Steam

123. Which of the following is not a secondary nuclear fuel?
(a) Pu_{239} (b) U_{233}
(c) U_{235} (d) None of above

124. The purpose of the moderator in a nuclear power plant is to
(a) control the flow of water inlet
(b) control the amount of nuclear fuel into the reactor
(c) control the nuclear fission or fission rate by slowing down the neutrons
(d) control the steam flow to the turbine

125. Rotating machines are protected against lightning surges by a combination of
(a) lightning conductor and capacitor
(b) lightning conductor and lightning arrester
(c) lightning arrester and capacitor
(d) none of these

126. The gas turbine power plant can be used in combination with steam power plants by
(a) using exhaust gases from gas turbine power plant in heating of feed water coming from the steam trubine condenser
(b) using exhaust gases from gas turbine power plant as combustion air in steam boiler
(c) using gas from a supercharged boiler for expansion in gas turbine
(d) any of the above

127. Skin effect
(a) increases the effective resistance and effective internal reactance
(b) reduces the effective resistance and effective internal reactance
(c) increases the effective resistance but reduces the effective internal reactance
(d) reduces the effective resistance but increases the effective internal reactance

128. The critical clearing time is related to
(a) steady state stability limit
(b) transient stability limit
(c) short-circuit current limit
(d) none of these

129. As compared to air the relative dielectric strength of sulphur hexafluoride is nearly
(a) 1.5 times (b) 2.5 times
(c) 4.0 times (d) 5.0 times

130. The relay best suited for phase fault relaying for medium transmission lines is
(a) mho relay (b) reactance relay
(c) impedance relay (d) none of these

131. In parallel operation of alternators, the synchronising power will be maximum when
(a) armatures have resistances equal to their reactances
(b) armatures have resistances more than their reactances
(c) armatures have resistances lesser than their reactances
(d) none of the above

132. An adjustable blade propeller turbine is called a
(a) Pelton turbine (b) Kaplan turbine
(c) Francis turbine (d) None of them

133. The criterion for selection of size of conductor for a feeder is
(a) Voltage drop (b) Corona loss
(c) Temperature rise (d) Radio interference

134. Inverse time-current relays are used for the protection of
(a) feeders (b) transformers
(c) alternators (d) both (a) and (b)

135. Surge voltage originate in power system due to
(a) lightening
(b) switching operations
(c) faults
(d) all of these

136. The proximate analysis of coal gives percentage by weight of
(a) moisture and volatile matter
(b) moisture, volatile matter, fixed carbon and ash
(c) carbon, hydrogen, oxygen, nitrogen, sulphur and ash
(d) carbon, hydrogen and oxygen

137. A gas turbine works on
(a) Carnot cycle (b) Brayton cycle
(c) Dual cycle (d) Rankine cycle
(e) Regenerative cycle

138. Which of the following protects the underground cables against mechanical injury?
(a) Armouring (b) Bedding
(c) Sheath (d) None of these

139. Coal and peat is not generally used in gas turbines as fuel because of
(a) coal handling and ash handling problems
(b) their higher costs
(c) their non-availability
(d) all of the above

140. A 1000 kVA transformer with 5% reactance will have a reactance of 10% at
(a) 1000 kVA base (b) 2000 kVA base
(c) 3000 kVA base (d) 4000 kVA base

141. In circuit breakers the contact space is ionized by
(a) field emission from the contact surface
(b) thermal emission from the contact surface
(c) thermal ionization of gas
(d) any of the above

142. When extra stop buttons are added to an existing starter control circuit they must be
(a) in series with the contactor coil
(b) parallel to the overload
(c) parallel to the start button
(d) in series with the motor

143. In a transmission line, if the load is suddenly increased in the receiving end of the system, the phase shift will
(a) decrease (b) become zero
(c) increase (d) not be affected

144. In case of inter-connected system for stable operation the passive element that can be used as interconnecting element is
(a) capacitor (b) reactor
(c) resistor (d) any of these

145. The rate of rise of restriking voltage depends upon
(a) the type of Circuit Breaker
(b) the inductance of the system only
(c) the capacitance of the system only
(d) the inductance and capacitance of the system

146. To increase the transmission capability of a high voltage long line
(a) the resistance can be increased
(b) the resistance can be decreased
(c) the series reactance can be reduced
(d) the shunt admittance can be reduced

147. In Van de Graff generator, output voltage is controlled by
(a) controlling the corona source voltage
(b) controlling the belt speed
(c) controlling the lower spray point
(d) all of these

148. In a dc 3-wire distributor using balancers and having unequal loads on the two sides
(a) both balancers operate as generators
(b) both balancers operate as motors
(c) balancer connected to lightly loaded side operates as a generator
(d) balancer connected to heavily loaded side operates as a generator

149. In context of corona which statement is not true?
(a) Corona is voltage effect.
(b) Corona takes place on short transmission lines.
(c) Corona is accompanied with power loss.
(d) Corona attenuates lightning surges.

150. The frequency of voltage generated can be increased by
(a) adjusting the governor
(b) increasing the excitation
(c) reducing the excitation
(d) any of the above

151. The advantage of transmitting power at high voltage is
(a) magnitude of current will be small
(b) it will reduce the voltage drop in the line impedance
(c) power loss will be less
(d) all of these

152. If the height of the transmission tower is changed, which of the following parameters is likely to change?
(a) Resistance (b) Inductance
(c) Capacitance (d) None of the above

153. The sag of a power line with 100 m span is 1m, what will be the sag if the height of the line is increased by 20%
(a) 1.6 m (b) 1.5 m
(c) 2 m (d) 2.5 m

154. A synchronous condenser is virtually a/an
(a) induction motor
(b) over excited synchronous motor
(c) under excited synchronous motor
(d) commutator motor

155. The thickness of insulation layer provided on the conductor in cables depends upon
(a) operating voltage (b) current to be carried
(c) power factor (d) none of these

156. A single phase line is transmitting 1,100 kW power to a factory at 11 kV and at 0.8 pf lagging. It has a total resistance of 2 Ω and a loop reactance of 3 Ω. The voltage at sending end, percentage regulation and transmission efficiency will be respectively.
(a) 11854 V; 7.76% and 94.62%
(b) 11426 V; 3.73% and 97.24%
(c) 11426 V; 3.87% and 97.24%
(d) 11426 V; 3.87% and 94.62%

157. The steepness of the wave front can be reduced by connecting
(a) an inductor in series with the line
(b) a capacitor between line and earth
(c) either (a) or (b)
(d) an inductor between line and earth or a capacitor in series with the line

158. Which of the following is correct statement regarding insulators and lightning arresters?
(a) The insulators and lightning arresters should have high impulse ratio.
(b) The insulators and lightning arresters should have low impulse ratio.
(c) The insulator should have high impulse ratio and lightning arrester low.
(d) The lightning arrester should have high impulse ratio but insulator low.

159. The distribution transformers is generally connected in
(a) Delta/Delta (b) Star/Delta
(c) Delta/Star (d) Star/Star

160. In a two stage gas turbine power plant intercooling and reheating
(a) improves the work ratio but reduces the thermal efficiency
(b) reduces the work ratio but improves the thermal efficiency
(c) improves both of the work ratio and thermal efficiency
(d) reduces both of the work ratio and thermal efficiency

161. Directional over-current relay is used for protection of
(a) long transmission line
(b) large power transformer
(c) ring main distribution line
(d) radial distribution line

162. What is the most serious problem in vacuum circuit breaker?
(a) Poor arc quenching
(b) Low thermal stability
(c) Current chopping
(d) All of these

163. If the dielectric strength of the medium between contacts builds up more rapidly than the restriking voltage. Then the arc will
(a) be extinguished
(b) not be extinguished
(c) increase
(d) none of these

164. The operation of thermo-electric generator is based on
(a) Seebeck effect (b) Hall effect
(c) Peltier effect (d) None of these

165. Oil filled cables have the advantage(s) of
(a) no ionisation, oxidation and formation of voids
(b) possibility of increased temperature range in service
(c) more maximum permissible stresses
(d) all of the above

166. In a static over-current relay, inverse time characteristics are obtained by
(a) a transistor amplifier
(b) an integrating circuit
(c) a transistor switch
(d) a differentiating circuit

167. In a transmission line sag depends upon
(a) span length
(b) tension in conductors
(c) weight of the conductor per unit length
(d) all of the above

168. The CANDU type reactor can be shut down by controlling
(a) safety rod (b) shim rod
(c) regulating rod (d) none of the above

169. Buchholz relay is used for protection in case of a
(a) transformer
(b) synchronous generator
(c) bus-bar
(d) induction motor

170. Run away speed of a pelton wheel is
(a) full load speed
(b) actual speed operating at no load
(c) no load speed when governor mechanism fails
(d) 80% greater than the normal speed

171. For a transmission line the standing wave ratio is the ratio of
(a) peak voltage to rms voltage
(b) maximum current to minimum current
(c) maximum voltage to minimum voltage
(d) maximum impedance to minimum impedance

172. In a steam power plant water is used for cooling purpose in
(a) condenser
(b) turbine only
(c) boiler tubes
(d) boiler tubes and turbine both

173. For low head and high discharge, the hydraulic turbine used is
(a) Francis turbine (b) Kaplan turbine
(c) Pelton wheel (d) None of these

174. A Kaplan turbine is
(a) inward flow, impulse turbine
(b) outward flow, reaction turbine
(c) a high head mixed flow turbine
(d) low head axial flow turbine

175. In which of the following circuits there may be zero sequence components?
(a) Line voltage of star circuit
(b) Phase voltage of star circuit
(c) Line current of delta circuit
(d) None of these

176. Which of the following relays does not make use of electromagnetic force?
(a) Attracted armature type relay
(b) Solenoid and plunger type impedance relay
(c) Static relay
(d) Induction type relay

177. The frequency of Trichel pulses
(a) increases with voltage and gap pressure
(b) increases with voltage and decreases with gap pressure
(c) decreases with increase in voltage and pressure
(d) none of these

178. Which of the following equipments is installed in steam power plants to reduce air pollution?
(a) Desuper heater
(b) Air filter
(c) Air electrostatic precipitator
(d) Stock

179. An air blast circuit breaker is usually employed for
(a) instantaneous duty
(b) intermittent duty
(c) repeated duty
(d) short duty

180. Thermal shielding is provided to
(a) absorb the fast neutrons
(b) protect the operating personnel from exposure to radiations
(c) prevent the reactor wall from getting heated
(d) all of the above

181. In medium transmission lines the shunt capacitance is taken into account in
(a) end condenser method
(b) π method
(c) T-method
(d) all of the above

182. Transient disturbances are caused by
(a) sudden load changes
(b) switching operations
(c) inadvertent tripping of lines and generators
(d) faults in the power system
(e) all of the above

183. Electromechanical breakdown of solid insulating materials occurs due to
(a) magnetic hum
(b) vibrations
(c) mechanical stresses produced by the electrical field
(d) electrical stresses produced by the voltage fluctuations

184. Coal rank classifies coal as per its
(a) specific gravity
(b) degree of metamorphism
(c) carbon percentage
(d) ash content

185. If the capacitance between two conductors of a 3-phase line is 6 μF, the capacitance of each conductor to neutral will be
(a) 3 μF (b) 12 μF
(c) 6 μF (d) 1.5 μF

186. If ACSR conductor has specification as 48/7, which of the following statement is correct for the conductor?
(a) The conductor has 48 strands.
(b) The conductor has 55 strands.

(c) The conductor has 48 aluminium and 7 steel strands.
(d) The conductor has 48 steel and 7 aluminium strands.

187. A generating station which has a high investment cost and low operating cost is usually operated as a
(a) peak load station
(b) base load station
(c) medium load station
(d) none of the above

188. The nuclear reactor starts generation when
(a) the safety rod is inserted into the core
(b) the safety rod is withdrawn from the core
(c) the shim rod is inserted into the core
(d) the shim rod is withdrawn from the core

189. When all the three phases are short circuited it gives rise to
(a) asymmetrical fault currents
(b) symmetrical fault current
(c) zero current
(d) none of these

190. The string efficiency of a string of suspension insulators is dependent on
(a) size of the insulators
(b) number of discs in the string
(c) size of tower
(d) none of these

191. SF_6 circuit breakers have the advantages of
(a) very much reduced electrical clearance, reduced moisture problem and minimum current chopping problem
(b) noiseless operation, less arcing time resulting in less contact erosion
(c) no reduction in dielectric strength of SF_6
(d) performance independent of ambient conditions
(e) all of the above

192. In order to have lower cost of electrical energy generation it is required to have
(a) low load factor and low diversity factor
(b) low load factor but high diversity factor
(c) high load factor but low diversity factor
(d) high load factor and high diversity factor

193. The rate of rise of restriking voltage depends on
(a) the type of circuit breaker
(b) the inductance of the system only
(c) the capacitance of the system
(d) the inductance and capacitance of the system only

194. The potential across the various discs of suspension string is different because of
(a) series capacitance
(b) shunt capacitance
(c) series and shunt capacitance
(d) none of these

195. The dielectric strength of air under normal conditions is around
(a) 30 kV/cm (b) 100 kV/cm
(c) 150 kV/cm (d) 200 kV/cm

196. For magnetic blow out of arc the magnetic field is produced
(a) in the load circuit
(b) at right angles to the axis of the arc
(c) in line with the axis of the arc
(d) any of the above

197. The most suitable material for transformer core is
(a) hot rolled grain oriented steel
(b) cold rolled grain oriented steel (CRGOS)
(c) cast steel
(d) aluminium

198. The torque developed by a 3-phase induction motor depends upon
(a) rotor phase resistance
(b) rotor standstill phase reactance
(c) applied voltage
(d) slip
(e) all of the above

199. The breaking capacity of a 3-phase circuit breaker is given as
(a) service line voltage in volts × rated symmetrical current in amperes × 10^{-6} MVA
(b) $\sqrt{3}$ service line voltage in volts × rated symmetrical curent in amperes × 10^{-6} MVA
(c) 1.1 × service line voltage in volts × rated symmetrical current in amperes × 10^{-6} MVA
(d) $\sqrt{2}$ service line voltage in volts × rated symmetrical current in amperes × 10^{-6} MVA

200. The factor that is not responsible for drop terminal voltage of a dc shunt generator load is
(a) commutation
(b) armature reaction
(c) armature resistance drop
(d) field weakening due to (b) and (c)

201. A 3-phase synchronous generator with constant excitation is supplying electrical power to an infinite bus-bar at lagging power factor. If the power input is reduced
(a) both power factor and power angle will increase
(b) both power factor and power angle will decrease
(c) power factor will increase but power angle will decrease
(d) power factor will decrease but power angle will increase

202. The medium sized induction motor will operate at maximum power factor while operating at
(a) full load
(b) 50 per cent full load
(c) 25 per cent full load
(d) any load

203. The draught produced by a chimney is called the
(a) forced draught (b) induced draught
(c) natural draught (d) balanced draught

204. Air used in air blast circuit breaker must
(a) be ionized
(b) be free from moisture
(c) have least CO_2
(d) have oil mist

ANSWERS

1	2	3	4	5	6	7	8	9	10
(d)	(a)	(b)	(d)	(b)	(e)	(a)	(c)	(b)	(a)
11	**12**	**13**	**14**	**15**	**16**	**17**	**18**	**19**	**20**
(a)	(e)	(c)	(d)	(c)	(a)	(a)	(b)	(c)	(a)
21	**22**	**23**	**24**	**25**	**26**	**27**	**28**	**29**	**30**
(d)	(d)	(d)	(d)	(c)	(a)	(d)	(a)	(e)	(b)
31	**32**	**33**	**34**	**35**	**36**	**37**	**38**	**39**	**40**
(d)	(a)	(c)	(c)	(a)	(a)	(a)	(a)	(a)	(a)
41	**42**	**43**	**44**	**45**	**46**	**47**	**48**	**49**	**50**
(a)	(b)	(a)	(b)	(d)	(b)	(c)	(a)	(d)	(c)
51	**52**	**53**	**54**	**55**	**56**	**57**	**58**	**59**	**60**
(c)	(a)	(b)	(c)	(c)	(a)	(d)	(a)	(c)	(d)
61	**62**	**63**	**64**	**65**	**66**	**67**	**68**	**69**	**70**
(a)	(a)	(d)	(b)	(d)	(a)	(b)	(b)	(d)	(b)
71	**72**	**73**	**74**	**75**	**76**	**77**	**78**	**79**	**80**
(a)	(b)	(c)	(d)	(d)	(b)	(a)	(a)	(a)	(a)
81	**82**	**83**	**84**	**85**	**86**	**87**	**88**	**89**	**90**
(e)	(a)	(a)	(b)	(a)	(c)	(d)	(a)	(b)	(b)

91	92	93	94	95	96	97	98	99	100
(a)	(c)	(b)	(b)	(b)	(a)	(a)	(c)	(c)	(c)
101	**102**	**103**	**104**	**105**	**106**	**107**	**108**	**109**	**110**
(c)	(c)	(c)	(a)	(a)	(a)	(c)	(c)	(a)	(b)
111	**112**	**113**	**114**	**115**	**116**	**117**	**118**	**119**	**120**
(d)	(c)	(c)	(c)	(b)	(b)	(d)	(b)	(c)	(b)
121	**122**	**123**	**124**	**125**	**126**	**127**	**128**	**129**	**130**
(a)	(c)	(c)	(c)	(c)	(d)	(c)	(b)	(b)	(a)
131	**132**	**133**	**134**	**135**	**136**	**137**	**138**	**139**	**140**
(a)	(b)	(c)	(b)	(d)	(b)	(b)	(a)	(a)	(b)
141	**142**	**143**	**144**	**145**	**146**	**147**	**148**	**149**	**150**
(d)	(a)	(c)	(b)	(d)	(c)	(a)	(d)	(b)	(a)
151	**152**	**153**	**154**	**155**	**156**	**157**	**158**	**159**	**160**
(d)	(c)	(a)	(b)	(a)	(c)	(c)	(c)	(c)	(a)
161	**162**	**163**	**164**	**165**	**166**	**167**	**168**	**169**	**170**
(c)	(c)	(a)	(a)	(d)	(b)	(d)	(d)	(d)	(c)
171	**172**	**173**	**174**	**175**	**176**	**177**	**178**	**179**	**180**
(c)	(a)	(b)	(d)	(b)	(c)	(a)	(c)	(c)	(d)
181	**182**	**183**	**184**	**185**	**186**	**187**	**188**	**189**	**190**
(d)	(e)	(c)	(b)	(b)	(c)	(b)	(c)	(b)	(b)
191	**192**	**193**	**194**	**195**	**196**	**197**	**198**	**199**	**200**
(e)	(d)	(d)	(c)	(a)	(b)	(b)	(e)	(b)	(a)
201	**202**	**203**	**204**						
(c)	(a)	(c)	(b)						

2. A.C. MACHINES AND D.C. MACHINES

TRANSFORMER

A transformer is a static device which transfers a.c. electrical power from one circuit to the other at the same frequency through magnetic flux linking both the circuits, by electro-magnetic induction (Fig. 1).

For step up transformer $V_2 > V_1$

For step down transformer $V_2 < V_1$

where

V_1 = voltage applied across primary
V_2 = voltage applied across secondary
E_1 = emf developed in primary
E_2 = emf developed in secondary
N_1 = no. of turns in primary
N_2 = no. of turns in secondary

$$\frac{V_2}{V_1} = \frac{E_2}{E_1} = \frac{N_2}{N_1} = \frac{I_1}{I_0} = n$$

When secondary winding is open circuited, *i.e.*, secondary current is zero, a very small exciting current I_0 is drawn by the primary. It supplies iron losses (hysteresis and eddy current) in the core and a very small amount of copper losses in the primary.

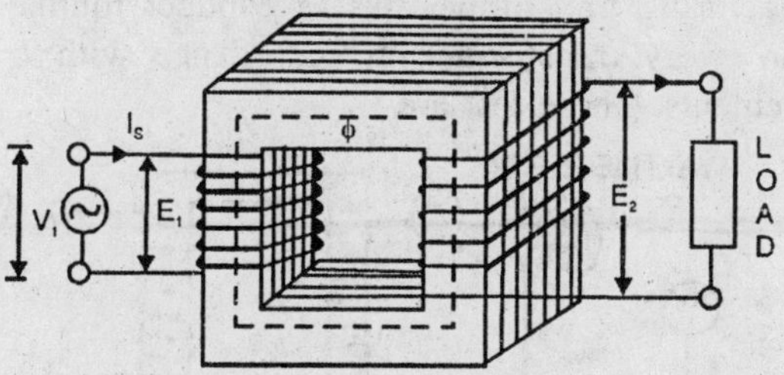

Fig. 1

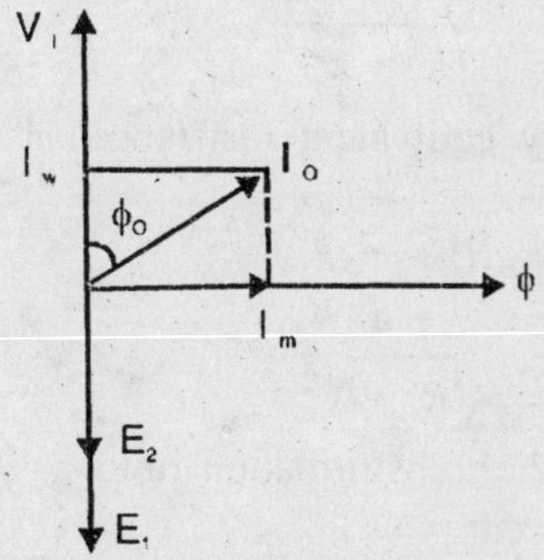

Fig. 2 : *Phasor diagram at no load*

Hence, I_0 lags the voltage V_1 by an angle ϕ (called the hysteresis angle).

(i) I_w in phase with the applied voltage V_1 called active or working component. It supplies the iron losses and a small primary copper loss.

(ii) I_m in qudrature with the applied voltage V_1 called reactive or magnetising component. It produces flux in the core and does not consume any power (Fig. 2).

Working component

$$I_w = I_0 \cos \phi_0$$

Magnetising component,

$$I_m = I_0 \sin \phi_0$$

No-load current

$$I_0 = \sqrt{I_w^2 + I_m^2}$$

Transformer Equation

E.m.f. induced in the transformer is given by the following equations

$$E_1 = 4.44 \, f \, N_1 \, \phi_m \text{ volts},$$

$$E_2 = 4.44 \, f \, N_2 \, \phi_m \text{ volts}$$

where E_1 and E_2 are induced emfs

f = frequency of ac in Hertz

N_1 and N_2 = number of turns and

ϕ_m = peak flux in webers.

Equivalent resistance of a transformer as referred to primary is

$$R_P = R_p + \frac{R_s}{n^2}$$

$$X_P = X_p + \frac{X_s}{n^2}$$

$$Z_P = \sqrt{R_p^2 + X_p^2}$$

Similarly equivalent resistance as referred to secondary is

$$R_s = R_s + n^2 R_p$$

$$X_s = X_s + n^2 X_p$$

$$Z_s = \sqrt{R_s^2 + X_s^2}$$

where n is the transformation ratio.

No load current

$$(I_0) = \sqrt{I_w^2 + I_m^2}$$

where I_m = magnetising current

I_w = working current

Losses in a Transformer

The losses in a transformer are:

(i) Copper losses: These occur due to resistance in winding and also eddy currents in the conductors. These losses are proportional to the square of the load current.

(ii) Iron losses: These occur due to hysteresis and eddy currents in the core. These losses are constant irrespective of the load current.

Transformer Efficiency

Transformer Efficiency is given by

$$\eta = \frac{\text{Output}}{\text{Output + losses}}$$

$$= \frac{\text{Output}}{\text{Output + copper losses + iron losses}}$$

For maximum efficiency of a transformer

Copper losses = Iron losses

All-day efficiency

All-day efficiency =

$$\frac{\text{Output kWh per 24 hours}}{\text{kWh output in 24 hours + kWh wasted in loses in 24 hours}}$$

Testing of Transformers

The performance of a transformer can be determined when the following parameters are known:

1. Equivalent resistance as referred to primary or as referred to the secondary.
2. Equivalent reactance as referred to the pimary or as referred to the secondary.
3. The core loss at no load due to resistance at no load.
4. The magnetising current I_m'and the reactance at no load.

For this purposes, two tests are commonly conducted on transformers. These are:

1. Open circuit test: In this one winding is kept open and the other connected to the supply of normal voltage and frequency. Due to small no load current, copper losses will be very small on the winding connected to voltage source. There will be no copper losses on open circuited winding. The watt-meter reading will give the iron losses. The voltmeter is so connected with the pressure coil of the watt-meter that the current through it does not pass through the current of the coil of the watt meter (see Fig. 3).

The applied voltage being a small fraction, only about (10 per cent of the normal voltage) the flux produced is also a small fraction of the normal flux. Hence, the core losses are negligible, and the watt-meter reading is equal to the copper losses.

Also power factor, $\cos \phi = \frac{P}{E_p I_p}$

where P is the watt-meter reading.

Other tests on transformers: A factory manufacturing transformer has to conduct routine test on every transformer in accordance with I_S requirements. These test are

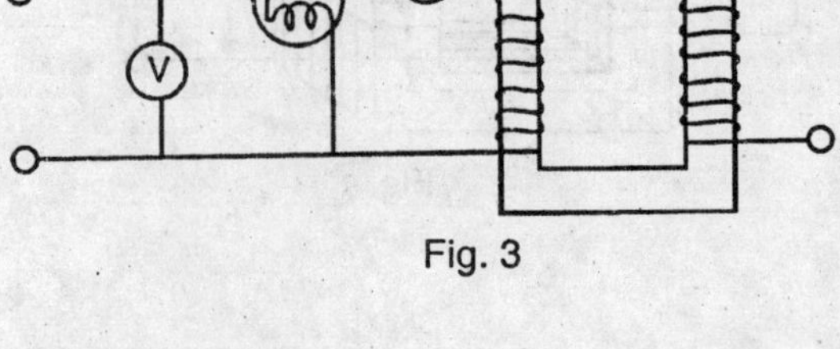

Fig. 3

1. Ratio and polarity test
2. Load losses test
3. Impedance test
4. Insulation resistance test
5. Resistane of winding
6. No load losses
7. No load current
8. Voltage tests
9. Core insulation voltage test

2. Short circuit test: Following parameters can be measured with the help of this test.

(i) Equivalent resistance and equivalent reactance and hence equivalent impedance.

(ii) Full load copper losses.

During this test, low voltage winding is short circuited and a reduced voltage of sufficient magnitude is applied to cause a certain rated current (full load current) to circulate in the short circuit. In case secondary is short circuited the voltage applied on the primary will be a small fraction of the normal voltage (otherwise the winding will burn out).

Every transformer is expected to satisfy the following types of test:

1. Temperature rise test
2. Impulse voltage test
3. Noise level test

These special tests are conducted whenever purchaser desires and in accordance with terms of agreement.

Saving of Copper in Auto Transformer

Weight of copper in AC section $\propto (N_1 - N_2)\, I_1$

Weight of copper in BC section $\propto (I_2 - I_1)\, N_2$

So, total weight of copper in auto-transformer is $\propto (N_1 - N_2).\, I_1 + N_2\,(I_2 - I_1)$

In a two winding transformer total weight of copper $\propto N_1 I_1 + N_2 I_2$

$$\frac{\text{weight of Cu in auto transformer}}{\text{weight of Cu in two winding transformer}}$$

$$= \frac{(N_1 - N_2)I_1 + N_2(I_2 - I_1)}{N_1 I_1 + N_2 I_2}$$

$$= 1 - \frac{2\times\dfrac{N_2}{N_1}}{\left(1+\dfrac{N_2}{N_1}.\dfrac{I_2}{I_1}\right)}$$

$$= 1 - \frac{2n}{2} = 1 - n$$

Weight of Cu in auto transformer

$= (1 - n)$ wt. of Cu in two winding transformer.

VOLTAGE REGULATION OF TRANSFORMER

At a constant supply voltage, the change in secondary terminal voltage from no-load to full-load with respect to no-load voltage is called voltage regulation of the transformer.

If E_2 = Secondary terminal voltage at no load

V_2 = Secondary terminal voltage at full load

$$\textbf{\% regulation} = \frac{E_2 - V_2}{E_2} \times 100$$

Approximate expression for voltage regulation

1. For inductive load:

$$E_2 = V_2 + I_2\,\text{Res}\cos\phi_2 + I_2\,\text{Xes}\sin\phi_2$$

or $$E_2 - V_2 = I_2\,\text{Res}\cos\phi_2 + I_2\,\text{Xes}\sin\phi_2$$

or $$\frac{E_2 - V_2}{E_2}\times 100 = \frac{I_2\text{Res}}{E_2}\times 100\cos\phi_2 + \frac{I_2\text{Xes}}{E_2}\times 100\sin\phi_2$$

where

$$\frac{I_2\text{Res}}{E_2}\times 100 = \text{percentage resistance drop}$$

and

$$\frac{I_2\text{Xes}}{E_2}\times 100 = \text{percentage reactance drop}$$

$\therefore$ % Reg = % resistance drop × cos ϕ_2 + % reactance drop × sin ϕ_2

2. *For resistive load:*

$$E_2 = V_2 + I_2 \text{ Res}$$

or, $$E_2 - V_2 = I_2 \text{ Res}$$

or, $$\frac{E_2 - V_2}{E_2} \times 100 = \frac{I_2\text{Res}}{E_2} \times 100$$

$$\% \text{ Reg} = \% \text{ resistance drop}$$

3. *For capacitive load*

$$E_2 = V_2 + I_2 \text{ Res} \cos \phi_2 - I_2 \text{ Xes} \sin \phi_2$$

or, $$E_2 - V_2 = I_2 \text{ Res } \phi_2 - I_2 \text{ Xes} \sin \phi_2$$

or, $$\frac{E_2 - V_2}{E_2} \times 100 = \frac{I_2\text{Res}}{E_2} \times 100 \cos \phi_2 - \frac{I_2\text{Xes}}{E_2} \times 100 \sin \phi_2$$

$\therefore$ $$\% \text{ Reg} = \% \text{ resistance drop} \times \cos \phi_2 - \% \text{ reactance drop} \times \sin \phi_2$$

EQUIVALENT CIRCUIT

The equivalent circuit of a transformer is shown in Fig. 7. In this resistances and leakage reactances of the windings are assumed to be external to the winding. No load current is simulated by a pure inductance X_0 and non-inductive resistance R_0. Thus, the value of E_1 is obtained by substracting I_1Z_1 from V_1E_1 and E_2 are related by the expression.

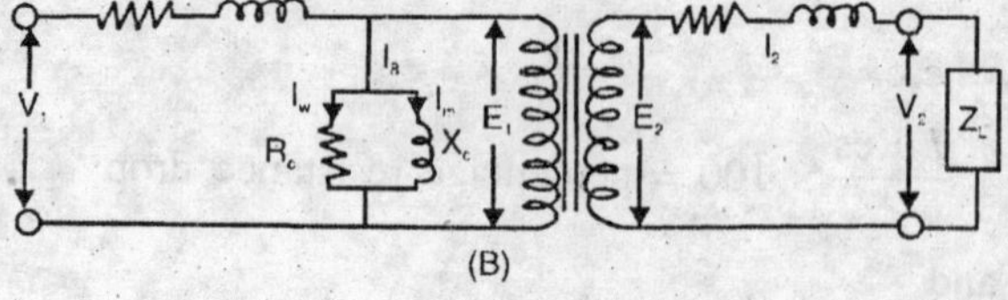

Fig. 4

Current transformers: Current transformers are used for reducing or stepping down a.c. current from higher value to a lower value for measurement (sometimes for protection or control). These transformers are used with ammeters, wattmeters, kVA meters, kWh meters.

A current transformer is specified as 20/10 P 10. In this, first number indicates output in VA, *i.e.*, 20 VA.

Second number indicates accuracy class (*e.g.*, 10 P). Third number indicates composite error (*e.g.*, 10).

Burden on CT: 'Burdens' of CTs and VTs refer to the maximum load in volt ampere (VA) which may be applied across the secondary terminals, without the ratio and phase angle exceeding the permissible limits.

In case of d.c. circuits whenever large currents are to be measured with the help of low-range ammeter, a shunt is used. Likewisely for measuring high voltages, low range voltmeters are used by connecting high resistance in series. In case of ac circuits above arrangement is not suitable and in place of that instrument transformers are used. These transformers are

1. Current transformers for measuring large alternating currents.
2. Potential transformers for measuring large alternating voltages.

Voltage transformers: These transformers are extremely accurate ratio step down transformers. Their primary is connected directly to power circuit between phase and ground. The voltage factor of the transformer is expressed as

$$T.F. = \frac{100\,(k_n V_s - V_s)}{V_p}$$

where k_n = normal ratio

V_s = secondary voltage

V_p = primary voltage

The burden on voltage transformer is expressed in volt amperes at a rated secondary voltage and at a particular power factor.

Induced E.M.F.

$$\boxed{e = B\, l\, v \text{ volts}}$$

where B = flux density Wb/sqm

v = velocity (m/s) of movement

l = length of conductors in metres

Frequency: The frequency of the voltage generated is given by

$$f = \frac{NP}{120}$$

where P is the total number of poles and N is the speed in r.p.m.

Breadth Factor

$$(K_b) = \frac{\text{Voltage obtained in multi-slots winding}}{\text{Voltage obtained if the windings were all concentrated in one slot}}$$

Thus, breadth factor is always less than unity. Mathematically,

$$K_b = \frac{\sin\frac{n\delta}{2}}{\pi \sin\frac{\delta}{2}}$$

where n is the number of slot and δ is the slot pitch

Pitch Factor

Shortening the pitch of the coil has the same effect as the distribution of the winding. When the turns of the windings do to span a complete pitch there occurs a slight loss in the induced emf. A pitch factor (K_p) is given by

$$K_p = \cos\frac{\theta}{2}$$

for a coil which extends over (180°–θ) instead of 180°.

Magnitude of Induced emf in alternators/phase

$$E_{RMS} = 4.44\ K_p\ K_b\ \phi\ f.T.\ \text{volts}$$

Synchronous Reactance:

$$X_S = X_L + X_A$$

where X_L = Leakage reactance

X_A = Armature reactance

Synchronous Impedance:

$$Z_S = \sqrt{R^2 + X_S^2}$$

SYNCHRONOUS GENERATOR CHARACTERISTICS

1. Open Circuit Characteristics: Magnetisation Curve.

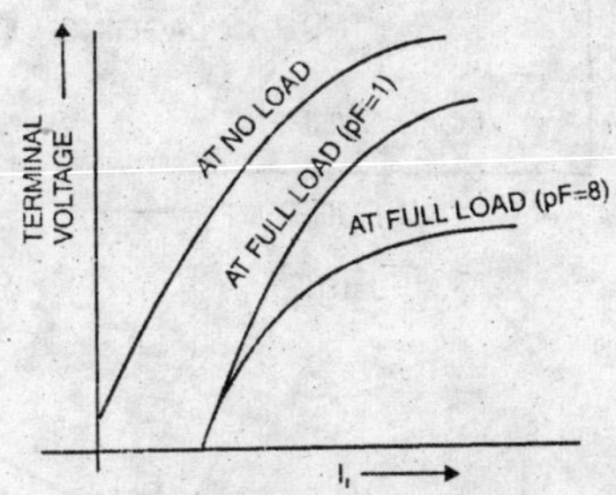

Fig. 5

2. Short Circuit Characteristics:

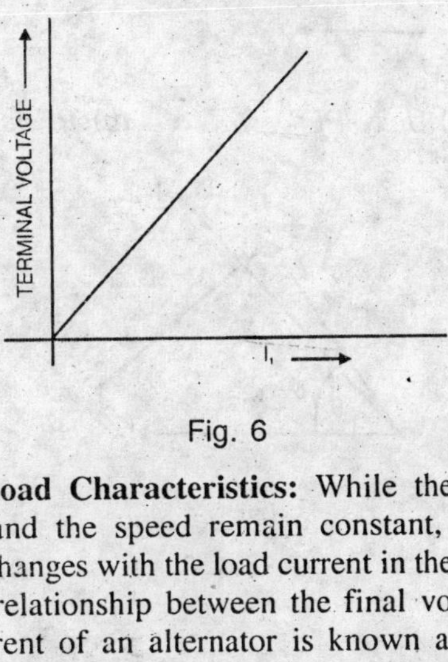

Fig. 6

3. Load Characteristics: While the exciting current and the speed remain constant, the final voltage changes with the load current in the armature and the relationship between the final voltage and load current of an alternator is known as its load characteristics.

When the armature current increases, the terminal voltage drops. This is mainly due to

(a) Resistance and reactance of armature winding, and

(b) Armature reaction

The load characteristics of an alternator is shown in Fig. 7.

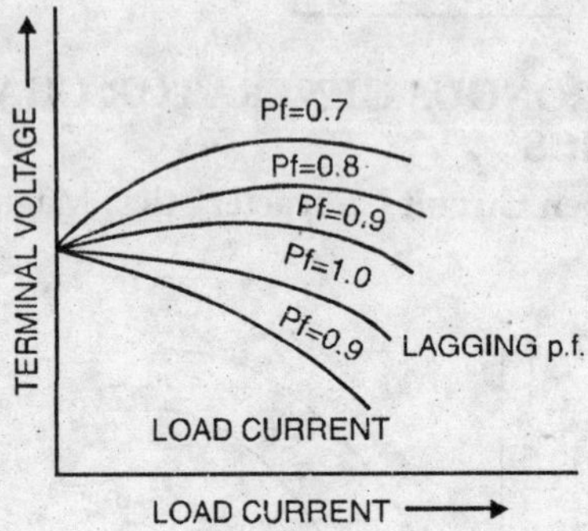

Fig. 7

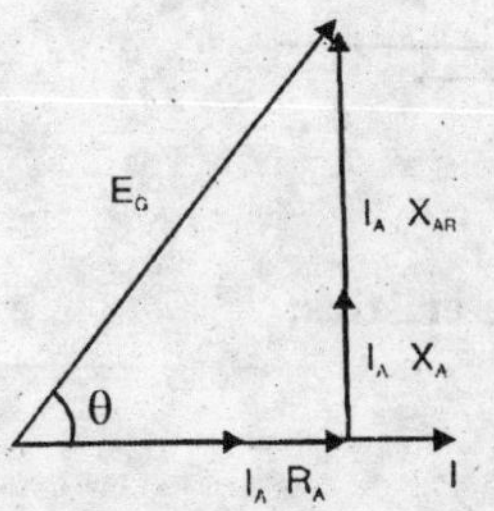

(a) Unity PF

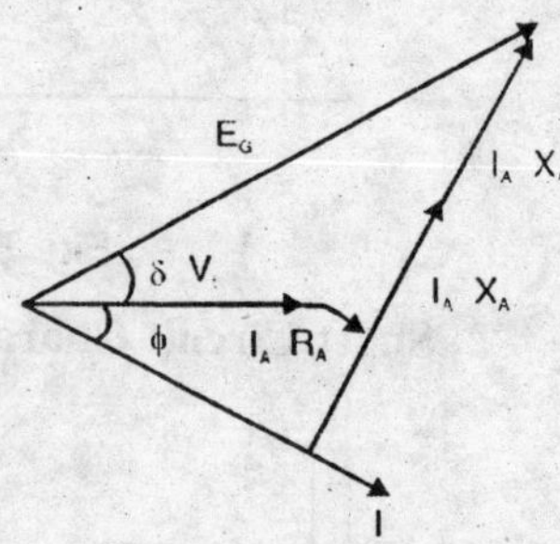

(b) PF lagging

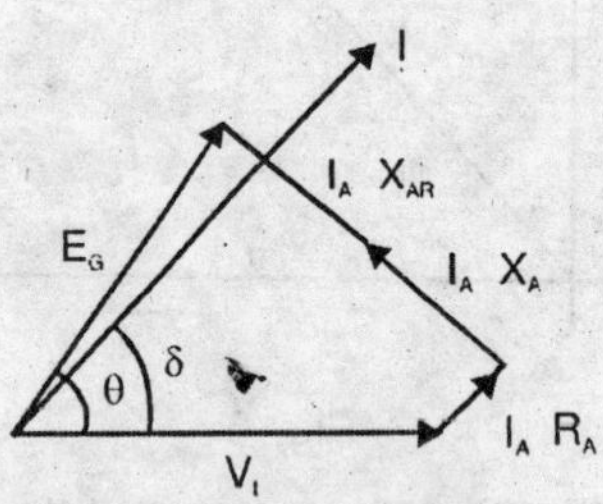

(c) PF leading

Fig. 8

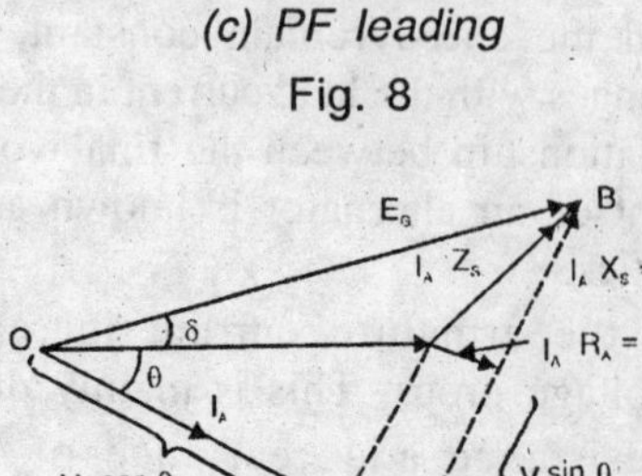

(a) Phasor diagrams

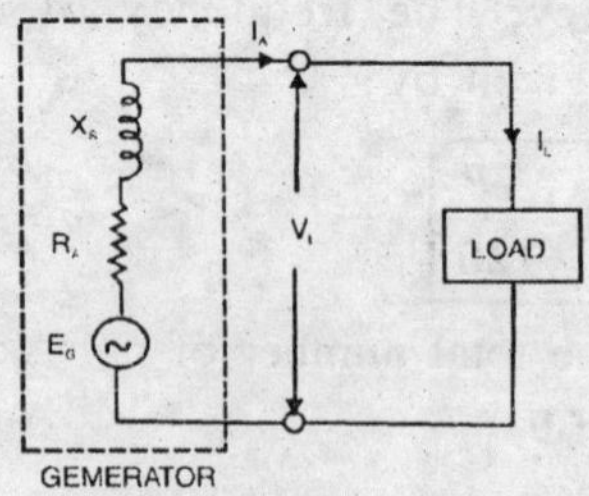

(b) Electric Circuit

Fig. 9: *Simplified equivalent ac circuit (per phase) for synchronous generator*

Phashor diagrams of a synchronous generator under three types of leading conditions (as shown in Fig. 8 and 9).

At Power Factor Lagging

(A) When R_A is very small

$$\alpha = \text{torque angle}$$

$$P = \frac{3\, V_\phi\, E_0 \sin\alpha}{Xs}$$

Torque induced

$$T_{ind} = \frac{3\, V_\phi\, E_\theta \sin\alpha}{\omega_m X_s}$$

where ω_m = speed

(B) General case:

$$P = \frac{3\, E_0}{Z_S}[E_0 \cos\theta - V(\cos\theta + \alpha)]$$

$$\cos\theta = \frac{R_a}{Z_S}$$

small Ra implies $\theta = 90$

For maximum power output:

$$\cos\phi = \frac{E_0}{\sqrt{E_0^2 + v\phi^2}}$$

$$\alpha = 90$$

$$3\ P_{max} = \frac{3\, V_\phi\, I_{max} E_0}{\sqrt{E_0^2 + V_\phi^2}} = \frac{3\, E_0\, V_\phi}{X_S}$$

BLONDELS TWO REACTION THEORY

The Blondel's two reaction theory considers the results of the cross and direct-reaction components separately and if saturation is neglected,

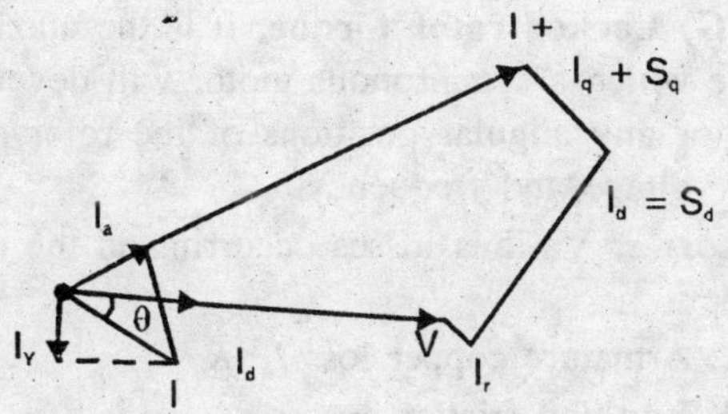

Fig. 10

accounts for their different effects by assigning to each an appropriate value for armature-reaction "reactive" respectively X_{aq} and X_{ad}.

Considering the leakage reactance, the combined reactance value becomes

$$X_{ad} = X + X_{aq} \text{ and}$$

$$X_{sq} = X_{aq}$$

$X_{sq} < X_{sd}$ as a given current component of the q-axis gives rise to a smaller flux due to the higher reluctance of the magnetic path.

Let I_q and I_d be the q and d-axis components of the current I in the armature reference to the phasor diagram in Figure.

We get the following relationships

$$I_q = I \cos (\sigma + \phi),\ I_a = I \cos \phi$$

$$I_d = I \sin (\sigma + \phi)$$

$$I_r = I \sin \phi$$

and $$I = \sqrt{I_d^2 + I_q^2} = \sqrt{I_a^2 + I_r^2}$$

where I_a and I_r are the active and reactive components of current I.

Voltage Regulation

Voltage Regulation of an alternator is defined as "the rise in voltage when full load is removed (field excitation and speed remaining unaltered) divided by the rated terminal voltage. Thus

$$\% \text{ regulation} = \frac{E_0 - V}{V} \times 100$$

In case of leading load pf the regulation is negative.

Difference Between Induction Motor and Synchronous Motor

Induction Motors	*Synchronous Motor*
1. These motors have wound rotor with slip rings or a squirrel cage rotor.	These motors have dc poles on rotor energised by excitation system.
2. Rotor current is ac and is induced by magnetic induction.	The field current (excitation current) can be changed to vary the power factors.
3. These motors run at less than synchronous speed. Full load slip is about 4%.	These motors always run at synchronous speed without slip.
4. These motors take lagging power factor current.	These motors take different pf currents depending upon the excitation level.
5. These motors have inherent starting torque.	These motors do not have any inherent starting torque.
6. These motors start unaided.	These motors have to be started by suitable means and brought to synchronous speed and ·ien synchronised.
7. These motors are used for variable speed and variable load drives.	These motors are used for constant speed and constant load drives.
8. For the same size, these motors are cheaper.	These motors are costly due to additional cost of excitation system.

TORQUE DEFINITIONS

(A) Synchronous torque: It is the steady state required to drive the motor and the load at the synchronous speed.

(B) Pull-in torque: It is the maximum constant load torque under which the motor will pull into synchronism at the rated rotor supply voltage and rated frequency, when the rated field current is applied.

(C) Nominal pull in torque: It is the value of pull in torque at 95 per cent of the synchronous speed with the rated voltage and frequency applied to the stator when the motor is running with the winding current.

(D) Pull out torque: It is the maximum sustained torque which the motor will develop at synchronous speed for 1 minute with rated frequency and with rated field current.

(E) Pull up torque: It is the minimum torque developed between standstill and pull in point. This torque must exceed the load torque by sufficient margin to ensure satisfactory acceleration of the load during starting.

(F) Reluctance torque: It is fraction of the total torque with the motor operating synchronously. It results from saliency of the poles. It is approximately 30% of the pull-out torque.

Effect of change of excitation: The real power is $P = VI \cos \phi$. The value of excitation for which back emf, E_b is equal to applied voltage V, is known as 100% excitation. An over excited motor (more than 100% excitation) takes leading power factor current. An under excited motor takes lagging power factor current.

Change in excitation currents does not change the load or power output of the synchronous motor. To change the power output, the mechanical load should change.

'Load angle' of 'Power angle': It is the space angle between the axis of stator revolving magnetic field and the rotor pole axis, both locked and running at synchronous speed.

Hunting: Due to sudden change of load, the angle changes causing oscillations of rotor about the mean position due to inertia of the rotor. Thus hunting is usually of low frequency oscillations superimposed on normal synchronous speed.

Synchronous reactance: A synchronous machine can be represented as an emf source in series with internal impedance of the machine. This internal impedance, Z_s is called synchronous impedance. The synchronous reactance takes into account the effect of armature reactions and the flux produced by the armature current. The emf takes into account the flux produced by field excitation.

(G) Locked rotor torque: It is the maximum torque which a synchronous motor will develop at rest, for any angular positions of the rotor at the rated voltage and frequency.

Losses: Various losses occurring in the motor are:

1. Armature copper loss $I_a^2 R_a$
2. Iron and friction losses.

Torque: In a synchronous motor, the power per phase

$$P_m = \frac{E_b . V}{Z_S} \cos (\theta - \alpha) - \frac{E_b^2}{Z_s} \cos \theta$$

Since the speed of the motor is always constant, above expression also expresses the torque developed by the motor.

The condition for the maximum power is

$$\theta = \alpha$$

Hence the value of maximum power

$$P_{max} = \frac{E_b . V}{Z_S} - \frac{E_b^2}{Z_s} \cos \theta$$

when $\theta = 90°$, $\cos \theta = 0$, so that

$$P_{max} = \frac{E_b . V}{Z_S}$$

OPEN CIRCUIT CHARACTERISTICS

The open circuit characteristics of a synchronous machine is a curve of the armature terminal voltage on open circuit as a function of the field excitation, when the machine is running at synchronous speed.

SHORT CIRCUIT CHARACTERISTICS

If the armature terminals of a synchronous machine (driven as a generator at synchronous speed) are short-circuited through suitable ammeter, and the field current is gradually increased until the armature current has reached a maximum safe value (about 1.5 times rated current), data can be obtained from which short circuit armature current can be plotted against the field current. Such a characteristic is known as short-circuit characteristic.

SPEED

For P poles in the machine, there will be $\frac{P}{2}$ pairs of poles and hence the magnetic field will rotate through $\frac{f}{P/2}$ or $\frac{2f}{P}$ rotations 'f' cycles of the current. Thus synchronous speed, N_s is given by

$$N_s = \frac{f}{P/2} = \frac{2f}{P} \text{ rps}$$

$$= \frac{120f}{P} \text{ rpm}$$

If the supply frequency is constant, the synchronous speed will also be constant. The rotor of the motor revolves at less than the synchronous speed, say N and the difference $(N_s - N)$ is called the slip of the motor. Thus

$$\% \text{ slip} = \frac{\text{Synchronous speed} - \text{Rotor speed}}{\text{Synchronous speed}} \times 100$$

or
$$s = \frac{N_s - N}{N_s} \times 100$$

The slip usually lies in the range 0 to 5%.

STARTING OF INDUCTION MOTORS

To start a motor from rest and to bring it to normal operating speed requires an input of energy (a) to supply the losses, and (b) to provide the rotating path with kinetic energy.

When the motor is directly switched on to a normal voltage supply, it draws a large starting current which is almost 6 to 7 times the rated full load current.

If T_s : starting torque

T_n : full load torque

S_n : full load slip

Then $\frac{T_s}{T_n} = \left(\frac{I_s}{I_n}\right)^2 \times S_n$

(i) Starting of slipring motors: A Rheostat is provided in the rotor circuit. During starting the rheostat will be in maximum resistance position and the resistance being gradually cut out as the motor speeds up (Fig. 11).

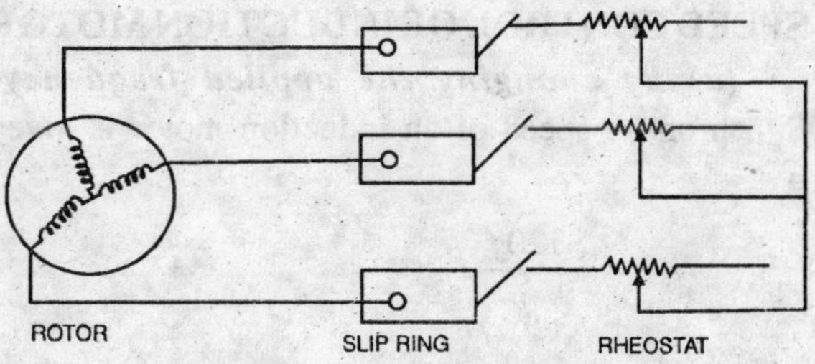

Fig. 11: *Rotor rheostat method*

(ii) Starting or squirrel cage induction motors:

(a) Stator rheostat method: A reduced voltage, is applied during starting. The voltage is gradually increased by reducing the resistance as the motor picks up speed (Fig. 12).

(b) Auto-transformer stator: An auto transformer with different tappings at a voltage lower than the rated voltage is used for starting.

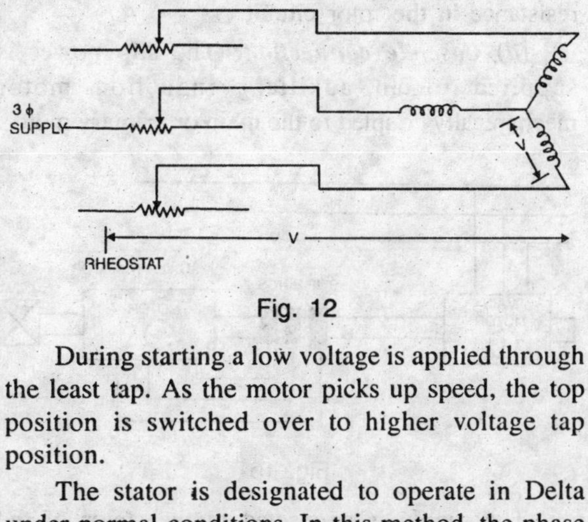

Fig. 12

During starting a low voltage is applied through the least tap. As the motor picks up speed, the top position is switched over to higher voltage tap position.

The stator is designated to operate in Delta under normal conditions. In this method, the phase connections are temporarily connected in star at start so that the voltage applied across is $V/\sqrt{3}$. The line current at start is then reduced to $\frac{1}{3}$ of the starting current and starting torque is one third of short circuit value.

When the motor picks up speed the connections are changed over from start to Delta by a change over switch.

SPEED CONTROL OF INDUCTION MOTOR

(a) By changing the applied frequency: Synchronous speed of an induction motor is given by

$$N_S = \frac{120f}{p}$$

where f = frequency

P = no of poles

(b) By changing the number of stator poles: Changing of number of poles is achieved by having two or more independent stator winding's in the same slots. Each winding gives a different number of poles and hence different synchronous speeds.

(c) Rotor rheostat control: Addition of external resistance in the rotor circuit. It is applicable to slip ring motors. The speed can be reduced by adding resistance in the rotor circuit.

(d) Cascade connection: The slip power is supplied to an auxiliary induction motor mechanically coupled to the main or primary motor.

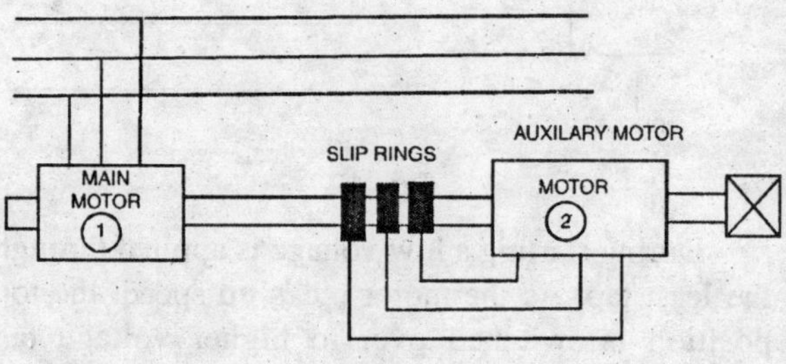

Fig. 13

The supply is connected to the stator of the main motor. The auxiliary motor 2 is fed from the rotor circuit of the motor 1.

If f is supply freq. and p_1 and p_2 are no. of poles of the 2 motors.

Then the following speeds can be obtained.

Main motor alone : f/p_1

Aux. motor along : f/p_2

Differential cascade : $f/(p_1 - p_2)$

Cumulative cascade : $f/(p_1 + p_2)$

Effect of Supply Voltage Variation on Characteristics of Induction Motor

Voltage	*Function of voltage V*	*90% V*	*110%V*
Synchronous speed	constant	constant	constant
% slip	$\frac{1}{V^2}$	increases by about 25%	reduces by 17%
Full load speed	—	decreases by 15%	increases by 10%
Starting current	αV	decreases	increases
Full load current	—	increases	decreases
Starting torque and maximum running torque	αV^2	decreases by 20%	increases by 20%
Temp. rise on full load	–	increases	decreases

Effect of Variation of Frequency on the Characteristics of Induction Motors

Frequency	*Function of frequency, f*	*95% f*	*105% f*
Synchronous speed	$\alpha\, f$	decreases by 5%	increases by 5%
% slip	–	No change	No change
Full load speed	$\alpha\, f$	decreases by 5%	increases by 5%
Starting current	$\alpha \frac{1}{f}$	increases by 5%	decreases slightly
Full load current	–	increases slightly	decreases slightly
Starting torque and maximum running torque	$\alpha \frac{1}{f^2}$	increases by 11%	decreases by 10%
Temp. rise on full load	–	increases slightly	decreases slightly

Crawling: Sometimes an induction motor when started on load does not accelerate upto full speed but continues to run at about 1/7th of the normal full speed. This is called *crawling* of induction motor. Crawling can be prevented by proper designing of the motor.

Clogging: Whenever there are equal number of teeth on stator and rotor, the reluctance of the magnetic circuit would be considerably less when the teeth were opposite to one another. Particularly at low voltages, magnetic locking of the teeth on the stator and the rotor may prevent the rotation of the rotor. This phenomenon is known as *clogging.*

For preventing 'crawling' and 'clogging' in induction motors, the motor should have

(i) Skewed (non-parallel) slots,

(ii) Fractional pitch winding,

(iii) Fractional slots winding,

(iv) Choice of stator slots and rotor slots having definite ratio.

Advantages/Limitations of Induction Mc/s having Squirrel Cage Type Rotors and over Slip-ring Type Rotors (phase wound)

Squirrel Cage Rotors	Phase Wound Rotors Slip-ring Motors
1. Rotor consists of a cylindrical laminated Core with parallel slots for Cu conductors (bars).	1. Rotor also has 3 ϕ windings similar to stator and wound for same number of poles as stator winding.
2. Cu bars are short circuited by *end rings.*	2. Rotor windings terminate *slip rings* mounted on rotor shaft.
3. Rotor conductors are not parallel to shaft but skewed. To provide: (a) more uniform torque (b) reduce noise during operation, (c) reducing locking tendency. (clogging action due to reluctance torque).	3. Brushes ride on the slip *rings.*
4. Winding adjusts itself to any no. on poles.	4. Permits the use of 3 ϕ external resistors to be added in series to the rotor wdg for starting purpose and providing speed control.
5. Since rotor bars are permanently *short circuited* by end rings, it is not possible to add any resistance (external) in series with motor circuit for starting purpose.	5. When running under normal conditions, slip-rings are short circuit by a metal collar and brushes are automatically lifted from slip rings.
6. No slip rings/carbon brushes construction maintenance free.	∴ Wound rotor is short circuited on itself just like squirrel cage rotor.

STEPPER MOTOR

It is an electromechanical device which actuates a train of step angular (or linear) movements in response to a train of input pulses on one to one basis i.e. one step actuation for each pulse input.

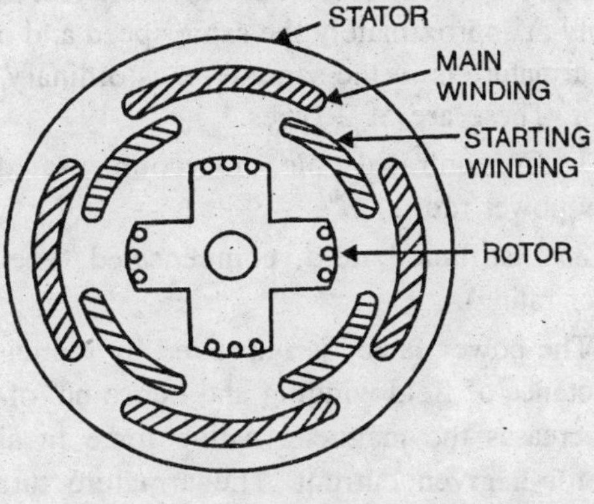

Fig. 14

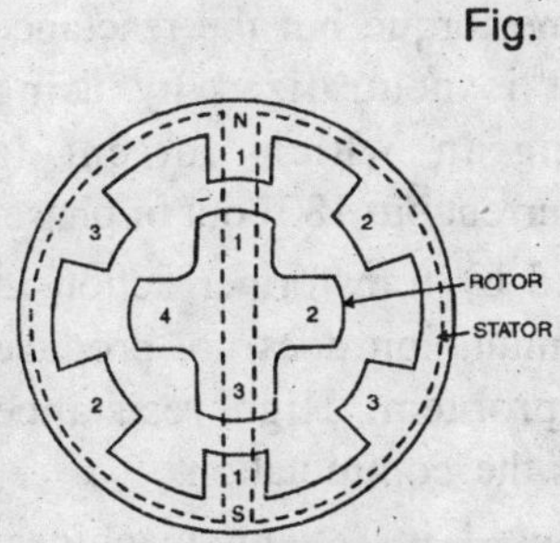

Fig. 15: *Variable reluctance motor*

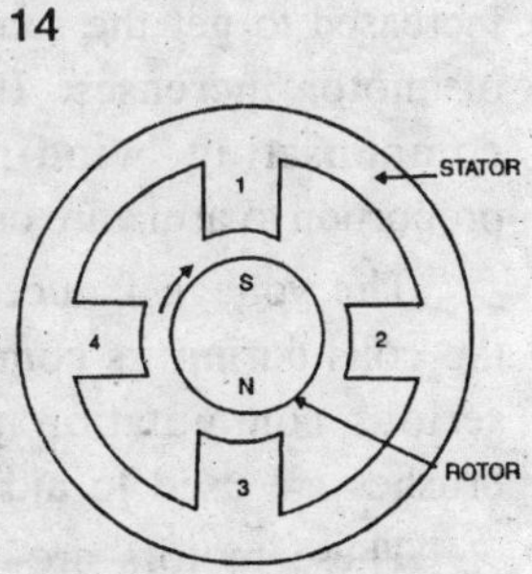

Fig. 16: *Permanent magnet stepper motor*

Depending upon the construction, there are 2 types of stepper motor.

(i) Variable reluctance motor: A 3 ϕ motor with 6 stator teeth and 4 rotor teeths are shown here. The 3 phases are excited in succession.

At the time when first phase is excited, the magnetic flux axis is shown. When 2nd phase is excited, the magnetic flux axis shifts and rotor rotates. Hence by changing the magnetic flux axis, rotor rotates in steps.

(ii) Permanent magnet stepper motor: A four phase permanent magnet motor is shown here. The rotor is a cylindrical permanent magnet and coils are wound on stator teeths.

When phases are excited in sequence, rotor rotates clockwise. Since it is a 4-phase motor, the step angle is 45°. For small step angles, no. of magnetic poles and stator teeths are increased.

UNIVERSAL MOTORS

They can be operated either on a.c. or d.c. supply at approximately the same speed and output. The armature is of the same type as ordinary series motor. These are of 2 types.

1. Concentrated-pole, non-compensated type (Low power rating).

2. Distributed field, compensated type (high power rating).

The power factor is improved by reducing the inductance of field winding and hence no. of turns. It decreases the magnetic native force in air-flux gap for a given current. The armature turns are increased to get the same torque but the reactance of motor increases. It is neutralized by using compensating winding in which current is proportion to armature current but 180° out of phase.

The voltage induced by transformer action in the coils during its commutation does not produce serious commutation problem. High resistance brushes are used to aid the commutation.

These motors are used in sewing machines, vacuum cleaners, kitchen appliances, drills hair dryers etc.

The speed torque characteristics for d.c. and a.c. input supply is shown in the Fig. 17.

HYSTERESIS MOTOR

These motors consist of a chrome-steel cylinder of high retentivity so that the hysteresis loss is high. It has no winding. Once the magnetic polarities are induced in the rotor, it revolves synchronously with the revolving magnetic field. Since the rotor has no slots or winding, the motor is noiseless free from vibrations. Such a motor is ideal for sound equipment.

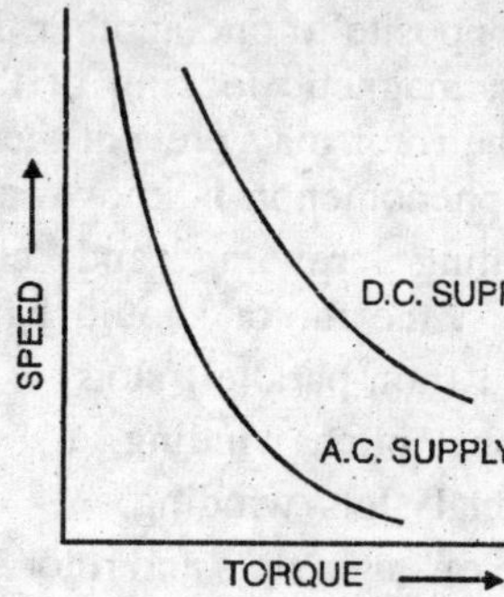

Fig. 17

Summary of Characteristics and Applications of Single Phase Motor

Motor type	*Main characteristics*	*Applications*
Split phase	Poor starting torque. Low power factor and efficiency. Shunt speed characteristics.	Non-reversing drives with light loads on starting.
Capacitor motor	Moderately good starting torque. Higher power factor and efficiency than split phase type. Quiet operation shunt speed characteristics.	Suitable for reversing as well as non reversing drives without heavy starting loads. Used in passenger lifts, domestic refrigerators, fans etc.
Repulsion	Good starting torque. Shunt speed characteristics.	Suitable for heavy starting. Additional winding needed for reversing.
Universal (Series)	Good starting torque. High power factor.	Vacuum cleaners, motorised hand tools.
Small Synchronous motor	Constant speed operation. Poor starting torque. Low power factor.	Non-reversing drives requiring absolutely constant speed, with light starting. Used in clocks, timing mechanisms, picture and sound reproduction.

DC GENERATOR

DC generator operates on the principle of the production of dynamically induced emf. To produce dynamically induced emf, a magnetic field and a conductor moving with respect to the field are essential. The current induced in the coil is collected and conveyed to the external load circuit by connecting the coil terminals to two continuous and insulated rings known as *slip rings* or *collector rings*.

DC machine mainly consists of four parts as shown in Fig. 18. Field magnets, armature, commutator and brushes.

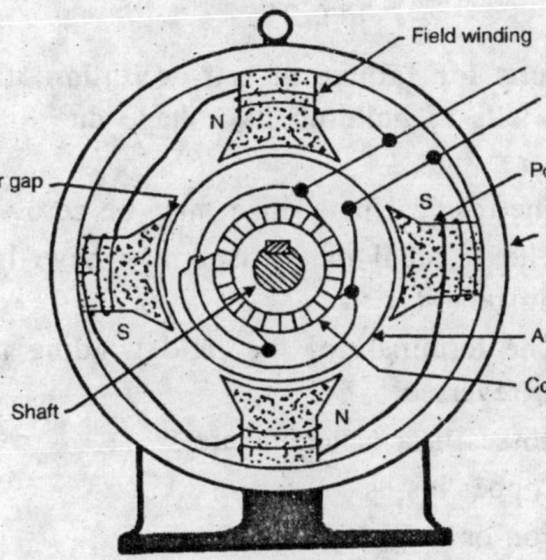

Fig. 18

The emf. generated within the armature of a dc generator,

$$E_g = \frac{\Phi ZN}{60}\left(\frac{P}{A}\right)\text{Volt}$$

where A = Number of parallel paths in armature
= 2 for wave – winding
= P for lap – winding
N = Speed in RPM
Z = Number of conductors in the armature
ϕ = Flux/pole in Wb.

Characteristics of DC Generators

The three important characteristics of a dc machine are shown in Fig. 19.

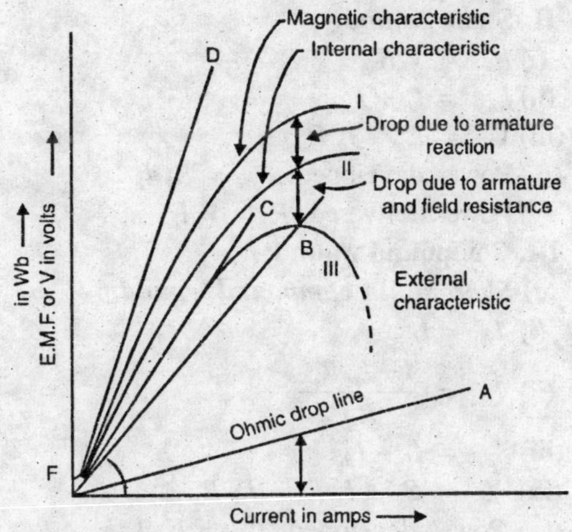

Fig. 19

1. Magnetic open-circuit characteristics: These show the relation between no-load generated emf in armature and field current at a given fixed speed.

2. External characteristics: These curves represent the relationship between the load current and terminal voltage.

3. Internal or total characteristics: These characteristics represent the relation between generated emf and armature current.

Critical resistance: It is the maximum resistance with which the generator can be excited.

Types of DC generators: Important types of dc generators are separately-excited, series-wound, shunt-wound, short-shunt compound-wound, and long-shunt compound-wound.

I. Series wound:

(i) $I_a = I_{Se} = I_L = I$
(ii) $V = E_g - I\ (R_a + R_{se})$
(iii) Power developed, $P_{dev} = E_g\ I$
(iv) Power delivered, $P_{dil} = V\ I$

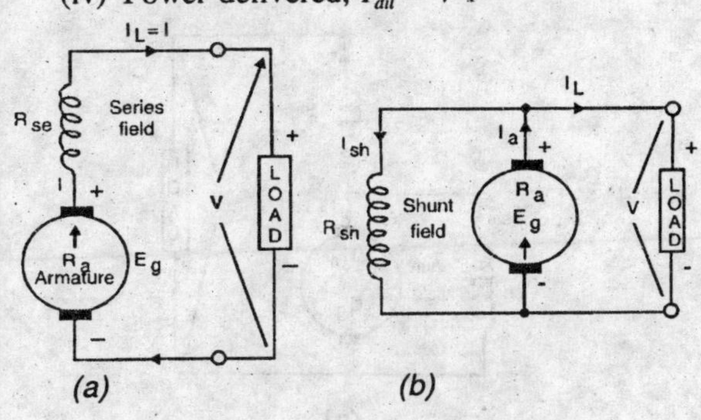

Fig. 20

II. Shunt wound:

(i) $I_{sh} = V/R_{sh}$

(ii) $I_a = I_L + I_{sh}$

(iii) $V_l = E_g - I_a R_a$

(iv) Power developed, $P_{dev} = E_g I_a$

(v) Power delivered, $P_{dil} = V I_L$

III. Compound wound:

(a) Short shunt compound wound:

(i) $I_{se} = I_L$

(ii) $I_{sh} = \dfrac{I + I_{se} R_{se}}{R_{sh}}$

(iii) $I_a = I_L + I_{sh}$

(iv) $V = E_g - I_a R_a - I_{se} R_{se}$

(v) Power developed, $P_{dev} = E_g I_a$

(vi) Power delivered, $P_{dil} = V I_L$

(b) Long shunt compound wound:

(i) $I_{sh} = V/R_{sh}$

(ii) $I_a = I_{se} = I_L + I_{sh}$

(iii) $V = E_g - I_a R_a - I_{se} R_{se}$
$= E_g - I_a (R_a + R_{se})$

(iv) Power developed, $P_{dev} = E_g I_a$

(v) Power delivered, $P_{dil} = V I_L$

Separately-excited generators are used in Ward Leonard system of speed control. Series generators are used for series arc lighting, series incandescent lighting and series booster.

Shunt generators with field regulators are used for light and power supply purposes and also used for charging of batteries.

Compound generators are used for power services and lighting

Differential-compound generator is used as arc welding generator (see Fig. 4).

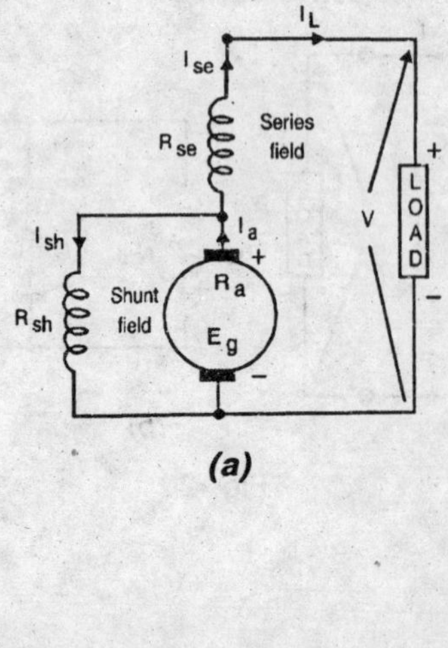

(a)

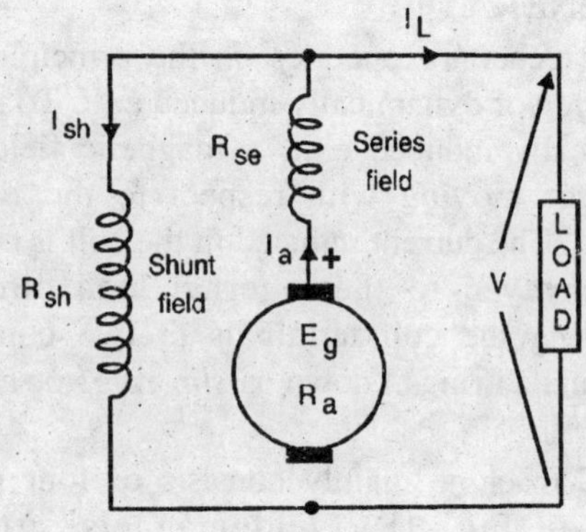

(b)

Fig. 21

Reasons for failure of self-excitation: D.C. generator fails to build-up its voltage due to the following reasons:

(1) The residual magnetism may be zero.

(2) The residual magnetism may have been reversed in polarity.

(3) The terminals of the field winding may have been reversed.

The losses in a generator are:

(1) Copper losses

(2) Iron or magnetic losses

(3) Mechanical losses

Magnetic and mechanical losses are collectively known as *stray losses*. In case of shunt generator, the shunt copper loss is practically constant. The condition for maximum efficiency of dc shunt generator is

Armature copper loss = Iron loss

The load current corresponding to maximum efficiency is given by

$$I = \sqrt{W_c / R_a}$$

where W_c is the copper losses and R_a is armature resistance.

Armature Reaction: It is the effect of the magnetic field set up by armature current on the distribution flux under the main poles, as shown in Fig. 22.

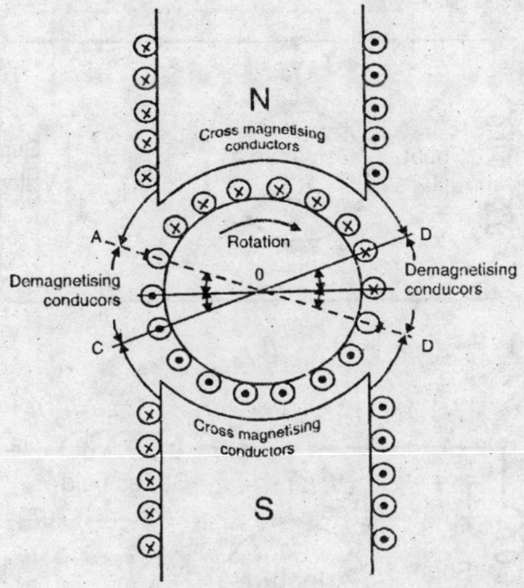

Fig. 22

Armature reaction has two effects—it weakens the main flux, and it distorts it.

The conductors lying between angles AOC and BOD carry current in such a direction so as to oppose the main mmf. This is known as *demagnetising effect* and thus corresponding conductors are called *demagnetising conductors*.

The conductors lying between angles AOD and BOD carry current in such a direction which causes mmf in the direction perpendicular to that of main mmf. This results in distortion of main field and is called *cross-magnetising effect*.

Demagnetising amp-turns per pole are given by:

$$AT_d\text{/pole} = ZI\frac{\theta}{360}$$

Cross-magnetising amp-turns per pole

$$= ZI\left[\frac{1}{2P}-\frac{\theta}{360}\right]$$

Compensating windings are placed in the pole shoes and their function is to neutralise the cross-magnetising effect of armature reaction.

Armature Reaction can be neutralized by

(i) increasing the length of air gap

(ii) providing the machine with a compensating winding

(iii) using commutating poles

(iv) reducing the cross-section of pole pieces.

$$\theta_m\text{ (mechanical)} = \frac{\theta\text{ (electrical)}}{\text{pair of poles}} = \frac{2\theta_e}{p}$$

where p is the number of poles

Commutation: The process by which the current in the short-circuited armature coil is reversed while it crosses the magnetic neutral axis is called commutation. The self-induced emf in the coil undergoing commutation is known as *reactance voltage*.

$$\text{Value of reactance voltage} = 1.11\text{ L}\frac{2I}{T_c}$$

where T_c is the commutation time

Methods of improving commutation: These are:

(1) Resistance commutation: In this, the low resistance copper brushes are replaced by comparatively high resistance carbon brushes.

(2) Emf commutation: In this method of improving commutation an arrangement is made to neutralise the reactance voltage by producing a reversing emf in the short circuited coil under commutation.

Principle of DC motor: When a conductor carrying current is placed in a magnetic field, emf is procured whose direction is opposite to the main voltage corresponding to Lenz's law. The mechanical force is experienced by the conductor, the direction of which is given by Fleming's left-hand rule.

Armature current of dc motor is

$$I = \frac{V-E_b}{R_a}$$

Voltage equation for shunt motor is,

$$V = E_b + I_aR_a + \text{brush drop}$$

where E_b is the back emf, I_a is the armature current, and R_a is the armature resistance.

Condition for maximum power developed in armature is

$$E_b = \frac{V}{2}$$

Armature torque of a motor is given by

$$T = 0.159\ \Phi\ ZI_a\ (P/A)\text{ Nm}$$
$$= 0.0162\ \Phi\ ZI_a\ (P/A)\text{ kgm}$$

$$\text{Useful torque} = \frac{\text{Output in watts}}{2\pi N} \text{ Nm}$$

Speed of dc motor

$$N = \frac{E_b}{\Phi}\left(\frac{A}{ZP}\right) \text{ revolution per sec.}$$

Rotation of a motor can be reversed by reversing the current through either the armature winding or the field coils. If the current through both are reversed, the motor will continue to rotate in the same direction.

Advantages and Disadvantages of Carbon Brushes

Advantages:

1. They have high contact resistance, a loss of 2 V is caused.
2. They lubricate and polish the commutator as it rotates.
3. In the event of separating, carbon brushes will damage two commutator less in comparison to copper brushes.

Disadvantages:

1. Due to high contact resistance, a loss of about 2 V is caused.
2. Because of large loss, the commutator has to be made somewhat larger than with copper brushes so as to dissipate heat efficiently.
3. Owing to lower current density, large brush holders are required.

Types of DC motors: Types of dc motors are listed below:

(I) Series-wound motors
(II) Shunt-wound motors
(III) Compound-wound motors
 (i) Commutative type
 (ii) Differential type

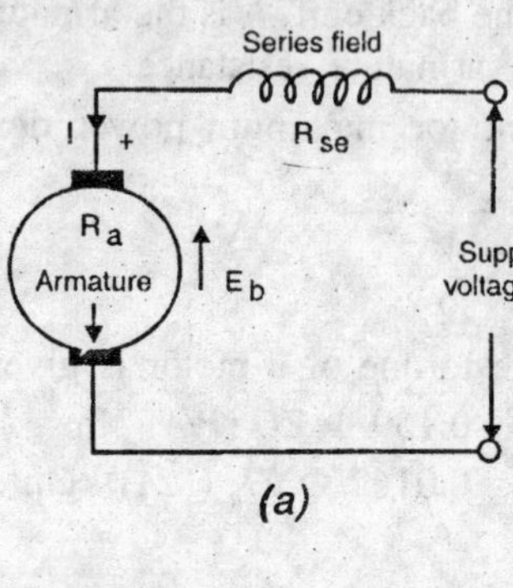

(a)

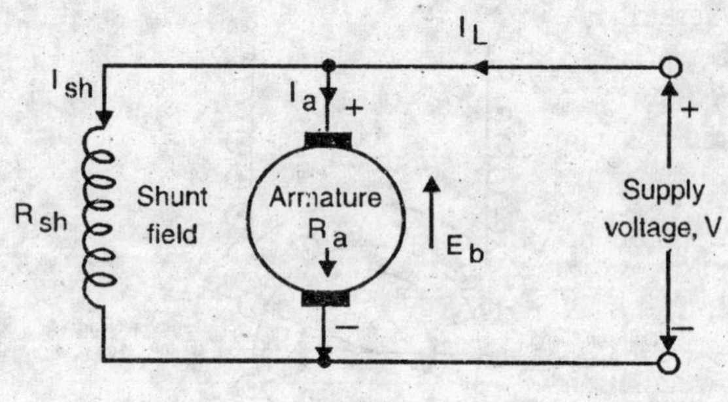

(b)

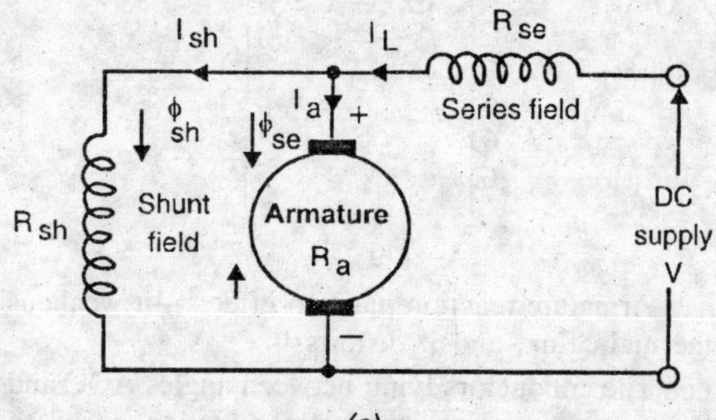

(c)

Fig. 23

(I) Series wound motor:

(i) Back emf.: $E_b = V - I(R_a + R_{se})$

(ii) $I_a = I_{se} = I$

(iii) Power Input = VI

(iv) Power developed,

$$P_{dev} = E_b I = VI - I^2(R_a + R_{se})$$

(II) Shunt wound motor:

(i) $I_L = I_a + I_{sh}$

(ii) $I_{sh} = V/R_{sh}$

(iii) Back emf,

$$E_b = V - I_a R_a$$

(iv) Power input = VI_L

(v) Power developed, $P_{dev} = VI_L - VI_{sh} - I_a^2 R_a$

(III) Compound wound motor: This is of two types:

(a) Cumulative Compound; and
(b) Differential Compound

Heating and Cooling Equations of DC machines are:

$$\theta = \theta_m (1 - e^{-t/T_h})$$

$$\theta = \theta_i (1 - e^{-t/T_c})$$

where q_m is the final temperature rise while heating, °C, q_i is the initial temperature rise over ambient medium °C, T_h and T_c are the heating and cooling time constants 't' is the time (sec).

Speed Regulation: Speed regulation of dc motor is defined as the change in speed when load on the motor is reduced from full load to zero and is expressed as

$$\% \text{ regulation } = \frac{N_0 - N_f}{N_f} \times 100$$

In a dc motor, speed is inversely proportional to flux per pole if supply voltage is constant. In case of dc shunt motor, the flux is constant, and the speed will approximately remain constant.

Conditions of Paralleling DC Generators

1. The polarities of the generators must be same.

2. The voltages should be nearly identical so that each machine will contribute.

3. The change of voltage with change of load should be of the same character.

4. The prime movers that drive the generators should have similar and stable rotational speed characteristics.

Functions of interpoles or compoles: It performs the following functions:

1. To make commutation sparkless and ensure automatic neutralisation of reactance voltage.

2. To neutralise the cross-magnetising effect of armature reaction.

Equaliser connections: These should be applied to the multi-pole lap windings and to the wave windings with more than two parallel circuits.

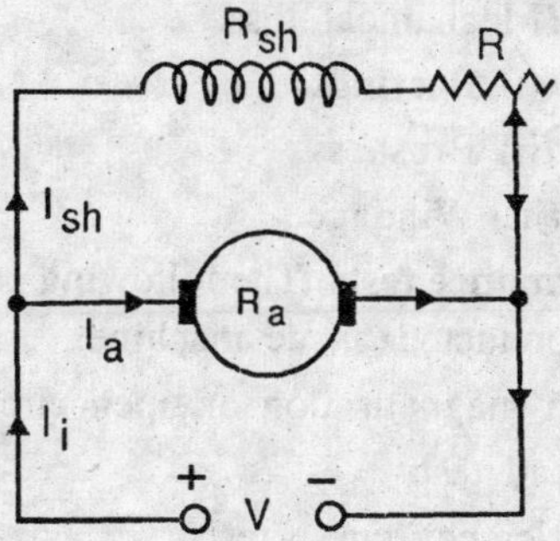

Fig. 24

Speed control of DC motors: The speed of dc motor is given by

$$N = \frac{V - I_a R_a}{\Phi} \cdot \frac{60\,A}{ZP}$$

It is clear from the above equation that the speed of dc motor can be varied by changing either flux or armature current or terminal voltage.

Speed of dc motors may be controlled by one of the following methods:

(a) Flux control method: For a dc motor, the speed is inversely proportional to flux. Therefore, if a variable resistance R is connected in series with a field winding, the flux can be varied thereby changing the speed. Fig. 24 shows the speed control by flux variation method.

(b) Rheostative control: In this method, a variable resistance R is inserted in series with the armature circuit. As variable resistance is increased, potential difference across the armature falls thereby decreasing the armature speed.

Torque and power characteristics of DC motors: Fig. 25 shows the constant torque and constant power characteristics of a separately-excited motor for adjustment by armature and field voltage control.

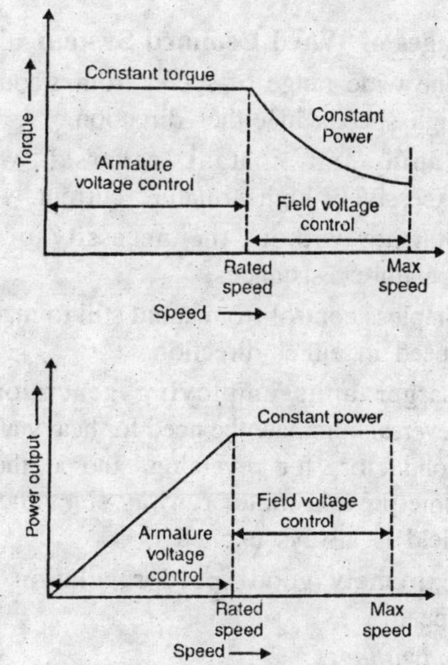

Fig. 25

Voltage control-method or ward leonard method: This system consists of simply running the motor with a constant excitation and applying a variable voltage to its armature to give required speed. The variable voltage supply is obtained from motor generator set as shown in Fig. 26. The advantages obtained from this method are:

1. Very fine speed control from 0 to normal in both directions.
2. Uniform acceleration can be obtained.
3. Speed regulation is good.

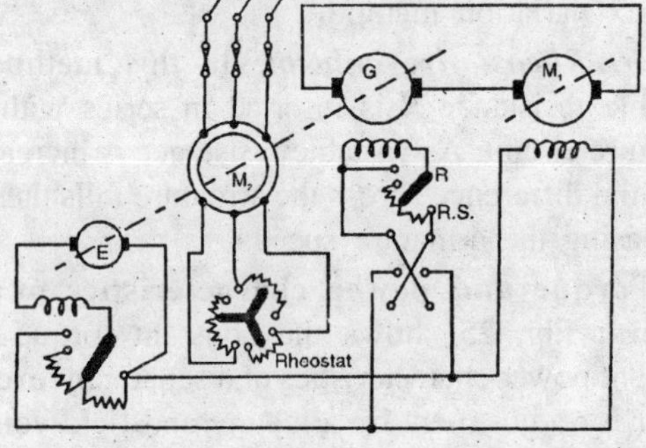

Fig. 26

Advantages of Ward Leonard System

1. The wide range of speed from standstill to high speeds in either direction.
2. Rapid and instant reversal without excessively high armature current.
3. Starting without the necessity of series armature resistances.
4. Stepless control from stand still to maximum speed in either direction.
5. Larger units employing generator field reversal eliminate the need for heavy armature conductors for reversing, and at the same time prevent motor runway since the motor field is always excited
6. Extremely good speed regulation at any speed.

Disadvantages:

1. High initial cost
2. Efficiency of this method is not as high as rheostat speed control by flux control method.

Electric braking: Electric braking of motors can be broadly classified as:

(a) Electromechanical

(b) Electrical

(a) Electro-mechanical brakes:

Electro-mechanical or friction brakes are operated by electromagnets.

(b) Electric brakes:

Electric braking is of three types:

(i) Plugging

(ii) Rheostatic braking

(iii) Regenerative braking

Efficiency of D.C. machine: This is defined as:

$$\text{Efficiency} = \frac{\text{Output}}{\text{Input}} = \frac{\text{Output}}{\text{Input} + \text{Losses}}$$

Losses in a DC Machine may be classified as follows:

(1) Electrical losses (copper loss)

- (i) Armature
- (ii) series field = $I_{se}^2 R_e$
- (iii) shunt field = (VI_{sh})
- (iv) Commutative field = $I^2 R_c$

(2) Rotational losses

- (a) Core loss:
  - (i) Hysteresis loss
  - (ii) Eddy currents
- (b) Mechanical loss
  - (i) Bearings
  - (ii) Brushes
  - (iii) Windage

Performance tests: The following performance tests are conducted on dc machine:

(i) the magnetisation or open circuit test

(ii) Load tests

(iii) efficiency curve tests

(iv) Temperature rise tests

EXERCISE

1. The large-sized induction motors are protected against over-load by
   (a) high-voltage fuses
   (b) automatic cutouts
   (c) thermal or magnetic relays
   (d) rewirable fuses
2. Which of the following statements associated with split phase motors is incorrect?
   (a) Auxiliary winding is wound of the fine wire and is placed in the top of the slots to give high resistance and low reactance.
   (b) Main winding has low resistance and high reactance.
   (c) Main winding current and auxiliary winding current are 90° out of phase.
   (d) Torque developed is proportional to sine of the angle between main winding and auxiliary winding currents.
   (e) Starting winding is connected through centrifugal switch.
3. Overheating of windings of generator
   (a) reduces the generated voltage
   (b) reduces the power factor
   (c) reduces the life of the machine
   (d) does not have any significant effect
4. The rotor slots in an induction motor are usually not kept parallel to the shaft as it
   (a) helps the rotor teeth to remain under the stator teeth
   (b) helps in reducing the tendency of the rotor teeth to remain under the stator teeth
   (c) improves pf
   (d) improves efficiency
5. In a single phase ac induction motor
   (a) stator is supplied with single phase ac
   (b) rotor is supplied with single phase ac
   (c) rotor is a cage rotor
   (d) rotor is a wound rotor
   (e) both (a) and (c)
6. In a ceiling fan employing permanent capacitor motor
   (a) secondary winding surrounds the primary winding
   (b) primary winding surrounds the secondary winding
   (c) both are usual arrangements
   (d) none of the above.
7. In an induction motor, the rotor input is 600 W and slip is 4%. The rotor copper-loss is
   (a) 700 W (b) 0.6 kW
   (c) 650 W (d) 24 W
8. When a transformer is operating on no load, the primary applied voltage is approximately balanced by
   (a) primary induced emf
   (b) secondary induced emf
   (c) terminal voltage across the secondary
   (d) voltage drop across the resistance and reactance
9. When measuring the no load input to an induction motor, using two wattmeter method, it is necessary to subtract wattmeter readings, because the no load power factor is
   (a) lagging (b) less than 0.5
   (c) unity (d) zero
10. What is the advantage of starting a slipring induction motor with the help of rotor resistances as compared to other methods?
    (a) The starting current is reduced.
    (b) The starting torque increase due to the rotor resistances.
    (c) The starter has to be designed for only a very low current.
    (d) The starter can be built directly into the motor.
11. The alternators are operated in parallel because it
    (a) increases the reliability of supply
    (b) makes the repairing economical and convenient

(c) is easy to instal an additional unit as and when required
(d) all of the above

12. In a repulsion motor
(a) stator usually carries a distributed winding similar to the main winding of an ordinary single phase induction motor
(b) the rotor or armature is similar to a dc motor armature with a drum type winding connected to the commutator
(c) the brushes fixed directly opposite to each other are connected to each other or short circuited
(d) the speed is function of load
(e) all of the above

13. A distribution transformer is required to supply
(a) variable load between no load to full load
(b) constant part full load throughout the day
(c) constant full load throughout the day
(d) variable load between no load to full load at a fixed power factor

14. The speed of the squirrel cage induction motor can be controlled from
(a) stator side
(b) rotor side
(c) stator and rotor sides both
(d) supply voltage side

15. If the armature current is in phase with generated emf, the effect of armature reaction is
(a) cross magnetising (b) magnetising
(c) demagnetising (d) none of above

16. Transformer zero voltage regulation occurs at
(a) unity p.f. (b) leading p.f.
(c) lagging p.f. (d) zero p.f. leading

17. One slip-ring connection of a 3-phase induction motor gets open-circuited. The motor will
(a) continue to run at the same speed
(b) run at a lower speed
(c) run at a higher speed
(d) stop

18. Spiral winding is suitable only for windings
(a) carrying very low current
(b) carrying very high current
(c) rated for high voltage
(d) rated for low voltage

19. If an induction motor hums during starting up, the possible cause could be
(a) open circuit
(b) unequal phase resistance
(c) inter-turn short-circuit on rotor
(d) any of the above

20. The iron-losses of a transformer can be calculated by knowing the weights of
(a) cores only
(b) yokes only
(c) copper winding only
(d) cores and yokes

21. Insulation resistance is measured between
(a) inter-turns of stator winding
(b) inter-turns of rotor winding
(c) windings and motor frame
(d) rotor and stator

22. Low voltage windings are placed nearer to the core in the case of concentric windings because it reduces
(a) hysteresis loss
(b) eddy current loss
(c) insulation requirement
(d) leakage fluxes

23. The core losses, and friction and windage losses in case of an induction motor are determined from the____ test.
(a) no-load (b) blocked rotor
(c) load (d) stator resistance

24. When a ceiling fan using a capacitor run motor is switched on, it hums but does not burn. When it is driven by some external means it runs in the direction in which it was made to run. The probable cause is
(a) open-circuited capacitor
(b) blown fuses
(c) short-circuited capacitor
(d) any of the above

25. In a synchronous motor
(a) the generated emf must always be less than the terminal voltage
(b) the generated emf must always be more than the terminal voltage
(c) the generated emf can be less than or greater than the terminal voltage
(d) none of these

26. Under no load operating condition, the speed of a universal motor is limited by
(a) windage and friction
(b) armature reaction
(c) armature weight
(d) supply frequency

27. An induction motor, in general, is analogous to
(a) an auto-transformer
(b) a two-winding transformer with its secondary open-circuited
(c) a two-winding transformer with its secondary winding short-circuited
(d) a three-winding transformer

28. In an induction motor the slip will be negative when
(a) stator magnetic field and rotor rotate in opposite directions
(b) rotor rotates at a speed less than synchronous speed and in the direction of rotation of stator field
(c) rotor rotates at a speed more than synchronous speed and in the direction of rotation of stator field
(d) none of the above

29. In a synchronous machine if the axis of the field flux coincides with that of armature flux, the machine
(a) will operate smoothly without any vibration
(b) is said to be floating
(c) is operating as a synchronous generator
(d) is operating as a synchronous motor

30. The purpose of skewing of rotor slots in induction motor is:
(a) to reduce the magnetic hum of motor
(b) to increase the distribution factor
(c) to reduce the locking tendency of rotor
(d) to increase the breadth factor

31. The power factor of an induction motor at low load is low due to
(a) high working component of 1 I_0
(b) high magnetising component of I_0
(c) high speed
(d) very low speed

32. Short-circuit test is performed on an induction motor to determine
(a) short-circuit current under rated voltage
(b) equivalent resistance and reactance
(c) transformation ratio
(d) power factor on short-circuit
(e) all of the above

33. Repulsion induction motor has
(a) single phase winding on its stator
(b) two separate windings on its rotor in common slots
(c) squirrel cage rotor and two separate windings on stator in common slots
(d) both (a) and (b)

34. In an induction motor, if the phase sequence of applied voltage is changed
(a) no back e.m.f. will be developed in rotor
(b) no torque will be developed by rotor
(c) speed will drop to zero
(d) direction of rotation of motor will change

35. In a 4 pole, 50 Hz, 3-phase induction motor, blocked rotor reactance per phase is four times the rotor resistance per phase. The speed at which maximum torque developed is
(a) 1500 r.p.m. (b) 1125 r.p.m.
(c) 1000 r.p.m. (d) none of these

36. When a 400-Hz transfromer is operated at 50 Hz, its kVA rating is
(a) reduced to 1/8
(b) increased 8 times
(c) unaffected
(d) determined by load on secondary

37. In an alternator, reactance emf
(a) leads the current by 90°
(b) lags behind the current by 90°
(c) is in phase with the current
(d) none of the above

38. A single phase transformer has a turn ratio of 10:1. The primary winding has a resistance of 2.1 ohm and the secondary winding has a resistance 0.02 ohm. The total resistance as referred to primary is
(a) 2.12 ohm (b) 4.1 ohm
(c) 0.041 ohm (d) 2.3 ohm

39. When applying a high-voltage test to the primary winding of a rebuilt transformer
(a) secondary winding must be short-circuited
(b) the secondary transformers case and core must be grounded
(c) one end of the primary must be grounded
(d) all other parts of the transformer must be grounded

40. Mark the wrong statement:
(a) In a given ideal transformer, volt/turn is constant for a given primary voltage.
(b) A transformer whose secondary current is greater than primary current is called step-up transformer.
(c) Hysteresis loss is proportional to supply frequency.
(d) Eddy current loss is reduced by laminating transformer core.

41. A synchronous motor develops synchronous torque only
(a) at synchronous speed
(b) on no-load
(c) on full-load
(d) while over-excited
(e) while under-excited

42. An ideal transformer is one which
(a) has a common core for its primary and secondary windings
(b) has no losses and magnetic leakage
(c) has core of stainless steel and windings of pure copper metal
(d) has interleaved primary and secondary windings

43. Cascade method of speed control involves the use of two coupled induction motors. The necessary condition for speed control is that
(a) both the motors are of the wound rotor type having the same number of poles
(b) both the motors are of the squirrel cage rotor type having different number of poles
(c) one motor is of the slip-ring type but both the motors have the same number of poles
(d) one motor is of the slip-ring type and the two motors have different number of poles

44. The nominal short-circuit voltage of the transformer is defined as the percentage of
(a) the test voltage
(b) the rated secondary voltage
(c) the rated primary voltage
(d) the nominal transformation ratio

45. Three number of 10:1 transformers are connected in Y–Δ to supply a load at 230 V. The supply voltage of this transformer must be
(a) 2300 V (b) 4000 V
(c) 23 V (d) 40 V

46. Which of the following motors is not a synchronous motor?
(a) Hysteresis (b) Repulsion
(c) Inductor (d) Reluctance

47. In an induction motor if the flux density is reduced to one-half of its normal value then the torque will
(a) reduce to one half
(b) reduce to one-fourth
(c) remain unchanged
(d) increase four times

48. Surface flash-over of the bushing insulators are often caused due to
(a) heavy external short-circuit
(b) moisture present in the transformer oil
(c) pollution of the bushing surfaces
(d) lining up of the suspended particles present in the oil

49. Which of the following motors is used most frequently?
(a) D.C. shunt motor
(b) A.C. induction motor
(c) Three phase commutator motor
(d) Three phase induction motor

50. A rotating magnetic field is produced by the current in the two windings displaced by 90 electrical degrees. This is the principle of
(a) phase timing (b) phase splitting
(c) phase sequence (d) phase relationship

51. When the frequency of the rotor of an induction motor is small it can be measured by
(a) galvanometer
(b) dc moving coil milli-voltmeter
(c) dc moving coil ammeter
(d) ac voltmeter

52. Which of the following motors is used for unity power factor?
(a) Squirrel-cage induction motors
(b) Slip ring induction motor
(c) Hysteresis motor
(d) Schrage motor

53. Squirrel cage induction motors have the advantages of
(a) cheaper in initial as well as in maintenance costs
(b) nearly constant speed, high over-load capacity, simple starting arrangement and high power factor
(c) lower copper losses and higher operation efficiency
(d) all of the above

54. The repulsion-start induction-run motor is used because of
(a) high efficiency (b) high starting torque
(c) minimum cost (d) good power factor

55. The speed of an induction motor is
(a) always less than the synchronous speed
(b) can be equal to or less than the synchronous
(c) always more than the synchronous speed
(d) none of these

56. Which of the following motors has highest starting torque?
(a) Split-phase motor
(b) Shaded pole motor
(c) Capacitor-start motor
(d) Repulsion motor

57. Synchronising torque will come into operation whenever
(a) there is a difference in the magnitude of voltages
(b) there is a phase difference in the voltages
(c) there is a frequency difference between the two voltages
(d) excitation of one of the alternators is changed
(e) in all of the above cases

58. Which of the following will improve the mutual coupling between primary and secondary circuits?
(a) Transformer oil of high breakdown voltage
(b) High reluctance magnetic core
(c) Winding material of high resistivity
(d) Low reluctance magnetic core

59. An unexcited single phase synchronous motor is
(a) reluctance motor (b) universal motor
(c) repulsion motor (d) a.c. series motor

60. In star-star connected transformers distortion in voltage wave shape due to third harmonic flux and voltage imbalance on single phase loads are minimum in case of three phase
(a) shell type
(b) five limb core type
(c) three limb core type
(d) none of these

61. If the voltage of one of the two machines operating in parallel suddenly falls
(a) both the machines will stop
(b) the machine whose voltage has suddenly decreased, will stop
(c) the synchronous torque will come into operation to restore synchronism
(d) none of the above

62. During short-circuit test, the iron loss of a transformer is negligible because
(a) the entire input is just sufficient to meet copper losses only
(b) voltage applied across the h.v. side is a small fraction of the rated voltage and so is the flux
(c) iron core becomes fully saturated
(d) supply frequency is held constant

63. Which of the following devices can be used as a phase advancer?
(a) 3-phase induction motor squirrel cage type
(b) 3-phase induction motor slip-ring type
(c) Synchronous motor working at leading power factor
(d) Synchronous motor working at lagging power factor

64. A 3-phase 400 V, 50 Hz synchronous motor is working at 50% load. In case an increase in the field current of the motor cause a reduction in the armature current, it can be concluded that
(a) the motor is delivering reactive power to the mains
(b) the motor is absorbing reactive power from the main
(c) the motor is neither absorbing nor delivering reactive power
(d) none of these

65. An induction motor has synchronous speed of 1,500 rpm. What will be slip when it is running on a speed of 1,450 rpm?
(a) +3.33%   (b) –3.33%
(c) +3%   (d) –3%

66. For a full pitch winding, the generated voltages in both coil sides are
(a) exactly in phase
(b) in quadrature
(c) exactly 180° out of phase
(d) approximately 180° out of phase

67. Slip-ring induction motor have the advantages of
(a) high starting torque and high over-load capacity
(b) nearly constant speed
(c) low starting current in comparison to squirrel cage induction motor
(d) all of the above

68. The doubly-excited magnetic systems are
(a) moving iron instruments
(b) electromagnetic relays
(c) solenoids
(d) synchronous motors

69. Decrease in supply voltage to a 3-phase induction motor will not cause
(a) any difficulty in accelerating the load
(b) increase in torque
(c) decrease in speed as well as in core loss
(d) increase in stator as well as rotor currents
(e) operating temperature abnormally high owing to increase in copper loss

70. In a synchronous motor
(a) the rotor mmf and stator mmf are stationary with respect to each other.
(b) the speed of rotor mmf is slightly less than the speed of stator mmf.
(c) the speed of rotor mmf is slightly more than the speed of stator mmf.
(d) none of these.

71. Alternator works on the principle of
(a) mutual induction
(b) Faraday's laws of electromagnetic induction
(c) self induction
(d) self and mutual induction

72. Decrease in length of air-gap between the stator and rotor of an induction motor will improve
(a) motor efficiency   (b) starting torque
(c) power factor   (d) pull-out torque

73. A capacitor motor has difficulty of starting. What is the probable cause?
(a) Reversed magnetic field
(b) Shorted commutator segments
(c) Shorted windings
(d) All of the above

74. Addition of tubes to the transformer tank improves heat dissipation capacity because of
(a) additional cooling surface
(b) additional dissipation by radiation only
(c) additional dissipation by convection only
(d) additional dissipation by radiation and convection both

75. Which of the following is minimized by laminating the core of a transformer?
(a) Hysteresis loss
(b) Eddy current loss
(c) Heat loss
(d) Mechanical vibrations

76. In an induction motor
(a) stator current, stator flux and rotor emf are in phase
(b) rotor current and rotor flux are in phase and both lag behind the rotor emf by 90°
(c) rotor current, rotor flux and rotor emf are in phase
(d) both (a) and (b) are correct

77. The most common mechanical method of providing speed reduction for universal motors is to use
(a) gearing (b) brakes
(c) chains (d) belts

78. Chording and distribution of armature windings for ac machines results in
(a) reduction in air gap mmf harmonics
(b) reduction in fundamental component or induced emf
(c) increase in fundamental component of induced emf
(d) reduction in noise and machine size
(e) both (a) and (b)

79. Star-delta and auto transformer starters are used with 3-phase induction motors because they
(a) have high starting torque
(b) may not run in reverse direction
(c) draw 5 to 7 times the full load current at the time of starting
(d) pick up high speed immediately

80. If a single phase induction motor runs at a speed lower than the rated one, the most likely defect is
(a) improper size fuses
(b) worn-out bearings or low voltage or over load
(c) open-circuit in the winding
(d) short-circuit in the winding

81. In a single-phase transformer, if leakage impedance drop is neglected, the flux in the magnetic core and the leakage flux linking a winding are
(a) proportional to the applied voltage and proportional to the winding current respectively
(b) both proportional to the applied voltage
(c) proportional to the applied voltage respectively
(d) both proportional to the winding current

82. The transformer efficiency, under heavy loads, is comparatively low due to
(a) large increase in copper losses in comparison to the output
(b) large increase in iron losses
(c) drop in power factor
(d) none of these

83. The difference between the number of stator slots and that of rotor in an induction motor should not be equal to P, 2P or 5P. It is essential in order to avoid
(a) synchronous cusps
(b) crawling
(c) magnetic locking
(d) noise and vibrations

84. By connecting reactance at the slip-ring leads of a rotary converter running at a leading power factor, the output d.c. voltage can be raised if
(a) the power factor is made more leading by increasing the excitation
(b) the power factor is made less leading or lagging by increasing the excitation
(c) the power factor is made more leading by decreasing the excitation
(d) the power factor is made less leading or lagging by decreasing the excitation

85. Synchronous impedance of a synchronous machine is given as phasor sum of
(a) armature resistance and armature reactance
(b) armature resistance and leakage reactance
(c) armature resistance and synchronous reactance
(d) armature reactance and leakage reactance

86. Which of the following statements is not true for an induction motor?
(a) If $(1 - s)$ is the power input to the rotor, the power lost in the rotors is $s\ (1 - s)$.
(b) Maximum torque of an induction motor is independent of the rotor resistance.
(c) An induction motor can supply the load stably from $s = 0$ to $s = R_2/X_2$.
(d) The efficiency of an induction motor is maximum, when $R_2 = X_2$.

87. A 3-phase synchronous motor hunts due to
(a) fluctuating load
(b) fluctuating supply voltage
(c) excessive field current
(d) faulty connections
(e) either fluctuating load or fluctuating supply voltage

88. If a dc series motor is operated on ac supply, it
(a) will not start at all
(b) will start and run but will have poor performance such as excessive sparking, poor efficiency and poor power factor
(c) will get damaged due to burning of its windings
(d) will run at excessively high speed

89. In a transformer if in place of sine wave, a peaked voltage is fed to the primary,
(a) the iron losses will be less
(b) the iron losses will be more
(c) the copper losses will be less
(d) the noise level will be low

90. What is meant by the leakage flux of transformer?
(a) It is the flux which is linked with the primary and the secondary winding.
(b) It is that part of the magnetic flux which is significant for radio interference.
(c) It is the magnetic flux which is linked either only with the primary or only with the secondary winding.
(d) The leakage flux in the transformer is the flux whose path is exclusively through the air.

91. In a 3-phase induction motor, the number of slots on stator is not kept an exact multiple of the number of rotor slots because it
(a) facilitates cooling
(b) avoids magnetic locking between stator field and rotor
(c) improves efficiency
(d) improves pf

92. In a transformer supplying inductive load
(a) the secondary current results in equivalent primary current in phase opposition
(b) the secondary terminal voltage is less than the secondary-induced emf
(c) the power factor on primary side will be lower than that of load
(d) all of the above

93. The open-circuit test on a transformer is meant for measuring its
(a) copper losses
(b) iron losses
(c) insulation resistance
(d) equivalent resistance

94. In star-delta starting, a 3-phase induction motor
(a) starts with delta connections and runs on star-connections
(b) starts with star-connections and runs on delta-connections
(c) remains throughout star-connected
(d) remains through out delta connected

95. Slots provided on the stator core of a synchronous machine are of ____ type.
(a) open
(b) semi-closed
(c) totally closed
(d) either open or semi-closed

96. An autotransformer is preferred to a conventional 2-winding transformer
(a) because it is much safer to use an autotransformer
(b) where large number of secondary taps are needed
(c) where it is required to electrically isolate the two windings
(d) where ratio of transformation is nearly one

97. Which of the following methods is employed for starting a 3-phase synchronous motor?
(a) Star-delta starter
(b) Damper winding
(c) Resistance starter in the stator circuit
(d) Damper winding in conjunction with a star-delta starter or an auto-transformer starter

98. The noise and tooth pulsation losses can be minimised by using
(a) large number of open slots in stator
(b) small number of open slots in stator
(c) large number of narrow slots in stator
(d) small number of narrow slots in stator

99. Burning out of windings is due to
(a) open circuited capacitor
(b) short-circuited capacitor
(c) capacitor of improper rating
(d) none of the above

100. In two induction motors, running at the same speed and having same number of poles, the physical dimensions are in the ratio of 3:2. The output of both the motors will be in the ratio of
(a) 3:2 (b) 9:4
(c) 27:8 (d) 81:16

101. The leakage impedances of primary and secondary windings of a transformer are (3 + j4)ohms and (1 + j4) ohms respectively. It can be concluded that the transformers have
(a) low voltage primary
(b) low voltage secondary
(c) high voltage secondary
(d) no conclusion can be drawn on the basis of information provided

102. A 3-phase synchronous motor is operating at a given load. If an increase in excitation reduces the armature current, it can be concluded that the motor is
(a) operating at lagging power factor and absorbing reactive power from the mains
(b) operating at leading power factor and delivering reactive power to the mains
(c) either (a) or (b)
(d) none of these

103. In a 3-phase wound rotor induction motor the short-circuit gear is used to short-circuit the
(a) stator phases of the motor
(b) rotor at slip-rings
(c) starting resistances in the starter
(d) none of the above

104. If a rotor of induction motor could be theoretically rotated at synchronous speed, the voltage that would be generated in the rotor, is
(a) zero
(b) equal to applied voltage
(c) more than applied voltage
(d) none of these

105. A three-ring synchronous converter supplying a d.c. 3-wire system must have the secondary of its transformer connected as
(a) delta only (b) delta or star
(c) zig-zag only (d) star or zig-zag

106. The most suitable rotor for a turbo-alternator designed to operate at high speed is
(a) salient pole type rotor
(b) smooth cylindrical type rotor
(c) squirrel cage rotor
(d) either of the above

107. A permanent-split capacitor motor does NOT have
(a) a starting winding
(b) a centrifugal switch
(c) a squirrel-cage rotor
(d) reversing capabilities

108. The crawling occurs in induction motors due to
(a) low supply voltage
(b) over load
(c) harmonics developed in the motor
(d) jammed bearings
(e) improper design of machine

109. An open-circuit test on a transformer is performed basically to determine
(a) copper loss
(b) iron loss
(c) regulation
(d) leakage impedance

110. Speeds higher than synchronous speed can be had by
(a) line voltage control
(b) rotor slip power control
(c) rotor resistance control
(d) frequency control

111. No-load test on a transformer is carried out to determine
(a) copper loss
(b) full-load current
(c) magnetising current
(d) efficiency of the transformer

112. Stability of a synchronous motor____with the increase in excitation.
(a) increases
(b) decreases
(c) remains unaffected
(d) none of these

113. The squirrel-cage rotor or a 4-pole induction motor
(a) can be used for only 4 pole induction motor
(b) can be used for motors having 2, 4 or 8 poles only
(c) can be used for motor with any number of poles
(d) none of these

114. Which one of the following statements is not true for an ac servo-motor?
(a) Has low inertia rotor
(b) Is a single phase motor
(c) Has slip torque characteristic as straight line with negative slope
(d) Reference voltage frequency is high compared to signal frequency

115. AC servo-motor has the drawback of
(a) commutation problem
(b) low starting torque
(c) poor reliability
(d) all of these

116. The generator which gives d.c. supply to the rotor is called
(a) convertor (b) exciter
(c) invertor (d) rectifier

117. Lesser the number of anodes in mercury arc rectifier
(a) more smoother will be the output
(b) less smoother will be the output
(c) output smoothness will have no effect
(d) none of these

118. The armature mmf. wave for a d.c. machine is
(a) sinusoidal and rotates w.r.t. armature
(b) sinusoidal and rotates w.r.t.field
(c) triangular and rotates w.r.t. armature
(d) triangular and stationary w.r.t. armature

119. Harmonics in the emf generated in an alternator can be reduced by
(a) skewing the slots
(b) chamfering the salient pole tips
(c) using distributed winding
(d) all of the above

120. In a polyphase mercury arc rectifier the utility factor is given as

(a) $\dfrac{\sqrt{2m}\sqrt{m}}{\pi}\sin\dfrac{\pi}{m}$

(b) $\dfrac{\sqrt{2m}}{\pi}\sin\dfrac{\pi}{m}$

(c) $\dfrac{\sqrt{2m}}{\pi}\sin\dfrac{\pi}{m}$

(d) $\dfrac{2}{\pi}\sin\dfrac{\pi}{m}$

121. If the centrifugal switch fails to open when the motor attains 70 to 80 per cent of synchronous speed, it would result in
(a) over-loading of main winding
(b) damage to centrifugal switch
(c) damage to the starting winding
(d) none of the above

122. In relation to a transformer, the ratio 20:1 indicates that
(a) there are 20 turns on primary and one turn on secondary
(b) secondary voltage is 1/20th of primary voltage
(c) primary current is 20 times greater than secondary current
(d) for every 20 turns on primary, there is one turn on secondary

123. For stability of an ac servo-motor
(a) a negative slope on the torque speed curve is necessary
(b) linearized torque-speed curve is essential
(c) the ratio of the rotor reactance to rotor resistance should be high
(d) none of these

124. In an induction motor with star-delta starter at star position
(a) the torque developed is three times as high as at the run position
(b) the torque developed is $\sqrt{3}$ times as high as at the run position
(c) the current is $\frac{1}{\sqrt{3}}$ times of the current at direct on line starting
(d) none of these

125. Short-circuit test is performed on a transformer with a certain impressed voltage at rated frequency. If the short-circuit test is now performed with the same magnitude of impressed voltage, but at a frequency higher than the rated frequency, then
(a) the magnitude of current and power factor will both increase
(b) the magnitude of current will decrease but the power factor will increase
(c) the magnitude of current will increase but power factor will decrease
(d) the magnitude of current as well as the power factor will decrease

126. The iron losses in a 10 kVA, 240/100 V single phase transformer are 100 watts. The maximum efficiency occurs at full load. When the secondary current is 50 A, the copper losses in the transformer will be
(a) 100 W (b) 50 W
(c) 25 W (d) 10 W

127. In a transformer when two or more dielectrics, having different permitivities are used in series, incorrect proportioning of their thickness may result in
(a) very poor heat dissipation
(b) very high leakage current
(c) very high dielectric loss
(d) failure of insulation due to excessive electric stresses

128. Closed windings may be
(a) single layer
(b) double layer
(c) both single layer and double layer
(d) all of these

129. The speed of a squirrel cage induction motor cannot be controlled by___ method.
(a) pole changing
(b) frequency control
(c) rotor resistance control
(d) line voltage control

130. For the applications requiring speed ratio other than 2:1, the speed control can be affected by varying the number of stator poles employing
(a) multiple stator winding
(b) pole amplitude modulation technique
(c) consequent pole technique
(d) any of the above

131. Which of the following statements regarding permanent capacitor motor is false?
(a) It does not have a centrifugal switch.
(b) It does not have a starting winding and a squirrel cage rotor.
(c) Its auxiliary winding is designed for continuous rating.
(d) It is more sensitive to voltage variations due to its poor running torque.

132. Skew of rotor bar eliminates
(a) the effect of space harmonics
(b) the entire effect of crawling
(c) magnetic noise
(d) vibration due to unequal force developed on rotor

133. The stator of an alternator gets overheated due to
(a) open phase
(b) unbalanced currents in the phases
(c) improper alignment of the rotor
(d) any one or more of the above

134. The self-induced voltage of a coil depends upon
(a) the voltage applied to the coil
(b) the shape of the iron core
(c) the shape of the bobbin
(d) the number of turns of the coil

135. In a three-phase induction motor, the power output is maximum when the equivalent load resistance is
(a) equal to the standstill resistance of the motor
(b) equal to the standstill impedance of the motor
(c) equal to the standstill reactance of motor
(d) none of the above

136. The phenomenon of oscillation of the rotor of a synchronous motor about its equilibrium position corresponding to new load on sudden throwing off or increasing of load is called the
(a) swinging (b) crawling
(c) hunting (d) none of these

137. The torque of a rotor in an induction motor under running condition is maximum
(a) at unity value of the slip
(b) at zero value of slip
(c) at the value of slip which makes the rotor reactance half of the rotor resistance
(d) at the value of slip which makes the rotor reactance per phase equal to its resistance per phase

138. A 3-phase induction motor is operating at its rated torque. If the supply voltage falls to 75% of its normal value,
(a) the motor will get heated up to inadmissible extent after some time
(b) the motor will stop
(c) the slip will decrease
(d) the stator and rotor current will decrease

139. In a shaded pole motor, the rotating field is developed by using
(a) salient poles (b) a capacitor
(c) shading coils (d) damper winding

140. In a comparative study of the torque-slip characteristic of a balanced polyphase induction motor and that of a single phase induction motor, it is found that for zero slip
(a) the torque for the former is zero and has a non-zero negative value for the latter
(b) the torque has a non-zero positive value on the former and has a non-zero negative value on the latter
(c) the torque is zero on both of the characteristics
(d) the torque has non-zero positive value on both of the characteristics

141. The speed of the slipring induction motor can be controlled by
(a) changing supply frequency
(b) changing number of poles
(c) changing the resistance of the rotor winding
(d) all of these

142. A machine is driven by an induction motor running at nominal speed. What happens if the counter torque of the machine becomes larger than the maximum torque of the motor?

(a) The induction motor heats up to an inadmissible extent.

(b) The induction motor stops.

(a) The speed of the induction motor is reduced to less than half of its nominal speed.

(d) The winding of the motor can be damaged because of high current strength.

143. In which of the following motors, the stator and rotor magnetic fields rotate at the same speed?

(a) Induction motors

(b) Synchronous motors

(c) Universal motors

(d) Reluctance motors

144. The power scale of circle diagram of an induction motor is determined from ______ test data only.

(a) open circuit (b) stator resistance

(c) short-circuit (d) slip

145. The maximum possible speed of a 3-phase squirrel cage induction motor running at a slip of 4% is

(a) 2,880 rpm (b) 3,000 rpm

(c) 1,440 rpm (d) 960 rpm

146. The direction of rotation in a shaded-pole motor is always toward the

(a) main pole (b) grease

(c) salient pole (d) consequent pole

147. An induction motor is running at its rated torque. The applied voltage is reduced from the rated value of 440 V to 300 V. What is the consequence of this?

(a) After some time the motor heats up to an inadmissible extent

(b) The current decreases

(c) The motor stops

(d) The speed reduces considerably

148. During a short circuit test, the iron losses are negligible because

(a) the mutual flux is small

(b) the power factor is low

(c) the current is high

(d) none of these

149. The short-pitch winding has the advantage(s) of

(a) increased mechanical strength

(b) reduced tooth ripples as fractional number of slots per pole can be used

(c) saving in copper requirement in the coil ends due to shorter span

(d) increased rating of the machine for a given size

(e) all of the above except (d)

150. The synchronous motor runs at

(a) less than synchronous speed

(b) synchronous speed

(c) more than synchronous speed

(d) none of the above

151. Which of the following statements associated with repulsion motor is wrong?

(a) Its direction of rotation depends upon the position of brushes.

(b) Its characteristics are similar to those of series motor.

(c) Its power factor is high.

(d) It is used where sturdy motor with large starting torque and adjustable but constant speed is required.

152. If H be the ratio of heating in the armature of a synchronous converter running as a converter to that while running as a d.c. generator with the same d.c. output then the ratio of outputs as a converter to that as a d.c. generator for the same armature heating is

(a) $1/\sqrt{H}$ (b) 1/H

(c) H (d) $\sqrt{H}$

153. In a 3-phase induction regulator, the output line voltages are in phase with the supply line voltage in

(a) maximum buck position only

(b) maximum boost position only
(c) both maximum boost and maximum buck positions
(d) all positions

154. Single phase synchronous motors
(a) are self starting motors
(b) do not need dc excitation
(c) operate at constant speed
(d) are built for a wider range of output
(e) all of the above

155. Electromagnetic force or torque developed in any physical system tends to
(a) increase the magnetic stored energy at constant flux
(b) decrease the magnetic stored energy at constant current
(c) decrease the reluctance
(d) decrease in inductance

156. The condition(s) to be fulfilled for proper synchronising of 3-phase alternators is/are
(a) the terminal voltage of the incoming machine must be approximately equal to bus-bar voltage
(b) the frequency of the incoming machine must be equal to that of bus-bars
(c) the phase of the incoming machine voltage must be the same as that of the bus-bar voltage relative to load (the phase voltage of the incoming machine and those of bus-bar should be in phase opposition)
(d) the phase sequence of incoming machine voltage must be the same as that of the bus-bars
(e) all of the above

157. Which of the following statements about the humming of transformer is true?
(a) The humming is caused by vibrations of the low voltage winding through which the high current flows.
(b) The humming is caused by the periodic force of attraction between the laminations of the core.
(c) The frequency of humming tone is 50 Hz.
(d) The frequency of humming tone is 2×50 Hz = 100 Hz.

158. The damping winding in a synchronous motor is generally used
(a) to provide starting torque only
(b) to reduce noise level
(c) to reduce eddy currents
(d) to prevent hunting and provide the starting torque

159. A 3-phase synchronous motor connected to an infinite bus is operating at half-full load with normal excitation. When the load on the synchronous motor is suddenly increased
(a) its speed will first decrease and then become synchronous
(b) its speed will first increase and then become synchronous
(c) its speed will fluctuate around synchronous speed and then become synchronous
(d) its speed will remain unchanged

160. If diameter and speed of the stator bore of the high-speed turbo-alternator and a low-speed hydel generator of identical ratings are compared, then
(a) the turbo-alternator has larger diameter and larger length
(b) the turbo-alternator has smaller diameter and smaller axial length
(c) the turbo-alternator has larger diameter and smaller axial length
(d) the turbo-alternator has smaller diameter and larger axial length

161. During starting of a double cage induction motor, the current induced in the rotor
(a) flows mostly through the lower cage
(b) flows mostly through the upper cage
(c) is equally divided between the two windings
(d) none of the above

162. The capacitor in a capacitor-start motor is connected in series with the
(a) running winding
(b) starting winding and centrifugal switch
(c) compensation winding
(d) split-phase winding

163. A 250 μF, 250 volt capacitor is defective. How many 250 μF, 150 volt capacitors are required and how are they connected to obtain 250 μF at 250 volts?
(a) Two connected in series
(b) Two connected in parallel
(c) Four connected in series
(d) Four connected in parallel

164. In a synchronous machine, the stator frame serves the purpose of
(a) holding the armature stampings in position and also in some cases for circulating cold water for cooling
(b) insulating the armature windings
(c) providing path to the magnetic flux
(d) protecting the whole machine

165. Which of the following statements about a transformer having a small short circuit voltage is true?
(a) The transformation ratio of the transformer is small.
(b) During operation the transformer has high iron losses.
(c) During operation the transformer has high copper losses.
(d) A high short-circuit current flows through the transformer.

166. In induction machines, it is usually a standard practice to employ
(a) integral-slot winding with full pitch coils
(b) integral slots winding with chorded coils
(c) fractional slot winding with fractional pitch coils
(d) fractional slot winding with full pitch coils

167. An induction motor always operates on lagging power factor. This is due to
(a) stator reactance
(b) rotor leakage reactance
(c) the large reactive lagging magnetizing current essential to produce the magnetic flux
(d) all of the above

168. The leakage flux of a transformer is defined as following
(a) it is the flux which is linked with the primary and the secondary winding
(b) it is magnetic flux which is linked either only with the primary or only with the secondary
(c) it is the flux whose path is exclusively through the air
(d) none of these

169. Reluctance torque is the
(a) torque developed in a given synchronous motor as a function of field excitation and the sine of the torque angle
(b) torque developed by salient pole synchronous or synchronous induction motors due to variations in air gap produced by armature reaction
(c) torque developed by non-salient pole asynchronous motor
(d) torque developed by none of the above

170. The distribution transformers are designed to keep the iron-losses minimum because
(a) iron-losses may destroy the insulation
(b) iron-losses will heat up the oil of the transformer
(c) the primary of distribution transformer is energized for all the twenty-four hours
(d) iron-losses produce time harmonics

171. Synchronous speed is defined as the speed at which the
(a) stator magnetic field rotates
(b) rotor rotates on no load
(c) rotor rotates on full load
(d) none of the above

172. The short-circuit characteristic of an alternator is
(a) always linear
(b) always non-linear
(c) sometimes linear and sometimes non-linear
(d) none of these

173. The short-circuit test on a transformer is conducted to obtain
(a) core losses at any load
(b) ohmic losses at any load
(c) hysteresis losses
(d) both core losses and ohmic losses

174. A set of resonant shunts is connected across the output terminals of a multi-anode mercury arc rectifier in order to
(a) reduce harmonic effect
(b) reduce noise level
(c) reduce internal losses
(d) improve the supply power factor

175. Synchronising current means
(a) the total current supplied to the load by the alternators operating in parallel
(b) the current supplied by the synchronous generator
(c) the current circulating in the local circuit of two alternators operating in parallel which brings the alternators in synchronism once they are out of it
(d) none of the above

176. The transformer oil should have
(a) low volatility
(b) high dielectric strength
(c) good resistance to emulsion with water
(d) low viscosity to provide good heat transfer
(e) all of the above

177. Sludging of transformer oil means
(a) continuous expansion and contraction due to heating and cooling
(b) formation of semi-solid hydrocarbon due to heat and oxidation
(c) decomposition of transformer oil under the influence of power arcs
(d) evaporation of transformer oil due to heating

178. In a shaded pole type motor, the revolving field is produced by the use of
(a) capacitor
(b) copper winding
(c) shading coils
(d) using damper winding

179. For induction motors, normally
(a) the rotor winding is connected to supply and the stator winding is short-circuited
(b) the stator winding is connected to supply and the rotor winding is short circuited
(c) both the stator and the rotor windings are connected to supply
(d) the stator winding is connected to supply and the rotor winding is open-circuited

180. For a simplex lap winding, the commutator pitch is equal to
(a) + 1 (b) ± 1
(c) – 1 (d) ± 2

181. Reluctance torque in rotating machines is present when
(a) airgap is not uniform
(b) reluctance seen by stator mmf is constant
(c) reluctance seen by rotor mmf varies
(d) reluctance seen by rotor mmf is constant

182. An alternator is connected to the bus bars and is supplying load. Its prime mover is suddenly shut down. The alternator will
(a) continue to work as an alternator
(b) continue to run as synchronous motor but direction of rotation will reverse
(c) continue to run as synchronous motor and the direction of rotation will remain the same
(d) none of above

183. When a salient pole 3-phase synchronous motor is started by induction motor action and its field is connected across a field discharge resistance, starting torque is developed by
(a) reluctance torque due to saliency of the rotor
(b) eddy current and hysteresis torque in pole faces
(c) induction motor torque in field and damper windings
(d) all of the above

184. The regulation of an alternator is defined as the
(a) increase in terminal voltage when full load is thrown off, assuming field current and speed remaining the same
(b) fall in terminal voltage when the full load is thrown off, assuming field current and speed remaining unchanged
(c) the change in terminal voltage under the conditions of maximum and minimum excitations
(d) none of the above

185. Electromagnetic torque is present in rotating machines when
(a) stator winding carries current
(b) rotor winding carries current
(c) both stator and rotor windings carry current
(d) none of the above

186. The efficiency of a power transformer is maximum at
(a) nearly full load (b) 1/2 full load
(c) 1/4 full load (d) 1/8 full load

187. The short-circuit test in a transformer is used to determine
(a) iron loss at any load
(b) copper loss at any load
(c) hysteresis loss
(d) eddy-current loss

188. In case of a split-phase motor, the phase shift between currents in the two windings is around
(a) 30° (b) 70°
(c) 90° (d) 120°

189. When an alternator designed for operation at 60 Hz is operated at 50 Hz
(a) kVA rating will increase in the ratio of 1:2
(b) operating voltage will reduce in the ratio of 5/6
(c) operating voltage will increase in the ratio of 1:2
(d) operating voltage will reduce in the ratio of $\left(\frac{5}{6}\right)^2$

190. What is the use of the bright lamp circuit?
(a) It is used during synchronization to indicate equal voltages of generator and line.
(b) It is used during synchronization to indicate that generator and line are having the same phase.
(c) It is used to start synchronous motors.
(d) It is used to indicate when the power factor of a synchronous motor is exactly 1.

191. Which of the following statements about a short-circuit power transformer is true?
(a) There is a fuse in its primary circuit.
(b) There is a bimetallic switch in its primary circuit.
(c) There is a fast magnetic switch in its primary circuit.
(d) The short-circuit current can continuously flow through it without causing a damage.

192. For core type power transformers, both primary and secondary windings have circular coil sections, because this section
(a) is easier to wind
(b) requires minimum copper and, therefore, less I^2R loss
(c) results in less core material and, therefore, less core loss
(d) 1 as the strongest mechanical shape

193. As compared to capacitor start motors two capacitor type induction motors have
(a) better power factor and better efficiency
(b) constant torque and so quite operation
(c) greater overload capacity
(d) high starting torque
(e) all of the above

194. In a capacitor-start, capacitor-run induction motor, the split phase angle can be adjusted to be nearly 90° by choosing the proper
(a) number of turns on the auxiliary winding
(b) value of capacitor for the auxiliary winding
(c) value of capacitor for the main working
(d) any of the above

195. The biggest size of alternators used in India is
(a) 200 MW (b) 350 MW
(c) 500 MW (d) 1000 MW

196. If a 3-phase, 60 Hz, 10-pole induction motor has a full load slip of 0.075, then the speed of rotor relative to revolving field will be
(a) 54 r.p.m. (b) 1000 r.p.m.
(c) zero r.p.m. (d) 720 r.p.m.

197. The direction of rotation of a split phase induction motor can be reversed by reversing the connections to the supply of
(a) auxiliary winding only
(b) main winding only
(c) either (a) or (b)
(d) both (a) and (b) simultaneously

198. A synchronous motor operating at leading power factor can be employed as a
(a) phase advancer
(b) voltage booster
(c) mechanical synchroniser
(d) synchronous reactor

199. In an ac series motor
(a) the starting current is about 2.5 times of full load current
(b) the starting torque is about 4 times of full load torque
(c) power factor varies from 0.9 to 0.95 lagging
(d) all of the above

200. The maximum temperature permitted for class A insulation is
(a) 180° C (b) 165° C
(c) 120° C (d) 105° C

201. A d.c. overcompounded generator was operating satisfactorily and supplying power to an infinite bus. When the prime-mover failed to supply any mechanical power, the machine would then run as a
(a) cumulatively compounded motor with speed reversed
(b) cumulatively compounded motor with direction of rotation as before
(c) differentially compounded motor with speed reversed
(d) differentially compounded motor with direction of rotation as before

202. The carbon brushes are generally used as they
(a) are self lubricating
(b) are soft
(c) have negative temperature coefficient
(d) possess all the above three properties

203. The core (or iron) losses, in a dc machine occur due to
(a) eddy current loss only
(b) hysteresis loss only
(c) both hysteresis and eddy current losses
(d) air friction only

204. In a dc motor the windage loss is proportional to
(a) supply voltage
(b) square of the supply voltage
(c) square of the flux density
(d) square of the armature speed

205 In a dc machine, the constant losses are
(a) armature copper loss
(b) series field copper loss
(c) commutator loss
(d) shunt field copper loss
(e) iron and mechanical loss
(f) (d) and (e)

206 Consider the following statements regarding the starting of a dc shunt motor.
1. External field resistance should be minimum
2. External field resistance should be maximum
3. Reduced voltage should be applied to the armature
4. Increased voltage should be applied to the armature

Of these statements
(a) 1 and 3 are correct
(b) 1 and 4 are correct
(c) 2 and 3 are correct
(d) 2 and 4 are correct

207. In a d.c. machine the armature reaction and the inductance of the commutating coils results in
(a) over-commutation
(b) sinusoidal commutation
(c) linear commutation
(d) under commutation

208. The emf generated by a d.c. generator is limited to 650 V. This is mainly due to limitations imposed by
(a) armature (b) brush material
(c) commutator (d) insulating materials

209. A d.c. motor is to drive a load which is almost nil for certain part of the load cycle and peak value for short duration. The most suitable d.c. motor is
(a) Series
(b) Shunt
(c) Differential compound
(d) Cumulative compound

210. The polarity of a d.c. generator is reversed by reversing the direction of
(a) field current as well as rotation
(b) rotation
(c) field current
(d) none of these

211. The armature core of a d.c. machine gets over heated due to
(a) copper loss occurring in armature wiring only
(b) eddy current loss only
(c) hysteresis loss only
(d) all of the above

212. If some of the switching devices in a convertor are controlled ones and others are simply diodes, the convertor is called
(a) dc convertor (b) semiconvertor
(c) full convertor (d) ac convertor

213. A dc shunt motor is driving a mechanical load at rated voltage with normal excitation. If the load torque is increased to double of the normal one, the speed of the motor will
(a) become half (b) become double
(c) increase slightly (d) fall slightly

214. Wave OAB is produced in _____ revolution(s) of conductor.

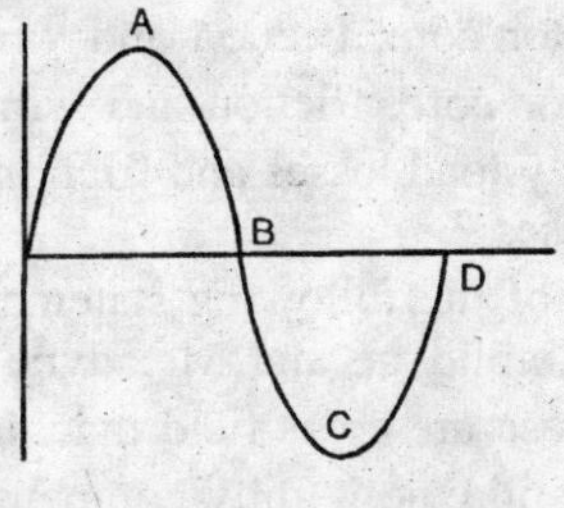

(a) two (b) one
(c) half (d) one quarter

215. The load current and flux of a d.c. motor are kept constant, if the supply voltage is increased by 20%, its speed will
(a) remain unchanged
(b) increases by 20%
(c) decreases by 20%
(d) depend upon the armature resistance

216. The commutator of a d.c. machine acts as a
(a) full-wave rectifier
(b) half-wave rectifier
(c) controlled full-wave rectifier
(d) controlled half-wave rectifier

217. A d.c. shunt motor runs at 200 V supply, if the armature current is 20 A and resistance of the armature is 0.5 ohm, the back e.m.f. develop will be
(a) 210 V (b) 200 V
(c) 190 V (d) 180 V

218. In a d.c. machine
(a) the current and emf in armature conductors are alternating while those at the terminals are unidirectional
(b) the current and emf in armature conductors are unidirectional while those at the terminals are alternating
(c) the current and emf in armature conductors and at the terminals are unidirectional
(d) the emf in armature conductors and at the terminals is alternating while current there is unidirectional

219. Rotational losses in electrical machines consist of
(a) friction and windage losses
(b) stator core, friction and windage losses
(c) rotor core, friction and windage losses
(d) stray load losses and friction and windage losses

220. Which of the following statements associated with Amplidyne and Metadyne are correct?
(a) These are cross-field machines.
(b) Amplidyne is fully compensated machine and Metadyne is under compensated machine.
(c) Commutating poles are also provided in these machines.
(d) Compensating winding is connected in series with the load output brush terminals.
(e) All of the above.

221. If field of one of two generators operating in parallel is made very weak, then it will
(a) not take any load
(b) take major share of load
(c) operate as a motor and run in the same direction
(d) operate as a motor and run in the opposite direction

222. Direct-on-line (DOL) starters are not suitable for starting large d.c. motors, because
(a) the starting current will be enormously high, which will cause large voltage drop in the supply mains
(b) the motor may not start
(c) the motor may run away
(d) the starting torque becomes low

223. In a d.c. machine how are the commutating pole winding connected?
(a) In series with the shunt winding
(b) Parallel to the shunt winding
(c) In series with the armature winding
(d) Parallel to the armature winding

224. The direction of rotation of a d.c. motor is reversed by
(a) reversing armature connections
(b) interchanging the armature and field connection
(c) adding resistance to the field circuit
(d) reversing supply connections

225. Which of the following winding is connected in series with armature winding of d.c. machine?
(a) Series winding
(b) Auxiliary series winding
(c) Compensating winding
(d) Commutating pole winding

226. A d.c. machine used as a generator has an efficiency of 90% when the output voltage and current are 220 V and 10 A respectively. If the machine is used as a motor and takes 10 A from 220 A supply the efficiency will be
(a) 90% (b) less than 90%
(c) more than 90% (d) none of these

227. In a d.c. motor if the brushes are given a backward shift, then
(a) commutation is worsened and speed decreases
(b) commutation is improved and speed decreases
(c) commutation is unaffected and speed increases
(d) commutation is improved and speed increases

228. The function of the starter in a d.c. machine is
(a) to avoid the excessive current at starting
(b) to control the speed
(c) to avoid armature reaction
(d) to avoid excess heating

229. The coil span
(a) must be exactly equal to pole pitch
(b) may or may not be exactly equal to pole pitch
(c) can never be equal to pole pitch
(d) none of these

230. The main disadvantage(s) of the Ward-Leonard system is/are
(a) high initial cost
(b) poor overall efficiency
(c) high maintenance cost
(d) all of the above

231. If the back emf of a d.c. motor is absent, then
(a) motor will run at very high speed
(b) motor will run at very slow speed
(c) motor will not run at all
(d) motor will burn

232. Air gap at the pole tips of a dc machine is kept more than that at the centre of the pole mainly to reduce
(a) reactance voltage
(b) effect of armature reaction
(c) losses of armature core
(d) noise of the machine

233. The rated speed of a given d.c. shunt motor is 1050 rpm. To run this machine at 1200 rpm, which of the following speed control scheme will be used
(a) Armature current resistance control
(b) Field resistance control
(c) Ward-Leonard control
(d) None of these

234. Shunt generator to the other operating in parallel is by
(a) adjustment of speeds
(b) adjustment of armature resistances
(c) adjustment of field rheostats
(d) using equalizer connections

235. The armature current in a dc shunt generator is given as
(a) $\frac{E_g + V}{R_a}$ (b) $\frac{E_g}{R_a}$
(c) $\frac{E_g - V}{R_a}$ (d) $I_L + I_{sh}$

236. D.C. series motors are best suited for traction work because
(a) torque is proportional to the square of armature current and speed is inversely proportional to torque
(b) torque is proportional to the square of armature current and speed is proportional to torque
(c) torque and speed are proportional to square of armature current
(d) none of these

237. Ward-Leonard system for controlling the speed of dc motor is used where
(a) the speed in both the directions is required
(b) very fine speed control over the whole range from zero to normal speed is required
(c) the accuracy in speed control is required
(d) all of the above

238. Interpole are used in
(a) lap wound machines
(b) wave wound machines
(c) both lap and wave wound machines
(d) none of above

239. An external resistance is added in the series with the field of a d.c. shunt motor. When the motor runs, the effect of resistance is
(a) to reduce the speed of the motor
(b) to increase the speed of the motor
(c) to reduce the armature current drawn by the motor
(d) to reduce the losses

240. Three point starters are not suitable for applications where speed variation by flux control is required because the motor may
(a) not start
(b) run away
(c) stop at very high speed
(d) stop at very slow speed

241. In Ward-Leonard system, the lower limit of speed is imposed by
(a) armature resistance
(b) field resistance
(c) residual magnetism of the generator
(d) none of the above

242. In dc shunt motors, at start, the field excitation is kept at maximum value in order to
(a) reduce starting torque
(b) increase acceleration duration
(c) reduce armature heating
(d) avoid voltage dip in the supply mains

243. In dc machines
(a) induced emf and torque are produced in both motor and generator

(b) emf is induced in generator and torque is developed in motor
(c) counter emf is induced in generator and counter torque is developed in motor
(d) none of the above

244. The efficiency of a d.c. machine is maximum when the variable losses is equal to
(a) the constant losses
(b) the square of the constant losses
(c) the square root of the constant losses
(d) zero

245. The brake test for the determination of efficiency of a d.c. machine is
(a) an indirect method
(b) a regenerative method
(c) a direct method
(d) none of these

246. Ohmic losses in a d.c. machine occur in
(a) the armature winding only
(b) the field winding only
(c) the brush contact only
(d) the armature winding, the field winding and also in the brush contact

247. In Ward Leonard method of speed control, the direction of rotation of the motor is reversed usually by reversing the connections of the
(a) generator field terminals
(b) generator armature terminals
(c) motor armature terminals
(d) motor field terminals

248. A d.c. series motor is driving a load with a divertor connected across its armature. If the diverter resistance is decreased, the speed of the motor
(a) increases
(b) decreases
(c) remains unchanged
(d) becomes zero

249. A lap wound armature winding, fitted with a commutator and a pair of brushes on it is rotated at a speed N_r in a rotating magnetic field having P poles and rotating at a speed N_f in space N_f and N_r both being in the same direction. The frequency of induced voltage across the brushes on the commutator is
(a) $\frac{N_f P}{120}$ (b) $\frac{(N_f - N_r)}{120} P$
(c) $\frac{(N_f + N_r)}{120} P$ (d) $\frac{N_r P}{120}$

250. The type of dc generator used for arc welding purposes is a
(a) series generator
(b) shunt generator
(c) cumulatively compounded generator
(d) differentially compounded generator

251. A dc series generator is employed
(a) as a booster to maintain constant voltage at the load end of the feeder
(b) for supplying traction load
(c) for supplying industrial load at constant voltage
(d) for battery charging

252. For reversing the direction of rotation of a d.c. motor
(a) the connections of both armature and field winding are required to be reversed
(b) either armature or field winding connection need to be reversed
(c) only field flux should be reversed
(d) only armature current should be reversed

253. If a current carrying coil is placed in a uniform magnetic field with its plane perpendicular to the direction of magnetic induction, then
(a) the net force and torque on the coil are both zero
(b) the net force is zero but torque is finite
(c) the net force is finite but torque is zero
(d) the net force and torque are both finite

254. The object of using compensation winding in d.c. machines is to neutralize the
(a) armature reaction in the interpolar zone
(b) armature reaction in the commutating zone
(c) armature reaction under the pole faces
(d) cross-magnetizing armature reaction

255. Pole shoe of a dc machine is laminated for the purpose of
(a) decreasing hysteresis loss
(b) decreasing eddy current loss
(c) decreasing both hysteresis and eddy current loss
(d) manufacturing ease

256. In a dc series motor, the torque developed is
(a) inversely proportional to armature current
(b) directly proportional to armature current
(c) proportional to the square of armature current
(d) proportional to the square root of the armature current

257. For efficient operation of a dc motor, the additional resistance inserted in the armature circuit should be
(a) increased in steps
(b) cut-out in steps
(c) left in the armature circuit
(d) removed immediately after start

258. A dc motor is running with a certain load. The effect of adding an external resistance in the shunt field circuit is
(a) to increase the motor speed
(b) to reduce the motor speed
(c) to reduce the armature current of motor
(d) to stop the motor

259. Speed control by variation of field flux results in
(a) constant power drive
(b) variable power drive
(c) constant torque drive
(d) none of these

260. The number of re-entrancy of a duplex lap winding is 2 only if the
(a) number of slots is odd
(b) commutator pitch is odd
(c) number of coils is even
(d) commutator pitch is 2

261. A duplex lap winding with equalizers and even number of pairs of poles is
(a) doubly re-entrant and number of coils per pair of poles is an odd integer
(b) double re-entrant and number of coils per pair of poles is an even integer
(c) singly entrant and number of coils per pair of poles is an even integer
(d) singly entrant and number of coils per pair of poles is an odd integer

262. The loss, which is independent of load as well as flux density in a dc machine, is
(a) windage loss (b) copper loss
(c) eddy current loss (d) hysteresis loss

263. The direction of rotation of a dc compound motor can be reversed by interchanging _____ connections.
(a) armature
(b) series field
(c) shunt field
(d) armature and series field both

264. In a dc generator having P number of poles and speed of N rpm, the frequency of magnetic reversals will be
(a) $\frac{PN}{60}$ (b) $\frac{PN}{120}$
(c) $\frac{PN}{240}$ (d) $\frac{PN}{2}$

265. Flashing of field of dc generator means
(a) neutralization of residual magnetism
(b) creation of residual magnetism by a dc source
(c) increasing flux density by providing extra ampere-turns in field
(d) none of the above

266. Reluctance torque in rotating machines is present, when
(a) airgap is not uniform
(b) reluctance seen by stator mmf varies
(c) reluctance seen by rotor mmf varies
(d) reluctances seen by the working mmf varies

267. The yoke of a large machine is invariably made of fabricated steel because of its
(a) high permeability (b) low permeability
(c) low cost (d) low specific gravity

268. Width of a carbon brush should be equal to
(a) less than the width of one commutator segment
(b) the width of 1 to 2 commutator segments
(c) the width of 2 to 3 commutator segments
(d) the width of more than 3 commutator segments

269. The emf generated by a dc generator may be increased by increasing the
(a) speed of rotation (b) excitation
(c) armature length (d) either (a) or (b)

270. In arc welding, in order to obtain steady arc one should use
(a) dc series generator
(b) dc shunt generator
(c) dc differentially compounded generator
(d) dc cumulatively compounded generator

271. Before connecting the motor to the supply mains it is necessary to ensure that
(a) there is a proper insulation between field winding, armature winding and earth
(b) protective devices have been adjusted at their proper settings
(c) all the necessary connections show continuity
(d) supply voltage is appropriate
(e) all of the above

272. The mmf necessary for establishment of flux in the magnetic circuit of a dc generator can be obtained by means of field coils excited by
(a) some separate source
(b) the generator itself
(c) either of the above methods
(d) none of these

273. A pair of similar dc shunt generator operate in parallel and supply a common load. It is required to switch off machine no. 1 and allow machine no. 2 to supply the circuit load. The following operations are to be used to achieve this
1. Switch off the main switch of machine no. 1
2. Reduce the field current of machine no. 1
3. Increase the field current of machine no. 2
4. Ensure that machine no. 1 just floats

The correct sequence of these operations is
(a) 4, 3, 2, 1 (b) 2, 3, 4, 1
(c) 2, 4, 3, 1 (d) 3, 2, 4, 1

274. Which of the following statement(s) associated with installation and preventive maintenance of dc machines is incorrect?
(a) Accumulation of carbon dust on the commutator surface may result in flash-over.
(b) The commutator should be lubricated in order to reduce brush friction.
(c) Accumulation of dust on the machine may result in overheating of the machine.
(d) Sufficient space is necessary all around the motor for movement of operational and maintenance personnels.
(e) Resistance of earth continuity conductor is to be checked periodically in order to ensure the effectiveness of the earthing system.

275. The terminal board of a motor is as shown in the diagram. Which type of motor is this?

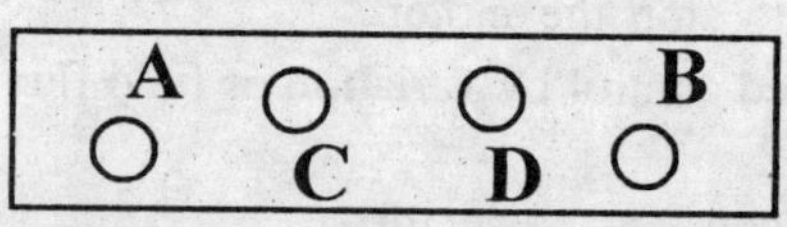

(a) A compound motor with commutating pole winding
(b) A shunt motor with commutating pole winding
(c) A shunt motor without commutating pole winding
(d) A series motor with commutating pole winding

276. Which of the following statement(s) associated with a Rosenberg generator is/are incorrect?
(a) It is an armature excited high speed machine.

(b) It provides constant current over wider limits of speed.
(c) It is a constant voltage generator at low speeds.
(d) It is essentially a 2-pole machine with two sets of brushes arranged on the axis at right angles to each other.
(e) Its voltage polarity is independent of direction of rotation.

277. The magnetic field which initially induces emf in the armature in a self excited dc generator is because of
(a) permanent magnets
(b) armature rotation
(c) residual magnetism
(d) none of the above

278. Short-circuiting is caused in the armature winding due to
(a) failure of insulation between two turns of a coil
(b) failure of insulation between two commutator bars
(c) grounding of two or more turns of the same coil
(d) any of the above

279. Two dc shunt generators having equal open circuit emfs but slight different load characteristics are operating in parallel, then
(a) the machines will share load equally
(b) the machine with more drooping characteristic will supply less load
(c) the machine with more drooping characteristic will supply more load
(d) none of these

280. Efficiency of a dc shunt machine can be computed by knowing
(a) output and input
(b) rating of machine and account of constant losses and armature resistance
(c) either (a) or (b)
(d) none of these

281. The Field's efficiency test of d.c. series motors overcomes the difficulty of obtaining readings relatively light loads by connecting
(a) the series field of the generator in series with the motor armature
(b) the series field of the motor in series with the generator armature
(c) the armature of the generator in series with the motor
(d) the armature of the motor in series with the generator

282. Core loss in a dc machine occurs in
(a) armature only
(b) pole shoe only
(c) yoke only
(d) in all the above three

283. The dc motor draws high current at the starting instant due to absence of back emf. In order to prevent this high inrush of current at start, a resistance is connected
(a) across the field
(b) across the armature
(c) in series with the armature
(d) in series with the field

284. The component of a dc generator which plays vital role in providing direct current is
(a) dummy coils (b) equalizer rings
(c) commutator (d) brushes

285. A separately excited dc generator has an open circuit voltage E_0 for a certain value of field current. If the field current is halved, the open circuit voltage will be
(a) $\frac{1}{2} E_0$
(b) less than $\frac{E_0}{2}$
(c) may be $\frac{E_0}{2}$ or more than $\frac{E_0}{2}$
(d) $2\ E_0$

286. Armature coil is short-circuited by brushes when it lies
(a) along field axis
(b) along neutral axis
(c) in any of the above position
(d) in none of the above positions

287. When a dc machine is connected to the dc supply main it will produce
(a) emf in opposition to applied voltage
(b) unidirectional torque
(c) pulsating torque
(d) copper losses in the windings
(e) all of the above except (c)

288. The magnitude of the back emf. depends upon
(a) flux per pole
(b) speed of the motor
(c) number of the parallel paths in the armature
(d) all of these

289. In cross-field generators
(a) the reversal of speed does not reverse the polarity of the output
(b) compensating winding is provided in order to increase the amplification factor
(c) the number of brush studs is double of that of poles
(d) all of the above

290. For preventive maintenance of a dc machine it is to be ensured that
(a) insulation resistances of the field and armature windings are proper
(b) commutator and brushes are in good condition
(c) bearings are properly greased
(d) motor and its control gear are free from oil and grease
(e) all of the above

291. A dc series motor develops a torque of 20 Nm at 3 A of load current. If the current is increased to 6 A, the torque developed will be
(a) 10 Nm (b) 20 Nm
(c) 80 Nm (d) 40 Nm

292. A cumulative compound long shunt motor is driving a load at rated torque and rated speed. If the series field is shunted by a resistance equal to the resistance of the series field, keeping the torque constant,
(a) the armature current increases.
(b) the motor speed increases.
(c) the armature current decreases.
(d) the motor speed decreases.
(e) both (a) and (b)

293. The function of a starter in a dc motor is to
(a) control its speed
(b) increase its starting torque
(c) limit the starting current to a safer value
(d) reduce armature reaction effect
(e) both (b) and (c)

294. When a current carrying coil (shown below) is placed within a magnetic field, a force will move the coil

(a) to the right (b) to the left
(c) clockwise (d) anti-clockwise

295. An emf is induced in the windings of an armature of a d.c. generator when the armature rotates in
(a) alternating magnetic flux
(b) magnetic field
(c) electrostatic field
(d) electromagnetic flux

296. In a coal mine, Ward Leonard method of speed control, as shown in the given fig., is used to lift coal from the pit through a crane and bucket arrangement. After lifting the coal to desired level and emptying at the dumping ground, the bucket has to be lowered into the pit. The action to be taken at this stage is to reverse the

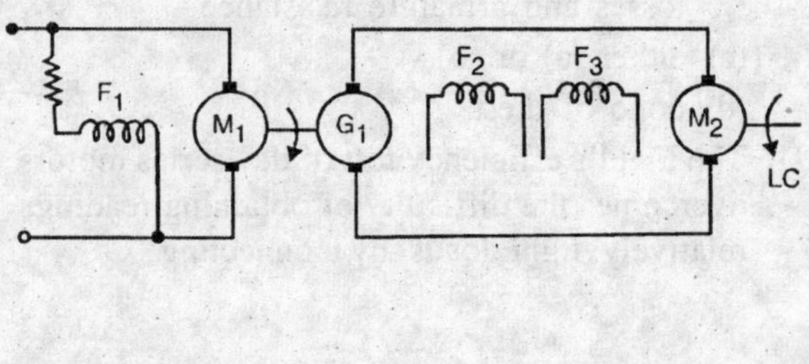

(a) direction of current in F_2 and slowly increase it
(b) current in F_3 and slowly increase it
(c) supply terminal of M_1
(d) direction of current in F_1 and slowly increase it

297. Consider the following statements:
The armature relation mmf. in a d.c. machine is
I. stationary with respect to the field poles
II. rotating with respect to the field poles
III. rotating with respect to the armature
State which of the following is correct
(a) only I (b) Only III
(c) both I and III (d) both II and III

298. A dc shunt generator has an armature resistance of 0.1 Ω and runs at 1200 rpm when delivering 50 kW at 250 V. The speed of the machine, when run as a motor fed from 250 V supply and drawing 50 kW will be approximately
(a) 1,410 rpm (b) 1,020 rpm
(c) 1,100 rpm (d) 1,320 rpm

299. In a Hopkinson test on a pair of shunt machines
(a) the armature currents of the motor and generator are equal
(b) the armature current of the motor is less than that of generator
(c) the armature current of the generator is less than that of the motor
(d) none of these

300. A shunt generator has a speed of 500 rpm when delivering 100 kW at 220 V. It runs as a motor taking an input of 100 kW from 220 V mains, the speed will be
(a) 500 r.p.m.
(b) less than 500 r.p.m.
(c) more than 500 r.p.m.
(d) none of these

301. The presence of equaliser bar
(a) is essential for parallel operation of compound generators
(b) is preferable for parallel operations of compound generators
(c) is unnecessary for parallel operation of compound generators
(d) none of these

302. In a dc machine, iron losses result in
(a) excessive heating of core
(b) loss of efficiency
(c) rise in temperature of ventilating air
(d) all of the above

303. The terminal board of a motor is as shown in the diagram. Which type of motor is this?

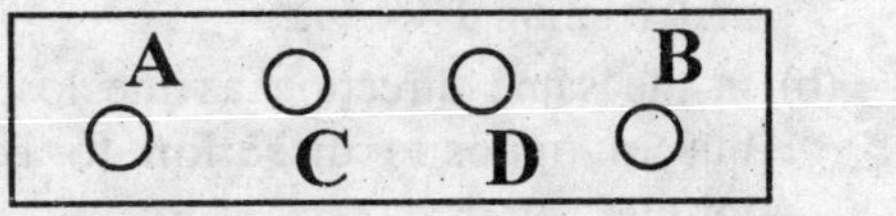

(a) A compound motor without commutating pole winding
(b) A shunt motor with distributed commutating pole winding
(c) A shunt motor without commutating pole winding
(d) A series motor with distributed commutating pole winding

304. To avoid formation of grooves in the commutator
(a) the brushes of opposite polarity should track each other
(b) the brushes of same polarity should track each other
(c) brush position has no effect on the commutator grooving
(d) none of these

305. In case of dc shunt motors, the regenerative braking is employed when the load
(a) has an overhauling characteristic
(b) is variable
(c) is constant
(d) also acts as a braking force
(e) is constantly reducing

306. The variable loss in a dc shunt machine is
(a) iron loss
(b) shunt field loss
(c) armature copper loss
(d) friction and windage loss

307. In a dc machine mechanical losses occur due to
(a) air resistance of rotation to armature and fan
(b) brush friction
(c) brearing friction
(d) all of the above

308. In an electric motor, the electromagnetic torque developed is
(a) in opposite direction to both load torque and frictional torque
(b) in the same direction as the load torque but in opposite direction to frictional torque
(c) in the same direction as the load torque and frictional torque
(d) in the same direction as the frictional torque but in the opposite direction to the load torque

309. For speed control of dc motors using controlled rectifiers, armature voltage control gives speed
(a) above rated speed
(b) below rated speed
(c) above as well as below rated speed
(d) none of these

310. The direction of emf generated in a dc generator can be found out by considering
(a) Fleming's right hand rule
(b) Fleming's left hand rule
(c) Lenz's law
(d) Kirchhoff's law

311. The terminal board of a motor is as shown in the diagram. Which type of motor is this?

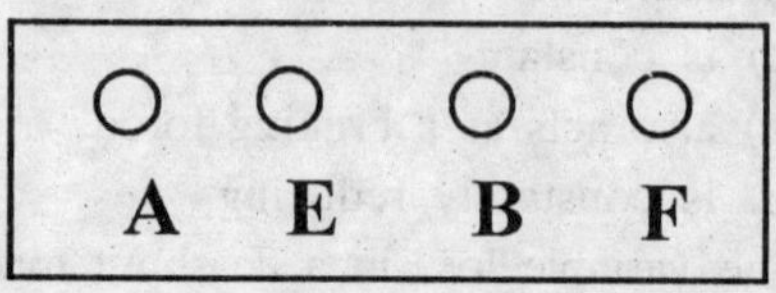

(a) A compound motor with commutating pole winding
(b) A shunt motor with distributed commutating pole winding
(c) A shunt motor with commutating pole winding
(d) A series motor with commutating pole winding

312. Under-commutation results in
(a) sparking at the middle of the brush
(b) sparking at the leading edge of the brush
(c) sparking at the trailing edge of the brush
(d) no sparking

313. If a self-excited dc generator after being installed fails to build up during its first trial, the remedy lies in
(a) increasing the prime-mover speed
(b) reversing the field connections
(c) increasing the field resistance
(d) reducing the field resistance

314. Variation in speed by Ward Leonard control of dc motors occurs due to variation in
(a) field excitation (b) armature current
(c) armature voltage (d) supply voltage

315. The function of a commutator in a d.c. generator is
(a) to collect current from conductors
(b) to change d.c. to a.c.
(c) to conduct the current to the brushes
(d) to change a.c. to d.c.

316. The efficiency of any electrical machine/apparatus will be high, if
(a) its losses are minimum
(b) its losses are more
(c) voltage applied is constant
(d) the current drawn is minimum

317. In a d.c. generator, the polarity of an inter pole is
(a) the polarity of the next main pole
(b) the polarity of the main pole immediately following the interpole
(c) the polarity of the main pole opposite to the interpole
(d) none of these

318. Plugging of d.c. motors is normally executed by
(a) reversing the field polarity
(b) reversing the armature polarity
(c) reversing both armature and field polarity
(d) connecting a resistance across the armature

319. Two d.c. series motors connected in series are driving the same mechanical load. If the motors are now connected in parallel the speed becomes
(a) slightly less than double
(b) slightly less than half
(c) slightly more than double
(d) slightly more than half

320. Eddy current loss in a dc machine is given as $k_e\ (B_{max})^2 f^2 t^2\ V$ where V is the
(a) voltage applied or generated
(b) volume of iron core
(c) peripheral velocity
(d) linear velocity of armature conductors

321. In a dc motor, energy conversion would not have been possible but for
(a) input energy from the supply
(b) production of back emf in the armature
(c) use of commutator
(d) rotation of the machine

322. A d.c. shunt motor is driving a mechanical load at rated voltage and rated excitation. If the load torque becomes double then the speed of the motor
(a) increase slightly (b) decreases slightly
(c) becomes double (d) becomes half

323. In d.c. generators, the polarity of interpoles is
(a) same as that of main pole behind
(b) same as that of main pole ahead
(c) opposite to that of the main pole
(d) none of these

324. The purpose of using interpoles in d.c. machines is to nullify
(a) the demagnetising effect of armature mmf.
(b) the cross-magnetising effect of armature mmf.
(c) the reactance voltage
(d) both the cross-magnetizing mmf. and the reactance voltage

325. If speed of a d.c. shunt motor increases, the back emf
(a) increases
(b) decreases
(c) remains constant
(d) first decreases and then increases

326. Which of the following statements is incorrect? If a starter is not used with large d.c. motor, it will draw a starting current which
(a) is many times its full-load current
(b) will produce excessive line voltage drop
(c) will damage the commutator
(d) will produce very low starting torque

327. The direction of armature current in a d.c. motor is
(a) the same as of the generated emf
(b) opposite to that of the generated emf
(c) not dependent upon the direction of the armature emf
(d) none of the above

328. In a Ward-Leo rd drive, if the field current of the dc generator is suddenly reduced, the controlled dc motor operates
(a) still in the motoring mode
(b) in dynamic braking mode
(c) in counter-current braking mode
(d) in regenerative braking mode

329. The speed of a d.c. shunt motor is required to be more than F.L. speed. This is possible by
(a) increasing the armature current
(b) decreasing the armature current
(c) increasing the excitation current
(d) reducing the field current

330. For non-reversing d.c. drives it is preferable to employ
(a) regenerative braking
(b) dynamic braking with separate excitation
(c) dynamic braking with self excitation
(d) plugging

331. An external resistance added in the field of a d.c. shunt generator will
(a) increase the speed of the generator
(b) increase the voltage of the generator
(c) decrease the voltage of the generator
(d) increase the power delivered

332. The function of equalizing connections in a lap wound d.c. generator is
(a) to neutralise the armature reaction effect
(b) to avoid unequal distribution of currents at brushes
(c) to avoid shunt circuit current
(d) none of these

333. In a d.c. machine the maximum losses occur due to
(a) iron losses (b) mechanical losses
(c) copper losses (d) none of above

334. In a dc shunt generator working on load, the brushes are moved forward in the direction of rotation, as a result of this, commutation will
(a) improve but terminal voltage will fall
(b) worsen and terminal voltage will fall
(c) improve and terminal voltage will rise
(d) none of these

335. The inductor of a three-wire generator should be iron-cored so as to
(a) increase the current through it
(b) reduce the voltage ripples in the output circuit
(c) reduce the current through it
(d) improve the voltage regulation of the machine

336. In the Kapp's modification of Hopkinson's efficiency test
(a) the power losses in the two machines are supplied mechanically
(b) the power output of the generator is dissipated in a resistor
(c) the two machines are mechanically decoupled
(d) the power losses in the two machines are supplied electrically

337. In Rosenberg generators,
(a) use of armature reaction is made
(b) the field coils are shunt connected
(c) the direction of load current is independent of direction of rotation and remains almost constant between wider limits of speed
(d) all of the above

338. Consider the following statements:
If the terminal voltage of a dc shunt motor is halved with the load torque varying as the square of speed, then
1. speed is halved
2. speed remains unaltered
3. armature current is doubled
4. armature current remains unaltered
Of these statements
(a) 1 and 3 are correct
(b) 1 and 4 are correct
(c) 2 and 3 are correct
(d) 2 and 4 are correct

339. A separately excited dc generator is feeding a dc shunt motor. If the load torque on the motor is halved approximately
(a) armature current of both motor and generator are halved
(b) armature current of motor is halved and that of the generator is unaltered
(c) armature current of generator is halved and that of motor is unaltered
(d) armature current of both motor and generator are unaltered

340. Torque developed in a dc motor depends upon
(a) magnetic field
(b) current flowing through the armature conductors
(c) active length of the conductors
(d) number of armature conductors
(e) radius of armature
(f) all of these factors

341. The ratio of the starting torque to full load torque is minimum in case of
(a) cumulative compound motors
(b) differential compound motors
(c) series motors
(d) shunt motors

342. Which of the following dc motors will have highest percentage increase of input current, for the same percentage increase in torque?
(a) Series
(b) Shunt
(c) Cumulative compound
(d) All equal

343. Dynamic braking is very effective if the dc motor
(a) is series excited
(b) is shunt excited
(c) is separately excited
(d) has cumulative compound excitation

344. During rheostatic braking of dc series motors,
(a) the speed is reduced
(b) the direction of rotation is reversed
(c) the machine operates as a generator
(d) none of above

345. In a lap wound dc generator, the equalizer rings are provided to
(a) neutralize the armature reaction effect
(b) avoid short-circuiting
(c) avoid unequal distribution of currents at brushes
(d) avoid harmonics generated in the emf
(e) provide mechanical balancing

346. If starter is not used with large dc motor for starting, it will draw a starting current which
(a) is many times its rated full load current
(b) will produce excessive voltage drop in line
(c) may damage the armature and commutator
(d) will produce very low starting torque
(e) all of the above except (d)

347. The polarity of the interpole is the
(a) same as that of main pole ahead in case of generators
(b) same as that of main pole ahead in case of motor
(c) same as that of main pole behind in case of motor
(d) same as that of main pole behind in case of generator
(e) both (a) and (c)

348. The self induced emf in the coil undergoing commutation is called the
(a) reactance voltage
(b) statically induced voltage
(c) dynamically induced voltage
(d) none of the above

349. Neglecting all losses, the developed torque (T) of a dc separately excited motor, operating under constant terminal voltage, is related to its output power (P) as under
(a) $T \propto \sqrt{P}$ (b) $T \propto P$
(c) $T^2 \propto P^3$ (d) T independent of P

350. If the field of a d.c. shunt motor is opened
(a) it will continue to run at its rated speed
(b) the speed of the motor will become very high
(c) the motor will stop
(d) the speed of motor will decrease

351. Which of the following losses occuring in a machine varies significantly with the load?
(a) Armature copper loss
(b) Shunt field copper loss
(c) Magnetic or iron losses
(d) Mechanical losses

352. Which of the following statements associated with a 3-wire generator are correct?
(a) It is an ordinary dc generator with a special provision for connecting the neutral wire to the armature winding.
(b) It is somewhat more expensive than the standard one.
(c) For operating 3-wire compound generators in parallel it is necessary that two equalizer connections are used to connect all series fields in parallel.
(d) There are two series fields on each 3-wire compound generator.
(e) all of the above.

353. The reactance voltage is
(a) directly proportional to armature current and commutation period

(b) directly proportional to commutation period and inversely proportional to armature current
(c) directly proportional to armature current and inversely proportional to commutation period
(d) none of the above

354. The field current flowing through shunt field in a short shunt compound wound generator is given as

(a) $I_{sh} = \dfrac{V + I_{se}R_{se}}{R_{sh}}$ (b) $I_{sh} = \dfrac{V}{R_{sh}}$

(c) $I_{sh} = \dfrac{E_g}{R_{sh}}$ (d) $I_{sh} = \dfrac{V - I_{se}R_{se}}{R_{sh}}$

355. In a dc shunt motor, the three point starter
(a) limits the starting current to a safer value
(b) provides over-load protection
(c) provides no-volt protection
(d) all of the above

356. The emf generated in a dc generator depends upon
(a) brush contact drop
(b) commutation
(c) number of parallel paths
(d) terminal voltage

357. The electrical efficiency of a dc machine given as the ratio of
(a) VI_L and $E_g\ I_a$ in case of generator
(b) E_bI_a and VI_L in case of motor
(c) output/input
(d) output/output + total loss
(e) both (a) and (b)

358. The speed of a dc motor is
(a) directly proportional to back emf and flux
(b) directly proportional to its back emf and inversely proportional to flux
(c) inversely proportional to both back emf and flux
(d) directly proportional to flux and inversely proportional to back emf

359. A d.c. series motor is running with a diverter connected across its field winding. If the diverter resistance is increased then the speed of the motor
(a) decreases
(b) increases
(c) remains unchanged
(d) becomes excessively high

360. The motor used for intermittent, high torque loads is
(a) d.c. shunt motor
(b) d.c. series motor
(c) differential compound motor
(d) cumulative compound motor

361. Current in a coil undergoing commutation is not able to get reversed completely by the end of commutation period. It is due to
(a) reactance voltage induced in the coil
(b) coil resistance
(c) armature emf
(d) none of the above

362. In Hopkinson's and field's tests, the main common thing is that
(a) both tests are regenerative
(b) both tests use two identical mechanically coupled dc machines
(c) the power drawn in both the tests is negligible to meet the internal losses only
(d) all of the above

363. The yoke of a small dc generator is made of cast iron as it
(a) is cheaper
(b) gives mechanical protection to the machine
(c) completes the magnetic path
(d) all of the above

364. The overall efficiency of a well designed machine may be expected to be around
(a) 99% (b) 92%
(c) 75% (d) 50%

365. In d.c. machines, the power of the interpole is
(a) same as that of the main pole behind for the generators and that of the main pole ahead for the motors

(b) same as that of the main pole ahead for both the generators and the motors
(c) same as that of the main pole ahead for the generators and that of the main pole behind for the motor
(d) none of these

366. The armature of a dc machine has a resistance of 0.1 Ω and is connected to a 230 V supply. What will be the emf of generator giving 80 A?
(a) 8 V (b) 22 V
(c) 238 V (d) 230 V

367. Which of the following dc motors has least drop in speed from no-load to rated full load?
(a) Series motors with interpoles
(b) Series motors without interpoles
(c) Shunt motors with interpoles
(d) Cumulative compound motors with interpoles

368. In a dc machine, the sparking between brushes and commutator surface may be due to
(a) under commutation
(b) over commutation
(c) too rapid reversal of current
(d) any of the above

369. The emf produced in a dc generator is _____ induced emf.
(a) statically (b) dynamically
(c) magnetically (d) electrostatically

370. In a dc machine, which loss increases rapidly with the increase in frequency of magnetic reversals?
(a) Copper loss (b) Hysteresis loss
(c) Eddy current loss (d) Mechanical loss

371. A dc shunt motor is driving a constant torque load with normal excitation. If the field current is halved then the motor will run at
(a) rated speed
(b) half or rated speed
(c) double of rated speed
(d) slightly less than double the rated speed

372. The armature current of a dc shunt motor under the condition of development of maximum power will be _____ full load current.
(a) more than (b) less than
(c) equal to (d) almost negligible

373. Which of the following is not a cross-field machine?
(a) Rosenberg generator
(b) Amplidyne
(c) Metadyne
(d) Three-wire generator

374. The induced voltage in a single loop reverses
(a) once each revolution
(b) once each half revolution
(c) once each one-quarter revolution
(d) 8 times each revolution

375. D.C. motors should be stopped by opening the line switches and not by forcing the starter handle back to the off position because
(a) heavy sparking occurs at the brushes
(b) heavy sparking occurs at the first stud of the starting resistance steps
(c) both (a) and (b)
(d) none of these

376. Commutation conditions at full-load for a large d.c. machine can be checked by
(a) the brake test
(b) the Swinburne's test
(c) the Hopkinson's test
(d) none of the above

377. In an over loaded machine, the main danger is due to overheating of
(a) bus-bars (b) bearings
(c) windings (d) none of these

378. Interpoles are connected in series with the
(a) line
(b) armature winding
(c) shunt field winding
(d) line and armature winding

379. When two dc series generators are operating in parallel, an equalizer bar is used
(a) to reduce armature reaction

(b) to increase emf
(c) to increase the speed
(d) to reduce the flux
(e) so that the two similar machines take approximately equal load current

380. When a shunt generator is delivering a certain load current, its terminal voltage
(a) will always be less than open circuit voltage
(b) will always be greater than open circuit voltage
(c) may be greater or less than the open circuit voltage
(d) none of these

381. For the production of induced e.m.f., field system of an electric machine
(a) must be on stator
(b) may be on stator or rotor
(c) must be on rotor
(d) none of these

382. If the voltage applied across the armature of a dc motor is reduced by 5 %, keeping the load current and field current unchanged, the speed of the motor will
(a) increase by about 5%
(b) reduce by about 5%
(c) remain unaltered
(d) unpredictable

383. When a dc cumulative compound wound motor is loaded,
(a) torque increases and speed decreases
(b) torque decreases and speed increases
(c) both speed and torque increase
(d) both speed and torque decrease

384. The interpole winding consists of
(a) a large number of turns of thin wire
(b) a small number of turns of thick wire
(c) a large number of turns of thick wire
(d) none of these

385. A shunt generator can self-excite
(a) only if the resistance of the field circuit is less than critical value
(b) only if the resistance of the field circuit is greater than critical value
(c) irrespective of the value of the resistance is the field circuit
(d) none of above

386. Two shunt generators having slightly different external characteristics are operating in parallel and their open circuit emf are equal. Then
(a) the machine with more drooping characteristic will supply greater load
(b) the machine with more drooping characteristic will supply less load
(c) the two machines will supply equal loads
(d) none of above

387. A series generator is provided with diverter and is delivering its rated current. If the diverter switch is opened
(a) the terminal voltage will increase
(b) the terminal voltage will decrease
(c) the terminal voltage will remain the same
(d) none of these

388. In a dc motor, if armature current is increased, keeping field current constant, the torque developed will
(a) remain unchanged
(b) decrease in inverse proportion
(c) increase proportionately
(d) increase in proportion to the square of the armature current

389. In a Hopkinson test on two shunt machines
(a) the field currents of the two machines are equal
(b) the field current of the generator is more than that of the motor
(c) the field current of the motor is more than that of the generator
(d) none of these

390. The mechanical output available at the dc motor shaft is equal to
(a) electrical power input to motor
(b) electrical power input less iron and friction losses
(c) electrical power input less copper losses
(d) electrical power input less total losses (copper loss. iron loss, friction and windage losses)

391. The back e.m.f. of the d.c. motor
(a) opposes the applied voltage
(b) has no effect on the applied voltage
(c) favours the applied voltage
(d) none of the above

392. If the flux of a dc motor approaches zero, its speed will
(a) approach infinity
(b) approach zero
(c) remain unchanged
(d) between 0 and ∞

393. In d.c. machines, the armature reaction m.m.f. is
(a) stationary with respect to armature
(b) rotating with respect to stator
(c) stationary with respect to stator
(d) rotating with respect to brushes

394. The parts of the armature electric circuit which take active part in emf generation are
(a) the commutator segments
(b) the overhangs
(c) the coil sides inside the slots
(d) both (b) and (c)

395. The e.m.f. generated in a d.c. generators is
(a) dynamically induced e.m.f.
(b) statically induced e.m.f.
(c) electrostatically induced e.m.f.
(d) magnetically induced e.m.f.

396. The speed of a d.c. motor can be altered
(a) only by varying the flux
(b) only by varying the armature voltage
(c) by varying both the flux and armature voltage
(d) none of the above

397. The essential condition for satisfactory parallel operation of two dc generators is that they should have same
(a) kW output rating
(b) drooping voltage characteristics
(c) percentage regulation
(d) speed of operation

398. Residual magnetism is the essential prerequisite for starting which type of d.c. generator?
(a) Separately excited generator
(b) Shunt generator
(c) Series generator
(d) All of these

399. The dummy coil in d.c. machines is used to
(a) eliminate reactance voltage
(b) eliminate armature reaction
(c) bring about mechanical balance of armature
(d) eliminate harmonics developed in the machine

400. It is preferable to start a d.c. series motor with some mechanical load on it because
(a) it will not run at no load
(b) it acts as a starter to the motor
(c) it may develop excessive speed and damage itself
(d) none of these

401. Laminations of core are generally made of
(a) Cast iron (b) Carbon
(c) Silicon steel (d) Stainless steel

402. The armature of D.C. generator is laminated to
(a) Reduce of bulk
(b) Provide passage for cooling air
(c) Insulate the core
(d) Reduce eddy current loss

403. In a commutator
(a) Copper is harder than mica
(b) Mica and copper are equally hard
(c) Mica is harder than copper
(d) None of these

404. In D.C. generator the pole shoes are fastened to the pole core by
(a) Rivets
(b) Counter sunk screws
(c) Brazing
(d) Welding

405. In lap winding, the number of brushes is always
(a) Double the number of poles
(b) Same as the number of poles
(c) Half the number of poles
(d) Two

406. In a four-pole D.C. machine
(a) All the four-poles are north poles
(b) Alternate poles are North and South
(c) All the four poles are South poles
(d) Two North poles follow two South poles

407. If B is the flux density, l the length of conductor and v is the velocity of conductor, then iduced e.m.f. is given by
(a) Blu (b) Blv^2
(c) Bl^2v (d) Bl^2v^2

408. In a D.C. generator the armature reaction results in
(a) Demagnetisation of the centres of poles
(b) Magnetisation of interpoles
(c) Demagnetisation of the leading pole tip and magnetisation of the trialing pole tip
(d) Magnetisation of the leading tip and demagnetisation of the trailing pole tip

409. Armature reaction of an unsaturated D.C. machine is
(a) Crossmagnetisation
(b) Demagnetising
(c) Magnetising
(d) None of the above

410. Equalizer rings are required in case armature is
(a) Wave wound (b) Lap wound
(c) Delta wound (d) Duplex wound

411. The demagnetisation component of armature reaction in a D.C. generator
(a) Reduces generator e.m.f.
(b) Increases armature speed
(c) Reduces interpoles flux density
(d) Results in sparking trouble

412. Magnetic field in a D.C. generator is produced by
(a) Electromagnets
(b) Permanent magnets
(c) Both (A) and (B)
(d) None of the above

413. The number of brushes in a commutator depends on
(a) Speed of armature
(b) Types of winding
(c) Voltage
(d) Amount of current to be collected

414. In a D.C. generator the actual flux distribution depends upon
(a) Size of air gap
(b) Shape of the pole shoe
(c) Clearance between tips of the adjacent pole shoes
(d) All of the above

415. Permeance is the reciprocal of
(a) Flux density (b) Reluctance
(c) Ampere-twins (d) Resistance

416. In D.C. generator on no-load, the air gap flux distribution in space is
(a) Sinusoidal (b) Triangular
(c) Pulsating (d) Flat topped

417. A shunt generator running at 1000 r.p.m. has generator e.m.f. as 200 V. If the speed increases to 1200 r.p.m. the generated e.m.f. will be nearly
(a) 150 V (b) 175 V
(c) 240 V (d) 290 V

418. In a D.C. generator in case the resistance of the field winding is increased, then output voltage will
(a) Increase
(b) Decrease
(c) Remain unaffected
(d) Fluctuate heavily

419. A 220 V D.C. generator is run at full speed without any excitation. The open circuit voltage will be
(a) Zero (b) About 2V
(c) About 50 V (d) 220 V

420. If residual magnetism is present in a D.C. generator, the induced e.m.f. at zero speed will be
(a) Zero
(b) Small
(c) The same as rated voltage
(d) High

421. A D.C. generator works on the principle of
(a) Lenz's law
(b) Ohm's law
(c) Faraday's law of electromagnetic induction
(d) None of these

422. A series generator can self-excite
(a) Only if the load current is zero
(b) Only if the load current is not zero
(c) Irrespective of the value of load current
(d) None of the above

423. The series field of a short-shunt D.C. generator is excited by
(a) External current (b) Armature current
(c) Shunt current (d) Load current

424. A simple method of increasing the voltage of a D.C. generator is
(a) To increase the length of the armature
(b) To decrease the length of the armature
(c) To increase the speed of rotation
(d) To decrease the speed of rotation

425. The .... generator has poorest voltage regulation
(a) Shunt (b) Series
(c) Compound (d) Over-compound

426. By looking at which part of the motor it can be easily confirmed that a particular motor is D.C. motor?
(a) Frame (b) Shaft
(c) Commutator (d) Stator

427. In which of the following applications D.C. series motor is invariably used?
(a) Starter for a car
(b) Drive for a water pump
(c) Fan motor
(d) Motor operation in A.C. or D.C.

428. In D.C. machines fractional pitch winding is used
(a) To improve cooling
(b) To reduce copper losses
(c) To increase the generated e.m.f.
(d) To reduce the sparking

429. Small D.C. motors upto 5 H.P. usually have
(a) 2 poles (b) 4 poles
(c) 6 poles (d) 8 poles

430. In D.C. motor which of the following can sustain the maximum temperature rise?
(a) Slip rings (b) Commutator
(c) Field winding (d) Armature winding

431. Which of the following load normally needs starting torque more than the rated torque?
(a) Blowers
(b) Conveyors
(c) Air compressors
(d) Centrifugal pumps

432. Which D.C. motor has got maximum self loading property?
(a) Series motor
(b) Shunt motor
(c) Comulatively compound motor
(d) Differentially compound motor

433. If the supply voltage for a D.C. motor is increased which of the following will decrease?
(a) Starting torque (b) Operating speed
(c) Full-load current (d) All of the above

434. Which of the following motor has the poorest speed regulation?
(a) Shunt motor
(b) Series motor
(c) Differential compound motor
(d) Cumulative compound motor

435. Which of the following method of speed control of D.C. machine will after minimum efficiency?
(a) Voltage control method
(b) Field control method
(c) Armature control method
(d) All of above methods

436. The speed regulation of a D.C. motor is
(a) $\frac{\text{Lowest speed}}{\text{Highest speed}}$
(b) $\frac{\text{Highest speed} - \text{lowest speed}}{\text{Average speed}}$
(c) $\frac{\text{No load speed} - \text{full load speed}}{\text{Full load speed}}$
(d) None of these

437. At the instant of starting when a D.C. motor is put on supply, it behaves like
(a) A highly resistive circuit
(b) A low resistance circuit
(c) A capacitive circuit
(d) None of these

438. The speed of a D.C. motor can be varied by varying
(a) Field current
(b) Applied voltage
(c) Resistance in series with armature
(d) Any of the above

439. Which one of the following is not necessarily the advantage of D.C. motors over A.C. motors?
(a) Low cost
(b) Wide speed range
(c) Stability
(d) High starting torque

440. The plugging gives the
(a) Zero torque braking
(b) Smallest torque braking
(c) Highest torque braking
(d) None of the above

441. The hysteresis loss in a D.C. generator varies with the frequency of magnetic reversals as
(a) $\frac{1}{f}$ (b) f
(c) $f^{1.6}$ (d) f^2

442. Which loss in a D.C. generator does not vary with load as well as flux density?
(a) Copper loss (b) Eddy current loss
(c) Hysteresis loss (d) Windage loss

443. Which of the following loss in a D.C. generator is dissipated in the form of heat?
(a) Mechanical loss (b) Core loss
(c) Copper loss (d) All of the above

444. Hopkinson's test on D.C. machines is conducted at
(a) No load (b) Part load
(c) Full load (d) Over load

445. During rheostatic braking the braking torque is proportional to
(a) Speed (b) $(\text{Speed})^2$
(c) $(\text{Speed})^{-1}$ (d) $(\text{Speed})^{-2}$

446. In the D.C. motor the iron-losses occur in
(a) The field (b) The armature
(c) The brushes (d) The commutator

447. In a D.C. motor if the back e.m.f. is absent
(a) Motor will burn
(b) Motor will not run at all
(c) Motor will run at very low speed
(d) Motor will run at very high speed

448. A face plate starter is employed for starting
(a) Induction motor
(b) Universal motor
(c) Synchronous motor
(d) D.C. series motor

449. In which of the following tests only one motor is required?
(a) Brake test (b) Hopkinson's test
(c) Field's test (d) All of the above

450. Hopkinson's test is conducted at
(a) No load (b) Part load
(c) Low load (d) Full load

ANSWERS

1	2	3	4	5	6	7	8	9	10
(c)	(c)	(c)	(b)	(e)	(d)	(d)	(a)	(b)	(b)
11	**12**	**13**	**14**	**15**	**16**	**17**	**18**	**19**	**20**
(d)	(e)	(a)	(a)	(a)	(b)	(b)	(b)	(d)	(d)
21	**22**	**23**	**24**	**25**	**26**	**27**	**28**	**29**	**30**
(c)	(c)	(a)	(a)	(c)	(a)	(c)	(c)	(b)	(c)

31	32	33	34	35	36	37	38	39	40
(b)	(e)	(d)	(d)	(b)	(a)	(a)	(b)	(b)	(b)
41	**42**	**43**	**44**	**45**	**46**	**47**	**48**	**49**	**50**
(a)	(b)	(d)	(c)	(c)	(b)	(a)	(c)	(d)	(b)
51	**52**	**53**	**54**	**55**	**56**	**57**	**58**	**59**	**60**
(b)	(d)	(d)	(b)	(a)	(c)	(e)	(b)	(a)	(c)
61	**62**	**63**	**64**	**65**	**66**	**67**	**68**	**69**	**70**
(c)	(b)	(c)	(b)	(a)	(a)	(d)	(d)	(b)	(a)
71	**72**	**73**	**74**	**75**	**76**	**77**	**78**	**79**	**80**
(b)	(c)	(c)	(a)	(b)	(d)	(a)	(e)	(c)	(b)
81	**82**	**83**	**84**	**85**	**86**	**87**	**88**	**89**	**90**
(a)	(a)	(a)	(a)	(c)	(d)	(e)	(b)	(a)	(c)
91	**92**	**93**	**94**	**95**	**96**	**97**	**98**	**99**	**100**
(b)	(d)	(b)	(b)	(d)	(d)	(d)	(c)	(b)	(d)
101	**102**	**103**	**104**	**105**	**106**	**107**	**108**	**109**	**110**
(b)	(a)	(b)	(a)	(c)	(b)	(b)	(c)	(b)	(b)
111	**112**	**113**	**114**	**115**	**116**	**117**	**118**	**119**	**120**
(c)	(a)	(c)	(b)	(b)	(b)	(b)	(c)	(d)	(c)
121	**122**	**123**	**124**	**125**	**126**	**127**	**128**	**129**	**130**
(c)	(d)	(a)	(b)	(d)	(c)	(d)	(b)	(c)	(b)
131	**132**	**133**	**134**	**135**	**136**	**137**	**138**	**139**	**140**
(b)	(a)	(d)	(d)	(b)	(c)	(d)	(a)	(c)	(a)
141	**142**	**143**	**144**	**145**	**146**	**147**	**148**	**149**	**150**
(d)	(b)	(b)	(c)	(a)	(b)	(a)	(a)	(e)	(b)
151	**152**	**153**	**154**	**155**	**156**	**157**	**158**	**159**	**160**
(c)	(a)	(c)	(e)	(c)	(e)	(d)	(d)	(c)	(d)
161	**162**	**163**	**164**	**165**	**166**	**167**	**168**	**169**	**170**
(b)	(b)	(c)	(a)	(d)	(b)	(d)	(b)	(b)	(c)
171	**172**	**173**	**174**	**175**	**176**	**177**	**178**	**179**	**180**
(a)	(a)	(b)	(a)	(c)	(e)	(b)	(d)	(b)	(b)
181	**182**	**183**	**184**	**185**	**186**	**187**	**188**	**189**	**190**
(c)	(c)	(d)	(a)	(c)	(a)	(b)	(a)	(b)	(b)
191	**192**	**193**	**194**	**195**	**196**	**197**	**198**	**199**	**200**
(d)	(d)	(e)	(c)	(c)	(a)	(c)	(a)	(d)	(d)
201	**202**	**203**	**204**	**205**	**206**	**207**	**208**	**209**	**210**
(d)	(d)	(c)	(d)	(f)	(a)	(d)	(c)	(d)	(c)
211	**212**	**213**	**214**	**215**	**216**	**217**	**218**	**219**	**220**
(d)	(b)	(d)	(b)	(b)	(a)	(a)	(a)	(b)	(e)
221	**222**	**223**	**224**	**225**	**226**	**227**	**228**	**229**	**230**
(c)	(a)	(c)	(a)	(d)	(b)	(d)	(a)	(b)	(d)
231	**232**	**233**	**234**	**235**	**236**	**237**	**238**	**239**	**240**
(a)	(b)	(b)	(c)	(c)	(a)	(d)	(c)	(b)	(b)

241	242	243	244	245	246	247	248	249	250
(c)	(c)	(c)	(a)	(a)	(c)	(d)	(a)	(b)	(a)
251	**252**	**253**	**254**	**255**	**256**	**257**	**258**	**259**	**260**
(d)	(a)	(b)	(a)	(c)	(a)	(c)	(b)	(a)	(a)
261	**262**	**263**	**264**	**265**	**266**	**267**	**268**	**269**	**270**
(c)	(a)	(a)	(a)	(b)	(d)	(a)	(c)	(d)	(c)
271	**272**	**273**	**274**	**275**	**276**	**277**	**278**	**279**	**280**
(e)	(c)	(b)	(b)	(c)	(c)	(c)	(d)	(b)	(c)
281	**282**	**283**	**284**	**285**	**286**	**287**	**288**	**289**	**290**
(a)	(a)	(c)	(c)	(c)	(b)	(e)	(d)	(d)	(e)
291	**292**	**293**	**294**	**295**	**296**	**297**	**298**	**299**	**300**
(c)	(e)	(c)	(d)	(b)	(a)	(c)	(b)	(c)	(b)
301	**302**	**303**	**304**	**305**	**306**	**307**	**308**	**309**	**310**
(a)	(d)	(b)	(a)	(a)	(c)	(d)	(a)	(b)	(a)
311	**312**	**313**	**314**	**315**	**316**	**317**	**318**	**319**	**320**
(d)	(c)	(b)	(d)	(d)	(a)	(a)	(b)	(c)	(b)
321	**322**	**323**	**324**	**325**	**326**	**327**	**328**	**329**	**330**
(b)	(b)	(b)	(d)	(a)	(d)	(b)	(d)	(d)	(b)
331	**332**	**333**	**334**	**335**	**336**	**337**	**338**	**339**	**340**
(c)	(b)	(c)	(a)	(c)	(d)	(d)	(c)	(a)	(f)
341	**342**	**343**	**344**	**345**	**346**	**347**	**348**	**349**	**350**
(b)	(b)	(c)	(c)	(c)	(e)	(e)	(a)	(b)	(b)
351	**352**	**353**	**354**	**355**	**356**	**357**	**358**	**359**	**360**
(a)	(e)	(c)	(a)	(d)	(c)	(e)	(b)	(a)	(d)
361	**362**	**363**	**364**	**365**	**366**	**367**	**368**	**369**	**370**
(a)	(b)	(a)	(b)	(c)	(c)	(c)	(d)	(b)	(c)
371	**372**	**373**	**374**	**375**	**376**	**377**	**378**	**379**	**380**
(d)	(a)	(d)	(b)	(b)	(c)	(c)	(b)	(e)	(a)
381	**382**	**383**	**384**	**385**	**386**	**387**	**388**	**389**	**390**
(b)	(b)	(a)	(b)	(a)	(b)	(a)	(c)	(b)	(d)
391	**392**	**393**	**394**	**395**	**396**	**397**	**398**	**399**	**400**
(a)	(a)	(c)	(c)	(a)	(c)	(b)	(c)	(c)	(c)
401	**402**	**403**	**404**	**405**	**406**	**407**	**408**	**409**	**410**
(c)	(d)	(c)	(b)	(b)	(b)	(a)	(c)	(a)	(b)
411	**412**	**413**	**414**	**415**	**416**	**417**	**418**	**419**	**420**
(a)	(a)	(d)	(d)	(b)	(d)	(c)	(b)	(a)	(c)
421	**422**	**423**	**424**	**425**	**426**	**427**	**428**	**429**	**430**
(b)	(d)	(b)	(b)	(c)	(a)	(d)	(a)	(c)	(b)
431	**432**	**433**	**434**	**435**	**436**	**437**	**438**	**439**	**440**
(d)	(c)	(c)	(b)	(c)	(c)	(b)	(d)	(a)	(c)
441	**442**	**443**	**444**	**445**	**446**	**447**	**448**	**449**	**450**
(b)	(d)	(d)	(c)	(b)	(b)	(a)	(d)	(a)	(d)

3. ELECTRIC CIRCUITS AND NETWORK

THE COULOMB'S LAW

Charges of same polarity repel one another and that of opposite polarity attract each other. The force (F) between the two charges q_1 and q_2 as shown in Fig. 1 is

(i) directly proportional to the product of the charges q_1 and q_2;

(ii) inversely proportional to the square of distance d between them;

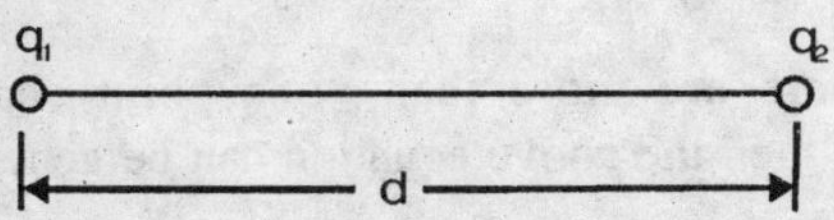

Fig. 1

(iii) depends on the nature of medium surrounding the charges. Mathematically

$$F \propto \frac{q_1 . q_2}{d^2} \bar{a}_r$$

$$F = \frac{q_1 . q_2}{4\pi \varepsilon_r \varepsilon_0 d^2} \bar{a}_r \text{ Newton}$$

where ε_0 is the permittivity of air and its value is 8.854×10^{-12} F/m, ε_r is the relative permittivity of surrounding medium with respect to air and $\bar{a}_r$ is the unit vector pointing in direction of line joining the two charges.

ELECTRIC FIELD INTENSITY

The space around the charge which is under stress, and experiences a force on another charge when placed there, is known as electrostatic field. This is illustrated in Fig. 2 (a).

If the force $\bar{F}$ experienced by a resting positive charge q_0 placed at a point as shown in Fig. 2 (b) at a distance R metres from the charge of q, then the field intensity is defined as:

$$\overline{E} = \frac{\overline{F}}{q_0}$$

Thus field intensity is a vector in the direction of the force. Its value is given by

$$\overline{E} = -\frac{q}{4\pi \varepsilon_r \varepsilon_0 R^2} \bar{i}_R \text{ Newton/Coulomb}$$

where $\bar{i}_R$ is the unit vector along the distance R and directed away from the charge.

ELECTRIC DIPOLE MOMENT

It is a vector p whose magnitude is $2aq$ and direction is from the negative to positive charge.

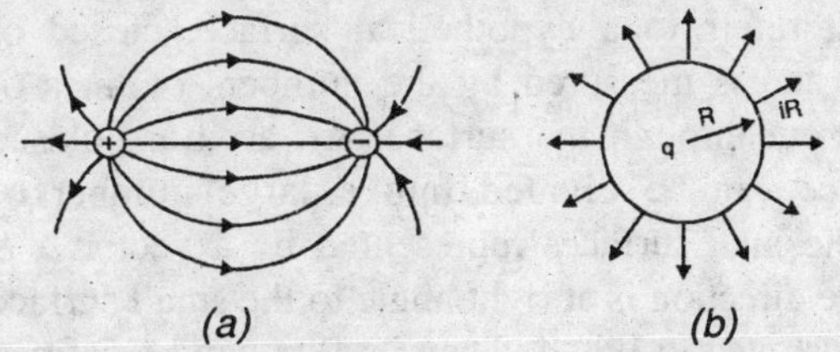

Fig. 2

When the dipole is placed in a uniform external electric field $\overline{E}$, as shown in Fig. 3, the two charges experience equal and opposite forces.

$$\overline{F} = q\overline{E}$$

Thus the net force on the dipole is zero but there is a net torque τ about an axis at point P at right angles to the plane of the paper.

$$\begin{aligned} \tau &= 2F\,(a \sin\theta) \\ &= 2\,(qE)\,(a \sin\theta) \\ &= 2aqE \sin\theta \\ &= pE \sin\theta \end{aligned}$$

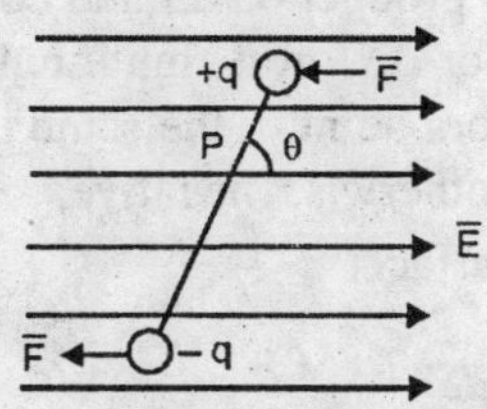

Fig. 3

Thus torque is the product of magnitude of force and the perpendicular distance between the forces. In vector from,

$$\bar{\tau} = \bar{p} \times \bar{E}$$

In order to change the orientation of the electric dipole placed in an external field, some amount of work is to be done and this work is stored as potential energy in the system.

If the dipole is to be rotated from its reference vertical position (*i.e.* $\theta = 90°$) to angle θ, the potential energy is given by

$$U = \int_{90°}^{\theta} \tau \, d\theta = \int_{90°}^{\theta} pE \sin\theta \, d\theta = -pE\cos\theta$$

or $$U = -\bar{p} \cdot \bar{E}$$

Flux of an Electric Field

It refers to a hypothetical surface, closed or open and is measured by the numbers of lines of force cut through the surface. An arbitrary closed surface can be divided into a large number of infinitesimal surfaces represented by a vector $\Delta\bar{S}$ whose direction is at right angle to the small surface as illustrated in Fig. 4. Then its flux can be defined as

$$\Delta\Phi_e = \bar{E} \cdot \Delta\bar{S} = E\,\Delta S\cos\theta$$

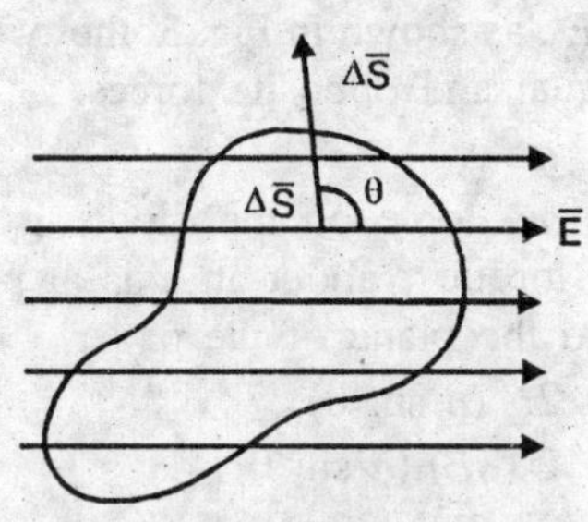

Fig. 4

which means it is the product of ΔS and component of $\bar{E}$ parallel to vector $\Delta\bar{S}$ or at right angles to the surface. If both vectors point in the same direction, the flux is positive otherwise negative.

For the whole surface,

$$\Phi_e = \oint_S \bar{E} \cdot d\bar{S}$$

The electric field intensity of a point charge is thus directed everywhere radically away from the point charge, and on any spherical surface at the point charge, its magnitude is constant.

The Gauss's Law of Electricity

The surface integral of the normal component of electric field intensity $\bar{E}$ over a closed surface containing point charge q is given by

$$\oint \bar{E} \cdot d\bar{S} = \frac{q}{\varepsilon_0}$$

This can be interpreted as the net flux of electric field emanating from the surface S containing a point charge q is equal to q/ε_0. If this arbitrary surface does not enclose the point charge, the net electric field flux emanating from the surface must be zero, *i.e.*

$$\oint \bar{E} \cdot d\bar{S} = 0$$

If there are more than one point charges enclosed, then the above equation can be generated as follows

$$\oint_S \bar{E} \cdot d\bar{S} = \oint_S \bar{E}_1 \cdot d\bar{S} + \oint_S \bar{E}_2 \cdot d\bar{S} + \oint_S \bar{E}_3 \cdot d\bar{S} + \ldots$$

$$= \frac{q_1 + q_2 + \ldots + q_n}{\varepsilon_0}$$

$$= \frac{\text{charge enclosed by the surface } S}{\varepsilon_0}$$

An important outcome of this law is that excess charge placed on an insulated conductor resides entirely on its outer surface.

Electric Potential due to a Charge

If point A is taken to be at infinity and potential at infinity is taken to be zero, then the potential V at a point B will be

$$V = -\int_{\infty}^{B} \bar{E} \cdot d\bar{l} = -\int_{\infty}^{r} \frac{q}{4\pi\varepsilon_r\varepsilon_0 r^2} dr$$

$$= -\frac{q}{4\pi\varepsilon_r\varepsilon_0}\left[\frac{1}{r}\right]_{\infty}^{r} = \frac{q}{4\pi\varepsilon_r\varepsilon_0 r}$$

Since field intensity is the variation of potential with the distance, it can also be visualised as potential gradient. If potential for all points of space are known, the components of E and thus E itself can be found by taking the following derivatives.

$$E_x = \frac{-\partial V}{\partial x},\ E_y = \frac{-\partial V}{\partial y},\ E_z = \frac{-\partial V}{\partial z}$$

Therefore,

$$\overline{E} = -\left(\bar{i}\frac{\partial V}{\partial x} + \bar{j}\frac{\partial V}{\partial y} + \bar{k}\frac{\partial V}{\partial z}\right)$$

Thus the unit of electric field is volt/metre.

Electric Potential Energy

For two charges $+q_1$ and $-q_2$ placed at a distance 'r' apart, energy is stored in the system because a definite amount of work has to be done to move away these charges. If the charges are of opposite polarity, their potential energy will change into kinetic energy and as a result, they will accelerate towards each other.

Thus potential energy of a system of point charges is the work required to assemble these charges by bringing them together from infinity.

Now, the potential due to q_1 is

$$V = \frac{1}{4\pi\varepsilon_0}\cdot\frac{q_1}{r}$$

The work done required to move q_2 from infinity to distance r by definition of potential will be

$$W = Vq_2$$

Therefore electric potential energy $U = Vq_2$

$$= \frac{1}{4\pi\varepsilon_0}\cdot\frac{q_1 q_2}{r}$$

Potential energy due to Group of Charges

The potential energy at a point due to a group of point charges q_1, q_2, q_n, is the algebraic sum of the potential energy due to each charge. That is

$$V = \frac{1}{4\pi\varepsilon_0}\left(\frac{q_1}{r_1} + \frac{q_2}{r_2} + \ldots\frac{q_n}{r_n}\right)$$

$$= \frac{1}{4\pi\varepsilon_0}\sum_n \frac{q_n}{r_n}$$

If the charge distribution is continuous, then the potential energy at point is given by

$$V = \frac{1}{4\pi\varepsilon_0}\int\frac{dq}{r}$$

where dq is infinitesimal element of charge at a distance r from the point.

Maxwell's Curl Equations for Static Field

Since the potential difference between two points A and B is independent of the path followed from A to B, therefore for two paths ACB and ADB, as shown in Fig. 5

$$\int_{ACB} \overline{E}.\overline{dl} = \int_{ADB} \overline{E}.\overline{dl}$$

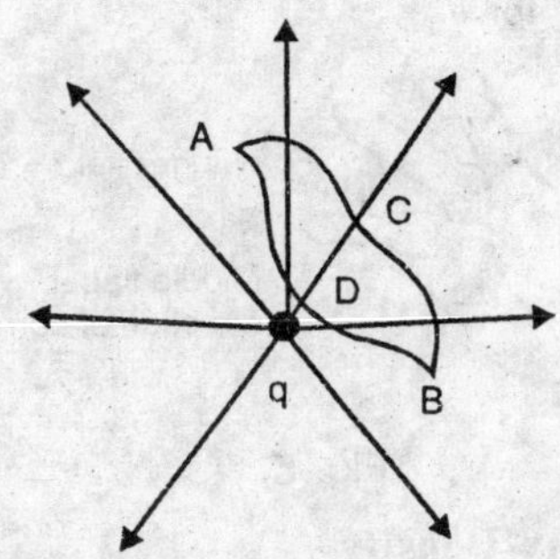

Fig. 5

or, $$\int_{ACB} \overline{E}.\overline{dl} - \int_{ADB} \overline{E}.\overline{dl} = 0$$

or, $$\int_{ACB} \overline{E}.\overline{dl} + \int_{BDA} \overline{E}.\overline{dl} = 0$$

or, $$\oint_{ACBDA} \overline{E}.\overline{dl} = 0$$

The integral is taken around a closed path. By superposition, the above result can be generalised for discrete or continuous charges as

$$\oint \overline{E}.\overline{dl} = 0$$

This implies that the work involved in moving a test charge around a closed path in a static electric field is equal to zero.

In differential form, this can be written as:

$$\nabla \times \overline{E} = 0$$

Force on a Conductor

Force on current carrying conductor in magnetic field is given by

$$\overline{F} = i\,\overline{l} \times \overline{B}$$

$$= Bil \sin\theta$$

The direction of force can be determined by applying Flemming's Left Hand Rule: The thumb, forefinger and middle finger of the left hand are stretched in such a way that they are at right angles to each other mutually. Then the forefinger points towards the direction of the magnetic field, middle finger towards the direction of the flow of current, and the thumb will be in the direction of force acting on the conductor (Fig. 6).

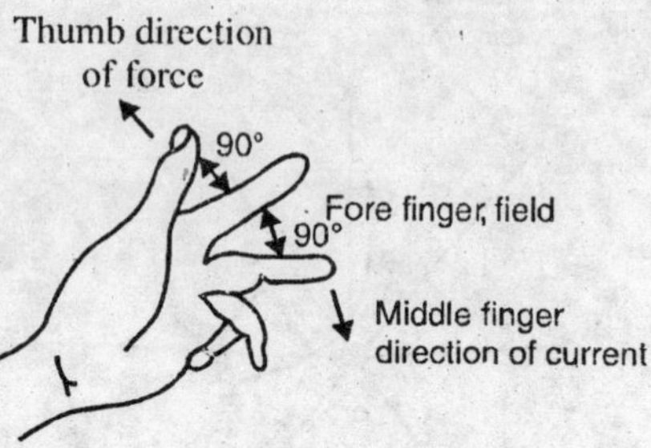

Fig. 6

Magnetic Flux Density

$\overline{F}_1$ and $\overline{F}_2$ are two non-zero forces for two velocities v_1 and v_2 in different directions in the magnetic field $\overline{B}$. Then

$$\overline{F}_1 \times \overline{F}_2 = (qv_1 \times \overline{B}) \times (qv_2 \times \overline{B})$$

$$= q^2 (\overline{v}_1 \times \overline{B}.\overline{B})\ \overline{v}_2 - (\overline{v}_1 \times \overline{B}.\overline{v}_2)\overline{B}$$

$$= -q\,(\overline{F}_1 . \overline{v}_2)\ \overline{B}$$

or $$\overline{B} = \frac{\overline{F}_2 \times \overline{F}_1}{q(\overline{F}_1 . \overline{v}_2)}$$

If the maximum force on q_0 is $\overline{F}_m$ and the direction of $\overline{v}$ is $\overline{i}_m$ then

$$\overline{B} = \frac{\overline{F}_m \times \overline{i}_m}{q\overline{v}}$$

Therefore unit of

$$\overline{B} = \frac{\text{Newton per Coulomb}}{\text{meter per second}}$$

$$= \frac{\text{Newton second}}{\text{Coulomb . meter}}$$

$$= \frac{\text{Newton . metre}}{\text{Coulomb}} \times \frac{\text{second}}{(\text{metre})^2}$$

Now since Newton metre per Coulomb is a Volt, unit of B = Volts-second per square metre, commonly known as Weber per metre^2 or Wb/m^2.

LORENTZ RELATION

When a charged particle q_0 is the subjected to an electric field $\overline{E}$ and magnetic field $\overline{B}$, the resultant force acting on it is given by

$$\overline{F} = q_0\,\overline{E} + q_0\,\overline{v} \times \overline{B}$$

For a continuous charge distribution of density ρ moving with a velocity v, the force per unit volume can be defined as

$$\overline{F} = \rho\overline{E} + \overline{J} \times \overline{B}$$

where $\overline{J}$ is the volume current density and is given by $\overline{J} = \rho\overline{v}$

(i) directly proportional to length δl;

(ii) directly proportional to the strength of current flowing;

(iii) inversely proportional to the square of the perpendicular distance of the point from δl.

Mathematically,

$$d\overline{B} = \frac{\mu_0\, I\, \delta l}{4\,\pi\, r^2} . \overline{i}_R$$

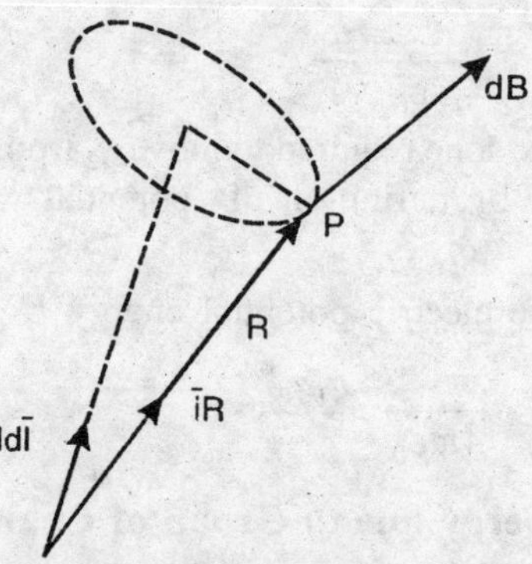

Fig. 7

This is known as *Biot-Savart Law* and is analogous to the electric field intensity of a point charge. According to this law, the magnetic flux density at a point *P* due to a current element is normal to the plane containing the element and the line joining the element and point (Fig. 7). Clearly it is circular to the straight line axis along the current element. The direction of flux density can be known by visualising right hand grabbing the filament wire and the thumb pointing in the direction of current. The direction in which the fingers curl is the direction of field. Alternately it is the same as the turning the right-hand screw as it advances in the direction of current.

The magnetic flux density due to a wire of any length is given by

$$\overline{B} = \frac{\mu_0}{4\pi}\int_C \frac{I\,\overline{dl}\times\overline{i_R}}{R^2}$$

where the integral is taken along the contour C of the wire.

MAGNETIC DIPOLE

Consider a rectangular loop of length a and width b placed at an angle θ with uniform magnetic field B as shown in Fig. 8.

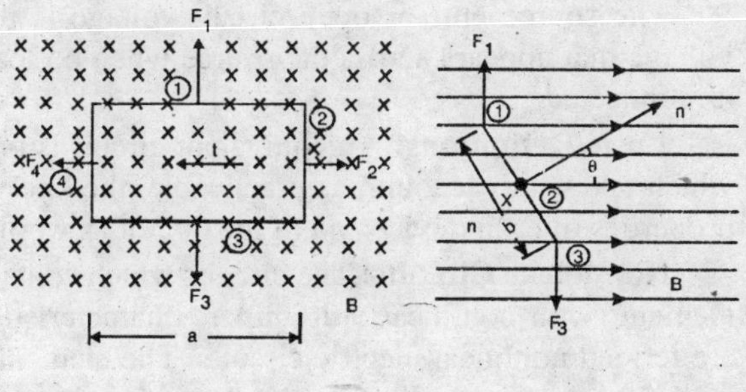

(a) (b)

Fig. 8

The forces $\overline{F}_2$, $\overline{F}_4$ on sides 2 and 4 are equal and opposite and therefore cancel each other.

The forces $\overline{F}_1$ and $\overline{F}_3$ on sides 1 and 3 are also equal and opposite. But since they do not have the same line of action, they produce a torque τ, on the loop and thus tends to rotate it in clockwise direction about the axis xx'. This torque is given by

$$\begin{aligned}\tau &= \text{Force} \times \text{Distane between the forces}\\ &= iaB\,.\,b\sin\theta\\ &= iAB\sin\theta\end{aligned}$$

where A is the area of the loop

If there are N turns in the loop, then

The term (NiA) is called the *magnetic dipole moment* μ of the loop. In vector form above equation becomes

$$\overline{\tau} = \overline{\mu}\times\overline{B}$$

The vector $\overline{\mu}$ lies along the axis of the loop. This torque acting on a current loop is the basis of operation of electric motors and many electric metres.

The Gauss's Law for Magnetism

According to this law, the flux Φ_B due to the magnetic field B through any closed gaussion surface must be zero. That is

$$\Phi_B = \oint \overline{B}.\overline{dS} = 0$$

The Biot-Savart Law

The field strength due to a small conductor of length δl carrying current I at any point P is given by following expression in (i) We know,

$$\begin{aligned}|\nabla\times\overline{B}\,| &= \text{maximum value of } \lim_{\Delta S\to 0}\frac{\int_{\Delta C}\overline{B}.\overline{dl}}{\Delta S}\\ &= \mu_0\,|\,\overline{J}\,|\end{aligned}$$

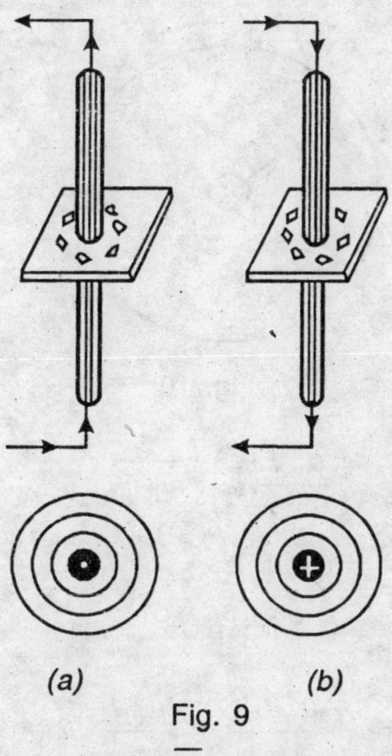

(a) (b)

Fig. 9

and Direction of $\nabla\times\overline{B}$ = direction of $\overline{J}$

so that

$$\nabla\times\overline{B} = \mu_0\overline{J} \qquad \text{...........(i)}$$

Magnetic Field due to Current Carrying Conductor

When current flows through a conductor, magnetic field is produced around it. If the direction of current is upwards as shown by a dot in Fig. 9, then the direction of lines of force is anti-clockwise. On the other hand, if the current is flowing downwards (shown by a cross), the direction of force is clockwise.

The direction of magnetic field around straight current carrying conductor may be determined by Cork Screw Rule: If the right-handed cork screw held with its axis parallel to the direction of flow of current, is rotated in such a direction that the hand of the screw moves in direction of flow of current, then the direction of rotation of the head will be the direction of magnetic field.

THE AMPERE'S LAW

Consider a circular path *C* of radius *r* in the plane normal to the wire and centred at the wire as shown in Fig. 10. Take an infinitesimal element of length *dl* on this path. Then

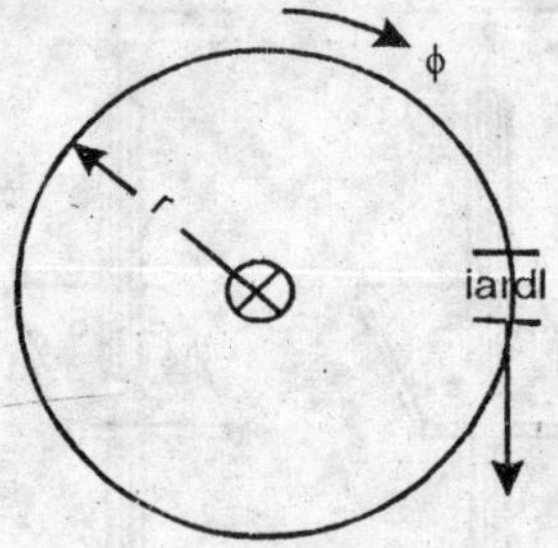

Fig. 10

$$\overline{B}\,.\,\overline{dl} = \left(\frac{\mu_0 I}{2\pi r}\bar{i}_\phi\right).\ \overline{dl}\ \bar{i}_\phi$$

$$= \frac{\mu_0\, Idl}{2\pi r}$$

Therefore,

$$\oint_C \overline{B}\,.\,\overline{dl} = \oint_C \frac{\mu_0\, I\overline{dl}}{2\pi r} = \frac{\mu_0 I}{2\pi r}\,.\,2\pi r$$

$$= \mu_0 I.$$

When generalised over any arbitrary closed path around the wire, this equation is known as *Ampere's Law.* It gives information about the current enclosed by the path *C*. If the arbitrary path does not enclose current, then

$$\oint_C \overline{B}\,.\,\overline{dl} = 0$$

FUNDAMENTALS OF CIRCUIT THEORY

An electric circuit (or network) is an interconnection of physical electrical devices.

An energy source (a primary or secondary cell, a generator) converts chemical, mechanical, thermal or any other form of energy into electrical energy.

An energy convertor, also called load, converts electrical energy into light, heat or mechanical work.

When electric energy is generated, transmitted and converted under condition such that the currents and voltages involved remain constant with time, the electric circuit is identified usually as direct current (dc) circuit. If the currents and the voltage do change with time, the circuit is identified as alternating current (ac) circuit.

The source emf or open circuit voltage is the voltage that appears across the source when no load is connected.

Basic Definitions: An equivalent circuit is one which takes into account, as practicable, the known properties of each device and of the circuit as whole.

Non-linear Circuits: The circuits which contain elements with nonlinear volt-ampere characteristics are termed nonlinear electric circuits. The elements, for example having non-linear characteristics, are vacuum valves and transistors, etc.

Lumped Parameter: A circuit containing a limited (finite) number of circuit elements is referred as 'lumped parameter'. A circuit containing an unlimited (infinite) number of circuit is called a 'distributed-parameter'. Transmission lines is an example of distributed parameter network.

Two-Port Network: If two branches are removed so that the network is left with four terminals or two-pair of terminals, the remainder network is termed *two-port network.* Usually one port accepts a source and the other port is coupled to a load, so that there is an input port and an output port in any two-port system.

Linear Circuit: The elements, those having an output that varies with respect to the input linearly, are called *linear elements*. The circuits having only linear elements are termed as *linear circuits* or *linear networks*.

Branch: This is defined as a portion of the network containing solely voltage or current sources and/or passive elements like resistances, etc., along which the current remains the same at any given instant of time.

'Junction' or 'Node': It is defined as a terminal where three or more branches meet.

Loop or Mesh: It is a closed path made by several branches of the network.

One-Port Network: In case, a branch is removed, the remainder of the network is left with a pair of terminals. The part of the network, which is considered with respect to the removed branch or terminal pair or port is termed as *one-port network.*

Ideal Current Source

This is a source whose internal conductance ($g_s = 0$ or $R_s = \infty$). The current of an ideal current source is independent of the load resistance *R*.

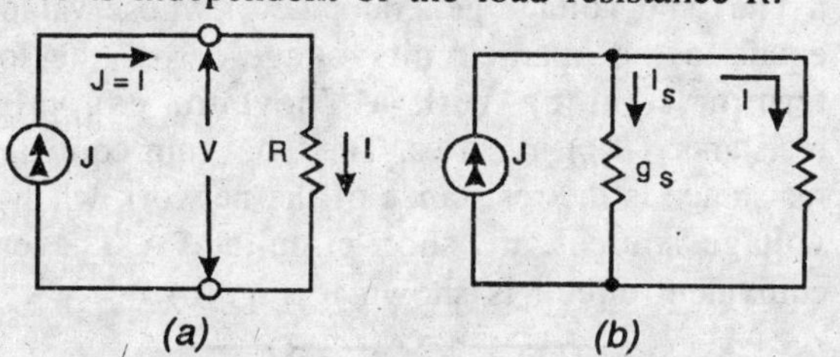

Fig. 11

A practical or impressed current source is one whose internal conductance is not zero. In such cases, the current supplied by the current source is dependent on the load resistance.

$$J = I + I_s$$

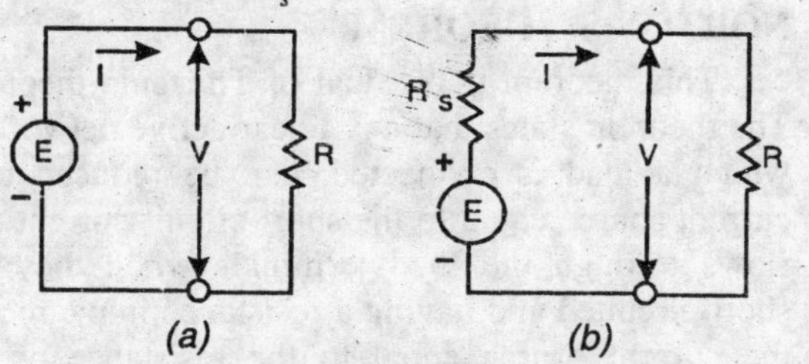

Fig. 12

Ideal voltage and current sources are active elements while resistance and conductance etc. are passive elements.

Ideal Voltage Source

If the internal resistance of a voltage source is zero, the voltage across the source (the source emf) is equal to the terminal voltage (across the load), and is independent of the amount of load current, or in other words the voltage of ideal voltage source is independent of load. Source is called *Ideal Voltage Source.*

A practical or impressed voltage source is one whose internal resistance is not zero. The terminal voltage in such cases is less than source emf by the drop across the internal resistance R_s as shown in Fig. 12

$$V = E - IR_s = IR$$

Inductance

The inductance *L* of a device is that characteristic of the device which accounts for the storage of energy in a magnetic field associated with the element. The energy stored in an inductance is given by $W_M = \frac{1}{2}Li^2$. As the current through an inductance changes (*di/dt*), an *emf* of self-induction, e_L, is induced in it, such that it opposes the change (according to Lenz's law), and expressed mathematically by

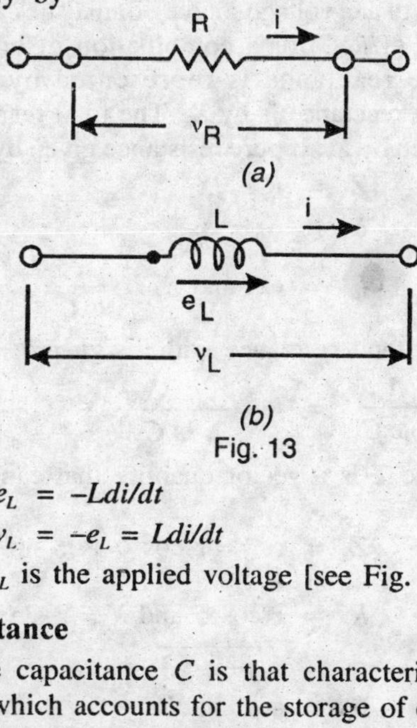

Fig. 13

$$e_L = -Ldi/dt$$

or, $$v_L = -e_L = Ldi/dt$$

where v_L is the applied voltage [see Fig. 13 (b)]

Capacitance

The capacitance *C* is that characteristic of a device which accounts for the storage of energy in the associated electric field. The stored energy is given by $CV_c^2/2$. The charge *q* taken by electrodes of the capacitance is, $q = Cv_c$, where v_c is the voltage across the capacitor.

The current entering the capacitance is

$$i = dq/dt$$

or $$i = Cdv_c/dt$$

or $$v_c = \frac{1}{C}\int idt$$

Kirchhoff's Current Law

As applied to d.c. circuit, it is stated as follows:

The algebraic sum of all the currents at a node is zero, *i.e.*, $\Sigma I = 0$

In case of a.c. circuits, KCL holds true as it is, except that now the instantaneous value of the current are taken into consideration. In other words, the algebraic sum of all the instantaneous currents at any junction of an ac circuit is zero.

Impedance

The ratio of the complex voltage across a circuit to the complex current is called impedance in complex vector notations.

In general, an impedance is the sum of pure resistance and reactance. The reactance may be inductive reactance ($j\omega L$ where $\omega = 2\pi f$, f being frequency of a.c. voltage source), or may be capacitive reactance ($1/j\omega C$) or a combination of both. The inductive reactance is represented by X_L and capacitive reactance is by X_c. The total reactance is represented by X_L. If pure resistance given by R, then

$$Z = R + jX$$

and $$X = X_L - X_c$$

where $$X_L = \omega L \text{ and } X_c = \frac{1}{\omega C}$$

Note that total reactance with j sign is

$$j\omega L + \frac{1}{j\omega C} = j\omega L - \frac{j}{\omega C}$$

Impedance Z is a vector quantity that can be given by

$$Z = ze^{j\phi} = z\cos\phi + jz\sin\phi$$
$$= R + jX$$

Here $$R = z\cos\phi \text{ and } X = z\sin\phi$$

Therefore $$Z = \sqrt{R^2 + X^2}$$

and $$\phi = \text{arc tan } X/R$$

In complex notation, for ac circuit, the Ohm's law states:

$$\dot{V} = \dot{I}Z \text{ or } Z = \dot{V}/\dot{I}$$

Network Analysis Loop/Mesh Method of Analysis: Applying KVL to all the loops of the given network, n number of equations equal to n number of loops with the same number of unknown loop currents can be written. After solving the n equations of $\Sigma IR = \Sigma E$ form, for n unknown variables (I), every branch current can be known.

THEVENIN THEOREM

Thevenin theorem reduces a linear electrical network to a voltage generator circuit which is called 'Thevenin Equivalent Circuit'. According to this theorem, any linear active network to which a load is connected can be reduced to a voltage generator whose generated voltage is equal to the open-circuit voltage that appears across the load terminals when load is disconnected and whose internal impedance is equal to the impedance of the network looking back into the load terminals when all the generators are replaced by their internal impedances. Or in other words, Thevenin equivalent circuit consists of a Thevenin voltage generator (E_{TH}) whose value is equal to the open-circuit voltage across the load terminals, along with a Thevenin equivalent resistance (R_{TH}) in series. The Thevenin equivalent resistance is the resistance of the network when all voltage sources are short-circuited. A Thevenin equivalent circuit is shown in Fig. 14.

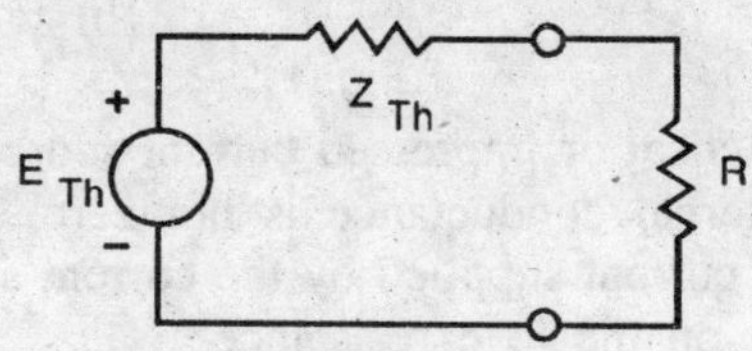

Fig. 14

NORTON'S THEOREM

This theorem is the dual of Thevenin theorem. The theorem states that any linear active network to which a load is connected, can be reduced to a current source equal to the short-circuit current that flows through the load terminals when they are short-circuited and having a resistance in parallel to the current source equal to the resistance of the active network. Likewise the Thevenin equivalent resistance, the Norton equivalent resistance is also equal to the resistance of the network when all voltage sources are short-circuited. A Norton's equivalent circuit is shown in Fig. 15.

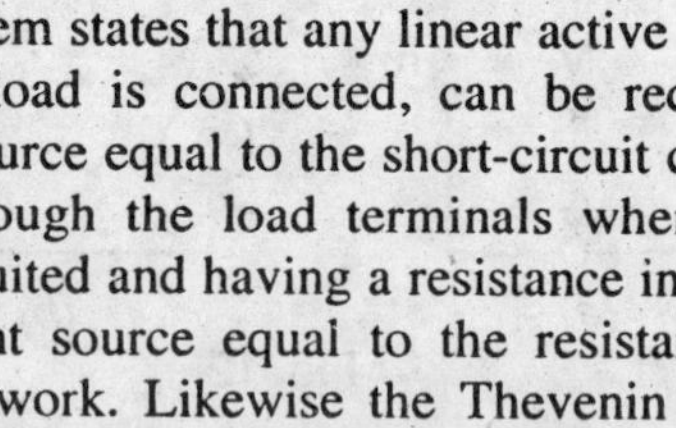

Fig. 15

Thus, the current through the load resistance remains unchanged.

THE SUPERPOSITION THEOREM

The superposition theorem states that in a linear system several causes (sources) acting simultaneously produce an effect which is the sum of all separate effects.

If in the network, more than one sources are acting, the net effect (usually in terms of current through any branch) is the algebraic sum of all the effects when one by one (only one source) is taken into consideration at a time and all others are neglected. The voltage source can be neglected by short circuiting it and the current source can be neglected by open circuiting it.

PARALLEL GENERATOR THEOREM

The several voltage connected in parallel can be replaced by a single generator of equivalent voltage and equivalent internal resistance as depicted in Fig. 16.

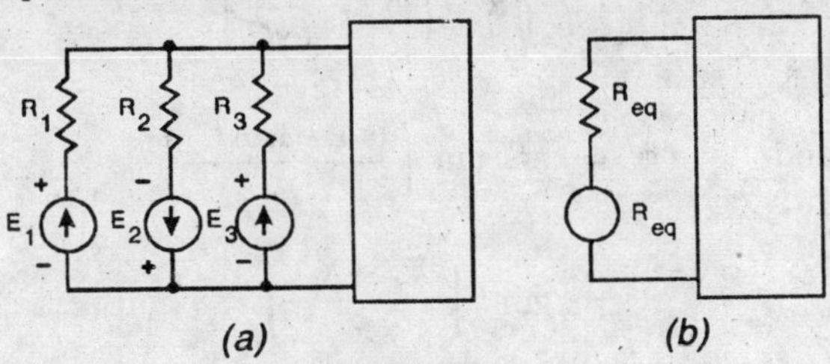

Fig. 16

$$E_{eq} = \frac{E_1 g_1 - E_2 g_2 + E_3 g_3}{g_1 + g_2 + g_3}$$

and $$R_{eq} = \frac{1}{g_1 + g_2 + g_3}$$

Generalising

$$E_{eq} = \frac{\sum_{n=1}^{\infty} E_n \times g_n}{\sum_{n=1}^{\infty} g_n}$$

$$R_{eq} = \frac{1}{\sum_{n=1}^{\infty} g_n}$$

where g is the internal conductance g = 1/R.

COMPENSATION THEOREM

Compensation theorem states that any resistance in a network may be replaced by a voltage source that has zero internal resistance and a generated voltage which is equal to the potential drop across the replaced resistance by current flowing through it and directed against this current.

As shown in Fig. 17(*a*), the resistance R through which current I flows can be replaced by voltage source E [Fig. 17 (*b*)] whose generated value is $E = I \times R$ and directed against the direction of current I.

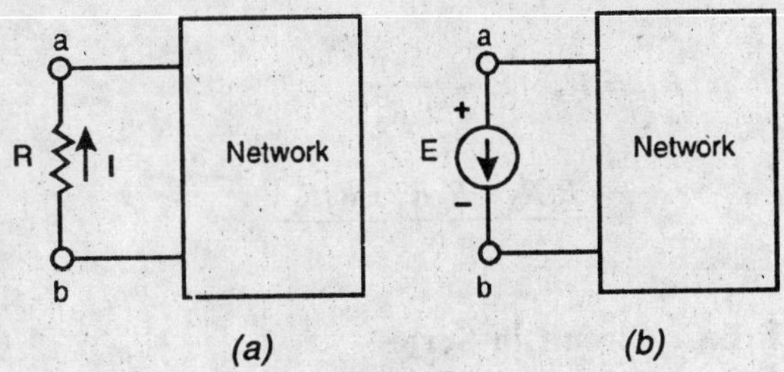

Fig. 17

Star-Delta Connection

Three resistances (or impedances) are connected in star or delta fashion as shown in the Fig. 17.

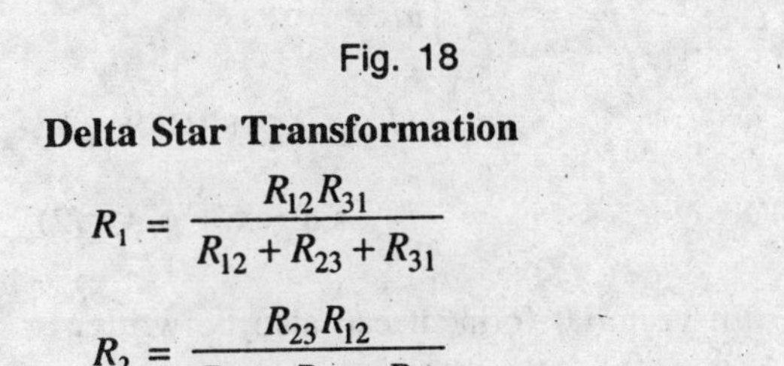

Fig. 18

Delta Star Transformation

$$R_1 = \frac{R_{12} R_{31}}{R_{12} + R_{23} + R_{31}}$$

$$R_2 = \frac{R_{23} R_{12}}{R_{12} + R_{23} + R_{31}}$$

$$R_3 = \frac{R_{31} R_{23}}{R_{12} + R_{23} + R_{31}}$$

Star to Delta Transformation

$$R_{12} = R_1 + R_2 + \frac{R_1 R_2}{R_3}$$

$$= \frac{R_1 R_2 + R_2 R_3 + R_3 R_1}{R_3}$$

$$R_{23} = R_2 + R_3 + \frac{R_2 R_3}{R_1}$$

$$= \frac{R_1 R_2 + R_2 R_3 + R_3 R_1}{R_1}$$

$$R_{31} = R_3 + R_1 + \frac{R_3 R_1}{R_2}$$

$$= \frac{R_1 R_2 + R_2 R_3 + R_3 R_1}{R_2}$$

R.L.C. Circuit in Series

Let the current through a series combination of resistance R, inductance L and capacitance C be

$$i = I_m \sin(\omega t + \phi_i)$$

Applying KVL

$$v_R + v_L + v_C = v$$

where

$$v_R = R \times i = R \times I_m \sin(\omega t + \phi_i)$$

$$v_L = L\frac{di}{dt} = \omega L\, I_m \cos(\omega t + \phi_i)$$

$$= \omega L I_m \sin(\omega t + \phi_i + \pi/2)$$

$$v_C = \frac{1}{C}\int i dt$$

$$= -(I_m/\omega C)\cos(\omega t + \phi_i)$$

$$= \frac{I_m}{\omega C}\sin(\omega t + \phi_i - \pi/2)$$

In vectorial form, it can also be written

$$\dot{V}_R + \dot{V}_l + \dot{V}_c = \dot{V}$$

In can also be represented by phasor-diagram as shown in Fig. 19.

$$R\dot{I} + j\omega L\dot{I} + \dot{I}/j\omega C = \dot{V}$$

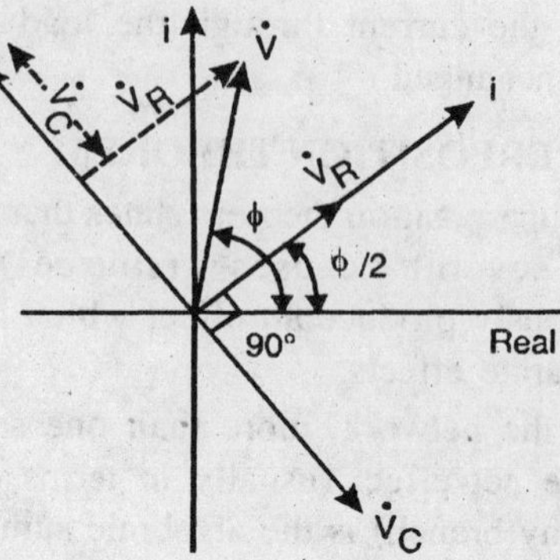

Fig. 19

$$\text{Therefore } \dot{V} = \left[R + j\left(\omega L - \frac{1}{\omega C}\right)\right] \times \dot{I}$$

$$\text{where} \quad V = I\sqrt{R^2 + \left(\omega L - \frac{1}{\omega C}\right)^2}$$

$$\text{or} \quad I = \frac{V}{\sqrt{R^2 + \left(\omega L - \frac{1}{\omega C}\right)^2}}$$

$$\text{and} \quad \phi = \text{arc tan}\left(\frac{\omega L - 1/\omega C}{R}\right)$$

$$= \tan^{-1}\left(\frac{X_L - X_C}{R}\right)$$

where ϕ is the phase single introduced by the impedance.

Therefore $v = V_m \sin(\omega t + \phi_i + \phi)$

$$\text{where} \quad V_m = I_m \times \sqrt{R^2 + \left(\omega L - \frac{1}{\omega C}\right)^2}$$

Maximum Power Transfer Theorem

Power transform from a source to a load is maximum when the load complex impedance is the conjugate vector to the complex impedance of the source. That is

$$Z_0 = Z_i$$

Let the load

$$Z_l = R_l + jX_l$$

$$\text{and} \quad Z_i = R_i + jX_i$$

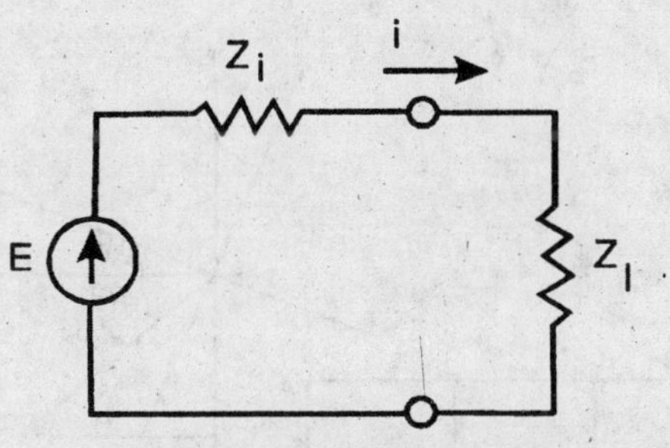

Fig. 20

The power transfer from the source to the load

$$P = R_l \times I^2$$

$$= R_l \times \left(\frac{E}{\sqrt{(R_i + R_l)^2 + (X_i + X_l)^2}} \right)^2$$

$$= \frac{R_l E^2}{(R_i + R_l)^2 + (X_i + X_l)^2}$$

For any value of R_l, the power P will be maximum when

$$X_i = -X_l$$

Thus $$P = \frac{R_l E^2}{(R_i + R_l)^2}$$

Taking derivative of the above expression with respect to R_l and equating to zero for P maximum,

$$\frac{dP}{dR_l} = 0$$

$$E^2 \left[\frac{(R_i + R_l)^2 - 2R_l\,(R_i + R_l)}{(R_i + R_l)^4} \right] = 0$$

$$(R_i + R_l)^2 - 2\,R_l (R_i + R_l) = 0$$

$$(R_i + R_l) - 2R_l = 0$$

$$R_i - R_l = 0$$

or $$R_i = R_l$$

Therefore the maximum power can be transferred only when

$$X_i = -X_l$$

and $$R_i = R_l$$

or $$Z_l = Z_i$$

RESONANCE

A passive network containing inductances and capacitances is said to be at resonance when its driving point reactance (in case of series combination) or driving point susceptance (in case of parallel combination) is zero.

Series Resonance

Resonance state in a series combination of resistance, inductance and capacitance is the state when inductive reactance becomes equal to capacitive reactance or the driving point reactance is zero and circuit behaves like a resistive one at resonance, *i.e.*

$$X = X_L - X_C = 0$$

$$\omega L = \frac{1}{\omega C}$$

so $$f = f_0 = \frac{1}{2\pi\sqrt{LC}}$$

The frequency, at which resonance occurs, is called resonant frequency and denoted by f_0.

At resonance

$$X = X_C - X_C = 0$$

Thus $$I = \frac{V}{R}$$

This follows that in a state of resonance the current flowing through the circuit is maximum and state of resonance could be achieved by either varying the frequency of the supply sources or the parameter L or C.

Frequency Resonance

The frequency resonance is shown in Fig. 21. The circuit behaves capacitive before the state of resonance, resistive at resonance and inductive after resonance as the frequency of supply is varied.

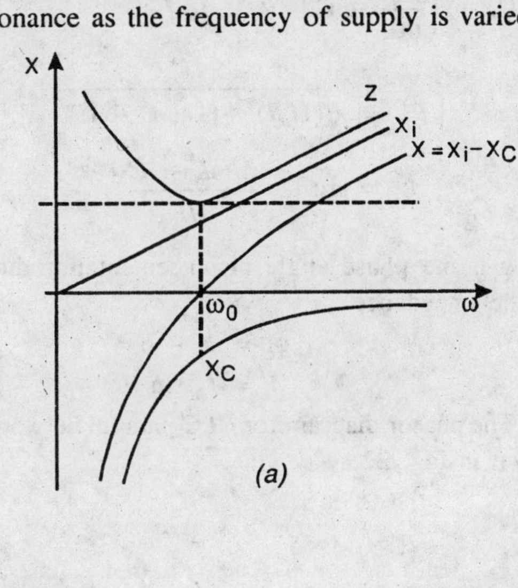

(a)

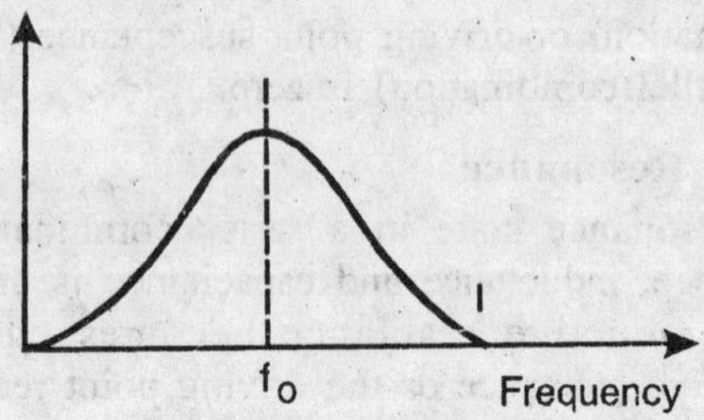

(b)

Fig. 21

The current in *RLC* series circuit increases with the increase in frequency and reaches to its maximum value at resonance (when the impedance of the circuit has minimum value as shown in Fig. 21 (*b*) and then decreases, with the further increase in frequency.

RLC in Parallel: In the circuit shown in Fig. 22 (a) applying *KCL*,

$$i_R + i_L + i_C = i \text{ or } \dot{I}_R + \dot{I}_L + \dot{I}_C = \dot{I}$$

$$\dot{I}_R = \dot{V}/R,\ \dot{I}_L = \dot{V}/j\omega L,$$

$$\dot{I}_C = \dot{V}\,(j\omega C)$$

$$v = V_m \sin(\omega t + \phi_v)$$

$$\dot{V}/R + \dot{V}/j\omega L + j\omega C\dot{V} = \dot{I}$$

$$\text{or, } \left[1/R + \frac{1}{j\omega L} + j\omega C\right]\dot{V} = \dot{I}$$

$$\text{or, } \left[1/R - j\left(\frac{1}{\omega L} - \omega C\right)\right]\dot{V} = \dot{I}$$

where $|I| = \sqrt{(1/R)^2 + (1/\omega L - \omega C)^2}\,.V$

and $\phi = \text{arc tan}\dfrac{1/\omega L - \omega C}{1/R}$

ϕ is the phase angle displacement introduced by the impedance

$$\phi_i = \phi_v - \phi$$

So $i = I_m \sin(\omega t + \phi_v - \phi)$

The phasor diagram for *RLC* parallel network is shown in Fig. 22.

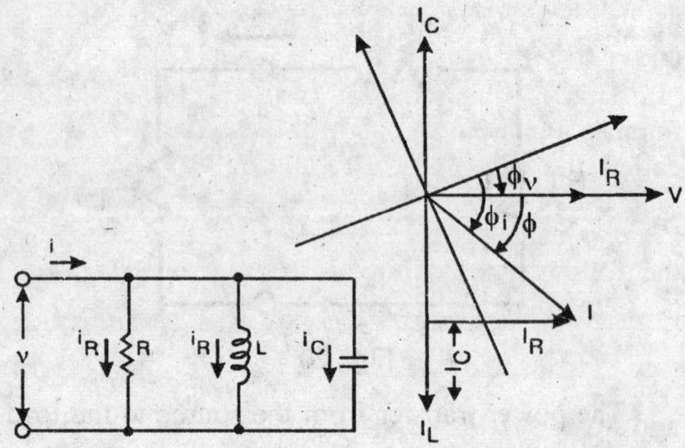

(a) (b)

Fig. 22

THE LAPLACE TRANSFORMATION

The Laplace transformation is denoted by the script letter *L*. The Laplace transform of any function of *f*(*t*) is given by the expression.

$$L[f(t)] = F(s) = \int_0^{\infty} f(t)\ e^{-st}\ dt$$

If there is an impulse function at $t = 0$, then $t = 0^-$ indicating the time just before the reference time must be used so that the impulse function is included as

$$L\,[f\,(t)] = F\,(s) = \int_{0^-}^{\infty} f(t)\,e^{-st}\ dt$$

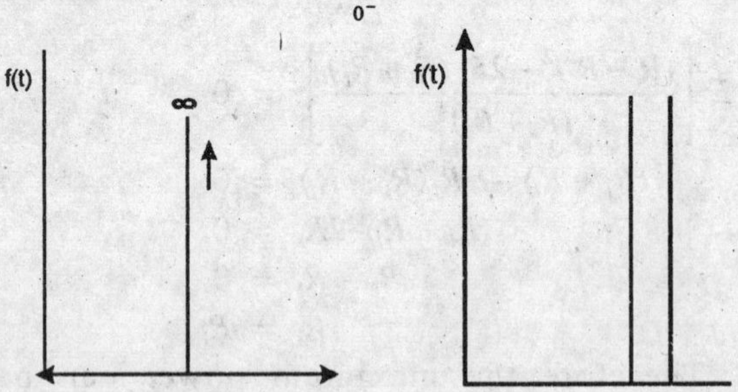

(a) (b)

Fig. 23

Unit impulse function is a special limiting case of a pulse function. The condition for a unit impulse function is that the area under the pulse should be unity. The simplest approach to define unit impulse or delta function is

$$f(t) \to \infty \qquad V \to \infty$$
$$\text{as} \quad \tau \to 0 \quad \text{or} \quad \text{as } \tau \to 0$$
$$\text{and } f(t) \times \tau = 1 \qquad V \cdot \tau = 1$$

This is illustrated in Fig. 23 (*b*). Thus, the impulse function whose area is equal to unity is called the unit-impulse function or *Dirac-delta function*. The unit impulse function occurring at $t = t_0$ is usually denoted by $\delta(t - t_0)$ and satisfies the following conditions:

$$\delta(t - t_0) = 0 \quad \text{for } t \neq t_0$$
$$\delta(t - t_0) = \infty \quad \text{for } t = t_0$$
$$\text{and } \int_{-\infty}^{\infty} \delta(t - t_0)\, dt = 1$$

To find the Laplace transform for unit impulse function, it is assumed that unit impulse occurring at $t = 0$ has width of τ sec so that

$$f(t).\ \tau = 1$$
$$\text{so} \quad f(t) = \frac{1}{\tau} \quad \text{for } 0 < t < \tau$$
$$\text{and} \quad f(t) = 0 \quad \text{for } t < 0,\ t > \tau$$
$$L[\delta(t)] = \int_0^{\infty} f(t)\, e^{-st}\, dt$$
$$= \int_0^{\tau} \frac{1}{\tau} e^{-st}\, dt$$
$$= \frac{1}{\tau}\left[\frac{-e^{-st}}{s}\right]_0^{\tau}$$
$$= \frac{1}{s\tau}[1 - e^{-s\tau}] \approx 1$$

FOURIER ANALYSIS

Any periodic function $f(t)$ can be expressed as a sum of a fundamental and harmonic terms. A Fourier series can be written for this expression if $f(t)$ is periodic and satisfies the Dirichlet conditions, which mainly reveals that $f(t)$ must be absolutely convergent, *i.e.*,

$$= \int_0^{T} |f(t)|\, dt < \infty$$

The other conditions require that in each period the function has a finite number of discontinuities and possesses a finite number of maxima and minima.

Inverse Laplace transformation

The mathematical process of passing from the complex variable expression to the time expression is called an inverse transformation. The notation for the inverse transformation is L^{-1}, so that

$$L^{-1}[F(s)] = f(t)$$

Mathematically

$$f(t) = \frac{1}{2\pi j} \int_{c-j\infty}^{c+j\infty} F(s)\, e^{st}\, ds \quad (t > 0)$$

EXERCISE

1. Kirchhoff's current law is applicable to only
(a) Junction in a network
(b) Closed loops in a network
(c) Electric circuits
(d) Electronic circuits

2. The concept on which Superposition Theorem is based on
(a) Reciprocity
(b) Duality
(c) Non-linearity
(d) Linearity

3. An ideal voltage source should have
(a) Large value of e.m.f.
(b) Small value of e.m.f.
(c) Zero source resistance
(d) Infinite source resistance

4. Kirchhoff's law is not applicable to circuits with
(a) Lumped parameters
(b) Passive elements
(c) Distributed parameters
(d) Non-linear resistances

5. In a circuit containing R, L and C power loss can take place in
(a) C only (b) L only
(c) R only (d) All of the above

6. The purpose of a parallel circuit resonance is to magnify
(a) Current (b) Voltage
(c) Power (d) Frequency

7. In an A.C. circuit power is dissipated in
(a) Resistance only
(b) Inductance only
(c) Capacitance only
(d) None of the above

8. In an A.C. Circuit I sin ϕ is called
(a) Active component
(b) Wattless component
(c) Any of the above
(d) None of the above

9. The value of operator j^2 is equal to
(a) Zero (b) + 1
(c) – 1 (d) $\sqrt{-1}$

10. Selectivities of different resonance circuits are compared in terms of their
(a) Impedances (b) Reactances
(c) Frequencies (d) Band widths

11. The ratio of bandwidth to the resonance frequency is called the............of the circuit.
(a) Impedance (b) Susceptance
(c) Quality factor (d) Selectivity

12. The series element of a band stop filter is
(a) Capacitive
(b) Inductive
(c) Parallel combination of L and C
(d) Series combination of L and C

13. The phase velocity *v* in a transmission line is
(a) LC (b) $\sqrt{C/L}$
(c) $\sqrt{L/C}$ (d) $1/\sqrt{L/C}$

14. The double energy transients occur in the
(a) Pure Inductive Coil
(b) R–L Circuit
(c) R–C Circuit
(d) R–L–C Circuit

15. The time constant of an R.C. Circuit increases if the value of resistance is
(a) Increased
(b) Decreased
(c) Either of the above
(d) None of the above

16. The shunt element in a band pass filter is
(a) Inductive
(b) Capacitive
(c) Shunt combination of L and C
(d) Series combination of L and C

17. The resistance of a wire depends on its
(a) Colour
(b) Humidity
(c) Number of neutrons
(d) Temperature

18. Fouriers series expansion of an odd periodic function contains
(a) Sine terms only
(b) Cosine term only
(c) Both (A) and (B)
(d) None of the above

19. In a linear network if all the *n* sources are multiplied by a constant *z* then the response gets multiplied by
(a) *z* (b) *z*/*n*
(c) *n*/2 (d) 2*n*

20. An impedance is capacitive if—
(a) only if $X_L = 0$ (b) $X_L < X_C$
(c) $X_L > X_C$ (d) R = 0

21. Fourier transform of even periodic functions contains only—
(a) Sine terms (b) Odd harmonics
(c) A constant (d) None of the above

22. A capacitor stores energy in—
(a) An electromagnetic field
(b) A magnetic field
(c) Dielectric dipole
(d) All of the above

23. In a R–L series circuit time constant is given by—
(a) L/R (b) LR
(c) LR^2 (d) L^2R

24. In a parallel resonance circuit the current is given by—

(a) V/R (b) VR/LC

(c) V/RC (d) $\frac{V}{L/CR}$

25. A circuit is called complex if—

(a) Electrons can flow

(b) A battery is present

(c) Electrons are present

(d) A voltage difference exits

26. The r.m.s. value of pure cosine function is—

(a) 0.5 of peak value

(b) 0.707 of peak value

(c) Same as peak value

(d) Zero

27. The time constant of a series R-C circuit is given by—

(a) R/C (b) RC^2

(c) RC (d) R^2C

28. Which of the following is bilateral element?

(a) Constant voltage source

(b) Constant current source

(c) Capacitance

(d) None of the above

29. An inductor store energy in—

(a) Electrostatic field

(b) Electromagnetic field

(c) Core

(d) Magnetic field

30. With zero initial conditions an inductor at $t=\infty$ will act as—

(a) Open circuit

(b) Short Circuit

(c) A source of voltage

(d) A source of current

31.

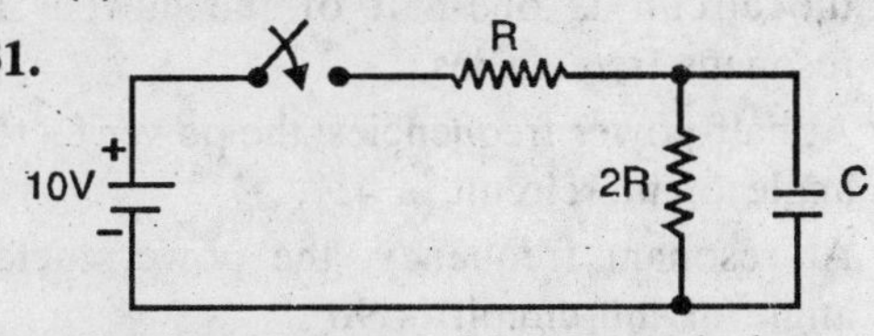

The time constant of the network shown in fig is

(a) 2 RC (b) 3 RC

(c) RC/2 (d) 2 RC/3

32. To a highly inductive circuit, a small capacitance is added in series. The angle between voltage and current will

(a) increase

(b) decrease

(c) remain nearly the same

(d) become indeterminant

33. Which of the following statements associated with capacitors is worng?

(a) A capacitor resists an abrupt change in the voltage across it in a manner analogous to the way a spring resists abrupt change in its displacement.

(b) A capacitor resists an abrupt change in the current flowing through it.

(c) It is impossible to change the voltage across a capacitor by a finite amount in zero time, for this requires infinite current through the capacitor.

(d) A finite amount of energy can be stored in a capacitor even if the current through the capacitor is zero, such as when the voltage across it is a constant.

34. Three equal impedances are first connected in delta across a 3–Φ balanced supply. If the same impedances are connected in star across the same supply

(a) phase currents will be one-third.

(b) line currents will be one-third.

(c) power consumed will be one-third.

(d) none of the above.

35.

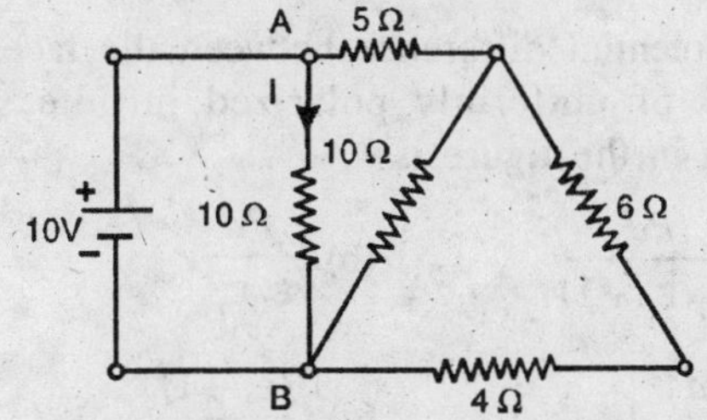

The resistance between points *A* and *B* of circuit shown above is

(a) 25 Ω (b) 15 Ω

(c) 5 Ω (d) 2.5 Ω

36. Three identical impedances are connected in delta to a 3-phase supply of 400 V. The line-current is 34.65 A and the total power taken is 14.4 kW. The resistance of the load in each phase (in ohm) is

(a) 20 (b) 16
(c) 12 (d) 10

37. Which of the following relations between apparent power (kVA), true power (kW) and reactive power (kvar) is true?

(a) $kVA = \sqrt{(kW)^2 + (kvar)^2}$
(b) kVA = kW + kVAr
(c) $kVA = \sqrt{(kW)^2 - (kvar)^2}$
(d) kVA = kW – kVAr

38. Two electrons moving parallel to each other at the same velocity will

(a) attract each other if they move in the same direction
(b) repel each other more strongly when moving in the same direction than when moving in opposite direction
(c) repel each other more strongly when moving in opposite direction
(d) repel each other with the same force when moving in the same or opposite direction

39.

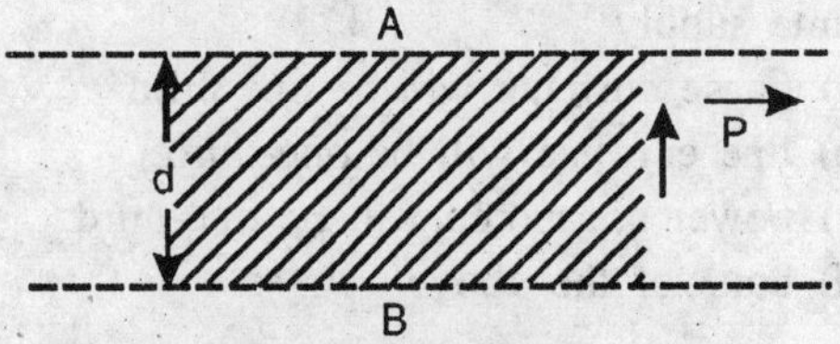

The potential difference between the faces *A* and *B* of uniformly polarized infinite slab shown in the figure is

(a) $\frac{Pd}{\varepsilon_0(\varepsilon_r - 1)}$ (b) $\frac{Pd}{\varepsilon_0 \varepsilon_r}$
(c) $\frac{Pd}{\varepsilon_0}$ (d) $\frac{(\varepsilon_r + 1)}{\varepsilon_0}$

40. Consider the following statements associated with parallel plate capacitor

1. Capacitance is proportional to area.
2. Capacitance is inversely proportional to distance of separation of plates.
3. The dielectric material is in a state of compression.

Of these statements

(a) 1, 2 and 3 are correct
(b) 1 and 2 are correct
(c) 1 and 3 are correct
(d) 2 and 3 are correct

41. An alternating current of frequency 50 Hz and maximum value 200 A is given as

(a) $i = 200 \sin 628\, t$
(b) $i = 200 \sin 314\, t$
(c) $i = 100\sqrt{2} \sin 314\, t$
(d) $i = 100\sqrt{2} \sin 157\, t$

42.

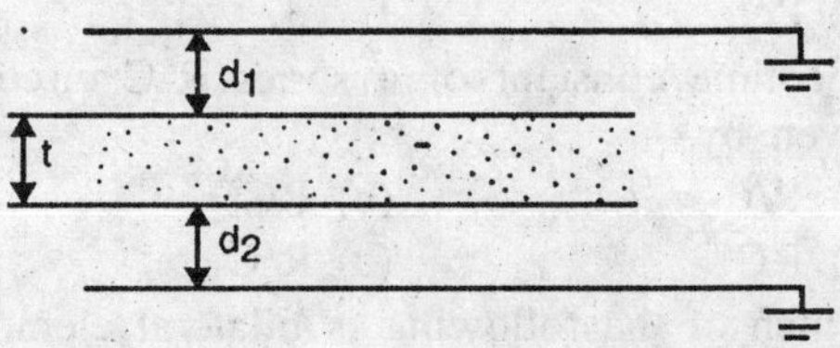

An infinite charged conducting plate is placed between and parallel to two infinite conducting grounded plates as shown. The ratio of charge densities σ_1 and σ_2 on the two sides of the plates will be

(a) $\frac{(d_1 + t)}{(d_2 + t)}$ (b) $\frac{(d_2 + t)}{(d_1 + t)}$
(c) $\frac{d_2}{d_1}$ (d) $\frac{d_1}{d_2}$

43. Consider the following statements regarding the frequency response curve of a series R-L-C circuit.

1. At half power frequencies, the current in the circuit is one-half of the current at resonant frequencies.
2. At half-power frequencies, the power factor angle of the circuit is 45°.
3. At resonant frequency, the power factor angle of the circuit is 90°.
4. Maximum power occurs at resonant frequency.

Of these statements
(a) 1, 2 and 4 are correct
(b) 1, 2 and 3 are correct
(c) 2 and 4 are correct
(d) 1 and 4 are correct

44. The watt-hour efficiency is always
(a) more than ampere hour efficiency
(b) equal to ampere-hour efficiency
(c) less than ampere-hour efficiency
(d) none of these

45. Specific resistance of a conductor depends upon
(a) dimensions of the conductor
(b) composition of the conductor material
(c) resistance of the conductor
(d) both (a) and (b)

46. Which of the following statements is true both for a series as well as a parallel circuit?
(a) Resistance's are additive.
(b) Powers are additive.
(c) Voltage drops are additive.
(d) Conductances are additive.

47. Mica capacitors are characterised by all of the following except
(a) accurate value
(b) low losses
(c) low leakage resistance
(d) stable operation

48. How are 500 Ω resistors connected so as to give an effective resistance of 750 Ω?
(a) Three resistors of 500 Ω each, in parallel
(b) Three resistors of 500 Ω each, in series
(c) Two resistors of 500 Ω each, in parallel
(d) Two resistors of 500 Ω each, in parallel and the combination in series with an other 500 Ω resistor

49. The theorem that enables a number of voltage (or current) sources to be combined directly into a single voltage (or current) source is the ______ theorem.
(a) compensation (b) reciprocity
(c) Millman's (d) Maxwell's

50. Twelve identical wires of resistance 6 Ω each are arranged to form the edges of a cube. The effective resistance between the opposite corners of the cube is
(a) 6 Ω (b) 5 Ω
(c) 8 Ω (d) 4.5 Ω

51. Two alternating currents represented as

$i_1 = 4 \sin \omega t$ and $i_2 = 10 \sin \left(\omega t + \frac{\pi}{3}\right)$ are fed

into a common conductor. The rms value of resultant current is
(a) 9.62 A (b) 8.83 A
(c) 12.48 A (d) 13.60 A

52. When a heater is connected to the power supply, the heater coil will glow but the supply wiring does not glow. This is because
(a) resistance of heater coils is very high in comparison to that of internal wiring
(b) internal wiring is of superior material
(c) the resistance of internal wiring is very high
(d) supply wires are covered with insulation

53. A Y arrangement of resistances has each resistance of 3 Ω. The equivalent delta arrangement will have each resistance of values
(a) 9 Ω (b) 6 Ω
(c) 3 Ω (d) 1 Ω

54. Coulomb's law for the force between electric charges most closely resembles with
(a) Newton's law of motion
(b) Law of conservation of energy
(c) Gauss's theorem
(d) Newton's law of gravitation

55. A steel bar needs 2000 AT to magnetise it. The voltage required for the magnetising coil of 100 turns and 20 ohms resistance will be
(a) 400 V (b) 200 V
(c) 100 V (d) 10 V

56. What capacitance must be placed in series with a 15 μF capacitor to give a total capacitance of 5 μF
(a) 4 μF (b) 7.5 μF
(c) 10 μF (d) 25 μF

57. Which of the following statements is incorrect?
(a) Whenever the flux linking with the coil or circuit changes, e.m.f is produced.
(b) The direction of dynamically induced emf can be determined by Fleming's right hand rule.
(c) The coefficient of self inductance is proportional to the square of number of turns on it.
(d) Coefficient of coupling for tightly coupled coil is zero.

58. In a 3-phase supply, floating neutral is undesirable because it may result in ______ across the load.
(a) unequal line voltages
(b) high voltage
(c) low voltage
(d) none of these

59. Two spheres of radii R_1 and R_2 ($R_2 > R_1$) are connected by a conducting wire. Each of the spheres has been given a charge q. Now
(a) sphere of radius R_1 will have greater potential
(b) sphere of radius R_2 will have less potential
(c) potentials of both the spheres will be equal
(d) sphere of radius R_1 will have zero potential

60. The phase difference between the two waveforms can be compared only when they
(a) have the same frequency
(b) have the same peak value
(c) have the same effective value
(d) are sinusoidal

61. A 0.1 μF capacitor has voltage increasing linearly at the rate of 100 volts each m sec. The current flowing through the capacitor will be
(a) zero (b) 10 mA
(c) 100 mA (d) 1 A

62. The design value of a prototype high pass filter with a design impedance R_0 and cut-off frequency f_c is given by
(a) $L = R_0/4\pi f_c$, $C = \dfrac{f_c}{4\pi R_0}$
(b) $L = R_0/4\pi f_c$, $C = \dfrac{1}{4\pi f_c R_0}$
(c) $L = \dfrac{1}{4\pi f_c R_0}$, $C = \dfrac{R_0}{4\pi f_c}$
(d) $L = \dfrac{R_0}{4\pi f_c}$, $C = \dfrac{R_0 f_c}{4\pi}$

63. An R-L-C parallel circuit in resonance will
(a) have a high impedance
(b) act like a resistor of low value
(c) have current in each branch equal to that of line current
(d) produce lot of noise and heat

64. An ideal voltage source should have
(a) zero source resistance
(b) infinite source resistance
(c) terminal voltage in proportion to current
(d) terminal voltage in proportion to load
(e) open-circuit voltage nearly equal to voltage on full load

65. Power loss in an electrical circuit can take place in
(a) inductance only
(b) capacitance only
(c) inductance and resistance
(d) resistance only

66. The capacitance of a cylindrical capacitor is given as
(a) $\dfrac{\varepsilon_0 \varepsilon_r}{\log_e \dfrac{D}{d}} F/m$ (b) $\dfrac{2\pi \varepsilon_0 \varepsilon_r}{\log_e \dfrac{D}{d}} F/m$
(c) $\dfrac{2\pi \varepsilon_0 \varepsilon_r}{\log_{10} \dfrac{D}{d}} F/m$ (d) $\dfrac{2\pi}{\varepsilon_0 \varepsilon_r \log_e \dfrac{D}{d}} F/m$

67. A tiny particle carrying a charge of 0.3 coulombs is accelerated through a potential difference of 1000 volts. The kinetic energy acquired by the particle will be
(a) 100 J (b) 200 J
(c) 300 J (d) 400 J

68. The series element of band-stop filter is
(a) inductive
(b) capacitive
(c) series combination of L and C
(d) parallel combination of L and C

69. During dielectric breakdown of a capacitor
(a) electrons cease to move from one plate to another
(b) permanent conduction path is established between plates
(c) dielectric stored energy rendering plates chargeless
(d) electrons get scattered

70. Internal heating of capacitor is usually attributed to
(a) dielectric charge
(b) plate vibration
(c) electron movement
(d) leakage resistance

71. When the two quantities are in quadrature the phase angle between them will be
(a) 45° or $\frac{\pi}{4}$ radians
(b) 90° or $\frac{\pi}{2}$ radians
(c) 135° or $\frac{3\pi}{4}$ radians
(d) 60° or $\frac{\pi}{3}$ radians

72. The Laplace transform of a ramp function is
(a) s (b) $1/s^2$
(c) $1/s$ (d) none of these

73. The Laplace transform of t^n is
(a) $\frac{n!}{s^{n+1}}$ (b) $\frac{1}{s^{2n}}$
(c) $\frac{n}{s-a}$ (d) $\frac{n^2}{s+a}$

74. For the circuit shown, the cut-off frequency is

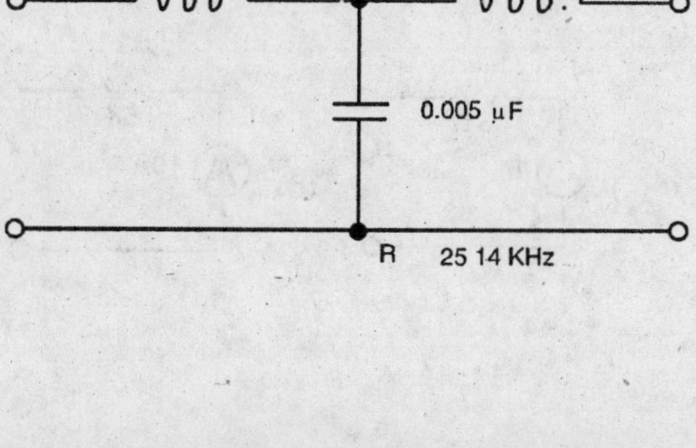

(a) 20.14 kHz (b) 25.14 kHz
(c) 10.14 kHz (d) 15.14 kHz

75. The frequency of operation and coëfficient of coupling in the circuit given below is 1 MHz and 0.1 respectively. The input impedance of the circuit is
(a) $(4 + j\ 3000)$ ohms
(b) $(5 + j\ 1886)$ ohms
(c) both
(d) none

76. The shunt element of a band-pass filter is
(a) inductive
(b) capacitive
(c) parallel combination of L and C
(d) series combination of L and C

77. A square wave is fed to an R-C circuit. Then
(a) voltage across R is square and across C is not square
(b) voltage across C is square and across R is not square
(c) voltage across both R and C is square
(d) voltage across both R and C is not square

78. A charge of 75 micro-coulombs is stored in a capacitor. The area of each of the two plates is 300 square centimeters. The flux density in milli-coulombs per square metre is
(a) 2.5 (b) 35
(c) 50 (d) 0

79. The direction of current in an ac circuit
(a) is from positive to negative
(b) is always in one direction
(c) varies from instant to instant
(d) cannot be determined

80. Two capacitors of capacity 32 μF and 16 μF are connected parallel, the total capacity will be
(a) 48 μF (b) 32 μF
(c) 2/32 μF D 32/3 μF

81. In a radio, a gang condenser is a type of
(a) Paper capacitor
(b) Air capacitor
(c) Electrolytic capacitor
(d) Ceramic capacitor

82. Like a series R-L-C resonant circuit, a parallel resonant circuit also

(a) magnifies current
(b) offers minimum impedance
(c) draws maximum current
(d) has unity power factor

83. The peak factor is the ratio of
(a) average value to rms value
(b) rms value to average value
(c) peak value to rms value
(d) peak value to average value

84. In case of ceramic capacitors, the tolerance is given in pF for capacitors values less than
(a) 5 pF (b) 10 pF
(c) 20 pF (d) 100 pF

85. Filament lamp makes use of
(a) chemical effect (b) heating effect
(c) magnetic effect (d) none of these

86. The current in a single element circuit leads the voltage by 50° at all times. The circuit element is
(a) a resistor (b) an inductor
(c) a capacitance (d) none of these

87. What will be the capacity of four capacitors of equal capacity "C" when connected in parallel
(a) 4 C (b) C/4
(c) 3/4 C (d) C

88. In a capacitor, the electric charge is stored in
(a) dielectric
(b) metal plates
(c) dielectric as well as metal plates
(d) neither dielectric nor metal plates

89. Generally an electrolytic capacitor is made to provide
(a) fixed capacitance
(b) variable capacitance
(c) low capacitance
(d) large value of capacitance

90. The electric field intensity between the plates of a parallel plate condenser is E. Now if a dielectric of medium of dielectric constant $\in$ is introduced between the plates, the electric field intensity will become
(a) $\in E$ (b) $E/\in$
(c) $\sqrt{\in E}$ (d) $\sqrt{E/\in}$

91. Which capacitor is preferred for high frequency circuits?
(a) Mica capacitor
(b) Air capacitor
(c) Electrolytic capacitor
(d) None of these

92. A 4000 μF capacitor of an electronic flash unit is charged to potential of 300 V. The charge stored in the capacitor will be
(a) 1.2 Coulombs (b) 12 Coulombs
(c) 120 Coulombs (d) 1200 Coulombs

93. Nichrome is used for
(a) overhead line wires
(b) heater coils
(c) lamp filaments
(d) none of these

94. Which of the following statements about the heating effect of the current is true?
(a) The heating effect appears only with large currents.
(b) The higher the current strength, the lower the heating effect.
(c) The heating effect is always desirable
(d) The heating effect always appears when a current flows through a resistor.

95. The circuit given below is equivalent to

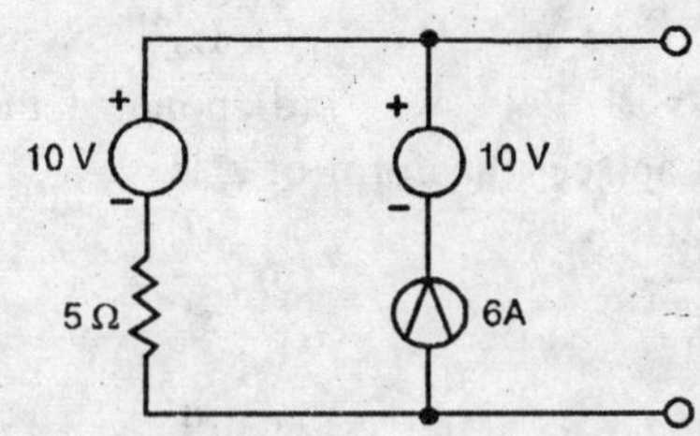

(a)
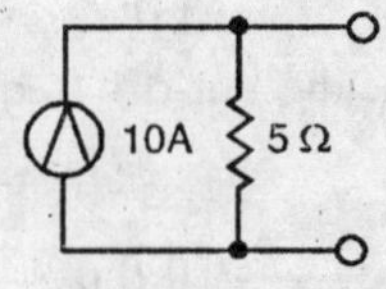

(b)
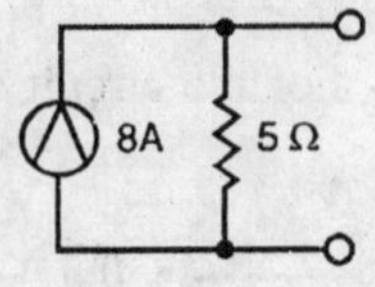

(c)
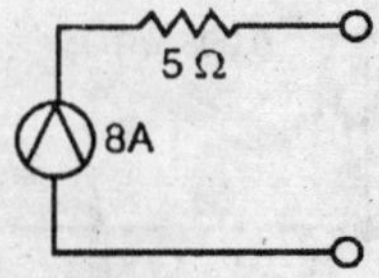

(d)
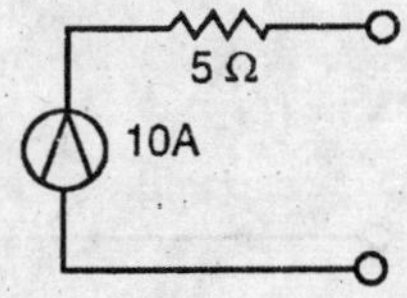

96. A parallel resonant circuit employs 50 μμF capacitor and has bandwidth of 250 kHz. The maximum impedance of the circuit would be

(a) 31.5 K ohm (b) (17 + *j*8) K ohm

(c) 22.5 K ohm (d) 12.7 K ohm

97. Two capacitors each of breakdown voltage 500 V are connected in parallel. The breakdown rating of the combination will be

(a) 500 V (b) 650 V

(c) 1000 V (d) 2500 V

98. The circuit given below can be reduced to a single source of

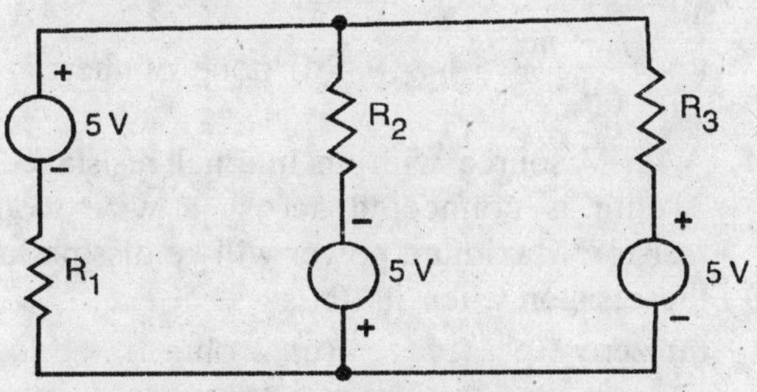

(a) 15 V in series with R_3

(b) 5 V in series with R_3

(c) 10 V in series with R_2

(d) 15 V in series with R_1

99. The density of the acid in a lead acid battery gives an indication of

(a) eventual damages caused to the plates

(b) the level of the acid

(c) the e.m.f. of the battery

(d) the charge of the battery

100. With which of the following types of capacitors care should be taken about the correct polarity while connecting it in a circuit?

(a) Paper capacitor

(b) Mica capacitor

(c) Ceramic capacitor

(d) Electrolytic capacitor

101. A capacitance is charged to 100 V and has 100 micro coulombs of charge. The value of capacitance will be

(a) 10 μF (b) 100 μF

(c) 10 pF (d) 100 pF

102. A series resonant circuit is capacitive at f = 100 Hz. The circuit will be inductive somewhere at

(a) f < 100 Hz

(b) f > 100 Hz

(c) f = 100 Hz by increasing the value of the resistance

(d) none of the above

103. To a series RLC circuit, a voltage of 10 V is applied. If Q of the coil at resonant frequency is 20, the voltage across the inductor at resonant frequency will be

(a) 200 V (b) 100 V

(c) 75 V (d) 50 V

104. The rms value of the periodic waveform e(t) shown in figure is

(a) $\sqrt{3/2}$ A (b) $\sqrt{2/3}$ A

(c) $\sqrt{3}$ A (d) $\sqrt{2}$ A

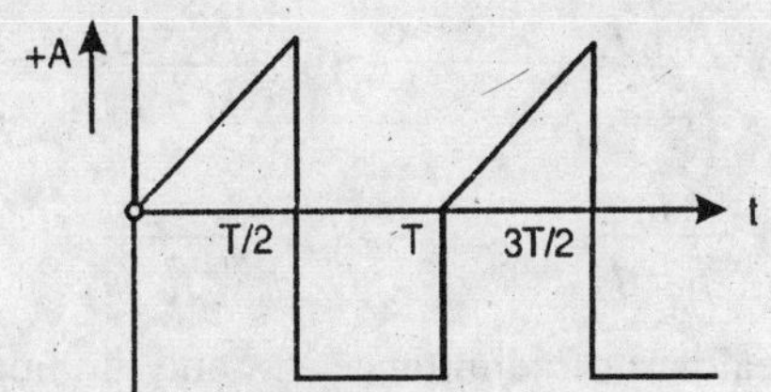

105. The electromotive force is

(a) the torque produced by a motor

(b) the force experienced by an electromagnet

(c) the force with which the current carrying conductors attract or repel each other

(d) the voltage produced by a voltage source

106. The capacitor, commonly used for ceiling fan motors has a value of 2.3 μF. The type of capacitor used is generally

(a) paper capacitor

(b) electrolyte capacitor

(c) parallel plate with mica dielectric

(d) none of these

107. The equivalent inductance of the parallel connection is

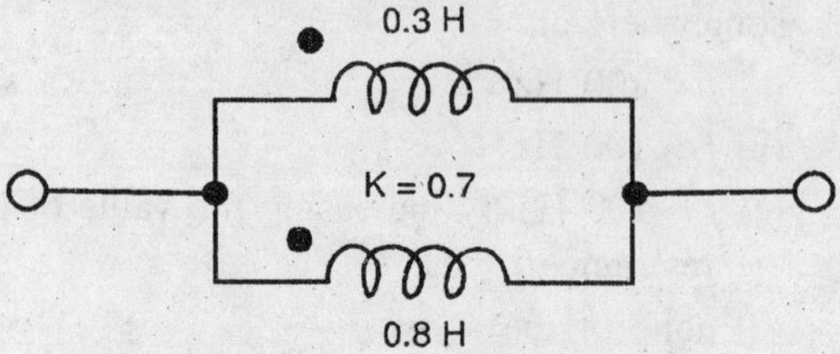

(a) 0.25 H (b) 0.32 H
(c) 0.34 H (d) 0.38 H

108. Two charges of equal magnitude are separated by some distance. If the charges are increased by 10%; to get the same force between them, their separation must be
(a) increased by 21%
(b) increased by 10%
(c) decreased by 10%
(d) none of the above is correct

109. An R-L-C series circuit has f_1 and f_2 as the half power frequencies and f_0 as the resonant frequency. The Q-factor of the circuit is given by

(a) $\frac{f_1+f_2}{2f_0}$ (b) $\frac{f_1-f_0}{f_2-f_0}$

(c) $\frac{f_0}{f_1-f_2}$ (d) $\frac{f_1-f_2}{f_0}$

110. Real part of admittance is... and the imaginary part is...
(a) impedance, resistance
(b) resistance, impedance
(c) susceptance, inductance
(d) conductance,susceptance

111. There are two wires A and B. A is 20 times longer than B and has half the x-section of that of B. If the resistance of B is 1 Ω, the resistance of conductor A will be
(a) 40 Ω (b) 1/40 Ω
(c) 20 Ω (d) 10 Ω

112. One commercial unit of energy equals
(a) One watt-hour
(b) one kilowatt-hour
(c) 1000 watt-seconds
(d) none of these

113. In an R-L circuit connected to an alternating sinusoidal voltage, the magnitude of transient current primarily depends on the
(a) instant in the voltage cycle at which circuit is closed
(b) impedance of the circuit
(c) frequency of the voltage
(d) peak value of steady state current

114. If f_1 and f_2 are half power frequencies and f_0 be resonance frequency, the selectivity of RLC series circuit is given by

(a) $\frac{f_2-f_1}{f_0}$ (b) $\frac{f_2-f_1}{2f_0}$

(c) $\frac{f_2-f_0}{f_1}$ (d) none of these

115. A 45-V source with an internal resistance of 2 ohm is connected across a wire wound resistor. Maximum power will be dissipated in the resistor when its R is
(a) zero (b) 2 ohm
(c) 45 ohm (d) infinitely large

116. When an R-L circuit is switched on across a dc source of supply of V volts, the expression for current is given as

(a) $i(t) = \frac{V}{R}\left(1-e^{-\frac{R}{L}t}\right)$

(b) $i(t) = \frac{V}{R}\left(1+e^{-\frac{R}{L}t}\right)$

(c) $i(t) = \frac{V}{R}\left(1+e^{\frac{R}{L}t}\right)$

(d) $i(t) = \frac{V}{R}\left(1-e^{\frac{R}{L}t}\right)$

117. An infinite number of charges, each equal to 'Q' are placed along the axis at $x = 1$, $x = 2$, $x = 3$... and so on. The electric field at the point $x = 0$ due to these charges will be

(a) Q (b) $\frac{2Q}{3}$

(c) $\frac{4Q}{3}$ (d) $\frac{4}{5}Q$

118. Which of the following is incorrect?
(a) The characteristic of impedance of prototype filters does not remain constant during pass band
(b) The attenuation does not rise sharply beyond cut-off frequency in prototype filters
(c) Composite filters are combination of prototype and m-derived type filters
(d) m-derived filters also suffer from the disadvantages given in (a) and (b)

119. Which of the following coils will have large resonant frequency?
(a) A coil with low resistance
(b) A coil with large resistance
(c) A coil with large distributed capacitance
(d) A coil with low distributed capacitance

120. If a piece of iron is placed in a magnetic field
(a) the magnetic field will not be affected
(b) the magnetic lines of force will bend away from their usual paths in order to pass through the piece
(c) the magnetic lines of force will bend away from their usual paths in order to go away from the piece
(d) none of these

121. The two quantities are said to be in phase with each other when
(a) the phase difference between two quantities is zero degree or radian
(b) each of them pass through zero values at the same instant and rise in the same direction
(c) each of them pass through zero values at the same instant but rises in the opposite directions

122. Two-wattmeter method is employed to measure power in a 3-phase balanced system with the current coils connected in the A and C lines. The phase sequence is ABC. If the wattmeter with its current coil in A-phase line reads zero, then the power factor of the 3-phase load will be
(a) zero lagging (b) zero leading
(c) 0.5 lagging (d) 0.5 leading

123. Which of the following comparisons between the metallic paper (MP) capacitor and the electrolytic capacitor is true?
(a) The MP capacitor cues itself after any puncture, while the electrolytic capacitor does not
(b) For the same volume the MP capacitor can have much more capacitances as compared to the electrolytic capacitor
(c) Both of these
(d) None of these

124. The most important advantage of using electrical energy in the form of ac is
(a) the construction cost per kW of ac generator is lower than that of dc generator
(b) conductor of smaller x-section is required in case of ac in comparison to dc for carrying the same current
(c) less insulation is required in case of ac
(d) transformation of voltage is possible in case of ac only

125. In a series RC circuit, the voltage across the capacitor and the resistor are 60 V and 80 V respectively. The input voltage should be
(a) $70 \angle 45°$V (b) $100 \angle -37°$V
(c) $105 \angle -42°$V (d) $108 \angle -60°$V

126. The drift velocity of electrons is
(a) equal to speed of light
(b) almost equal to speed to light
(c) very small as compared to speed of light
(d) none of these

127. The frequency at which maximum voltage occurs across the inductance in an R-L-C circuit is

(a) $\dfrac{1}{2\pi\sqrt{LC}}$

(b) $\dfrac{1}{2\pi\sqrt{LC - C^2R^2/2}}$

(c) $\dfrac{1}{2\pi}\sqrt{\dfrac{1}{LC} - \dfrac{R^2}{2L^2}}$

(d) $\dfrac{1}{2\pi\sqrt{LC - R^2}}$

128. Which of the following should have low value for the contacts and their material?

(a) Thermal capacity

(b) Contact resistance

(c) Thermal conductivity

(d) None of these

129. The shunt element of band-stop filter is

(a) inductive

(b) capacitive

(c) series combination of L and C

(d) parallel combination of L and C

130. In an R-L-C circuit

(a) power is consumed in resistance only and is equal to $I^2 R$

(b) exchange of power does not take place between resistance and supply mains

(c) exchange of power takes place between capacitor and supply mains

(d) all of the above

131. A cloud is at a potential of 10^6 V relative to the ground. A charge of 6 coulombs is transferred in a lighting stroke between the cloud and the earth. The energy dissipated is

(a) 10^6 J (b) 3×10^6 J

(c) 6×10^6 J (d) 12×10^6 J

132. Which of the following statements associated with a pure capacitive circuit is not true?

(a) Power consumed is zero

(b) Heat produced is zero

(c) Power factor is unity

(d) Work done is zero

(e) Power factor is zero

133. In resistor, if there is no colour band for tolerance, it implies that the tolerance is

(a) ± 10 ohms (b) ±10%

(c) ± 20% (d) infinite

134. In a.c. inductive circuit, condenser is used

(a) for decreasing the power factor

(b) for improving the power factor

(c) for keeping the power factor constant

(d) none of these

135. The point to be kept in mind with parallel resonance is

(a) a very high voltage appears across the capacitor

(b) a very high voltage appears across the inductive coil

(c) although the line current is small but the current passing through inductive and capacitance branches is very high

(d) all of the above

136. Internal heating of a capacitor is usually attributed to

(a) leakage resistance

(b) dielectric charge

(c) electron movement

(d) plate vibration

137. During charging and discharging of an Edison cell

(a) electrolyte does not take part in chemical reaction

(b) emf remains the same

(c) corrosive fumes are produced

(d) none of these

138. The electrons revolve around the nucleus with high velocity. Which type of force acts against the centrifugal force and keeps the electrons in their orbits?

(a) Electrostatic force of attraction

(b) Electromagnetic force of attraction

(c) Gravitational force

(d) Adhesive force

139. Four 100 W bulbs are connected in parallel across 200 V supply line. If one bulb gets fused

(a) no bulb will light

(b) all the four bulbs will light

(c) rest of the three bulbs will light

(d) none of the above

140. Voltage applied across a ceramic dielectric produces an electrostatic field 100 times greater than in air. The dielectric constant ε of the ceramic equals

(a) 100/3 (b) 50

(c) 100 (d) 1/100

141. The best indication about the state of charge on a lead acid battery is given by
(a) specific gravity of electrolyte
(b) temperature of electrolyte
(c) output voltage
(d) none of these

142. In a series R-C circuit current_____ with the increase in frequency.
(a) increases (b) decreases
(c) remains unaltered (d) none of these

143. The depolarizer in a carbon zinc cell
(a) absorbs the oxygen produced in the cell
(b) prevents the fast chemical action on the zinc container
(c) converts the hydrogen produced into water
(d) all of the above

144. The phasor *C* can be represented in exponential form as
(a) $\sqrt{a^2+b^2}\, e^{j\theta}$ (b) $(a + b)\, e^{j\theta}$
(c) $(a^2 + b^2)e^{j\theta}$ (d) $e^{(a + jb)}$

145. The resistance of a parallel circuit consisting of two resistors is 12 Ω. One of the resistance wire breaks and the effective resistance becomes 18 Ω. The resistance of the broken wire is
(a) 48 Ω (b) 18 Ω
(c) 36 Ω (d) 24 Ω

146. The equivalent current source branch for the voltage source branch given below is

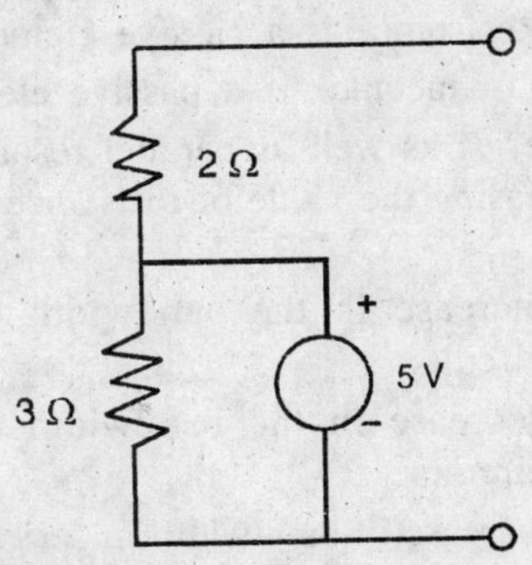

(a) 2 A, 5 ohm (b) 5 A, 3 ohm
(c) 1 A, 5 ohm (d) 2.5 A, 2 ohm

147. In a series R-L circuit
(a) voltage drop across R and L are in phase
(b) voltage drop across L leads the voltage drop across R by 90°
(c) voltage drop across L lags behind the voltage drop across R by 90°
(d) voltage drops across R and L are in phase opposition

148. At a frequency less than the resonant frequency
(a) series circuit is capacitive and parallel circuit is inductive.
(b) series circuit is inductive and parallel circuit is capacitive
(c) both circuits are inductive
(d) both circuits are capacitive

149. The point to be kept in mind with series resonance is
(a) the current is practically zero
(b) the current can increase infinitely
(c) the voltage across resistance can become much larger than applied voltage
(d) the voltage across the coil and across the capacitor becomes much larger than applied voltage

150. Three equal resistances are connected in delta. If this delta is converted into star
(a) the resistances of the star network will be lower than the resistances of delta network
(b) the resistances of both the networks will be equal
(c) the resistances of the star network will be larger than the resistances of delta network
(d) none of these

151. Q-factor of a parallel resonant circuit is
(a) $\dfrac{2\pi f_1}{\text{band width}}$
(b) $2\pi \times \dfrac{\text{maximum stored energy}}{\text{energy dissipated per cycle}}$
(c) $\dfrac{\text{maximum stored energy}}{\text{energy dissipated per cycle}}$
(d) none of the above

152. Non-sinusoidal waveforms are made up of
(a) different sinusoidal waveforms
(b) fundamental and odd harmonics
(c) fundamental and even harmonics
(d) none of these

153. In a 3-phase, 4-wire load circuit shown below, line voltage is indicated by arrow

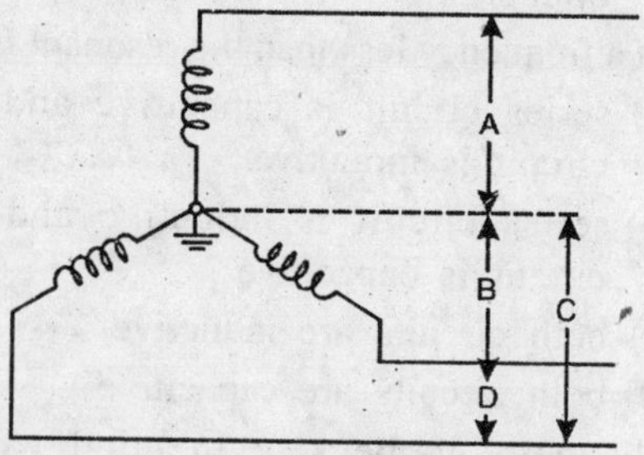

(a) A (b) B
(c) C (d) D

154. For a voltage source
(a) the source e.m.f. and terminal voltage are always equal
(b) terminal voltage is always lower than source e.m.f.
(c) terminal voltage cannot be higher than source e.m.f.
(d) none of these

155. The bandwidth of a resonant circuit is given by
(a) $\frac{R}{2\pi L}$ Hz (b) $\frac{f_r}{Q}$ Hz
(c) $\frac{2\pi R}{L}$ Hz (d) $2\pi f_r/Q$ Hz
(e) both (a) and (b)

156. When an uncharged body is placed near a charged body, then uncharged body
(a) is attracted first and then charged by induction
(b) gets charged by induction and then attracted towards the charging body
(c) gets charged by conduction
(d) remains as such

157. A series circuit having a resonant frequency of 60 kHz is connected in series with a signal generator which produces signals of frequencies 20, 30, 40, and 60 kHz. The signals experiencing minimum and maximum impedances will be
(a) 60 kHz and 20 kHz respectively
(b) 20 kHz and 60 kHz respectively
(c) 30 kHz and 60 kHz respectively
(d) 20 kHz and 40 kHz respectively

158. If three 30 μF capacitors are connected in series, the net capacitance is
(a) 10 μF (b) 60 μF
(c) 90 μF (d) none of these

159. According to Faraday's law of electromagnetic induction an emf is induced in a conductor whenever it
(a) lies in a magnetic field
(b) lies perpendicular to the magnetic field
(c) cuts the magnetic flux
(d) moves parallel to the direction of magnetic field

160. Which of the following is correct?
(a) $B = \mu_0 H + M$ (b) $B = \mu_0 M + H$
(c) $B = \mu_0 (H + M)$ (d) $B = \frac{M}{\mu_0}$

161. Which of the following statement is not correct?
(a) Voltage source is an active element.
(b) Current source is a passive element.
(c) Resistance is a passive element.
(d) Conductance is a passive element.

162. In series as well as parallel resonant circuits, increasing the value of resistance would lead to
(a) increase in the bandwidth of both the circuits
(b) decrease in the bandwidth of both the circuits
(c) increase in bandwidth in series circuit and decrease in parallel circuit
(d) decrease in bandwidth in series circuit and increase in parallel circuit

163. During electroplating the weight of a substance deposited depends upon
(a) shape of the article
(b) quantity of electricity
(c) room temperature
(d) all of the above

164. For dielectric, flux is proportional to
(a) potential difference between electrodes
(b) resistivity of medium
(c) rate of change of potential difference
(d) rate of change of current

165. A leading power factor implies that
(a) current leads the voltage
(b) current lags behind the voltage
(c) voltage leads the current
(d) none of the above

166. An R-L circuit is fed from an ac source of voltage V_{max} (sin ωt + α). The transient component of the current, when the circuit is switched on, will be zero if
(a) $\alpha = 0$ (b) $\alpha = 90°$
(c) $\alpha = \tan^{-1} \frac{\omega L}{R}$ (d) $\alpha = 135°$

167. A coil is tuned to a certain frequency by a 220 μμF capacitor. A capacitor of 20 μμF is required to tune the same coil to the third harmonic of this frequency. The self capacitance of this coil is
(a) 10 μμF (b) 2.5 μμF
(c) 5 μμF (d) 20 μμF

168. The only sure proof of testing the polarity of magnetism is
(a) attraction and repulsion both
(b) attraction
(c) repulsion
(d) none of these

169. A voltage wave containing 20% third harmonic, is applied to an inductor. The percentage of third harmonic in the current wave will be
(a) much less than 20%
(b) much more than 20%
(c) 20%
(d) 10%

170. In an ac circuit, low reactive power in comparison to true power indicates
(a) low power factor (b) low efficiency
(c) high power factor (d) high efficiency

171. A parallel plate capacitor with air an dielectric is charged and then disconnected from the supply. The force between the plates is F. If the capacitor is now immersed in a liquid of dielectric constant $\in$, then the force between the plates will be
(a) $\in^2$F (b) $\in$F
(c) F (d) F/$\in$

172. A parallel plate capacitor with air dielectric is connected to a constant voltage source. The force between its plates is *F*. If the capacitor is immersed in a liquid of dielectric constant $\in$ without disconnecting it from the power supply, then the force between the plates would be
(a) $\in^2$F (b) $\in$F
(c) F (d) F/$\in$

173. Which of the following equations is valid for a 3-phase 4-wire balanced star- connected load?
(a) $I_R + I_Y + I_B = I_N = 0$
(b) $I_R + I_Y - I_B = I_N$
(c) $I_R - I_Y + I_B = I_N$
(d) $\frac{V_B + V_R + V_Y}{Z} = I_N$

174. Resonant frequency f_r of a series R-L-C circuit is related to half power frequencies f_1 and f_2 as
(a) $f_r = \frac{f_1 + f_2}{2}$ (b) $f_r = \sqrt{f_1 f_2}$
(c) $f_r = f_2 - f_1$ (d) $f_r = \sqrt{f_1} + \sqrt{f_2}$

175. Mutual inductance between two magnetically coupled coils depends on the
(a) permeability of the core material
(b) number of turns of the coils
(c) cross-sectional area of their common core
(d) all of the above

176. Which of the following statements is true about two-wattmeter method for power measurement in 3-phase circuit?

(a) Power can be measured using two wattmeter method only for star-connected 3-phase circuits.

(b) When two wattmeters show identical readings, the power factor is 0.5

(c) When power factor is unity, one of the wattmeter reads zero

(d) When the readings of the two wattmeters are equal but of opposite sign, the power factor is zero

177. A variable capacitor of 50 μF carries a charge of 0.175 micro-coulombs. The capacitance is subsequently reduced to 20 pF. The voltage appearing across the capacitor after reduction of its capacitance will be

(a) 350 V (b) 700 V

(c) 2050 V (d) 8750 V

178. The phase difference between the two quantities in degrees is

(a) 75° (b) 105°

(c) 60° (d) 15°

179. When a charge is given to a conductor,

(a) it distributes uniformly all over the surface

(b) it distributes uniformly all over the volume

(c) it distributes on the surface, inversely proportional to the radius of curvature

(d) it stays where it was placed

180. In a parallel capacitor of capacitance *C* and electric field *E* if a mica slab ($\in_r = 6$) is introduced to fill capacitor completely then the new capacitance and electric field will be

(a) 6 C and 6 E (b) C/6 and 6 E

(c) 6 C and E/6 (d) C/6 and E/6

181. For removing static charge from machinery the

(a) machinery is insulated

(b) insulated cabins are constructed

(c) framework is earthed

(d) any of the above

182. The colour code on a carbon resistance is yellow-brown-red. The value of resistance is

(a) 4100 ohm

(b) 4100 ± 20% ohm

(c) 41000 ± 20% ohm

(d) none of these

183. Which effect of the electric current is utilized in a filament lamp?

(a) The heating effect

(b) The magnetic effect

(c) The collision ionization of the gases

(d) The chemical effect

184. Which of the following statement is not correct?

(a) Ideal voltage source is one whose internal conductance is zero.

(b) Ideal current source is one whose internal conductance is zero.

(c) Ideal voltage source is one whose internal resistance is zero.

(d) Ideal voltage source is one whose generated voltage is equal to the available terminal voltage.

185. A parallel plate capacitor has capacitance of 10 μF. If the linear dimensions of the plates are doubled and the separation between them is also doubled the value of the capacitor would be

(a) 10 μF (b) 20 μF

(c) 5 μF (d) 40 μF

186. Three capacitors of 1, 2 and 3 μF respectively are connected in series to a 60-volt d.c. source. How many capacitors will have voltage drop of more than 20 volts across themselves?

(a) None (b) One

(c) Two (d) None of these

187. The ratio of total flux (flux in the iron path) to useful flux (flux in the air gap) is known as ____ factor.

(a) utilisation (b) fringing

(c) leakage (d) depreciation

188. Which of the following devices draws inductive reactive power also?

(a) Filament lamp (b) Electric heater

(c) Induction motor (d) All of these

189. In a multilayer dielectric material on either side of a boundary

(a) the normal component of electrical displacement is same

(b) the normal component of electrical field is same

(c) the tangential component of electrical displacement is necessarily zero

(d) the tangential component of electrical field is necessarily zero

190. Three resistances of 30 ohms, 20 ohms and 10 ohms are connected in parallel. The combined resistance will be

(a) less than 10 ohms

(b) greater than 10 ohms but less than 20 ohms

(c) greater than 20 ohms but less than 30 ohms

(d) none of these

191. In a series resonant circuit, with the increase in L

(a) resonant frequency will decrease

(b) bandwidth will decrease

(c) Q will increase

(d) all of the above

192. To determine the polarity of the voltage drop across a resistor, it is necessary to know

(a) value of resistor

(b) value of current through resistor

(c) direction of current through the resistor

(d) none of these

193. If a copper conductor is moved across a magnetic field

(a) the wire will become magnetic

(b) a voltage will be induced in the wire

(c) a current will be induced in the wire

(d) nothing will happen

194.

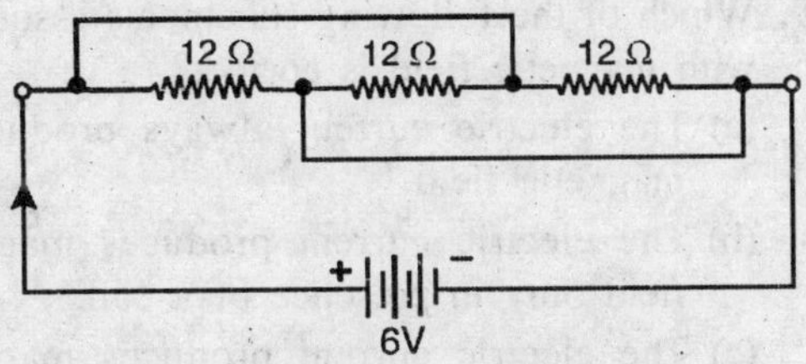

For the circuit shown above the equivalent resistance will be

(a) 36 Ω (b) 12 Ω

(c) 4 Ω (d) 6 Ω

195. If four 10 μF capacitors are connected in parallel, the net capacitance is

(a) 2.5 μF (b) 40 μF

(c) 20 μF (d) none of these

196. The overall inductance of two coils connected in series, with mutual inductance aiding self inductance is L_1 with mutual inductance opposing self-inductance the overall inductance is L_2. The mutual inductance M is given by

(a) $L_1 + L_2$ (b) $L_1 - L_2$

(c) $\frac{1}{4}(L_1 - L_2)$ (d) $\frac{1}{2}(L_1 + L_2)$

197. The figure shown represents Bohr's model of the oxygen atom. Which particles constitute the nucleus and which revolve around it?

(a) In nucleus: protons; around the nucleus: electrons

(b) In nucleus: protons; around the nucleus: neutrons

(c) In nucleus: ions; around the nucleus: electrons

(d) In nucleus: neutrons; around the nucleus: electrons.

198. The phasor C can be represented in trigonometrical form as

(a) $(a \cos\theta + jb \sin\theta)$

(b) $(a + b)(\cos\theta + j\sin\theta)$

(c) $\sqrt{(a^2 + b^2)}\,(\cos\theta + j\sin\theta)$

(d) $ab\,(\cos\theta + j\sin\theta)$

199. Which of the following statements associated with magnetic field is correct?
(a) The electric current always produces a magnetic field.
(b) The electric current produces magnetic field only in presence of a coil.
(c) The electric current produces magnetic field only in presence of an iron core.
(d) Only large currents produce a magnetic field.

200. When two coils having self inductances of L_1 and L_2 are coupled through a mutual inductance M, the coefficient of coupling, K is given by
(a) $K = \frac{M}{\sqrt{2L_1L_2}}$ (b) $K = \frac{M}{\sqrt{L_1L_2}}$
(c) $K = \frac{2M}{\sqrt{L_1L_2}}$ (d) $K = \frac{L_1L_2}{M}$

201. The Laplace transform of $t \sin \omega t$ is
(a) $\frac{2\omega s}{(s^2+\omega^2)^2}$ (b) $\frac{s^2-\omega^2}{(s^2+\omega^2)^2}$
(c) $\frac{2\omega s}{(s^2-\omega^2)^2}$ (d) $\frac{s^2+\omega^2}{(s^2-\omega^2)^2}$

202. Phase reversal in a 4-wire unbalanced load supplied from a balanced 3-phase supply causes change in
(a) the power consumed
(b) magnitude of phase currents
(c) only the magnitude of the neutral current
(d) magnitude as well as phase angle of the neutral current

203. The rating given on the name plate of a transformer indicates the
(a) true power which it can supply
(b) apparent power which it can supply
(c) apparent power which it draws from the supply mains
(d) true power which it draws from the supply mains

204. Current velocity through a copper conductor is
(a) nearly 3×10^9 m/s
(b) of the order of a few μm/s
(c) independent of current strength
(d) the same as propagation velocity of electric energy

205. A choke coil of inductance L and series resistance R is shunted by a capacitor C. The dynamic impedance of the resonant circuit would be
(a) $\frac{R}{LC}$ (b) $\frac{C}{RL}$
(c) $\frac{L}{RC}$ (d) $\frac{1}{RLC}$

206. If $e_1 = A \sin(\omega t + \theta_1)$ and $e_2 = B \sin(\omega t + \theta_2)$ then
(a) e_2 is leading e_1 by an angle $(\theta_1 - \theta_2)$
(b) e_1 is lagging e_2 by an angle $(\theta_1 - \theta_2)$
(c) e_2 is leading e_1 by an angle $(\theta_2 - \theta_1)$
(d) e_2 is lagging e_1 by an angle $(\theta_2 - \theta_1)$

207. The magnetic reluctance of a magnetic circuit decreases with the
(a) decrease in x-sectional area
(b) increase in x-sectional area
(c) increase in length of magnetic path
(d) decrease in relative permeability of the magnetic material of the circuit

208. What are the minimum requirements to cause the flow of current?
(a) A voltage source and a conductor
(b) A voltage source, a conductor an insulator
(c) A voltage source, a switch and a resistor
(d) A voltage source, an ammeter, a conductor and an insulator

209. Which of the following is not a non-linear element?
(a) Electric ore with unlike electrodes
(b) Diode
(c) Transistor
(d) Heater coil

210. In series LCR circuit, at resonance
(a) current is maximum, power factor is zero
(b) current is maximum, power factor is unity
(c) current is minimum, power factor is unity
(d) none of the above

211. The electrons revolve around the nucleus with high velocity. The force which acts against the centrifugal force and keeps the electrons in their orbits is
(a) electrostatic force of attraction
(b) adhesive force
(c) electromagnetic force of attraction
(d) none of the above

212. The nodal analysis is primarily based on the application of
(a) Ohm's law
(b) Kirchhoff's current law
(c) Kirchhoff's voltage law
(d) both (a) and (b)
(e) both (a) and (c)

213. Two plates each with an area 2 square metre are separated by 1 cm with air as dielectric. The value of capacitance will be
(a) 10 μF (b) 1200 μF
(c) 17 μF (d) 1770 μF

214. The capacitance of a parallel plate capacitor is not affected by
(a) area of plates
(b) thickness of plates
(c) separation between plates
(d) nature of dielectric

215. Dielectric strength of air is nearly
(a) 3 kV/mm (b) 30 kV/mm
(c) 300 kV/mm (d) 3000 kV/mm

216. Which of the following statements about the zinc-carbon cell is true?
(a) The zinc container has a potential of 1.5 V against the carbon electrode.
(b) The air in the air space is needed for the oxidation of zinc.
(c) When current is drawn from the cell the carbon rod is partly consumed.
(d) The depolarizer mainly contains brown iron ore and carbon powder.

217. A floating battery is one
(a) which is charged and discharged simultaneously
(b) in which battery voltage is equal to charger voltage
(c) which supplies current intermittently and also during idle period gets charged
(d) none of the above

218. The three resistances each of value 3 Ω are connected in delta. Their value in each branch of equivalent star connection will be
(a) 9 Ω (b) 6 Ω
(c) 3 Ω (d) 1 Ω

219. A network is said to be nonlinear if it does not satisfy
(a) superposition condition
(b) homogeneity condition
(c) both superposition and homogeneity conditions
(d) associative condition

220. The capacitance of a capacitor is not affected by
(a) area of plates
(b) thickness of plates
(c) distance between plates
(d) none of these

221. An electron having mass m kg and charge e coulomb travels from rest through a potential difference of V volts. It has a kinetic energy of
(a) mV joules (b) m eV joules
(c) eV joules (d) m/e joules

222. Rust, scales and oxides can be removed from a surface with the help of
(a) various acids
(b) alkali and salt solution
(c) mechanical abrasion
(d) electrolytic cleaning
(e) any of the above

223. If in an R-L-C series circuit the supply current lags behind the applied voltage by 60° then
(a) $X_L - X_C = \frac{R}{\sqrt{3}}$ (b) $X_L - X_C = \sqrt{3}R$
(c) $R = X_L - X_C$ (d) $X_L = X_C$

224. A coil is tuned to a certain frequency by a 250 μμF capacitor. To tune the coil to the second harmonic of this frequency a capacitor of 55 μμF is required. The self-capacitance of the coil is

(a) 10 μμF (b) 15 μμF

(c) 20 μμF (d) 40 μμF

225. For making a capacitors, it is better to select a dielectric having

(a) high permittivity

(b) low permittivity

(c) permittivity same as that of air

(d) none of these

226. Three resistors have the following ratings.

R_1 = 200 ohm ± 5%

R_2 = 100 ohm ± 5%

R_3 = 50 ohm ± 5%

The percentage error when the resistors are connected in series, would be

(a) + 5% (b) ± 5%

(c) + 5/3% (d) ± 15%

227. When a piece of iron is placed in a magnetic field

(a) there will be no effect on the magnetic field

(b) the magnetic lines of force will bend away from the piece

(c) the magnetic lines of force will bend away from their usual paths so as to pass through the piece

(d) none of the above

228. Three unequal impedances are connected in delta to a 3-phase, 3 wire system.

(a) The voltages across the three phases will be different.

(b) Both of the phase currents and line currents will be unbalanced.

(c) Phase currents will be unbalanced but the line currents will be balanced.

(d) None of these.

229. Electric supply for electro-deposition should be

(a) dc voltage

(b) low voltage ac

(c) low frequency ac voltage

(d) either (a) or (b)

230. The combined capacity of the parallel combination of two capacitors is four times their combined capacity when connected in series. It can be concluded that

(a) their capacities are equal

(b) their capacities are 1 μF and 2 μF

(c) their capacities are 0.5 μF and 1 μF

(d) their capacities are infinite

ANSWERS

1	2	3	4	5	6	7	8	9	10
(a)	(d)	(c)	(c)	(c)	(b)	(a)	(b)	(c)	(d)
11	12	13	14	15	16	17	18	19	20
(d)	(c)	(d)	(d)	(a)	(c)	(d)	(a)	(a)	(b)
21	22	23	24	25	26	27	28	29	30
(d)	(c)	(a)	(d)	(c)	(b)	(c)	(c)	(d)	(b)
31	32	33	34	35	36	37	38	39	40
(d)	(b)	(b)	(c)	(c)	(b)	(a)	(a)	(a)	(a)
41	42	43	44	45	46	47	48	49	50
(b)	(c)	(c)	(c)	(b)	(b)	(c)	(d)	(c)	(b)

51	52	53	54	55	56	57	58	59	60
(b)	(a)	(a)	(d)	(a)	(b)	(d)	(b)	(c)	(a)
61	**62**	**63**	**64**	**65**	**66**	**67**	**68**	**69**	**70**
(a)	(b)	(a)	(a)	(d)	(b)	(c)	(d)	(b)	(d)
71	**72**	**73**	**74**	**75**	**76**	**77**	**78**	**79**	**80**
(b)	(b)	(a)	(a)	(b)	(c)	(d)	(a)	(c)	(a)
81	**82**	**83**	**84**	**85**	**86**	**87**	**88**	**89**	**90**
(b)	(d)	(c)	(b)	(b)	(c)	(a)	(a)	(d)	(b)
91	**92**	**93**	**94**	**95**	**96**	**97**	**98**	**99**	**100**
(a)	(a)	(a)	(d)	(b)	(d)	(a)	(c)	(d)	(d)
101	**102**	**103**	**104**	**105**	**106**	**107**	**108**	**109**	**110**
(a)	(b)	(a)	(b)	(d)	(a)	(c)	(b)	(c)	(d)
111	**112**	**113**	**114**	**115**	**116**	**117**	**118**	**119**	**120**
(a)	(b)	(a)	(a)	(b)	(a)	(c)	(d)	(d)	(b)
121	**122**	**123**	**124**	**125**	**126**	**127**	**128**	**129**	**130**
(c)	(c)	(a)	(d)	(b)	(c)	(b)	(b)	(c)	(d)
131	**132**	**133**	**134**	**135**	**136**	**137**	**138**	**139**	**140**
(b)	(c)	(c)	(b)	(c)	(a)	(a)	(a)	(c)	(c)
141	**142**	**143**	**144**	**145**	**146**	**147**	**148**	**149**	**150**
(a)	(a)	(c)	(a)	(c)	(d)	(b)	(a)	(d)	(a)
151	**152**	**153**	**154**	**155**	**156**	**157**	**158**	**159**	**160**
(b)	(a)	(d)	(c)	(e)	(b)	(a)	(a)	(c)	(c)
161	**162**	**163**	**164**	**165**	**166**	**167**	**168**	**169**	**170**
(b)	(d)	(b)	(a)	(a)	(c)	(c)	(c)	(a)	(c)
171	**172**	**173**	**174**	**175**	**176**	**177**	**178**	**179**	**180**
(d)	(b)	(a)	(a)	(d)	(d)	(d)	(a)	(a)	(c)
181	**182**	**183**	**184**	**185**	**186**	**187**	**188**	**189**	**190**
(c)	(b)	(a)	(a)	(b)	(b)	(c)	(c)	(d)	(a)
191	**192**	**193**	**194**	**195**	**196**	**197**	**198**	**199**	**200**
(d)	(c)	(b)	(d)	(b)	(c)	(a)	(c)	(a)	(b)
201	**202**	**203**	**204**	**205**	**206**	**207**	**208**	**209**	**210**
(a)	(a)	(b)	(b)	(c)	(c)	(b)	(a)	(d)	(b)
211	**212**	**213**	**214**	**215**	**216**	**217**	**218**	**219**	**220**
(a)	(d)	(d)	(b)	(a)	(d)	(c)	(d)	(c)	(b)
211	**222**	**223**	**224**	**225**	**226**	**227**	**228**	**229**	**230**
(c)	(e)	(b)	(a)	(a)	(b)	(c)	(b)	(a)	(a)

4. BASIC ELECTRONICS

EXTRINSIC SEMICONDUCTOR

In order to increase the conductivity of a semiconductor, an impurity is added to it and this process is called *doping*. The materials is known as extrinsic semiconductor.

An acceptor material accepts electrons from the valence band of silicon since it has only three valence electrons. Example of donor impurity are Boron, Indium, Gallium, and Aluminium.

PN-Junction

When a *PN*-junction is formed, holes from *P*-type material tend to diffuse towards *N*-types. Similarly, electrons move from *N*-side to *P*-side. Due to this phenomena, most of holes and electrons near the junction get neutralised and a small region on both side of the junction gets devoid of any mobile carriers with the result that impurity ions in this region become electrically un-neutralised. This region, called *depletion region* or *layer*, now acts like battery or potential barrier V_0 which opposes the further diffusion of majority carriers.

When an external voltage V_f is applied across the junction with *P*-side positive and *N*-side negative so as to reduce the potential barrier V_0, the junction is said to be forward biased and the majority carrier of each side can go over to other side more easily leading to external current as shown in Fig. 1.

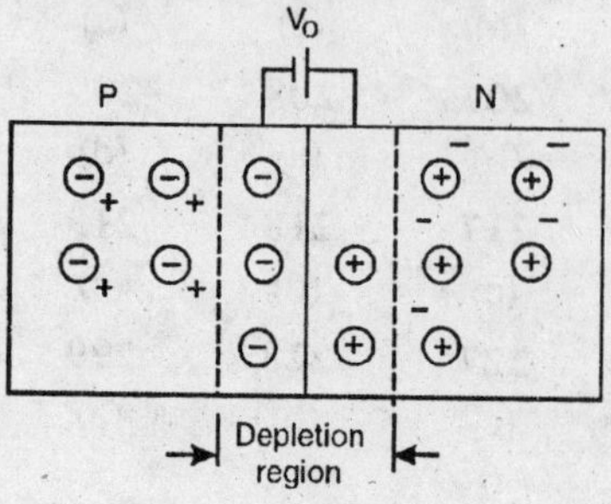

Fig. 1

When an external voltage V_R is connected in the reverse way, the potential barrier increases and the majority carriers find it difficult to cross to the other side. Only a very small reverse current I_0 flows in this reverse biased *PN*-junction. This current is not affected by potential barrier and depends on temperature, material and construction of the junction. Therefore *PN*-junction allows large current only in forward bias direction and only small reverse current I_0 in the reverse bias direction.

Collector-to-Base Bias

This arrangement shown in Fig. 2 leads to an improvement in bias stability because of *Q*-point shifts upwards, I_{CQ} will increase leading to decrease in V_{CEQ}. Thus by the above equation, I_{BQ} will decrease resulting in a corresponding decrease in I_{CQ}, thus arresting its increasing tendency.

In this arrangement, the resistance R_b is not connected to supply voltage V_{CC} but is returned to the collector. The biasing current is

$$I_{BQ} = \frac{V_{CEQ} - V_{BE}}{R_b}$$

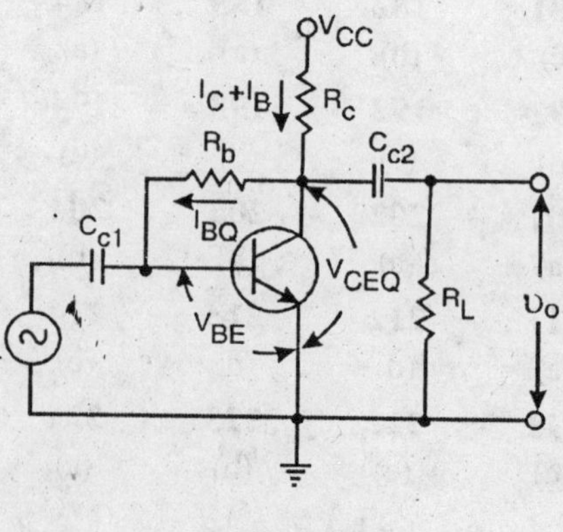

Fig. 2

Small Signal Low Frequency Analysis

For small collector signal swing, the transistor is considered to be linear and can be replaced by a small-signal equivalent circuit model. Prior to this, it is assumed that d.c. analysis, *i.e.,* getting the proper Q-point has been done and now the transistor amplifier is ready for amplification of small a.c. signals. Therefore, even if there is no a.c. input, d.c. currents and voltages are present in the circuit and d.c. power is being dissipated. When a.c. amplification is being done, then d.c. as well as a.c. signals are present at any moment of times so that total collector current is

$$i_C = I_{CQ} + i_b$$

This is shown in Fig. 3

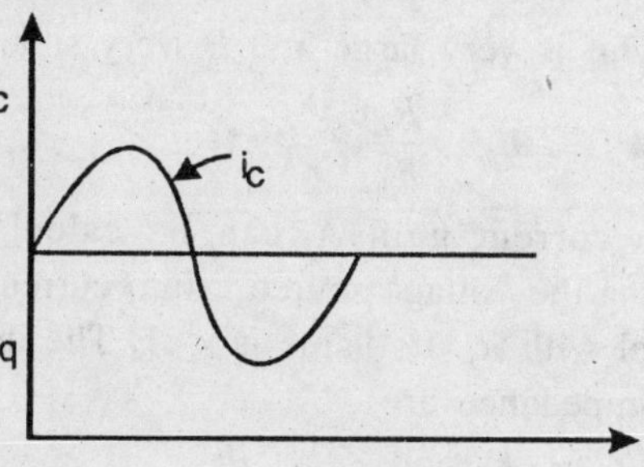

Fig. 3

Common-Emitter Configuration

This equivalent circuit can be used to evaluate the important quantities of a common-emitter amplifier as shown in Fig 4. The capacitors are assumed of zero reactance at the signal frequency.

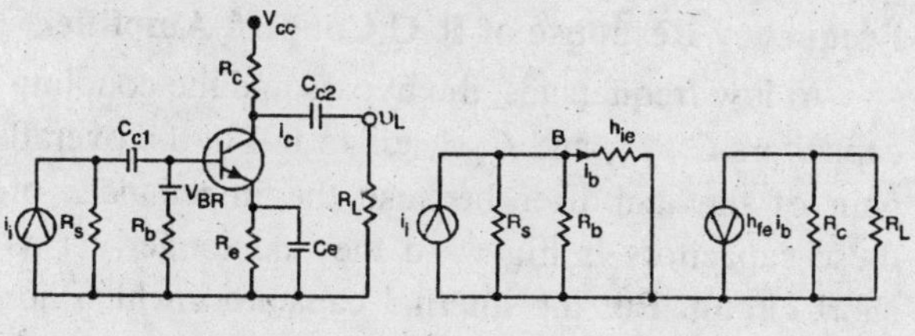

Fig. 4

Current gain

$$A_i = \frac{i_L}{i_i} = \frac{i_L}{i_b} \times \frac{i_b}{i_i}$$

$$i_L = -h_{fe}\, i_b \cdot \frac{R_C}{R_C + R_L}$$

$$i_b = i_i \cdot \frac{R_S \parallel R_b}{R_S + R_b + h_{ie}}$$

Therefore

$$A_i = -h_{fe} \cdot \frac{R_C}{R_C + R_L} \cdot \frac{R_S \parallel R_b}{R_S + R_b + h_{ie}}$$

The input and output impedances Z_i and Z_0 as seen by the source and load respectively are

$$Z_i = R_s \parallel R_b \parallel h_{ie}$$

$$Z_0 = R_C$$

If h_{oe} is not neglected, then

$$Z_0 = R_C \parallel 1/h_{oe}$$

The voltage gain A_v can also be calculated by converting the current source into a voltage source *i.e.,* v_i in series with R_s.

Common-Collector Configuration

In the CC configuration shown in Fig. 5, the collector is directly connected to V_{CC} and thus grounded for ac signals. The output is taken across R_e. The equivalent circuit is drawn by reflecting R_e in the base circuit with modified value of $(h_{fe} + 1)\, R_e$.

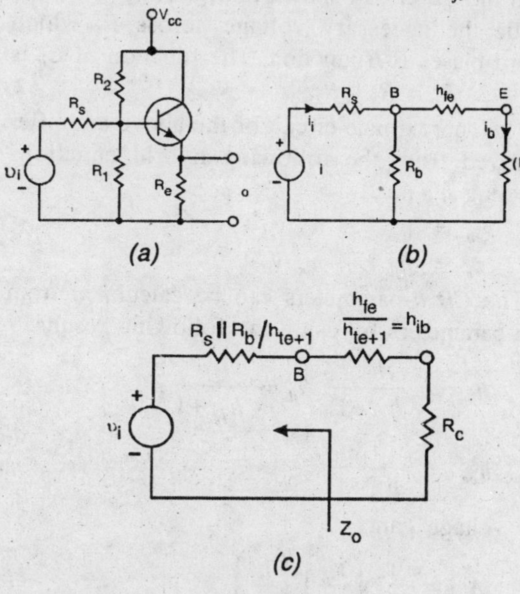

Fig. 5

The voltage gain of CC amplifier is

$$A_v \cong 1$$

Input impedance

$$Z_i = h_{ie}(h_{fe}+1)R_e$$

It can be shown that if base circuit is reflected into the emitter circuit, the resistance values get divided by $(h_{fe}+1)$. Then, the equivalent circuit becomes of the from in Fig. 5(c). Thus, the output impedance $Z_o = h_{ib} + \dfrac{R_S \parallel R_b}{h_{fe}+1}$. Thus, CC configuration gives nearby unity voltage gain some current gain, very high Z_i [because $(h_{fe}+1)R_e$ is quite large] and very low Z_o. The output voltage at the emitter terminal is in phase with the input voltage and therefore the circuit is also emitter follower.

Due to its above features, emitter follower is generally used as an impedance transformer in the input circuits of amplifiers. That is, when it is placed in the input circuit, it reduces the unnecessary loading of the source because of its high Z_i. In the output circuit, it helps to connect the amplifier with high Z_o to a load of low Z_i.

Common-Base Configuration

In the CB circuit shown in Fig. 6(a). R_1 and R_2 provide the necessary voltage across R_1 which forward biases B-E junction. The function of C_b is to by-pass $R_b = R_1 \parallel R_2$.

The approximate circuit of the above amplifier is derived from the following hybrid equations neglecting h_{rb} i.e.,

$$v_{eb} = h_{ib}\, i_e + h_{rb}\, v_{cb}$$

$$i_c = h_{fb}\, i_e + h_{ob}\, v_{cb}$$

The CB h-parameters can be calculated from CE h-parameters by using the following results:

$$h_{ib} = \frac{h_{ie}}{h_{fe}+1},\; h_{fb} = \frac{h_{fe}}{h_{fe}+1},$$

$$h_{oe} = \frac{h_{oe}}{h_{fe}+1}$$

Now voltage gain

$$A_v = \frac{v_L}{v_i}\left(\frac{v_L}{i_e}\right)\cdot\left(\frac{i_e}{v_i}\right)$$

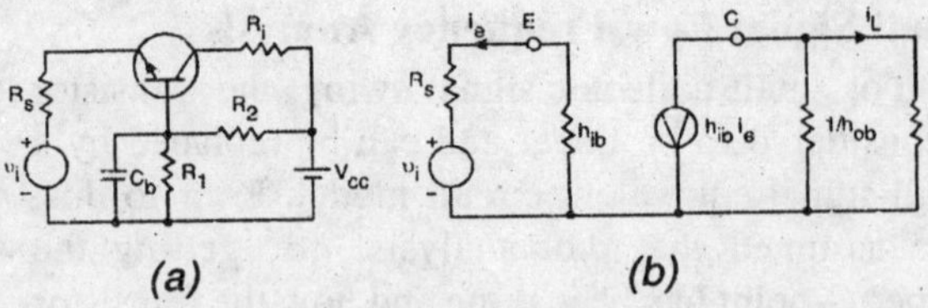

(a) (b)

Fig. 6

$$v_L = i_L \,.\, R_L = -\frac{h_{fb}.i_e.1/h_{ob}}{1/h_{ob}+R_L}R_L$$

$$v_i = -i_e \,.\, (h_{ib}+R_s)$$

Therefore,

$$A_v = h_{fb}\,.\left(\frac{1/h_{ob}.R_L}{1/h_{ob}+R_L}\right)\left(\frac{1}{h_{ib}+R_S}\right)$$

If $1/h_{ob}$ is very large and R_s very small, then

$$A_v = h_{fb}\,.\,\frac{R_L}{h_{ib}}$$

The current gain A_i can be calculated by converting the voltage source v_i into current source i_i parallel with R_s. Its value is <<1. The input and output impedance are

$$Z_i = h_{ib} \text{ and } Z_0 = 1/h_{ob}$$

The CB configuration provides no current gain, some voltage gain, very low input impedance and very high output impedance (this is because h_{oe} is usually very small and therefore $h_{ob} = \dfrac{h_{oe}}{h_{fe}+1}$ will still be smaller).

Frequency Response of R-C Coupled Amplifier

At low frequencies, the bypass and the coupling capacitors C_e, C_{c1} and C_{c2} leads to fall in the overall gain of the amplifier because the impedances of these capacitors is high and they no longer act as short circuit. But the internal capacitors which are of small value are open circuit and thus do not affect the gain at the low frequencies.

As the input frequency is increased to the middle frequency range, the external capacitors (C_e, C_{c1} and C_{c2}) act like nearly a short circuit, and the internal capacitors remain open circuit.

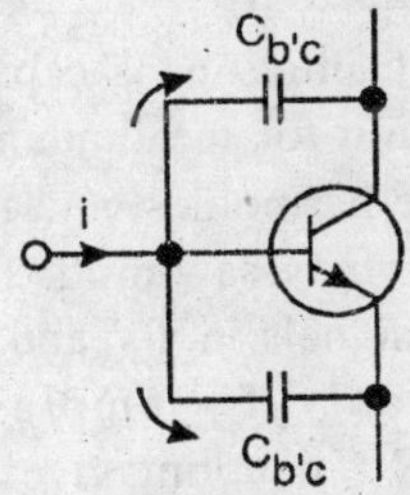

Fig. 7

At high frequencies, the external capacitors remain short circuit, but the external capacitors act as short circuit. As shown Fig. 7, the high frequency signal tends to flow via C'_{be} and C'_{bc} instead of flowing through the transistor.

The complete frequency response is shown in Fig. 8.

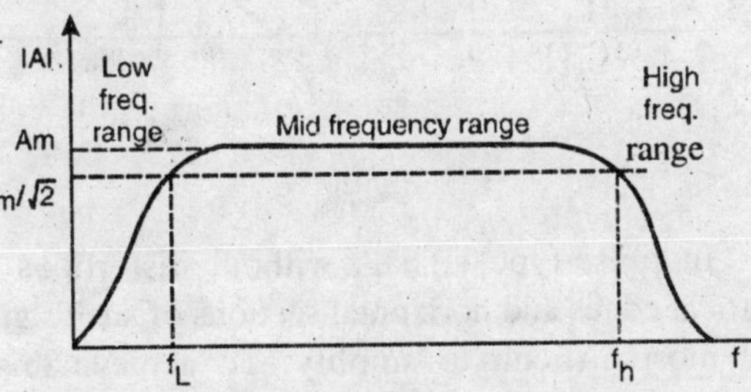

Fig. 8

The mid-frequency range is determined by the low cut-off frequency (f_l), and high cut off frequency (f_h). At these frequencies, the gain of the amplifier is $A_m/\sqrt{2}$, which means that the gain in decibels fall by 3*dB*. This is because

$$A_m/\sqrt{2}\,|d_B = \log_{10} A_m - \log_{10} 2 = A_m\,|dB - 3dB$$

Therefore, these cut-off frequencies are also called 3*dB frequencies*.

The mid frequency range is called *bandwidth* of the amplifier because at all frequencies in this range, the gain A_m is maximum and constant. Therefore,

$$BW = f_h - f_l$$

It is basically the half-power bandwidth. Integrated circuits and d.c. amplifier have zero low cut-off frequency, *i.e.*, they amplify uniformly low frequencies down to d.c.

Emitter-Base Capacitance

Now consider the forward bias *E-B* junction. Since there is local space-charge neutrality and because of the flow of electron add, hole currents in the transistor, there is a distribution of excess holes which is coupled with an equal distribution of electrons. Theses exces holes and electrons are those charge carriers which are present over their number present in equilibrium or in a situation where there is no net flow of current.

Now, if the junction voltages increase by ΔV, this will lead to excess hole charge of ΔQ_p and an equal excess electron charge ΔQ_n. Since the currents producing these excess charges enter the junction from opposite directions, these charges add leading to a net charge $(\Delta Q_p + \Delta Q_n)$ trapped in the region. This corresponds to the presence of a capacitance of C'_{be} across the *B-E* junction.

Another way to explain the presence of C'_{be} is in terms of time delay involved when an impurity carrier (say hole in *PNP* transistor) moves from emitter to collector. Now, when the a.c. input voltage at emitter goes positive, hole starts diffusing across the base. But by the time it crosses the base, the a.c. signal charges its polarity, the hole could be attracted back by the emitter and thus would not contribute to the collector current. Thus as the frequency of the a.c. signal increases, more and more number of holes will be trapped near the junction and thus collector current will be decreasing.

This decrease in current with increase in input frequency can be accounted by the presence of the capacitance C'_{be}. Moreover, as the number of charge carriers increase C'_{be} increases linearly with I_{EQ}. The C'_{be} lies in the range of 100-5000 *pF* and thus much larger than C'_{bc}.

The current gain of the amplifier can be deduced to

$$A_i = \frac{i_L}{i_i} = \frac{g_m R'_{be}}{1 + j\,\omega\, R'_{be}(C'_{be} + C_m)}$$

where $R'_{be} = r'_{bc} \,||\, (R_b + r'_{bb})$

From this, mid-frequency gain

$$A_{im} = -g_m\, R'_{be}$$

and high $3dB$ frequency

$$f_h = \frac{1}{2\pi R'_{be}(C'_{be}+C_m)}$$

$\cong$ $3dB$ bandwidth of the amplifier

Note that f_h will be approximately equal to f_β if

$$C'_{be} >> C'_{bc}\,(1 + g_m R_L) \text{ and } R'_{be} \cong r'_{bc}$$

Gain Bandwidth Product will be

$$GBW = A_{im} \times f_h = \frac{g_m}{2\pi (C'_{be}+C_m)}$$

For an ideal CE amplifier, A_{im} is approximately h_{fe} and upper $3dB$ frequency is f_β.

Therefore,

$GBW = h_{fe} \cdot f_\beta = f_T$.

The actual gain is low due to miller capacitance.

or $$\frac{\omega_h}{\omega_{h1}} = \sqrt{2^{1/n}-1}$$

The expression implies that as the number of stages is increased, the bandwidth of the cascaded amplifier decreases.

Collector-Base Capacitance

In a transistor, the C-B junction is reverse biased which means that in a PNP transistor the electrons in the base and holes in the collector move away from the junction thus leading to the promotion of depletion region. The length of this region increases as the reverse bias voltage is increased. Since there are no mobile carriers in the depletion region, base side in this region becomes positively charged while collector side becomes negatively charged. Thus the junction acts like a capacitor C'_{bc} whose value is inversely proportional to $(V_{CB})^{1/2}$ for alloy transistor, and $(V_{CB})^{1/3}$ for grown junction transistor. This capacitor is very small and varies from $1pF$ to $30\,pF$.

Tuned Amplifiers

Ideal response of a tuned amplifier provides constant gain over the complete pass band $(\omega_h - \omega_L)$ centered around a resonant freqency ω_o. It rejects all frequencies $< \omega_L$ and $> \omega_h$ as shown in Fig. 9(a). The actual response is shown in Fig. 9(b), where ω_h and ω_L are defined in terms of $3dB$ frequencies.

Wide-Band Amplifier

This type of amplifier is capable to providing equal amplification for the fundamental frequency, as well as all the harmonics, and thus causing very little distortion. Many saw-tooth signals such as in CRO and pulse signals in TV and radar circuit can be amplified only by employing wideband amplifiers. The R-C coupling gives better frequency response than transformer coupling for the design of these amplifiers.

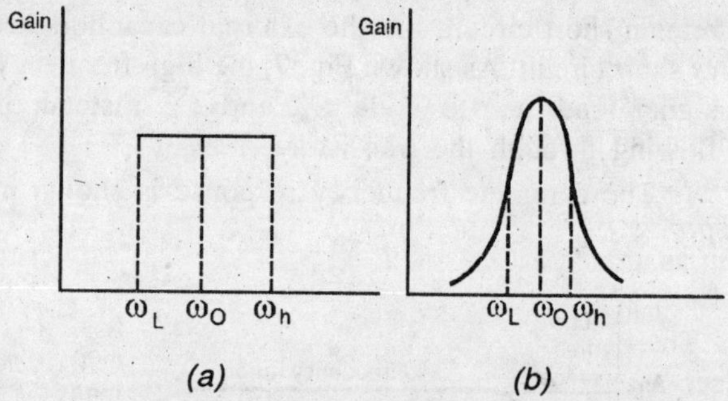

Fig. 9

In pulse-type signals without distortions the vertical edges and horizontal sections of such signals are most difficult to amplify. To achieve this, a good high frequency response of the amplifier is required. The upper limit of the bandwidth f_{max} is given by $f_{max} \cong \frac{1}{2t}$, where t is the rise line of the edge. The low frequency extreme, f_{min} of the bandwidth is governed by the need to reproduce horizontal parts of wave accurately and given by

$$f_{min} = \frac{1}{2\pi} \times \%\text{ sag in half-cycle of 50 Hz square wave}$$

The necessary low frequency response can be achieved by using direct coupling. But it is difficult to control drift in high gain d.c. amplifiers. Therefore, usually an amplifier with limited low frequency response is used. The zero-frequency component is restored by the techniques of d.c. restoration or d.c. clamping.

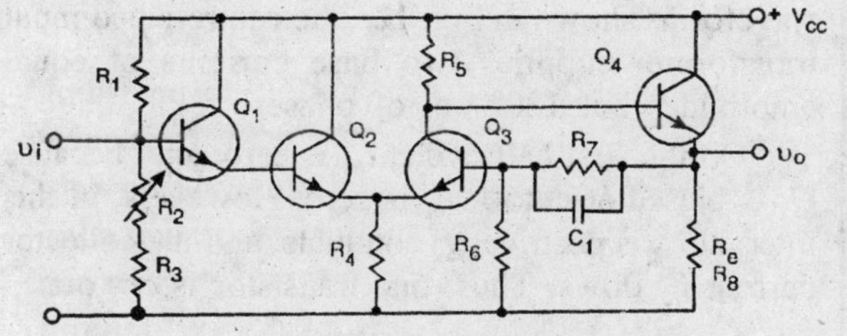

Fig. 10

In a typical wide-band amplifier shown in Fig. 10, Q_1, is an *EF* stage providing high input impedance and Q_3 is also an *EF* stage which gives a slow output impedance.

Transistors Q_2 and Q_3 are direct emitter-coupled pair called long-tail pair. Q_2 is an *EF* and drives Q_3 as a *CB* stage. A high value of R_4 gives good d.c. stability while at the same time losing considerable gain as a result of signal frequency feedback in the resistor.

The base of Q_3 provides a convenient point to inject a negative feedback signal which is made frequency depended by including $R_6 - R_7 - C_1$ network designed to make the frequency response of the amplifier fall off above the required bandwidth.

Single-Tuned Amplifier

It consists of a CE amplifier in which a parallel-tuned circuit has been included as shown in Fig. 11(a).

In the equivalent circuit shown in Fig. 11(b),

$$C = C' + C'_{be} + (1 + g_m R_L) C'_{bc}$$

The inductor has been replaced by its equivalent admittance *i.e.*,

$$Y_C = \frac{1}{rc + j\omega_L} = \frac{1}{R_p} + \frac{1}{j\omega_L}$$

where $R_P = r_e Q_c^2$

Let $R = r_i \parallel R_p \parallel r'_{be}$ ($r_{bb'}$ is neglected)

The current gain

$$A_i = \left(\frac{i_L}{v'_{be}}\right)\left(\frac{v'_{be}}{i_i}\right)$$

$$= \frac{-g_m R}{1 + jQ_i(\omega/\omega_o - \omega_o/\omega)}$$

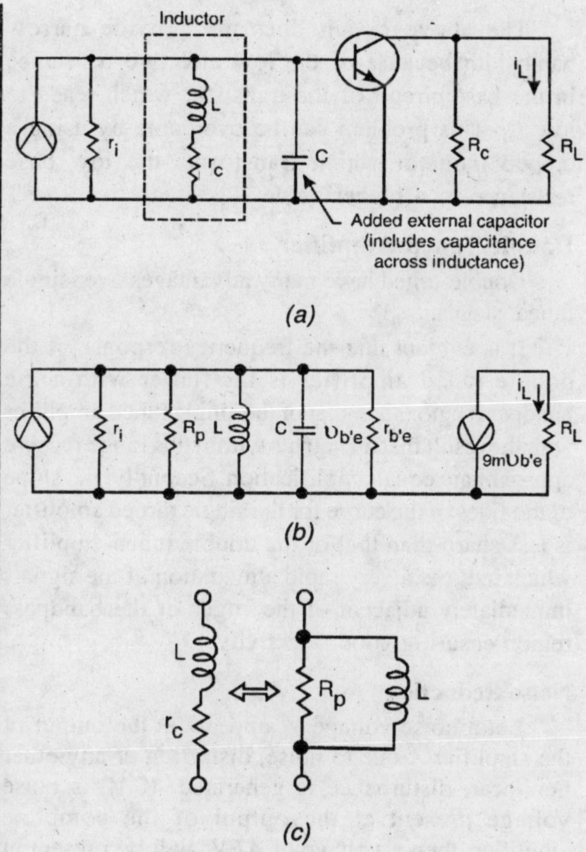

Fig. 11

where $\omega_o = \frac{1}{LC}$ and Q_i of the turned input circuit at ω_o is

$$Q_i = \frac{R}{\omega_o L} = \omega_o RC$$

The gain is maximum at

$$\omega = \omega_o$$

i.e., $A_{im} = -g_m R$

The bandwidths of amplifiers $= \frac{A_{im}}{\sqrt{2}}$

$$BW = f_h - f_L = \frac{\omega_o}{2\pi Q_i} = \frac{1}{2\pi R_C}$$

Gain bandwidths products

$$GBW = \frac{g}{2\pi C}$$

The above circuit does not provide narrow bandwidth because of the low effective resistance in the base circuit of the transistor which leads to low Q_i. This problem can be overcome by using a tapped inductor which transforms the low base resistance to a higher value.

Double-Tuned Amplifier

Double-tuned have many advantages over single tuned stages.

It is evident that the frequency response of the double tuned amplifier is far flatter within the bandpass region than that of the single tuned amplifier with the result that all signals within this range receive approximate equal amplification. Secondly, the slope of the sides of the curve for the single turned amplifier is less sharp than that of the double tuned amplifier which induces a very rapid attenuation of the signals immediately adjacent of the edges of the bandpass region ensuring good selectivity.

Noise Reduction

Let a noise voltage V_n appears at the output of the amplifier A due to noise, distortion or any other nonlinear, disturbance is generated. If V_{nf} is noise voltage present at the output of the complete amplifier, then a voltage of AFV_{nf} will be present at the output. Thus, the total amount of noise voltage will be

$$V_{nf} = V_n + AFV_{nf}$$

or $$V_{nf} = \frac{V_n}{1-AF} = \frac{V_n}{1-T}$$

Thus, any internally generated disturbance will be reduced by the desensitivity factor $(1 - T)$.

But it must be noticed that feedback can not improve the signal-to-noise ratio if the noise signal enters at the amplifier's input.

Class-B Push-Pull Amplifiers

The maximum attainable efficiency in Class-A operation is 50 percent, because the peak a.c. collector current never exceeds the quiescent collector current. In Class-B amplifier shown in Fig. 12, the d.c. collector current is less than the peak a.c. current. Thus, less collector dissipation results, and the efficiency increases. Circuit operation can be explained in terms of the waveforms shown in Fig. 12. The centre-taped input transformer supplies two base currents of equal amplitudes but 180° out of phase.

On the first half cycle, i_{B1} is zero, and, because Q_1 is biased at cutoff, i_{c1} is zero. Howevers, in this interval i_{B2} is positive Q_2 conducts, and the collector current i_{c2} flows. Thus, one transistor is cut off,

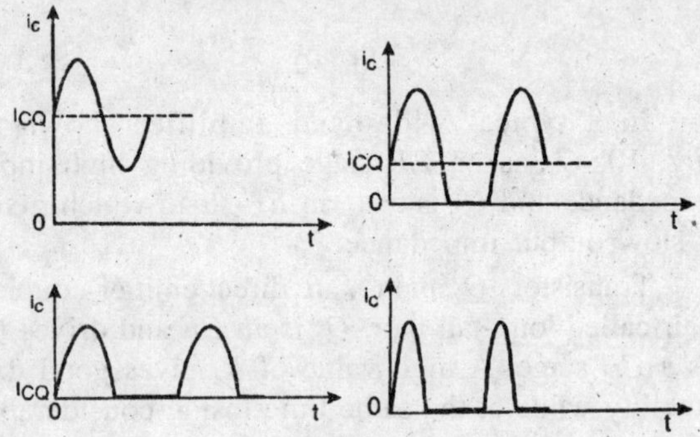

Fig. 12

while the other is conducting. On the second half cycle, the roles are reversed, Q_2 is cut off and Q_1 conducts. When Q_2 conducts the current of Q_2 flows through the upper half of the primary winding, and the resulting time-varying flux in the transformer core induces a voltage in the secondary winding. The voltage, in turn produces the first half cycle of the current through the load. When Q_1 conducts, the current i_{c1} induces flux in the core in a direction opposite to the flux of previous half-cycle of load current. The final load current under these ideal conditions is thus directly proportional to the signal current i_i. The load current i_L is related to the individual current by

$$i_L = N\,(i_{C1} - i_{C2})$$

Power transferred to the load

$$P_L = I_{LRMS}^2\, R_L$$

$$= \frac{I_{cm}^2}{2} RL'$$

Field Effect Transistor

Diffused junction field effect transistor (JFET) consists of a thin layer of n–type material on which p–type material is diffused. Ohmic contacts called the source S, the drain D and gate G are then taken out. The conducting path between the source and drain is called the channel.

When the source and the gate are at zero potential, and drain is made positive, electrons flow from S to D, but negligible current flows between S or D and G since the *pn*–junctions are reversed biased. The current I_{DS} depends upon V_{DS} and resistance of the channel.

As V_{DS} is increased, the *pn*-junctions are more heavily reverse biased and the area of depletion region increases leading to narrowing of the channel. This leads to inrease in channel resistance. This process continues until at some voltage, V_{PO} called the *pinch-off* voltage since it cuts off the channel between S and D. The drain current I_D remains constant because potential of point A essentially remains equal to V_{PO}. When $V_{DS} > V_{PO}$, the current remains I_{PO}, and then rises slowly. When $V_{DS} = BV_{DSS}$, the breakdown voltage, an avalanche breakdown occurs and i_D rises very fast.

Frequency Response of Amplifiers

Generally speaking, A, F and hence T can vary with frequency. The loop gain T may be positive in one frequency range and negative in another with the result that if $T(\omega) \to +1$, $A_f(\omega) \to \infty$ and the amplifier becomes highly unstable.

Uncondition stability of the amplifier is usually desired so that it is stable for all frequencies and gain, and not affected adversely by aging of components, and transient signals etc.

The loop gain T is given by

$$T \angle \phi = AF$$

Since, feedback F is usually resistive, the phase responses of T and A are identical stability can be assured if $T \leq 1$, when $\phi = 180°$ or (2) $\phi \leq 180°$, when $T = 1$.

Amplitude or Gain Margin is defined as the amount by which T is less than 1 when $\phi = 180°$.

Phase Margin is the amount by which ϕ is less than 180° when $T = 1$. Generally a $PM = 45°$ is used to ensure stability which means that T should be ≤ 1 when its phase angle is $-(180° - 45°)$ or $-135°$.

For larger bandwidths or greater desensitivity, a larger value of T is required leading to low A_f. This is achieved by using phase compensation networks which may lead to stability for all values of T or for specified ranges of T.

Power Amplifiers

Power amplifiers are required to furnish large amounts of power economically and meet other specifications on size, weight, d.c. supply voltage and distortion, etc. The transistors used may be driven to the limit of their operating range and therefore excessive heating and thus physical damage is to be avoided.

The criterion for classification of power amplifiers is the portion of the input sine wave during which the load current flows as given below. The corresponding waveforms are shown in Fig. 12.

Thus, apparently only Class-A provides complete cycles and low distortion. In push-pull configuration, Class-B provide linear amplification. In Class-C amplifiers used at radio frequencies, tuned circuits remove the distortion due to their non-linear operation.

IGFET or MOSFET

Insulated Gate FET consists of definite layer of insulating silicon dioxide formed between gate and channel. Thus, it does not has a junction and consequently, the disadvantage of leakage current and the need for reverse bias are eliminated. This insulated gate can be forward-biased without any flow in the gate.

In Fig. 13 (a), a channel of n-material has been diffused on an p-type semiconductor and enlarged ends of the n-channel form the source and drain. The gate is only a layer of conducting metal. It is insulated from the channel by a layer of silicon dioxide. If the gate is made more negative, its voltage produces a field effect. This enlarges the depletion region in the n-channel with the result that the flow of electrons decreases through the channel. This mode of operation of MOSFET is called *depletion mode*.

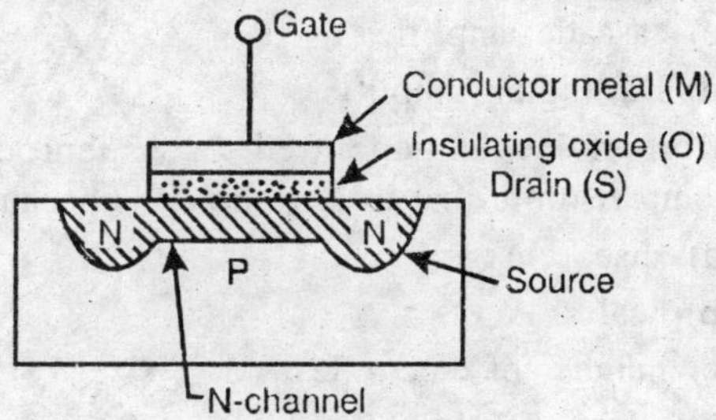

Fig. 13 (a)

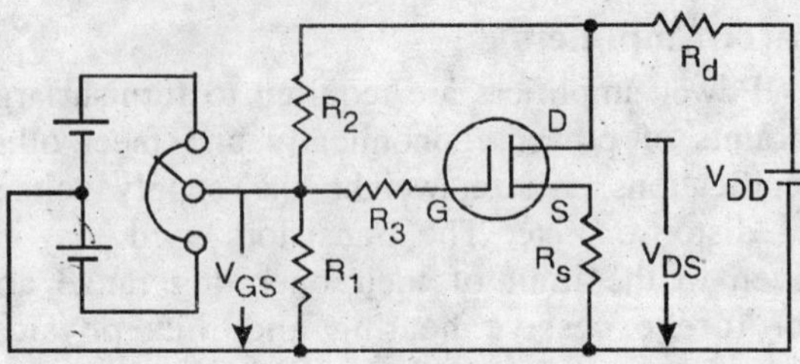

Fig. 13 *(b)*

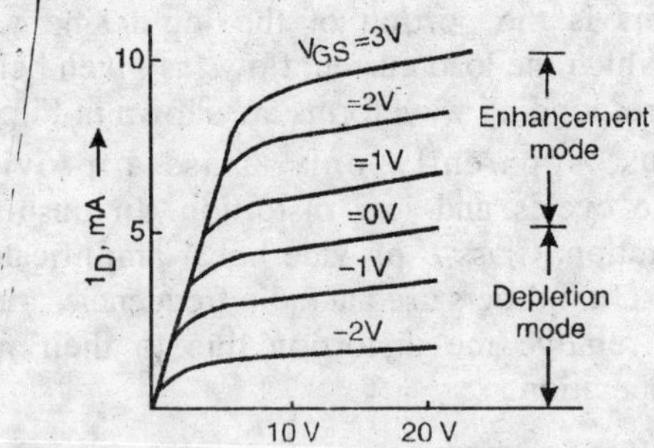

Fig. 13 *(c)*

In the enhancement mode of operation, the MOSFET is usually operated with a positive gate-source potential which leads to increase in drain current.

In this saturation region, the drain current is given by

$$i_D = I_{PO}\left(1+\frac{V_{GS}}{V_{PO}}\right)^2$$

The MOSFET is symmetrical in the sence that its drain and sourse connections can be interchanged with only minor changes in its performance.

A basic amplifier and the characteristics of MOSFET are shown in Fig. 13 (b) and (c).

In IGFET, the gate is most often forward biased. The d.c. load line equation is

$$V_{DD} = V_{DS} + i_D\,(R_d + R_S)$$

and $$V_{GS} = \left(\frac{R_1}{R_1+R_2}\right) \cdot V_{DD} - i_D\,R_S$$

$$= V_{GG} - i_D\,R_S$$

The resistance R_3 does not affect the *dc* bias since the gate current is negligible. Its function is to make a.c. input impedance high.

The main disadvantage of MOSFET is that it is easily damaged by static charges. With very small gate capacitance and gate current, a small amount of charge is sufficient to develop a gate voltage of 35 to 50 V, large enough to cause a destructive avalanche breakdown of the insulating layer which gets punctured. Static current even in pico-ampere may lead to high voltage across r_{gs}. To avoid this, it is packaged to include a metal ring that is in contact with its external connection between the gate and source to prevent the development of static charges.

EXERCISE

1. The bandwidth of a difference amplifier is comparable to that of a
   (a) single-stage CE amplifier
   (b) double-stage CE amplifier
   (c) cascade amplifier
   (d) Darlington amplifier
2. More noise is generated in a pentode in comparison to that in a triode. It is because of
   (a) space charge
   (b) heater
   (c) number of electrodes
   (d) all of the above
3. SCR can be turned ON by applying
   (1) very large anode voltage
   (2) sufficiently large gate current
   (3) anode voltage at a sufficiently fast rate
   (4) increased temperature of SCR to a sufficiently large value

   Of these statements
   (a) (1) and (2) are correct
   (b) (1) and (3) are correct
   (c) (2) and (4) are correct
   (d) (1), (2), (3) and (4) are correct

4. Which of the following transistors can be used in enhancement mode?
   (a) UJT (b) JFET
   (c) MOSFET (d) NPN transistor
5. In a CE transistor amplifier, if collector-emitter voltage increases, the instantaneous operating point
   (a) moves up the load line
   (b) moves down the load line
   (c) moves at right angles to the load line
   (d) remains stationary
6. Zener diodes
   (a) have breakdown voltage of less than 5 V and have a –ve temperature coefficient
   (b) have breakdown voltage of less than 5 V and have a +ve temperature coefficient
   (c) have breakdown voltage of more than 5 V and have a +ve temperature coefficient
   (d) have breakdown voltage of 5 V and have a zero temperature coefficient
7. A bleeder resistor is used in a d.c. power supply because
   (1) it keeps the supply ON
   (2) it improves voltage regulation
   (3) it improves filtering action
   Of these statements
   (a) (1) and (2) are correct
   (b) (2) and (3) are correct
   (c) (1) and (3) are correct
   (d) (1), (2) and (3) are correct
8. On the pole-zero diagram of an amplifier, the low cut-off frequency f_l will be determined by
   (a) the pole farthest from the origin
   (b) the pole closest to the origin
   (c) the zero farthest from the origin
   (d) the zero closest to the origin
9. Modern electronic multimeters measure resistance by
   (a) using bridge circuit
   (b) using an electronic bridge compensator for nulling
   (c) forcing a constant current and measuring the voltage across the unknown resistor
   (d) applying a constant voltage and measuring the current through the unknown resistor
10. In a semiconductor, the movement of holes is due to
    (a) movement of electrons in conduction band
    (b) movement of holes in conduction band
    (c) movement of holes in valence band
    (d) movement of electrons in valence band
11. When a P-N junction is forward biased
    (a) the width of the depletion layer is decreased
    (b) the width of depletion layer is increased
    (c) the width of the depletion layer remains the same
    (d) none of above
12. Dynamic resistance is the ratio of
    (a) change in drain-source voltage and change in drain current at constant V_{GS}
    (b) change in gate-source voltage and change in drain current at constant V_{DS}
    (c) drain-source voltage and drain current
    (d) gate-source voltage and drain current
13. The addition of trivalent impurity to an intrinsic semiconductor creates
    (a) N-type semiconductor
    (b) excess free electrons
    (c) excess holes
    (d) electron-hole pairs
14. The theoretical maximum efficiency of class B operation of an amplifier is
    (a) 50% (b) 78.5%
    (c) 62.5% (d) None of above
15. In a properly biased transistor
    (a) both depletion regions are large
    (b) both depletion regions are small
    (c) the emitter to base depletion region is small and collector to base depletion region is large
    (d) the emitter to base depletion region is large and collector to base depletion region is small

16. In a full wave rectifier circuit the peak inverse voltage per diode is
(a) the same as that in a half wave circuit
(b) half the value in a half wave circuit
(c) double the value in a half wave circuit
(d) none of above

17. The ratio of diffusion constant for electrons D_e to the mobility for electrons μ_e is
(a) independent of T
(b) inversely proportional to T
(c) proportional to T^2
(d) proportional to T

18. A UJT has
(a) stable negative resistance characteristics
(b) low firing current
(c) use as a waveform generator
(d) all of these characteristics

19. In an SCR, the anode current
(a) is independent of gate current
(b) decreases with the increase in gate current
(c) increases with the increase in gate current
(d) none of the above

20. One disadvantage of directly coupled transistor amplifier is that
(a) identicai transistors are required
(b) both NPN transistors are required
(c) variations in current due to temperature changes in one stage are amplified by other stages
(d) the low frequency response is poor

21. Modulation is a process to vary
(a) carrier signal by signal to be transmitted
(b) signal to be transmitted
(c) both of these
(d) none of these

22. A UJT is a
(a) current controlled device
(b) voltage controlled device
(c) a relaxation oscillator
(d) none of these

23. Push-pull amplifier circuit is used as
(a) power amplifier (b) audio amplifier
(c) RF amplifier (d) None of above

24. Assuming carrier mobility to be temperature independent, it can be shown that pure *Si* (E_g = 1.1eV) and Ge (E_g = 0.7eV) have the same conductivity at a temperature of
(a) 191° K (b) 300° K
(c) 471° K (d) 1,470° K

25. Lower cut-off frequency of an amplifier is primarily determined by
(a) stray capacitance between its wiring and ground
(b) ac β value of its active devices
(c) internal capacitance of the active device used
(d) capacitances of coupling and bypass capacitors

26. On of the methods to increase the frequency response of a transistor is to
(a) make base region as thin as possible
(b) employ graded-base doping
(c) dope the transistor as lightly as possible
(d) dope the base heavily

27. The type of multivibrator used for generation of clock pulses is
(a) monostable multivibrator
(b) astable multivibrator
(c) bistable multivibrator
(d) none of the above

28. Tunnel diode
(a) is a power diode
(b) has light doping
(c) has heavy doping
(d) is a reverse recovery diode

29. In an N-P-N transistor, the leakage current is due to
(a) flow of minority carriers from collector to emitter
(b) flow of holes from base to emitter
(c) flow of electrons from collector to base
(d) flow of holes from collector to base

30. In FM transmission, amplitude of modulating signal determines
(a) rate of frequency variations
(b) broadcast distance
(c) amount of deviation in frequency
(d) all of the above

31. The positive swing of the output signal in a transistor circuit starts clipping first when Q-point of the circuit moves
(a) towards the saturation point
(b) towards the cut-off point
(c) to the centre of the load line
(d) one-third way up the load line

32. In a properly biased, JFET will act as a
(a) current controlled current source
(b) voltage controlled voltage source
(c) voltage controlled current source
(d) current controlled voltage source

33. In amplifier circuits the impedance matching is done to
(a) achieve high efficiency
(b) reduce distortion
(c) ensure maximum power transfer to the load
(d) none of above

34. The main advantage of the same circuit is that
(a) d.c. as well as a.c. current can flow in R_L
(b) the current gain is twice the gain of a single transistor
(c) d.c. current through R_L is eliminated
(d) no center-tapped transformer is required

35. Feed back regulators are used to provide
(a) high load current
(b) low load current
(c) medium load current
(d) very low load current

36. For correct working of a P-N-P bipolar junction transistor, the different electrodes should have the polarities with respect to emitter as below:
(a) collector – ve and base – ve
(b) collector + ve and base + ve
(c) collector + ve and base – ve
(d) collector – ve and base + ve

37. To increase bandwidth, the distributed amplifier utilizes
(a) cascade amplifier
(b) common-base configuration
(c) tuned circuits
(d) transmission lines

38. In the circuit shown below, an emitter follower drives a capacitive load C_L. The charging and discharging time constants will be

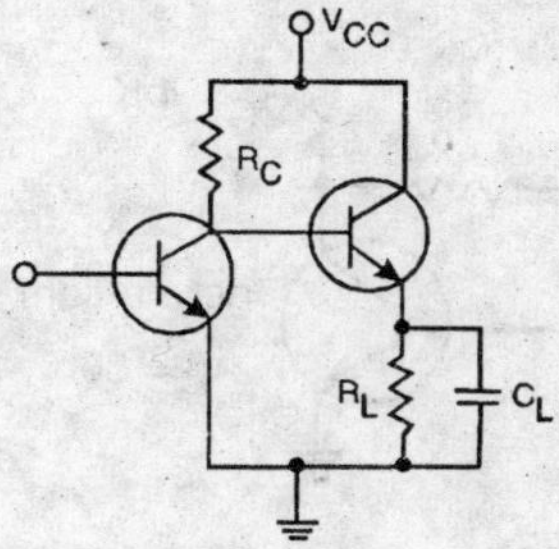

(a) $(R_c + h_{oe})\, C_L$, $(R_L + h_{ie})\, C_L$
(b) $(R_c + R_L)\, C_L$, $(R_C + R_L)\, C_L$
(c) $(R_c / \beta \,||\, R_L)\, C_L$, $R_L\, C_L$
(d) $R_c\, C_L$, $R_L\, C_L$

39. Which of the following statements is not correct?
(a) In a pentode, the control grid is used to control the plate current.
(b) In a pentode, the screen grid is used to reduce the capacitance from control grid to plate.
(c) In a pentode, the suppressor grid is used to suppress the secondary emission.
(d) Pentode finds wide application as a rectifier

40. The heater filament of a vacuum tube is usually supplied with ac (not dc) for heating. It is so because
(a) it gives uniform heating resulting in uniform electron emission
(b) d.c. voltage required will be of higher magnitude than that of ac voltage
(c) a.c. voltage is easily available from the a.c. supply mains
(d) expensive filament is needed in case of d.c. heating

41. A Hartley oscillator uses
(a) a tapped inductor
(b) a tapped capacitor
(c) both of the above
(d) none of the above

42. In the biasing circuit shown below, if I_{CQ} increases, the I_{BQ} will

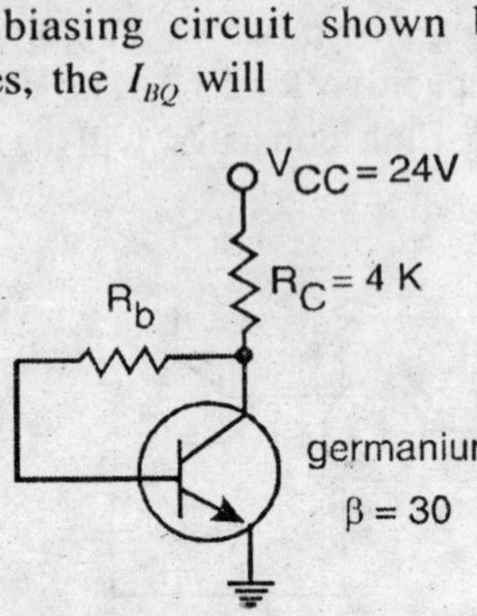

(a) increase (b) decrease
(c) remain the same (d) become zero

43. Fermi level represents the energy level with probability of its occupation of
(a) zero (b) 50%
(c) 75% (d) 100%

44. When diodes are connected in series to increase the voltage rating?
(a) The peak inverse voltage per junction should not exceed half the breakdown voltage.
(b) The peak inverse voltage per junction should not exceed half the breakdown voltage.
(c) The peak inverse voltage per junction should not exceed one third the breakdown voltage.
(d) None of above.

45. For generating a 1 kHz signal, the most suitable circuit is
(a) Hartley oscillator
(b) Colpitts oscillator
(c) untuned collector oscillator
(d) Wien-bridge oscillator

46. The bandwidth of a feedback amplifier
(a) increases by a factor of $(1 - T)$
(b) decreases by a factor of T
(c) increases by a factor of T
(d) decreases by a factor of $(1 - T)$

47. An RC-coupled amplifier has a gain of 500. Without feedback the distortion is 5%. If negative feedback with feedback factor of 0.01 is used the distortion will be
(a) 1% (b) 3%
(c) 4.5% (d) 10%

48. The addition of indium to pure semi-conductors results in
(a) *n*-type semi-conductor
(b) *p*-type semi-conductor
(c) *p*-n semi-conductor
(d) none of above

49. Which of the following statements is correct?
(a) Oxide coated emitters are used in X-ray tubes.
(b) Secondary emission does not affect the operation of vacuum tubes having more than two electrodes.
(c) Photo-electric emission is used in photo-tubes forming the basis of TV and sound films.
(d) The force, which prevents the electrons from leaving surface is called the work function of the metal.

50. Transformer coupling is used to cascade two such stages of which the first has
(a) high collector impedance and succeeding has low input impedance
(b) low collector resistance and succeeding has high input impedance
(c) low collector impedance and succeeding has high input impedance
(d) high collector impedance and succeeding has high input impedance

51. Peak value of a collector current P_{CC} is
(a) $I_{CQ}/2$ (b) I_{CQ}
(c) $2\ I_{CQ}$ (d) $V_{CC}/2\ R_L$

52. One advantage of transformer coupling in transistor amplifiers is that
(a) it provides excellent frequency response
(b) it is simple and less expensive than other coupling methods
(c) low power supply may be used
(d) high efficiency and high power output is obtained

53. R-C coupling is proper in low-level AF amplifier because it
(a) is inexpensive and needs no adjustment
(b) has better low frequency response
(c) needs low voltage battery
(d) provides an output signal in phase with input signal

54. The current stability of a common collector amplifier can be improved by
(a) decreasing emitter and base resistances
(b) increasing emitter and base resistances
(c) decreasing emitter resistance and increasing base resistance
(d) increasing emitter resistance and decreasing base resistance

55. For faster switching action of a transistor,
(a) a capacitor may be connected across the base resistance
(b) a capacitor may be connected in series with the base resistance
(c) a capacitor may be connected across R_E
(d) the value of the coupling capacitor may be increased

56. The zener diode shown in the circuit (Fig. given below) has a reverse breakdown voltage of 10 V. The power dissipation in R_S would be

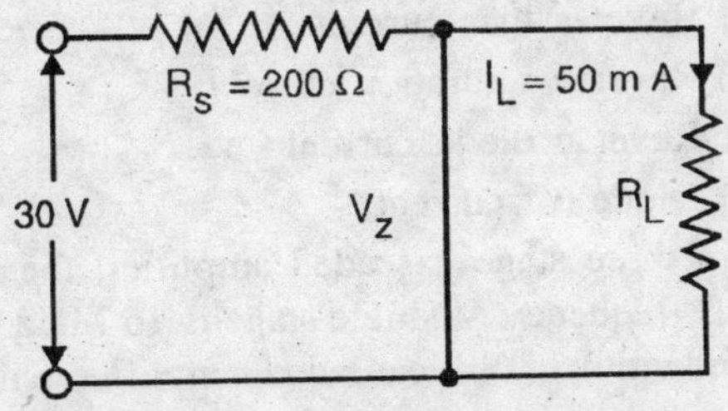

(a) 2.0 W (b) 1.5 W
(c) 1.0 W (d) 0.5 W

57. The advantage of using a series resistance R_s in the emitter-base circuit of the amplifier shown below is that
(a) bias stability increases
(b) base current can be controlled
(c) input resistance remains nearly constant
(d) current gain of the amplifier increases

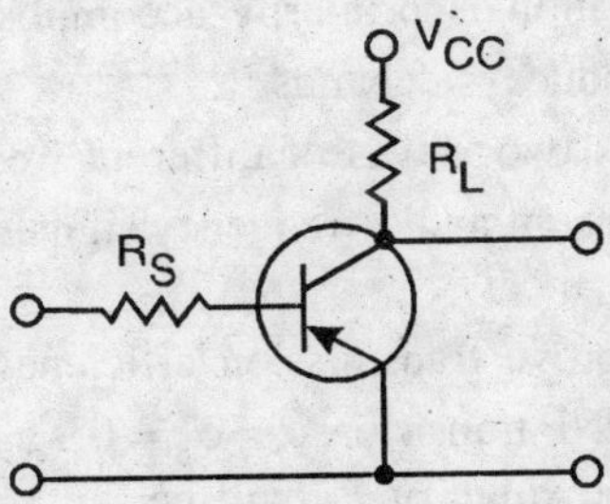

58. N-channel FETs are superior to P-channel FETs because of
(a) their high input impedance
(b) their high switching time
(c) less power consumption
(d) higher mobility of electrons in comparison to that of holes

59. In a feedback amplifier, the feedback improves the signal-to-noise ratio for noise signal
(a) internally generated in the amplifier
(b) present with the amplifier input
(c) both internally generated and present with the input
(d) present at the output

60. In a P-N-P transistor with normal bias
(a) the collector junction is of low resistance
(b) only majority carriers cross the collector junction
(c) only holes cross the collector junction
(d) the emitter-base junction is forward biased and collector-base junction is reverse biased

61. The main advantage of a point contact diode is that
(a) its reverse resistance is infinite
(b) the ratio of forward current to reverse current is very high
(c) its cut-in voltage is zero
(d) none of the above

62. Which of the following valves cannot be used as an amplifier
(a) triode (b) diode
(c) pentode (d) none of above

63. Modulation is primarily accomplished to
(a) produce sidebands
(b) mix two waves of different frequencies
(c) transmit audio-frequency signals over long distances
(d) improve transmission efficiency

64. For a PNP transistor, $\alpha = \alpha_R = 0.9$ and $I_{CO} = 10$ μA. The value of I_{CS} will be
(a) 15.2 μA (b) 52.6 μA
(c) 72.5 μA (d) 1.2 μmA

65. The reason of prefering FETs to bipolar transistors in integrated circuits is that
(a) they occupy very small space
(b) it has become a tradition
(c) fabrication of circuit is easy
(d) it is cheaper

66. Which one of the following statements is not ture?
(a) Capacitance is a measure of a capacitor's capability to store charge.
(b) A capacitor offers high impedance to ac but very low impedance to dc.
(c) A capacitor is also used as bypass capacitor.
(d) Capacitors are used to couple alternating voltages from one circuit to another and at the same time to block dc voltage from reaching the next circuit.

67. In order to convert RC-coupled amplifier to a wide-band amplifier, it is necessary
(a) to compensate for low frequency drop off
(b) to compensate for high frequency drop-off
(c) to compensate harmonic phase shifts that are not proportional to the frequency of the harmonics
(d) all of these

68. The primary function of a clamper circuit is to
(a) introduce a dc level into ac signal
(b) suppress variations in signal voltage
(c) raise +ve half cycle of the signal
(d) lower –ve half cycle of the signal

69. In a properly biased N-P-N transistor, most of the electrons from the emitter
(a) pass to the collector through the base
(b) recombine with holes in base
(c) recombine with holes in emitter itself
(d) are stopped by the function barrier

70. Which one of the following parameters is used for distinguishing between a small signal and a large-signal amplifier?
(a) Voltage gain
(b) Frequency response
(c) Harmonic distortion
(d) Input/output impedances

71. The most stable sine-wave oscillator is
(a) Colpitts (b) Armstrong
(c) Phase shift (d) Crystai

72. The biasing that provides good stability of the operation point but fails to provide good amplification is said to be
(a) fixed bias
(b) collector to base bias
(c) self bias
(d) collector to emitter bias

73. A certain amount of diode current still flows when diode is under reverse bias condition. What is this current called?
(a) Reverse bias current
(b) Reverse saturation current
(c) Reverse diode current
(d) Diode off current

74. In a three stage cascaded amplifier, the high 3dB frequency of single stage is 16 MHz. The bandwidth of the cascaded amplifier will be about
(a) 41 MHz (b) 16 MHz
(c) 10 MHz (d) 8.2 MHz

75. Which of the following statements is not true, regarding negative feedback in amplifiers?
(a) Gain stability is improved
(b) Distortion is reduced
(c) Frequency response is improved
(d) Gain bandwidth product is increased

76. The symbol I_{CBO} signifies the current that flows when some d.c. voltage is applied
(a) in the forward direction to the collector junction with the emitter open-circuited
(b) in the reverse direction to the collector junction with the emitter open-circuited
(c) in the reverse direction to the emitter junction with the collector open-circuited
(d) in the foward direction to the emitter junction with the collector open-circuited

77. The emitter must have the following characteristics
(a) high melting point
(b) low value of work function
(c) immunity to reaction from residual gasses and water vapours
(d) all of these

78. The transistors have the following advantages over thermionic tubes
(1) Compact size and light in weight
(2) Quite low operating voltage
(3) Instantaneous operation
(4) No energy loss in heating
(5) Long life if operated within permissible limits of temperature
(6) More resistant to shocks and vibrations
(7) No hum noise
Of these statements
(a) only (1), (2), (3) are correct
(b) all (1), (2), (3), (4), (5), (6) and (7) are correct
(c) only (6) and (7) are correct
(d) all except (7) are correct

79. Which of the following statements is not true for balance control in difference amplifier?
(a) It can only be used in discrete amplifier.
(b) It reduces offset due to β mismatching of the transistors.
(c) It reduces offset due VBE mismatching of the transistors.
(d) It improves CMRR of the amplifier.

80. Consider the following statements. From a sine wave one can obtain square wave by using
(1) Schmitt trigger circuit
(2) Zero crossing detector
(3) Clippers and amplifiers
Of these statements
(a) (1) and (2) are correct
(b) (1) and (3) are correct
(c) (2) and (3) are correct
(d) (1), (2) and (3) are correct

81. Which one of the following pairs is not correctly matched
(a) DSB-SC modulation : balanced modulator
(b) PCM : Pre-emphasis
(c) FM : Reactance modulator
(d) SSB modulation : Weaver's method

82. In modern electronic multimeters, a FET or MOSFET is preferred over BJT, because
(a) its input resistance is high
(b) its input resistance is high and does not vary with the change of range
(c) its input resistance is low
(d) it is cheaper

83. A monostable multivibrator is widely used
(a) in counting circuits
(b) in memory and timing circuits
(c) for regeneration of distorted waves
(d) for generating square waveforms

84. Schmitt trigger is basically
(a) an astable multivibrator
(b) a monostable multivibrator
(c) a bistable multivibrator
(d) an oscillator

85. In the circuit given below, in order to get an a.c. current through the load R_L it is necessary that input 1 and input 2 should be

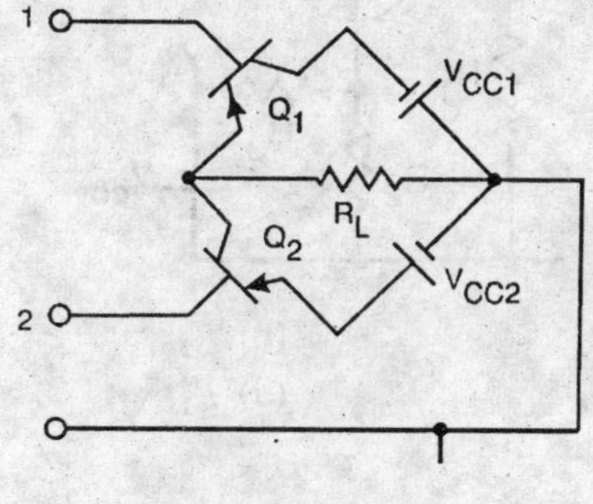

(a) 180° out of phase
(b) in phase
(c) of opposite polarity
(d) 90° out of phase

86. For the transistor AF115 shown below, emitter, base, collector terminals are

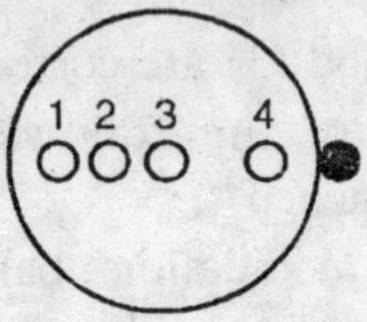

(a) 1, 2, 3 (b) 1, 2, 4
(c) 2, 3, 4 (d) 4, 3, 2

87. Which of the following type is most suitable for high frequency circuits?
(a) Grown-diffusion transistor
(b) Alloy transistor
(c) Rate-grown transistor
(d) hermetically sealed transistor

88. In an intrinsic semiconductor, the mobility of electrons in the conduction band is
(a) zero
(b) less than the mobility of holes in the valence band
(c) equal to mobility of holes in the valence band
(d) greater than the mobility of holes in the valence band

89. In the CB circuit shown below, the base emitter bias is obtained from

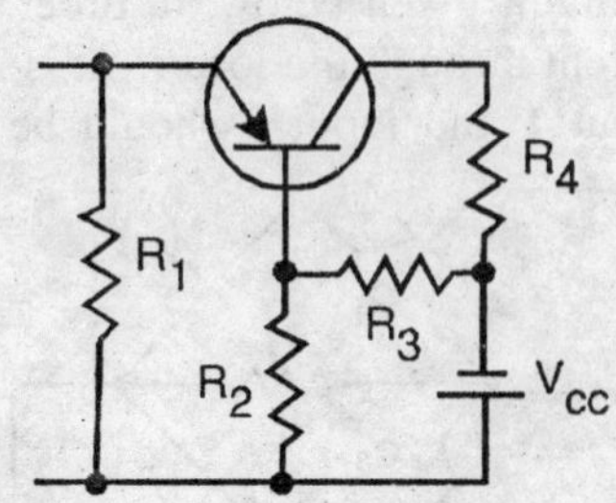

(a) R_3 (b) R_2
(c) R_4 (d) R_1

90. On the pole-zero diagram of an amplifier, the high cut-off frequency f_h will be determined by
(a) the pole farthest from the origin
(b) the polse closed to the origin
(c) the zero farthest from the origin
(d) none of these

91. The input bias-current offset I_{io} of a different amplifier is
(a) the difference in input bias currents that results in a specified output offset current
(b) the difference in input bias currents that must be supplied to make output-offset zero
(c) the difference in input bias currents that must be supplied to make input-offest zero
(d) none of these

92. As the reverse bias in a P-N junction is increased the reverse saturation current
(a) increases (b) remains constant
(c) decreases (d) none of above

93. The most desirable feature of transformer coupling is its
(a) ability to eliminate hum from the output
(b) ability to provide impedance matching between stages
(c) higher voltage gain
(d) wider frequency range

94. An electron tube can only operate when
(a) anode is negative with respect to cathode
(b) anode is positive with respect to cathode
(c) anode must be at zero potential with respect to cathode
(d) anode must be earthed

95. The main disadvantage of FM is
(a) low operating range
(b) complex circuitry
(c) limited line of-sight-range
(d) adjacent channel interference

96. A relaxation oscillator is one which
(a) produces sinusoidal output
(b) produces non-sinusoidal output
(c) relaxes indefinitely
(d) oscillates continuously

97. Once the SCR starts conducting its gate current loses control over
(a) anode current (b) anode voltage
(c) anode resistance (d) all of the above

98. Which of the following statements is not correct in regard to UJT?
(a) It exhibits a negative resistance.
(b) It is operated with emitter junction reverse biased.
(c) It has no ability to amplify while it has stability to control a large a.c. power with a small signal.
(d) It has one P-N junction and three leads.

99. Current density in a conducting media is
(a) $J = nq\mu$ (b) $J = \sigma E$
(c) $J = b\mu\in$ (d) $J = nq\in$

100. A transistor terminal current is considered positive if
(a) the electrons flow into the transistor at the terminal
(b) the current is because of flow of electrons only
(c) the current is because of flow of holes only
(d) the electrons flow out of the transistor at the terminal

101. In AM wave
(a) RF and AF waves are sent alternately
(b) carrier wave magnitude varies with AF signal
(c) RF signal should be an even multiple of AF signal
(d) none of these

102. Zener diode is usually operated
(a) in forward bias mode
(b) in reverse bias mode
(c) in forward linear region
(d) near cut-in voltage

103. Square-wave generator is a special type of
(a) variable frequency oscillator
(b) sweep frequency generator
(c) function generator
(d) pulse generator
(e) both (c) and (d)

104. The *h*-parameters are called hybrid parameters because
(a) they are obtained from different characteristics
(b) they have mixed dimensions
(c) they are mixed with other parameters
(d) all of the above

105. Which of the following classes of amplifiers has maximum distortion?
(a) Class A (b) Class B
(c) Class AB (d) Class C

106. The negative feedback in an amplifier
(a) reduces the voltage gain
(b) increases the voltage gain
(c) increases the gain bandwidth products
(d) reduces the input impedance

107. The conduction of electricity, in semiconductors, takes place due to movement of
(a) +ve ions only
(b) –ve ions only
(c) +ve and –ve ions only
(d) electrons and holes

108. A silicon wafer (intrinsic carrier concentration $1 \times 10^{16} m^{-3}$) is doped with 2×10^{22} aluminium atoms/m^3 and 1×10^{22} arsenic atoms per m^3. Assume complete dopantionization, the minority carrier concentration will be
(a) $1 \times 10^{22}/m^3$ (b) $1 \times 10^{10}/m^3$
(c) $2 \times 10^{6}/m^3$ (d) $0.5 \times 10^{-6}/m^3$

109. The reverse saturation current in a P-N junction diode is the current that flows when
(a) only minority carriers are crossing the junction
(b) only majority carriers are crossing the junction
(c) when potential barrier is zero
(d) the junction is unbiased

110. In a vacuum tetrode secondary emission is because of emission of
(a) electrons from the filament due to heat energy
(b) high velocity electrons from the cathode

(c) electrons from the plate due to bombardment of the fast moving electrons emitted from the cathode
(d) electrons belonging to the second orbit of the atoms of cathode

111. A transistor terminal voltage is considered positive if
(a) the terminal is more negative than the common terminal
(b) the terminal is more positive than the common terminal
(c) the terminal is the output terminal
(d) the terminal is connected to the P-type material

112. The voltage gain of a given common source FET amplifier depends upon its
(a) drain load resistance
(b) input impedance
(c) dynamic drain resistance
(d) amplification factor

113. When the reverse voltage across a P-N junction is gradually decreased, the depletion region inside the diode
(a) does not change in width
(b) initially increases upto a certain width and then decreases
(c) continuously increases in width
(d) continuously decreases in width

114. The maximum efficiency of an half-wave rectifier is
(a) 20.3% (b) 40.6%
(c) 50% (d) 81.2%

115. UJT oscillators are used for gate triggering of thyristor for
(a) better phase control
(b) snap action
(c) being cheap and simple
(d) none of these

116. Forward biasing of a P-N junction
(a) reduces the majority carrier current to zero
(b) reduces the minority carrier current to zero
(c) raises the potential barrier
(d) reduces the potential barrier

117. An intrinsic semiconductor at the absolute zero temperature
(a) behaves like a metallic conductor
(b) behaves like an insulator
(c) has a large number of holes
(d) has a large number of electrons

118. The amplifier gain varies with frequency. This happens mainly due to
(a) Miller effect
(b) logarithmic increase in its output power
(c) interstage transformers
(d) presence of external and internal capacitances

119. A transistor circuit employing base bias with collector feedback has greater stability than the one without feedback. It is because of
(a) reduction of I_C in magnitude
(b) reduction of V_{BE}
(c) I_C becoming independent of β
(d) negative feedback effect

120. The internal resistance of a vacuum tube is because of
(a) space charge (b) plate potential
(c) vacuum (d) air in tube

121. When a high reverse voltage is applied to a P-N junction
(a) zener breakdown occurs
(b) avalanche breakdown occurs
(c) it becomes a transistor
(d) none of above

122. Trigger pulses are essential for the operation of a bistable multivibrator because
(a) there are no R-C timing circuits
(b) the circuit cannot switch between its two states automatically
(c) transistor operation is controlled by the triggering pulses
(d) all of the above

123. A Colpitt's oscillator uses
(a) a tapped inductor
(b) a tapped capacitor
(c) both the above
(d) none of the above

124. The Hall angle θ of a metal sample is
(a) independent of the magnetic flux density B
(b) independent of the carrier mobility
(c) independent of the density of free carriers
(d) dependent on magnetic flux density, carrier mobility and density of free carriers

125. IGFET is a
(a) square-law device
(b) half-power device
(c) 3/2 power-law device
(d) linear device

126. For transistor operation
(a) emitter-base diode is always forward-biased and the collector-base diode is always reverse-biased
(b) emitter-base diode is reverse-biased and collector-base diode is forward biased
(c) both the emitter-base diode and the collector-base diode are forward-biased
(d) both the emitter-base diode and the collector-base diode are reverse-biased

127. The Q-point in a voltage amplifier is selected in the middle of the active region so that
(a) it may give distortionless output
(b) it may need a small d.c. voltage
(c) the operating point becomes very stable
(d) less number of resistor is required

128. The emitter region in N-P-N junction transistor is more heavily doped than the base region so that
(a) the flow across the base region will be mainly due to electrons
(b) the flow across the base region will be mainly due to holes
(c) base current will be high
(d) there will be increased recombination in base region

129. Silicon is preferred over germanium for use in semiconductor devices. The reasons is/are:
(a) Silicon crystal has fewer electrons than germanium crystal at room temperature. So silicon has much smaller collector cut-off current (I_{CBO}) than that of germanium
(b) ICBO approximately doubles with each 6°C rise of temperature in germanium while it doubles with each 10°C rise of temperature for silicon
(c) The normal operating temperature of germanium is approximately 70°C while it is 150°C in case of silicon
(d) all the above three

130. The high and low frequency response of an RC coupled circuit can be increased by
(a) increasing load resistance
(b) decreasing load resistance
(c) increasing coupling capacitor
(d) decreasing coupling capacitor

131. The function of control grid in a pentode tube is to
(a) collect electrons from the space charge
(b) control the secondary emission from the plate
(c) accelerate the electrons emitted from the cathode
(d) control the number of electrons moving from cathode to plate

132. Low frequency response of an RC coupled amplifier can be improved by
(a) increasing the coupling capacitors only
(b) increasing the by-pass capacitors only
(c) increasing the by-pass capacitor as well as coupling capacitor
(d) decreasing the by-pass capacitor

133. The 3 dB cut-off frequency of a transistor amplifier is the frequency at which
(a) the current gain increases by 3dB
(b) the current gain becomes 3 dB
(c) the current gain becomes 0.707 of its mid range value
(d) the power gain decreases by 3 dB

134. In the circuit given below, which statement is true?

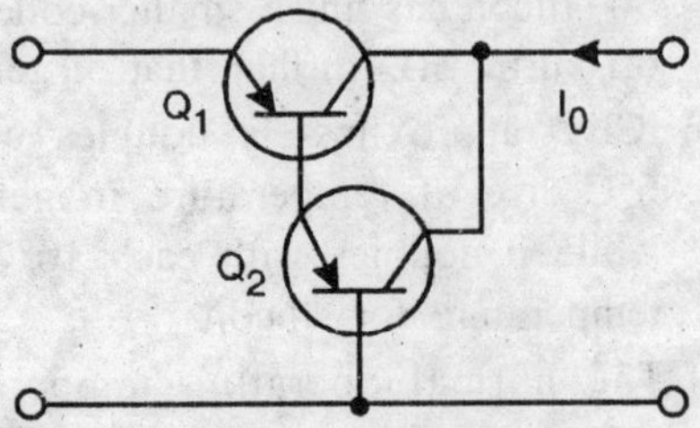

(a) $I_{B2} = I_{C2} - I_{E1}$ (b) $I_{E1} = I_{C1} + I_{E2}$
(c) $I_{E2} = I_{B1}$ (d) $I_0 = I_{C1} - I_{C2}$

135. Cross-over distortion occurs in
(a) class A amplifiers
(b) class B amplifiers
(c) class C amplifiers
(d) push-pull amplifiers

136. To generate a 1 MHz signal, the most suitable oscillator is
(a) Colpitt's oscillator
(b) Phase-shift oscillator
(c) Wien-bridge oscillator
(d) none of these

137. In TV transmission, picture signal is amplitude modulated and sound signal is frequency modulated. This is done because
(a) it is not possible to frequency modulate the picture signal
(b) bandwidth requirement is minimised
(c) sound signal is more susceptible to noise than picture signal
(d) synchronisation of picture frames becomes easier

138. Feedback in amplifier always helps in
(a) controlling its output
(b) increasing its gain
(c) reducing its input impedance
(d) stabilizes its gain

139. Zener diode when used in a circuit, is always
(a) connected in series
(b) troubled due to heating
(c) forward biased
(d) reverse biased

140. Astable multivibrator has
(a) a stable state
(b) two quasi stable states
(c) an oscillator
(d) none of these

141. The Hall effect voltage in intrinsic silicon
(a) is positive
(b) is zero
(c) is negative
(d) changes sign on application of magnetic field

142. A large sacrifice factor in a negative feedback amplifier leads to
(a) precise control over output
(b) reduced input impedance
(c) increased output impedance
(d) characteristics which cannot be achieved without feedback

143. N-type semi-conductors
(a) are negatively charged
(b) are produced when indium is added as an impurity to germanium
(c) are produced when phosphorus is added as an impurity to silicon
(d) none of the above

144. The output time period of a transistorised monostable multivibrator using base resistor R_b and coupling capacitor C_b for the output transistor is given by
(a) R_bC_b (b) 0.69 R_bC_b
(c) 2 R_bC_b (d) 1.38 R_bC_b

145. Conduction electrons have more mobility than holes because they
(a) have –ve charge
(b) they need less energy to move them
(c) are lighter
(d) experience collisions less frequently

146. The negative output swing in a transistor circuit starts clipping first when Q-point
(a) has optimum value
(b) is in the active region of load line
(c) is near cut-off point
(d) is near saturation point

147. The potential-divider method of biasing is employed in amplifiers in order to
(a) reduce the cost of the circuit
(b) reduce the d.c. base current
(c) limit the input a.c. signal going to the base
(d) make the operating point almost independent of β

148. In a JFET, drain current will be maximum when gate-source voltage is
(a) equal to V_p (b) positive
(c) negative (d) zero

149. Turn-off time of a thyristor
(a) depends upon junction temperature and forward current
(b) is a constant
(c) depends on load
(d) none of these

150. For junction isolation of P-type resistor in I.C. chip, the N-type isolation island is connected to most
(a) +ve bias (b) –ve bias
(c) floating bias (d) unbiased

151. Which one is not the advantage of push-pull amplifier?
(a) More output
(b) Improved linearity
(c) All harmonics (even and odd) removed
(d) Balanced out effect of ripple in power supply

152. A diode have breakdown voltage of greater than 5 V and a +ve temperature coefficient is
(a) Zener diode (b) Avalanche diode
(c) Tunnel diode (d) P-N junction diode

153. In an R-C coupled amplifier, the voltage gain
(a) remains almost constant over a range of frequency
(b) always increases with frequency
(c) always decreases with frequency
(d) none of these

154. Closed-loop gain of a feedback amplifier is the gain achieved when
(a) feedback factor exceeds unity
(b) feedback loop is closed
(c) its output terminals are closed
(d) negative feedback is applied

155. For an amplifier, the coupling method which gives the highest gain is
(a) capacitance coupling
(b) resistance coupling
(c) impedance coupling
(d) transformer coupling

156. When audio-signal controls the amplitude of the carrier wave, it is called
(a) amplitude modulation
(b) frequency modulation
(c) pulse modulation
(d) pulse-amplitude modulation

157. For constructing a full-wave rectifier
(a) atleast two diodes are needed
(b) more than two diodes are needed
(c) atleast four diodes are needed
(d) none of these

158. The addition of impurity atoms to a pure semiconductor material
(a) creates a new energy band
(b) creates many new energy bands
(c) does not create any new energy band
(d) none of above

159. In RLC circuit can be synthesised using only
(a) L element and amplifier
(b) L, C elements and amplifiers
(c) R, L elements and amplifiers
(d) R, C elements and amplifiers

160. In order to achieve good stabilization in potential divider method, current through R_1 and R_2 should be at least
(a) twice that of I_B (b) 5 times of I_B
(c) 10 times of I_B (d) 20 times of I_B

161. A photocell is illuminated by a small bright source placed 1m away. When the same source of light is placed two metres away, the electrons emitted by the photocathode
(a) each carry one quarter of their previous energy
(b) each carry one quarter of their previous moments
(c) are half as numerous
(d) are one-quarter as numerous

162. A major advantage of an emitter-follower is that provides
(a) maximum gain
(b) maximum efficiency
(c) maximum output impedance
(d) minimum distortion

163. In an R-C coupled common emitter the following is true.
(a) Coupling capacitance affects the h_f response and bypass capacitance affects the I_f response.
(b) Both coupling and bypass capacitances affect the I_f response only.
(c) Both coupling and bypass capacitances affect the h_f response only.
(d) Coupling capacitance affects the I_f response and bypass capacitance affects the h_f response.

164. The potential-barrier across a PN junction corresponds to
(a) height of the barrier
(b) width of the barrier
(c) forward bias of the junction
(d) reverse bias of the junction

165. In a P-type semiconductor with acceptor atom concentration of N_A, the electron concentration in terms of intrinsic concentration is given as
(a) $n_i - N_A$ (b) $n_i + N_A$
(c) n_i^2/N_A (d) n_i/N_A

166. The maximum power rating of a transistor is not exceeded if
(a) *Q*-point lies in the area bounded by the two axes of output characteristics and the constant power dissipation line
(b) the load line lies in the area bounded by the two axis and the constant power dissipation line
(c) the load line intersects the constant dissipation line
(d) none of these

167. On applying a +ve voltage signal to the base of a normally biased N-P-N CE transistor-amplifier
(a) collector voltage will become less +ve
(b) base current will fall
(c) emitter current will fall
(d) collector current will fall

168. When transistor is operating in active region, the emitter junction is
(a) forward biased in both P-N-P and N-P-N transistor
(b) reverse biased in both P-N-P and N-P-N transistors
(c) both of these
(d) none of these

169. The most popular form of an IC package is
(a) dual-in-line (DIL) pack
(b) flat pack
(c) TO-5 package
(d) both (a) and (b)

170. Acceptor type impurities
(a) must have three valence electrons
(b) must have five valence electrons
(c) both of these
(d) none of these

171. A cascade amplifier will have higher cut-off frequency
(a) same as that a single stage amplifier
(b) higher than single stage amplifier
(c) lower than single stage amplifier
(d) none of the above

172. A choke wound with many turns of fine wire on an iron core made of laminated sheet is used
(a) as a filter choke
(b) as an AF choke
(c) as a RF choke
(d) in micro-wave systems

173. The arrow head on the transistor symbol always shows the direction of
(a) electron flow in emitter region
(b) conventional current flow
(c) majority carrier flow in the emitter region
(d) minority carrier flow in the emitter region

174. In FM transmission, if frequency of modulating signal is doubled, the deviation will
(a) remain unchanged
(b) be doubled
(c) be halved
(d) be 4 times

175. A class B push-pull amplifier has the main advantage of being free from
(a) unwanted noise
(b) even order harmonic distortion
(c) amplitude distortion
(d) circuit imbalance

176. The frequency of oscillation in case of an astable multivibrator depends mainly on the
(a) value of transistor β
(b) R.C. values of the circuit
(c) value of V_{CC} power supply
(d) collector resistors

177. Which of the following statements is not true for an intrinsic semiconductor?
(a) The number of holes is less than the number of electrons.
(b) The number of holes is equal to number of electrons.
(c) The net charge density of the material is zero.
(d) The product of hole concentration and electron concentration is constant.

178. For N-type semiconductor the doping material is
(a) a tetravalent material
(b) a pentavalent material
(c) a trivalent material
(d) germanium

179. In an intrinsic semiconductor
(a) there are no holes in the material
(b) the number of holes is too small
(c) electrons in the material are neutralized by holes
(d) there are no electrons in the material

180. In a semiconductor material doping is done to
(a) decrease the number of charge carriers
(b) change the chemical properties of semiconductor
(c) make semiconductor less than 100% pure
(d) increase the conductivity of the semiconductor

181. Donor type impurities
(a) have five valence electrons
(b) create excess free electrons
(c) are used to make N-type semiconductors
(d) all of the above

182. Flat plate collector
(a) has plate blackened in order to absorb maximum amount of direct radiations
(b) is placed at a proper inclination to the Sun so as to absorb solar radiations
(c) is mainly used for water heating, space-heating, and drying
(d) all of the above

183. If a small amount of arsenic is added to silicon
(a) the resistance will increase
(b) the arsenic becomes an acceptor type impurity
(c) the silicon will become a P-type semiconductor
(d) there will be more free electrons than holes in the semiconductor

184. Which of the following not decrease as a result of introduction of negative feedback?
(a) Instability (b) Bandwidth
(c) Overall gain (d) Distortion

185. An N-channel JFET has pinch off voltage $V_p = -4$ volts. Given $V_{GS} = -1$V, the minimum V_{DS} for the device to operate in the pinch-off region will be
(a) + 1 V (b) + 3 V
(c) + 4 V (d) + 5 V

186. In a JFET, drain current is primarily controlled by
(a) size of depletion region
(b) channel resistance
(c) gate reverse bias
(d) voltage drop across channel

187. Which of the following configurations has invariably high cut-off frequency?
(a) Common-emitter (b) Common-base
(c) Both of these (d) None of these

188. The bandwidth of an amplifier may be increased by
(a) reducing the stray capacitances to the minimum possible
(b) cascading it
(c) reducing the capacitance of bypass capacitors
(d) increasing input signal frequency

189. The most preferred high power output stage for hi-fi AF amplifier is of the
(a) class B push type
(b) class B single ended type
(c) class A type
(d) class C type

190. A transistor in CB configuration transfers
(a) a current from low impedance circuit to high impedance circuit
(b) current from high impedance circuit to high impedance circuit
(c) voltage from low impedance circuit to high impedance circuit
(d) voltage from high impedance circuit to low impedance circuit

191. A bistable multivibrator
(a) has no stable state
(b) has two stable states
(c) has one energy storage element
(d) none of these

192. Which one of the following is used as a passive component in an electronic circuit?
(a) Vacuum diode
(b) Zener diode
(c) Inductor
(d) Silicon controlled rectifier (SCR)

193. The addition of antimony to pure semiconductor results in
(a) n-type-semiconductor
(b) p-type semiconductor
(c) p-n semiconductor
(d) none of above

194. The best method of bias is
(a) base resistor method
(b) potential divider method
(c) collector to base bias
(d) base bias with collector and emitter feedbacks

195. A signal of 10 mV at 75 MHz is to be measured. Which of the following instrument can be used?
(a) VTVM
(b) Cathode ray oscilloscope
(c) Moving iron voltmeter
(d) Digital multimeter

196. Major part of the current in an intrinsic semiconductor is because of
(a) valence band electrons
(b) conduction band electrons
(c) thermally generated electrons
(d) holes in the valence band

197. Which of the following statements is not correct?
(a) Gas filled diodes can be used for charging the storage batteries.
(b) Thyratrons are widely used as amplifiers.
(c) Thyratrons are very useful in switching and relay applications.
(d) Thyratrons can be used as grid controlled rectifiers when voltage control is needed.

198. Which of the following statements is not correct?
(a) Electron emission takes place in vacuum.
(b) The amount of energy required for the escape of electrons varies with different materials.
(c) Metals with lower work function will emit electrons at lower temperatures.
(d) At ordinary temperature, the energy of free electrons in the metal is more than the work function of the metal.

199. A triode having $\mu = 25$ and $r_p = 10$ k is used as an amplifier. The load resistance is 10 k. The voltage gain will be
(a) –25 (b) –12.5
(c) +2.3 (d) None of these

200. Which of the following statements is correct in regard to broadcast superhetrodyne receiver?
(a) RF is of no use.
(b) Mixer is tuned to signal frequency.
(c) Intermediate frequency is variable.
(d) Local oscillator frequency is below the signal frequency.

201. The potential barrier existing across PN junction
(a) facilitates recombination of electrons and holes
(b) prevents flow of minority carriers
(c) prevents total recombination of holes and electrons
(d) prevents neutralisation of acceptor and donor ions

202. A zener diode
(a) is useful as an amplifier
(b) has a –ve resistance
(c) has a sharp breakdown at low reverse voltage
(d) has a high forward voltage rating

203. The outstanding characteristic of a direct coupled amplifier is its
(a) temperature stability
(b) utmost economy
(c) ability to amplify d.c. and low frequency signals
(d) avoidance of frequency-sensitive components

204. A half wave rectifier has a load resistance R and a capacitance filter connected across the load. The capacitance of the filter is C. It is desired that the output voltage should have small ripple. Then
(a) RC should be very large
(b) RC should be very low
(c) C should be reciprocal of R
(d) none of these

205. To turn a conducting SCR to off state, it is necessary to make
(a) the anode current less than holding current
(b) the gate current zero
(c) the anode voltage less than the break over voltage
(d) the gate voltage zero

206. One of the advantages of hermetically sealed transistor is that
(a) frequency response is better
(b) no heat sink is required
(c) thermal stability is more
(d) contamination of the material is avoided

207. Heat sink is used in the power amplifier circuit
(a) to increase the output power
(b) to reduce the heat loss in a transistor
(c) to increase the voltage gain of the power amplifier
(d) to increase the collector dissipation ratings of the transistor

208. FET is a device which has
(a) high input impedance and is voltage controlled
(b) high input impedance and is current controlled
(c) low input impedance and is voltage controlled
(d) low input impedance and is current controlled

209. Which of the following statements is not true not an intrinsic semiconductor?
(a) The number of holes is less than the number of electrons.
(b) The product of hole concentration and electron concentration is a constant.
(c) The net charge density of the material is zero.
(d) All of these

210. A transformer audio-amplifier is found to have an overall efficiency of the order of 70%. It is
(a) class A push-pull amplifier
(b) class B push-pull amplifier
(c) single stage class C amplifier
(d) direct coupled amplifier

211. The semiconductors are replacing electron tube because they are
(a) light in weight
(b) smaller in size
(c) longer in life and greater in ruggedness
(d) all of these

212. In the self-bias CE transistor amplifier, a single battery V_{CC} is used because
(a) of the voltage divider action of biasing resistance
(b) the emitter base junction is of low resistance
(c) the collector base junction is reverse biased by V_{CC}
(d) all of these

213. JFET has main drawback of
(a) having low input impedance
(b) having high output impedance
(c) being noisy
(d) having small gain-bandwidth product

214. In a transistor with normal bias, the emitter junction
(a) is of high resistance
(b) is reverse biased
(c) is of low resistance
(d) emits such carriers into the base region which are in majority in the base

215. The theoretical maximum efficiency of a full wave rectifier circuit is
(a) the same as that of a half wave circuit
(b) double as that of a half wave circuit
(c) definitely more but less than double as that of a half wave circuit
(d) none of these

216. An RC-coupled amplifier has an open loop gain of 100 and an upper cut of frequency of 100 kHz. If negative feedback with a feedback factor of 0.02 is used, the upper cut off frequency will be
(a) 100 kHz (b) 33.3 kHz
(c) 300 kHz (d) 1000 kHz

217. The P-N Junction diode is a
(a) passive device (b) vacuum tube
(c) unilateral device (d) bilateral device

218. A circuit in which the output voltage remains constant irrespective of the value of load resistance, uses
(a) Silicon diode (b) Zener diode
(c) SCR (d) None of above

219. In an unbiased P-N junction, the junction current at equilibrium is
(a) zero, because no charge crosses the junction
(b) zero, because equal but opposite carriers cross the junction
(c) because of minority carriers only
(d) because of majority carriers only

220. In Class-C operation of an amplifier, the collector current exists for
(a) 180° of the input signal cycle
(b) more than 180° of the input signal cycle
(c) less than 180° of the input signal cycle
(d) none of above

221. In a correctly biased N-P-N transistor
(a) the base is +ve with respect to collector
(b) the base is +ve with respect to emitter
(c) the collector is –ve and base is –ve
(d) the base is +ve with respect to both emitter and collector

222. Which of the following amplifier operations has the highest efficiency
(a) Class A (b) Class B
(c) Class C (d) None of these

223. In a correctly biased NPN transistor
(a) the base is positive with respect to collector
(b) the base is positive with respect to emitter
(c) the base is positive with respect of both emitter and collector
(d) none of these

224. When a voltage is applied to an intrinsic semiconductor at room temperature
(a) electrons move to +ve terminal and holes move to –ve terminal
(b) electrons move to –ve terminal and holes move to +ve terminal
(c) both electrons and holes move to +ve terminal
(d) both electrons and holes move to –ve terminal

225. A digital voltmeter uses a 10 MHz clock and has a voltage controlled generator which provides a width of 10 μ s/V of unit signal. 10 V of input of signal would correspond to a pulse count of

(a) 500 (b) 750
(c) 1000 (d) 1500

226. A 10 bit A/D convertor is used to digitise an analog signal in the 0 to 5 V range. The maximum peak to peak ripple voltage that can be allowed in the d.c. supply voltage is

(a) nearly 100 mV (b) nearly 50 mV
(c) nearly 25 mV (d) nearly 5 mV

227. In a P-N-P transistor with normal bias

(a) the collector junction is of low resistance
(b) only majority carriers cross the collector junction
(c) only holes cross the collector junction
(d) the emitter-base junction is forward biased and collector-base junction is reverse biased

228. The liberation of electrons from the surface of a substance is called

(a) bombardment of electrons
(b) electronic emission
(c) movement of free electrons
(d) ions emission

229. Ripple frequency of the output waveform of a bridge rectifier when fed with a 50 Hz sine wave is

(a) 100 Hz (b) 25 Hz
(c) 50 Hz (d) none of these

230. Which of the following transistors are symmetrical in the sense that emitter and collector, or source and drain terminals can be interchanged?

(a) JFET (b) MOSFET
(c) NPN transistor (d) PNP transistor

231. In a tetrode the plate resistance is –ve when

(a) plate voltage is more than the screen grid voltage
(b) plate voltage is less than the screen grid voltage
(c) control grid is at +ve potential w.r.t. screen grid
(d) control grid is at +ve potential w.r.t. to cathode

232. In the context of IC fabrication, metallisation means

(a) covering with a metal cap
(b) depositing SiO_2 layer
(c) connecting metal wires
(d) forming interconnecting conduction pattern and bonding pads

233. In an indirectly heated cathodes

(a) filament is not used
(b) filament heater is used
(c) filament heater may or may not be used
(d) high voltage is used

234. For a transistor amplifier operating in the mid-frequency range

(a) external capacitors are open circuit; internal capacitor short circuit
(b) external capacitors short circuit; internal capacitors also short circuit
(c) external capacitors short circuit; internal capacitors open circuit
(d) none of these

235. The staggered tuned amplifier generally employs

(a) common emitter configuration
(b) common collector configuration
(c) common base configuration
(d) FET

236. Latching current of an SCR is

(a) below 10% (b) 10-20%
(c) 20-25% (d) 25-30 %

of rated current

237. For the power transistor AD149 shown below, emitter, base and collector terminals are

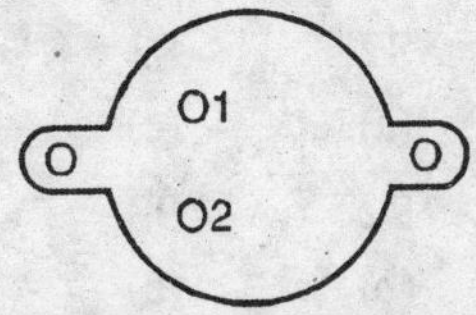

(a) 2, 1 and cap (b) 1, 2 and cap
(c) 1, cap, 2 (d) None of these

238. Which of the following statements is not true for hole?

(a) Holes may constitute an electric current.

(b) Holes can be considered as a net positive charge.

(c) Holes can exist in any material including conductors.

(d) Holes can exist in certain semiconductor materials only.

239. Which is a pair of acceptor elements?

(a) Arsenic and boron

(b) Antimony and indium

(c) Phosphorous and aluminium

(d) Gallium and boron

240. The frequency response of an amplifier is given below (in Figure). If the amplifier is to be stable with a phase margin of 45°, the maximum permissible loop gain will be

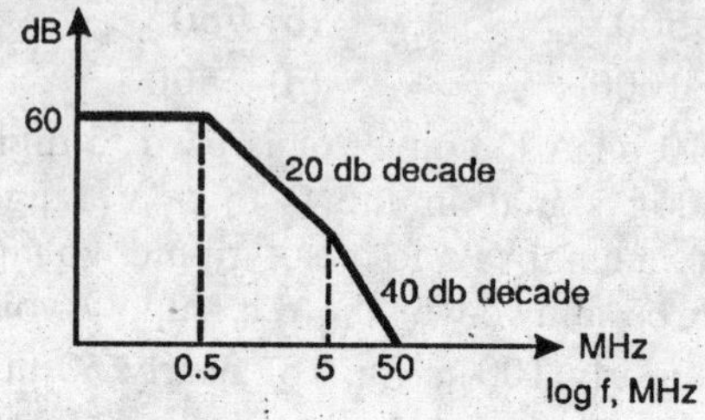

(a) 40 dB
(b) 37 dB
(c) 23 dB
(d) 20 dB

ANSWERS

1	2	3	4	5	6	7	8	9	10
(c)	(d)	(d)	(c)	(a)	(a)	(b)	(a)	(c)	(d)
11	**12**	**13**	**14**	**15**	**16**	**17**	**18**	**19**	**20**
(a)	(a)	(c)	(b)	(c)	(c)	(d)	(a)	(a)	(c)
21	**22**	**23**	**24**	**25**	**26**	**27**	**28**	**29**	**30**
(a)	(b)	(a)	(d)	(d)	(b)	(a)	(c)	(d)	(c)
31	**32**	**33**	**34**	**35**	**36**	**37**	**38**	**39**	**40**
(b)	(c)	(c)	(c)	(a)	(a)	(d)	(c)	(b)	(c)
41	**42**	**43**	**44**	**45**	**46**	**47**	**48**	**49**	**50**
(a)	(b)	(b)	(c)	(d)	(a)	(a)	(b)	(c)	(a)
51	**52**	**53**	**54**	**55**	**56**	**57**	**58**	**59**	**60**
(b)	(d)	(a)	(d)	(a)	(a)	(c)	(d)	(a)	(d)
61	**62**	**63**	**64**	**65**	**66**	**67**	**68**	**69**	**70**
(b)	(b)	(c)	(b)	(a)	(b)	(d)	(a)	(a)	(b)
71	**72**	**73**	**74**	**75**	**76**	**77**	**78**	**79**	**80**
(d)	(b)	(b)	(d)	(d)	(b)	(d)	(d)	(c)	(b)
81	**82**	**83**	**84**	**85**	**86**	**87**	**88**	**89**	**90**
(b)	(a)	(c)	(c)	(a)	(b)	(a)	(d)	(b)	(b)
91	**92**	**93**	**94**	**95**	**96**	**97**	**98**	**99**	**100**
(b)	(b)	(b)	(b)	(c)	(b)	(d)	(b)	(b)	(d)
101	**102**	**103**	**104**	**105**	**106**	**107**	**108**	**109**	**110**
(b)	(b)	(e)	(b)	(d)	(a)	(d)	(b)	(a)	(c)

111	112	113	114	115	116	117	118	119	120
(b)	(a)	(d)	(b)	(b)	(d)	(b)	(d)	(d)	(a)
121	**122**	**123**	**124**	**125**	**126**	**127**	**128**	**129**	**130**
(a)	(d)	(b)	(d)	(a)	(a)	(a)	(a)	(d)	(b)
131	**132**	**133**	**134**	**135**	**136**	**137**	**138**	**139**	**140**
(c)	(c)	(c)	(b)	(d)	(a)	(b)	(a)	(d)	(b)
141	**142**	**143**	**144**	**145**	**146**	**147**	**148**	**149**	**150**
(c)	(d)	(c)	(b)	(b)	(d)	(d)	(d)	(a)	(a)
151	**152**	**153**	**154**	**155**	**156**	**157**	**158**	**159**	**160**
(c)	(b)	(a)	(b)	(d)	(a)	(a)	(c)	(b)	(c)
161	**162**	**163**	**164**	**165**	**166**	**167**	**168**	**169**	**170**
(d)	(d)	(b)	(a)	(c)	(b)	(a)	(a)	(a)	(a)
171	**172**	**173**	**174**	**175**	**176**	**177**	**178**	**179**	**180**
(c)	(a)	(b)	(a)	(b)	(b)	(a)	(b)	(c)	(d)
181	**182**	**183**	**184**	**185**	**186**	**187**	**188**	**189**	**190**
(d)	(d)	(d)	(b)	(c)	(c)	(b)	(a)	(d)	(a)
191	**192**	**193**	**194**	**195**	**196**	**197**	**198**	**199**	**200**
(b)	(b)	(a)	(b)	(b)	(c)	(c)	(d)	(b)	(b)
201	**202**	**203**	**204**	**205**	**206**	**207**	**208**	**209**	**210**
(c)	(c)	(c)	(a)	(a)	(d)	(d)	(a)	(a)	(b)
211	**212**	**213**	**214**	**215**	**216**	**217**	**218**	**219**	**220**
(d)	(d)	(d)	(c)	(b)	(c)	(c)	(b)	(a)	(c)
221	**222**	**223**	**224**	**225**	**226**	**227**	**228**	**229**	**230**
(b)	(c)	(b)	(a)	(c)	(d)	(d)	(b)	(a)	(b)
231	**232**	**233**	**234**	**235**	**236**	**237**	**238**	**239**	**240**
(c)	(d)	(b)	(c)	(c)	(a)	(b)	(c)	(d)	(b)

5. ELECTRICAL AND ELECTRONIC MEASUREMENTS

Direct-Current Indicating Instruments

The suspension galvanometer, being neither a practical nor portable instrument, is essentially the permanent-magnet moving-coil mechanism (PMMC). Figure 1 shows the construction of the PMMC mechanism. A coil is suspended in the magnetic field of a permanent magnet of the shape of a horse-shoe. The coil is suspended so that it can rotate freely in the magnetic field. When current flows in the coil, the developed electromagnetic torque causes the coil to rotate. This torque is counterbalanced by the mechanical torque of control springs attached to the movable coil. The balance of torques, and therefore the angular position of the movable coil, is indicated by a pointer against a fixed reference, called the scale.

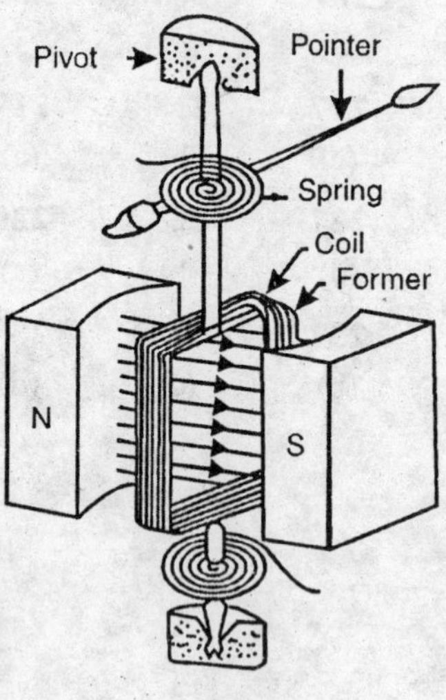

Fig. 1

$T = B \times A \times I \times N$

Where

T = torque, newton metre (N-m)

B = flux density in the air gap, weber/square metre (Wb/m^2)

A = effective coil area, square meter (m^2)

I = current in the movable coil, amperes (A) and

N = turns of wire on the coil.

This equation shows that the developed torque is directly proportional to the flux density of the field in which the coil rotates, the current in the coil, and the coil constants (area and number of turns).

Permanent Magnet Moving Coil Movement

The basic PMMC movement, also called the d' Arsonval movement, offers a large magnet in a given space and is used when maximum flux in the air gap is required. It provides an instrument with very low power consumption and low current required for full-scale deflection (*fsd*). The permanent magnet is of horse-shoe form with soft iron pole pieces attached to it. Between the pole pieces is a cylinder of soft iron which serves to provide a uniform magnetic field in the air gap between the pole pieces and the cylinder. The coil is wound on a light metal frame and is mounted so that it can rotate freely in the air gap. The pointer, attached to the coil, moves over a graduated scale and indicates the angular deflection of the coil and therefore the current through the coil.

Temperature Compensation Movement

The basic PMMC, though inherently insensitive to temperature, may be further temperature-compensated by the appropriate use of series and shunt-resistors of copper and manganin. Both the magnetic field strength and spring tension decrease with an increase in temperature. The coil resistance increases with an increase in temperature. These changes tend to make the pointer read low for a given current with respect to magnetic field strength and coil resistance.

Temperature compensation is obtained with the help of *swamping resistors* in series with the movable coil. The swamping resistor is made of manganin (which has a temperature coefficient of practically zero) combined with copper in the ratio of 20/1 to 30/1. The total resistance of coil and swamping resistor increases slightly with a rise in temperature, but only just enough to counteract the change in the springs and magnet so that the overall temperature effect is zero.

Galvanometer Sensitivity

The sensitivity of galvanometer can be specified in terms of current sensitivity, voltage sensitivity and megohm sensitivity.

Current Sensitivity may be defined as the ratio of the deflection of the galvanometer to the current producing this deflection, *i.e.*,

$$S_I = \frac{d}{I} \frac{mm}{\mu A}$$

Where

d = deflection of the galvanometer in scale division in mm, and

I = galvanometer current in μA.

Voltage Sensitivity may be defined as the ratio of the galvanometer deflection to the voltage producing this deflection. Therefore

$$S_v = \frac{d}{V} \frac{mm}{mV}$$

Where

d = deflection of the galvanometer in scale divisions in mm, and

V = voltage applied to the galvanometer in mV.

Megohm Sensitivity may be defined as the number of megohms required in series with the (CRDX shunted) galvanometer to produce one scale division deflection when 1 V is applied to the circuit. Numerically it is equal to current sensitivity.

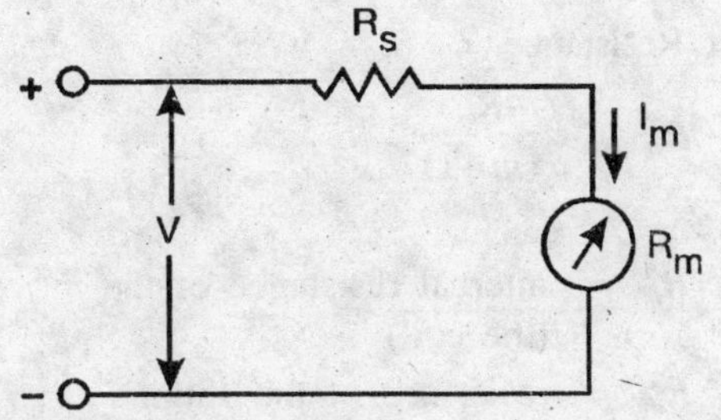

Fig. 2

DC Voltmeter

The basic d' Arsonal movement can be converted into a d.c. voltmeter with the addition of a series resistor, or multiplier, as shown in Fig. 2. The multiplier limits the current through the movement so as not to exceed the value of the full-scale deflection current (I_{fsd}).

It is connected across a source of e.m.f. or a circuit component. The meter terminals are generally marked positive and negative since polarity must be observed.

The value of a multiplier, required to extend the voltage ranges is given below

$$R_s = (m - 1) R_m$$

Where

I_m = deflection current of the movement (I_{fsd})

R_m = internal resistance of the movement

R_s = multiplier resistance, and

V = full-range voltage of the instrument

DC Ammeter

The coil winding of the PMMC movement is small and light and it can carry only very small currents. When large currents are to be measured, it is necessary to bypass the major part of the current through a resistance called a shunt, as shown in Fig. 3. Clearly,

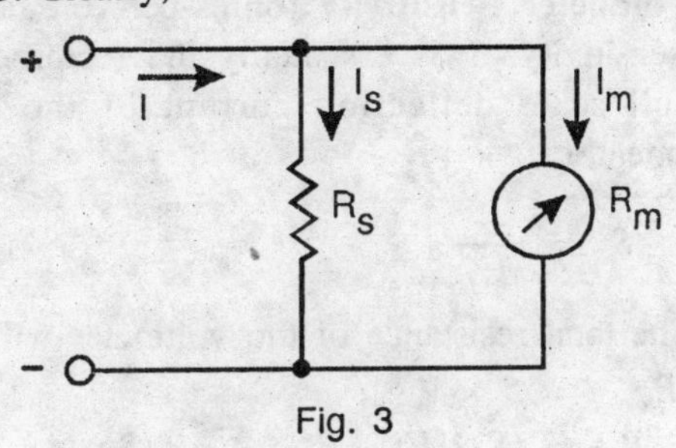

Fig. 3

Shunt Resistance

$$R_{sh} = \frac{R_m}{(m-1)}$$

Where

R_m = internal resistance of the movement (the coil)

R_{sh} = resistance of the shunt

I_m = full-scale deflection current of the movement

I_s = shunt current, and

I = full-scale current of the ammeter including the shunt

m = Total current/current for full scale deflection

Precautions

(a) An ammeter should never be connected across a source of e.m.f., otherwise it would draw damaging high currents as its resistance is low and as a result the delicate movement would be destroyed. It is always connected in series with a load so that the current is limited.

(b) The correct polarity should be observed. Reverse polarity causes the meter to deflect against the mechanical stop and this may damage the pointer.

(c) When using a multi-range meter, first the highest current range should be used. Then decrease the current range until substantial deflection is obtained. To increase accuracy of the observation, use the range that will give a reading as near to full-scale as possible.

Voltmeter Sensitivity (ohms-per-volt rating): The sensitivity, S, is essentially the reciprocal of the full scale deflection current of the basic movement, or

$$S = \frac{1}{I_{fsd}}$$

The total resistance of the voltmeter will be

$$R_{total} = S \times V$$

And $R_s = (S \times V) - R_m$

where

S = sensitivity of the voltmeter, in Ω/V

V = the voltage range as set by the range switch

R_m = internal resistance of the movement (plus the previous series resistors)

R_s = resistance of the multiplier

Alternating-Current Indicating Instruments

If the PMMC movement carries an alternating current with positive and negative half cycles, the driving torque would be in one direction for the positive alternation, and in the other direction for the negative alternation. If the frequency of the a.c. is very low, the pointer would swing back and forth around the zero point on the meter scale.

To measure a.c. on a d' Arsonval movement, the signal can be made unidirectional by rectification of the a.c. Other methods use the heating effect of the alternating current to produce an indication of its magnitude.

Ohm-meter

These are the instruments used to measure resistance. It is mainly of two types:

1. Series-type ohm-meter.
2. Shunt-type ohm-meter.

The Series-type Ohm-meter: It essentially consists of d' Arsonval movement connected in series with a resistance and a battery to a pair of terminals to which the unknown resistance is connected. The current through the movement then depends on the magnitude of the unknown resistor and the meter indication is proportional to the value of the unknown resistance provided that calibration problems are taken into account. Fig.4 shows the elements of single-range series ohm-meter.

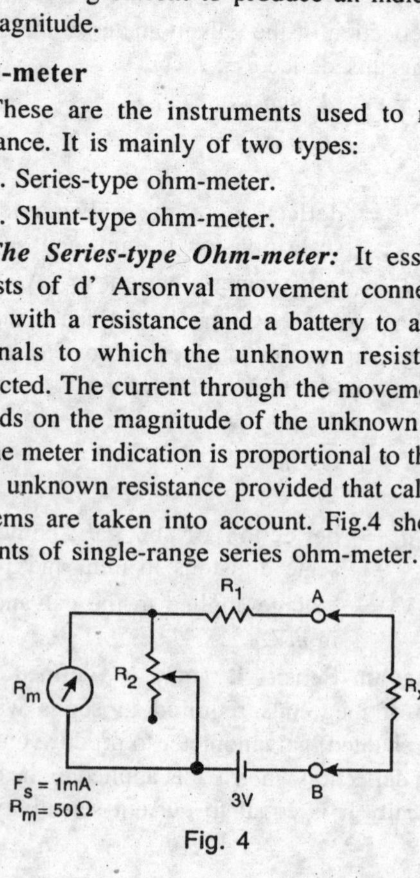

Fig. 4

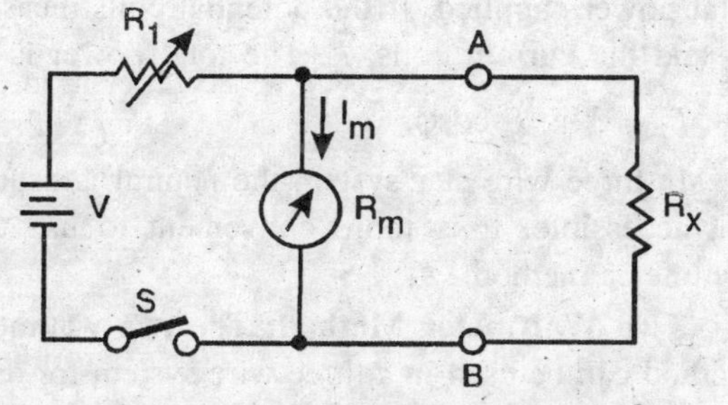

Fig. 5

When $R_c = 0$ (terminals *A* and *B* shorted), maximum current flows in the circuit under this condition and shunt resistor R_2 is adjusted until the movement indicates full-scale current. The full-scale current position of the pointer is marked 0 ohm on the scale. When $R_x = \infty$ (terminals *A* and *B* open), the current drops to zero and movement indicates zero current which is marked '∞' on the scale. Intermediate markings may be placed on the scale by connecting different known values of R_x to the instrument.

Shunt-type Ohm-meter: The circuit diagram of a shunt type ohmmeter is shown in Fig 5. In this circuit, it is necessary to have an off-on switch to disconnect the battery from the circuit when the circuit is not used. When $R_x = 0$ (*A* and *B* shorted), the meter current is zero. If $R_x = \infty$ (*A* and *B* open), a current finds a path only through the meter and by appropriate selection of the value of R_1, the pointer can be made to read full scale. This ohm-meter has zero mark at the left hand of scale (no current) and infinite mark at the right hand side of the scale. It is particularly used for low value resistors.

Electrodynamometer

It is one of the most important a.c. movement and is often used in accurate a.c. voltmeters and ammeters, not only at the power line frequency but also in the lower audience frequency range. With some slight modifications the electrodynamometer can be used as a wattmeter, varmeter, a power-factor, or a frequency meter.

The electrodynamometer uses the current under measurement to produce the necessary field flux.

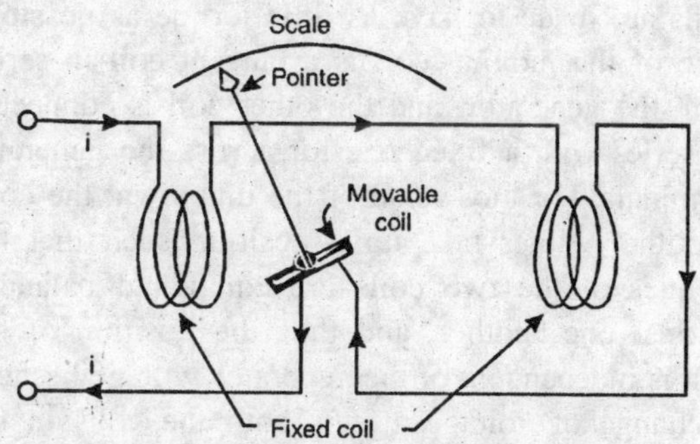

Fig. 6

Fig. 6 shows a schematic arrangement of the parts of this movement. A fixed coil, split into two equal halves, provides the magnetic field in which the movable coil rotate. The two coil halves are connected in series with the moving coil and are fed by the current under measurement. The fixed coils are spaced far enough apart to allow passage of the shaft of the movable coil. The movable coil carriers a pointer which is balanced by counterweight. Its rotation is controlled by springs, similar to the d' *Arsonval* movement construction. The complete assembly is surrounded by a laminated shield to protect the instrument from stray magnetic fields which may affect its operation. Damping is provided by aluminium air vanes, moving in sector-shaped chambers. The entire movement is very solid and rigidly constructed in order to keep its mechanical dimensions stable and its calibration intact.

The torque developed by a coil suspended in a magnetic field is given by

$$T = B \times A \times I \times N$$

The scale of the electrodynamometer is usually calibrated in terms of the r.m.s. or effective value of the a.c.

Megger (Insulation Tester)

It consists of a permanent magnet, closed-coil meter and a power supply that may be either a hand driven generator or a rectified a.c. supply as shown in the Fig. 7. The two torque opposing coils are mounted rigidly together on a shaft that carries the pointer. The spirals that conduct current from the coils are made to have as little torque as possible. One of the moving coil is a current coil in series with the generator, and the other coil is connected in series with a fixed resistor across the generator terminals. For any value of the unknown, the coils and the pointer take up a position such that the torques of the two coils are equal and balanced against one another, and thus the position of the coil is independent of the generator voltage because a change of voltage affects both the coils in the same proportion. The scale of the meter can be calibrated directly in the resistance value, with zero at one end and infinity at the other. The scale distribution depends upon the series resistor and on the shape of the magnet poles.

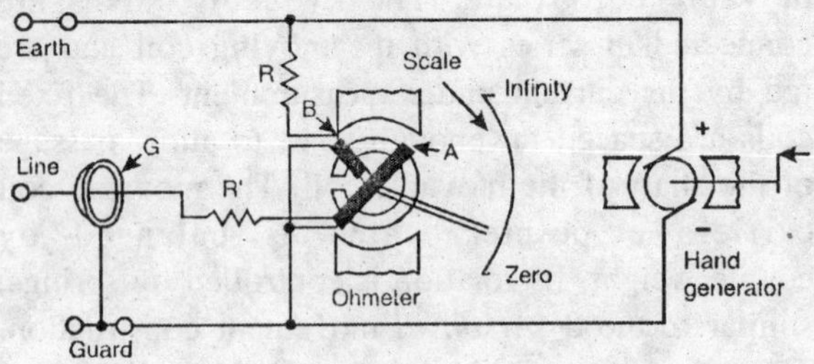

Fig. 7

The megger is used very commonly to measure the insulation resistance of electrical machinery insulators, insulation bushings, and so on. The test is made with a moderately high voltage stress on the insulation. The generator (or the rectified a.c. supply) are made in different models for 100, 500, 1000, 2500 or 5000 volts.

Polyphase Wattmeter

Power measurement in a polyphase system require the use of two or more wattmeters. The total real power is then found by algebraically adding the readings of the individual wattmeters. If the neutral wire of the three-phase system is also present as in case of four-wire star-connected load, three wattmeters would be needed to make the total real power measurement.

Three Wattmeter Method: In this method, three wattmeters are connected, one in each phase. The three wattmeter readings add upto give the total power supplied. If the potential coils measure V_p and the current coils, I_p. The total power is

$$P_T = 3\ V_p\ I_p\ \cos\varphi.$$

In three wire star system the neutral is usually not accessible. It is more convenient to use two wattmeter method.

Two Wattmeter Method: The two wattmeter method can be used in a three wire system for delta or star connected load.

The total power in a three-phase system = $\sqrt{3}\ V_L I_L\ \cos\ \phi$. This can prove that the power in three wire system is the sum of the readings of the two wattmeters. This method is also used to calculate the phase angle φ.

$$\tan\varphi = \sqrt{3}\ \frac{P_2 - P_1}{P_2 + P_1} \quad \text{for balanced load.}$$

Reactive Power Measurements: The reactive power is given by

$$P_r = VI \sin\varphi$$

It indicates the exchange of power between the source and the load due to the reactance of the circuit. *Reactive* power can be measured by an instrument called the **varmeter**.

A varmeter is in effect a wattmeter in which the current in its potential coil has been shifted to lag the applied potential by 90°. Fig. 8 shows the modified circuit of the varmeter. The current in the potential moving coil has been shifted 90° by means of a tapped inductor and a shunt resistor. The meter is now sensitive to reactive power and is calibrated in vars.

In three-phase three-wire system, the reactive power is given by

$$P_r = V_L I_L \sin\varphi$$

The reactive power in single phase varmeter is connected as shown in Fig 8. The meter reading must be multiplied by $\sqrt{3}$ when the meter is not calibrated for three-phase measurements.

Watt-Hour Meter or Energy Meter

It is used for the commercial measurement of electrical energy. Fig. 8 shows the element of a single-phase watt-hour meter.

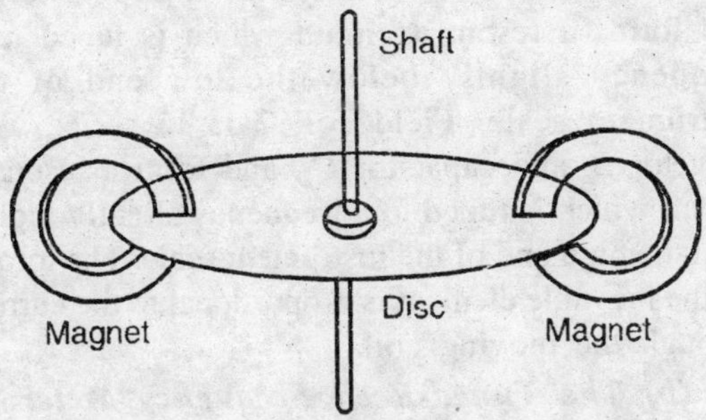

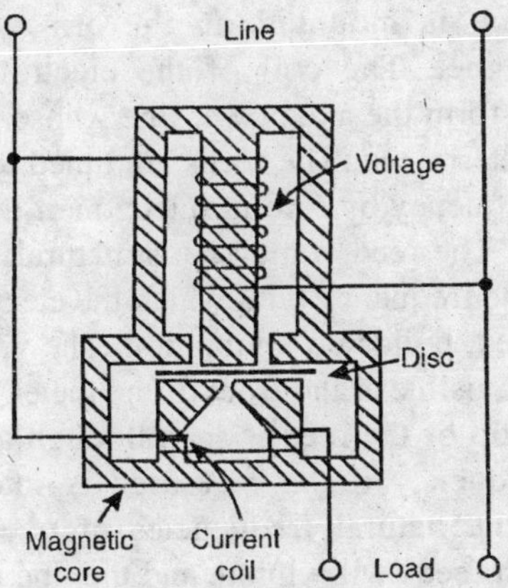

Fig. 8

The current coil is connected in series with the line and the voltage coil is connected across the line. Both coils are wound on a metal of special design providing two magnetic circuits. A light aluminium disc is suspended in the air gap of the current coil field which causes eddy currents to flow in the disc. The reaction of the eddy currents and the field of voltage coil creates a torque on the disc, causing it to rotate. The number of rotations of the disc is proportional to the energy consumed by the load in certain time interval.

At very light loads, the voltage component of the field produces zero torque that is not directly proportional to the load. Compensation for error is provided by inserting a shading coil with the meter operating at 10 per cent of rated load. Two holes are drilled in the disc of energy meter on the opposite side of the spindle to eliminate creeping on no load.

Power-Factor Meter

It essentially measures the cosine of phase angle between voltage and current. The most common type is *crossed coil* power-factor meter. This instrument is basically an electrodynamometer movement where the moving element consists of two coils, mounted on the same shaft but at right angles to each other. The moving coils rotate in the magnetic field provided by the field coil that carries the line current.

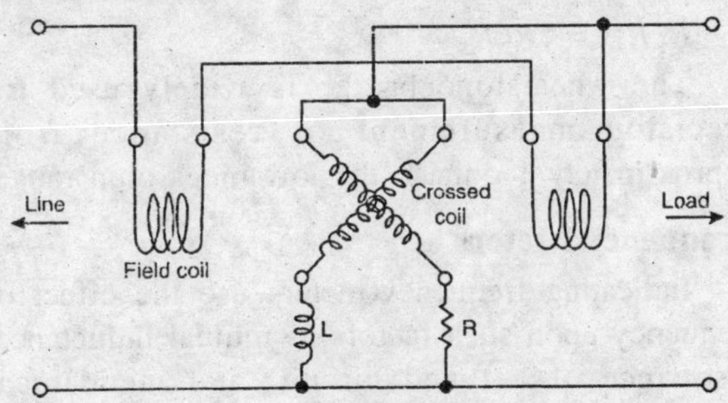

Fig. 9

The connections for this meter in a single-phase circuit are shown in Fig. 9. The field coil is connected as usual in series with the line and carries the line current. One coil of the movable element is connected in series with an inductor across the lines. Since no control springs are used, the balance position of the movable element depends on the resulting torque developed by the two crossed coils. When the movable element is in a balanced position, the contribution to the total torque by each element must be equal but of opposite sign.

The developed torque in each coil is a function of the current through the coil and therefore depends on the impedance of that coil circuit. The torque is also proportional to the mutual inductance between each part of the crossed coil and the stationary field coil. This mutual inductance depends on the angular position of the crossed-coil elements with respect to the position of the stationary field coil. When the movable element is at balance, it can be shown that its angular displacement is a function of the phase angle between line current (field coil) and line voltage (crossed coil). The indication of the pointer which is connected to the movable element, is calibrated directly in terms of the phase-angle or power-factor.

Wheatstone Bridge

It is used for the measurement of d.c. resistance and a simple version is shown in Fig. 10. The bridge has four resistor arms together with a source of emf and a null detector (usually a galvanometer). The bridge is said to be balanced when the potential difference across the galvanometer is zero volt so that there is no current through the galvanometer. Hence the bridge is balanced.

When,

$$R_1 R_4 = R_2 R_3$$

The wheatstone bridge is widely used for precision measurement of resistance from approximately 1 ohm to the low mega-ohm range.

Frequency Meters

Indicating frequency-meters use the effect of frequency upon such factors as mutual inductance, resonance of a tuned circuit, and mechanical resonance.

(a) Electrodynamometer type Frequency Meter: It is shown in Fig. 11. Here the field coil form part of two separated resonant circuits. Field

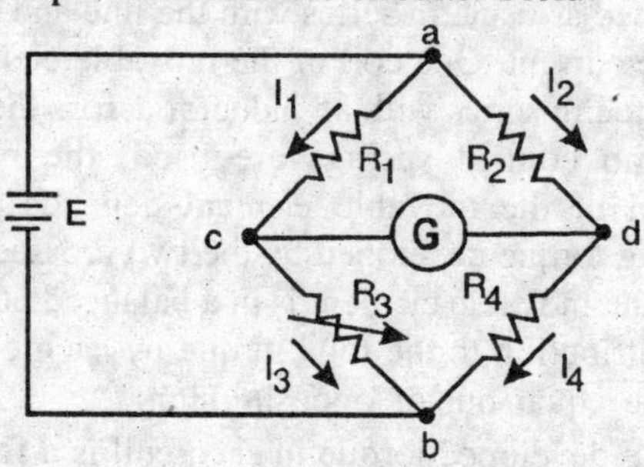

Fig. 10

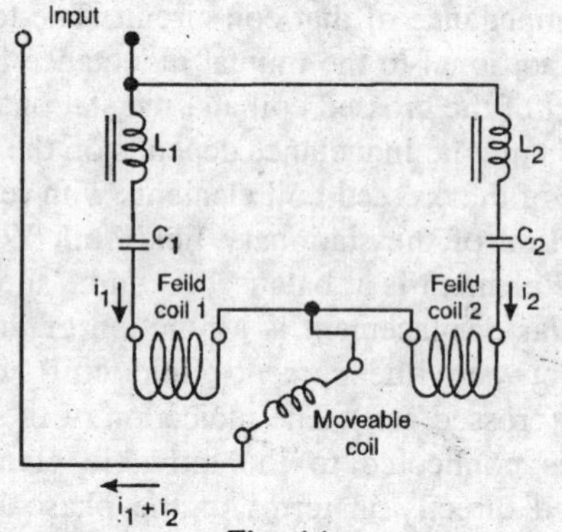

Fig. 11

coil 1 is in series with inductor L_1 and capacitor C_2 and forms a resonant circuit which is tuned to a frequency slightly below the low end of the instrument scale. Field coil 2 is in series with inductor L_2 and capacitor C_2, and form a resonant circuit which is tuned to a frequency slightly higher than the high end of the instrument scale. The torque on the movable element is proportional to the current through the moving coil.

(b) The Tuned-Reed Frequency Meter: It operates on the principle of mechanical resonance. A series of reeds is fastened to a flexible common base which is mounted on the armature of an electromagnet. The coil of the electromagnet is energized form the a.c. power line whose frequency is to be determined. The reeds are tuned to an exact natural frequency by careful selection of their length and mass. The reed, which has a natural frequency equal to the frequency with which the electromagnet is energized, builds up a vibration. The vibration of the reed is visible at the front of the meter where the vibrating tip of the reed is seen through a window. If the frequency to be measured is intermediate between the natural frequencies of two adjacent reeds, both reeds will vibrate and the line frequency will be closest to the reed with the largest vibration. Interpolation between the natural frequencies of the reeds can be made very easily and accurately, since the reed frequencies are exact.

Oscilloscope

An oscilloscope (referred to as a *CRO*) is a universal measuring instrument capable of measuring a wide variety of rapidly changing electrical signals. The signals may be repetitive or may occur only once and last for a fraction of a microsecond. It presents a picture of the exact signal as a function of time. The oscilloscope graphs the changes in signal amplitude on its vertical axis and time, *i.e.*, how long the event lasts on its horizontal axis. With the oscilloscope, the user can determine the signal's polarity, amplitude and duration. Oscilloscopes are also available which can store the signal trace until observed or in some units a second signal can be stored for direct comparison. These oscilloscopes are called *storage scopes.*

Frequency Measurement

1. Direct Method: A signal frequency is determined by measuring its time period T and calculating the frequency by $f\,(\text{hertz}) = \dfrac{1}{T}$ (seconds). The input waveform is fed into the vertical input, with vertical sensitivity sweep speed and triggering controls are adjusted for at least one complete stable cycle of waveform.

2. Lissajous Method: In this method the unknown signal waveform is fed into vertical input of the scope, and horizontal input of the oscilloscope is fed through a known frequency oscillator. With the sweep generator set to off, if both inputs are at same frequency, a circular pattern will appear on the screen. If the frequency to be measured is higher than the known frequency range, Lissajous pattern will result as shown in Fig 12.

The frequency ratio is found by

$$f_v = \frac{n_h \cdot f_h}{n_v}$$

where f_v = unknown frequency

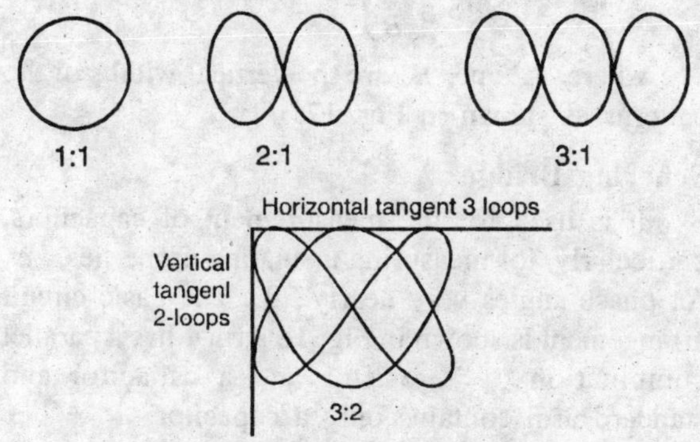

Fig. 12

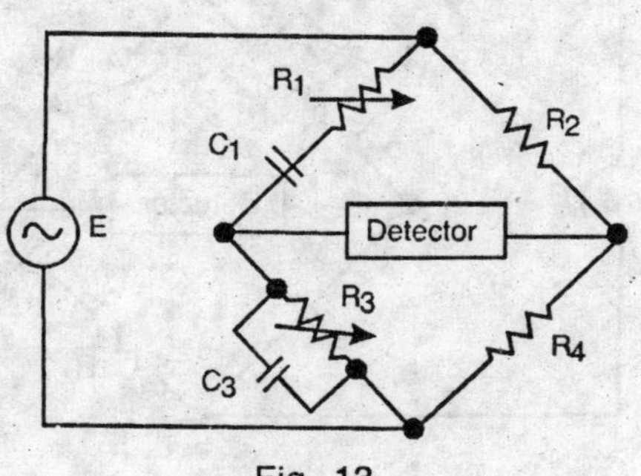

Fig. 13

f_h = known frequency

n_h = number of loops touching the horizontal tangent line, and

n_v = number of loops touching the vertical tangent line.

Wien Bridge: The Wein bridge has a series RC combination in one arm and a parallel RC combination in the adjoining arm as shown in Fig. 13. The frequency of the applied voltage is

$$f = \frac{1}{2\,\pi\,RC}$$

Wien bridge is used as a notch filter in harmonic distortion analyzer. It is used in audio and HF oscillators as frequency- determining elements.

Hay Bridge

Hay Bridge shown in Fig. 14, differs from the Maxwell bridge in having resistor R_1 in series with standard capacitor C_1 instead of being in parallel.

The value of R_x and L_x are given by

$$R_x = \frac{\omega^2 C_1^2 R_1 R_2 R_3}{1+\omega^2 C_1^2 R_1^2}$$

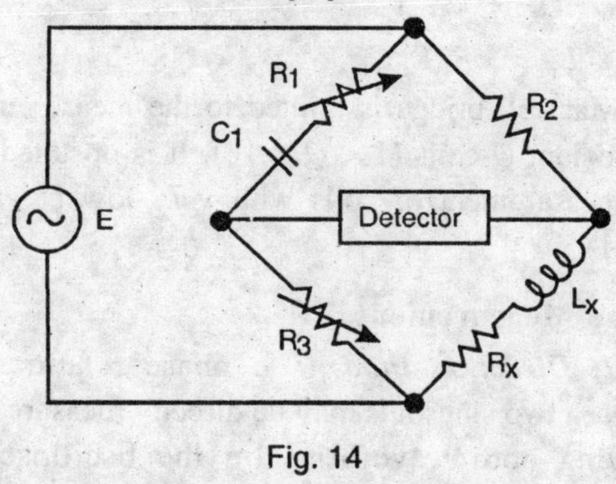

Fig. 14

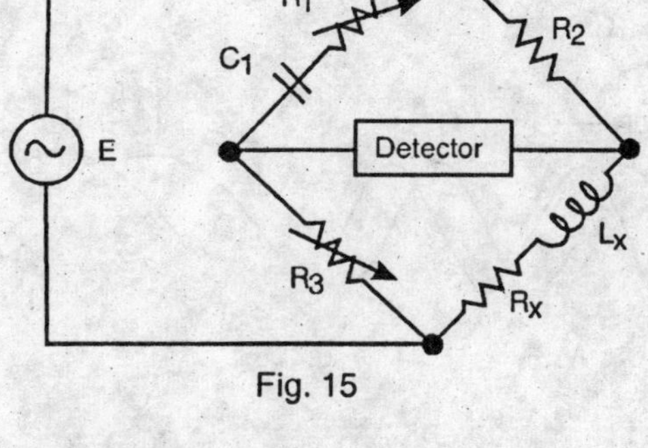

Fig. 15

$$L_x = \frac{R_2 R_3 C_1}{1+\omega^2 C_1^2 R_1^2}$$

Hay bridge is suited for the measurement of high-Q inductors having Q more than 10.

Null Detectors: There are basically three types of null detectors:

1. The pointer type galvanometer having sensitivity from 1 μA to 0.1 μA per scale division.

2. The reflecting galvanometer with enclosed lamp and scale. It has high sensitivity range of 0.1 μA to 0.01 μA per scale division.

3. Electronic null detector having excellent sensitivity at high input impedance.

Maxwell Bridge: It is shown in Fig. 15 and it measures an unknown inductance in terms of known capacitance. One of the ratio arms has a resistance and capacitance in parallel.

$$R_x = \frac{R_2 R_3}{R_1}$$

$$L_x = R_1 R_3 C_1$$

Maxwell bridge is limited to the measurement of medium Q-coils ($1 < Q < 10$). It is unsuited for the measurement of coils with very low Q value $Q < 1$).

Phase Measurement

1. Direct Method: The phase relationship between two sinusoids may be directly measured by viewing both waveforms on the oscilloscope and the delay line T_d between the two waveforms and the time period T is determined as shown in Fig. 16.

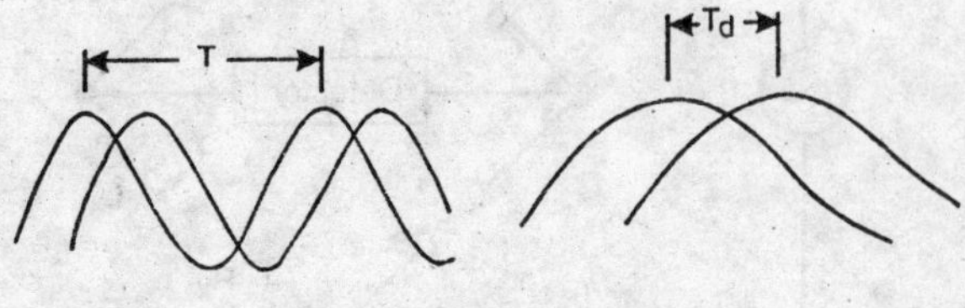

Fig. 16

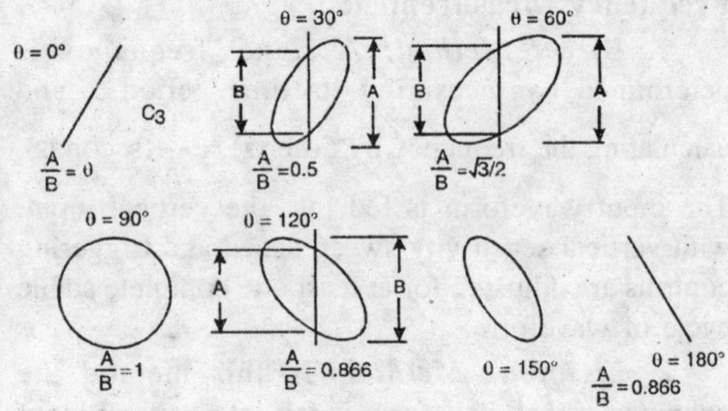

Fig. 17

The phase is determined by

$$\text{phase delay in (deg)} = \frac{T_d}{T} \times 360$$

2. Lissajous Method: In this method, one waveforms is fed into the vertical input, while the other fed into horizontal input. The sweep generator is set to the off position. The vertical and horizontal gains are adjusted for a reasonable pattern. The phase shift θ is determined by.

$$\theta = \sin^{-1}\left(\frac{A}{B}\right)$$

where 'A' and 'B' are the vertical widths of the patterns as shown in Fig. 17.

Schering Bridge

It is used for the measurement of capacitors, particularly, for measuring insulating properties, *i.e.*, for phase angles very nearly 90°. The basic circuit arrangement is shown in Fig. 18 Arm 1 has a parallel combination of a resistor and a capacitor and standard arm contains only a capacitor.

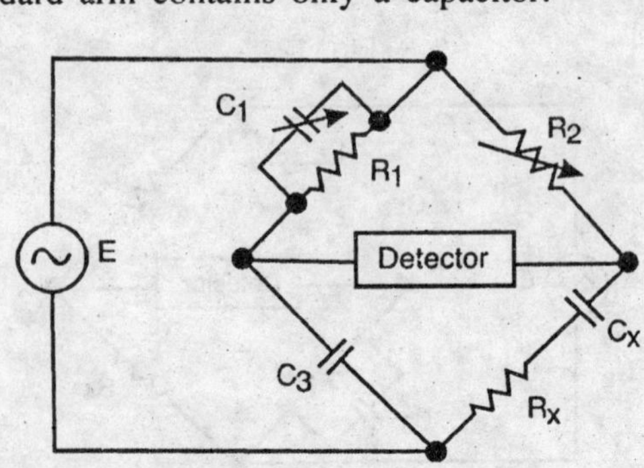

Fig. 18

The value for R_x and C_x are given by

$$R_x = \frac{R_2 C_1}{C_3}$$

$$C_x = C_3 \frac{R_1}{R_2}$$

Power factor

$$\cong \frac{R_x}{X_x} = \omega C_x R_x$$

AC Bridges

AC bridge shown in Fig. 19 consists of four bridge arms, a source of excitation and a null detector. The power source supplies an a.c. voltage to the bridge at the desired frequency. At higher frequencies, an oscillator generally supplies the excitation voltage. The null detector must respond to a.c. unbalance currents and in its cheapest form consists of a pair of headphones. Other null detectors may be a.c. amplifier with an output meter or an electron ray tube indicator.

The condition for bridge balance is

$$\overline{Z}_1 \overline{Z}_4 = \overline{Z}_2 \overline{Z}_3$$

Q-Meter

The Q meter is an instrument designed to measure some of the electrical properties of coils and capacitors. Its operation is based on the familiar characteristics of a series resonant circuit that the voltage across the coil or capacitor is equal to the applied voltage times the Q of the circuit (see Fig. 20).

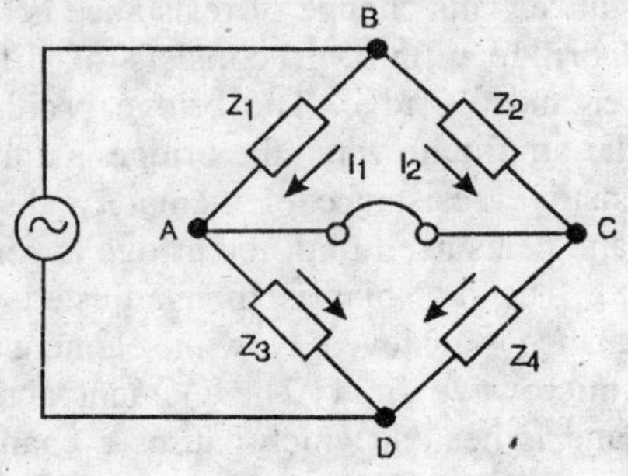

Fig. 19

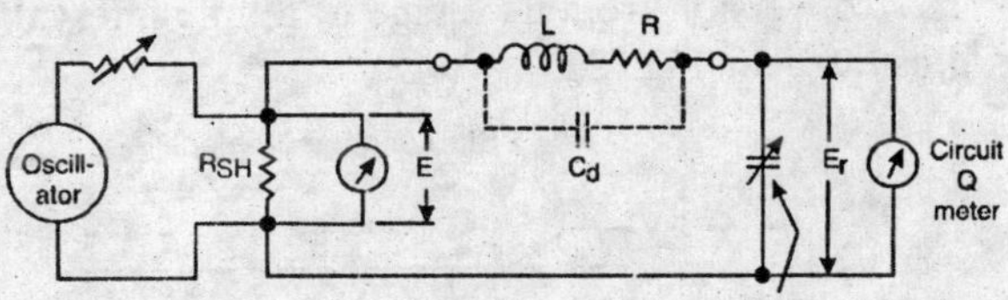

Fig. 20

To make a measurement, the unknown coil is connected to the test terminals of the instrument and the circuit is tuned to resonance either by setting the oscillator to a given frequency and varying the internal resonating capacitor. The reading Q on the output meter must be multiplied by the index setting of the Q meter to obtain the actual Q value.

The inductance of the coii can be calculated from the known values of frequency f and resonating capacitance C. Since

$$X_L = X_C \text{ and } L = \frac{1}{(2\pi f)^2 C} \text{ Henry}$$

Digital Voltmeters

The digital voltmeter (DVM) displays measurements of d.c. or a.c. voltages or discrete numerals instead of a pointer deflection on a continuous scale as in analog devices.

Advantages of digital voltmeter are:

1. It reduces human reading and Interpolation errors.
2. It eliminates parallax error.
3. It increases reading speed.
4. It provides output in digital form suitable for reading.

Digital voltmeters can be classified as

(a) Ramp-type *DVM*
(b) Integrating *DVM*
(c) Continuous balance *DVM*
(d) Successive approximation *DVM*

Ramp-type DVM: The operating principle of the ramp-type *DVM* is based on the measurement of the time it takes for a linear ramp voltage to raise from zero to the level of the input voltage or to decrease from the level of the input voltage to zero. This time interval t is measured with an electronic time-interval counter and the count is displayed as a number of digits on electronic indicating devices.

Conversion from a voltage to a time interval is illustrated in Fig. 21

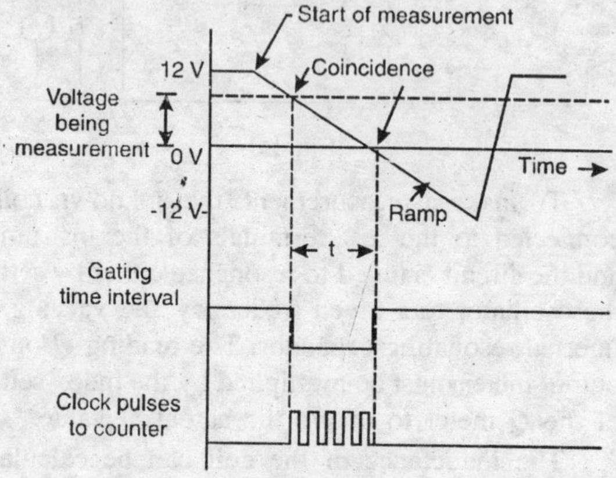

Fig. 21

At the start of the measurement cycle, a ramp voltage is initiated. This voltage can be positive-going or negative going. The negative-going ramp is continuously compared with the unknown input voltage. At the instant the ramp voltage equals the unknown voltage, a coincidence circuit generates a pulse which opens a gate as shown in Fig 22.

The ramp voltage continues to decrease with time until finally it reaches zero voltage and a second comparator generates clock pulse which closes the gate. An oscillator generates clock pulses which are allowed to pass through the gate to a number of decade counting units which totalize the number of pulses passed through the gate. The decimal number displayed by the display system associated with the counter is a measure of magnitude of input voltage.

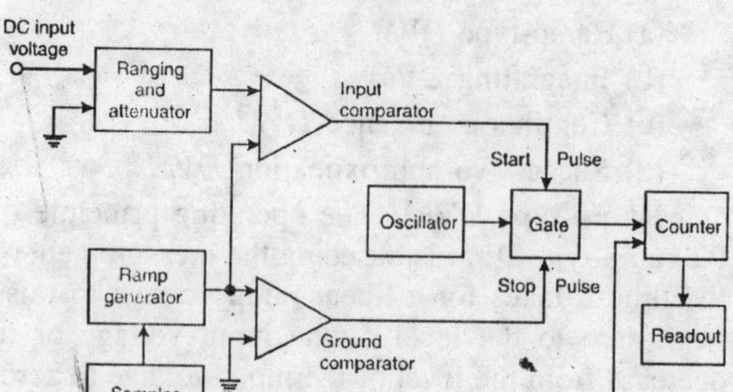

Fig. 22

Calorimeter Type Power Meter

The basic principle of operation of the calorimeter type power meter is quite simple as illustrated in Fig. 23. A resistor is heated by the signal to be measured. The resistor is in a completely enclosed, well insulated fluid bath. The insulation of the walls of the bath are such that very little heat is allowed to radiate from the bath. If the bath temperature is measured before and after the signal is applied, the difference in temperature is a measure of the heat developed by the resistor. Knowing the volume, the specific heat of the fluid and the characteristics of the bath, the power can be calculated. The need to know the exact mass and specific heat of calorimeter bath material restricts the usage of the basic calorimeter power meter.

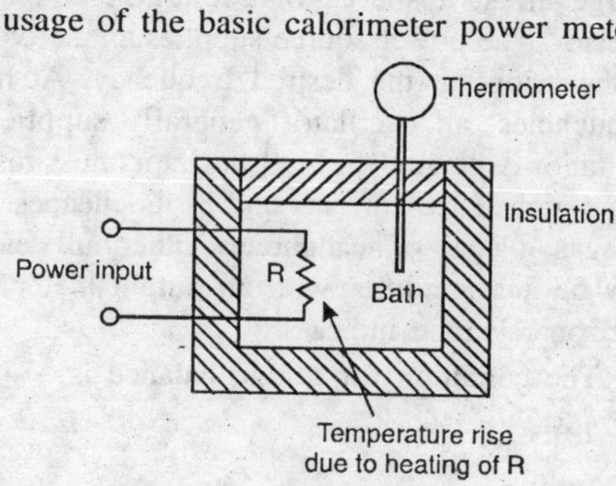

Fig. 23

Bolometer

The bolometer is basically a bridge circuit where one of the arms contains a temperature sensitive resistor. The temperature-sensitive resistor is balanced in the field of microwave signal whose power is to be measured. The power is absorbed by the resistor and the heat generated causes a change in resistance. This change of resistance is measured with a bridge circuit. It consists of differential amplifier and a bridge. The bridge oscillates at a particular amplitude when the bridge is unbalanced. The sensitive resistance elements R_T absorbs the power and heats itself until the bridge is very nearly balanced. The d.c. bias is then adjusted until the exact balance is achieved. Now the element is placed in the microwave field. The element absorbs the power and is heated, which causes a change in its resistance, thereby unbalancing the bridge. The unbalance is in a direction opposite to that of initial cold resistance. This action causes the output form the oscillator to decrease so as to effect the balance. The EVM circuit measures the amount of this power-decrease from the oscillator and displays the measurement as a power which is supplied by the microwave field.

EXERCISE

1. The source of energy for operating an ohmmeter is obtained from
(a) the line being measured
(b) any 120 volt source
(c) a rectifier cell
(d) a battery

2. Two voltmeters of 0-300 V range are connected in parallel to an ac circuit. One voltmeter is moving iron type and reads 200 V. If the other voltmeter is moving coil type, its reading will be
(a) $200\sqrt{3}$ V
(b) 200×1.41 V
(c) slightly less than 200 V
(d) zero

3. Electrostatic instruments
(a) can be used on dc only
(b) when used on ac measure rms value whatever the waveform
(c) are highly sensitive to eddy current errors
(d) none of these

4. An accurate ammeter must have a resistance of
(a) high value (b) low value
(c) very low value (d) none

5. In a two wattmeter method of measuring power in a 3-phase system one of the wattmeters reads negative implying
(a) wattmeter connection is faulty
(b) load is unbalanced
(c) power flow is in the reverse direction
(d) power factor is less then 0.5

6. Two 200 V D.C. voltmeters having resistances of 15 k-ohm and 10 k-ohm are connected in series. The safe voltage which can be measured by this combination will be
(a) 400 V (b) $200\sqrt{2}$ V
(c) 200 V (d) 100 V

7. Quadrant type electrostatic instruments can be used for measurement of ac voltage
(a) only when heterostatically connected.
(b) only when idiostatically connected.
(c) in either heterostatic connection or idiostatic connection
(d) not at all

8. To measure 2 volts, if one selects 0-100 volt range voltmeter which is accurate within ±1%, the error in his/her measurement may be upto
(a) ± 0.02 % (b) ± 1 %
(c) ± 2 % (d) ± 50 %

9. The ratio of maximum displacement deviation to full scale deviation of the instrument is called the
(a) static sensitivity (b) accuracy
(c) linearity (d) precision
(e) dynamic deviation

10. Before connecting a meter to measure an unknown current or voltage, it is best to
(a) start with the highest range and work down
(b) start with the lowest range and work up
(c) select an estimated mid-range
(d) use the trial and error method

11. The rectifier instrument is not free from
(a) temperature error (b) frequency error
(c) Wave shape error (d) all of the above

12. Which of the following is not the method for reducing residual inductance in resistors?
(a) Faraday's winding method
(b) Card wound resistor
(c) Chaperon winding method
(d) Curtis and Arower winding method

13. Electrodynamometers are used extensively for the measurement of
(a) magnetic lines of force
(b) resistivity
(c) capacitor networks
(d) power

14. Which of the following meter mechanisms is adaptable to a greater variety of measurement?
(a) Inclined coil
(b) Moving-iron vane
(c) Electrodynamometer
(d) Permanent magnet-moving coil

15. Which of the following does not have the same units as the others? The symbols have their usual meanings.
(a) $\frac{L}{R}$ (b) R C
(c) $\sqrt{LC}$ (d) $\frac{1}{\sqrt{LC}}$

16. An alternator is being synchronized to the bus-bars of frequency 50 Hz. The synchroscope lamp flickers at a frequency of 5Hz. The frequency of the alternator is
(a) 45 Hz (b) 55 Hz
(c) 45 of 55 Hz (d) none of the above

17. For measuring a low resistance by ammeter-voltmeter method, the voltmeter is connected directly across the resistance under measurement
(a) there is an error in measurement as the ammeter measures current flowing through the voltmeter in addition to the current flowing through the resistance under measurement
(b) there is an error in measurement as the voltmeter measures voltage drop across the ammeter in addition to that across the resistance under measurement
(c) both (a) and (b)
(d) none of above

18. Which of the following is not an advantage of semi-conductor gauges as compared to conventional strain gauges?
(a) Excellent hysteresis characteristics
(b) Least sensitive to temperature changes
(c) High fatigue life
(d) Smaller size

19. Using a C.T. has
(a) poorer overload capacity than a P.T.
(b) the same overload capacity as a P.T.
(c) a higher overload capacity than a P.T.
(d) none of these

20. Capacitor potential transformers are used
(a) for primary voltage exceeding 100 kv (phase)
(b) because these are cheaper than the conventional type above a certain voltage
(c) for keeping the transformation ratio constant irrespective of the burden with certain adjustments
(d) all of the above

21. Half wave rectifier type AC meters are used as voltmeters. They cannot be used as ammeters because
(a) pointer would oscillate with AC
(b) AC current would be too small to read
(c) AC current would be excessive
(d) AC is changed to DC

22. In indicating instruments the damping is usually adjusted
(a) at critical value
(b) to the value slightly below critical value
(c) to the value slightly higher than critical value
(d) to any value

23. On testing an electric iron on megger, the reading of the megger is infinity. This indicates
(a) short circuit of the heating element
(b) short circuit of the supply terminal
(c) loose terminal connections
(d) open circuit of the heating element

24. W_1 and W_2 are the readings of two wattmeters used to measure power of a 3-phase balanced load. The reactive power drawn by the load is
(a) $W_1 + W_2$ (b) $W_1 - W_2$
(c) $\sqrt{3}(W_1 + W_2)$ (d) $\sqrt{3}(W_1 - W_2)$

25. A man holds both the terminals of a 500 V megger, but still safe due to
(a) high voltage
(b) very low current
(c) high resistance of the body
(d) low resistance of the body

26. The function of a shunt in an ammeter is to
(a) increase the instrument resistance
(b) bypass the current
(c) reduce the voltage drop across the instrument coil
(d) increase the current flowing through the instrument coil

27. The reading of the megger is 30 Mega ohms while testing the insulation resistance of the wire. The wire can be
(a) suitable for installation
(b) not suitable for installation
(c) semi-suitable for the installation
(d) none of these

28. In a single phase induction type energy meter, the lag adjustment is affected to
(a) make the series magnet flux to lag behind the applied voltage by 90°
(b) the shunt magnet flux to lag behind the applied voltage by 90°
(c) the shunt magnet flux in phase with the applied voltage
(d) the series magnet flux in phase with the applied voltage

29. The most commonly used type of single phase energy meter is
(a) dynamometer type (b) electrostatic type
(c) induction type (d) moving coil type

30. Piezo-electric transducers work when we apply to it
(a) heat (b) mechanical force
(c) vibrations (d) illumination

31. For testing of energy meters phantom load is used to
(a) isolate the current and voltage circuits
(b) test meters of low current rating
(c) reduce power losses during testing
(d) test meters of large current rating for which loads may not be available in the testing laboratory and reduce power losses during testing

32. The sensitivity of a potentiometer can be improved by
(a) reducing the current flowing through the potentiometer wire
(b) reducing the length of potentiometer wire
(c) increasing the length of potentiometer wire
(d) reducing the resistance of the rheostat connected in series with the battery

33. Which of the following are piezo-electric substances?
1. Barium titanate
2. Lead titanate
3. Lead Zirconate
4. Cadmimum sulphate
(a) 1, 2 and 4 (b) 1, 3 and 4
(c) 1, 2 and 3 (d) 2, 3 and 4

34. Piezometer is used to measure
(a) pressure in pipes and channels
(b) very high pressure
(c) very low pressure
(d) difference of pressure between two points

35. The bridge used for the measurement of dielectric loss of capacitance is
(a) Anderson bridge (b) Maxwell bridge
(c) Hay bridge (d) Schering bridge

36. Certain types of materials generate an electrostatic charge or voltage when mechanical force is applied across them. Such materials are called the
(a) piezo-electric (b) photo-electric
(c) thermo-electric (d) none of these

37. The dissipation factor of capacitor can be measured by using a
(a) Potentiometer (b) Campbell bridge
(c) Schering bridge (d) Galvanometer

38. Capacitive transducers have the advantages of
(a) very high input impedance, excellent frequency response, high sensitivity, and not being affected by stray magnetic fields
(b) very high output impedance
(c) both (a) and (b)
(d) none of the above

39. The most suitable transducer for monitoring continuously variations in very fine thickness (say of paper in paper industry) is

(a) inductive (b) capacitive
(c) ultrasonic (d) nuclear radiation

40. The main drawbacks of dc generator tachometers are

(a) maintenance problem of commutator and brushes
(b) distortion of main magnetic field giving rise to non-linear relationship between output voltage and rotational speed
(c) presence of a small superimposed ripple voltage because of finite number of conductors or coils
(d) all of the above

41. The oscilloscope is used to check what elements of a circuit?

(a) voltage, current, and resistance
(b) Voltage, current, and power
(c) Frequency, phase, and waveshape
(d) Frequency, power, and waveshape

42. Electric utility companies require frequency meters that indicates frequency within

(a) one cycle-per-second
(b) two cycles-per-second
(c) 60 cycles-per-second
(d) a fraction of a cycle-per-second

43. Inductive method can be used for measuring thickness of

(a) magnetic but non-conducting materials
(b) conducting but non-magnetic materials
(c) conducting and magnetic materials
(d) non-conducting and non-magnetic materials
(e) both magnetic and non-magnetic materials, as well as non-conducting and conducting materials

44. The inductance of the coil using Q-meter can be calculated by the expression

(a) $\frac{1}{2\pi fC}$ henry (b) $\frac{1}{(2\pi f)^2 C}$ henry
(c) $2\pi fC$ henry (d) $(2\pi f)^2 C$ henry

45. A thermo-couple arrangement is to be used to measure temperature in the range of 700-800°C. select the pair that would be most suitable for this application.

(a) copper-constantan
(b) iron-constantan
(c) chromel-alumel
(d) platinum-platinum rhodium

46. The speed transducer using a drag cup rotor has the main advantage of

(a) very high accuracy
(b) low energy requirement
(c) cheaper construction
(d) none of above

47. Moving iron instruments are usually used as

(a) standard instruments for calibration of other instruments owing to their higher accuracy and lower cost
(b) transfer type instruments as they indicate the same values for dc as well as ac measurements and are cheaper
(c) ordinary indicating instruments because of their robust construction
(d) none of these

48. In a dynamometer type moving coil instrument a swamping resistance is provided in order to

(a) control the deflecting torque
(b) reduce the bulk of the moving system
(c) reduce the current flowing through the moving coil
(d) provide equal time constant for moving coil and fixed coil, when used for ac measurement

49. In a force-balance transducer

(a) the output of the sensing element is amplified
(b) the output is fed back to an element which causes a force-summing member to return to its zero position
(c) the magnitude of the feedback determines the output of the transducer
(d) all of these

50. Low resistors are provided with four terminals in order to
(a) eliminate the thermo-electric emf effect
(b) facilitate the connection of current and voltage circuits
(c) make the resistance value definite irrespective of the nature of contacts at the current terminals
(d) eliminate the effect of connecting leads

51. In measurement of resistance by Carey Foster bridge no error is introduced due to
(a) contact resistance
(b) connecting leads
(c) thermo-electric emfs
(d) all of these

52. The sensitivity of a Wheatstone bridge depends upon
(a) galvanometer current sensitivity
(b) galvanometer resistance
(c) bridge supply voltage
(d) all of the above

53. The best method for the measurement of temperatures of hot bodies radiating energy in the visible spectrum is
(a) bolometer (b) optical pyrometers
(c) thermocouples (d) thermopile

54. The direction of current in case of antimony-bismuth thermocouple will be
(a) from antimony to bismuth at the cold junction
(b) from antimony to bismuth at the hot junction
(c) from bismuth to antimony at cold junction
(d) none of these

55. A Wheatstone bridge cannot be employed for measurement of very low resistance as it introduces error on account of
(a) contact resistance
(b) resistance of connecting leads
(c) thermo-electric emfs
(d) all of the above

56. Alternating current cannot be measured directly by
(a) hot-wire ammeter
(b) moving-iron ammeter
(c) moving-coil ammeter
(d) thermocouple type ammeter

57. A wattmeter is reading backwards in an experiment. Upscale reading can be obtained by reversing
(a) pressure coil connection only
(b) current coil connection only
(c) both pressure as well as current coil connections
(d) either the pressure connection or the current connection

58. Thermal zero-shift in an instrument refers to
(a) inaccuracy in measurement due to temperature
(b) maximum change in pen zero due to temperature
(c) shift in zero-adjustment due to expansion of springs due to temperature
(d) none of these

59. Swamping resistance is connected
(a) in series with a voltmeter coil and have the lowest temperature coefficient of resistance in order to reduce temperature error
(b) in series with an ammeter coil in order to reduce temperature error
(c) in series with a voltmeter coil and have the high temperature coefficient in order to reduce the temperature error
(d) in series with the ammeter to increase its range

60. A very accurate voltmeter gives inaccurate reading when used for measuring voltage across a low resistance because
(a) the meter sensitivity is too low
(b) the meter sensitivity is too high
(c) the voltmeter is taking too low current
(d) the higher scale has been selected

61. The position telemetering system using synchros is
(a) a pulse telemetering system
(b) an rf telemetering system
(c) a dc telemetering system
(d) an ac telemetering system

62. The non-contact method of measuring thickness or density of cold or hot materials while in motion or when stationary is
(a) inductive (b) capacitive
(c) nuclear radiation (d) ultrasonic

63. The Grassot fluxmeter has the following advantage(s) over ballistic galvanometer.
(a) The instrument is very portable and the scale is calibrated directly in wb-turns.
(b) The deflection is independent of the length of time taken for the change in flux causing the deflection.
(c) The instrument is more sensitive and more accurate.
(d) both (a) and (b)

64. Which of the following bridges is frequency sensitive?
(a) Wheatstone (b) Maxwell
(c) Anderson (d) Wien

65. A PMMC instrument can be used as a fluxmeter by
(a) using a low resistance shunt
(b) removing the control springs
(c) making the control springs of large moment of inertia
(d) using a high series resistance

66. What values are measured by the two separate bimetallic elements of a thermal wattmeter?
(a) Heater temperature and ambient temperature
(b) Voltage and current values
(c) kW and kVAR
(d) Kilowatts and kVA

67. The picture on an oscilloscope screen is produced by
(a) A Electron beam
(b) a moving vane
(c) a T-V type camera
(d) an intensity control

68. The main advantage of a strip-chart recorder is that it provides a
(a) record you can see at a glance
(b) record for long unattended periods
(c) daily record on a single sheet
(d) record of voltage and current, using the same instrument

59. A bridge used for measurement of dielectric loss and power factor is
(a) Maxwell's bridge (b) Wien's bridge
(c) Schering bridge (d) Owen bridge

70. When current transformers are not in use, the secondary should be
(a) fused
(b) open-circuited
(c) short-circuited
(d) grounded with the primary

71. Which of the following disturbance may permanently affect instrument accuracy?
(a) A short circuit on a nearby conductor
(b) Operating near an unshielded instrument
(c) Passing through a stray magnetic field
(d) All of the above

72. Volt-Box is basically a device used to
(a) measure the voltage
(b) measure the power
(c) extend the range of potentiometer
(d) measure the current

73. Induction type single-phase energymeter is
(a) an ampere-hour meter
(b) true watt-hour meter
(c) wattmeter
(d) none of these

74. Hysteresis error, in moving iron instruments, may be reduced by using
(a) mumetal or permalloy
(b) stainless steel
(c) silver coating
(d) high speed steel

75. Electrostatic voltmeters are particularly suitable for measuring high voltages because the construction is simplified due to
(a) large electrostatic forces
(b) small electrostatic forces
(c) large value of current
(d) small value of current

76. The zero-suppression control is different from pen-position control in the sense that static component is removed
(a) prior to attenuation
(b) after attenuation
(c) before amplification
(d) after amplification

77. The instrument used to measure frequency in waveguides is
(a) bolometer (b) cavity resonator
(c) galiometer (d) klystron

78. Q-meter is an instrument to measure
(a) mechanical properties of the coils only
(b) electrical properties of the coils only
(c) electrical properties of the capacitors only
(d) electrical properties of both the coils and capacitors

79. In indicating instruments, the springs are mainly used to
(a) hold the pivot in position
(b) conduct the current to the coils
(c) control the movement of the pointer
(d) reduce the vibrations of the pointer

80. Sensitivity of a potentiometer can be increased by
(a) decreasing the length of potentiometer wire
(b) increasing the length of potentiometer wire
(c) decreasing the current in potentiometer wire
(d) decreasing the resistance in the rheostat in series with the battery

81. A non-triggered oscilloscope
(a) has a continuously running time-base generator
(b) has no sweep generator
(c) cannot produce a stable stationary screen display
(d) can display a portion of the input signal waveform

82. The essential requirements of a sawtooth wave generator, in addition to a dc power source, are
(a) a switching device
(b) a resistor
(c) a capacitor
(d) all of the above

83. The potentiometer wire should have
(a) high specific resistance and high temperature coefficient
(b) high specific resistance and low temperature coefficient
(c) low specific resistance and high temperature coefficient
(d) low specific resistance and low temperature coefficient

84. Commonly used standard capacitor is
(a) concentric sphere type
(b) parallel plate type
(c) concentric cylinder type with guard rings
(d) multiple parallel plate type

85. One of the method to measure power output of a radio transmitter while it is radiating is
(a) electrostatic meter
(b) three-wattmeter method
(c) three-ammeter method
(d) two-wattmeter method

86. In comparison to monolithic ICs, film ICs have the advantage of
(a) smaller in size
(b) cheaper in cost
(c) better high frequency performance
(d) higher reliability

87. In the two-wattmeter method for balanced load, the readings of the wattmeters are 3 kW and 1 kW respectively, the latter being obtained after reversing the connections to the current coil of one-wattmeter, the power measured is
(a) 4 W (b) 2 W
(c) 1 W (d) 0.5 W

88. For measurement and control, instruments should preferably have
(a) dead zone and dead time
(b) linear output and fast response
(c) non-linear output
(d) a highly damped response

89. Piezo-electric crystals are used for measurement of __________ changes.
(a) static
(b) dynamic
(c) static and dynamic
(d) none of these

90. Low resistance is measured by
(a) De Sauty's bridge
(b) Maxwell's bridge
(c) Kelvin's double bridge
(d) Wien bridge

91. Zero adjust control is provided in a VOM for
(a) correcting zero point
(b) changing the sensitivity
(c) tightening the moving components to the casing
(d) all of the above

92. Digital instruments, particularly digital voltmeters and multimeters, are ordinarily used for measurement of
(a) analog quantities such as current, voltage, resistance
(b) digital quantities
(c) both analog and digital quantities
(d) none

93. If the zero-adjust screw of a moving coil meter is turned to the left, the pointer moves
(a) upscale to the right
(b) off scale to the left
(c) half-scale in the center
(d) full-scale to the right

94. ADC
(a) stands for analog-to-digital converter
(b) is often referred to an encoding device
(c) is often referred to a decoding device
(d) both (a) and (b)

95. On which of the following factors the sensitivity inaccuracy of an instrument does not depend?
(a) Hysteresis or dead bond
(b) Amplitude distortion
(c) Frequency response
(d) All of these

96. A waveguide acts as a
(a) low pass filter (b) high pass filter
(c) band pass filter (d) none of these

97. The static error band of an instrument implies
(a) the accuracy of the instrument
(b) the error produced when the pen is stopped at some deflection
(c) the irrepeatibility of the instrument
(d) the error introduced in low varying inputs

98. In an instrument, the error when reading at half-scale is
(a) less than full-scale error
(b) equal to full-scale error
(c) greater than-full scale error
(d) equal to half of full-scale error

99. For surface temperature measurement one can use
(a) strain gauge (b) diaphragm
(c) RTD (d) thermo-couple

100. Which of the following instruments is the best choice to measure a dc potential difference of about 0.5 V, the current being 20 μA?
(a) Multimeter (b) Rectifier type meter
(c) VTVM (d) Potentiometer

101. For sustained oscillations it is essential that
(a) the loop gain of the circuit must be equal to (or greater than) unity
(b) the phase shift around the circuit must be zero
(c) the loop gain of the circuit must be smaller than unity
(d) both (a) and (b)

102. Tansformers are tested for impulse testing for determining their ability of
(a) insulation to withstand transient voltage
(b) windings to withstand voltage fluctuations
(c) bushings to withstand vibrations
(d) all of the above

103. The resolution of an indicating instrument is
(a) the smallest change in the output reading due to drifting of pointer
(b) the smallest change in applied stimulus that will indicate a detectable change in deflection

(c) the difference between various reading for the same applied stimulus
(d) none of these

104. What does the reading of the first dial on the right of a 4-dial watthourmeter indicate?
(a) Number of single units
(b) Total watts each hour
(c) Maximum value the meter can register
(d) Multiplier value of the preceding dial

105. High ac voltages are usually measured with
(a) magnetic voltmeter
(b) inductive voltmeter
(c) potential transformers with voltmeters
(d) current transformers and voltmeters

106. In the measurement of 3-phase power by two-wattmeter method, if the two wattmeter readings are equal, the power factor of the circuit is
(a) 0.8 lagging (b) 0.8 leading
(c) zero (d) unity

107. In a thermocouple temperature transducer, the output voltage is generally measured by a
(a) high resistance voltmeter
(b) high resistance milli-voltmeter
(c) low resistance voltmeter
(d) none of these

108. Error may be caused by braking system in an induction type energy meter due to
(a) change in brake magnet strength
(b) change in resistance of the meter disc
(c) self braking effect of series magnet flux
(d) all of the above

109. Hydrometer is used to determine
(a) specific gravity of liquids
(b) relative humidity
(c) specific gravity of solids
(d) specific gravity of gases

110. In an energy meter the braking device is provided to produce braking torque so that the
(a) energy meter can be brought to standstill
(b) meter creeping be checked
(c) moving system of the instrument
(d) none of these

111. A delay line is used in high speed CRO to introduce time delay in
(a) vertical channel
(b) horizontal channel
(c) in the cathode Z-axis of CRT
(d) none of these

112. Ballistic tests are used in magnetic measurements for determination of
(a) iron losses in the specimen
(b) B-H curve of the specimen
(c) hysteresis loop of the specimen
(d) flux density B, magnetizing force H and B-H curve and hysteresis loop of the specimen

113. If a large number of restrictions are installed along a pipe, the pressure at the pipe output will become
(a) less (b) more
(c) remains constant (d) varies randomly

114. Sustained low frequency tests are carried on installation, switchgear circuits and other equipment on a frequency of the order of
(a) 5 Hz (b) 50 Hz
(c) 200 Hz (d) 500 Hz

115. In measuring iron losses in an iron specimen by ac potentiometer method the magnetizing component of no-load current is read by
(a) in-phase potentiometer
(b) quadrature potentiometer
(c) either by inphase or quadrature potentiometer
(d) none of the above

116. FET input stage is used in an amplifier to increase its
(a) output impedance
(b) input impedance
(c) frequency bandwidth
(d) power handling capacity

117. The ratio of voltage reflected from the load to the voltage applied to the load is called the
(a) reflection loss (b) SWR
(c) return loss (d) none of these

118. A thermal meter differs from a thermocouple meter in that a thermal meter
(a) produces a small D-C current
(b) has heaters
(c) can be used for current or voltage measurement
(d) produces pointer deflection directly by heat

119. Routine tests are performed on porcelain insulators for
(a) ascertaining their electrical performance individually
(b) ascertaining their mechanical performance individually
(c) determining their flash-over voltage
(d) weeding out defective insulators and includes proof load and corrosion tests

120. Non-sinusoidal waveforms
(a) are departures from sinusoidal waveforms
(b) are much easier to generate
(c) are not suitable for digital operation
(d) have low mark-to-space ratio

121. The most suitable instrument for measurement of alternating currents and voltages in radio-frequency range is
(a) moving iron (b) electro-thermic
(c) electrostatic (d) dynamometer type

122. The power delivered to a 3-phase load can be measured by the use of 2 wattmeters only when the
(a) load is balanced
(b) load is unbalanced
(c) 3-phase load is connected to the source through 3-wires
(d) 3-phase load is connected to the source through 4-wires

123. In which of the following situations does a round-chart recorder have the greatest advantage?
(a) Each day's record must be kept individually
(b) The instrument is left unattended
(c) A record is needed over a long period of time
(d) Values fluctuate rapidly

124. Various adjustments in an energy meter include
(a) temperature compensation
(b) overload and voltage compensation
(c) lag and creep
(d) friction or light load
(e) all of the above

125. Which of the following instruments can be used both for ac and dc?
(a) PMMC type (b) Induction type
(c) Moving-iron type (d) None of the above

126. Rectifier instruments are generally not free from
(a) wave shape errors
(b) frequency and wave shape errors
(c) frequency, wave shape, and temperature errors
(d) none of these

127. Holes are drilled on the opposite sides of the disc of an induction type energy meter to
(a) avoid creep on no load
(b) balance the disc
(c) dissipate the energy due to eddy currents
(d) increase the deflecting torque

128. Piezo-electric crystals produce an emf
(a) when external mechanical force is applied to it
(b) when external magnetic field is applied
(c) when radiant energy stimulates the crystal
(d) when the junction of two such crystals is heated

129. The resistance of a shunt for a precision grade ammeter can be best measured by
(a) Kelvin's double-bridge
(b) Schering's bridge
(c) De Sauty's bridge
(d) Maxwell's bridge

130. A dynamometer type wattmeter responds to the
(a) average value of active power
(b) average value of reactive power
(c) peak value of a active power
(d) peak value of reactive power

131. The advantage of zero-suppression control over pen-position control is that full gain capability is available for
(a) dynamic part of a signal
(b) static part of the signal
(c) the whole signal
(d) none of these

132. Dead time of the instrument is
(a) the time required by an instrument to begin to respond to a change in the measurand
(b) the time required by an instrument to warm up initially
(c) the largest change of input quantity for which there is no output of the instrument
(d) none of the above

133. Use of metallic parts should be avoided in the construction of inductors because
(a) they are uneconomical
(b) inductance gets affected by external magnetic field
(c) inductance gets affected by electric field
(d) inductance gets affected due to eddy currents set up in the metallic parts

134. Dead zone of an instrument is
(a) the time required by an instrument to warm up initially
(b) the largest change of input quantity for which there is no output of the instrument
(c) the time required by an instrument to begin to respond to a change in measurand
(d) the unmeasured quantity which exceeds the maximum range of the instrument
(e) none of the above

135. In a strain measuring equipment, using a resistance strain gauge, the output quantity is
(a) resistance (b) voltage
(c) current (d) impedance

136. In moving- coil instruments, the scale used is
(a) non-linear scale (b) linear scale
(c) square law scale (d) log scale

137. The important advantages of electrical methods of measuring non-electrical quantities are
(a) automatic measurement and constant readiness of the apparatus for measurement
(b) possibility of non-inertial reproduction of a varying value of quantity under measurement
(c) possibility of automatic mathematical processing of the results of measurement.
(d) wide measurement range
(e) all of the above

138. A 0-25 A ammeter has a guaranteed accuracy of 1 percent of full scale reading. The current measured by this instrument is 5 A. The limiting error in percentage is
(a) 5 (b) 2.5
(c) 2 (d) 1

139. The bridge used for the measurement of capacitance is
(a) Schering bridge (b) Wheatstone bridge
(c) Wein' s bridge (d) Hay' s bridge

140. The relative error is the
(a) difference of measured value and true value
(b) ratio of absolute error to the measured value of the quantity under measurement
(c) ratio of absolute error to the true value of the quantity under measurement
(d) ratio of probable error to the true value of quantity under measurement

141. A moving iron voltmeter is connected across the voltage source whose instantaneous value is $v(t) = 5 + 10 \cos (314\, t + 30°)$. The reading of the meter is
(a) 15 V (b) 5 V
(c) $\sqrt{125}$ V (d) $\sqrt{75}$ V

142. Precautions are essential for ensuring that the secondary of a CT is not open circuited when the primary circuit carries a current because
(a) a dangerously high voltage might develop across the secondary
(b) the ferromagnetic core may develop residual magnetism
(c) the reflected impedance may prevent the flow of current in the primary circuit
(d) none of these

143. A differential amplifier essentially consists of
(a) two input and two output terminals
(b) only resistors and transistors
(c) two transistors
(d) two CE amplifiers having their emitters directly coupled to each other

144. A moving iron type instrument has
(a) a linear scale (uniform scale)
(b) a nonlinear scale
(c) its deflection directly proportional to the current
(d) its deflection directly proportional to the voltage

145. The accelerometer using LVDT has the advantage of
(a) high natural frequency
(b) being-contactless device
(c) better resolution
(d) all of the above

146. The main reason for using springs in a measuring instrument is
(a) to conduct the current to the coils
(b) to hold the pivot in position
(c) to control the pointer movement
(d) to minimize the vibration of the pointer

147. The ballast circuit employs a capacitor to act as high pass filter for measurement of
(a) static strains
(b) dynamic strains
(c) both static and dynamic strains
(d) none of the above

148. In dynamometer type of wattmeter, which of the coil is split up into two parts
(a) pressure coil
(b) current coil
(c) pressure coil and current coil both
(d) none of the above

149. Pulse modulation essentially is a process of
(a) multiplexing
(b) message processing
(c) pulse modulation
(d) none of these

150. Temperature compensation in bridge arrangement is affected by
(a) using dummy strain gauges
(b) using strain gauges of smaller gauge factor
(c) reversing strain gauge
(d) any of the above

151. In restriction type flow measuring devices, if the differential pressure is ΔP the flow will be proportional to
(a) ΔP (b) $\sqrt{\Delta P}$
(c) $\frac{1}{\Delta P}$ (d) $\frac{1}{\sqrt{\Delta P}}$

152. A slide wire potentiometer has 10 wires of 1m each. With the help of a standard voltage source of 1.018 V it is standardized by keeping the jockey at 101.8 cm. If the resistance of the potentiometer wire is 1000 Ω, then the value of the working current is
(a) 0.1 A (b) 0.5 mA
(c) 1 mA (d) 10 mA

153. In a force-balance transducer
(a) the output and the sensing element is amplified
(b) the output is feed back to an element which causes a force-summing member to return to its zero position
(c) the magnitude feed back determines the output of the transducer
(d) all of these

154. A temperature sensitive transducer is subjected to a sudden temperature change. It takes 10 seconds for the transducer to reach equilibrium condition (five time constants). The time taken by the transducer to read half of the temperature difference will be nearly
(a) 1.38 seconds (b) 5 seconds
(c) 8.62 seconds (d) 10 seconds

155. What is the function of the zero-adjust control in multimeter?
(a) It serves to conduct the current
(b) With this control, the sensitivity of the meter can be changed

(c) The zero point is corrected with the help of this control

(d) The moving parts can be tightened to the casing with the help of this control-screw

156. The accelerometer used for measurement of vibration of large structures is

(a) servo-accelerometer

(b) piezo-electric accelerometer

(c) potentiometric accelerometer

(d) strain gauge accelerometer

157. The secondary of a current transformer is never left open-circuited because otherwise

(a) heat dissipation in the core will be very high

(b) the core will be saturated and permanently magnetized rendering it useless

(c) secondary voltage will be very large

(d) all of these

158. The total power delivered to a three-phase load is equal to

(a) algebraic difference of two-wattmeter readings

(b) algebraic sum of two-wattmeter readings

(c) vectorial difference of two-wattmeter readings

(d) vectorial sum of the two-wattmeters readings

159. Two meters X and Y require 40 mA and 50 mA respectively, to give full-scale deflection, then

(a) X is more sensitive

(b) Y is more sensitive

(c) both are equally sensitive

(d) sensitivity can not be judged with the given information

160. The drawbacks of radiation pyrometers are that

(a) their initial as well as installation costs are high

(b) they need maintenance

(c) each pyrometer needs individual calibration

(d) all of the above

161. Which of the following instruments is used to measure current in a long extension wire?

(a) Ammeter with a shunt

(b) Thermocouple type meter

(c) Current transformer

(d) Voltage transformer

162. The electrical transducers used for continuous recording and control of humidity are

(a) resistive hygrometers

(b) electrolytic hygrometers

(c) aluminium oxide hygrometers

(d) all of the above

163. In VTVMs the ac voltage measurements corresponds to

(a) saw-tooth wave input

(b) square-wave input

(c) sine-wave input

(d) any waveform at the input

164. The disadvantage associated with an electro-dynamic instrument is that

(a) it consumes more power

(b) it has low torque-to weight ratio

(c) its frequency range is low

(d) all of these

165. The errors committed by a person in the measurement are

(a) gross errors

(b) random errors

(c) instrumental errors

(d) environmental errors

166. Damping provides

(a) braking action on a meter pointer

(b) good accuracy

(c) starting torque on the meter pointer

(d) counter torque to deflection torque

167. To reduce the effect of a voltmeter upon the circuit under test, we should

(a) decrease the multiplier resistance

(b) get an instrument with higher internal resistance

(c) use a parallel resistor

(d) use an ac meter with rectifier

168. Which one of the following is the main reason for insertion of two strain gauges in the adjacent arms of a bridge circuit?

(a) Achievement of higher sensitivity.

(b) Elimination of radio-frequency interference.

(c) Elimination of effect environmental temperature.

(d) To facilitate quick balancing of the bridge.

169. A rotation tester is used to determine the phase sequence of leads for a/an

(a) single phase motor

(b) d-c motor

(c) 3-phase motor

(d) a-c or d-c motor

170. A capacitive transducer working on the principle of change of capacitance with change of displacement exhibits non-linear characteristics. The response of these transducers can be made linear by using

(a) differential arrangement

(b) use of an op-amp

(c) working them over a small displacement range

(d) all of the above

171. Synchros and resolvers have the following advantages

(a) infinite resolution

(b) much operating speeds

(c) high reliability and accuracy

(d) all of the above

172. Capacitive transducers are normally employed for

(a) static measurements

(b) dynamic measurements

(c) both static and dynamic measurements

(d) transient measurements

173. Consider the following statements. DC potentiometer is the best means available for measurement of dc voltages because

1. the precision in measurement is independent of the type of detector used
2. it is based on null-balance technique
3. it is possible to standardize before a measurement is undertaken
4. it is possible to measure dc voltages ranging in value from mV to hundreds of volts

Of these statements

(a) 2 and 3 are correct

(b) 1 and 4 are correct

(c) 2 and 4 are correct

(d) 3 and 4 are correct

174. The braking torque provided by a permanent magnet in a single phase induction type energy meter can be varied by

(a) changing the position of the magnetic shunt provided for this purpose

(b) changing the position of brake magnet with respect to the meter disc

(c) both (a) and (b)

(d) none of the above

175. Complex waveforms are most accurately measured with

(a) rms responding electronic voltmeter

(b) average responding electronic voltmeter

(c) peak responding electronic voltmeter

(d) both average and peak responding electronic voltmeters

176. An electro-dynamic instrument can be employed for measurement of

(a) dc voltages

(b) ac voltages

(c) dc as well as ac voltages

(d) dc voltages but for ac voltages rectification is necessary

177. In comparison to PPM, which of the following statements is/are true for PDM?

(a) The pulse amplitude in PDM remains constant

(b) The PDM transmitter should be able to handle maximum width pulse

(c) PDM will still work if synchronization between transmitter and receiver fails

(d) all of the above

178. The accuracy of a 0–10 mA meter is ±10 percent. A full scale reading of 10 mA may be due to a current of

(a) 9 mA

(b) 11 mA

(c) either 9 mA or 11 mA

(d) 12 mA

179. Four voltmeters W, X, Y, Z are specified as follows:
Voltmeter W: 100 V , 2 mA
Voltmeter X: 100 V, 100 Ω/V
Voltmeter Y: 10000 Ω, 1 mA
Voltmeter Z: 100 V, 1 mA
The most suitable voltmeter for measurement of 100 V is
(a) W (b) X
(c) Y (d) Z

180. Moving iron instrument can be used as
(a) an ammeter for measuring direct as well as alternating current
(b) a voltmeter for measuring direct as well as alternating voltage
(c) for measuring direct currents and voltages only
(d) for measuring alternating currents and voltages only
(e) both (a) and (b)

181. Creeping is observed in
(a) watt-hour meter (b) power factor meters
(c) wattmeter (d) ammeter

182. The braking torque provided by a permanent magnet in a motor meter is
(a) proportional to the square of the flux of the permanent magnet
(b) proportional to the rotational speed of the disc
(c) inversely proportional to the resistance of induced current path
(d) all of the above

183. Multimeter can be used for measuring
(a) alternating current quantities
(b) D.C. quantities
(c) A.C. and D.C. quantities both
(d) pulsating D.C. quantities

184. The errors in current transformers can be reduced by designing them with
(a) large primary ampere-turns
(b) primary and secondary windings wound closed together
(c) primary and secondary windings wound with large x-section
(d) core made from high permeability and low loss magnetic materials avoiding any joint in the core and using low values of flux density
(e) both (a) and (b)

185. Which of the following statements is true about two wattmeter method for power measurement in 3-phase circuit?
(a) Power can be measured using two wattmeter method only for star-connected 3- phase circuits.
(b) When two wattmeters show identical readings, the power factor is 0.5.
(c) When power factor is unity, one of the wattmeter reads zero.
(d) When the readings of the two wattmeters are equal but opposite sign, the power factor is zero.

186. The current coil of a wattmeter is connected to the C.T. of *R*-phase. The potential coil is connected across *Y* and *B* phases. The wattmeter measures
(a) active power in *R* phase
(b) active power of *Y* phase
(c) reactive power in *R* phase
(d) power proportional to 3-phase power if the load is balanced

187. The errors in C.T. are mainly due to
(a) leakage flux
(b) excitation emf required
(c) core losses
(d) copper losses

188. Though electro-dynamometer instruments can be used both, for dc and ac measurements but most of its practical uses are in
(a) dc because of their lower cost in comparison to PMMC
(b) ac because of their higher cost, higher power consumption, lower torque-weight ratio, non-uniform scale and other several drawbacks in comparison to PMMC
(c) dc and ac equally
(d) laboratory and shop measurements at power frequencies

189. A shunt in conjunction with a shunt type ammeter is used in measuring D.C. current where
(a) it is desired to isolate the instrument from main circuit
(b) the current fluctuates greatly in value
(c) it is not practical to carry the full load current through the instrument
(d) the accompanying D.C. voltage is high

190. The main requirements of voltage multipliers to be used for dc measurements are
(a) low temperature coefficient
(b) the resistance should not change with time of usage
(c) there should be ample provision for cooling to dissipate the heat developed
(d) all of the above

191. Which of the following statements is correct?
(a) Frictional error in moving iron instruments is quite high because of small torque-weight ratio.
(b) Frictional error in moving iron instruments is quite small because of high torque-weight ratio.
(c) Frictional error is reduced in moving iron instruments when used on dc circuits.
(d) None of the above

192. Which of the following set torques is provided in deflection galvanometer?
(a) Deflecting and controlling
(b) Controlling and damping
(c) Deflecting and damping
(d) Deflecting, controlling and damping

193. A PMMC type ammeter and a moving iron type ammeter are connected in series in a resistive circuit fed from output of a half wave rectifier voltage source. If the moving iron type reads 5A, the PMMC type instrument is likely to read
(a) zero (b) 2.5 A
(c) 3.18 A (d) 5 A

194. Megger is an instrument to measure
(a) very low resistance
(b) insulation resistance
(c) Q of a coil
(d) inductance of a coil

195. Which one of the following statements about internal resistance of measuring instruments is true?
(a) The internal resistance of ammeters should be very small and that of voltmeters very high.
(b) The internal resistance of ammeters should be very high and that of voltmeters very low.
(c) The internal resistance of ammeters and voltmeters should be very high.
(d) None of these

196. Error due to change in frequency in moving iron instrument is reduced by connecting a condenser across the swamping resistance. The reading of the instrument will be independent of frequency only when
(a) $C = L/r^2$ (b) $C = L^2r$
(c) $C = \sqrt{Lr^2}$ (d) $C = L/r$

197. Large currents in D.C. circuit are practically always measured with
(a) an ammeter and shunts
(b) a miliiammeter and multiplier
(c) an ammeter and current transformer
(d) a millivoltmeter and shunt

198. Bonded strain gauges are
(a) exclusively used for construction of transducers
(b) exclusively used for stress analysis
(c) used for both stress analysis and for construction of transducers
(d) none of the above

199. What will happen if a voltmeter is connected like an ammeter in series to the load?
(a) The meter will burn out
(b) The measurement will be too high
(c) An inadmissably high current will flow
(d) There will be almost no current in the circuit

200. In semiconductor strain gauges, the change in resistance on application of strain is mainly on account of
(a) change in length of wire
(b) change in diameter of wire
(c) change in resistivity
(d) both (a) and (b)

201. VTVM provides more accurate readings in high resistance circuits as compared to voltmeter because of its
(a) high V/ohm ratings
(b) high ohms/V ratings
(c) low meter resistance
(d) high resolution

202. In a balanced Wheatstone bridge $R_1 = 33$ kΩ, $R_2 = 47$ kΩ, $R_3 = R_x$ and $R_4 = 94$ kΩ, the value of R_x is
(a) 14.7 kΩ (b) 47 kΩ
(c) 66 kΩ (d) 157 kΩ

203. Inductive transducers are employed in differential configurations because differential outputs are less affected by
(a) external magnetic fields
(b) temperature variations
(c) variations of bridge supply voltage and frequency
(d) all of the above

204. Which of the following statement is not a disadvantage of digital voltmeter?
(a) It cannot measure non-linear parameters.
(b) It is comparatively high priced.
(c) Its circuitery is more complex.
(d) Its accuracy changes with the reading taken.

205. Thermocouples
(a) are most commonly employed for indication of rapidly changing temperature and for use in localized and in otherwise accessible positions
(b) need reference junction compensation
(c) have a low output voltage level
(d) all of the above

206. In modern electronic multimeters, a FET or MOSFET is preferred over BJT, because
(a) its input resistance is high
(b) its input resistance is high and does not vary with the change of range
(c) its input resistance is low
(d) it is cheaper

207. Electrodynamic types of instruments are used commonly for the measurement of
(a) voltage (b) current
(c) resistance (d) power

208. Instrumental errors may be avoided by
(a) selecting a proper measuring device for the particular application
(b) applying correction factor after determining the magnitude of instrumental error
(c) calibrating the measuring device or instrument against a standard
(d) all of the above

209. The FETVM employes FETs' in
(a) cascade mode (b) differential mode
(c) cascode mode (d) commod mode

210. In a VTVM of various ranges, the voltage difference between the plates corresponds to
(a) half-scale deflection of the water
(b) full-scale deflection of the meter
(c) rms value of the maximum voltage
(d) dc value of the maximum voltage

211. Over wire strain gauges foil strain gauges have the advantages of
(a) higher heat dissipation capacity and better bonding
(b) superior mechanical stability under prolonged strained and high temperature conditions, low hysteresis and creeping effects
(c) excellent reproducibility and longer life
(d) all of the above

212. In wire wound strain gauges, the change in resistance under strained condition is mainly on account of
(a) change in diameter of wire
(b) change in length of wire
(c) change in both length and diameter of wire
(d) change in resistivity

213. Two wattmeter method is employed to measure power in a 3-phase balanced system with current coils connected in the A and C lines. The phase sequence in ABC. If the wattmeter with its current coil in A-phase line reads zero, then the power factor of the 3-phase load will be

(a) zero lagging (b) zero leading
(c) 0.5 lagging (d) 0.5 leading

214. How should a D-C voltmeter be connected in a circuit being tested?

(a) In series with the multiplier, in parallel with the circuit
(b) In series with the circuit, in parallel with the multiplier
(c) In series with both the multiplier and the circuit
(d) In parallel with both the multiplier and the circuit

215. While using a CT it is essential to maintain at all times a closed circuit on the secondary side in order to

(a) reduce power losses
(b) avoid demagnetization
(c) avoid dangerously high emfs for both the operator and the transformer insulation
(d) all of the above

216. In case of a PT with the increase in load on secondary side

(a) both of the ratio error and phase angle increase
(b) the ratio error increases but phase angle decreases
(c) the ratio error decreases but phase angle increases
(d) both of the ratio error and phase angle error decrease

217. The type of multivibrator used for generation of clock pulses is

(a) monostable multivibrator
(b) astable multivibrator
(c) bistable multivibrator
(d) none of the above

218. The pocket-type tester, sometimes called the "Wiggy", is used to indicate approximate

(a) current (b) resistance
(c) voltage (d) impedance

219. LVDT is always used as

(a) secondary transducer
(b) primary transducer
(c) primary signal generator
(d) none of these

220. In a Marx's circuit

(a) the capacitors are charged in parallel and discharged in series
(b) the capacitors are charged in series and discharged in parallel
(c) the capacitors are charged in series and discharged in series
(d) the capacitors are charged in parallel and discharged in parallel

221. An instrument will have uniform scale only when

(a) deflecting torque varies directly as the magnitude of the quantity under measurement
(b) controlling torque varies directly as the deflection angle
(c) damping torque varies directly as the deflection angle
(d) both (a) and (b)

222. A rectifier is used in an instrument for the purpose of

(a) measuring high voltage values
(b) measuring high current values
(c) converting ac into dc
(d) making the instrument more stable

223. Electro-dynamometer type moving coil instruments are mainly used as

(a) indicator type instruments
(b) standard instruments for calibration of other instruments
(c) transfer instruments only
(d) both as standard instruments and transfer instruments

224. The arms of a Wheatstone bridge are shown in the given figure. For the balanced condition, the least tolerance value of R_4 will be

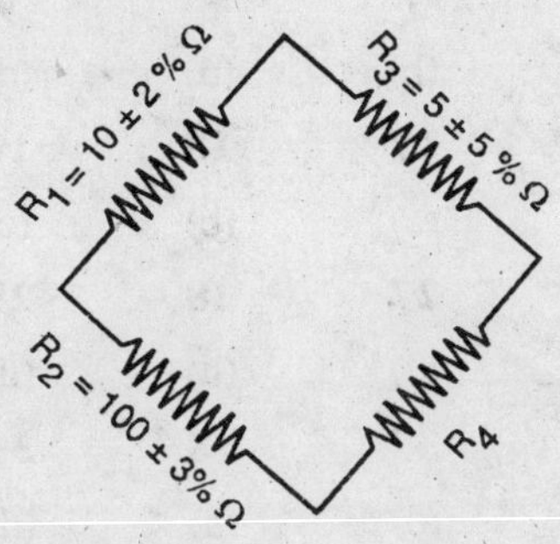

(a) 50 ± 2% Ω (b) 50 ± 3% Ω
(c) 50 ± 5% Ω (d) 50 ± 10% Ω

225. A moving iron voltmeter reads correctly on 250 V dc. If 250 V, 50 Hz ac is applied to it, what will be the reading of the voltmeter? The instrument coil has a resistance of 500 Ω and an inductance of 1 H and series non-inductive resistance is 2000 Ω.

(a) 248 V (b) 250 V
(c) 252 V (d) 255 V

226. Which of the following statements is wrong for thermocouple measuring instruments?

(a) They read rms values.
(b) If calibrated on D.C., they cannot be used for AC. signals.
(c) They are incapable of standing any overloads.
(d) Their calibration does not change with time or temperature.

227. The reading of the voltmeter connected in the circuit given below would be nearest to

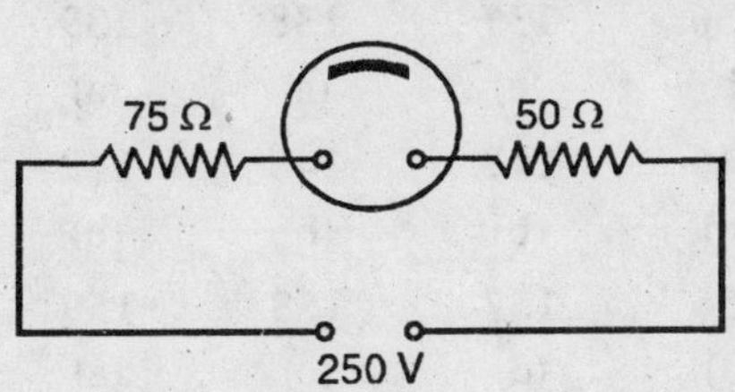

(a) 0 V (b) 50 V
(c) 75 V (d) 250 V

228. Induction type instruments are not usually used as ammeters and voltmeters because

(a) their indications are affected by stray magnetic field considerably
(b) variation in supply frequency and temperature may cause serious errors unless compensating device is used
(c) these instruments are costlier and consume more power in comparison to other instruments
(d) both (b) and (c)

229. LVDT is a

(a) displacement transducer
(b) velocity transducer
(c) acceleration transducer
(d) pressure transducer

230. Error due to change in frequency in moving iron instruments, may be reduced by using a/an

(a) induction coil
(b) condenser of suitable value in parallel with the swamping resistance
(c) condenser of suitable value in series with the swamping resistance
(d) balancing circuit

231. Thermocouple used in radio micrometer and thermo-galvanometer is

(a) antimony-bismuth couple
(b) copper constantan couple
(c) copper-iron couple
(d) iron-copper couple

232. The energy meter used for measuring energy of a D.C. circuit is

(a) ampere hour type
(b) wattmeter type
(c) induction type
(d) energy meter type

ANSWERS

1	2	3	4	5	6	7	8	9	10
(d)	(d)	(b)	(c)	(d)	(c)	(b)	(d)	(d)	(a)
11	**12**	**13**	**14**	**15**	**16**	**17**	**18**	**19**	**20**
(d)	(a)	(d)	(c)	(d)	(c)	(a)	(b)	(c)	(d)
21	**22**	**23**	**24**	**25**	**26**	**27**	**28**	**29**	**30**
(a)	(b)	(d)	(d)	(b)	(b)	(c)	(b)	(d)	(b)
31	**32**	**33**	**34**	**35**	**36**	**37**	**38**	**39**	**40**
(b)	(c)	(c)	(c)	(d)	(a)	(c)	(a)	(d)	(d)
41	**42**	**43**	**44**	**45**	**46**	**47**	**48**	**49**	**50**
(c)	(d)	(e)	(b)	(b)	(b)	(c)	(d)	(d)	(b)
51	**52**	**53**	**54**	**55**	**56**	**57**	**58**	**59**	**60**
(d)	(d)	(b)	(a)	(d)	(c)	(d)	(b)	(a)	(a)
61	**62**	**63**	**64**	**65**	**66**	**67**	**68**	**69**	**70**
(c)	(c)	(d)	(d)	(b)	(b)	(a)	(b)	(c)	(c)
71	**72**	**73**	**74**	**75**	**76**	**77**	**78**	**79**	**80**
(a)	(b)	(c)	(a)	(a)	(a)	(c)	(b)	(c)	(b)
81	**82**	**83**	**84**	**85**	**86**	**87**	**88**	**89**	**90**
(a)	(d)	(b)	(c)	(c)	(c)	(b)	(b)	(b)	(d)
91	**92**	**93**	**94**	**95**	**96**	**97**	**98**	**99**	**100**
(a)	(a)	(a)	(d)	(d)	(b)	(b)	(c)	(d)	(d)
101	**102**	**103**	**104**	**105**	**106**	**107**	**108**	**109**	**110**
(d)	(a)	(b)	(a)	(c)	(d)	(b)	(d)	(a)	(c)
111	**112**	**113**	**114**	**115**	**116**	**117**	**118**	**119**	**120**
(a)	(b)	(b)	(b)	(b)	(b)	(b)	(b)	(d)	(a)
121	**122**	**123**	**124**	**125**	**126**	**127**	**128**	**129**	**130**
(b)	(c)	(a)	(e)	(b)	(c)	(a)	(a)	(a)	(a)
131	**132**	**133**	**134**	**135**	**136**	**137**	**138**	**139**	**140**
(a)	(c)	(d)	(b)	(b)	(b)	(e)	(a)	(a)	(c)
141	**142**	**143**	**144**	**145**	**146**	**147**	**148**	**149**	**150**
(d)	(a)	(a)	(b)	(d)	(c)	(b)	(b)	(b)	(a)
151	**152**	**153**	**154**	**155**	**156**	**157**	**158**	**159**	**160**
(b)	(d)	(a)	(a)	(c)	(a)	(d)	(c)	(a)	(d)
161	**162**	**163**	**164**	**165**	**166**	**167**	**168**	**169**	**170**
(c)	(b)	(c)	(c)	(a)	(a)	(b)	(a)	(c)	(b)

171	**172**	**173**	**174**	**175**	**176**	**177**	**178**	**179**	**180**
(d)	(b)	(a)	(c)	(a)	(c)	(d)	(c)	(d)	(e)
181	**182**	**183**	**184**	**185**	**186**	**187**	**188**	**189**	**190**
(a)	(d)	(c)	(e)	(d)	(c)	(c)	(b)	(c)	(d)
191	**192**	**193**	**194**	**195**	**196**	**197**	**198**	**199**	**200**
(b)	(d)	(c)	(b)	(a)	(a)	(a)	(c)	(d)	(c)
201	**202**	**203**	**204**	**205**	**206**	**207**	**208**	**209**	**210**
(b)	(c)	(d)	(d)	(d)	(a)	(d)	(d)	(b)	(b)
211	**212**	**213**	**214**	**215**	**216**	**217**	**218**	**219**	**220**
(d)	(c)	(c)	(a)	(c)	(a)	(a)	(c)	(a)	(a)
211	**222**	**223**	**224**	**225**	**226**	**227**	**228**	**229**	**230**
(d)	(c)	(d)	(d)	(a)	(b)	(d)	(d)	(a)	(b)
231	**232**								
(a)	(a)								

6. DIGITAL AND MICROPROCESSOR

POSTULATES

Postulates 1: (a) An operator '+' is defined such that if $c = a + b$, $c \in X$, for every pair of elements a, $b \in X$. This operation replaces the 'union' (∪) operation of set theory, and in switching theory, it is known as *OR* operation.

(b) An operator '.' (dot, replacing intersection (∪) operation of set theory), is defined as $d = a \cdot b$, then $d \in X$ for every pair if a, $b \in X$. In switching theory, it is known as *AND* operation.

Postulate 2: (a) There exists an element '0' in X such that $a + 0 = a$ for every element $a \in X$.

(b) There exists an element '1' in X such that $a \cdot 1 = a$ for every element $a \in X$.

Postulate 3: It holds commutative law true:

(i) $a + b = b + a$

(ii) $a \cdot b = b \cdot a$

Postulate 4: It holds the distributive law true.

(i) $a \cdot (b + c) = a \cdot b + a \cdot c$

(ii) $a + (b \cdot c) = (a + b) \cdot (a + c)$

Postulate 5: The complementary set $\overline{a}$, for every element $a \in X$, is defined as

(i) $a + \overline{a} = 1$

(ii) $a \cdot \overline{a} = 0$

Postulate 6: There are at least two elements a, $b \in X$, such that $a \neq b$

Based on these postulates, one can define now *AND*, *OR* and *NOT* operation. For example, the absorption law stated earlier, now can be written as

$$A \cdot (A + B) = A$$

$$A + A \cdot B = A$$

Venn-Diagram Representation

To fix the ideas of Boolean algebra, pictorial model known as the Venn-Diagram is useful. The diagram consists of a rectangle inside which, one circle for each variable is drawn. Points inside the circle belong to the variable, while points outside the circle are assumed belonging to the bar of that variable. Few examples are shown in Figure 1.

BOOLEAN THEOREM

To understand the combinational logic system more deeply, some basic, Boolean theorems can be derived. Let set X has two elements '0' and '1'. This can also be taken as logical '0' and logical '1'.

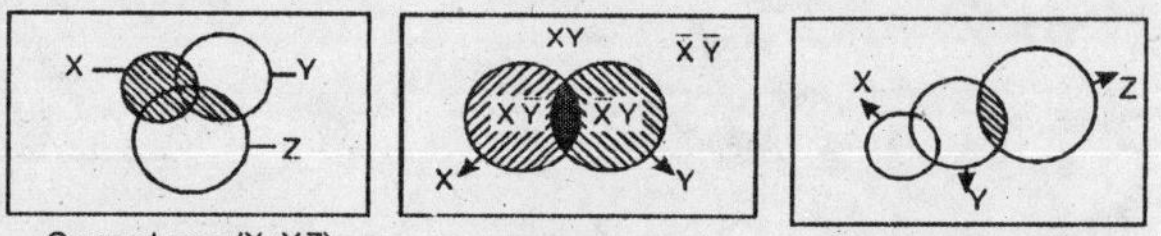

Covered area (X+Y.Z)   Covered area is $\overline{X}YZ$

Fig. 1

The rules for '+' and '.' operations can be listed as shown in Table 1 and Table 2 given below.

Table 1: *OR* operation			Table 2: *AND* operation		
a	b	$a + b$	a	b	$a \cdot b$
0	0	0	0	0	0
0	1	1	0	1	0
1	0	1	1	0	0
1	1	1	1	1	1

This gives us *OR* and *AND* operations when applied to binary system. Table 1 shows *OR* operation as

$$0 + 0 = 0$$
$$0 + 1 = 1$$
$$1 + 0 = 1 \quad \text{or } X = A + B$$
$$1 + 1 = 1$$

AND operation is

$$0 \cdot 0 = 0$$
$$0 \cdot 1 = 0$$
$$1 \cdot 0 = 0 \quad \text{or } X = A \cdot B$$
$$1 \cdot 1 = 1$$

where X is the output of logic gate and A and B are two input binary variables.

The *complements operation* or NOT operation is defined as

$$\overline{0} = 1$$

and $\overline{1} = 0$

or $X = \overline{A}$

Now on the basis of these three fundamental operations (*OR*, *AND* and *NOT*), the various basic relations can be understood and proved as follows.

1*a*. $A + A = A$	1*b*. $A \,.\, A = A$
2*a*. $A + 1 = 1$	2*b*. $A \,.\, 0 = 0$
3*a*. $A + (A.B) = A$	3*b*. $A \,.\, (A + B) = A$
4*a*. $\overline{\overline{A}} = A$	
5*a*. $A + (\overline{A} \,.\, B) = A + B$	5*b*. $A \,.\, (\overline{A} + B) = A \,.\, B$
6*a*. $\overline{A+B} = \overline{A} \,.\, \overline{B}$	6*a*. $\overline{A \,.\, B} = \overline{A} + \overline{B}$

The relation (6) is known as De-Morgon's Law and is very helpful in solving Boolean expression. All of these basic relations can be proved true by using the fundamental operations.

Boolean Function

It is defined as a set of Boolean variables, which are independent, and assigned by another Boolean variable which is dependent on the set of Boolean variables by some specific rule. In mathematical notion, we can write.

$$z = f(a, b, c)$$

THE TRUTH TABLE

This is a list of the true values of the function for all possible values (0 and 1) of its variables. Thus, n variable, each having two states, give 2^n combinations leading to 2^n rows in the truth table

A	B	$X = A+B$	$X = A.B$	$X = \overline{A+B}$	$X = \overline{A \,.\, B}$
0	0	0	0	1	1
0	1	1	0	0	1
1	0	1	0	0	1
1	1	1	1	0	0

Resistor Transistor Logic (RTL)

The basic *RTL* gate is a *NOR* gate. As shown in Fig. 2, the inputs A and B are connected to the base of Q_1 and Q_2 whose collectors are connected to V_{CC} through R_L. If all inputs are low *i.e.* $V_i \le V_{iL}$ (logical '0'), all the transistors remain off. Thus the common collector potential goes high so that $V_o \ge V_{OH}$ (logical '1'). If any one of the inputs goes high, the respective transistor becomes *ON*, the output becomes low *i.e.*, logical '0' value. So if all the inputs are high, the output remains at low because of conduction of the transistors. Thus *RTL* gate behaves as *NOR* gate.

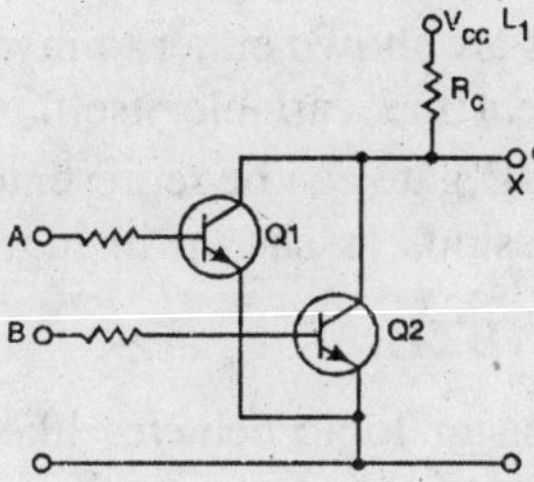

A	B	X
0	0	1
0	1	0
1	0	0
1	1	0

Fig. 2

DIGITAL LOGIC SYSTEMS

Positive and Negative Logic

A wire carrying a POSITIVE LOGIC signal (also known as ASSERTED HIGH LIGIC is equivalent to the complement of NEGATIVE LOGIC (also known as ASSERTED LOW LOGIC signal. In ASSERTED HIGH or POSITIVE LOGIC, the ASSERTED state (logic 1) is at higher voltage level than the NOT-ASSERTED state (logic 0), while in ASSERTED-LOW or NEGATIVE LOGIC, the ASSERTED state (logic 1) is at lower voltage level than the NOT ASSERTED state (logic 0).

From the above discussion, the logic gates can be manipulated by manipulating the logic of the Boolean variables. One example, is shown in Fig. 3

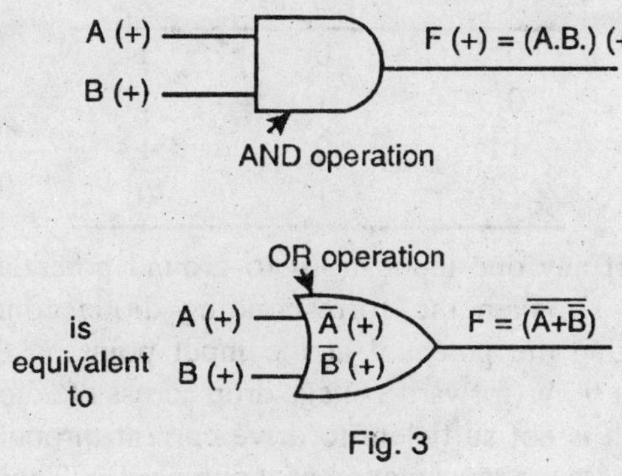

Fig. 3

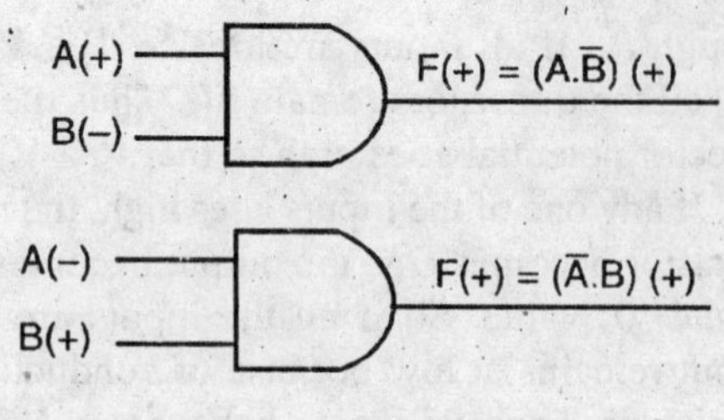

Fig. 4

Note that bubbles are shown either to invert the logic or to complement the variable itself.

In mixed logic, an AND gate can be represented by different output expressions as shown in Fig. 4

Diode Transistor Logic (DTL)

The basis diode transistor logic behaves like a NAND gate. As shown in the circuit of Fig. 5, if all the inputs are kept high, the diodes D_1 and D_2 cannot pass any current. The series diode D_S now passes current through the base emitter junction of the transistor and holds it into saturation. The V_{CE} of this transistor during saturation being of the order of 0.1 V, the output potential remains at low $V_0 \geq V_{OL}$ i.e., logical '0'.

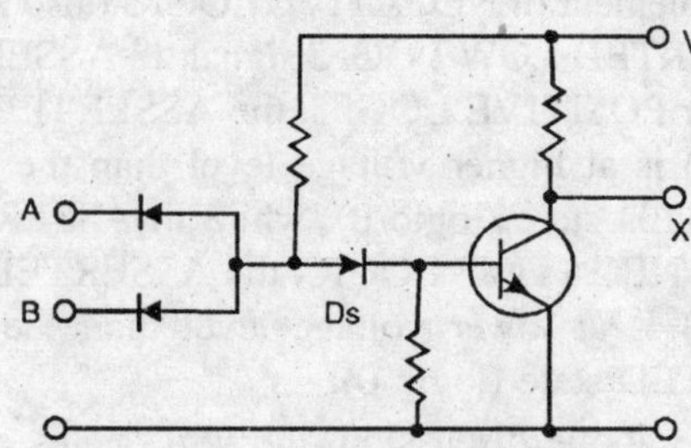

Fig. 5

A	B	X
0	0	1
0	1	1
1	0	1
1	1	0

If any one input drops to ground potential or $V_i \leq V_{iL}$, then the corresponding diode conduct bringing the potential at the input point of D_1 t_0 about 0.7V (forward voltage drop across the diode), which is not sufficient to drive current through D_s and base-emitter junction of the transistor. Thus the transistor remains off and collector potential becomes high.

Transistor Transistor Logical (TTL).

In Fig. 6 (a), the input transistor Q_1 has multiple emitters for multiple input connections. When any of the input goes low, Q_1 saturates making the base of Q_2 low and hence causing Q_2 as well as Q_3 to be cut-off. Thus, the output goes high with Q_4 acting as emitter follower, supplying output current to the load. When all the inputs become high, Q_1 becomes off, forcing Q_2 and Q_3 to be saturated so that the output goes low at logical '0'.

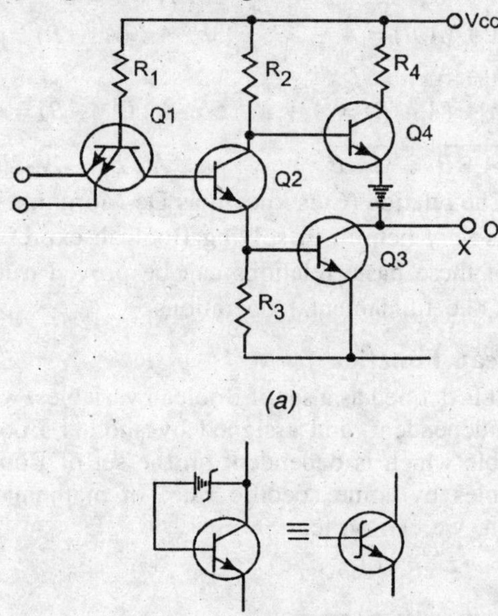

Fig. 6

The function of the diode is to prevent Q_4 from turning *ON* when Q_3 is saturated. The V_{BE} of Q_3 (approximately 0.7 V), and V_{CE} of Q_2 ($\cong$0.1 V) a total of about 0.8 V, is applied to the base of Q_4. Without the diode, Q_4 will turn *ON*.

The truth table for *TTL-NAND* gate given below:

A	B	X
0	0	1
0	1	1
1	0	1
1	1	0

To provide low impedance the output sides of Q_3 and Q_4 make up what is referred to as a *totem-pole* or *active pull-up output*. Depending upon speed, power requirement and operating temperature range, *TTL* circuiting is available in different families. The series 54/74 are normal *TTL* families. But the operating temperature range for 54 series is – 55°C to + 125°C while for 74 series, it is 0°C to 70°C.

NUMBER SYSTEMS

The decimal counting system is an example of a positional notation. The name decimal implies ten unique symbols :0,1,2,3,4,5,6,7,8 and 9. Thus, the radix or base of the systems is 10. The value of the number represented is given by the sum of the digits values, each weighted by a power of 10 determined by its position. For example, $(6278.35)_{10}$ is

$$6 \times 10^3 + 2 \times 10^2 + 7 \times 10^1 + 8 \times 10^0 + 3 \times 10^{-1} + 5 \times 10^{-2}$$

Similarly, in binary counting, the radix is two, and the value can be determined by the digit values weighted by a power of 2. For example, $(10010.11)_2$ is equivalent to

$$1 \times 2^4 + 0 \times 2^3 + 0 \times 2^2 + 1 \times 2^1 + 0 \times 2^0 + 1 \times 2^{-1} + 1 \times 2^{-2}$$

Conversion of Decimal Number to Binary Number

The successive remainders obtained by division (by 2) yield the bits of the binary number.

Example: Convert $(19)_{10}$ to binary number

	Remainder	
19/2 = 9	1	Least significant digit
9/2 = 4	1	↓
4/2 = 2	0	
2/2 = 1	0	
1/2 = 0	1	

$(19)_{10} = (10011)_2$ Most Significant digit

Binary Subtraction

In binary subtraction, we follow the principle that addition of a negative number to a positive number is subtraction. As in case of addition process, in subtraction we can also make a table of borrow bit.

0 – 0 = 0 with a borrow 0

0 – 1 = 1 with a borrow 1

1 – 0 = 1 with a borrow 0

1 – 1 = 0 with a borrow 0

This is half subtraction. The full subtraction is one which also takes care of borrow of previous digit to give the difference of that digit.

Example:

Borrow	1 1 . 1	1 1
Minuend	1 0 . 0 0	1 1 0
Subtrahend	0 1 . 1 1	0 1 1
	0 0 . 0 1	0 1 1

Sign Bit

Negative sign is represented by '1' and positive sign by '0'. Sign bit is placed first along with a comma before the binary code of that number. As +5 is represented by 0,101 but – 5 is represented by 1,101 (or 0,0101 and 1,0101 respectively in BCD)

Negative numbers are also represented in the complement way. Any negative number can be conveniently represented by either in one's complement form or in two's complement form. One's complement representation is obtained by replacing every '1' by '0' and every '0' by '1' of that binary number. Thus –5 is represented by 1,010 (or 1,0010 in *BCD*). The bit appearing in front of comma is sign bit. Thus one's complement of n bit (binary bit) number X is given by $[(2^n - 1) - X]$.

The *Two's complement* representation of a negative number is obtained by adding a '1' to the one's complement. Thus, the 2's complement for –14 is 0001 + 1 = 0010 and with sign bit it is 1,0010. With the help of 1's complement or 2's complement, the addition/subtraction of number can be done more easily, but correctness is obtained only to those computations, where the answer does not exceed the limit of binary numbers.

Self-Checking/Correcting Codes

A parity bit is introduced in the side of a code to detect the error. It can follow either odd parity code or even parity code. This is an extra 1 bit depending on whether the total number of ones in the code is even or odd. In case of even parity code, '0' is put when the total number of ones are even and '1' is put when the total number of ones are odd, so to get the total number of ones in the code is even or odd. In case of even parity code, '0' is put when the total number of ones are even and '1' is put when the total number of ones are odd, so to get the total number of ones always even, when the

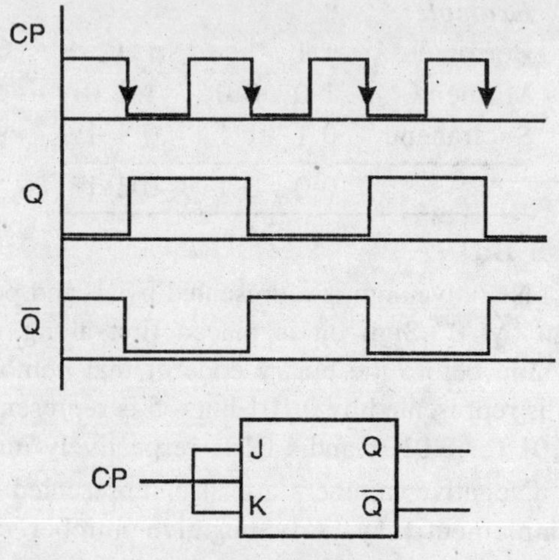

Fig. 7

parity bit is included. Similarly, '1' or '0' is put in the odd parity code to make the total number of ones odd, when the parity bit is included. For Example

Decimal Number	*odd parity bit*	*even parity bit*
0	0000 1	0000 0
1	0001 0	0001 1
5	0101 1	0101 0
8	1000 0	1000 1

A self-correcting code is one in which a parity check bit is given for both columns and rows. In this system, if there is an error, it will be corrected by itself provided the error is of singular bit.

Digital ICs

Digital *ICs* using *MOS* (Metal Oxide Semiconductor) technology were introduced around 1969. The *MOS* technology has several advantages over bipolar devices.

1. *MOS* devices require fewer manufacturing cycles.
2. *MOS* gates dissipate less power per gate.
3. *MOS* gates require less space on the silicon wafer.

Bipolar *TTL* ICs continue to dominate in *SSI* and *MSI* because of their high speed, wide acceptance and long history of reliable operations. Most *LSI* (Large Scale Integration) devices, including memories and microprocessors that require even thousands of gates in a single *IC*, use *MOS* rather than bipolar technology.

MOS technology is divided into two types- *PMOS* which is based on *p*-doped silicon, and *NMOS*, which is based on *n*-doped silicon. These two types of implementation can be used individually or can be combined effectively to form a third category known as *CMOS* (Complementary *MOS*).

PMOS circuit speed is much slower (about one tenth) than bipolar devices, but has lower power dissipation per gate and reduced geometry to accommodate more complexity on a single chip.

NMOS is basically three times faster than *PMOS*. As a result *NMOS* has emerged the most popular process for microprocessor production. It is the process used for *M 6800*, Intel 8080, Fairchild *F* 8 and Zilog 80 etc.

CMOS combines a *n*-channel and a *p*-channel *MOS* transistor in each gate. It has the advantage of extremely low power dissipation when it is static.

Megnetic Devices and Memories: The ability to store information in two different states is available in ferromagnetic material. A large class of binary elements has been devised using the process, of magnetization. One of the most widely used magnetic element is magnetic core.

Magnetic Cores: The typical core is of toroidal shape and of two types. The metal-ribbon core, which is constructed by winding a very thin metallic ribbon on a ceramic core form, and a ferrite core, which is constructed from a finely powdered mixture of magnetic, various bivalent metals like magnesium or maganese, and a binder material. The ferrite cores can be constructed in smaller dimension than metal-ribbon cores. They have sensitivities greater than 10^5 ohm-cm which means eddy current losses are negligible, and thus the core heating is reduced. For these reasons, they are widely used in digital computers.

A magnetic core material can be magnetized in a particular direction by the application of a suitable magnetising force (a magnetic flux resulting from a current flow). The material remains magnetised in that direction after removal of the excitation. Application of magnetizing force of the opposite polarity will switch the material, and it will remain magnetized in the opposite direction after removal of the excitation. Thus, the information in two different states is stored.

A pulse at the 1 input sets a '1' in the core, and a pulse at the 0 input sets a '0' in the core. During the advance pulse, a pulse appears at the output only if the core previously held at 1. By using cores, basic logic functions can also be implemented.

Integrated Circuit Packages: It can be subdivided into three basic groups, based on the size of integration of the package:

1. *SSI* (Small Scale Integration)
2. *MSI* (Medium Scale Integration)
3. *LSI* and *VLSI* (Large Scale Integration and Very Large Scale Integration).

Small Scale Integration Package: It contains fewer than 12 gates. Examples of *SSI* are *NAND* gates (7400, 7410, 7420, 7430), *AND* gates (7408, 7411, 7421), *OR* gates (7432), hex inverters (7404, 7405, 7406, 7407) etc.

Medium Scale Integrator: Depending on the technology used (bipolar or *MOS*) and the chip size, much more complicated *IC* package containing 12 to 100 gates have Full *BCD* encoder 74147 or *BCD* to 7-segment decoder-driver 7446, 7447, 7448 etc.

Large Scale Integration: When the circuit complexity crosses the limit of 100 logic gates, by using Large Scale integration techniques, highly completed circuits are manufactured on a single *IC* chip known as *LSI* or *VLSI* package. For example, *TMS* 2300, 2560 bit dynamic *ROM* or microprocessor chips Intel 8080, Intel 8085, *CP* 1600 etc.

The Integrated Circuit Timer: The 555 monolithic timing circuit is highly stable controller capable of producing accurate time delays or oscillation. Additional terminals are provided for triggering or resetting, if desired. The circuit may be triggered at falling waveforms and the output structure can source or sink up to 200 mA or drive *TTL circuits*.

Read Only Memory: There is another type of arrangement which is known as Read Only Memory (*ROM*). The information stored in a *ROM* can be read out, but new information cannot be written into it. Thus, the information stored is permanent in nature. *ROMs* are *LSI* components with a high degree of programmability and are useful in the design of combination and sequential digital systems. A *ROM* which can be programmed by the user is called *PROM* (Programmable Read Only Memory). To permit modifications, *PROMs* are also available which can be erased and reprogrammed. They are called *EPROMs* (Erasable Programmable Read Only Memory). The erasing may be Ultra Violet (*UV*) radiation based in *U-VEPROMs* (for example, Intel 2716) or done electrically in *EE PROM* (Electrically Erasable Programmable Read Only Memory) or *EAROM* (Electrically Alterable *ROM*).

MOS devices are somewhat simpler than bipolar devices; as a result, *MOS* memories can be constructed with more bits in a chip. They are less expensive than bipolar memories but slower than bipolar units.

Magnetic Drum Storage: A magnetic drum is a cylindrical shaped drum, the surface of which has been coated with a magnetic material. The drum is rotated on its axis, and the read/write heads are used to record the information on the drum or read the information from the drum. Magnetic drums and disks provide larger storage capacities. But the disadvantage of using magnetic drums or disks is the increased access time.

Static Memory: It is composed of cells capable of storing binary information indefinitely. For example, bipolar or *MOS* memory units remain set or reset as long as power is applied to the circuit. Magnetic core remains set or reset even if the power is removed. These basic cells are used to construct static memory. But 'dynamic memory' is one whose contents tend to decay over a period of time.

Memory Devices: A memory device is an array of *m*-bit registers in a single chip (*i.e.*,) which shares a common set of inputs and outputs. Internally, a memory chip has an array of one-bit cells, logic to address one bit, and read/write control circuits. Also, there must be address inputs, data outputs, and chip select input to enable tristate output drivers. A general schematic diagram of a memory device (16 *k ROM* in *X-Y* coincidence mode is shown in Fig. 8). A classification of different types of semiconductor memories is given in Fig. 9.

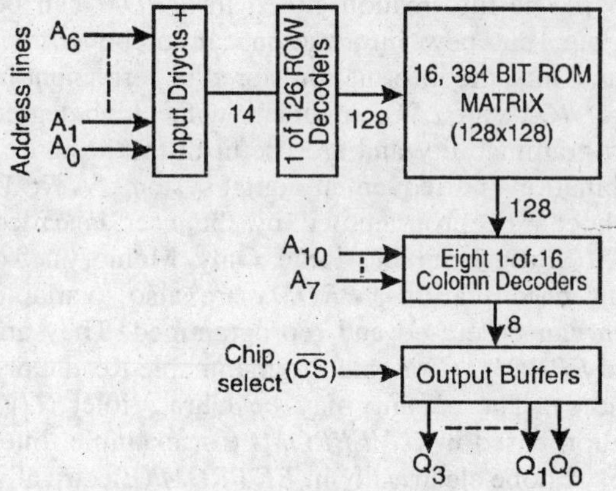

Fig. 8

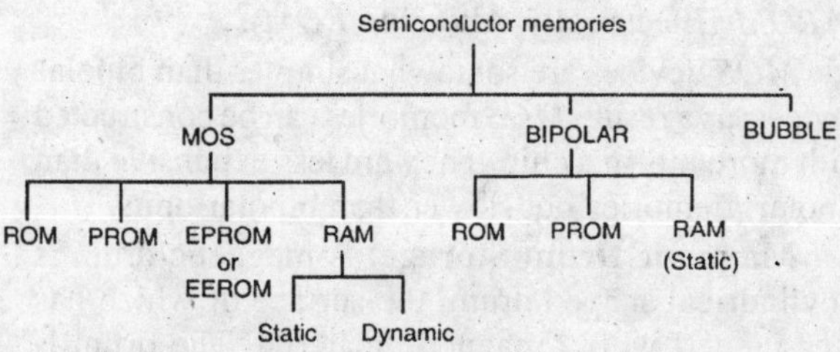

Fig. 9

Implementation of a Boolean Function Using MSI Devices. Multiplexers, decoders, etc, can be used to implement Boolean expression or to design digital logic system with or without the help of individual gates. A multiplexer selects one of the many inputs at a given time. For example, a four-to-one line multiplexer has two select lines to select one of the four inputs, as shown in Fig.10. The input lines are selected by selecting their equivalent minterm coded by select-lines variables. This is clear from the table in Fig. 11, which shows a 4×1 line multiplexer.

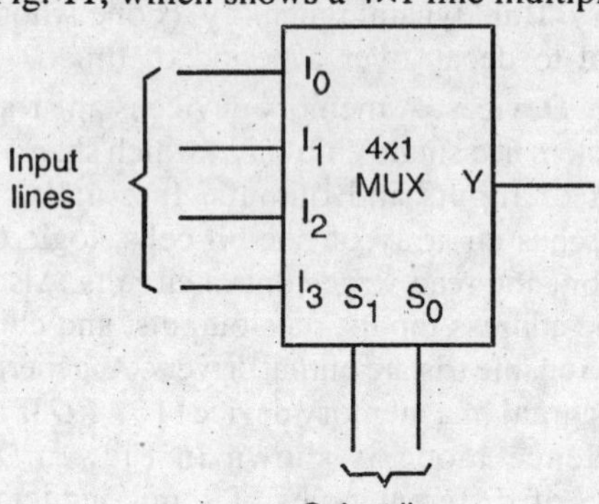

Fig. 10

S_1	S_0	*Minterm*	*OUTPUT selected*
0	0	$\overline{S}_1\ \overline{S}_0$	I_0
0	1	$\overline{S}_1\ S_0$	I_1
1	0	$S_1\ \overline{S}_0$	I_2
1	1	$S_1\ S_0$	I_3

Thus, if the Boolean expression is given as

$$F(A, B) = \overline{A}\ \overline{B} + A\ \overline{B} + AB$$
$$= m_0 + m_2 + m_3$$

A four-to-one line *MUX* chip can be used, as shown in Fig. 11, for the implementation.

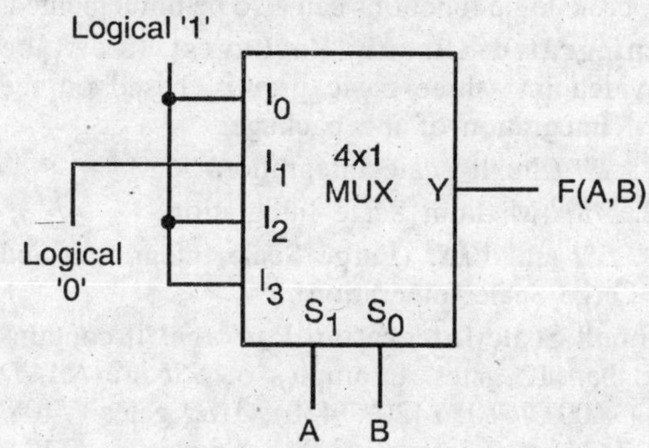

Fig. 11

Random Access Memory: If the cells are arranged in such a fashion that each bit is individually addressable by selecting one X line and one Y line, the arrangement is referred to as a Random Access Memory (*RAM*). This is *NDRO* (non-destructive read-out). This memory is widely used for reading or writing. For this reason, this is also called *RWM* (Read/Write Memory).

Optical Encoder: This provides a convenient means for the digitising shaft-position information or angular position information. Gray code is used to code the optical encode wheel to eliminate the large-ambiguity error found in binary coded wheels. If the light areas on the wheel are transparent and the dark are opaque, the digital information can be obtained by placing light sources and photo-sensors on opposite sides of the disc. The output of photo-sensor is 'high' if light is sensed and 'low' if no light is sensed.

EXERCISE

1. The central processing unit of a small computer system, including *ALU* and control functions on a single *LSI* chip is called
   (a) hardware (b) memory
   (c) microprocessor (d) Peripheral device
2. A digital computer can memorize indefinitely
   (a) only numerical data
   (b) only non-numerical data
   (c) both numerical and non-numerical data
   (d) neither numerical nor non-numerical data
3. The program which translates the instructions in assembly language into the corresponding binary machine language instruction is called a/an
   (a) assembler (b) loader
   (c) compiler (d) interpreter
4. Which of the following control signal does not belong to a printer interface?
   (a) DAV (b) DACC
   (c) NEW LINE ACK (d) TRACK 00
5. A system of letters, numbers and symbols adopted as an abbreviated form of instruction sets is called
   (a) mnemonic (b) mask
   (c) module (d) machine
6. The bit size of first practical microprocessor was
   (a) 2 bit (b) 4 bit
   (c) 8 bit (d) 4 bytes
7. Which of the following circuit converts a *JK* flip-flop to *T* flip-flop?

(a) 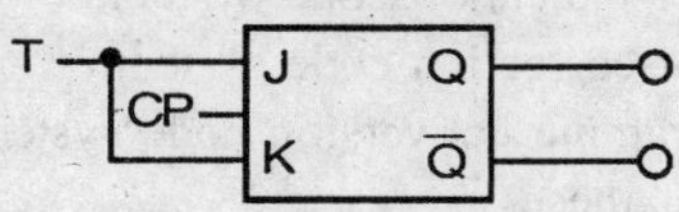

(b) 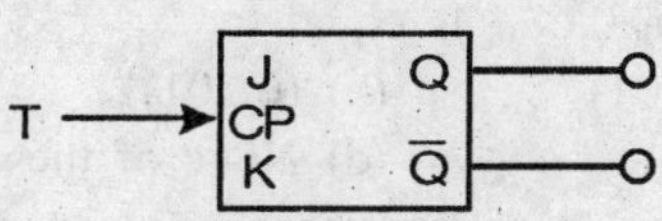

(c) 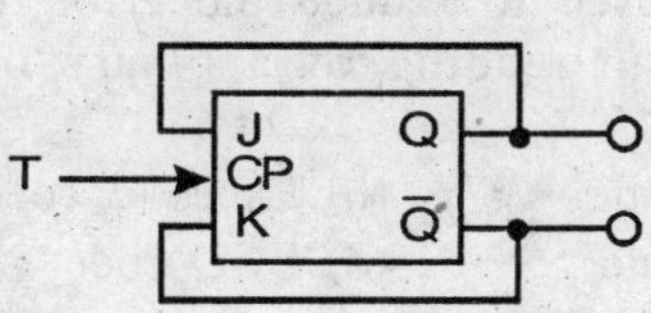

(d) 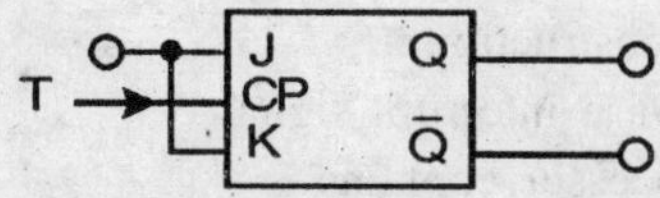

8. A DAD H instruction is same as
   (a) shifting each bit one position to the left
   (b) shifting each bit one position to the right
   (c) shifting each bit one position to the left with a zero inserted in Isb position
   (d) shifting each bit one position to the right with a zero inserted in Isb position
9. Correction in decimal adder is required because
   (a) sums are represented wrongly in binary code
   (b) sums are represented wrongly in *BCD code*
   (c) the numbers to be added are not represented in *BCD* code
   (d) none of these
10. Muemonic symbols are used
    (a) to denote address
    (b) to employ hamming code
    (c) to denote errors
    (d) to assist human memory
11. A micro-computer is a small computer and has the following basic elements.
    (a) Microprocessing unit, memory and input/output devices
    (b) Microprocessing unit, input/output devices and control unit
    (c) Microprocessing unit, input/output devices and program counter
    (d) Microprocessing unit, memory, input/output devices and arithmetic logic unit
12. The function of strobe pulse in digital system is
    (a) to reset memory registers
    (b) to check the functioning of a logic gate
    (c) to avoid race problem
    (d) to shift data in registers
13. In a microcomputer, microprocessor is its
    (a) brain (b) heart
    (c) control unit (d) memory

14. Return from a subroutine is affected by
(a) a jump instruction
(b) an RST instruction
(c) a RET instruction
(d) a hardware interrupt signal

15. A microprocessor contains
(a) most of the control and arithmetic logic functions of a computer
(b) most of the RAM
(c) most of the ROM
(d) peripherial drivers

16. Which of the following is not a magnetic memory?
(a) Flip-flop (b) Tape
(c) Drum (d) Disk

17. A program structure that permits the repeated operation of a particular sequence of instructions until a specified termination is reached is called
(a) subroutine (b) module
(c) loop (d) template

18. The circuit given below is a

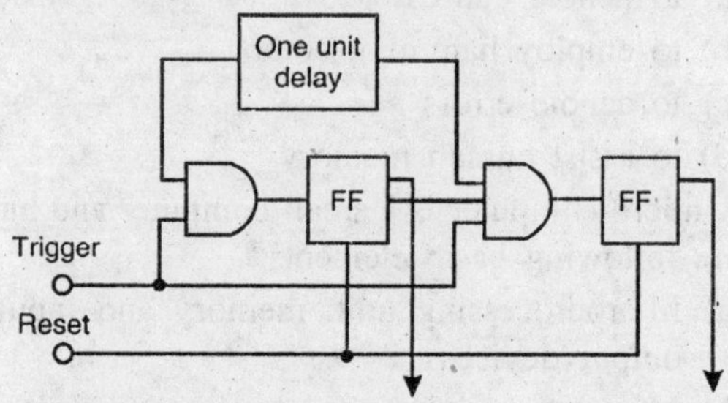

(a) two-bit binary counter
(b) analog-to-digital converter
(c) two-bit series-to parallel converter
(d) two-bit parallel-to-series converter

19. Registers and counters are similar in the sense that they both
(a) are made from an array of flip-flops and gates integrated on a single chip
(b) store binary information
(c) count pulses
(d) are, in fact, shift registers

20. Programmable Logic Array (*PLA*) uses
(a) ROM matrices (b) PROM matrices
(c) RAM matrices (d) Silo memory

21. What is the function of control unit in the CPU?
(a) Decoding of program instructions.
(b) Transfer of data to primary storage.
(c) Performing logical operations.
(d) Storage of program instructions.

22. Which of the following statements is true for 2-out-of-5 code?
(a) It is an unweighted code.
(b) It has even parity.
(c) It has exactly two I's in each code group.
(d) All of these.

23. Loader in a computer is
(a) hardware (b) software
(c) auxiliary (d) none of these

24. Which of the following logics has excellent noise margin?
(a) *TTL* (b) *ECL*
(c) *CMOS* (d) All of these

25. The number of comparator circuits required to build a three-bit simultaneous A/D converter is
(a) 7 (b) 8
(c) 15 (d) 16

26. What type of construction is used for most stator poles of a shaded-pole motor?
(a) Sailent pole (b) Consequent pole
(c) Alternate pole (d) Compensated pole

27. A magnetic drum of 8 inch diameter has 100 tracks and storage density of 200 bits/inch. Its storage capacity will be
(a) 502400 bits (b) 8402 bits
(c) both (d) none of these

28. Hamming code is
(a) an error-indication code system.
(b) an error-correction code system.
(c) a programme conversion code system
(d) none of these

29. The fraction 0.68_{10} is equal to
(a) $(0.010101)_2$ (b) $(0.101)_2$
(c) $(0.10101)_2$ (d) None of these

30. The code used to reduce the error due to ambiguity in reading of a binary optical encoder is
(a) Octal code (b) Excess-3 code
(c) Gray code (d) BCD code

31. *Call* in computer system means
(a) to execute a part of main programme
(b) to call a sub-programme to be executed
(c) to transfer control to specified closed sub-routine
(d) none of these

32. In grand-scale integration (*GSI*) a chip contains more than
(a) 1500 gates (b) 1000 gates
(c) 5000 gates (d) 10,000 gates

33. What is the function implemented by the following circuit
(a) $F_2 (A, B, C, D) = ABCD - \overline{A}\ BC\overline{D}$
(b) $F_2 (A, B, C, D) = CD + AB + BC$
(c) $F_2 (A, B, C, D) = \overline{A}\ B + \overline{B}\ \overline{C} + \overline{C}\ \overline{D}$
(d) $F_2 (A, B, C, D) = AB + BC + \overline{C}\ \overline{D}$

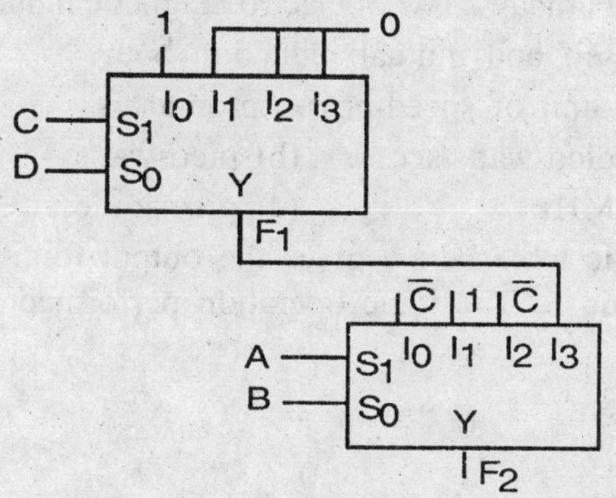

34. The voltage levels for a four-input resistive divider are 0 = 0 V, 1 = +10 V. The analog output voltage for a digital input of 1001 will be
(a) 3 V (b) 6 V
(c) 8 V (d) 9 V

35. Which of the following codes is a weighted code?
(a) Excess-3 code (b) Shift-counter code
(c) Gray code (d) 5111 code

36. The disadvantage of magnetic drum storage is that
(a) its size is very large
(b) only read out is possible
(c) access time is high
(d) access time is less

37. Decimal number 9 in 50 43210 code (biquinary code) is represented as
(a) 00 01001 (b) 10 10000
(c) 10 01001 (d) 11 00000

38. The maximum time required to perform a division using 12-bit numbers and a clock of 2 MHz is
(a) 12 μ sec (b) 19 μ sec
(c) 31 μ sec (d) 48 μ sec

39. Which of the following parameters is not specified for digital *ICs*
(a) Gate dissipation (b) Propagation delay
(c) Noise margin (d) Bandwidth

40. A decade counter requires
(a) 2 flip-flops (b) 3 flip-flops
(c) 4 flip-flops (d) 100 flip-flops

41. Decimal number 59 with odd parity will be represented in 8421 *BCD* code as
(a) 0101 1001 1 (b) 0101 1111 0
(c) 1001 0110 1 (d) 0100 1011 0

42. An electronic wrist-watch has a clock of frequency 32 kHz. To divide this frequency down to 1 Hz. It is necessary to have
(a) two decade counters, one two-bit binary counter and a *T* flip-flop
(b) three decade counters, one four-bitbinary counter and one *T* flip-flop
(c) one four-bit binary counter and *T* flip-flop and one decade counter
(d) four four-bit binary counter and decade counter

43. The deselect to output float time is
(a) the delay between application of proper chip select signal and the stable output data
(b) the delay between the previous valid output data and the next change in address
(c) the time for which the output data remains valid when the device is no longer selected
(d) maximum time for which the valid address can be changed

44. Which of the following is not valid in case of binary product?
(a) 0 × 0 (b) 0 × 1 = 1
(c) 1 × 1 = 1 (d) All of these

45. The Boolean expression for the lower network shown in the above question is

(a) $A(B+C)$ (b) $A+BC$

(c) $A+BC+AC+AB$ (d) $A(A+B+C)$

46. As compared to fixed-point machine, a floating-point machine has

(a) a floating position for the binary point

(b) no provision for power of 2

(c) provision for power of 2

(d) no position for the binary point

47. Which of the following characteristics is not true for *TTL* logic?

(a) Good speed

(b) Low power dissipation per gate

(c) High cost

(d) None of these

48. Generally, the unit of propagation delay is

(a) sec (b) m-sec

(c) p-sec (d) n-sec

49. The *CMOS* ICs can be operated at power supply of value

(a) 5 V (b) 5.2 V

(c) 3-18 V (d) 3-9 V

50. PSW stands for

(a) accumulator contents

(b) flag byte

(c) accumulator and the flag byte

(d) accumulator and temporary register byte

51. The number of flip-flops required to build a mod-19 counter is

(a) 4 (b) 5

(c) 6 (d) 7

52. The gates required to build an half adder are

(a) *Ex. OR* gate and *NOR* gate

(b) *Ex. OR* gate and *OR* gate

(c) *Ex. OR* gate and *AND* gate

(d) Four *NAND* gate

53. The output of the circuit shown below for the input T will be (Assume Q is '0' at the start and F/F is negative edge triggered)

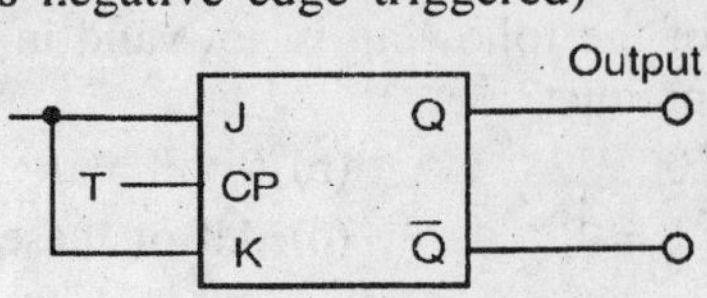

(a)
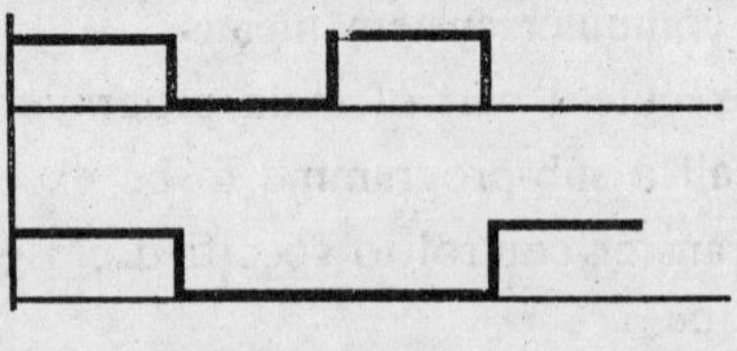

(b)

(c)

(d)

54. Transformer works on the principle of

(a) self-induction

(b) mutual induction

(c) Faraday's law of electro magnetic induction

(d) self and mutual induction both

55. The unit of speed-power product is

(a) pico-watts/sec (b) pico-watts

(c) MHz (d) pico-joules

56. Logic table below gives the output for inputs *A* and *B*. The logic operation performed is

A	*B*	*C*
0	0	1
0	1	0
1	0	0
1	1	1

(a) Negative of *NOR*

(b) Ex. *OR*

(c) *NAN*

(d) Negative of Ex. *OR*

57. The Boolean expressions for the circuits shown below is

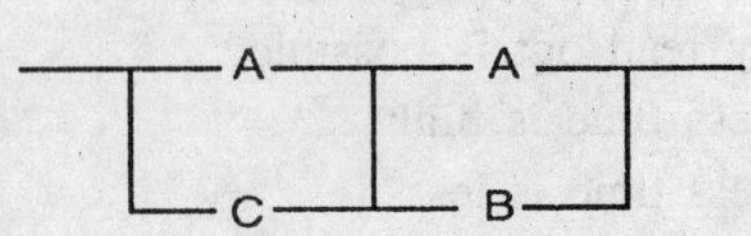

(a) identical
(b) complementary
(c) dual
(d) different from each other

58. Access time of a storage is the time required
(a) to write one word into the memory
(b) to read one word from the memory
(c) to write one word into and to read one word from the memory
(d) either to write one word or to read one word

59. The decimal number 29 in binary form is
(a) 11001 (b) 11101
(c) 10001 (d) 11111

60. Benchmark problem is used to evaluate the performance of
(a) hardware
(b) software
(c) both hardware and software
(d) all of these

61. After completing the execution, microprocessor returns to
(a) Halt state (b) Fetch state
(c) Execute state (d) Interrupt state

62. The Binary number 10.1 100.110 in octal numbers is
(a) 152.6 (b) 154.6
(c) 145.6 (d) 174.6

63. The most widely used universal gates are
(a) *OR* and *AND* gates
(b) *NOR* and *NAND* gates
(c) *NOR* and *AND* gates
(d) *NAND* and *OR* gates

64. A device that works in conjunction with a computer but not as part of it is called
(a) hardware (b) memory
(c) microprocessor (d) peripheral device

65. In positive logic, the transistor gate in the circuit below is an

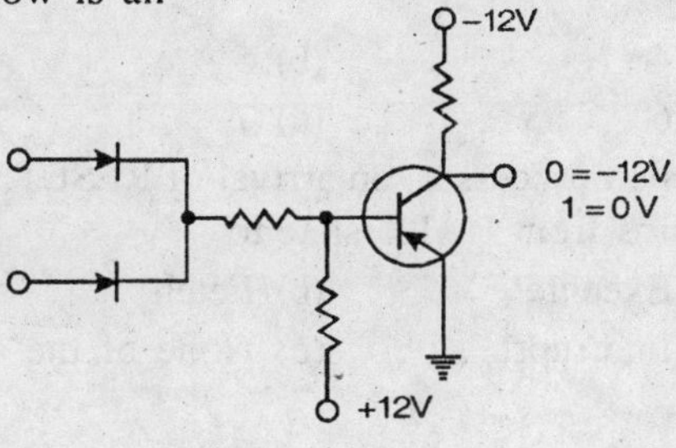

(a) *AND* gate (b) *NOR* gate
(c) *NAND* gate (d) *OR* gate

66. 10 in BCD code is represented as
(a) 10100 (b) 1100
(c) 010111 (d) None of these

67. In the Schmitt trigger shown below, the threshold voltages V_1 and V_2 are

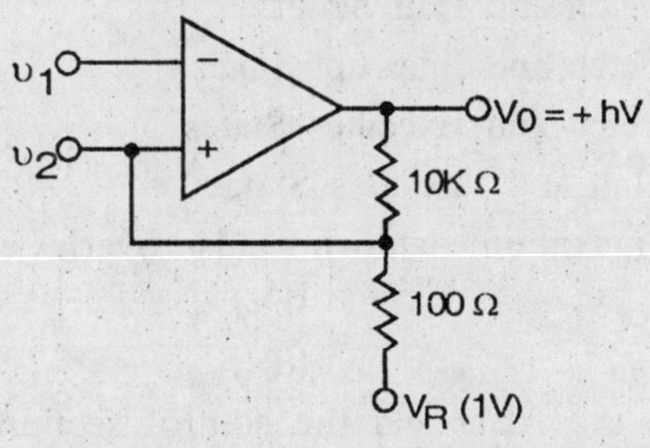

(a) 2.5V, 1.5V (b) 1.04V, 0.94V
(c) 1.5V, 1V (d) 1.85V, 1.15V

68. In another number system e.g., 6, a "decade" counter has to recycle to "0" at the sixth count. Which of the connections indicated below will realise this resetting? (a logic "0" at the *R* inputs resets the counters)

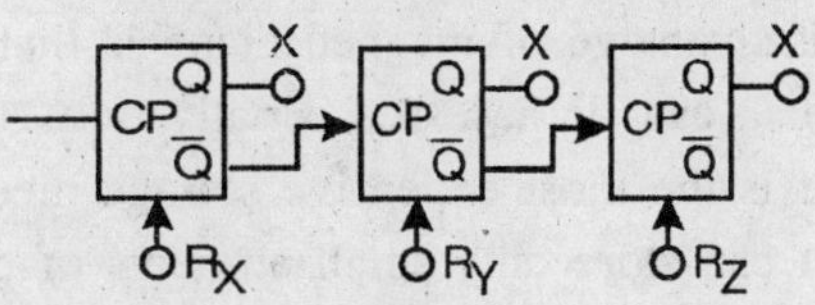

(a)
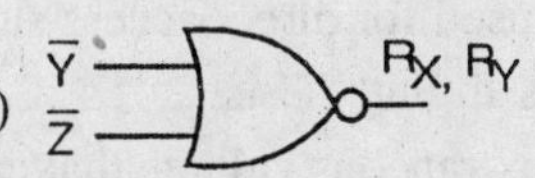

(b)
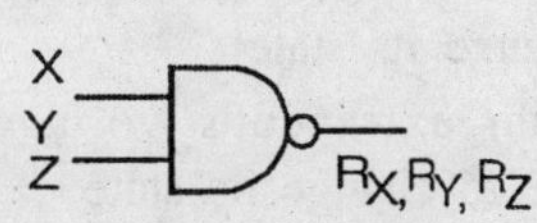

(c)
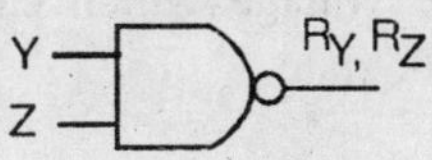

(d) None of these

69. An *D/A* converter uses a ladder of + 10 V full scale output. The number of bits required at its input for a resolution of 5 mV will be
(a) 7 (b) 8
(c) 9 (d) 11

70. The function of Interleave is to assign successive storage location numbers to
(a) physically separated memory locations
(b) physically adjacent memory locations
(c) altenate memory location
(d) none of these

71. Normally a microprocessor cycles between
(a) Fetch and Halt States
(b) Fetch and Interrupt States
(c) Fetch and Executes States
(d) Halt and Executes States

72. The maximum data/wire pulse overlays is
(a) t_{CR} (b) t_{CW}
(c) t_{DH} (d) t_{WR}

73. Both the ALU and the control section have special-purpose storage location called
(a) address (b) accumulators
(c) registers (d) decoders

74. The binary fraction 0.0111 in decimal form is equal to
(a) 0.4375 (b) 0.6225
(c) 0.8325 (d) 0.1105

75. A disadvantage of magnetic tape is that
(a) data can be accessed serially only
(b) it is the most expensive storage medium
(c) it can store only small amounts of data
(d) it can only be used for direct access storage

76. Noise margin of a digital *IC* is
(a) the minimum extraneous voltage that causes a gate to change its state
(b) the maximum extraneous voltage that causes a gate to change its state
(c) the thermal noise voltage which causes a gate to change its state
(d) none of these

77. An assembler does not perform the task of
(a) providing storage allocation
(b) translating a program written in high level language to machine code program
(c) doing assembly time arithmetic
(d) none of these

78. For a Schmitt trigger, the upper and lower trip voltages are 3 V and 1 V, and high and low states are 15 V and 2 V. The output for a sinusoidal input of 10 V peak will lie between.
(a) 1 V and 3 V (b) 2 V and 15 V
(c) 3 V and 15 V (d) 10 V and 15 V

79. *ACK* indicates reception of
(a) correct data (b) incorrect data
(c) insufficient data (d) sufficient data

80. The circuit shown below is a

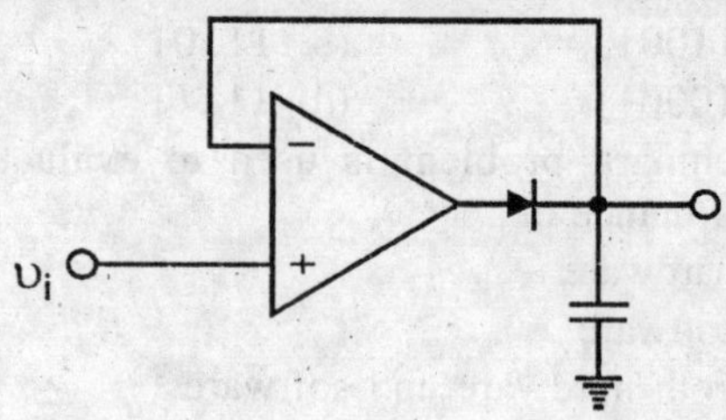

(a) half-wave rectifier
(b) average detector
(c) peak detector
(d) clamping circuit

81. In a digital computer, monostable vibrator finds main application of
(a) triggering (b) wave-shaping
(c) wave-analysis (d) all of these

82. In a digital system, the maximum clock frequency that can be used with Master/Slave Clocked flip-flops having total propagation delay of 200 μ sec is
(a) 20 MHz (b) 50 MHz
(c) 100 MHz (d) 200 MHz

83. Sixty capsules are to be filled in bottles automatically employing an electronic counter. The number of flip-flop in such a counter will be
(a) 4 (b) 5
(c) 6 (d) 7

84. A microprocessor, on arrival of RESET signal returns from HALT state to
(a) Execute (b) Fetch
(c) Interrupt (d) None of the above

85. The translator program that converts source code in high level language into machine code line by line is called

(a) Assembler (b) Compiler
(c) Loader (d) Interpreter

86. The number of 7490s of obtain positive half cycle of 10 m sec is

(a) 3 (b) 4
(c) 5 (d) 7

87. What is the state of the bus at *X*?

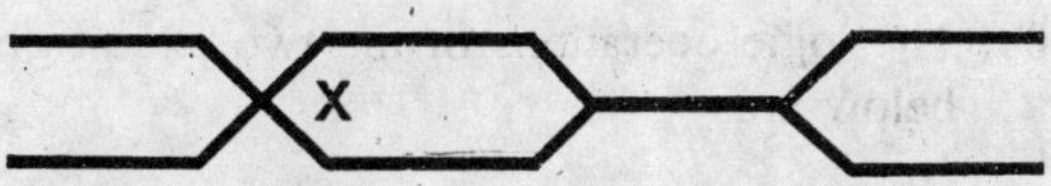

(a) Bus is High.
(b) All wires are Low.
(c) Some wires are floating.
(d) Signals are changing their states.

88. If the negative logic is used, the diode gate in the circuit below represents an

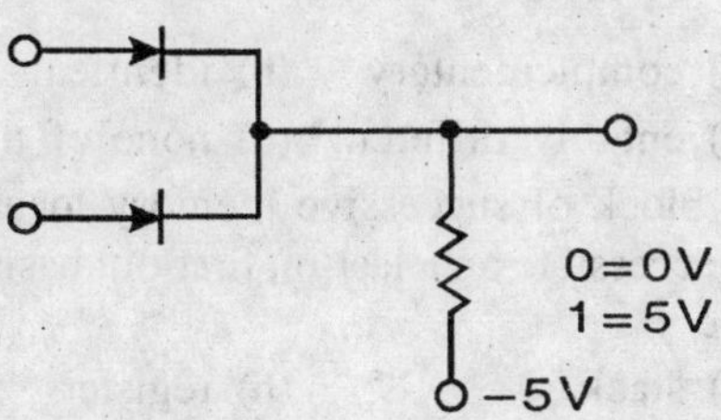

(a) AND gate (b) OR gate
(c) NOR gate (d) NAND gate

89. The disadvantage of an open-shift register is that

(a) both shift-left and shift-right operations cannot be performed
(b) the quantity stored is lost at every shift pulses
(c) the register is reset when read-out is over
(d) all of these

90. The disadvantage of a counter-type A/D converter as compared to simultaneous A/D converter is that

(a) the resolution is low
(b) longer conversion time is required
(c) the circuitry is more complex
(d) its stability is low

91. Data management system may be implemented as

(a) system software
(b) computer program
(c) application software
(d) all of the above

92. The first practical microprocessor was introduced by

(a) Motorola
(b) National Semiconductors
(c) Intel
(d) Fairchild

93. The common name given to a program written in any one of the high level languages is

(a) source program (b) system program
(c) compiler program (d) object program

94. Which of the following integrated circuit type provides Ex-*OR* operation?

(a) 7404 (b) 7486
(c) 7470 (d) 7476

95. Output circuit of a computer is used for

(a) storing the data till it is converted into analog form
(b) converting the digital data into digital form acceptable to the readout or display
(c) either of the above
(d) none of the above

96. Which of the following logics has the fan-out of more than 50?

(a) *TTL* (b) *5-nsec ECL*
(c) *8-nsec ECL* (d) *CMOS*

97. Which of the following is the redundancy check character?

(a) Double Precision (b) Multiple Precision
(c) Parity bit (d) *CRC*

98. The thickness of magnetic tape is
(a) 1 μm (b) 10 μm
(c) 5 μm (d) 40 μm

99. A high on RESET OUT line signifies that
(a) all the registers of the CPU are being reset
(b) all the registers and counters are being reset
(c) all the registers and counters are being reset and in addition this signal can be used to reset external support chips
(d) processing can begin when this signal goes high

100. Which of the following devices automatically interrupts the supply in the event of surges?
(a) Earthing switch (b) Isolator
(c) Lightning switch (d) Circuit breaker

101. Which of the following statements is true for dynamic memory?
(a) It has low speed as compared to static memory.
(b) It has low power dissipation.
(c) Its contents tend to decay over period of time.
(d) All of these.

102. Currently the most popular form of secondary storage is
(a) magnetic tape (b) disk
(c) magnetic core (d) semiconductor

103. The resolution of a 12-bit D/A converter using a binary ladder with + 10V as the full scale output will be
(a) 2.44 mV (b) 3.50 mV
(c) 4.32 mV (d) 5.12 mV

104. In the circuit shown below, the output Y_1 and Y_2 for the given initial condition $Y_1 = Y_2 = 1$ and after four input pulses will be

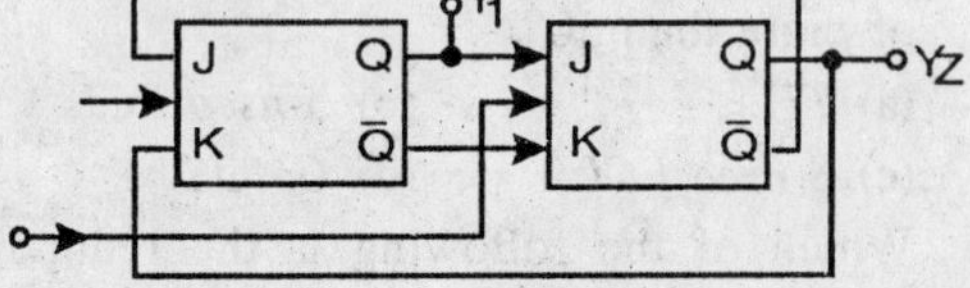

(a) $Y_1 = 1, Y_2 = 0$ (b) $Y_1 = 0, Y_2 = 1$
(c) $Y_1 = 0, Y_2 = 0$ (d) $Y_1 = 1, Y_2 = 1$

105. The minimum time between writing operation is specified by
(a) t_{CW} (b) t_{WCY}
(c) t_{WR} (d) t_{DH}

106. Consider two normally open contacts in series for a normally closed relay. The logic operation performed by this circuit is
(a) *AND* (b) *NAND*
(c) *NOR* (d) None of these

107. Compatibility concerns
(a) only hardware
(b) only software
(c) only peripheral devices
(d) only operating systems
(e) both hardware and software

108. The logic operations of the two circuit given below are

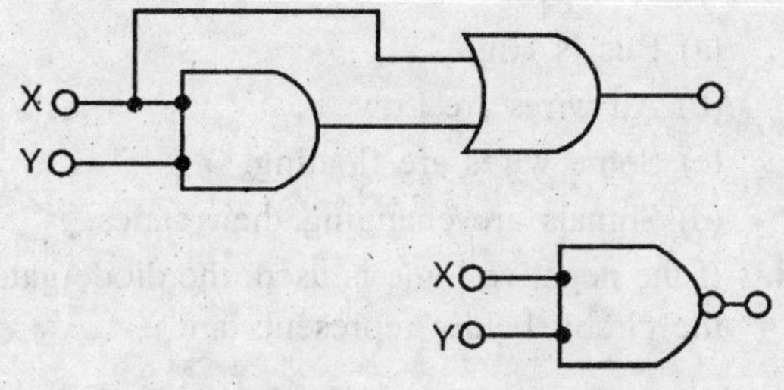

(a) complementary (b) identical
(c) entirely different (d) none of these

109. A block of successive memory locations that is accessible on a last-in, first-out basis is called the
(a) stack (b) register
(c) program counter (d) accumulator

110. The maximum allowable delay between address change and 1→0 transition of write pulse is
(a) t_{AW} (b) t_{WR}
(c) t_{DH} (d) t_{DW}

111. Digital computers have the application(s) of
(a) stimulation
(b) business and specific problems
(c) line control or real time control
(d) all of the above

112. For the op amp, the gain is 10,000. The exact output voltage will be

(a) –5.11 V (b) –5.003 V
(c) –4.997 V (d) –4.910 V

113. The processing of causing an unplanned branching operation to occur, usually initiated by external system is called

(a) masking (b) interrupt
(c) iteration (d) debugging

114. A microcomputer is a minimum combination of

(a) μP and clock
(b) μP clock, ROMs
(c) μP, clock, RAMs and ROMs
(d) μP, clock, RAM, ROM, PIA and ACIA

115. The *ECL* can be used to switch frequencies as high as

(a) 1 MHz (b) 100 MHz
(c) 500 MHz (d) 1 GHz

116. Which of the following is the peripheral device?

(a) Graph plotter (b) Assembler
(c) Program (d) Arithmetic unit

117. Which of the following logic is the fastest?

(a) *TTL* (b) *ECL*
(c) *CMOS* (d) *LSI*

118. Which of the following circuit represents the shaded area of the accompanying Venn diagram?

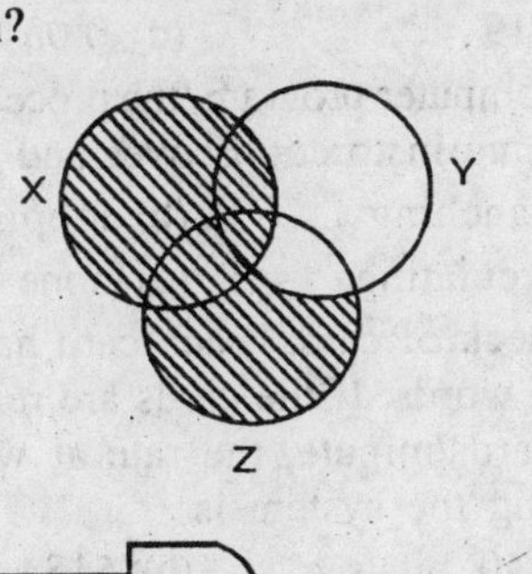

(a)
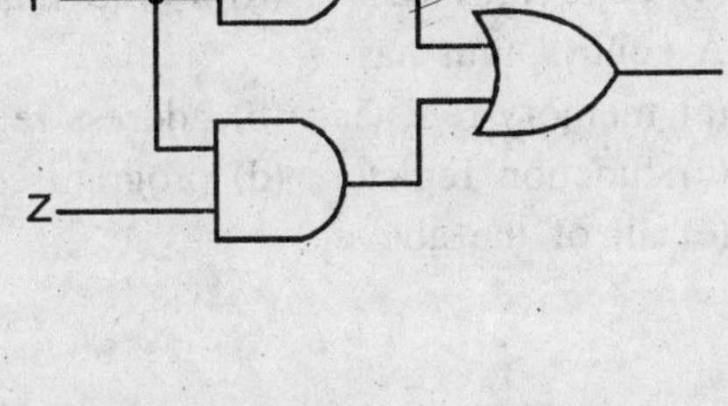

(b)
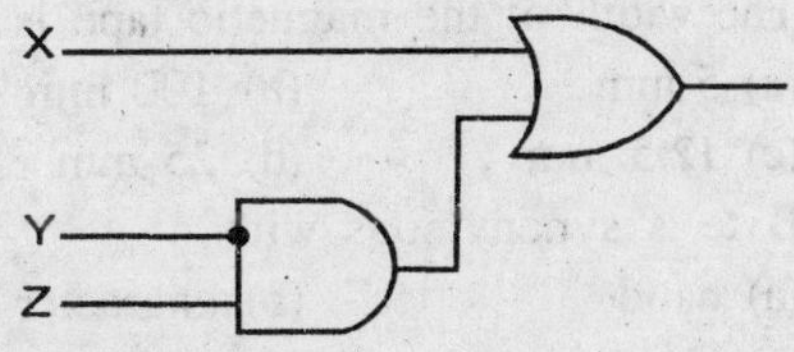

(c)
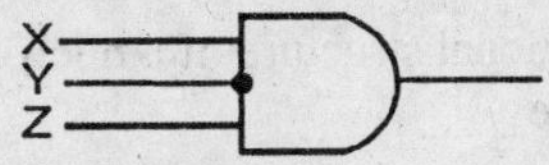

(d) none of these

119. Which of the following does not represent peripheral data storage device?

(a) Punched tape (b) Magnetic tape
(c) Magnetic card (d) Magnetic drum

120. In Schottky-clamped *TTL*, the purpose of Schottky diode is

(a) to increase propagation delay
(b) to achieve efficient non-saturated switching
(c) to improve noise margin
(d) to decrease dissipation

121. To a great extent, computer in function is similar to

(a) CPU (b) Buffer
(c) Assembler (d) PLA

122. Which of the following storages has greatest capacity with less cost per bit?

(a) coincidence-current memory
(b) magnetic tape
(c) magnetic drum
(d) semi-conductor memory

123. Which of the following can be used as an inverter?

(a) *AND* gate (b) *OR* gate
(c) *NOR* gate (d) None of these

124. American Standard Code for Information Interchange (ASCII) employs a coded character set consisting of

(a) 7 bits
(b) 7 bits with parity check
(c) 8 bit
(d) 8 bit with parity check

125. The width of the magnetic tape is usually
(a) 5 mm (b) 100 mm
(c) 12.5 mm (d) 25 mm

126. Byte is synonymous with
(a) band (b) character
(c) bit (d) word

127. An organisational structure of a micro-processor is called the
(a) organiser (b) architecture
(c) manager (d) none of these

128. A transistor is operated as a non-saturated switch to eliminate
(a) turn-on time (b) turn-off time
(c) storage time (d) delay time

129. A 12-bit binary counter has the following state. Which is the octal number represented?

(a) 677 (b) 7163
(c) 7183 (d) 7128.

130. Magnetic tape falls under the category of
(a) main memory
(b) core memory
(c) RAM memory
(d) catche memory
(e) auxiliary storage device

131. Which of the following circuit represents a subtractor to subtract A from B?

(a) 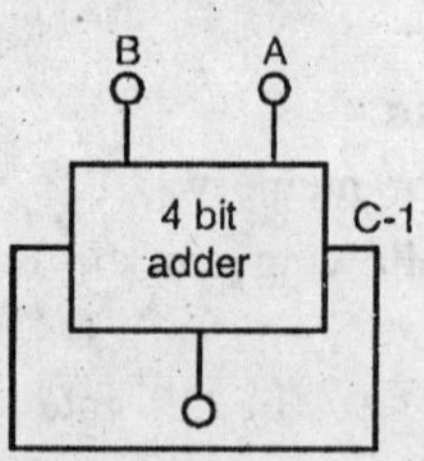

(b) 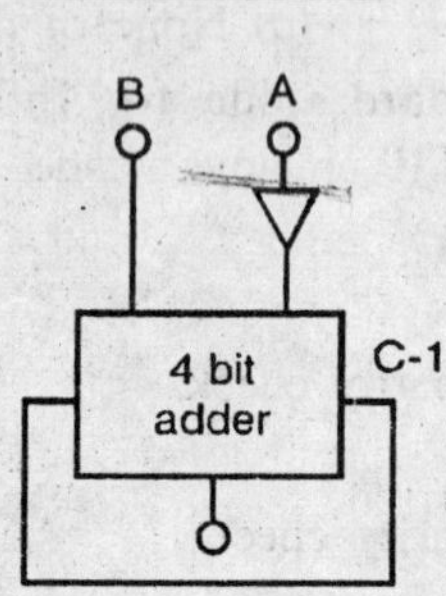

(c) 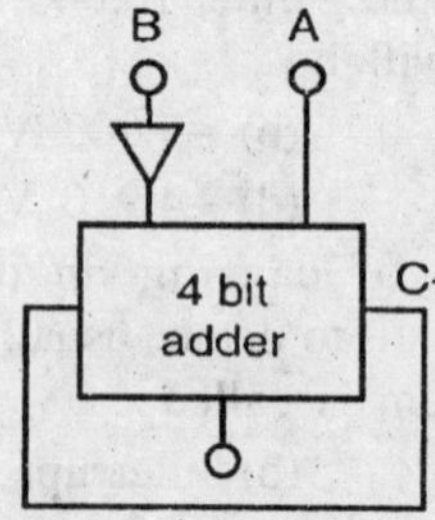

(d) None of these

132. The CPU
(a) is controlled by input data as it enters the system
(b) is controlled by the auxiliary storage unit
(c) controls the program
(d) controls all input, output and processing

133. In a train of binary signals, 1 *baud* is equal to
(a) ¼ bit/sec (b) ½ bit/sec
(c) 1 bit/sec (d) 2 bits/sec

134. Sequential circuits are
(a) clocked or synchronous
(b) unlocked or asynchronous
(c) either of the above
(d) none of the above

135. Data are recorded on a 2,400-ft reel of magnetic tape at a density of 556 characters per inch. If the record length is of 100 characters and 0.75 inch of record gap, the tape utilization factor is
(a) 0.85 (b) 0.67
(c) 0.19 (d) 0.08

136. In a computer program, the process of executing the same instructions over and over is called
(a) branching (b) looping
(c) circulating (d) none of these

137. In a deck of cards, each card has twenty four 36-bit words. If the cards are read at a rate of 600 cards/minute, the rate at which data are entering the system is
(a) 1440 bits/sec (b) 5184 bits/sec
(c) 8640 bits/sec (d) 14400 bits/sec

138. A control unit has
(a) memory register (b) address register
(c) function register (d) program counter
(e) all of the above

139. Flag is a character for
(a) identification of a word
(b) occurance of some condition
(c) marking or tagging
(d) all of these

140. Which of the following is used for serial access storage only?
(a) RAM (b) Magnetic tape
(c) Magnetic disk (d) Core memory

141. In large-scale integration (*LSI*) a chip contains
(a) more than 100 but less than 1000 gates
(b) more than 500 but less than 1000 gates
(c) more than 1000 gates
(d) more than 5000 gates

142. In a digital computer, an index register is used for
(a) address modification
(b) performing arithmetic and logic operations
(c) temporary storage of results
(d) indirect addressing

143. The output of the circuit shown below for a digital input of 1010 would be proportional to

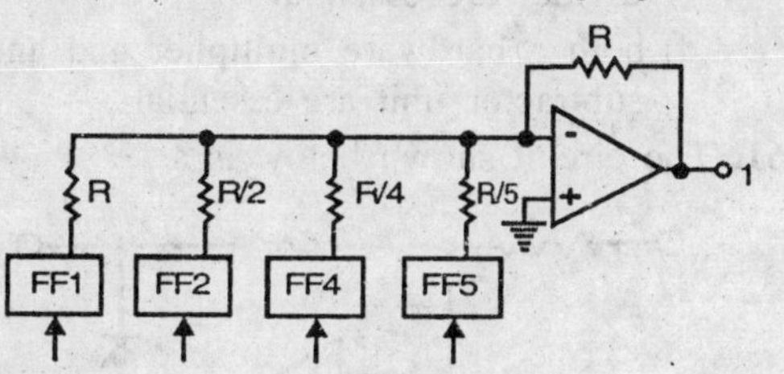

(a) 15 (b) −10
(c) $-\dfrac{-10V}{R}$ (d) $\dfrac{-15V}{R}$

144. The function implemented by the following circuit

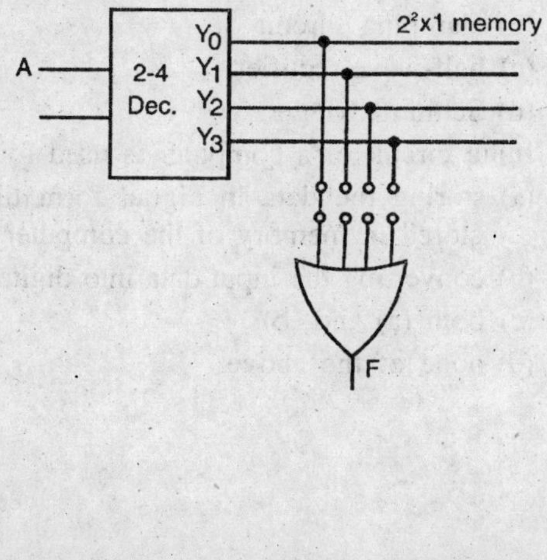

(a) $F(A, B) = A+B$ (b) $F(A, B) = \overline{A}\,B+AB$
(c) $F(A, B) = A$ (d) $F(A, B) = A.B$

145. A digital computer system consists of a CPU interfaced with
(a) input devices (b) output devices
(c) auxiliary storage (d) all of these

146. A central processing unit (CPU) of a computer consists of
(a) control and arithmetic logic unit and primary storage
(b) control, clock and ROM
(c) control, clock and RAM
(d) control, ALU, RAM and ROM

147. What is the maximum number (in decimal notation) that can be counted with above counter?
(a) 999 (b) 4096
(c) 4095 (d) 9999

148. The degree of resolution that can be obtained using an eight-bit optical encoder will be
(a) 1.4° (b) 2.8°
(c) 3.2° (d) 4.8°

149. Accumulator is a
(a) storage battery for supplying necessary power to the system
(b) hardware which stores one of the operand to be manipulated by the ALU
(c) hardware which stores memory in the memory unit
(d) hardware used to link the control unit with I/O unit

150. "In all cases of electromagnetic induction, an induced voltage will cause a current to flow in a closed circuit in such a direction that the magnetic field which is caused by that current will oppose the change that produces the current" is the original statement of
(a) Lenz's law
(b) Faraday's law of magnetic induction
(c) Fleming's law of induction
(d) Ampere's law

151. A USART chip provides
(a) half duplex operation
(b) full duplex operation
(c) duplex operation
(d) full duplex operation but cannot work in asynchronous mode

152. Magnetic records have the advantage(s) of
(a) large storage capacity
(b) short access time
(c) repeated use
(d) high speed of transmission
(e) all of the above

153. The minimum time output data will be valid after address changes is called
(a) t_{DF} (b) t_{RC}
(c) t_{OH} (d) t_A

154. The output of the circuit for the given inputs '*a*' and '*b*' will be

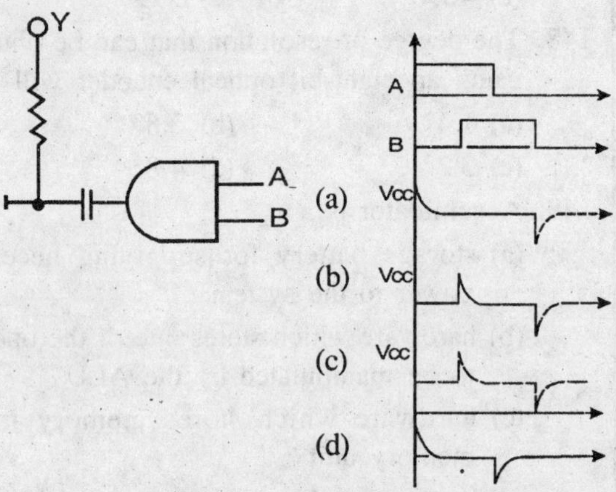

155. Digital differential analyser is employed for solving
(a) linear differential equations
(b) non-linear differential equations
(c) set of linear differential equations
(d) set of non-linear differential equations
(e) any of the above

156. Modem is a
(a) code changing system
(b) programme conversion system
(c) modulator-demodulator system
(d) demodulator-modulator system

157. Bootstrap is a technique designed
(a) to transfer control to specified closed subroutine
(b) to suspend the main programme for a while
(c) to bring itself into a desired state by means of its own action
(d) none of above

158. The input code of the compiler as well as assembler is called
(a) assembler code (b) machine code
(c) source code (d) object code

159. *Carry-Look-Ahead* is a type of adder in which
(a) inputs to several stages are examined
(b) carries are produced simultaneously
(c) carries are produced before hand
(d) none of these

160. In a digital computer, for multiplying two binary numbers, in the computer
(a) a hardware divider is essential
(b) a hardware multiplier is essential
(c) both a hardware multiplier and a hardware divider are essential
(d) both a hardware multiplier and an adder subtractor unit are essential

161. The circuit shown below is a

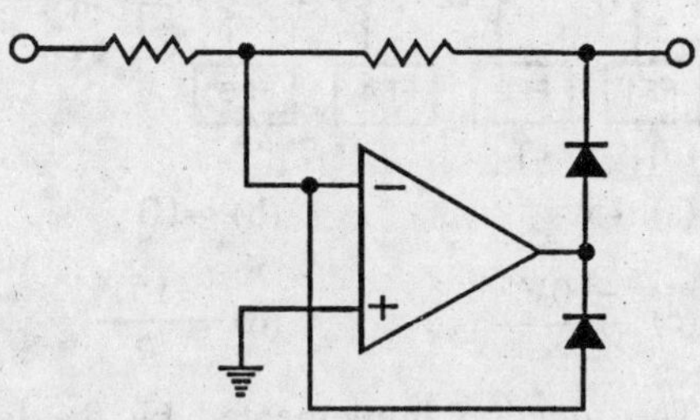

(a) average detector
(b) clamping circuit
(c) half-wave rectifier
(d) Schimitt trigger

162. Input circuit of a computer is used for
(a) storing the data in digital form till it is stored in memory of the computer
(b) converting the input data into digital form
(c) both (a) and (b)
(d) none of the above

163. The number -34 is represented in Excess-3 *BCD* code is
(a) 1.1001 1000 (b) 0.1001 1001
(c) 1.0110 0111 (d) none of the above

164. The output of a *JK* flip-flop toggles when
(a) $J = 1, K = 0$ (b) $J = 0, K = 1$
(c) $J = 1, K = 1$ (d) $J = 0, K = 0$

165. A microprocessor consists of
(a) arithmetic logic unit (ALU)
(b) memories
(c) input/output devices
(d) all of the above

166. Which of the following codes is an unweighted code?
(a) 8421 (b) Excess-3 code
(c) 2421 (d) 63210

167. A device in which computer information and data are stored and relieved at a later time is called
(a) hardware (b) memory
(c) microprocessor (d) peripheral device

168. Transaction processing was made possible by the development of
(a) direct access storage
(b) magnetic tape
(c) mini computers
(d) cash register input

169. An Input Port is
(a) Tri-state buffer with register
(b) Select logic
(c) Input device
(d) R/W memory

170. In a train of signals each of which can assume one out of eight different states, 1 baud is equal to
(a) 2 bits/sec (b) 3 bits/sec
(c) 4 bits/sec (d) 8 bits/sec

171. Which of the following does not represent input device?
(a) Punched tape (b) Magnetic drum
(c) Magnetic tape (d) Matrix printer

172. In writing mode of R/W memory, we can not begin writing until following time has elapsed
(a) t_{CW} (b) t_{WCY}
(c) t_{DH} (d) t_{AW}

173. The block diagram that outlines, step by step, working of a computer program is called the
(a) program flow chart
(b) program layout
(c) logical planning
(d) structured programming

174. Which code is suitable for input-output devices and analog-to-digital converters?
(a) 8421 code
(b) Excess-3 code
(c) Four bit BCD code
(d) Gray code

175. A six-bit alpha-numeric code is able to code
(a) 36 characters (b) 48 characters
(c) 64 characters (d) 128 characters

176. Current transformers for meters and relays usually have
(a) 10-A secondaries (b) 5-A secondaries
(c) 10:1 ratio (d) 1:1 ratio

177. The multiplication time for 10-bit numbers with 1 MHz clock will be
(a) 32 μ sec (b) 20 μ sec
(c) 21 μ sec (d) 22 μ sec

178. Two point charges of 10^{-8} Coul, each are located at points (0,1,2) and (1,0,2). The electric field at point (2,2,0) will be
(a) $(\bar{I}_x) + (\bar{I}_y) + (\bar{I}_z)$
(b) $(3\,\bar{I}_x + 3\,\bar{I}_y + 3\,\bar{I}_z)$
(c) $(3\,\bar{I}_x + 3\,\bar{I}_y - 4\,\bar{I}_z)$
(d) $10/3\,[3\,\bar{I}_x + 3\,\bar{I}_y - 4\,\bar{I}_z]$

179. 2's complement of-7 is
(a) 1,1001 (b) 1,1000
(c) 1,0111 (d) 0,0111

180. LSI usually contains
(a) 10 gates
(b) 10 to 100 gates
(c) more than 100 gates
(d) more than 10,000 gates

181. The decimal fraction 0.375 in binary form is
(a) 0.0011 (b) 0.011
(c) 0.0111 (d) 0.111

182. How many 7490 *ICs* are to be cascaded to count upto 999?
(a) 1 (b) 2
(c) 3 (d) 4

183. The advantage of serial transfer compared with parallel transfer for data transmission is that
(a) it needs only one wire
(b) it is faster
(c) *BCD* is compatible
(d) all of these

184. Which of the following binary addition is incorrect?
(a) 1001 + 1101 = 10110
(b) 10101 + 10011 = 101000
(c) 11111 + 11111 = 100000
(d) 11111 + 10001 = 110000

185. The maximum power dissipated in the collector
(a) $V_{CC}^2/4\ R_L$ (b) $V_{CC}^2/2\ R_L$
(c) $V_{CC}^2/\ R_L$ (d) $2\ V_{CC}^2/R_L$

186. Dynamic memory cells are constructed using
(a) transistors (b) flip-flops
(c) MOSFETs (d) FETs

187. The value of commutating capacitor is of the order of
(a) 10 *pF* (b) 50 *pF*
(c) 0.5 μ*F* (d) 10 μ*F*

188. Which of the following motors are used in largest number?
(a) Fractional horse power motors
(b) 3-phase induction motors
(c) DC shunt motors
(d) Synchronous motors

ANSWERS

1	2	3	4	5	6	7	8	9	10
(c)	(c)	(a)	(b)	(a)	(b)	(a)	(c)	(b)	(d)
11	12	13	14	15	16	17	18	19	20
(a)	(c)	(b)	(c)	(a)	(a)	(c)	(c)	(a)	(c)
21	22	23	24	25	26	27	28	29	30
(a)	(d)	(b)	(c)	(a)	(c)	(a)	(b)	(c)	(c)
31	32	33	34	35	36	37	38	39	40
(c)	(b)	(c)	(b)	(d)	(c)	(b)	(b)	(d)	(c)
41	42	43	44	45	46	47	48	49	50
(a)	(b)	(c)	(b)	(b)	(c)	(c)	(d)	(c)	(c)
51	52	53	54	55	56	57	58	59	60
(b)	(b)	(c)	(d)	(d)	(d)	(c)	(d)	(b)	(d)
61	62	63	64	65	66	67	68	69	70
(b)	(b)	(b)	(d)	(b)	(d)	(b)	(c)	(d)	(a)
71	72	73	74	75	76	77	78	79	80
(c)	(c)	(c)	(a)	(a)	(b)	(b)	(b)	(a)	(c)
81	82	83	84	85	86	87	88	89	90
(b)	(b)	(c)	(b)	(b)	(c)	(d)	(a)	(c)	(b)

91	92	93	94	95	96	97	98	99	100
(d)	(c)	(a)	(b)	(b)	(d)	(d)	(c)	(c)	(d)
101	**102**	**103**	**104**	**105**	**106**	**107**	**108**	**109**	**110**
(c)	(b)	(a)	(d)	(b)	(c)	(e)	(b)	(a)	(a)
111	**112**	**113**	**114**	**115**	**116**	**117**	**118**	**119**	**120**
(d)	(c)	(b)	(d)	(c)	(a)	(b)	(b)	(c)	(b)
121	**122**	**123**	**124**	**125**	**126**	**127**	**128**	**129**	**130**
(c)	(c)	(c)	(d)	(c)	(b)	(b)	(c)	(b)	(e)
131	**132**	**133**	**134**	**135**	**136**	**137**	**138**	**139**	**140**
(b)	(d)	(c)	(c)	(c)	(b)	(c)	(e)	(d)	(b)
141	**142**	**143**	**144**	**145**	**146**	**147**	**148**	**149**	**150**
(a)	(a)	(b)	(d)	(d)	(a)	(c)	(a)	(b)	(a)
151	**152**	**153**	**154**	**155**	**156**	**157**	**158**	**159**	**160**
(b)	(e)	(c)	(c)	(e)	(c)	(c)	(c)	(c)	(a)
161	**162**	**163**	**164**	**165**	**166**	**167**	**168**	**169**	**170**
(c)	(c)	(c)	(c)	(a)	(b)	(b)	(a)	(a)	(b)
171	**172**	**173**	**174**	**175**	**176**	**177**	**178**	**179**	**180**
(b)	(d)	(a)	(d)	(c)	(b)	(d)	(d)	(a)	(c)
181	**182**	**183**	**184**	**185**	**186**	**187**	**188**		
(b)	(c)	(a)	(c)	(c)	(c)	(b)	(a)		

7. CONTROL SYSTEM

BASIC CONTROL SYSTEM

A control sytem is an arrangement of physical components connected or related in such a manner as to command, direct or regulate itself to another system. This can be of two types:

(1) Open loop control system: In this system, the control action is somehow independent on the output.

(2) Closed-loop control system: In this system the control action is somehow dependent on the output.

Feedback

This is that property of a closed-loop system which permits the outpput to be compared with the input to the system so that the appropriate control action may be formed as some function of the output and input.

Characteristics of Feedback

The most important features imparted by the presence of feedback to a system are the following

(1) Increased accuracy.

(2) Reduced sensitivity of the ratio of output to input to variations in system characteristics.

(3) Reduced effects of nonlinearities and distortion.

(4) Increased bandwidth (the bandwidth is that range of frequencies over which the system will respond satisfactorily.

(5) Tendency towards oscillation or instability.

Terminology of the Closed-loop Block Diagram

The terms used in the closed-loop block diagram shown in Fig 1.

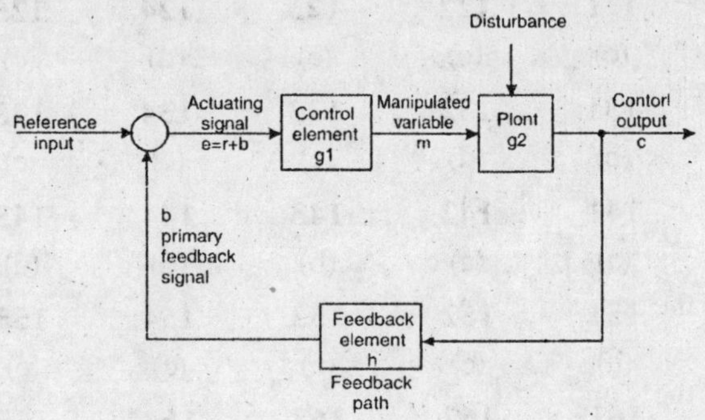

Fig. 1

The g_2, also called the controlled system is the body, process or machine of which a particular quantity or condition is to be controlled.

The control elements g_1, also called the controller, are the components required to generate the appropriate control signal *m* applied to the plant.

The *feedback elements h* are the components required to establish the functional relationship between the primary feedback signal *b* and the controlled output *c*.

The *reference input r* is an external signal applied to a feedback control system in order to command a specified action of the plant.

The *controlled output c* is that quantity or condition of the plant which is controlled.

The *primary feedback signal b* is a signal which is a function of the controlled output *c,* and which is algebraically summed with the reference input r to obtain the actuating signal *e.*

The *actuating signal e,* also called the *error or control action,* is the algebraic sum of the reference input *r* and (plus or minus) the primary feedback b.

The *manipulated variable m,* (control signal)

is that quantity which the control element g_1 apply to the plant g_2.

A *disturbance u*, is an undesired input signal which affects the value of the controlled output *c*.

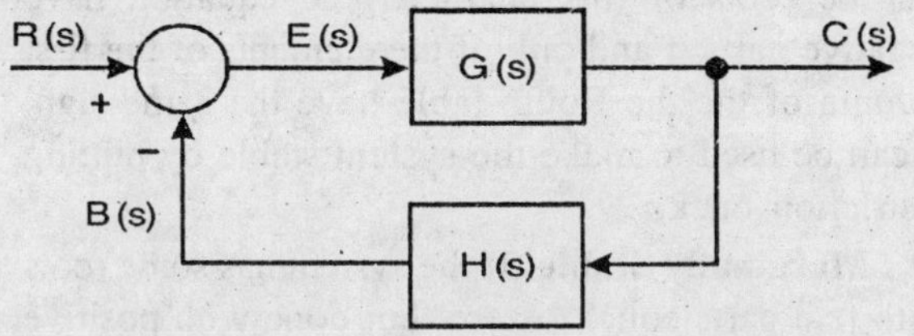

Fig. 2

The *forward path* is the transmission path from the actuating signal *e* to the controlled output *c*.

The *feedback path* is the transmission path from the controlled output *c* to the primary feedback signal *b*.

Transfer function

It is the ratio of output to input expressed in terms of Laplace Transform.

$$G(S) = \frac{C(s)}{R(s)} = \frac{b_m s^m + b_{m-1}s^{m-1} + \ldots b_0}{a_n s^n + a_{n-1}s^{n-1} + \ldots a_0}$$

Transfer Function of a Closed-loop System

Fig. 2 shows the block diagram of a closed loop system. Part of the ouput $C(s)$ is fed back to the summing point where it is compared with reference input $R(s)$.

The feedback signal $B(s)$ is

$$B(s) = H(s)\,C(s)$$

Ratio of feedback signal to actuating error signal $E(s)$ is open loop transfer function.

Open loop transfer function

$$= \frac{B(s)}{E(s)}$$

$$= G(s)\,H(s)$$

Ratio of ouput $C(s)$ to actuating error signal $E(s)$ is called feed forward transfer function

$$\text{or,} \quad \frac{C(s)}{E(s)} = G(s)$$

Thus the output of closed loop system depends on both the closed loop transfer function and the nature of input.

Block Reduction

Any finite number of blocks in series may be algebraically combined by multiplication. That is *n* blocks with transfer functions G_1, $G_2 \ldots G_n$ connected in cascade are equivalent to single element *G* with transfer function given by

$$G = G_1, G_2, G_3 \ldots\ldots\ldots G_n$$

Analogous Quantities in Control System

These are tabulated below:

Analogous Quantities in Force-Voltage Analogy

Mechanical System	*Electrical System*
Force	Voltage
Mass	Inductance
Viscous friction coefficient	Resistance
Spring constant	Reciprocal of capacitance
Displacement	Charge
Velocity	Current

Analogous Quantities in Force-Current Analogy

Mechanical System	*Electrical System*
Force	Current
Mass	Capacitance
Viscous-friction coefficient	Reciprocal of Resistance
Mechanical System	*Electrical System*
Spring constant	Reciprocal of inductance
Displacement	Magnetic flux linkage
Velocity	Voltage

STABILITY

The stability of a system is determined by its response to input or disturbances. A stable system is one that will remain at rest unless excited by an external sources and will return to rest if all the excitations are removed.

A system is stable if its impulse response approaches zero as time approaches infinity.

Figure 3 shows the stability of the system for different locations of poles and zeros.

A necessary condition for the system to be stable is that the real parts of the roots of the characteristic equation have negnative real parts. This ensures that the impulse response will decay exponentially with time.

Routh Stability Criterion

It is a method for determining system stability that can be applied to on *n*th order characteristic equation of the form

$a_n s^n + a_{n-1} s^{n-1} + ... + a_1 s + a_0 = 0$

The criterion is applied through the use of Routh table defined as follows:

s^n	a_n	a_{n-2}	a_{n-4}....
s^{n-1}	a_{n-1}	a_{n-3}	a_{n-5}....
:	b_1	b_2	b_3
:	c_1	c_2	c_3

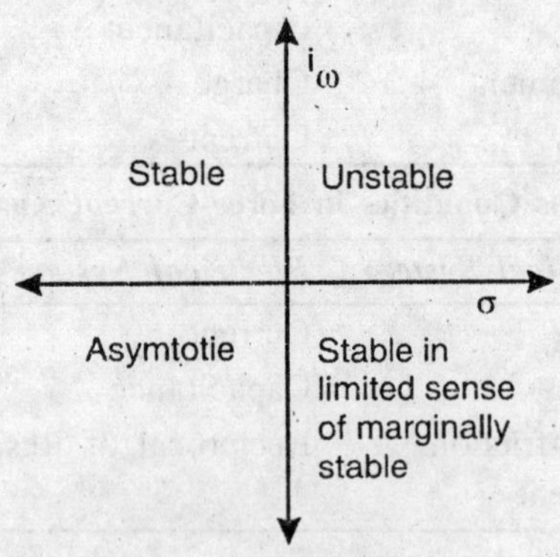

Fig. 3

Where a_n, a_{n-1}, a_0 are the coefficients of the characteristic equation and

$$b_1 = \frac{a_{n-1}a_{n-2} - a_n a_{n-3}}{a_{n-1}}$$

$$b_2 = \frac{a_{n-1}a_{n-4} - a_n a_{n-5}}{a_{n-1}}$$

$$c_1 = \frac{b_1 a_{n-3} - a_{n-1} b_2}{b_1}$$

$$c_2 = \frac{b_1 a_{n-5} - a_{n-1} b_3}{b_1}$$

The table is continued horizontally and vertically until only zero are obtained. Any row can be multiplied by a constant before the next row is computed without disturbing properties of the table. All the roots of this characteristic equation have negative parts if and only if the elements of the first column of the the Routh table have the same sign. It can be used to make the system stable by putting restriction on k.

Marginally Stable: If the system has some roots with real parts equal to zero, but none with positive real parts, the system is said to be *marginally stable* which is unstable.

Frequency Response

In time domain analysis, the nature of the inputs are either step, ramp or parabolic inputs. But, sometimes, system has inputs other than the above such as sinusoidal inputs whose amplitude and frequency may vary.

Frequency Response of a Closed-loop System

Let the forward path transfer function be $G(s)$ and the feedback path transfer function is $H(s)$. Closed loop transfer function will be

$$C(s) = \frac{G(s)}{1+G(s)\,H(s)} R(s)$$

Since the input is sinusoidal having amplitude and variable frequency ω

$$C(s) = \frac{G(s)}{1+G(s)\,H(s)} \cdot \frac{\omega}{\omega^2 + s^2}$$

$$\text{Let } T(s) = \frac{G(s)}{1+H(s)\,G(s)}$$

Thus, the output

$$c(t) = \pounds^{-1}\left[\frac{\omega}{s^2+\omega^2} . T(s)\right].$$

Since $R(s)$ may be assumed to be a stable system, the steady state response $y_{ss}(t)$ is that component of the response $y(t)$ which is due to the input poles $(j\omega)$ and $(-j\omega)$. Thus,

$$y_{ss}(t) = \alpha \sin(\omega t + \theta).$$

These can be plotted in any one of the following ways:

(1) $|G(j\omega)|$ *vs* frequency has phase angle *vs* frequency

(2) Magnitude $|G(j\omega)|$ and phase angle in polar plot

(3) Magnitude *vs phase shift*

The three predominant objectives of feedback control systems analysis are the determination of the following system characteristics:

(1) The degree or extent of system stability

(2) The steady state performance

(3) The transient response

There are primarily four graphical methods available to control systems analysis which are simpler and more direct than the time domain method for practical linear models of feedback control systems. These are:

(1) Bode's-Plot representation

(2) Nyquist Diagrams

(3) Nichols Charts

(4) The Root Locus method

The first three are frequency-domain techniques.

Bode's Plot

A sinusoidal function may be represented by two separate plots. One giving the magnitude versus frequency and the other the phase angle versus frequency. A logarithmic plot of Bode's plot of logarithm of the magnitude of a sinusoidal transfer function, and the other is a plot of the phase angle, both are plotted against the frequency in logarithmic scale.

The main advantage of Bode's plot is that multiplication of magnitudes can be converted into addition. It is the simplest method. Transfer function can be determined easily by Bode's plot, the low frequency and high frequency characteristics of the transfer function can be determined.

Phase Margin: It is a measure of relative stability, is defined as 180 degrees plus the phase angle ϕ_1 of the open-loop transfer function at unity gain, *i.e.*

$$\phi_{PM} = [180 + arg\ GH\ (j\omega_1)] \text{ degrees}$$

where

$|GH\ (j\omega_1)|$ = 1 and ω_1 is called gain crossover frequency

Gain Margin: It is a measure of relative stability, is defined as the magnitude of the reciprocal of the open-loop transfer function, evaluated at the frequency ω_π at which the phase angle is –180 degrees.

i.e. Gain Margin = $\dfrac{1}{|GH(j\omega_\pi)|}$

where arg $GH\ (j\omega_\pi) = -180$ degrees

The frequency ω_π is called *phase crossover frequency*.

Bandwidth (BW)

For a system, this is defined as that range of frequencies over which the system will respond satisfactorily.

Cut-off Rate: This is the frequency rate at which the magnitude ratio decreases beyond the cut-off frequency ω_c.

Resonance Peak M_p: This is a measure of relative stability, is the maximum value of the magnitude of the closed-loop frequency response. That is,

$$M_p = \max \left|\frac{C}{R}(j\omega)\right|$$

Resonant Frequency ω_p: This is the frequency at which *Mp* occurs.

The Nyquist Method

The Nyquist method handles systems with time delay without the necessity of approximations and hence yields exact results about both absolute and relative stability of the system. This is also useful for obtaining information about transfer functions of components or systems from experimental frequency response data.

Polar Plots

The polar plot of a sinusoidal transfer function $G(j\omega)$ is a plot of the magnitude of $G\ (j\omega)$ *vs* phase angle of $G(j\omega)$ on polar coordinates as ω is varied from 0 to infinity. Thus the ploar plot is the locus of vectors $|G\ (j\omega)|\ \angle G\ (j\omega)$ as ω is varied from zero to infinity. A positive angle is measured from counter-clockwise from positive real axis. Polar plot is called Nyquist plot. Both magnitude $|G(j\omega)|$ and phase angle $\angle (G(j\omega))$ must be calculated directly for each frequency ω in order to construct polar plot.

Relative Stability: The relative stability of a feedback control system is determined from the polar of Nyquist stability plot.

The phase crossover frequency ω_π is that frequency at which the phase angle of $GH(j\omega)$ is −180°, that is, the frequency at which the polar plot crosses the negative real axis, the gain margin is given by

$$\text{gain margin} = \frac{1}{|GH(j\omega_\pi)|}$$

Gain crossover frequency ω is that frequency at which $|GH(j\omega)| = 1$

Phase margin ϕ_{PM} is the angle by which polar plot must be rotated to cause it to pass through the (−1, 0) point. It is given by

$$\phi_{PM} = [180 + arg\ GH(j\omega)] \text{ degrees}$$

Time Response of Control-System

For a unit step input, the transient response of a second order system is shown in Fig. 4. Its salient featu1es are:

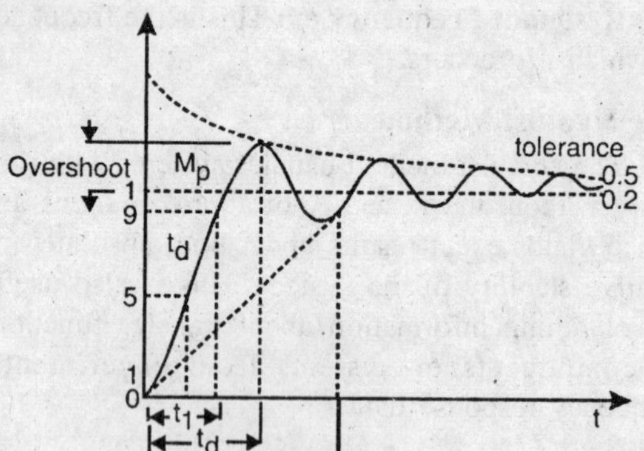

Fig. 4

(1) *Delay time* t_d is the time required for the response to reach the half the final value.

(2) *Rise time* t_r, is the time required for the response to rise from 10 to 90% of its final value.

(3) *Peak time* t_p, is the time required for the response to reach the first peak of the over shoot.

(4) *Maximum overshoot* M_p is the maximum value of the response curve measured from unity.

(5) *Overshoot* is the maximum difference between the transient and steady state solutions for a unit-step function input. It is a measure of relative stability and is represented as percentage of final value of the output.

(6) *Settling time* t_s, is defined as the time required for the response to unit-step function input to reach and remain within, a specified percentage of its final value.

Typical Test Signals Commonly used test signals are step function, ramp function, impulse function and sinusoidal functions.

Root-Locus Method

The closed-loop transfer function of this system is

$$\frac{C}{R} = \frac{G}{1+GH}$$

Centre of asymptotes σ_c is given by

$$\sigma_i = \frac{-1}{n-m}\left[\sum_{i=1}^{n} p_i - \sum_{i=1}^{m} z_i\right]$$

where p_i are the poles z_i are the zeros, n is the number of poles and m the number of zeros of GH

Angle between the asymptotes and real axis are given by

$$\beta = \begin{cases} \dfrac{(2l+1)180}{n-m} \text{ degree for } k > 0 \\ \dfrac{(2l)\,180}{n-m} \text{ degree for } k > 0 \end{cases}$$

for $l = 0, 1, 2, \ldots n - m - 1$

Breakaway point can be determined by solving the following equation

$$\sum_{i=1}^{n} \frac{1}{\sigma_b + p_i} = \sum_{i=1}^{m} \frac{1}{\sigma_b + z_i}$$

where $-p_i$ and $-z_i$ are the poles and zero of GH respectively.

Control System Components

Synchros: Synchros are small motor components widely used for the remote transmission of shaft position in a.c. servomechanism. The basic structure consists of a wound rotor and wound stator concentrically arranged to give adjustable mutual coupling between windings of two members. The magnetic winding circuits are designed to give a substantially sinusoidal variation in magnetic coupling as a function of shaft position.

Tachometers: Tachometers are electro-mechanical device that convert mechanical energy into electrical energy. The device works essentially as a generator with the output voltage proportional to the magnitude of the angular velocity.

In control systems, tachometers are used for the sensing of shaft velocity and for the improvement of system performance.

D.C. Tachometer: A d.c. tachometer is a generator which produces a voltage proportional to the rotating speed. It is used as a transducer, converting the velocity of the rotating shaft into a proportional voltage. In a d.c. tachometer induced voltage e can be written as:

$$e = k\phi \frac{d\theta}{dt}$$

where k is the constant, ϕ is the air gap flux and θ is the rotating speed.

Transfer function $\dfrac{E(s)}{\theta(s)} = k_t s$

A d.c. tachometer can replace an a.c. tachometer in a control system by use of a modulator converting its d.c. output signal into a.c. Similarly, a d.c. tachometer can be replaced by an a.c. if a phase sensitive demodulator is used to convert the a.c. output to d.c.

A.C. Tachometer: In a.c. tachometer an a.c. voltage is applied to the primary winding of the tachometer. The secondary winding is placed 90 degrees apart in space from the primary winding. Thus, when the rotor is stationary, the output voltage is zero. When the rotor shaft is rotating, the output voltage at the secondary winding, is proportional to the rotor velocity. The polarity of the output voltage is determined by the direction of rotation. The transfer function of an a.c. tachometer is:

$$\frac{E(s)}{\theta(s)} = ks$$

where $E(s)$ is the Laplace Transform of the output voltage, $\theta(s)$ is the Laplace transform of the rotor position and k is a constant.

Two Phase Servo-Motors

These motors transform electric signals into equivalent speed, angle or torque quantities. Accuracy, speed and reliability of signal transmission are more important than the efficiency. Thus two phase servo motors can be identified by their operating characteristics from the normal fractional H.P. two-phase capacitor motor, etc. The typical characteristics of servo motors are the decreasing speed torque characteristics. Rotors are specially designed to have low inertia. That is why they are usually long and have small diameters.

Armature Controlled D.C. Motor

A d.c. motor is often employed in a control system where an appreciable amount of shaft power is required. The d.c. motors are much more efficient than two-phase a.c. servomotor.

The d.c. motors have separately excited fields. They are armature controlled with fixed field controlled with fixed armature current.

D.C. Servo-motors

Among various d.c. servomotors are series motor, split-phase motor, shunt control motor and permanent magnet shunt motor. These units develop high output power in a given size and in the case of field controlled shunt motor require little control power, the problems are radio interference, brush wear and d.c. amplifier drift.

The series motor has high starting torque and draws large current and has poor speed regulation. Reversal can be obtained by reversing field voltage polarity with split series winding. A typical speed torque curve shows a high starting torque and rapid reduction of torque with increasing speed. This results in good damping and large velocity error.

The shunt motor has good starting torque and good speed regulation. Reversibility is possible by reversing armature of field polarity. Performance is similar to shunt motor with armature control and fixed field.

Potentiometers

Since the output voltage of a potentiometer is proportional to the shaft displacement, when a voltage is applied across its fixed terminals, the device can be used to compare two shaft positions. In this case, one shaft may be fastened to the potentiometer can and other to shaft of the potentiometer. When a constant voltage is applied to the fixed terminals of the potentiometer, the voltage across the variable and the reference terminals will be proportional to the difference between the two shaft positions.

Proportional Control Action (P-Action)

It is defined as the action of a controller in which the output signal *m(t)* is proportional to the measured actuating error signal *e(t)* as shown in Fig. 5.

$$m(t) = k_p\, e(t)$$

$$\frac{M(s)}{E(s)} = K_p$$

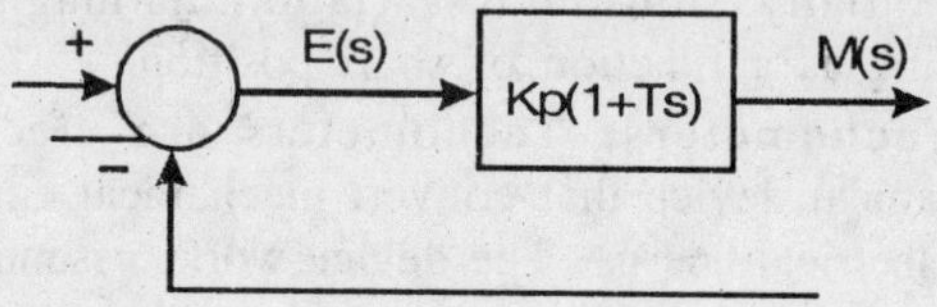

Fig. 5

where K_p is termed the proportional sensitivity or the gain. The proportional controller is essentially an amplifier with an adjustable gain *A*.

EXERCISE

1. If a conventional servomotor is used for servo applications, the system becomes unstable because
   (a) the applied voltages are always to be balanced
   (b) the rotor resistance is low
   (c) the rotor resistance is high
   (d) the rotor's diameter is large
2. Given that D = rotor diameter and L = axial length, a high perfromance ac servo-motor is characterized by
   (a) large D, large L (b) large D, small L
   (c) small D, large L (d) small D, large L
3. Backlash in a stable control system can cause
   (a) overdamping
   (b) low-level oscillations
   (c) underdamping
   (d) poor stability at reduced values of open-loop gain
4. The sensitivity of a closed loop control system to variations in gain and load disturbance depends upon
   (a) loop gain (b) frequency
   (c) forward gain (d) all of these
5. In pneumatic systems, electrical resistance is analogous to a
   (a) restriction to flow (b) volume of air
   (c) filled helical tube (d) none of these
6. An AC servomotor (2-phase induction motor) has a rotor with
   (a) high resistance winding
   (b) very small diameter to reduce inertia
   (c) very small axial length to reduce inertia
   (d) both (a) and (b)
   (e) both (a) and (c)
7. In pneumatic systems, electrical capacitance is analogous to
   (a) restriction to flow
   (b) volume of air
   (c) filled helical tube
   (d) none of these
8. The transfer function of a system is used to determine
   (a) the output for a given input
   (b) the type of system
   (c) the input for a given output
   (d) the steady state gain

9. Proportional band of a controller is defined as the range of
(a) measured variables from set value
(b) measured variables through which the air output changes from maximum to minimum
(c) air output as measured variable varies from maximum to minimum
(d) none of these

10. Which one of the following statements regarding state space method is NOT TRUE?
(a) It gives compact and convenient form.
(b) It reduces complexity.
(c) Direct programming is possible on analog computer.
(d) None of these

11. In force-current analogy, displacement is analogous to
(a) magnetic flux linkage
(b) capacitance
(c) voltage
(d) inductance

12. For the minimum phase system to be stable
(a) phase margin should be negative and gain margin positive
(b) phase margin should be positive and gain margin negative
(c) both gain margin and phase margin should be positive
(d) both gain margin and phase margin should be negative

13. The Laplace Transform of unit step function and ramp functions respectively are
(a) $\frac{1}{s^2}, \frac{1}{s}$ (b) $\frac{1}{s}, \frac{1}{s^2}$
(c) $\frac{1}{s}, \frac{1}{s^3}$ (d) $\frac{1}{s^3}, \frac{1}{s}$

14. In a hybrid feedback control system carrier signals are
(a) d.c. only (b) a.c. only
(c) both d.c. and a.c. (d) none of these

15. Damping due to back emf is observed in
(a) armature controlled d.c. motor
(b) field controlled d.c. motor
(c) a.c. servomotor
(d) none of these

16. Two blocks having respective functions as G_1 and G_2 are connected in series cascade. Their resultant will be
(a) $G_1 G_2$ (b) $G_1 + G_2$
(c) G_1/G_2 (d) G_2/G_1

17. The transfer function technique is considered inadequate with systems having
(a) stability problems
(b) multiple input disturbances
(c) complexities and non-linearities
(d) all of the above

18. Laplace Transform of the functions e^{-t} and e^{-2t} are
(a) $\frac{1}{s+1}, \frac{1}{s+2}$ (b) $\frac{1}{s-1}, \frac{1}{s-2}$
(c) $\frac{1}{s+1}, \frac{1}{s-2}$ (d) None of these

19. In a system non-linearity may be introduced due to
(a) backlash in gears
(b) end positions in detectors
(c) saturation effects in amplifiers
(d) any of the above

20. The function $u(t - t_0) = \begin{bmatrix} 1 & t > t_0 \\ 0 & t \le t_0 \end{bmatrix}$ defines
(a) unit step function
(b) unit ramp function
(c) unit impulse function
(d) none of these

21. A system has the transfer function $(1-s)/(1+s)$. What is its gain at 1 rad/sec?
(a) 1 (b) 0
(c) –1 (d) None of these

22. A system has the transfer function $(1-s)/(1+s)$. It is known as a
(a) low-pass system (b) high-pass system
(c) all-pass system (d) none of these

23. 5 percent-proportional band means control output
(a) change by 5 percent
(b) change from maximum to minimum for 5 percent change in measured variable
(c) changes by 95 percent
(d) none of these

24. ...... has some roots with real parts equal to zero but none with positive real parts.
(a) Marginally stable
(b) Absolutely stable
(c) Absolutely unstable
(d) Stable

25. Human system can be considered as a
(a) open-loop system
(b) closed-loop system with single feedback
(c) closed-loop system with multivariable input
(d) none of these

26. A free gyro with no restraining forces is used in space to measure
(a) velocity of a vehicle
(b) acceleration
(c) angular momentum
(d) angular position of vehicle with respect to gyro axis

27. Given that $G(s) = \dfrac{K}{s^2(1+sT)}$ when this system is operated in a closed-loop with unity feedback, what is the order and type of the closed-loop system?
(a) 3 and 2 (b) 2 and 3
(c) 3 and 1 (d) 3 and 0

28. The root locus plot is symmetrical about the real axis because
(a) complex roots occur in conjugate pairs
(b) all roots occur in pairs
(c) roots occur simultaneously in left hand and right hand plane
(d) none of the above

29. The frequency and time domain are relate through
(a) Laplace Transform
(b) Fourier Integral
(c) Laplace Transform or Fourier Integral
(d) Laplace Transform and Fourier Integral

30. If any root of the characteristic equation has a positive real part, then the system is
(a) limitedly stable (b) stable
(c) unstable (d) absolutely unstable

31. A signal flow graph is a
(a) special type of graph for analysing modern control systems
(b) pictorial representation of the simultaneous equations describing a system
(c) polar graph
(d) log log graph

32. A linear time invariant system initially at rest when subject to a unit step input gave a response $c(t) = te^{-2t}$ $(t \geq 0)$. The transfer function is given by
(a) $\dfrac{1}{s(s+2)^2}$ (b) $\dfrac{1}{s(s+2)}$
(c) $\dfrac{1}{(s+2)^2}$ (d) none of these

33. A unity feedback system has transfer function $G(s) = \dfrac{9}{s(s+3)}$, its
(a) Natural frequency = 9
(b) Natural frequency = 3
(c) Natural frequency = 1
(d) Natural frequency = 0

34. .....signal starts at zero and increases linearly with time
(a) Ramp (b) Step
(c) Impulse (d) Parabolic

35. The expression for the direct transmission function will be
(a) $40/(s + 10)$ (b) $40/(s^2 + 10s)$
(c) $40/(s^2 + 10)$ (d) none of these

36. ....are the starting points for root loci.
(a) Open loop poles (b) Closed loop poles
(c) Open loop zeros (d) Closed loop zeros

37. The system with transfer function $\frac{K}{s^2(1+sT)}$ is operated in closed-loop with unity feedback. The closed-loop system is

(a) stable (b) unstable
(c) marginally stable (d) conditionally stable

38. A type-1 system under steady state will have position error when there is

(a) ramp input
(b) step displacement input
(c) either (a) or (b)
(d) none of these

39. Given the transfer function $G(s) = \frac{K}{s^2(1+sT)}$

State the type and order of the system

(a) 2 and 3 (b) 3 and 2
(c) 3 and 3 (d) none of these

40. The characteristic equation for the differential equation $\frac{d^2y}{dt} + 3\frac{dy}{dt} + 2y = x$ is given by

(a) $D^2 + 3D + 2 = 0$ (b) $D^2 + 3D + 2 = x$
(c) $D^2 + 3D = 0$ (d) $D^2 + 2D + 3 = 0$

41. For a linear transfer function of the variable, the transfer function of the system

(a) has no relation at all
(b) changes
(c) does not change
(d) depends on other factors also

42. For the system shown, the transfer function $C(s)/R(s)$ is equal to

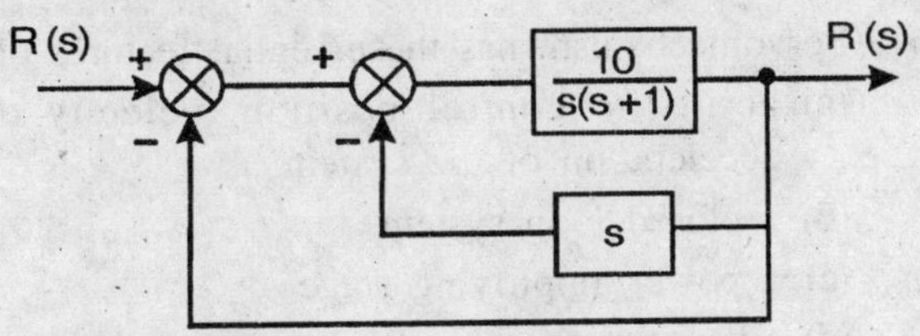

(a) $\frac{10}{s^2+s+10}$ (b) $\frac{10}{s^2+11s+10}$
(c) $\frac{10}{s^2+9s+10}$ (d) $\frac{10}{s^2+2s+10}$

43. According to the Routh-Hurwitz Criterion the roots of a polynominal $F(s) = 0$ all lie in the left half of the s-plane if

(a) all the elements of the first row of the Routh's tabulation are of the same sign
(b) all the elements of the first column are of the same sign
(c) elements of the arc of opposite sign alternatively
(d) elements of the first column are of opposite sign alternatively

44. Two blocks having respective transfer functions as G_1 and G_2 are connected in series cascade. Their resultant will be

(a) $G_1 + G_2$ (b) $G_1 G_2$
(c) $\frac{G_1G_2}{G_1+G_2}$ (d) $\frac{G_1}{G_2}$

45. For underdamped second order system, the poles are

(a) negative and real
(b) imaginary and complex
(c) complex conjugates with negative real parts
(d) positive and real

46. When deriving the transfer function of a linear element

(a) both initial conditions and loading are taken into account
(b) initial conditions are taken into account, but the element is assumed to be not loaded
(c) initial conditions are assumed to be zero, but loading is taken into account
(d) initial conditions are assumed to be zero and the element is assumed to be not loaded

47. Laplace Transform of damped cosine wave $e^{-at}\cos\omega t$ is

(a) $\frac{\omega}{(s+a)^2+\omega^2}$ (b) $\frac{s+a}{(s+a)^2+\omega^2}$
(c) $\frac{s}{(s+a)^2+\omega^2}$ (d) $\frac{1}{(s+a)^2+\omega^2}$

48. The overshoot (an indication of the largest error between the actual and desired output) is the ratio of

(a) transient error to peak error
(b) dynamic error to peak error
(c) maximum overshoot to final desired value
(d) none of the above

49. The field of a d.c. servomotor is separately excited by a d.c. amplifier of gain $K = 90$. If the field has an inductance of 2 H and a resistance of 50 ohms the value of the field constant will be

(a) 0.01 sec (b) 0.02 sec
(c) 0.04 sec (d) 0.5 sec

50. A servomechanism is called a proportional error device when the system output is a

(a) function of error only
(b) function of error and first derivative error
(c) function of first derivative of error
(d) none of the above

51. The transient response of a system is mainly due to

(a) internal forces (b) inertia forces
(c) friction (d) stored energy

52. The open loop transfer function represents

(a) Type - 0 system (b) Type - I system
(c) Type - II system (d) Type - III system

53. Steady state error is the difference of input and output at t =

(a) 0 (b) ∞
(c) T (d) 2 T

54. Analysis of control systems by Laplace transform technique is not possible for.... systems.

(a) linear
(b) discrete-time
(c) time-invariant
(d) unstable continuous time

55. The transfer function of the system whose input and output are related by the following differential equation is given by
$d^2y/dt^2 + 3dy/dt + 2y = x + dx/dt$

(a) $\dfrac{s}{s^2+3s+2}$ (b) $\dfrac{1}{s^2+3s+2}$

(c) $\dfrac{s+1}{s^2+3s+2}$ (d) $\dfrac{s+2}{s^2+3s+2}$

56. The root locus are the plots of the variations of the poles of the closed loop system function with variations in

(a) open loop poles (b) open loop gain
(c) closed loop zeros (d) none of these

57. The open loop control system is one in which

(a) output is dependant on control input
(b) output is independent of control input
(c) only system parameters have effect on the control output
(d) none of these

58. A phase lag-lead network introduces in the output

(a) lag at high frequencies and lead at low frequencies
(b) lead at high frequencies and lag at low frequencies
(c) lag at all frequencies
(d) lead at all frequencies

59. The main application of transfer function is the study of

(a) steady state behaviour of systems
(b) steady state as well as transient behaviour of systems
(c) only transient behaviour of system
(d) none of these

60. In pneumatic systems the medium used is

(a) hydrogen (b) air
(c) liquid (d) oil

61. Servomechanism has the essential features of

(a) ability to control position, velocity or acceleration of the system
(b) a closed loop system
(c) a power amplifying stage
(d) all of the above

62. The value of K for which the system $s^3 + 3s^2 + 3s + 1 + K = 0$ becomes stable is

(a) $K > 8$ (b) $K = 8$
(c) $K = 7$ (d) None of these

63. For a second-order differential equation if the damping ratio is 1 then
(a) the poles are imaginary and complex conjugate
(b) the poles are in the right half of the s-plane
(c) the poles are equal, negative and real
(d) both poles are negative and real

64. The inherent capability of a feedback control system is adjustability of its parameters to alter its
(a) steady state conditions
(b) transient conditions
(c) both (a) and (b)
(d) none of these

65. The poles of $F(s) = \dfrac{s^2 - 16}{s^5 - 7s^4 - 30s^3}$ are located at
(a) $s = 0$ (triple pole), –3 and 10
(b) $s = 0$ (triple pole), –3 and 20
(c) $s = -4, 4$
(d) $s = 0, 4, 16$

66. Viscous friction can be added to a servo-mechanism by
(a) increasing speed of shaft
(b) reducing speed of shaft
(c) coupling a disc to shaft which is immersed in a viscous medium
(d) any of the above method

67. The maximum overshoot of a second order system can be increased by
(a) reducing damping frequency
(b) increasing damping frequency
(c) increasing damping factor
(d) none of the above

68. A position-control system is a
(a) automatic regulating system
(b) process control system
(c) servomechanism
(d) stochastic control system

69. Which of the following is/are the examples of the open loop control system?
(a) An automatic toaster
(b) Field controlled d.c. motor
(c) Human eye
(d) Metadyne
(e) Ward Leonard control system
(f) both (a) and (b)

70. A regulator that contains four phase lags, at $t_1 = 1$ sec, $t_2 = 0.1$ sec, $t_3 = 0.02$ sec, $t_4 = 0.01$ sec, is stable if its steady-state gain is
(a) 10 dB (b) 20 dB
(c) 30 dB (d) none of these

71. A servo-system with step displacement input is type .... system.
(a) 0 (b) 1
(c) 2 (d) none of these

72. The linear equation describing the motion of pendulum for small values of displacement θ is given by
(a) $\dfrac{d^2\theta}{dt^2} + \dfrac{g}{l}\sin\theta = 0$
(b) $\dfrac{d^2\theta}{dt^2} + \dfrac{g}{l}\theta = 0$
(c) $\dfrac{d^2\theta}{dt^2} + \dfrac{l}{g}\sin\theta = 0$
(d) $\dfrac{d^2\theta}{dt^2} + \dfrac{l}{g}\theta = 0$

73. For handling multiple input, multiple output system..... is used.
(a) state variable approach
(b) Bode plot
(c) Nyquist plot
(d) root locus technique

74. The resolution of a potentiometer depends on
(a) composition of wire material
(b) size of wire
(c) type of contacts
(d) none of these

75. Well designed first order control systems have a
(a) small bandwidth
(b) negative time constant
(c) a large negative transfer function pole
(d) none of the above

76. In Force-Current Analogy, indicate the true statement

(a) Force is analogous to voltage

(b) Mass is analogous to inductance

(c) Spring constant is analogous to reciprocal of capacitance

(d) Viscous friction coefficient is analogous to reciprocal of resistance

77. Feedback control systems are

(a) band-pass filters (b) low-pass filters

(c) high-pass filters (d) none of the above

78. Transfer function $G(s) = \dfrac{K}{s^2(1+sT)}$. This open-loop system is

(a) stable (b) unstable

(c) marginally stable (d) conditionally stable

79. Root locus diagram exhibits the

(a) frequency response of a system

(b) poles of the transfer function for a set of parameter values

(c) bandwidth of the system

(d) all of the above

80. In Force-Voltage Analogy which one is the true statement?

(a) Force is analogous to current

(b) Mass is analogous to capacitance

(c) Velocity is analogous to current

(d) Displacement is analogous to magnetic flux linkage

81. A root locus is symmetrical about

(a) real axis

(b) imaginary axis

(c) both real and imaginary axis

(d) none of these

82. Adding of poles in the transfer function causes

(a) lag compensation

(b) lead compensation

(c) lead-lag compensation

(d) none of these

83. The position and velocity errors of a type-2 system are

(a) zero, zero (b) zero, constant

(c) constant, zero (d) zero, infinity

84. The poles of $F(s) = \dfrac{1}{1-e^{-s}}$ are located at

(a) $s = 0$ and 1

(b) $s = 1$ only

(c) $s = \pm j2n\pi$ (n = 0, 1, 2,....)

(d) none of these

85. The time required for the response to reach and stay within a specified tolerance band is called the

(a) rise time (b) pickup time

(c) settling time (d) transient time

86. Proportional band of a controller is expressed as a

(a) ratio

(b) gain

(c) percentage

(d) range of the control variable

87. The output of a feedback control system must be a function of

(a) reference and input

(b) reference and output

(c) input and feedback signal

(d) output and feedback signal

88. In the system if the poles lie off the real axis, then the system is

(a) overdamped (b) critically damped

(c) under-damped (d) none of these

89. If the bandwidth of a system is increased, the system response will

(a) remain unaffected (b) become faster

(c) become slower (d) none of these

90. A second order differential equation is given by $\dfrac{d^2x}{dt^2} + 5\dfrac{dx}{dt} + 7x = 7y$. The undamped natural frequency and damping ratio are

(a) 1, 5 (b) 5, 7

(c) 1, $\sqrt{7}$ (d) $\sqrt{7}$ rad/sec, 0.94

91. Reduction gear is employed for increasing
(a) viscous friction (b) moment of inertia
(c) torque developed (d) driven shaft speed

92. The phase lag produced by transportation delays
(a) decreases linearly with frequency
(b) increases linearly with frequency
(c) inversely proportional to frequency
(d) independent of frequency

93. An impulse function is the derivative of a...... function.
(a) parabolic (b) step
(c) ramp (d) linear

94. A gyroscope operates on the principle of
(a) law of conservation of energy
(b) law of conservation of momentum
(c) electro-mechanical conversion
(d) Newton's third law of motion

95. If a zero appears in the first column of the Routh table, the system is
(a) marginally stable
(b) necessarily stable
(c) necessarily unstable
(d) conditionally stable

96. Laplace Transform of damped sine wave $e^{-at} \sin \omega t$ is
(a) $\frac{1}{(s+a)^2+\omega^2}$ (b) $\frac{s}{(s+a)^2+\omega^2}$
(c) $\frac{\omega}{(s+a)^2+\omega^2}$ (d) $\frac{\omega^2}{(s+a)^2+\omega^2}$

97. Bias winding is provided in a magnetic amplifier to
(a) weaken d.c. flux in the core
(b) weaken a.c. flux in the core
(c) produce initial saturation in the core for high amplification
(d) strengthen a.c. flux in the core

98. The state transition matrix for the system $x = Ax + Bu$ is given by
(a) e^{At} (b) e^{-At}
(c) $\frac{1}{2} e^{At}$ (d) $\frac{1}{2} e^{-At}$

99. Which of the following systems provides excellent transient as well as steady-state response?
(a) Proportional action
(b) Proportional + Integral action
(c) Proportional + Differential action
(d) Proportional + Integral + Differential action

100. In the transfer function of a system, there is zero in the mirror image position for every pole in the left half plane. Such a system is called
(a) minimum phase system
(b) non-minimum phase system
(c) all-stop system
(d) all-pass system

101. By the use of..... the power amplification of a magnetic amplifier is increased
(a) resistive load circuit
(b) negative feedback
(c) positive feedback
(d) direct current in control winding

102. One of the disadvantages of a servomotor is that
(a) it has low starting torque
(b) it develops commutation problem
(c) it has low reliability
(d) it can handle only light loads

103. Inductance is not employed in fabrication of lag-network as it
(a) is of big size
(b) does not provide sufficient reactance
(c) produces time delay and hysteresis losses
(d) does not operate satisfactorily at high frequencies

104. Which one of the following statements regarding open control system is incorrect?
(a) Less expensive
(b) Simple construction and ease of maintenance
(c) No requirement of recalibration for maintaining the required quality of the output
(d) Stability can be ensured
(e) The control adjustment depends upon human judgement and estimate

105. The order of the system is determined by number of
(a) stable roots of the system
(b) multiplying terms in the denominator
(c) poles at the origin
(d) none of the above

106. The percentage resolution of the potentiometer of 1000 turns of excitation voltage 5V, is
(a) 0.1% (b) 0.2 %
(c) 0.5% (d) 1.0%

107. A control system in which control action is somehow dependent on the output is called the.... control system.
(a) open loop (b) closed loop
(c) stable (d) unstable

108. Which of the following sequences is correct for a three-term controller?
(a) *IDP* controller
(b) *PID* controller
(c) *PDI* controller
(d) *PID* as well as *PID* controller

109. In pneumatic systems a restriction volume combination is equivalent to
(a) rectifier (b) R–C circuit
(c) R–L circuit (d) resonant circuit

110. A servosystem with unit step input can be categorized as type..... system.
(a) 2 (b) 0
(c) 1 (d) none of these

111. The transfer function for an a.c. tachometer is
(a) $\frac{E(s)}{\theta(s)} = Ks$ (b) $\frac{E(s)}{\omega_m(s)} = Ks$
(c) $\frac{E(s)}{\theta(s)} = K$ (d) none of these

where $E(s)$, $\theta(s)$, $\omega_m(s)$ are the Laplace transforms of the tacho output voltager $E(t)$, rotor angular displacement $\theta(t)$ and rotor speed $\omega_m(t)$ respectively, and K is the tachometer constant in volts per radian second.

112. Which of the statements is not a function of reservoir in a compressor air plant?
(a) It filters air
(b) It cools air
(c) It removes pressure ripples
(d) It stores air

113. The transfer function has the main application in the study of.... behaviour of systems.
(a) steady as well as transient
(b) only steady
(c) only transient
(d) neither steady nor transient

114. The output of the controller in a control system is given to
(a) senor
(b) comparator
(c) amplifier
(d) final control element

115. ....is/are the example(s) of international non-linear systems.
(a) On-off transducers
(b) Contractor servos
(c) Non-linear pitch or dampers in aircraft control
(d) all of the above

116. The resolution of a potentiometer depends upon
(a) size of wire
(b) shape of wire cross-section
(c) composition of the wire material
(d) type of contact

117. The number of operational amplifier required to design an electronic *PID*-controller is
(a) 1 (b) 2
(c) 3 (d) 4

118. The thermocouple directly converts temperature into
(a) d.c. voltage
(b) a.c. voltage
(c) direct current
(d) alternating current

119. Which of the following statement is not true for a two-phase servo-motor?
(a) Torque-speed characteristics are linear.
(b) The rotor diameter is small.
(c) The rotor resistance is low.
(d) None of these.

120. Over electronic devices, magnetic amplifiers have the advantage(s) of
(a) being mechanically sturdy and inherently shock proof
(b) relatively low cost, compactness and lighter in weight
(c) more flexibility
(d) all of the above

121. Which of the following systems provides good performance if off-set is to be eliminated?
(a) Proportional action
(b) Proportional + Integral action
(c) Proportional + Differential action
(d) None of these

122. In a feedback system, the bandwidth
(a) increases by the same amount as the gain decreases
(b) decreases by the same amount as the gain decreases
(c) is independent of gain
(d) none of the above

123. The loop gain that makes the damping ratio equal to 0.5 will be
(a) 3 (b) 4
(c) 5 (d) 6

124. Settling time of a second-order system for damping ratio ξ and frequency ω_n is given by
(a) $4\,\xi\,\omega_n$ (b) $4\,\omega_n/\xi$
(c) $\frac{4}{\xi\omega_n}$ (d) $\xi\omega_n$

125. ....is employed for indicating angular position of an aircraft
(a) Rotary differential transformer
(b) Rotary capacitor
(c) Rotary inductor
(d) Rotary transformer

126. The frequency and time domain are related through
(a) Laplace Transform
(b) Fourier Integral
(c) Laplace Transform of Fourier Integral
(d) Laplace Transform and Fourier Integral

127. Type-0 system has steady state error, for unit step function of
(a) k_p (b) $1/1+ k_p$
(c) $1/1- k_p$ (d) $1/k_p$

128. Bandwidth is used as means of specifying performance of a control system related to
(a) relative stability of the system
(b) the speed of response
(c) the constant gain
(d) all of these

129. Magnetic amplifiers are used to amplify
(a) current (b) voltage
(c) power (d) none of these

130. Which compensator will be used to increase the damping of a badly under-damped system?
(a) phase-lag (b) phase-lead
(c) phase lag-lead (d) none of these

131. Phase margin of a system is used to specify
(a) relative stability (b) absolute stability
(c) time response (d) frequency response

132. A physical system is a collection of..... objects connected in such a way to give the desired output response.
(a) mechanical (b) physical
(c) control (d) electrical

133. ....gives indication how fast the system tends to attain the final value.
(a) Delay time (b) Rise time
(c) Time constant (d) Settling time

134. In Force-Voltage Analogy, mass is analogous to
(a) voltage (b) inductance
(c) resistance (d) current

135. LVDT is an....device.
(a) electro-dynamic
(b) electro-magnetic
(c) electro-mechanical
(d) electrostatic

136. In Force-Current Analogy, mass is analogous to
(a) current (b) resistance
(c) capacitance (d) voltage

137. Tyep-1 system under parabolic input will have
(a) parabolic output
(b) actuating signal increasing with time
(c) actuating signal decreasing with time
(d) constant actuating signal

138. Damping is proportional to
(a) gain (b) 1/gain
(c) $\sqrt{\text{gain}}$ (d) $1/\sqrt{\text{gain}}$

139. The steady state acceleration error for a type-1 system is
(a) infinity (b) unity
(c) zero (d) $1/k_p$

140. Control systems are normally designed with damping factor
(a) less than unity (b) of unity
(c) of zero (d) more than unity

141. In a system if the poles lie off the real axis, then the system is
(a) underdamped (b) overdamped
(c) critically damped (d) none of these

142. A system with gain margin close to unity or a phase margin close to zero is
(a) highly stable (b) oscillatory
(c) relatively stable (d) none of these

143. For an nth order system the state equations will be of the order of
(a) n (b) 1
(c) $\frac{n}{2}$ (d) $\frac{n+1}{2}$

144. The resolution of potentiometer should be
(a) zero (b) low
(c) very high (d) infinity

145. Inherent characteristic of a digital controller is that it accepts.....data.
(a) analog
(b) sampled
(c) sampled or discrete
(d) intermittent

146. When the gain margin is positive and the phase margin is negative, the system is
(a) stable (b) unstable
(c) oscillatory (d) highly stable

147. The mathematical model is solved for various types of inputs to obtain
(a) automation
(b) control system
(c) the physical model
(d) the dynamic response of the system

148. The Bode plot for the circuit given below will be of the type

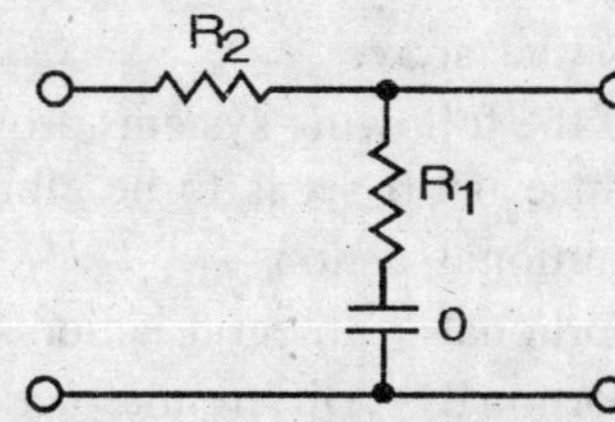

(a)
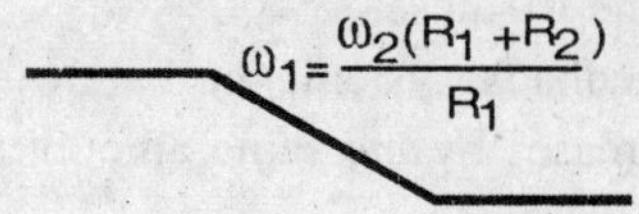

(b)
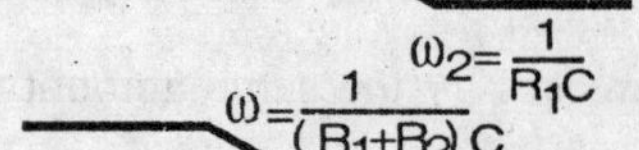

(c)
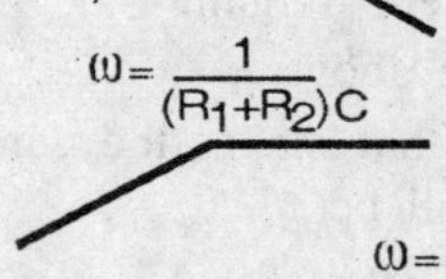

(d)
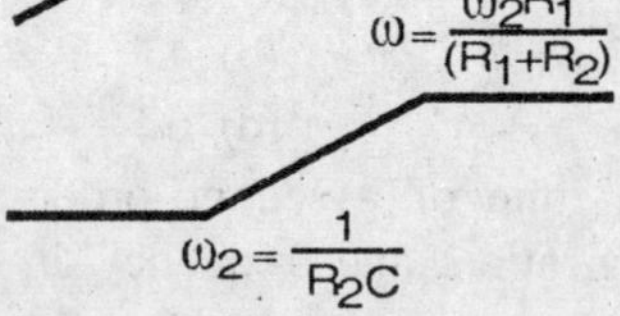

149. Output rate control is used to improve the damping of the system given below. If the closed-loop system has to have a damping factor of 0.5, what is the value of K_0?

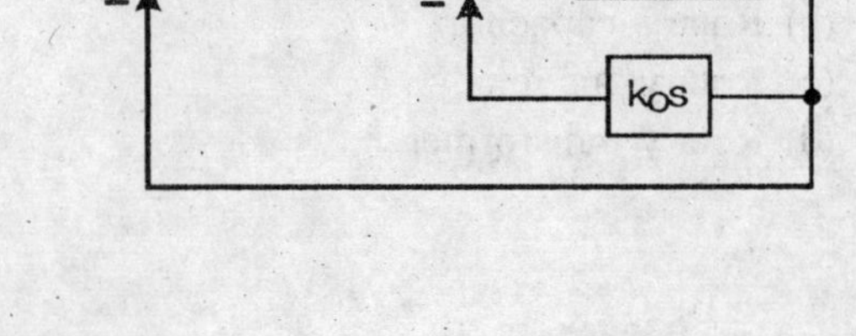

(a) 4 (b) 19

(c) $\frac{1}{4}$ (d) 6

150. In the unity feedback system shown below the value of derivative feedback constant *a*, which will increase the damping-ratio of the system to 0.7 is

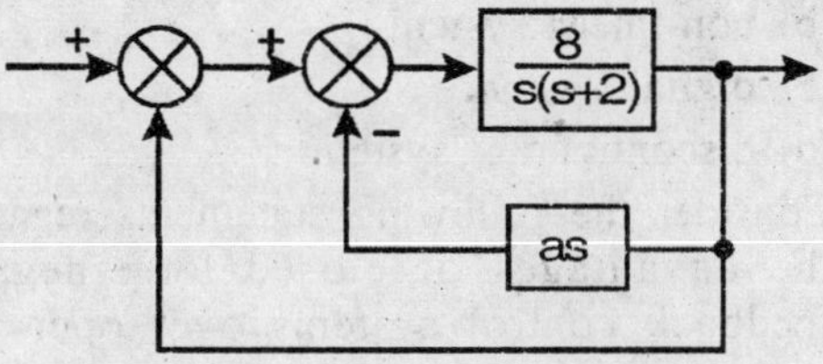

(a) 0.152 (b) 0.245
(c) 0.353 (d) 0.558

151. ....are commonly employed as error detectors in instruments.

(a) Resolvers (b) Vernistats
(c) Microsyns (d) None of these

152. The characteristics equation for the second order differential equation of the form

$$\frac{d^2y}{dt^2} + 2\,\xi\,\omega_n\,\frac{dy}{dt} + \omega_n^2 y = \omega_n^2 x$$

(a) $D^2 + 2\,\xi\,\omega_n\,D + \omega_n^2 = 0$
(b) $D^2 + \xi\,\omega_n\,D + \omega_n^2 = 0$
(c) $D^2 + 2\,\xi\,\omega_n\,D + \omega_n^2 = 0$
(d) $D^2 + \xi\,\omega_n + \omega_n^2 = 0$

153. In pneumatic control system, the compressed air is not

(a) filtered (b) regulated
(c) lubricated (d) any of these

154. If a system has only two poles (each having a negative real part) then its damping ratio is

(a) zero (b) non-zero
(c) infinity (d) none of these

155. Factors imparted by feedback to a system are

1. Increased accuracy and reduced sensitivity of output/input ratio to variations in system characteristics.
2. Reduced effect of non-linearities and increased bandwidth.
3. Tendency towards oscillation or instability.

The correct choice for this equation is

(a) (1) and (2) only (b) (1) and (3) only
(c) (2) and (3) only (d) (1), (2) and (3)

156. The stator of a synchros is made of

(a) laminated silicon steel
(b) cast iron
(c) stainless steel
(d) none of these

157. Root locus technique is important because

(a) it gives complete dynamic response of the system
(b) it indicates the effects of varying various parameters of the system on the root locations
(c) both (a) and (b)
(d) none of these

158. When integral action is included in a proportional controller, the proportional band

(a) decreases
(b) remains unaffected
(c) increases
(d) depends upon the integral time constant

159. Regenerative feedback

(a) implies feedback with positive sign
(b) is sometimes used for increasing the loop gain of feedback systems
(c) has a transfer function with a negative sign in the denominator
(d) all of the above

160. A 2nd order system with no zeros has its poles located at $-3 + j4$ and $-3 - j4$ in the *s*-plane. The undamped natural frequency and the damping factor of the system are respectively

(a) 4 rad/sec and 0.75
(b) 3 rad/sec and 0.60
(c) 5 rad/sec and 0.80
(d) 5 rad/sec and 0.60

161. The transfer function of a system is defined as the

(a) Laplace transform of the impulse response
(b) step response

(c) response due to an exponentially varying input
(d) none of these

162. Which of the following statements is not correct for servomechanism?
(a) Steady-state accuracy of a servo is better than that of a regulator.
(b) Some servos do not need to be stable, since they are intended for use with steady signals.
(c) A motor, may be added to convert a regulator into a servo.
(d) A servo with better frequency response need not be stable.

163. In a servo-control bridge and positioning loop system, the direction in which the load is driven depends on the
(a) ratio of bridge arms
(b) load shaft position
(c) error voltage polarity
(d) supply voltage polarity

164. The state-variable representation is preferred
(a) to make a plant simple and to control the transient response
(b) to reduce the sensitivity to the plant parameter variations
(c) to increase the sensitivity to the plast parameter variations
(d) none of these

165. In Routh-Hurwitz criterion, if all the elements in one row are zero, then there are
(a) pairs of conjugate roots on imaginary axis
(b) pairs of equal roots with opposite signs
(c) conjugate roots forming a quadrate in the s-plane
(d) all of the above

166. In a force-balance type pneumatic controller, the number of bellows required for *PID*-action is
(a) 1 (b) 2
(c) 3 (d) 4

167. Assumption(s) made in Laplace technique in sampled data control is/are
(a) Sampler is ideal having make and break contacts operating instantly.
(b) Sampler is operating on periodic duty cycle.
(c) Sampler is having small pulse duration.
(d) Sampler is having sampled information fed to a linearly released system.
(e) All of the above.

168. The on-off controller is a
(a) linear system
(b) non-linear system
(c) digital system
(d) discontinuous system

169. Consider the following statements regarding the advantages of closed loop negative feedback control systems over open loop systems.
1. The overall reliability of the closed loop system is more than that of open loop system.
2. The transient response in a closed-loop system decays more quickly than in the open-loop system.
3. In an open-loop system, closing of the loop increases the overall gain of the system.
4. In the closed-loop system, the effect of variation of component parameters on its performances is reduced.

Of these statements
(a) 1 and 3 are correct
(b) 1 and 2 are correct
(c) 2 and 4 are correct
(d) 3 and 4 are correct

170. Which of the following element is not a final control element?
(a) Electro-pneumatic convertor
(b) Potentiometer
(c) Servo motor
(d) Control valve

171. For stability of an AC servo-motor
(a) a negative slope on the torque speed curve is necessary
(b) linearized torque-speed curve is essential
(c) the ratio of the rotor reactance to rotor resistance should be high
(d) none of these

172. The output of a flapper-nozzle mechanism in pneumatic control system corresponds to a
(a) flow-range
(b) pressure-range
(c) mechanical movement
(d) voltage-range

173. Concept of a phase margin and gain margin is applicable to.....systems only.
(a) open loop unstable
(b) open loop stable
(c) closed loop unstable
(d) closed loop stable

174. In a negative feedback system with loop gain T, the noise generated within the basic amplifier
(a) decreases by a factor (1 + T)
(b) decreases by a factor (1 – T)
(c) increases by a factor (1 + T)
(d) increases by a factor (1 – T)
(e) is independent of feedback

175. Excessive noise in control systems can cause
(a) reduction in bandwidth
(b) reduction in gain
(c) saturation in amplifying stages
(d) oscillations

176. When gain k of the loop transfer function is varied from zero to infinity the closed loop system
(a) may become unstable
(b) stability is not affected
(c) always become unstable
(d) stability is improved

177. Error constants of system are a measure of
(a) steady-state response
(b) transient-state response
(c) relative stability
(d) steady-state as well as transient response

178. Root locus diagram can be used to determine
(a) absolute stability
(b) relative stability
(c) conditional stability
(d) none of the above

179. A state variable approach can be applied to.... system(s).
(a) time variant
(b) non-linear
(c) linear and time invariant
(d) all of the above

180. Knowing the state space representation, the transfer function of a system
(a) cannot be determined
(b) can be determined partly
(c) can be determined completely
(d) none of these

181. A state variable approach is applicable to.... system(s).
(a) continuous time
(b) discrete time
(c) periodic time
(d) continuous time and discrete time

182. The basic property(ies) of signal flow graph is/are
(a) it is applicable to linear system only
(b) nodes are arranged from left to right in a sequence
(c) signals travel along branches only in the marked direction and is multiplied by the branch gain
(d) the algebraic equations must be in the form of cause and effect relationship
(e) all of the above

183. The type-0 system has a finite non-zero value of
(a) K_p (b) K_v
(c) K_a (d) either of these

184. If the gain of the open-loop control system is halved, the gain margin will
(a) remain the same (b) become half
(c) become double (d) become four times

185. In control systems, excessive bandwidth should be avoided because
(a) noise is proportional to bandwidth
(b) it leads to low relative stability
(c) it leads to slow speed of response
(d) none of these

186. A servo-motor has the drawback of
(a) commutation problem
(b) low starting torque
(c) poor reliability
(d) all of these

187. Gain-cross over frequency is defined as
(a) $|G(j\omega) H(j\omega)| = 1$
(b) $|G(j\omega) H(j\omega)| = 0$
(c) $|G(j\omega) H(j\omega)| = \alpha$
(d) $|G(j\omega) H(j\omega)| = \frac{1}{\sqrt{2}}$

188. An ideal potentiometer should have
(a) zero resolution
(b) infinite resolution
(c) a fine wire
(d) a thick wire

189. Static error coefficients are used as a measure of the effectiveness of closed-loop systems for specified
(a) position input signal
(b) velocity input signal
(c) acceleration input signal
(d) all of these

190. The sensitivity of a closed-loop system to gain changes and load disturbances depends upon
(a) forward gain (b) loop gain
(c) frequency (d) all of these

191. For the system gain to be zero, the roots move towards
(a) zeros (b) origin
(c) poles (d) none of these

192. Natural frequency of a unity feedback control system of transfer function $G(s) = 10/(s+1)s$ is
(a) 3.16 rad/sec (b) 0.5 rad/sec
(c) 4.6 rad/sec (d) none of these

193. For any given closed-loop system
(a) only one of the static error coefficients has a finite non-zero value
(b) all the coefficients are always non-zero
(c) all the coefficients can have zero value
(d) none of these

194. Servo-actuators are designed to produce either
(a) a d.c. output or a.c. output
(b) linear motion or rotary motion
(c) constant speed or variable speed
(d) none of these

195. For the differential equation in the above question the damping coefficient is equal to
(a) $\omega_d \sqrt{1-\xi^2}$ (b) $\sqrt{\omega_n(1-\xi^2)}$
(c) $\omega_n \sqrt{1-\xi^2}$ (d) $\xi \omega_n$

196. The phase margin is defined as the amount of additional phase-lag at the gain crossover frequency required to bring the system to the verge of
(a) stability (b) instability
(c) critical damping (d) oscillating

197. For the characteristic equation, $s^2 + 4.8s + 72 = 0$ the damping ratio and natural frequency respectively are
(a) 0.212, 8.1 rad/sec
(b) 0.283, 8.48 rad/sec
(c) 0.299, 8.66 rad/sec
(d) none of these

198. Gain margin is the reciprocal of gain at the frequency at which the phase angle becomes
(a) 0° (b) 90°
(c) 180° (d) 270°

199. In a physically realizable system, number of poles is....the number of zeros.
(a) equal to
(b) less than
(c) more than
(d) equal to or more than
(e) equal to or less than

200. The type-1 system has
(a) no net pole at the origin
(b) net pole at the origin
(c) simple pole at the origin
(d) two poles at the origin

201. Velocity error constant of a system is measured when the input to the system is
(a) unit step function
(b) unit ramp function
(c) unit impulse function
(d) unit parabolic function

202. If a type-2 system is subjected to acceleration input, the steady state error will be
(a) zero (b) k_a
(c) $1/k_a$ (d) ∞

203. In a feedback system the transient response
(a) decays at a constant rate
(b) gets magnified
(c) decays slowly
(d) decays more quickly

204. Phase lag network
(a) reduces bandwidth
(b) increases system stability
(c) maintains velocity gain constant
(d) all of the above

205. The physical requirements for a servo-motor are
(a) low inertia and low starting torque
(b) low inertia and high starting torque
(c) large inertia and high starting torque
(d) large inertia and low starting torque

206. Which of the following terms are not a form of non-linearity for a control system?
(a) Saturation
(b) Backlash
(c) Square-law transfer characteristics
(d) All of these

207. Error constants of a system are measure of
(a) relative stability
(b) transient state response
(c) steady state response
(d) steady state as well as transient state response

208. Saturation in a stable control system can cause
(a) conditional stability
(b) overdamping
(c) low-level oscillations
(d) high-level oscillations

209. Electronic control systems have the serious drawbacks of
(a) low reliability
(b) operational difficulty
(c) temperature sensitiveness
(d) all of the above

210. Bimetallic thermostat is a
(a) zero-term controller
(b) one-term controller
(c) two-term controller
(d) on-off controller

211. If a system has only two poles each having a negative real part, then its damping ratio is
(a) zero (b) non-zero
(c) more than unity (d) less than unity

212. The open loop transfer function of a control system is $G(s) = \dfrac{K}{1\,(s+5)}$, the number of asymptotes and the angles of the asymptotes are
(a) two, 90° (b) two, 60°
(c) four, 90° (d) none of these

213. A system is said to be....when any one of the real roots is positive, or if any of the complex roots has a positive real part, the transient term associated with these roots increase with time.
(a) stable
(b) unstable
(c) absolutely unstable
(d) absolutely stable

214. Spring force is a non-linear function of the displacement 'x' measured from the rest position. The equation of motion of mass M is
(a) $M \dfrac{dx}{dt} + fs\,(x) = 0$
(b) $M \dfrac{d^2x}{dt^2} + fs\,(x) = 0$
(c) $M \dfrac{d^2x}{dt^2} + \dfrac{dx}{dt} = 0$
(d) none of these

215. In a feedback system, lead compensator
(a) speeds up the transient response
(b) increases the margin of stability
(c) increases the system error constant to some extent
(d) all of these

216. In thermal-electrical analogy charge is considered analogous to
(a) reciprocal of heat flow
(b) reciprocal of temperature
(c) temperature
(d) heat flow

217. The inductance is not used in lag network because of
(a) big size
(b) time delay and hysteresis losses
(c) high reactance
(d) none of these

218. In a non-linear control system limit cycle is self sustained oscillations of
(a) variable amplitude
(b) variable frequency
(c) fixed frequency
(d) fixed frequency and amplitude

219. The control valve used as final control element in pneumatic control systems converts
(a) pressure signal to position change
(b) position change to pressure signal
(c) pressure signal to electric signal
(d) electric signal to pressure signal

220. The characteristic equation of a system has roots with negative real parts if and only if elements of the first column of the Routh's table have .... sign(s).
(a) positive (b) negative
(c) same (d) none of these

221. Adding in the zeros in the transfer function causes
(a) lag-compensation
(b) lead-compensation
(c) lead-lag compensation
(d) none of these

222. The drag cup rotor is employed in a two phase induction motor to give
(a) low inertia (b) high inertia
(c) low torque (d) high torque

223. An ideal potentiometer should have
(a) fine wire
(b) infinite resolution
(c) zero resolution, proportion to reference voltage
(d) none of these

224. In pneumatic control system, the compressed air is not
(a) filtered (b) lubricated
(c) regualted (d) all of these

225. Diodes are connected in series with a.c. source of the magnetic amplifier primarily to
(a) avoid desaturation of the core on account of negative half cycle
(b) act as filter
(c) act as rectifier
(d) act as demodulator

226. Compensation in pneumatic control systems is provided by
(a) extension tubes
(b) restriction-volume combinations
(c) flapper-nozzle mechanism
(d) none of these

227. The time required for the response to rise from 10% to 90% of the final value for over-damped systems and 0 to 100% of the final value for under-damped systems is called the
(a) rise time (b) pick up time
(c) settling time (d) transient time

228. In a flapper-nozzle mechanism, if flapper moves close to nozzle, the nozzle back pressure will
(a) decrease
(b) increase
(c) remain constant
(d) depend upon the construction

229. Any physical system which does not automatically correct for variation in its output, is called a/an

(a) open loop system
(b) closed loop system
(c) unstable system
(d) none of the above

230. The bandwidth of a control system can be increased by
(a) phase lag compensator
(b) phase lead compensator
(c) phase lag-lead compensator
(d) all of these

231. Gyroscopes are employed for measuring or indicating...... in inertial navigation systems.
(a) water pressure
(b) moisture
(c) inclination of frames
(d) all of the above

232. In the following, indicate the time-invariant systems

1. $\frac{dy(t)}{dt} + 5y(t) = u(t)$

2. $t\frac{d^2y(t)}{dt^2} + \frac{dy(t)}{dt} + 2y(t) = v(t)$

3. $\frac{d^2y(t)}{dt^2} + 5\frac{dy(t)}{dt} + 6y(t) = w(t)$

(a) 1 and 3 (b) 1 and 2
(c) 2 and 3 (d) 1 only

233. The second derivative input signals modify
(a) the gain of the system
(b) damping of the system
(c) the time constant of the system
(d) the time constant and suppress the oscillations

234. Transfer function can be obtained from
(a) output-input ratio
(b) analogous table
(c) signal flow graph
(d) standard block diagram

235. The type-1 system steady state error for unit ramp function equal to
(a) $1/K_p$ (b) $1/(1 + K_b)$
(c) $1/K_v$ (d) $1/K_a$

236. Small coefficient of friction
(a) gives less steady state error
(b) gives more steady state error
(c) has no effect on steady state error
(d) none of the above

237. In the s-plane, the unstable region is
(a) second and third quadrants including imaginary axis
(b) first and fourth quadrants including imaginary axis except the origin
(c) first and second quadrants including real axis
(d) second and fourth quadrants including real axis except the origin

238. A system is said to be....when the roots are negative real or in the case of complex roots have negative real parts, the transient terms all decay with time.
(a) marginally stable
(b) absolutely stable
(c) absolutely unstable
(d) limitedly stable

239. Phase margin of a system is used to specify
(a) relative stability
(b) absolute stability
(c) time response
(d) frequency response

240. A pneumatic amplifier amplifies
(a) differential pressure
(b) flow
(c) change in air volume
(d) none of the above

241. When a step function is applied to the input of a system, the output remains below a certain level for all the time. The system is
(a) stable
(b) unstable
(c) not necessarily stable
(d) always unstable

242. The transfer function of a proportional controller is of the type
(a) K_c (b) T_s
(c) $\frac{1}{T_s}$ (d) $\frac{1}{T_s + 1}$

243. Open loop control system is one in which the control action

(a) depends on the input signal
(b) is independent of the desired output
(c) depends on system variables
(d) depends on system size

244. The position error coefficient for a unity feedback system is defined as

(a) $\lim_{s\to 0} \frac{G(s)}{s}$ (b) $\lim_{s\to 0} G(s)$
(c) $\lim_{s\to 0} sG(s)$ (d) none of these

245. The time required for the response to reach half the final value for the first time is called the

(a) rise time (b) decay time
(c) delay time (d) settling time

246. The transformer function of a system is $\frac{100\,(1+0.25s)}{(1+0.5s)}$. The phase shift at $\omega = 0$ and $\omega = \alpha$ will be

(a) 0° and –90° (b) 90° and –90°
(c) 90° and 180° (d) 0° and 180°

247. In a sampled data system, the data should be

(a) of the form of a pulse train at some points in the system
(b) modulated at some points in the system
(c) modulated at all points in the system
(d) unmodulated at all points in the system

248. The transfer function of a rate controller is of the type

(a) K_c (b) T_s
(c) $\frac{1}{T_s}$ (d) $\frac{1}{T_s+1}$

249. A type-0 system under step input has step output with...... actuating signal.

(a) zero (b) constant
(c) decreasing (d) increasing

250. The velocity-error coefficient for a unity feedback system is defined as

(a) $\lim_{s\to 0} \frac{G(s)}{s}$ (b) $\lim_{s\to 0} G(s)$
(c) $\lim_{s\to 0} s\,G(s)$ (d) none of these

251. Bandwidth is used as a means for specifying the performance of a control system related to the

(a) speed of response (b) constant gain
(c) relative stability (d) all of the above

252. The acceleration coefficient of a unity feedback system is defined as

(a) $\lim_{s\to 0} \frac{G(s)}{s}$ (b) $\lim_{s\to 0} G(s)$
(c) $\lim_{s\to 0} G(s)$ (d) none of these

253. In a compressed air plant, the reservoir does not perform the function of

(a) cooling of air
(b) air filteration
(c) air storage
(d) removal of pressure ripples

254. The transfer function of an integral controller is of the type

(a) K_c (b) T_s
(c) $\frac{1}{T_s}$ (d) $\frac{1}{T_s+1}$

255. An idealized physical system is called the

(a) physical model
(b) mathematical model
(c) electrical model
(d) control model

256. The type-2 system has

(a) no net pole at the origin
(b) net pole at the origin
(c) simple pole at the origin
(d) two poles at the origin

257. Tachogenerator is employed to measure

(a) rotational speed (b) displacement
(c) velocity (d) acceleration

258. The type-0 system has steady state error for unit step function equal to
(a) $1/K_p$ (b) $1/(1 + K_p)$
(c) $1/K_v$ (d) $1/K_a$

259. The open loop transfer function represents..... system.
(a) type-1 (b) type-2
(c) type-0 (d) none of these

260. If a simple system has inertia of 5 slug-ft² and a damping torque of 20 lb/ft/rad/sec, a gain of 20 will lead to a damping ratio of
(a) 0.5 (b) 1.0
(c) 2.0 (d) 3.0

261. A system has some roots with real parts equal to zero, but none with positive real parts is
(a) absolutely stable (b) relatively stable
(c) marginally stable (d) absolutely unstable

262. A temperature control system is known as
(a) process control system
(b) servomechanism
(c) cascade control system
(d) none of these

263. .... is used for improving both the transient and steady state responses of a control system.
(a) Integrator
(b) Comparator
(c) Lag-lead compensator
(d) Any of the above

264. A system has the transfer function $(1-s)/(1+s)$. It is a
(a) non-minimum phase system
(b) minimum-phase system
(c) low-pass system
(d) none of these

265. The frequency at which the phase angle is 180° is called the...... frequency.
(a) phase cross over (b) cut-off
(c) break (d) critical

266. Addition of zeros in transfer function causes..... compensation.
(a) lag (b) lead
(c) lag-lead (d) none of these

267. The Inverse Laplace Transform of $\frac{2}{s+1}$ is
(a) $2(t + 1)$ (b) $2e^{-t}$
(c) $2e^{t}$ (d) e^{-2t}

268. Introduction of integral action changes a system from type..... to type ....
(a) 0, 1 (b) 1, 2
(c) 2, 1 (d) 1, 0

269. The output of a linear system for a unit step input is given by $t^2 e^{-2t}$. The transfer function is given by
(a) $\frac{s}{(s+1)^3}$ (b) $\frac{2s}{(s+1)^3}$
(c) $\frac{1}{s^2(s+1)}$ (d) $\frac{2}{s(s+1)^2}$

270. The phase shift of the second order system with transfer function, $\frac{1}{s^2}$, is
(a) 90° (b) 180°
(c) –90° (d) –180°

271. Routh Hurwitz criterion gives
(a) roots in right half of s-plane
(b) roots in left half of s-plane
(c) roots in left half of s-plane and /or roots on imaginary axis
(d) roots in right half of s-plane and/or roots on imaginary axis

272. A rotational system is described by the first order differential equation $2\frac{d\omega}{dt} + \omega = 5$, where the right-hand side gives the constant torque acting on the system and 'ω' represents the angular velocity. The solution for ω is given by
(a) $5(1 - e^{t/2})$ (b) $5e^{-t/2}$
(c) $5(1 + e^{-t/2})$ (d) None of these

273. The phase lag caused by transportation delays
(a) reduces linearly with frequency
(b) increases linearly with frequency
(c) is independent of frequency
(d) none of the above

274. A step function is applied to the input of a system and output is of the form $y = t$ the system is
(a) stable
(b) unstable
(c) not necessarily stable
(d) conditionally stable

275. An effect of phase-lag compensation on servo-system performance is that
(a) for a given relative stability, the velocity constant is increased
(b) for a given relative stability the velocity constant is decreased
(c) the bandwidth of the system is increased
(d) none of these

276. Gain margin and phase margin can be computed by using
(a) Bode plot
(b) direct and inverse polar plots
(c) log-magnitude verses phase angle plot
(d) any of the above

277. The closed-loop gain of the system shown below is

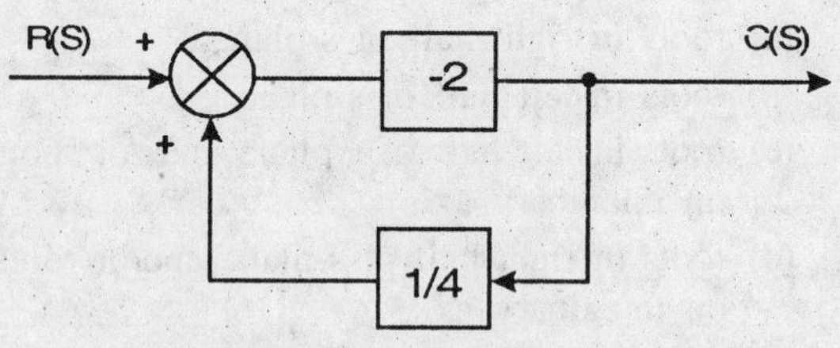

(a) $-\frac{4}{3}$ (b) –4
(c) 4 (d) None of these

278. Gain margin may be defined as the reciprocal of the gain at the frequency at which the phase angle becomes
(a) 0° (b) 90°
(c) 180° (d) 225°

279. A unity feedback system has open-loop transfer function $G(s) = 1/(1 + s)$. The pole of the closed loop system is located on the real axis in the s-plane at
(a) –5 (b) 2
(c) –2 (d) –1

280. If unit step function is applied to first order system, the steady state error will be
(a) T (b) zero
(c) unity (d) varying with time

281. In the same system if $\xi = 0$ the system's response will be
(a) damped oscillatory
(b) critically-damped oscillatory
(c) constant-amplitude sinusoidal
(d) zero

282. The steady-state error coefficients which system are given as $k_p = 0$, k_v = finite constant, $k_a = \infty$. The system is..... system.
(a) type - 0 (b) type - 1
(c) type - 2 (d) none of these

283. The poles of $F(s) = \frac{s^2 - 16}{s^5 - 7s^4 - 30s^3}$ are located at
(a) $s = 0$ (triple pole), 3 and 10
(b) $s = 0$ (triple pole), –3 and 10
(c) $s = 4, 4$
(d) $s = 0, 4, 16$

284. The servo-system with step acceleration input is a..... system.
(a) type - 0 (b) type - 1
(c) type - 2 (d) type - 3

285. A system has some roots with real parts equal to zero but none with positive real parts is
(a) absolutely stable
(b) relatively stable
(c) marginally stable
(d) absolutely unstable

286. Lag compensator
(a) causes faster transient response
(b) causes slower transient response
(c) does not affect transient response
(d) none of the above

287. If the open loop transfer function $G(j\omega)$ of a unity feedback system has a phase angle of $-150°$ at the gain cross-over frequency, the phase margin of the system is equal to

(a) $-150°$ (b) $+ 210°$

(c) $30°$ (d) None of these

288. For good degrees of relative stability, the values of gain margin and phase margin respectively should be

(a) 10 db, 30° – 35° (b) 6 db, 30° – 35°

(c) 6 db, 15° (d) 10 db, 15°

289. If the gain margin of a certain feedback system is given as 20 db, the Nyquist plot will cross the negative real axis at the point

(a) $s = -0.05$ (b) $s = -0.02$

(c) $s = -0.1$ (d) None of these

290. A phase-lag compensation will

(a) improve relative stability

(b) increase the speed of response

(c) increase bandwidth

(d) increase overshoot

ANSWERS

1	2	3	4	5	6	7	8	9	10
(b)	(d)	(b)	(d)	(a)	(d)	(b)	(a)	(b)	(b)
11	**12**	**13**	**14**	**15**	**16**	**17**	**18**	**19**	**20**
(a)	(c)	(b)	(a)	(a)	(a)	(d)	(a)	(d)	(a)
21	**22**	**23**	**24**	**25**	**26**	**27**	**28**	**29**	**30**
(a)	(b)	(b)	(a)	(c)	(d)	(a)	(a)	(d)	(c)
31	**32**	**33**	**34**	**35**	**36**	**37**	**38**	**39**	**40**
(b)	(a)	(b)	(a)	(c)	(a)	(b)	(a)	(a)	(a)
41	**42**	**43**	**44**	**45**	**46**	**47**	**48**	**49**	**50**
(c)	(b)	(a)	(b)	(c)	(d)	(b)	(c)	(c)	(a)
51	**52**	**53**	**54**	**55**	**56**	**57**	**58**	**59**	**60**
(b)	(c)	(b)	(b)	(c)	(b)	(b)	(b)	(b)	(b)
61	**62**	**63**	**64**	**65**	**66**	**67**	**68**	**69**	**70**
(d)	(d)	(c)	(c)	(a)	(c)	(a)	(a)	(f)	(b)
71	**72**	**73**	**74**	**75**	**76**	**77**	**78**	**79**	**80**
(b)	(b)	(a)	(b)	(c)	(d)	(b)	(b)	(b)	(c)
81	**82**	**83**	**84**	**85**	**86**	**87**	**88**	**89**	**90**
(a)	(b)	(a)	(c)	(c)	(c)	(b)	(c)	(b)	(d)
91	**92**	**93**	**94**	**95**	**96**	**97**	**98**	**99**	**100**
(c)	(b)	(b)	(b)	(c)	(c)	(b)	(a)	(d)	(d)
101	**102**	**103**	**104**	**105**	**106**	**107**	**108**	**109**	**110**
(c)	(a)	(c)	(c)	(c)	(a)	(a)	(d)	(b)	(c)
111	**112**	**113**	**114**	**115**	**116**	**117**	**118**	**119**	**120**
(a)	(a)	(a)	(d)	(d)	(a)	(a)	(a)	(c)	(d)
121	**122**	**123**	**124**	**125**	**126**	**127**	**128**	**129**	**130**
(b)	(a)	(c)	(c)	(a)	(d)	(b)	(b)	(c)	(b)

131	**132**	**133**	**134**	**135**	**136**	**137**	**138**	**139**	**140**
(a)	(b)	(c)	(b)	(c)	(c)	(b)	(b)	(a)	(a)
141	**142**	**143**	**144**	**145**	**146**	**147**	**148**	**149**	**150**
(a)	(b)	(a)	(d)	(c)	(b)	(d)	(a)	(b)	(b)
151	**152**	**153**	**154**	**155**	**156**	**157**	**158**	**159**	**160**
(c)	(c)	(c)	(b)	(d)	(c)	(c)	(b)	(d)	(d)
161	**162**	**163**	**164**	**165**	**166**	**167**	**168**	**169**	**170**
(b)	(b)	(c)	(a)	(d)	(d)	(e)	(b)	(c)	(b)
171	**172**	**173**	**174**	**175**	**176**	**177**	**178**	**179**	**180**
(a)	(b)	(b)	(b)	(c)	(c)	(a)	(b)	(c)	(c)
181	**182**	**183**	**184**	**185**	**186**	**187**	**188**	**189**	**190**
(d)	(e)	(a)	(c)	(a)	(b)	(a)	(b)	(d)	(d)
191	**192**	**193**	**194**	**195**	**196**	**197**	**198**	**199**	**200**
(c)	(a)	(a)	(b)	(d)	(b)	(b)	(c)	(d)	(c)
201	**202**	**203**	**204**	**205**	**206**	**207**	**208**	**209**	**210**
(b)	(c)	(d)	(d)	(b)	(d)	(c)	(a)	(c)	(d)
211	**212**	**213**	**214**	**215**	**216**	**217**	**218**	**219**	**220**
(b)	(a)	(c)	(b)	(d)	(d)	(b)	(d)	(a)	(c)
221	**222**	**223**	**224**	**225**	**226**	**227**	**228**	**229**	**230**
(a)	(a)	(b)	(b)	(a)	(b)	(a)	(b)	(a)	(b)
231	**232**	**233**	**234**	**235**	**236**	**237**	**238**	**239**	**240**
(c)	(a)	(d)	(c)	(c)	(a)	(b)	(b)	(a)	(a)
241	**242**	**243**	**244**	**245**	**246**	**247**	**248**	**249**	**250**
(c)	(a)	(b)	(b)	(c)	(a)	(a)	(b)	(b)	(c)
251	**252**	**253**	**254**	**255**	**256**	**257**	**258**	**259**	**260**
(a)	(d)	(b)	(c)	(a)	(d)	(a)	(b)	(b)	(b)
261	**262**	**263**	**264**	**265**	**266**	**267**	**268**	**269**	**270**
(c)	(b)	(c)	(a)	(a)	(a)	(b)	(b)	(d)	(b)
271	**272**	**273**	**274**	**275**	**276**	**277**	**278**	**279**	**280**
(a)	(a)	(b)	(b)	(a)	(d)	(a)	(c)	(c)	(b)
281	**282**	**283**	**284**	**285**	**286**	**287**	**288**	**289**	**290**
(c)	(b)	(b)	(c)	(c)	(c)	(c)	(b)	(c)	(a)

8. ELECTRICAL ENERGY UTILIZATION AND ELECTRIC TRACTION

Resistance Heating

When electric current passes through a resistance, power loss takes place therein, which appears in the form of heat.

Power loss $= I^2 R = IV = \dfrac{V^2}{R}$ watts

where R is the effective resistance of the element.

Different Types of Heating Materials

Types of Alloy	*Composition*	*Max. Temp. of Operation*	*Specific Resistance at Room Temp.*	*Specific Gravity*
Nickel-Copper	45% Ni 55% Cu	400°C	49 μ ohm/cm^3	8.88
Nickel-Chromium Iron	60% Ni, 16% Cr, 24% Fe	950°C	10 μ ohm/cm^3	8.28
Nickel-Chromium	80% Ni, 20% Cr	1150°C	190 μ ohm/cm^3	8.36
Iron-Chromium Aluminium	65-75% Fe, 20-30% Cr, 5% Al	1150–1350°C	140 μ ohm/cm^3	7.2

Requirements of a Good Heating Material

Material best suited for heating element should have following properties:

(1) It should have high resistance so that small length of wire may be required to produce given amount of heat.

(2) It should have high melting point.

(3) It should not oxidise at the temperature of the furnace.

(4) It should have low temperature coefficient so that resistance may not vary with the change in temperature otherwise starting current would be high.

Temperature Control of Resistance Furnace

There are three ways by which the temperature can be controlled.

1. By varying the applied voltage or current
2. By varying the resistance of the element
3. By varying the ratio of 'ON' and 'OFF' times of supply.

These three methods are used to control the heat loss in the oven. Voltage can be varied by using tapped transformer for supply to the ovens or by using a series resistance so that some voltage is dropped across this series resistor. The latter method is, of course, utilized for controlling temperatures of smaller capacity oven. An ON-OFF switch can be used to control the temperature. The time for which the oven is connected to the supply and the time for which it remains isolated from the supply will determine the temperature.

$$= \frac{\text{Ratio of Time for which the switch is ON}}{\text{Total time for an ON - OFF cycle}}$$

is an indication of temperature. The higher the ratio, the larger will be the temperature of the oven.

Design of Resistance Heating Elements

When the element has reached a steady temperature, all the electrical input is given out as heat. They produced according to Stefan's Law is

$$H = 5.72 \times 10^4\ ke \left[\left(\frac{T_1}{1000}\right)^4 - \left(\frac{T_2}{1000}\right)^4\right] \frac{\text{watts}}{\text{m}^2}$$

If circular wire is used for the element, electrical input $P = V^2/R$ watts; V is the supply voltage and R is resistance in ohms.

But $\quad R = \frac{\rho l}{a} = \frac{\rho . l}{\pi d^2/4} = \frac{4 \rho l}{\pi d^2}$

where l is the length of wire, d the diameter of wire and, ρ the specific resistance

$$P = \frac{V^2}{4 \rho l / \pi d^2} = \frac{\pi d^2 V^2}{4 \rho l}$$

At steady temperature, Electrical Power Input = Heat Power

Since $\pi.\ d.\ l$ is the total surface area from which heat radiation takes place, therefore

$$P = H. \pi\ d.\ l \qquad \text{...(i)}$$

$$\therefore \frac{\pi d^2 V^2}{4 \rho l} = \pi.\ d.\ lH$$

$$\frac{d}{l^2} = \frac{4 \rho H}{V^2} \qquad \text{...(ii)}$$

Also $\quad R = \frac{V^2}{P} = \frac{4 \rho l}{\pi d^2}$

$$\frac{l}{d^2} = \frac{V^2}{P} . \frac{\pi}{4 \pi . \rho} \qquad \text{...(iii)}$$

High Frequency Heating

The main difference between conventional methods of heating and high frequency methods of heating is that in the former case, heat is transferred either by conduction, convection or radiation while in later case conversion of electromagnetic energy into heat energy takes place inside the material. Heat transfer by conventional methods is very limited as given below:

(1) By conduction 20 watts/sq. cm.

(2) By convection 0.5 watt/sq. cm.

(3) By radiation 8.0 watts/sq. cm.

(4) By conduction from intense flame 1000 watts/sq.cm.

As against, this heat transfer rate by high frequency either by induction or by dielectric heating methods is as much as 10,000 watts/sq. cm.

High frequency heating can be applied to two classes of material. (1) Conducting materials which can be ferromagnetic or nonmagnetic. (2) Insulating materials.

Heating process to first class of materials is called *induction heating* and to the second class of materials is *dielectric heating*.

Oscillator Frequencies

The table given below shows the frequencies required for various heating processes and equipment used to generate these frequencies.

Type of Heating	*Frequency used*	*Equipment*
1. Induction heating		
(a) Low temperature heating of metals, annealing	60–600 Hz	Diode Frequency Converter or Rotating Generator
(b) Deep heat penetration melting	600–10,000 Hz	– do –
(c) Surface hardening of metals	10 – 200 kHz	Spark-gap Converter
(d) Heating of small pieces wire, metal strips	400 – 1000 kHz	Vacuum-Tube Oscillator (electronic heating)
2. Dielectric Heating	1–50 MHz	– do –

Electron Bombardment Heating

In electron bombardment heating, controlled stream of electrons is produced between an emitter and the material to be heated. When the fast moving electrons hit the material they release their kinetic energy which appears as heat in the material to be heated. Power released by electron beam is $P = nqV$ watts where n is the number of charges hitting per second, q is the charge in coulombs per particle and V, voltage through which charges have been accelerated from rest.

Electric Arc Heating

When voltage across two electrodes separated by an air gap is increased, a stage is reached when voltage gradient in the air gap is such that the air in the gap becomes good conductor of electricity. An arc is said to exist when electric current passes through air gap. It should be noted that is required a very high voltage to establish an arc across the air gap, but to maintain the arc small voltage may be sufficient. An electric arc provides a large quantity of power in a small volume. This concentration of heat developed at high temperature of about 3500°C from carbon arc, forms a good heating source. This principle is made use in an electric arc furnace.

Dielectric Heating

Dielectric heating sometimes called high frequency capacitance heating, is employed for heating non-metal like wood, plastic, etc. Dielectric heating operates on the principle that when a capacitor is placed in an electric field, its molecules are subjected to stress and are disturbed. The current drawn by it is never leading the voltage by exactly 90°. The angle between the current and voltage is slightly less with the result that there is a small phase component of the current which produces power loss in the dielectric of the capacitor. At ordinary frequency of 50 Hz, such loss may be small enough to be negligible but at high frequencies, the loss becomes large enough to heat the dielectric. It is the loss that is utilised in heating the dielectric. The material to be heated is placed between two electrodes which may be of two parallel plates across which high frequency voltage is applied. The material acts as the dielectric between two electrodes and heat is produced inside the material. Thus the art of dielectric heating consists in utilising the dielectric loss in any poorly conducting material for the production of heat.

Theory of Dielectric Heating

Consider an infinite small cube of dielectric material placed in an ac electrostatic field as shown in Fig. 1. The potential difference between two faces of the cube is V. Let the side of cube be '*a*'. The capacitance of the cube is given by

$$C = \varepsilon_0\, \varepsilon_r \frac{\text{Area of the face}}{\text{Thickness}}$$

$$= \varepsilon_0\, \varepsilon_r \frac{a^2}{a} = \varepsilon_0\, \varepsilon_r\, a \text{ Farad}$$

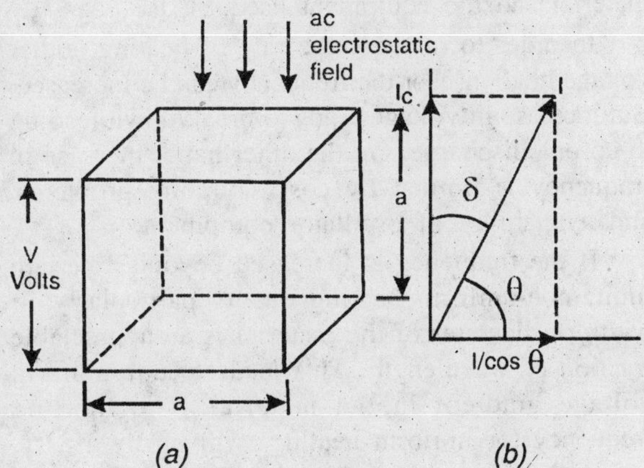

Fig. 1

where ε_r is the relative permittivity of the material. The resulting current makes an angle θ with the voltage V across the capacitor. θ is slightly less than 90°. The small in-phase component I is given by

$$I \cos\theta = \frac{|V|}{Z_C} \cos\theta$$

where Z_C is the impedance of elementary capacitor and nearly equals $X_C = 1/2\pi fC$.

The power dissipated in the cube

$$P = VI \cos\theta$$

$$= VI \text{ . power factor}$$

$$= V.\ \frac{|V|}{Z_C} . (pf)$$

$$= 2\,\pi\, f\,.\, CV^2 . (pf)$$

$$= 2\,\pi\, f\,.\, \varepsilon_0\, \varepsilon_r\, a\, V^2\, (pf)$$

Power per unit volume can be obtained by dividing both sides by a^3.

$$P_v = \frac{2\pi f_2.\varepsilon_0\varepsilon_r a.(pf)V^2}{a^3}$$

$$= 2\,\pi\, f\,.\,\varepsilon_0\,\varepsilon_r\,.\,(pf)\,\frac{V^2}{a^2}$$

$$P_v = 2\,\pi\, f\,.\,\varepsilon_0\,\varepsilon_r\,(pf)\,v^2 \text{ watt/m}^2$$

where v is the applied voltage per unit length. The product of dielectric constant ε_r and power factor (pf) *i.e.*, ($\varepsilon_r\ pf$) is called the *loss factor*. Thus the power can be calculated accurately as the quantities to be measured are the properties of dielectric material and the equipment used.

In order to increase the rate of heating, either voltage gradient v or the frequency can be increased. But increase in voltage tends to break down leading to corona discharge. On the other hand, increase in frequency is limited by cost, coupling problems, and availability of oscillator equipment.

If the frequency is increased beyond a certain limit, non-uniform heating occurs particularly, if width or diameter of the material is an appreciable fraction of wavelength. This leads to non-uniform voltage gradient in the material. The limiting frequency for uniform heating is given by

$$f_c = \frac{14.31}{a\sqrt{\varepsilon_r}} \text{ MHz}$$

where a is the radius of material

Applications of Dielectric heating

Dielectric heating has a large number of applications in industry. Some applications of dielectric heating are given below:

(a) Heating of Raw Plastics: The raw material in the form of tablets is put in the moulds which are heated by steam. When cold tablets are put into hot moulds, the core of material does not melt by the time the outermost portions have started setting and solidifying. Once the outer parts start setting, it is not easy to soften them again. This results in mould where corners are not sharp and also the mould may break on account of premature and unequal hardening of the plastic. To avoid this, the tablets are heated uniformly before being put into hot moulds. Dielectric heating of such tablets is done in few seconds.

(b) Gluing of Wood: Gluing of wooden pieces is universal in wood industry. If animal glue is used, it takes 24 hours to dry up. The edges of the pieces to be glued are applied with plastic type glue that hardens when heated up to a certain temperature. This is done by dielectric heating, Mechanical pressure may be applied to secure better adhesion. The pieces can be removed from the press in about 30 seconds as most of the heat goes into the glue and very little heat is wasted.

(c) Electronic Sewing: Electronic sewing machine using dielectric heating may be used for sewing of plastic film materials into articles such as rain coats, umbrellas, food packets, tobacco containers and medicine containers, etc. The machine simply seals two or more pieces together along a line using dielectric heating. This is superior to conventional sewing using dielectric heating. If these films are stitched with ordinary thread, they are no longer water tight and also become weak at the seam. The use of adhesive instead of electronic sewing is inferior because of higher cost and longer drying time. With the help of an electronic sewing machine, the films to be stitched together pass between rollers to which radio frequency voltage is applied. The heat produced in the material seals it along the line where pressure is applied making a water proof joint. The cold wheel electrodes do not allow the outer surfaces to melt.

(d) Food Processing : Dielectric heating has been applied in the food processing industry. Some applications are:

(i) Pasteurising milk and beer inside the bottles

(ii) Cooking foods without removing the outer shells.

(iii) Dehydrating fruits, vegetables, eggs, etc.

(iv) Defrosting frozen foods in large bakeries and restaurants.

(e) Disinfestation of Cereals and Grains: By dielectric heating, the eggs of insects and pests can be killed saving grain and cereals from damage and also preventing these eggs and larva to pass on to cereal processing equipment and develop into dangerous worms later on under favourable conditions of temperature and humidity.

Resistance Welding

Resistance welding is the process of fusing two or more metal pieces together by passing heavy currents through the areas of contact to be welded. The duration of the current may vary from a few milliseconds to several seconds depending upon the job requirement. Spot welding implies a succession of spaced welded spots joining two metal sheets, whereas seam welding is produced by succession of overlapping and timed spots, using water-cooled roller electrodes. Pulsation welding applies a number of successive current pulses to the same weld, used mainly to prevent electrode overheating in the welding of thick plate. Electronic control of the duration and magnitude of the welding current has made precise welding possible, and the materials such as aluminium and stainless steel can be satisfactorily welded in production.

This process is based on the resistance to a current flow between the two metal pieces where weld heat is produced. The welding heat is given by

$$H = \int_0^{t_w} i^2 r\, dt$$

where r is the resistance between the pieces to be welded and t_w, time during which weld current flows. Either alternating current or short pulses of unidirectional current may be used.

Types of Resistance Welding

Following are the principal types of resistance welding processes.

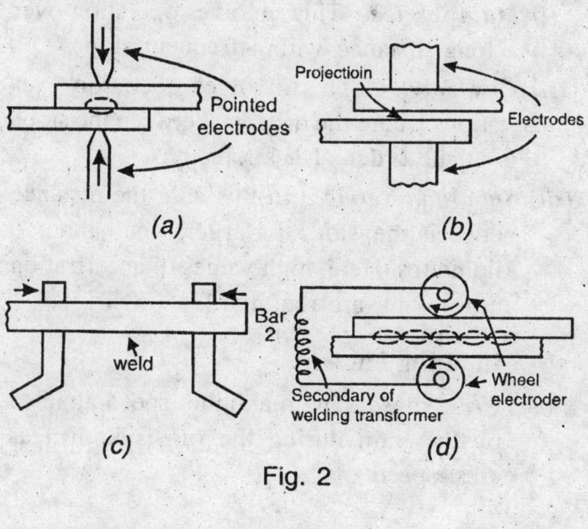

Fig. 2

(a) Spot Welding: Spot welding is done by clamping two or more pieces of metal in the form of sheets together between two pointed electrodes. The electrode tips are made of copper or copper alloy and are water-cooled. The welding current depends on the thickness and the composition of the plates. Fig. 2 (a) shows the arrangement.

(b) Projection Welding: In projection welding, instead of using pointed electrode for concentration of heat, use is made of either an embossing on or both of the pieces at a location where welding is desired. Fig. 2 (b) shows the general arrangement.

(c) Butt Welding: In butt welding, one bar is held in a fixed clamp and the other is held in a moving clamp. The two bars are brought together as shown in Fig. 2 (c). A heavy current is passed from the welding transformer or raise the temperature when the desired temperature is reached, the two pieces are ramped together either manually or automatically resulting in a weld. Rods, pipes and wires are welded in this way.

(d) Seam Welding: In seam welding, two overlapping sheets of metal are welded together along a continuous line by moving them between wheel-shaped electrodes through which the welding current flows at short intervals. Fig. 2(d) illustrates the principle. This process can produce continuous pressure tight seams at high speeds.

(e) Pulsation Welding: In pulsation welding, the welding current flows inermittently unlike spot welding in which current flows continuously until the weld is formed. This intermittent flow of current permits the water cooled electrodes to remove heat from the surface of the materials and thereby causes temperature gradient near the weld. This method is used for pieces thicker than 1 cm.

Electronic Control in Resistance Welding

Electronic controls are very accurate and precise in operation. Some of the electronic controls are:

(a) Ignitron Contactor: It connects the welding transformer primary to the a.c. supply for intervals controlled by the control signals from control circuits.

(b) Heat Control: This is an electronic circuit which delays the firing of the ignitrons in the line contactor by specific angle in each half cycle of the voltage and thus controls the amount of heat given to the weld.

(c) Non-Synchronous Weld Timer: This is an electronic circuit which governs the number of cycles for which the line contactor remains closed. It can control the conduction to nearest integral number of cycles.

(d) Synchronous Weld Timer: This is more elaborate electronic timing circuit which not only controls full cycles of conduction accurately but also controls the firing of the contactor precisely at the desired angle in each cycle so as to avoid production of undesired welding current transients.

(e) Sequence Timer: This is the circuit which includes: (i) timer to determine the 'squeeze time' *i.e.*, the time required for pressure to build up before the line contactor closes; (ii) weld-time; (iii) hold-time; and (iv) off-time.

ELECTRIC TRACTION

Advantages of Electric Traction

Advantages of electric traction over steam traction are:

(1) Cleanliness: Electric traction is free from smoke and flue gases etc.

(2) Maintenance cost: The maintenance cost of electric traction system is 50% of that of steam traction system.

(3) Starting time: Electric locomotive can be starts without any loss of time.

(4) High starting torque: The motor used in electric traction is DC series/AC series motor which has a very starting torque.

(5) Higher acceleration rate: It makes the traffic handling capacity almost double.

(6) Braking: Regenerative braking is used in electric traction which feeds back 80% of the energy required during current back during decent.

(7) Centre of gravity: Centre of gravity of electric locomotive is quite low which makes it quite stable and as a result it is able to take curves even at higher speeds quite safely.

(8) Absence of unbalanced forces: Due to absence of unbalanced forces produced by reciprocating, co-efficient of adhesion is more in case of electric traction. This reduces the weight to HP ratio of the locomotive.

Disadvantages of Electric Traction

(1) The capital cost of overall electric traction system is quite high.

(2) Failure of power disturbs the traction.

(3) Communication lines which run parallel to the power lines face interference.

(4) Electric traction can be used only at places which are electrified.

Systems of Traction Electrification

There are four types of track electrification systems normally used

(i) Direct current system

(ii) Single phase low frequency system

(iii) Three phase a.c. system

(iv) Composite system

Railway Service

Railway service may be classified into following categories:

(i) Main service : This involves operation over a long distance within frequent stops.

(ii) City Service: This involves operation over stations where the distance between the stops is of the order of a kilometre.

(iii) Suburban Service: In this case the distance between the stops is larger, upto about 6 kilometres. Here, high values of acceleration and braking are required.

Limiting Factors

(1) Crest speed: The maximum speed attained by the train during the run is known as crest speed.

(2) *Average speed*

$$= \frac{\text{Total distance}}{\text{Running time (excluding stops)}}$$

(3) *Scheduled Speed*

$$= \frac{\text{Total distance}}{\text{Total time (including stops)}}$$

ILLUMINATION ENGINEERING

Terms used in Illumination are described below:

Light: Light is defined as the radiant energy from a hot body causing visual sensation on the human eye.

Flux: It is also known as luminous flux. It is defined as the total quantity of light energy radiated or emitted per second from a luminous body in the form of light waves. It is measured in lumens and is denoted by F or Φ. It is defined as the rate of luminous energy.

If Q lumens-hour is the luminous output of source of light and energy radiated for t hours, then flux is $\Phi = Q/t$ lumens.

Plane Angle: Plane angle is subtended in a plane by two converging lines. This angle is measured in radians or degrees.

One radian is the angle subtended at the centre of a circle by an arc whose value is equal to the radians of the circle.

$$\theta = \frac{\text{Arc}}{\text{radians}}$$

and one Radian = $180/\pi$ degree

The largest plane angle subtended at a point may be 2π radians.

Solid angle: Solid angle is the angle generated by the line passing through the point in space and the periphery of the area. In other words, a solid angle encloses a volume by an infinite number of lines lying on a surface and meeting at a point. It is measured in steradians and is denoted by ω and

$$\omega = \frac{\text{Area}}{(\text{Radius})^2} \text{ steradians}$$

Luminous Intensity: Luminous intensity in any particular direction is the luminous flux emitted by per unit solid angle by a point source and is denoted by I.

$$I = \frac{F}{\omega} = \frac{\Phi}{\omega} \text{ lumens/steradian or}$$

Candela

It is the ratio of the brightness of a source of light to that of standard candle. One candle gives out luminous flux of 4π lumens in space. Thus lumens emitted by one candle source of light is one lumen/steradian.

In scientific terms, candle is defined as the luminous intensity in the perpendicular direction of a surface of 1/600,000 sq. metre of a full radiator at the temperature of freezing platinum under a pressure of 101,325 N/sq. metre.

Light Energy: It is the energy contained in visual radiations in a given time and is expressed in lumen-hour and is denoted by Q.

Luminous Efficiency or Radiant Efficiency: It is defined as the output in lumens per watt of the power consumed by the source of light. It is measured in lumens per watt. If a bulb is rated at 500 watts and 250 volts, has an efficiency of 13 lumens/watt. Then total flux produced by bulb = 500 × 13 = 6500 lumens.

Lumen: Lumen is defined as the amount of luminous flux given out in space represented by one unit of solid angle by a source having an intensity of one candle power in all directions.

$$\text{Lumens} = \text{Candle power} \times \text{Solid angle}$$
$$= C.P. \times \omega$$

Total lumens given out by the source of one candle is 4π lumens.

Mean Spherical Candle Power (MSCP): It is defined as average of candle powers in all directions and in all plane from the source of light, *i.e.*

$$MSCP = \frac{\text{Total flux in lumens}}{4\pi}$$

Mean Hemispherical Candle Power (MHSCP): It is defined as average of candle powers in all directions above or below the horizontal plane passing through the source of light.

Mean Horizontal Candle Power (MHCP): It is average of all the candle power in all directions in the horizontal plane containing the source of light.

Reduction Factor: Reduction factor of a source of light is defined as the ratio of its mean spherical candle power to its mean horizontal candle power.

$$\text{Reduction factor} = \frac{\text{MSCP}}{\text{MHCP}}$$

Candle Power (PC): Candle power is the light rendering capacity of a source in a given direction and is defined as number of lumens given out by the source in a unit solid angle in a given direction. It is denoted by symbol CP, *i.e.,*

$$\text{CP} = \frac{\text{Lumens}}{\omega}$$

Illumination: When the light falls upon any surface, the phenomenon is called the illumination. It is defined as the number of lumens, falling on the surface per unit area. It is denoted by symbol E and is measured in lumens per square metre or lux or metre candle.

If a flux of F lumens falls on a surface of area A, then the illumination of that surface is $E = F/A$ lumens/m^2 or lux.

Bigger unit of illumination is *phot.*

One phot = 10^4 lux

Centimetre Candle: It is also a unit of illumination and is defined as the luminous flux falling per square centimetre on the surface which everywhere is perpendicular to the rays of light from a source of one CP and one cm away from it.

Metre Candle: It is also known as lux. It is the unit of illumination and is defined as the luminous flux falling per sq. metre on the surface which is everywhere perpendicular to the rays of light from a source of one Candle Power and one metre away form it. Or it is the illumination produced by a source of one candle power on the inner surface of a sphere of one metre radius.

Adhesive Weight: This is total weight to be carried on the driving wheels is called adhesive weight.

Coefficient of Adhesion (μ)

$$= \frac{\text{Tractive effort to stop the wheels}}{\text{Adhesive weight}}$$

Tractive Effort: The effective force, necessary to propel the train at the wheels of vehicle is called tractive effort. It is tangential to the driving wheels and measured in Newtons.

Specific Energy Output: Energy output of the driving wheels is the energy output in watt hour per ton km.

Specific Energy Consumption: It is the total energy input to all the traction motors in a train.

Factors which effects the Energy Consumption: (i) Distance between stops; (ii) Acceleration

Reflection Factor: It is defined as the ratio of reflected light to incident light. It is always less than unity.

$$\text{Reflection factor} = \frac{\text{Reflected light}}{\text{Incident light}}$$

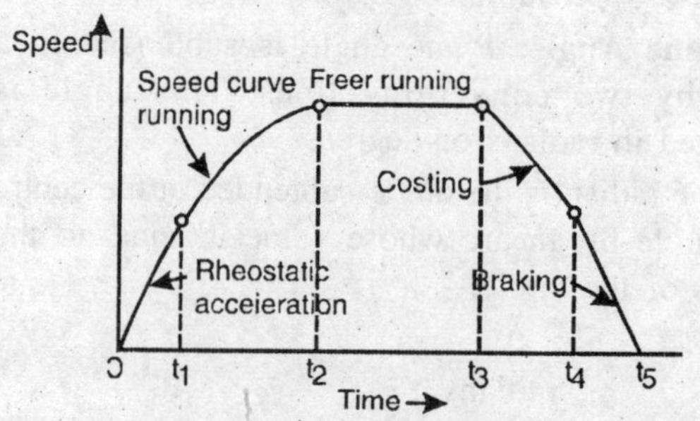

Fig. 3

A polished surface like mirror reflects light incident over it. The part of light absorbed by such a surface is too small in comparison with the reflected part. Since all the incident light is not reflected, reflection factor is always less than one. Following are some typical values of RF

Source	:	R.F.
Mirror	:	0.80 to 0.85
Steel stainless	:	0.60 to 0.65
Chromium plating	:	0.55 to 0.60

Lamp Efficiency: It is defined as the ratio of luminous flux to the power input. It is expressed as lumens/watt or watts/candle power.

$$\text{Lamp efficiency} = \frac{\text{Lumens emitted to source}}{\text{Wattage of source of light}}$$

Speed-Time Curves of Suburban Run

A typical speed-Time curve is shown in Fig. 3.

(i) Acceleration while notching up or constant acceleration: During this period of run (0 to t_1), starting resistance is gradually cut off so that the motor current is limited to a certain value and the voltage across the motor is gradually increased.

(ii) Speed curve running : During speed curve running (t_1 to t_2), the current starts decreasing with the increase in speed.

(iii) Free running (t_2 to t_3) : This period occurs, on level track, when the power output from the driving axels balances the rate at which energy is expended against the resistance to motion.

(iv) Coasting period (t_3 to t_4) : At the end of free running period, supply to the motors is cut off and train is allowed to run under its own momentum.

(v) Braking period (t_4 to t_5): At the end of coasting period, brakes are applied to bring the train to stop.

Space Height Ratio: It is defined as the ratio of horizontal distance between two adjacent lamps and height of lamps from the working plane.

Space height ratio

$$= \frac{\text{Horizontal distance between two adjacent lamps}}{\text{Height of lamps above working plane}}$$

Maintenance Factor: It is merely reverse of the depreciation factor. So it is always less than unity.

Specific Consumption: It is the ratio of power input to the source of light to its luminous intensity. Its unit is watts per candela.

Absorption Factor: In case of factories or places where atmosphere is full of smoke fumes, there is a possibility of absorption of light energy. The absorption factor is defined as

Absorption factor

$$= \frac{\text{Net lumens available after absorption}}{\text{Total lumens emitted by source of light}}$$

Depreciation Factor: Due to accumulation of dirt, dust and smoke, lamps emit less light as compare to they emit when they are new ones. Similarly, ceilings and walls, etc., after being covered by dust etc., reflect less light as compare to that when they are new.

Therefore, the ratio of illumination under everything is perfectly clean to the illumination under normal working condition is known as depreciation factor.

Depreciation factor

$$= \frac{\text{Illumination when everything is clean}}{\text{Illumination under normal working condition}}$$

It is more then unity.

Co-efficient of Utilisation: All the light emitted by the source does not reach the surface to be illuminated. Some portion of light directly falls upon surface and some light falls upon surface after reflection from wall and ceilings. All the light falling upon the walls and ceiling does not reach the surface because some light is absorbed.

Therefore, coefficient of utilisation is the ratio of lumens reaching the working plane to the total lumens given out by lamp.

Coefficient of utilisation

$$= \frac{\text{Lumens reaching on working plane}}{\text{Total lumens emitted by source of light}}$$

Waste Light Factor: In flood lighting scheme, a number of projector lamps is employed so the light of each projector not only overlaps that of its adjacent projector but at the edges of the area, some light falls outside. In order to compute total lumens required, theoretical lumens required are multiplied by waste light factor. Value of this factor is about 1.2 for rectangular areas and 1.5 for irregular objects such as statues, monuments, etc.

Beam Factor: It is used in turns of projector lamps. It is the ratio of lumens in the beam of a projector to lamp lumens. This factor takes into account the absorption of light by reflector and front glass of the projector lamp. Its value lies between 0.3 to 0.6.

LAWS OF ILLUMINATION

There are two laws of Illumination:

(i) First Law : It is also known as Law of Inverse Square.

According to this law, the illumination of a surface is inversely proportional to square of distance between the source and surface provided that the distance between the surface and the source is sufficiently large so that the source can be regarded as a point source.

(ii) Lambert's Cosine Law: According to this law, illumination of a surface varies directly as the cosine of the angle between the normal to the surface and direction of incident light.

EXERCISE

1. Wound rotor and squirrel-cage motors with high slip which develop maximum torque at stand still are used for
(a) presses and punches
(b) machine tools
(c) elevators
(d) all of these

2. Which of the following devices is necessarily required for automatic temperature control in a furnace?
(a) Thermocouple
(b) Thermostat
(c) Auto-transformer
(d) Heating elements of variable resistance material

3. Which of the following site will be preferred for earthing?
(a) wet mashy ground
(b) clay soil
(c) loam mixed with small quantities of sand
(d) damp and wet sand pit

4. Which of the following heating elements can give highest temperature in resistance heating?
(a) Copper (b) Nickel copper
(c) Nichrome (d) Silicon carbide

5. A locomotive exerts a tractive effort of 40,000 N in pulling a train at 60 kmph on a level track. If the same train is to be hauled at the same speed but on gradient, the tractive effort required will be 60,000 N. The output delivered by the motor will be more if it is driven by
(a) a 3-phase induction motor
(b) a dc series motor
(c) an ac series motor
(d) equal in all the three cases

6. Nichrome wires can be safely used for heating to temperature around 1500°C. Which of the following materials for heating element should be selected?
(a) Eureka
(b) Kanthal
(c) Platinum molybdenum, carbon compound
(d) Nichrome

7. Utilisation factor depends upon
(a) size of the room
(b) space height ratio of the lamps
(c) colour of walls/ceiling
(d) all of the above

8. The electric locomotives run faster at curved routes as compared to steam locomotives as:
(a) the centre of gravity of electric locomotive is higher than that of steam locomotive
(b) the centre of gravity of electric locomotive is lower than that of steam locomotive
(c) the speed at curved routes is independent of location of centre of gravity
(d) none of these

9. The dc series motor is most suitable for traction services but more particularly for urban/suburban services because
   (a) dc series motors are suitable for regenerative braking
   (b) dc series motors are capable of withstanding rapid fluctuations in supply voltage
   (c) dc series motors are capable of developing high torque at start
   (d) dc series motors are capable of withstanding temporary interruption of supply without undue rush of current

10. For 600 V d.c. line for tram cars
    (a) track is connected to negative of the supply
    (b) track is connected to positive of the supply
    (c) track is connected to mid voltage of 300 V
    (d) none of these

11. Which of the following statements about illumination is true?
    (a) If the distance from the source doubles, the illumination becomes half
    (b) If the distance from the source doubles, the illumination reduces to one fourth
    (c) The greater the illumination, the better one sees
    (d) The finer the work, the less the required illumination

12. Motor used for elevators is generally
    (a) synchronous motor
    (b) induction motor
    (c) capacitor start single-phase induction motor
    (d) any of these

13. A single phase reluctance motor
    (a) has salient pole rotor structure and runs at subsynchronous speed
    (b) has salient pole rotor structure and runs at super-synchronous speed
    (c) has salient pole rotor structure and runs at synchronous speed
    (d) has non-salient pole rotor structure and runs at synchronous speed

14. Belted slip ring induction motor is almost invariably used for
    (a) centrifugal blowers
    (b) water pumps
    (c) jaw crushers
    (d) heavy load

15. Electric traction in comparison to other traction systems has the advantage(s) of
    (a) higher acceleration and braking retardation
    (b) cleanest system and so ideally suitable for the underground and tube railways
    (c) better speed control
    (d) all of the above

16. The device necessarily used for automatic temperature control in a furnace is
    (a) thermostat (b) auto-transformer
    (c) thermo-couple (d) any of the above

17. The diameter of a 50-SWG wire is closer to
    (a) 0.0253 mm (b) 0.05 mm
    (c) 0.16 mm (d) 0.52 mm

18. The illumination level required for precision work is about
    (a) 500–1000 lux (b) 250 lux
    (c) 100 lux (d) 50 lux

19. Inside the earth or pit, the earthing electrode should be placed
    (a) vertical (b) horizontal
    (c) inclined at 45° (d) none of these

20. In Kando system of track electrification
    (a) single phase a.c. is converted into d.c.
    (b) single phase a.c. is converted into 3-phase a.c.
    (c) 3 phase a.c. is converted into d.c.
    (d) 3 phase a.c. is converted into single phase a.c.

21. The amount of energy returned to the line during regeneration depends on
    (a) the initial and final speeds during regenerative braking
    (b) efficiency of the system
    (c) the train resistance and gradient of track also in case the train is moving down the gradient
    (d) all of the above

22. Applied voltage across the motor terminals during starting is not reduced in case of
(a) star-delta starting
(b) rotor-resistance starting
(c) auto-transformer starting
(d) stator resistance starting

23. The power factor at which the direct arc furnace operates is
(a) low lagging (b) low leading
(c) unity (d) high leading

24. In a domestic baking oven, the temperature is controlled by
(a) voltage
(b) series-parallel operation
(c) thermostat
(d) star-delta connections

25. The basic elements of an electric drive are
(a) electric motor and the transmission system
(b) electric motor, the transmission and control system
(c) the transmission and control system
(d) electric motor and conversion equipment

26. The load power factor using welding transformer depends on
(a) arc length
(b) material to be welded
(c) type of electrode to be used
(d) all of the above

27. Luminous flux is
(a) the rate of energy radiation in the form of light waves
(b) the part of light energy, radiated by sun that is received on earth
(c) measured in lux
(d) none of the above

28. Glare is caused due to
(a) excessive luminance
(b) excessive lighting contrast in the field of vision
(c) either (a) and (b)
(d) none of the above

29. The motor used in motor-generator set is
(a) d.c. series motor
(b) plain-squirrel cage induction motor
(c) 3-phase synchronous motor
(d) pole-changing induction motor

30. In neon signs argon gas is used to give
(a) red colour (b) blue colour
(c) pink colour (d) green colour

31. For power factor correction of welding transformer, a capacitor is usually connected on
(a) pimary side
(b) secondary side
(c) parallel to arcing electrodes
(d) parallel to mains

32. The load taken by a welding transformer is
(a) purely inductive (b) non-inductive
(c) highly inductive (d) none of these

33. Which of the following is not resistance welding?
(a) Projection welding (b) MIG welding
(c) Seam welding (d) Flash-butt welding

34. A perfect diffuser surface is one that
(a) transmits all the incident light
(b) absorbs all the incident light
(c) diffuses all the incident light
(d) all of the above

35. In series motor the method used for controlling the flux per pole is/are
(a) divertor field control
(b) series-parallel control
(c) tapped field control
(d) all of the above

36. Arc blow is a welding defect which is encountered in
(a) arc welding using d.c. current
(b) arc welding using a.c. current
(c) gas welding
(d) thermit welding

37. In Argon arc welding the purpose of using Argon is
(a) to prevent oxidation of metal by coming in contact with oxygen of air
(b) to create inert atmosphere around the job to be welded
(c) to obviate the necessity for using flux
(d) all of these

38. Method of speed control used on 25 kV, 50 Hz single-phase traction is
(a) Tap changing control of transformer
(b) Reduced current method
(c) Series parallel operation of motors
(d) Any of these

39. The speed can be controlled by injecting emf in the rotor circuit in case of
(a) squirrel-cage induction motor
(b) wound rotor induction motor
(c) synchronous motor
(d) Schrage motor

40. In case of travelling cranes, the motor preferred for boom hoist is
(a) slip ring induction motor
(b) squirrel cage induction motor
(c) synchronous motor
(d) single phase motor

41. In start-delta starting
(a) applied voltage across motor terminals is reduced
(b) starting current is reduced
(c) operation speed is reduced
(d) both (a) and (b)

42. The transformer used for a.c. welding sets is
(a) Booster type
(b) Step-up transformer
(c) Step-down transformer
(d) None of these

43. As the thickness of the part to be welded increases, which of the following parameter (s) for a.c. welding should also increase?
(a) Voltage (b) Current
(c) Frequency (d) All of these

44. Steel rails are welded by
(a) Resistance welding (b) Thermit welding
(c) Argon arc welding (d) Gas welding

45. In ultrasonic welding, the frequency range is generally
(a) 100 - 4000 Hz
(b) 4000 - 20,000 Hz
(c) 20,000 - 80,000 Hz
(d) 80,000 - 200,000 Hz

46. The welding load
(a) is always intermittent load
(b) is always continuous and constant
(c) is always continuous but varying
(d) may be any one of the above

47. A rectifier for welding has voltage/current characteristics as
(a) drooping (b) rising
(c) static (d) variable

48. In electric discharge lamps, light is produced by
(a) magnetic effect of current
(b) heating effect of current
(c) cathode ray emission
(d) ionisation in a gas or vapour

49. Low frequency supply is necessary for direct core type induction furnaces because
(a) magnetic coupling between the primary and secondary circuit is poor
(b) with normal frequency supply the electro-magnetic forces cause severe stirring action in the molten metal
(c) both (a) and (b)
(d) none of the (a) and (b)

50. In induction heating, the depth upto which the current will penetrate is proportional to?
(a) frequency (b) $(\text{frequency})^2$
(c) 1/(frequency) (d) $1/\sqrt{\text{frequency}}$

51. For regenerative braking, the regenerated power should have
(a) the same frequency as that of the main supply
(b) frequency 1/3 that of the main supply
(c) frequency 1/2 of that of the main supply
(d) any frequency

52. Two shunt motors having identical characteristics are used to drive a car with unequal wheel diameters. The two motors share load equally if they are connected in
(a) series
(b) parallel
(c) the loading will always be unequal
(d) none of these

53. High frequency power supply for coreless induction furnaces is obtained by converting normal supply frequency into higher value by means of
(a) motor-generator set with salient pole-alternator
(b) motor-generator set with inductor alternator
(c) valve oscillator
(d) any of the above

54. For rheostatic braking of two series motors connected in parallel,
(a) equaliser connection is better
(b) cross-connection is better
(c) both are equally good
(d) none of these

55. The rate of heat flow through a 40 mm thick wall of material having thermal conductivity of 50 W/m/°C for a temperature difference of 16°C will be
(a) 2,000 W/m^2
(b) 20,000 W/m^2
(c) 20,000 W/m^2/hour
(d) 112.5 × 10^{-3} W/m^2

56. The motors used alongwith flywheels for fluctuating loads are
(a) dc shunt motors
(b) dc cumulative compound motors and 3 phase induction motors
(c) synchronous motors
(d) all of the above

57. A pony motor is used for starting a
(a) slip-ring induction motor
(b) squirrel cage induction motor
(c) synchronous motor
(d) Schrage motor

58. In case of bow and pantograph current collectors,
(a) the bow collector is used for large current at higher speeds
(b) the pantograph collector is used for large currents at higher speeds
(c) the bow collector is used for large currents at lower speeds
(d) the pantograph collector is used for large currents at lower speeds

59. Induction furnaces are used for
(a) heat treatment of castings
(b) heating of insulators
(c) melting of aluminium
(d) all of the above

60. A train having inertial weight of 220 tonnes uses regenerative braking when the speed is changed from 60 kmph to 20 kmph, the electric energy returned to supply is (assume 100% efficiency)
(a) 7.546 kWh (b) 8.32 kWh
(c) 5.6595 kWh (c) None of these

61. Which of the following motors has the lowest ratio of starting torque to full load torque?
(a) DC series motor
(b) Wound rotor induction motor
(c) DC cumulative compound motor
(d) Squirrel cage induction motor

62. In dielectric heating current flows through
(a) air
(b) dielectric
(c) metallic conductor
(d) ionic discharge between dielectric medium and metallic conductor

63. In induction heating, which of the following is of high value?
(a) Frequency (b) Current
(c) Voltage (d) Power factor

64. For supply of 25 kV, 50 Hz single-phase, suitable motor for electric traction is
(a) a.c. single-phase split phase motor
(b) a.c. single-phase universal motor
(c) d.c. shunt motor
(d) d.c. series motor

65. In induction heating, the depth up to which current will penetrate is proportional to
(a) 1/(frequency)½ (b) 1/frequency
(c) frequency (d) (frequency)^2

66. The advantage of a synchronous motor in addition to its constant speed is
(a) high power factor
(b) better efficiency
(c) lower cost
(d) all of these

67. Blinking of a fluorescent tube may be on account of
(a) low circuit voltage
(b) loose contact
(c) defective starter
(d) any of the above

68. The luminous flux reaching the working plane least depends on
(a) proportion of the room
(b) the lumen output of the lamps
(c) colour of the working plane surface
(d) reflectance of internal surfaces

69. In upset butt welding
(a) the faces of the metal pieces to be joined are prepared for even contact
(b) heating is obtained by the contact resistance of metal pieces to be welded
(c) the voltage required is 2-8 V and current required ranges from 50 A to several hundred amperes depending upon material and the area to be welded at a time
(d) all of the above

70. The supply frequency usually employed for high frequency eddy current heating is
(a) 10 MHz
(b) 10 kHz to 400 kHz
(c) 5 kHz
(d) 1 kHz

71. The preparation of an object for electroplating involves the
(a) removal of oil, grease or other organic material
(b) removal of dust, smoke, oxides, or other inorganic coatings adhering to the metal
(c) mechanical preparation of the metal surface by polishing, buffing etc.
(d) any or all of the above operations

72. Radio interference from a fluorescent tube can be reduced by
(a) eliminating choke
(b) connecting a small capacitor across starter terminals
(c) putting two tubes in parallel
(d) any of the above

73. In resistance welding, the magnitude of current is controlled
(a) by varying the primary voltage of the welding transformer using an auto transformer between supply and welding transformer
(b) by changing the primary turns of the welding transformer
(c) by varying the magnitude and waveform of the primary as well as secondary current by using thyratron or ignitron
(d) any of the above

74. Radiant heating is used for
(a) melting of ferrous metals
(b) annealing of metals
(c) drying of paints and varnishes
(d) any of the above

75. Which of the following is not used as earth continuity conductor?
(a) water pipes
(b) gas pipes
(c) structural steel members
(d) any of these

76. The specific energy consumption for main line services is around
(a) 20-30 watt hours per tonne-km
(b) 30-45 watt hours per tonne-km
(c) 50-75 watt hours per tonne-km
(d) 100-150 watt hours per tonne-km

77. A body reflecting entire radiations incidenting on it is called the
(a) white body (b) gray body
(c) black body (d) transparent body

78. Which of the following motors has least range of speed control?
(a) DC shunt motor
(b) Wound rotor induction motor
(c) Schrage motor
(d) Synchronous motor

79. For power factor correction in a welding circuit, a capacitor is usually connected
(a) across the mains
(b) across secondary side of welding transformer
(c) across primary side of welding transformer
(d) across arcing electrodes

80. In a mercury vapour lamp light, red objects appear black. This is on account of
(a) colour mixing
(b) high wavelengths of red colour
(c) absence of red light from lamp radiations
(d) absorption of red light by the lamp

81. The shunt motor with armature shunted through a resistance as compared to with armature not shunted, has no load speed
(a) higher (b) lower
(c) equal (d) none of these

82. Which of the following is a constant speed motor?
(a) DC series motor
(b) Squirrel cage induction motor
(c) Synchronous motor
(d) Universal motor

83. The dielectric loss in a dielectric is proportional to
(a) voltage impressed on the dielectric
(b) the square of the voltage impressed on the dielectric
(c) the square root of the voltage impressed on the dielectric
(d) none of the above

84. In case of 3-phase slip ring induction motor, as the rotor resistance is increased, the starting torque
(a) increases
(b) decreases
(c) increases upto certain value of resistance and remains constant
(d) increases upto certain value of resistance and then decreases

85. Ward-Leonard controlled d.c. drives are generally used for
(a) light duty excavators
(b) medium duty excavators
(c) heavy duty excavators
(d) all of these

86. Which electromagnet is preferred for noiseless operation?
(a) DC operated (b) AC operated
(c) Any of these (d) None of these

87. A 3-phase delta connected squirrel cage induction motor when started with D.O.L. stater has a starting torque of 600 NM. Its starting torque when star-delta is used, is
(a) 600 NM (b) 200 NM
(c) 300 NM (d) none of these

88. The advantage(s) of eddy current heating is/are
(a) easy temperature control, little wastage of heat and possibility of heating in vacuum or other special atmosphere
(b) heat can be made to penetrate into metal surface to any desired depth
(c) the area of surface over which heat is produced can be accurately controlled
(d) all of the above

89. The motor suitable for a reciprocating pump required to start under load is
(a) plain squirrel cage induction motor
(b) double-squirrel cage induction motor
(c) synchronous motor
(d) dc shunt motor

90. For automatic drives the preference is for
(a) synchronous motors
(b) Ward-Leonard controlled dc shunt motors
(c) plain squirrel cage induction motors
(d) any of the above

91. A reluctance motor
(a) is a self-starting synchronous motor
(b) operates as an induction motor when overloaded
(c) has power factor between 0.3 and 0.4 and operation efficiency of the order of 70%
(d) all of the above

92. Which of the following motors has series characteristics?
(a) Capacitor start induction motor
(b) Repulsion motor
(c) Shaded-pole motor
(d) Reluctance motor

93. The squirrel cage induction motor cannot be started by using
(a) resistance in rotor circuit
(b) resistance in stator circuit
(c) both of these
(d) none of these

94. An ideal traction system should have
(a) high starting tractive effort and self contained and compact locomotive or train unit
(b) equipment capable of withstanding large temporary overloads, of high efficiency and low initiai as well as maintenance cost
(c) easy speed control
(d) all of the above

95. Heavy-duty steel-works cranes having wide load variations are equipped with
(a) dc series motors
(b) plain squirrel cage induction motors
(c) wound-rotor induction motors
(d) synchronous motors

96. During starting, the energy consumed by the armature of a d.c. series motor
(a) equals the K.E. stored by the rotor and increases with increase in armature resistance
(b) equals the K.E. stored by the rotor and decreases with increase in armature resistance
(c) equals the K.E. stored by the rotor and is independent of armature resistance
(d) none of these

97. During starting, the energy consumed by the armature of a d.c. shunt motor
(a) equals the K.E. stored by the rotor and increases with increase in armature resistance
(b) equals the K.E. stored by the rotor and decreases with increase in armature resistance
(c) equals the K.E. stored by the rotor and is independent of armature resistance
(d) none of these

98. A piece of steel is to be heated to a predetermined temperature, in which of the following furnace it will attain the desired temperature in the shortest possible time?
(a) Oil fired furnace with heat exchanger
(b) Electric resistance furnace
(c) Induction heating furnace
(d) Electric arc furnace

99. When a bogie negotiates a curve, reduction in adhesion occurs resulting in sliding. This sliding is acute when
(a) degree of curvature is more
(b) wheel base of axles is more
(c) none of the above
(d) both (a) and (b)

100. In Kando system
(a) single-phase supply is converted into three-phase system
(b) single-phase a.c. is converted into d.c.
(c) three-phase a.c. is converted into d.c.
(d) d.c. supply is to run d.c. motors

101. Nichrome wires can be safely used for heating upto
(a) 2000°C (b) 1600°C
(c) 1450°C (d) 1050°C

102. The electric resistance welding has the advantage(s) of
(a) reduced distortion, higher production rates, suitability for large quantity production and comparatively lesser skill need
(b) heat is localized where required
(c) no filler material is required
(d) all of the above

103. Highest power factor can be expected in which method of heating?
(a) Electric arc heating
(b) Dielectric heating
(c) Induction heating
(d) Resistance heating

ANSWERS

1	**2**	**3**	**4**	**5**	**6**	**7**	**8**	**9**	**10**
(a)	(b)	(a)	(d)	(a)	(c)	(d)	(b)	(c)	(a)
11	**12**	**13**	**14**	**15**	**16**	**17**	**18**	**19**	**20**
(b)	(b)	(c)	(c)	(d)	(a)	(a)	(a)	(a)	(b)
21	**22**	**23**	**24**	**25**	**26**	**27**	**28**	**29**	**30**
(b)	(b)	(a)	(c)	(b)	(b)	(a)	(b)	(c)	(a)
31	**32**	**33**	**34**	**35**	**36**	**37**	**38**	**39**	**40**
(a)	(c)	(b)	(c)	(d)	(b)	(d)	(a)	(d)	(a)
41	**42**	**43**	**44**	**45**	**46**	**47**	**48**	**49**	**50**
(d)	(c)	(b)	(b)	(b)	(a)	(a)	(d)	(c)	(d)
51	**52**	**53**	**54**	**55**	**56**	**57**	**58**	**59**	**60**
(a)	(a)	(d)	(b)	(b)	(b)	(c)	(d)	(a)	(a)
61	**62**	**63**	**64**	**65**	**66**	**67**	**68**	**69**	**70**
(d)	(b)	(a)	(d)	(a)	(a)	(d)	(c)	(d)	(b)
71	**72**	**73**	**74**	**75**	**76**	**77**	**78**	**79**	**80**
(d)	(b)	(d)	(c)	(d)	(a)	(a)	(d)	(c)	(c)
81	**82**	**83**	**84**	**85**	**86**	**87**	**88**	**89**	**90**
(b)	(c)	(b)	(d)	(c)	(a)	(b)	(d)	(b)	(b)
91	**92**	**93**	**94**	**95**	**96**	**97**	**98**	**99**	**100**
(d)	(b)	(a)	(d)	(a)	(a)	(c)	(c)	(d)	(a)
101	**102**	**103**							
(b)	(d)	(d)							

9. ENGINEERING MATERIALS

Exterinsic Semiconductors

In order to increase the conductivity of a semiconductor, an impurity is added to it and this process is called *doping*. The material is known as *extrinsic semiconductor*.

An acceptor material accepts electrons from the valence band of silicon, since it has only three valence electrons. Example of donor impurity are Boron, Indium, Gallium, and Aluminium.

At room temperature, the electrons from the valence band of silicon fill the acceptor space of the boron.

Since the probability of the valence-electrons having sufficient energy at room temperature to bridge the small gap is very high, an extremely large number of holes are present. When electric field is applied across this material, the hole current is very high, and the material becomes a good conductor. This is called *P-type* semiconductor and conduction is primarily due to the movement of holes.

When a donor impurity (with five valence electrons) is added to silicon, it donates electrons to the conductor band of silicon. Examples of donors are Arsenic, Phosphorous, Antimony and Bismuth.

When an electric field is applied, current flows which is primarily due to electrons. This is called *N-type* semiconductor.

The forbidden energy gaps of germanium and silicon are 0.72 eV and 1.12 eV respectively. Therefore silicon devices may be operated at higher temperatures than germanium as silicon requires higher thermal energy for breaking of valence bands.

Semiconductors: Semiconductor is a material whose conductivity lies between conductors and insulators. Silicon and Germanium are most important semiconductors and both have four valence electrons, *i.e.*, electrons in the outer most shell of the atom.

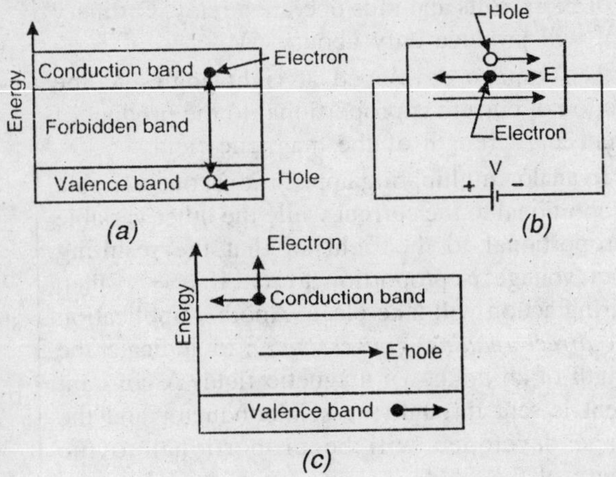

Fig. 1

Valence electrons are bound in an energy band in which valence band positions are filled or unoccupied. This filled band is separated from a normally unoccupied higher energy band by a forbidden energy gap ΔE.

At room temperature, very few electrons exist in the conduction band. Since the current is proportional to the number of electrons in motion, the current is small, and hence the material has a higher resistance.

An occasional electron has enough energy to escape from the valence band and move to the conduction band as shown by the dots in Fig. 1.

When an energy band is completely filled, its electrons do not contribute to electrical conductivity as there are no open energy level to which they can move after absorbing energy from an electric field. Therefore, conductivity of a semiconductor at absolute zero temperature is zero.

Hall Effect

It deals with the effect produced by a magnetic field upon an electron or other current carrier. The magnetic field causes these current carriers to move exerting a force at right angles to both the field and the direction of motion of the particles. If the material is a semiconductor placed in magnetic field and current is passed, the carriers move to one side of the crystal, producing a difference of potential of one or more volts and thus operate a relay. Ordinary metal will produce only about $1\mu V$.

The voltage developed at right angles to the direction of current is proportional to the product of current and strength of the magnetic field.

In analog multiplying applications, one variable is proportional to the current while the other variable is proportional to the field so that the resulting output voltage is proportion to xy. If $p = y$, then squaring action will take place. Another application is of *direct reading gauses meter* to indicate the strength of an unknown magnetic field. A constant current is sent through the semiconductor and the voltage developed will be proportional to the strength of the field.

Hall Coefficient

R_H of a semiconductor material is defined as the ratio of electric field strength produced per unit current density to the transverse magnetic field strength. It is given by

$$R_H = \frac{3\pi\,(n_h\,u_h^2 - n_e\,u_e^2)}{(8\,n_h\,u_h + n_e\,u_e)^2}$$

Where n_e, n_h are electron and hole density, and u_e, u_h are electron and hole mobilities.

The Diode Characteristics

The diode current i_D and diode voltage V_D related by

$$i_D = I_0\,(e^{qV_D/KT} - 1)$$

where q = electron charge,

K = Boltzmann constant; and

T = absolute temperature °K

At room temperature (T = 300°K),

$$\frac{KT}{q} = V_T = 25\ mV$$

If V_D is negative and large (in case of reverse biasing), then

$$i_D \cong I_0$$

If V_D is positive,

$$i_D = I_0\,e^{V_D/V_T}$$

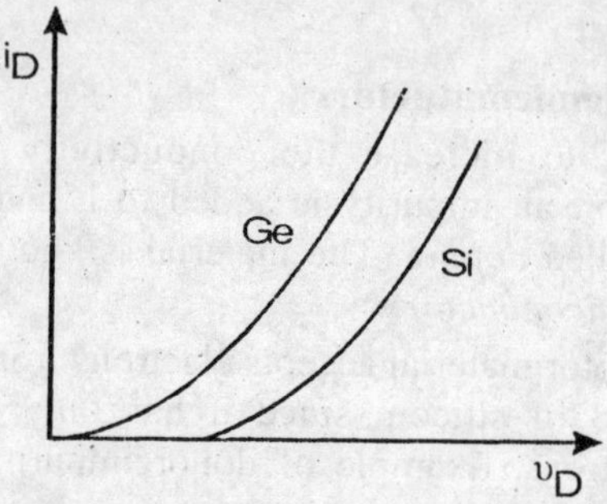

Fig. 2

The graphical representation of this equation is shown in Fig. 2.

The dynamic resistance of the diode is given by

$$\frac{1}{r_D} = \frac{di_D}{dv_D} = I_0\,\frac{1}{V_T}\,e^{V_D/V_T}$$

$$\cong \frac{i_D}{V_T}\ \text{(because } v_D/V_T >> 1)$$

$$r_D = \frac{V_T}{i_D} = \frac{25\ mV}{i_D}\ \text{(at 25° C)}$$

Transistors

A transistor essentially consists of two *PN*-junctions connected back to back. Basically, it is a current sensitive device *i.e.*, it shifts current from a low impedance circuit to an high impedance circuit thus leading to power amplification. That is why the name transfer-resistor or transistor.

Current Flow Mechanism

The junction transistor consists two *PN*-junctions obtained by formation of three regions of *P*, *N* and *P* or *N*, *P* and *N*. These regions are called emitter *E*, base *B*, and collector *C*. Thus, there are two types of transistors *PNP*, *NPN* shows the biasing arrangement of a *PNP* transistor.

Avalanche Breakdown

When a *PN*-junction is reverse biased, the

minority carriers flowing through the junction acquire a kinetic energy which increases as the reverse voltage increases. At sufficiently high reverse voltage, the kinetic energy of carriers becomes so large that they knock out electrons from the covalent bonds of the semiconductor material. As a result of collisions, the liberated electrons in turn liberate more electrons and the current becomes very large leading to the breakdown of the crystal structure itself. This phenomenon is called *Avalanche breakdown*. Then the current is not controlled by the junction voltage but rather by the external circuits.

Zener Breakdown

Under a very high reverse voltage, the depletion region expands and the potential barrier increases leading to a very high electric field across the junction. This electric field will break some of the covalent bonds of the semi-conductor atoms leading to a large number of free minority carriers. As a result, the reverse current increases tremendously.

In actual practice, avalanche breakdown is more pronounced than the zener *breakdown voltage*. Therefore, this phenomenon can be utilised to provide constant reference voltage against variation of current within a considerable range. A *PN*-junction made to perform this function is called *zener diode*.

The point on the characteristics where break down occurs, is called the knee-point and is more sharp in case of silicon diode.

PN-junction

When a *PN*-junction is formed, holes from *P*-type material tend do diffuse towards *N* types material due to density gradient *i.e.*, concentration of holes is higher on *P*-side than on *N*-side. Similarly, electrons move from *N*-side to *P*-side. Due to this phenomena, most of holes and electrons near the junction get neutralised and a small region on both side of the junction gets devoid of mobile carriers with the result that impurity ions in this region become electrically unneutralised. This region, called *depletion region* or *layer*, now acts like battery or potential barrier V_0 which opposes the further diffusion of majority carriers.

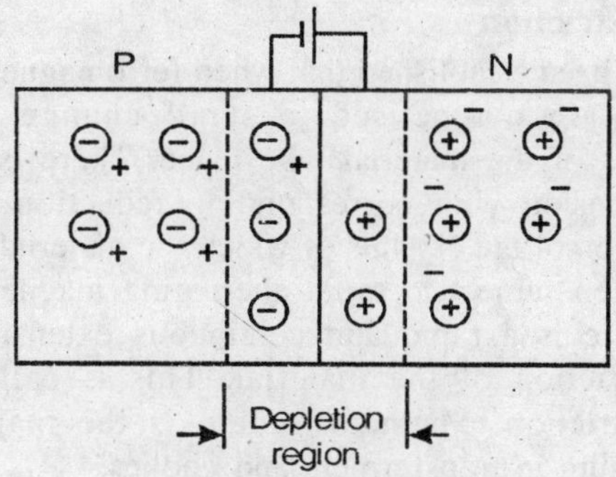

Fig. 3

When an external voltage V_p is applied across the junction with *P*-side positive and *N*-side negative so as to reduce the potential barrier V_0, the junction is said to be *forward biased* and the majority carrier of each side can go over to other side more easily leading to external current as shown in Fig. 3

When an external voltage V_R is connected in the reverse way, the potential barrier increases and the majority carriers find it difficult to cross to the other side. Only a very small reverse current I_0 flows in this *reverse biased PN*-junction. This current is not affected by potential barrier and depends on temperature, material and construction of the junction. Therefore *PN*-junction allows large current only in forward bias direction and only small reverse current I_o in the reverse bias direction.

Electrical Behaviour of Polymers

Polymers are extensively used for electrical insulation. The polymers may be applied on unpolymerised or partially polarized liquid to form a uniform coating which can be polymerised. The covalent bonds of all polymers prevent electrical conduction. The dielectrics behaviour of polymer is due to polarizable structure of polymers. *PVC* possesses a high dielectric constant at low frequencies because it has high molecular polarization in an unsymmetric polymer. At high frequency, the resulting larger dipole cannot maintain alignment with the alternating field. Polytetra flouroethylene (*PTFE*) is a symmetrical mer and its polarisation is only electronic and atomic.

Magnetostriction

It has been established that when ferromagnetic materials are magnetised, a small change of dimensions of the material take place. There is a small extension with corresponding reduction of cross-section of the crystals of which the material is made. When subject to rapid alternating magnetic fields, there is a rapid and continuous extension and contraction of the material. This is called magnetostriction. Magnetostriction is the major cause of hum in transformers and chokes.

Electronic Components

Major types are as follows:

(a) Resistors: In carbon resistors, thin layer of carbon is deposited on the surface of a ceramic rod. The resistance value required determines the thickness of the carbon film. The exact value is obtained by cutting a groove in the form of a spiral in the carbon film.

A solid type carbon resistor consists of solid rod of special material composed of carbon and binding agent. Carbon pile resistors are made up of a number of carbon plates maintained under pressure. Its resistance value can be changed by changing the pressure on the carbon discs.

In wire-wound resistor, ceramic tubes having cap and lead assemblies are used as insulated bobbins. During winding, the machine allows a regular pitch and uniform tension to be applied to the wire of desirable resistance such as copper, constantan, nichrome and aluminium. The end connections to terminals are accomplished by welding or soldering. The coating is applied by dipping the resistor after the curing is done.

(b) Transformers: It is a static device to convert voltage from higher to low or vice-versa. It consists of mainly core; bobbin and winding. Bobbin is made of any plastic material to hold the core. Core is made of grain- oriented silicon steel or hot-rolled grain oriented silicon steel. It gives the easy path to the magnetic field. It has two windings—one is called primary winding and the other is called secondary winding, having different number of turns in both the windings. These windings are of insulated, hot- rolled annealed enamel copper. The winding of hot- rolled annealed copper is of different gauges depending upon the requirement. Over the winding, insulating glazed paper is wrapped. The terminals are soldered at the bobbin on both sides *i.e.*, primary and secondary.

(c) Rectifiers: Rectifiers convert ac into dc. It is mainly of two types - (i) Copper oxide rectifier, and (2) Selenium rectifier. Copper oxide rectifier is a plate of 99.98% pure copper on which a film of cuprous oxide is produced by special purpose. One side of plate is cleaned with cuprous oxide and an electrode is soldered directly to copper. The second electrode is soldered to cuprous oxide film. When positive potential is applied to the oxide layer and negative to the copper , and it corresponds to forward biasing of a P-N Junction. These rectifiers hence have low permissible current density. Selenium rectifiers use more than 99.9% pure selenium. Crystalline selenium which has a melting point of 220°C is used for making rectifiers. It is constructed by using Nickel-plated steel plate. Selenium under pressure at 130°C is raised to 180°C to 215°C and put on the nickel plate making a layer of 1 mm on it. Crystalline selenium will change to grey crystallic selenium. Over this electrode of tin, an alloy is sprayed. This makes the active disc of the rectifiers and thus makes the selenium rectifier.

(d) Chokes: This is a device used to give blast of voltage. It consists of mainly bobbin, stamping and winding. Bobbin is made up of insulating material such as plastic to hold the stampings which are made up of mild steel of thin lamination which reduce the eddy current loss. Winding is done on these stampings of definite number of turns and a particular gauge. The input and output terminals are fixed on the insulating materials such as bakelite. Whole assembly is insulated by insulating paper. This assembly is put in a box of metallic sheet.

Composite Materials

It is often possible to produce a superior material by combining two or more materials, with properties unattainable in each of them separately. The material so produced is termed as a composite material. The combination is made up of material with complementary properties. For example, concrete is strong in compression and steel is strong in tension. Therefore, a situation may require food strength both in tension and compression in structure. The concrete is reinforced with steel to combine the two strengths in one material-reinforced cement concrete. Other examples are glass fibre, reinforced plastics and carbon fibre, reinforced plastic and expanded polymers.

EXERCISE

1. In Hall's Effect, the output voltage produced across the crystal is due to
   (a) induced voltage by the applied magnetic field
   (b) drop across the crystal due to the current passed through it
   (c) movement of charge carriers towards one end
   (d) all of these
2. In the absence of external magnetic field
   (a) the net magnetization is zero
   (b) the domains are aligned in one direction
   (c) the domains are not magnetized
   (d) none of the above
3. The impurity atoms in semiconductors
   (a) reduce the energy gap
   (b) increase the kinetic energy of valence electrons
   (c) inject more charge carriers
   (d) all of these
4. At very high frequency (of the order of 10 Hz) the permittivity of a dielectric is due to __________ polarisation.
   (a) magnetic (b) ionic
   (c) electronic (d) none of these
5. The conductivity of an extrinsic semiconductor ________ with the increase in temperature.
   (a) decreases
   (b) increases
   (c) remains unaffected
   (d) none of these
6. In a depletion region of a *PN* junction,
   (a) *P*-side is positively charged and *N*-side is negatively charged
   (b) *N*-side is positively charged and *P*-side is negatively charged
   (c) there is hole concentration on *P*-side and electron concentration *N*-side
   (d) none of these
7. ______ has the lowest temperature coefficient of resistance.
   (a) Nichrome (b) Constantan
   (c) Molybdenum (d) Kanthal
8. The velocity of an electron at the Fermi level of 5.0 eV is
   (a) 1.33×10^5 m/sec (b) 3×10^3 m/sec
   (c) 1.33×10^6 m/sec (d) None of these
9. In the Modern Periodic Table, elements are arranged in order of increasing
   (a) atomic weight (b) atomic number
   (c) molecular weight (d) none of these
10. Austenite is
    (a) FCC iron with nearly 2% (max) carbon in solid solution
    (b) BCC iron with nearly 0.025% (max) carbon in solid solution
    (c) BCC iron with nearly 1% carbon in solid solution
    (d) None of these
11. In the depletion region of a *PN* junction, there are
    (a) no charge (b) no mobile charges
    (c) no currents (d) all of these
12. The most important factor which can influence the operation of a *PN* junction is
    (a) impurity atom concentration
    (b) temperature
    (c) mobility of charge carriers
    (d) all of these
13. The Half's Coefficient for a particular material was found to be zero. The material is
    (a) metal
    (b) intrinsic semi-conductor
    (c) insulator
    (d) any of these

14. Resistivity of copper at absolute zero is
(a) 1.76×10^{-8} Ω-m (b) 1.64×10^{-8} Ω-m
(c) negligibly small (d) zero

15. Thermosetting polymers are
(a) injection mouided (b) cast moulded
(c) exruded (d) none of these

16. The conductivity of a metal is determined by
(a) the number of valence electrons per atom
(b) the electronic concentration and the mobility of the free electrons
(c) both (a) and (b)
(d) none of these

17. The materials having permanent electric moment are known as
(a) electrets (b) Dielectrics
(c) semiconductors (d) none of the above

18. Resistivity of electrical conductors is most affected by
(a) temperature (b) pressure
(c) composition (d) none of these

19. An element used in semiconductors whose atoms have three valence electrons is
(a) germanium (b) a donor
(c) an acceptor (d) silicon

20. It is possible to obtain *P*-type or *N*-type semiconductor from a single compound by adding Ge. That compound is
(a) InSb (b) GaP
(c) GaAs (d) None of these

21. High-frequency transformers cores are generally made from
(a) Ferrites (b) Mu-metal
(c) Mone-metal (d) None of these

22. The ______ polarization vanishes at Curie temperature of the material.
(a) dipolar (b) spontaneous
(c) ionic (d) polar

23. Hard magnetic materials have
(a) high retentivity
(b) high coercivity
(c) high energy loss per cycle of magnetization
(d) all of the above

24. Which of the following is/are used in electrical systems?
(a) Pyrex
(b) Silican glass
(c) Fibre glass insulation
(d) All of the above

25. The Miller Indices are the same for
(a) perpendicular planes
(b) crystal planes
(c) parallel planes
(d) none of these

26. The capacity of a single orbital is
(a) 2 (b) 6
(c) 10 (d) 18

27. Polar dielectrics are normally employed for
(a) dc and power frequencies
(b) microwaves
(c) high frequencies
(d) none of the above

28. The conductivity of ferrites is
(a) less than that of ferromagnetic materials
(b) equal to that of ferromagnetic materials
(c) greater than that of ferromagnetic materials
(d) very high than that of ferromagnetic materials

29. The magnetic materials, in which the permanent magnet moment (due to electron spin) are already aligned because of bonding forces, are called the ______ materials.
(a) ferro-magnetic (b) diamagnetic
(c) para-magnetic (d) ferri-magnetic

30. Which of the following metals have maximum magnetic permeability?
(a) Pure iron
(b) 4% silicon steel
(c) Grain-oriented silicon tell
(d) None of these

31. Super-conductivity is due to
(a) all electrons having Fermi energy at 0°K.
(b) all electrons interacting in the super-conducting state
(c) crystal structure having no atomic vibration at 0°K
(d) crystal structure having infinite atomic vibrations at 0°K

32. For silicon the intrinsic concentration is approximately 10^{10} carries/cm³ respectively. If an impurity concentration of 10^{14} donor atoms/ cm², the electron concentration will be

(a) 10^6 (b) 10^{10}

(c) 10^{16} (d) 10^{20}

33. In ferro-magnetic materials, the spin moments associated with two sets of atoms are aligned

(a) in a random fashion

(b) antiparallel to each other

(c) parallel to each other

(d) antiparallel but equal in magnitude

34. The mass of an electron can be found if we know

(a) Charge (b) $\frac{e}{m}$

(c) $\frac{e}{m}$ and charge (d) $e \times m$

35. The unit of magnetisation vector $\overline{M}$ is

(a) ampere-m² (b) ampere/m²

(c) ampere/m (d) ampere/-m³

36. In ferromagnetic materials, the spin moments associated with two sets of atoms are aligned

(a) antiparallel to each other

(b) parallel to each other

(c) random to each other

(d) antiparallel but of unequal magnitude

37. A pure semiconductor, under ordinary conditions, acts as a/an

(a) insulator

(b) conductor

(c) super conductor

(d) ferro-electric material

38. The drift velocity of an electron under the action of applied electric field is of the order of

(a) 10^{-14} (b) 10^{-7}

(c) 10^7 (d) None of these

39. Which one of following does not constitute a point defect in a crystal

(a) self interstitial (b) slip lines

(c) vacancies (d) none of these

40. Insulating liquids are generally employed for potential stresses of upto

(a) 500 V/mm (b) 5 kV/mm

(c) 50 kV/mm (d) 500 kVmm

41. Conductivity is measured in

(a) Ω-m (b) ℧-m

(c) ℧/m (d) Ω/m

42. Which of the following ceramic materials are used as electric ceramics?

(a) Chromite (b) Ba IO_3

(c) Alamandite (d) None of these

43. A dielectric of relative permittivity ε_r is introduced in an air capacitor of capacitance C_0 its capacitance will become.

(a) $\frac{C_0}{\varepsilon_r}$ (b) $\varepsilon_r C_0$

(c) $\frac{\varepsilon_r}{C_0}$ (d) $(1 + \varepsilon_r) C_0$

44. Electrons will collide with lattice atoms, if the atoms are

(a) very large

(b) displaced from their regular position

(c) close together

(d) none of these

45. Silicon devices are preferred at high temperature operations as compared to germanium because

(a) silicon is more thermally stable

(b) silicon can dissipate more power

(c) reverse saturation current is less in case of silicon

(d) all of these

46. Cadmium is added to copper primarily to

(a) reduce its cost

(b) improve its mechanical strength

(c) improve electrical conductivity

(d) all of the above

47. Electrical contact resistance is better between

(a) metal and insulator

(b) metal and carbon

(c) metal and metal

(d) carbon and carbon

48. In a differential synchro-transmitter the stator and rotor windings are connected in
(a) star (b) delta
(c) series (d) parallel

49. What is the type of bonding in SO_2?
(a) Ionic (b) Covalent
(c) Vander waals (d) None of these

50. When a *PN* junction is reverse-biased, then
(a) holes and electrons are attracted towards the junction
(b) majority carriers are not affected
(c) holes and electrons move away from the junction
(d) none of these

51. The electron and hole concentration in an *N*-type semiconductor is $10^{16}/cm^2$ and $10^{16}/cm^2$. If the mobilities of electrons and holes are 400 and 600 cm^2/C-sec respectively, the conductivity of the material approximately is
(a) $10^{32} \times e$ (b) $10^{19} \times e$
(c) $4 \times 10^{18} \times e$ (d) $6 \times 10^{8} \times e$

52. Which of the following statements is not true for a hole?
(a) Holes may constitute an electric current.
(b) Holes can be considered as a net positive charge.
(c) Holes can exist in any material including conductors.
(d) Holes can exist in certain semiconductor materials only.

53. Magnetization vector M is expressed in
(a) Tesla (b) A/m
(c) A/m^2 (d) A-m

54. Ferro-electric materials are characterized by
(a) very high degree of polarization
(b) a sharp dependence of polarization on temperature
(c) non-linear dependence of the charge on the applied voltage
(d) all of these

55. The potential barrier existing across a PN junction
(a) facilitates recombination of electrons and holes
(b) prevents flow of minority carriers
(c) prevents total recombination of holes and electrons
(d) prevents neutralisation of acceptor and donor ions

56. The mobility of an electron in a metal is expressed as
(a) $\frac{em}{t}$ (b) $\frac{et}{m}$
(c) $\frac{mt}{e}$ (d) None of these

57. The conductors have transport phenomenon due to
(a) electric field
(b) magnetic field
(c) electromagnetic field
(d) none of the above

58. Ferro-electrics are widely used as ______ transducers.
(a) active
(b) passive
(c) electro-mechanical
(d) none of the above

59. Soft magnetic materials have
(a) steeply rising magnetization curve
(b) relatively small and narrow hysteresis loop
(c) small energy loss per cycle of magnetisation
(d) all of the above

60. In ferromagnetic materials, the spin moments of two sets of atoms are aligned
(a) antiparallel to each other
(b) strong magnetic fields
(c) very strong magnetic fields
(d) alternating magnetic fields

61. In electrical machines varnish is mainly used in
(a) impregnation (b) coating
(c) adhesion (d) all of these

62. When a semiconductor is doped with a *P*-type impurity, each impurity atom will
(a) acquire negative charge
(b) acquire positive charge
(c) remain electrically neutral
(d) give away one electron

63. The ferro-electric materials, above the Curie temperature lose ferro-electric properties and become ordinary ______ materials.
(a) insulating (b) dielectric
(c) ferromagnetic (d) super conducting

64. Ferro-electric materials are the dielectrics and analogous to _______ materials.
(a) diamagnetic (b) paramagnetic
(c) ferromagnetic (d) antiferromagnetic

65. The relative permeability of a material is 0.95. The material is
(a) diamagnetic (b) paramagnetic
(c) ferromagnetic (d) none of these

66. Exposure of insulating material to moisture causes increase in
(a) dielectric loss
(b) dielectric constant
(c) dielectric strength
(d) insulation resistance

67. The current passed through a semiconductor placed in a magnetic field is proportional to x. The magnetic field intensity is proportional to y. Then the voltage developed across the semiconductor will be proportional to
(a) $x - y$ (b) x/y
(c) $x + y$ (d) xy

68. Materials, whose specific resistance abruptly falls at very low temperature, are called
(a) conductors (b) super conductors
(c) semiconductors (d) insulators

69. Insulators have a/an
(a) large energy gap
(b) empty conduction band
(c) full valence band
(d) all of the above

70. A set of four quantum numbers describe
(a) energy level only
(b) energy state only
(c) energy level and energy state
(d) all of these

71. With increase in temperature, electrical resistance of a semiconductor
(a) increases (b) decreases
(c) remains constant (d) none of these

72. In transistor, if electrons flow into the emitter
(a) holes flow out of the emitter
(b) electrons flow into the collector
(c) electrons flow out of the collector
(d) holes flow out of the collector

73. The electric breakdown strength of an insulating material depends on
(a) composition of the material
(b) moisture content
(c) thickness of material
(d) temperature
(e) all of the above

74. The donor atoms in an n-type semiconductor at normal temperature
(a) carry a positive charge
(b) carry a negative charge
(c) are neutral
(d) none of the above

75. Presence of even a trace of water in transformer oil_________ its dielectric strength considerably.
(a) increases (b) reduces
(c) does not affect (d) none of these

76. The Hall coefficient of an intrinsic semi-conductor is
(a) positive under all conditions
(b) negative under all conditions
(c) zero under all conditions
(d) zero at 0°K

77. In correctly biased NPN transistor
(a) the base is positive with respect to collector
(b) the base is positive with respect to emitter
(c) the base is positive with respect to both emitter and collector
(d) none of these

78. The major advantage of a point-control diode is that
(a) the ratio of forward current to reverse current is very high
(b) its cut-in voltage is zero
(c) its reverse resistance is infinite
(d) none of these

79. At zero degree Kelvin, germanium acts as
(a) superconductor (b) dielectric
(c) insulator (d) semiconductor

80. The potential-barrier across a *PN* junction corresponds
(a) height of the barrier
(b) width of the barrier
(c) forward bias of the junction
(d) reverse bias of the junction

81. The intensity of magnetization of a ferro-magnetic solid_____ with the increase in temperature.
(a) increases
(b) decreases
(c) remains unaffected
(d) none of these

82. The dielectric strength of ferro-electric materials depends to a large extent on
(a) frequency of applied voltage
(b) intensity of electric field
(c) presence of magnetic materials in the vicinity
(d) hysteresis loop area for the material

83. When a *PN* junction is reverse-biased, then
(a) depletion region decreases
(b) minority carriers are not affected
(c) holes and electrons move away from the junction
(d) barrier breaks down

84. Hard magnetic materials are suitable for making
(a) transformer core
(b) electromagnets
(c) permanent magnets
(d) reactor core

85. In a metal, there are 1028 electrons per cubic metre and mean free time is 10–14 sec. When a field of 10^4 V/m is applied, the current density will be
(a) 3.8×10^6 A/m^2 (b) 2.8×10^6 A/m^2
(c) 2.8 A/m^2 (d) None of these

86. The conductivity of a metal is determined by
(a) the number of valence electrons per atom
(b) the electron concentration and the mobility of the free electrons
(c) both (a) and (b)
(d) none of these

87. The dielectric strength of gaseous dielectrics depends on
(a) polarity of electrodes
(b) pressure
(c) frequency of applied field
(d) uniformity of applied electric field
(e) all of the above

88. The permeability and permittivity of a medium are
(a) independent of each other
(b) related by the velocity of electromagnetic waves
(c) related by the Boltzmann's constant
(d) all of these

89. In a properly biased transistor
(a) both depletion regions are small
(b) both depletion regions are large
(c) the emitter-to-base depletion region is large and collector-to-base depletion region is small
(d) the emitter-to-base depletion region is small and collector-to-base depletion region is large

90. Ferri-magnetic materials are used as
(a) super conductors (b) conductors
(c) semiconductors (d) insulators

91. In a semiconductor, the movement of holes is due to movement of
(a) electrons in conduction band
(b) electrons in valence band
(c) holes in conduction band
(d) holes in valence band

92. The relative permeability of paramagnetic material is
(a) less than unity (b) equal to unity
(c) greater than unity (d) none of these

93. Energy formation of Schottky defect in a metal is of the order of
(a) 1 joule (b) 1 eV
(c) 1.6×10^{-19} eV (d) 2 eV

94. The dielectric strength of high voltage porcelain is
(a) 10–16 kV/mm (b) 20–25 kV/mm
(c) 30–40 kV/mm (d) 60–80 kV/mm

95. The impurity atoms in semiconductors
(a) increase the energy gap
(b) reduce the energy gap
(c) increase the kinetic energy of valence electrons
(d) inject more charge carriers

96. A good electrical contact material should have the properties of
(a) high melting point
(b) good thermal conductivity
(c) high-resistance to corrosion
(d) high conductivity
(e) all of the above

97. The relative permeability of super-conducting materials is
(a) zero (b) +1
(c) –1 (d) infinity

98. The minority carrier concentration is largely a function of
(a) temperature
(b) amount of doping
(c) forward biasing voltage
(d) reverse biasing voltage

99. The conductivity of semiconductors depends upon the
(a) number of current carriers present per unit volume
(b) mobility of the current carriers
(c) both (a) and (b)
(d) none of these

100. The material used for photo conductive cell is
(a) ZnS (b) PbS
(c) CdS (d) None of these

101. The materials which are used for storing electrical energy are classified as ________ materials
(a) insulating (b) dielectric
(c) super conducting (d) paramagnetic

102. A *PN* junction is
(a) a rectifier (b) an amplifier
(c) an insulator (d) none of these

103. Which of the following dielectric is not preferred for high frequency applications?
(a) Teflon (b) Butyl rubber
(c) Polysterene (d) Polyethylene

104. For ferromagnetic materials the susceptibility is
(a) constant, positive and very high
(b) positive and very high but not constant
(c) always negative
(d) positive but very low

105. High frequency transformer core are generally made from
(a) Alnico (b) ferrites
(c) Mu-metal (d) silicon steel

106. ________ insulators are employed for high frequency applications.
(a) Stellite (b) Forsterite
(c) Stealite (d) None of these

107. The factor that generally affects the resistivity of electrical conductors is
(a) composition (b) size
(c) temperature (d) pressure

108. ________ is employed as an electric ceramic.
(a) Chromite (b) Alamandite
(c) $BaIO_3$ (d) None of these

109. Which one of the following is the poorest electrical conductor?
(a) Steel (b) Carbon
(c) Copper (d) Aluminium

110. Sludge formation in insulating oil causes
(a) increase in operating temperature
(b) reduction in rate of heat transfer
(c) clogging of ducts
(d) all of the above

111. The formula that determines the number of electrons which can be accommodated in any level is

(a) $2n^2$ (b) n^2

(c) 4n (d) $4n^2$

112. Thermo-plastic and thermoset polymers differ in

(a) thermal behaviour

(b) mechanical behaviour

(c) glass transition temperature

(d) all of these

113. A material is said to be super-conductor when its resistance is

(a) zero (b) very small

(c) negative (d) none of these

114. The electrical conductivity of metals is typically of the order of (in ohm^{-1} m^{-1})

(a) 10^7 (b) 10^{-4}

(c) 10^5 (d) 10^{-6}

115. The material which obstructs the flow of current without any appreciable loss of power is called the ________ material.

(a) dielectric

(b) insulating

(c) antiferromagnetic

(d) super conducting

ANSWERS

1	2	3	4	5	6	7	8	9	10
(c)	(a)	(a)	(c)	(b)	(b)	(a)	(c)	(b)	(a)
11	**12**	**13**	**14**	**15**	**16**	**17**	**18**	**19**	**20**
(b)	(b)	(b)	(c)	(b)	(b)	(a)	(a)	(c)	(c)
21	**22**	**23**	**24**	**25**	**26**	**27**	**28**	**29**	**30**
(a)	(b)	(d)	(d)	(a)	(a)	(a)	(a)	(a)	(c)
31	**32**	**33**	**34**	**35**	**36**	**37**	**38**	**39**	**40**
(c)	(b)	(c)	(c)	(c)	(b)	(a)	(b)	(a)	(b)
41	**42**	**43**	**44**	**45**	**46**	**47**	**48**	**49**	**50**
(c)	(b)	(b)	(b)	(c)	(b)	(b)	(a)	(b)	(c)
51	**52**	**53**	**54**	**55**	**56**	**57**	**58**	**59**	**60**
(c)	(c)	(b)	(d)	(c)	(b)	(a)	(c)	(d)	(c)
61	**62**	**63**	**64**	**65**	**66**	**67**	**68**	**69**	**70**
(d)	(a)	(a)	(c)	(a)	(a)	(d)	(a)	(b)	(b)
71	**72**	**73**	**74**	**75**	**76**	**77**	**78**	**79**	**80**
(b)	(c)	(e)	(b)	(b)	(c)	(b)	(a)	(c)	(a)
81	**82**	**83**	**84**	**85**	**86**	**87**	**88**	**89**	**90**
(b)	(b)	(a)	(c)	(b)	(b)	(e)	(b)	(d)	(c)
91	**92**	**93**	**94**	**95**	**96**	**97**	**98**	**99**	**100**
(b)	(c)	(b)	(a)	(d)	(d)	(a)	(a)	(c)	(c)
101	**102**	**103**	**104**	**105**	**106**	**107**	**108**	**109**	**110**
(b)	(a)	(b)	(b)	(b)	(b)	(a)	(c)	(b)	(d)
111	**112**	**113**	**114**	**115**					
(a)	(a)	(a)	(a)	(b)					

ENGLISH LANGUAGE

1. Comprehension Passages

ENGLISH LANGUAGE COMPREHENSION

The objective of language comprehension test is to ascertain the ability of the candidates to understand the passage properly. Therefore candidates are required to take notice of the following points:

1. Read the full passage very attentively and intelligently.
2. Try to comprehend the gist of it.
3. Make a mental note of all the important details and points given in the passage.
4. Read the passage for the second time in case you have not been able to understand it satisfactorily.
5. Divide the time proportionately for all the passages.
6. Answer the questions on the basis of facts, as given in the paragraph.
7. Don't waste much time in answering the questions of any one passage.
8. Check all the answers once again, very carefully, to see whether any question is left unanswered by mistake.

MODEL QUESTIONS (FOR PRACTICE)

Directions: *Each of the following passages is followed by five questions. Read the passage carefully and then answer the questions that follow each. For each question, four probable answers A, B, C and D are given. Only one out of these is correct. Choose the correct answer.*

PASSAGE-1

The use of words like 'welcome', 'thank you', 'please', etc., at the right moment reflects a polite nature. The civic sense also lies within the scope of good manners. We should not shout or talk loudly in public places like hospitals and libraries and create disturbance. We should not cheat people or make fun of them. Cleanliness is also necessary. We must not throw the waste on roads and make use of dustbins. We should not harm the public property as it belongs to all of us. While in a queue, discipline should be maintained. We must give fair chance to others.

1. Expressions like 'welcome' 'thank you' and 'please' reflect
   A. happiness B. discipline
   C. civic sense D. polite nature
2. While in a library, we should
   A. respect others B. avoid arguments
   C. talk in low tone D. be courteous
3. A public property belongs to
   A. nobody
   B. all of us
   C. government
   D. one who maintains it

4. Discipline is
   A. the rule of proper conduct or action
   B. the rule of road sense
   C. making use of dustbins
   D. forming a queue
5. The most appropriate title for this passage would be
   A. Polite Nature
   B. Courtesy
   C. Good Manners
   D. Civic Sense

PASSAGE-2

There is an old proverb 'Early to bed and early to rise makes a man healthy and wise.' I am in the habit of getting up early in the morning and have formed the habit of taking long morning walks in the past two years. It is a light exercise and best for physical fitness. The morning air which is fresh and pure is beneficial for the lungs. The early rays of the rising sun are good for healthy skin. 'Health is wealth' and doctors also recommend morning walk to their patients for gaining sound health and freshness of energy.

1. What is good for lungs?
   A. Sunrays B. Fresh air
   C. Sound sleep D. Light exercise
2. What is a light exercise?
   A. Early to bed
   B. Early to rise
   C. Morning walk
   D. Gaining sound health
3. What is good for skin?
   A. Fresh air
   B. Morning air
   C. Morning walk
   D. Rising sun's rays
4. What is best for physical fitness?
   A. Light exercise
   B. Long morning walk
   C. Early to rise
   D. Fresh and pure air
5. Long morning walk
   A. bring sound sleep
   B. ensures physical fitness
   C. ensures healthy skin
   D. keeps healthy, wealthy and wise

PASSAGE-3

Mahatma Gandhi lived a splendid long life and has set great moral standards before us. He showed to the world the true way to peace. He wished to see India prosper but he became a martyr for the noble cause of Hindu-Muslim unity at the time of partition when a religious fanatic, Nathuram Godse, shot him dead on January 30, 1948. His last words were 'Hey Ram'. He lived and died for his country and countryman.

1. Mahatma Gandhi showed the world the true way to
   A. prosperity B. love
   C. truth D. peace
2. Mahatma Gandhi became a martyr for the noble cause of
   A. truth
   B. non-violence
   C. freedom of India
   D. Hindu-Muslim unity
3. Mahatma Gandhi was shot dead
   A. before India achieved independence
   B. by a mad man
   C. by an intolerant religious person
   D. by a non-religious person
4. Mahatma Gandhi set great moral standards. It means
   A. he was a great religious teacher
   B. he was a great moralist
   C. he made India morally stronger
   D. moral was everything to him
5. Gandhiji lived and died for his country and countryman. It means
   A. he was born in India and died in India
   B. he was a patriot
   C. he was a great moralist
   D. he sacrified his life for India and her people

PASSAGE-4

On one hot day a crow felt very thirsty. He flew from one place to another in search of water. After long hours of labour he found a pitcher. Eagerly, he perched on the mouth of the pitcher. He found that the water was at the bottom of the vessel. He tried his best to dip his beak but did not succeed. He did not know what to do. Suddenly some pebbles lying nearby gave him an idea. One by one he dropped the pebbles with his beak into the pitcher. The level of water slowly came up to the mouth of the pitcher. The crow then drank the water and quenched his thirst.

1. The crow found a pitcher
   A. as it flew
   B. after many hours of labour
   C. full of water
   D. which was empty
2. What is the moral of the passage?
   A. No pains, no gains
   B. God helps those who help themselves
   C. Necessity is the mother of invention
   D. Try and try again, you will succeed at last
3. The crow flew from place to place
   A. in search of pitcher
   B. in search of pebbles
   C. in search of water
   D. in search of a vessel
4. The pitcher, the crow found
   A. was full of water
   B. was dry
   C. had little water in the bottom
   D. had water up to its mouth
5. As the crow dropped pebbles into the pitcher, what happend?
   A. The pitcher broke down
   B. The water leaked one of the pitcher
   C. The level of water into the pitcher rose up slowly
   D. Water level immediately rose to the mouth of the pitcher

PASSAGE-5

Once upon a time a crane and a fox lived in a forest. They were good friend. One day the fox invited the crane to a feast. He made a tasty food and served it before the crane on a plate. The crane could not eat anything because of the long beak. But the fox licked all his food. The crane felt insulted. He decided to teach the fox a lesson. Next day he invited the fox. He prepared the same tasty food and placed it in front of the fox inside a narrow glass. The crane ate easily while the fox looked on. Now, it was the fox's turn to remain hungry.

1. What is the moral of the passage?
   A. Beware of the wicked
   B. One good turn deserves another
   C. Be contented with what you have
   D. Tit for tat
2. The crane could not eat tasty food because the
   A. food was served in a shallow plate
   B. food was very hot
   C. food was served in a long jar
   D. crane was not hungry
3. The fox had to remain hungry because
   A. the food served was not enough in quantity
   B. the food was served inside a narrow glass
   C. the food served was not tasty
   D. the food was all liquid
4. Why did the crane feel insulted?
   A. Because he was invited to feast but he could not eat anything
   B. Because the food was served in a shallow plate and he could not eat
   C. Because the food was too hot
   D. Because the fox gulped all the food quickly
5. The crane successfully taught a lesson to the fox when he invited the fox to a feast and served the food
   A. in a narrow glass
   B. in a large plate
   C. in a broken plate
   D. in a long jar

PASSAGE-6

The family set down at the table and began to talk about the summer holidays. They had to decide a place to visit during the vacation. Should they go to their village or to a hill station? The parents preferred the village while the children wished to go the hill station. After few moments of discussion the elders decided to visit both the places. First they shall go to the village for a week and then stay at the hill station for the remaining days. For the first time the family shall be together during the holidays. The children were happy with the holiday plan.

1. The purpose for which the family set down at the table was
   A. to decide a place to visit during the vacation
   B. to educate the children how to carry articles during a visit to a hill station
   C. to decide the date when they should start their journey
   D. to tell the children that they will visit a hill station during this vacation
2. The final plan was to visit
   A. their village
   B. a hill station
   C. their village as well as a hill station
   D. their home town
3. The final decision was made by
   A. the boys B. the girls
   C. the women D. the elders
4. They decided first to go to their village and stay there for
   A. a day B. a week
   C. ten days D. a fortnight
5. Why were children happy?
   A. Because a hill station was included in their holiday plan
   B. Because a visit to their village was excluded from their holiday plan
   C. Because their choice prevailed
   D. Because they were going all alone to the hill station

PASSAGE-7

Once Govind intended to go on pilgrimage with his family. He asked Mirind to accompany. But for his trade's reason, he did not go with him. So Govind thought it safe to leave the box of his jewellery with him, as it was dangerous to leave it in a lone house or take it on the journey. So he went to him with the box. He took him to a lonely place under a tree and handed it over to him. He told Mirind, "Keep it safe with you. I shall return from the journey after six month then I shall take it back from you." Mirind said, "Don't worry, I shall keep it as safe as own."

1. Govind intended to go
   A. for a business trip
   B. to a hill station
   C. on a long journey to a sacred place
   D. to his home town for a long period
2. Why did Govind leave his box of jewellery with Mirind?
   A. Because it was not safe to take the box with him on a long journey
   B. Because Mirind was his fast friend
   C. Because the box was very heavy
   D. Because his house was unsafe
3. Why did Govind take Mirind to a lonely place?
   A. To tell him that the box contained valuable jewellery
   B. So that no third person could see box
   C. To show him what was within the box
   D. To tell him that the box will remain with him
4. Where did Govind hand over the box of jewellery to Mirind?
   A. At Mirind's house
   B. At his own house
   C. In a lonely place
   D. In a lonely place under a tree
5. It was not safe to leave the box in a lone house. Here the word 'lone house' means
   A. a house in a deserted place
   B. a house where none lives
   C. a house without door and lock
   D. a house near the forest

PASSAGE-8

Zahir-ud-din Babar was the first Mughal emperor of India. A descendent of Timur on father's side and Changez Khan on his mother's side, Babar was a brave warrior. After defeating Ibrahim Lodhi in the First Battle of Panipat in 1526 he entered Delhi and soon gained control over Agra. After many more battles with Rajputs he extended his empire over Punjab, Uttar Pradesh and north Bihar. He died at a young age of 48 years in 1530 at his capital Agra without getting much time to consolidate his victories.

1. Zahir-ud-din Babar was the first
   A. Muslim ruler of India
   B. Mughal ruler of India
   C. Afghan ruler of India
   D. Turk ruler of India
2. Babar was born in the years
   A. 1480 B. 1482
   C. 1492 D. 1962
3. Babar first occupied
   A. Punjab B. Agra
   C. Delhi D. Panipat
4. Babar was a brave warrior. Here brave warrior means
   A. courageous soldier
   B. a kind hearted soldier
   C. a clever fighter
   D. a victorious general
5. Babar extended his empire over Punjab and Uttar Pradesh after many more battles with the
   A. Afghans B. Rajputs
   C. Mughals D. Lodhies

PASSAGE-9

Our National Flag is tricolour. It has three equal horizontal strips. The strip at the top is saffron, in the middle is white and at the bottom is green. The ratio of width to length of the flag is 2 : 3. In the centre of the white strip is a wheel in navy blue. The wheel represents the *chakra.* Its design is similar to the wheel which appears on the abacus of the Sarnath Lion Capital of Ashoka. Its diameter approximates to the width of the white strip. The wheel has 24 spokes. It was adopted by Constituent Assembly on July 22, 1947. We love our national flag. We respect it. We are ready to sacrifice our life to protect its honour. It represents the nation. So it is a symbol of national honour.

1. In our national flag the wheel is located in the centre of
   A. saffron strip B. white strip
   C. green strip D. blue strip
2. In our national flag which of the strips is at the bottom in our national flag
   A. blue C. saffron
   B. white D. green
3. Why do we love our national flag?
   A. Because it is tricolour
   B. Because it has three strips
   C. Because it has a wheel at the centre
   D. Because it is a symbol of national honour
4. Our national flag was approved by
   A. President
   B. Lok Sabha
   C. Parliament
   D. Constituent Assembly
5. The diameter approximates to the width of the white strip. Here the word 'approximates' means
   A. is more or less equal
   B. is exactly equal
   C. is not equal
   D. is related

PASSAGE-10

Distance in large cities are long. All the people do not have their own means of transport. They have to depend upon the state or private buses. The number of bus users is very large. Every bus stop is, therefore, crowded. The number of buses is not adequate. Thus people suffer the torture of long wait at the bus stop. Some bus stops are quite orderly. People form queues and get into the buses turn by turn. However, often this order is forgotten and confusion spreads when the bus comes and the law of jungle prevails.

1. Why are the bus stops crowded?
   A. Because they are small is size
   B. Because the number of passengers is very large
   C. Because they are situated at some busy centre
   D. Because people do not form queues
2. Long wait at the bus stop is the result of
   A. over-crowding in the buses
   B. late running of buses
   C. shortage of buses
   D. slow speed of buses
3. Some bus stops are quite orderly where
   A. there is no crowd
   B. the number of buses is adequate

C. people do not have to wait for long
D. people form queues and enter the buses one by one

4. Most of the people who travel by buses are
A. non-working
B. do not have their own vehicles
C. have to go a long distance
D. live in large cities

5. What happens when people do not have their own transport?
A. They have to wait for a bus at a bus stop
B. They have to depend upon the state or private buses
C. They have to travel long distances
D. They form queues and get into buses one by one

PASSAGE-11

A certain king once fell ill and doctors said that only a sudden fright would restore his health but the king was not a man for anyone to play tricks on, except his fool. One day, when the fool was with him in his boat he cleverly pushed the king into water but he was rescued and put to bed. The fright, the bath and bed cured the diseased king, but he was so angry with the fool that he turned him out of the country.

1. What did the doctor say about the king?
A. Only a sudden fright would restore the king's health
B. Only fool would cure the king
C. Only a boat trick could cure the king
D. The king had suffered a sudden fright

2. He cleverly pushed the king into water but *he* was rescued and put to bed. In this sentence *he* refers to
A. the king B. the fool
C. the doctor D. the river

3. When the fool pushed the king into water they were
A. in the palace B. in the bed
C. in the garden D. in a boat

4. Who played the trick on the king?
A. The doctor B. The boatman
C. The fool D. The fright

5. The fool who cured the king was
A. rewarded
B. thrown into water
C. turned out of the country
D. put into jail

ANSWERS

Passage	1	2	3	4	5
Passage 1.	D	C	B	A	C
Passage 2.	B	C	D	B	B
Passage 3.	D	D	C	B	D
Passage 4.	B	C	C	C	C
Passage 5.	D	A	B	B	A
Passage 6.	A	C	D	B	A
Passage 7.	C	A	B	D	B
Passage 8.	B	B	C	A	B
Passage 9.	B	D	D	D	A
Passage 10.	B	C	D	B	B
Passage 11.	A	A	D	C	C

2. English Grammar

PARTS OF SPEECH

Part of speech	Definition or Function	Examples
Noun	Name of a person, place, animal, quality or thing	Ram, boy, dog pen, sun, Delhi, truth, honesty
Pronoun	Used in place of a noun	I, you, he she, they
Articles & Determiners	Points out indefinite and definite nouns	a, an, the, few, some
Adjective	Describes a noun or pronoun	big, honest, wooden valuable, quiet, deep, soft, narrow
Adverb	Describes a verb, an adjective or another adverb	silently, widely, softly, quietly, very, carefully
Verb	Tells about action or state of something or someone	is, am, was, have, do, like, walk, work, make, throw, tell
Conjuction	Joins words, clauses or sentences	and, but, when, yet, while, else
Preposition	Links a noun or pronoun to another word	at, to, after, on for, under, over, with
Interjection	Expresses sudden feelings or emotions	Ah!, Alas!, oh!, ouch!, hi!, well!, Hurrah!

NOUNS

A word which denotes a person, a thing, an animal or a place is said to be a noun.

There are two noun numbers in English — the *Singular* and the *Plural*.

Singular Numbers : A noun that denotes one person or one thing, is said to be in the Singular number. For example — book, pencil, bird, dog, hen etc. are in singular number.

Plural Number : A noun that denotes more than one person or one thing is said to be in plural number. For example — boys, pens, lions, girls, men etc. are in plural number.

REMEMBER

Singular	*Plural*
Cat	Cats
Book	Books
Pen	Pens
Room	Rooms
Tree	Trees
Bus	Buses
Bush	Bushes
Box	Boxes
Glass	Glasses
Dish	Dishes
Judge	Judges
Tax	Taxes
Watch	Watches
Calf	Calves
Thief	Thieves
Knife	Knives

Singular	Plural
Scarf	Scarves
Wife	Wives
Leaf	Leaves
Wolf	Wolves
Half	Halves
Monarch	Monarchs
Roof	Roofs
Hoof	Hoofs
Gulf	Gulfs
Staff	Staffs
Radio	Radios
Bamboo	Bamboos
Folio	Folios
Hero	Heroes
Volcano	Volcanoes
Mango	Mangoes
Potato	Potatoes
Photo	Photos
Piano	Pianos
Baby	Babies
Fly	Flies
Country	Countries
Lady	Ladies
Boy	Boys
Monkey	Monkeys
Ox	Oxen
Child	Children
Man	Men
Woman	Women
Tooth	Teeth
Axis	Axes
Basis	Bases
Foot	Feet
Goose	Geese
Englishman	Englishmen
Radius	Radii
Vertex	Vertices
Stimulus	Stimuli

1. Note the plurals of the following nouns:

Singular	*Plural*	*Singular*	*Plural*
copy	copies	cry	cries
baby	babies	duty	duties
body	bodies	country	countries
family	families	diary	diaries
fly	flies	fairy	fairies
city	cities	spy	spies
army	armies	storey	storeys
bay	bays	monkey	monkeys

2. The following nouns do not undergo any change in plural form, in general.

Singular	*Plural*	*Singular*	*Plural*
deer	deer	sheep	sheep
thousand	thousand	pair	pair
hundred	hundred	score	score
dozen	dozen	gross	gross

Note: We can write—

(*a*) thousands of men; (*b*) two pairs of shoes; (*c*) dozens of mangoes; (*d*) scores of people etc.

But—

(*a*) two thousand rupees; (*b*) three hundred men; (*c*) five dozen eggs, etc.

3. The following nouns are usually used in plural forms. They take a plural verb after them—

eatables	fetters	surroundings
riches	alms	spectacles
trousers	pants	scissors
premises	thanks	annals
congratulations	goods	shorts
tongs	pains	arms
breeches	(for troubles)	

4. The following are the nouns which are plural in appearance but are usually used in singular number. They are followed by a singular verb—

news	politics	physics
mathematics	economics	ethics
politics	classics	gallows
statistics	athletics	innings
mechanics	summons	mumps

5. Collective nouns often used as plurals—

public	police	cattle
audience	clergy	folk
people	poultry	nation
elite	gentry	glitterati

6. The nouns that are usually used in singular forms—

advice	hair	rice
fuel	alphabet	machinery
offspring	issue	furniture
mischief	stationery	luggage
bedding	information	abuse

7. Material nouns are always used in singular number—

gold	copper	milk
water	silk	wool

Note: They may be used in plural with a different meaning.

copper coins (coppers), chains or fetters (irons), cans made of tin (tins).

GENDERS

The difference in sex is denoted by Gender in grammar. The various genders are as follows :

1. **Masculine Gender :** A noun that denotes a male is said to be of the masculine gender, as man, uncle, ox, boy etc.
2. **Feminine Gender :** A noun that denotes a female is said to be of feminine gender, as woman, aunt, princess, cow etc.
3. **Common Gender :** Nouns which denote both males and females are said to be of the common gender, as friend, cousin, person, parent, baby etc.
4. **Neuter Gender :** A noun that denotes the name of object without life is said to be of neuter gender, as file, table, pencil.

REMEMBER

Masculine	***Feminine***
Boy	Girl
Son	Daughter
Brother	Sister
Murderer	Murderess
Sorcerer	Sorceress
Son-in-law	Daughter-in-law
Father-in-law	Mother-in-law
Man-servant	Maid-servant
Land-lord	Land-lady
Bachelor	Maid
Gentleman	Lady
Monk	Nun
Earl	Countess
Lad	Lass
Sir	Madam
Duke	Dutchess
Emperor	Empress
Milk-man	Milk-maid
Pea-cock	Pea-hen

Masculine	***Feminine***
Step-father	Step-mother
Hero	Heroine
Viceroy	Vicerine
Mr.	Mrs.
Governor	Governess
Master	Mistress
Wizard	Witch
Heir	Heiress
Host	Hostess
Lion	Lioness
Mayor	Mayoress
Actor	Actress
Buck	Doe
Colt	Filly
Dog	Bitch
Horse	Mare
Count	Countess
Hunter	Huntress
Prince	Princess
Abbot	Abbess
God	Goddess
Author	Authoress
Ox	Cow
Widower	Widow
Grand-father	Grand-mother
He-goat	She-goat
Milk-man	Milk-woman
Bridegroom	Bride
Tiger	Tigress
Priest	Priestess
Poet	Poetess
Shepherd	Shepherdess
Nephew	Niece
Stag	Hind

PRONOUNS

The repetition of a noun in a sentence or a set of sentences is really boring. So, instead of repeating the noun, we can use a word (for that noun) called the pronoun.

"A pronoun is a word that we use instead of a noun".

Example:

This is *Sachin. He* plays cricket.

Note: *He* is the pronoun used in place of *Sachin.*

Kinds of Pronouns

1. **Personal pronouns :** A pronoun which is used instead of the name of a person is known as a 'Personal Pronoun'. A list of the 'Personal pronouns' is listed below :

   I, my, mine, me, we (First Person)
   You, your, yours (Second Person)
   He, his, him, she, her, hers, it,
   its, they, their, theirs, them (Third Person)

2. **Demonstrative, Indefinite and Distributive Pronouns :**

   (a) Demonstrative Pronouns : Pronouns used to point out the objects to which they refer are called Demonstrative Pronouns.

   Examples :
   (i) *This* is a present from my uncle.
   (ii) *These* are merely excuses.
   (iii) Bembay mangoes are better than *those* of Bangaluru.

   (b) Indefinite Pronouns : All pronouns which refer to persons or things in a general way and do not refer to any particular person or thing are called Indefinite Pronouns.

   Examples :
   (i) *Somebody* has stolen my watch.
   (ii) *Few* escaped unhurt.
   (iii) Did you ask *anybody* to come?

   (c) Distributive Pronouns : Each, either, neither are called distributive pronouns because they refer to persons or things one at a time. For this reason they are always singular and followed by the verb in singular.

   Examples :
   (i) *Each* of the men received a reward.
   (ii) *These* men received *each* a reward.
   (iii) *Either* of you can go.

3. **Relative Pronouns :** A relative pronoun refers or relates to some noun going before, which is called its Antecedent.

   Examples :
   (i) I met Hari *who* used to live here.
   (ii) I have found the pen *which* I had lost.
   (iii) Here is the book *that* you lent me.

4. **Interrogative Pronouns :** These pronouns, are used for asking questions.

   Examples :
   (i) *Whose* book is this?
   (ii) *What* will all the neighbours say?
   (iii) *Which* do you prefer, tea or coffee?

Note : Interrogative pronouns can also be used in asking indirect questions. Consider the following examples :
(i) I asked *who* was speaking.
(ii) Tell me *what* you have done.
(iii) Say *which* you would like best.

Behaviour of the Pronouns

1. If three pronouns are used together in the same sentence they are arranged in the following order :

   2 + 3 + 1
   ↓ ↓ ↓
   Second Person, Third Person, First Person

   Examples :
   I, you and he must help *that* poor man. (Incorrect)
   You, he and I must help *that* poor man. (Correct)

2. When two or more singular nouns are joined by and, the pronoun used for them should be plural.

   Examples :
   Mohan and Sohan are friends. *They* play football. *They* live at Lajpat Nagar.

3. But if these nouns joined by and refer to the same person or thing, the pronoun used should be singular.

   Examples :
   (i) Delhi, the beautiful city and the capital of India, is famous for *its* historical monuments.
   (ii) The manager and owner of the firm expressed *his* views on the demands of the workers.

4. When two nouns are used with as well as, the pronoun agrees with the first subject.

   Examples :

   (a) Mohan as well as his friends is doing *his* work.

   (b) The students as well as their teachers are doing *their* work.

5. When two singular nouns joined by 'and' are preceded by *each* or *every*, the pronoun used must be singular and should agree in gender with the second noun.

   Examples :

   (a) Every man and every woman will do *her* best for the nation.

   (b) Each boy and each girl went to *her* house.

6. When two nouns are joined by using 'with', the pronoun agrees with the noun coming before 'with'.

   Examples :

   (a) The boy with *his* parents has gone to see a movie.

   (b) The children with *their* parents have gone to picnic.

7. When two different nouns are joined by either.......... or; neither .... nor, the pronoun is used according to the number and gender of the second noun.

   Examples :

   (a) Either your sister or you have done *your* work.

   (b) Neither the students nor the teacher was in *his* class.

8. The pronoun coming after '*than*' must be in the same case as that coming before '*than*'.

   Examples :

   (a) She plays better than *me*. (Incorrect)
   She plays better than *I*. (Correct)

   (b) His elder brother is more intelligent than *him*. (Incorrect)
   His elder brother is more intelligent than *he*. (Correct)

9. 'Many a' always takes a singular pronoun and singular verb.

   Example :

   Many a soldier has met *his* death in the battle field.

10. 'Who', 'Whose', 'Whom' are used only for persons.

    Examples :

    (a) *Who* is knocking at the door?

    (b) *Whose* pen is this?

    (c) *What* do you want?

11. 'Which' is used for things.

    Example :

    Which game do you like?

MULTIPLE CHOICE QUESTIONS

Directions: *In the following questions choose the correct options to fill the blanks.*

1. The place was so dirty that ..... wished to run away from there.

A. everybody B. anybody
C. few D. some

2. ..... was there to help me.

A. Somebody B. Anything
C. Anybody D. Nobody

3. Is there .... to eat?

A. some B. something
C. any D. few

4. ..... of the students were making a great noise.

A. Anyone B. Somebody
C. Many D. Nobody

5. ..... of the students can solve this sum.

A. Someone B. Anybody
C. Somebody D. None

6. ...... of us should try our best to make India a heaven.

A. Any B. Somebody
C. Anybody D. All

7. ...... of us do not know the real meaning of our lives.

A. Any B. Something
C. Several D. Many

8. My .... black.

A. hairs are B. hair is
C. hairs shall D. hair will

9. She saw two .... on the last Sunday.
A. thiefs B. theifs
C. thieves D. theives

10. My sister is a ....
A. bacheloress B. bachelor
C. unmaried D. spinster

11. One is supposed to do ....
A. our duty B. their duty
C. one's duty D. his duty

12. Take anything .... you want.
A. that B. which
C. than D. then

13. I cannot tolerate ....
A. separated you
B. your separation
C. separation from you
D. you separated

14. He is .... faithful partner.
A. Yours B. You
C. Your D. Your's

15. Ajay is more smart than ....
A. her B. hers
C. herself D. she

16. Vivek works harder than ....
A. me B. I
C. her D. his

17. They should help ....
A. the poor people B. the poor
C. the poor persons D. the poor peoples

18. .... are mad.
A. All his sons B. His all sons
C. Sons all his D. All sons his

19. The poor fellow .... to fate.
A. resigned
B. resigned himself
C. resigned itself
D. resigned themselves

20. Nobody will help you but ....
A. I B. me
C. ours D. his

21. It is a good chance, You must avail .... this opportunity.
A. of B. yourself of
C. for D. from

22. The person who is elected .... my relative.
A. is B. he is
C. his D. him

23. He made ....
A. yours mention B. mention of you
C. mention for you D. mention about you

24. .... I know, he is quite faithful.
A. As far as B. So far as
C. So far this D. So far so

25. It is a duty of a person to take .... for his family.
A. pain B. pains
C. pain-killers D. pained

26. She does not love .... husband.
A. his B. her
C. its D. their

27. Let .... work together.
A. him and me B. he and I
C. he and him D. I and me

28. Copper, Silver and Gold ....
A. each will do B. either will do
C. any one will do D. any will do

29. Jessica and Roma are very irregular .... habits.
A. in her B. in their
C. in its D. in every

30. One likes to enjoy .... who was a great poet.
A. The sonnets of Shakespeare
B. Shakespeare's sonnets
C. Sonnets
D. Shakespeare

31. That is the boy .... everybody loves.
A. whom B. who
C. that D. whose

32. That is the girl .... won the first prize.
A. whom B. who
C. whose D. which

33. That is the man .... purse was lost.
A. who B. whom
C. whose D. their

ANSWERS

1	2	3	4	5	6	7	8	9	10
A	D	B	C	D	D	D	B	C	D
11	**12**	**13**	**14**	**15**	**16**	**17**	**18**	**19**	**20**
C	A	C	C	D	B	B	A	B	B
21	**22**	**23**	**24**	**25**	**26**	**27**	**28**	**29**	**30**
B	A	B	A	B	B	A	C	B	A
31	**32**	**33**							
A	B	C							

ARTICLES

The family of the articles has only three members. They are : A, An and The. However, they fall under two groups :

(a) Definite Article *(b)* Indefinite Article

'The' is known as definite article whereas 'a' and 'an' are known as indefinite articles.

Use of the Definite Article 'The'

'The' is used before

1. The superlative degree :
   He is the ablest man of the town.
   (ablest is a superlative degree)
2. The name of states, countries etc. having a descriptive name :
   (i) The J & K is a small state. (J & K is a descriptive name)
   (ii) He lives in the U.S.A. (U.S.A. is a descriptive name)
   (But the Delhi and the America are wrong because neither Delhi nor America is a descriptive name)
3. The names of the scriptures :
   The Gita is a holy book. (Gita is a scripture)
4. Name of newspapers :
   The Tribune is published from Chandigarh.
5. Name of rivers, canals, seas, oceans, bays, gulfs, groups of islands etc. :
   (i) The Ganga is a holy river.
   (ii) The Indian Ocean is the deepest ocean.
   (iii) The Persian Gulf is a narrow gulf.
6. The name of famous buildings :
   The Taj is one of the best buildings in India.
7. The names of nationals, sects and communities:
   (i) The English defeated the Germans in the World War.
   (ii) The rich should help the poor.
   (iii) The Hindus believe in the caste system.
8. Proper nouns used as common nouns :
   (i) Kalidas is the Shakespeare of India.
   (ii) Delhi is the London of India.
9. Famous historical events :
   The Industrial Revolution changed the face of England.
10. The directions and the celestial bodies:
    The sun rises in the east.
11. Titles :
    Akbar, the Great was loved by his subjects.

Do not use 'the'

1. Before languages :
   The English is an international language. (Incorrect)
   English is an international language. (Correct)
2. Before the names of games :
   The hockey is a popular game. (Incorrect)
   Hockey is a popular game. (Correct)

Use of the Indefinite Articles 'A' and 'An'

'A' is used before :

1. All singular common nouns beginning with a consonant :
   (i) A boy sings a song.

(ii) A black and a white cow were grazing in the field.

2. If a word begins with a vowel but gives the sound of a consonant, 'a' should be used before it :
   (i) He was helped in his work by a European.
   (ii) He is a one-eyed man.
   (iii) It is a useful work.

'An' is used as follows :

1. All singular common nouns beginning with a vowel (*i.e.*, a, e, i, o, u) :
   (i) He is an artist.
   (ii) He is an old man.
   (iii) I intend to buy an umbrella.
2. If a word starts with a consonant but gives the sound of a vowel, "an" should be used before it :
   (i) Brutus is an honourable man.
   (ii) He is an honour to his profession.
   (iii) He is an L.L.B.
   (iv) He is an M.A.
   (v) You will reach there in an hour.

Demonstratives, that, these and those

1. The demonstrative adjectives and pronouns are for objects nearby the speaker:
   this (singular) those (plural)
   and for objects far away from the speaker.
   That (singular) those (plural)
2. Demonstratives are the only adjectives that agree in number with their nouns.
   That hat is nice.
   Those hats are nice.
3. When there is the idea of selection, the pronoun "one" (or "ones") often follows the demonstrative.
   I want a book. I'll get this (one).
   If the demonstrative is followed by an adjective, "one"(or "ones") must be used.
   I want a book. I'll get this big one.

MULTIPLE CHOICE QUESTIONS

Directions: *In the following questions choose the correct options to fill the blanks.*

1. .... will have to be paid for this material.
A. Half rupee B. Half a rupee
C. A half rupee D. An half rupee

2. .... is taking keen interest in India.
A. The USA B. USA
C. An USA D. A USA

3. Only .... can save our country.
A. the Hitler B. a Hitler
C. Hitler D. an Hitler

4. I can run for ....
A. hundred miles B. the hundred miles
C. a hundred miles D. an hundred miles.

5. .... man-eater has been killed.
A. The B. A
C. An D. Either A or B

6. What .... fine idea!
A. the B. an
C. a D. No article

7. .... earth is moving around the sun.
A. An B. A
C. The D. No article

8. This is .... first example while I got.
A. the B. a
C. an D. No article

9. This is .... house which was built during earthquake.
A. a B. an
C. the D. No article

10. .... America is a rich country.
A. The B. An
C. A D. No article

11. .... U.S.A. is a developed country.
A. A B. An
C. The D. No article

12. .... Bible is a holy book.
A. A B. The
C. An D. No article

13. .... rich should help the poor.
A. The B. A
C. An D. No article

14. .... Gold is a costly metal.
A. The B. A
C. An D. No article

15. Kalidas is .... Shakespeare of India.
A. a B. an
C. the D. No article

16. I cannot do .... difficult work.
A. a such B. the such
C. such the D. such a

17. How foolish .... plan it is!
A. a B. an
C. the D. No article

18. An ink is .... useful article.
A. an B. a
C. the D. No article

19. There are .... husband and wife.
A. a B. an
C. the D. No article

20. He is learning .... French
A. the B. a
C. an D. No article

ANSWERS

1	2	3	4	5	6	7	8	9	10
B	A	B	C	D	C	C	A	C	D
11	**12**	**13**	**14**	**15**	**16**	**17**	**18**	**19**	**20**
C	B	A	D	C	D	A	B	D	D

ADJECTIVES & ADVERBS

An Adjective is a word which adds something to the meaning of a noun or a pronoun.

Mridula is an *intelligent* girl.
He has a *black* goat.
He is a *brilliant* student.
She is a *clever* girl.
It is a *beautiful* picture.

In the sentences given above, the words in italics are adjectives.

An Adverb is a word which qualifies the meaning of a Verb, an Adjective or another Adverb.

(*i*) He talks *slowly*.
(*ii*) He is a *very* good student.
(*iii*) He talks *very* slowly.

In sentence (*i*), *slowly* qualifies the verb *talks*.

In sentence (*ii*), *very* qualifies the adjective *good*.

In sentence (*iii*), *very* qualifies the adverb *slowly*.

Adjectives have three degrees of comparison :

1. **Positive Degree :** It expresses the common form of an adjective.
   Example :
   Ram is a *tall* boy.
   In the above sentence *tall* is an adjective and expresses the common form.
2. **Comparative Degree :** It expresses the more of the same form.
   Example :
   Ram is *taller* than Mahesh.
   In the above sentence *taller* is an adjective that expresses the more of the common form of the adjective *tall*.

"When and How to Use" Comparative Degree?

(a) Comparative Degree is used when two persons or two groups of persons or things are compared.
Examples :
(a) He is *wiser* than his younger brother.
(b) This glass is *cleaner* than the other.

(b) When two different qualities in the same person are compared, more is used instead of 'er' to form the comparative. The formula used in this case should be :
More + Positive Degree
She is *fairer* than polite. (Incorrect)
She is *more fair* than polite. (Correct)

(c) When selection of one out of two persons or things is meant, the degree of comparison is followed by of and *the* is used before it.
Example :
Zia is abler of *the* two sisters.

(d) If two comparatives are used in the same sentence to impress upon an idea, both should be preceded by the definite article.

Examples :

(i) The higher you go, the cooler it is.

(ii) The more we get, the more we desire.

(e) When one person or thing is compared with another of the same kind, other is used after the comparative degree. In such sentences other is normally preceded by any or all.

Examples :

(i) Kalidas is greater than any dramatist. (Incorrect)

Kalidas is greater than any other dramatist. (Correct)

(ii) Lead is heavier than all metals. (Incorrect)

Lead is heavier than all other metals. (Correct)

(f) Senior, junior, superior, inferior, prior, anterior (earlier than) and posterior (later than) are always followed by 'to'.

Examples :

(i) Ram is senior *to* Mohan by three years.

(ii) That pen is inferior *to* that.

(iii) He is junior *to* me in rank.

(iv) This event was posterior *to* that.

Note: Never use *than* after the above mentioned adjectives.

Important Information

(a) 'Preferable' is also used as an adjective of the comparative degree. As such, it is always followed by *to* and not *a.*

Death is preferable than dishonour. (Incorrect)

Death is preferable *to* dishonour. (Correct)

(b) To intensify the Degree of comparison, we use *far* or *much* before the comparative.

Examples :

(i) This book is *far* better than that.

(ii) His performance was *much* better than Mohan's.

Warning : Always avoid the use of double comparatives.

Don't say : Ram is more cleverer than his younger brother.

Say: Ram is cleverer than his younger brother.

3. Superlative Degree : It expresses the most of the common form of an adjective.

Example :

He is the ablest man of the town.

How and when to use the Superlative Degree?

(a) The Superlative Degree is used when more than two persons or things are compared.

(b) The Superlative Degree is generally preceded by 'the' and followed by 'of' in most of the cases or otherwise.

(c) When an adjective of the superlative degree is preceded by a Possessive Adjective or a Noun in the Possessive case, 'the' should not be used before it.

Example :

Which is Kalidas' best play?

It will be a blunder to use 'the' before the Superlative Degree in such cases.

Don't say : Which is Kalidas' the best play.

(d) To intensify the degree of comparison, *by far* is used before the superlative degree.

Example :

India is *by far* the most beautiful country of the world.

Note: Always avoid the use of double superlatives.

Don't say : He is the most strongest boy in the class.

Say : He is the strongest boy in the class.

Use of some Important Adjectives

1. (a) '**Some**' is used as follows :

(i) With countable nouns where it means—a little, a small quantity.

(ii) In a question which shows some request.

Examples :

(i) There is some water in the bottle.

(ii) Some of the students were absent yesterday.

(iii) Will you have some milk?

(iv) Will you buy some fruit for me?

(b) **'Any'** is used as follows :

(i) In negative sentences.

(ii) In interrogative sentences.

(iii) After 'Hardly', 'Scarcely' and 'Barely'.
(iv) After 'If'.

Examples :

(i) There is not any sugar in the pot.
(ii) We haven't any rice in the house.
(iii) I have hardly any money.
(iv) There are scarcely any plants in this field.
(v) If there is any danger, blow the whistle.

2. (a) **Older :** Older (and oldest) are used for persons animals and things. But 'Older' and 'Oldest' refer to the persons who do not belong to the same family.

Examples :

(i) Radha is older than Shyama.
(ii) John is the oldest member of the staff. 'Older' and 'Oldest' refer to the persons who do not belong to the same family.

(b) **Elder** (and **eldest**) are used in respect of the members of the same family like sons, daughters, brothers, sisters.

Examples :

(i) My elder sister is a lecturer.
(ii) Meenakshi is the eldest of the three sisters.

Note :

(i) 'Elder' is not followed by 'than'.
(ii) 'Elder' and 'Eldest' cannot be used for things.

3. (a) **'Few'** is negative and is the opposite of 'Many'. It means 'not many'.
(b) **'A few'** is positive and means 'some at least'. It is the opposite of 'None'.
(c) **'The few'** means 'minority' and suggests 'whether there is'.

Examples :

(i) We have few holidays in school.
(ii) Only a few boys will fail in the examination.
(iii) The few poems that he wrote are very popular.

4. (a) **Further** means 'something additional'.
(b) **Farther** means 'a greater distance'.

Examples :

(i) Further discussion will be held in the office of the principal.
(ii) Amritsar is farther from Delhi than Ambala.

5. (a) **Little** is negative. It means, 'not much', or 'hardly any'.
(b) **A little** is positive. It means 'some quantity'.
(c) **The little** denotes quantity. It means, 'not much but all that is, or whatever quantity there is'.

Examples :

(i) There is little hope of his success.
(ii) He knows a little of everything.
(iii) I have spent the little money I had.
(iv) The little knowledge of shoe-making proved very useful to me.

6. (a) **'Much'** expresses 'quantity'.
(b) **'Many'** expresses 'number'.
(c) **'Many a'**—'Singular noun' and 'Singular verb' are used with 'many a'.

Examples :

(i) There is not *much* water in the jug.
(ii) *Many* boys are absent today.
(iii) *Many* a battle has been fought on the soil of India.

7. (a) **'Less'** denotes 'in a small degree'.
(b) **'Fewer'** denotes 'number'.

Examples :

(i) He devotes less time to his studies.
(ii) There are no fewer than ten chairs in this room.

8. (a) **'Each'** is used for a single number of 'two persons' or 'things'.
(b) **'Every'** is used for a single number of 'many persons' or 'things'.

Examples :

(i) Each boy must take part in games.
(ii) There are only two poets. Each poet recited his poem.
(iii) Every man dies in this world.
(iv) Every man is expected to do his duty.

9. (a) **'Either'** means one of the two or both.
(b) **'Neither'** is negative of the either.

Examples :

(i) You may buy either of these two chairs.
(ii) Neither of them could speak on the stage.

10. (a) '**Later**' expresses 'late in time'.
(b) '**Latter**' means 'second in position or order'.
Examples :
(i) My father reached later than I expected.
(ii) The latter position was better than the former.

Use of some Important Adverbs

1. (a) Also, too, enough:
(i) He taught English. Also, he edited the school magazine
(ii) He is a writer and also he is a painter.
(iii) He is too obstinate to listen to any reason.
(iv) This is too difficult a piece for the junior students.
(v) Sarla was kind enough to help the poor.
(vi) He is brave enough to help the truth.
Note: 'Too' is used in a negative sense, but enough is used in a positive sense.
(b) Fairly and rather: Both suggest the meaning 'moderately'. But, mainly 'fairly' is used with the words that denote a positive meaning and rather is used with the words that denote a negative meaning:
(i) Rita did fairly well in that competition, but her performance was rather poor in sports.
(ii) Mona is fairly rich, but she is rather stingy.
Note: 'Rather' can also be used in a positive sense.
(i) This is a rather interesting job.
(ii) That boy is rather smart.
(c) Hardly, barely, scarcely: These words mostly convey the negative suggestions and are almost similar.
(i) I have hardly any strength now.
(ii) There was barely any supply to the township,
(iii) There were scarcely a hundred guests present.
Note: With slight variance in the meaning, the words given above convey the idea of 'very little', 'not enough', 'lack of quantity and number'.
(d) Yet, Still: These adverbs can often be used to connect the sentence units:
(i) He has been defeated many times in the contest; still he wants to be a competitor.
(ii) Mona was sick; yet she went on doing her work.
(e) Alone:
(i) He alone (none else) is capable of handling that fire,
(ii) He hunted all alone in the forest. (not in any company)

Special Note:
(a) Apart from their conventional positions the adverbs might be used in different positions with different meanings and angles.
(i) He had only four books.
(ii) John only contacted his friend in need.
(iii) He greeted me only.
(iv) Only he greeted me there.
(b) Inversion: Some adverbs can be inverted *i.e.* placed in the beginning of the sentence and then be followed by an interrogative form. The most common of these adverb are: so, seldom, never, nowhere, under no circumstances, hardly, scarcely etc.
(i) So big was the bus that it could not enter the narrow lane.
(ii) Hardly had he reached the station when he received the message.

MULTIPLE CHOICE QUESTIONS

Directions: *In the following questions choose the correct options to fill the blanks.*

1. The girl whom you met is the .... sister of Ravi.
A. eldest B. elder
C. older D. oldest

2. The historical place is ....
A. seeing worth

B. worthy of seeing
C. worth seeing
D. worthy seeing

3. These flowers smell ....
A. sweet B. sweetly
C. more sweetly D. sweetest

4. .... aspirant cannot pass the entrance examination.
A. Each B. Every
C. All D. No

5. Harivansh Rai .... second Shakespeare.
A. is a B. is
C. is the D. is an

6. .... student in the class got prizes.
A. Each and every B. Every and each
C. Every D. Never

7. It is .... picture than the one we saw last Monday.
A. interesting B. much interesting
C. more interesting D. most interesting

8. She is clever ....
A. that her mother is
B. as her mother is
C. to her mother is
D. than her mother is

9. They will get ....
A. Red, green and black paper
B. Red, green black paper
C. Red and green and black paper
D. Red green black paper

10. Health is .... wealth.
A. preferable to
B. more preferable than
C. more preferable to
D. most preferable then

11. .... water that was in the jug evaporated.
A. Little B. The little
C. Small D. A small

12. He has not sung .... songs.
A. much B. most
C. more D. many

13. Srishti has searched .... office.
A. whole the B. the whole
C. a whole D. some whole

14. Premchand was .... best and .... famous writer.
A. a, the most B. the, a most
C. the, more D. the, the most

15. William Shakespeare is famous as ....
A. a poet and a dramatist
B. a poet and dramatist
C. the poet and the dramatist
D. a poet and the dramatist

16. What does .... leader suggest?
A. other B. another
C. others D. anothers

17. He .... money.
A. has few B. have few
C. has little D. have little

18. The .... boys are rewarded.
A. first two B. two first
C. firsts two D. two's first

19. He is .... brave.
A. stronger than
B. stronger then
C. more strong then
D. more strong than

20. No sooner said ....
A. so done B. and done
C. then done D. but done

21. She returned .... than I had thought.
A. quickly B. more quicker
C. more quickly D. quicker

22. He is .... foolish person.
A. rather the B. a rather
C. rather a D. rather

23. This pen .... rupees.
A. costs twenty
B. twenty costs only
C. costs only twenty
D. only costs twenty

24. It is .... pride.
A. nothing else but
B. nothing else than
C. else nothing than
D. but

25. This tea is .... to drink.
A. too hot B. very hot
C. enough hot D. much hot

ANSWERS

1	2	3	4	5	6	7	8	9	10
A	C	A	B	A	C	C	C	A	A
11	**12**	**13**	**14**	**15**	**16**	**17**	**18**	**19**	**20**
B	D	B	D	B	B	C	A	D	C
21	**22**	**23**	**24**	**25**					
C	C	C	A	A					

DETERMINERS

Determiners are actually Adjectives. They are always followed by nouns.

Determiners are of the following kinds:

1. Demonstrative Determiners

this, that, these, those

2. Possessive Determiners

my, our, your, his, her, its, their

3. Quantitative Determiners

some, any, much, enough, sufficient, whole, a little, the little, little, all, both

4. Numerical Determiners

a few, some, few, the few, any, several, many, no, etc.

One, two, three ... (Cardinals)

First, second, third ... (Ordinals)

5. Distributive Determiners

either, neither

6. Articles

Indefinite: a, an

Definite: the

MULTIPLE CHOICE QUESTIONS

Directions: *In the following questions choose the correct options to fill the blanks.*

1. Give me .... rice.
   A. some B. few
   C. a few D. any
2. .... sheep grazing on the slope of the hill had gone away.
   A. Any B. The few
   C. This D. Much
3. Have you got .... magazines to read?
   A. all B. much
   C. some D. little
4. I have .... money that I want to spend on shares.
   A. any B. much
   C. less D. some
5. There is .... owl on the branch of the tree.
   A. a B. the
   C. an D. some
6. My brother is .... MBA.
   A. a B. an
   C. the D. any
7. Have you got .... cheese?
   A. some B. many
   C. a few D. few
8. No, I have not got .... cheese.
   A. many B. few
   C. any D. some
9. There is only .... milk left in the bottle.
   A. enough B. few
   C. much D. a little
10. There is .... hope of his recovery.
    A. any B. little
    C. many D. few
11. .... dogs were barking at the strangers.
    A. Some B. Any
    C. Much D. Less

12. The girl bought her father .... juice.
A. few B. some
C. any D. many

13. You should take .... honey everyday.
A. any B. many
C. a little D. a few

14. .... boy was punished by the teacher.
A. Either B. All
C. Any D. Many

15. .... girl was asked to join the army.
A. None B. Neither
C. All D. Any

16. .... water in the jug has been drunk by Mohan.
A. The little B. The few
C. A few D. Few

17. I shall play .... piano at the party.
A. some B. any
C. the D. few

18. .... labourers were found dead in the mine.
A. Any B. Fewer
C. Many D. Less

19. Could I borrow .... umbrella?
A. our B. your
C. yours D. my.

20. My brother is standing in the .... row.
A. any B. many
C. some D. first

ANSWERS

1	2	3	4	5	6	7	8	9	10
A	B	C	D	C	B	A	C	D	B
11	**12**	**13**	**14**	**15**	**16**	**17**	**18**	**19**	**20**
A	B	C	A	B	A	C	C	B	D

THE VERB

A Verb is a word that tells something about the action or state of or happenning to a person or thing.

A Verb tells the following:

1. What a person or thing does.
Sachin goes to school daily.
The bell *rang* loudly.
Many birds fly in the sky.
She *sang* a song.

2. What a person or thing is.
India *is* the biggest democracy in the world.
Ram Mehar *is* very rich.
They *are* happy.

3. What is done to a person or thing.
You *are liked* by all.
Two thieves *were arrested.*
Four students *were punished* by the teacher.

4. What happens to a person or thing.
His maternal uncle *died* last week.
Two ships *sank* yesterday.
Leaves *turn* yellow in autumn.

5. What a person or thing has, had, and so on.
I *have* a new car.
He *had* a scooter last year.
He *has* several cows and goats.

It goes without saying that a verb is the most important part of a sentence. No sentence is complete without a Verb.

Important Information

1. If two or more singular nouns are joined by 'and' the verb used will be plural.

Example:
(i) He and I were going to the market.
(ii) Ram and Mohan are friends.

2. If two singular nouns joined by 'and' points out to the same thing or person, the verb used must be singular.

Example:
(i) Rice and curry is the favourite food of the Punjabis.
(ii) The Collector and District Magistrate is away.

3. In case two subjects are joined by 'as well as' the verb agrees with the first subject.

Example :
(i) Kanta as well as her children is playing.
(ii) Children as well as their mother are playing.

In the case of first sentence the verb (is) agrees with Kanta and in the case of second sentence the verb (are) agrees with the children.

4. 'Neither', 'Either', 'Every', 'Each', 'Everyone', and 'Many a' are followed by a singular verb.
   Example :
   (i) Either of the plans is to be adopted.
   (ii) Neither of the two brothers is sure to pass.
   (iii) Every student is expected to be obedient.
   (iv) Everyone of them desires this.
   (v) Many a person is drowned in the sea.
5. If two subjects are joined by 'Either .... or' / 'Neither .... nor', the verb agrees with the subject near to it.
   Example :
   (i) Either my brother or I am to do this work.
   (ii) Neither he nor they are prepared to do this work.
6. 'A great many' is always followed by a 'plural noun' and a 'plural verb'. For example :
   A great many students have been declared successful.
7. Similarly if two subjects are joined by 'with', 'together with', 'no less than', in addition to 'and not', etc. the verb agrees with the first subject.
   Example :
   (i) The boy with his parents has arrived.
   (ii) He, no less than I, is to blame.
8. Nouns, plural in form, but singular in meaning, take a singular verb.
   Example :
   This news was broadcast from television yesterday.

MULTIPLE CHOICE QUESTIONS

Directions: *In the following questions choose the correct options to fill the blanks.*

1. The bus with all its passengers .... lost.
A. were B. was
C. are D. would

2. You as well as I .... responsible for this work.
A. am B. are
C. was D. is

3. Raghava like all his companions .... a spoiled child.
A. are B. were
C. is D. will be

4. Pen and ink .... required for me.
A. are B. were
C. is D. has required

5. Every girl and every boy .... attended the seminar.
A. have B. has
C. is D. are

6. Not only she but all her sisters ...... been married.
A. has B. have
C. is D. are

7. There .... nothing but miseries in life.
A. is B. are
C. were D. will be

8. Neither prose nor poem .... given.
A. were B. was
C. has D. have

9. Either he or I .... wrong.
A. is B. are
C. am D. were

10. Either Sulekha or Rekha .... coming here.
A. are B. is
C. were D. have

11. .... the child or his parents to blame?
A. Is B. Are
C. Were D. Has

12. You and I .... neighbours.
A. am B. are
C. was D. has

13. The house with all its belongings ..... sold away.
A. were B. are
C. was D. must

14. Either water or juice .... required.
A. is B. are
C. were D. has

15. There were not as many tables as .... required.
A. was B. were
C. is D. are

16. They each .... a book.
A. have B. are
C. has D. is

17. He and I .... class friends.
A. is B. am
C. was D. are

18. She as well as I .... guilty.
A. is B. are
C. am D. must be

19. Purushottam .... not read more on this chapter.
A. needs B. has been need
C. need D. had been need

20. He came .... to his aunt.
A. run B. running
C. to run D. in run

21. She dislikes .... meat.
A. eat to B. to eat
C. eating D. to eating

22. He likes ....
A. sing to B. singing
C. to sing D. to singing

23. We are ready .... the match.
A. play to B. to playing
C. playing D. to play

24. .... is injurious to health.
A. Smoking B. To smoke
C. To smoking D. Smoke to

25. He loves .... raw vegetables.
A. eaten B. eating
C. to eating D. eat to

26. He seemed .... finished his homework.
A. have to B. to have
C. having D. to having

ANSWERS

1	2	3	4	5	6	7	8	9	10
B	B	C	C	B	B	A	B	C	B
11	**12**	**13**	**14**	**15**	**16**	**17**	**18**	**19**	**20**
A	B	C	A	B	A	D	A	C	B
21	**22**	**23**	**24**	**25**	**26**				
C	B	D	A	B	B				

CONJUNCTIONS

A conjunction is a word which connects words, clauses or sentences.

Look at the following sentences.

(i) He bought apples *and* mangoes.
(ii) God made the country *and* man made the town.
(iii) The door was open *but* there was no one in the house.
(iv) He knows that I am here *and* that I want to see him.

In the sentence (i), *and* connects two words—*apples* and *mangoes.*

In the sentence (ii), *and* connects two sentences—*God made the country* and *man made the town.*

In the sentence (iii), *but* connects two sentences—*The door was open* and *there was no one in the house.*

In the sentence (iv), *and* connects two clauses—*that I am here* and *that I want to see him.*

The main coordinating conjunctions are:

and, but, for, or, nor, also, either ..... or, neither ..... nor.

There are some conjunctions which are used in pairs. They are:

either .... or, ... neither .... nor, both .... and, though .... yet, whether .... or, not only .... but also.

Example: *Either* take it *or* leave it.

It is *neither* useful *nor* ornamental.

They *both* like *and* respect me.

Though he is suffering from high fever, *yet* he does not cry.

He does not care *whether* you go *or* stay.

He is *not only* doltish, *but also* obstinate.

The conjunctions which are used in pairs in this way, are called correlative conjunctions, or merely correlatives.

Use of Important Conjunctions

1. **As soon as :** As soon as denotes simultaneous time.
   Example : As soon as he saw his enemy, he took to his heels.
2. **No sooner .... than :**
   (a) 'No sooner' is always followed by 'than'.
   (b) Please remember that 'No sooner' is always followed by do/does/did. As such only first form of the verb should be used after the subject.
   Example :
   No sooner did he see his enemy than he took to his heels.
3. **Hardly :** Hardly is followed by when.
   Examples :
   (i) Hardly had I left the house when it started raining.
   (ii) We had hardly come into the room when his father began chastising him.
   Note :
   A. Hardly is never followed by than.
   B. 'Scarcely' can also be used in the sense and manner of 'Hardly'.
4. **Lest :** Lest is used in the sense of so that .... not. It is always followed by should. Lest is negative in sense. Hence 'not' should never be used with it.
   Example :
   Work hard lest you should fail.
   Note : 'Lest' is always followed by 'should' and not 'may'.
5. **Unless :** Unless expresses condition. It is also used in the negative sense. Use of 'not' is not allowed with unless because unless is already in the negative sense.
   Example :
   Unless you labour hard you will not pass.
6. **Until :** 'Until' expresses time. It means 'till not'.
   Example :
   Wait here until I return.
   Note : Until is in the negative sense. So 'not' should not be used with it. Example :
   Wait here until I do not return. (Incorrect)
   Wait here until I return. (Correct)
7. **As well as :** When two subjects are joined by 'as well as', the verb always agrees with the first subject.
   Examples :
   (i) The teacher as well as students is playing.
   (ii) Students as well as the teacher are playing.
   Note : 'Both' and 'as well as' cannot be used together in the same sentence.
   Examples :
   Both Sita as well as Kanta are beautiful. (Incorrect)
   Sita as well as Kanta is beautiful. (Correct)
   Both Sita and Kanta are beautiful. (Correct)
8. **As if :** 'As if' is used in the sense of pretension. While using 'as if' in a sentence, we should see that even the third person singular subject gets 'were'.
   Example :
   He talks as if he were mad.
9. **Till :** Till expresses time. Till is always used in the affirmative.
   Example :
   We did not come back till sunset.
10. **Rather than :** 'Rather than' is used in the sense of 'preference'. 'Rather' is always followed by 'than'.
    Example :
    I would rather die than submit.
11. **As long as/so long as :** Both express time during which an action or event takes place.
    Example :
    As long as there is life, there is hope.
12. **However :** It is both a subordinate and co-ordinate clause.
    Examples :
    (a) Mala worked hard, she however, failed.
    (b) However hard he may work, he cannot pass.
13. **Such as :** 'Such as' gives us the sense of 'like'. Such is always followed by 'as'.
    Example :
    Life is such a puzzle as cannot be solved.

MULTIPLE CHOICE QUESTIONS

Directions: *In the following questions choose the correct options to fill the blanks.*

1. Neither he .... his friend is good.
A. or B. and
C. but D. nor

2. The officer asked the peon .... why he was late.
A. that B. if
C. but D. No word needed

3. Both Ajay .... Vijay are intelligent.
A. or B. nor
C. and D. No word needed

4. No Sooner did the thief see the public .... he ran away.
A. then B. and
C. but D. than

5. Abhinav .... his brothers was going to Mumbai.
A. but B. yet
C. No word needed D. together with

6. He behaves .... he were the captain of the team.
A. as if B. as
C. No word needed D. that

7. Either Rupali .... Sonali is going to attend the meeting.
A. and B. but
C. nor D. or

8. Neither Nirmal .... Ashwinee is going to listen the speech.
A. and B. but
C. nor D. or

9. Ravi .... Prakash are going to Kolkata.
A. or B. nor
C. but D. and

10. Rice .... curry is my usual breakfast.
A. and B. but
C. then D. than

11. Hardly had he left .... his brother came.
A. then B. than
C. when D. that

12. I would rather have a copy .... a book.
A. then B. than
C. when D. that

13. He is no other .... my friend.
A. then B. than
C. when D. but

14. He saw a snake ....he awoke.
A. then B. when
C. than D. No word needed

15. Ten years have passed .... my grandmother died.
A. since B. when
C. then D. than

16. She is .... good .... bad.
A. either, not B. neither, or
C. neither, nor D. neither, than

17. The cellphone is both cheap .... best.
A. than B. and
C. then D. or

18. No sooner did the rogue see the police .... he disappeared.
A. then B. than
C. so D. because

19. Srishti will go .... Sanju goes.
A. if B. than
C. then D. although

20. She is wise .... timid.
A. and B. yet
C. but D. however

21. Make hay .... the sun shines.
A. though B. while
C. after D. before

22. He is so weak .... he cannot walk.
A. but B. that
C. then D. so

23. Although he is rich, ... he is unhappy.
A. but B. yet
C. so D. still

24. Wait here .... I come back.
A. till B. until
C. before D. after

25. He is my friend .... I shall help him.
A. so
B. hence
C. that is why
D. therefore

26. He must go away .... he will be beaten.
A. otherwise B. and
C. or D. else

27. God loves good men .... good men love God.
A. and B. or
C. that D. those

28. He was late .... he was not punished.
A. but B. yet
C. still D. therefore

29. Walk slowly ...., you may fall.
A. and B. or
C. so D. otherwise

30. Work hard, ... you will fail.
A. and B. or
C. otherwise D. else

ANSWERS

1	2	3	4	5	6	7	8	9	10
D	D	C	D	D	A	D	C	D	A
11	**12**	**13**	**14**	**15**	**16**	**17**	**18**	**19**	**20**
C	B	B	B	A	C	B	B	A	C
21	**22**	**23**	**24**	**25**	**26**	**27**	**28**	**29**	**30**
B	B	B	A	B	C	A	C	D	D

PREPOSITIONS

A *Preposition* is a word which is placed before a noun or a pronoun to show its relation to some other word in the sentence.

1. I saw a goat *in* the field.
2. I am fond *of* hot coffee.

In sentence 1, the word *in* shows the relation between two things—*goat* and *field.*

In sentence 2, the word *of* shows the relation between the attribute expressed by the adjective *found* and *tea.*

The words *in* and *of* are here used as prepositions.

The noun or pronoun which is used with a preposition is called its object. The noun or pronoun is in the objective case. It is governed by the preposition. Now it is absolutely clear that in sentence 1, the noun *field* is in the objective case. The word *field* is governed by the preposition *in.*

A preposition may have two or more objects.

The road runs over *hill* and *plain.*

Here, the words *hill* and *plain* are used as objects.

Use of Important Prepositions

1. Among, Between

'**Among**' is used for more than two persons or things; '**Between**' is used only for two.

Examples :

(i) Distribute these sweets *among* the poor students of the class.

(ii) Distribute these books *between* Ram and Shyam.

2. Among, In

'**Among**' is used before collective plural nouns. '**In**' is used before collective singular nouns.

Examples :

(i) I found him standing *among* the crowd.

(ii) I saw him in the crowd.

3. Beside, Besides

'**Beside**' means 'by the side of'. '**Besides**' means 'in addition to'.

Examples :

(i) The daughter was sitting *beside* her mother.

(ii) *Besides* his relatives, he invited his friends also.

4. In, Within

'**In**' means at the expiry of a period of time in future, '**Within**' means before the expiry of a period of time in any tense.

Examples :

(i) She will return *in* a week.

(ii) I shall finish my work *within* a weak.

5. On, Upon

'On' is used for things at rest; **'Upon'** is used for things in motion.

Examples :

(i) He is sitting *on* the floor.

(ii) The dog sprang *upon* the table.

6. By, With

'By' denotes the agent or doer, **'With'** denotes the instrument with which anything is done.

Examples :

(i) The bird was killed *by* the hunter with an arrow.

(ii) He beat the dog *with* a stick.

(iii) I shall reach here *by* five o'clock.

7. After, In

'After' means at the end of a period of time in the past. **'In'** means at the end of a period of time in future.

Examples :

(i) I shall return your book *in* a week.

(ii) He returned the book *after* a week.

8. For, From, Since

'For' is used before a noun denoting a period of time with all the tenses. **'From'** is used before a noun or phrase denoting a point of time, it is used in all the tenses. **'Since'** is used before a noun or phrase denoting some point of time and is always produced by a verb in the perfect continuous tense or third form of a verb.

Examples :

(i) We have been playing cards *for* two hours.

(ii) She stayed with her uncle *from* the 15th of March to the 15th of May.

(iii) I have been reading this book *since* morning.

9. Above, Over

'Above' means 'higher from', **Over** is used in the following four senses :

(i) In the sense of 'above' :
At noon, the sun is *over* our heads.

(ii) In the sense of 'beyond' :
I cannot get *over* my disappointment.

(iii) In the sense of 'Superiority' :
God *over* all blesses for ever more.

(iv) In the sense of 'Conclusion' :
It is all *over* with me.

10. At, Towards

'At' denotes the idea of aim, **'Towards'** denotes the idea of destination.

Examples :

(i) He threw the stone *at* the cat.

(ii) He went *towards* the house.

11. At, In, On

'At' is used as follows :

(i) **'At'** is used with small towns and villages.

Examples :

(a) He was born *at* Sonepat.

(b) He lives *at* village Bangra. (Bangra is a village)

(ii) **'At'** is used before a noun denoting a definite point of time.

Example :

He called on me *at* 9 p.m. yesterday.

'In' is used as follows :

(iii) **'In'** is used with the names of big cities, provinces and countries.

Examples :

(a) His father lives *in* England.

(b) His younger brother lives *in* Calcutta.

(iv) **'In'** is used before the names of months and years.

Example :

His elder sister was born *in* 1972 *in* the month of May.

'On' is used with dates and names of days.

Examples :

(a) I joined college *on* the 26th April.

(b) He will leave for Kolkata *on* Wednesday next.

Important Information

1. **'In'** is also used in the following phrases : In the morning; In the evening, In winter, In summer.

2. '**In**' also denotes a place inside anything.
   He travelled *in* a crowded bus.
3. '**At**' is used in the following phrases :
   At home, *At* the station, *At* work, *At* play.

12. Below, Beneath

Below means 'of lower level in position, dignity and expectation' etc. *Beneath* means 'under'.

Examples :

(i) It is *below* my dignity to talk to her.
(ii) They rested *beneath* the shade of a tree.

13. In, Into, To

'**In**' expresses Rest or Motion inside anything. '**Into**' expresses Motion towards the inside of anything or change from one medium to another. '**To**' denotes motion from one place to another.

Examples :

(i) The boys are *in* the room.
(ii) Translate this passage from English *into* Hindi.
(iii) Every morning he goes *to* the temple.

14. Till, By, Of, Off

- 'Till' means upto or not earlier than.
- 'By' means not later than.
- 'Of' shows cause, source, separation, quality, contents, possession, apposition, point of reference, space in time etc.
- 'Off' shows separation at a near distance, and detached condition.

Consider the following examples:

(i) I shall work *till* 5 a.m.
(ii) Madhu died *of* cancer.
(iii) The nib *of* the pen is made *of* gold.
(iv) He presented me a bottle *of* perfume.
(v) Our principal is a man *of* principle.
(vi) He lived in the house *of* his friend.
(vii) *By* this time tomorrow, I'll have finished my job.
(viii) My house is *off* the road.
(ix) The book fell *off* the table.

MULTIPLE CHOICE QUESTIONS

Directions: *Tick the correct preposition for the blank in each of the following sentences.*

1. He applied ...... the manager.
A. for B. to
C. with D. by

2. Trust ...... God and do the right.
A. in B. for
C. to D. with

3. She is worthy ...... a prize.
A. with B. for
C. to D. of

4. Mr. Gomes has no taste ...... music.
A. of B. for
C. with D. to

5. You are hard ...... hearing.
A. at B. of
C. with D. for

6. He is sure ...... his success
A. for B. with
C. on D. of

7. Preeti was warned ...... the danger ahead.
A. for B. at
C. of D. about

8. I am thankful ...... you for a good advice.
A. for B. with
C. to D. of

9. Deepak would not surrender ...... the police.
A. with B. to
C. for D. on

10. The small plant in your lawn is very sensitive ...... touch.
A. on B. with
C. to D. about

11. Divya was sure to succeed ..... the examination.
A. for B. in
C. to D. with

12. Geeta was jealous ...... Ravina's beauty.
A. to B. with
C. for D. of

13. He was ignorant ..... what was happening there.
A. for B. of
C. to D. with

14. Your pen is inferior ...... mine.
A. than B. with
C. from D. to

15. Reenu is no match ...... Meenu.
A. to B. for
C. with D. upon

16. It is necessary ...... you to apply for this job.
A. on B. with
C. for D. to

17. Be loyal ...... your country.
A. for B. to
C. on D. with

18. Mukesh is junior ...... me.
A. than B. to
C. from D. of

19. Deepika was innocent ...... the crime.
A. of B. with
C. from D. to

20. I am desirous.... joining the Indian cricket team.
A. for B. of
C. to D. on

ANSWERS

1	2	3	4	5	6	7	8	9	10
B	A	D	B	B	D	D	D	B	D
11	**12**	**13**	**14**	**15**	**16**	**17**	**18**	**19**	**20**
B	D	B	D	B	D	B	B	A	B

SYNONYMS

A synonym is a word which conveys a meaning similar to the given word.

REMEMBER

Words	*Synonyms*
Add	Increase
Adequate	Enough
Adjust	Adapt
All	Aggregate
Allow	Permit
Abode	Dwelling
Apt	Proper
Assess	Appraise
Accuse	Calumniate
Abashed	Timid
Annoy	Displease
Ample	Enough, Sufficient
Amplify	Increase
Apathetic	Unenthusiastic
Accost	Address
Authentic	True
Adjust	Fit
Approve	Assent, Allow, Accept
Adapt	Conform
Adversary	Opponent, Rival, Competitor
Beat	Whack
Benign	Kind
Breeze	Zephyr
Baffle	Puzzle
Booty	Spoil
Beauty	Charm
Beast	Animal
Bandit	Robber
Blaze	Shine
Bond	Tie
Bend	Twist
Bate	Diminish
Beg	Plead
Barbaric	Wild, Savage
Bashful	Shy, Reserved

Words	*Synonyms*
Begin	Start
Blend	Mix, Mingle
Bizarre	Funny
Below	Under
Bedevil	Confuse
Bemoan	Lament
Babble	Nonsense
Blame	Fault
Behaviour	Demeanour
Call	Accost
Copy	Imitate
Close	Shut
Caress	Love
Camp	Stay
Connect	Attach
Cut	Injure, Curtail
Cling	Stick
Conical	Funny
Convey	Carry
Conspicuous	Prominent
Cheerful	Happy, Pleasant
Curtail	Decrease
Cheerless	Sad, Dejected
Curious	Strange
Circumstance	Factor, Situation, Condition
Competent	Capable
Congruent	Overlapping
Cope	Deal, Endure
Confident	Sure
Complex	Intricate
Cajole	Coax, Flatter
Cunning	Crafty
Delectable	Joyful, Delightful
Devilish	Diabolical
Delicate	Soft
Devil	Fiend
Delay	Postpone
Dislike	Repugnance
Destroy	Ruin

Words	*Synonyms*
Dwell	Live, Dilate
Declare	Pronounce
Drunk	Flushed
Deficient	Lacking
Damn	Condemn, Curse
Decrease	Diminish
Destruction	Devastation
Efficient	Competent
Ethnic	Racial
Enthral	Enslave
Earnest	Serious
Envious	Jealous
Ending	Final
Egg	Incite
Extempore	At once
Extensive	Far-ranging
Extra	Surplus
Existence	Life
Exceed	Overstep
Enormous	Vast
Excessive	Superfluous
Free	Unhindered
Frigid	Cold
Feed	Cater
Fame	Reputation
Frame	Make
First	Initial
Frighten	Terrorise, Intimidate
Fervent	Fervid
Fall	Decline
Feeble	Frail
Fickle	Changeable
Finish	Conclude
Fraud	Deception
Forgiving	Placable
Grow	Develop
Greed	Avidity
Greet	Welcome
Grave	Serious
Group	Constellation

Words	*Synonyms*
Given	Bestowed
Gratitude	Thankfulness
Have	Possess
Hire	Rent
Hit	Strike
Handsome	Beautiful
Hinder	Prevent
Heap	Pile
Hope	Expect
Hard	Harsh
Help	Aid
Hymn	Song
Henpecked	Enslaved
Hoodwink	Mystify, Cheat
Humble	Polite, Urbane, Modest
Harass	Vex, Trouble
Impart	Instil
Intact	Untouched
Instal	Establish
Indict	Impeach
Imitate	Ape
Instigate	Incite
Initiate	Start, Introduce
Inimical	Unfriendly
Insufferable	Intolerable
Impartiality	Justice
Jolly	Merry
Joyful	Delectable
Join	Conjoin
Kind	Benign
Kill	Murder
Kindred	Similar
Kinship	Relationship
Keen	Sharp
Knowledge	Scholarship
Lazy	Slothful
Large	Substantial, Gargantuan
Listless	Careless, Lackadaisical
Lax	Loose
Little	Small
Lifelike	Realistic

Words	*Synonyms*
Lofty	High
Lenient	Soft, Gentle
Lacking	Deficient, Wanting
Lessen	Decrease
Middleclass	Bourgeois
Mitigate	Lessen, Abate
Modesty	Humility, Lowliness
Mix	Mingle, Blend
Mixture	Mingling
Mixed	Assorted
Modify	Decrease
Mean	Imply
Multifarious	Varied
Miscarry	Abort
Note	Notice
Noble	Stately
Native	Indigenous
Needful	Necessary
Notify	Declare
Nervous	Shaky, Tremulous, Timid
Natural	Spontaneous
Near	Close
Normal	Natural
Offend	Displease
Oppress	Persecute, Tyrannize
Opponent	Adversary
Obstruct	Hinder, Check
Offence	Fault
Offender	Villain
Overstep	Exceed
Overlapping	Congruent
Occult	Mystic
Profane	Unholy
Patience	Forbearance
Pornographic	Obscene
Plenitude	Abundance
Prominent	Important
Prodigal	Spender
Procrastinate	Postpone
Promote	Develop, Honour
Persecute	Tyrannise

Words	*Synonyms*
Profess	Claim
Pliant	Flexible
Plebian	Common
Polished	Sophisticated
Quake	Shake
Quit	Leave
Queer	Eccentric
Quell	Suppress
Quantify	Allot
Reply	Answer
Relinquish	Retire
Read	Peruse
Relation	Reference
Render	Do
Remainder	Residuals
Repeat	Reiterate
Repentant	Contrite
Retaliative	Retaliatory
Rumour	Hearsay
Reveal	Divulge
Ritualistic	Ceremonious
Soft	Delicate
Sort	Kind, Choose, Select
Selfish	Egoistic
Sensual	Earthly
Suppress	Quell, Check
Stimulate	Provoke
Tasteless	Insipid
Travel	Journey
True	Authentic, Faithful, Truthful
Turbulence	Turmoil
Tragedy	Calamity
Tasteful	Tasty, Delicious
Touching	Painful
Thankful	Grateful
Tremendous	Great, Huge
Tough	Strong
Terminate	Conclude, End
Theory	Doctrine
Tell	Relate
Tremble	Shake, Shiver
Urge	Spur

Words	*Synonyms*
Unbeaten	Unsubdued
Use	Utilize, Practise
Underhand	Unfair, Undue
Unfair	Unjust
Unravel	Reveal, Divulge
Unimportant	Common
Unconcerned	Apathetic
Unimitated	Inimitable
Unfortunate	Unlucky
Understand	Perceive, Comprehend
Vain	Proud, Haughty, Conceited, Shameless
Vale	Valley, Dale, Dell
Vice	Fault
Virtue	Quality
Veracity	Reality
Value	Price, Prize
Vex	Tease
Vibrate	Quiver, Shake
Violent	Excessive
Vivid	Clear, Lucid
Victory	Triumph
Vulgar	Indecent
Virtuous	Honest
Variegated	Varied, Multifarious
Well	Good
Yell	Cry, Shout
Yonder	There
Yearn	Wish, Desire
Yoke	Slavery
Zest	Earnestness, Enthusiasm
Zealous	Earnest

ANTONYMS

A antonym is a word which conveys a meaning opposite to the given word.

REMEMBER

Words	*Antonyms*
Abhor	Love
Abnormal	Normal
Able	Unable
Acceptable	Unacceptable
Adequate	Inadequate
Amusing	Boring

Words	Antonyms
Angry	Calm
Apex	Bottom
Attract	Repel
Bad	Good
Barren	Fertile
Beautiful	Ugly
Bitter	Sweet
Brave	Cowardly
Brief	Lengthy
Bright	Dull
Calm	Violent
Careful	Careless
Clear	Vague, Cloudy
Cold	Hot
Cruel	Kind
Dear	Cheap
Deep	Shallow
Difficult	Easy
Direct	Indirect
Dishonest	Honest
Disobey	Obey
Encourage	Discourage
Enormous	Tiny
Excellent	Bad
Expensive	Cheap
Eat	Fast
Fair	Unfair
Fake	Authentic
False	True
Famous	Notorious
Fool	Genius
Generous	Miserly
Genius	Fool
Genuine	Unauthentic
Gigantic	Tiny
Glad	Depressed
Good	Bad
Great	Little
Happy	Sad

Words	Antonyms
Hard	Soft
Hate	Love
Honest	Dishonest
Idle	Busy
Immoral	Moral
Include	Exclude
Incorrect	Correct
Intelligent	Unintelligent
Kind	Cruel
Like	Dislike
Long	Short
Lucid	Vague
Major	Minor
Naive	Experienced
Nadir	Apex
Neat	Clumsy
Obedient	Disobedient
Obscure	Clear
Oppose	Support
Optimistic	Pessimistic
Out	In
Patience	Impatience
Peaceful	Belligerent
Pious	Impious
Polite	Impolite
Potent	Impotent
Prominent	Unimportant
Proper	Improper
Pure	Impure
Quick	Slow
Quiet	Disturbance
Real	False, Unreal
Reject	Select, Choose
Reliable	Unreliable
Respect	Disrespect
Right	Wrong
Robust	Feeble, Weak
Sad	Happy

Words	Antonyms
Secret	Open
Sensible	Insensible
Severe	Mild
Sharp	Blunt
Simple	Complex
Sociable	Unsociable
Tall	Short
Tidy	Untidy
Uncanny	Canny
Violent	Calm
Vivid	Vague

Words	Antonyms
Strong	Weak
Big	Small
Easy	Difficult
Fast	Slow
High	Low
Catchy	Unattractive
Ugly	Handsome, Beautiful, Tidy
Tasty	Insipid
Sonorous	Harsh

MULTIPLE CHOICE QUESTIONS

Directions (Qs. 1 to 20): *In the following questions choose the word which best expresses the meaning of the given word.*

1. ABSURD
   A. Foolish B. Simple
   C. Courageous D. Silly
2. ABANDON
   A. Lose B. Profit
   C. Vacate D. Foil
3. CAJOLE
   A. Pause B. Lenient
   C. Blast D. Lure
4. COMBAT
   A. Fight B. Conflict
   C. Shoot D. Quarrel
5. LAMENT
   A. Condone B. Console
   C. Complain D. Contribution
6. DEBACLE
   A. Disgrace B. Defeat
   C. Collapse D. Decline
7. SHIVER
   A. Fear B. Tremble
   C. Shake D. Ache
8. TORTURE
   A. Terror B. Harassment
   C. Torment D. Tranquility
9. LAUDABLE
   A. Lovable B. Commendable
   C. Profitable D. Oblivious
10. FIXED
    A. Sterile B. Static
    C. Stubborn D. Parennial
11. QUEER
    A. Unfamiliar B. Cute
    C. Curious D. Strange
12. SUFFICIENT
    A. Fit B. Proper
    C. Adequate D. Vast
13. GLOSS
    A. Brightness B. Soothing
    C. Rubbing D. Miracle
14. LONGING
    A. Prune B. Apathy
    C. Curtail D. Craving
15. JEER
    A. Applaud B. Magnanimity
    C. Avoid D. Scoff
16. ZENITH
    A. Minimum B. Nadir
    C. Plant D. Peak
17. GARB
    A. Distort B. Dress
    C. Trivial D. Rage

18. ABHOR
A. Rude B. Reconcile
C. Crave D. Detest

19. YIELD
A. Shum B. Incisive
C. Retain D. Surrender

20. YOKE
A. Twist B. Release
C. Link D. Extra

Directions (Qs. 21 to 38): *In the following questions choose the word which best expresses the opposite of the given word.*

21. TRAGIC
A. Dramatic B. Strong
C. Gentle D. Comic

22. ORAL
A. Verbal B. Sane
C. Minor D. Written

23. ADMIRE
A. Hate B. Unlike
C. Dislike D. Enough

24. VIOLENT
A. Gentle B. Savage
C. Haughty D. Decline

25. ADVERSITY
A. Windfall B. Inprosperity
C. Prosperity D. Slave

26. GENUINE
A. Spurious B. Obscure
C. Countless D. Apathetic

27. GRUDGE
A. Essence B. Guile
C. Goodwill D. Ill-will

28. STIFF
A. Soft B. Courteous
C. Lively D. Flexible

29. VANITY
A. Conceit B. Pride
C. Ostentious D. Humility

30. FRONT
A. Upper B. Unusual
C. Back D. Rear

31. ATTRACT
A. Lured B. Longing
C. Repel D. Disguise

32. COMFORT
A. Discomfort B. Discontent
C. Uncomfort D. Miscomfort

33. WELCOME
A. Repel B. Accept
C. Resist D. Fight

34. TACTFUL
A. Naive B. Loose
C. Strict D. Uncivilized

35. DUTIFUL
A. Harmful B. Watchful
C. Forgetful D. Remiss

36. RIGID
A. Flux B. Adoptable
C. Yielding D. Adaptable

37. RARE
A. Petty B. Poor
C. Small D. Common

38. ZEAL
A. Despair B. Calmness
C. Passiveness D. Indifference

ANSWERS

1	2	3	4	5	6	7	8	9	10
D	C	D	A	C	C	B	C	B	B
11	12	13	14	15	16	17	18	19	20
D	C	A	D	D	D	B	D	D	C
21	22	23	24	25	26	27	28	29	30
D	D	C	A	C	A	C	D	D	D
31	32	33	34	35	36	37	38		
C	A	C	A	D	D	D	D		

3. Sentence Completion

It is such an exercise which starts with the primary schools and continues in the highest level of competitive examinations. One must practise it regularly to score well.

Directions (Qs. 1 to 15): *Pick out the most effective word(s) from the given words to fill in the blanks to make the sentence meaningfully complete.*

1. The student ...... that book from the library to study at home.
A. issued B. borrowed
C. hired D. lent

2. I wish I ...... a king.
A. was B. am
C. should be D. were

3. He ...... to listen to my arguments and walked away.
A. denied B. disliked
C. objected D. refused

4. The flow of blood was so ...... that the patient died.
A. intense B. adequate
C. profuse D. extensive

5. When I met her yesterday, it was the first time I ...... her since Christmas.
A. saw B. have seen
C. had seen D. have been seing

6. Can you pay ...... all these articles?
A. for B. of
C. off D. out

7. I ...... you to be at the party this evening.
A. expect B. hope
C. look forward to D. desire

8. ...... being a handicapped person, he is very cooperative and self-reliant.
A. Because B. Although
C. Since D. Despite

9. The child broke ...... from his mother and ran towards the painting.
A. away B. after
C. down D. with

10. With his ...... income, he finds it difficult to live a comfortable life.
A. brief B. sufficient
C. meagre D. huge

11. He could ...... a lot of money in such a short time by using his intelligence and working hard.
A. spend B. spoil
C. exchange D. accumulate

12. Though the brothers are twins; they look ......
A. alike B. handsome
C. indifferent D. different

13. Unfavourable weather conditions can ...... illness.
A. cure B. detect
C. treat D. enhance

14. No sooner did the bell ring, ... the actor started singing.
A. when B. than
C. after D. before

15. If I ...... realised it, I would not have acted on his advice.
A. was B. had
C. were D. have

Directions (Qs. 16 to 25): *In each question, an incomplete statement (Stem) followed by four fillers* *is given. Pi·k out the best one which can complete the incomplete stem correctly and meaningfully.*

16. Unless you work harder you will fail, means .....
A. if you fail you will work harder.
B. you must at least plan well than you will not fail.
C. hardly you will fail if you do not desire so.
D. if you do not put more efforts, then you will fail.

17. Even if it rains I shall come, means .....
A. if I come it will not rain.
B. if it rains I shall not come.
C. I will certainly come whether it rains or not.
D. whenever there is rain I shall come.

18. Dinesh is as stupid as he is lazy means .....
A. Dinesh is stupid because he is lazy.
B. Dinesh is lazy because he is stupid.
C. Dinesh is either stupid or lazy.
D. Dinesh is equally stupid and lazy.

19. He is so lazy that he .....
A. cannot depend on others for getting his work done.
B. cannot delay the schedule of completing the work.
C. can seldom complete his work on time.
D. dislike to postpone the work that he undertakes to do.

20. He always stammers in public meetings, but his today's speech .....
A. was fairly audible to everyone present in the hall.
B. was not received satisfactorily.
C. could not be understood properly.
D. was free from that defect.

21. In order to raise the company's profit, the employees .....
A. demanded two additional increments.
B. decided to go on paid holidays.
C. requested the management to implement new welfare schemes.
D. offered to work overtime without any compensation.

22. Although, he is reputed for making very candid statements, ...
A. his today's speech was not fairly audible.
B. his promises had always been realistic.
C. his speech was very interesting.
D. his today's statements were very ambiguous.

23. I felt somewhat more relaxed .....
A. but tense as compared to earlier.
B. and tense as compared to earlier.
C. as there was already no tension at all.
D. and tension-free as compared to earlier.

24. With great efforts his son succeeded in convincing him not to donate his entire wealth to an orphanage .....
A. and lead the life of a wealthy merchant.
B. but to a home for the forsaken children.
C. and make an orphan of himself.
D. as the orphanage needed a lot of donations.

25. Even though it is a very large house, ...
A. there is a lot of space available in it for children.
B. there is hardly any space available for children.
C. there is no dearth of space for children.
D. the servants take a long time to clean it.

ANSWERS

1	2	3	4	5	6	7	8	9	10
B	D	D	C	C	A	A	D	A	C
11	**12**	**13**	**14**	**15**	**16**	**17**	**18**	**19**	**20**
D	D	D	B	B	D	C	D	C	D
21	**22**	**23**	**24**	**25**					
D	D	D	C	B					

4. Spotting Errors

The most common errors in English are of spellings, grammar and usage of words. By regular practice, the errors can be easily spotted and minimised.

MULTIPLE CHOICE QUESTIONS

Directions: *In the following questions some of the sentences have errors and some are correct. Find out which part of a sentence has an error, the number of that part is your answer. If a sentence is free from errors, then your answer is D i.e., No error.*

1. (A) Either Ram or/(B) you is responsible/(C) for this action./(D) No error.

2. (A) The student flatly denied/(B) that he had copied/(C) in the examination hall./(D) No error.

3. (A) By the time you arrive tomorrow/(B) I have finished/(C) my work./(D) No error.

4. (A) The captain with the members of his team/ (B) are returning/(C) after a fortnight./(D) No error.

5. (A) After returning from/(B) an all-India tour/ (C) I had to describe about it./(D) No error.

6. (A) The teacher asked his students/(B) if they had gone through/(C) either of the three chapters included in the prescribed text./(D) No error.

7. (A) Do you know/(B) how old were you/(C) when you came here?/(D) No error.

8. (A) Beware of/(B) a fair-weather friend/(C) who is neither a friend in need nor a friend indeed./ (D) No error.

9. (A) Copernicus proved/(B) that Earth/(C) moves round the Sun./(D) No error.

10. (A) The property/(B) was divided/(C) among the two brothers./(D) No error.

11. (A) I am quite certain/(B) that the lady is not only greedy/(C) but miserly./(D) No error.

12. (A) The brilliant success in the examination/ (B) as well as his record in sports/(C) deserves high praise./(D) No error.

13. (A) I cannot find/(B) where has he gone/(C) though I have tried may best./(D) No error.

14. (A) If I was/(B) the Prime Minister of India/(C) I would work wonders/(D) No error.

15. (A) If it weren't/(B) for you,/(C) I wouldn't be alive today./(D) No error.

16. (A) He looked like a lion/(B) baulked from/ (C) its prey./(D) No error.

17. (A) Widespread flooding/(B) is affecting/(C) large areas of the villages./(D) No error.

18. (A) If we really set to/(B) we can get the whole house/(C) cleaned in an afternoon./(D) No error.

19. (A) It's arrogant for you/(B) to assume you'll/ (C)win every time./(D) No error.

20. (A) The two books are the same/(B) except for the fact that this/(C) has an answer in the back./(D) No error.

21. (A) Your husband doesn't/(B) believe that you are older/(C) than I./(D) No error.

22. (A) I could not/(B) answer to/(C) the question./(D) No error.

23. (A) Two years passed/(B) since/(C) my cousin died./(D) No error.

24. (A) I am learning English/(B) for ten years/(C) without much effect./(D) No error.

25. (A) Ramesh has agreed/(B) to marry with the girl/(C) of his parent's choice./ (D) No error.

26. (A) When he was arriving./(B) the party was/(C) in full swing./(D) No error.

27. (A) The most studious boy/(B) in the class/(C) was made as the captain./(D) No error.

28. (A) I am participating/(B) in the two-miles race/(C) tomorrow morning./(D) No error.

29. (A) When the boy committed a mistake/(B) the teacher made him to do/(C) the sum again./(D) No error.

30. (A) Whenever a person lost anything/(B) the poor folk around/(C) are suspected./(D) No error.

ANSWERS

1	2	3	4	5	6	7	8	9	10
B	D	B	B	C	C	D	D	B	C
11	**12**	**13**	**14**	**15**	**16**	**17**	**18**	**19**	**20**
C	D	B	A	C	C	C	A	A	C
21	**22**	**23**	**24**	**25**	**26**	**27**	**28**	**29**	**30**
C	B	A	A	B	A	C	B	B	A

EXPLANATORY ANSWERS

1. Replace 'is' by 'are'.
2. No error.
3. Replace 'have' by 'would have'.
4. Replace 'are' by 'is'.
5. Replace 'had to describe' by 'described'.
6. Replace 'either' by 'any'.
7. No error.
8. No error.
9. Omit 'that'.
10. Replace 'among' by 'between'.
11. Add 'also'.
12. No error.
13. Replace 'has he' by 'he has'.
14. Replace 'was' by 'were'.
15. Replace 'wouldn't be' by 'would not have been'.
16. Replace 'its' by 'his'.
17. Replace 'areas' by 'area'.
18. Replace 'set to' by 'set on'.
19. Replace 'for' by 'of'.
20. Replace 'in' by 'on'.
21. Replace 'I' by 'me'.
22. Omit 'to'.
23. Replace 'passed' by 'have passed'.
24. Replace 'am' by 'have been'.
25. Omit 'with'.
26. Replace 'was arriving' by 'arrived'.
27. Omit 'as'.
28. Replace 'in' by 'at'.
29. Omit 'to'.
30. Replace 'lost' by 'loses'.

5. One Word Substitution

There are many single words in English language which can be perfectly used for a number of words. These words help in expressing ideas in a short and correct manner for the right occasion. Such words not only increase the vocabulary but also enable you to economise in the use of words to a great extent.

Multiple Word Expression	*Substitution*
One who always looks towards the bright side of things	Optimist
One who always looks towards the dark side of things	Pessimist
The time when one develops from a child into an adult	Adolescence
The process of growing more plants in order to form a forest.	Afforestation
The science which deals with farming	Agriculture
From some other country or place etc.	Alien
A term, etc. giving more than one meaning	Ambiguous
A vehicle which is used to carry sick persons	Ambulance
An animal which can live both in water and on land	Amphibian
A lawless situation when there is no government	Anarchy
Belonging to the history of thousands of years old	Ancient
Once a year	Annual
A very old object but still valuable	Antique
Words of opposite meanings	Antonyms
Words of similar meanings	Synonyms
Signatures of a famous person	Autograph
A government led by one person with absolute authority	Autocracy
A written work of one's own life history	Autobiography
A person who has never been married	Bachelor
A person usually having no hair on his head	Bald
A place where one can deposit money and get interest	Bank
A person who cuts our hair	Barber
A building/group of buildings where soldiers live	Barracks
A person who makes buns and biscuits	Baker
A person who lives by asking people for food and money without doing any useful job	Beggar
The crime of having married to two persons at the same time	Bigamy
The branch of science which deals with the study of plants	Botany
Able to speak two languages	Bilingual

Multiple Word Expression	*Substitution*
Able to speak more than two languages	Polyglot
The branch of science which deals with the living organisms	Biology
A powerful snow storm	Blizzard
A great successful book or movie	Blockbuster
A short news on the radio or TV	Bulletin
A system in which the most important works are organised by the government officials	Bureaucracy
A person who has no vision in his eyes	Blind
A page or a series of pages on which the information of days, weeks, months, etc. is given	Calendar
A person who eats human flesh	Cannibal
A complete list of items often arranged alphabetically	Catalogue
A sudden disaster	Catastrophe
A period of 100 years	Century
A branch of science which deals with chemicals	Chemistry
A printed leaf usually issued by banks that we sign to carry certain financial deal	Cheque
A person who makes or mends shoes	Cobbler
A group of people who has been chosen by others to make decisions on their own	Committee
A building in which nuns live	Convent
An animal which feeds on other animals	Carnivorous
A person who does criticism	Critic
A person who cannot hear	Deaf
A condition in which one loses a lot of water from one's body because of vomiting, etc.	Dehydration
A system of government in which the people cast their votes to elect their leaders	Democracy
The study of skin problems	Dermatology
A long piece of land covered with sand	Desert
The art of managing relationships between countries	Diplomacy
A piece of information about the words in a book form	Dictionary
A piece of information about the telephone numbers of the people in a book from	Directory
A person in charge of a newspapers, magazine etc.	Editor
A person who thinks he is better than the others	Egoist
To leave your country and settle in some other country	Emigrate
A book or series of books giving almost all knowledge about an area or some persons etc.	Encyclopaedia
Study of insects	Entomology
Time when day and night are of the same duration	Equinox
To sell things out of the country	Export
To purchase things from some other country	Import
A plant or animal no longer in existence	Extinct
A situation when there is a shortage of food for a long period of time	Famine
An amount of money that we pay for some action or services	Fee
Related to women	Feminine
An animal strong and aggressive	Ferocious

Multiple Word Expression	*Substitution*
A piece of land where plants grow easily from the soil that is favourable to them	Fertile
A work of literature having some imaginary events	Fiction
A large amount of water covering certain area	Flood
A person who sells flowers	Florist
A religious ceremony for burying or cremating a dead person	Funeral
A substance which kills fungus	Fungicide
A person studying or having studied the diseases and the related things of female reproductory system	Gynaecologist
The murder of the person of the same group race or country	Genocide
A substance which kills germs	Germicide
A situation in which many people die because of fire during war	Holocaust
The act of killing a person deliberately	Homicide
A word having the pronunciation as the other one does but it differs in meaning	Homophone
A word having the same spelling as the other one does but it is pronounced in some other way	Homonym
A person who is attracted towards the person of the same sex	Homosexual
Go across and parallel to the ground	Horizontal
A substance which kills the insects	Insecticide
That cannot be corrected	Incorrigible
That cannot be defeated	Invincible
That cannot be eaten	Inedible
That cannot be seen	Invisible
A place in a school or college where books are kept for the benefit of students, teachers etc.	Library
A place in a school or college where scientific experiments are performed	Laboratory
An official who is a judge in the lowest court	Magistrate
A piece of music or a book before it is printed	Manuscript
Related to men	Masculine
One who believes in the existence of God	A theist
One who does not believe in the existence of good	An atheist
That can be believed	Credible
That cannot be believed	Incredible
That which dissolves in a solvent	Soluble
That which does not dissolves in a solvent	Insoluble
Hard writing that can be read	Legible
Hard writing that cannot be read	Illegible
A person who does jobs beneficial to mankind	Philanthropist
A person who goes on foot	Pedestrian
A person who fights for his own country	Patriot
An act of killing oneself	Suicide
A woman whose husband is dead	Widow
A man whose wife is dead	Widower
A person who eats vegetarian and non-vegetarian diets	Omnivorous

Multiple Word Expression	*Substitution*
Something which is everywhere at the same time	Omnipresent
One who knows everything	Omniscient
A child who does not have parents	Orphan
An award etc. given after the death of the person	Posthumous
The place where animals are kept for amusement and to increase the knowledge of the public	Zoo
The science which deals with the study of animals	Zoology

MULTIPLE CHOICE QUESTIONS

Directions: *In questions given below, out of the four alternatives, choose the one which can be substituted for the given words/sentences.*

1. Something that relates to everyone in the world
A. General B. Common
C. Usual D. Universal

2. An expression of mild disapproval
A. Warning B. Denigration
C. Impertinence D. Reproof

3. One who is not easily pleased by anything
A. Maiden B. Medieval
C. Precarious D. Fastidious

4. Murder of a king
A. Infanticide B. Matricide
C. Genocide D. Regicide

5. A remedy for all diseases
A. Stoic B. Marvel
C. Panacea D. Recompense

6. A dramatic performance
A. Mask B. Mosque
C. Masque D. Mascot

7. Study of birds
A. Orology B. Optology
C. Ophthalmology D. Ornithology

8. Ready to believe
A. Credulous B. Credible
C. Creditable D. Incredible

9. Incapable of being seen through
A. Ductile B. Opaque
C. Obsolete D. Potable

10. One who eats everything
A. Omnivorous B. Omniscient
C. Irresistible D. Insolvent

11. A place where bees are kept is called
A. An apiary B. A mole
C. A hive D. A sanctuary

12. One who cannot be corrected
A. Incurable B. Incorrigible
C. Hardened D. Invulnerable

13. One who is in charge of a museum
A. Curator B. Supervisor
C. Caretaker D. Warden

14. Continuing fight between parties, families, clans, etc.
A. Enmity B. Feud
C. Quarrel D. Skirmish

15. A voice loud enough to be heard
A. Audible B. Applaudable
C. Laudable D. Oral

16. A paper written by hand
A. Handicraft B. Manuscript
C. Handiwork D. Thesis

17. Habitually silent or talking little
A. Serville B. Unequivocal
C. Taciturn D. Synoptic

18. To slap with a flat object
A. Chop B. Hew
C. Gnaw D. Swat

19. A person who speaks many languages
A. Linguist B. Monolingual
C. Polyglot D. Bilingual

20. A light sailing-boat built specially for racing
A. Canoe B. Yacht
C. Frigate D. Dinghy

21. A fixed orbit in space in relation to earth
A. Geological B. Geo-synchronous
C. Geo-centric D. Geo-stationary

22. A style in which a writer makes a display of his knowledge
A. Pedantic B. Verbose
C. Pompous D. Ornate

23. A religious discourse
A. Preach B. Stanza
C. Sanctorum D. Sermon

24. A place that provides refuge
A. Asylum B. Sanatorium
C. Shelter D. Orphanage

25. Detailed plan of a journey
A. Travelogue B. Travelkit
C. Schedule D. Itinerary

26. A person who insists on something
A. Disciplinarian B. Stickler
C. Instantaneous D. Boaster

27. A drawing on transparent paper
A. Red print B. Blue print
C. Negative D. Transparency

28. One who believes that all things and events in life are predetermined is a
A. Fatalist B. Puritan
C. Egoist D. Tyrant

29. A school boy who cuts classes frequently is a
A. Defeatist B. Sycophant
C. Truant D. Martinet

30. The act of violating the sanctity of the church is
A. Blasphemy B. Heresy
C. Sacrilege D. Desecration

31. A place where monks live as a secluded community
A. Cathedral B. Diocese
C. Convent D. Monastery

32. One who is fond of fighting
A. Bellicose B. Aggressive
C. Belligerent D. Militant

33. Tending to move away from the centre or axis
A. Centrifugal B. Centripetal
C. Axiomatic D. Awry

34. Words inscribed on tomb
A. Epitome B. Epistle
C. Epilogue D. Epitaph

35. Leave or remove from a place considered dangerous
A. Evade B. Evacuate
C. Avoid D. Exterminate

36. Original inhabitants of a country
A. Abroge B. Aborger
C. Aborgory D. Aborigins

37. Government by the officials
A. Theocracy B. Plutocracy
C. Bureaucracy D. Democracy

38. Incapable of being exhausted
A. Inexhaustible B. Inaexhaustible
C. Exhaustable D. Non-tired

39. A person of good understanding, knowledge and reasoning power
A. Expert B. Intellectual
C. Snob D. Literate

40. One absorbed in his own thoughts and feelings rather than in things outside
A. Scholar B. Recluse
C. Introvert D. Intellectual

ANSWERS

1	2	3	4	5	6	7	8	9	10
D	D	D	D	C	C	D	A	B	A
11	12	13	14	15	16	17	18	19	20
A	B	A	B	A	B	C	D	A	B
21	22	23	24	25	26	27	28	29	30
D	A	D	A	D	B	D	A	C	C
31	32	33	34	35	36	37	38	39	40
D	A	A	D	B	B	C	A	B	C

6. Spelling Errors

There are thousands of words in English language. It is difficult to remember the spellings and meanings of all at once. Try to learn as many as you can. Use a dictionary regularly.

Directions: *Find the correctly spelt words.*

1. A. Damage B. Dammage C. Damaige D. Dammege
2. A. Efficiant B. Effecient C. Efficient D. Eficient
3. A. Schedule B. Schdule C. Schedale D. Schedeule
4. A. Occurad B. Occurred C. Ocurred D. Occured
5. A. Grieff B. Grief C. Grieef D. Grrief
6. A. Guarantee B. Garuntee C. Guaruntee D. Gaurantee
7. A. Meddicine B. Medicine C. Medicene D. Medicinne
8. A. Benefeted B. Benefitted C. Benifited D. Benefited
9. A. Acommodation B. Acomodation C. Accomodation D. Accommodation
10. A. Querrelsome B. Quarrelsame C. Quarrelsome D. Querralsome
11. A. Sympathetic B. Smypathetic C. Sympothetic D. Sympethetic
12. A. Prograssive B. Progressive C. Progresive D. Prograsive
13. A. Uncivilized B. Uncevilized C. Uncivillized D. Uncevelized
14. A. Extravagant B. Extreragent C. Extreregant D. Extravegent
15. A. Missunderstood B. Miesunderstood C. Misunderstood D. Misunderstod
16. A. Belligerent B. Beligirent C. Belligarant D. Belligerrent
17. A. Astonished B. Astronished C. Astoneshed D. Asstonished
18. A. Sincerely B. Sencerely C. Sincerelly D. Sincerrely
19. A. Rigourous B. Rigerous C. Rigorous D. Regerous
20. A. Satellite B. Sattellite C. Satelite D. Sattelite
21. A. Pesanger B. Passenger C. Pessenger D. Pasanger
22. A. Humurous B. Humorous C. Humoreus D. Humorrous
23. A. Exeggerate B. Exaggerate C. Exadgerate D. Exagerate
24. A. Fariegn B. Forein C. Foriegn D. Foreign
25. A. Excesive B. Excessive C. Exccessive D. Exccesive
26. A. Forcaust B. Forcast C. Forecast D. Forecaste
27. A. Paralleted B. Paralelled C. Parralleled D. Parallelled

28. A. Ocasion B. Occassion
C. Occasion D. Ocassion

29. A. Boquet B. Bouquet
C. Bouquéte D. Bouquette

30. A. Chettering B. Chaterring
C. Chattering D. Chatering

31. A. Discourage B. Disscourage
C. Discourege D. Discaurage

32. A. Curageous B. Courageous
C. Courrageous D. Couregeous

33. A. Abandon B. Abanddon
C. Abendon D. Abbandon

34. A. Embarassment
B. Emberrassement
C. Embarrassment
D. Embbaresment

35. A. Eccintric B. Eccentrie
C. Eccentric D. Eccintrie

36. A. Occasional B. Occassional
C. Occesional D. Occessional

37. A. Querrel B. Querral
C. Quarrel D. Quarel

38. A. Contrebution B. Contribution
C. Contributtion D. Conterbution

39. A. Desgrace B. Disgrece
C. Disgrice D. Disgrace

40. A. Harassment B. Herassment
C. Harasment D. Harassmient

41. A. Imaginative B. Imeginative
C. Imagenative D. Imaginetive

42. A. Suficient B. Suficiant
C. Sufficient D. Sufficiant

43. A. Adequate B. Edequate
C. Adaquete D. Edaquete

44. A. Exparienced B. Experianced
C. Experienced D. Experrienced

45. A. Flatering B. Fletering
C. Flattering D. Fletaring

46. A. Cuttiveted B. Culltrivated
C. Cultivated D. Caltivated

47. A. Praiceworthy B. Peiseworthy
C. Praiseworthy D. Praisaworthy

48. A. Profesional B. Professionel
C. Professional D. Profissional

49. A. Ameteur B. Amateur
C. Amataur D. Amateor

50. A. Unfevourable B. Unfevaurable
C. Unfavourable D. Unfivourable

ANSWERS

1	2	3	4	5	6	7	8	9	10
A	C	A	B	B	A	B	B	D	C
11	**12**	**13**	**14**	**15**	**16**	**17**	**18**	**19**	**20**
A	B	A	A	C	A	A	A	C	A
21	**22**	**23**	**24**	**25**	**26**	**27**	**28**	**29**	**30**
B	B	B	D	B	C	A	C	B	C
31	**32**	**33**	**34**	**35**	**36**	**37**	**38**	**39**	**40**
A	B	A	C	C	A	C	B	D	A
41	**42**	**43**	**44**	**45**	**46**	**47**	**48**	**49**	**50**
A	C	A	C	A	C	C	C	B	C

ARITHMETICAL AND NUMERICAL ABILITY

NUMBER SYSTEM

1. There are four numbers A, B, C and D. Average of the first three i.e., A, B and C is 15 and that of B, C and D is 16. If the last number, i.e., D is 19, then the first number is—

A. 15 B. 16
C. 17 D. 18

2. Of the three numbers, the first is twice the second and thrice the third. If the average of three is 22, the three numbers are—

A. 12, 18, 36 B. 18, 12, 36
C. 36, 12, 18 D. 36, 18, 12

3. If a person is standing on the sixth number in the queue from both the ends, the total persons in the queue are—

A. 9 B. 11
C. 12 D. 13

4. A number 'x' when multiplied by 5 and added to three times its own gives 64, the number is—

A. 8 B. 12
C. 14 D. 18

5. A number which when multiplied by 11 is as much above 180 as it was originally below it. The number is—

A. 25 B. 30
C. 40 D. 45

6. The sum of a number and its reciprocal is thrice the difference of the number and its reciprocal. Find the number.

A. $\sqrt{2}$ B. $\sqrt{3}$
C. $\sqrt{5}$ D. $\sqrt{7}$

7. A boy was asked to find $\frac{7}{9}$ of a fraction. He made a mistake of dividing the fraction by $\frac{7}{9}$ and so got an answer which exceeded the correct answer by $\frac{8}{21}$. Find the correct answer.

A. $\frac{2}{3}$ B. $\frac{5}{7}$
C. $\frac{7}{12}$ D. $\frac{7}{15}$

8. There are 408 boys and 312 girls in a school, which are to be divided into equal sections of either boys or girls alone. Find the maximum number of boys or girls that can be placed in a section. Also find the total number of sections thus formed.

A. 10, 20 B. 24, 30
C. 24, 40 D. 30, 30

9. The sum of all possible two-digit number formed from three different one-digit natural numbers, when divided by the sum of the original three numbers is equal to—

A. 11 B. 18
C. 22 D. 36

10. There are four prime numbers written in ascending order. The product of the first three is 385 and that of the last three is 1001. The last number is—

A. 19 B. 17
C. 13 D. 11

11. If the number 357 ★ 25 ★ is divisible by both 3 and 5, then the missing digits in the unit's place and thousandth place respectively are—

A. 0, 4 B. 5, 4
C. 5, 6 D. 0, 6

12. The difference between two numbers is 1365. When the larger number is divided by the smaller one, the quotient is 6 and the remainder is 15. The smaller number is:

A. 360 B. 295
C. 270 D. 240

13. When a number is divided by 31, the remainder is 29. When the same number is divided by 16, what will be the remainder?
A. 15 B. 13
C. 11 D. Data inadequate

14. In dividing a number by 585, a student applied the method of short division. He divided the number successively by 5, 9 and 13 (factor of 585) and got the remainders 4, 8 and 12. If he had divided the number by 585, the remainder would have been:
A. 584 B. 292
C. 144 D. 24

15. When a number divided by 6 leaves a remainder 3. When the square of the same number is divided by 6, the remainder is:
A. 3 B. 2
C. 1 D. zero

ANSWERS

1	2	3	4	5	6	7	8	9	10
B	D	B	A	B	A	C	B	C	C
11	**12**	**13**	**14**	**15**					
C	C	D	A	A					

SOME SELECTED EXPLANATORY ANSWERS

1. $\frac{A+B+C}{3} = 15,$

or, $A + B + C = 15 \times 3 = 45$ ... (*i*)

$\frac{B+C+D}{3} = 16,$

or $B + C + D = 48$ ... (*ii*)

$D = 19$

$\therefore B + C + 19 = 48$

or, $B + C = 48 - 19 = 29$

But, $A + B + C = 45$

Putting the value of $B + C = 29$ in the above equation (*i*), we get $A + 29 = 45$

$\therefore A = 45 - 29 = 16.$

2. Let the third number $= x$

$\therefore$ First number $= 3x$

Second number $= \frac{3x}{2}$

$\therefore \frac{1}{3}\left[x+3x+\frac{3x}{2}\right] = 22 \Rightarrow \frac{11}{2}x = 66$

$\Rightarrow x = \frac{66\times 2}{11} = 12 =$ Third number,

$12 \times 3 = 36 =$ First number,

$\frac{12\times 3}{2} = 18 =$ Second number.

3. If the person is standing at sixth number in the queue from both sides, that means there are five persons ahead and five persons behind him. Hence, total number of persons in the queue is $5 + 1 + 5 = 11$.

4. $5 \times x + 3x = 64 \Rightarrow 8x = 64$

$\therefore x = \frac{64}{8} = 8.$

5. Let the number is x

$\therefore 180 - x = 11x - 180$

$\Rightarrow 180 + 180 = 11x + x$

$\Rightarrow 360 = 12x,$

$\Rightarrow x = \frac{360}{12} = 30.$

6. Let the no. $= x$ then its reciprocal $= \frac{1}{x}$

By the question, $\left(x+\frac{1}{x}\right) = 3\left(x-\frac{1}{x}\right)$

$$\Rightarrow \quad \frac{x^2+1}{x} = \frac{3(x^2-1)}{x}$$

$$\Rightarrow \quad x^2 + 1 = 3x^2 - 3$$

$$\Rightarrow \quad 3x^2 - x^2 = 3 + 1$$

$$\therefore \quad x = \sqrt{2}.$$

7. Let the required fraction = x

then, by the question $x \div \frac{7}{9} - x \times \frac{7}{9} = \frac{8}{21}$

$$\Rightarrow \quad x \times \frac{9}{7} - \frac{7x}{9} = \frac{8}{21}$$

$$\Rightarrow \quad \frac{32x}{63} = \frac{8}{21}$$

$$\Rightarrow \quad x = \frac{8}{21} \times \frac{63}{32} = \frac{3}{4}$$

Hence, the correct answer = $\frac{3}{4} \times \frac{7}{9} = \frac{7}{12}$.

8.
```
312) 408(1
     312
     ---
      96) 312 (3
          288
          ---
           24) 96 (4
               96
               --
                ×
```

$\therefore$ Maximum number of girls or boys that can be placed in a section = 24 and total number of such section = $\frac{408}{24} + \frac{312}{24}$

$$= 17 + 13 = 30$$

9. Let three different one digit natural numbers be x, y and z.

Then, sum of all possible two digits numbers

$= (10x + y) + (10y + x) + (10x + z) + (10z + x) + (10y + z) + (10z + y)$

$= 22x + 22y + 22z = 22 (x + y + z)$

Hence, required number = 22.

10. Let four prime numbers be a, b, c and d respectively.

Now, $\frac{abc}{bcd} = \frac{385}{1001} \quad \Rightarrow \frac{c}{d} = \frac{5}{13}$

Hence, $a = 5$ and $d = 13$

11. 357 ★ 25 ★

For divisible by 5, the last digit must be either 0 or 5.

If last digit is 0, then other required digit will be 2 or 5 or 8

Hence, the numbers are (0, 2) or (0, 5) or (0, 8)

If last digit is 5, then other required digit will be 0 or 3 or 6 or 9

Hence, the numbers are (5, 0) or (5, 3) or (5, 6) or (5, 9)

So, correct option is (c).

12. Here, $(x + 1365) = 6x + 15$

$\Rightarrow 5x = 1350$

$\therefore x = \frac{1350}{5} = 270$

Hence, the smaller number = 270.

13. The number = $31x + 29$.

Here, given data is inadequate.

14.

5	a
9	$b - 4$
13	$c - 8$
	$1 - 12$

Now, $c = 13 \times 1 + 12 = 25$

$b = 9c + 8 = 9 \times 25 + 8 = 233$

$a = 5b + 4 = 5 \times 233 + 4$

$= 1165 + 4 = 1169$

$1169 = 585 \times 1 + 584$

Hence, required remainder = 584.

15. The number = $6x + 3$

Now, $(6x + 3)^2 = 36x^2 + 36x + 9$

$= (36x^2 + 36x + 6) + 3$

$= 6(6x^2 + 6x + 1) + 3$

Hence, required remainder = 3.

LCM AND HCF

1. The L.C.M. and H.C.F. of two numbers are 4284 and 32 respectively. If one of the numbers is 204, the other is
   A. 672 B. 576
   C. 676 D. 572
2. Two numbers are in the ratio of 8 : 15. If their H.C.F. is 4, the numbers are
   A. 32 and 60 B. 16 and 30
   C. 80 and 150 D. 64 and 120
3. The greatest number that will divide 366, 513 and 324 leaving the same remainder in each case is
   A. 21 B. 18
   C. 27 D. 42
4. The L.C.M. of two numbers is 45 times their H.C.F. If the sum of the L.C.M. and the H.C.F. of these two numbers is 1150 and one of the numbers is 125, then the other number is
   A. 256 B. 225
   C. 250 D. 255
5. The H.C.F. and the L.C.M. of two numbers are 50 and 250 respectively. On dividing one of these numbers by 2, 50 is obtained as quotient. The numbrs are
   A. 100, 125 B. 80, 100
   C. 125, 100 D. 200, 250
6. Three bells ring respectively at an interval of 15 seconds, 20 seconds and 24 seconds. If they ring continuously for 12 minutes then how many times, during this period, will they ring together?
   A. 2 times B. 6 times
   C. 5 times D. 3 times
7. If the sum of two numbers is 55 and the H.C.F. and L.C.M. of these numbers are 5 and 120 respectively. Find the sum of their reciprocals.
   A. $\frac{120}{11}$ B. $\frac{11}{120}$
   C. $\frac{601}{55}$ D. $\frac{55}{601}$
8. The LCM of two numbers is 48. The numbers are in the ratio of 2 : 3. The sum of the numbers is
   A. 64 B. 40
   C. 32 D. 28
9. Find the greatest number that will divide 43, 91 and 183 so as to leave the same remainder in each case.
   A. 13 B. 9
   C. 7 D. 4
10. The greatest possible length which can be used to measure exactly the length 7m, 3m 85cm, 12m 95 cm is
    A. 42 cm B. 35 cm
    C. 25 cm D. 15 cm
11. A, B and C start at the same time in the same direction to run around a circular park. A completes a round in 252 seconds, B in 308 seconds and C in 198 seconds, all starting at the same point, After what time will they meet again at the starting point?
    A. 46 minutes 12 seconds
    B. 45 minutes
    C. 42 minutes 36 seconds
    D. 26 minutes 18 seconds

12. Which of the following has most numbers of divisors?

A. 182 B. 176

C. 101 D. 99

13. Which is of the following is a co-primes?

A. (23, 92) B. (21, 35)

C. (18, 25) D. (16, 62)

14. Let N be the greatest number that will divide 1305, 4665 and 6905, leaving the same remainder in each case. Then find the sum of the digits in N.

A. 8 B. 6

C. 5 D. 4

15. The greatest number which one dividing 1657 and 2037 leaves remainder 6 and 5 respectively, is:

A. 305 B. 235

C. 127 D. 123

ANSWERS

1	2	3	4	5	6	7	8	9	10
A	A	A	B	A	B	B	B	D	B
11	**12**	**13**	**14**	**15**					
A	B	C	D	C					

SOME SELECTED EXPLANATORY ANSWERS

1. 1st number × 2nd number = LCM × HCF

$\therefore$ 204 × 2nd number = 4284 × 32

$\therefore$ 2nd number $= \frac{4284 \times 32}{204} = 672$

$\therefore$ 2nd number = 672

2. Let the numbers be $8x$ and $15x$

$8x = 2 \times 2 \times 2 \times x$

$15x = 3 \times 5 \times x$

$\therefore$ LCM of $8x$ and $15x = 2 \times 2 \times 2 \times x \times 3 \times 5 = 120x$

Now, 1st number × 2nd number = HCF × LCM

$\Rightarrow 8x \times 15x = 4 \times 120x$

$\Rightarrow 120x^2 = 4 \times 120x$

$\Rightarrow x = 4$

$\therefore$ Numbers are $8 \times 4 = 32$ and $15 \times 4 = 60$

3. Difference between 366 and 513 = 513 − 366 = 147

and difference between 513 and 324 = 513 − 324 = 189

$\therefore$ HCF of 147 and 189

```
147) 189 (1
     147
     × 42) 147 (3
           126
           × 21) 42 (2
                 42
                 ×
```

$\therefore$ The required largest number is 21.

4. LCM of the two numbers = 45 × HCF

and LCM + HCF = 1150

$\Rightarrow$ 45 × HCF + HCF = 1150

$\Rightarrow$ HCF(45 + 1) = 1150

$\Rightarrow$ HCF $= \frac{1150}{46} = 25$

$\therefore$ LCM = 45 × 25 = 1125

$\because$ 1st number × 2nd number = LCM × HCF

$\therefore$ 125 × 2nd number = 1125 × 25

$\therefore$ 2nd number $= \frac{1125 \times 25}{125} = 225.$

5. According to the condition of the problem, 50 is obtained on dividing one of the numbers by 2

$\therefore$ One of the numbers = 50 × 2 = 100

Now, 1st number × 2nd number = LCM × HCF

$\therefore$ 100 × 2nd number = 250 × 50

$\therefore$ 2nd number $= \frac{250 \times 50}{100} = 125$

Hence, numbers are 100 and 125.

6. LCM of 15, 20 and 24

5	15, 20, 24
4	3, 4, 24
3	3, 1, 6
	1, 1, 2

LCM = 5 × 4 × 3 × 2 = 120

$\because$ 12 minutes = 12 × 60 = 720 seconds
$\therefore$ Number of times the bells will ring together during 12 minutes

$$= \frac{720}{120} = 6 \text{ times.}$$

7. Let the number be x and y.
Then, $x + y = 55$;
xy = HCF × LCM = 5 × 120
$\therefore$ Sum of their reciprocals

$$= \frac{1}{x} + \frac{1}{y} = \frac{x+y}{xy} = \frac{55}{5 \times 120} = \frac{11}{120}.$$

8. Let the two numbers be $2x$ and $3x$;
their LCM = $6x$
Now, $6x = 48$ $\therefore$ $x = 8$
Hence, the numbers are 2 × 8, 3 × 8 = 16, 24
Their sum = 16 + 24 = 40.

9.
```
2240) 3360 (1          1120) 5600 (5
      2240                   5600
      1120 ) 2240 (2         ×
             2240
              ×
```

Hence, N = HCF of 3360, 2240 and 5600 = 1120
Sum of digits in N = 1 + 1 + 2 + 0 = 4.

10. 7m = 700 cm;
3m 85 = 385 cm;
12m 95cm = 1295 cm

```
385) 700 (1
     385
     315) 385 (1
          315
           70) 315 (4
               280
                35 ) 70 (2
                     70
                      ×

35) 1295 (37
    105
     245
     245
      ×
```

Hence, required length = HCF of 700 cm, 385 cm, 1295 cm = 35 cm.

11.

2	252, 308, 198
2	126, 154, 99
3	63, 77, 99
3	21, 77, 33
7	7, 77, 11
11	1, 11, 11
	1, 1, 1

Hence, LCM = 2 × 2 × 3 × 3 × 7 × 11 = 2772
Hence, A, B, C will meet again at the starting point after 2772 sec. = 46 min 12 sec.

12.

Numbers	***Their divisors***
182	→ 1, 2, 7, 13, 14, 26, 91 and 182
176	→ 1, 2, 4, 8, 16, 22, 44, 88 and 176
101	→ 1 and 101
99	→ 1, 3, 9, 11, 33 and 99

Therefore, 176 has the most number of divisors.

13. HCF of 23 and 92 = 23
HCF of 21 and 35 = 7
HCF of 18 and 25 = 1
HCF of 16 and 62 = 2
Hence, 18 and 25 are co-prime numbers.

14. N = HCF of (4665 – 1305), (6905 – 4665) and (6905 – 1305)
= HCF of 3360, 2240 and 5600 = 112
Sum of digit of 1 + 1 + 2 = 4.

15. Required number = HCF of (1657 – 6) and (2037 – 5) = HCF of 1651 and 2032 = 127.

```
1651) 2032 (1
      1651
       381) 1651 (4
            1524
             127) 381 (3
                  381
                   ×
```

AVERAGE

1. One-third of a certain journey was covered at the rate of 25 km per hour, one-fourth at the rate of 30 km per hour and the rest at the 50 km per hour. What is the average speed per hour for whole journey?

A. $33\frac{1}{3}$ kmph B. $44\frac{1}{4}$ kmph

C. $22\frac{1}{2}$ kmph D. 33 kmph

2. A batsman has a certain average of runs for 16 innings. In the 17th innings, he makes a score of 85 runs thereby increasing his average by 3. What is the average after the 17th inning?

A. 33 runs B. 34 runs

C. 37 runs D. 36 runs

3. The average of 6 observations is 12. A new seventh observation is included and the new average is decreased by 1. The seventh observation is

A. 1 B. 3

C. 5 D. 6

4. The average age of 30 students in a class is 12 years. The average age of a group of 5 of the students is 10 years and that of another group of 5 of them is 14 years. The average age of the remaining students is

A. 8 years B. 10 years

C. 12 years D. 14 years

5. Out of the three given numbers, the first number is twice the second and thrice the third. If the average of three numbers is 121, what is the difference between the first and third number?

A. 144 B. 77

C. 99 D. 132

6. If the average marks of three batches of 55, 60 and 45 students is 50, 55 and 60, then average marks of all the students is:

A. 55 B. 54

C. 54.68 D. 55.68

7. The average of 8 numbers is 20. The average of first two numbers is $15\frac{1}{2}$ and that of the next three is $21\frac{1}{3}$. If the sixth number is less than the seventh and eighth numbers by 4 and 7 respectively, then the eighth number is:

A. 27 B. 25

C. 22 D. 18

8. A pupil's marks were wrongly entered as 83 instead of 63. Due to that the average marks for the class got increased by half. What is the number of pupils in the class?

A. 73 B. 40

C. 40 D. 10

9. A cricketer whose bowling average is 12.4 runs per wicket takes 5 wickets for 26 runs and thereby decreases his average by 0.4. The number of wickets taken by him till the last match was:

A. 85 B. 80

C. 72 D. 64

10. The average weight of a class of 24 students is 35 kg. If the weight of the teacher is included, the average rises by 400 g. What is the weight of the teacher?

A. 55 kg B. 53 kg

C. 50 kg D. 45 kg

11. Nine men went to a hotel. Eight of them spent Rs. 3 for each over their meals and the ninth spent Rs. 2 more than the average expenditure of all the nine. What is the total money spent by them?

A. Rs. 29.25 B. Rs. 29.50
C. Rs. 29 D. Rs. 30

12. The average age of 24 students in a class is 10. If the teacher's age is included, the average increases by one. The age of the teacher is

A. 25 B. 30
C. 35 D. 40

13. The average of 5 consecutive even numbers A, B, C, D and E is 34. What is the product of B and D?

A. 1152 B. 1368
C. 1224 D. 1088

14. The average of 50 numbers is 30. If two numbers, 35 and 40 are discarded, then the average of the remaining numbers is nearly:

A. 29.68 B. 29.27
C. 28.78 D. 28.32

15. The average monthly salary of 20 employees of an organisation is Rs. 1500. If the manager's salary is added, then the average salary increases by Rs. 100. Find the manager's monthly salary?

A. Rs. 4800 B. Rs. 3600
C. Rs. 2400 D. Rs. 2000

ANSWERS

1	2	3	4	5	6	7	8	9	10
A	C	C	C	D	C	B	B	A	D
11	**12**	**13**	**14**	**15**					
A	C	A	A	B					

SOME SELECTED EXPLANATORY ANSWERS

1. Let the total distance covered during journey = 60 km

$\frac{1}{3}$ of the distance covered during journey

$$= 60 \times \frac{1}{3} = 20 \text{ km}$$

$\frac{1}{4}$ of the distance covered during journey

$$= \frac{1}{4} \times 60 = 15 \text{ km}$$

∴ The distance covered during the rest of journey = 60 – (20 + 15) = 25 km

Time taken to cover 20 km at 25 km/h

$$= \frac{20}{25} \text{ hours} = \frac{4}{5} \text{ hour}$$

Time taken to cover 15 km at 30 km/h

$$= \frac{15}{30} \text{ hours} = \frac{1}{2} \text{ hour}$$

Time taken to cover 25 km at 50 km/h

$$= \frac{25}{50} \text{ hours} = \frac{1}{2} \text{ hour}$$

$$\text{Total time taken} = \frac{4}{5} + \frac{1}{2} + \frac{1}{2}$$

$$= \frac{9}{5} \text{ hours}$$

$$\text{Hence average speed per hour} = 60 \div \frac{9}{5}$$

$$= \frac{60 \times 5}{9} = \frac{100}{3} \text{ km/h}$$

$$= 33\frac{1}{3} \text{ km/h}$$

2. Average increase in the score of 17 innings = 3 runs

Total increase in the score of 17 innings = 3 × 17 = 51 runs

∴ His average of 16 innings = 85 – 51 = 34 runs

Hence, average after the 17th innings
$= 34 + 3 = 37$ runs

3. Seventh observation $= (7 \times 11 - 6 \times 12) = 5$

4. Let, the required average age be x
Then, $5 \times 10 + 5 \times 14 + 20 \times x = 30 \times 12$
$\Rightarrow \quad 20x = 360 - 120$
$\Rightarrow \quad 20x = 240$
$\Rightarrow \quad x = 12$

5. Let the three numbers be x, $\frac{x}{2}$ and $\frac{x}{3}$ respectively,

Now, $\frac{1}{3}\left(x+\frac{x}{2}+\frac{x}{3}\right)=121$

$\Rightarrow \frac{11x}{6} = 121 \times 3$

$\therefore \ x = \frac{121\times3\times6}{11} = 198$

Hence, required difference $= x-\frac{x}{3} = \frac{2x}{3}$

$=\frac{2}{3} \times 198 = 132$

6. Required average Marks

$=\frac{55\times50+60\times55+45\times60}{55+60+45}=\frac{8750}{160} = 54.68$

7. Let the sixth, seventh and eighth numbers are x, $x + 4$ and $x + 7$.
Sum of last three numbers

$= 8 \times 20 - (2 \times \frac{31}{2}+3\times\frac{64}{3})$

$\Rightarrow x + x + 4 + x + 7 = 160 - 95$
$\Rightarrow 3x + 11 = 65$
$\Rightarrow 3x = 54 \qquad \therefore x = 18$
New eighth number $= x + 7 = 18 + 7 = 25$

8. Let the total number of pupils in the class be x; then,

$\frac{83-63}{x}=\frac{1}{2} \quad \Rightarrow \frac{20}{x}=\frac{1}{2} \quad \therefore x = 40$

9. Let the number of wickets taken by him be x till the last match.

Then, $\frac{x\times12.4+26}{x+5}=12$

$\Rightarrow 12.4x + 26 = 12x + 60$

$\Rightarrow 0.4x = 34 \quad \therefore \ x = \frac{340}{4}= 85$

10. Let the weight of the teacher be x kgs, then

$\frac{24\times35+x}{25}= 35.4$

$\Rightarrow \ 840 + x = 885 \qquad \therefore \quad x = 45$ kgs

12. Age of the teacher $= (25 \times 11 - 24 \times 10)$ years
$= 35$ years

13. Let 5 consecutive even numbers A, B, C, D and E be x, $x + 2$, $x + 4$, $x + 6$ and $x + 8$ respectively.

Now, $\frac{x+x+2+x+4+x+6+x+8}{5} = 34$

$\Rightarrow 5x + 20 = 170$
$\Rightarrow 5x = 150 \qquad \therefore x = 30$
Then, $B = x + 2 = 30 + 2 = 32$;
$D = x + 6 = 30 + 6 = 36$
Hence, their product $= 32 \times 36 = 1152$

14. The average of remaining 48 numbers

$=\frac{50\times30-(35+40)}{48}=\frac{1500-75}{48}$

$=\frac{1425}{48}= 29.68$

15. Let manager's salary be Rs. x, then

$\frac{20\times1500+x}{21}=1600$

$\Rightarrow \ 30{,}000 + x = 33600$
$\therefore \ x =$ Rs. 3600

PROBLEMS BASED ON AGES

1. The ratio of ages of A and B is 3 : 11. After 3 years the ratio becomes 1 : 3. What are the ages of A and B?

A. 9 years, 33 years B. 10 years, 40 years
C. 9 years, 27 years D. None of these

2. Two years ago, the ratio of Ram's and Mohan's age was 3 : 2 and at present 7 : 5. What are their present ages?

A. 14 years, 10 years B. 15 years, 10 years
C. 13 years, 9 years D. None of these

3. The ages of Samir and Saurabh are in the ratio of 8 : 15 respectively. After 9 years the ratio of their ages will be 11 : 18. What is the difference between their ages in years?

A. 20 years B. 21 years
C. 22 years D. 24 years

4. The present age of father is 34 years more than that of his son. 12 years ago, father's age was 18 times the age of his son. The present age of son in years is:

A. 12 B. 14
C. 16 D. 18

5. A mother is 25 years older than her daughter. Five years ago, the age of the mother was 6 times the age of the daughter. What is the present age of mother?

A. 25 years B. 29 years
C. 32 years D. 35 years

6. The difference between the present ages of P and Q is 4 years. The ratio of their ages after 5 years will be 9 : 8. The present age of P is:

A. 24 years B. 30 years
C.. 32 years D. None of these

7. Ten years ago, the age of Divya was half of the age of Namrata. If the ratio of present ages of both is 3 : 4, the sum of their present ages is:

A. 35 years B. 30 years
C. 25 years D. 18 years

8. The ratio between the present ages of A and B is 5 : 3 respectively. The ratio between A's age 4 years ago and B's age 4 years hence is 1 : 1. The ratio between A's age 4 years hence and B's age 4 years ago is:

A. 4 : 1 B. 3 : 1
C. 2 : 1 D. 1 : 3

9. Ram got married 8 years ago. His present age is $\frac{6}{5}$ times his age at the time of marriage. Ram's sister was 10 years younger to him at the time of his marriage. What is the present age of Ram's sister?

A. 40 years B. 38 years
C. 36 years D. 32 years

10. A father said to his son, "I was as old as you are at present at the time of your birth." If the father's age is 38 years now. Five years ago the age of son was:

A. 38 years B. 33 years
C. 19 years D. 14 years

ANSWERS

1	2	3	4	5	6	7	8	9	10
A	A	B	B	D	D	A	B	B	D

SOME SELECTED EXPLANATORY ANSWERS

1. Let the ages of A and B be $3x$ and $11x$ years; then

$$\frac{3x+3}{11x+3}=\frac{1}{3} \quad \Rightarrow \quad 9x + 9 = 11x + 3$$

$\Rightarrow 2x = 6 \qquad \therefore \; x = 3$

Hence, their present age, $3x = 3 \times 3 = 9$ years; $11x = 11 \times 3 = 33$ years

2. Let the present ages of Ram and Mohan are $7x$ and $5x$ years; then

$$\frac{7x-2}{5x-2}=\frac{3}{2} \quad \Rightarrow \quad 14x - 4 = 15x - 6$$

$\therefore \; x = 2$

Hence, their present ages : $7 \times 2 = 14$ years and $5 \times 2 = 10$ years

3. Let the present ages of Samir and Saurabh are $8x$ and $15x$ years respectively; then

$$\frac{8x+9}{15x+9}=\frac{11}{18} \quad \Rightarrow \quad 144x + 162 = 165x + 99$$

$\Rightarrow 21x = 63 \quad \therefore \; x = 3$

Hence, difference of their ages $= 15x - 8x = 7x$ $= 7 \times 3 = 21$ years

4. Let the present ages of father and his son be $x + 34$ and x years respectively; then

$18(x - 12) = x + 34 - 12$

$\Rightarrow 18x - 216 = x + 22$

$\Rightarrow 17x = 238 \qquad \therefore \; x = 14$

Hence, present age of his son = 14 years

5. Let the present ages of mother and her daughter are $(x + 25)$ and x years respectively; then

$6(x - 5) = x + 25 - 5$

$\Rightarrow \quad 6x - 30 = x + 20$

$\Rightarrow \quad 5x = 50 \qquad \therefore \; x = 10$

Hence, the age of the mother $= 10 + 25$ $= 35$ years

6. Let the present ages of P and Q be $(x + 4)$ and x years;

then, $\dfrac{x+4+5}{x+5}=\dfrac{9}{8} \quad \Rightarrow \quad 8x + 72$ $= 9x + 45 \qquad \therefore \; x = 27$

Hence, present age of P $= 27 + 4 = 31$ years

7. Let the present ages of Divya and Namrata are $3x$ and $4x$ years respectively; then

$$\frac{3x-10}{4x-10}=\frac{1}{2}$$

$\Rightarrow \quad 6x - 20 = 4x - 10$

$\Rightarrow \quad 2x = 10 \quad \therefore \; x = 5$

Hence, sum of their ages $= 3x + 4x = 7x$ $= 7 \times 5 = 35$ years

8. Let the present ages of A and B are $5x$ and $3x$ years respectively; then,

$$\frac{5x-4}{3x+4}=1 \quad \Rightarrow \quad 5x - 4 = 3x + 4$$

$\Rightarrow 2x = 8 \qquad \therefore \; x = 4$

Hence, their present ages are 20 years and 12 years.

So, required ratio $= (20 + 4) : (12 - 4)$ $= 24 : 8 = 3 : 1$

9. Let the present age of Ram be x years; then

$$\frac{x}{x-8}=\frac{6}{5} \quad \Rightarrow \quad 5x = 6x - 48$$

$\therefore \quad x = 48$

Hence, present age of Ram's sister $= 48 - 10 = 38$ years.

10. Let the age of father was x years at the time of his son's birth, then present age of father and his son will be $2x$ and x years,

Now, $\quad 2x = 38 \qquad \therefore \; x = 19$ years

Hence, 5 years ago the age of son was $19 - 5$ $= 14$ years

CHAIN RULE

1. A fort has provision for 50 days. After 15 days a reinforcement of 150 men arrives and the provision now lasts 25 days. How many men were there in the fort?
   A. 300 B. 225
   C. 275 D. 200
2. In a fort there is provisions for 40 days for 275 persons. If after 16 days 125 persons leave the fort for how many more days the provisions will last?
   A. 35 days B. 44 days
   C. 45 days D. 53 days
3. 60 men could complete a work in 250 days. They worked together for 200 days. After that the work had to be stopped for 10 days due to bad weather. How many more men should be engaged to complete the work in time?
   A. 20 B. 18
   C. 15 D. 10
4. A contractor undertook to complete a project in 90 days and employed 60 men on it. After 60 days, he found that $\frac{3}{4}$ of the work has already been completed. How many men can he discharge so that the project may completed exactly on time?
   A. 15 B. 20
   C. 30 D. 40
5. A flagstaff 17.5 m high casts a shadow of length 40.25 m. The height of the building, which casts a shadow of length 28.75m under similar condition will be:
   A. 21.25 m B. 17.5 m
   C. 12.5 m D. 10 m
6. If 5 men or 9 women can do a piece of work in 19 days, then 3 men and 6 women will do the same work in how many days?
   A. 21 B. 18
   C. 15 D. 12
7. A certain number of men can finish a piece of work in 100 days. If there were 10 men less, it will take 10 days more for the work to be finished. How many men were there originally?
   A. 110 B. 100
   C. 82 D. 75
8. Some persons can do a piece of work in 12 days. Two times the number of such persons will do half of that work in:
   A. 12 days B. 3 days
   C. 6 days D. 4 days
9. 2 men and 7 boys can do a piece of work in 14 days; 3 men and 8 boys can do the same in 11 days. Then 8 men and 6 boys can do three times of this work in
   A. 30 days B. 4 days
   C. 21 days D. 18 days
10. If 3 men or 6 boys, working 7 hours a day can do a piece of work in 10 days; how many days will it take to complete a piece of work twice as large with 6 men and 2 boys working together for 8 hours a day?
    A. 9 B. $8\frac{1}{2}$
    C. $7\frac{1}{2}$ D. $6\frac{1}{2}$

11. If 15 men can do a certain amount of work in 20 days working 8 hours a day, in how many days will 10 men do three times the work working 6 hours a day?

A. 120 days B. 70 days
C. 100 days D. None of these

12. 40 men consume 60 kgs of rice in 15 days, then in how many days will 30 men consume 12 kgs of rice?

A. 9 days B. $6\frac{1}{4}$ days
C. 4 days D. $3\frac{1}{4}$ days

13. 56 men can complete a piece of work in 24 days. In how many days can 42 men complete the same piece of work?

A. 48 B. 32
C. 20 D. 16

14. Running at the same constant rate, 6 identical machines can produce a total of 270 bottles per minute. At this rate, how many bottles could 10 such machines produce in 4 minutes?

A. 1400 B. 1600
C. 1800 D. 2000

15. 400 persons, working 9 hours a day complete $\frac{1}{4}th$ of the work in 10 days. The number of additional persons, working 8 hours a day, required to complete the remaining work in 20 days, is:

A. 275 B. 250
C. 675 D. 200

ANSWERS

1	2	3	4	5	6	7	8	9	10
B	B	C	B	C	C	A	B	C	C
11	**12**	**13**	**14**	**15**					
A	C	B	C	C					

SOME SELECTED EXPLANATORY ANSWERS

1.

Days	Men
35 ↑	x
25	$x + 150$ ↓

$$\Rightarrow \frac{x+150}{x} = \frac{35}{25} \quad \Rightarrow 1 + \frac{150}{x} = \frac{35}{25}$$

$$\Rightarrow \frac{150}{x} = \frac{10}{25}$$

$$\therefore\ x = \frac{25}{10} \times 150 = 375$$

Required number of men = 375 – 150 = 225

2.

Persons	Days
275 ↑	24
150	x ↓

$$\Rightarrow \frac{x}{24} = \frac{275}{150} \quad \therefore\ x = \frac{275}{150} \times 24 = 44 \text{ days}$$

3.

Days	Men
50 ↑	60
40	x ↓

$$\Rightarrow \frac{x}{60} = \frac{50}{40} \quad \therefore\ x = \frac{50}{40} \times 60 = 75 \text{ men}$$

Hence, number of additional men = 75 – 60
= 15

4.

Work	Days	Men
$\frac{3}{4}$	60 ↑	60
$\frac{1}{4}$ ↓	30	x ↓

$$\Rightarrow \frac{x}{60} = \frac{60}{30} \times \frac{1/4}{3/4}$$

$$\therefore\ x = \frac{60}{30} \times \frac{1}{3} \times 60 = 40 \text{ days}$$

Hence, number of men to be discharged
= 60 – 40 = 20

5. Shadow (m) — Object (m)

40.25 ↓   17.5 ↓
28.75 x

$$\Rightarrow \frac{x}{17.5} = \frac{28.75}{40.25}$$

$$\therefore x = \frac{28.75 \times 17.5}{40.25} = 12.5 \text{ m}$$

6. 5 men $\equiv$ 9 women

$$\therefore 3 \text{ men} = \frac{9}{5} \times 3 = \frac{27}{5} \text{ women}$$

$$\text{Hence, 3 men and 6 women} = \frac{27}{5} + 6 = \frac{57}{5} \text{ women}$$

Women — Days

9 ↑   19 ↓
$\frac{57}{5}$ x

$$\Rightarrow \frac{x}{19} = \frac{9 \times 5}{57}$$

$$\therefore x = \frac{9 \times 5}{57} \times 19 = 15 \text{ days}$$

7. Days — Men

100 ↑ x ↓
110    $x - 10$

$$\Rightarrow \frac{x-10}{x} = \frac{100}{110} \quad \Rightarrow \quad 110x - 1100 = 100x$$

$$\Rightarrow 10x = 1100 \quad \therefore x = 110$$

Hence, initially the number of men = 110

8. Work — Persons — Days

1 ↓ x ↑   12 ↓
$\frac{1}{2}$ $2x$ a

$$\Rightarrow \frac{a}{12} = \frac{x}{2x} \times \frac{1}{2} \quad \therefore a = \frac{1}{4} \times 12 = 3 \text{ days}$$

9. Here, 14×2 men + 14×7 boys $\equiv$ 11×3 men + 11×8 boys

$\Rightarrow$ 28 men + 98 boys $\equiv$ 33 men + 88 boys

$\Rightarrow$ 5 men = 10 boys $\therefore$ 1 man = 2 boys

Then, 2 men and 7 boys $\equiv$ 4 boys + 7 boys = 11 boys

& also, 8 men and 6 boys $\equiv$ 16 boys + 6 boys = 22 boys

Work — Boys — Days

1 ↓   11 ↑   14 ↓
3   22 x

$$\Rightarrow \frac{x}{14} = \frac{11}{22} \times \frac{3}{1}$$

$$\therefore x = \frac{1}{2} \times 3 \times 14 = 21 \text{ days}$$

12. Men — Rice (kgs) — Days

40 ↑   60 ↓   15 ↓
30   12 x

$$\Rightarrow \frac{x}{15} = \frac{12}{60} \times \frac{40}{30}$$

$$\therefore x = \frac{12}{60} \times \frac{40}{30} \times 15 = 4 \text{ days}$$

14. Machines — Time (minutes) — Bottles

6 ↓   1 ↓   270 ↓
10   4 x

$$\Rightarrow \frac{x}{270} = \frac{4}{1} \times \frac{10}{6}$$

$$\therefore x = \frac{4 \times 10}{6} \times 270 = 1800 \text{ bottles}$$

15. Work — Hours — Days — Persons

$\frac{1}{4}$ ↓   9 ↑   10 ↑   400 ↓
$\frac{3}{4}$ 8   20 x

$$\Rightarrow \frac{x}{400} = \frac{10}{20} \times \frac{9}{8} \times \frac{3/4}{1/4}$$

$$\therefore x = \frac{1}{2} \times \frac{9}{8} \times 3 \times 400 = 675$$

Hence, number of additional persons = 675 – 400 = 275

TIME AND DISTANCE

1. Starting from a point at a speed of 4 km/hr a man reaches at a cerain place and returns back to the point from where he had started journey on bicycle at the speed of 16 km/hr. His average speed during the entire journey will be :
   A. 6.4 km/h B. 8.4 km/h
   C. 5.4 km/h D. 10 km/h

2. A motorist covers a certain distance at a average speed of 48 km/h in 45 minutes. What speed in km/h he must maintain to cover the same distance in 30 minutes?
   A. 66 km/h B. 79 km/h
   C. 80 km/h D. 72 km/h

3. A policeman saw a thief at a distance of 200 m. The policeman and the thief started running at the same time. If the policeman runs at a speed of $4\frac{1}{6}$ m per second and the thief at a speed of $3\frac{1}{3}$ m per second, after what time the policeman will catch the thief?
   A. 12 min B. 10 min
   C. 9 min D. 4 min

4. A monkey wants to climb up a glazed pole. He climbs 12 metres in 1 minute and then he slips back 3 metres in the next minute. If the pole is 63 metre high, how long does he take to climb at the top of the pole?
   A. $11\frac{1}{4}$ min B. $12\frac{1}{2}$ min
   C. $12\frac{3}{4}$ min D. $14\frac{3}{4}$ min

5. The distance between two stations A and B is 300 km. A train leaves the station A with a speed of 40 km/hr. At the same time another train departs from the station B with a speed of 50 km/hr. How much time will these two trains take to cross each other?
   A. 3 hrs 40 min B. 3 hrs 20 min
   C. 2 hrs 20 min D. 3 hrs 45 min

6. Nilesh goes to school from his village at the speed of 4 km/hr and returns from school to village at the speed of 2 km/hr. If he takes 6 hours in all, then what is the distance between the village and the school?
   A. 8 km B. 6 km
   C. 5 km D. 4 km

7. By increasing the speed of the bus by 10 km/hr the time of journey for 72 km is reduced by 36 minutes. What was the original speed of the bus?
   A. 30 km/hr B. 35 km/hr
   C. 40 km/hr D. 45 km/hr

8. A train covers a distance in 50 minutes, if it runs at a speed of 48 km/hr on an average. The speed at which the train must run to reduce the time of journey to 40 minutes will be:
   A. 70 km/hr B. 60 km/hr
   C. 55 km/hr D. 50 km/hr

9. A certain distance is covered by a vehicle at a certain speed. If half of this distance is covered by another vehicle in double the time, the ratio of the speeds of the two vehicles is:
   A. 4 : 1 B. 1 : 4
   C. 2 : 1 D. 1 : 2

10. A is faster than B. A and B each walk 24 km. The sum of their speeds is 7 km/hr and sum of times taken by them is 14 hours. What is the speed of A?
    A. 7 km/hr B. 5 km/hr
    C. 4 km/hr D. 3 km/hr

ANSWERS

1	2	3	4	5	6	7	8	9	10
A	D	D	C	B	A	A	B	A	C

SOME SELECTED EXPLANATORY ANSWERS

1. Average speed during the entire journey

$= \frac{2xy}{x+y} = \frac{2 \times 4 \times 16}{4+16} = \frac{8 \times 16}{20} = 6.4$ km/hr.

2. Let required speed be x km/hr; then

$x \times \frac{1}{2} = 48 \times \frac{3}{4} \quad \therefore \; x = 48 \times \frac{3}{4} \times 2$

$= 72$ km/hr

3. Suppose the policeman will catch the thief after t seconds

then, $\left(\frac{25}{6} - \frac{10}{3}\right) t = 200 \Rightarrow \frac{5}{6} t = 200$

$\therefore \; t = \frac{200 \times 6}{5} = 240$ sec $= 4$ min.

4. The monkey climbs 12 metres in 1 minute and then he slips back 3 metres in the next minute
$\therefore$ The monkey climbs in the first 2 minutes $= 12 - 3 = 9$ metres
$\therefore$ In the first 12 minutes the monkey climbs $= 9 \times 6 = 54$ metres
Remaining height of the pole to be covered by the monkey $= 63 - 54 = 9$ metre
$\therefore$ The monkey will climb the height of 9 metres in the 13th minute
$\because$ The monkey climbs 12 metres in 1 minute
$\therefore$ The monkey will climb 9 metres in $\frac{1}{12} \times 9$

$= \frac{3}{4}$ minute

$\therefore$ Time spent in climbing at the top of the pole $= \left(12 + \frac{3}{4}\right)$ minutes $= 12\frac{3}{4}$ minutes

5. The two trains are moving in the opposite directions

$\therefore$ Relative speed $= 40 + 50 = 90$ km/hr.

$\therefore$ Time taken to cross each other $= \frac{300}{90} = 3\frac{1}{3}$ hours or, 3 hours 20 minutes.

6. Let x km be the distance between village and the school; then

$\frac{x}{4} + \frac{x}{2} = 6 \qquad \Rightarrow \frac{3x}{4} = 6$

$\therefore \; x = \frac{6 \times 4}{3} = 8$ km

8. Let x km/hr be the required speed of the train; then

$x \times \frac{40}{60} = 48 \times \frac{50}{60}$

$\therefore \; x = \frac{48 \times 50}{40} = 60$ km/hr

9. Let x km/hr and t hr be the certain speed and certain time.

Then, ratio of their speeds $= \frac{x}{t} : \frac{x}{2 \times 2t} = 1 : \frac{1}{4}$

$= 4 : 1$

10. Let speeds of A and B are x_1 and x_2 km/hr and times taken by them are t_1 and t_2 hrs, then

$x_1 + x_2 = 7$ km/hr ...(i)

$t_1 + t_2 = 14$ hrs ...(ii)

Now, $\frac{24}{x_1} + \frac{24}{x_2} = 14 \Rightarrow \frac{24(x_1 + x_2)}{x_1 x_2} = 14$

$\therefore \; x_1 x_2 = \frac{24 \times 7}{14} = 12$

Then, $x_1 - x_2 = \sqrt{(x_1 + x_2)^2 - 4x_1 x_2}$

$= \sqrt{(7)^2 - 4 \times 12} = 1$ ...(iii)

Solving *(i)* and *(iii)* we get $x_1 = 4$ km/hr

TIME AND WORK

1. A and B working together complete a work in 35 days. If A takes 60 days to complete it, how long would B alone take to complete it?

A. 64 days B. 72 days
C. 81 days D. 84 days

2. A few children working together can do a piece of work in 18 days. If the number of children employed on the work is made double, how long would they take to complete half of the work?

A. $4\frac{1}{2}$ days B. $2\frac{1}{3}$ days
C. $8\frac{3}{4}$ days D. $6\frac{1}{2}$ days

3. 10 men or 18 boys can do a piece of work in 15 days. In how many days would 25 men and 15 boys complete the same work working together?

A. $5\frac{1}{2}$ days B. $4\frac{1}{2}$ days
C. $6\frac{2}{3}$ days D. $2\frac{1}{3}$ days

4. A cistern is filled by a tap in $3\frac{1}{2}$ hours. Due to a leak in the bottom of the cistern, it takes half an hour longer to fill the cistern. If the cistern is full, how long will it take the leak to empty it?

A. 28 hours B. 29 hours
C. $31\frac{1}{3}$ hours D. 38 hours

5. A is twice as good a workman as B and thrice as good a workman as C. If C alone can do a piece of work in 24 days, how long would the three persons take to finish the work working together?

A. $3\frac{3}{11}$ days B. $4\frac{4}{7}$ days
C. $4\frac{4}{11}$ days D. $3\frac{4}{11}$ days

6. If 3 men and 5 women can do a piece of work in 8 days and 2 men and 7 boys can do the same work in 12 days. Find the number of boys, the work done by whom can equate the work done by 10 women.

A. 19 boys B. 21 boys
C. 23 boys D. 15 boys

7. 8 men alone can complete a piece of work in 12 days. 4 women alone can complete the same piece of work in 48 days and 10 children alone can complete the piece of work in 24 days. In how many days can 10 men, 4 women and 10 children together complete the piece of work?

A. 6 B. 8
C. 10 D. 15

8. A works twice as fast as B. If B can complete a piece of work independently in 12 days. Find in how many days A and B together can complete the work?

A. 8 days B. 6 days
C. 4 days D. 18 days

9. A contractor undertook to complete a project in 90 days and employed 60 men on it. After 60 days, he found that $\frac{3}{4}$ of the work has already been completed. How many men can he discharge so that the project may be completed exactly on time?

A. 15 B. 20
C. 30 D. 40

10. A can do a piece of work in 25 days and B can do it in 20 days. They work together for 5 days and then A goes away. In how many days will B finish the remaining work?

A. 33 days B. 20 days
C. 11 days D. 10 days

ANSWERS

1	2	3	4	5	6	7	8	9	10
D	A	B	A	C	B	A	C	B	C

SOME SELECTED EXPLANATORY ANSWERS

1. (A + B)'s 1 day's work = $\frac{1}{35}$

and also, A's 1 day's work = $\frac{1}{60}$

Hence, B's 1 day's work = $\frac{1}{35} - \frac{1}{60} = \frac{5}{420} = \frac{1}{84}$

So, B will do the whole work in 84 days.

3. 10 men $\equiv$ 18 boys

25 men $\equiv$ $\frac{18}{10} \times 25 = 45$ boys

Hence, 25 men + 15 boys = 45 + 15 = 60 boys

Now, 18 boys can do a piece of work in 15 days.

Hence, 60 boys will do a piece of work in

$\frac{15 \times 18}{60} = \frac{9}{2}$ days = $4\frac{1}{2}$ days.

4. In 1 hour $\frac{2}{7}$ cistern is filled by the tap.

Hence, in $\frac{1}{2}$ hour $\frac{2}{14} = \frac{1}{7}$ cistern is filled by the tap.

So, $\frac{1}{7}$ cistern is emptied by the leakage in 4 hours.

So, 1 cistern will be emptied by the leakage in 28 hours.

6. Here, (3 men + 5 women) × 8

$\equiv$ (2 men + 7 boys) × 12

$\Rightarrow$ 40 women $\equiv$ 84 boys

$\therefore$ 10 women $\equiv \frac{84}{40} \times 10 = 21$ boys

Hence, work done by 10 women

= work done of 21 boys.

7. B's 1 day's work = $\frac{1}{4} - \frac{1}{12} = \frac{2}{12} = \frac{1}{6}$

Hence, B alone will complete the work in 6 days.

8. Ratio of efficiency of A and B = 2 : 1

Then, ratio of their time taking = 1 : 2

Hence, if B can complete the work in 12 days, then A in 6 days.

Now, (A + B)'s 1 day's work = $\frac{1}{6} + \frac{1}{12} = \frac{3}{12} = \frac{1}{4}$

So, A and B together can complete the work in 4 days.

9. After 60 days remaining work = $1 - \frac{3}{4} = \frac{1}{4}$

In 60 days $\frac{3}{4}$ work has been done by 60 men

In 30 days $\frac{1}{4}$ work will be done by

$60 \times \frac{4}{3} \times \frac{1}{4} \times \frac{60}{30} = 40$ men.

Hence, required number of men = 60 – 40 = 20 (which are to be discharged).

BOATS AND STREAMS

1. A boat goes 6 km upstream and back to the starting point in 2 hours. If the current of the stream runs at the rate of 4 km/hr, find the speed of the boat in still water.

A. 6 km/hr B. 8 km/hr
C. 10 km/hr D. 12 km/hr

2. A boat covers 24 km upstream and 36 km downstream in 6 hours, while it covers 36 km upstream and 24 km downstream in 6½ horus. Find the speed of the current.

A. 2 km/hr B. 4 km/hr
C. 6 km/hr D. 8 km/hr

3. A man can row 5 km/hr in still water and the speed of the stream is 1.5 km/hr. He takes an hour when he travels upstream to a place and back again to the starting point. How far is the place from the starting point?

A. 2.275 km B. 3.5 km
C. 1.5 km D. None of these

4. The speed of a boat in still water is 6 km/hr and the speed of the stream is 1.5 km/hr. A man rows to a place at a distance of 22.5 km and comes back to the starting point. Find the total time taken by him.

A. 8 hours B. 10 hours
C. 12 hours D. 4 hours

5. A boat covers 20 km downstream and 6 km upstream in 3 hours, while it covers 30 km downstream and 12 km upstream in 5 hours. What is the speed of boat in still water?

A. 6 km/hr B. 8 km/hr
C. 10 km/hr D. 12 km/hr.

6. Samir can travel 12 miles downstream in a certain river in 6 hours less than it takes him to travel the same distance upstream. But when he could double his rowing rate for his 24-mile round trip, the downstream 12 miles would then take only one hour less than the upstream 12 miles. Find the speed of the current in miles/hour.

A. $2\frac{2}{3}$ B. $2\frac{1}{3}$
C. $1\frac{2}{3}$ D. $1\frac{1}{3}$

7. A boat takes 6 hours to travel from place M to N downstream and back from N to M upstream. If the speed of the boat in still water is 4 km/hr; what is the distance between two places?

A. 6 kms B. 8 kms
C. 12 kms D. Data inadequate

8. A man can row upstream at 8 km/hr and downstream at 13 km/hr. The speed of the stream is:

A. 2.5 km/hr B. 4.2 km/hr
C. 5 km/hr D. 10.5 km/hr

9. A man's speed with the current is 15 km/hr and the speed of the current is 2.5 km/hr. The man's speed against the current is:

A. 12.5 km/hr B. 10 km/hr
C. 9 km/hr D. 8.5 km/hr

10. A motorboat, whose speed is 15 km/hr in still water goes 30 km downstream and comes back in a total of 4 hours 30 minutes. What is the speed of the stream (in km/hr)?

A. 10 B. 6
C. 5 D. 4

ANSWERS

1	2	3	4	5	6	7	8	9	10
B	A	A	A	B	B	D	A	B	C

SOME SELECTED EXPLANATORY ANSWERS

1. Let the speed of a boat in still water = x km/hr; then

$$\frac{6}{x-4}+\frac{6}{x+4}=2 \quad \Rightarrow \quad \frac{2x}{x^2-16}=\frac{1}{3}$$

$\Rightarrow x^2 - 6x - 16 = 0$

$\Rightarrow (x - 8)(x + 2) = 0$

Hence, the speed of the boat = 8 km/hr.

2. Let x km/hr and y km/hr be the speeds of the boat in still water and the speed of the current respectively, then

$$\frac{24}{x-y}+\frac{36}{x+y}=6 \Rightarrow \frac{4}{x-y}+\frac{6}{x+y}=1 \quad ...(i)$$

And, $$\frac{36}{x-y}+\frac{24}{x+y}=\frac{13}{2} \quad ...(ii)$$

Solving these two equations, we get

$x + y = 12$; $x - y = 8$

Hence, $y = \frac{1}{2}(12-8) = 2$ km/hr.

3. Let required distance be x km, then

$$\frac{x}{5-1.5}+\frac{x}{5+1.5}=1 \Rightarrow \frac{x\times 2}{7}+\frac{x\times 2}{13}=1$$

$\Rightarrow 40x = 91 \qquad \therefore x = 91/40 = 2.275$ km

4. Required time period $= \frac{22.5}{6+1.5}+\frac{22.5}{6-1.5}$

$= \frac{45}{15}+\frac{45}{9} = 8$ hours.

5. Let x km/hr and y km/hr be the speed of boat in still water and speed of current respectively; then

$$\frac{20}{x+y}+\frac{6}{x-y}=3 \quad ...(i)$$

and also, $$\frac{30}{x+y}+\frac{12}{x-y}=5$$

$$\Rightarrow \frac{15}{x+y}+\frac{6}{x-y}=\frac{5}{2} \quad ...(ii)$$

Solving equations *(i)* & *(ii)*, we get $x + y = 10$ and $x - y = 6$

Since, $x = \frac{1}{2}(10 + 6) = 8$ km/hr.

6. Let x km/hr and y km/hr be the speed of rowing in still water and speed of the current respectively; then

$$\frac{12}{x-y}-\frac{12}{x+y}=6 \quad \Rightarrow \frac{24y}{x^2-y^2}=6$$

$\Rightarrow x^2 = y^2 + 4y \quad ...(i)$

Again, $$\frac{12}{2x-y}-\frac{12}{2x+y}=1$$

$$\Rightarrow \frac{24y}{4x^2-y^2}=1 \quad \Rightarrow x^2 = \frac{y^2+24y}{4} \quad ...(ii)$$

From equations (i) and (ii), we get

$$y^2 + 4y = \frac{y^2+24y}{4} \Rightarrow 3y^2 = 8y$$

$\therefore \quad y = \frac{8}{3} = 2\frac{1}{3}$ miles/hr.

8. The speed of the stream $= \frac{1}{2}(13 - 8) = \frac{5}{2}$

$= 2.5$ km/hr.

9. The man's speed in still water

$= 15 - 2.5 = 12.5$ km/hr

Hence, the men's speed against the current

$= 12.5 - 2.5 = 10$ km/hr

10. Let speed of the stream be x km/hr, then

$$\frac{30}{15+x}+\frac{30}{15-x}=4\frac{1}{2} \quad \Rightarrow \frac{30\times 30}{225-x^2}=\frac{9}{2}$$

$\Rightarrow \frac{200}{225-x^2}=1 \qquad \Rightarrow x^2 = 225 - 200$

$\Rightarrow x^2 = 25 \qquad \therefore \quad x = 5$ km/hr.

ALLIGATION OR MIXTURE

1. A shopkeeper buys 26 kgs of milk @ Rs. 16 per kg. He also buys from another source an inferior quality of milk @ Rs. 10 per kg. How much quantity of the latter should he buy to mix it with the former so that he can sell the mixture @ Rs. 14 per kg without making any loss?

A. 13 kgs B. 12 kgs
C. 14 kgs D. 16 kgs

2. Two vessels A and B contain mixture of milk and water in the ratio 4 : 1 and 9 : 11 respectively. They are mixed in the ratio of 3 : 2. Find the ratio of milk : water in the resulting mixture.

A. 34 : 16 B. 33 : 17
C. 16 : 34 D. 17 : 33

3. A shopkeeper has 50 kgs of rice. He sells a part of it at 20% profit and the rest at 40% profit. If he gains 25% on the whole, find the quantity of each part.

A. 12.5 kgs and 37.5 kgs
B. 37.5 kgs and 12.5 kgs
C. 23.5 kgs and 21.5 kgs
D. 21.5 kgs and 23.5 kgs

4. A man bought a certain quantity of sugar for Rs. 8000. He sells one-fourth of it at 20% loss. At what per cent profit should he sell the remainder stock so as to make an overall profit of 20%?

A. 20% B. 30%
C. 35% D. 40%

5. Rs. 675 was divided among 75 boys and girls. Each boy gets Rs. 20 whereas a girl gets Rs. 5. Find the number of boys and girls.

A. 20, 55 B. 15, 60
C. 25, 50 D. 30, 45

6. A vessel contains mixture of liquids A and B in the ratio 3 : 2. When 20 litres of the mixture is taken out and replaced by 20 litres of liquid B, the ratio changes to 1 : 4. How many litres of liquid A was there initially present in the vessel?

A. 12 litres B. 18 litres
C. 24 litres D. 22 litres

7. A container is full of milk. One-third of milk is taken out of it and replaced by same quantity of water. Then again one-third of the mixture is taken out of it and replaced by the same quantity of water. The process is repeated 4 times. If 16 litres of milk is left in the container at the end of 4th operation, find the capacity of the container.

A. 76 litres B. 81 litres
C. 82 litres D. 85 litres

8. The cost of type-I rice is Rs. 15 per kg and type-II is Rs. 20 per kg. If both type I and type II are mixed in the ratio of 2 : 3, then find the price per kg of the mixed variety.

A. Rs. 19.50 B. Rs. 19
C. Rs. 18.50 D. Rs. 18

9. In what ratio must a grocer mix two varieties of tea worth Rs. 60 a kg and Rs. 65 a kg so that by selling the mixture at Rs. 68.20 a kg he may gain 10%?

A. 4 : 5 B. 3 : 5
C. 3 : 4 D. 3 : 2

10. A vessel contains 80 litres of milk. 16 litres of milk was taken out of the vessel and replaced by water. Then 16 litres of mixture was withdrawn and again replaced by water. The operation was repeated for third time. How much milk is now left in the vessel?

A. 96.40 litres B. 50.36 litres
C. 40.96 litres D. 32.76 litres

ANSWERS

1	2	3	4	5	6	7	8	9	10
A	B	B	B	A	B	B	D	D	C

SOME SELECTED EXPLANATORY ANSWERS

1.

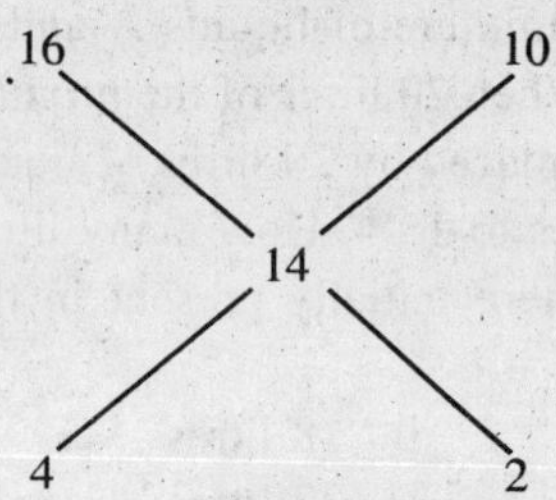

or 2 : 1 $\dfrac{\text{Quantity of milk @ Rs.10 per kg}}{\text{Quantity of milk @ Rs. 16 per kg}} = \dfrac{1}{2}$

So, quantity of milk @ Rs. 10 per kg. $= \dfrac{26}{2}$

$= 13$ kgs.

2. Fraction is

	Milk	*Water*
A :	$\dfrac{4}{5}$	$\dfrac{1}{5}$
B :	$\dfrac{9}{20}$	$\dfrac{11}{20}$

$(3A + 2B) = A$ and $B : \left(\dfrac{12}{5}+\dfrac{9}{10}\right) \left(\dfrac{3}{5}+\dfrac{11}{10}\right)$

$\dfrac{33}{10}$ $\dfrac{17}{10}$

So, Ratio of milk : water in the resulting mixture $= 33 : 17$.

3.

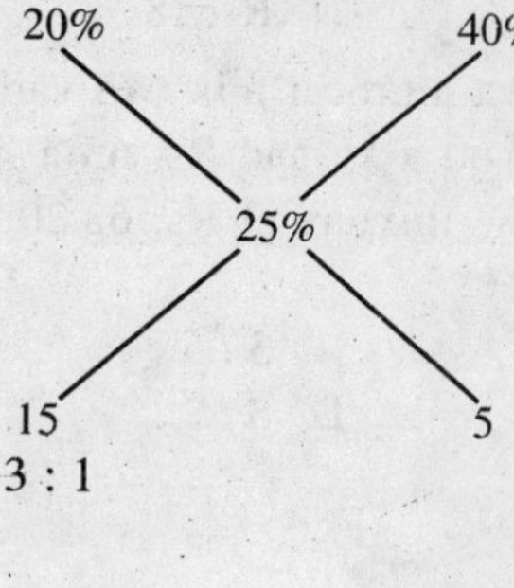

or 3 : 1

Quantity sold at 20% profit $= \dfrac{3}{3+1} \times 50$

$= 37.5$ kgs.

Quantity sold at 40% profit $= (50 - 37.5)$

$= 12.5$ kgs.

4. Let the remainder stock be sold at x% profit.

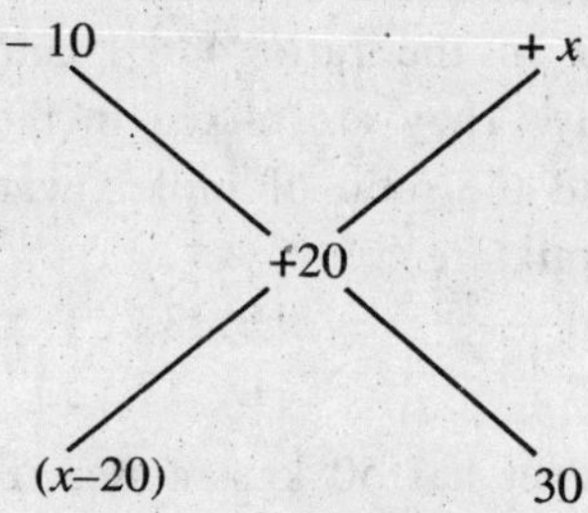

$$\frac{x-20}{30} = \frac{1/4}{3/4}$$

or $x - 20 = 30 \times \dfrac{1}{3}$

or $x = 20 + 10$

$x = 30\%$ profit.

5. Average money per head (boy or girl)

$= \text{Rs. } \dfrac{675}{75} = \text{Rs. } 9$

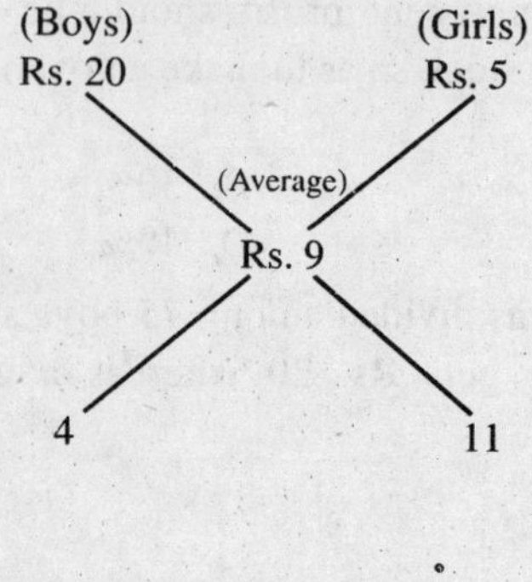

Number of boys $= \dfrac{4}{4+11} \times 75 = 20$

Number of girls $= \dfrac{11}{4+11} \times 75 = 55.$

6. % of liquid B initially present in the vessel

$$= \frac{2}{3+2} \times 100 = 40\%$$

% of liquid B finally present in the vessel

$$= \frac{4}{1+4} \times 100 = 80\%$$

The second solution is liquid B which is being mixed and it has 100% liquid B.
80% of liquid B present in the resultant mixture may be taken as average percentage. So, using rule of alligation on liquid B per cent, we can write,

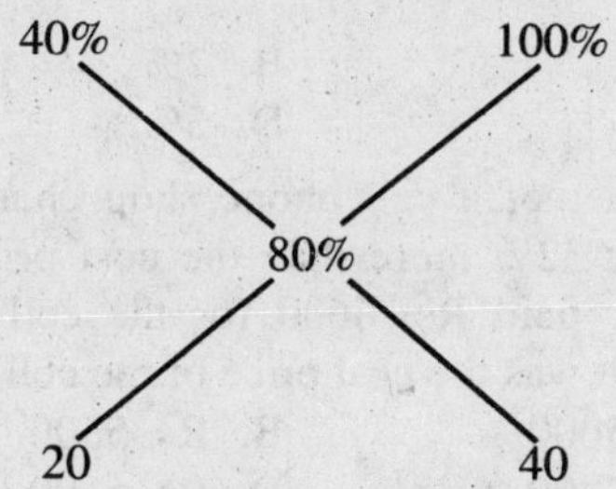

or 1 : 2
The ratio of liquid left in the vessel to liquid B being mixed = 1 : 2
Since the quantity of liquid B being mixed is 20 litres, the quantity of liquid left in the vessel is 10 litres.
Therefore, the total quantity of liquid initially present in the vessel

$= 10 + 20 = 30$ litres

Quantity of liquid A $= \dfrac{3}{2+3} \times 30$

$= 18$ litres.

7. Let capacity of the container be x litre; then

$x(1 - 1/3)^4 = 16 \Rightarrow x\left(\dfrac{2}{3}\right)^4 = 16$

$\Rightarrow x \times \dfrac{16}{81} = 16 \quad \therefore \; x = 81$ litres

8. Let the price per kg of mixed variety be Rs. x; then

By the rule of alligation,

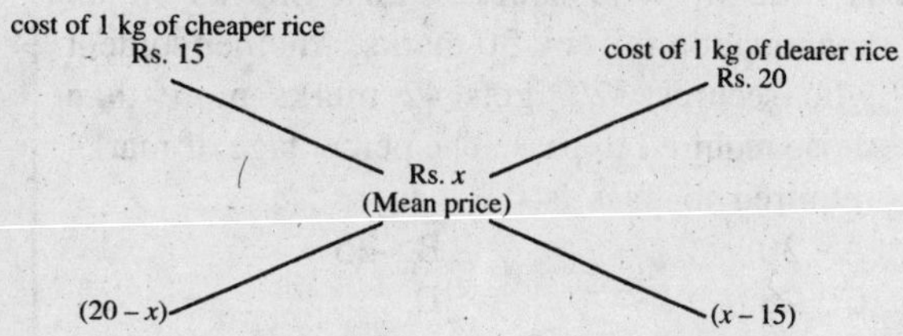

Now, $\dfrac{20-x}{x-15} = \dfrac{2}{3} \Rightarrow 60 - 3x = 2x - 30$

$\Rightarrow 5x = 90 \quad \therefore \; x =$ Rs. 18

9. S.P. of 1 kg mixture = Rs. 68.20,
Gain % = 10%

Hence, C.P. of 1 kg mixture $= \dfrac{100}{110} \times$ Rs. 68.20

= Rs. 62

By the rule of alligation

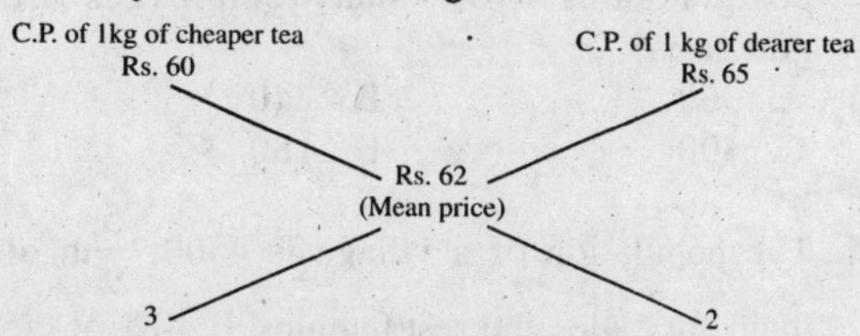

Hence, required ratio = 3 : 2

10. Amount of milk left $= 80\left(1 - \dfrac{16}{80}\right)^3$

$= 80\left(\dfrac{4}{5}\right)^3$

$80 \times \dfrac{64}{125} = 40.96$ litres.

PERCENTAGE

1. A student who secures 20% marks in an examination fails by 30 marks. Another student who secures 32% gets 42 marks more than those required to pass. The percentage of marks required to pass is:

A. 20 B. 25
C. 28 D. 30

2. In a college election, a candidate secured 62% of the votes and is elected by a majority of 144 votes. The total number of votes polled is:

A. 600 B. 800
C. 925 D. 1200

3. In an organisation, 40% of the employees are matriculates, 50% of the remaining are graduates and the remaining 180 are postgraduates. How many employees are graduates?

A. 360 B. 240
C. 300 D. 180

4. The population of a village is 4500. $\frac{5}{9}$th of them are males and rest females. If 40% of the males are married, then the percentage of married female is :

A. 35 B. 40
C. 50 D. 60

5. A's income is 10% more than B's. How much per cent is B's income is less than A's?

A. 10% B. 7%
C. $9\frac{1}{11}\%$ D. $6\frac{1}{2}\%$

6. If the price of a television set is increased by 25%, then by what percentage should the new price be reduced to bring the price back to original level?

A. 15% B. 20%
C. 25% D. 30%

7. In an election one of the two candidates gets 40% votes and loses by 100 votes. Total number of votes is :

A. 500 B. 400
C. 600 D. 1000

8. The gross income of a person is Rs. 20000. 10% of his income is exempted from income tax and his net income is Rs. 19100. The rate of income tax is :

A. 3% B. 2%
C. 4% D. 5%

9. The owner of a cell phone shop charges his customer 32% more than the cost price. If a customer paid Rs. 6600 for the cell phone, then what was the cost price of the cell phone?

A. Rs. 5000 B. Rs. 5500
C. Rs. 5800 D. Rs. 6100

10. If the cost of pins reduced by Rs. 4 per dozen, 12 more pins can be purchased for Rs. 48. The cost of pins per dozen after reduction is:

A. Rs. 8 B. Rs. 12
C. Rs. 16 D. Rs. 20

11. In an examination 80% of the students passed in Mathematics and 70% passed in English, while 10% students failed in both the subjects. If 360 students passed in both the subjects, find the total number of students who appeared in the examination.

A. 400 B. 600
C. 630 D. 640

12. Electric tax is increased by 20% and its consumption is decreased by 20%. The change in the expenditure is:

A. 4% decrease B. 4% increase
C. 5% decrease D. 5% increase

13. The selling price of certain commodity was reduced by 25%. As a result of it, the sales increased by 30%. What was the effect of it on cash collected by daily sales?

A. 2.5% decrease B. 2.5% increase
C. 5% decrease D. 5% increase

14. The wheat sold by a grocer contained 10% low quality wheat. What quantity of good quality wheat should be added to 150 kgs of wheat so that the percentage of low quality wheat becomes 5%?

A. 50 kgs B. 85 kgs
C. 135 kgs D. 150 kgs

15. Nilam spends 15% of her monthly income on household expenses. She spends 17% of the monthly income in travelling and 6% on medical expenses and saves the rest Rs. 15,500. What is her monthly income?

A. Rs. 20,000
B. Rs. 25,000
C. Rs. 30,000
D. Rs. 35,000

ANSWERS

1	2	3	4	5	6	7	8	9	10
B	A	D	C	C	B	A	D	A	B
11	**12**	**13**	**14**	**15**					
B	A	A	D	B					

SOME SELECTED EXPLANATORY ANSWERS

1. 20% of $x + 30 = 32\%$ of $x - 42$

$\Rightarrow$ 12% of $x = 72$

$$\Rightarrow \quad x = \frac{72 \times 100}{12} = 600$$

Pass Mark $= 20\%$ of $600 + 30 = 150$

$$\text{Pass percentage} = \left(\frac{150}{600} \times 100\right)\% = 25\%$$

2. (62% of $x - 38\%$ of x) $= 144$

$$\Rightarrow 24\% \text{ of } x = 144 \quad \Rightarrow x = \frac{144 \times 100}{24} = 600$$

3.
$$\text{Matriculates} = \frac{40}{100}x = \frac{2x}{5}$$

$$\text{Remaining} = \left(x - \frac{2x}{5}\right) = \frac{3x}{5}$$

$$\text{Graduates} = \frac{50}{100} \times \frac{3x}{5} = \frac{3x}{10}$$

$$\text{Remaining} = \frac{3x}{5} - \frac{3x}{10} = \frac{3x}{10}$$

$$\text{Now, } \frac{3x}{10} = 180$$

$$\therefore \; x = \frac{10 \times 180}{3} = 600$$

$$\therefore \; \text{Graduates} = \frac{3 \times 600}{10} = 180.$$

4. $\text{Males} = \left(\frac{5}{9} \times 4500\right) = 2500$

Females $= 2000$

$$\therefore \quad \text{Married males} = \frac{40}{100} \times 2500 = 1000$$

and married females $= 1000$

$\therefore$ Percentage of married females

$$= \left(\frac{1000}{2000} \times 100\right)\% = 50\%.$$

5. $$\text{Required percentage} = \left[\frac{10}{(100+10)} \times 100\right]\%$$

$$= 9\frac{1}{11}\%.$$

6. $$\text{Required reduction} = \frac{25}{100+25} \times 100 = 20\%.$$

7. Out of 100, difference in votes = (60 – 40) = 20

20% of x = 100

$$\therefore x = \frac{100 \times 100}{20} = 500.$$

8. Gross income = Rs. 20000

Income exempted from income tax = 10% of gross income

∴ Income on which income tax is chargeable = (100 – 10%) = 90% of gross income

$$= 20000 \times \frac{90}{100} = \text{Rs. } 18000$$

∴ Total income tax paid on

= Rs. 20000 – Rs. 19100

= Rs. 900

$$\therefore \text{Rate per cent of income tax} = \frac{900}{18000} \times 100 = 5\%$$

9. Let cost price of the cell phone be Rs. x; then

$$x + \frac{32}{100} \times x = 6600 \quad \Rightarrow \frac{132x}{100} = 6600$$

$$\therefore x = \frac{100 \times 6600}{132} = \text{Rs. } 5000.$$

10. Let reduced price by Rs. x per dozen, then

$$\frac{48}{x} - \frac{48}{x+4} = 1 \quad \Rightarrow \frac{48 \times 4}{x^2 + 4x} = 1$$

$\Rightarrow \quad x^2 + 4x - 192 = 0$

$\Rightarrow (x + 16)(x - 12) = 0$

$\therefore \quad x = \text{Rs. } 12.$

11. Here, percentage of students failed in Mathematics and English be 30% and 20% respectively.

Percentage of students failed either one or both subjects = 30 + 20 – 10 = 40%

Hence, percentage of pass students = 100 – 40 = 60%

Now, 60% = 360

$$\therefore 100\% = \frac{360}{60} \times 100 = 600.$$

12. Let initially electric tax is Rs. 100 and consumption = 100 units

Decrease in consumption

= 100 × 100 – 120 × 80 = Rs. 400

$$\text{Hence, decrease percentage} = \frac{400 \times 100}{100 \times 100} = 4\%.$$

13. Let the selling price of a commodity be Rs. 100 and number of sales = 100 units

Decrease in daily cash = 100 × 100 – 75 × 130 = Rs. 250

Hence, decrease percentage

$$= \frac{250 \times 100}{100 \times 100} = 2.5\%.$$

14. Let x kg of good wheat be added; then

$$\frac{10}{100} \times 150 = \frac{5}{100}(150 + x)$$

$\Rightarrow 150 + x = 300 \quad \therefore x = 150$ kg.

15. Let her monthly income be Rs. x; then

$$x - \left(\frac{15}{100} \times x + \frac{17}{100} \times x + \frac{6}{100} \times x\right) = 15{,}500$$

$$\Rightarrow x - \frac{38x}{100} = 15500 \quad \Rightarrow \frac{62x}{100} = 15500$$

$$\therefore x = \frac{15500 \times 100}{62} = \text{Rs. } 25000.$$

PROFIT AND LOSS

1. Ashok bought 25 kg of rice at the rate of Rs. 6 per kg and 35 kg of rice at the rate of Rs. 7 per kg. He mixed the two and sold the mixture at the rate of Rs. 6.75 per kg. What was his gain or loss in the transaction?
   A. Rs. 16 gain B. Rs. 16 loss
   C. Rs. 10 gain D. None of these
2. Profit after selling a commodity for Rs. 425 is same as loss after selling it for Rs. 355. The cost of the commodity is :
   A. Rs. 285 B. Rs. 390
   C. Rs. 295 D. Rs. 400
3. Ram bought 4 dozen apples at Rs. 12 per dozen and 2 dozen at Rs. 16 per dozen. He sold all of them to earn 20%. At what price per dozen did he sell the apples?
   A. Rs. 14.40 B. Rs. 16.00
   C. Rs. 16.80 D. Rs. 16.20
4. At what price must Kantilal sell a mixture of 80 kg sugar at Rs. 6.75 per kg with 120 kg at Rs. 8 per kg to gain 20%?
   A. Rs. 7.50 per kg B. Rs. 8.20 per kg
   C. Rs. 8.35 per kg D. Rs. 9 per kg
5. A person bought an article and sold it at a loss of 10%. If he had bought it for 20% less and sold it for Rs. 55 more, he would have had a profit of 40%. The C.P. of the article is :
   A. Rs. 200 B. Rs. 225
   C. Rs. 250 D. None of these
6. A dealer sold a machine to a shopkeeper at 20% profit. The shopkeeper sold the machine to a customer so as to get 25% profit for himself. The difference between the selling price of the dealer and that of the shopkeeper was found to be Rs. 129. What is the initial price of the machine?
   A. Rs. 410 B. Rs. 420
   C. Rs. 430 D. Rs. 440
7. A man bought a horse and cart. If he sold the horse at 10% loss and the cart at 20% gain he would not loss anything. If he sold the horse at 5% loss and the cart at 5% gain he would lose Rs. 10 in the bargain. What did he pay for each?
   A. Rs. 400, Rs. 200 B. Rs. 300, Rs. 300
   C. Rs. 250, Rs. 350 D. Rs. 350, Rs. 250
8. The marked price of a radio is 20% more than its cost price. If a discount of 10% is given on the marked price, the gain percentage is:
   A. 8 B. 10
   C. 12 D. 15
9. A dishonest dealer sells his goods at the cost price and still earns a profit of 60% by underweight. What weight does he use for a kg?
   A. 625 gms B. 750 gms
   C. 800 gms D. 850 gms
10. A man sells two horses for Rs. 990 each. On one he gains 10% and the other he loses 10%. What is his total percentage of gain or loss in the transaction?
   A. 1% gain B. 1% loss
   C. 2% gain D. 2% loss

ANSWERS

1	2	3	4	5	6	7	8	9	10
C	B	B	D	C	C	A	A	A	B

SOME SELECTED EXPLANATORY ANSWERS

1. C.P. of 60 kg mixture = Rs. $(25 \times 6 + 35 \times 7)$ = Rs. 395

S.P. of 60 kg mixtire = Rs. (60×6.75) = Rs. 405

$\therefore$ Gain = Rs. $(405 - 395)$ = Rs. 10

2. Let C.P. = Rs. x

Then, $425 - x = x - 355 \Rightarrow 2x = 780$

$\therefore$ x = Rs. 390

3. C.P. of 6 dozen apples = Rs. $(12 \times 4 + 16 \times 2)$ = Rs. 80

$\therefore$ S.P. = Rs. $\left(\frac{120}{100} \times 80\right)$ = Rs. 96

$\therefore$ S.P. per dozen = Rs. $\left(\frac{96}{6}\right)$ = Rs. 16

4. C.P. of 1 kg sugar = $\frac{80 \times 6.75 + 120 \times 8}{200}$ = Rs. 7.50

$\therefore$ S.P. of 1 kg = Rs. $\left(\frac{120}{100} \times 7.50\right)$ = Rs. 9 per kg

5. Let C.P. = Rs. x,

then S.P. = $\frac{90}{100} \times x$ = Rs. $\frac{9x}{10}$

Now, when C.P. = Rs. $\frac{80x}{100}$ = Rs. $\frac{4x}{5}$;

then S.P. = $\frac{140}{100} \times \frac{4x}{5}$ = Rs. $\frac{28x}{25}$

But, $\frac{28x}{25} - \frac{9x}{10} = 55 \Rightarrow \frac{11x}{50} = 55$

$\therefore$ x = Rs. 250

6. Let the initial price = Rs. x; then C.P. for dealer

$= \frac{120}{100} \times x$ = Rs. $\frac{6x}{5}$

Again, C.P. for shopkeeper = $\frac{125}{100} \times \frac{6x}{5}$ = Rs. $\frac{3x}{2}$

Now, $\frac{3x}{2} - \frac{6x}{5} = 129 \Rightarrow \frac{3x}{10} = 129$

$\therefore x = \frac{10 \times 129}{3}$ = Rs. 430

7. Here, 10% C.P. of horse = 20% C.P. of cart;
Hence, C.P. of horse = 2 × C.P. of cart;
Let C.P. of cart and horse be Rs. x and Rs. $2x$ respectively; then,

$\frac{5}{100} \times 2x - \frac{5}{100} \times x = 10 \Rightarrow \frac{1}{20} x = 10$

$\therefore x = 200$

Hence, C.P. of a cart = Rs. 200 and C.P. of a horse = 2 × 200 = Rs. 400

8. Let C.P. be Rs. 100; then marked price = Rs. 120

Since, S.P. = $\frac{90}{100} \times 120$ = Rs. 108

$\therefore$ Profit = 108 – 100 = Rs. 8, Hence, gain = 8%.

9. Required weight = $\frac{100}{160} \times 1000$ = 625 gms.

10. Here, loss % = $\left(\frac{10}{10}\right)^2$ = 1%.

SIMPLE INTEREST

1. A lent a sum of Rs. 1250 to B at a certain rate of interest for 3 years and a sum of Rs. 1500 to C at the same rate of interest for 2 years. If he was paid total Rs. 258.75 as interest in both cases, find the rate of interest at which money was lent by him.

   A. $4\frac{1}{6}\%$ B. $6\frac{1}{4}\%$

   C. $2\frac{1}{7}\%$ D. $3\frac{5}{6}\%$

2. A invested Rs. 5000 at a certain rate of simple interest and Rs. 4000 for the same period at 1% higher rate of interest. If the interest in both cases is same, the former rate of interest is :

   A. 3% B. 4%

   C. 6% D. 5%

3. If a certain sum of money at simple interest amounts to Rs. 1900 in 3 years and to Rs. 2050 in 5 years, the rate per cent per annum is :

   A. 4½% B. 3½%

   C. 2½% D. 5¼%

4. A certain sum of money lent out on simple interest amounts to Rs. 1760 in 2 years and to Rs. 2000 in 5 years. Find the sum.

   A. Rs. 1650 B. Rs. 1500

   C. Rs. 1580 D. Rs. 1600

5. Out of the sum of Rs. 1550, a part was lent out at 5% p.a. simple interest and the remaining at 8% p.a. simple interest. If the total interest in both cases after 3 years is Rs. 300, the sum of money lent out at 8% p.a. simple interest was:

   A. Rs. 760 B. Rs. 775

   C. Rs. 750 D. Rs. 780

6. If simple interest on a certain sum of money for 4 years at 5% p.a. is same as the simple interest on Rs. 840 for 10 years at the rate of 4% p.a., the sum of money is:

   A. Rs. 1780 B. Rs. 1660

   C. Rs. 1680 D. Rs. 1620

7. What equal instalment of annual payment will discharge a debt which is due as Rs. 848 at the end of 4 years at 4% per annum simple interest?

   A. Rs. 200 B. Rs. 212

   C. Rs. 225 D. Rs. 250

8. Madhavi lent Rs. 5000 to Kamla for 5 years and Rs. 3000 to Vimla for 4 years. Find the rate of interest, if Madhavi gets an interest of Rs. 600 in the end.

   A. 1.62% B. 2.5%

   C. 3% D. 4%

9. A sum of money doubles itself in 7 years at simple interest. In how many years it will become four fold?

   A. 10 years B. 14 years

   C. 21 years D. 35 years

10. An amount doubles itself at the end of 8 years with a certain rate of simple interest. What will be the total simple interest on Rs. 8000 at that rate at the end of 4 years?

    A. Rs. 2000 B. Rs. 4000

    C. Rs. 6000 D. None of these

ANSWERS

1	2	3	4	5	6	7	8	9	10
D	B	A	D	C	C	A	A	C	B

SOME SELECTED EXPLANATORY ANSWERS

1. $\frac{1250 \times R \times 3}{100} + \frac{1500 \times R \times 2}{100} = 258.75$

$\Rightarrow 6750\ R = 25875$

$\therefore \quad R = \frac{25875}{6750} = \frac{23}{6} = 3\frac{5}{6}\%$

2. Here, $\frac{5000 \times R \times T}{100} = \frac{4000 \times (R+1) \times T}{100}$

$\Rightarrow 5R = 4R + 4 \quad \therefore \quad R = 4\%$

3. Simple interest for 2 years
= Rs. 2050 − Rs. 1900 = Rs. 150

$\therefore$ Simple interest for 1 year = Rs. $\frac{150}{2}$
= Rs. 75

Since simple interest for 3 years = Rs. 75 × 3
= Rs. 225

$\therefore$ Principal = Rs. 1900 − Rs. 225
= Rs. 1675

Hence, Rate = $\frac{75 \times 100}{1675 \times 1}$ = 4½%

4. Interest for 3 years = Rs. 2000 − Rs. 1760
= Rs. 240

$\therefore$ Interest for 1 year = Rs. $\frac{240}{3}$ = Rs. 80

And interest for 2 years = Rs. 80 × 2 = Rs. 160

$\therefore$ Principal = Rs. 1760 − Rs. 160 = Rs. 1600

5. Let Rs. x and Rs $(1550 - x)$ were lent out at 8% and 5% respectively; then

$\frac{x \times 8 \times 3}{100} + \frac{(1550 - x) \times 5 \times 3}{100} = 300$

$\Rightarrow 24x + 23250 - 15x = 30000$

$\Rightarrow 9x = 6750 \quad \therefore \quad x = \frac{6750}{9}$ = Rs. 750

6. Here, $\frac{P \times 5 \times 4}{100} = \frac{840 \times 4 \times 10}{100} \Rightarrow 5P = 8400$

$\therefore P = \frac{8400}{5}$ = Rs. 1680

7. Let equal instalment be Rs. x; then

$x + \frac{x \times 4 \times 3}{100} + x + \frac{x \times 4 \times 2}{100} + x + \frac{x \times 4 \times 1}{100} + x = 848$

$\Rightarrow 4x + \frac{24x}{100} = 848 \quad \Rightarrow \quad \frac{106x}{25} = 848$

$\therefore x = \frac{848 \times 25}{106}$ = Rs. 200

8. $\frac{5000 \times R \times 5}{100} + \frac{3000 \times R \times 4}{100} = 600$

$\Rightarrow \quad 250\ R + 120\ R = 600$

$\Rightarrow \quad 370R = 600$

$\therefore \quad R = \frac{600}{370} = 1.62\%$

9. Let principal be Rs. x; then amount = Rs. $2x$,
Hence, I = $2x - x$ = Rs. x.

$R = \frac{x \times 100}{x \times 7} = \frac{100}{7}\%$ p.a.

Now, amount = Rs. $4x$; then I = $4x - x$
= Rs. $3x$

Hence, $T = \frac{3x \times 100}{x \times \frac{100}{7}} = \frac{3 \times 100 \times 7}{100} = 21$ years

10. Let principal = Rs. x; then amount = Rs. $2x$;
I = $2x - x$ = Rs. x

$R = \frac{x \times 100}{x \times 8} = \frac{25}{2}\%$

Again, $I = \frac{8000 \times 25 \times 4}{100 \times 2}$ = Rs. 4000

COMPOUND INTEREST

1. The compound interest on a certain sum of money invested for 3 years at 5% per annum is Rs. 1891.50. What will be the simple interest on the same sum at the same rate for 2 years?
   A. Rs. 1700 B. Rs. 1200
   C. Rs. 1500 D. Rs. 2100

2. A sum of money lent out at a certain rate of simple interest amounts to Rs. 6600 in 2 years and to Rs. 6900 in 3 years. What will be the compound interest on the same sum of money if lent out at the same rate for 2 years?
   A. Rs. 605 B. Rs. 715
   C. Rs. 615 D. Rs. 595

3. A man deposits Rs. 1200 in a bank on the 1st day of each year. If the bank pays 5% per annum compound interest on deposited sum of money, what will be the amount to his credit on the 10th day of the second year?
   A. Rs. 2560 B. Rs. 2460
   C. Rs. 2370 D. Rs. 2860

4. If the difference between compound and simple interest on a certain sum of money for 3 years at 5% per annum is Rs. 244, the sum is :
   A. Rs. 40000 B. Rs. 25000
   C. Rs. 30000 D. Rs. 32000

5. A man purchased a sewing machine for Rs. 5000. If due to sustained use value of this sewing machine depreciates by 6% annually, find its value after 3 years.
   A. Rs. 3775.67 B. Rs. 4152.92
   C. Rs. 4250.25 D. Rs. 4356.25

6. Find the sum on which the difference between compound and simple interest for 3 years at 10% per annum will be Rs. 868.
   A. Rs. 29500 B. Rs. 27625
   C. Rs. 28500 D. Rs. 28000

7. Samir invested Rs. 15000 at the rate of interest 10% p.a. for 1 year. If the interest compound six months. What amount will Samir get at the end of the year?
   A. Rs. 16,500 B. Rs. 16525.50
   C. Rs. 16537.50 D. Rs. 18,150

8. The compound interest on a certain sum for 2 years at 10% per annum is Rs. 525. The simple interest on the same sum for double the time at half the rate per cent per annum is:
   A. Rs. 800 B. Rs. 600
   C. Rs. 500 D. Rs. 400

9. The least number of complete years in which a sum of money put at 20% compound interest will be more than doubled is:
   A. 6 B. 5
   C. 4 D. 3

10. On a sum of money, the simple interest for 2 years is Rs. 660, while the compound interest is Rs. 696.30, the rate of interest being the same in both cases. Find the rate of interest.
    A. Rs. 12% B. 11%
    C. 10% D. 9%

ANSWERS

1	2	3	4	5	6	7	8	9	10
B	C	B	D	B	D	C	C	C	B

SOME SELECTED EXPLANATORY ANSWERS

1. Here, $1891.50 = P\left[\left(1+\frac{5}{100}\right)^3 - 1\right]$

$\Rightarrow \quad 1891.50 = P\left[\left(\frac{21}{20}\right)^3 - 1\right]$

$\Rightarrow \quad 1891.50 = P\left(\frac{1261}{8000}\right)$

$\therefore\ P = \frac{1891.50 \times 8000}{1261} = \text{Rs. } 12000$

Now, $\quad \text{S.I.} = \frac{12000 \times 5 \times 2}{100} = \text{Rs. } 1200$

2. Here, 1 year's S.I. = Rs. 6900 – Rs. 6600 = Rs. 300

$\therefore$ 2 year's S.I. = 300 × 2 = Rs. 600

$\therefore$ Principal = Rs. 6600 – Rs. 600 = Rs. 6000

Hence, $\quad \text{Rate} = \frac{600 \times 100}{6000 \times 2} = 5\%$

$\therefore \quad \text{C.I.} = 6000\left[\left(1+\frac{5}{100}\right)^2 - 1\right]$

$= 6000\left[\left(\frac{21}{20}\right)^2 - 1\right] = \frac{6000 \times 41}{400} = \text{Rs. } 615$

3. Required amount $= 1200\left(1+\frac{5}{100}\right) + 1200$

$= 1200 \times \frac{21}{20} + 1200 = 1260 + 1200 = \text{Rs. } 2460$

4. Here, $P\left[\left(1+\frac{5}{100}\right)^3 - 1\right] - \frac{P \times 5 \times 3}{100} = 244$

$\Rightarrow P \times \frac{1261}{8000} - \frac{3P}{20} = 244 \Rightarrow P \times \frac{61}{8000} = 244$

$\therefore\ P = \frac{244 \times 8000}{61} = \text{Rs. } 32000$

5. Here, value of the machine after 3 years

$= 5000\left(1-\frac{6}{100}\right)^3 = 5000 \times \frac{47}{50} \times \frac{47}{50} \times \frac{47}{50}$

= Rs. 4152.92.

6. Here, $P\left[\left(1+\frac{10}{100}\right)^3 - 1\right] - \frac{P \times 10 \times 3}{100} = 868$

$\Rightarrow P \times \frac{331}{1000} - \frac{3P}{10} = 868$

$\Rightarrow P \times \frac{31}{1000} = 868 \quad \therefore\ P = \frac{868 \times 1000}{31}$

= Rs. 28000

7. $A = 15000\left(1+\frac{5}{100}\right)^2 = 15000 \times \frac{441}{400}$

= Rs. 16537.50

8. Here, $P\left[\left(1+\frac{10}{100}\right)^2 - 1\right] = 525$

$\Rightarrow P\left[\frac{121}{100} - 1\right] = 525 \Rightarrow P \times \frac{21}{100} = 525$

$\therefore\ P = \frac{525 \times 100}{21} = \text{Rs. } 2500$

Hence, required S.I. $= \frac{2500 \times 5 \times 4}{100} = \text{Rs. } 500$

9. Here, $P\left(1+\frac{20}{100}\right)^n > 2P \Rightarrow \left(\frac{6}{5}\right)^n > 2$

Hence, if $n = 4$ then, $\left(\frac{6}{5}\right)^4 = \frac{1296}{625} > 2$

So, $n = 4$ years

10. Here, S.I. for 1 year = Rs. 330

Since, simple interest of Rs. 330 for 1 year = 696.30 – 660 = Rs. 36.30

Hence, required rate $= \frac{36.30 \times 100}{330 \times 1} = \frac{3630}{330}$

= 11%

AREA AND PERIMETER

1. If side of a square is reduced by 50%, its area will be reduced by

A. 50% B. 75%
C. 80% D. 60%

2. If each side of a square is doubled, its area will become

A. double
B. four times
C. three times
D. eight times

3. Three sides of a triangle are in the ratio of 17 : 15 : 8. If the perimeter of this triangle is 40 m, find its area

A. 50 sq. m. B. 49 sq. m.
C. 60 sq. m. D. 69 sq. m.

4. If the length of a rectangle is increased by 20% and width is decreased by 15%, then its area

A. decreases by 4% B. increases by 2%
C. decreases by 2% D. increases by 3%

5. If the length of a rectangle is increased by 20%, then by how much per cent its breadth must be decreased so as to keep its area unaltered?

A. 25% B. $8\frac{1}{3}\%$
C. $16\frac{2}{3}\%$ D. 20%

6. The ratio of length and breadth of a rectangular plot is 71 : 61 respectively. The area of the plot is 17324 m^2. What is perimeter of the plot?

A. 264 m B. 284 m
C. 528 m D. 614 m

7. If the length and breadth of a rectangular field are increased, the area increases by 50%. If the increase in length was 20%, by what percentage was the breadth increased?

A. 20% B. 25%
C. 30% D. 40%

8. The length and breadth of a varandah is 40 m and 15 m respectively. How many stone slabs of size 6 decimetre × 5 decimetre each are needed in flooring it:

A. 1000 B. 2000
C. 3000 D. 4000

9. The circumference of a circular plot is 396 m. What is the area of the circular plot?

A. 9,446 m^2 B. 9,856 m^2
C. 12,474 m^2 D. 18,634 m^2

10. If the sides of an equilateral triangle are increased by 20%, 30% and 50% respectively to form a new triangle, the increase in the perimeter of the equilateral triangle is:

A. 25% B. $33\frac{1}{3}\%$
C. 50% D. 100%

ANSWERS

1	2	3	4	5	6	7	8	9	10
B	B	C	B	C	C	B	B	C	B

SOME SELECTED EXPLANATORY ANSWERS

1. Area of the square = x^2 sq. m.

Side of the new square = x – 50% of $x = \frac{x}{2}$ m

$\therefore$ Area of the new square = $\left(\frac{x}{2}\right)^2 = \frac{x^2}{4}$ sq. m.

$\therefore$ Reduction in area of the square = $x^2 - \frac{x^2}{4}$

$= \frac{3x^2}{4}$ sq. m.

$\therefore$ Percentage reduction = $\frac{3x^2/4}{x^2} \times 100 = 75\%$

2. Area of the square = x^2 sq. m

Now, area of the new square = $(2x)^2 = 4x^2$ sq. m

Hence, it is clear that if side of a square is doubled, its area becomes four times.

3. Suppose sides of the triangle are $17x$ m, $15x$ m and $8x$ metres

$\therefore$ Perimeter $= 17x + 15x + 8x = 40x$

Now, $40x = 40$

$\Rightarrow$ $x = 1$ m

Therefore, the sides are $17 \times 1 = 17$ m, $15 \times 1 = 15$ m and $8 \times 1 = 8$ m

$\because$ $(17)^2 = (15)^2 + (8)^2$,

i.e., it is a right angled triangle

$\therefore$ Area of the right angled triangle

$= \frac{1}{2} \times 8 \times 15 = 60$ sq. m.

4. Area of the rectangle = xy sq. metre

Area of the new rectangle = $\frac{120}{100} x \times \frac{85}{100} y$

$= 1.020\, xy$ sq. metre

$\therefore$ Increase in the area = $1.02\, xy - xy$

$= .02\, xy$ sq. m.

$\therefore$ Percentage increase = $\frac{.02xy}{xy} \times 100 = 2\%$

5. Area of the rectangle = xy

On reducing the breadth by A% and increasing the length by 20%

Length of the new rectangle = $\frac{120x}{100}$ $x = 1.2x$

Breadth of the new rectangle = y – A% of y

$= y\left(1 - \frac{A}{100}\right)$

$\therefore$ Area of the new rectangle = $1.2x \times y\left(1 - \frac{A}{100}\right)$

Now, $xy = 1.2\, xy\left(1 - \frac{A}{100}\right) \Rightarrow 1 = 1.2\frac{(100 - A)}{100}$

$\Rightarrow$ $1.2\,A = 120 - 100$

$\therefore$ $A = \frac{20}{1.2} = 16\frac{2}{3}\%$

6. Let length and breadth of a rectangle be $71x$ and $61x$ m; then

$71x \times 61x = 17324 \Rightarrow x^2 = \frac{17324}{71 \times 61} = 4$

$\therefore$ $x = 2$

Hence, length = $71 \times 2 = 142$ m; breadth $= 61 \times 2 = 122$ m

Since, perimeter $= 2(142 + 122) = 2 \times 264$

$= 528$ m

7. Here, $20 + x + \frac{20 \times x}{100} = 50 \Rightarrow x + \frac{x}{5} = 30$

$\Rightarrow \frac{6x}{5} = 30 \quad \therefore x = \frac{5 \times 30}{6} = 25$

Hence, breadth was increased by 25%

8. Required number of stone slabs = $\frac{40 \times 15}{\frac{6}{10} \times \frac{5}{10}}$

$= \frac{40 \times 15 \times 100}{6 \times 5} = 2000$

9. Radius of circular plot = $\frac{396 \times 7}{2 \times 22} = 63$ m

Area of the circular plot = $\frac{22}{7} \times 63 \times 63$

$= 12{,}474$ m^2

VOLUME AND SURFACE AREA

1. If a solid sphere of 3 cm radius is melted and recast into a right circular cone whose base radius is same as that of the sphere, the height of the cone will be

   A. 8 cm   B. 12 cm
   C. 6 cm   D. 5 cm

2. Diameter of a roller is 2.4 m and it is 1.68 m long. If it takes 1000 complete revolutions once over to level a field, the area of the field is

   A. 12672 sq. m   B. 12671 sq. m
   C. 12762 sq. m   D. 11768 sq. m

3. If each edge of a cube is increased by 10%, then by how much per cent will the surface area of this cube be increased?

   A. 21%   B. 18%
   C. 15%   D. 20%

4. Height and base radius of a solid cylinder are 14 m and 4 m respectively. It is melted and recast into a solid cone of the same base radius as that of the cylinder, what will be the height of the cone?

   A. 21 m   B. 42 m
   C. 48 m   D. 54 m

5. A room is in the form of a cube of side 10 m. How many bales of cotton can be kept in it if each bale covers 5 cu m space?

   A. 100   B. 175
   C. 200   D. 225

6. Three cubes having side 2 cm, 3 cm and 4 cm respectively are melted together to form a new cube. The side of the new cube will be

   A. 3.526 cm   B. 4.628 cm
   C. 4.626 cm   D. 4.528 cm

7. If base diameter of a cylinder is increased by 50%, then by how much per cent its height must be decreased so as to keep its volume unaltered?

   A. 45.56%   B. 55.56%
   C. 50.16%   D. 62.33%

8. The surface area of a cube is 600 sq. m. Its diagonal is

   A. $10\sqrt{3}$ cm   B. $5\sqrt{3}$ cm
   C. $4\sqrt{2}$ cm   D. $10\sqrt{2}$ cm

9. The base diameter of a conical tomb is 28 m and its slant height is 50 m. Find the cost of white washing its curved surface at the rate of 80 paise per sq. m?

   A. Rs. 1860   B. Rs. 1760
   C. Rs. 1950   D. Rs. 1875

10. The volume of a cuboid is 1120 cu cm and its height is 5 cm while the length and the breadth of the cuboid are in the ratio 8 : 7. The length of this cylinder exceeds the breadth by

    A. 4 cm   B. 2 cm
    C. 7 cm   D. 5 cm

ANSWERS

1	2	3	4	5	6	7	8	9	10
B	A	A	B	C	C	B	A	B	B

SOME SELECTED EXPLANATORY ANSWERS

1. Volume of the cone = Volume of the sphere

$\therefore \quad \frac{1}{3}\pi(3)^2 \times h = \frac{4}{3}\pi \times 3^3 \Rightarrow h = 12$ cm

Hence, height of the cone = 12 cm.

2. Surface area of the roller = $2\pi rh$

$= 2\times\frac{22}{7}\times 1.2\times 1.68 = 12.672$ sq. m

In one complete revolution, the roller covers 12.672 sq. m.

$\therefore$ It will cover in 1000 revolutions

$= 12.672 \times 1000 = 12672$ sq. m

Hence, area of the field = 12672 sq. m.

3. Percentage increase in the surface area of the cube $= \left(x+y+\frac{xy}{100}\right)\%$

$= \left(10+10+\frac{10\times 10}{100}\right)\% = 21\%.$

4. Here,

volume of the cone = Volume of the cylinder

$\Rightarrow \quad \frac{1}{3}\pi r^2 \times \text{height} = \pi r^2 \times 14$

$\therefore \quad$ Height $= 14 \times 3 = 42$ m

Thus, height of the cone = 42 m.

5. Volume of the cubical room $= (10)^3$

$= 1000$ cu m

Number of cotton bales which can be placed in the room

$= \frac{\text{Volume of the room}}{\text{Volume of each cotton bale}} = \frac{1000}{5} = 200.$

6. Volume of the new cube $= 2^3 + 3^3 + 4^3$

$= 8 + 27 + 64 = 99$cu cm

$\therefore$ Side of the new cube $= \sqrt[3]{99} = 4.626$ cm.

7. Change in the volume of the cylinder

$= \left(x+y+(-z)+\frac{xy+y(-z)+(-zx)}{100}+\frac{xy(-z)}{100^2}\right)\%$

Since volume of the cylinder remains unchanged.

$\therefore \quad$ Change = 0%

Now, $\left(50+50+(-z)+\frac{50\times 50-50z-50z}{100}+\frac{50\times 50\times(-z)}{100^2}\right)=0$

$\therefore \quad 100 - z + 25 - z - .25z = 0$

$\Rightarrow 2.25z = 125 \Rightarrow z = \frac{125}{2.25} = 55.56$

$\therefore$ Height of the cylinder should be decreased by 55.56%.

8. Here, $\quad 6 \times (\text{side})^2 = 600$

$\Rightarrow \quad \text{side}^2 = 100$

$\Rightarrow \quad \text{side} = \sqrt{100} = 10$ cm

$\therefore$ Diagonal of the cube $= \sqrt{3}\times\text{side}$

$= \sqrt{3}\times 10$

$= 10\sqrt{3}$ cm.

9. Area of the curved surface of the cone

$= \frac{22}{7}\times\frac{28}{2}\times 50 = 2200$ sq. m.

$\therefore$ Cost of white washing at 80 paise per sq. m

$= 2200\times\frac{80}{100} = $ Rs. 1760.

10. Suppose the length and the breadth of the cuboid are $8x$ cm and $7x$ cm

$\therefore$ Here, $\quad 8x \times 7x \times 5 = 1120$

$\Rightarrow x^2 = \frac{1120}{280} = 4 = (2)^2 \quad \Rightarrow \quad x = 2$

$\therefore$ Length of the cuboid $= 8 \times 2 = 16$ cm

Breadth of the cuboid $= 7 \times 2 = 14$ cm

Hence, it is clear that length of the cuboid exceeds the breadth by 2 cm.

ALGEBRIC OPERATION

1. If $x + \frac{1}{x} = 15$, then the value of $x^2 + \frac{1}{x^2}$ will be:

A. 228 B. 230
C. 323 D. 223

2. If $x = 12$ and $y = 4$, the value of $(x+y)^{x/y}$ will be:

A. 4096 B. 3896
C. 4196 D. 5086

3. If $x = 9$, $y = \sqrt{17}$, then the value of $\left(x^2 - y^2\right)^{-1/2}$ will be:

A. 2^{-4} B. 2^2
C. 3^{-3} D. 2^{-3}

4. What should be added to $\frac{x}{y}$ to get $\frac{y}{x}$?

A. $\frac{x^2 - y^2}{xy}$ B. $\frac{y^2 - x^2}{xy}$
C. $\frac{2xy}{x^2 - y^2}$ D. $\frac{y^2 - x^2}{2xy}$

5. If $x + y = 2z$, then the value of $\left(\frac{x}{x-z} + \frac{z}{y-z}\right)$ will be:

A. 1 B. 4
C. 3/2 D. 2

6. If $x + y + z = 0$, then the value of $\frac{(x+y)(y+z)(z+x)}{xyz}$ will be:

A. −3 B. −2
C. 0 D. −1

7. If $x + \frac{1}{x} = 3$, the value of $x^4 + \frac{1}{x^4}$ will be:

A. 49 B. 47
C. 37 D. 42

8. If $\left(x + \frac{1}{x}\right)^2 = 0$, then the value of $\left(x^2 + \frac{1}{x^2}\right)$ will be:

A. 1 B. −1
C. 2 D. −2

9. If $\left(a + \frac{2}{a}\right) = 3$, then the value of $\left(a - \frac{2}{a}\right)$ will be:

A. ± 4 B. ± 5
C. ± 2 D. ± 1

10. If $\sqrt{a} + \frac{1}{\sqrt{a}} = 4$, then the value of $a^2 + \frac{1}{a^2}$ will be:

A. 194 B. 199
C. 178 D. 192

ANSWERS

1	2	3	4	5	6	7	8	9	10
D	A	D	B	A	D	B	D	D	A

EXPLANATORY ANSWERS

1. $\because \quad x + \frac{1}{x} = 15$

$\Rightarrow \quad \left(x+\frac{1}{x}\right)^2 = (15)^2$

$\Rightarrow \quad x^2 + \frac{1}{x^2} + 2.x\frac{1}{x} = 225$

$\therefore \quad x^2 + \frac{1}{x^2} = 225 - 2$

$= 223.$

2. $(x+y)^{x/y} = (12+4)^{12/4}$

$= (16)^3 = 4096.$

$[\because x = 12, y = 4]$

3. $\left(x^2-y^2\right)^{-1/2} = (81-17)^{-1/2}$

$= (64)^{-1/2} = \frac{1}{\sqrt{64}} = \frac{1}{8} = 2^{-3}.$

4. Suppose A is added to $\frac{x}{y}$, then $\frac{x}{y} + \text{A} = \frac{y}{x}$

$\Rightarrow \text{A} = \frac{y}{x} - \frac{x}{y} = \frac{y^2-x^2}{xy}$

$\therefore$ when $\frac{y^2-x^2}{xy}$ is added to $\frac{x}{y}$, the sum so obtained will be $\frac{y}{x}$.

5. $\because \quad x + y = 2z$

$\Rightarrow \quad x - z = z - y = -(y - z)$

$\therefore \quad \frac{x}{x-z} + \frac{z}{y-z} = \frac{x}{-(y-z)} + \frac{z}{y-z} = \frac{z-x}{y-z} = 1.$

$[\because x - z = z - y]$

6. $\because \quad x + y + z = 0$

$\Rightarrow \quad x + y = -z$

$x + y + z = 0$

$\Rightarrow \quad y + z = -x$

and $\quad x + y + z = 0 \Rightarrow z + x = -y$

$\therefore \quad \frac{(x+y)(y+z)(z+x)}{xyz} = \frac{-z.-x.-y}{xyz} = -1.$

7. $\because \quad x + \frac{1}{x} = 3 \Rightarrow \left(x+\frac{1}{x}\right)^2 = (3)^2$

$\Rightarrow \quad x^2 + \frac{1}{x^2} + 2.x.\frac{1}{x} = 9$

$\Rightarrow \quad x^2 + \frac{1}{x^2} = 9 - 2 = 7$

$\because \quad x^2 + \frac{1}{x^2} = 7$

$\Rightarrow \quad \left(x^2+\frac{1}{x^2}\right)^2 = (7)^2$

$\Rightarrow x^4 + \frac{1}{x^4} + 2.x^2.\frac{1}{x^2} = 49$

$\therefore \quad x^4 + \frac{1}{x^4} = 49 - 2 = 47.$

8. $\left(x+\frac{1}{x}\right)^2 = 0$

$\Rightarrow \quad x^2 + \frac{1}{x^2} + 2x.\frac{1}{x} = 0 \Rightarrow x^2 + \frac{1}{x^2} = -2.$

9. $\because \quad \left(a-\frac{2}{a}\right)^2 = \left(a+\frac{2}{a}\right)^2 - 4.a.\frac{2}{a}$

$= (3)^2 - 8 = 9 - 8 = 1$

$\therefore \quad \left(a-\frac{2}{a}\right) = \sqrt{1} = \pm 1.$

10. $\because \quad \sqrt{a}+\frac{1}{\sqrt{a}} = 4 \Rightarrow \left(\sqrt{a}+\frac{1}{\sqrt{a}}\right)^2 = (4)^2$

$= a + \frac{1}{a} + 2.\sqrt{a}.\frac{1}{\sqrt{a}} = 16$

$\because \quad \left(a+\frac{1}{a}\right) = 14 \Rightarrow \left(a+\frac{1}{a}\right)^2 = (14)^2.$

$\Rightarrow \quad a^2 + \frac{1}{a^2} + 2.a.\frac{1}{a} = 196$

$\therefore \quad a^2 + \frac{1}{a^2} = 196 - 2 = 194.$

GENERAL INTELLIGENCE AND REASONING

SERIES

Directions : *In each of the following series determine the order of the letters. Then from the given options select the one which will complete the given series.*

1. BMK, DLM, FKO, HJQ, ?

A. JIR B. JIT
C. JHS D. JIS

2. A, CD, FGH, ?

A. IJKL B. KLMN
C. JKLM D. LMNO

3. BXJ, ETL, HPN, KLP, ?

A. PHR B. NIR
C. NHR D. MHR

4. PUF, QVG, RWH, ?

A. SXI B. SYZ
C. SXJ D. SVI

5. DEF, HIJ, MNO, ?

A. RTV B. STU
C. PTU D. SRU

Directions : *Which of the following groups of letters will complete the given series?*

6. ab---b-bbaa-

A. babba B. abaab
C. abbab D. baaab

7. aa-ab--aaa-a

A. baaa B. abab
C. aaab D. aabb

8. -baa-aab-a-a

A. baab B. abab
C. aaba D. aabb

9. -a cca-ccca-acccc-aaa

A. ccaa B. acca
C. caac D. caaa

10. c-bbb--abbbb-abbb-

A. abccb B. bacbb
C. aabcb D. abacb

Directions : *In the following questions, select the number(s) from the given options for completing the given series.*

11. 3, 9, 27, 81, 243, ?

A. 486 B. 729
C. 972 D. 359

12. 1, 6, 12, 19, 27, ?

A. 38 B. 35
C. 36 D. 54

13. 2, 6, 14, 30, 62, ?

A. 126 B. 128
C. 120 D. 130

14. 8, 48, 16, 96, 32, ?

A. 192 B. 150
C. 64 D. 288

15. 2, 8, 14, 24, 34, 48, ?

A. 66 B. 62
C. 58 D. 64

Directions : *In the given series find the number which is wrong.*

16. 5, 25, 120, 625, 3125, 15625

A. 15625 B. 625
C. 120 D. 5

17. 4, 8, 11, 22, 18, 36, 24, 50

A. 8 B. 22
C. 36 D. 24

18. 2, 4, 12, 24, 72, 142, 432

A. 432 B. 12
C. 142 D. 72

19. 2, 3, 4, 4, 6, 8, 9, 12, 16

A. 3 B. 9
C. 6 D. 12

20. 97, 91, 86, 83, 79, 77, 76, 76

A. 86 B. 76
C. 91 D. 83

ANSWERS

1	2	3	4	5	6	7	8	9	10
D	C	C	A	B	D	C	B	D	A
11	**12**	**13**	**14**	**15**	**16**	**17**	**18**	**19**	**20**
B	C	A	A	B	C	D	C	B	D

SOME SELECTED EXPLANATORY ANSWERS

1. The letters in one group correspond to the letters in the next group in the manner +2, –1, +2 respectively.

BMK DLM FKO HJQ JIS

+2 +2 +2 +2

–1 –1 –1 –1

+2 +2 +2 +2

2. The letters are in natural sequence and from one group to the next one letter is dropped. Also the number of letters in groups is increased by one.

A CD FGH JKLM

↓ ↓ ↓

B E I

3. The letters in one group correspond to the letters in the next group in the manner +3, – 4, +2 respectively, *i.e.*,

BXJ ETL HPN KLP NHR

+3 +3 +3 +3

–4 –4 –4 –4

+2 +2 +2 +2

4. The three letters in each group are moved one step forward.

PUF QVG RWH SXI

+1 +1 +1

+1 +1 +1

+1 +1 +1

5. The letters are in natural order. The number of letters dropped in between the groups is increased by one at each step.

DEF HIJ MNO STU

↓ ↓ ↓

G KL PQR

6. The series is abbaab, abbaab

7. The series is aaaaba, aaaaba

8. The series is aba, aba, aba, aba

9. The series is c,a,cc,aa, ccc, aaa, cccc, aaaa

10. The series is cabbbb, cabbbb, cabbbb

11. The numbers in the series are multiplied by 3 to get the next numbers.

12. The difference between the numbers in the series increases by 1, after beginning from 5, *i.e.*,

1 6 12 19 27 36

+5 +6 +7 +8 +9

13. The difference between the numbers in the series doubles each time, after beginning from 4, *i.e.*,

2 6 14 30 62 126

+4 +8 +16 +32 +64

14. *Explanation I* : The sequence in the series is × 6, ÷ 3 which is repeated.

8 48 16 96 32 192

× 6 ÷ 3 × 6 ÷ 3 × 6

Explanation II : There are two alternate series and the numbers are multiplied by 2.

× 2 × 2

8 48 16 96 32 192

× 2 × 2

Series I : 8, 16, 32

Series II : 48, 96, 192

15. The sequence in the series is :

2 8 14 24 34 48 62

+6 +6 +10 +10 +14 +14

The difference increases by 4 at alternate step.

16. The numbers in the series are multiplied by 5 to get the next number.

∴ 125 should be in place of 120.

17. Two numbers form a pair. The first number increases by 7 for the next pair and the second number is the double of first number.

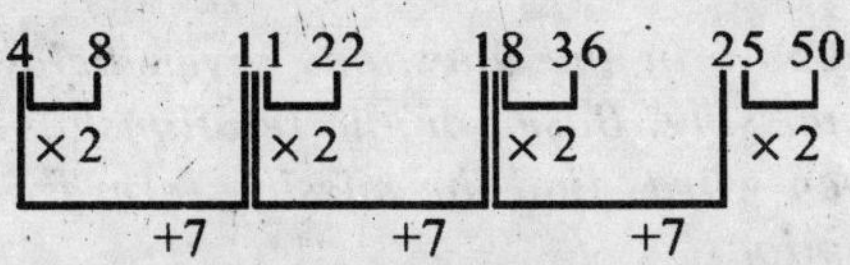

∴ 25 should be in place of 24.

18. There are two alternate series and in each series, the numbers are multiplied by 6 to get the next number.

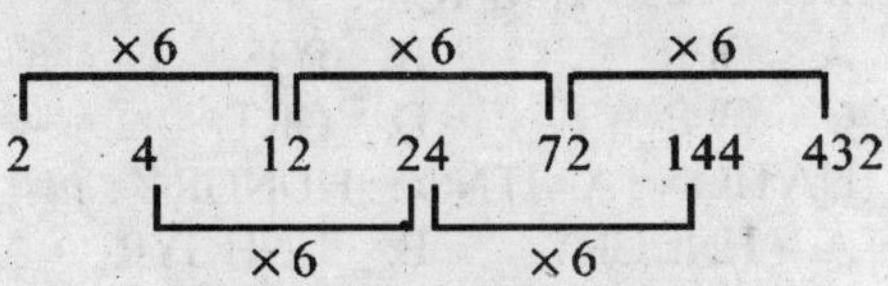

∴ 144 should be in place of 142.

19. There are three alternate series and in each series, the numbers are multiplied by 2 to get the next number.

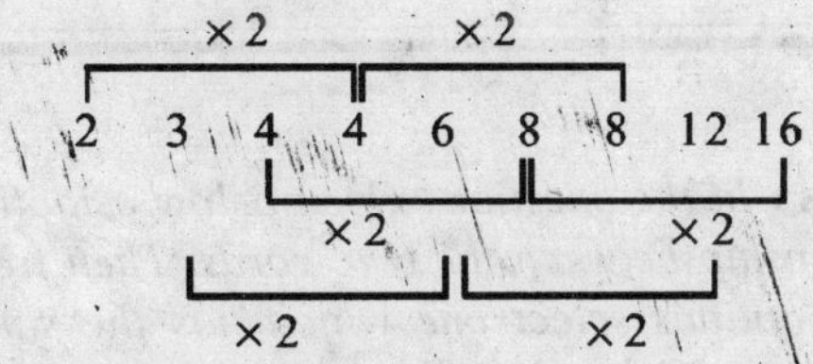

Series I : 2, 4, 8

Series II : 3, 6, 12

Series III : 4, 8, 16

∴ 8 should be in place of 9.

20. The difference between the consecutive numbers in the series decreases by 1 at each step.

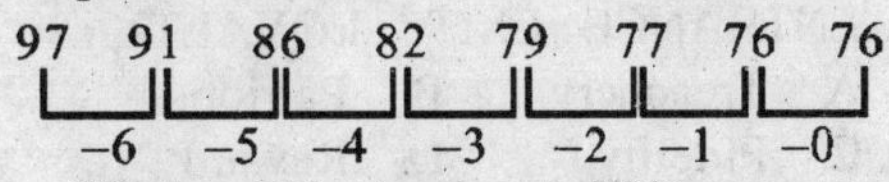

∴ 82 should be in place of 83.

ANALOGIES OR RELATIONSHIPS

Directions : *In the questions given below establish the relationship between the two words. Then from the given options select one which has the same relationship as of the given two words.*

1. ADULT : BABY : : FLOWER : ?

A. Seed B. Bud
C. Fruit D. Butterfly

2. WRITER : READER : : PRODUCER : ?

A. Creator B. Contractor
C. Creature D. Consumer

3. ENTRANCE : EXIT : : LOYALTY : ?

A. Treachery B. Patriotism
C. Fidelity D. Reward

4. MOTHER : MATERNAL : : FATHER : ?

A. Eternal B. Detrimental
C. Paternal D. Formidable

Directions : *In the questions given below one term is missing. Based on the relationship of the two given words find the missing term from the given options.*

5. GFC : CFG : : RPJ : ?

A. JRP B. JPR
C. PJR D. RJP

6. BCF : DEG : : MNQ : ?

A. OPR B. PQS
C. OPP D. QRT

7. NATION : ANITNO : : HUNGRY : ?

A. HNUGRY B. UNHGYR
C. YRNGUH D. UHGNYR

8. SSTU : MMNO : : AABC : ?

A. GGHH B. IJKK
C. XXYZ D. NOOP

ANSWERS

1	2	3	4	5	6	7	8
B	D	A	C	B	A	D	C

SOME SELECTED EXPLANATORY ANSWERS

1. The youngone of an adult is a baby and that of a flower is a bud.

2. A writer aims to please the readers by his writings, a producer aims to please the consumers by his products.

3. The related words are opposites.

4. Relations on the mother's side are maternal and on the father's side paternal.

5. The letters of the first group are reversed.

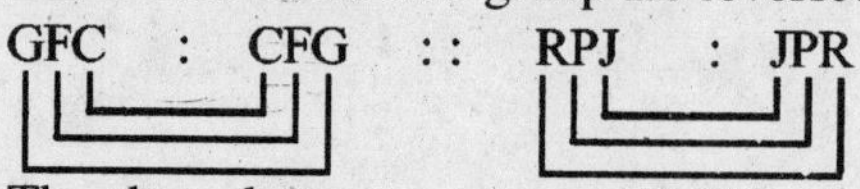

6. The three letters are moved 2, 2 and 1 steps forward respectively.

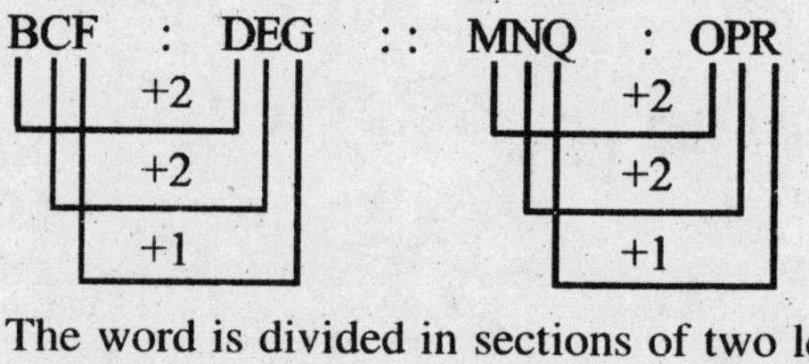

7. The word is divided in sections of two letters and the letters are reversed.

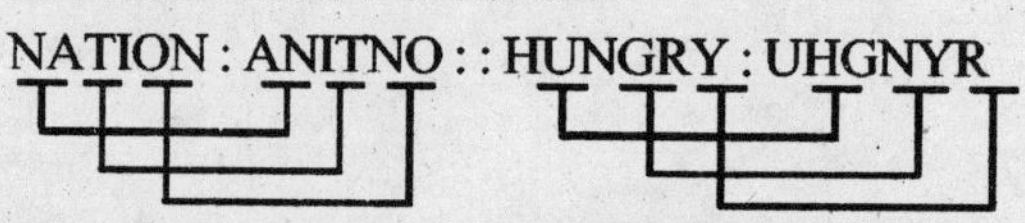

8. The first letter in each group is repeated and followed by two consecutive letters.

ODD ONE OUT

Directions : *Three of the following four in each question are alike in a certain way and so form a group. Select the group of letters that does not belong to that group.*

1. A. ACE B. LOR
C. GIK D. VXZ

2. A. TSR B. LKJ
C. PQO D. HGF

3. A. EF LM B. KJ SR
C. XW HG D. ED YX

4. A. JOPK B. BOPC
C. QOPR D. TOPS

5. A. DfH B. MoQ
C. UwY D. lnO

6. A. JKkL B. OPpQ
C. DEEf D. VWwX

7. A. BdfH B. FHJL
C. RTvX D. uVwX

8. A. DFHEG B. TWXUV
C. OQSPR D. JLNKM

9. A. FEUV B. DCXW
C. BAZY D. HGTS

10. A. UTSR B. XYZW
C. ONML D. IHGF

ANSWERS

1	2	3	4	5	6	7	8	9	10
B	C	A	D	D	C	D	B	A	B

SOME SELECTED EXPLANATORY ANSWERS

1. The sequence in each group is +2. Only option B has sequence in +3, *i.e.,*

ABCDE (+2 +2) LMNOPQR (+3 +3)

GHIJK (+2 +2) VWXYZ (+2 +2)

2. The sequence of alphabet in each group is in reverse order. Only option C has sequence in disturbed order.

3. Two consecutive alphabet in each group are in reverse sequence (–1), *i.e.,*

KJ (–1) SR (–1); XW (–1) HG (–1); ED (–1) YX (–1)

Only in option (A) the sequence is in natural order (+1), *i.e.,*

E F (+1) L M (+1)

4. In each group, letters 'OP' are common. The two corner alphabet are in natural order (+1); *i.e.,*

JOPK (+1) ; BOPC (+1) ; QOPR (+1)

Only in option (D) they are in reverse order (–1); *i.e.,*

TOPS (–1)

5. In other groups, only the alphabet in the centre is of lower case. In this option letter 'L' on the left is also in lower case.

6. In other groups, the third letter which is a repeat of the second alphabet is in lower case.

7. In each group, the sequence of the alphabet, irrespective of the case, is +2; *i.e.*,

B D f H ; F H J L ; R T v X

+2 +2 +2   +2 +2+2   +2 +2 +2

Only in option (D) the sequence is in natural order (+1), *i.e.*,

u V w X

+1 +1 +1

8. In each group; the alphabet at positions-first, fourth, second, fifth and third, form a natural sequence.

In option (B), the alphabet at positions first, fourth, fifth, second and third, form the natural sequence.

9. In each group, two alphabets in the corner and two alphabets in the centre correspond to their reverse order positioned alphabet. *i.e.*,

natural order → A B C D E F G H I J K L M
reverse order → Z Y X W V U T S R Q P O N
natural order → N O P Q R S T U V W X Y Z
reverse order → M L K J I H G F E D C B A

As such—

D corresponds with W and
C corresponds with X.
B corresponds with Y and
A corresponds with Z.
H corresponds with S and
G corresponds with T.

Similarly,

F should correspond with U and
E should correspond with V;
i.e. letters 'UV' should be written as 'VU'

10. In each group, the alphabet are in reverse order. In option (B), the order is disturbed.

CODING AND DECODING

Directions : *In the following questions select the right option which indicates the correct code for the word or letter given in the question.*

1. If CHAIR is coded as FKDLU then RAID is coded as :

   A. ULGD B. ULKG
   C. ULDG D. UDLG

2. If CONDEMN is coded as CNODMEN, then TEACHER is coded as :

   A. TEACHER B. TAEECHR
   C. TCAEEHR D. TAECEHR

3. In a code language COME is written as XLNV and ABLE as ZYOV. How will MOLLY be written in that code?

   A. NLOBO B. NLBOO
   C. LNOOB D. NLOOB

4. In a certain code PROFESSION is written as EFORPNOISS. In the same code DICTIONARY will be written as :

   A. YRANOITCID
   B. ITCIDYRANO
   C. ITCIDYRNAO
   D. ITCDIYARNO

5. JUNE is coded as NXPF, how will STAY be coded in the same manner?

   A. WWCZ B. WVCZ
   C. WWDB D. VWZC

Directions : *In the following questions study the coded patterns and then select the right option from the given alternatives.*

6. In a certain language, (a) 'go ju mi' stands for 'plenty of money'; (b) pao ju go nei vu' for 'money creates lots of problems'; (c) 'kol vu nei' for 'problems create tension'; and (d) 'sol tun ju haw' for 'still money is needed'. Which of the following words stand for 'money'?

   A. nei B. ju
   C. haw D. go

7. In a certain language, (a) 'FOR' stands for 'old is gold'; (b) 'ROT' stands for 'gold is pure'; (c) 'ROM' stands for 'gold is costly'. How will 'pure old gold is costly' be written?

   A. TFROM B. FOTRM
   C. FTORM D. TOMRF

8. In a certain code '415' means 'milk is hot'; '18' means 'hot soup'; and '895' means 'soup is tasty'. What number will indicate the word 'tasty'?

   A. 9 B. 8
   C. 5 D. 4

9. In a certain code '643' means 'she is beautiful', '593' means 'he is handsome', and '567' means 'handsome meets beautiful'. What number will indicate the word 'meets'?

   A. 5 B. 3
   C. 7 D. 6

10. In a certain code language, (a) 'dugo hui mul zo' stands for 'work is very hard'; (b) 'hui dugo ba ki' for 'Bingo is very smart'; (c) 'nano mul dugo' for 'cake is hard', and (d) 'mul ki qu' for 'smart and hard'. Which of the following words stand for 'Bingo'?

    A. jalu B. dugo
    C. ki D. ba

ANSWERS

1	2	3	4	5	6	7	8	9	10
D	D	D	B	A	B	A	A	C	D

SOME SELECTED EXPLANATORY ANSWERS

2. In this word, the second and third letters interchange their places and the fifth and sixth letters do the same. Other letters retain their position.

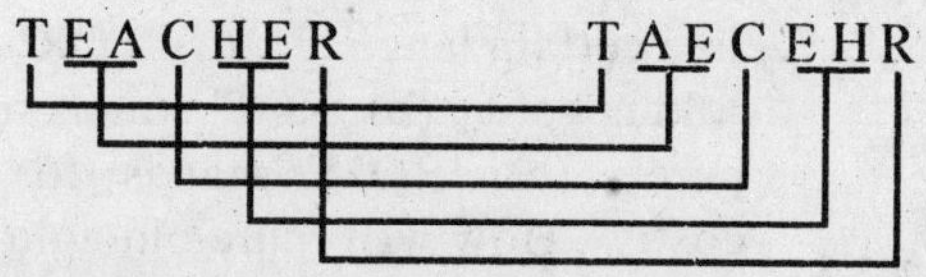

3. The letters of the word are coded by their represented letters in the reverse series.

C O M E → letters in natural series
X L N V → letters in reverse series
↓ ↓ ↓ ↓
3rd 15th 13th 5th → position of letters
A B L E → letters in natural series
Z Y O V → letters in reverse series
↓ ↓ ↓ ↓
1st 2nd 12th 5th → position of letters

Similarly,

M O L L Y → letters in natural series
N L O O B → letters in reverse series
↓ ↓ ↓ ↓ ↓
13th 15th 12th 12th 25th → position of letters

4. The word is divided into two equal parts and the letters of each part are written backwards.

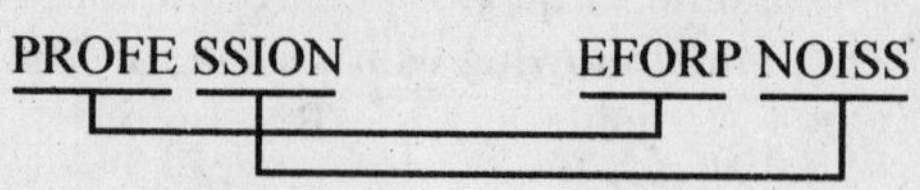

Similarly,

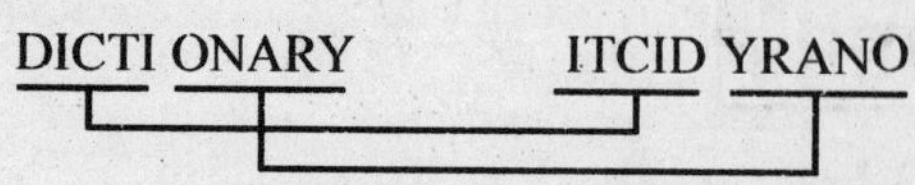

5. The word is coded by moving the letters +4, +3, +2, and +1 steps respectively.

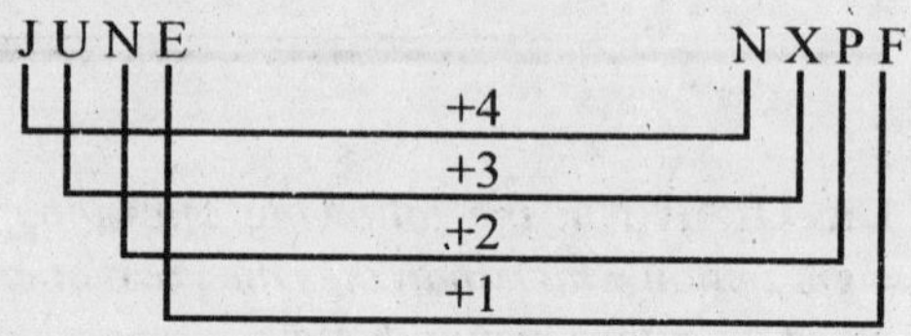

Similarly,

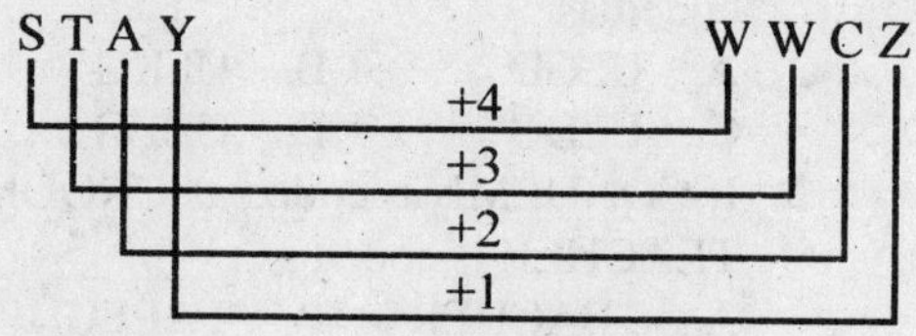

6.

Code	Sentence
1. go *ju* mi	plenty of *money*
2. pao *ju* go nei vu	*money* creates lots of problems
3. kol vu nei	problems create tension
4. sol tun *ju* haw	still *money* is needed

In 1st, 2nd and 4th codes and their sentences the word 'ju' is repeated and so is 'money'.

8.

Code	Sentence
1. 415	milk is hot
2. 18	hot soup
3. 895	soup is *tasty*

From 3rd code and its sentence neither number '9' is repeated nor the word 'tasty'.

9.

Code	Sentence
1. 643	she is beautiful
2. 593	he is handsome
3. 567	handsome *meets* beautiful

From 3rd code and its sentence, neither number '7' nor the word 'meets' is repeated.

10.

Code	Sentence
1. *dugo hui* mul zo	work *is very* hard
2. *hui dugo* **ba** *ki*	**Bingo** *is very smart*
3. nano mul *dugo*	cake is *hard*
4. mul *ki* qu	*smart* and hard

From 2nd code and its sentence, neither 'ba' nor 'Bingo' is repeated.
(Words repeated are in italics)

STATEMENT ANALYSIS

1. Among five friends, A is heavier than B; C is lighter than D; B is lighter than D but heavier than E. Who among them is the heaviest?
   A. B B. C
   C. A D. Can't say
2. Pune is bigger than Jhansi, Sitapur is bigger than Chittor. Raigarh is not as big as Jhansi, but is bigger than Sitapur. Chittor is not as big as Sitapur. Which is the smallest?
   A. Jhansi B. Pune
   C. Chittor D. Sitapur
3. Ajay works more than Ram. Alok works as much as Raju. Pankaj works less than Alok. Ram works more than Alok. Who works the most of all?
   A. Ajay B. Ram
   C. Alok D. Raju
4. Vipul is taller than Hans. Hans is taller than Anand. Alok is taller than Ashok. Ashok is taller than Hans. Who among them is the tallest?
   A. Vipul
   B. Alok
   C. Ashok
   D. Cannot be determined
5. Pramod is taller than Gopal. Gopal is shorter than Madhu. To find out who among them is the tallest, which of the following further informations is necessary?
   A. Madhu is taller than Gopal.
   B. Madhu is shorter than Pramod's brother
   C. Pramod is taller than Madhu.
   D. Pramod is taller than Madhu's brother.
6. Among five friends P, Q, R, S and T, who is the youngest? To arrive at the answer which of the following information given in the statements (*a*) and (*b*) is sufficient?
   (*a*) R is younger than P and T.
   (*b*) S is younger than Q.
   A. Only (*a*) alone is sufficient
   B. Either (*a*) or (*b*) is sufficient
   C. Both (*a*) and (*b*) together are needed
   D. Both (*a*) and (*b*) together are not sufficient
7. Sushma is richer than Rashmi whereas Anand is richer than Priya. Arun is as rich as Rashmi. Shoba is richer than Sushma. Which of the following statements is correct according to the above propositions?
   A. Rashmi is poorer than Priya.
   B. Priya is richer than Arun
   C. Arun is poorer than Sushma.
   D. Anand is richer than Rashmi
8. A is elder to B while C and D are elder to E who lies between A and B. If C be elder to B, which one of the following statements is necessarily true?
   A. E is elder to B
   B. A is elder to C
   C. C is elder to D
   D. D is elder to C
9. Vikram is taller than Rajan but shorter than Annie. Jamal is taller than Annie. Sita is taller than Vikram. Rajan is shorter than Sita. Who is the shortest of all in the group?
   A. Sita
   B. Rajan
   C. Vikram
   D. Cannot be determined
10. Suresh is as much older than Kamal as he is younger than Prabodh. Navin is as old as Kamal. Which of the following statements is wrong?
    A. Suresh is older than Navin
    B. Kamal is younger than Suresh
    C. Prabodh is not the oldest
    D. Navin is younger than Prabodh

ANSWERS

1	2	3	4	5	6	7	8	9	10
D	C	A	D	C	D	C	A	B	C

SOME SELECTED EXPLANATORY ANSWERS

1. The five friends in descending order of weight are : A/D, B/C, E or A/D, B, C/E. Either A or D is the heaviest.

2. The order of cities in descending order of size is : Pune, Jhansi, Raigarh, Sitapur, Chittor.

3. On the basis of doing work, the descending order will be : Ajay, Ram, Alok/Raju, Pankaj.

4. On the basis of height, the descending order will be Vipul/Alok, Ashok, Hans, Anand. Either Vipul or Alok is the tallest.

5. According to the information both Pramod and Madhu are taller than Gopal. Option (c) decides who is the tallest.

6. Statements are not inter-related.

7. On the basis of wealth, the descending order will be :

1. Shobha, Sushma, Rashmi/Arun
2. Anand, *and* Priya

(The two statements are not inter-related.)

8. The order in descending seniority will be : A/C/D, E, B.

9. On the basis of height the descending order will be :

Jamal/Sita, Annie, Vikram, Rajan.

or

Jamal, Sita/Annie, Vikram, Rajan.

10. On the basis of age the descending order will be : Prabodh, Suresh, Kamal/Navin.

PLACE ARRANGEMENT

Directions : *In the following questions, understand the arrangement pattern and then select the right answer from the given options :*

1. Five boys are sitting in a row. Raghu is not adjacent to Shyam or Amit. Ajay is not adjacent to Shyam. Raghu is adjacent to Mayank. If Mayank is at the middle in the row, then Ajay is adjacent to whom out of the following?

A. Amit B. Raghu
C. Mayank D. Shyam

2. Mini is to the right of Rajni but to the left of Ananta. Saya is to the right of Mini but to the left of Jaya. Who is on the extreme left if all the girls are facing North?

A. Jaya B. Mini
C. Rajni D. Saya

3. Kittu is in-between Mohan and Sohan. Raju is to the left of Sohan and Shyam is to the right of Mohan. If all of the friends are sitting facing South, then who is on their extreme right?

A. Mohan B. Sohan
C. Kittu D. Shyam

4. A, B, C, D and E are running one behind the other. C is not near E and A is not near D. B is next to A and E is not near D. Who is in the middle?

A. B B. E
C. A D. Cannot be said

5. O, P, Q, R, S and T are standing on a bench according to their height. P is taller than O but shorter than S. Only S is taller than T. R is shorter than P but taller than Q. Who is the shortest?

A. O B. Q
C. P D. Cannot be said

ANSWERS

1	2	3	4	5
B	C	D	A	D

SOME SELECTED EXPLANATORY ANSWERS

1. The order of sitting is :
Amit, Shyam, Mayank, Ajay, Raghu
or
Ajay, Raghu, Mayank, Amit, Shyam

2. The order in which the girls are positioned is :
Rajni, Mini, Ananta, Saya, Jaya
or
Saya, Jaya, Ananta
or
Saya, Ananta, Jaya

3. The order of sitting while facing South is:
Shyam, Mohan, Kittu, Sohan, Raju.

4. The positions while running behind the other is :

E E
A A
B *or* B
C D
D C

5. In descending order of height, the standing positions are :

S S
T T
P *or* P
R R
O Q
Q O

Either O or Q is the shortest. The information given is not enough to clarify the answer.

DIRECTION SENSE

Directions : *In the following questions, select the right answer from the given options to depict the correct direction/distance.*

1. Kittu walks towards East and then towards South. After walking some distance he turns towards West and then turns to his left. In which direction is he walking now?

A. North B. South
C. East D. West

2. A person is driving towards West. What sequence of directions should he follow so that he is driving towards South?

A. left, right, right B. right, right, left
C. left, left, left D. right, right, right

3. Richa drives 8 km to the South, turns left and drives 5 km. Again, she turns left and drives 8 km. How far is she from her starting point?

A. 3 km B. 5 km
C. 8 km D. 13 km

4. Dingi runs 40 km towards North then turns right and runs 50 km. He turns right and runs 30 km, and once again turns right and runs 50 km. How far is he from his starting point?

A. 90 km B. 50 km
C. 10 km D. 5 km

5. Debu walks towards East then towards North and turning 45° right walks for a while and lastly turns towards left. In which direction is he walking now?

A. North B. East
C. South-East D. North-West

ANSWERS

1	2	3	4	5
B	D	B	C	D

SOME SELECTED EXPLANATORY ANSWERS

1.

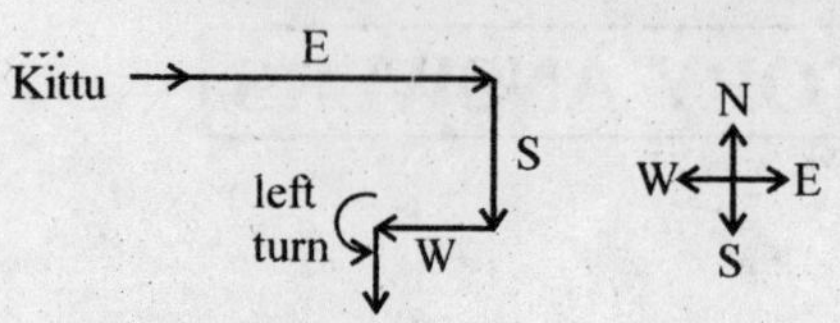

2.

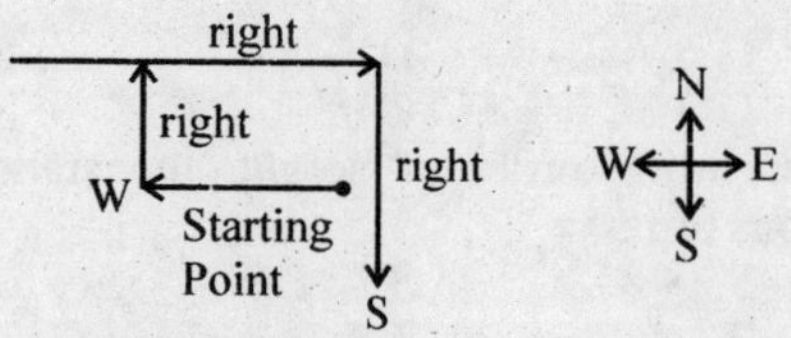

3.

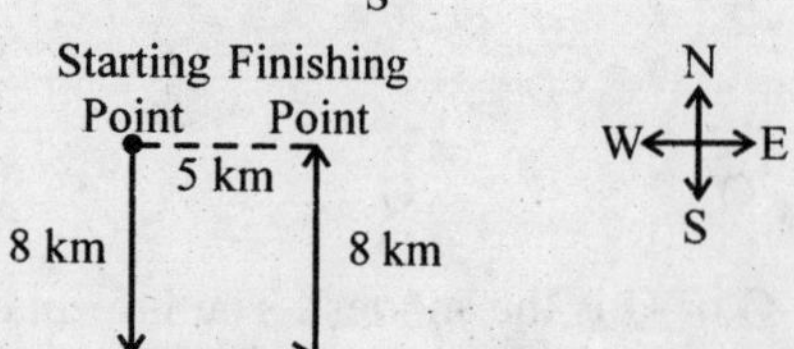

4.

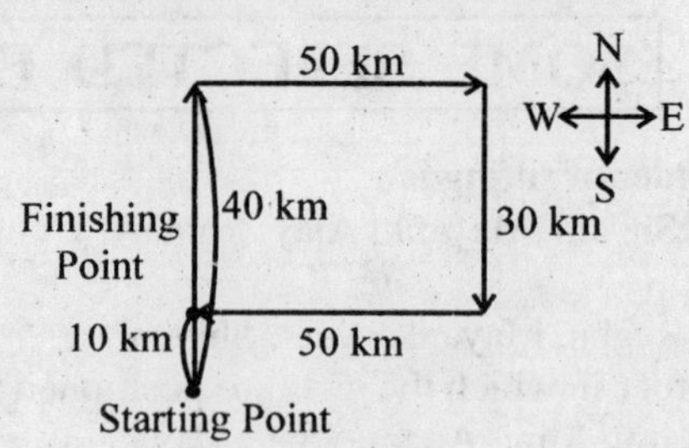

5.

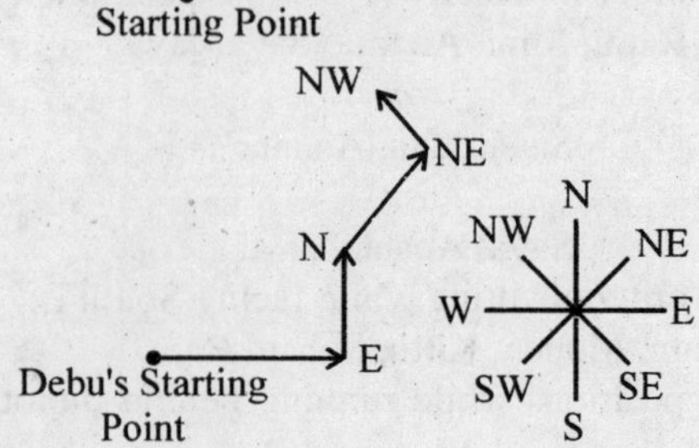

BLOOD RELATIONSHIPS

Directions : *In each of the following questions keenly study the relationship mentioned between the persons, and then from the given options select the right relationship as the answer.*

1. 'A' is the father of 'B' and 'C'. 'B' is the son of 'A' but 'C' is not the son of 'A'. What is 'C's' relation with 'A'?

A. Daughter B. Son
C. Niece D. Nephew

2. A lady said, "The person standing there is my grandfather's only son's daughter". How is the lady related to the standing person?

A. Sister B. Mother
C. Aunt D. Cousin

3. Ravi is the brother of Amit's son's son. What is Amit's relation to Ravi?

A. Cousin B. Father
C. Grandfather D. Son

4. Mayank said, "My mother is the sister of Rajat's brother." What is Rajat's relation with Mayank?

A. Cousin B. Maternal uncle
C. Uncle D. Brother-in-law

5. Introducing Lily, Raghav said, "Her father is my mother's only son". How is Lily related to Raghav?

A. Aunt B. Daughter
C. Mother D. Sister

ANSWERS

1	2	3	4	5
A	A	C	B	B

SOME SELECTED EXPLANATORY ANSWERS

1.

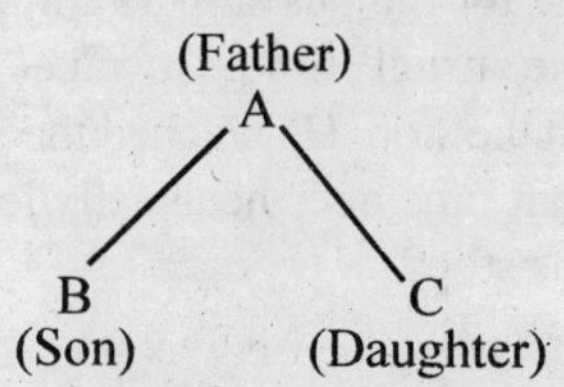

'C' is not the son of 'A', but 'A' is the father of 'C'. So, 'C' is the daughter of 'A'.

2.

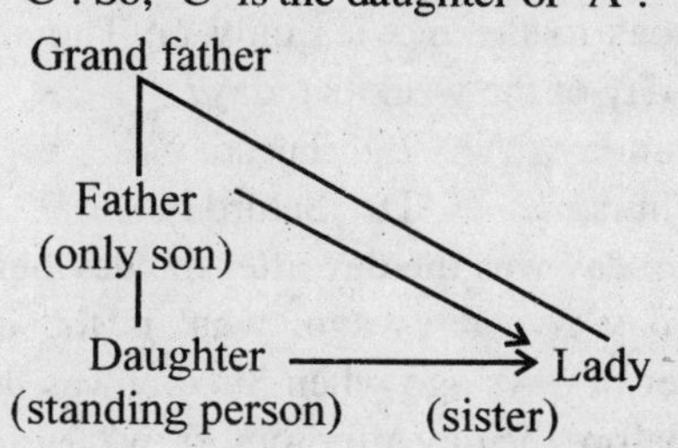

Lady's grandfather's son is lady's father and father's daughter will only be lady's sister.

4.

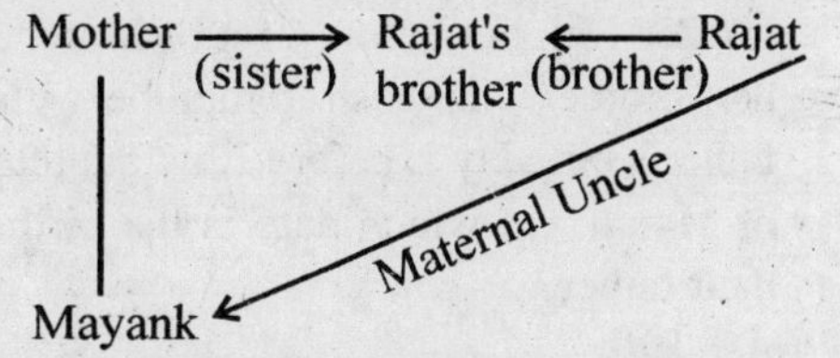

Mayank's mother is the sister of Rajat's brother. So Rajat is also the brother of Mayank's mother. Relation of the brother with his sister's child is maternal. So Rajat is Mayank's maternal uncle.

CALENDAR, CLOCK, TIME, DISTANCE

1. If the day before yesterday was Thursday, when will Sunday be?
   A. Tomorrow B. Day after tomorrow
   C. Today D. Two days after today
2. There are twenty people working in an office. The first group of five works between 8:00 A.M. and 2:00 PM. The second group of ten works between 10:00 AM to 4:00 PM. And the third group of five works between 12 noon to 6:00 PM. There are three computers in the office which all the employees frequently use. During which of the following hours the computers are likely to be used most?
   A. 1:00 PM - 3:00 PM
   B. 12 noon - 2:00 PM
   C. 2:00 PM - 4:00 PM
   D. 10:00 AM - 12 noon
3. If the seventh day of a month is three (3) days earlier than Friday, what day will it be on the nineteenth day of the month?
   A. Sunday B. Monday
   C. Wednesday D. Friday
4. Radha remembers that her father's birthday is after 16th but before 21st of March, while her brother Mangesh remembers that his father's birthday is before 22nd but after 19th of March. On which date is the birthday of their father?
   A. 19th
   B. 20th
   C. 21st
   D. Cannot be determined
5. A man is three (3) years older than his wife and four (4) times as old as his son. If the son attains an age of fifteen (15) years after three (3) years, what is the present age of the mother?
   A. 60 years B. 51 years
   C. 48 years D. 45 years
6. A clock is so placed that at 12 noon its minute hand points towards north-east. In which direction does its hour hand point at 1.30 P.M.?
   A. East B. West
   C. North D. South
7. If in the above question clock is turned through an angle of 135° in an anticlockwise direction, in which direction will its minute hand point at 8.45 P.M.?
   A. East B. West
   C. North D. South
8. A couple married in 1980 had two children, one in 1982 and the other in 1984. Their combined ages will equal the years of the marriage in?
   A. 1986 B. 1985
   C. 1987 D. 1988
9. Manoj left home for the bus stop 15 minutes earlier than the usual time. It takes 10 minutes to reach the stop. He reached the stop at 8.40 a.m. What time does he usually leave home for the bus stop?
   A. 8.30 a.m. B. 8.55 a.m.
   C. 8.45 p.m. D. None of these
10. Mamuni went to the movies nine days ago. She goes to the movies only on Thursday. What day of the week is today?
   A. Sunday B. Tuesday
   C. Thursday D. Saturday
11. If Thursday was the day after the day before yesterday five days ago, what is the least number of days ago when Sunday was three days before the day after tomorrow?
   A. Two days ago
   B. Three days ago

C. Four days ago
D. Five days ago

12. 1.12.91 is the first Sunday. Which is the fourth Tuesday of December 91?
A. 31.12.91 B. 24.12.91
C. 17.12.91 D. 26.12.91

13. If the third day of a month is Monday, which of the following will be the fifth day from 21st of that month?
A. Tuesday B. Monday
C. Wednesday D. Thursday

14. Keshav runs a factory in three shifts of eight hours each with 210 employees. In each shift minimum of 80 employees are required to run the factory effectively. No employee can be allowed to work for more than 16 hours a day. At least how many employees will be required to work for 16 hours every day?
A. 30
B. 60
C. Data inadequate
D. None of these

15. If 15 horses eat 15 bags of gram in 15 days, in how many days will one horse eat one bag of grain?
A. 15 days B. 1/15 days
C. 1 day D. 30 days

16. A century leap year is divisible by :
A. 4 B. 16
C. 40 D. 400

17. If the fifth day of a month is Friday, which of the following will be the Seventh day from 10th of that month?
A. Tuesday B. Monday
C. Wednesday D. Thursday

18. Day after tomorrow is my birthday. On the same day next week falls 'Holi'. Today is Monday. What will be the day after 'Holi'?
A. Wednesday B. Thursday
C. Friday D. Saturday

19. A clock shows the time as 3 : 30 p.m. If the minute hand gains 2 minutes every hour, how many minutes will the clock gain by 4 a.m.?
A. 23 Minutes B. 24 Minutes
C. 25 Minutes D. 26 Minutes

20. Two brothers were expected to return home on the same day. Rajat returned 3 days earlier but Rohit returned 4 days later. If Rajat returned on Thursday, what was the expected day when both the brothers were to return home and when did Rohit Return?
A. Wednesday, Sunday
B. Thursday, Monday
C. Sunday, Thursday
D. Monday, Friday

ANSWERS

1	2	3	4	5	6	7	8	9	10
A	B	A	B	A	A	D	A	D	D
11	**12**	**13**	**14**	**15**	**16**	**17**	**18**	**19**	**20**
A	B	C	D	A	D	C	B	C	C

SOME SELECTED EXPLANATORY ANSWERS

1. Thursday —Day-before-yesterday
Friday —Yesterday
Saturday —Today
Sunday — Tomorrow

2. 1. 5 people work between 8 a.m. to 2 p.m.
2. 10 people work between 10 a.m. to 4 p.m.
3. 5 people work between 12 noon to 6 p.m.

So, computers are used most between 12 noon to 2 p.m.

3. 7th day is 3 days earlier than Friday so, 10th day is Friday, so also is 17th.

∴ 19th day will be 2nd day ahead of Friday, *i.e.,* Sunday.

4. Father's birthday

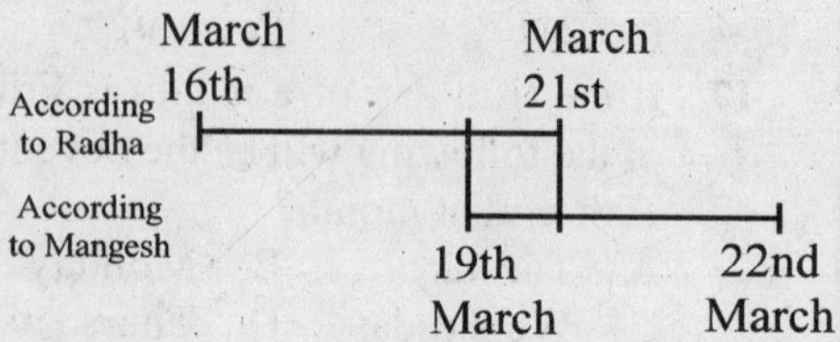

$\therefore$ Their father's birthday is on 20th March.

5. Present age of son is 15 – 3 = 12 years. Age of the man is 4 times the age of son, *i.e.*,
12 × 4 = 48 years
Man is 3 years elder to his wife/son's mother.
So Age of the mother is 48 – 3 = 45 years

6.

At 12 noon

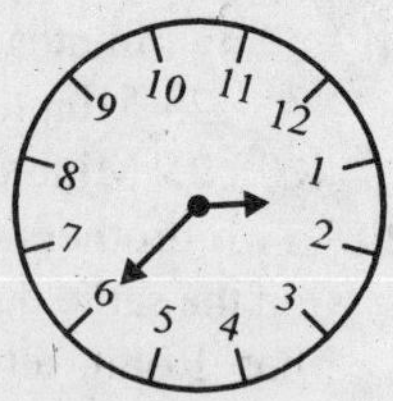

At 1.30 p.m. the hour hand will point towards East.

7.

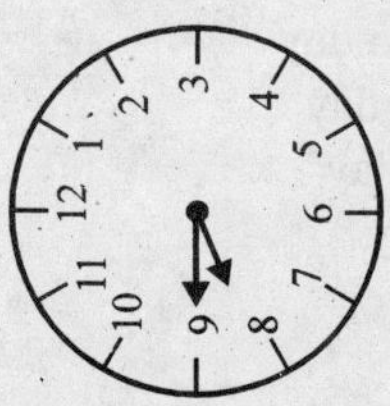

After rotating the clock in earlier question, its minute hand will point towards South at 8:45 p.m.

8. 1982 — 2 years later — 1st child
1984 — 4 years later — 2nd child
Total age of children — 2 years.
1985 — 5 years later — Total age of children: 4 years.
1986 — 6 years later — Total age of children : 6 years.

9. Manoj reached the bus stop at 8.40 a.m. He left his home at 8:40 – 10 minutes = 8:30 a.m. He left 15 minutes earlier than usual, so his actual time of leaving home is 8:30 am + 15 minutes = 8:45 a.m.

10. Mamuni goes to the movies on Thursday, so nine days ago was Thursday.
$\therefore$ Two days ago was also Thursday. So, today is Saturday.

11. Day after the day-before-yesterday five days ago is the 6th day which is Thursday. And so, the 3rd day will be Sunday. Three days before the day-after-tomorrow is Yesterday which is the 1st day of the five days. So, two days ago was Sunday.

12. First Sunday is on 1st December
First Tuesday is on 3rd December
3 weeks later, Fourth Tuesday will be on 3 + (7 × 3) = 24th December.

13. 3rd day of the month is Monday
5th day from 21st is 26th
26 – 3 = 23 days
23 days later, 23/7 leaves 2 days.
So, two days ahead of Monday will be Wednesday.

14. 80 employees are required for double shift.

15. 15 horses eat 15 bags of grain in 15 days
15 horses eat 1 bag of grain in 1 day
1 horse eats 1 bag of grain in 15 days

16. A leap year is divisible by 4 and a century leap year is divisible by 400.

17. Seventh day from 10th is 17th.
5th day is Friday. Next Friday is on 12th, 17 – 12 = 5, 5 days ahead of Friday will be Wednesday. So, 17th is Wednesday.

18. Today is Monday
Day-after-tomorrow is Wednesday
Next week 'Holi' is also on Wednesday
So, Day after Holi is Thursday.

19. Hours between 3:30 p.m. and 4 a.m. are — 12½ hours. Number of minutes gained will be 12½ × 2 = 25 minutes.

20. Rajat returned on Thursday. 3 days later was the day of expected return, *i.e.*, Sunday. Rohit returned 4 days after Sunday, *i.e.*, Thursday.

ROWS AND RANKS

1. In a row of trees, one tree is fifth from either end of the row. How many trees are in the row?
   A. 11 B. 8
   C. 10 D. 9
2. Jaya ranks 5th in a class of 53. What is her rank from the bottom in the class?
   A. 49th B. 48th
   C. 47th D. 50th
3. Mohan ranks twenty-first in a class of sixty-five students. What will be his (Mohan's) rank if the lowest candidate is assigned rank 1?
   A. 44th B. 45th
   C. 46th D. Data inadequate
4. If Rahul finds that he is 12th from the right in a line of boys and 4th from the left, how many boys should be added to the line such that there are 28 boys in the line?
   A. 12 B. 14
   C. 20 D. 13
5. In a row of boys, Rajan is tenth from the right and Suraj is tenth from the left. When Rajan and Suraj interchange their positions, Suraj will be twenty-seventh from the left. Which of the following will be Rajan's position from the right?
   A. Tenth
   B. Twenty-sixth
   C. Twenty-ninth
   D. None of these
6. Mahesh and Suresh are ranked 11th and 12th respectively from the top in a class of 41 students. What will be their respective ranks from the bottom?
   A. 32nd and 33rd
   B. 29th and 30th
   C. 30th and 31st
   D. 31st and 30th
7. Uma ranked 8th from the top and 37th from bottom in a class. How many students are there in the class?
   A. 47 B. 46
   C. 45 D. None of these
8. In a queue, Sadiq is 14th from the front and Joseph is 17th from the end, while Jane is in between Sadiq and Joseph. If Sadiq be ahead of Joseph and there be 48 persons in the queue, how many persons are there between Sadiq and Jane?
   A. 5 B. 6
   C. 7 D. 8
9. Rohan ranked eleventh from the top and twenty-seventh from the bottom among the students who passed the annual examination in a class. If the number of students who failed in the examination was 12, how many students appeared for the examination?
   A. 48
   B. 49
   C. 50
   D. Cannot be determined
10. Some boys are sitting in a row. P is sitting fourteenth from the left and Q is seventh from the right. If there are four boys between P and Q, how many boys are there in the row?
    A. 19 B. 21
    C. 25 D. 23

ANSWERS

1	2	3	4	5	6	7	8	9	10
D	A	B	D	D	D	D	C	B	C

SOME SELECTED EXPLANATORY ANSWERS

1. 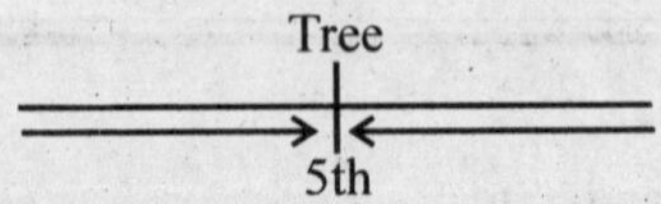

Total number of trees in the row are :
$(5 + 5) - 1 = 9$

2. 

Jaya's rank from the bottom is :
$(53 - 5) + 1 = 49$th.

3. 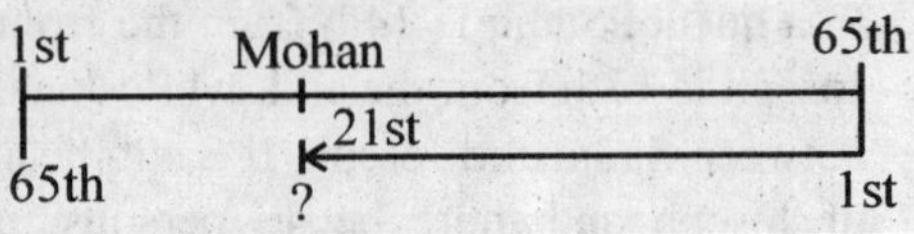

Note : Mohan's rank from the last or the question asked means the same.

Mohan's rank is $(65 - 21) + 1 = 45$th

4. 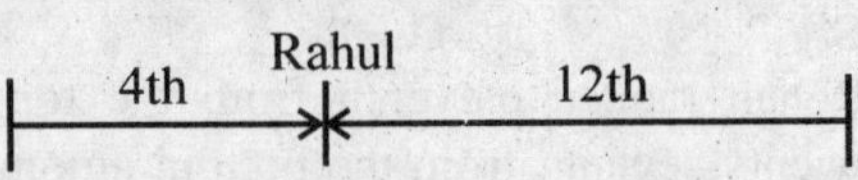

The number of boys in the line are :
$(4 + 12) - 1 = 15$
To make a line of 28 boys, $(28 - 15)$ *i.e.* 13 more boys are needed.

5. 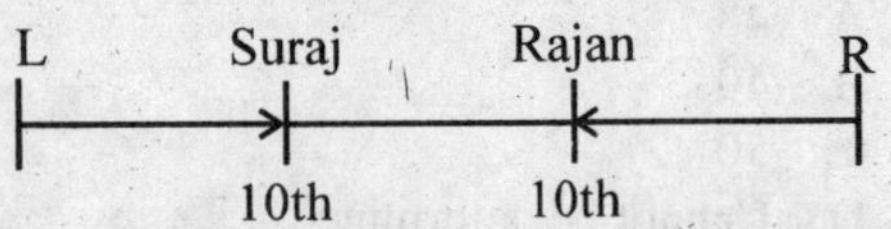

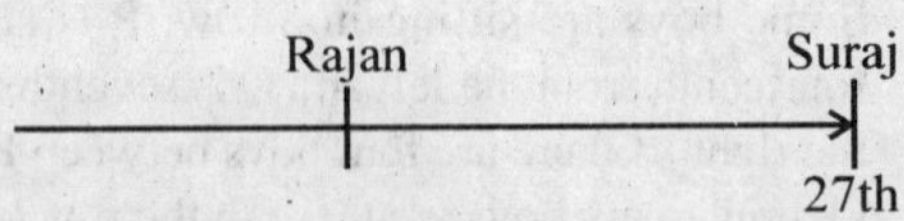

As the position of boys is equal from both ends, Rajan will also be 27th from the right after changing positions.

6. 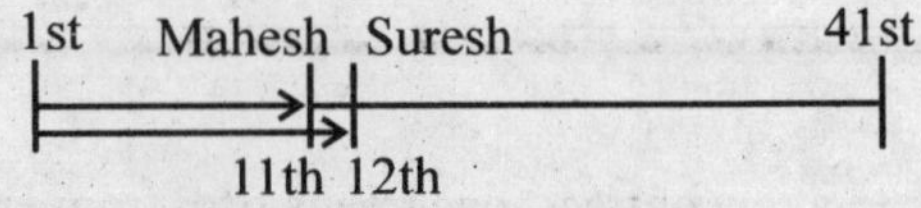

Mahesh's position from bottom is :
$(41 - 11) + 1 = 31$st
Suresh's position from bottom is :
$(41 - 12) + 1 = 30$th

7. 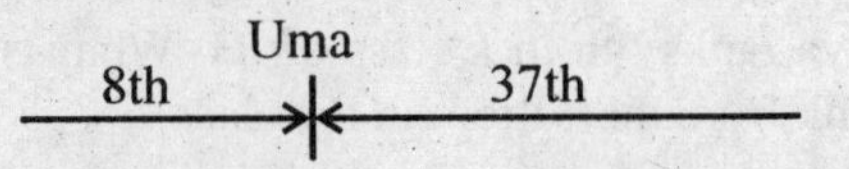

Total number of students in the class are :
$(8 + 37) - 1 = 44$

8. 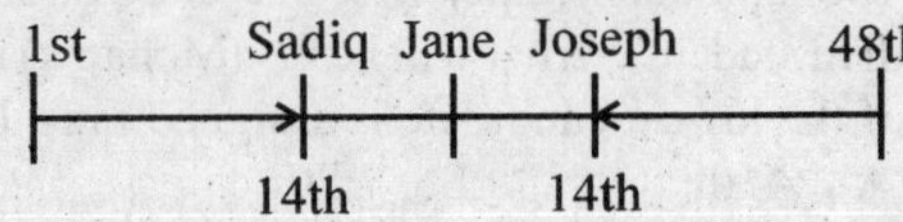

Sadiq's position from last is :
$(48 - 14) + 1 = 35$th
Number of persons between Sadiq and Joseph are $(35 - 17) - 1 = 17$
Jane is in-between Sadiq and Joseph *i.e.,* she's at 9th position from both the boys.
∴ there are 8 persons between Sadiq and Jane.
Note : $(8 + 8) - 1 = 17$

9. 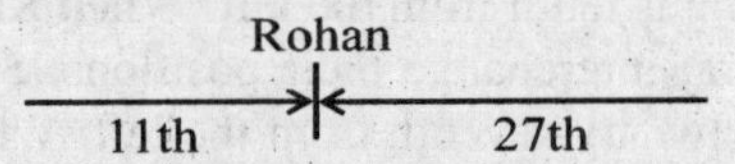

Number of students who passed the examination $(11 + 27) - 1 = 37$
Those who failed = 12
Total number of students who appeared in the examination = $37 + 12 = 49$.

10. 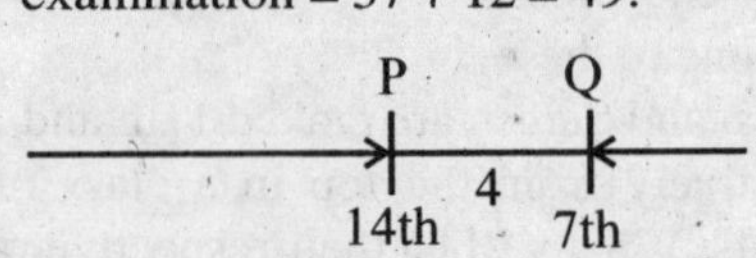

The number of boys in the row are :
$(14 + 4 + 7) = 25$

NUMBER PROBLEMS

1. How many 6's are there in the following series of numbers which are preceded by 7 but not immediately followed by 9?
6 7 9 5 6 9 7 6 8 7 6 7 8 6 9 4 6 7 7 6 9 5 7 6 3
A. One B. Two
C. Three D. Four

2. In a chess tournament each of six players will play every other player exactly once. How many matches will be played during the tournament?
A. 12 B. 15
C. 30 D. 36

3. How many 4's are there in the following series which are preceded by 7, but are not preceded by 8?
3 4 5 7 4 3 7 4 8 5 4 3 7 4 9 8 4 7 2 7 4 1 3 6
A. 1 B. 2
C. 3 D. 4

4. How many even numbers are there in the following series of numbers, each of which is immediately preceded by an odd number, but not immediately followed by an even number?
5 3 4 8 9 7 1 6 5 3 2 9 8 4 3 5
A. Nil B. 1
C. 2 D. 3

5. If all the numbers from 1 to 51 which are exactly divisible by 3 are arranged in descending order, which of the following numbers will come at the seventh and tenth places from the top?
A. 33 & 27 B. 33 & 21
C. 21 & 30 D. 33 & 24

ANSWERS

1	2	3	4	5
C	B	D	C	D

SOME SELECTED EXPLANATORY ANSWERS

1. 6 7 9 5 6 9 7 6 8 7 6 7 8 6 9 4 6 7 7 6 9 5 7 6 3
1 2 3

2. When all the players have to play with each other then the method of calculating the number of matches to be played is $\frac{n(n-1)}{2}$ where 'n' is the number of players playing the match. So, the number of matches played will be :
$(6 \times 5) \div 2 = 30 \div 2 = 15$

3. 3 4 5 7 4 3 7 4 8 5 4 3 7 4 9 8 4 7 2 7 4 1 3 6
1 2 3 4

4. 5 3 4 8 9 7 1 6 5 3 2 9 8 4 3 5
1 2

5. The numbers divisible by 3 in descending order are :
51, 48, 45, 42, 39, 36, 33, 30, 27, 24, 21,
7th 10th
18, 15, 12, 9, 6, 3.

SYMBOL SUBSTITUTION

1. If "+" means "–"; "–" means "×"; "×"means "÷" and "÷" means "+", then $15 \times 5 \div 10 + 5 - 3 = ?$
   A. 9.5 B. 0
   C. – 2 D. 24

2. If "+" means "–"; "–" means "×"; "×"means "÷" and "÷" means "+", then $15 \times 3 \div 15 + 5 - 2 = ?$
   A. 0 B. 10
   C. 20 D. 6

3. If "+" means "÷"; "×" means "–"; "÷"means "+" and "–" means "×", then $16 \div 8 \times 6 - 2 + 12 = ?$
   A. 22 B. 24
   C. 23 D. 20

4. If "+" means "×"; "–" means "÷"; "÷"means "+" and "×" means "–", then what will be the value of $20 \div 40 - 4 \times 5 + 6 = ?$
   A. 60 B. 1.67
   C. 150 D. 0

5. If "+" means "×"; "–" means "÷"; "×"means "–" and "÷" means "+", then $5 + 8 - 4 \times 2 \div 9 = ?$
   A. 15 B. 13
   C. 17 D. 11

ANSWERS

1	2	3	4	5
C	B	C	D	C

SOME SELECTED EXPLANATORY ANSWERS

1. $15 \div 5 + 10 - 5 \times 3$
   $3 + 10 - 15 = -2$
2. $15 \div 3 + 15 - 5 \times 2$
   $5 + 15 - 10 = 10$
3. $16 + 8 - 6 \times 2 \div 12$
   $16 + 8 - 1 = 23$
4. $20 + 40 \div 4 - 5 \times 6$
   $20 + 10 - 30 = 0$
5. $5 \times 8 \div 4 - 2 + 9$
   $10 - 2 + 9 = 17$

MISSING NUMBERS

Directions : *In each question given below which one number can be placed at the sign of interrogation?*

1. 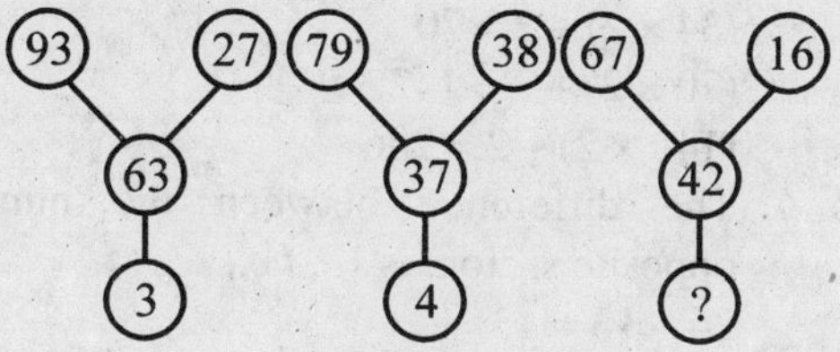

A. 5　　B. 6
C. 8　　D. 9

2. 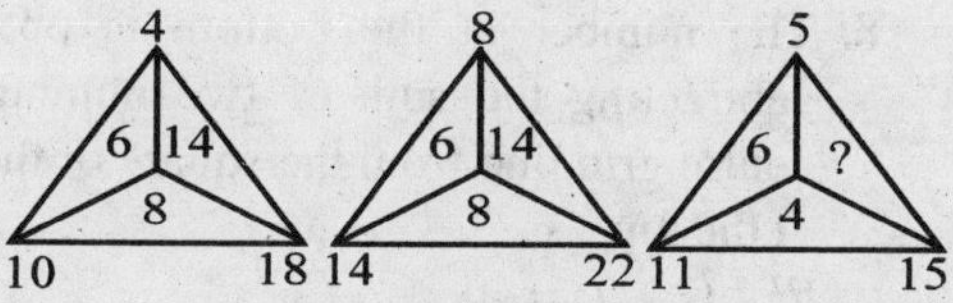

A. 8　　B. 14
C. 10　　D. 6

3. 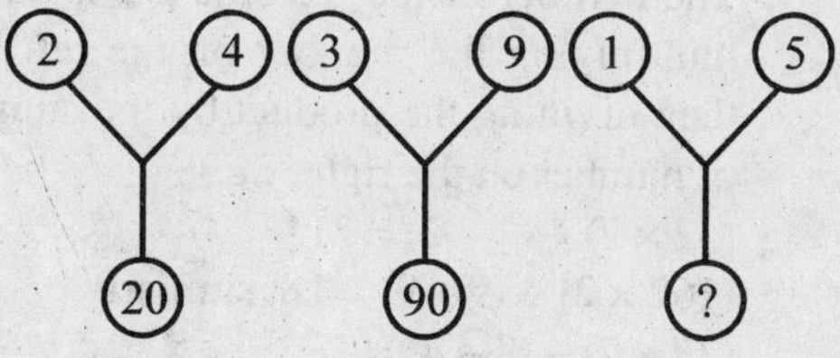

A. 20　　B. 25
C. 26　　D. 75

4.

27	22	50
13	12	26
9	2	?

A. 12　　B. 39
C. 18　　D. 24

5. 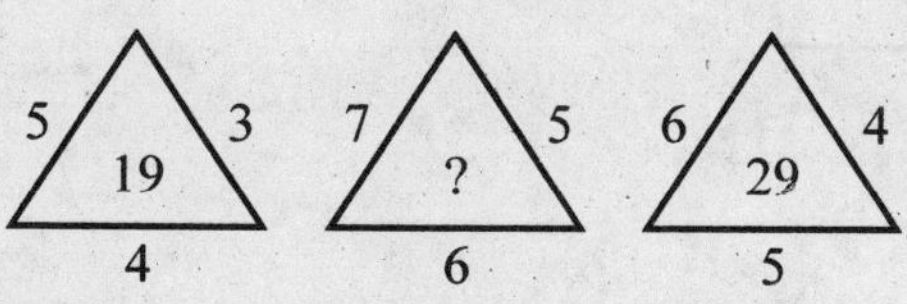

A. 25　　B. 47
C. 37　　D. 41

6. 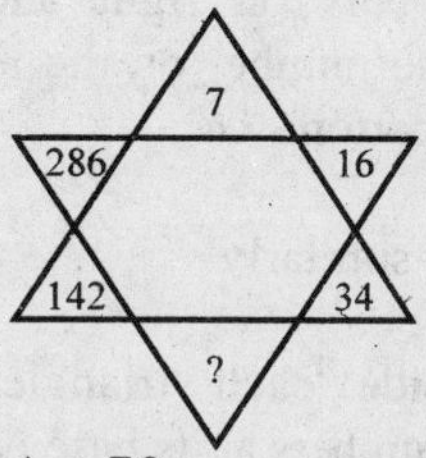

A. 70　　B. 68
C. 56　　D. 92

7. 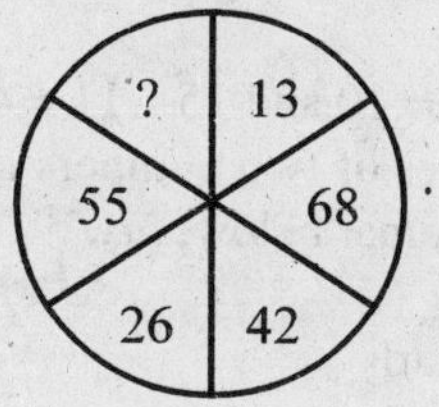

A. 41　　B. 37
C. 29　　D. 25

8. 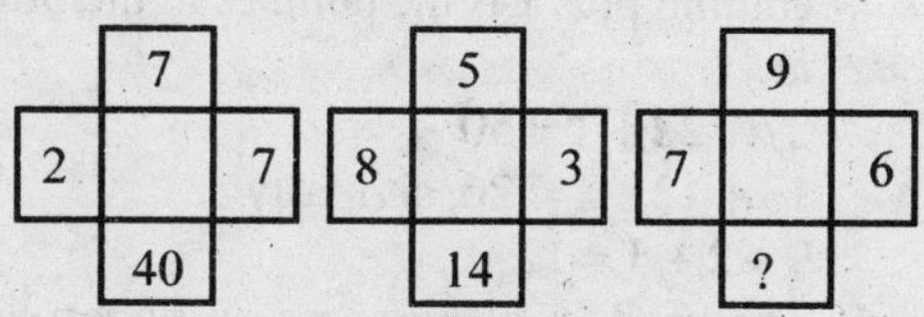

A. 72　　B. 68
C. 82　　D. 96

9.

42	(21)	22
78	(?)	84
162	(18)	99

A. 12　　B. 13
C. 60　　D. 72

10. 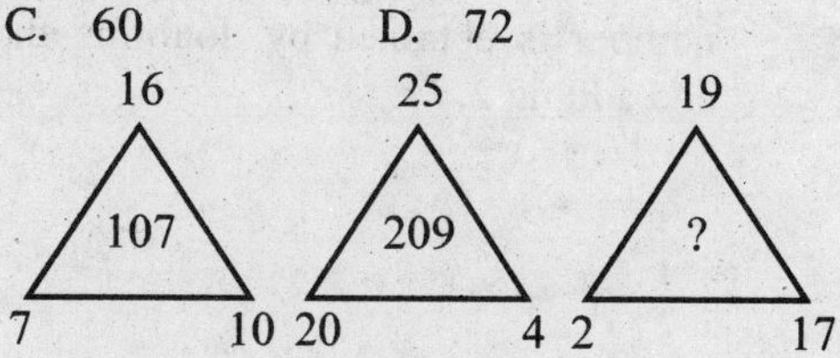

A. 68　　B. 93
C. 175　　D. 217

ANSWERS

1	2	3	4	5	6	7	8	9	10
D	C	C	A	D	A	C	B	B	A

SOME SELECTED EXPLANATORY ANSWERS

1. The sum of numbers on right and centre subtracted from the number on the left gives the number at the bottom, *i.e.,*
$93 - (27 + 63) = 3$
$79 - (38 + 37) = 4$, similarly
$67 - (16 + 42) = 9$
2. The number inside each triangle is the difference of the numbers at its base *i.e.*
$10 - 4 = 6$, $18 - 4 = 14$ and $18 - 10 = 8$
$14 - 8 = 6$, $22 - 8 = 14$ and $22 - 14 = 8$, similarly
$11 - 5 = 6$, $15 - 5 = 10$ and $15 - 11 = 4$.
3. The sum of squares of two numbers at the top gives the third number below, *i.e.,*
$2^2 + 4^2 = 20$
$3^2 + 9^2 = 90$, similarly
$1^2 + 5^2 = 26$
4. The sum of numbers in 1st and 2nd column plus 1 is the number in the 3rd column, *i.e.,*
$27 + 22 + 1 = 50$
$13 + 12 + 1 = 26$, similarly
$9 + 2 + 1 = 12$
5. The product of numbers on either side of the triangle plus the number at the base is the number inside the triangle, *i.e.,*
$(5 \times 3) + 4 = 19$
$(6 \times 4) + 5 = 29$, similarly
$(7 \times 5) + 6 = 41$
6. Clockwise starting from number 7, the next number is obtained by doubling the number and adding 2, *i.e.,*
$(7 \times 2) + 2 = 16$
$(16 \times 2) + 2 = 34 \ldots$, similarly
$(34 \times 2) + 2 = 70$
$(70 \times 2) + 2 = 142$
$(142 \times 2) + 2 = 286$
7. The difference between the numbers in opposite sectors is 13, *i.e.,*
$26 - 13 = 13$
$68 - 55 = 13$, similarly
The missing number is $42 - 13 = 29$
($42 + 13 = 55$ is not given as option)
8. The number at the bottom is obtained by subtracting the sum of two numbers in the centre grid line from the square of the number at the top, *i.e.,*
$7^2 - (2 + 7) = 40$
$5^2 - (8 + 3) = 14$, similarly
$9^2 - (7 + 6) = 68$
9. The number inside the brackets is obtained by multiplying the number on the left by 2 and then dividing the product by the sum of digits of number on the right, *i.e.,*
$(42 \times 2) \div (2 + 2) = 21$
$(162 \times 2) \div (9 + 9) = 18$, similarly
$(78 \times 2) \div (8 + 4) = 13$
10. Subtracting the sum of squares of two numbers at the base from the square of number at the apex gives the number inside the triangle, *i.e.,*
$16^2 - (7^2 + 10^2) = 107$
$25^2 - (20^2 + 4^2) = 209$, similarly
$19^2 - (2^2 + 17^2) = 68$

ALPHABET PROBLEMS

Directions : *The following questions are based on alphabet series in natural or reverse order and the combinations that can be made by changing the position of alphabet in given words.*

1. Which alphabet comes immediately before the sixth alphabet from the left extreme in alphabetical series?

A. U B. E
C. F D. V

2. Which letter is midway between G and S?

A. L B. N
C. M D. No letter

3. Which letter should be ninth letter to the left of ninth letter from the right if the first half of the alphabet is reversed?

A. I B. D
C. F D. E

4. If the alphabet is in reverse order, which letter will be eighth letter to the left of the seventh letter counting from the right end?

A. O B. P
C. N D. Q

5. What will be the fifth letter to the right of the thirteenth letter from the right?

A. R B. S
C. I D. O

ANSWERS

1	2	3	4	5
B	C	D	A	B

SOME SELECTED EXPLANATORY ANSWERS

1.

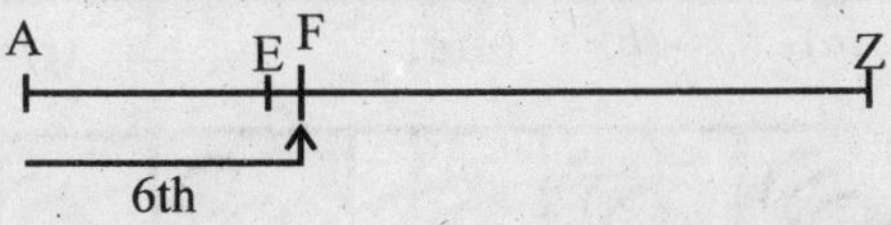

Sixth letter from left is 'F' and letter immediately before 'F' is 'E'.

2.

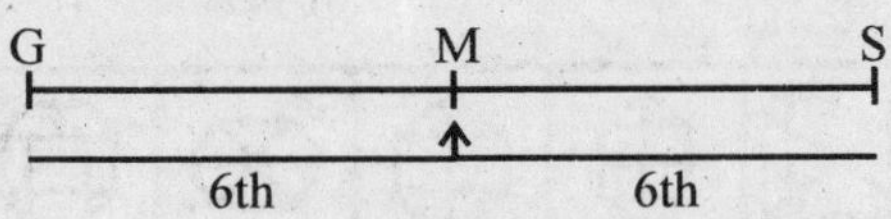

'M' is midway between G and S.

3. MLKJIHGFEDCBANOPQRSTUVWXYZ

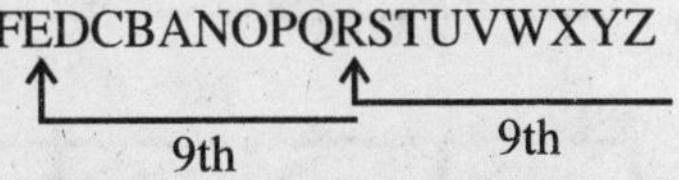

4. ZYXWVUTSRQPONMLKJIHGFEDCBA

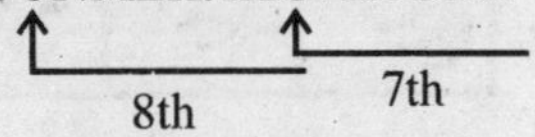

5.

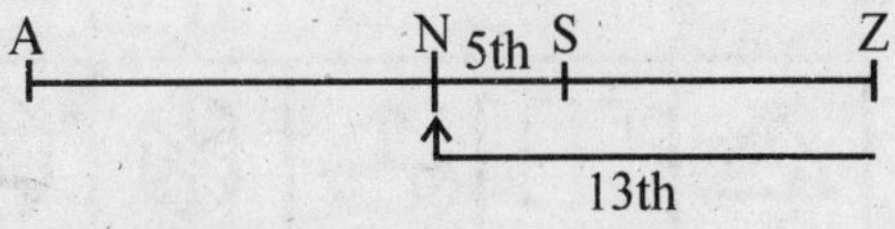

13th letter from right is 'N' and 5th letter to the right of 'N' is 'S'.

NON-VERBAL SERIES

Directions (Q. 1–10) : *In each of the following questions which one of the five answer figures given below should come after the problem figures if the sequence are continued?*

Problem Figures | **Answer Figures**

1.  

(a) *(b)* *(c)* *(d)* *(e)*

2. 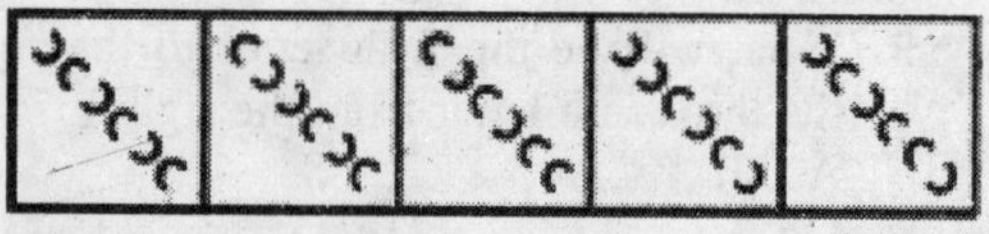 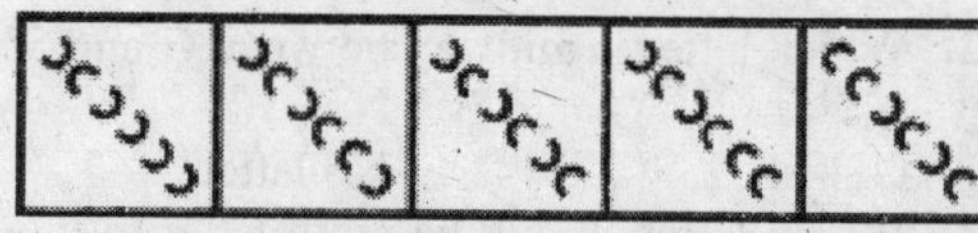

(a) *(b)* *(c)* *(d)* *(e)*

3. 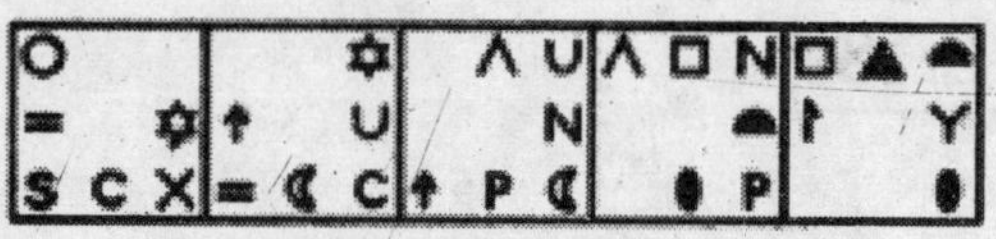 

(a) *(b)* *(c)* *(d)* *(e)*

4.  

(a) *(b)* *(c)* *(d)* *(e)*

5.  

(a) *(b)* *(c)* *(d)* *(e)*

6.  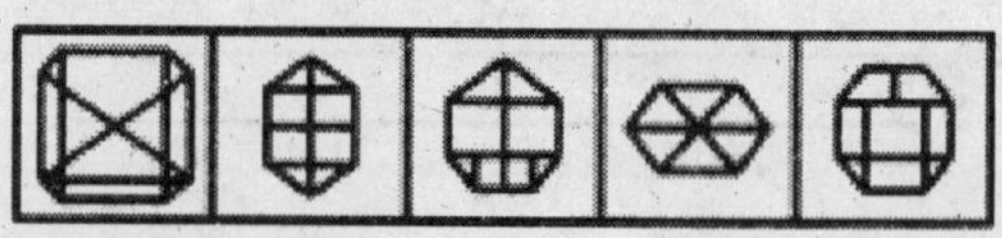

(a) *(b)* *(c)* *(d)* *(e)*

7.  

(a) *(b)* *(c)* *(d)* *(e)*

Problem Figures **Answer Figures**

8.  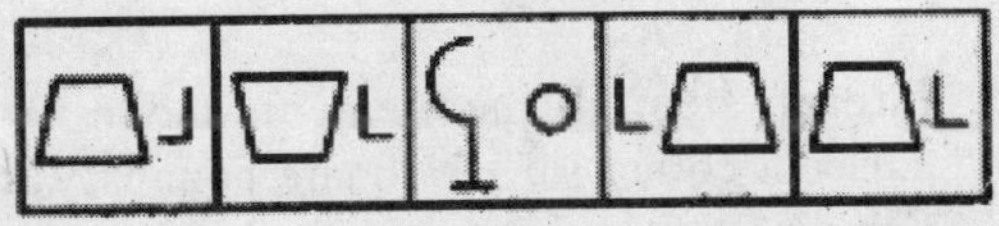

(a) (b) (c) (d) (e)

9.  

(a) (b) (c) (d) (e)

10. 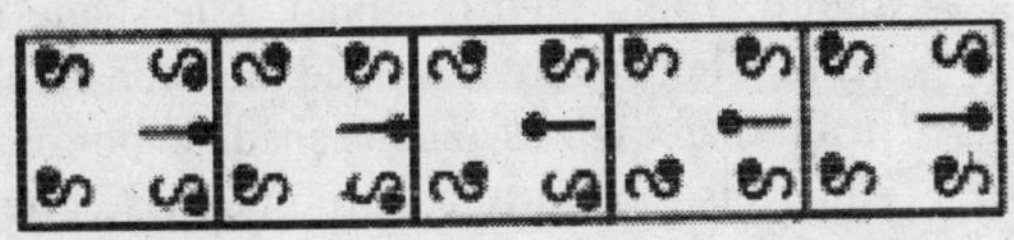 

(a) (b) (c) (d) (e)

Directions (Q. 11-20) : *In each of these questions, a series begins with an unmarked figure on the extreme left in the row of figures. One and only one of the five lettered figures in the series does not fit into the series. The two unmarked figures, one on the extreme left and the other on the extreme right fit into the series. Take as many aspects into account as possible of the figures in the series and find out the one and only of the five marked figures which does not fit into the series. The letter of that figure is the answer.*

11. 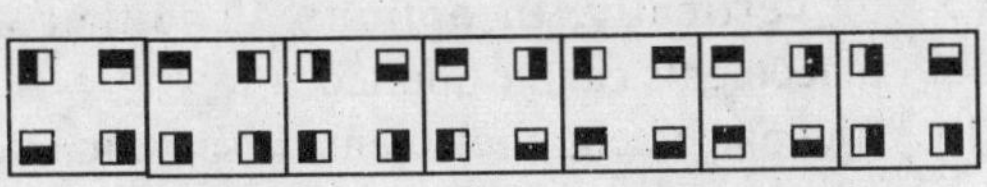

(a) (b) (c) (d) (e)

12. 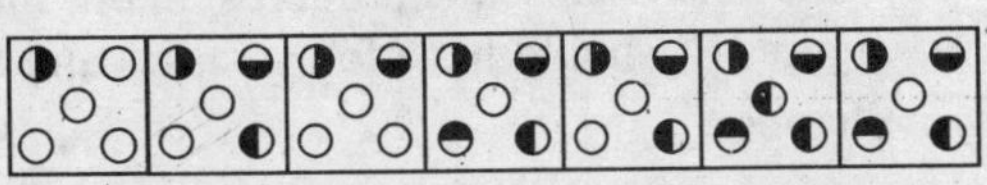

(a) (b) (c) (d) (e)

13. 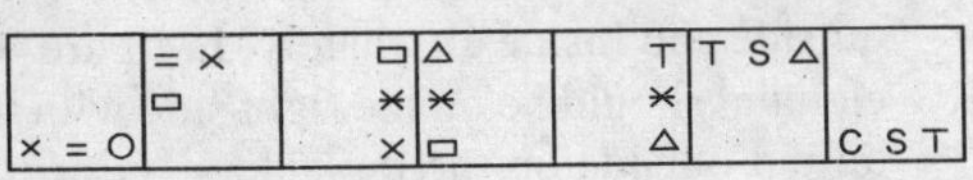

(a) (b) (c) (d) (e)

14. 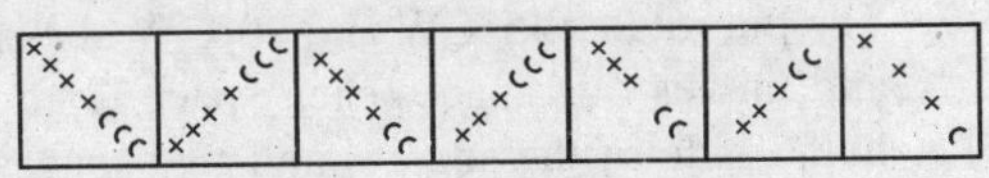

(a) (b) (c) (d) (e)

15. 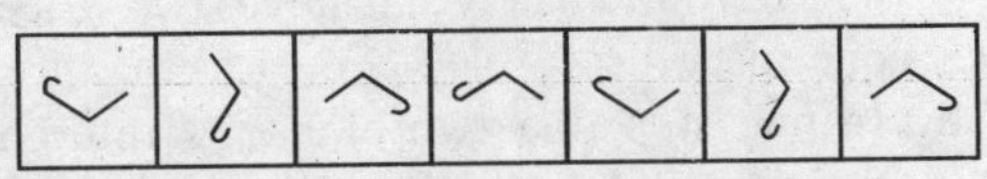

(a) (b) (c) (d) (e)

16. 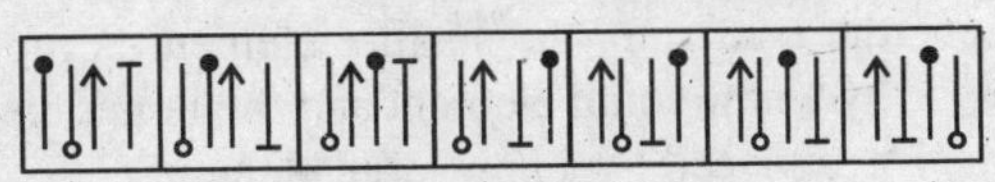

(a) (b) (c) (d) (e)

ANSWERS

1	2	3	4	5	6	7	8	9	10
D	C	D	A	C	E	C	E	C	B
11	**12**	**13**	**14**	**15**	**16**				
A	E	A	C	C	E				

SOME SELECTED EXPLANATORY ANSWERS

1. In each step, all the elements move to the adjacent corner (of the square boundary) in a CW direction and the element that reaches the upper-left corner gets vertically inverted.
2. We can label the arcs as shown 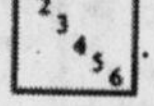

. The arcs get inverted in the sequence (1 & 2), (3, 4 & 5), (6 & 1), (2, 3 & 4), (5 & 6), ...
3. All the elements move half-a-side of the square boundary in ACW direction in each step. Also, first, third and fifth elements are replaced by new elements in one step and second, fourth and sixth elements are replaced by new elements in the next step. The two steps are repeated alternately.
4. In each step, the dot moves one space CW and the arrow moves two spaces CW.
5. One arc and four arcs get inverted alternately.
6. The number of parts increases by one along with the number of sides in the figure.
7. The pin rotates 45°CW and 90°CW alternately and moves one space (each space is equal to half-a-side of the square) and two spaces CW alternately. The arrow rotates 90°ACW and 45°ACW alternately and moves two spaces and one space.
8. In one step, the two elements interchange positions and the smaller element gets enlarged while the larger element gets reduced in size. In the next step, the smaller element is replaced by a new small element and the larger element is replaced by a new large element.
9. In each step, the elements move in the order .
10. The upper-left element gets laterally inverted in first, third, fifth. .... steps; the upper-right element gets rotated through 180° is first, fourth, seventh,.... steps; the lower-left element gets laterally inverted in second, fourth, sixth, ... steps; the lower-right element gets rotated through 180° in third, sixth,... steps and the pin at the middle-right position gets laterally inverted in every second step.
11. The shade in the top left square is moved one step clockwise till figure B and then reversed, the process is repeated. The shade in the top right square is moved one step anticlockwise till figure D and then reversed. The shade in the bottom left square is moved one step clockwise in alternate figures and the shade in bottom right square is moved one step clockwise after two figures. In figure 'A' the rule is isolated by the shade in the bottom left square.
12. In alternate figures a new circle is shaded clockwise. The pattern of the shade is also moved clockwise. In figure 'E' right half of the circle in the centre should have been shaded.
13. The three elements are placed either horizontally or vertically. In option 'A' neither of the placements can be applied.
14. The placement of elements is same in alternate figures. The number and type of elements is same in two subsequent figures. In this manner, figure 'C' should have four crosses and two C shapes.
15. *(c)*: The element is moved one step anticlockwise and the arc at one end is turned outside and inside alternately. In figure 'C' the element should be on the right side with the arc turned outside on the top side.
16. The left most element, line segment with the dot is moved one step towards right till figure C where it reaches the extreme right position. This process is repeated from figure D where the element on the extreme left, line segment with a circle, is moved. In figure 'E' the placement of the elements does not follow the rule of the series.

General Knowledge

INDIAN HISTORY AND CULTURE

1. Which of the following throws light on Harappan Culture?
A. Rock edicts
B. The writings on terracotta seals
C. Archaeological excavations
D. All of the above

2. The idol worship in India can be traced to:
A. the Pre-Aryan period
B. the Later Vedic period
C. the Mauryan period
D. the Kushan period

3. Who was the court poet of Samudra Gupta?
A. Asvaghosha B. Nagarjuna
C. Harishena D. Aryabhatta

4. The ruins of the glory of Vijayanagar and a place of historical importance for its architectural style is now found at:
A. Belur B. Hampi
C. Srirangapattanam D. Tanjore

5. The world famous rock cut Kailas Temple at Ellora was built by the:
A. Mauryas B. Pallavas
C. Chalukyas D. Rashtrakutas

6. Which one of the following Silsilas of Sufism was against music:
A. Chishtiya B. Suhrawardiya
C. Qadiriya D. Naqshbandiya

7. From the excavations of which ancient site informations are gathered regarding brisk trade relations between India and Rome during early centuries of Christian era:
A. Madurai B. Tamralipti
C. Tondi D. Arikamedu

8. Greeko-Roman Art has found a place in:
A. Ellora B. Gandhara
C. Kalinga D. Buddhist Art

9. How many 'Mandals' (Books) does the *Rig Veda* contain?
A. 7 B. 10
C. 11 D. 21

10. Which one of the following trees is shown in seals of the Indus Valley Civilisation in association with a deity?
A. Neem tree B. Pipal tree
C. Banyan tree D. Mango tree

11. Chinese pilgrim who visited India during Harshavardhan's period was:
A. Fa-hien B. Itsing
C. Nishka D. Hiuen Tsang

12. Chalukya King Pulakesin-II was defeated by:
A. Mahendra Varman-I
B. Narasimha Varman-I
C. Parameswara Varman-I
D. Parantaka-I

13. Lumbini, the birth place of Gautam Buddha, is in:
A. Bihar B. Sikkim
C. Nepal D. None of these

14. Which one of the following Sufis regarded Krishna among the awliyas:
A. Shah Mohammad Ghaus
B. Shah Waliullah
C. Shah Abdul Azeez
D. Khwaja Mir Dard

15. The Mughals borrowed the celebration of 'Nauroz' from:
A. Parsis B. Jews
C. Mangols D. Turks

16. The temple built in 1100 AD and dominating all other temples in Bhubaneshwar is:
A. Raja Rani Temple
B. Kandariya Mahadev
C. Tribhuvaneshwara Lingaraja
D. Mukteshwara

17. The paintings in the Ajanta and Ellora caves are indicative of development of art under the:
A. Rashtrakutas B. Pallavas
C. Pandyas D. Chalukyas

18. Match List-I with List-II and select the correct answer with the help of the codes given below:

List-I	*List-II*
(*a*) Rigveda	1. Musical hymns
(*b*) Yajurveda	2. Hymns and rituals
(*c*) Samaveda	3. Charms and spells
(*d*) Atharvaveda	4. Hymns and prayers

Codes:

	(*a*)	(*b*)	(*c*)	(*d*)
A.	4	2	1	3
B.	3	2	4	1
C.	4	1	2	3
D.	2	3	1	4

19. Mughal painting reached its zenith under:
A. Shahjahan B. Akbar
C. Jahangir D. Aurangzeb

20. Who among the following Sikh Gurus compiled the 'Adi Granth'?
A. First Guru
B. Fifth Guru
C. Ninth Guru
D. Tenth and the last Guru

21. 'Mongols' intruded into India for the first time during the reign of:
A. Iltutmish B. Firoz Shah Tughlaq
C. Balban D. Alauddin Khilji

22. Which dynasty was well-known for excellent village administration?
A. Pallavas B. Cholas
C. Pandyas D. Chalukyas

23. Who of the following was the biographer of Akbar?
A. Abul Fazl B. Faizi
C. Abdun Nabl Khan D. Birbal

24. Match the following:

List-I	*List-II*
(*a*) Sanchi	1. Chandela Art
(*b*) Khajuraho	2. Great Stupa
(*c*) Thanjavur	3. Pallava Temples
(*d*) Kanchipuram	4. Chola Temples

Codes:

	(*a*)	(*b*)	(*c*)	(*d*)
A.	1	2	3	4
B.	2	1	4	3
C.	3	4	2	1
D.	4	1	2	3

25. Who was called the "Second Founder of the Maratha Kingdom"?
A. Raja Ram B. Balaji Viswanath
C. Baji Rao I D. Balaji Baji Rao

26. The Mughal emperor who discouraged *Sati* was:
A. Babur B. Humayun
C. Akbar D. Jahangir

27. Which one of the following Saints' name is associated with Shivaji?
A. Ramanand B. Ram Das
C. Chaitanya D. Tukaram

28. Tansen, the greatest musician of Akbar's court, belonged to:
A. Gwalior B. Kannauj
C. Delhi D. Agra

29. The tomb of Sufi saint Sheikh Salim Chishti is at:
A. Jaunpur B. Sikandara
C. Fatehpur Sikri D. Ajmer

30. Islam was abolished as the State religion during the rule of:
A. Akbar
B. Balban
C. Ibrahim Lodi
D. Ghias-ud-din Tughlaq

31. Who among the following founded the 'Sunga' dynasty?
A. Bimbisara B. Agnimitra
C. Ajatshatru D. Pushyamitra

32. Who among the following founded the 'Brahmo Samaj'?
A. Keshab Chandra Sen
B. Ramakrishna
C. Dayanand Saraswati
D. Raja Ram Mohan Roy

33. Akbar built Ibadatkhana at Fatehpur Sikri to:
A. conduct mass prayer
B. hold darbar
C. hold religious discussions
D. hear public grievances

34. Which one of the following Mughal buildings bears the inscription "If on Earth be the Eden of Bliss it is this, it is this none but this"?
A. Diwan-i-Aam B. Diwan-i-Khas
C. Taj Mahal D. Buland Darwaza

35. 'Mansabdars' during the Mughal period were:
A. Landlords and zamindars
B. Militia men
C. Officials of the state
D. Revenue collectors

36. During Aurangzeb's reign which of the following were not employed by his government?
A. Rajputs B. Pathans
C. Marathas D. All of the above

37. The first Europeans who started trade with India were:
A. British B. Danish
C. Portuguese D. Dutch

38. The fulsome development of Mughal painting was the achievement of:
A. Humayun B. Akbar
C. Babur D. Jahangir

39. Moti Masjid in the Red Fort at Delhi was built by:
A. Akbar B. Jahangir
C. Shahjahan D. Aurangzeb

40. Who among the following Sultans of Delhi has been described by the historians as the 'mixture of opposites'?
A. Balban
B. Alauddin Khilji
C. Muhammad Bin Tughlaq
D. Ibrahim Lodi

41. Who was the last ruler of Lodi Dynasty?
A. Bahlol Lodi B. Ibrahim Lodi
C. Daulat Khan Lodi D. Sikander Lodi

42. Which of the following Mughal emperors has vividly described Indian flora & fauna, seasons, fruits, etc. in his diary?
A. Akbar B. Jahangir
C. Babur D. Aurangzeb

43. The greatness of Shershah lies in his:
A. victories against Humayun
B. superior generalship
C. adminstrative reforms
D. religious tolerance

44. Who among the following Mughal emperors wrote his autobiography in Persian?
A. Babur B. Akbar
C. Jahangir D. Aurangzeb

45. Taxila was a famous site of:
A. Early Vedic Art B. Mauryan Art
C. Gandhara Art D. Gupta Art

46. The gold coins were introduced first time in India by:
A. The Kushanas B. The Greeks
C. The Sakas D. The Parthians

47. Which of the following dynasties conquered Sri Lanka and South-East Asian countries?
A. The Pandyas B. The Chalukyas
C. The Cholas D. The Rashtrakutas

48. Match the capitals of the ruling dynasties of early Medieval India:

List-I	***List-II***
(*a*) Pratiharas	1. Kannauj
(*b*) Chandelas	2. Khajuraho
(*c*) Paramaras	3. Dhar
(*d*) Chalukyas	4. Anhilwad

Codes:

	(*a*)	(*b*)	(*c*)	(*d*)
A.	1	2	3	4
B.	1	3	4	2
C.	2	4	1	3
D.	2	1	3	4

49. 'Al Hilal' was a newspaper started for propagating nationalism by:
A. Abul Kalam Azad B. Mohammed Ali
C. Zafar Ali Khan D. Dr. Syed Mahmud

50. The famous monastery of Vikramsila was founded by the:
A. Guptas B. Senas
C. Palas D. Rashtrakutas

51. Fahein, the first Chinese pilgrim, visited India during the reign of:
A. Chandragupta Maurya
B. Chandragupta Vikramaditya
C. Harshavardhana
D. Ashoka the Great

52. The Kuka Movement was founded in:
A. Uttar Pradesh B. Malabar
C. Punjab D. Bihar

53. Who levied the tax known by the name "Chauth"?
A. Marathas B. Mughals
C. Cholas D. Chandelas

54. The most important feature in the economic measures pursued by Allauddin Khilji was:
A. Foreign trade
B. Minting of new coins
C. Development of agriculture
D. Market control

55. The era which is counted from 78 AD is the:
A. Kollam Era B. Vikrama Era
C. Saka Era D. Salivahana Era

56. Provincial Autonomy was a significant feature of:
A. The Indian Independence Act, 1947
B. The Government of India Act, 1919
C. The Government of India Act, 1909
D. The Government of India Act, 1935

57. The Simon Commission was appointed in:
A. 1927 B. 1929
C. 1930 D. 1926

58. Swarajya was declared as the goal of the Congress at its session in 1906 at:
A. Bombay B. Calcutta
C. Lucknow D. Madras

59. Gandhiji started the Dandi March from:
A. Ahmedabad B. Allahabad
C. Dandi D. Calcutta

60. The Congress adopted the Quit India Resolution in the year:
A. 1940 B. 1938
C. 1946 D. 1942

61. The art style which combines Indian and Greek features is called:
A. Sikhara B. Verna
C. Nagara D. Gandhara

62. Match the following:

List-I	List-II
(*a*) Fascism	1. Adolf Hitler
(*b*) Democracy	2. Lenin
(*c*) Nazism	3. Mussolini
(*d*) Socialism	4. Woodrow Wilson

Codes:

	(*a*)	(*b*)	(*c*)	(*d*)
A.	1	4	2	3
B.	4	3	2	1
C.	3	4	1	2
D.	3	1	4	2

63. Which battle laid the foundation of Mughal rule in India?
A. Battle of Plassey
B. Battle of Talikota
C. First battle of Panipat
D. Battle of Haldighati

64. The site of Amritsar was bestowed by Mughal emperor Akbar upon:
A. Guru Tegh Bahadur
B. Guru Ram Das
C. Guru Amar Das
D. Guru Hari Kishan

65. Alexander advanced in India up to the river:
A. Ravi B. Satluj
C. Beas D. Yamuna

66. Who introduced permanent settlement in 1793?
A. Lord Cornwallis
B. Lord Wellesley
C. William Bentinek
D. Lord Dalhousie

67. The Partition of Bengal was effected in 1905 by:
A. Lord Minto B. Lord Lyton
C. Lord Curzon D. Lord Lawrence

68. Revival of Vedas is associated with:
A. Swami Dayanand Saraswati
B. Swami Vivekananda
C. Acharya Rajneesh
D. Raja Ram Mohan Roy

69. At the time of independence of India in 1947, the Prime Minister of England was:
A. Lord Mountbatten
B. Clement Attlee
C. Winston Churchill
D. Neville Chamberlain

70. Who is known as the 'Iron man' of India?
A. Lala Lajpat Rai
B. Gopal Krishna Gokhale
C. Sardar Vallabhbhai Patel
D. Dr. B.R. Ambedkar

71. Iqtas were organised in India by:
A. Qutubuddin Aibak B. Balban
C. Alauddin Khilji D. Iltutmish

72. Literature in the Gupta period was written mostly in:
A. Sanskrit B. Telugu
C. Tamil D. Kannada

73. Who among the following was impeached on return to Britain for accepting bribes and committing atrocities on Indian rulers?
A. Warren Hastings B. Sir John Shore
C. Lord Clive D. Lord Cornwallis

74. Gandhiji started Satyagraha in 1919 in protest against the:
A. Salt Law
B. Rowlatt Act
C. Act of 1909
D. Jallianwala Bagh Massacre

75. The immediate cause for the outbreak of the First World War was:
A. the assassination of Archduke Francis Ferdinand
B. the imprisonment of Lenin
C. the ambition of America to dominate the world
D. the sudden death of Lloyd George

76. The Opium Wars were fought between:
A. Britain and China B. Britain and India
C. India and China D. Britain and Japan

77. Of the following who was not a signatory to the historic Poona Pact of 1932?
A. B.R. Ambedkar
B. Madan Mohan Malviya
C. C. Rajagopalachari
D. M.K. Gandhi

78. On the first occasion, the Prime Minister of India was appointed by:
A. The Governor-General
B. The British Emperor
C. Mahatma Gandhi
D. The Viceroy

79. The American publicist who was with Mahatma Gandhi during his 'Quit India' movement was:
A. Louis Fischer B. William L. Shiver
C. Web Miller D. Negley Farson

80. The most decisive battle that led to the establishment of supremacy of the British in India was:
A. The battle of Plassey
B. The battle of Buxar
C. The battle of Wandiwash
D. The third battle of Panipat

81. The person who returned his Token of Honour to Government of India on May 30, 1919 was:
A. Jamnalal Bajaj
B. Tej Bahadur Sapru
C. Mahatma Gandhi
D. Rabindranath Tagore

82. Match the following Lists I and II and select the correct answer from the codes given below:

List-I *(Authors)*	List-II *(Books)*
(*a*) Mahatma Gandhi	1. India Divided
(*b*) Ram Manohar Lohia	2. India Wins Freedom
(*c*) Dr Rajendra Prasad	3. Hind Swaraj
(*d*) Abul Kalam Azad	4. The Wheel of History

Codes:

	(*a*)	(*b*)	(*c*)	(*d*)
A.	1	3	4	2
B.	4	3	2	1
C.	3	4	1	2
D.	2	3	4	1

83. Karamchand Gandhi was a Dewan of:
A. Porbandar
B. Rajkot
C. Wakaner
D. All of the above states

84. The Asiatic Society of Bengal (founded in 1784) owes its origin to:
A. Warren Hastings
B. Sir William Jones

C. Sir James Mackintosh
D. James Princep

85. A prominent leader of the Ghadar Party was:
A. P. Mitra B. Hardayal
C. B.G. Tilak D. Bipin Chandra Pal

86. Who propounded the theory of 'Drain of Wealth' from India to Great Britain?
A. Gopal Krishna Gokhale
B. Dadabhai Naoroji
C. Surendranath Banerjee
D. Lala Lajpat Rai

87. Which one of the following was the first to impose censorship of the Press:
A. Wellesley B. Hastings
C. John Adams D. Dalhousie

88. MacDonald's Communal Award did not provide separate electorates and reserved seats in provincial legislatures to:
A. Muslims B. Sikhs
C. Scheduled Castes D. Buddhists

89. On November 1, 1858 Queen Victoria Proclamation was read out at Allahabad by:
A. Lord William Bentinck
B. Lord Canning
C. Lord Burnham
D. Sir Harcourt Butler

90. The first census in India during the British period was held during the tenure of:
A. Lord Dufferin B. Lord Lyton
C. Lord Mayo D. Lord Ripon

91. Which one of the following names cannot be associated with the Revolt of 1857?
A. Begum Hazarat Mahal
B. Maulavi Ahmadullah
C. Peshwa Baji Rao II
D. Bahadur Shah II

92. The call 'Dilli Challo' was given by:
A. Lala Lajpat Rai
B. Dr Rajendra Prasad
C. Subhash Chandra Bose
D. Mahatma Gandhi

93. Who among the following attended all the three Round Table Conferences?
A. Jawaharlal Nehru B. Dr B.R. Ambedkar
C. Vallabhbhai Patel D. Dr Rajendra Prasad

94. The British Viceroy who took a number of measures for preserving ancient buildings and monuments of India was:
A. Lord Ripon B. Lord Curzon
C. Lord Minto D. Lord Irwin

95. Find the correct match:

List-I	*List-II*
(*a*) Abdul Gaffar Khan	1. Mahatma
(*b*) Dadabhai Naoroji	2. Frontier Gandhi
(*c*) Mohandas Karamchand Gandhi	3. Grand Old Man of India
(*d*) Rabindranath Tagore	4. Gurudev

Codes:

	(*a*)	(*b*)	(*c*)	(*d*)
A.	3	1	4	2
B.	2	3	1	4
C.	4	1	2	3
D.	2	1	3	4

96. The first Governor-General of the East India Company in India was:
A. Robert Clive
B. Sir John Shore
C. Warren Hastings
D. Marquis of Hastings

97. The Stupa of Sanchi was built by:
A. Ashoka B. Kanishka
C. Harshvardhan D. Dharmapala

98. The prefix 'Mahatma' was added with the name of Gandhi:
A. During Champaran Satyagraha
B. During the Satyagraha against Rowlatt Act
C. In the Amritsar Session of the Indian National Congress 1919
D. At the beginning of Khilafat movement

99. The Harappans were the earliest people to produce:
A. Rice B. Maize
C. Cotton D. Barley

100. The Megalithic culture (500 BC-AD 100) brings us to the historical period in South India. The Megaliths used:
A. weapons made of stone
B. tools and implements made of stone
C. graves encircled by big pieces of stones
D. articles of daily use made of stone

101. Which one of the following persons called Irwin and Gandhi as 'the two Mahatmas':
A. Mira Behn
B. Sarojini Naidu
C. Madan Mohan Malviya
D. Jawaharlal Nehru

102. Gandhi suspended his first non-cooperation movement because:
A. it turned violent suddenly
B. most of the leaders had been arrested and were in prison
C. his experiment on all-India strike had succeeded
D. he saw no chances of success for the movement

103. Indian National Army was headed by:
A. Netaji Subhash Chandra Bose
B. General Cariappa
C. Field Marshal Manekshaw
D. Chandra Shekhar Azad

104. 'Purna Swaraj' day was first celebrated in India on:
A. 26 January, 1930 B. 15 August, 1930
C. 15 August, 1947 D. 26 January, 1950

105. Who was the Viceroy of British India when Attlee's government decided to grant Independence to India?
A. Lord Mountbatten B. Lord Linlithgow
C. Lord Wavell D. Lord Wellington

106. When did the 'Quit India' movement begin?
A. March 1930 B. August 1942
C. August 1945 D. August 1947

107. The Mausoleum of Sher Shah Suri is at:
A. Allahabad B. Agra
C. Jaunpur D. Sasaram

108. The slogan 'Inquilab Zindabad' was given by:
A. Chandra Shekhar Azad
B. Mohammed Iqbal
C. Bhagat Singh
D. Mahatma Gandhi

109. 'Red Shirts' movement aimed at:
A. creation of an independent Pakhtoonistan
B. ensuring the creating of Pakistan
C. making India a communist country at the dawn of independence
D. throwing out the British from India

110. Bhagwad Gita was originally written in the language:
A. Pali B. Prakrit
C. Sanskrit D. Hindi

111. Megasthenes was sent by Seleukos Nikator to the court of
A. Chandragupta Maurya
B. Ashoka
C. Chandragupta I
D. Bimbisara

112. The aim of the Cripps Mission to India was to:
A. appease the Indian public opinion
B. decide the future of India immediately
C. grant independence to India in stages
D. decentralise power to provinces

113. Which party was in power in the UK when India became independent?
A. Labour
B. Conservative
C. Liberal
D. No party, since a National Government was there

114. Who evolved the national consciousness as a formal concept?
A. Bal Gangadhar Tilak
B. Mahatma Gandhi
C. Jawaharlal Nehru
D. Surendranath Banerjee

115. The Swaraj Party was founded by:
A. Motilal Nehru
B. Bal Gangadhar Tilak
C. C. Rajagopalachari
D. Vallabhbhai Patel

116. The aim of the Swaraj Party was to:
A. boycott the foreign goods
B. declare independence and establish a provisional Indian government
C. enter the Legislative Councils through elections in order to wreck the legislature from within
D. All of the above

117. The cause of the immediate precipitation of the Sepoy mutiny was:
A. the spread of Christianity
B. the Doctrine of Lapse
C. the disparity between the European soldiers and the native Sepoys in service conditions
D. The compulsion on the Sepoys to use cartridges greased with fat

118. When did Vikram era start?
A. 19 BC B. 58 BC
C. 78 AD D. 73 AD

119. Which of the following was a consequence of the invasion of Amir Timur?
A. Decline of the Mughal Empire
B. Fall of Lodi Dynasty
C. Decline of Tughlaq Dynasty
D. End of Khilji Dynasty

120. What is the correct chronological sequence of the following?
I. Gandhi-Irwin Pact
II. Nehru Report
III. Non-cooperation Movement
IV. Quit India Movement
A. III, IV, I, II B. III, II, I, IV
C. II, III, IV, I D. I, III, II, IV

121. What is the correct chronological order in which the following four appeared on the political scenario in India?
I. Lord Minto II. Lord Reading
III. Lord Curzon IV. Lord Irwin
A. II, III, I, IV B. IV, I, III, II
C. I, III, II, IV D. III, I, II, IV

122. Who was the first Governor-General of free India?
A. Lord Mountbatten
B. C. Rajagopalachari
C. Pandit Jawaharlal Nehru
D. Babu Rajendra Prasad

123. 'Jatakas' are the sacred books of the:
A. Vaishnavas B. Jains
C. Buddhists D. Shaivas

124. The Ajanta paintings belong to the:
A. Harappan period B. Mauryan period
C. Buddhist period D. Gupta period

125. The famous King legendary Bhoja, belonged to the dynasty of:
A. the Pratiharas B. the Chauhanas
C. the Paramaras D. the Chandelas

126. The Gandhara School of Art was influenced most by the:
A. Greeks B. Kushans
C. Persians D. Sakas

127. Rock cut temples have been discovered in:
A. Elephanta Caves B. Ajanta Caves
C. Ellora Caves D. None of the above

128. 'Sufi Sect' developed in the religion:
A. Hinduism B. Islam
C. Christianity D. Sikhism

129. The great Indian philosopher Sankara advocated:
A. Dvaita B. Advaita
C. Vishishtadvaita D. None of the above

130. The influence of Chaitanya was mainly confined to:
A. The Eastern India B. The Southern India
C. Gujarat D. North India

131. Which of the following classes participated the least in the Indian National Movement?
A. Capitalists
B. Princes of States
C. Government officials
D. The peasants

132. Who said first 'Swaraj is my birth right, and I shall have it'?
A. Bal Gangadhar Tilak
B. Gopal Krishna Gokhale
C. M.K. Gandhi
D. Lala Lajpat Rai

133. Who led the extremists before the arrival of Gandhi on the political scene for India's freedom struggle?
A. Dadabhai Naoroji
B. Surendranath Banerjee
C. Gopal Krishna Gokhale
D. Bal Gangadhar Tilak

134. The Home Rule movement was launched by:
A. Annie Besant and Bal Gangadhar Tilak together

B. Annie Besant and Bal Gangadhar Tilak separately
C. Annie Besant and Mahatma Gandhi together
D. The Congress when Mrs Besant was its President

135. Which of the following caves has the 'Trimurti' statue with the faces of Brahma, Vishnu and Mahesh?
A. Kanheri B. Ajanta
C. Elephanta D. Ellora

ANSWERS

1	**2**	**3**	**4**	**5**	**6**	**7**	**8**	**9**	**10**
C	A	C	B	D	D	D	B	B	B
11	**12**	**13**	**14**	**15**	**16**	**17**	**18**	**19**	**20**
D	B	C	A	A	C	A	A	C	B
21	**22**	**23**	**24**	**25**	**26**	**27**	**28**	**29**	**30**
A	B	A	B	B	C	B	A	C	A
31	**32**	**33**	**34**	**35**	**36**	**37**	**38**	**39**	**40**
D	D	C	B	C	C	C	D	D	C
41	**42**	**43**	**44**	**45**	**46**	**47**	**48**	**49**	**50**
B	B	C	C	C	A	C	A	A	C
51	**52**	**53**	**54**	**55**	**56**	**57**	**58**	**59**	**60**
B	C	A	D	C	D	A	B	A	D
61	**62**	**63**	**64**	**65**	**66**	**67**	**68**	**69**	**70**
D	C	C	B	C	A	C	A	B	C
71	**72**	**73**	**74**	**75**	**76**	**77**	**78**	**79**	**80**
D	A	A	B	A	A	B	A	A	B
81	**82**	**83**	**84**	**85**	**86**	**87**	**88**	**89**	**90**
D	C	B	B	B	D	A	D	B	C
91	**92**	**93**	**94**	**95**	**96**	**97**	**98**	**99**	**100**
C	C	B	B	B	C	A	B	C	B
101	**102**	**103**	**104**	**105**	**106**	**107**	**108**	**109**	**110**
C	A	A	A	C	B	D	B	D	C
111	**112**	**113**	**114**	**115**	**116**	**117**	**118**	**119**	**120**
A	A	A	D	A	C	D	B	C	B
121	**122**	**123**	**124**	**125**	**126**	**127**	**128**	**129**	**130**
D	A	C	D	A	A	A	B	B	A
131	**132**	**133**	**134**	**135**					
B	A	D	B	C					

INDIAN POLITY AND CONSTITUTION

1. The Constituent Assembly was presided over by:
   A. Dr Rajendra Prasad
   B. Dr B.R. Ambedkar
   C. Pandit Jawaharlal Nehru
   D. Dr K.M. Munshi
2. Under which article of the Constitution of India, a citizen can go to the Supreme Court for the enforcement of his Fundamental Rights?
   A. Article 31 B. Article 29
   C. Article 32 D. Article 10
3. Which of the following two words were added to the Preamble of the Indian Constitution by the 42nd Amendment?
   A. Sovereign and Democratic
   B. Secular and Socialist
   C. Secular and Democratic
   D. Democratic and Republic
4. By which Constitutional Amendment Bill was the voting age reduced from 21 years to 18 years?
   A. 48th B. 57th
   C. 61st D. 63rd
5. Which among the following is not a Fundamental Right now?
   A. Right to Equality
   B. Right to Property
   C. Right to Constitutional Remedies
   D. None of these
6. Secularism in the Constitution of India stands for:
   A. equal respect to all religions
   B. non-interference of the State in religious affairs
   C. Both A and B
   D. None of the above
7. Which of the following is not a condition for Indian citizenship?
   A. Property B. Birth
   C. Heredity D. Nationality
8. The President calls the joint sitting of both Houses of Parliament when:
   A. any constitutional amendment bill is to be passed
   B. a money bill is rejected by the Rajya Sabha
   C. an ordinary bill is not passed by both Houses of Parliament
   D. the President wished to do so
9. The Indian Constitution was adopted and enacted by the Constituent Assembly of India on:
   A. 9 December, 1949
   B. 26 January, 1946
   C. 26 November, 1949
   D. 26 January, 1950
10. The Preamble of our Constitution reads—India is a:
    A. Sovereign, Socialist, Secular, Democratic Republic
    B. Sovereign, Democratic, Socialist, Secular Republic
    C. Socialist, Democratic, Secular, Republic
    D. Democratic, Sovereign, Secular, Socialist Republic
11. The main feature of the Panchayati Raj in India is:
    A. Rolling plan
    B. Decentralisation of power
    C. Money plan
    D. Sharing of power between the Centre and the States
12. The President of India is elected by:
    A. the people of India
    B. all the members of Parliament
    C. all the elected Members of Parliament
    D. all the elected Members of the Parliament and of State Legislative Assemblies
13. The maximum strength of the Rajya Sabha is:
    A. 250 B. 270
    C. 300 D. 545

14. Who conducts elections to the Lok Sabha and Legislative Assemblies of the States?
A. President and Governor respectively
B. Prime Minister and Chief Minister respectively
C. Speakers of the Lok Sabha and the Legislative Assemblies
D. Chief Election Commissioner

15. The Comptroller and Auditor General of India may be removed:
A. by the President in his discretion
B. by the President on the advice of the Union Council of Ministers
C. by the President on the advice of the UPSC
D. by the President on an address by both Houses of Parliament

16. Salaries and allowances of the High Court judges are charged upon the:
A. Consolidated Fund of India
B. Consolidated Fund of the State
C. Contingency Fund of India
D. Contingency Fund of the State

17. Who was appointed as the Prime Minister without being a member of a House of the Parliament?
A. Gulzarilal Nanda
B. Rajiv Gandhi
C. Chandrashekhar
D. P.V. Narasimha Rao

18. What can be the maximum period of gap between any two sessions of the Indian Parliament?
A. Three months B. Six months
C. One year D. Ten weeks

19. The High Court comes under:
A. Union List B. State List
C. Concurrent List D. None of these

20. Which democratic country is said to be federal in form but unitary in character?
A. USA B. India
C. Ireland D. UK

21. Which of the following is not a charged expenditure on the Consolidated Fund of India?
A. Expenditure of Five-Year Plans
B. Expenditure on the Chairman and Members of the UPSC
C. Expenditure on the Judges of the Supreme Court
D. Debt charges of the Government of India

22. Which one of the following subjects is not contained in the Union list?
A. Currency B. Agriculture
C. Foreign Affairs D. Union Duties

23. The Speaker of the Lok Sabha is:
A. nominated by the President
B. nominated by the Prime Minister
C. nominated by the Vice-President
D. elected by the members of the Lok Sabha

24. Which writ is issued by a superior court to an individual or institution directing him to perform a public duty?
A. Habeas Corpus B. Quo Warranto
C. Mandamus D. Certiorari

25. The Council of Ministers of an Indian State is collectively responsible to the:
A. Legislative Council
B. Legislative Assembly
C. Governor of the State
D. Both houses of the State legislature

26. Who can legislate on those residual matters which are not mentioned in Central/State/Concurrent lists?
A. State legislatures exclusively
B. Parliament alone
C. Parliament after State legislatures concur
D. Parliament or State legislatures as adjudicated by the Supreme Court

27. The salary of the Members of Parliament is decided by:
A. the Parliament B. the Central Cabinet
C. the President D. the Speaker

28. Which one of the following Fundamental Rights was described by Dr B.R. Ambedkar as the heart and soul of the Constitution?
A. Right to Religion
B. Right to Constitutional Remedies
C. Right to Property
D. Right to Education

29. The President of India addresses both Houses of Parliament assembled together at the commencement of the first session:
A. of each year
B. after each general election to the House of the People
C. Both A and B
D. Neither A nor B

30. Of the following, who held the offices of judge of the Supreme Court and the Speaker of Lok Sabha?
A. M. Hidayatullah B. K.S. Hegde
C. Subba Rao D. P.N. Bhagwati

31. No person shall be a citizen of India if he has:
A. lived in a foreign country for more than five years
B. been convicted by a foreign court of law
C. voluntarily acquired citizenship of another country
D. accepted employment in another country

32. The Balwant Rai Mehta Committee made important recommendations concerning:
A. Industrial policy towards the small scale industries
B. Policy towards foreign capital
C. Panchayati raj
D. Foodgrain policy

33. The Constituent Assembly of India was set up under the:
A. Simon Commission Proposals
B. Cripps' Mission Proposals
C. Mountbatten Plan
D. Cabinet Mission Plan

34. A Judge of the Supreme Court retires at the age of:
A. 65 years B. 55 years
C. 60 years D. 58 years

35. Match List-I with List-II and select your answer from the code given below:

List-I *(Articles of the Constitution)*	**List-II** *(Subject Matter)*
(*a*) Art. 40	1. Organisation of village panchayat
(*b*) Art. 41	2. Right to work
(*c*) Art. 44	3. Uniform Civil Code
(*d*) Art. 48	4. Organisation of agriculture and animal husbandry

Codes:

	(*a*)	(*b*)	(*c*)	(*d*)
A.	1	2	3	4
B.	2	3	1	4
C.	1	3	4	2
D.	3	2	4	1

36. The introduction of "No Confidence" motion in the Lok Sabha requires the support of at least:
A. 70 members B. 60 members
C. 50 members D. 80 members

37. When the office of the President of India falls vacant, it must be filled by an election within:
A. eight months B. six months
C. two months D. nine months

38. The provisions as to disqualification on grounds of defection by a member of Parliament are contained in:
A. Article 191
B. Article 102
C. The Seventh Schedule
D. The Tenth Schedule

39. According to our Constitution, the Rajya Sabha:
A. is dissolved once in 2 years
B. is dissolved every 5 years
C. is dissolved every 6 years
D. is not subject to dissolution

40. Fundamental Duties were introduced in the Constitution by:
A. 40th Amendment B. 42nd Amendment
C. 43rd Amendment D. 44th Amendment

41. The jurisdiction of a High Court may be extended by the:
A. President
B. Governor of the State
C. Parliament
D. State Legislature

42. Linguistic reorganisation of state took place in:
A. 1947 B. 1950
C. 1956 D. 1971

43. The Union Council of Ministers is collectively responsible to the:
A. President
B. Lok Sabha
C. Rajya Sabha and Lok Sabha
D. Prime Minister

44. Who administers the oath of the office to the President in India?
A. Prime Minister
B. Speaker of Lok Sabha
C. Chief Justice of India
D. Vice-President

45. Which of the following qualifications is not essential for a person to become the Vice-President of India?
A. He must be an Indian citizen
B. He should be a graduate
C. He must not be less than 35 years of age
D. He must be qualified to be a member of the Rajya Sabha

46. The term "Fourth Estate" is used for:
A. The Press and Newspaper
B. Parliament
C. Judiciary
D. The Executive

47. Implementing Laws is the function of:
A. Executive B. Legislature
C. Judiciary D. Cabinet

48. Which one of the following is a Fundamental Right guaranteed by the Constitution of India?
A. Right to Govern
B. Right to Property
C. Right to Information
D. Right to Equality

49. Education is included in which of the following lists?
A. Central list B. State list
C. Concurrent list D. Local list

50. The Chief Jusitce of a High Court is appointed by:
A. The President
B. Chief Justice of the Supreme Court
C. Governor of the State
D. Chief Minister of the State

51. Can a person who is not a member of Parliament be appointed as a minister?
A. No
B. Yes
C. Yes, if the Parliament approves of such an appointment
D. Yes, but he has to become a member of Parliament within six months of his appointment

52. Through which Constitutional Amendment was the Nagarpalika Bill passed?
A. 70th B. 72nd
C. 73rd D. 74th

53. The fourth schedule of the Constitution of India contains:
A. Directive Principles of State Policy
B. the Anti Defection Act
C. Fundamental Duties
D. Allocation of seats in the Council of State

54. Which of the following Article/Articles read with the word 'Socialist' used in the Preamble of the Indian Constitution enabled the Supreme Court to deduce a fundamental right to equal pay for equal work?
A. Article 14
B. Article 14 and 15
C. Article 14, 15 and 16
D. Article 14 and 16

55. Under the Cabinet Mission Plan, the total number of seats allotted to each province in the Constituent Assembly was roughly in the ratio of one representative to the population of:
A. 8 lakh persons B. 10 lakh persons
C. 12 lakh persons D. 15 lakh persons

56. Which Article of the Constitution of India deals with the appellate jurisdiction of the Supreme Court in connection with constitutional cases:
A. Article 131
B. Article 132
C. Article 132 read with Article 134 A
D. Article 133 read with Article 134 A

57. Article 356 of the Constitution of India deals with:
A. autonomy of States

B. the proclamation of President's Rule in a State
C. the removal of a Chief Minister
D. the appointment of a Governor

58. Which one of the following constitutional amendments gives a constitutional status of the Panchayati Raj institutions?
A. 72nd B. 73rd
C. 78th D. 75th

59. Panchayati Raj system involves a three-tier arrangement. Which one of the following correctly represents this system?
A. Village level, corporation level, block level
B. Village level, block level, district level
C. Village level, town level, district level
D. Village level, district level, State level

60. The Election Commission is:
A. A legislative body
B. A constitutional body
C. An executive body
D. A non-formal body

61. Who is normally the Chancellor of the State Universities?
A. Chief Minister of the State
B. Governor of the State
C. Education Minister of the State
D. Advocate-General of the State

62. The *ex officio* Chairman of the NITI Aayog of India is the:
A. Planning Minister B. Finance Minister
C. Prime Minister D. President

63. In which part of the Constitution the concept of Welfare State finds elaboration?
A. Preamble
B. Fundamental Rights
C. Fundamental Duties
D. Directive Principles of State Policy

64. Judges of the High Courts cannot practise, after retirement, in:
A. The Supreme Court
B. Any of the High Courts
C. The High Courts served by them
D. Any court in the country

65. The election of the President can be challenged:
A. before the Chief Election Commissioner
B. in the Supreme Court
C. before Union Parliament
D. before the Ministry of Law

ANSWERS

1	**2**	**3**	**4**	**5**	**6**	**7**	**8**	**9**	**10**
A	C	B	C	B	A	A	C	C	A
11	**12**	**13**	**14**	**15**	**16**	**17**	**18**	**19**	**20**
B	D	A	D	D	A	B	B	A	B
21	**22**	**23**	**24**	**25**	**26**	**27**	**28**	**29**	**30**
A	B	D	C	B	D	A	B	C	B
31	**32**	**33**	**34**	**35**	**36**	**37**	**38**	**39**	**40**
C	C	D	A	A	C	B	D	D	B
41	**42**	**43**	**44**	**45**	**46**	**47**	**48**	**49**	**50**
C	C	B	C	B	A	C	D	C	A
51	**52**	**53**	**54**	**55**	**56**	**57**	**58**	**59**	**60**
D	D	D	C	B	B	B	B	B	B
61	**62**	**63**	**64**	**65**					
B	C	D	C	B					

GEOGRAPHY OF INDIA AND WORLD

1. Which of the following soils in India is most fertile?
A. Regur B. Alluvial soil
C. Laterite soil D. Red soil

2. In which of the following States is the site of Jawaharlal Nehru (Nhava Sheva) Port located?
A. Kerala B. Karnataka
C. Andhra Pradesh D. Maharashtra

3. Density of Earth's atmosphere is highest in the:
A. Troposphere B. Stratosphere
C. Mesosphere D. Ionosphere

4. Which one of the following is the driest region in India?
A. Telengana B. Marwar
C. Vidarbha D. Marathwada

5. The Equatorial Forests of the Amazon Basin in South America are known as:
A. Selva B. Taiga
C. Tundra D. Pampas

6. Which is a tropical food crop requiring a temperature of 27°C and a rainfall more than 100 cm?
A. Wheat B. Maize
C. Rice D. Barley

7. After which one of the following tribes of India; has a large continent of ancient geological history of the world been named?
A. Santhals B. Bhils
C. Marias D. Gonds

8. Which one of the following characteristics is associated with the 'Bread Basket' area of the USA?
A. Moderate rainfall in winter
B. Heavy rainfall throughout the year
C. Low rainfall in summer
D. Long winter with snow

9. Which of the following is largely used in textile industries in India?
A. Cotton B. Wool
C. Synthetic fibres D. Jute

10. Sun belt of USA is important for which one of the following industries?
A. Cotton textile B. Petrochemical
C. Hi-tech electronics D. Food processing

11. Coffee is a:
A. Sub-tropical shrub
B. Warm temperate shrub
C. Tropical shrub
D. Cool temperate shrub

12. The best variety of world's cotton is known as:
A. Sea Island B. Upland American
C. Egyptian D. Short staple Indian

13. How much land area in India is under forests?
A. About 17% B. About 24%
C. About 18% D. About 22%

14. Which one of the following statements is not true for laterite soils?
A. they are the soils of the humid tropical regions
B. they are highly leached soils
C. their fertility is low
D. they are rich in lime

15. Which of the following is known as 'White Coal'?
A. Hydro Power B. Nuclear Power
C. Thermal Power D. All types of Power

16. The Industry for which Nepanagar is known is:
A. cement B. fertilizer
C. handloom D. newsprint paper

17. Which of the following is known as the morning star?
A. Saturn B. Jupiter
C. Venus D. Mars

18. The Nagarjuna Sagar project is constructed on the river:
A. Couvery B. Krishna
C. Godavari D. Indus

19. The innermost layer of the earth is known as:
A. Lithosphere B. Mesosphere
C. Asthenosphere D. Barysphere

20. Which one of the following is not a cold ocean current?
A. California B. Oyashio
C. Kuroshio D. Canaries

21. The highest tropic level in an ecosystem is obtained by:
A. herbivores B. carnivores
C. decomposers D. omnivores

22. Which of the following absorbs part of the insolation and preserves earth's radiated heat?
A. Oxygen B. Nitrogen
C. Water vapour D. Carbon dioxide

23. Arakan Yoma is the extension of the Himalayas located in:
A. Baluchistan B. Myanmar
C. Nepal D. Kashmir (India)

24. The largest estuary in India is at the mouth of river:
A. Hooghly B. Bhagirathi
C. Godavari D. Krishna

25. Match Lists I and II and mark the correct answer using the codes given below:

List-I *(Places)*	**List-II** *(Minerals)*
(*a*) Ankaleshwar	1. Iron ore
(*b*) Dolli-Rajhara	2. Petroleum
(*c*) Kodarma	3. Copper
(*d*) Khetri	4. Mica

Codes:

	(*a*)	(*b*)	(*c*)	(*d*)
A.	1	2	3	4
B.	2	1	4	3
C.	4	3	2	1
D.	3	2	1	4

26. When it is noon at IST meredian, what would be the local time at 120° East longitude?
A. 09.30 B. 14.30
C. 17.30 D. 20.00

27. Which one of the following is correctly matched?
A. Eskimo–Canada B. Oran–Japan
C. Lapps–India D. Gonds–Africa

28. The coniferous forests are not found in:
A. Amazon B. Scandinavia
C. Canada D. Finland

29. Which of the following is not a cash crop?
A. Jute B. Cashewnut
C. Paddy D. Sugarcane

30. Which food crop in India is sown in October-November and reaped in April?
A. Coconut B. Coffee
C. Rice D. Wheat

31. Which one of the following is the longest river in the world?
A. Amazon B. Yangtze-Kiang
C. Nile D. Mississipi-Missouri

32. The Alamatti Dam is constructed on the river:
A. Kaveri B. Seeleru
C. Krishna D. Tungabhadra

33. Which of the following States is most famous for its beautiful sea beaches?
A. Gujarat B. Goa
C. Tamil Nadu D. Odisha

34. Grassland is called 'Pampas' in:
A. Africa B. South America
C. United Kingdom D. the USA

35. The coastal part of water bodies of the oceans which is structurally part of the mainland of the continents is called the:
A. Isthmus B. Oceanic Ridge
C. Continental Shelf D. Continental Slope

36. Which one of the following is not the result of underground water action?
A. Stalactites B. Stalagmites
C. Sink holes D. Fiords

37. Which one of the following practices is adopted for restoring the fertility of soil?
A. Weeding B. Levelling
C. Fallowing D. Harrowing

38. The Eastern Coast of India is known as:
A. Eastern Plateau B. Bengal Coast
C. Coromandel Coast D. Cyclonic Coast

39. Which of the following dams is the highest?
A. Mython Dam
B. Tehri Dam
C. Hirakud Dam
D. Nagarjuna Sagar Dam

40. Which of the following States is the largest producer of lignite?
A. Odisha B. Bihar
C. West Bengal D. Tamil Nadu

41. The International date line passes through:
A. Gibraltar strait B. Bering strait
C. Florida strait D. Malacca strait

42. The direction of ocean currents is reversed with seasons:
A. in the Pacific ocean
B. in the Indian ocean
C. in the Atlantic ocean
D. in the Mediterranean sea

43. The importance of ozone layer is that it shields:
A. plants from radiation
B. life on earth from cosmic bombardment
C. earth from meteorites
D. life on earth from the ultraviolet rays of the sun

44. The ideal monsoon system is developed in:
A. Mexico B. India
C. Thailand D. China

45. The State which occupies the first place in India in the production of Tobacco is:
A. Tamil Nadu B. West Bengal
C. Andhra Pradesh D. Maharashtra

46. The greatest mass of ice on the earth's surface is found at ......
A. Canada B. Greenland
C. Sibexia D. Antarctica

47. The largest brackish water lake of India is in the State of:
A. Jammu & Kashmir
B. Maharashtra
C. Odisha
D. West Bengal

48. Which of the following represents the zone between Tropic of Cancer and Tropic of Capricorn?
A. Frigid Zone B. Torrid Zone
C. Temperate Zone D. Sub-tropical Zone

49. Maharashtrian Plateau is made up of:
A. alluvial soil B. coral reef
C. sandstone D. lava

50. Which gets first monsoon in summer?
A. Western Ghats B. Himalayas
C. Eastern Ghats D. Gangetic Plains

51. Which country is called the Sugar Bowl of the world?
A. Cuba B. India
C. Argentina D. Brazil

52. What is the maximum known depth of an ocean?
A. 8 km B. 10 km
C. 11 km D. 22 km

53. A line drawn on a weather map connecting places that receive equal amounts of sunshine is called:
A. Isohyet B. Isotherm
C. Isobar D. Isohel

54. Palk Strait connects:
A. India and Sri Lanka
B. North Korea and South Korea
C. Saudi Arabia and Burma (Myanmar)
D. Britain and France

55. Black Pagoda is found at:
A. Konark B. Khajuraho
C. Madurai D. Egypt

56. Earthquakes occur owing to:
A. changes in earth crust
B. movements in the interior layers of the earth
C. volcanic eruptions
D. None of the above

57. What is the International Date Line?
A. A line connecting places of the same longitude as Greenwich
B. The line near 180° longitude, while crossing which date changes
C. The line of the Globe which will have daytime throughout the year
D. None of the above

58. In which region do we find the belt of doldrum?
A. Polar region B. Sub-tropical region
C. Temperate region D. Equatorial region

59. The grasslands of Argentina are called:
A. Steppes B. Pampas
C. Campos D. Prairies

60. On which one of the following longitudes is the Indian Standard Time determined?
A. 68½ °E B. 68½ °W
C. 82½ °E D. 82½ °W

61. The origin of earth dates back to approximately:
A. 3.6 billion years B. 4.6 billion years
C. 5.6 billion years D. 6.6 billion years

62. The period by which the entire country in India comes under southwest monsoon is:
A. 1st - 10th June B. 10th - 20th June
C. 20th - 30th June D. 1st - 15th July

63. The most extensive soil cover of India comprises:
A. laterite soils B. black soils
C. alluvial soils D. marshy soils

64. Evergreen rain forest is mainly found in regions having well distributed annual rainfall:
A. below 50 cm B. 50 - 100 cm
C. 100 - 200 cm D. more than 200 cm

65. Which one of the following organisations is responsible for publishing topographical sheets?
A. Geological Survey of India (GSI)
B. National Atlas & Thematic Mapping Organisation (NATMO)
C. Indian Meteorological Department (IMD)
D. Survey of India (SOI)

66. Humidity is measured by:
A. Lactometer B. Polarimeter
C. Thermometer D. Hygrometer

67. The State having the largest density of population per square kilometre in India is:
A. Kerala B. Uttar Pradesh
C. Bihar D. West Bengal

68. Access to raw material is the main basis for the location of:
A. sugarcane industry B. aluminium industry
C. electronic industry D. hi-tech industry

69. Which of the following Himalayan peaks is situated in Assam?
A. Nanda Devi B. Namche Barwa
C. Dhaulagiri D. Kedarnath

70. Among the world oceans, the widest continental shelves are observed around the:
A. Atlantic ocean B. Arctic ocean
C. Indian ocean D. Pacific ocean

71. Mozambique current forms part of currents of:
A. North Pacific B. South Pacific
C. Indian Ocean D. South Atlantic

72. The average time interval between successive high and low tides is:
A. 3 hours and 13 minutes
B. 6 hours and 26 minutes
C. 12 hours and 36 minutes
D. 24 hours and 52 minutes

73. Which of the following shipping canals joins the North sea and the Baltic sea?
A. Suez B. Keil
C. Soo D. Manchester

74. High temperature and low pressure over the Indian subcontinent during the summer season, draws air from the Indian ocean leading to the in blowing of the:
A. South-east monsoon
B. South-west monsoon
C. Trade winds
D. Westerlies

75. Through which of the following countries does the river Tigris flow?
A. Egypt B. Iran
C. Italy D. Iraq

76. Imaginary lines drawn on a global map from pole-to-pole and from the perpendicular to the equator are called:
A. Contours B. Isobars
C. Meridians D. Steppes

77. The 23½° South latitude is known as:
A. the Tropic of Cancer
B. the Tropic of Capricorn
C. the Equator
D. the Prime Meridian

78. 'Equinox' means:
A. days are longer than nights
B. days and nights are equal
C. days are shorter than nights
D. None of these

79. The hills that have the Dodda Bettah Peak are:
A. Annamalai B. Nilgiri
C. Palani D. Kutralam

80. The great Barrier Reef is a ......
A. Plateau B. Coral formation
C. Mountain D. Tidal bore

81. The food crop sown in the largest area in India is:
A. maize B. paddy
C. wheat D. jowar

82. Find the mismatched pair:
A. Mathura—Oil refinery
B. Visakhapatnam—Aircraft
C. Sindri—Fertiliser
D. Kapurthala—Railway coaches

83. Which one of the following is the largest lake in the world?
A. Lake Superior B. Caspian Sea
C. Lake Baikal D. Lake Victoria

84. Chilka Lake is located in:
A. Bihar B. West Bengal
C. Assam D. Odisha

85. Seasonal movement of people from mountains to plains and vice versa is called:
A. migration B. transhumance
C. commutation D. transportation

86. What do you call a narrow neck of land that connects two large landmarks?
A. Peninsula B. Isthmus
C. Cape D. Strait

87. What is the colour of laterite soil?
A. Yellow B. Brown
C. Red D. Pink

88. What are Doldrums?
A. The trade winds
B. Area of great humidity
C. A low pressure belt round the Equator where there are very light winds and calm seas
D. Area where seas are calm

89. The Thermal Equator coincides with the Tropic of Cancer on:
A. 21st March B. 21st June
C. 23rd September D. 22nd December

90. The total length of India's coastline is approximately:
A. 5500 km B. 6500 km
C. 7500 km D. 8500 km

ANSWERS

1	2	3	4	5	6	7	8	9	10
B	D	A	B	A	C	D	A	A	B
11	**12**	**13**	**14**	**15**	**16**	**17**	**18**	**19**	**20**
A	D	D	D	A	D	C	B	D	B
21	**22**	**23**	**24**	**25**	**26**	**27**	**28**	**29**	**30**
D	C	B	A	B	B	A	A	C	D
31	**32**	**33**	**34**	**35**	**36**	**37**	**38**	**39**	**40**
C	C	B	B	C	D	C	C	B	D
41	**42**	**43**	**44**	**45**	**46**	**47**	**48**	**49**	**50**
B	B	D	B	C	D	C	C	D	A
51	**52**	**53**	**54**	**55**	**56**	**57**	**58**	**59**	**60**
A	A	D	A	A	B	B	D	B	C
61	**62**	**63**	**64**	**65**	**66**	**67**	**68**	**69**	**70**
B	D	C	C	B	D	C	A	B	D
71	**72**	**73**	**74**	**75**	**76**	**77**	**78**	**79**	**80**
C	C	B	B	D	C	B	B	B	B
81	**82**	**83**	**84**	**85**	**86**	**87**	**88**	**89**	**90**
B	B	B	D	A	B	B	C	B	C

INDIAN ECONOMY

1. According to the 2011 Census the population of India is:
   A. 1 billion 21 crore
   B. 1 billion 2 crore
   C. 1 billion 2 crore 7 lakh
   D. 1 billion
2. What is the approximate density of population in India?
   A. 273 B. 382
   C. 416 D. 216
3. The sex ratio (females per thousand males) in India is approximately:
   A. 927 B. 963
   C. 943 D. 993
4. The annual growth rate of population during the decade 2001-2011:
   A. 1.64 per cent B. 1 per cent
   C. 2 per cent D. 3 per cent
5. The principal means of transport of goods in India is:
   A. Railways B. Roadways
   C. Inland waterways D. Airways
6. Which one of the following is the most densely populated state of India?
   A. UP B. Bihar
   C. West Bengal D. Kerala
7. Which of the following states has the highest literacy rate?
   A. Kerala B. Arunachal Pradesh
   C. Nagaland D. Maharashtra
8. Which one of the following Union Territories has the highest literacy rate?
   A. Puducherry B. Daman and Diu
   C. Lakshadweep D. Chandigarh
9. Unemployment in India is due to:
   A. poor manpower planning
   B. population explosion
   C. inappropriate educational system
   D. All of the above
10. The policy of family planning was adopted by the government in:
    A. 1947 B. 1952
    C. 1956 D. 1962
11. The Second Five Year Plan focussed on:
    A. agriculture B. education
    C. heavy industries D. health
12. Which one of the following measures has been taken to modernise Indian agriculture?
    A. Area under irrigation increase
    B. High yielding variety seeds
    C. Credit and facilities to villages
    D. All of the above
13. Seasonal unemployment refers mainly to:
    A. Private sector industry
    B. Public sector industry
    C. Agriculture
    D. Banks
14. Open unemployment refers to people:
    A. who are not willing to work
    B. who are willing but do not get work
    C. who leave their jobs in search of better ones
    D. who have been dismissed because of incorrect practices
15. Which one of the following is not a source of revenue of the Union Government?
    A. Income tax B. Corporation tax
    C. Land revenue D. Customs duties
16. Bank rate means:
    A. the official rate of interest charged by the Central Bank of the country
    B. rate of profit of the banking institutions
    C. interest rate charged by the scheduled banks
    D. interest rate charged by the moneylenders
17. Marginal revenue will be zero if the elasticity of demand is:
    A. negative B. unity
    C. greater than one D. equal to zero

18. The term "market" in Economics means:
A. a central place
B. presence of competition
C. place where goods are stored
D. shops and superbazars

19. Commercial banking system in India is:
A. mixed banking B. unit banking
C. branch banking D. None of the above

20. The gilt-edged market in the capital market of India refers to:
A. long term private securities
B. market dealing in existing securities
C. market for corporate securities
D. market for Government securities

21. Operation Flood Programme was introduced in:
A. 1951 B. 1970
C. 1975 D. 1985

22. Sustainable agriculture means:
A. Self-sufficiency
B. To be able to export and import under WTO norms
C. To utilise land so that its quality remains intact
D. To utilise waste land for agricultural purposes

23. Which one of the following crops is the greatest beneficiary of the Green Revolution in both production and productivity?
A. Jowar B. Maize
C. Rice D. Wheat

24. Per capita income means:
A. average income of the wage-earners
B. income necessary for an individual to meet his daily expenses
C. total income of the group divided by the number of the people in the group
D. average income of family

25. The Railway gets the maximum income from ......
A. Goods freight
B. Passenger fares
C. Advertisement
D. None of these

26. The most serious economic problems of India are:
A. underdevelopment, not poverty
B. poverty and unemployment
C. unemployment, not poverty
D. stagnation, not poverty

27. National product includes goods:
A. only those consumed by the producers
B. all whether exchanged or not
C. both exchanged in markets and retained by producers for addition to their stock
D. only exchanged in markets but not those consumed by producers

28. Marginal utility is:
A. total minus average utility
B. addition to total utility because of one unit increase in commodity
C. total utility divided by the number of units
D. total plus average utility

29. Demand of a commodity mainly depends on:
A. desire to purchase B. power to purchase
C. tax policy D. advertisement

30. GST was introduced in India with effect from:
A. 1-7-2017 B. 1-1-2017
C. 1-4-2017 D. 1-1-2018

31. In a highly developed country the relative contribution of agriculture to Gross Domestic Product (GDP) is:
A. relatively high
B. relatively low
C. the same as that of other sectors
D. zero

32. Match List-I with List-II and select the correct answer using the codes given below:

List-I *(Industry)*	List-II *(Production Centre)*
(*a*) Jute Textile	1. Bhadohi
(*b*) Silk Textile	2. Ludhiana
(*c*) Woollen Hosiery	3. Bengaluru
(*d*) Woollen Carpet	4. Titagarh

Codes:

	(*a*)	(*b*)	(*c*)	(*d*)
A.	3	4	2	1
B.	4	3	2	1
C.	1	3	4	2
D.	4	1	3	2

33. The credit control operation in India is performed by:
A. Rural Banks
B. Commercial Banks
C. Reserve Bank of India
D. State Bank of India

34. Division of labour is limited by:
A. the number of workers
B. hours of work
C. extent of the market
D. working space

35. The four factors of production are:
A. land, labour, capital, organisation
B. land, electricity, water, labour
C. labour, capital, land, rainfall
D. labour, climate, land, tools

36. What is the main purpose of currency?
A. Currency Chest
B. Standard of Postponed Payments
C. Standard of Money
D. Medium of Exchange

37. National Income accounting is the study of the income and expenditure of the entire:
A. family B. state
C. economy D. organisation

38. The problem of Economics arises from:
A. plenty of goods
B. scarcity of goods
C. more wants and less goods
D. All of these

39. Agricultural income-tax is a source of revenue to:
A. Central Government
B. State Government
C. Local Administration
D. Central and State Governments

40. Beyond a certain point, deficit financing will certainly lead to:
A. inflation
B. deflation
C. recession
D. economic stagnation

41. In public budgets, zero-based budgeting was first introduced in:
A. USA B. UK
C. France D. Sweden

42. To achieve economic self-reliance was the main objective of which of the following Five-Year Plans?
A. First Plan B. Second Plan
C. Third Plan D. Fourth Plan

43. The preparation of National Income Estimates is the responsibility of the:
A. NITI Aayog
B. National Development Council
C. National Sample Survey
D. Central Statistical Office

44. Which one of the following is the most sensitive indicator of the health of a community?
A. Birth rate
B. Infant mortality rate
C. Death rate
D. Maternal mortality rate

45. Banks in India were nationalised for the first time in the year:
A. 1950 B. 1960
C. 1969 D. 1979

46. The objectives of Indian Planning are:
A. increasing national income
B. reducing inequalities in income wealth
C. elimination of poverty
D. All of the above

47. The Gandhian economy was based on the principle of:
A. State control B. Competition
C. Trusteeship D. Rural cooperation

48. Fiscal policy is concerned with:
A. public revenue
B. public expenditure and debt
C. bank rate policy
D. Both A and B

49. Devaluation of a currency refers to:
A. decrease in the internal value of money
B. decrease in the external value of money
C. decrease both in the external and internal values of money
D. Government withdrawal of a currency not of a denomination

50. Which was the first country in the world to introduce Goods and Services Tax (GST)?
A. France B. Italy
C. U.K. D. Japan

51. To get the Net National Product we deduct what from the Gross National Product?
A. Direct Taxes B. Imports
C. Interim Payments D. Loss

52. 'Protection' means:
A. restrictions imposed on import trade
B. protection to home industries
C. no free exchange of goods and services between two countries
D. All of these

53. The Reserve Bank of India:
A. provides direct finance to agriculture
B. provides finance to primary cooperative societies
C. provides finance to State cooperative banks
D. does not provide finance to agriculture

54. 'Food for work Programme' was renamed as:
A. RLEGP B. IRDP
C. NREP D. MNP

55. Which of the following is not a method of estimating national income?
A. Income method
B. Value-added method
C. Expenditure method
D. Export-import method

56. As per the 2011 Census, the literacy rate in India has gone up to:
A. 52% B. 56%
C. 62% D. 73%

57. Population explosion in a country means:
A. high birth rate and high death rate
B. high birth rate and low death rate
C. low birth rate and high death rate
D. low birth rate and low death rate

58. The measurement of poverty line is based on the criteria of:
A. their dwelling houses
B. the nature of employment
C. caloric consumption
D. level of education

59. Elasticity of demand is a tendency of demand to:
A. increase or decrease on the change of price
B. increase on the rising of price
C. decrease on the falling of price
D. consistency of demand on rising and falling prices

60. Capital is that wealth:
A. which is used for the production of wealth
B. which is kept in boxes and lockers
C. which is buried in the land
D. which is stored for consumption

61. Function of an entrepreneur is:
A. organisation of labour
B. collection of capital
C. showing efficiency in collection of loans from the banks and the market
D. risk-taking

62. How many banks were nationalised on 19th July, 1969?
A. 14 B. 20
C. 19 D. 23

63. The poverty line has been defined in the:
A. Seventh Five-Year Plan
B. Sixth Five-Year Plan
C. Eighth Five-Year Plan
D. Fifth Five-Year Plan

64. In Centre-State financial relations in India, the Gadgil Formula is used in:
A. division of tax revenue
B. formulating the policy for fresh borrowings
C. writing off states indebtedness to the Centre
D. allocating Central Plan assistance between States

65. Which of the following is a cash crop?
A. Wheat B. Rice
C. Maize D. Sugarcane

66. According to the Reserve Bank of India, the term 'Open Market Operation' means sale and purchase of:
A. gold
B. government securities
C. iron and steel
D. foreign exchange

67. Reserve Bank of India was established on:
A. January 1, 1934
B. April 1, 1934
C. January 1, 1935
D. April 1, 1935

68. What is India's trade policy?
A. Increase in both exports and imports
B. Decrease in both exports and imports
C. Neither increase nor decrease in both imports and exports
D. Export promotion and import substitution

69. The Centre gives grants-in-aid to States:
A. to augment the financial resources of the States
B. to maintain good relations with the States
C. to ensure balanced and quick economic growth throughout the country
D. to ensure social justice in India

70. Temporary tax levied to obtain additional revenue is called:
A. Cess B. Rate
C. Fee D. Surcharge

71. Finance Commission is constituted every:
A. three years B. six years
C. four years D. five years

72. 'Mixed economy' means co-existence of:
A. heavy industries and light industries
B. agrarian economy and industrialised economy
C. the poor and the rich
D. public sector and private sector

73. Which of the following is not a regional Block in the global economic order?
A. ASEAN B. SAFTA
C. WTO D. NAFTA

74. Which one of the following taxes is levied by the State Government only?
A. Entertainment tax B. Wealth tax
C. Income tax D. Corporation tax

75. ECOMARC is a symbol related to:
A. Export goods
B. Goods safe for Environment
C. Import goods
D. Best quality

ANSWERS

1	2	3	4	5	6	7	8	9	10
A	B	C	A	A	B	A	C	D	B
11	**12**	**13**	**14**	**15**	**16**	**17**	**18**	**19**	**20**
C	D	C	D	C	A	B	B	C	C
21	**22**	**23**	**24**	**25**	**26**	**27**	**28**	**29**	**30**
B	C	D	A	A	B	B	B	B	A
31	**32**	**33**	**34**	**35**	**36**	**37**	**38**	**39**	**40**
B	B	C	B	A	D	C	B	B	A
41	**42**	**43**	**44**	**45**	**46**	**47**	**48**	**49**	**50**
A	D	D	B	C	D	C	D	B	A
51	**52**	**53**	**54**	**55**	**56**	**57**	**58**	**59**	**60**
D	D	D	C	D	D	B	C	A	A
61	**62**	**63**	**64**	**65**	**66**	**67**	**68**	**69**	**70**
D	A	D	A	D	B	D	D	A	D
71	**72**	**73**	**74**	**75**					
D	D	C	A	B					

SCIENCE

1. Which of the following is the hardest metal?
A. Gold B. Iron
C. Platinum D. Tungsten

2. Bakeries use yeast in bread-making because it:
A. makes the bread hard
B. makes the bread soft and spongy
C. enhances the food values
D. keeps the bread fresh

3. The chemical name of 'laughing gas' is:
A. nitric oxide B. nitrogen dioxide
C. nitrogen pentoxide D. nitrous oxide

4. Brass is an alloy of:
A. lead and tin
B. zinc and copper
C. antimony, tin and lead
D. zinc, tin and copper

5. The length of its day and tilt of its axis are almost identical to those of the earth. This is true of:
A. Uranus B. Neptune
C. Saturn D. Mars

6. The milky way is classified as:
A. spiral Galaxy B. electrical Galaxy
C. irregular Galaxy D. round Galaxy

7. The energy of the sun is produced by:
A. ionisation B. nuclear fusion
C. nuclear fission D. oxidation

8. Which one of the following is not correctly matched?
A. Decibel—unit of loudness of sound
B. Horse power—unit of power
C. Nautical mile—unit of distance in navigation
D. Celsius—unit of heat

9. The common name of Sodium Bicarbonate is:
A. baking soda B. washing soda
C. caustic soda D. soda lime

10. Which variety of glass is heat resistant?
A. Flint glass B. Hard glass
C. Bottle glass D. Pyrex glass

11. Which of the following is a source of ready energy that one athlete can use after strenuous exercises?
A. Milk B. Glucose
C. Sucrose D. Tomato soup

12. Which part of an eye is transplanted?
A. Retina B. Sciera
C. Iris D. Cornea

13. The filament of an electric bulb is made of:
A. copper B. soft iron
C. cast iron D. tungsten

14. The natural wax and lac are obtained as:
A. petroleum products
B. resins of forest plants
C. by-products of sugar industry
D. insect secretions

15. Which hormone is known as 'fight or flight hormone':
A. insulin B. adrenaline
C. estrogen D. oxytocin

16. "Pacemaker" is associated with:
A. kidney B. brain
C. heart D. lungs

17. The velocity of sound is more in:
A. water B. air
C. steel D. wood

18. Which planet orbits closest to the earth?
A. Mars B. Jupiter
C. Venus D. Mercury

19. It causes clotting of blood:
A. thrombin B. haemoglobin
C. pectin D. All of the above

20. Hardness of water is caused by soluble salts of:
A. sodium and potassium
B. potassium and ammonium

C. sodium and calcium
D. calcium and magnesium

21. The purification of a substance which evaporates without melting can be carried out by:
A. Crystallisation B. Distillation
C. Steam distillation D. Sublimation

22. Which of the following is the largest part of the human brain?
A. Cerebellum B. Midbrain
C. Cerebrum D. Medulla Oblongata

23. The total number of ear bones are:
A. 2 B. 4
C. 6 D. 8

24. An element in the form of gaseous atoms is converted into negative ions is called:
A. bond energy B. electron affinity
C. electronegativity D. ionization energy

25. Match the following:

List-I *(Name of Instruments)*	**List-II** *(The Quantities they Measure)*
(*a*) Anemometer	1. Speed rotation
(*b*) Ammeter	2. High temperature
(*c*) Tachometer	3. Wind speed
(*d*) Pyrometer	4. Electric current
	5. Pressure difference

Codes:

	(*a*)	(*b*)	(*c*)	(*d*)
A.	4	3	1	5
B.	3	4	1	2
C.	3	5	2	1
D.	1	4	5	2

26. Diamond is a form of:
A. carbon B. nitrogen
C. oxygen D. hydrogen

27. The method used to obtain alcohol from molasses is called:
A. Distillation B. Hydrolysis
C. Fermentation D. Oxidation

28. Which of the following is the least inflammable fabric?
A. Cotton B. Nylon
C. Rayon D. Silk

29. Which of the following is required to build new tissues in the human body?
A. Carbohydrates B. Fat
C. Protein D. Water

30. The Vitamin which is required for proper clotting of blood in human body is:
A. vitamin E B. vitamin A
C. vitamin B_{12} D. vitamin K

31. Electron was discovered by:
A. Ernest Rutherford B. Max Planck
C. Joseph Thomson D. Albert Einstein

32. The number of amino acids which are found in nature is:
A. 20 B. 10
C. 15 D. 105

33. Bacteria were first seen, described and sketched by:
A. Jenner B. Linnaeus
C. Pasteur D. Leeuwenhock

34. The outstanding discovery of J.C. Bose, the Indian Scientist, is:
A. crescograph B. boson
C. cosmic rays D. ionograph

35. Density of a metal—when it is heated:
A. remains the same B. increases
C. decreases D. melts

36. Which of the following elements has been known to man from prehistoric times?
A. Sulphur B. Uranium
C. Platinum D. Arsenic

37. Our Solar system is a small unit of:
A. milky way galaxy
B. crab nebula galaxy
C. an independent galaxy
D. None of the above

38. Nights are cooler in the deserts because:
A. the sky is generally clear
B. the sky is generally cloudy
C. sand radiates heat less quickly as compared to earth
D. sand radiates heat more quickly as compared to the earth

39. Storage batteries commonly contain:
A. copper B. mercury
C. lead D. iron

40. Which of the following is a polymer?
A. Vinyl chloride B. Urea
C. Starch D. Styrene

41. What is common between a whale and a monkey?
A. Both have an external ear
B. Both have a long balancing tail
C. Both have body-hair throughout life
D. Both give birth to young ones

42. The hormone which regulates the basal metabolism in our body is secreted from:
A. pituitary B. thyroid
C. adrenal cortex D. pancreas

43. The acid used in car battery is:
A. hydrochloric acid B. boric acid
C. sulphuric acid D. carbonic acid

44. The boiling point of water is unaffected by:
A. the external pressure
B. the temperature of heat source
C. the kind of dissolved substances
D. the amount of dissolved substances

45. What is the velocity of sound in the air?
A. 330 cms per sec. B. 330 metres per sec.
C. 760 metres per sec. D. 1120 cms per sec.

46. The gas used in discharge tubes for optical decoration and advertising is:
A. carbon dioxide B. ammonia
C. sulphur dioxide D. neon

47. The substances present at the centre of the sun are in:
A. solid, liquid and gaseous states
B. liquid state only
C. gaseous state only
D. Both B and C

48. Blank capsules used in dispensing are made of:
A. egg-white B. gum
C. starch D. gelatine

49. Which one of the following is not an explosive?
A. trinitrotoluene
B. trinitroglycerine
C. cyclotrimethylene trinitramine
D. nitrochloroform

50. An ordinary clock loses time in summer; this is because:
A. the length of the pendulum increases and time period decreases
B. the length of the pendulum increases and time period increases
C. the length of the pendulum decreases and time period increases
D. the length of the pendulum decreases and time period decreases

51. When ice cubes floating in a beaker of water melt, the level of water in the beaker:
A. goes up
B. goes down
C. remains same
D. fall or rise depending on the number of ice cubes present in the beaker

52. Which of the following is an element?
A. Silica B. Magnesia
C. Glass D. Graphite

53. A characteristic gas smells near the unclear public urinals. Which is this gas?
A. Ammonia B. Chlorine
C. Sulphur dioxide D. Carbon monoxide

54. Kilowatt is a unit to measure:
A. power B. work
C. energy D. current

55. The apparent weight of a man in a lift will be less than his real weight:
A. when the lift is stationary
B. at no time
C. when the lift is going up with uniform acceleration
D. when the lift is going down with uniform acceleration

56. A natural sweetening agent obtained from a plant (but not sugar) is:
A. saccharin B. santonine
C. cyclomates D. None of these

57. Alkaloids are by-products of the metabolism of:
A. animals B. bacteria
C. plants D. viruses

58. Atom bomb is based on:
A. artificial radioactivity
B. nuclear fission
C. nuclear fusion
D. chemical reaction

59. Which gas in the atmosphere absorbs ultraviolet rays?
A. Methane B. Nitrogen
C. Ozone D. Helium

60. Which of the following is essential for the plants to help them in the formation of chlorophyll?
A. Potassium B. Magnesium
C. Calcium D. Phosphorus

61. The material used for bleaching paper pulp is:
A. lime
B. alum
C. caustic soda
D. sodium hypochlorite

62. Which of the following is used as a preservative of food articles?
A. sodium bicarbonate
B. sodium benzoate
C. sodium carbonate
D. sodium chloride

63. Milk in natural form has a certain amount of sugar. This sugar is called:
A. fructose B. glucose
C. sucrose D. lactose

64. Blood is classified biochemically as a:
A. cell B. liquid
C. tissue D. cartilage

65. Foxglove plant yields a drug which is a stimulant to:
A. kidney B. brain
C. lungs D. heart

66. The function of a catalyst in a reaction is to:
A. decrease the rate of the reaction
B. increase the rate of the reaction
C. increase the pressure of the reactants
D. decrease the pressure of the reactants

67. Which of the following gases is used for refrigeration?
A. Sulphur dioxide B. Chlorine
C. Freon D. Phosphine

68. Which plant stores food in the stem?
A. Ginger B. Carrot
C. Raddish D. Groundnut

69. When a ship enters a sea from a river, its level:
A. remains same
B. falls
C. rises
D. rises or falls depending on the condition and material of the ship

70. The sky is blue in colour because of:
A. combination of various lights producing blue colour
B. the moisture present in the air
C. the accumulation of smoke in the sky
D. the scattering of light by dust particles or air molecules

71. If a body is taken from the earth to the moon:
A. its mass will not be affected
B. its mass will decrease
C. its weight will become more
D. Both its mass and weight will decrease

72. An iron nail floats on mercury but sinks in water because:
A. mercury is a metal and water is not
B. upper layer of mercury is strong
C. mercury is a liquid metal and iron is a solid metal
D. iron is less dense than mercury

73. An electric bulb produces a loud sound when broken, because:
A. the glass is brittle
B. the gas inside the bulb suddenly expands
C. the gas makes the explosion
D. the air rushes into the partial vacuum in the bulb

74. A person climbing a hill bends forward so as to:
A. reduce chances of slipping
B. increase his stability
C. increase his stamina
D. move faster

75. The freezer in a refrigerator is fitted near the top:
A. without any specific and particular purpose
B. because it is convenient
C. so that it can cool the whole interior by setting up convection current
D. to keep it away from the hot compressor

76. The cover of a solar cooker is made of glass:
A. because glass allows heat radiation from the sun into the container but not out of it
B. to enable us to see the food cooking
C. because heat is radiated without absorption by glass
D. as glass is a good conductor of heat and cheap

77. Chlorine is a/an:
A. halogen B. alloy
C. metal D. noble gas

78. Which of the following is not an alloy?
A. brass B. bronze
C. steel D. zinc

79. Which of the following is an insecticide?
A. TNT B. DDT
C. Urea D. Alcohol

80. 'IC chips' for computers are usually made of:
A. chromium B. lead
C. silicon D. gold

81. Which of the following is used as dry ice?
A. Carbon dioxide B. Ammonia
C. Oxygen D. Ice with raw dust

82. The normal unit of measurement of distance of a star is:
A. kilometre B. light year
C. nautical mile D. knot

83. Solution of washing soda in water will be:
A. alkaline B. acidic
C. neutral D. None of these

84. Vitamin C is also called:
A. ascorbic acid B. nucleic acid
C. lactic acid D. hydrochloric acid

85. Pearls are found in:
A. turtles B. snails
C. tortoises D. oysters

86. Coal burns in air because air contains:
A. hydrogen B. oxygen
C. nitrogen D. carbon dioxide

87. A substance which glows and is used in watch dials is:
A. sodium B. sulphur
C. phosphorus D. chlorine

88. Which of the following chemical is used by photographers?
A. Sodium sulphide B. Silver bromide
C. Potassium cyanide D. Ivory powder

89. The process of coating iron with zinc is known as:
A. vulcanisation B. electroplating
C. polishing D. galvanising

90. The best source of iron is:
A. milk B. egg
C. cauliflower D. green vegetables

91. Vitamins are useful to the body for:
A. replacing the energy lost
B. the body growth
C. regulating the functions of the body
D. maintaining the body temperature

92. The metals used for the manufacture of stainless steel are:
A. chromium and carbon
B. aluminium and carbon
C. copper and nickel
D. chromium and zinc

93. In refrigerator, the refrigerant liquid is:
A. carbon dioxide B. nitrogen
C. liquid helium D. ammonia

94. Which of the following is the least inflammable fabric?
A. Cotton B. Nylon
C. Rayon D. Silk

95. Which of the following contains carbon?
A. Chromite B. Bauxite
C. Lignite D. Phosphorite

96. Which of the following blood groups is the universal donor?
A. A B. B
C. AB D. O

97. Which of the following fight infections in the body?
A. WBCs B. RBCs
C. Blood plasma D. Haemoglobin

98. The term 'refraction of light' means:
A. bending of light rays when they enter from one medium to another medium
B. splitting of white light into seven colours when it passes through the prism

C. bending of light round the corners of obstacles and apertures
D. coming back of light from a bright smooth surface

99. In the visible spectrum, the colour having the shortest wavelength is:
A. green B. red
C. violet D. blue

100. What is used to disintegrate bladder stones?
A. Infrared B. Ultraviolet rays
C. X-rays D. Ultrasonics

101. Mica is used in an electric iron, because it is a:
A. bad conductor of heat
B. good conductor of heat
C. good conductor of electricity
D. bad conductor of electricity

102. A line on a map joining places having equal atmospheric pressure is called:
A. Isotherm B. Isobar
C. Isocryme D. Isoheline

103. On addition of salt to water, its:
A. boiling point increases
B. boiling point decreases
C. boiling point is not affected
D. freezing point increases

104. If the velocity of a particle is reduced to half of its initial value, then the kinetic energy of the particle will:
A. get doubled
B. become four times
C. reduce to half of its original value
D. reduce to one-fourth of its original value

105. A lunar eclipse occurs when:
A. Sun, Moon and Earth are not in the same line
B. Earth comes between the Sun and the Moon
C. Moon comes between the Sun and the Earth
D. Sun comes between the Earth and the Moon

106. Red light is used in traffic signals because:
A. it has the longest wavelength
B. it is beautiful
C. it is visible to people even with bad eyesight
D. None of these

107. The oil in the wick of a lamp rises up due to:
A. pressure difference B. low viscosity of oil
C. capillary action D. gravitational force

108. A thick glass tumbler cracks more easily than a thin one when hot water is poured into it. Why?
A. Thick glass is more brittle than thin glass
B. Thick glass is of inferior quality
C. The inner surface of the tumbler expands more than its outer surface
D. The outer surface of the tumbler expands more than its inner surface

109. How many cells are there in the hen's egg?
A. 1 B. 10
C. 100 D. 1000

110. The mirror placed near the driver of a bus is:
A. plane mirror B. convex mirror
C. concave mirror D. cooling mirror

111. Beri-Beri is a disease, caused by the deficiency of:
A. vitamin B B. vitamin C
C. vitamin K D. protein

112. Following are the great discoveries in physics:
1. X-rays
2. Theory of Relativity
3. Super Conductivity
4. Raman Effect

The chronological order in which they were discovered is:
A. 1, 3, 2, 4 B. 1, 2, 3, 4
C. 2, 1, 4, 3 D. 4, 1, 2, 3

113. Heliotropism is:
A. harmful effects of helium
B. helicopter flight control
C. medicine used to cure heart diseases
D. movement of plant organs towards sunlight

114. The isotope of uranium which is very much radioactive is:
A. U^{235} B. U^{238}
C. U^{233} D. All of the above

115. The human skull consists of:
A. 8 bones B. 14 bones
C. 21 bones D. 42 bones

ANSWERS

1	2	3	4	5	6	7	8	9	10
D	B	D	D	D	A	B	D	A	D
11	12	13	14	15	16	17	18	19	20
B	D	D	D	B	C	A	C	A	D
21	22	23	24	25	26	27	28	29	30
D	C	C	B	B	A	C	A	C	D
31	32	33	34	35	36	37	38	39	40
C	A	D	A	C	A	A	D	C	C
41	42	43	44	45	46	47	48	49	50
D	B	C	B	B	D	C	C	D	B
51	52	53	54	55	56	57	58	59	60
C	D	C	A	D	D	C	B	C	B
61	62	63	64	65	66	67	68	69	70
D	B	D	C	D	B	C	A	C	D
71	72	73	74	75	76	77	78	79	80
A	D	D	B	C	A	A	D	D	C
81	82	83	84	85	86	87	88	89	90
A	B	A	A	D	B	C	B	D	D
91	92	93	94	95	96	97	98	99	100
C	A	D	A	C	D	A	A	C	C
101	102	103	104	105	106	107	108	109	110
A	A	A	D	B	A	C	C	A	C
111	112	113	114	115					
A	B	D	A	C					

SCIENCE & TECHNOLOGY

1. Which one of the following techniques can be used to establish the paternity of child?
   A. Protein analysis
   B. Chromosome counting
   C. Quantitative analysis of DNA
   D. DNA finger printing
2. The first Indian artificial satellite was named:
   A. Aryabhatta B. Explorer-I
   C. Sputnik-I D. Luna-3
3. The first computer of India is known as:
   A. Dharam B. Siddharth
   C. Param D. Gati
4. The symptom of anaemia is:
   A. loose or wrinkled skin
   B. difficulty in breathing
   C. yellowish eyes
   D. Oedema of liver
5. In surgery, what is arthroplasty:
   A. open heart surgery
   B. kidney transplant
   C. hip-joint replacement
   D. blood transfussion
6. The intermediate range nuclear-capable missile developed indigenously is named:
   A. Agni B. Prithvi
   C. Nag D. Trishul
7. The computer was invented by:
   A. Faraday B. Maxwell
   C. Babbage D. Bill Gates
8. Which of the following is the name of the first indigenously developed Indian Super Computer?
   A. Param B. Shakti
   C. Dharam D. Gati
9. The instrument which measures the movement of clouds by casting their images through a peephole on to a black mirrored surface is called:
   A. Periscope B. Nephoscope
   C. Stethoscope D. Gyroscope
10. Genetic engineering is possible only due to the role of certain specific enzymes that cut DNA at particular points of the sequence. These enzymes are called:
   A. nucleuses B. restriction enzymes
   C. DNA polymerases D. nitrogenases
11. The intensity of the waves generated by an earthquake and its time of occurrence is recorded by a:
   A. Barometer B. Thermometer
   C. Seismograph D. Galvanometer
12. A genetic disorder characterised by poor blood circulation and abnormal haemoglobin molecules is better known as:
   A. Sickel-cell anaemia
   B. Haemophilia
   C. Phenyl ketonuria
   D. Huntington's chorea
13. The process of preparation of soap is known as:
   A. Saponification B. Calcification
   C. Hydroxylation D. Methylation
14. Who amongst the following initiated the age of genetic engineering in 1973 by inserting an amphibian ribosomal RNA gene into a bacterial plasmid?
   A. Cohen and Boyer B. J.C. Sanford
   C. Watson and Crick D. Roger Beachy
15. Superconductivity results when matter is:
   A. heated to very high temperature
   B. compressed to very high pressure
   C. subjected to very low pressure
   D. cooled to very low temperature
16. All of the following diseases are caused by viruses except:
   A. jaundice B. influenza
   C. mumps D. typhoid
17. Penicillin is given a patient in order to:
   A. cure hereditary disease
   B. cure all diseases
   C. prevent any rise in body temperature
   D. prevent the growth of several types of diseases caused by bacteria

18. BCG is:
A. curative medicine for tuberculosis
B. a preventive medicine for tuberculosis
C. a disinfectant
D. an antiseptic

19. What is "Lakshya"?
A. Pilotless target aircraft
B. Missile
C. Radar
D. Satellite Launch Vehicle

20. What is a 'Robot'?
A. a type of rocket
B. a bomb
C. a machine that resembles a person and does mechanical routine tasks on command
D. an animal found in the jungles of Africa

21. MAB stands for:
A. Man and Biosphere Programme
B. Man and Biology Programme
C. Mammals and Biosphere Programme
D. None of the above

22. Element used for atomic power is:
A. calcium B. sodium
C. beryllium D. uranium

23. A pure semiconductor:
A. has low resistance
B. is called an intrinsic semi-conductor
C. Both of the above
D. None of the above

24. AIDS disease is caused by:
A. virus B. sexual contact
C. bacteria D. protozoa

25. The first indigenously built missile boat is named as:
A. INS Vibhuti B. INS Vikrant
C. INS Shilpi D. INS Mana

26. Which of the following is an example of Bio-technology?
A. Using electron microscope
B. Using technology to stabilise the life processes
C. Using modern techniques to understand the evolution of life
D. Using micro-organisms to synthesis insulin

27. Autopsy means:
A. curing a disease through self-medication
B. postmortem examination of a human body
C. curing a disease through auto-suggestion
D. becoming diseased through abuse of drugs

28. India's Chandrayaan-3 soft landed on 23 August, 2023 at which area of the Moon?
A. South Pole
B. Centre of the Moon
C. North Pole
D. East of the Moon surface

29. For appropriate technology what factors are of immediate concern?
I. skilled manpower II. capital
III. infrastructure IV. latest innovation
A. I and II B. III and IV
C. I and IV D. II and IV

30. Eco mark is given to Indian products that are:
A. pure and unadulterated
B. rich in protein
C. environment friendly
D. economically viable

31. 'Dolly' is the first clone mammal in the world of:
A. buffalo B. goat
C. sheep D. monkey

32. India's biggest nuclear research reactor is known as:
A. Apsara B. Dhruva
C. Cirus D. Purnima

33. We use the term 'mach number' in connection with:
A. sound B. submarines
C. aircraft D. spacecraft

34. Which of the following units measures the memory of the computer?
A. Volts B. Amperes
C. Ohms D. Bits

35. Maximum 'gobar gas' is produced during:
A. summer B. winter
C. rainy season D. All seasons

36. The first Indian satellite, Aryabhatta, was launched into space from a cosmodrome of:
A. France B. USA
C. USSR D. West Germany

37. The Vikram Sarabhai Space Centre is at:
A. Ahmedabad
B. Bengaluru
C. Sriharikota
D. Thiruvananthapuram

38. The science dealing with the study of inheritance and variation is called:
A. Genetics B. Evolution
C. Morphology D. Cytology

39. Acetamide is
A. Neutral B. Basic
C. Acidic D. Amphotenic

40. Which is the first artificial satellite to be put into orbit on October 4, 1957?
A. Sputnik-1 B. Apollo-7
C. Explorer-1 D. Solar Max

41. CNG (Compressed Natural Gas) is used for:
A. protecting pollution
B. saving diesel
C. avoiding the use of petrol
D. All of the above

42. Bronchitis is a disease of:
A. blood B. liver
C. intestine D. respiratory tract

43. The molecules responsible for storing the genetic code are:
A. DNA B. RNA
C. protein D. chromosome

44. Test tube baby means:
A. ovum fertilised and developed in test tube
B. ovum fertilised in test tube and developed in test tubes
C. ovum fertilised in test tubes and developed in uterus
D. ovum developed without fertilisation in test tubes

45. What is the basic characteristic of antigens:
A. They are capable of stimulating the formation of haemoglobin in the blood
B. They destroy haemoglobin
C. They are capable of defending themselves against attack by antibodies
D. They are capable of stimulating the formation of antibodies

46. What was the disease that led to the discovery of first anti viral vaccine?
A. Cancer B. Tetanus
C. Polio D. Small pox

47. Which is the most fast spreading disease?
A. Malaria B. Plague
C. Poliomyelitis D. Leprosy

48. The Central Food Technological Research Institute is located at:
A. Kolkata B. Kanpur
C. Mysore D. Ranchi

49. The International Rice Research Institute is located in:
A. Philippines B. Thailand
C. Indonesia D. Malaysia

50. "AIDS" affects:
A. blood cells of human body
B. immune system of human body
C. growth of human body
D. All of the above

51. Which of the following fertilisers is used after sowing the seeds:
A. nitrate B. potash
C. green manure D. phosphorus

52. Swelling of a strained foot is reduced by soaking in hot water containing a large amount of common salt. This is because of phenomenon called:
A. Osmosis B. Plasmolysis
C. Electrolysis D. None of these

53. Match List-I with List-II and select the correct answer using the codes given below the lists:

List-I	List-II
(*a*) Trishul	1. Anti-tank missile
(*b*) Prithvi	2. Intermediate range ballistic system
(*c*) Agni	3. Short range surface to air missile
(*d*) Nag	4. Surface to surface missile

Codes:

	(*a*)	(*b*)	(*c*)	(*d*)
A.	1	2	3	4
B.	4	3	2	1
C.	3	4	2	1
D.	2	1	4	3

54. In paints, the pigment is responsible for:
A. durability B. colour
C. smoothness D. glossy face

55. The working principle of a washing machine is:
A. centrifugation B. dialysis
C. reverse osmosis D. diffusion

56. Who invented 'radar':
A. J.H. Van Tassell
B. Wilhelm K. Roentgen
C. P.T. Farnsworth
D. A.H. Taylor and Zeo C. Young

57. Which one of the following is a useful functional association between fungi and the roots of higher plants?
A. Biofertiliser B. Coralloid root
C. Lichen D. Mycorrhiza

58. Low temperatures (cryogenics) find application in:
A. space travel, surgery and magnetic levitation
B. surgery, magnetic levitation and telemetry
C. space travel, surgery and telemetry
D. space travel, magnetic levitation and telemetry

59. Pure silicon is used as a:
A. conductor B. insulator
C. non-conductor D. semiconductor

60. The most common type of fingerprint encountered are:
A. whorls B. loops
C. arches D. composites

61. Indian farmers are unhappy over the introduction of 'Terminator Seed Technology' because the seeds produced by this technology are expected to:
A. show poor germination
B. form low-yielding plants despite the high quality
C. give rise to sexually sterile plants
D. give rise to plants incapable of forming viable seeds

62. Which one of the following genetic diseases is sex linked?
A. Royal haemophilia B. Tay Sachs disease
C. Cystic fibrosis D. Hypertension

63. Guided missiles are:
A. missiles that guide the soldiers in the army
B. unmanned self-propelled space or air vehicles carrying explosive war head
C. missiles that are launched by the gliders
D. ordinary war planes with a very sharp striking power and deep thrust

64. Prithvi is:
A. indigenously developed intermediate range ballistic missile
B. indigenously developed nuclear bomb
C. indigenously developed nuclear reactor
D. indigenously developed surface to surface missile

65. National Institute of Immunology and National Institute of Science, Technology and Development Studies are located in:
A. Hyderabad B. Bangalore
C. Mumbai D. New Delhi

ANSWERS

1	2	3	4	5	6	7	8	9	10
C	A	B	D	C	A	C	A	B	B
11	**12**	**13**	**14**	**15**	**16**	**17**	**18**	**19**	**20**
C	A	C	A	D	D	D	B	A	C
21	**22**	**23**	**24**	**25**	**26**	**27**	**28**	**29**	**30**
A	D	B	A	A	B	B	A	A	C
31	**32**	**33**	**34**	**35**	**36**	**37**	**38**	**39**	**40**
C	B	C	D	C	C	D	A	D	A
41	**42**	**43**	**44**	**45**	**46**	**47**	**48**	**49**	**50**
D	D	A	C	D	D	B	C	A	B
51	**52**	**53**	**54**	**55**	**56**	**57**	**58**	**59**	**60**
A	A	C	B	A	D	A	A	B	B
61	**62**	**63**	**64**	**65**					
D	A	B	D	D					

AWARDS AND HONOURS

1. Who among the following is the first person to receive the Bharat Ratna award?
A. C. Rajagopalachari B. S. Radhakrishnan
C. C.V. Raman D. M. Visweswaraiya

2. Who among the following is the first person who was given the Bharat Ratna award posthumaously?
A. K. Kamraj B. Lal Bahadur Shastri
C. B.R. Ambedkar D. Vallabhbhai Patel

3. Which of the following is the highest order of gallantry award in India?
A. Mahavir Chakra B. Vir Chakra
C. Paramveer Chakra D. Ashok Chakra

4. The Arjuna awards are given to outstanding persons in the field of:
A. science B. sports
C. social services D. literature

5. The Bhartiya Jnanpith award is given to:
A. sportspersons B. scientists
C. coaches D. creative writers

6. Dada Saheb Phalke award is given in the field of:
A. social services B. cinema
C. creative writing D. politics

7. Who among the following is the first to receive 'Dada Saheb Phalke award'?
A. Sivaji Ganesan B. Dr. Raj Kumar
C. Devika Rani D. Majrooh Sultanpuri

8. Which of the following awards is given to the eminent coaches who successfully trained international sportspersons and teams:
A. Dronacharya Award
B. K.K. Birla Foundation Sports Award
C. Jamnalal Bajaj Award
D. Arjuna Award

9. Lata Mangeshkar award is given by Madhya Pradesh Government in the field of:
A. music B. cinema
C. drama D. dance

10. The Kalinga Prize is given for the popularisation of Science and Research, by which of the following:
A. UNICEF B. UNESCO
C. Odisha Govt. D. Indian Govt.

11. Indira Gandhi International award is given in the field of:
A. peace B. disarmament
C. development D. All of the above

12. Which of the following prizes is considered to be the most prestigious in the world?
A. Magsaysay award B. Nobel prize
C. Japan prize D. Pulitzer award

13. Dhanvantari prize is given in which of the following fields:
A. medicine
B. agriculture
C. journalism
D. international understanding

14. The Nobel prize is not given in which of the following fields:
A. peace B. physics
C. economics D. agriculture

15. Match the following:

List-I (Nobel Prize Recipients)	*List-II (Fields in which given)*
(*a*) C.V. Raman	1. Economics
(*b*) Hargobind Khorana	2. Peace
(*c*) Mother Teresa	3. Medicine
(*d*) Amartya Sen	4. Literature
(*e*) Rabindra Nath Tagore	5. Physics

Codes:

	(*a*)	(*b*)	(*c*)	(*d*)	(*e*)
A.	5	3	2	1	4
B.	5	2	3	1	4
C.	3	4	2	1	5
D.	3	4	2	5	1

16. How many Oscar awards did the film Slumdog Millionaire win?

A. 7 B. 8
C. 9 D. 11

17. Which of the following is not a Civilian award?
A. Padma Vibhushan
B. Bharat Ratna
C. Padma Bhushan
D. Param Vishist Seva Medal

18. Which of the following is not a Gallantry award?
A. Paramveer Chakra B. Mahavir Chakra
C. Padma Shri D. Ashoka Chakra

19. Vikram Sarabhai Puraskar is given for:
A. outstanding contribution in science and technology
B. the popularisation of science and research
C. outstanding contribution in space and research
D. significant contribution in medicine

20. Which of the following is the highest order of Scientific award in India?
A. Shanti Swaroop Bhatnagar Puraskar
B. Homi Jahangir Bhabha Puraskar
C. Vikram Sarabhai Puraskar
D. G.D. Birla Science Puraskar

21. Which of the following awards is not conferred by Indian Government?
A. Ambedkar International award
B. Mahatma Gandhi Peace award
C. Padma Bhushan
D. Mahatma Gandhi award

22. C.K. Naidu award is given to a person for:
A. excellence in athletics
B. outstanding performance in games
C. outstanding contribution in cricket
D. best performance in hockey

23. Who among the following cinestars is awarded Pakistan's highest civil award in recognition of his services in improving Indo-Pak relations?
A. Manoj Kumar B. Dilip Kumar
C. Raj Kumar D. Ashok Kumar

24. The Saraswati Samman the highest and most prestigious literary award of the country is given by:
A. Bharatiya Jnanpith
B. K.K. Birla Foundation
C. Sahitya Akademi
D. Human Resources Ministry, Indian Government

25. The Nobel prize for economics was awarded for the first time in 1969 by:
A. Swedish Central Bank
B. World Bank
C. International Monetary Fund
D. Nobel Foundation Committee

26. The UNESCO peace award is regarded as little Nobel prize conferred by:
A. UNESCO
B. Nobel Foundation Committee, Sweden
C. US Government
D. None of these

27. Govind Ballabh Pant award is given to:
A. the honestman of the year
B. the best parliamentarian
C. the best sportsman of the year
D. None of these

28. Which of the following samman is not conferred by Madhya Pradesh Government?
A. Tansen Samman B. Kalidas Samman
C. Tulsi Samman D. Vyas Samman

29. What name is given to the highest award for self-sacrifice or brave, daring and prominent act of valour?
A. Param Vishist Seva Medal
B. Mahavir Chakra
C. Paramveer Chakra
D. Vir Chakra

30. 'Global 500' awards are given for achievements in:
A. population control
B. campaign against terrorism
C. protection of environment
D. campaign against drugs

31. The first Indian to win Nobel prize was:
A. C.V. Raman
B. Rabindra Nath Tagore
C. Hargobind Khorana
D. Amartya Sen

32. In which one of the following scientific fields Borlaug award is given?
A. medicine B. space research
C. agriculture D. atomic physics

33. Highest sports award of our country is:
A. Arjuna Award
B. Dronacharya Award
C. Major Dhyan Chand Khel Ratna Award
D. Indira Gandhi Award

34. The highest civilian award of India, Bharat Ratna has been awarded to only two foreigners so far. One of them is Khan Abdul Ghaffar Khan, the other is:
A. Mikhail Gorbachev B. George Bush
C. Nelson Mandela D. Helmut Kohl

35. Match the following:

I. Arjuna award	(*a*) Persons of cine world
II. Oscar award	(*b*) Journalists
III. Dronacharya award	(*c*) Sports persons
IV. Pulitzer prize	(*d*) Coaches

Codes:
A. I-(*a*), II-(*b*), III-(*d*), IV-(*c*)
B. I-(*c*), II-(*a*), III-(*d*), IV-(*b*)
C. I-(*b*), II-(*a*), III-(*c*), IV-(*d*)
D. I-(*c*), II-(*d*), III-(*a*), IV-(*b*)

36. Match List-I with List-II and select the correct answer by using the codes given below the lists:

List-I ***(Field in which given)***	**List-II** ***(Name of Award)***
(*a*) Science	1. Ghalib award
(*b*) Films	2. Arjuna award
(*c*) Poetry and prose	3. Phalke award
(*d*) Sports	4. Shanti Swarup Bhatnagar Memorial award

Codes:

	(*a*)	(*b*)	(*c*)	(*d*)
A.	4	3	2	1
B.	3	4	1	2
C.	3	4	2	1
D.	4	3	1	2

37. Which India-born scientist was awarded the Nobel prize in Astrophysics?
A. Prof. Chandrasekhar
B. Sir C.V. Raman
C. Satyendra Nath Bose
D. Vikram Sarabhai

38. Which of the following awards is not conferred by K.K. Birla Foundation?
A. Bihari Award
B. Shankar Award
C. Bharat Bharti Samman
D. Vyas Samman

39. The Vachaspati award is given for the outstanding contribution in the field of:
A. Hindi literature
B. Sanskrit literature
C. Bengali literature
D. Malayalam literature

40. The Ramon Magsaysay award, considered to be the Asia's Nobel prize is given by which of the following country:
A. India
B. Indonesia
C. Mauritius
D. Philippines

ANSWERS

1	2	3	4	5	6	7	8	9	10
A	B	C	B	D	B	C	A	A	B
11	**12**	**13**	**14**	**15**	**16**	**17**	**18**	**19**	**20**
D	B	A	D	A	B	D	C	C	A
21	**22**	**23**	**24**	**25**	**26**	**27**	**28**	**29**	**30**
D	C	B	C	A	A	B	D	C	C
31	**32**	**33**	**34**	**35**	**36**	**37**	**38**	**39**	**40**
B	C	C	C	B	D	A	C	B	D

GAMES AND SPORTS

1. Which is the national game of America?
A. Football B. Cricket
C. Baseball D. Kabaddi

2. Who among the following sportsmen is called the 'magician of Hockey'?
A. Dhyanchand
B. Dhanraj Pillai
C. Pargat Singh
D. Baljit Singh Dhillon

3. Which one of the following teams won the First One-Day Cricket World Cup held in 1975?
A. England B. Australia
C. Pakistan D. West Indies

4. In India the game of polo was introduced by the:
A. Greeks B. Englishmen
C. Turks D. Mughals

5. The term 'Tricks' is associated with which of the following games?
A. Polo B. Billiards
C. Bridge D. Croquet

6. Novak Djokovic is associated with which of the following sport?
A. Badminton B. Swimming
C. Weightlifting D. Tennis

7. The name of Abhinav Bindra is associated with this sport?
A. Shooting B. Cricket
C. Football D. Basketball

8. 'Deodhar Trophy' is associated with which of the following games?
A. Hockey B. Cricket
C. Football D. Basketbal!

9. 'Free-throw' is given in which of the following sports?
A. Volleyball B. Basketball
C. Badminton D. Cricket

10. Match the following:

List-I *(Countries)*	**List-II** *(Sports)*
1. Australia	(*a*) Bull fighting
2. USA	(*b*) Ice hockey
3. Spain	(*c*) Cricket
4. Pakistan	(*d*) Baseball
	(*e*) Hockey

Codes:
A. 1-(*c*), 2-(*d*), 3-(*b*), 4-(*a*)
B. 1-(*d*), 2-(*b*), 3-(*c*), 4-(*e*)
C. 1-(*c*), 2-(*d*), 3-(*a*), 4-(*e*)
D. 1-(*c*), 2-(*b*), 3-(*a*), 4-(*e*)

11. How many players participate in a polo team?
A. 7 B. 8
C. 11 D. 4

12. In a cricket game when the umpire raises his right hand's index finger high:
A. batsman is not out
B. batsman is out
C. batsman is retired
D. batsman scores a six

13. What is the maximum duration of playing a football match?
A. 60 minutes B. 90 minutes
C. 80 minutes D. 70 minutes

14. The longest swimming course in the world is:
A. Dardenelles strait B. Palk strait
C. English channel D. Magellan strait

15. 'Subroto Cup' is associated with which of the following games?
A. Hockey B. Football
C. Basketball D. Cricket

16. Which of the following is the distance of running in a Marathon race?
A. 26 miles
B. 26 miles, 385 yards
C. 26 miles, 225 yards
D. 26 miles, 365 yards

17. Which is the correct weight of the cricket ball?
A. 4¼ oz B. 5¾ oz
C. 4 oz D. 6 oz

18. The term 'butterfly stroke' is associated with which of the following games?
A. Swimming B. Cricket
C. Gliding D. Football

19. The term 'put' is associated with the sport:
A. Billiards B. Golf
C. Cricket D. Baseball

20. The Olympic Symbol (Summer Games) comprises of five rings or circles linked together to represent:
A. the sporting friendship of all
B. the five continents
C. Both A and B
D. None of these

21. Select a pair which is not properly matched:
A. Diego Maradona—Hockey
B. Gary Kasparov—Chess
C. Pete Sampras—Tennis
D. Ronaldo—Football

22. Santosh Trophy is associated with this sport:
A. Hockey B. Cricket
C. Badminton D. Football

23. Who was the first Indian woman to swim across the English channel?
A. Rita Faria
B. Shanta Rangaswami
C. Arati Saha
D. P.T. Usha

24. The 'Hall of Fame' tournament is associated with which of the following games?
A. Cricket B. Football
C. Hockey D. Tennis

25. The term 'Silly Point' is associated with the sport:
A. Billiards B. Bridge
C. Chess D. Cricket

26. The term 'Bunker' is associated with:
A. Polo B. Golf
C. Basketball D. Table Tennis

27. 'Arthur Walker Trophy' is associated with the sport:
A. Basketball B. Billiards
C. Boat rowing D. Bridge

28. Geet Sethi is associated with the sports:
A. Athletics B. Billiards
C. Shooting D. Weightlifting

29. Saina Nehwal is associated with the sport:
A. Shooting B. Badminton
C. Boxing D. Weightlifting

30. How many players participate in a volleyball team?
A. 6 B. 7
C. 8 D. 9

31. The Sports Day is observed on:
A. August 27 B. August 29
C. October 25 D. October 27

32. The first Asian Games were held in 1951 at:
A. Tokyo, Japan B. Jakarta, Indonesia
C. Bangkok, Thailand D. New Delhi, India

33. India won the world cup cricket in 1983 by defeating which of the teams?
A. England B. Australia
C. West Indies D. None of these

34. 'Checkmate' is associated with which of the following sports?
A. Boxing B. Bridge
C. Chess D. Golf

35. Eden Garden is a famous place associated with which of the following games?
A. Football B. Hockey
C. Lawn Tennis D. Cricket

36. The first Modern Olympic Games were held in 1896 in which of the following places?
A. Athens B. Paris
C. Los Angeles D. Sarajevo

37. The Winter Olympic Games came into being in 1924 was held at:
A. Chamonix (France)
B. St. Moritz (Switzerland)
C. Lake Placid (New York)
D. Oslo (Norway)

38. In the game of Baseball, distance between each base in a Diamond shaped ground is:
A. 56 ft B. 72 ft
C. 80 ft D. 90 ft

39. The Davis Cup is associated with which of the following games?
A. Lawn Tennis B. Tennis
C. Cricket D. Soccer

40. The Olympic Games are held every:
A. two years B. four years
C. five years D. six years

41. In which of the following years, the Olympic Games were not held:
A. 1916 B. 1940
C. 1944 D. All of these

42. Baron Pierre de Coubertin, father of the modern Olympic Games, belongs to:
A. Greece B. USA
C. France D. Italy

43. What is the national sport of England?
A. Karate B. Sumo
C. Cricket D. Mikado

44. Which of the following cups is not associated with Hockey?
A. Agha Khan Cup
B. Azlan Shah Cup
C. Singer Cup
D. Indira Gandhi Gold Cup

45. Match the following:

List-I ***(Game)***	***List-II*** ***(Term)***
1. Badminton	(*a*) Dribbling
2. Basketball	(*b*) Smash
3. Baseball	(*c*) Cue
4. Billiards	(*d*) Strike

Codes:
A. 1-(*b*), 2-(*a*), 3-(*d*), 4-(*c*)
B. 1-(*a*), 2-(*b*), 3-(*c*), 4-(*d*)
C. 1-(*d*), 2-(*b*), 3-(*a*), 4-(*c*)
D. 1-(*b*), 2-(*a*), 3-(*c*), 4-(*d*)

46. Who among the following has become the first women in the world to swim across seven seas?
A. Shikha Tandon B. Bula Chowdhury
C. Amanda Beard D. Arati Saha

47. In which of the following years were women athetes admitted to Olympic Games?
A. 1900 B. 1904
C. 1908 D. 1912

48. The term 'Gambit' is associated with the game of:
A. Golf B. Boating
C. Bridge D. Chess

49. 'Thomas Cup Trophy' is associated with which of the following sports?
A. World Chess B. World Badminton
C. World Cricket D. World Hockey

50. Match the following:

List-I ***(Sportsmen)***	**List-II** ***(Sports)***
I. Pele	(*a*) Ocean swimming
II. Sachin Tendulkar	(*b*) Athletics
III. Anju B. George	(*c*) Cricket
IV. Bula Chowdhury	(*d*) Football

Codes:
A. I-(*a*), II-(*b*), III-(*c*), IV-(*d*)
B. I-(*d*), II-(*c*), III-(*b*), IV-(*a*)
C. I-(*d*), II-(*c*), III-(*a*), IV-(*b*)
D. I-(*c*), II-(*d*), III-(*b*), IV-(*a*)

ANSWERS

1	2	3	4	5	6	7	8	9	10
C	A	D	C	C	D	A	B	B	C
11	**12**	**13**	**14**	**15**	**16**	**17**	**18**	**19**	**20**
D	B	B	C	B	B	B	A	B	C
21	**22**	**23**	**24**	**25**	**26**	**27**	**28**	**29**	**30**
A	D	C	D	D	A	B	B	B	A
31	**32**	**33**	**34**	**35**	**36**	**37**	**38**	**39**	**40**
B	D	C	C	D	A	A	D	A	B
41	**42**	**43**	**44**	**45**	**46**	**47**	**48**	**49**	**50**
D	C	C	C	A	B	A	D	B	B

MISCELLANEOUS

1. Who is popularly known as the 'Nightingale of India'?
   A. Sarojini Naidu B. M.S. Subbulakshmi
   C. Mahadevi Verma D. Lata Mangeshkar
2. The first Speaker of the Lok Sabha was:
   A. Rabi Ray
   B. M. Ananthasayanam Ayangar
   C. Hukam Singh
   D. G.V. Mavalankar
3. The book *Prison Diary* was written by:
   A. Mahatma Gandhi B. V.D. Savarkar
   C. Jaya Prakash NarainD. Morarji Desai
4. The new name given to Calcutta city is:
   A. Kalighat B. Kalicutta
   C. Kolkatta D. Kolkata
5. ISI mark is not given to which of the following products?
   A. Electrical goods B. Hosiery goods
   C. Biscuits D. Cloth
6. Which day will be celebrated as 'National Space Day' in India?
   A. May 13 B. June 30
   C. August 23 D. September 30
7. The origin of the phrase "United Nations" is associated with which one of the following personalities?
   A. Jawaharlal Nehru B. Franklin Roosevelt
   C. Charles de Gaulle D. Woodrow Wilson
8. The Economic and Social Commission for Asia and Pacific (ESCAP) is located at:
   A. Kuala Lumpur B. Bangkok
   C. Manila D. Singapore
9. Which of the following is the headquarters of the World Bank?
   A. The Hague B. Washington
   C. Paris D. London
10. Badrinath is in which state?
    A. Gujarat B. Odisha
    C. Himachal Pradesh D. Uttarakhand
11. What is the currency of South Africa?
    A. Guilder B. Pound
    C. Shekel D. Rand
12. Who was the first woman to become the Prime Minister of a country in the world?
    A. Benazir Bhutto
    B. Indira Gandhi
    C. Margaret Thatcher
    D. Sirimavo Bandarnaika
13. Which animal is the symbol of the World Wildlife Fund?
    A. Tiger B. Giant Panda
    C. Hornbill D. White Bear
14. Who was the first President of All India Trade Union Congress?
    A. Dewan Chaman Lal B. Lala Lajpat Rai
    C. N.G. Ranga D. Swami Sahajanand
15. Which one of the following is an important tribe of the Dhauladhar Range?
    A. Abor B. Gaddi
    C. Lepcha D. Tharu
16. 'Pravada' is a famous newspaper of which country?
    A. America B. Russia
    C. Britain D. China
17. Which one of the following cities does not have the special economic zone?
    A. Chennai B. Kandla
    C. Kochi D. Surat
18. Which one of the following programmes is not included in the Swarna Jayanti Gram Swarojgar Yojna?
    A. IRDP B. TRYSEM
    C. DWCRA D. JRY
19. Who took the charge of Prime Ministership immediately after the death of Jawaharlal Nehru?
    A. Indira Gandhi B. Morarji Desai
    C. Gulzarilal Nanda D. Lal Bahadur Shastri

20. Which one among the following is least like the others?
A. Kathakali B. Bhangra
C. Kuchipudi D. Bharat Natyam

21. Which one of the following is not correctly matched?
A. Fiji—Suva
B. Finland—Oslo
C. Guyana—George Town
D. Lebanon—Beirut

22. The author of the book "Animal Farm" is:
A. Leo Tolstoy B. George Orwell
C. John Dryden D. S.M. Ali

23. Which one of the following is referred to as the 'Golden Hand Shake'?
A. Honouring VIP's
B. Voluntary Retirement Scheme
C. Wishing Bon voyage
D. Receiving Distinguished Guests

24. "India House" is located in:
A. New Delhi B. Kolkata
C. London D. NewYork

25. The largest flightless bird which can run at a great speed:
A. Penguin B. Kiwi
C. Ostrich D. Emu

26. International Finance Corporation is the ancillary institution of the:
A. UNO B. IDO
C. IMF D. IBRD

27. The Pradhan Mantri Gram Sadak Yojna is:
A. to augment road connectivity and provide foodgrains to the poorest of the poor at cheaper rates.
B. to facilitate patrolling of the area to prevent misuse of electricity by unauthorised persons
C. to help the police to reach the place of crime more swiftly to control crime-spurt
D. to develop community life in villages which are not well connected

28. Losoong is a festival which is celebrated in:
A. Tibet B. Arunachal Pradesh
C. Sikkim D. Kerala

29. Which of the following countries is now known as Myammar?
A. Kampuchea B. Northern Rhodesia
C. Burma D. Laos

30. Who said 'Man is a political animal'?
A. Socrates B. Plato
C. Aristotle D. Dante

31. "Persons may change but rules should not change" is the principle of:
A. Absolute Monarchy
B. Constitutional Government
C. Unwritten Constitution
D. Republic

32. 'Kuchipudi' is a dance style which originated from:
A. Kerala B. Andhra Pradesh
C. Manipur D. Tamil Nadu

33. Currency of Japan is called:
A. Yen B. Dollar
C. Pound D. Lira

34. The first Secretary-General of the United Nations was:
A. Dag Hammarskjoeld
B. U. Thant
C. Kurt Waldheim
D. Trygve Lie

35. Padma Subramaniam is an exponent of classical dance:
A. Kuchipudi B. Odissi
C. Bharatnatyam D. Manipuri

36. Shiv-Hari, the popular musical duo, plays which of the following instruments?
A. Tabla and Guitar B. Santoor and Flute
C. Piano and Drums D. None of these

37. Which of the following is called the 'Mother of Parliaments'?
A. The German Parliament
B. The American Parliament
C. The French Parliament
D. The British Parliament

38. Which of the following places is not in Pak-occupied Kashmir?
A. Gilgit B. Skardu
C. Muzaffarabad D. Kargil

39. Who amongst the following was not a Vice-President before becoming President of India?
A. V.V. Giri B. R. Venkataraman
C. S. Radhakrishnan D. Giani Zail Singh

40. Which one of the following projections is used chiefly in navigation?
A. Mercator's B. Mollweid's
C. Bonne's D. Lambert'

41. Which of the following years is known as the "Year of great divide" with regard to population growth in India?
A. 1911 B. 1921
C. 1947 D. 1951

42. Which one of the following is the World Environment Day?
A. 22nd April B. 1st May
C. 31st May D. 5th June

43. The cost of next-best alternative is known as:
A. Real Cost B. Social Cost
C. Opportunity Cost D. Over-head Cost

44. "Kamasutra" is written by:
A. Kalamandalam Nair
B. Ananda Coomaraswamy
C. Birju Maharaj
D. S.H. Vatsyayan

45. December 10, is regarded as a red-letter-day for the whole world because it is the:
A. International Labour Day
B. Human Rights Day
C. United Nations Day
D. Science Day

46. Given below is a list of traditional dresses of women along with States. Which one of them is not correctly matched?
A. Boku–Sikkim
B. Mekhala–Assam
C. Mundu–Chhattisgarh
D. Pheran–Kashmir

47. The book "The Proudest Day" deals with the story of:
A. Integration of Indian States
B. India's independence
C. Pokhran nuclear explosion
D. Formation of the NDA Government at the Centre

48. March 8th, is observed as:
A. World Environment Day
B. Heritage Day
C. International Women's Day
D. Youth Day

49. The 'Kumbha Mela' comes round once in:
A. 7 years B. 5 years
C. 10 years D. 12 years

50. Who among the following has written the book entitled 'Autobiography of an Unknown Indian'?
A. Kuldip Nayyar
B. V.S. Naipaul
C. Nirad C. Choudhuri
D. N.A. Palkhivala

51. The abbrivation IGNOU stands for:
A. Indian Government's Nuclear Option Ultimatum
B. Indira Gandhi National Open University
C. Inter-Governmental and Non-Official Understandings
D. Informal Group on National Occupational Utilities

52. The author of the book 'The Gin Drinkers' is:
A. Arundhati Roy B. Anita Desai
C. Sagarika Ghose D. Shobha De

53. 1st December, of every year is observed to mark:
A. World Habitat Day
B. Universal Children's Day
C. World AIDS Day
D. Anniversary of United Nations

54. The famous Salar Jung Museum is situated in:
A. Assam
B. Telangana
C. Jammu and Kashmir
D. Uttar Pradesh

55. The International Nautical Mile is equal to:
A. 1852 metres B. 1825 metres
C. 2000 metres D. 1582 metres

56. Consumer Day is celebrated every year on:
A. April 1 B. October 23
C. March 15 D. December 5

57. Subhas Mukhopadhyay is associated with which one of the following fields?
A. Politics B. Sports
C. Literature D. Social service

58. The Asian Development Bank has its headquarters in:
A. Kathmandu B. Manila
C. Colombo D. Tokyo

59. Who among the following Indians has presided over the UNESCO?
A. Dr. Zakir Hussain
B. Dr. Ramaswami Mudaliar
C. Dr. S. Radhakrishnan
D. Maulana Abul Kalam Azad

60. World Health Day is observed on:
A. April 7 B. April 9
C. April 18 D. April 20

61. Which of the following countries is now known as Cambodia?
A. Northern Rhodesia B. Laos
C. Kampuchea D. Comoros

62. Who was the first Indian to become the member of British Parliament?
A. W.C. Bannerjee B. M. Malabari
C. D.N. Wacha D. Dadabhai Naoroji

63. Who is the writer of the book 'Interpreter of Maladies'?
A. Jhumpa Lahiri B. Arundhati Roy
C. Vikram Seth D. Geeta Mehta

64. Which of the following is a morning 'Raag'?
A. Sohini B. Bhairavi
C. Kalabati D. Sarang

65. Who is the writer of the poetry 'Deep Shikha'?
A. Ramdhari Singh Dinkar
B. Shankar Dayal Sharma
C. Subhadara Kumari Chauhan
D. None of these

66. The compilation of 'Meri Ekawan Kavitayen' (My 51 Poems) is written by:
A. Atal Behari Vajpayee
B. Harivanshrai Bachchan
C. Dharam Vir Bharati
D. Shivmangal Singh 'Suman'

67. Who among the following is the writer of 'Anand Math'?
A. Harindra Nath Chattopadhyay
B. Rabindranath Tagore
C. Mulk Raj Anand
D. Bankim Chandra Chatterjee

68. In which Shakespearean drama is *Desdemona* a character?
A. Hamlet B. Othello
C. Merchant of Venice D. As You Like It

69. The famous work of Leo Tolstoy is:
A. Merchant of Venice
B. Illiad
C. War and Peace
D. Great Expectations

70. Who said, "Fools rush in where angels fear to tread"?
A. The Bible B. John Milton
C. Alexander Pope D. Dr. Samuel Johnson

71. Who is the writer of the novel "God of Small Things"?
A. Arundhati Roy
B. Jhumpa Lahiri
C. Kamal Subramaniyam
D. Mahashweta Devi

72. The capital of Mizoram is:
A. Imphal B. Shillong
C. Kohima D. Aizawl

73. Who is the author of the book 'The Namesake'?
A. Shashi Desh B. Jhumpa Lahiri
C. Kapil Dev D. Benazir Bhutto

74. Which of the following is the 28th State of India?
A. Jharkhand B. Uttarakhand
C. Chhattisgarh D. Gorkhaland

75. Guernica was painted by:
A. Leonardo da Vinci B. Michelangelo
C. Picasso D. Raphael

76. The 'Last Supper' is a world famous painting by:
A. Paul Gaugin B. Leonardo da Vinci
C. Raphael D. Rembrandt

77. 'Bhogali Bihu' is a festival of:
A. Assam B. Odisha
C. Gujarat D. Rajasthan

78. Classical dance having its roots in Tamil Nadu is:
A. Kathakali B. Kathak
C. Kuchipudi D. Bharat Natyam

79. Jamini Roy distinguished himself in:
A. dancing B. colour photography
C. instrumental music D. painting

80. Which of the following countries is not a member of the UNO?
A. Sweden B. Taiwan
C. Australia D. Norway

81. Which Indian jurist held the office of the President of International Court of Justice?
A. H.R. Khanna B. K.S. Hegde
C. Nagendra Singh D. R.S. Pathak

82. Who was the first Indian to be the President of UN General Assembly?
A. Natwar Singh
B. V.K. Krishna Menon
C. Mrs. Vijayalakshmi Pandit
D. Romesh Bhandari

83. What is the correct sequence of the formation of the following States of India?
1. Andhra Pradesh 2. Haryana
3. Kerala 4. Meghalaya
A. 1, 3, 2, 4 B. 1, 3, 4, 2
C. 3, 1, 2, 4 D. 3, 1, 4, 2

84. The 'first lady' of the Indian silver screen is:
A. Madhubala B. Devika Rani
C. Durga Khote D. Nargis Dutt

85. Arunachal Pradesh has borders with:
A. Bhutan, China and Myanmar
B. Bhutan, Bangladesh and Myanmar
C. Bangladesh, China and Myanmar
D. Bhutan, China and Bangladesh

86. The talkie film Alam Ara was produced in:
A. 1912 B. 1913
C. 1931 D. 1934

87. The headquarters of UNESCO is:
A. Paris B. Washington DC
C. Geneva D. Switzerland

88. The headquarters of WHO is:
A. Paris B. Geneva
C. Washington DC D. Rome

89. The author of the book 'India Wins Freedom' is:
A. Abul Kalam Azad B. Rajendra Prasad
C. Annie Besant D. Lala Lajpat Rai

90. Television was introduced in India in:
A. 15 September, 1959
B. 5 September, 1959
C. 25 September, 1959
D. 30 September, 1959

ANSWERS

1	2	3	4	5	6	7	8	9	10
A	D	C	D	D	C	B	B	B	D
11	**12**	**13**	**14**	**15**	**16**	**17**	**18**	**19**	**20**
D	D	B	B	B	B	A	D	C	B
21	**22**	**23**	**24**	**25**	**26**	**27**	**28**	**29**	**30**
B	B	B	C	C	D	D	C	C	C
31	**32**	**33**	**34**	**35**	**36**	**37**	**38**	**39**	**40**
B	B	A	D	C	B	D	D	D	A
41	**42**	**43**	**44**	**45**	**46**	**47**	**48**	**49**	**50**
B	D	C	D	B	C	C	C	D	C
51	**52**	**53**	**54**	**55**	**56**	**57**	**58**	**59**	**60**
B	C	C	B	B	C	C	B	C	A
61	**62**	**63**	**64**	**65**	**66**	**67**	**68**	**69**	**70**
C	D	A	B	D	A	D	B	C	C
71	**72**	**73**	**74**	**75**	**76**	**77**	**78**	**79**	**80**
A	D	B	A	C	B	A	D	D	B
81	**82**	**83**	**84**	**85**	**86**	**87**	**88**	**89**	**90**
C	C	A	B	A	C	A	B	A	A